44th
SOUTH AFRICAN R

Edited by Duane Heath & Eddie Grieb

Springbok Season Correspondent: Stephen Nell

Statisticians: Eddie Grieb, Piet Landman, Paul Dobson, Stuart Farmer,
Ashley Berry & Johanna de Vos

Production Manager: Alison Ward

Designer: Ryan Manning

Text by the Editor, Stephen Nell, or as credited

Photographs by Gallo Images, or as credited

© 2015 – South African Rugby Union & MWP Media
Printed & bound by Creda Communications, Eliot Ave, Eppindust II, Cape Town
ISBN: 978-0-620-62087-1 SA Rugby Annual 2015

All rights reserved. No part of this publication may be reproduced, stored in a retrieval system, or transmitted in any form or by any means electronic, mechanical or photocopied, recorded or otherwise without prior consent of the publishers.

Disclaimer: The views expressed in this book are those of the editors & contributors and not necessarily those of the South African Rugby Union.

The Editors welcome suggestions as well as notification of any errors or omissions.
Duane Heath: *PO Box 22643 Fish Hoek 7974; 021 928 7055 (office); duaneh@sarugby.co.za*
Eddie Grieb: *PO Box 989 Olifantsfontein 1665; 086 559 0744 (fax); eddieg@sarugby.co.za*

South Africa's 14 Provincial Unions

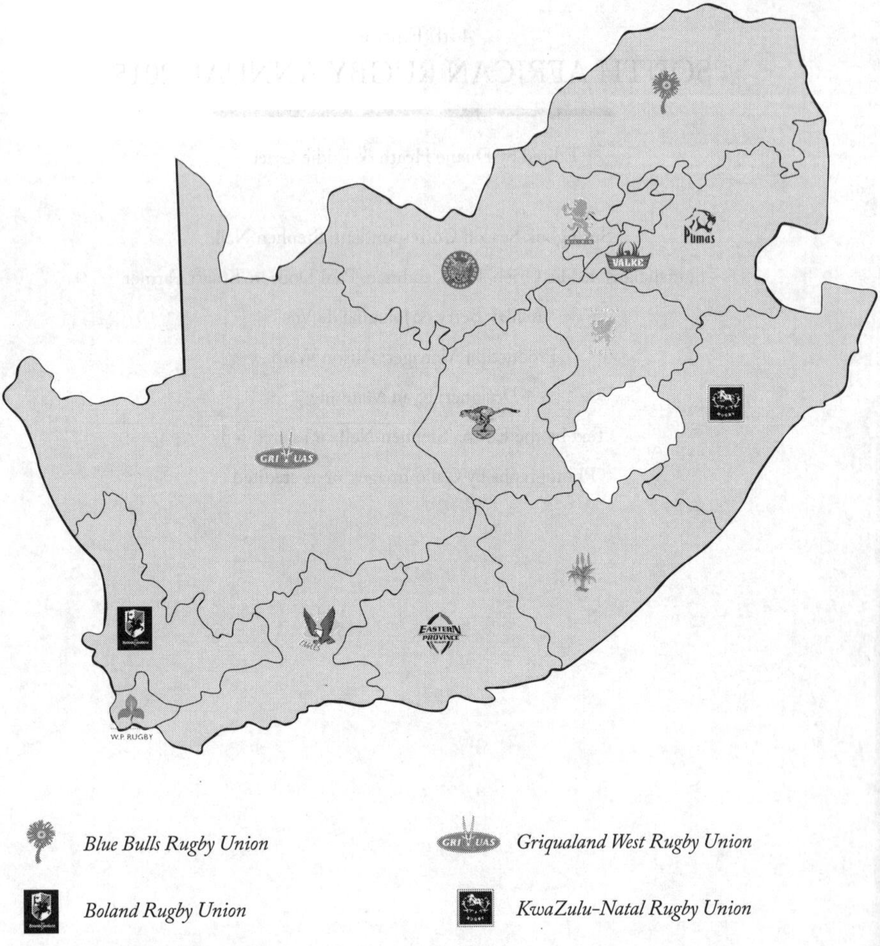

 Blue Bulls Rugby Union

 Boland Rugby Union

 Border Rugby Football Union

 Eastern Province Rugby Union

 Free State Rugby Union

 Golden Lions Rugby Union

 Griffons Rugby Union

 Griqualand West Rugby Union

 KwaZulu-Natal Rugby Union

 Leopards Rugby Union

 Mpumalanga Rugby Union

 South Western Districts Rugby Football Union

 Valke Rugby Union

 Western Province Rugby Football Union

Contents

SOUTH AFRICAN RUGBY ANNUAL 2015

UPFRONT
Foreword	5
Preface	6
Player of the Year	7
Previous Winners	8
Young Player of the Year	9
Previous Winners	10
SA Rugby Award Winners 2014	11

THE 2014 SEASON
Season Records	12
First-Class Matches	17
South Africans at Overseas Clubs	22
Who's Who of First-Class Players	25
Notable Obituaries	64
Referees	66

INTERNATIONAL RUGBY
Worldwide Test Results	71
South Africans Capped by Other Countries	76

RUGBY WORLD CUP 2015
Opinion: State of World Rugby	78
Interview: Morné du Plessis looks back at 1995	80
Scene-setter: Fortress Twickenham	83
Feature: African Qualification Race	86
Rugby World Cup Records & Statistics	88

THE SPRINGBOKS
Season Review & Statistics	98
Springbok Players 1891-2014	146
Springbok Records	176

OTHER NATIONAL TEAMS
Junior Springboks	243
Springbok Sevens	252
Springbok Women	258
South African Schools	267

FIRST-CLASS RUGBY
South African First-Class Records	276
Provincial First-Class Records	277
Vodacom Super Rugby	292
Vodacom Cup	382
Absa Currie Cup	440

JUNIOR PROVINCIAL RUGBY
Absa Under-21 & Under-19 Championships	548
Youth Weeks	555

CLUB & AMATEUR RUGBY
Cell C Community Cup	569
FNB Varsity Cup	614
Other Amateur Tournaments	627
Obituaries	630

Notes

KEY TO TEAM APPEARANCE LISTS:
R = Replacement
X = Unused replacement
c = Captain
A dash (–) denotes player not named in match-day squad for that particular match.

1. All records are correct as at 1 January 2015, unless otherwise stated.
2. All teams listed are in the order of fullback (15) to loosehead prop (1).
3. For record purposes, team names at the time of the establishment of the record have been used.
4. Union names and the names of their senior teams in 2014 were as follows:

Blue Bulls Rugby Union (formerly Northern Transvaal) – playing as Blue Bulls.
Boland Rugby Union – playing as Boland Cavaliers.
Border Rugby Football Union – playing as Border Bulldogs.
Eastern Province Rugby Union – playing as Eastern Province Kings.
Free State Rugby Union (formerly Orange Free State) – playing as Free State Cheetahs or Free State XV (Vodacom Cup).
Golden Lions Rugby Union (formerly Transvaal & Gauteng Lions) – playing as Golden Lions.
Griffons Rugby Union (formerly Northern Free State) – playing as Griffons.
Griqualand West Rugby Union – playing as Griquas.
Leopards Rugby Union (formerly Western Transvaal & North West) – playing as Leopards or Leopards XV (Vodacom Cup).
Mpumalanga Rugby Union (formerly South Eastern Transvaal) – playing as Pumas.
KwaZulu-Natal Rugby Union (formerly Natal) – playing as Sharks or Sharks XV (Vodacom Cup)
South Western Districts Rugby Football Union – playing as SWD Eagles.
Valke Rugby Union (formerly Eastern Transvaal, Gauteng Falcons & Falcons) – playing as the Valke.
Western Province Rugby Football Union – playing as Western Province.

5. Definition of a 'first-class match' and 'first-class appearance':
i) To qualify as a first-class match, it must be played strictly according to the Laws of the game (no more than seven or eight players on the bench, depending on the tournament or match).
ii) The following categories of matches qualify for first-class status if point i) is fulfilled:
a) All matches featuring the South African national team (Springboks) and the South African national under-20 team (Junior Springboks);
b) All matches in senior tournaments sanctioned by SARU;
c) All matches against touring international teams;
d) All matches between senior provincial teams & touring teams of the same or a higher status;
e) All matches between senior provincial teams outside of SARU tournaments where the strongest possible teams are fielded;
f) All matches played by senior teams carrying the name of a South African national team;
g) All matches played by senior composite teams in IRB approved tournaments.
iii) Any player appearing in one of the above matches (either in the starting XV or as a replacement – blood replacements and yellow-card replacements included) will be deemed to have made a first-class appearance.

Team Abbreviations

SOUTH AFRICAN TEAMS: BB – Blue Bulls, Bol – Boland, Bor – Border, EP – Eastern Province, ETvl – Eastern Transvaal, F – Falcons (if province), FS – Free State, GF – Gauteng Falcons, GL – Golden Lions, GW – Griqualand West, Mpu – Mpumalanga, NEC – North Eastern Cape, NED – North Eastern Districts, NNtl – Northern Natal, NOFS – Northern Orange Free State, NTvl – Northern Transvaal, OFS – Orange Free State, SWD – South Western Districts, SETvl – South Eastern Transvaal, Tvl – Transvaal, WP – Western Province, WTvl – Western Transvaal.

MAJOR INTERNATIONAL TEAMS: A – Australia, Arg – Argentina, BI – British & Irish Lions, E – England, F – France, I – Ireland, It – Italy, NZ – New Zealand, S – Scotland, Sam – Samoa, W – Wales.

OTHER TEAMS: Bots – Botswana, C – Canada, Cam – Cameroon, Fj – Fiji, G – Georgia, Gulf – Gulf States, IC – Ivory Coast, J – Japan, Ken – Kenya, Mad – Madagascar, Mor – Morocco, Nam – Namibia, Neth – Netherlands, Nor – Norway, NZC – New Zealand Cavaliers (1986), P – Portugal, PI – Pacific Islanders, R – Romania, Russ – Russia, SAm – South America, Sp – Spain, SWA – South West Africa, Swazi – Swaziland, T – Tonga, Tan – Tanzania, Tun – Tunisia, U – Uruguay, Ug – Uganda, WS – Western Samoa, WT – World XV, Z – Zimbabwe, Zam – Zambia

FOREWORD

London Calling in 2015

THE Rugby World Cup is woven deeply into the tapestry of South African life – and for good reason.

People of all backgrounds can recall instantly where they were on 24 June 1995, when the Springboks beat the All Blacks at Ellis Park in Johannesburg to lift the Webb Ellis Cup for the first time. Our new 'Rainbow Nation' was in its infancy and rugby reflected everything that was good about our country. In many ways, it still does.

Twelve years later the men in green and gold were at it again, winning the Rugby World Cup for a second time, this time on the fields of France. It could be argued that, in pure rugby terms, the class of 2007's achievement was perhaps even greater than that of their predecessors of '95, for the job was done far away from home.

The 1995 vs 2007 debate will surely go on for as long as there are braai fires to congregate around, but what is certain is that there is another team desperate to become part of that debate: the Springboks of 2015. To players and fans alike, a Rugby World Cup year just feels different. Preparation is that much more intense, the stakes that much higher, the anticipation and excitement that much more unbearable.

Can South Africa become the first team to win the World Cup three times? Only time will tell, but what is undeniable is the effect that victory will surely have on rugby in South Africa, 20 years after the heroics of 1995.

I am sure that winning is at the forefront of the mind for each and every one of those hopefuls who dream of taking their place on the aeroplane to England later this year. Between now and then, the pressure will increase to breaking point – and it is up to us to give them all our support as the clock ticks down inexorably to September.

The Springboks might not have finished off the 2014 season the way they would have wanted to, but the Webb Ellis Cup has a way of bringing out the best in South Africans, and I have no doubt 2015 will be no different.

But while the focus this year will be understandably on the Rugby World Cup, let us not forget that rugby is never only about the Springboks, but also about those tens of thousands of schoolboys and club players in every village and town dotted across our vast land – for whom the Springboks represent a measuring stick of quality they themselves aim to emulate each time they take to the field.

The health of South African rugby should never be be measured only by success in a World Cup tournament that comes around once every four years – prestigious as that may be. No; to feel the pulse of South African rugby one must only drive into its heartlands on any given Saturday, and witness just what this game means to the majority of its people – from Malmesbury to Malelane and everywhere in between.

This deep love for rugby, on display in the big cities and in every platteland *dorpie*, is what makes South African rugby strong, and long may it continue. Victory in the 2015 Rugby World Cup later this year will merely deepen that love.

Oregan Hoskins
President – South African Rugby Union

Preface

"THERE are many ways of going forward, but only one way of standing still," wrote Franklin D Roosevelt, the thirty-second president of the United States. FDR might not have had rugby in mind when he penned this famous line sometime during his unprecedented four terms in office, but it nevertheless rings true, not only for our sport but also for those who attempt to document its unfolding history.

This 2015 edition of the *South African Rugby Annual*, like its 43 predecessors, take a statistical snapshot of a season in our national sport and attempts to diligently and carefully record, in words, photographs and numbers, each one of its twisting turns. But in doing so we must heed Roosevelt's advice, and always strive to find new ways of "going forward". To this end, we have given the 2015 *Annual* a facelift: it's more compact and user-friendly size is complemented by subtle cosmetic changes in paper type and, inside, you will find a refreshed design that is cleaner and less cluttered.

A book such as the *Annual* is however measured by its content, and this has not escaped our attention. At 640 pages, this edition is by far the biggest ever. The ups and downs of the Springbok team are covered in unprecedented detail, with over 100 pages devoted to the men in green and gold. And befitting its stature as our most cherished tournament, the Absa Currie Cup and all its drama is detailed in over 100 pages as well.

But South African rugby, at its heart, is about far more than the professional game. Ninety-nine percent of all players are amateurs, and the immense importance of the grassroots game is reflected in our decision to devote a large section of the book to club rugby, which continues to undergo a revival after years in the doldrums.

My thanks, as always, go out to everyone involved in the *Annual*'s production, so that we are able to act as the eyes and ears for future generations for whom South African rugby will become as much a part of the fabric of their lives as it is ours.

Thank you to my co-editor Eddie Grieb and his statistical A-team of Piet Landman, Paul Dobson, Heinrich Schulze, Gideon Nieman, Ashley Berry, Johanna de Vos and Frikkie van Rensburg. Thanks as always to Herman le Roux and our overseas stalwarts – John Griffiths (World Rugby statistician), Geoff Miller (NZRU), Matthew Alvarez (ARU) and Stuart Farmer (Stuart Farmer Media Services Ltd, England).

Thank you to Gallo Images for their efforts to again visually document our sport, and to the writers whose words make the Annual the respected document of record it is: John Bishop, Simon Borchardt, Paul Dobson, Stephen Nell, Craig Ray, Dan Retief & Ken Borland. JJ Harmse and Zeena Isaacs of SARU also deserve thanks for their contributions, as does Andy Colquhoun, the *Annual*'s editor for many years and now, in his position at SARU, the person who continues, with the admirable support of the organisation, to ensure its continued survival.

Thanks also to our friends at the provincial unions: Saartjie Olivier (Blue Bulls), AK Warnick (Boland), Trevor Barnes (KZN), Marius van Rensburg (Mpumalanga), Emil Oelrich & Gesie van der Merwe (Valke), Revenne Maritz (WP), Rynhardt van As (SWD), Karen Crafford (Leopards), Leah van Wyk & Michael Herbert (Griffons), Debbie Ellis (EP), Lizette Viviers (Free State), Akhona Mgijima (Border) and Martin Coetzee (Griquas).

Special thanks to Alison Ward of co-publishers MWP, Linda Kay and Lesley Ackermann of Creda Communications; and Natasha Store, Mark Hackney and everyone at Blue Weaver. Finally, thanks to Eddie Grieb, designer extraordinaire Ryan Manning, and respected author Stephen Nell – the first name on the team sheet, as it were, when it comes to meeting the challenge of recording the Springboks' season in concise yet insightful detail.

And, for the sixth year running, on behalf of them thanks to our family members: Alida Grieb and Lee & Edrich; Vanessa Manning and Hannah & Joshua; and, finally, to my wife Aisling, our son Kian and daughter Emma.

Duane Heath
Cape Town, December 2014

PLAYER OF THE YEAR

Duane Vermeulen

(DHL Stormers, South Africa)

UNCOMPROMISING Springbok eighthman Duane Vermeulen was unanimously crowned South Africa's Player of the Year for the first time following a season of sustained excellence.

Such was Vermeulen's form throughout 2014 for all the teams he represented – and in particular the matches of real consequence in which he was involved – that when all was said and done he easily saw off the challenges of fellow finalists and Springbok team-mates **Nizaam Carr** (Stormers, Western Province, South Africa), **Marcell Coetzee** (Sharks, South Africa), **Willie le Roux** (Cheetahs, South Africa), and **Handré Pollard** (South Africa Under-20, Bulls, Blue Bulls, South Africa).

That the 1.93m, 108kg Vermeulen, a finalist in 2013, won by the proverbial couple of lengths does not detract in any way from the quality of the other four finalists, nor their individual performances during an oftentimes difficult season. It's just that the rugged loose forward was exceptional during a year in which his personal form rarely dipped below a consistently high level.

And yet it is difficult to believe that Vermeulen only truly made the Springbok No 8 jersey indisputably his own in 2014, at the relatively advanced age of 28, after a number of years of near-misses, false starts and untimely injuries.

Yes, he did have 16 Tests under his belt by the time the season began, including consecutive starts in the Springboks' last nine Tests of 2013, but many observers saw Vermeulen as merely doing a holding job until the 53-Test-capped Pierre Spies, who started the first three Tests of that year before getting injured, regained his fitness.

That Spies did not return to the Springbok fold in 2014 however should not be seen as paving the way for Vermeulen to start in all 13 of South Africa's Tests – the only one of 45 players eventually used to do so.

Such was the head of steam that Vermeulen built up for the DHL Stormers in Vodacom Super Rugby – he started all 16 of their matches and captained them on three occasions – that even had Spies been fully fit and firing on all cylinders, the Blue Bulls back-rower would have found it difficult to win back his place against a stubborn incumbent whose farm-raised physique and confrontational style seems tailor-made for Springbok rugby.

Daniel Johannes (Duane) Vermeulen, Springbok #840, who attended Nelspruit High School before made his first-class debut in 2005 for the Pumas, played 30 first-class matches in 2014 – 13 Tests, 16 Super Rugby games, and South Africa vs the World XV. He has represented South Africa in 29 Tests, scoring two tries, having made his Test debut in 2012 against Australia.

Previous Players of the Year

2013: Jean de Villiers (Winner, WP), Bismarck du Plessis (KZN), Eben Etzebeth (WP), Willie le Roux (FS), Duane Vermeulen (WP).
2012: Bryan Habana (Winner, WP), Keegan Daniel (KZN), Patrick Lambie (KZN), Eben Etzebeth (WP), JP Pietersen (KZN).
2011: Schalk Burger (Winner, WP), Bismarck du Plessis (KZN), Patrick Lambie (KZN), Francois Hougaard (BB), Victor Matfield (BB).
2010: Gurthrö Steenkamp (Winner, BB), Gio Aplon (WP), Schalk Burger (WP), Juan de Jongh (WP), Francois Hougaard (BB).
2009: Fourie du Preez (Winner, BB), Heinrich Brüssow (FS), Victor Matfield (BB), John Smit (KZN), Morné Steyn (BB).
2008: Jean de Villiers (Winner, WP), Tendai Mtawarira, Bismarck du Plessis, Ryan Kankowski, Adrian Jacobs (all KZN).
2007: Bryan Habana (Winner), Fourie du Preez, Victor Matfield (all BB), Percy Montgomery (KZN), Juan Smith (FS).
2006: Fourie du Preez (Winner, BB), Os du Randt (FS), Victor Matfield (BB), Pierre Spies (BB), Luke Watson (WP).
2005: Bryan Habana (Winner), Bakkies Botha, Victor Matfield (all BB), Jean de Villiers (WP), Ricky Januarie (GL).
2004: Schalk Burger (Winner), Os du Randt (FS), De Wet Barry, Marius Joubert (WP), Bakkies Botha (BB).
2003: Ashwin Willemse (Winner, GL), Juan Smith (FS), Richard Bands, Bakkies Botha (BB), Joe van Niekerk (GL).
2002: Joe van Niekerk (Winner), Jannes Labuschagne, André Pretorius, Lawrence Sephaka (all GL), Werner Greeff (WP).
2001: André Vos (Winner, GL), Braam van Straaten (WP), Victor Matfield (BB), Lukas van Biljon (Natal), Conrad Jantjes (GL).
2000: Breyton Paulse (Winner, WP), Thinus Delport, Rassie Erasmus (both GL), Kennedy Tsimba (FS), Corné Krige (WP).
1999: André Venter (Winner, FS), Breyton Paulse, Cobus Visagie (both WP), Joost van der Westhuizen (BB), Hennie le Roux (GL).
1998: Gary Teichmann (Winner, Natal), Joost van der Westhuizen, Krynauw Otto (BB), Gaffie du Toit (GW), Bobby Skinstad (WP).
1997: Os du Randt (Winner, FS), Pieter Rossouw, Percy Montgomery, Dick Muir (all WP), Johan Roux (GL).
1996: André Joubert (Winner, Natal), Henry Honiball, Gary Teichmann (both Natal), Ruben Kruger, Joost van der Westhuizen (both NTvl).
1995: Ruben Kruger (Winner), Joost van der Westhuizen (both NTvl), Francois Pienaar (Tvl), Joel Stransky (WP), André Joubert (Natal).
1994: Chester Williams (Winner, WP), Mark Andrews, André Joubert (both Natal), Ruben Kruger, Joost vd Westhuizen (both NTvl).
1993: Gavin Johnson (Winner), Francois Pienaar (both Tvl), James Small (Natal), Tiaan Strauss (WP), Joost vd Westhuizen (NTvl).
1992: Tiaan Strauss (Winner), Danie Gerber (both WP), Jacques Olivier, Naas Botha, Adriaan Richter (all NTvl).
1991: Uli Schmidt (Winner), Naas Botha, Gerbrand Grobler (all NTvl), André Joubert (OFS), Wahl Bartmann (Natal).
1990: Uli Schmidt (Winner), Robert du Preez (both NTvl), Wahl Bartmann, Joel Stransky (both Natal), Tiaan Strauss (WP).
1989: Johan Heunis (Winner), Robert du Preez, Burger Geldenhuys (all NTvl), André Joubert (OFS), Carel du Plessis (WP).
1988: Calla Scholtz (Winner), Tiaan Strauss (both WP), Naas Botha, Adolf Malan (both NTvl), Gerhard Mans (SWA).
1987: Naas Botha (Winner), Adri Geldenhuys (both NTvl), Gysie Pienaar (OFS), John Robbie, Jannie Breedt (both Tvl).
1986: Jannie Breedt (Winner), Wahl Bartmann (both Tvl), Carel du Plessis (WP), Uli Schmidt (NTvl), Garth Wright (EP).
1985: Naas Botha (Winner, NTvl), Jannie Breedt (Tvl), Schalk (SWP) Burger (WP), Danie Gerber (EP), Gerrie Sonnekus (OFS).
1984: Danie Gerber (Winner, EP), Rob Louw, Calla Scholtz (both WP), Ray Mordt (NTvl), Errol Tobias (Bol).
1983: Hennie Bekker (Winner), Divan Serfontein, Carel du Plessis (all WP), Liaan Kirkham (Tvl), Ray Mordt (NTvl).
1982: Divan Serfontein (Winner), Colin Beck, Hennie Bekker (both WP), Naas Botha, Johan Heunis (both NTvl).
1981: Naas Botha (Winner), Johan Heunis (both NTvl), Ray Mordt (Tvl), Divan Serfontein, De Villiers Visser (both WP).
1980: Gysie Pienaar (Winner, OFS), Naas Botha, Louis Moolman (both NTvl), Morné du Plessis (WP), Gerrie Germishuys (Tvl).
1979: Naas Botha (Winner), Louis Moolman (both NTvl), Morné du Plessis, Rob Louw, De Villiers Visser (all WP).
1978: Thys Lourens (Winner), Tommy du Plessis, Pierre Edwards (all NTvl), De Wet Ras (OFS), Ian Robertson (Rhodesia).
1977: Moaner van Heerden (Winner), Thys Lourens (both NTvl), Morné du Plessis (WP), Hermanus Potgieter, Theuns Stofberg (both OFS).
*1976: Morné du Plessis (WP), Moaner van Heerden (NTvl), Bryan Williams, Sid Going, Peter Whiting (all NZ).
*1975: Gerald Bosch (Tvl), Gerrie Germishuys (OFS), Pierre Spies, Thys Lourens (both NTvl), Johan Oosthuizen (WP).
*1974: Gareth Edwards, Willie John McBride, JPR Williams (all British Lions), Willem Stapelberg, John Williams (both NTvl).
*1973: Gerald Bosch (Tvl), Dirk de Vos, Moaner van Heerden, Pierre Spies (all NTvl), Johan Oosthuizen (WP).
*1972: Kevin de Klerk (Tvl), Sam Doble (England), Jan Ellis (SWA), Carel Fourie (NE Cape) John Pullin (England).
*1971: Benoit Dauga (France), Frik du Preez (NTvl), Jan Ellis (SWA), Hannes Marais (EP), Hannes Viljoen (Natal).
*1970: Piet Greyling (Tvl), Joggie Jansen (OFS), Ian McCallum (WP), Alan Sutherland, Bryan Williams (both NZ).

*: *Before 1977, no single player of the year was named.*

YOUNG PLAYER OF THE YEAR

Handré Pollard

(South Africa Under-20, Bulls, Blue Bulls, South Africa)

FLYHALF Handré Pollard's meteoric, if wholly expected, rise to the top of the Springbok charts during a memorable season culminated in the 20-year-old being named South Africa's Young Player of the Year for 2014.

Pollard, who earlier in the season was named world junior player of the year after stellar performances for the Junior Springboks, saw off the challenges of **Nizaam Carr** (Stormers, Western Province, South Africa), **Cheslin Kolbe** (Stormers, Western Province), **Seabelo Senatla** (Western Province, Springbok Sevens) and **Jan Serfontein** (Bulls, Blue Bulls, South Africa).

Springbok coach Heyneke Meyer has always maintained that he saw greatness in Pollard ever since first seeing him play as a schoolboy for Paarl Gymnasium. The rugby world was in agreement after Pollard, while still at school, helped South Africa Under-20 to the IRB Junior World Championship (JWC) title in 2012 with victory over New Zealand in the final at Newlands.

In 2014, Pollard very nearly nabbed his second JWC winner's medal in New Zealand, the Junior Springboks losing 21-20 to England in the final. The tournament will however be remembered for the two defeats inflicted on the Baby Blacks – with Pollard playing a central role in proceedings.

No sooner had the 1.89m, 97kg outside half arrived back in South Africa than Meyer threw him into the cauldron of Test rugby, albeit against lowly-ranked Scotland. It was to be the first of nine Test Pollard would play in 2014 – seven of those as a starter – with the undoubted highlight being his two first-half tries against the All Blacks at Ellis Park en route to a famous 27-25 victory.

It's perhaps unfair to expect a young player – even one of Pollard's prodigious talents – to fly through his first season of international rugby without encountering some turbulence along the way, and so it proved on the Springboks' unsuccessful end-of-year tour.

Pollard was given the No 10 jersey against Ireland but his inability to come to terms with foreign conditions during a near-record defeat cost him his place. For a young man of Pollard's pedigree, the tour would have been a steep learning curve and there is little doubt that he will return in 2015 far wiser. With a Rugby World Cup in England looming, the hopes of a nation might just rest on his 20-year-old shoulders.

Handré Pollard, Springbok #857, who attended Paarl Gymnasium before making his first-class debut in 2012, played a total of 29 first-class matches in 2014, scoring 217 points. This figure included 65 points in nine Tests in his first season of international rugby.

Previous Young Players of the Year

2013: **Eben Etzebeth** (Winner, WP), Pieter-Steph du Toit (KZN), Cheslin Kolbe (WP), Siya Kolisi (WP), Jan Serfontein (BB).
2012: **Eben Etzebeth** (Winner, WP), Elton Jantjies (GL), Marcell Coetzee (KZN), Johan Goosen (FS), Raymond Rhule (FS).
2011: **Patrick Lambie** (Winner, KZN), Elton Jantjies (GL), Johan Goosen (FS), Jaco Taute (GL), Francois Hougaard (BB).
2010: **Elton Jantjies** (Winner, GL), Bjorn Basson (BB), Juan de Jongh (WP), Francois Hougaard (BB), Patrick Lambie (KZN).
2009: **Heinrich Brüssow** (Winner, FS), Juan de Jongh (WP), Francois Hougaard (BB), Lionel Mapoe (FS), Frans Steyn (KZN).
2008: **Robert Ebersohn** (Winner, FS), Heinrich Brüssow (FS), Nick Koster (WP), Tendai Mtawarira, Bismarck du Plessis (both KZN).
2007: **Francois Steyn** (Winner), JP Pietersen, Ryan Kankowski (all KwaZulu-Natal), Heinke van der Merwe (GL), Richardt Strauss (FS).
2006: **Pierre Spies** (Winner, BB), JP Pietersen, Keegan Daniel (KwaZulu-Natal), Hilton Lobberts (Blue Buls), Gio Aplon (Western Province).
2005: **Jongi Nokwe** (Winner, Boland), Wynand Olivier, Morné Steyn (BB), Ruan Pienaar, JP Pietersen (KwaZulu-Natal).
2004: **Bryan Habana** (Winner, GL), Schalk Burger (WP), Schalk Brits (GL), Fourie du Preez (BB), Luke Watson (Natal).
2003: **Ashwin Willemse** (Winner, GL), Schalk Burger (WP), John Mametsa (BB), Jaque Fourie (GL), Fourie du Preez (BB).
2002: **Pedrie Wannenburg** (Winner, BB), Brent Russell (Pumas), Hanyani Shimange (FS), Jaque Fourie (GL), Derick Hougaard (BB).
2001: **Conrad Jantjes** (Winner), Gcobani Bobo, Joe van Niekerk (all GL), Adi Jacobs (Falcons), Wylie Human (FS).

2000: Marius Joubert (Bol), Conrad Jantjes (GL), De Wet Barry, Adri Badenhorst (both WP), Wylie Human (FS).
1999: John Smit (Natal), Kaya Malotana (Border), Jannes Labuschagne (GL), Wayne Julies (Boland), Torros Pretorius (Pumas).
1998: Lourens Venter, Robert Markram (both Griquas), Grant Esterhuizen, Nicky van der Walt (both BB), André Vos (GL).
1997: Thinus Delport (Gauteng GL), Breyton Paulse, Louis Koen, Bobby Skinstad (all WP), Jan-Harm van Wyk (FS).
1996: Dawie du Toit, Hannes Venter (both NTvl), Marius Goosen (Boland), MJ Smith (FS), André Vos (EP).
1995: Stephen Brink, Jorrie Kruger (both OFS), Robbie Kempson (Natal), Danie van Schalkwyk, Joggie Viljoen (both NTvl).
1994: Frikkie Bosman (ETvl), Braam Els (OFS), Harold Karele (EP), André Snyman (NTvl), Justin Swart (WP).
1993: Krynauw Otto, FP Naude (both NTvl), Ryno Oppermann (OFS), Johan Roux (Tvl), Christiaan Scholtz (WP).
1992: Jannie de Beer, Hentie Martens, Brendan Venter, André Venter (all OFS), Joost van der Westhuizen (NTvl).
1991: Pieter Hendriks (Tvl), Hennie le Roux (EP), Pieter Müller (OFS), Johan Nel, Jacques Olivier (both NTvl).
1990: Andrew Aitken (Natal), Jannie Claassens, Theo van Rensburg (both NTvl), Bernard Fourie (WTvl), Ian Macdonald (Tvl).
1989: Stompie Fourie (OFS), Pieter Nel, Verwoerd Roodt (both NTvl), Joel Stransky, Jeremy Thomson (both Natal).
1988: Kobus Burger, Christian Stewart (WP), Jacques du Plessis (EP), André Joubert (OFS), JJ van der Walt (NTvl).
1987: Chris Badenhorst (OFS), Robert du Preez (WTvl), Jan Lock, Charles Rossouw (both NTvl), Andrew Paterson (EP).
1986: Keith Andrews, Tiaan Strauss (both WP), Martin Knoetze (WTvl), Hendrik Kruger (NTvl), Frans Wessels (OFS).
1985: Schalk (SW) Burger, Faffa Knoetze (both WP), Deon Coetzee (Tvl), Christo Ferreira (OFS), Giepie Nel (NTvl).
1984: Paul Botes, Uli Schmidt (both NTvl), Niel Burger (WP), Wessel Lightfoot, Helgard Müller (both OFS).
1983: Wahl Bartmann (Tvl), Jannie Dreyer, Adolf Malan (both NTvl), Calla Scholtz (WP), Gert Smal (WTvl).
1982: Wilfred Cupido (South African Rugby Federation), Michael du Plessis (WP), Liaan Kirkham (Tvl), Piet Kruger (NTvl), Rudie Visagie (OFS).
1981: Harry Viljoen, Jannie Breedt, André Skinner (all NTvl), Jan du Toit, Ernest Viljoen (both OFS).
1980: Colin Beck (WP), Cliffie Brown (Natal), Johan Maräis (NTvl), Chris Rogers (Zimbabwe), Japie Wessels (OFS).
1979: Darius Botha (NTvl), Willie du Plessis (WP), Doug Jeffrey (OFS), André Markgraaff (WTvl), Gawie Visagie (Griquas).
1978: Burger Geldenhuys, Okkie Oosthuizen (both NTvl), Eben Jansen (OFS), Ray Mordt, David Smith (both Rhodesia).
1977: Naas Botha, Thys Burger (both NTvl), Agie Koch, Flippie van der Merwe (both WP), Gysie Pienaar (OFS).
1976: Dirk Froneman, Wouter Hugo (both OFS), Divan Serfontein, Nick Mallet (both WP), LM Rossouw (NTvl).
1975: Tommy du Plessis, Christo Wagenaar (both NTvl), Corrie Pypers (Tvl), Hermanus Potgieter, De Wet Ras (both OFS).
1974: Gavin Cowley (EP), Peter Kirsten (WP), John Knox, Louis Moolman (both NTvl), Johan Strauss (Tvl).
1973: Dave Frederickson (Tvl), Wilhelm Landman (WP), Martiens le Roux (OFS), Keith Thoresson (Natal), Barry Wolmarans (Boland).
1972: Paul Bayvel, Gerald Bosch (both Tvl), Pikkie du Toit (OFS), Dugald Macdonald (WP), Jackie Snyman (OFS).
1971: Kevin de Klerk, Gert Schutte (both Tvl), Piet du Plessis (NTvl), Buddy Swartz (Griquas), Johan Wagenaar (OFS).
1970: Francois de Villiers, Johan Walters (both WP), Peter Cronje (Tvl), Jannie van Aswegen (Griquas), John Williams (NTvl).

2014 Award Winners

Player of the Year:
Duane Vermeulen
Other finalists: Nizaam Carr, Marcell Coetzee, Willie le Roux, Handré Pollard

Young Player of the Year:
Handré Pollard
Other finalists: Nizaam Carr, Cheslin Kolbe, Seabelo Senatla, Jan Serfontein

Team of the Year:
DHL Western Province (Currie Cup champions)
Other finalists: Junior Springboks, Springboks, Springbok Sevens, Xerox Golden Lions

Coach of the Year:
Johan Ackermann

Springbok Sevens Player of the Year:
Seabelo Senatla

SA Under-20 Player of the Year:
Handré Pollard

Super Rugby Player of the Year:
Duane Vermeulen (DHL Stormers)
Other finalists: Warren Whiteley (Lions), Marcell Coetzee (Cell C Sharks), Nizaam Carr (DHL Stormers), Cobus Reinach (Cell C Sharks)

Currie Cup Player of the Year:
Nizaam Carr (DHL Western Province)
Other finalists: Jaco Kriel (Xerox Golden Lions), Juan de Jongh (DHL Western Province), Demetri Catrakilis (DHL Western Province), Warren Whiteley (Xerox Golden Lions)

First Division Player of the Year:
Boela Abrahams (Griffons)

Vodacom Cup Player of the Year:
Renaldo Bothma (Pumas)

Cell C Community Cup Player of the Tournament:
Michael Nienaber (Rustenburg Impala)

Coca-Cola Craven Week Player of the Tournament:
Curwin Bosch

Referee of the Year:
Craig Joubert

Women's Player of the Year:
Fundiswa Plaatjie

FIRST-CLASS TEAMS BY WINNING PERCENTAGE

TEAM	TOURNAMENT	P	W	L	D	PF	PA	TF	TA	Win %
Springboks XV	International Friendly	1	1	0	0	47	13	6	1	100%
Junior Springboks	U20 Junior World Championships	5	4	1	0	167	83	22	10	80%
Sharks XV	Vodacom Cup	8	6	2	0	235	147	27	17	75%
Western Province	Vodacom Cup/Currie Cup	20	15	5	0	608	396	77	43	75%
Springboks (Tests)	Incoming/Rugby Champs/EOY Tour	13	9	4	0	332	237	35	19	69,2%
Griquas	Vodacom Cup/CC Qual/Currie Cup	26	18	8	0	854	602	108	70	69,2%
Leopards	First Div./Currie Cup Qualifiers	12	8	4	0	570	318	83	40	66,7%
Sharks	Super Rugby	18	12	6	0	443	358	32	30	66,7%
Golden Lions	Currie Cup	12	8	4	0	428	245	51	25	66,7%
Sharks	Currie Cup	11	7	3	1	307	272	29	26	63,6%
Pumas	Vodacom Cup/Currie Cup	19	12	7	0	586	397	68	43	63,2%
Free State XV	Vodacom Cup	8	5	3	0	298	170	42	18	62,5%
Golden Lions	Vodacom Cup	10	6	4	0	305	243	40	28	60%
Blue Bulls	Vodacom Cup/Currie Cup	20	12	8	0	644	414	75	39	60%
SWD Eagles	Vodacom Cup/CC Qual/ First Div.	20	11	9	0	606	667	78	84	55%
Griffons	Vodacom Cup/CC Qual/ First Div.	20	10	10	0	588	677	77	92	50%
Bulls	Super Rugby	16	7	8	1	365	335	28	29	43,8%
Stormers	Super Rugby	16	7	9	0	290	326	30	29	43,8%
Lions	Super Rugby	16	7	9	0	367	413	31	46	43,8%
Leopards XV	Vodacom Cup	7	3	4	0	227	178	29	22	42,9%
Valke	Vodacom Cup/CC Qual/ First Div.	20	7	13	0	560	672	76	96	35%
Boland Cavaliers	Vodacom Cup/CC Qual/First Div.	18	6	12	0	436	496	56	65	33,3%
Free State Cheetahs	Currie Cup	10	3	6	1	249	271	34	29	30%
Cheetahs	Super Rugby	16	4	11	1	372	527	38	59	25%
Eastern Province Kings	Vodacom Cup/Currie Cup/Tour Match	18	4	14	0	389	602	51	78	22,2%
Border Bulldogs	Vodacom Cup/CC Qual/First Div.	18	2	16	0	340	750	43	112	11,1%
Tusker Simba XV	Vodacom Cup	7	1	6	0	102	283	14	45	14%
Limpopo Blue Bulls	Vodacom Cup	7	0	0	0	47	578	6	90	0%

SEASON IN 2014

LEADING SCORERS IN FIRST-CLASS RUGBY

ALL POINTS – TOP 10

PLAYER	TEAM	M	T	C	P	DG	Pts
Marnitz Boshoff	Lions, G Lions, SA, Barbarians	25	1	39	57	9	281
Jacques-Louis Potgieter	Bulls, Blue Bulls	23	1	29	65	3	267
Handre Pollard	Bulls, Blue Bulls, SA, SA U20	29	6	44	31	2	217
Willie du Plessis	Golden Lions, Free State	20	3	41	29	2	190
Gouws Prinsloo	Griquas	15	4	33	31	0	179
Demetri Catrakilis	Stormers, WP	19	0	34	32	1	167
Francois Steyn	Sharks	18	0	16	43	1	164
Fred Zeilinga	Sharks, Sharks XV	14	1	17	38	0	153
Johan Goosen	Cheetahs	14	2	23	30	2	152
Jaun Kotze	Valke	13	5	32	19	2	152

TRIES – 10 OR MORE

PLAYER	TEAM	Matches	Tries
Marnus Schoeman	Griquas	24	17
George Tossel	Leopards XV, Leopards	17	15
Sylvain Mahuza	Leopards XV, Leopards	11	14
Ederies Arendse	Griquas	22	13
Carel Greeff	Griquas	22	13
Alshaun Bock	SWD	13	12
Cornal Hendricks	SA, Cheetahs	26	11
Norman Nelson	Griffons	18	11
Juan de Jongh	Stormers, WP, Barbarians	25	11
Sampie Mastriet	Bulls, Blue Bulls	16	11
Sarel Pretorius	Cheetahs, Free State, Barbarians	25	10
Jaco Kriel	Lions, Golden Lions	28	10
Luther Obi	Leopards XV, Leopards	9	10

Most First-Class Appearances

Bismarck du Plessis	Sharks, SA	30
Duane Vermeulen	Stormers, SA	30

Made a 100th appearance for their province in 2014

Jaco Bouwer	Pumas vs Griquas	09/05/2014
Thembani Mkokeli	Border vs Griffons	11/07/2014
Ryno Barnes	Griquas vs Blue Bulls	11/10/2014

Made a 100th appearance for their franchise in 2014

Akona Ndungane	Bulls vs Blues	08/03/2014
Jean de Villiers	Stormers vs Chiefs	14/03/2014
JP Pietersen	Sharks vs Bulls	22/03/2014
Odwa Ndungane	Sharks vs Lions	12/04/2014
Keegan Daniel	Sharks vs Highlanders	26/04/2014
Jannie du Plessis	Sharks vs Crusaders	17/05/2014
Tendai Mtawarira	Sharks vs Crusaders	17/05/2014
Peter Grant	Stormers vs Force	17/05/2014

SEASON IN 2014

Youngest and oldest first-class players in 2014

Duhan van der Merwe	SA U20 vs England, 20 June	19 years 16 days
Victor Matfield	SA vs Wales, 29 November	37 years 202 days

Tallest, shortest, heaviest and lightest players in 2014

Lood de Jager	Cheetahs	2.05m
Percy Williams	Leopards	1.60m
Kalvano King	EP Kings	1.60m
Christo van Wyk	Western Province	144kg
Kalvano King	EP Kings	62kg

FIRST-CLASS CAREER POINTS - PLAYERS ACTIVE IN 2014

500 POINTS OR MORE*

PLAYER	TEAM/S	Matches	Tries	Conversions	Penalties	Drop Goals	Total
M Steyn	Bulls, SA	285	50	541	534	45	3069
AS Pretorius	Leopards	215	29	428	286	43	1988
LI Strydom	Griffons	208	16	330	317	13	1730
J-L Potgieter	Bulls, Blue Bulls	157	18	209	218	13	1201
PJ Grant	Stormers	169	19	190	241	1	1195
PJ Lambie	Sharks, SA	133	21	159	220	5	1092
D Catrakilis	Stormers, WP	74	1	114	183	10	812
ET Jantjies	Lions, Golden Lions	106	7	124	171	3	800
BG Habana	Stormers, SA	275	148	0	0	0	740
R Pienaar	SA	206	28	122	102	3	699
EG Watts	FS Cheetahs	132	37	151	81	1	733
JC Roos	Pumas	50	3	110	91	3	514

50 TRIES – PLAYERS ACTIVE IN 2014*

PLAYER	TEAM	Tries	PLAYER	TEAM	Tries
BG Habana	Stormers, SA	148	J-PR Pietersen	Sharks, SA	71
J de Villiers	Stormers, SA	94	LA Watson	EP	67
OM Ndungane	Sharks	88	RR Jansen	Griqualand West	61
AZ Ndungane	Bulls, Blue Bulls	87	W Olivier	Bulls, SA	58
NT Nelson	EP	86	NPJ Steyn	Griffons	58
AG Bock	SWD	85	PF du Preez	Bulls, SA	57
SJ Pretorius	Free State	77			

250 APPEARANCES – PLAYERS ACTIVE IN 2014*

PLAYER	TEAM	Matches	PLAYER	TEAM	Matches
V Matfield	Bulls, SA	370	BG Habana	Stormers, SA	275
JN du Plessis	Sharks, SA	305	JP Botha	Bulls, SA	272
LJ Botes	Sharks	294	J de Villiers	Stormers, SA	273
M Steyn	Bulls, SA	285			

*for South African teams only

SEASON IN 2014

The Blue Bulls on the charge during the Vodacom Cup.

MATCH FEATURES

Most points scored by a team (Top 5)

114	Blue Bulls vs Limpopo BB (114-0)	Vodacom Cup
110	Golden Lions vs Limpopo BB (110-0)	Vodacom Cup
103	Leopards vs Border (103-15)	Currie Cup Qualifying
88	Pumas vs Limpopo BB (88-0)	Vodacom Cup
84	Griquas vs SWD (84-15)	Vodacom Cup

Most tries scored by a team (10 or more)

18	Blue Bulls vs Limpopo BB (114-0)	Vodacom Cup
16	Golden Lions vs Limpopo BB (110-0)	Vodacom Cup
15	Leopards vs Border (103-15)	Currie Cup Qualifying
14	Pumas vs Limpopo BB (88-0)	Vodacom Cup
13	Free State XV vs Tusker Simba XV (75-10)	Vodacom Cup
11	Leopards XV vs Limpopo BB (71-10)	Vodacom Cup
11	Griquas vs SWD (84-15)	Vodacom Cup
10	Griquas vs Limpopo BB (68-13)	Vodacom Cup
10	Griffons vs Limpopo BB (62-10)	Vodacom Cup
10	Griquas vs Valke (64-34)	Vodacom Cup
10	Pumas vs Griffons (69-5)	Vodacom Cup
10	Leopards vs Griffons (70-25)	Currie Cup Qualifying

Biggest winning margin (by 50 points or more)

114	Blue Bulls vs Limpopo BB (114-0)	Vodacom Cup
110	Golden Lions vs Limpopo BB (110-0)	Vodacom Cup
88	Pumas vs Limpopo BB (88-0)	Vodacom Cup
88	Leopards vs Border (103-15)	Currie Cup Qualifying
69	Griquas vs SWD (84-15)	Vodacom Cup

SEASON IN 2014

65	Free State XV vs Tusker Simba XV (75-10)	Vodacom Cup
64	Pumas vs Griffons (69-5)	Vodacom Cup
61	Leopards XV vs Limpopo BB (71-10)	Vodacom Cup
55	Griquas vs Limpopo BB (68-13)	Vodacom Cup
52	Griffons vs Limpopo BB (62-10)	Vodacom Cup
51	Valke vs Limpopo BB (65-14)	Vodacom Cup

Most points by a single player

30	Willie du Plessis, GL vs Limpopo BB (15c)	Vodacom Cup

Most tries by a single player (3 or more)

4	Luther Obi	Leopards vs Border	Currie Cup Qualifying
4	Sylvain Mahuza	Leopards vs Border	Currie Cup Qualifying
4	Alshaun Bock	SWD vs Border	Vodacom Cup
4	Devon Williams	WP vs Tusker Simba XV	Vodacom Cup
3	Carel Greeff	Griquas vs Griffons	Currie Cup Qualifying
3	Marnus Schoeman	Griquas vs Border	Currie Cup Qualifying
3	Rayn Smid	WP vs EP Kings	Vodacom Cup
3	Jacques Verwey	Valke vs Limpopo BB	Vodacom Cup
3	Carel Greeff	Griquas vs Valke	Vodacom Cup
3	Sampie Mastriet	Blue Bulls vs Limpopo BB	Vodacom Cup
3	Hillford Clarke	Griquas vs Limpopo BB	Vodacom Cup
3	Ashwin Scott	Pumas vs Limpopo BB	Vodacom Cup
3	Bjorn Basson	Blue Bulls vs Griquas	Currie Cup

Most conversions by a single player (7 or more)

15	Willie du Plessis	Golden Lions vs Limpopo BB	Vodacom Cup
14	Andre Pretorius	Leopards vs Border	Currie Cup Qualifying
10	Gouws Prinsloo	Griquas vs SWD	Vodacom Cup
8	Gerhard Nortier	Leopards XV vs Limpopo BB	Vodacom Cup
8	Tiaan Schoeman	Blue Bulls vs Limpopo BB	Vodacom Cup
8	Andre Pretorius	Leopards vs Border	Currie Cup Qualifying
7	Jaun Kotze	Valke vs Border	Currie Cup Qualifying
7	Elton Jantjies	Lions vs Cheetahs	Super Rugby
7	JC Roos	Pumas vs Griffons	Vodacom Cup
7	Dustin Jinka	Griquas vs Limpopo BB	Vodacom Cup

Most penalties by a single player

8	Gouws Prinsloo	Griquas vs Pumas	Currie Cup

Most drop goals by a single player

2	Marnitz Boshoff	Lions vs Blues	Super Rugby

Scored in all four ways

21 Pts	Jacques-Louis Potgieter [1T, 2C, 3P, 1DG]	Bulls vs Blues	Super Rugby
13 Pts	Gerhard Nortier [1T, 1C, 1P, 1DG]	Leopards XV vs Blue Bulls	Vodacom Cup
15 Pts	Jaun Kotze [1T,2C,1P,1DG]	Valke vs Griquas	Currie Cup Qualifiers

FIRST-CLASS MATCHES

A list of all 224 first-class matches played by South African teams during 2014

#	Date	Team 1	Score	Team 2	Score	Competition	Venue	Referee
1	Sat 15 Feb	Cheetahs	20	Lions	21	Super Rugby	Bloemfontein	Craig Joubert
2	Sat 15 Feb	Sharks	31	Bulls	16	Super Rugby	Durban	Jaco Peyper
3	Fri 21 Feb	Cheetahs	15	Bulls	9	Super Rugby	Bloemfontein	Stuart Berry
4	Sat 22 Feb	Sharks	27	Hurricanes	9	Super Rugby	Durban	Andrew Lees
5	Sat 22 Feb	Lions	34	Stormers	10	Super Rugby	Johannesburg	Jaco Peyper
6	Fri 28 Feb	Rebels	35	Cheetahs	14	Super Rugby	Melbourne	Angus Gardner
7	Fri 28 Feb	Stormers	19	Hurricanes	18	Super Rugby	Cape Town	Steve R Walsh
8	Sat 1 Mar	Bulls	25	Lions	17	Super Rugby	Pretoria	Chris Pollock
9	Fri 7 Mar	Reds	43	Cheetahs	33	Super Rugby	Brisbane	Garratt Williamson
10	Fri 7 Mar	Valke	6	Pumas	26	Vodacom Cup	Kempton Park	Jaco van Heerden
11	Fri 7 Mar	Border	24	Sharks XV	46	Vodacom Cup	East London	Francois Pretorius
12	Fri 7 Mar	Leopards XV	16	Golden Lions	18	Vodacom Cup	Potchefstroom	Quintin Immelman
13	Sat 8 Mar	Crusaders	14	Stormers	13	Super Rugby	Christchurch	Rohan Hoffman
14	Sat 8 Mar	Blue Bulls	24	Griquas	26	Vodacom Cup	Pretoria	Marius vd Westhuizen
15	Sat 8 Mar	Free State XV	52	SWD	17	Vodacom Cup	Heidedal	Marius Jonker
16	Sat 8 Mar	Griffons	62	Limpopo BB	10	Vodacom Cup	Bultfontein	Jaco Kotze
17	Sat 8 Mar	Simba XV	17	EP Kings	10	Vodacom Cup	Cape Town	Rodney Bonaparte
18	Sat 8 Mar	WP	16	Boland	8	Vodacom Cup	Cape Town	Pro Legoete
19	Sat 8 Mar	Bulls	38	Blues	22	Super Rugby	Pretoria	Andrew Lees
20	Sat 8 Mar	Sharks	37	Lions	23	Super Rugby	Durban	Jaco Peyper
21	Fri 14 Mar	Chiefs	36	Stormers	20	Super Rugby	Hamilton	Craig Joubert
22	Sat 15 Mar	Hurricanes	60	Cheetahs	27	Super Rugby	Wellington	Angus Gardner
23	Sat 15 Mar	Golden Lions	23	Valke	22	Vodacom Cup	Johannesburg	Christie du Preez
24	Sat 15 Mar	Griquas	20	Griffons	12	Vodacom Cup	Kimberley	Oregopotsi Rametsi
25	Sat 15 Mar	Sharks XV	25	WP	7	Vodacom Cup	Durban	Jaco van Heerden
26	Sat 15 Mar	Lions	39	Blues	36	Super Rugby	Johannesburg	Stuart Berry
27	Sat 15 Mar	EP Kings	60	Border	6	Vodacom Cup	Grahamstown	Pro Legoete
28	Sat 15 Mar	Pumas	22	Blue Bulls	20	Vodacom Cup	Nelspruit	Tahla Ntshakaza
29	Sat 15 Mar	Limpopo BB	10	Leopards XV	71	Vodacom Cup	Polokwane	Gerrie de Bruin
30	Sat 15 Mar	Boland	20	Free State XV	28	Vodacom Cup	Malmesbury	Quintin Immelman
31	Sat 15 Mar	Simba XV	7	SWD	51	Vodacom Cup	Cape Town	Stephan Geldenhuys
32	Sat 15 Mar	Sharks	35	Reds	20	Super Rugby	Durban	Lourens vd Merwe
33	Fri 21 Mar	Griffons	5	Pumas	69	Vodacom Cup	Welkom	Christie du Preez
34	Fri 21 Mar	Free State XV	22	Sharks XV	23	Vodacom Cup	Heidedal	Quintin Immelman
35	Fri 21 Mar	Griquas	68	Limpopo BB	13	Vodacom Cup	Kimberley	Marius Jonker
36	Sat 22 Mar	Blues	40	Cheetahs	30	Super Rugby	Auckland	Francisco Pastrana
37	Sat 22 Mar	Brumbies	25	Stormers	15	Super Rugby	Cape Town	Glen Jackson
38	Sat 22 Mar	Valke	29	Leopards XV	40	Vodacom Cup	Kempton Park	Pro Legoete
39	Sat 22 Mar	Border	18	Simba XV	17	Vodacom Cup	East London	Stephan Geldenhuys
40	Sat 22 Mar	WP	56	EP Kings	22	Vodacom Cup	Cape Town	Rodney Bonaparte
41	Sat 22 Mar	SWD	46	Boland	17	Vodacom Cup	Swellendam	Tahla Ntshakaza
42	Sat 22 Mar	Blue Bulls	22	Golden Lions	20	Vodacom Cup	Pretoria	Craig Joubert
43	Sat 22 Mar	Lions	23	Reds	20	Super Rugby	Johannesburg	Stuart Berry
44	Sat 22 Mar	Bulls	23	Sharks	19	Super Rugby	Pretoria	Mike Fraser
45	Fri 28 Mar	Border	16	WP	29	Vodacom Cup	East London	Christie du Preez
46	Fri 28 Mar	Pumas	25	Griquas	16	Vodacom Cup	Nelspruit	Pro Legoete
47	Sat 29 Mar	Reds	22	Stormers	17	Super Rugby	Brisbane	Chris Pollock
48	Sat 29 Mar	Sharks XV	27	SWD	10	Vodacom Cup	Durban	Quintin Immelman

FIRST-CLASS MATCHES IN 2014

#	Date	Team 1	Score	Team 2	Score	Competition	Venue	Referee
49	Sat 29 Mar	Bulls	34	Chiefs	34	Super Rugby	Pretoria	Craig Joubert
50	Sat 29 Mar	Leopards XV	26	Blue Bulls	30	Vodacom Cup	Leeudoringstad	Tahla Ntshakaza
51	Sat 29 Mar	EP Kings	3	Free State XV	31	Vodacom Cup	Cradock	Jaco van Heerden
52	Sat 29 Mar	Golden Lions	40	Griffons	37	Vodacom Cup	Johannesburg	Marius vd Westhuizen
53	Sat 29 Mar	Simba XV	19	Boland	24	Vodacom Cup	Cape Town	Cwengile Jadezweni
54	Sat 29 Mar	Sharks	32	Waratahs	10	Super Rugby	Durban	Mike Fraser
55	Fri 4 Apr	Blue Bulls	54	Valke	7	Vodacom Cup	Pretoria	Stuart Berry
56	Fri 4 Apr	Griffons	15	Leopards XV	35	Vodacom Cup	Welkom	Stephan Geldenhuys
57	Fri 4 Apr	SWD	23	EP Kings	21	Vodacom Cup	George	B Crouse
58	Sat 5 Apr	Hurricanes	25	Bulls	20	Super Rugby	Napier	Steve R Walsh
59	Sat 5 Apr	Limpopo BB	0	Pumas	88	Vodacom Cup	Polokwane	Oregopotsi Rametsi
60	Sat 5 Apr	Free State XV	54	Border	17	Vodacom Cup	Bloemfontein	Rodney Bonaparte
61	Sat 5 Apr	Griquas	33	Golden Lions	18	Vodacom Cup	Kimberley	Jaco Peyper
62	Sat 5 Apr	Cheetahs	43	Chiefs	43	Super Rugby	Bloemfontein	Craig Joubert
63	Sat 5 Apr	Boland	27	Sharks XV	43	Vodacom Cup	Ceres	Jaco Kotze
64	Sat 5 Apr	WP	65	Simba XV	29	Vodacom Cup	Cape Town	Tahla Ntshakaza
65	Sat 5 Apr	Lions	7	Crusaders	28	Super Rugby	Johannesburg	M vd Westhuizen
66	Sat 5 Apr	Stormers	11	Waratahs	22	Super Rugby	Cape Town	Glen Jackson
67	Fri 11 Apr	Highlanders	27	Bulls	20	Super Rugby	Dunedin	Rohan Hoffman
68	Fri 11 Apr	Border	26	SWD	40	Vodacom Cup	East London	Jaco van Heerden
69	Fri 11 Apr	Griquas	64	Valke	34	Vodacom Cup	Kimberley	Rasta Rasivhenge
70	Fri 11 Apr	Griffons	10	Blue Bulls	49	Vodacom Cup	Welkom	Federico Anselmi
71	Fri 11 Apr	EP Kings	28	Boland	21	Vodacom Cup	Port Elizabeth	Juan Sylvestre
72	Sat 12 Apr	Simba XV	3	Sharks XV	40	Vodacom Cup	Cape Town	Francois Pretorius
73	Sat 12 Apr	Pumas	44	Leopards XV	31	Vodacom Cup	Middelburg	Quintin Immelman
74	Sat 12 Apr	Limpopo BB	0	Golden Lions	110	Vodacom Cup	Polokwane	Gerrie de Bruin
75	Sat 12 Apr	WP	28	Free State XV	15	Vodacom Cup	Cape Town	Ben Crouse
76	Sat 12 Apr	Cheetahs	31	Crusaders	52	Super Rugby	Bloemfontein	Glen Jackson
77	Sat 12 Apr	Lions	12	Sharks	25	Super Rugby	Johannesburg	Craig Joubert
78	Sat 19 Apr	Waratahs	19	Bulls	12	Super Rugby	Sydney	Rohan Hoffman
79	Sat 19 Apr	Sharks	19	Cheetahs	8	Super Rugby	Durban	Jaco Peyper
80	Sat 19 Apr	Stormers	18	Lions	3	Super Rugby	Cape Town	Stuart Berry
81	Fri 25 Apr	Blue Bulls	114	Limpopo BB	0	Vodacom Cup	Pretoria	Eduan Nel
82	Fri 25 Apr	Valke	17	Griffons	41	Vodacom Cup	Kempton Park	Juan Sylvestre
83	Fri 25 Apr	Sharks XV	11	EP Kings	27	Vodacom Cup	Durban	Federico Anselmi
84	Fri 25 Apr	SWD	23	WP	14	Vodacom Cup	George	Rasta Rasivhenge
85	Fri 25 Apr	Sharks	18	Highlanders	34	Super Rugby	Durban	Jaco Peyper
86	Sat 26 Apr	Force	15	Bulls	9	Super Rugby	Perth	Angus Gardner
87	Sat 26 Apr	Free State XV	75	Simba XV	10	Vodacom Cup	Bloemfontein	Marius vd Westhuizen
88	Sat 26 Apr	Golden Lions	27	Pumas	48	Vodacom Cup	Alberton	Ben Crouse
89	Sat 26 Apr	Leopards XV	8	Griquas	32	Vodacom Cup	Klerksdorp	Lourens vd Merwe
90	Sat 26 Apr	Boland	41	Border	17	Vodacom Cup	Piketberg	Daniel Fortuin
91	Sat 26 Apr	Cheetahs	35	Stormers	22	Super Rugby	Bloemfontein	Craig Joubert
92	Fri 2 May	Rebels	16	Sharks	22	Super Rugby	Melbourne	Andrew Lees
93	Fri 2 May	Sharks XV	20	Golden Lions	27	Vodacom Cup	Durban	Francois Pretorius
94	Fri 2 May	Pumas	13	WP	8	Vodacom Cup	Nelspruit	Stephan Geldenhuys
95	Sat 3 May	Chiefs	38	Lions	8	Super Rugby	Hamilton	Chris Pollock
96	Sat 3 May	Griquas	84	SWD	15	Vodacom Cup	Kimbeley	Christie du Preez

SEASON IN 2014

FIRST-CLASS MATCHES IN 2014

#	Date	Team 1	Score	Team 2	Score	Competition	Venue	Referee
97	Sat 3 May	Free State XV	21	Blue Bulls	22	Vodacom Cup	Bloemfontein	Rodney Bonaparte
98	Sat 3 May	Stormers	29	Highlanders	28	Super Rugby	Cape Town	Craig Joubert
99	Sat 3 May	Bulls	26	Cheetahs	21	Super Rugby	Pretoria	Marius vd Westhuizen
100	Fri 09 May	Pumas	14	Griquas	15	Vodacom Cup	Nelspruit	Pro Legoete
101	Sat 10 May	Highlanders	23	Lions	22	Super Rugby	Dunedin	Angus Gardner
102	Sat 10 May	Brumbies	16	Sharks	9	Super Rugby	Canberra	Glen Jackson
103	Sat 10 May	Blue Bulls	15	Golden Lions	16	Vodacom Cup	Pretoria	Quintin Immelman
104	Sat 10 May	Cheetahs	16	Force	23	Super Rugby	Bloemfontein	Chris Pollock
105	Sat 10 May	Bulls	28	Stormers	12	Super Rugby	Pretoria	Craig Joubert
106	Fri 16 May	Griquas	30	Golden Lions	6	Vodacom Cup	Kimberley	Jaco van Heerden
107	Sat 17 May	Crusaders	25	Sharks	30	Super Rugby	Christchurch	Rohan Hoffman
108	Sat 17 May	Stormers	24	Force	8	Super Rugby	Cape Town	Chris Pollock
109	Sat 17 May	Cheetahs	27	Brumbies	21	Super Rugby	Bloemfontein	Marius vd Westhuizen
110	Sun 18 May	Waratahs	41	Lions	13	Super Rugby	Sydney	Nick Briant
111	Fri 23 May	Blues	23	Sharks	29	Super Rugby	Albany	Nick Briant
112	Fri 23 May	Bulls	44	Brumbies	23	Super Rugby	Pretoria	Craig Joubert
113	Sat 24 May	Force	29	Lions	19	Super Rugby	Perth	Steve R Walsh
114	Sat 24 May	Stormers	33	Cheetahs	0	Super Rugby	Cape Town	Stuart Berry
115	Sat 31 May	Lions	32	Bulls	21	Super Rugby	Johannesburg	Craig Joubert
116	Sat 31 May	Sharks	19	Stormers	21	Super Rugby	Durban	Jaco Peyper
117	Mon 2 Jun	SA U/20	61	Scotland U/20	5	JWC	Albany	Jaquin Montes
118	Fri 6 Jun	SA U/20	33	NZ U/20	24	JWC	Albany	Alexandre Ruiz
119	Fri 6 Jun	Griquas	52	Border	5	CC Qualifiers	Kimberley	Christie du Preez
120	Sat 7 Jun	Leopards	51	SWD	23	CC Qualifiers	Potchefstroom	Ben Crouse
121	Sat 7 Jun	Griffons	27	Boland	25	CC Qualifiers	Welkom	Pro Legoete
122	Sat 7 Jun	Springboks	47	World XV	13	Int. friendly	Cape Town	George Clancy
123	Tue 10 Jun	SA U/20	21	Samoa U/20	8	JWC	Pukekohe	Ben O'Keefe
124	Tue 10 Jun	EP Kings	12	Wales	34	Tour match	Port Elizabeth	Lourens vd Merwe
125	Fri 13 Jun	Valke	22	Leopards	45	CC Qualifiers	Kempton Park	Rasta Rasivhenge
126	Fri 13 Jun	SWD	40	Griffons	37	CC Qualifiers	George	Christie du Preez
127	Sat 14 Jun	Boland	3	Griquas	21	CC Qualifiers	Wellington	Ben Crouse
128	Sat 14 Jun	South Africa	38	Wales	16	Test	Durban	Romain Poite
129	Fri 20 Jun	Border	12	Boland	37	CC Qualifiers	East London	Ben Crouse
130	Fri 20 Jun	SWD	34	Valke	52	CC Qualifiers	George	Quintin Immelman
131	Sat 21 Jun	Griquas	33	Leopards	32	CC Qualifiers	Kimberley	Marius Jonker
132	Sat 21 Jun	South Africa	31	Wales	30	Test	Nelspruit	Steve R Walsh
133	Sat 28 Jun	Griffons	24	Griquas	43	CC Qualifiers	Welkom	Rasta Rasivhenge
134	Sat 28 Jun	Boland	17	SWD	21	CC Qualifiers	Wellington	Jaco van Heerden
135	Sat 28 Jun	Valke	54	Border	49	CC Qualifiers	Kempton Park	Marius vd Westhuizen
136	Sat 28 Jun	South Africa	55	Scotland	6	Test	Port Elizabeth	Glen Jackson
137	Fri 4 Jul	Border	31	SWD	33	CC Qualifiers	East London	Jaco van Heerden
138	Fri 4 Jul	Lions	34	Rebels	17	Super Rugby	Johannesburg	Jaco Peyper
139	Sat 5 Jul	Valke	20	Boland	35	CC Qualifiers	Kempton Park	Pro Legoete
140	Sat 5 Jul	Leopards	70	Griffons	25	CC Qualifiers	Potchefstroom	Marius vd Westhuizen
141	Sat 5 Jul	Stormers	16	Bulls	0	Super Rugby	Cape Town	Craig Joubert
142	Sat 5 Jul	Cheetahs	27	Sharks	20	Super Rugby	Bloemfontein	Rohan Hoffman
143	Fri 11 Jul	Border	15	Griffons	41	CC Qualifiers	East London	Pro Legoete
144	Fri 11 Jul	Bulls	40	Rebels	7	Super Rugby	Pretoria	Rohan Hoffman

www.sarugby.co.za

FIRST-CLASS MATCHES IN 2014

#	Date	Team 1	Score	Team 2	Score	Competition	Venue	Referee
145	Sat 12 Jul	Boland	23	Leopards	55	CC Qualifiers	Wellington	Rasta Rasivhenge
146	Sat 12 Jul	Griquas	40	Valke	25	CC Qualifiers	Kimberley	Ben Crouse
147	Sat 12 Jul	Lions	60	Cheetahs	25	Super Rugby	Johannesburg	Marius vd Westhuizen
148	Sat 12 Jul	Stormers	10	Sharks	34	Super Rugby	Cape Town	Jaco Peyper
149	Fri 18 Jul	Griffons	29	Valke	20	CC Qualifiers	Welkom	Quintin Immelman
150	Sat 19 Jul	SWD	12	Griquas	57	CC Qualifiers	George	Lourens vd Merwe
151	Sat 19 Jul	Leopards	103	Border	15	CC Qualifiers	Potchefstroom	Ben Crouse
152	Sat 19 Jul	Sharks	31	Highlanders	27	Super Rugby	Durban	Steve R Walsh
153	Sat 26 Jul	Crusaders	38	Sharks	6	Super Rugby	Christchurch	Glen Jackson
154	Fri 8 Aug	EP Kings	16	WP	35	Currie Cup	Port Elizabeth	Jaco Peyper
155	Sat 9 Aug	Griquas	24	Sharks	31	Currie Cup	Kimberley	Craig Joubert
156	Sat 9 Aug	Golden Lions	41	Blue Bulls	13	Currie Cup	Johannesburg	Jaco van Heerden
157	Sat 9 Aug	Pumas	28	Free State	21	Currie Cup	Nelspruit	Marius v/d Westhuizen
158	Fri 15 Aug	Sharks	34	Pumas	17	Currie Cup	Durban	Christie du Preez
159	Sat 16 Aug	WP	41	Blue Bulls	17	Currie Cup	Cape Town	Rasta Rasivhenge
160	Sat 16 Aug	Golden Lions	60	EP Kings	19	Currie Cup	Johannesburg	Craig Joubert
161	Sat 16 Aug	Free State	34	Griquas	27	Currie Cup	Bloemfontein	Marius Jonker
162	Sat 16 Aug	South Africa	13	Argentina	6	Test	Pretoria	John Lacey
163	Fri 22 Aug	Pumas	33	Griquas	15	Currie Cup	Nelspruit	Quinton Immelman
164	Sat 23 Aug	Blue Bulls	30	EP Kings	25	Currie Cup	Pretoria	Lesego Legoete
165	Sat 23 Aug	WP	27	Golden Lions	14	Currie Cup	Cape Town	Craig Joubert
166	Sat 23 Aug	Sharks	19	Free State	16	Currie Cup	Durban	Rasta Rasivhenge
167	Sat 23 Aug	Argentina	31	South Africa	33	Test	Salta	Steve R Walsh
168	Fri 29 Aug	Border	19	Valke	14	1st Div.	East London	Stuart Berry
169	Fri 29 Aug	SWD	29	Leopards	21	1st Div.	George	Lesego Legoete
170	Fri 29 Aug	Pumas	32	Sharks	22	Currie Cup	Nelspruit	Ben Crouse
171	Sat 30 Aug	Boland	19	Griffons	27	1st Div.	Wellington	Lourens vd Merwe
172	Sat 30 Aug	Griquas	25	Free State	36	Currie Cup	Kimberley	Jaco van Heerden
173	Sat 30 Aug	Blue Bulls	18	WP	23	Currie Cup	Pretoria	Craig Joubert
174	Sat 30 Aug	EP Kings	22	Golden Lions	41	Currie Cup	Port Elizabeth	Marius v/d Westhuizen
175	Fri 5 Sep	WP	49	EP Kings	14	Currie Cup	Cape Town	Stuart Berry
176	Sat 6 Sep	Australia	24	South Africa	23	Test	Perth	George Clancy
177	Sat 6 Sep	Free State	17	Pumas	31	Currie Cup	Bloemfontein	Craig Joubert
178	Sat 6 Sep	Leopards	54	Boland	32	1st Div.	Potchefstroom	Federico Anselmi
179	Sat 6 Sep	Sharks	18	Griquas	21	Currie Cup	Durban	Lourens vd Merwe
180	Sat 6 Sep	Griffons	37	Border	32	1st Div.	Welkom	Marius Jonker
181	Sat 6 Sep	Valke	24	SWD	19	1st Div.	Kempton Park	Rasta Rasivhenge
182	Sat 6 Sep	Blue Bulls	36	Golden Lions	26	Currie Cup	Pretoria	Marius v/d Westhuizen
183	Fri 12 Sep	SWD	31	Border	22	1st Div.	George	Lourens vd Merwe
184	Fri 12 Sep	EP Kings	13	Blue Bulls	28	Currie Cup	Port Elizabeth	Quintin Immelman
185	Sat 13 Sep	New Zealand	14	South Africa	10	Test	Wellington	Jerome Garces
186	Sat 13 Sep	Griffons	37	Leopards	31	1st Div.	Welkom	Marius v/d Westhuizen
187	Sat 13 Sep	Griquas	31	Pumas	27	Currie Cup	Kimberley	Craig Joubert
188	Sat 13 Sep	Free State	30	Sharks	30	Currie Cup	Bloemfontein	Stuart Berry
189	Sat 13 Sep	Boland	25	Valke	32	1st Div.	Wellington	Lesego Legoete
190	Sat 13 Sep	Golden Lions	35	WP	33	Currie Cup	Johannesburg	Jaco Peyper
191	Fri 19 Sep	Border	19	Leopards	34	1st Div.	East London	Jaco Peyper
192	Fri 19 Sep	Golden Lions	29	Pumas	15	Currie Cup	Johannesburg	Jaco van Heerden

FIRST-CLASS MATCHES IN 2014

#	Date	Team 1	Score	Team 2	Score	Competition	Venue	Referee
193	Sat 20 Sep	SWD	24	Boland	35	1st Div.	George	Ben Crouse
194	Sat 20 Sep	Valke	36	Griffons	27	1st Div.	Kempton Park	Federico Anselmi
195	Sat 20 Sep	WP	36	Griquas	12	Currie Cup	Cape Town	Lesego Legoete
196	Sat 20 Sep	EP Kings	22	Free State	37	Currie Cup	Port Elizabeth	Marius Jonker
197	Sat 20 Sep	Blue Bulls	15	Sharks	26	Currie Cup	Pretoria	Quinton Immelman
198	Fri 26 Sep	Boland	27	Border	6	1st Div.	Wellington	Lesego Legoete
199	Fri 26 Sep	Pumas	22	WP	37	Currie Cup	Nelspruit	Jaco van Heerden
200	Fri 26 Sep	Free State	22	Blue Bulls	31	Currie Cup	Bloemfontein	Marius v/d Westhuizen
201	Sat 27 Sep	Sharks	53	EP Kings	24	Currie Cup	Durban	Ben Crouse
202	Sat 27 Sep	Leopards	50	Valke	29	1st Div.	Potchefstroom	Marius Jonker
203	Sat 27 Sep	Griquas	8	Golden Lions	46	Currie Cup	Kimberley	Jaco Peyper
204	Sat 27 Sep	Griffons	27	SWD	42	1st Div.	Welkom	Quintin Immelman
205	Sat 27 Sep	South Africa	28	Australia	10	Test	Cape Town	Nigel Owens
206	Fri 3 Oct	Griffons	45	SWD	43	1st Div. (SF)	Welkom	Ben Crouse
207	Fri 3 Oct	Leopards	24	Valke	31	1st Div. (SF)	Potchefstroom	Quintin Immelman
208	Fri 3 Oct	Sharks	26	Golden Lions	23	Currie Cup	Durban	Lesego Legoete
209	Fri 3 Oct	Pumas	6	Blue Bulls	37	Currie Cup	Nelspruit	Jaco Peyper
210	Sat 4 Oct	Free State	29	WP	34	Currie Cup	Bloemfontein	Marius Jonker
211	Sat 4 Oct	Griquas	45	EP Kings	25	Currie Cup	Kimberley	Stuart Berry
212	Sat 4 Oct	South Africa	27	New Zealand	25	Test	Johannesburg	Wayne Barnes
213	Fri 10 Oct	EP Kings	26	Pumas	25	Currie Cup	Port Elizabeth	Marius Jonker
214	Sat 11 Oct	Golden Lions	47	Free State	7	Currie Cup	Johannesburg	Stuart Berry
215	Sat 11 Oct	WP	20	Sharks	28	Currie Cup	Cape Town	Jaco Peyper
216	Sat 11 Oct	Blue Bulls	46	Griquas	12	Currie Cup	Pretoria	Lesego Legoete
217	Fri 17 Oct	Griffons	23	Valke	21	1st Div. (Fin)	Welkom	Ben Crouse
218	Sat 18 Oct	Golden Lions	50	Sharks	20	Currie Cup (SF)	Johannesburg	Jaco van Heerden
219	Sat 18 Oct	WP	31	Blue Bulls	23	Currie Cup (SF)	Cape Town	Lesego Legoete
220	Sat 25 Oct	WP	19	Golden Lions	16	Currie Cup Final	Cape Town	Craig Joubert
221	Sat 8 Nov	Ireland	29	South Africa	15	Test	Dublin	Romain Poite
222	Sat 15 Nov	England	28	South Africa	31	Test	London	Steve R Walsh
223	Sat 22 Nov	Italy	6	South Africa	22	Test	Padova	Jerome Garces
224	Sat 29 Nov	Wales	12	South Africa	6	Test	Cardiff	John Lacey

SEASON IN 2014

South Africans Playing Abroad
Compiled by Stuart Farmer

South Africans appearing for leading clubs overseas at some point during the 2014 calendar year.
* Springbok   + Overseas international

	Player	Club	Country
+	NJ (Nick) Abendanon	Bath	England
		Clermont Auvergne	France
	HJ (Heini) Adams	Bordeaux-Begles	France
	JP (Jacobie) Adriaanse	Scarlets	Wales
	CG (Chris) Alcock	Western Force	Australia
		Gr. Sydney Rams	Australia
	DZ (Zane) Ansel	Petrarca Padova	Italy
*	GG (Gio) Aplon	Grenoble	France
	PC (Pat) Barnard	Brive	France
+	BM (Brad) Barritt	Saracens	England
	CJ (Coenie) Basson	Lyon O.U.	France
	S (Stefan) Basson	FemiCZ Rovigo	Italy
*	A (Andries) Bekker	Kobe Kobelco Steelers	Japan
	R (Roland) Bernard	Grenoble	France
	RM (Rynier) Bernardo	Ospreys	Wales
	JF (Jannie) Bester vd Berg	Macclesfield Blues	England
	N (Naude) Beukes	Grenoble	France
	C (Carl) Bezuidenhout	Edinburgh	Scotland
	JDB (Jannie) Bornman	Castres Olympique	France
*	HM (Meyer) Bosman	Stade Francais Paris	France
+	WT (Tobie) Botes	Benetton Treviso	Italy
	BJ (Berend) Botha	Mont-de-Marsan	France
		Bordeaux-Begles	France
*	BJ (BJ) Botha	Munster	Ireland
*	JP (Bakkies) Botha	Toulon	France
+	MJ (Mouritz) Botha	Saracens	England
	RL (Rinus) Bothma	Perpignan	France
	R (Rudi) Brits	Colomiers	France
*	SB (Schalk) Brits	Saracens	England
*	HW (Heinrich) Brussow	NTT Docomo	
		Red Hurricanes	Japan
	AM (Albertus) Buckle	Grenoble	France
	CB (Craig) Burden	Toulon	France
*	SWP (Schalk) Burger	Suntory Sungoliath	Japan
	K (Kevin) Buys	Brive	France
+	D (Dario) Chistolini	Zebre	Italy
*	PM (Pat) Cilliers	Montpellier	France
+	AD (Antonie) Claassen	Castres Olympique	France
		Racing-Metro 92	France
	EF (Errie) Claassens	London Scottish	England
*	M (Michael) Claassens	Toulon	France
	ML (Michael) Coetzee	Castres Olympique	France
	R (Rudi) Coetzee	Grenoble	France
	C (Cilliers) Coetzer	Tarbes	France
	SD (Stuart) Commins	Ealing Trailfinders	England
		Esher	England
*	J (Jacques) Cronje	Racing-Metro 92	France
	L (Lionel) Cronje	ACT Brumbies	Australia
*	KR (Keegan) Daniel	Kubota Spears	Japan
	HJ (Hennie) Daniller	Zebre	Italy
	SJ (Sebastian) de Chaves	Leicester Tigers	England
+	B (Benjamin) de Jager	Cammi Calvisano	Italy
	N (Nick) de Jager	Saracens	England
		Old Albanians	England
	RP (Rossouw) de Klerk	Glasgow Warriors	Scotland
*	NA (Neil) de Kock	Saracens	England
+	CA (Carlo) del Fava	Newcastle Falcons	England
	AME (Allan) Dell	Edinburgh	Scotland
	JR (Jean) Deysel	Toyota Verblitz	Japan
+	RJE (Robbie) Diack	Ulster	Ireland
	WJ (Hanno) Dirksen	Ospreys	Wales
	MG (Matthew) Dobson	London Welsh	England
	J (Justin) Downey	Suntory Sungoliath	Japan
	WR (Wesley) Dunlop	Montauban	France
	C (Chris) du Plessis	Rugby Viadana	Italy
	PVW (Petrus) du Plessis	Saracens	England
	CG (Cornell) du Preez	Edinburgh	Scotland
*	PF (Fourie) du Preez	Suntory Sungoliath	Japan
	R (Ruaan) du Preez	Oyonnax	France
*	WH (Wian) du Preez	Lyon O.U.	France
	JJ (Jaco) du Toit	Pau	France
	DO (Dewalt) Duvenage	Perpignan	France
	GW (George) Earle	Scarlets	Wales
	JM (Sias) Ebersohn	Western Force	Australia
	RT (Robert) Ebersohn	Montpellier	France
+	J (Jaco) Erasmus	Lafert San Dona	Italy
+	IR (Ian) Evans	Ospreys	Wales
		Bristol	England
	MM (Mat) Evans	Ealing Trailfinders	England
	NS (Nick) Fenton-Wells	Bedford Blues	England
		Saracens	England
	AS (Andries) Ferreira	Zebre	Italy
	SJP (Schalk) Ferreira	Toulouse	France
	SR (Sebastian) Ferreira	Saracens	England
	LDVZ (Louis) Fouche	Ricoh Black Rams	Japan
	DA (Deon) Fourie	Lyon O.U.	France
*	J (Jaque) Fourie	Kobe Kobelco Steelers	Japan
	BK (Burton) Francis	Agen	France
+	Q (Quintin) Geldenhuys	Zebre	Italy
	R (Ross) Geldenhuys	Tasman Makos	New Zealand
	D (Dandre) Gerber	Beziers	France
	D (Durandt) Gerber	IMA Lazio	Italy
	RAM (Roy) Godfrey	Perpignan	France
	R (Reggie) Goodes	Hurricanes	New Zealand
		Wellington	New Zealand
*	JL (Johan) Goosen	Racing-Metro 92	France
	W (Wes) Goosen	Wellington	New Zealand
	K (Kieran) Goss	Cornish Pirates	England

SEASON IN 2014

	Player	Club	Country
*	PJ (Peter) Grant	Kobe Kobelco Steelers	Japan
*		La Rochelle	France
	M (Michael) Green	Canterbury	New Zealand
	JA (Cobus) Grobler	La Rochelle	France
	JH (Hans) Grobler	Tarbes	France
	BG (Bryan) Habana	Toulon	France
	T (Thor) Halvorsen	Marchiol Mogliano	Italy
	D (Dean) Hammond	Worcester Warriors	England
*	AJ (Alistair) Hargreaves	Saracens	England
	WJ (Wikus) Harmse	Bourg-en-Bresse	France
	J (Brok) Harris	Newport Gw. Dragons	Wales
	PJ (Petrus) Hauman	Brive	France
	DS (Dane) Haylett-Petty	Toyota Shokki Shuttles	Japan
		Western Force	Australia
		Perth Spirit	Australia
	R (Ross) Haylett-Petty	Perth Spirit	Australia
	C (Chris) Heiberg	Perth Spirit	Australia
	WJ (Wiehahn) Herbst	Ulster	Ireland
+	RW (Rob) Herring	Ulster	Ireland
	EW (Edwin) Hewitt	Biarritz Olympique	France
	WAJ (Willem) Heymans	I Cavalieri Prato	Italy
	CO (Cliffie) Hodgson	Coventry	England
	CF (Conrad) Hoffmann	ACT Brumbies	Australia
+	T (Tyrone) Holmes	Glasgow Warriors	Scotland
	JP (Joubert) Horn	Rugby Viadana	Italy
	A (Andre) Hough	Pau	France
		Albi	France
	PB (Pat) Howard	Munster	Ireland
	A (Alten) Hulme	Grenoble	France
	EA (Rassie) Jansen v Vuuren	La Rochelle	France
	JC (JC) Janse van Rensburg	Bayonne	France
*	ET (Elton) Jantjies	NTT Shining Arcs	Japan
*	ER (Ricky) Januarie	Lyon O.U.	France
	J (Jody) Jenneker	Oyonnax	France
	AF (Ashley) Johnson	Wasps	England
	G (Gavin) Jones	Blaydon	England
	R (Ross) Jones-Davies	Jersey	England
	EW (Wessel) Jooste	Agen	France
	CM (Chris) Jordaan	Petrarca Padova	Italy
	E (Ernst) Joubert	Saracens	England
*	R (Ryan) Kankowski	Toyota Shokki Shuttles	Japan
	JB (Kobus) Kemp	Aurillac	France
*	Z (Zane) Kirchner	Leinster	Ireland
	C (Clynton) Knox	Queensland Country	Australia
+	RM (Rory) Kockott	Castres Olympique	France
	RN (Nick) Koster	Bristol	England
+	DM (Dan) Kotze	Clermont Auvergne	France
	M (Marco) Kotze	Brisbane City	Australia
	AG (Andries) Kruger	Carcassonne	France
	OC (Okkie) Kruger	Dax	France
*	PJJ (Juandre) Kruger	Racing-Metro 92	France
	B (Brad) Lacey	Perth Spirit	Australia
	RJ (Rynard) Landman	Newport Gw Dragons	Wales
+	B (Bernard) le Roux	Racing-Metro 92	France
+	JE (Jacques) le Roux	Coventry	England
	DY (Dill) Leyds	Western Force	Australia
		Perth Spirit	Australia
	PL (Vickus) Liebenberg	Mont-de-Marsan	France

	Player	Club	Country
*	LFP (Francois) Louw	Bath	England
	L (Louis) Ludik	Agen	France
		Ulster	Ireland
	A (Ali) Lyon	Richmond	England
*	C (Charl) McLeod	Grenoble	France
	SJ (Shaun) Malton	Nottingham	England
	T (Thabo) Mamojele	Montauban	France
	JA (Jandre) Marais	Bordeaux-Begles	France
	PC (Peet) Marais	Brive	France
+	K (Kotaro) Matsushima	Suntory Sungoliath	Japan
+	RJG (Justin) Melck	Saracens	England
	WG (Jakes) Mjekevu	Perpignan	France
	W (Wouter) Moore	Beziers	France
*	G (Gerhard) Mostert	Stade Francais Paris	France
	GH (Gert) Muller	Bayonne	France
*	GJ (Johann) Muller	Ulster	Ireland
	J (Jacques) Naude	Dax	France
	WP (WP) Nel	Edinburgh	Scotland
*	W (Wynand) Olivier	Montpellier	France
	RJ (Richard) Palframan	Ealing Trailfinders	England
		Worthing Raiders	England
		Rosslyn Park	England
		London Irish	England
	J (Jeff) Perkins	Colomiers	France
	BJM (Ben) Pienaar	London Welsh	England
		Rosslyn Park	England
*	R (Ruan) Pienaar	Ulster	Ireland
	JC (Joe) Pietersen	Biarritz Olympique	France
*	JPR (JP) Pietersen	Panasonic Wild Knights	Japan
	DJ (Danie) Poolman	Connacht	Ireland
*	DJ (Dewald) Potgieter	Yamaha Jubilo	Japan
	JL (Jacques-Louis) Potgieter	Dax	France
*	UJ (Jacques) Potgieter	NSW Waratahs	Australia
		Fukuoka Sanix Blues	Japan
*	AS (Andre) Pretorius	Carcassonne	France
*	MC (Chiliboy) Ralepelle	Toulouse	France
+	C (Clyde) Rathbone	ACT Brumbies	Australia
	BC (Bryan) Rennie	Bristol	England
	E (Ethienne) Reynecke	Pau	France
	SMK (Shannon) Rick	Albi	France
	R (Reuben) Rolleston	Melbourne Rising	Australia
	HL (Hendrik) Roodt	Grenoble	France
*	DJ (Danie) Rossouw	Toulon	France
	A (Armand) Roux	Dorking	England
	Q (Quinn) Roux	Leinster	Ireland
		Connacht	Ireland
	J (Johann) Sadie	NTT Docomo	
		Red Hurricanes	Japan
	JA (Jarrod) Saffy	Bourg-en-Bresse	France
	JJ (Jared) Saunders	Saracens	England
		Plymouth Albion	England
		Bedford Blues	England
	NP (Nick) Schonert	Worcester Warriors	England
	DM (Dewald) Senekal	Bayonne	France
	BC (Brett) Sharman	Saracens	England
	RC (Ross) Skeate	Agen	France
		Grenoble	France
	R (Rayn) Smid	I Cavalieri Prato	Italy

SEASON IN 2014

	Player	Club	Country
	AJ (Riaan) Smit	Oyonnax	France
*	JH (Juan) Smith	Toulon	France
	JP (Jean-Pierre) Smith	ACT Brumbies	Australia
		Canberra Vikings	Australia
	RH (Ruan) Smith	ACT Brumbies	Australia
		Canberra Vikings	Australia
	BM (Brendon) Snyman	Montauban	France
	J (Joe) Snyman	Scarlets	Wales
+	SL (Scott) Spedding	Bayonne	France
	B (Brynard) Stander	Western Force	Australia
		Perth Spirit	Australia
	CJ (CJ) Stander	Munster	Ireland
*	GG (Gurthro) Steenkamp	Toulouse	France
	JWA (Wilhelm) Steenkamp	Western Force	Australia
+	MJH (Matt) Stevens	Saracens	England
	AJ (Braam) Steyn	Cammi Calvisano	Italy
		Zebre	Italy
*	FPL (Frans) Steyn	Toshiba Brave Lupus	Japan
*	M (Morne) Steyn	Stade Francais Paris	France
	AJ (Andries) Strauss	Edinburgh	Scotland
+	CR (Richardt) Strauss	Leinster	Ireland
	JZ (Josh) Strauss	Glasgow Warriors	Scotland
	NJ (Nic) Strauss	Narbonne	France
	M (Mark) Swanepoel	Gr. Sydney Rams	Australia
	M (Meyer) Swanepoel	Marchiol Mogliano	Italy
		Benetton Treviso	Italy
	R (Riaan) Swanepoel	Brive	France
+	RM (Rhys) Thomas	Carmarthen Quins	Wales
	MJ (Morgan) Thompson	Ealing Trailfinders	England
	M (Martin) Thomsen	Fiamme Oro Roma	Italy
+	GA (Greig) Tonks	Edinburgh	Scotland
	JS (Justin) Turner	Western Force	Australia
		Perth Spirit	Australia
	GJ (Gerhard) vd Heever	Munster	Ireland
*	CJ (CJ) van der Linde	London Irish	England
+	DTH (DTH) van der Merwe	Glasgow Warriors	Scotland
*	F (Franco) van der Merwe	Ulster	Ireland
	FC (Francois) vd Merwe	Racing-Metro 92	France
*	HS (Heinke) vd Merwe	Stade Francais Paris	France
	CP (Philip) van der Walt	Biarritz Olympique	France
	PW (Wimpie) vd Walt	NTT Docomo	
		Red Hurricanes	Japan
	S (Stephan) vd Walt	ACT Brumbies	Australia
	IP (Izak) vd Westhuizen	Edinburgh	Scotland
	MRS (Pellow) vd Westhuizen	Colomiers	France
	JP (Johan) van Heerden	Bucuresti Wolves	Romania
	RJ (Roan) van Heerden	Coventry	England
		Broadstreet	England
	R (Ruahan) van Jaarsveld	Rugby Viadana	Italy
		Dax	France
	J (Joe) van Niekerk	FemiCZ Rovigo	Italy
		Benetton Treviso	Italy
*	JC (Joe) van Niekerk	Toulon	France
	AJ (Dries) van Schalkwyk	Zebre	Italy
	E (Eugene) van Staden	Biarritz Olympique	France
	GJ (GJ) van Velze	Northampton Saints	England
		Worcester Warriors	England
	M (Michael) van Vuuren	Zebre	Italy
		Marchiol Mogliano	Italy
	MT (Mike) van Vuuren	Stade Francais Paris	France
	FD (Francois) van Wyk	Western Force	Australia
	A (Anton) van Zyl	Stade Francais Paris	France
+	CC (Cornelius) van Zyl	Benetton Treviso	Italy
	KD (Kayle) van Zyl	Marchiol Mogliano	Italy
	D (Darryl) Veenendaal	Bedford Blues	England
	DLR (De la Rey) Veenendaal	Cambridge	England
*	J (Jano) Vermaak	Toulouse	France
	FJN (Frans) Viljoen	Lyon OU	France
	R (Riaan) Viljoen	NTT Docomo	
		Red Hurricanes	Japan
	G (Gerhard) Vosloo	Clermont Auvergne	France
		Toulon	France
	B (Brandon) Walker	Esher	England
*	PJ (Pedrie) Wannenburg	Castres Olympique	France
		Oyonnax	France
	LR (Lorne) Ward	Rosslyn Park	England
	C (Carl) Wegner	Stade Francais Paris	France
	G (Gerhard) Wessels	Shelford	England
	PJ (Johan) Wessels	La Rochelle	France
	B (Brett) Wilkinson	Connacht	Ireland
	P (Paul) Willemse	Grenoble	France
	MJ (Matt) Williams	Moseley	England
	C (Cameron) Zeiss	Esher	England

SEASON IN 2014

Who's Who of First-Class Rugby

*A complete list of all 866 players who appeared in a first-class match for a South African team in 2014.
Note: The list also includes those players who represented the Springbok Sevens team.*

Abrahams, Keenan Marc (Klein Nederburg HS, Paarl) b 07/08/1991, Paarl. 1.89m. 140kg. Prop. FC DEBUT: 2013. PROV CAREER: Boland 2013-14 4-0-0-0-0-0. FC RECORD: 4-0-0-0-0-0. RECORD IN 2014: (Boland) 3-0-0-0-0-0.
Abrahams, Yuseph Williams (Boela) (Hentie Cilliers HS, Virginia) b 23/07/1988, Port Elizabeth. 1.63m. 65kg. Scrumhalf. FC DEBUT: 2007. PROV CAREER: Griffons 2007-08 & 14 14-5-0-0-1-28. EP Kings 2011-13 20-0-0-0-0-0. REP HONOURS: SA Kings 2011 2-0-0-0-0-0. SA Barbarians 2012 1-0-0-0-0-0. FC RECORD: 37-5-0-0-1-28. RECORD IN 2014: (Griffons) 10-5-0-0-1-28.
Ackerman, Justin (Paarl Boys"HS) b 17/03/1992, Johannesburg. 1.83m. 112kg. Prop. FC DEBUT: 2014. PROV CAREER: WP 2014 2-0-0-0-0-0. FC RECORD: 2-0-0-0-0-0. RECORD IN 2014: (WP) 2-0-0-0-0-0.
Adendorff, Jonathan Wallis (Napier HS & US) b 23/08/1985, Napier. 1.91m. 102kg. Flank. FC DEBUT: 2011. PROV CAREER: Pumas 2011 5-0-0-0-0-0. Griquas 2012-14 38-5-0-0-0-25. FC RECORD: 43-5-0-0-0-25. RECORD IN 2014: (Griquas) 19-3-0-0-0-15.
Adendorff, Shaun (Glenwood HS, Durban & UP) b 28/05/1992, Durban. 1.85m. 100kg. Flank. FC DEBUT: 2012. PROV CAREER: Blue Bulls 2013 3-0-0-0-0-0. REP HONOURS: SA U20 2012 3-2-0-0-0-10. SA Sevens 2014. FC RECORD: 6-2-0-0-0-10. RECORD IN 2014: (SA Sevens).
Adriaanse, Lourens Cornelius (Paarl Gym. & US) b 05/02/1988, Cape Town. 1.80m. 115kg. Prop. FC DEBUT: 2009. PROV CAREER: Griquas 2011-13 37-3-0-0-0-15. KZN 2014 11-3-0-0-0-15. SUPER RUGBY: Cheetahs 2011-13 30-0-0-0-0-0. Sharks 2014 18-0-0-0-0-0. REP HONOURS: SA 2013 1-0-0-0-0-0. SA Students 2009 2-0-0-0-0-0. Barbarians 2014 2-0-0-0-0-0. MISC INFO: Brother of Jacobie Adriaanse (Golden Lions). FC RECORD: 101-6-0-0-0-30. RECORD IN 2014: (Sharks, KZN, Barbarians) 31-3-0-0-0-15.
Afrika, Cecil Sebastian (Hentie Cilliers HS, Virginia) b 03/03/88, Port Elizabeth. 1.77m. 65kg. Fullback. FC DEBUT: 2006. PROV CAREER: Griffons 2006-09 48-36-2-0-1-187. REP HONOURS: SA U20 2008 4-1-0-0-0-5. SA Sevens 2009-14. SA Schools 2006. MISC INFO: IRB Sevens PoY 2010 -11. SARU Sevens PoY 2012. FC RECORD: 52-37-2-0-1-192. RECORD IN 2014: (SA Sevens).
Agaba, Timothy Ernest Victor Kwizera (Stirling HS, East London & NMMU) b 23/07/1989, Kampala. 1.93m. 106kg. Eighthman. FC DEBUT: 2013. PROV CAREER: EP Kings 2013-14 15-2-0-0-0-10. REP HONOURS: SA Univ 2013 1-0-0-0-0-0. FC RECORD: 16-2-0-0-0-10. RECORD IN 2014: (EP Kings) 3-0-0-0-0-0.
Alberts, Gert Dirk Jacobus (Jacques) (Helpmekaar HS, Johannesburg) b 17/01/1991, Johannesburg. 2.02m. 98kg. Lock. FC DEBUT: 2011. PROV CAREER: Valke 2011-14 48-1-0-0-0-5. FC RECORD: 48-1-0-0-0-5. RECORD IN 2014: (Valke) 16-0-0-0-0-0.
Alberts, Willem Schalk (Monument HS, Krugersdorp) b 05/11/1984, Pretoria. 1.91m. 119kg. Flank. FC DEBUT: 2005. PROV CAREER: Lions 2005 & 07-09 35-7-0-0-0-35. Lions XV 2007-08 2-1-0-0-0-5. Young Lions 2005 3-0-0-0-0-0. KZN 2010-13 19-4-0-0-0-20. Sharks XV 2013 2-2-0-0-0-10. SUPER RUGBY: Lions 2007-09 37-4-0-0-0-20. Sharks 2010-14 66-8-0-0-0-40. REP HONOURS: SA 2010-14 Tests: 32-7-0-

0-0-35. Tour: 1-0-0-0-0-0. Total: 33-7-0-0-0-35. Springbok XV 2014 1-0-0-0-0-0. FC RECORD: 198-33-0-0-0-165. RECORD IN 2014 (SA, Springbok XV, Sharks) 21-3-0-0-0-15.
Am, Lukhanyo (De Vos Malan HS, King William's Town) b 28/11/1993, King William's Town. 1.86m. 93kg. Centre. FC DEBUT: 2013. PROV CAREER: Border 2013 2-0-0-0-0-0. Valke 2014 2-1-0-0-0-5. FC RECORD: 4-1-0-0-0-5. RECORD IN 2014: (Valke) 2-1-0-0-0-5.
Annandale, Gavin Barnard (Brandwag HS, Benoni) b 27/04/1989, Welkom. 1.94m. 112kg. Lock. FC DEBUT: 2009. PROV CAREER: Valke 2009 5-0-0-0-0-0. Griffons 2010-12 27-2-0-0-0-10. Young Lions 2013 2-0-0-0-0-0. Leopards 2013 1-0-0-0-0-0. Boland 2014 10-0-0-0-0-0. WP 2014 1-0-0-0-0-0. FC RECORD: 46-2-0-0-0-10. RECORD IN 2014: (WP, Boland) 11-0-0-0-0-0.
Aplon, Gio Giaan (Hawston HS) b 06/10/1982, Hermanus. 1.75m. 78kg. Fullback. FC DEBUT: 2005. PROV CAREER: WP 2005-13 95-32-2-0-0-164. SUPER RUGBY: Stormers 2007-08 & 10-14 84-17-0-1-1-91. REP HONOURS: SA 2010-12 Tests: 17-5-0-0-0-25. Tour: 1-0-0-0-0-0. Total: 18-5-0-0-0-25. SA Sevens 2006-07. WP XV 2006 1-2-0-0-0-10. MISC INFO: Try of the Year 2006 (WP vs B Bulls). Super PoY 2011 nominee. FC RECORD: 198-56-2-1-1-290. RECORD IN 2014: (Stormers) 8-1-0-0-0-5.
April, Brendon Terence (Bergrivier HS, Wellington) b 20/12/1983, Paarl. 1.80m. 75kg. Wing. FC DEBUT: 2005. PROV CAREER: Valke 2005-06 32-12-0-0-0-60. Griffons 2007 2-0-0-0-0-0. Boland 2010-14 67-34-0-0-0-170. FC RECORD: 101-46-0-0-0-230. RECORD IN 2014: (Boland) 1-0-0-0-0-0.
April, Garth Graham (Bergrivier HS, Wellington) b 16/07/1991, Cape Town. 1.70m. 74kg. Fullback/Flyhalf. FC DEBUT: 2012. PROV CAREER: Young Lions 2012 5-2-0-0-0-10. Boland 2013-14 6-0-2-0-0-4. FC RECORD: 11-2-2-0-0-14. RECORD IN 2014: (Boland) 2-0-0-0-0-0.
April, Zingisa Nelson (Ithembelihle HS, Port Elizabeth) b 19/06/1990, Port Elizabeth. 1.8m. 100kg. Flank. FC DEBUT: 2014. PROV CAREER: Free State XV 2014 7-6-0-0-0-30. FC RECORD: 7-6-0-0-0-30. RECORD IN 2014: (Free State XV) 7-6-0-0-0-30.
Arends, Riaan Allister (Brandwag HS, Uitenhage, UJ & Wits) b 31/01/1989, Uitenhage. 1.86m. 86kg. Wing. FC DEBUT: 2012. PROV CAREER: Valke 2014 5-5-0-0-0-25. REP HONOURS: SA Students 2012 2-0-0-0-0-0. FC RECORD: 7-5-0-0-0-25. RECORD IN 2014: (Valke) 5-5-0-0-0-25.
Arendse, Ederies (Aloe HS, Cape Town) b 25/11/1987, Cape Town. 1.84m. 78kg. Wing. FC DEBUT: 2009. PROV CAREER: Valke 2009 6-3-0-0-0-15. WP 2011-13 15-5-0-0-0-25. Griquas 2014 22-13-0-0-0-65. FC RECORD: 43-21-0-0-0-105. RECORD IN 2014: (Griquas) 22-13-0-0-0-65.
Arendse, Junaid (Durbanville HS) b 09/07/1988, Cape Town. 1.70m. 82kg. Flyhalf. FC DEBUT: Boland 2014 2-0-0-0-0-0. FC RECORD: 2-0-0-0-0-0. RECORD IN 2014: (Boland) 2-0-0-0-0-0.
Aspeling, Karlo Gericke (Outeniqua HS, George & TUT) b 13/12/1987, George. 1.79m. 88kg. Flyhalf. FC DEBUT: 2012. PROV CAREER: Valke 2012 14-4-25-10-2-106. Border 2013 20-1-11-23-1-

SEASON IN 2014

99. SWD 2014 13-0-33-14-2-114. FC RECORD: 47-5-69-47-5-319. RECORD IN 2014: (SWD) 13-0-33-14-2-114.

Astle, John-Charles (Pionier HS, Vryheid & UFS) b 30/08/1990, Queenstown. 1.98m. 92kg. Lock. FC DEBUT: 2010. PROV CAREER: Cheetahs 2010-11 12-0-0-0-0-0. Free State XV 2012 4-0-0-0-0-0. Boland 2013-14 25-2-0-0-0-10. KZN 2014 8-0-0-0-0-0. FC RECORD: 49-2-0-0-0-10. RECORD IN 2014: (KZN, Boland) 20-1-0-0-0-5.

Baard, Gerard (Outeniqua HS, George) b 29/01/1991, Moorreesburg. 1.83m. 105kg. Prop. FC DEBUT: 2014. PROV CAREER: Griffons 2014 6-0-0-0-0-0. FC RECORD: 6-0-0-0-0-0. RECORD IN 2014: (Griffons) 6-0-0-0-0-0.

Bali, Mlungisi (St Alban's HS, Pretoria) b 01/06/1990, East London. 1.96m. 105kg. Lock. FC DEBUT: 2010. PROV CAREER: Griffons 2013-14 25-0-0-0-0-0. REP HONOURS: SA U20 2010 4-0-0-0-0-0. FC RECORD: 29-0-0-0-0-0. RECORD IN 2014: (Griffons) 12-0-0-0-0-0.

Banda, Masixole (Ithembelihle HS, Port Elizabeth) b 11/06/1988, Port Elizabeth. 1.65m. 69kg. Fullback. FC DEBUT: 2014. PROV CAREER: EP Kings 2014 5-2-3-1-0-21. Border 2014 11-2-16-13-0-81. FC RECORD: 16-4-19-14-0-102. RECORD IN 2014: (EP Kings, Border) 15-4-19-14-0-102.

Barnard, Eben Philip (Brandwag HS, Uitenhage) b 29/01/1992, Paarl. Wing. FC DEBUT: 2013. PROV CAREER: EP Kings 2013-14 9-2-0-0-0-10. FC RECORD: 9-2-0-0-0-10. RECORD IN 2014: (EP Kings) 5-2-0-0-0-10.

Barnes, Ryno Joseph (Paarl Gym.) b 05/11/81, Cape Town. 1.86m. 110kg. Hooker. FC DEBUT: 2006. PROV CAREER: WP 2006 13-0-0-0-0-0. Valke 2007-08 41-5-0-0-0-25. Griquas 2009-14 100-11-0-0-0-55. Cheetahs XV 2010 1-0-0-0-0-0. SUPER RUGBY: Cheetahs 2010-14 34-1-0-0-0-5. REP HONOURS: Royal XV 2009 1-1-0-0-0-5. FC RECORD: 190-18-0-0-0-90. RECORD IN 2014: (Cheetahs SR, Griquas) 22-3-0-0-0-15.

Bashiya, Yves Mulengi Tshiumbi (Capricorn HS) b 13/02/1987, Kinshasa. 1.85m. 107kg. Flanker. FC DEBUT: 2009. PROV CAREER: Valke 2009-10 14-2-0-0-0-10. EP Kings 2009-10 12-1-0-0-0-5. EP Inv XV 2010 1-0-0-0-0-0. Boland 2014 5-0-0-0-0-0. FC RECORD: 32-3-0-0-0-15. RECORD IN 2014: (Boland) 5-0-0-0-0-0.

Basson, Bjorn Alberic (Dale Coll., King William's Town) b 11/02/87, King William's Town. 1.87m. 82kg. Wing. FC DEBUT: 2008. PROV CAREER: Griquas 2008-10 56-47-0-0-0-235. Blue Bulls 2011-14 19-17-0-0-0-85. SUPER RUGBY: Cheetahs 2009-10 9-6-0-0-0-30. Bulls 2011-14 62-23-0-0-0-115. REP HONOURS: SA 2010-13 Tests: 11-3-0-0-0-15. Emerging Springboks 2008-09 4-1-0-0-0-5. Royal XV 2009 1-0-0-0-0-0. MISC INFO: Holds SA record for most tries in a Currie Cup season (21 in 2010 for Griquas). Brother of Logan & Cody Basson. Holds Bulls record for most tries in a season (10 in 2012). FC RECORD: 163-97-0-0-0-435. RECORD IN 2014: (Bulls, Blue Bulls) 20-7-0-0-0-35.

Basson, Cody Anthony (Dale Coll., King William's Town) b 02/07/1991, King William's Town. 1.87m.90kg. Flank. FC DEBUT: 2014. PROV CAREER: Border 2014 2-0-0-0-0-0. MISC INFO: Brother of Bjorn Basson. FC RECORD: 2-0-0-0-0-0. RECORD IN 2014: (Border) 2-0-0-0-0-0.

Basson, Logan Andrew (Dale Coll., King William's Town) b 09/03/1989, King William's Town. 1.91m. 77kg. Flyhalf. FC DEBUT: 2010. PROV CAREER: Border 2010 & 12 19-9-13-13-0-110. Griquas 2010-11 & 13 12-2-8-1-0-29. SWD 2011 2-0-0-0-0-0. Free State XV 2014 3-1-0-0-0-5. MISC INFO: Brother of Bjorn Basson. FC RECORD: 36-12-21-14-0-144. RECORD IN 2014: (Free State XV) 3-1-0-0-0-5.

Bastew, Keelin Weldon Cyril (Maritzburg Coll.) b 06/05/1992, Pietermaritzburg. 1.78m. 85kg. Fullback. FC DEBUT: 2014. PROV CAREER: Sharks XV 2014 2-0-0-0-0-0. FC RECORD: 2-0-0-0-0-0. RECORD IN 2014: (Sharks XV) 2-0-0-0-0-0.

Bax, Liam (Tiger) (St Andrew's Coll., Grahamstown & UCT) b 10/04/1988, East London. 1.84m. 84kg. Centre. FC DEBUT: 2009. PROV CAREER: WP 2009-10 & 14 11-1-0-0-0-5. Super 14: Stormers 2009 1-0-0-0-0-0. FC RECORD: 12-1-0-0-0-5. RECORD IN 2014: (WP) 6-0-0-0-0-0.

Bell, John-Wessel (JW) (Eldoraigne HS, Pretoria & UP) b 18/01/1990, Cape Town. 1.75m. 73kg. Fullback. FC DEBUT: 2011. PROV CAREER: Valke 2011-12 29-12-0-0-0-60. Pumas 2013-14 42-17-0-0-0-85. FC RECORD: 71-29-0-0-0-145. RECORD IN 2014: (Pumas) 17-2-0-0-0-10.

Benjamin, Ryno Shannon (Weston HS, Vredenburg) b 03/08/83, St Helena Bay. 1.84m. 83kg. Wing. FC DEBUT: 2004. PROV CAREER: Boland 2004-06 42-35-0-0-0-175. Lions 2007-08 23-13-0-0-0-65. Lions XV 2008 1-1-0-0-0-5. Cheetahs 2011-14 26-6-0-0-0-30. Emerging Cheetahs 2011 1-1-0-0-0-5. SUPER RUGBY: Stormers 2006 11-2-0-0-0-10. Lions 2008 12-2-0-0-0-10. Cheetahs 2011-14 41-10-0-0-0-50. REP HONOURS: SA Sevens 2005-07 & 13-14. FC RECORD: 157-70-0-0-0-350. RECORD IN 2014: (Cheetahs SR, Cheetahs) 20-7-0-0-0-35.

Bernardo, Rynier Mark (Framesby HS, Port Elizabeth) b 27/08/1991, Pretoria. 1.99m. 102kg. Lock. FC DEBUT: 2012. PROV CAREER: EP Kings 2012-14 19-0-0-0-0-0. SUPER RUGBY: Southern Kings 2013 10-0-0-0-0-0. FC RECORD: 29-0-0-0-0-0. RECORD IN 2014: (EP Kings) 2-0-0-0-0-0.

Bernardt, Michael Rudger Gerardus (Oakdale HS, Riversdale) b 19/03/1993, Cape Town. 1.85m. 94kg. Centre. FC DEBUT: 2014. PROV CAREER: EP Kings 2014 2-0-0-0-0-0. FC RECORD: 2-0-0-0-0-0. RECORD IN 2014: (EP Kings) 2-0-0-0-0-0.

Bester, Alwyn (Boland Agric HS, Paarl) b 15/04/87, Vredendal. 1.93m. 105kg. Eighthman. FC DEBUT: 2009. PROV CAREER: Boland 2009 & 2011-13 64-10-0-0-0-50. Pumas 2010 7-1-0-0-0-5. SWD 2014 19-4-0-0-0-20. FC RECORD: 90-15-0-0-0-75. RECORD IN 2014: (SWD) 19-4-0-0-0-20.

Bester, Jan-Francois (Campbell Coll. & UFS) b 12/11/1993, Bloemfontein. 1.84m. 114kg. Hooker. FC DEBUT: 2014. PROV CAREER: Griffons 2014 2-0-0-0-0-0. FC RECORD: 2-0-0-0-0-0. RECORD IN 2014: (Griffons) 2-0-0-0-0-0.

Beukman, Rowayne Elrich (Outeniqua HS, George & NWU) b 05/03/1992, Mossel Bay. 1.77m. 88kg. Wing. FC DEBUT: 2014. PROV CAREER: Leopards 2014 2-0-0-0-0-0. Leopards XV 2014 7-3-0-0-0-15. FC RECORD: 9-3-0-0-0-15. RECORD IN 2014: (Leopards, Leopards XV) 9-3-0-0-0-15.

Beyers, Ulrich (Ermelo HS) b 22/01/1991, Pretoria. 1.89m. 87kg. Fullback. FC DEBUT: 2011. PROV CAREER: Blue Bulls 2011-14 34-4-1-0-1-25. SUPER RUGBY: Bulls 2013-14 10-0-0-0-0-0. REP HONOURS: SA U20 2011 4-0-0-0-0-0. FC RECORD: 48-4-1-0-1-25. RECORD IN 2014: (Bulls, Blue Bulls) 15-1-0-0-0-5.

Bezuidenhout, Martin Johannes (Klerksdorp HS & UJ) b 21/08/1989, Orkney. 1.82m. 102kg. Hooker. FC DEBUT: 2010. PROV CAREER: Golden Lions 2010-13 33-1-0-0-0-5. Young Lions 2010-11 10-1-0-0-0-5. Griquas 2014 23-3-0-0-0-15. SUPER RUGBY: Lions 2011-12 24-3-0-0-0-15. Lions P/R 2013 2-0-0-0-0-0. Stormers 2013 8-0-0-0-0-0. FC RECORD: 100-8-0-0-0-40. RECORD IN 2014: (Griquas) 23-3-0-0-0-15.

Bezuidenhout, Stephanus Marthinus (Stephan) (HTS Potchefstroom) b 10/05/1986, Vereeniging. 1.85m. 128kg. Prop. FC DEBUT: 2011. PROV CAREER: Leopards 2011-14 43-1-0-0-0-5. Leopard XV 2013-14 9-1-0-0-0-5. FC RECORD: 52-2-0-0-0-10. RECORD IN 2014:

(Leopards, Leopard XV) 12-1-0-0-0-5.

Bholi, Thembelani (Jamangile HS, Maclear) b 18/01/1990, East London. 1.95m. 92kg. Eighthman. FC DEBUT: 2013. PROV CAREER: EP Kings 2013-14 19-0-0-0-0-0. FC RECORD: 19-0-0-0-0-0. RECORD IN 2014: (EP Kings) 15-0-0-0-0-0.

Binneman, Frederick Johannes (FJ) b 13/11/1991. Hooker. FC DEBUT: 2012. PROV CAREER: Border 2012 1-0-0-0-0-0. Valke 2014 5-0-0-0-0-0. FC RECORD: 6-0-0-0-0-0. RECORD IN 2014: (Valke) 5-0-0-0-0-0.

Blignaut, Hendrik Nikolai (Boys'ville HS) b 10/01/1985, East London. 1.95m. 101kg. Lock. FC DEBUT: 2005. PROV CAREER: KZN 2005-09 16-1-0-0-0-5. Sharks XV 28-2-0-0-0-10. KZN XV 2007 1-0-0-0-0-0. Boland 2010 14-1-0-0-0-5. REP HONOURS: Emerging Springboks 2007 2-0-0-0-0-0. SA U21 2005-06 10-0-0-0-0-0. FC RECORD: 71-4-0-0-0-20. RECORD IN 2014: (Sharks XV) 4-0-0-0-0-0.

Blommetjies, Clayton (New Orleans SSS, Paarl & UP) b 30/08/1990, Paarl. 1.85m. 75kg. Wing. FC DEBUT: 2009. PROV CAREER: Blue Bulls 2011-14 41-12-0-0-0-60. Cheetahs 2014 7-2-0-0-0-10. REP HONOURS: SA Students 2009 1-2-0-0-0-10. SA U20 2009 2-0-0-0-0-0. SA Sevens 2012. FC RECORD: 51-16-0-0-0-80. RECORD IN 2014: (Blue Bulls, Cheetahs) 16-6-0-0-0-30.

Bock, Alshaun Gerswon (Weltevrede HS, Wellington) b 16/05/1982, Wellington. 1.79m. 78kg. Wing. FC DEBUT: 2002. PROV CAREER: Boland 2002-04 & 07-08 38-19-0-0-0-95. Griquas 2005-06 22-13-0-0-0-65. WP 2009 1-1-0-0-0-5. SWD 2012-14 48-41-0-0-0-205. REP HONOURS: SA Pres XV 2013 3-2-0-0-0-10. SA Sevens 2003; SA U21 2003 5-9-0-0-0-45. FC RECORD: 117-85-0-0-0-425. RECORD IN 2014: (SWD) 13-12-0-0-0-60.

Boloko, Ofense Arthur (Selborne Coll., East London) b 12/05/1992, Pretoria. 1.80m. 85kg. Wing. FC DEBUT: 2014. PROV CAREER: EP Kings 2014 2-0-0-0-0-0. FC RECORD: 2-0-0-0-0-0. RECORD IN 2014: (EP Kings) 2-0-0-0-0-0.

Bondesio, Michael (Lichtenburg HS) b 10/03/85, Middelburg. 1.76m. 84kg. Scrumhalf. FC DEBUT: 2008. PROV CAREER: Leopards 2008-10 52-13-0-0-0-65. Lions 2011-13 25-0-0-0-0-0. Young Lions 2011 & 13-14 17-4-0-0-0-20. SUPER RUGBY: Lions 2012 7-1-0-0-0-5. FC RECORD: 101-18-0-0-0-90. RECORD IN 2014: (Young Lions) 3-0-0-0-0-0.

Booi, Ayabonga Ludwe (Pretoria THS & UFH) b 14/05/1987, Butterworth. 1.79m. 90kg. Wing. FC DEBUT: 2010. PROV CAREER: Border 2010 & 14 12-0-0-0-0-0. FC RECORD: 12-0-0-0-0-0. RECORD IN 2014: (Border) 10-0-0-0-0-0.

Boonzaaier, Abraham Johannes Stefanus (Barnie) b 19/04/1992. Hooker. FC DEBUT: 2014. PROV CAREER: Limpopo 2014 6-0-0-0-0-0. FC RECORD: 6-0-0-0-0-0. RECORD IN 2014: (Limpopo) 6-0-0-0-0-0.

Bosch, Christopher (Paarl Gym.) b 27/03/1992, Pretoria. 1.83m. 90kg. Centre. FC DEBUT: 2013. PROV CAREER: Blue Bulls 2013 1-0-0-0-0-0. Boland 2014 10-0-0-0-0-0. FC RECORD: 11-0-0-0-0-0. RECORD IN 2014: (Boland) 10-0-0-0-0-0.

Boshoff, Marnitz Louis (Nelspruit HS & UP) b 11/01/89, Nelspruit. 1.76m. 78kg. Flyhalf. FC DEBUT: 2009. PROV CAREER: Blue Bulls 2009-11 24-3-23-21-2-130. Griquas 2012 13-0-11-5-0-37. Lions 2013-14 17-2-33-28-1-163. Young Lions 2013 6-0-18-16-4-96. SUPER RUGBY: Lions 2014 16-0-18-43-8-189. Lions P/R 2013 1-0-0-0-0-0. REP HONOURS: SA 2014 Tests: 1-0-1-0-0-2. Barbarians 2014 2-1-7-0-0-19. FC RECORD: 80-6-111-113-15-636. RECORD IN 2014: (SA, Lions SR, Lions, Barbarians) 25-1-39-57-9-281.

Botes, Louis Jacques (Jacques) (Potchefstroom Gym.) b 12/04/80, Johannesburg. 1.81m. 97kg. Loose forward. FC DEBUT: 2002. PROV CAREER: Pumas 2002-04 42-6-0-0-0-30. KZN 2005-14 130-43-0-0-0-215. Sharks XV 3-1-0-0-0-5. Sharks Inv XV 2009-10 2-5-1-0-0-27. SUPER RUGBY: Sharks 2005-14 115-27-0-0-0-135. REP HONOURS: Emerging Springboks 2009 1-0-0-0-0-0. Barbarians 2014 1-1-1-0-0-5. FC RECORD: 294-83-2-0-0-419. RECORD IN 2014: (Sharks, KZN, Sharks XV, Barbarians) 14-3-1-0-0-17.

Botes, Wietz Tobias (Tobie) (Boland Agric., Paarl) b 26/04/1984, Worcester. 1.81m. 86kg. Scrumhalf. FC DEBUT: 2004. PROV CAREER: Boland 2004 2-0-0-0-0-0. Griquas 2006-08 45-11-21-1-0-100. EP Kings 2014 8-1-1-0-0-7. SUPER RUGBY: Cheetahs 2008 3-0-0-0-0-0. FC RECORD: 58-12-22-1-0-107. RECORD IN 2014: (EP Kings) 8-1-1-0-0-7.

Botha, Bernardo Carl (Florida HS, Roodepoort) b 04/07/88, Oudtshoorn. 1.81m. 86kg. Wing. FC DEBUT: 2009. PROV CAREER: Young Lions 2009-10 8-4-0-0-0-20. Griffons 2013 5-0-0-0-0-0. Pumas 2014 6-2-1-0-0-12. SUPER RUGBY: Lions 2010 2-0-0-0-0-0. Rep. honours: SA Sevens 2010-13. FC RECORD: 21-6-1-0-0-32. RECORD IN 2014: (Pumas) 6-2-1-0-0-12.

Botha, John Philip (Bakkies) (Vereeniging THS/Middelburg THS) b 22/09/79, Newcastle. 2.02m. 118kg. Lock. FC DEBUT: 1999. PROV CAREER: Valke 1999-2000 22-2-1-0-0-12. Blue Bulls 2001-02 & 04-05 & 09-10 53-10-0-0-0-50. SUPER RUGBY: Bulls 2002-11 100-11-0-0-0-55. REP HONOURS: SA 2002-05 & 07-11 & 13-14 Tests: 85-7-0-0-0-35. 2010 Tour: 1-1-0-0-0-5. Total: 86-8-0-0-0-40. Springbok XV 2014 1-1-0-0-0-5. SA 'A' 2001-03 6-1-0-0-0-5; SA U23 2001 3-1-0-0-0-5; SA Schools 1998 (captain); CW Pumas 1997. Barbarians 2008 1-0-0-0-0-0. MISC INFO: PoY nominee 2003, 2004, 2005. Locked together with Victor Matfield in 63 Tests (world record). FC RECORD: 272-33-1-0-0-167. RECORD IN 2014: (SA, Springbok XV) 8-0-0-0-0-0.

Botha, Chrysander Antonio (Walvis Bay HS) b 13/07/1988, Walvis Bay. 1.88m. 72kg. Fullback. SA FC DEBUT: 2010. PROV CAREER: Valke 2010 11-3-0-3-0-24. Lions 2013 6-0-0-0-0-0. Young Lions 2013-14 9-7-1-0-0-37. SUPER RUGBY: Lions 2014 9-0-0-0-0-0. Lions P/R 2013 2-0-0-0-0-0. SA FC RECORD: 37-10-1-3-0-61. REP HONOURS: Namibia. RECORD IN 2014: (Lions SR, Young Lions) 13-2-0-0-0-10.

Botha, Justin Joan (Monument HS, Krugersdorp & NWU) b 29/04/1989, Germiston. 1.77m. 87kg. Flyhalf. FC DEBUT: 2014. PROV CAREER: Leopards XV 2014 3-0-0-0-1-3. FC RECORD: 3-0-0-0-1-3. RECORD IN 2014: (Leopards XV) 3-0-0-0-1-3.

Botha, Philip Rudolph (Grey Coll., Bloemfontein & UFS) b 15/01/1993, Johannesburg. 1.85m. 119kg. Prop. FC DEBUT: 2014. PROV CAREER: Cheetahs 2014 6-0-0-0-0-0. FC RECORD: 6-0-0-0-0-0. RECORD IN 2014: (Cheetahs) 6-0-0-0-0-0.

Botha, Pieter Willem (PW) (Ficksburg HS) b 24/05/1991, Durban. 1.85m. 105kg. Prop. FC DEBUT: 2014. PROV CAREER: Griffons 2014 11-0-0-0-0-0. FC RECORD: 11-0-0-0-0-0. RECORD IN 2014: (Griffons) 11-0-0-0-0-0.

Botha, Renier (Diamantveld HS, Kimberley) b 28/09/1992, Bloemfontein. 1.73m. 73kg. Scrumhalf. FC DEBUT: 2014. PROV CAREER: Free State XV 2014 8-3-0-0-0-15. FC RECORD: 8-3-0-0-0-15. RECORD IN 2014: (Free State XV) 8-3-0-0-0-15.

Botha, Ruan (Jeugland HS, Kempton Park) b 10/01/1992, Brakpan. 2.03m. 113kg. Lock. FC DEBUT: 2012. PROV CAREER: Young Lions 2012 1-0-0-0-0-0. WP 2013-14 8-1-0-0-0-5. SUPER RUGBY: Lions 2012 5-0-0-0-0-0. Stormers 2014 12-1-0-0-0-5. REP HONOURS: SA U20 2012 5-0-0-0-0-0. FC RECORD: 31-2-0-0-0-10. RECORD IN 2014: (Stormers, WP) 19-1-0-0-0-5.

Botha, Tom (Paul Roos Gym., Stellenbosch) b 31/08/1990, Belville.

1.79m. 110kg. Prop. FC DEBUT: 2011. PROV CAREER: WP 2011-12 17-0-0-0-0-0. EP Kings 2014 6-0-0-0-0-0. FC RECORD: 23-0-0-0-0-0. RECORD IN 2014: (EP Kings) 6-0-0-0-0-0.
Bothma, Renaldo (Volkskool Heidelberg) b 18/09/1989, Alberton. 1.87m. 100kg. Flank. FC DEBUT: 2010. PROV CAREER: Golden Lions 2010 7-2-0-0-0-10. Young Lions 2011 6-1-0-0-0-5. Leopards 2011 1-0-0-0-0-0. Pumas 2012-14 54-22-0-0-0-110. REP HONOURS: SA Pres XV 2013 2-1-0-0-0-5. FC RECORD: 70-26-0-0-0-130. RECORD IN 2014: (Pumas) 17-7-0-0-0-35.
Bouwer, Molotsi Elias (Potchefstroom HS & NWU) b 11/08/1991, Potchefstroom. 1.9m. 109kg. Flank. FC DEBUT: 2014. PROV CAREER: Leopards 2014 4-0-0-0-0-0. Leopards XV 2014 7-0-0-0-0-0. FC RECORD: 11-0-0-0-0-0. RECORD IN 2014: (Leopards, Leopards XV) 11-0-0-0-0-0.
Bouwer, Willem Sterrenberg Jacobus Marais (Jaco) (Waterkloof HS, Pretoria) b 04/09/85, Kempton Park, 1.84m. 97kg. Flank. FC DEBUT: 2007. PROV CAREER: Leopards 2007-08 34-8-0-0-0-40. Pumas 2009-14 109-46-0-0-0-230. REP HONOURS: SA Pres XV 2013 4-0-0-0-0-0. SA Barbarians 2012 1-0-0-0-0-0. FC RECORD: 148-54-0-0-0-270. RECORD IN 2014: (Pumas) 12-2-0-0-0-10.
Brandt, Alvin b 30/09/1991. Wing. FC DEBUT: 2014. PROV CAREER: Free State XV 2014 4-2-0-0-0-10. FC RECORD: 4-2-0-0-0-10. RECORD IN 2014: (Free State XV) 4-2-0-0-0-10.
Bredenkamp, Eital (Affies, Pretoria) b 28/01/1993, Pretoria. 1.79m. 92kg. Flank. FC DEBUT: 2014. PROV CAREER: WP 2014 6-0-0-0-0-0. FC RECORD: 6-0-0-0-0-0. RECORD IN 2014: (WP) 6-0-0-0-0-0.
Breedt, Jan b 08/07/1988. Flank. FC DEBUT: 2014. PROV CAREER: Griffons 2014 12-0-0-0-0-0. FC RECORD: 12-0-0-0-0-0. RECORD IN 2014: (Griffons) 12-0-0-0-0-0.
Bresler, Anton (Durban HS) b 16/02/1988, Windhoek. 1.97m. 106kg. Lock. FC DEBUT: 2010. PROV CAREER: KZN 2010-12 28-1-0-0-0-5. Sharks XV 2010-11 15-0-0-0-0-0. Sharks Inv XV 2010 1-0-0-0-0-0. SUPER RUGBY: Sharks 2011-14 42-1-0-0-0-5. FC RECORD: 86-2-0-0-0-10. RECORD IN 2014: (Sharks) 8-0-0-0-0-0.
Briedenhann, Marnus (Jim Fouche HS, Bloemfontein) b 24/08/87, Kempton Park. 1.92m. 106kg. Lock. FC DEBUT: 2008. PROV CAREER: Cheetahs 2008-09 15-1-0-0-0-5. Griffons 2009-11 & 13 40-3-0-0-0-15. Free State XV 2013-14 8-0-0-0-0-0. MISC INFO: Brother of Gys Briedenhann. FC RECORD: 63-4-0-0-0-20. RECORD IN 2014: (Free State XV) 2-0-0-0-0-0.
Brink, Cyle Justin (KES, Johannesburg) b 16/01/1994, Johannesburg. 1.83m. 112kg. Flank. FC DEBUT: 2014. PROV CAREER: Young Lions 2014 8-3-0-0-0-15. REP HONOURS: SA U20 2014 5-0-0-0-0-0. FC RECORD: 13-3-0-0-0-15. RECORD IN 2014: (Young Lions, SA U20) 13-3-0-0-0-15.
Brits, Schalk Burger (Paul Roos Gym., Stellenbosch & US) b 16/05/81, Empangeni. 1.82m. 98kg. Hooker. FC DEBUT: 2002. PROV CAREER: WP 2002-03 & 06-08 39-6-0-0-0-30. Lions 2004-05 35-11-0-0-0-55. SUPER RUGBY: Cats 2005 11-0-0-0-0-0. Stormers 2006-09 & 2011 52-4-0-0-0-20. REP HONOURS: SA 2008 & 12 & 14 Tests: 7-0-0-0-0-0. Springbok XV 2014 1-0-0-0-0-0. Emerging Springboks 2007 3-2-0-0-0-10. SA 'A' 2004 3-2-0-0-0-10. WP XV 2006. Barbarians 2007, 09,10,13 5-1-0-0-0-5. SA Schools 1999. MISC INFO: YPoY nominee 2004. FC RECORD: 157-26-0-0-0-130. RECORD IN 2014: (SA, Springbok XV) 3-0-0-0-0-0.
Britz, Rudolph Martinus (Rudi) (Hentie Cilliers HS, Virginia) b 03/03/1989, Virginia. 1.89m. 126kg. Prop. FC DEBUT: 2012. PROV CAREER: Griffons 2012-14 36-2-0-0-0-10. FC RECORD: 36-2-0-0-0-10.

RECORD IN 2014: (Griffons) 6-0-0-0-0-0.
Britz, Willem Stephanus (Willie) (Diamantveld HS, Kimberley & UFS) b 31/08/88, Cape Town. 1.91m. 98kg. FC DEBUT: 2009. PROV CAREER: Cheetahs 2009 & 2011 5-2-0-0-0-10. Griffons 2010-12 28-8-0-0-0-40. Lions 2012-14 32-4-0-0-0-20. Young Lions 2013 7-1-0-0-0-5. Emerging Cheetahs 2011 1-0-0-0-0-0. SUPER RUGBY: Lions 2014 13-0-0-0-0-0. Lions P/R 2013 2-0-0-0-0-0. FC RECORD: 88-15-0-0-0-75. RECORD IN 2014: (Lions SR, Lions) 25-1-0-0-0-5.
Brown, Kyle Gie (SACS, Cape Town & UCT) b 06/02/1987, Cape Town. 1.82m. 96kg. REP HONOURS: SA Sevens 2008-14. RECORD IN 2014: (SA Sevens).
Brüssow, Heinrich Wilhelm (Grey Coll., Bloemfontein) b 21/07/86, Bloemfontein. 1.81m. 103kg. Flank. FC DEBUT: 2006. PROV CAREER: Cheetahs 2006-09 & 2011-12 59-25-0-0-0-125. Cheetahs XV 2010 1-0-0-0-0-0. Free State XV 2014 1-0-0-0-0-0. SUPER RUGBY: Cheetahs 2007-14 76-6-0-0-0-30. REP HONOURS: SA 2008-09 & 2011 Tests: 20-1-0-0-0-5. SA Sevens 2006, SA Schools 2004. Barbarians 2014 2-1-0-0-0-5. MISC INFO: YPoY nominee 2008, PoY Nominee 2009. FC RECORD: 159-33-0-0-0-165. RECORD IN 2014: (Cheetahs SR, Free State XV, Barbarians) 9-1-0-0-0-5.
Brummer, Francois (Waterkloof HS, Pretoria) b 17/05/1989, Pretoria. 1.82m. 90kg. Flyhalf. FC DEBUT: 2008. PROV CAREER: Blue Bulls 2008-11 49-6-66-91-15-480. Griquas 2012-14 56-5-48-34-7-244. SUPER RUGBY: Bulls 2010 1-0-1-0-0-2. Cheetahs 2013 1-0-0-1-0-3. REP HONOURS: SA U20 2008-09 9-3-24-13-1-105. FC RECORD: 116-14-139-139-23-834. RECORD IN 2014: (Griquas) 23-2-10-1-5-48.
Bullbring, David James (Alexander Road HS, Port Elizabeth & UJ) b 12/09//89, Port Elizabeth. 1.98m. 104kg. Lock. FC DEBUT: 2009. PROV CAREER: Golden Lions 2010 7-0-0-0-0-0. Young Lions 2009-11 19-4-0-0-0-20. EP Kings 2012 & 14 30-1-0-0-0-5. Blue Bulls 2013-14 15-3-0-0-0-15. SUPER RUGBY: Lions 2010-11 3-0-0-0-0-0. Southern Kings 2013 16-0-0-0-0-0. P/R 2013 2-0-0-0-0-0. REP HONOURS: SA Barbarians 2012 1-0-0-0-0-0. SA U20 2009 5-0-0-0-0-0. FC RECORD: 98-8-0-0-0-40. RECORD IN 2014: (Blue Bulls, EP Kings) 15-2-0-0-0-10.
Burger, Martinus Abraham (Grey Coll., Bloemfontein & UFS) b 01/11/1993, Rosendal. 1.93m. 104kg. Flank. FC DEBUT: 2014. PROV CAREER: Cheetahs 2014 10-2-0-0-0-10. Free State XV 2014 2-1-0-0-0-5. FC RECORD: 12-3-0-0-0-15. RECORD IN 2014: (Cheetahs, Free State XV) 12-3-0-0-0-15.
Burger, Schalk Willem Petrus (Paarl Gym.) b 13/04/83, Port Elizabeth. 1.93m. 114kg. Flank. FC DEBUT: 2002. PROV CAREER: WP 2003-05 & 08-11 & 13 37-7-0-0-0-35. SUPER RUGBY: Stormers 2004-12 & 14 97-7-0-0-0-35. REP HONOURS: SA 2003-11 & 14 Tests: 75-14-0-0-0-70. Springbok XV 2014 1-0-0-0-0-0. SA U21 2002-03 8-4-0-0-0-20; Barbarians 2004 & 08, 09,13 4-0-0-0-0-0. S Hemisphere XV 2005 1-1-0-0-0-5. MISC INFO: SA PoY 2004. IRB PoY 2004. IRPA PoY & YPoY 2004. Super PoY nominee 2011. SARU PoY 2011. SA YPoY nominee 2003, 2004. Holds SA record for most Tests as a Flank - 73 (also two at No. 8). Son of 1984-86 Springbok SWP (Schalk) Burger. FC RECORD: 223-33-0-0-0-165. RECORD IN 2014: (SA, Springbok XV, Stormers): 17-1-0-0-0-5.
Buys, Ashley Schutte (George HS) b 01/06/79, Blanco. 1.80m. 112kg. Prop. FC DEBUT: 2005. PROV CAREER: SWD 2005-08 & 14 71-3-0-0-0-15. Pumas 2009-12 79-2-0-0-0-10. REP HONOURS: SA Barbarians 2012 1-0-0-0-0-0. FC RECORD: 151-5-0-0-0-25. RECORD IN 2014: (SWD) 13-0-0-0-0-0.
Buys, Jaco (Northern Cape HS, Kimberley & NWU) b 08/01/1993,

Kimberley. 1.86m. 94kg. Eighthman. FC DEBUT: 2014. PROV CAREER: Leopards XV 2014 3-0-0-0-0-0. FC RECORD: 3-0-0-0-0-0. RECORD IN 2014: (Leopards XV) 3-0-0-0-0-0.

Buys, Jarryd Andrew (Selborne Coll., East London & US) b 02/02/1990, Elliot. 1.89m. 91kg. Fullback. FC DEBUT: 2013. PROV CAREER: Leopards 2013 8-4-1-0-0-22. SWD 2014 2-0-0-0-0-0. FC RECORD: 10-4-1-0-0-22. RECORD IN 2014: (SWD) 2-0-0-0-0-0.

Campbell, Duncan (Westville Boys" HS) b 13/02/1992, Westville. 1.78m. 83kg. Flyhalf. FC DEBUT: 2014. PROV CAREER: Sharks XV 2014 1-0-1-0-0-2. FC RECORD: 1-0-1-0-0-2. RECORD IN 2014: (Sharks XV) 1-0-1-0-0-2.

Carizza, Manuel b 23/08/1984, Rosario, Argentina. 2.01m. 117kg. Lock. SA FC DEBUT: 2014. SA PROV CAREER: WP 2014 11-0-0-0-0-0. SUPER RUGBY: Stormers 2014 5-0-0-0-0-0. REP HONOURS: Argentina 2004-13. SA FC RECORD: 16-0-0-0-0-0. RECORD IN 2014: (Stormers, WP) 16-0-0-0-0-0.

Carmichael, Ryan Stuart (Monument HS, Krugersdorp) b 20/04/1993, Roodepoort. 1.70m. 75kg. Scrumhalf. FC DEBUT: 2014. PROV CAREER: Valke 2014 3-0-0-0-0-0. FC RECORD: 3-0-0-0-0-0. RECORD IN 2014: (Valke) 3-0-0-0-0-0.

Carney, Deon (Northern Cape HS, Kimberley) b 30/08/1991, Brits. 1.80m. 84kg. Eighthman. FC DEBUT: 2013. PROV CAREER: Griquas 2013 8-2-0-0-0-10. Leopards 2014 1-1-0-0-0-5. FC RECORD: 9-3-0-0-0-15. RECORD IN 2014: (Leopards) 1-1-0-0-0-5.

Carr, Nizaam (Bishops HS, Rondebosch) b 04/04/1991, Cape Town. 1.84m. 93kg. Flank. FC DEBUT: 2011. PROV CAREER: WP 2011-14 28-5-0-0-0-25. SUPER RUGBY: Stormers 2012-14 37-4-0-0-0-20. REP HONOURS: SA 2014 Tests: 2-0-0-0-0-0. SA U20 2011 4-2-0-0-0-10. MISC INFO: PoY nominee 2014. FC RECORD: 71-11-0-0-0-55. RECORD IN 2014: (SA, Stormers, WP) 29-8-0-0-0-40.

Cassiem, Uzair (Strand HS, Cape Town & Boland Coll.) b 17/03/1990, Strand. 1.89m. 98kg. Flank. FC DEBUT: 2011. PROV CAREER: Young Lions 2012 4-0-0-0-0-0. Golden Lions XV 2011 1-1-0-0-0-5. Valke 2012 3-2-0-0-0-10. Pumas 2012-14 51-13-0-0-0-65. REP HONOURS: SA Pres XV 2013 4-2-0-0-0-10. FC RECORD: 63-18-0-0-0-90. RECORD IN 2014: (Pumas) 18-2-0-0-0-10.

Catrakilis, Demetri (St John's Coll., Johannesburg, UJ & UCT) b 06/09/1989, Johannesburg. 1.76m. 82kg. Flyhalf. FC DEBUT: 2011. PROV CAREER: WP 2011-14 51-1-96-131-9-617. SUPER RUGBY: Southern Kings 2013 14-0-14-37-1-142. P/R 2013 1-0-0-3-0-9. Stormers 2014 8-0-4-12-0-44. MISC INFO: VC PoY 2012. FC RECORD: 74-1-114-183-10-812. RECORD IN 2014: (Stormers, WP) 19-0-34-32-1-167.

Chadwick, Dale Michael (Westville Boys" HS) b 20/06/89, Westville. 1.83m. 105kg. Prop. FC DEBUT: 2009. PROV CAREER: KZN 2009 & 2011-14 43-2-0-0-0-10. Sharks XV 2010-12 13-2-0-0-0-10. Sharks Inv XV 2009 1-0-0-0-0-0. SUPER RUGBY: Sharks 2012 & 14 26-1-0-0-0-5. FC RECORD: 83-5-0-0-0-25. RECORD IN 2014: (Sharks, KZN) 25-1-0-0-0-5.

Chavhanga, Tonderai (Prince Edward, Harare) b 24/12/83, Masvingo, Zimbabwe. 1.84m. 86kg. Wing. FC DEBUT: 2003. PROV CAREER: Cheetahs 2003-04 3-1-0-0-0-5. WP 2005 & 07-09 40-16-0-0-0-80. Golden Lions 2010 1-0-0-0-0-0. Young Lions 2010-11 7-1-0-0-0-5. KZN 2014 8-1-0-0-0-5. Sharks XV 2014 4-0-0-0-0-0. SUPER RUGBY: Stormers 2004-06 & 08-09 37-14-0-0-0-70. Lions 2010 11-2-0-0-0-10. Sharks 2014 5-1-0-0-0-5. REP HONOURS: SA Tests: 2005 & 07-08 4-6-0-0-0-30. Emerging Springboks 2007 2-2-0-0-0-10. SA Sevens 2003. SA U21 2003 3-2-0-0-0-10. Zimbabwe CW 2000-01. FC

RECORD: 125-46-0-0-0-230. RECORD IN 2014: (Sharks, KZN, Sharks XV) 17-2-0-0-0-10.

Chonco, Lungelo (Maritzburg Coll. & US) b 06/08/1992, Pietermaritzburg. 1.87m. 99kg. Lock. FC DEBUT: 2014. PROV CAREER: WP 2014 1-0-0-0-0-0. FC RECORD: 1-0-0-0-0-0. RECORD IN 2014: (WP) 1-0-0-0-0-0.

Chowles, Deacon Godfrey (Hermanus HS & UCT) b 17/10/1993, Hermanus. 1.79m. 107kg. Prop. FC DEBUT: 2014. PROV CAREER: WP 2014 4-0-0-0-0-0. FC RECORD: 4-0-0-0-0-0. RECORD IN 2014: (WP) 4-0-0-0-0-0.

Cilliers, Patric Michael (Michaelhouse HS, Balgowan) b 03/03/87, Pietermaritzburg. 1.85m. 101kg. Prop. FC DEBUT: 2007. PROV CAREER: KZN 2007-10 34-5-0-0-0-25. Sharks XV 2007-10 18-3-0-0-0-15. Sharks Inv XV 2009-10 2-0-0-0-0-0. Lions 2011-12 17-4-0-0-0-20. WP 2013-14 23-1-0-0-0-5. SUPER RUGBY: Sharks 2007 & 09-10 3-0-0-0-0-0. Lions 2011-12 28-1-0-0-0-5. Stormers 2013-14 23-0-0-0-0-0. REP HONOURS: SA 2012 Tests: 6-0-0-0-0-0. Emerging Springboks 2009 1-0-0-0-0-0. FC RECORD: 155-14-0-0-0-70. RECORD IN 2014: (Stormers, WP) 21-1-0-0-0-5.

Claassen, Neil (Daniel Pienaar HS, Uitenhage) b 26/09/1992, Pretoria. 1.94m. 85kg. Lock/Flank. FC DEBUT: 2012. PROV CAREER: Free State XV 2012-14 12-2-0-0-0-10. Cheetahs 2014 10-0-0-0-0-0. FC RECORD: 22-2-0-0-0-10. RECORD IN 2014: (Cheetahs, Free State XV) 13-1-0-0-0-5.

Clarke, Hilford Monray (Northern Cape HS, Kimberley) b 01/01/1994, Paternoster. 1.87m. 76kg. Wing. FC DEBUT: 2014. PROV CAREER: Griquas 2014 1-3-0-0-0-15. FC RECORD: 1-3-0-0-0-15. RECORD IN 2014: (Griquas) 1-3-0-0-0-15.

Cleophas, Angus Andrew (Durbanville HS, Cape Town) b 02/03/1993, Belville. 1.83m. 90kg. Fullback. FC DEBUT: 2014. PROV CAREER: Valke 2014 7-0-4-7-0-29. FC RECORD: 7-0-4-7-0-29. RECORD IN 2014: (Valke) 7-0-4-7-0-29.

Cloete, Wesley Wyndham (Selborne Coll., East London) b 08/02/1990, East London. 1.77m. 100kg. Prop. FC DEBUT: 2012. PROV CAREER: Border 2012-13 34-0-0-0-0-0. Valke 2014 5-0-0-0-0-0. Griquas 2014 1-0-0-0-0-0. FC RECORD: 40-0-0-0-0-0. RECORD IN 2014: (Valke, Griquas) 6-0-0-0-0-0.

Coertzen, Adriaan Jacobus Van der Berg (AJ) (Jim Fouche HS, Bloemfontein & UFS) b 16/10/1990, Bethlehem. 1.85m. 85kg. Fullback/Wing. FC DEBUT: 2011. PROV CAREER: Cheetahs 2011 & 14 9-1-0-0-0-5. FC RECORD: 9-1-0-0-0-5. RECORD IN 2014: (Cheetahs) 6-0-0-0-0-0.

Coetzee, Andre b 28/12/1989. FC DEBUT: 2014. PROV CAREER: Boland 2014 1-0-0-0-0-0. FC RECORD: 1-0-0-0-0-0. RECORD IN 2014: (Boland) 1-0-0-0-0-0.

Coetzee, Andries (Middelburg THS) b 01/03/1990, Bethal. 1.81m. 86kg. Fullback. FC DEBUT: 2011. PROV CAREER: Lions 2012-14 26-6-1-0-0-32. Young Lions 2012-14 3-2-5-0-0-20. Golden Lions XV 2011 1-0-0-0-0-0. SUPER RUGBY: Lions 2012 & 14 15-1-0-0-1-8. Sharks 2013 1-0-0-0-0-0. FC RECORD: 46-9-6-0-1-60. RECORD IN 2014: (Lions SR, Lions, Young Lions) 12-4-0-0-0-20.

Coetzee, Floris Petrus (Marlow Agric. HS, Cradock) b 16/04/1991, Steynsburg. 1.87m. 98kg. Eighthman. FC DEBUT: 2014. PROV CAREER: 5-4-0-0-0-20. FC RECORD: 5-4-0-0-0-20. RECORD IN 2014: (Free State XV) 5-4-0-0-0-20.

Coetzee, Marcell Cornelius (Port Natal HS, Durban) b 08/05/1991, Potchefstroom. 1.90m. 106kg. Loose Forward. FC DEBUT: 2011. PROV CAREER: KZN 2011-13 24-1-0-0-0-5. Sharks XV 2011 8-3-0-0-0-15.

SUPER RUGBY: Sharks 2011-14 54-8-0-0-0-40. **REP HONOURS:** SA 2012-14 Tests: 26-6-0-0-0-30. **MISC INFO:** YPoY 2012 nominee. Super PoY 2012 nominee. PoY nominee 2014. **FC RECORD:** 112-18-0-0-0-90. **RECORD IN 2014:** (SA, Sharks) 26-8-0-0-0-40.

Coetzee, Robin Leendert (Robbie) (Eldoraigne HS, Pretoria) b 02/05/1989, Pretoria. 1.85m. 105kg. Hooker. **FC DEBUT:** 2012. **PROV CAREER:** Blue Bulls 2012 11-1-0-0-0-5. Lions 2013-14 18-2-0-0-0-10. Young Lions 2013 6-1-0-0-0-5. **SUPER RUGBY:** Lions 2014 1-0-0-0-5. Lions P/R 2013 2-0-0-0-0-0. **FC RECORD:** 51-5-0-0-0-25. **RECORD IN 2014:** (Lions SR, Lions) 22-2-0-0-0-10.

Coetzee, Ryno (THS Middelburg & TUT) b 07/09/1988, Middelburg. 1.87m. 105kg. Flank. **FC DEBUT:** 2014. **PROV CAREER:** Boland 2014 8-2-0-0-0-10. **FC RECORD:** 8-2-0-0-0-10. **RECORD IN 2014:** (Boland) 8-2-0-0-0-10.

Coetzee, Stephanus Hendrik (Paarl Boys' HS) b 09/01/1982, Worcester. 1.85m. 105kg. Hooker. **FC DEBUT:** 2013. **PROV CAREER:** WP 2013-14 17-0-0-0-0-0. **SUPER RUGBY:** Stormers 2014 7-0-0-0-0-0. **FC RECORD:** 24-0-0-0-0-0. **RECORD IN 2014:** (Stormers, WP) 16-0-0-0-0-0.

Coetzer, Johannes Machiel b 24/11/1985. Prop. **FC DEBUT:** 2013. **PROV CAREER:** Limpopo 2013-14 13-0-0-0-0-0. **FC RECORD:** 13-0-0-0-0-0. **RECORD IN 2014:** (Limpopo) 6-0-0-0-0-0.

Coetzer, Marius (Waterkloof HS, Pretoria) b 04/04/84, Pretoria. 2.00m. 104kg. Lock. **FC DEBUT:** 2005. **PROV CAREER:** Blue Bulls 2005 1-0-0-0-0-0. WP 2006 5-0-0-0-0-0. Valke 2007-08 26-0-0-0-0-0. Pumas 2009-11 & 13-14 85-10-0-0-0-50. **SUPER RUGBY:** Lions 2012 5-0-0-0-0-0. Stormers 2013 1-0-0-0-0-0. **FC RECORD:** 123-10-0-0-0-50. **RECORD IN 2014:** (Pumas) 18-1-0-0-0-5.

Coleman, Kurt Kendall (Grey HS, Port Elizabeth & US) b 29/01/1990, Knysna. 1.77m. 82kg. Flyhalf. **FC DEBUT:** 2011. **PROV CAREER:** WP 2011-14 52-7-44-50-0-273. SWD 2012 4-0-7-7-0-35. **SUPER RUGBY:** Stormers 2011 & 13-14 15-2-12-16-0-82. **FC RECORD:** 71-9-63-73-0-390. **RECORD IN 2014:** (Stormers, WP) 22-2-21-21-0-115.

Combrink, Ruan Jacobus (Michaelhouse HS, Balgowan) b 10/05/1990, Vryheid. 1.83m. 96kg. Wing. **FC DEBUT:** 2010. **PROV CAREER:** WP 2010 1-0-0-0-0-0. Lions 2012 & 14 21-10-20-14-0-132. Young Lions 2012 & 14 6-3-0-0-0-15. **SUPER RUGBY:** Lions 2012 & 14 13-0-0-1-0-3. P/R 2013 2-0-0-0-0-0. **FC RECORD:** 43-13-20-15-0-150. **RECORD IN 2014:** (Lions SR, Lions, Young Lions) 19-6-20-12-0-106.

Conradie, Ryno Janrich (Langeberg HS) b 08/07/1993, Robertson. 1.75m. 73kg. Wing. **FC DEBUT:** 2014. **PROV CAREER:** Boland 2014 1-0-0-0-0-0. **FC RECORD:** 1-0-0-0-0-0. **RECORD IN 2014:** (Boland) 1-0-0-0-0-0.

Constant, Ashton (Voortrekker HS, Cape Town, UWC) b 28/09/83, Cape Town. 1.82m. 110kg. Hooker. **FC DEBUT:** 2004. **PROV CAREER:** WP 2004-05 5-0-0-0-0-0. Pumas 2006-08 47-6-0-0-0-30. SWD 2009 11-1-0-0-0-5. Boland 2010-14 58-7-0-0-0-35. **REP HONOURS:** Emerging Springboks 2007 3-1-0-0-0-5. SA Pres XV 2013 3-0-0-0-0-0. SA U21 2004 5-1-0-0-0-5. **FC RECORD:** 132-16-0-0-0-80. **RECORD IN 2014:** (Boland) 10-1-0-0-0-5.

Cook, Jean George (Grey Coll., Bloemfontein & UCT) b 14/08/1991, Pietermaritzburg. 1.93m. 102kg. Flank. **FC DEBUT:** 2011. **PROV CAREER:** Cheetahs 2011 & 14 6-1-0-0-0-5. Blue Bulls 2012-13 17-3-0-0-0-15. **SUPER RUGBY:** Bulls 2013 1-1-0-0-0-5. Cheetahs 2014 13-1-0-0-0-5. **REP HONOURS:** SA U20 2011 5-0-0-0-0-0. **FC RECORD:** 42-6-0-0-0-30. **RECORD IN 2014:** (Cheetahs SR, Cheetahs) 18-2-0-0-0-10.

Cooke, Ronald John (Ronnie) (Noord-Kaap HS, Kimberley) b 05/01/85, Pretoria. 1.83m. 79kg. Centre. **FC DEBUT:** 2004. **PROV CAREER:** Leopards 2004-05 26-14-0-0-0-70. Griquas 2006-07 14-3-0-0-0-15. EP Kings 2013-14 15-2-0-0-0-10. **SUPER RUGBY:** Cheetahs 2006-07 24-5-0-0-0-25. Southern Kings 2013 15-2-0-0-0-10. P/R 2013 2-0-0-0-0-0. **REP HONOURS:** SA U21 2005 3-0-0-0-0-0. **FC RECORD:** 99-26-0-0-0-130. **RECORD IN 2014:** (EP Kings) 11-2-0-0-0-10.

Cooper, Kyle Lorran (Glenwood HS, Durban) b 10/02/1989, Johannesburg. 1.77m. 107kg. Hooker. **FC DEBUT:** 2010. **PROV CAREER:** KZN 2010-14 48-2-0-0-0-10. Sharks XV 2010-12 27-2-0-0-0-10. Sharks Inv XV 2010 1-1-0-0-0-5. **SUPER RUGBY:** Sharks 2012-14 30-2-0-0-0-10. **REP HONOURS:** SA U20 2009 5-0-0-0-0-0. **FC RECORD:** 111-7-0-0-0-35. **RECORD IN 2014:** (Sharks, KZN) 23-1-0-0-0-5.

Cornelius, Lionel Curtis (Hermanus HS) b 29/10/86, Hermanus. 1.75m. 91kg. Fullback. **FC DEBUT:** 2007. **PROV CAREER:** Boland 2007-10 56-9-15-18-0-129. SWD 2013-14 5-0-0-0-0-0. **FC RECORD:** 61-9-15-18-0-129. **RECORD IN 2014:** (SWD) 3-0-0-0-0-0.

Crocker, Quinton (Port Natal HS, Durban) b 26/06/1987, Kempton Park. 1.87m. 96kg. Centre. **FC DEBUT:** 2012. **PROV CAREER:** Border 2012-13 32-4-5-2-0-36. Sharks XV 2014 4-0-0-0-0-0. **FC RECORD:** 36-4-5-2-0-36. **RECORD IN 2014:** (Sharks XV) 4-0-0-0-0-0.

Cronje, Coert Frederick (Jeugland HS, Kempton Park & UJ) b 11/05/1988, Vereeniging. 1.82m. 86kg. Centre. **FC DEBUT:** 2010. **PROV CAREER:** Valke 2010-14 72-31-0-0-0-155. **FC RECORD:** 72-31-0-0-0-155. **RECORD IN 2014:** (Valke) 15-5-0-0-0-25.

Cronje, Divan b 16/12/1993. Flank. **FC DEBUT:** 2014. **PROV CAREER:** Limpopo 2014 3-1-0-0-0-5. **FC RECORD:** 3-1-0-0-0-5. **RECORD IN 2014:** (Limpopo) 3-1-0-0-0-5.

Cronje, Guy (Michaelhouse HS, Balgowan) B 26/07/89, Johannesburg. 1.76m. 75kg. Flyhalf. **FC DEBUT:** 2009. **PROV CAREER:** KZN 2009 7-0-3-0-0-6. Sharks XV 2009 & 2011 12-2-16-4-0-54. Sharks Inv XV 2009 1-0-0-0-0-0. Lions 2012-14 10-0-1-0-0-2. Young Lions 2012-14 11-2-26-10-0-92. **SUPER RUGBY:** Lions P/R 2013 2-0-0-0-0-0. **MISC INFO:** Twin brother of Ross Cronje. **FC RECORD:** 43-4-46-14-0-154. **RECORD IN 2014:** (Lions, Young Lions) 7-0-2-1-0-7.

Cronje, Lionel (Queens Coll., Queenstown & UOFS) b 25/05/1989, Bloemfontein. 1.84m. 90kg. Flyhalf. **FC DEBUT:** 2010. **PROV CAREER:** WP 2010-11 21-6-33-13-0-135. Blue Bulls 2012 5-0-0-0-0-0. Lions 2013 5-0-0-0-0-0. Young Lions 2013 5-3-2-0-0-19. KZN 2014 11-1-12-14-0-71. **SUPER RUGBY:** Stormers 2010-11 7-0-4-8-0-32. **REP HONOURS:** SA U20 2009 4-5-2-0-0-29. **MISC INFO:** Vodacom Cup POY 2011. **FC RECORD:** 58-15-53-35-0-286. **RECORD IN 2014:** (KZN) 11-1-12-14-0-71.

Cronje, Ross (Michaelhouse HS, Balgowan) b 26/7/89, Johannesburg. 1.81m. 79kg. Scrumhalf. **FC DEBUT:** 2009. **PROV CAREER:** KZN 2009 & 2011 14-0-0-0-0-0. Sharks XV 2009-11 22-3-11-4-0-49. Lions 2012-14 26-2-0-0-0-10. Young Lions 2012-13 7-0-3-0-0-6. **SUPER RUGBY:** Sharks 2009 1-0-0-0-0-0. Lions 2012 & 14 22-1-0-0-0-5. Lions P/R 2013 1-0-0-0-0-0. **REP HONOURS:** SA U20 2009 5-1-0-0-0-5. **MISC INFO:** Twin brother of Guy Cronje. **FC RECORD:** 98-7-14-4-0-75. **RECORD IN 2014:** (Lions SR, Lions) 26-2-0-0-0-10.

Cummins, Steven b 29/03/1992. 2.01m. 113kg. Lock. **FC DEBUT:** 2014. **PROV CAREER:** EP Kings 2014 8-0-0-0-0-0. **FC RECORD:** 8-0-0-0-0-0. **RECORD IN 2014:** (EP Kings) 8-0-0-0-0-0.

Cupido, Lucien Ronwil (Paarl Boys' HS & NWU) b 21/11/1991, Paarl. 1.74m. 80kg. Wing. **FC DEBUT:** 2014. **PROV CAREER:** Leopards 2014 1-0-0-0-0-0. Leopards XV 2014 2-0-0-0-0-0. **FC RECORD:** 3-0-0-0-0-0. **RECORD IN 2014:** (Leopards, Leopards XV) 3-0-0-0-0-0.

SEASON IN 2014

Cyster, Luke (HTS Louis Botha, Bloemfontein) b 26/12/1994, Cape Town. 1.78m. 79kg. Fullback. FC DEBUT: 2014. PROV CAREER: Free State XV 2014 8-1-0-0-0-5. FC RECORD: 8-1-0-0-0-5. RECORD IN 2014: (Free State XV) 8-1-0-0-0-5.

Dames, Hendrik Daniel Petrus (Danie) (Duineveld HS, Upington) b 07/02/86, Pretoria. 1.90m. 84kg. Utility back. FC DEBUT: 2008. PROV CAREER: Sharks XV 2008-09 12-0-0-0-0-0. Leopards 2009-13 58-22-0-0-0-110. Leopard XV 2013 7-5-0-0-0-25. Griquas 2014 16-2-0-0-0-10. MISC INFO: Represented Namibia at RWC 2011. FC RECORD: 83-29-0-0-0-145. RECORD IN 2014: (Griquas) 16-2-0-0-0-10.

Damon, Mohammed Ridhaa (Spine Road HS, Cape Town & UWC) b 14/05/85, Cape Town. 1.71m. 71kg. Scrumhalf. FC DEBUT: 2006. PROV CAREER: WP 2006 & 14 3-1-0-0-0-5. FC RECORD: 3-1-0-0-0-5. RECORD IN 2014: (WP) 1-0-0-0-0-0.

Daniel, Keegan Rhys (Dale Coll., King William's Town) b 05/03/81, Humansdorp. 1.85m. 100kg. Flank. FC DEBUT: 2006. PROV CAREER: KZN 2006-13 104-33-0-0-0-165. Sharks XV 2006-09 & 14 11-7-0-0-0-35. Sharks Inv XV 2009 10 2-2-1-0-0-12. SUPER RUGBY: Sharks 2006-14 105-16-0-0-0-80. REP HONOURS: SA 2010 & 12 Tests: 5-0-0-0-0-0. Tour: 1-0-0-0-0-0. Total: 6-0-0-0-0-0. SA U21 2006 5-3-0-0-0-15. MISC INFO: U21 PoY 2006, VC PoY 2006, YPoY nominee 2006, IRB YPoY nominee 2006. SARU PoY 2012 nominee. Super PoY 2012. FC RECORD: 233-61-1-0-0-307. RECORD IN 2014: (Sharks, Sharks XV) 11-4-0-0-0-20.

Daniller, Hendrick Joseph (Hennie) (Paarl Gym.) b 05/04/84, Cape Town. 1.95m. 95kg. Fullback. FC DEBUT: 2003. PROV CAREER: Blue Bulls 2003 & 05-06 19-1-0-0-0-5. Boland 2006-07 19-1-0-0-0-5. Cheetahs 2008-13 71-11-0-0-0-55. Griffons 2008 5-0-0-0-0-0. Cheetahs XV 2010 1-0-0-0-0-0. SUPER RUGBY: Bulls 2004 7-0-0-0-0-0. Cheetahs 2008-14 90-9-0-0-0-45. REP HONOURS: SA U21 2004-05 9-3-0-0-0-15. SA U19 2003. SA Schools 2002. FC RECORD: 221-25-0-0-0-125. RECORD IN 2014: (Cheetahs SR) 14-2-0-0-0-10.

Davel, Cornelius Andries (Nollie) (DF Malan HS, Cape Town & UP) b 09/11/1988, Vereeniging. 1.70m. 75kg. Scrumhalf. FC DEBUT: 2013. PROV CAREER: Limpopo 2013-14 8-0-0-0-0-0. FC RECORD: 8-0-0-0-0-0. RECORD IN 2014: (Limpopo) 3-0-0-0-0-0.

Davel, Louw Lodewickus b 24/08/1985. Flank. FC DEBUT: 2013. PROV CAREER: Limpopo 2013-14 10-0-0-0-0-0. FC RECORD: 10-0-0-0-0-0. RECORD IN 2014: (Limpopo) 4-0-0-0-0-0.

Davids, Clyde Eathan (Paarl Gym. & UP) b 17/04/1993, Paarl. 1.94m. 105kg. Eighthman. FC DEBUT: 2014. PROV CAREER: Blue Bulls 2014 9-2-0-0-0-10. FC RECORD: 9-2-0-0-0-10. RECORD IN 2014: (Blue Bulls) 9-2-0-0-0-10.

Davids, Selvyn (Nico Malan HS, Humansdorp) b 26/03/1994, Jeffreys Bay. 1.69m. 70kg. Flyhalf. FC DEBUT: 2014. PROV CAREER: EP Kings 2014 4-2-0-0-0-10. FC RECORD: 4-2-0-0-0-10. RECORD IN 2014: (EP Kings) 4-2-0-0-0-10.

Davis, Aidon (Daniel Pienaar THS, Uitenhage) b 29/04/1994, Uitenhage. 1.89m. 102kg. Flank. FC DEBUT: 2013. PROV CAREER: EP Kings 2013-14 16-3-0-0-0-15. SUPER RUGBY: Southern Kings 2013 1-0-0-0-0-0. REP HONOURS: SA U20 2013-14 8-2-0-0-0-10. FC RECORD: 25-5-0-0-0-25. RECORD IN 2014: (EP Kings, SA U20) 14-3-0-0-0-15.

Davis, Lodewyk (Wikus) (Pionier & Vryheid HS) b 06/03/1992, Empangeni. 1.98m. 118kg. Lock. FC DEBUT: 2014. PROV CAREER: 3-0-0-0-0-0. FC RECORD: 3-0-0-0-0-0. RECORD IN 2014: (Griffons) 3-0-0-0-0-0.

De Allende, Damian (Milnerton HS) b 25/11/1991, Cape Town. 1.89m. 96kg. Centre. FC DEBUT: 2012. PROV CAREER: WP 2012-13 24-6-0-0-0-30. SUPER RUGBY: Stormers 2013-14 28-4-0-0-0-20. REP HONOURS: SA 2014 Tests: 3-0-0-0-0-0. FC RECORD: 55-10-0-0-0-50. RECORD IN 2014: (SA, Stormers) 17-4-0-0-0-20.

De Bruin, Christiaan Pieter (Waterkloof HS, Pretoria) b 20/01/1993, Centurion. 1.98m. 107kg. Flank. FC DEBUT: 2014. PROV CAREER: Blue Bulls 2014 4-0-0-0-0-0. FC RECORD: 4-0-0-0-0-0. RECORD IN 2014: (Blue Bulls) 4-0-0-0-0-0.

De Bruin, Luan (Affies, Pretoria) b 13/02/1993, Pretoria. 1.83m. 124kg. Prop. FC DEBUT: 2013. PROV CAREER: Cheetahs 2014 2-0-0-0-0-0. Free State XV 2014 5-0-0-0-0-0. SUPER RUGBY: Cheetahs 2014 1-0-0-0-0-0. REP HONOURS: SA U20 2013 4-1-0-0-0-5. FC RECORD: 12-1-0-0-0-5. RECORD IN 2014: (Cheetahs SR, Cheetahs, Free State XV) 8-0-0-0-0-0.

De Jager, Lodewyk (Hugenote HS, Springs & NWU) b 17/12/1992, Alberton. 2.05m. 118kg. Lock. FC DEBUT: 2013. PROV CAREER: Cheetahs 2013-14 11-0-0-0-0-0. SUPER RUGBY: Cheetahs 2013-14 28-1-0-0-0-5. REP HONOURS: SA 2014 Tests: 9-2-0-0-0-10. FC RECORD: 48-3-0-0-0-15. RECORD IN 2014: (SA, Cheetahs SR, Cheetahs) 21-3-0-0-0-15.

De Jongh, Juan Leon (Hugenot HS, Wellington) b 15/04/88, Paarl. 1.77m. 85kg. Centre. FC DEBUT: 2009. PROV CAREER: WP 2009-14 50-20-0-0-0-100. SUPER RUGBY: Stormers 2010-14 69-12-0-0-0-60. REP HONOURS: SA 2009-12 Tests: 14-3-0-0-0-15. Tour 2009 2-1-0-0-0-5. Total: 16-4-0-0-0-20. Barbarians 2014 2-2-0-0-0-10. MISC INFO: YPOY Nominee 2009. FC RECORD: 137-38-0-0-0-190. RECORD IN 2014: (Stormers, WP, Barbarians) 25-11-0-0-0-55.

De Klerk, Francois (Waterkloof HS, Pretoria) b 19/10/1991, Nelspruit. 1.69m. 66kg. Scrumhalf. FC DEBUT: 2012. PROV CAREER: Pumas 2012-13 46-3-0-0-0-15. SUPER RUGBY: Lions 2014 16-3-0-0-0-15. FC RECORD: 62-6-0-0-0-30. RECORD IN 2014: (Lions SR) 16-3-0-0-0-15.

De Klerk, Johannes Cornelis (Jan) (Pietersburg HS, Waterkloof HS, Pretoria & US) b 10/02/1991, Polokwane. 1.98m. 110kg. Lock. FC DEBUT: 2014. PROV CAREER: WP 2014 4-0-0-0-0-0. FC RECORD: 4-0-0-0-0-0. RECORD IN 2014: (WP) 4-0-0-0-0-0.

De Klerk, Pieter Rossouw (Paarl Gym.) b 21/08/89. Vredenburg. 1.86m. 110kg. Prop. FC DEBUT: 2009. PROV CAREER: Blue Bulls 2009-12 33-0-0-0-0-0. Cheetahs 2013 7-0-0-0-0-0. Griffons 2013 1-0-0-0-0-0. Free State XV 2013-14 8-1-0-0-0-5. SUPER RUGBY: Bulls 2010-11 14-0-0-0-0-0. Cheetahs 2014 7-0-0-0-0-0. FC RECORD: 70-1-0-0-0-5. RECORD IN 2014: (Cheetahs SR, Free State XV) 8-0-0-0-0-0.

De Kock, Jacobus Johannes (Kobus) (Paarl Boys' HS) b 29/03/1988, Paarl. 1.89m. 98kg. Fullback. FC DEBUT: 2011. PROV CAREER: Sharks XV 2011 8-7-7-0-0-49. Lions 2013 2-0-0-0-0-0. Young Lions 2013-14 4-0-1-0-0-2. Leopards 2014 9-4-0-0-0-20. FC RECORD: 23-11-8-0-0-71. RECORD IN 2014: (Leopards, Young Lions) 10-4-0-0-0-20.

De Koker, Jovelian (Worcester Gym. & CPUT) b 28/02/1992, Worcester. 74kg. Scrumhalf. FC DEBUT: 2014. PROV CAREER: Boland 2014 9-1-0-0-0-5. FC RECORD: 9-1-0-0-0-5. RECORD IN 2014: (Boland) 9-1-0-0-0-5.

De Swardt, Albertus Jacobus (Albe) (Outeniqua HS, George) b 10/08/1990, George. 1.86m. 98kg. Hooker. FC DEBUT: 2011. PROV CAREER: WP 2011 1-0-0-0-0-0. EP Kings 2013-14 24-0-0-0-0-0. FC RECORD: 25-0-0-0-0-0. RECORD IN 2014: (EP Kings) 13-0-0-0-0-0.

De Villiers, Jean (Paarl Gym.) b 24/02/81, Paarl. 1.90m. 99kg. Centre. FC DEBUT: 2001. PROV CAREER: WP 2001-05 & 08 & 10-13 50-30-0-0-0-150. SUPER RUGBY: Stormers 2005-09 & 11-14 105-28-0-0-0-140. REP HONOURS: SA 2002 & 2004-14 Tests: 106-27-0-0-0-135. SA XV: 2006 1-0-0-0-0-0. SA Sevens 2002. SA U21s 2001-02 9-7-0-0-0-35;

SEASON IN 2014

SA U19 2000. SA Schools 1999; CW WP Academy 1999. Barbarians 2008 & 13 2-2-0-0-0-10. MISC INFO: SA Rugby PoY 2008. PoY nominee 2005. Holds SA Record for most Tests as a centre - 91. Son of former WP lock André de Villiers. FC RECORD: 273-94-0-0-0-470. RECORD IN 2014: (SA, Stormers) 19-3-0-0-0-15.
De Wee, Artur Bobby (Southdowns Coll., Centurion & UP) b 04/02/1994, Klerksdorp. 1.96m. 95kg. Flank. FC DEBUT: 2014. PROV CAREER: Young Lions 2014 4-0-0-0-0-0. FC RECORD: 4-0-0-0-0-0. RECORD IN 2014: (Young Lions) 4-0-0-0-0-0.
De Wet, Philip Albert (Grey Coll., Bloemfontein & NWU) b 14/02/1989, Kuruman. 1.87m. 98kg. Flank. FC DEBUT: 2011. PROV CAREER: Leopards 2011-14 32-15-0-0-0-75. FC RECORD: 32-15-0-0-0-75. RECORD IN 2014: (Leopards) 3-2-0-0-0-10.
De Wet, Pieter-Steyn (Paarl Gym.) b 08/01/1991, Caledon. 1.75m. 83kg. Flyhalf. FC DEBUT: 2012. PROV CAREER: Cheetahs 2014 4-0-6-1-0-15. Free State XV 2012 & 14 7-0-5-0-0-10. Griquas 2013 5-0-13-6-1-47. Griffons 2014 4-0-7-2-0-20. FC RECORD: 20-0-31-9-1-92. RECORD IN 2014: (Cheetahs, Griffons, Free State XV) 11-0-18-3-0-45.
De Wit, Allen Stephan (Transvalia HS, Vanderbijlpark & UJ) b 01/01/1992, Vereeniging. 1.86m. 104kg. Flank. FC DEBUT: 2012. PROV CAREER: Young Lions 2012 & 14 14-6-0-0-0-30. SUPER RUGBY: Lions 2014 2-0-0-0-0-0. FC RECORD: 16-6-0-0-0-30. RECORD IN 2014: (Lions SR, Young Lions) 9-5-0-0-0-25.
Delo, Layle Antonio (Outeniqua HS, George) b 28/10/1989, George. 1.86m. 115kg. Hooker. FC DEBUT: 2011. PROV CAREER: SWD 2011-14 37-2-0-0-0-10. FC RECORD: 37-2-0-0-0-10. RECORD IN 2014: (SWD) 10-0-0-0-0-0.
Demas, Danwel (New Orleans HS, Paarl) b 15/10/81, Paarl. 1.86m. 79kg. Wing. FC DEBUT: 2004. PROV CAREER: Pumas 2004 & 12-13 19-8-0-0-0-40. Blue Bulls 2005-08 27-8-0-0-0-40. Boland 2008 & 2011 & 14 27-25-0-0-0-125. Cheetahs 2009 12-3-0-0-0-15. Cheetahs XV 2010 1-0-0-0-0-0. Griffons 2013 2-1-0-0-0-5. SUPER RUGBY: Bulls 2006 & 08 4-0-0-0-0-0. Cheetahs 2009-10 21-2-0-0-0-10. REP HONOURS: Emerging Springboks 2009 1-1-0-0-0-5. SA Barbarians 2012 1-0-0-0-0-0. SA Sevens 2003-06. FC RECORD: 115-48-0-0-0-240. RECORD IN 2014: (Boland) 8-4-0-0-0-20.
Des Fountain, Dylan (Paarl Gym.) b 07/06/85. 1.87m. 84kg. Centre. FC DEBUT: 2004. PROV CAREER: Blue Bulls 2004 1-0-0-0-0-0. WP 2007-10 24-4-0-0-0-20. Lions 2011-13 17-1-0-0-0-5. Young Lions 2011 & 13-14 9-2-0-0-0-10. SUPER RUGBY: Stormers 2007-09 18-3-0-0-0-15. Lions 2011 6-1-0-0-0-5. Lions P/R 2013 2-0-0-0-0-0. FC RECORD: 77-11-0-0-0-55. RECORD IN 2014 (Young Lions) 1-0-0-0-0-0.
Deysel, Jean Roy (Hentie Cilliers HS, Virginia) b 05/03/85, Virginia. 1.92m. 103kg. Flank. FC DEBUT: 2005. PROV CAREER: Lions 2005-07 21-1-0-0-0-5. KZN 2007-13 61-7-0-0-0-35. Sharks XV 2007-08 & 2011-12 8-1-0-0-0-5. Sharks Inv XV 2007,09 2-3-0-0-0-15. SUPER RUGBY: Sharks 2008-14 67-1-0-0-0-5. REP HONOURS: SA 2009, 2011 Tests 4-0-0-0-0-0. Tour: 2009 2-0-0-0-0-0. Total: 6-0-0-0-0-0. Emerging Springboks 2009 1-0-0-0-0-0. SA Students 2007 1-0-0-0-0-0. MISC INFO: CC PoY 2008. FC RECORD: 167-13-0-0-0-65. RECORD IN 2014: (Sharks) 13-1-0-0-0-5.
Deysel, Johan (Windhoek HS & NWU) b 26/09/1991, Windhoek. 1.84m. 92kg. Centre. FC DEBUT: 2014. PROV CAREER: Leopards 2014 6-4-0-0-0-20. Leopards XV 2014 4-1-0-0-0-5. FC RECORD: 10-5-0-0-0-25. RECORD IN 2014: (Leopards, Leopards XV) 10-5-0-0-0-25.
Dippenaar, Dirk Hendrik Francois (Augsberg Agric. HS, Clanwilliam & UP) b 18/11/1989, Pretoria. 1.87m. 103kg. Wing. FC DEBUT: 2014.

PROV CAREER: Valke 2014 5-4-0-0-0-20. FC RECORD: 5-4-0-0-0-20. REP HONOURS: SA Sevens 2012. RECORD IN 2014: (Valke) 5-4-0-0-0-20.
Dippenaar, Stephanus Christiaan (Stephan) (Paul Roos Gym., Stellenbosch) b 03/01/88, Moorreesburg. 1.88m. 88kg. Centre. FC DEBUT: 2008. PROV CAREER: Blue Bulls 2008-11 32-6-0-0-0-30. SUPER RUGBY: Bulls 2008 & 10-11 21-1-0-0-0-5. REP HONOURS: SA U20 2008 2-1-0-0-0-5. SA Sevens 2012-14. FC RECORD: 55-8-0-0-0-40. RECORD IN 2014: (SA Sevens).
Dolo, Maputhla Stephen (Ben Vorster HS, Tzaneen & UFS) b 13/03/1992, Polokwane. 1.78m. 82kg. Fullback. FC DEBUT: 2013. PROV CAREER: Free State XV 2013-14 7-2-0-0-0-10. Cheetahs 2014 1-0-0-0-0-0. FC RECORD: 8-2-0-0-0-10. RECORD IN 2014: (Cheetahs, Free State XV) 3-2-0-0-0-10.
Downey, Justin (Northwood HS) b 11/11/86, Johannesburg. 1.93m. 102kg. Flank. FC DEBUT: 2008. PROV CAREER: KZN 2009 & 13 7-0-0-0-0. Sharks XV 2008-10 & 14 22-4-0-0-0-20. Sharks Inv XV 2009-10 2-0-0-0-0-0. Griquas 2010-13 48-4-0-0-0-20. SUPER RUGBY: Cheetahs 2012 12-0-0-0-0-0. FC RECORD: 91-8-0-0-0-40. RECORD IN 2014: (Sharks XV) 4-1-0-0-0-5.
Dreyer, Marthinus Chrisstoffel (Martin) (Wonderboom HS, Pretoria & NWU) b 25/08/1988, Rustenburg. 1.85m. 112kg. Prop. FC DEBUT: 2011. PROV CAREER: Leopards 2011 & 13 13-1-0-0-0-5. Leopard XV 2013 4-0-0-0-0-0. Boland 2014 12-1-0-0-0-5. SUPER RUGBY: Stormers 2014 5-0-0-0-0-0. REP HONOURS: SA Univ 2013 1-0-0-0-0-0. SA Pres XV 2013 4-0-0-0-0-0. FC RECORD: 39-2-0-0-0-10. RECORD IN 2014: (Stormers, Boland) 17-1-0-0-0-5.
Dreyer, Ruan Martin (Ruan)((Monument HS, Krugersdorp) b 16/09/1990, Carletonville. 1.86m. 113kg. Prop. FC DEBUT: 2010. PROV CAREER: Lions 2012-14 25-4-0-0-0-20. Young Lions 2010-13 17-1-0-0-0-5. Golden Lions XV 2011 1-0-0-0-0-0. SUPER RUGBY: Lions 2012 & 14 19-1-0-0-0-5. Lions P/R 2013 2-0-0-0-0-0. REP HONOURS: SA U20 2010 5-0-0-0-0-0. FC RECORD: 69-6-0-0-0-30. RECORD IN 2014: (Lions SR, Lions) 27-2-0-0-0-10.
Dry, Christopher Adriaan (Grey Coll., Bloemfontein & CUT.) b 13/02/88, Cape Town. 1.91m. 95kg. FC DEBUT: 2009. PROV CAREER: Cheetahs 2009-10 5-0-0-0-0-0. Rep. Honours: SA Sevens 2010-14. FC RECORD: 5-0-0-0-0-0. RECORD IN 2014: (SA Sevens).
Du Plessis, Andries (Piet Potgieter HS, Mokopane & TUT) b 07/04/1991, George. 1.74m. 83kg. Wing. FC DEBUT: 2014. PROV CAREER: Limpopo 2014 1-0-0-0-0-0. FC RECORD: 1-0-0-0-0-0. RECORD IN 2014: (Limpopo) 1-0-0-0-0-0.
Du Plessis, Bismarck Wilhelm (Grey Coll., Bloemfontein & UFS) b 22/05/1984, Bethlehem. 1.89m. 113kg. Hooker. FC DEBUT: 2003. PROV CAREER: Cheetahs 2003 2-0-0-0-0-0. KZN 2005-11 & 13 39-10-0-0-0-50. Sharks XV 2005-08 3-2-0-0-0-10. SUPER RUGBY: Sharks 2005-14 120-17-0-0-0-85. REP HONOURS: SA 2007-14 Tests: 70-9-0-0-0-45. Tour: 2007 2-0-0-0-0-0. Total: 72-9-0-0-0-45. Springbok XV 2014 1-2-0-0-0-10. SA U21 2005 1-1-0-0-0-5. British Barbarians 2009 & 13 2-2-0-0-0-10. MISC INFO: PoY nominee 2008, 2011. Super PoY 2011 and 2012 nominee. Brother of Sharks prop Jannie du Plessis. Son of former EOFS prop Francois du Plessis. FC RECORD: 240-43-0-0-0-215. RECORD IN 2014: (SA, Springbok XV, Sharks) 31-5-0-0-0-25.
Du Plessis, Charl Francois (Monument HS, Krugersdorp) b 08/04/87, Cape Town. 1.87m. 113kg. Prop. FC DEBUT: 2008. PROV CAREER: Young Lions 2008-10 7-0-0-0-0-0. Valke 2009 9-0-0-0-0-0. Boland 2010-12 31-0-0-0-0-0. EP Kings 2012-14 31-0-0-0-0-0. SUPER RUGBY: Southern Kings 2013 2-0-0-0-0-0. P/R 2013 1-0-0-0-0-0.

SEASON IN 2014

FC RECORD: 81-0-0-0-0-0. RECORD IN 2014: (EP Kings) 4-0-0-0-0-0.

Du Plessis, Christo John (George HS) b 02/06/1989, George. 1.86m. 92kg. Flanker. FC DEBUT: 2010. PROV CAREER: SWD 2010 & 12-14 49-9-0-0-0-45. FC RECORD: 49-9-0-0-0-45. RECORD IN 2014: (SWD) 16-4-0-0-0-20.

Du Plessis, Francois Theodorus (Grey Coll., Bloemfontein & UFS) b 10/12/1992, Bethlehem. 1.83m. 114kg. Prop. FC DEBUT: 2014. PROV CAREER: EP Kings 2014 3-0-0-0-0-0. FC RECORD: 3-0-0-0-0-0. RECORD IN 2014: (EP Kings) 3-0-0-0-0-0.

Du Plessis, Hans (Hans Strijdom HS, Naboomspruit) b 13/07/1988, Warmbaths. 1.65m. 65kg. Centre. FC DEBUT: 2014. PROV CAREER: Limpopo 2014 5-0-0-0-0-0. FC RECORD: 5-0-0-0-0-0. RECORD IN 2014: (Limpopo) 5-0-0-0-0-0.

Du Plessis, Jan Nathaniël (Jannie) (Grey Coll., Bloemfontein) b 16/11/82, Bethlehem. 1.87m.119kg. Prop. FC DEBUT: 2003. PROV CAREER: Cheetahs 2003-07 69-3-0-0-0-15. KZN 2008-13 35-3-0-0-0-15. SUPER RUGBY: Cheetahs 2006-07 26-0-0-0-0-0. Sharks 2008-14 106-0-0-0-0-0. REP HONOURS: SA 2007-14 Tests: 62-1-0-0-0-5. Tour: 2007, 09 2-0-0-0-0-0. Total: 64-1-0-0-0-5. Springbok XV 2014 1-0-0-0-0-0. SA U21 2003 4-0-0-0-0-0. MISC INFO: Brother of Natal Sharks hooker Bismarck du Plessis. Son of former EOFS prop Francois du Plessis. Medical doctor. FC RECORD: 305-7-0-0-0-35. REP HONOURS: CW Free State 2000. RECORD IN 2014: (SA, Springbok XV, Sharks) 30-0-0-0-0-0.

Du Plessis, Jean-Luc (Paarl Boys' HS & Varsity Coll.) b 07/05/1994, Cape Town. 1.79m. 87kg. Flyhalf. FC DEBUT: 2014. PROV CAREER: Sharks XV 2014 2-1-1-2-0-13. REP HONOURS: SA U20 2014 2-0-1-0-0-2. FC RECORD: 2-1-2-2-0-15. RECORD IN 2014: (Sharks XV, SA U20) 4-1-2-2-0-15.

Du Plessis, Nico Visser (Florida HS) b 22/09/93, Pretoria. 1.86m. 109kg. Prop. FC DEBUT: 2014. PROV CAREER: Young Lions 2014 3-2-0-0-0-10. FC RECORD: 3-2-0-0-0-10. RECORD IN 2014: (Young Lions) 3-2-0-0-0-10.

Du Plessis, Phillipus Jacobus Snyman (JP) (Paul Roos Gym., Stellenbosch) b 29/04/1991, Kroonstad. 1.84m. 89kg. Centre. FC DEBUT: 2012. PROV CAREER: WP 2012 16-3-0-0-0-15. Cheetahs 2014 10-1-0-0-0-5. SUPER RUGBY: Stormers 2012 2-0-0-0-0-0. MISC INFO: Son of former Transvaal & Eastern Free State utility back Charl du Plessis. FC RECORD: 28-4-0-0-0-20. RECORD IN 2014: (Cheetahs) 10-1-0-0-0-5.

Du Plessis, Willem Hendrik Jacques (Jacques) (Ermelo HS & UP) b 12/08/1993, Pongola. 2.01m. 119kg. Flank. FC DEBUT: 2013. PROV CAREER: Blue Bulls 2013-14 22-4-0-0-0-20. SUPER RUGBY: Bulls 2013-14 15-2-0-0-0-10. REP HONOURS: SA U20 2013 5-1-0-0-0-5. FC RECORD: 42-7-0-0-0-35. RECORD IN 2014: (Bulls, Blue Bulls) 24-4-0-0-0-20.

Du Plessis, Willem Nicolaas Frederik (Willie) (Affies, Pretoria & UP) b 05/06/1990, Pretoria. 1.86m. 90kg. Flyhalf. FC DEBUT: 2012. PROV CAREER: Blue Bulls 2012-13 7-4-33-0-0-86. Cheetahs 2013-14 19-2-18-18-1-103. Young Lions 2014 10-1-26-11-1-93. FC RECORD: 36-7-77-29-2-282. RECORD IN 2014: (Cheetahs, Young Lions) 20-3-41-29-2-190.

Du Plooy, Johannes Le Roux (Ellisras HS) b 28/04/1992, Ellisras. 1.85m. 112kg. Prop. FC DEBUT: 2014. PROV CAREER: Limpopo 2014 1-0-0-0-0-0. FC RECORD: 1-0-0-0-0-0. RECORD IN 2014: (Limpopo) 1-0-0-0-0-0.

Du Preez, Branco Bewinn Nazeem (PW Botha Coll., George) b 08/05/1990, George. 1.66m. 72kg. Flyhalf. REP HONOURS: SA U20 2010 4-1-0-0-0-5. SA Sevens 2010-14. FC RECORD: 4-1-0-0-0-5. RECORD IN 2014: (SA Sevens).

Du Preez, Hermanus Carel (Noordkaap HS, Kimberley.) b 30/04/1983, Hartswater. 1.98m. 100kg. Eighthman. FC DEBUT: 2013. PROV CAREER: WP 2013-14 10-2-0-0-0-10. FC RECORD: 10-2-0-0-0-10. RECORD IN 2014: (WP) 7-2-0-0-0-10.

Du Preez, Ivan-John (Brandwag HS, Uitenhage) b 23/06/1994, Port Elizabeth. 1.87m. 94kg. Flank. FC DEBUT: 2014. PROV CAREER: EP Kings 2014 5-2-0-0-0-10. FC RECORD: 5-2-0-0-0-10. RECORD IN 2014: (EP Kings) 5-2-0-0-0-10.

Du Preez, Jean-Luc (Kearsney Coll., Botha's Hill) b 05/08/1995, Durban. 1.93m. 110kg. Flank. FC DEBUT: 2014. REP HONOURS: SA U20 2014 3-0-0-0-0-0. FC RECORD: 3-0-0-0-0-0. RECORD IN 2014: (SA U20) 3-0-0-0-0-0.

Du Preez, Petrus Fourie (Affies, Pretoria) b 24/03/82, Pretoria. 1.83m. 88kg. Scrumhalf. FC DEBUT: 2001. PROV CAREER: Blue Bulls 2001-05 & 08-09 52-19-0-0-0-95. SUPER RUGBY: Bulls 2003-11 112-22-0-0-0-110. REP HONOURS: SA 2004-09 & 2011 & 13-14 70-15-0-0-0-75. SA U21 2002-03 9-1-0-0-0-5. SA U19 2001. Springbok XV 2014 1-0-0-0-0-0. British Barbarians 2008,09 2-0-0-0-0-0. MISC INFO: YPoY nominee 2003, 2004, PoY 2006 PoY nominee 2007. S14 PoY 2007. SA Rugby POY 2009. IRB Rugby POY Nominee 2009. Son of former Northern Transvaal No. 8 Fourie du Preez (Snr). FC RECORD: 246-57-0-0-0-285. RECORD IN 2014: (SA, Springbok XV) 4-0-0-0-0-0.

Du Preez, Phillip (Monument HS, Krugersdorp) b 01/08/1993, Roodepoort. 1.99m. 112kg. Lock. FC DEBUT: 2014. PROV CAREER: Free State XV 2014 3-0-0-0-0-0. FC RECORD: 3-0-0-0-0-0. RECORD IN 2014: (Free State XV) 3-0-0-0-0-0.

Du Preez, Robert James (Kearsney Coll., Botha's Hill) b 30/07/1993, Durban. 1.92m. 95kg. Scrumhalf. FC DEBUT: 2013. PROV CAREER: WP 2014 4-1-2-0-0-9. REP HONOURS: SA U20 2013 4-0-8-4-0-28. FC RECORD: 8-1-10-4-0-37. RECORD IN 2014: (WP) 4-1-2-0-0-9.

Du Toit, Francois (Florida HS, Roodepoort & UJ) b 17/08/1990, Johannesburg. 1.78m. 103kg. Hooker. FC DEBUT: 2011. PROV CAREER: Lions 2012-13 3-0-0-0-0-0. Young Lions 2011-13 14-3-0-0-0-15. Pumas 2013-14 20-1-0-0-0-5. REP HONOURS: SA Students 2012 2-0-0-0-0-0. SA U20 2010 4-0-0-0-0-0. FC RECORD: 43-4-0-0-0-20. RECORD IN 2014: (Pumas) 10-0-0-0-0-0.

Du Toit, Francois Cornelius (Franna) (Grey Coll., Bloemfontein & UFS) b 16/03/1990, Vryburg. 1.83m. 84kg. Flyhalf. FC DEBUT: 2011. PROV CAREER: Cheetahs 2011 1-1-0-0-0-5. Griffons 2013-14 17-0-24-14-0-90. REP HONOURS: SA Students 2012 2-0-2-1-0-7. FC RECORD: 20-1-26-15-0-122. RECORD IN 2014: (Griffons) 13-0-14-14-0-90.

Du Toit, Ockert Jacobus Jacques (Grey Coll., Bloemfontein & UFS) b 19/11/1993, Bloemfontein. 1.86m. 102kg. Hooker. FC debut: 2013. PROV CAREER: Free State XV 2014 1-0-0-0-0-0. REP HONOURS: SA U20 2013 5-1-0-0-0-5. FC RECORD: 6-1-0-0-0-5. RECORD IN 2014: (Free State XV) 1-0-0-0-0-0.

Du Toit, Ozard Martin (Hottentots Holland HS, Somerset West) b 27/06/1989, Welkom. 1.82m. 80kg. Fullback. FC DEBUT: 2012. PROV CAREER: SWD 2012-14 38-6-0-0-0-30. FC RECORD: 38-6-0-0-0-30. RECORD IN 2014: (SWD) 16-2-0-0-0-10.

Du Toit, Pieter Stephanus (Swartland HS, Malmesbury) b 20/08/1992, Cape Town. 2m. 115kg. Lock. FC DEBUT: 2012. PROV CAREER: Sharks 2012-14 22-0-0-0-0-0. REP HONOURS: SA 2013 Tests: 2-0-0-0-0-0. SA U20 2012 5-1-0-0-0-5. FC RECORD: 39-2-0-0-0-10. RECORD IN 2014: (Sharks) 3-0-0-0-0-0.

Du Toit, Thomas Joubert (Paarl Boys' HS) b 05/05/1995, Cape Town. 1.89m. 130kg. Prop. FC DEBUT: 2014. PROV CAREER: KZN 2014 7-1-0-0-0-5. Sharks XV 2014 7-2-0-0-0-10. SUPER RUGBY: Sharks 2014 4-0-

SEASON IN 2014

0-0-0-0-0. REP HONOURS: SA U20 2014 4-0-0-0-0-0. British Barbarians 2014 2-1-0-0-0-5. FC RECORD: 24-4-0-0-0-20. RECORD IN 2014: (Sharks, KZB, Sharks XV, British Barbarians, SA U20) 24-4-0-0-0-20.

Dubase, Onke Sydwell (Hudson Park HS, East London & UFH) b 06/08/1989, East London. 1.8m. 94kg. Flank. FC DEBUT: 2010. PROV CAREER: Border 2010-11 & 14 27-3-0-0-0-15. FC RECORD: 27-3-0-0-0-15. RECORD IN 2014: (Border) 8-0-0-0-0-0.

Dukisa, Ntabeni (Loyolo HS) b 25/07/1988. Wing. FC DEBUT: 2010. PROV CAREER: Border 2010-12 26-5-19-34-0-165. Griffons 2012 5-0-0-0-0-0. EP Kings 2013-14 32-6-17-14-1-109. REP HONOURS: SA Barbarians 2012 1-1-0-0-0-5. FC RECORD: 64-12-36-48-1-279. RECORD IN 2014: (EP Kings) 14-3-11-6-0-55.

Dumond, Cecil (Orkney HS) b 08/04/87, Klerksdorp. 1.82m. 84kg. Flyhalf. FC DEBUT: 2007. PROV CAREER: Leopards 2007 & 09-11 26-2-18-29-2-139. SWD 2011-12 13-1-1-4-0-19. Border 2013 7-0-2-1-0-7. Valke 2014 9-1-2-4-0-21. MISC INFO: Brother of Monty Dumond. FC RECORD: 55-4-23-38-1-186. RECORD IN 2014: (Valke) 9-1-2-4-0-21.

Dweba, Joseph (Florida HS, Roodepoort & HTS Louis Botha, Bloemfontein) b 25/10/1995, Carletonville. 1.72m. 103kg. Hooker. FC DEBUT: 2014. REP HONOURS: SA U20 2014 2-0-0-0-0-0. FC RECORD: 2-0-0-0-0-0. RECORD IN 2014: (SA U20) 2-0-0-0-0-0.

Dyanti, Mzoxolo (Willie) (Kwezi Lomso HS, Port Elizabeth) b 10/10/85, Port Elizabeth. 1.65m. 75kg. Scrumhalf. FC DEBUT: 2006. PROV CAREER: Griffons 2006 11-0-0-0-0-0. SWD 2007-09 & 2011-14 65-8-0-0-0-40. FC RECORD: 76-8-0-0-0-40. RECORD IN 2014: (SWD) 10-1-0-0-0-5.

Ebersohn, Arno (Framesby HS, Port Elizabeth & NWU) b 30/03/1992, Port Elizabeth. 1.83m. 112kg. Prop. FC DEBUT: 2014. PROV CAREER: Leopards XV 2014 5-0-0-0-0-0. FC RECORD: 5-0-0-0-0-0. RECORD IN 2014: (Leopards XV) 5-0-0-0-0-0.

Ehlers, Chris Erich (Wesvalia HS, Klerksdorp) b 22/05/1988, Kroonstad. 1.99m. 95kg. Lock. FC DEBUT: 2010. PROV CAREER: Valke 2010-11 30-1-0-0-0-5. Griffons 2012-14 37-5-0-0-0-25. FC RECORD: 67-6-0-0-0-30. RECORD IN 2014: (Griffons) 5-2-0-0-0-10.

Eksteen, Leighton (Outeniqua HS, George) b 15/09/1994, Riversdale. 1.7m. 70kg. Flyhalf. FC DEBUT: 2014. PROV CAREER: SWD 2014 5-1-0-0-0-5. FC RECORD: 5-1-0-0-0-5. RECORD IN 2014: (SWD) 5-1-0-0-0-5.

Eksteen, Ryno (Affies, Pretoria) b 03/10/1984, Centurion. 1.82m. 84kg. Flyhalf. FC DEBUT: 2014. SUPER RUGBY: Stormers 2014 1-0-0-0-0-0. FC RECORD: 1-0-0-0-0-0. RECORD IN 2014: (Stormers) 1-0-0-0-0-0.

Els, Cornelius Wilhelmus (Corniel) (Grey Coll., Bloemfontein) b 19/01/1994, Polokwane. 1.83m. 102kg. Hooker. FC DEBUT: 2014. REP HONOURS: SA U20 2014 4-1-0-0-0-5. FC RECORD: 4-1-0-0-0-5. RECORD IN 2014: (SA U20) 4-1-0-0-0-5.

Elstadt, Rynhardt (Montagu HS) b 02/12/1989, Johannesburg. 1.98m. 112kg. Lock. FC DEBUT: 2010. PROV CAREER: WP 2010 & 12-14 32-1-0-0-0-5. SUPER RUGBY: Stormers 2011-14 39-0-0-0-0-0. REP HONOURS: SA U20 2009 3-0-0-0-0-0. FC RECORD: 74-1-0-0-0-5. RECORD IN 2014: (Stormers, WP) 10-1-0-0-0-5.

Engelbrecht, Adriaan Erasmus (Volkskool, Potchefstroom) b 14/09/1990, Pretoria. 1.85m. 98kg. Centre. FC DEBUT: 2011. PROV CAREER: Leopards 2011-14 42-9-54-25-0-228. Leopard XV 2013 7-2-2-0-0-14. REP HONOURS: SA Pres XV 2013 4-1-0-0-0-5. FC RECORD: 53-12-56-25-0-247. RECORD IN 2014: (Leopards) 6-0-6-2-0-18.

Engelbrecht, Gabriel Joubert (Upington HS & NWU) b 27/06/1989, Kimberley. 1.89m. 90kg. Centre. FC DEBUT: 2010. PROV CAREER: Leopards 2010-12 36-14-0-0-0-70. Griffons 2013-14 14-2-5-1-0-23. Cheetahs 2013-14 10-1-0-0-0-5. Free State XV 2013-14 11-5-0-0-0-25. REP HONOURS: SA Students 2012 1-0-0-0-0-0. SA Barbarians 2012 1-1-0-0-0-5. FC RECORD: 73-23-5-1-0-128. RECORD IN 2014: (Cheetahs, Griffons, Free State XV) 18-3-0-0-0-15.

Engelbrecht, Gerhardus Petrus (Affies, Pretoria & UP) b 30/05/1991, Pretoria. 1.9m. 118kg. Prop. FC DEBUT: 2014. PROV CAREER: Valke 2014 3-0-0-0-0-0. FC RECORD: 3-0-0-0-0-0. RECORD IN 2014: (Valke) 3-0-0-0-0-0.

Engelbrecht, Jacques Jacobus (Monument HS, Krugersdorp) b 10/06/85, Cape Town. 1.94m. 105kg. Flank. FC DEBUT: 2007. PROV CAREER: WP 2007-08 2-0-0-0-0-0. SWD 2008-10 48-3-0-0-0-15. EP Kings 2011-12 24-5-0-0-0-25. Blue Bulls 2013-14 15-0-0-0-0-0. SUPER RUGBY: Southern Kings 2013 15-1-0-0-0-5. P/R 2013 2-0-0-0-0-0. Bulls 2014 13-0-0-0-0-0. REP HONOURS: SA Kings 2011 2-0-0-0-0-0. SA Barbarians 2012 1-1-0-0-0-5. SA Sevens 2010-11. FC RECORD: 122-10-0-0-0-50. RECORD IN 2014: (Bulls, Blue Bulls) 20-0-0-0-0-0.

Engelbrecht, Johannes Jacobus (JJ) (Grey HS, PE) b 22/02/1989, Port Elizabeth. 1.90m. 94kg. Wing/Centre. FC DEBUT: 2009. PROV CAREER: WP 2009-11 38-24-0-0-0-120. Blue Bulls 2012-14 15-0-0-0-0-0. SUPER RUGBY: Bulls 2012-13 49-8-0-0-0-40. REP HONOURS: SA 2012-13 Tests: 12-4-0-0-0-20. FC RECORD: 114-36-0-0-0-180. RECORD IN 2014: (Bulls, Blue Bulls) 22-1-0-0-0-5.

Erasmus, Lourens Jacobus (Garsfontein HS, Pretoria & UJ) b 14/06/1993, Pretoria. 2m. 105kg. Lock. FC DEBUT: 2014. PROV CAREER: Young Lions 2014 9-2-0-0-0-10. FC RECORD: 9-2-0-0-0-10. RECORD IN 2014: (Young Lions) 9-2-0-0-0-10.

Erasmus, Sheldon (Voortrekker HS, Bethlehem & UFS) b 21/10/1993, Nelspruit. 1.87m. 93kg. Wing. FC DEBUT: 2014. PROV CAREER: Griffons 2014 4-2-0-0-0-10. FC RECORD: 4-2-0-0-0-10. RECORD IN 2014: (Griffons) 4-2-0-0-0-10.

Esterhuizen, Adriaan Pieter (Andre) (Klerksdorp HS) b 30/03/1994, Potchefstroom. 1.91m. 106kg. Centre. FC DEBUT: 2013. PROV CAREER: Sharks XV 2013-14 9-2-0-0-0-10. KZN 2014 6-3-0-0-0-15. SUPER RUGBY: Sharks 2014 1-0-0-0-0-0. REP HONOURS: SA U20 2014 4-2-0-0-0-10. FC RECORD: 20-7-0-0-0-35. RECORD IN 2014: (Sharks, KZN, Sharks XV, SA U20) 17-7-0-0-0-35.

Esterhuizen, John-Ronald Andrew (Paarl Gym. & UJ) b 24/02/1991, Worcester. 1.80m. 90kg. Wing. FC DEBUT: 2011. PROV CAREER: Lions 2012 4-0-0-0-0-0. Young Lions 2012-14 11-4-0-0-0-20. Golden Lions XV 2011 1-0-0-0-0-0. REP HONOURS: SA Univ 2013 1-1-0-0-0-5. FC RECORD: 17-5-0-0-0-25. RECORD IN 2014: (Young Lions) 7-1-0-0-0-5.

Etzebeth, Eben (Tygerberg HS, Cape Town) b 29/10/1991, Cape Town. 2.03m. 117kg. Lock. FC DEBUT: 2012. PROV CAREER: WP 2012-14 7-0-0-0-0-0. SUPER RUGBY: Stormers 2012-13 21-2-0-0-0-10. REP HONOURS: SA 2012-14 Tests: 33-0-0-0-0-0. SA U20 2011 5-1-0-0-0-5. MISC INFO: SARU PoY 2012 nominee. YPoY 2012. Super PoY 2012 nominee. FC RECORD: 66-3-0-0-0-15. RECORD IN 2014: (SA, WP) 11-0-0-0-0-0.

Faasen, Daniel Cornelius (Danie) (Affies, Pretoria) b 11/11/1989, Middelburg. 1.74m. 70kg. Scrumhalf. FC DEBUT: 2010. PROV CAREER: Blue Bulls 2010 7-1-0-0-0-5. EP Kings 2011-12 23-2-0-0-0-10. SWD 2014 10-0-0-0-0-0. REP HONOURS: SA Kings 2011 3-0-0-0-0-0. FC RECORD: 43-3-0-0-0-15. RECORD IN 2014 (SWD) 10-0-0-0-0-0.

Fahey, Dexter Seanancy (Glenwood HS, Durban & NMMU) b 14/10/1989, Johannesburg. 1.83m. 114kg. Prop. FC DEBUT: 2012.

PROV CAREER: EP Kings 2012 1-0-0-0-0-0. SWD 2014 5-0-0-0-0-0. FC RECORD: 6-0-0-0-0-0. RECORD IN 2014: (SWD) 5-0-0-0-0-0.
Ferreira, Andries Stephanus (Affies, Pretoria & TUT) b 29/03/1990, Despatch. 1.97m. 117kg. Lock. FC DEBUT: 2012. PROV CAREER: Cheetahs 2012 3-1-0-0-0-5. Griffons 2013 1-0-0-0-0-0. Free State XV 2013 3-0-0-0-0-0. SUPER RUGBY: Cheetahs 2012 & 14 20-1-0-0-0-5. FC RECORD: 27-2-0-0-0-10. RECORD IN 2014: (Cheetahs SR) 6-0-0-0-0-0.
Ferreira, Martin (Grey HS, PE & NMMU & UFS) b 24/01/1989, Port Elizabeth. 1.88m. 115kg. Hooker. FC DEBUT: 2011. PROV CAREER: SWD 2011 & 13 22-6-0-0-0-30. EP Kings 2014 4-0-0-0-0-0. Border 1-0-0-0-0-0. REP HONOURS: SA Univ 2013 1-2-0-0-0-10. FC RECORD: 28-8-0-0-0-40. RECORD IN 2014: (EP Kings, Border) 5-0-0-0-0-0
Fikster, Kelvin Wikus (Bergrivier HS) b 16/07/1992, Paarl. 1.7m. 97kg. Hooker. FC DEBUT: 2014. PROV CAREER: Boland 2014 2-0-0-0-0-0. FC RECORD: 2-0-0-0-0-0. RECORD IN 2014: (Boland) 2-0-0-0-0-0.
Fortuin, Arno Franco (Hawston HS) b 10/11/1993, Hawston. 1.7m. 70kg. Wing. FC DEBUT: 2014. PROV CAREER: Boland 2014 7-4-0-0-0-20. FC RECORD: 7-4-0-0-0-20. RECORD IN 2014: (Boland) 7-4-0-0-0-20.
Fouche, Johan Neethling (Rustenburg HS, Grey Coll., Bloemfontein & UP) b 10/01/1993, Rustenburg. 1.87m. 114kg. Prop. FC DEBUT: 2014. PROV CAREER: Blue Bulls 2014 1-0-0-0-0-0. FC RECORD: 1-0-0-0-0-0. RECORD IN 2014: (Blue Bulls) 1-0-0-0-0-0.
Fouche, Louis Daniel van Zyl (Rustenburg HS) b 04/01/1990, Pretoria. 1.86m. 92kg. Flyhalf. FC DEBUT: 2011. PROV CAREER: Blue Bulls 2011-12 & 14 28-2-47-63-5-308. SUPER RUGBY: Bulls 2012-14 23-2-5-8-1-47. FC RECORD: 51-4-52-71-6-355. RECORD IN 2014: (Bulls, Blue Bulls) 6-0-4-11-1-44.
Fourie, Corne (Waterkloof HS, Pretoria) b 02/09/1988, Roodepoort. 1.87m. 116kg. Prop. FC DEBUT: 2010. PROV CAREER: Blue Bulls 2010-11 16-3-0-0-0-15. Pumas 2012-14 62-6-0-0-0-30. SUPER RUGBY: Lions 2014 12-1-0-0-0-5. REP HONOURS: SA Barbarians 2012 1-0-0-0-0-0. SA U20 2008 4-0-0-0-0-0. FC RECORD: 95-10-0-0-0-50. RECORD IN 2014: (Lions SR, Pumas) 22-1-0-0-0-5.
Fourie, Deon André (Pietersburg HS) b 25/09/86, Pretoria. 1.76m. 97kg. Hooker. FC DEBUT: 2006. PROV CAREER: WP 2006-13 90-22-0-0-0-110. SUPER RUGBY: Stormers 2008-14 84-12-0-0-0-60. REP HONOURS: SA Sevens 2007. MISC INFO: CC PoY 2014. FC RECORD: 174-34-0-0-0-170. RECORD IN 2014: (Stormers) 14-2-0-0-0-10.
Fourie, Louis Johannes (Pearson HS & NMMU) b 28/01/1991, Bloemfontein. 1.96m. 114kg. Lock. FC DEBUT: 2014. PROV CAREER: EP Kings 2014 2-0-0-0-0-0. FC RECORD: 2-0-0-0-0-0. RECORD IN 2014: (EP Kings) 2-0-0-0-0-0.
Fourie, Marius (Outeniqua HS, George & NWU) b 15/10/1990, Cape Town. 1.83m. 108kg. Hooker. FC DEBUT: 2011. PROV CAREER: Leopards 2011-12 & 14 30-2-0-0-0-10. FC RECORD: 30-2-0-0-0-10. RECORD IN 2014: (Leopards) 2-0-0-0-0-0.
Francke, Jonathan Charles (Strand HS, Cape Town & Boland Coll.) b 17/05/1986, Strand. 1.80m. 92kg. Fullback. FC DEBUT: 2011. PROV CAREER: Boland 2011-13 55-16-0-0-0-80. Griquas 2013-14 26-4-0-0-0-20. FC RECORD: 81-20-0-0-0-100. RECORD IN 2014: (Griquas) 25-4-0-0-0-20.
Franklin, Johannes (Hannes) (Bekker HS, Magaliesberg) b 06/10/81, Randfontein. 1.82m. 99kg. Hooker. FC DEBUT: 2003. PROV CAREER: Valke 2003-04 22-1-0-0-0-5. Pumas 2005,09-10 53-12-0-0-0-60. SWD 2006-08 & 14 64-18-0-0-0-90. EP Kings 2011-13 53-3-0-0-0-15. SUPER RUGBY: Lions 2010 12-2-0-0-0-10. Southern Kings 2013 8-1-0-0-0-5. P/R 2013 2-0-0-0-0-0. REP HONOURS: SA Kings 2011

3-0-0-0-0-0. SA Barbarians 2012 1-1-0-0-0-5. FC RECORD: 218-38-0-0-0-190. RECORD IN 2014: (SWD) 6-0-0-0-0-0.
Fraser, Jason-Collin (Sutherland HS) b 15/04/1991, Amanzimtoti. 1.96m. 100kg. Eighthman. FC DEBUT: 2014. PROV CAREER: Boland 2014 8-0-0-0-0-0. FC RECORD: 8-0-0-0-0-0. RECORD IN 2014: (Boland) 8-0-0-0-0-0.
Frylinck, Dylon (Wynberg Boys' HS) b 15/01/1992, Cape Town. 1.71m. 80kg. Scrumhalf. FC DEBUT: 2014. PROV CAREER: Pumas 2014 7-0-0-0-0-0. WP 2014 5-0-0-0-0-0. SUPER RUGBY: Stormers 2014 1-0-0-0-0-0. FC RECORD: 13-0-0-0-0-0. RECORD IN 2014: (Stormers, Pumas) 13-0-0-0-0-0.
Fuzani, Mthetheleli Godfrey (Bellville HS) b 18/01/1991, Uitenhage. 1.97m. 118kg. Lock. FC DEBUT: 2013. PROV CAREER: WP 2013-14 15-0-0-0-0-0. FC RECORD: 15-0-0-0-0-0. RECORD IN 2014: (WP) 6-0-0-0-0-0.
Ganto, Sinovuyo (Winterberg Agric. HS, Fort Beaufort) b 24/07/1987, Alice. 1.80m. 85kg. Wing. FC DEBUT: 2010. PROV CAREER: Border 2010 9-1-0-0-0-5. Valke 2011-12 16-4-0-0-0-20. Free State XV 2014 6-1-0-0-0-5. Boland 2014 1-0-0-0-0-0. FC RECORD: 32-6-0-0-0-30. RECORD IN 2014: (Boland, Free State XV) 7-1-0-0-0-5.
Gardner, Wayne (Brandwag HS, Uitenhage) b 13/08/1993, Uitenhage. 1.89m. 85kg. Flyhalf. FC DEBUT: 2014. PROV CAREER: Valke 2014 5-0-1-0-0-2. FC RECORD: 5-0-1-0-0-2. RECORD IN 2014: (Valke) 5-0-1-0-0-2.
Gates, Shane Edward (Muir Coll., Uitenhage & Boys' HS) b 27/09/1993, Port Elizabeth. 1.82m. 91kg. Flyhalf. FC DEBUT: 2011. PROV CAREER: EP Kings 2012-14 21-7-0-0-0-35. SUPER RUGBY: Southern Kings 2013 5-0-0-0-0-0. P/R 2013 2-0-0-0-0-0. REP HONOURS: SA Kings 2011 1-0-0-0-0-0. FC RECORD: 29-7-0-0-0-35. RECORD IN 2014: (EP Kings) 11-5-0-0-0-25.
Gavor, Selom (Rondebosch HS) b 18/09/1993. 1.92m. 90kg. Wing. FC DEBUT: 2014. PROV CAREER: Young Lions 2014 5-3-0-0-0-15. FC RECORD: 5-3-0-0-0-15. RECORD IN 2014: (Young Lions) 5-3-0-0-0-15.
Geduld, Justin Gilberto (Tygerberg HS, Cape Town) b 01/10/1993, Cape Town. 1.75m. 70kg. Centre. FC DEBUT: 2013. PROV CAREER: WP 2014 4-2-0-0-0-10. REP HONOURS: SA U20 2013 3-2-0-0-0-10. SA Sevens 2013-14. FC RECORD: 7-4-0-0-0-20. RECORD IN 2014: (WP, SA Sevens) 4-2-0-0-0-10.
Gelant, Warrick Wayne (Outeniqua HS, George) b 20/05/1995, Knysna. 1.79m. 86kg. Fullback. FC DEBUT: 2014. REP HONOURS: SA U20 2014 5-2-0-0-0-10. FC RECORD: 5-2-0-0-0-10. RECORD IN 2014: (SA U20) 5-2-0-0-0-10.
Gilbert, Warren James (Affies, Pretoria) b 19/03/1992, Nelspruit. 1.80m. 90kg. Flyhalf. FC DEBUT: 2013. PROV CAREER: Leopards 2013-14 7-0-1-0-0-2. Leopard XV 2013 4-0-0-4-0-12. FC RECORD: 11-0-1-4-0-14. RECORD IN 2014: (Leopards) 1-0-0-0-0-0.
Godfrey, Roy Andrew Michael (Selborne Coll., East London & NMMU) b 11/09/1989, East London. 1.88m. 118kg. Prop. FC DEBUT: 2013. PROV CAREER: SWD 2013-14 26-6-0-0-0-30. REP HONOURS: SA Univ 2013 1-1-0-0-0-5. FC RECORD: 27-7-0-0-0-35. RECORD IN 2014: (SWD) 12-1-0-0-0-5.
Goeda, Cheslin (Humansdorp HS) b 10/02/1991, Jeffreys Bay. 87kg. Hooker. FC DEBUT: 2014. PROV CAREER: Border 2014 2-0-0-0-0-0. FC RECORD: 2-0-0-0-0-0. RECORD IN 2014: (Border) 2-0-0-0-0-0.
Goliath, Robin Vernon (Middelburg HTS) b 24/10/1990, Cape Town. 1.75m. 67kg. Fullback. FC DEBUT: 2013. PROV CAREER: Limpopo 2013-14 12-0-0-0-0-0. FC RECORD: 12-0-0-0-0-0. RECORD IN 2014: (Limpopo) 7-0-0-0-0-0.

SEASON IN 2014

Goosen, Johannes Lodewikus (Johan) (Grey Coll., Bloemfontein) b 27/07/1992, Burgersdorp. 1.85m. 85kg. Flyhalf. FC DEBUT: 2011. PROV CAREER: Cheetahs 2011-13 17-2-23-26-3-143. Emerging Cheetahs 2011 1-0-0-0-0-0. SUPER RUGBY: Cheetahs 2012-14 27-4-46-70-3-331. REP HONOURS: SA 2012 & 14 Tests: 6-0-1-2-0-8. SA U20 2011 5-0-23-10-1-79. Springbok XV 2014 1-1-2-0-0-9. MISC INFO: YPoY 2011 and 2012 nominee. FC RECORD: 57-7-95-108-7-571. RECORD IN 2014: (SA, Springbok XV, Cheetahs SR) 17-2-23-30-2-152

Gouws, Gideon Petrus (Grey Coll., Bloemfontein & CUT) b 24/09/1990, Bloemfontein. 1.79m. 99kg. Hooker. FC DEBUT: 2013. PROV CAREER: Griffons 2013-14 3-0-0-0-0-0. FC RECORD: 3-0-0-0-0-0. RECORD IN 2014: (Griffons) 2-0-0-0-0-0.

Gqoboka, Lizo Pumzile (Ntabankuku HS, Butterworth) b 24/03/1990, Mount Free. 1.83m. 115kg. Prop. FC DEBUT: 2012. PROV CAREER: EP Kings 2012-14 43-3-0-0-0-15. FC RECORD: 43-3-0-0-0-15. RECORD IN 2014: (EP Kings) 13-1-0-0-0-5.

Graaff, Johannes Petrus Jacobus (Hansie) (Wonderboom HS, Pretoria & TUT) b 10/09/1989, Pretoria. 1.9m. 94kg. Wing/Fullback. FC DEBUT: 2012. PROV CAREER: Griffons 2012-13 27-7-46-15-2-178. Sharks XV 2014 2-1-0-0-0-5. EP Kings 2014 1-0-0-0-0-0. Border 2014 1-0-1-1-0-5. MISC INFO: CC First Div PoY 2012. FC RECORD: 31-8-47-16-2-188. RECORD IN 2014: (EP Kings, Border, Sharks XV) 4-1-1-1-0-10.

Grant, Dean (Rondebosch HS & US & UCT) b 18/03/1989, Johannesburg. 1.82m. 91kg. Flyhalf. FC DEBUT: 2010. PROV CAREER: Boland 2010 4-1-9-7-0-44. Griquas 2014 7-1-7-3-0-28. FC RECORD: 11-2-16-10-0-72. RECORD IN 2014: (Griquas) 7-1-7-3-0-28.

Grant, Peter John (Maritzburg Coll.) b 15/08/84, Durban. 1.88m. 90kg. Flyhalf. FC DEBUT: 2004. PROV CAREER: WP 2004-09 55-9-52-43-1-281. SUPER RUGBY: Stormers 2006-14 104-10-126-188-0-866. REP HONOURS: SA 2007-08 Tests: 5-0-0-0-0-0. Emerging Springboks 2007 3-0-10-8-0-44. WP XV 2006 1-0-2-0-0-4. British Barbarians 2007 1-0-0-0-0-0. SA U19 2003. SA Schools 2002. CW KZN 2002. FC RECORD: 169-19-190-241-1-1195. RECORD IN 2014: (Stormers) 14-0-10-9-0-47.

Greeff, Carel Fredrick Kirstein (Schoonspruit HS, Malmesbury) b 20/05/1990, Klerksdorp. 1.83m. 99kg. Flank. FC DEBUT: 2011. PROV CAREER: Golden Lions XV 2011 1-0-0-0-0-0. Griquas 2013-14 30-16-0-0-0-80. SUPER RUGBY: Cheetahs 2014 1-0-0-0-0-0. FC RECORD: 32-16-0-0-0-80. RECORD IN 2014: (Cheetahs SR, Griquas) 23-13-0-0-0-65.

Greeff, Lloyd Dirk (Transvalia HS, Vanderbijlpark & NWU) b 03/01/1994, Vanderbijlpark. 1.93m. 103kg. Wing. FC DEBUT: 2014. REP HONOURS: SA U20 2014 3-3-0-0-0-15. FC RECORD: 3-3-0-0-0-15. RECORD IN 2014: (SA U20) 3-3-0-0-0-15.

Greeff, Stephan (Gill Coll., Somerset East) b 24/12/1989, Cape Town. 1.98m. 103kg. Lock. FC DEBUT: 2010. PROV CAREER: WP 2010-11 6-0-0-0-0-0. Lions 2013 2-0-0-0-0-0. Young Lions 2012-13 2-0-0-0-0-0. Leopards 2013 2-0-0-0-0-0. Griquas 2014 11-0-0-0-0-0. SUPER RUGBY: Lions 2012 5-0-0-0-0-0. FC RECORD: 28-0-0-0-0-0. RECORD IN 2014: (Griquas) 11-0-0-0-0-0.

Grey, Siyanda (Hlumani HS, Komga) b 16/08/1989, Komga. 1.79m. 79kg. Centre. FC DEBUT: 2010. PROV CAREER: EP Kings 2010-14 33-15-0-0-0-75. SUPER RUGBY: Southern Kings 2013 4-0-0-0-0-0. REP HONOURS: SA Kings 2011 3-6-0-0-0-30. FC RECORD: 40-21-0-0-0-105. RECORD IN 2014: (EP Kings) 3-1-0-0-0-5.

Greyling, Henco (Grey Coll., Bloemfontein) b 01/01/1993, Bloemfontein. 1.86m. 100kg. Flank. FC DEBUT: 2014. PROV CAREER: Free State XV 2014 7-2-0-0-0-10. FC RECORD: 7-2-0-0-0-10. RECORD IN 2014: (Free State XV) 7-2-0-0-0-10.

Greyling, MacGuyver Dean (Affies, Pretoria) b 01/01/86, Potgietersrus. 1.92m, 122kg. Prop. FC DEBUT: 2005. PROV CAREER: Blue Bulls 2005,07-14 79-9-0-0-0-45. SUPER RUGBY: Bulls 2008 & 10-14 54-5-0-0-0-25. REP HONOURS: SA 2011-12 Tests: 3-0-0-0-0-0. S/Kings 2009 1-0-0-0-0-0. FC RECORD: 137-14-0-0-0-70. RECORD IN 2014 (Bulls, Blue Bulls) 26-3-0-0-0-15.

Griesel, Abraham Jacobus (Grey Coll., Bloemfontein) b 15/01/1992, Bloemfontein. 1.83m. 85kg. Scrumhalf. FC DEBUT: 2012. PROV CAREER: Griquas 2014 4-1-0-0-0-5. Free State XV 2014 4-0-0-0-0-0. REP HONOURS: SA U20 2012 3-0-0-0-0-0. FC RECORD: 11-1-0-0-0-5. RECORD IN 2014: (Griquas, Free State XV) 8-1-0-0-0-5.

Griesel, Werner (Welkom Gym.) b 01/07/86, Welkom. 1.80m. 90kg. Centre. FC DEBUT: 2008. PROV CAREER: Griffons 2008-14 123-26-0-0-0-130. Cheetahs 2011 1-1-0-0-0-5. FC RECORD: 124-27-0-0-0-135. RECORD IN 2014: (Griffons) 9-0-0-0-0-0.

Grobbelaar, Hendrik (Dirk) (Hans Strijdom HS, Naboomspruit) b 08/02/1992, Benoni. 1.89m. 106kg. Flank. FC DEBUT: 2013. PROV CAREER: Griffons 2013-14 4-0-0-0-0-0. FC RECORD: 4-0-0-0-0-0. RECORD IN 2014: (Griffons) 2-0-0-0-0-0.

Grobler, Francois Jacobus (Jaco) (Framesby HS, PE & NWU) b 11/06/1992, Newton Park. 1.72m. 84kg. Scrumhalf. FC DEBUT: 2012. PROV CAREER: Leopards 2012-13 18-2-0-0-0-10. Leopard XV 2013 2-0-0-0-0-0. EP Kings 2014 5-0-0-0-0-0. FC RECORD: 25-2-0-0-0-10. RECORD IN 2014: (EP Kings) 5-0-0-0-0-0.

Grobler, Douw Gerbrandt (Affies, Pretoria) b Nelspruit. 1.99m. 95kg. Lock. FC DEBUT: 2012. PROV CAREER: WP 2012-14 17-0-0-0-0-0. SUPER RUGBY: Stormers 2013 5-0-0-0-0-0. FC RECORD: 22-0-0-0-0-0. RECORD IN 2014: (WP) 2-0-0-0-0-0.

Groenewald, Brendon (Glenwood Boys' HS, Durban & UCT) b 2705/1991, Springs. 1.93m. 108kg. Flank. FC DEBUT: 2011. PROV CAREER: Cheetahs 2011 & 14 9-2-0-0-0-10. Sharks XV 2012 2-0-0-0-0-0. FC RECORD: 11-2-0-0-0-10. RECORD IN 2014: (Cheetahs) 1-0-0-0-0-0.

Groenewald, John Adriaan (Ian) (Nico Malan HS, Humansdorp & US) b 07/11/1992, Middelburg. 1.98m. 113kg. Lock. FC DEBUT: 2014. PROV CAREER: WP 2014 2-0-0-0-0-0. FC RECORD: 2-0-0-0-0-0. RECORD IN 2014: (WP) 2-0-0-0-0-0.

Groenewald, Lambert Smith (Paul Roos Gym., Stellenbosch) b 01/02/1989, Worcester. 1.89m. 106kg. Flanker. FC DEBUT: 2010. PROV CAREER: Sharks XV 2010-11 14-1-0-0-0-5. Lions 2013 6-0-0-0-0-0. Young Lions 2014 1-0-0-0-0-0. SUPER RUGBY: Sharks 2011 1-0-0-0-0-0. FC RECORD: 22-1-0-0-0-5. RECORD IN 2014: (Young Lions) 1-0-0-0-0-0.

Groenewald, Marcel Breytenbach (Oudtshoorn HS) b 10/03/1990, Pretoria. 1.89m. 88kg. Eighthman. FC DEBUT: 2012. PROV CAREER: Leopards 2012 2-0-0-0-0-0. Leopard XV 2013 1-0-0-0-0-0. SWD 2014 3-0-0-0-0-0. FC RECORD: 6-0-0-0-0-0. RECORD IN 2014: (SWD) 3-0-0-0-0-0.

Groenewald, Wilmar Romano (Hentie Cilliers HS, Virginia) b 30/04/1992, George. 1.84m. 81kg. Flanker. FC DEBUT: 2010. PROV CAREER: Griffons 2010-14 25-3-0-0-0-15. FC RECORD: 25-3-0-0-0-15. RECORD IN 2014: (Griffons) 10-1-0-0-0-5.

Gronum, Anthonie Johannes (Oakdale Agricultural HS, Riversdale) b 15/06/85, Knysna. 2.02m. 112kg. Lock. FC DEBUT: 2006. PROV CAREER: Blue Bulls 2006 2-0-0-0-0-0. Leopards 2007-10 55-2-0-0-0-10. Border 2011-14 40-0-0-0-0-0. FC RECORD: 97-2-0-0-0-10. RECORD IN

SEASON IN 2014

2014: (Border) 6-0-0-0-0-0.
Groom, Nicholas James (Rondebosch Boys' HS & UCT) b 21/02/1990, King William's Town. 1.71m. 81kg. Scrumhalf. FC DEBUT: 2011. PROV CAREER: WP 2011-14 58-8-0-0-0-40. SUPER RUGBY: Stormers 2011 & 13-14 27-1-0-0-0-5. FC RECORD: 85-9-0-0-0-45. RECORD IN 2014: (Stormers, WP) 25-1-0-0-0-5.
Gunter, Juan Janco (Waterkloof HS, Pretoria) b 09/03/1993, Pretoria. 1.81m. 85kg. Centre. FC DEBUT: 2014. PROV CAREER: WP 2014 3-0-0-0-0-0. FC RECORD: 3-0-0-0-0-0. RECORD IN 2014: (WP) 3-0-0-0-0-0.
Gwavu, Lubabalo Vincent (Daniel Pienaar HTS, Uitenhage) b 04/09/87, Port Elizabeth. 1.84m. 99kg. Flank. FC DEBUT: 2008. PROV CAREER: Blue Bulls 2008-11 23-2-0-0-0-10. SWD 2009 2-1-0-0-0-5. Valke 2013-14 20-3-0-0-0-15. REP HONOURS: SA Pres XV 2013 1-0-0-0-0-0. FC RECORD: 46-6-0-0-0-30. RECORD IN 2014: (Valke) 6-2-0-0-0-10.
Habana, Bryan Gary (KES, Johannesburg & RAU) b 12/06/83, Johannesburg. 1.80m. 93kg. Wing. FC DEBUT: 2003. PROV CAREER: Lions 2003-04 21-17-0-0-0-85. Blue Bulls 2005 & 08-09 14-9-0-0-0-45. WP 2010-12 8-2-0-0-0-10. SUPER RUGBY: Bulls 2005-09 61-37-0-0-0-185. Stormers 2010-13 57-19-0-0-0-95. REP HONOURS: SA Tests: 2004-14 106-57-0-0-0-285. Tour: 2007 2-0-0-0-0-0. Total: 108-57-0-0-0-285. Springbok XV 2014 1-1-0-0-0-5. SA Sevens 2004. SA U21 2004 3-3-0-0-0-15. British Barbarians 2008,09,11 3-3-0-0-0-15. MISC INFO: SARU PoY 2005, 2007, 2012 . YPoY 2004, S12 PoY 2005. IRB PoY 2007. IRB PoY nominee 2005. IRPA YPoY 2005. Try of the year 2012 (SA vs All Blacks). Leading FC try-scorer 2004, 2005, 2007. Holds SA record for most tries in a season (13 in 2007) Holds SA record for most tries in Tests - 57. Holds SA record for most Tests as a wing - 105 (also one at centre). Holds SA record for most tries in SUPER RUGBY (56 - Bulls 37 & Stormers 19) FC RECORD: 275-148-0-0-0-740. RECORD IN 2014: (SA, Springbok XV, Stormers) 12-5-0-0-0-25.
Hadebe, Monde Sakhile (Westville HS) b 09/12/1990, Durban. 1.77m. 102kg. Hooker. FC DEBUT: 2011. PROV CAREER: KZN 2011-14 17-1-0-0-0-5. Sharks XV 2011-14 27-1-0-0-0-5. REP HONOURS: SA U20 2010 5-0-0-0-0-0. FC RECORD: 49-2-0-0-0-10. RECORD IN 2014: (KZN, Sharks XV) 12-2-0-0-0-10.
Hamman, Stephan (Os) (Paul Roos Gym., Stellenbosch & US) b 14/10/1988, Cape Town. 1.84m. 130kg. Prop. FC DEBUT: 2012. PROV CAREER: WP 2014 1-0-0-0-0-0. REP HONOURS: SA Students 2012 2-0-0-0-0-0. SA Univ 2013 1-1-0-0-0-5. FC RECORD: 4-1-0-0-0-5. RECORD IN 2014: (WP) 1-0-0-0-0-0.
Hanekom, Morne (Boland Agric. HS, Paarl & Stellenbosch Univ.) b 15/02/88, Malmesbury. 1.94m. 112kg. FC DEBUT: 2009. PROV CAREER: WP 2009 1-0-0-0-0-0. EP Kings 2010-11 7-2-0-0-0-10. Leopards 2011-14 36-8-0-0-0-40. Leopard XV 2013-14 11-4-0-0-0-20. FC RECORD: 55-14-0-0-0-70. RECORD IN 2014: (Leopards, Leopard XV) 11-3-0-0-0-15.
Hanekom, Nicolaas Johannes (Stokkies) (Paarl Gym.) b 17/05/1989, Citrusdal. 1.93m. 101kg. Centre. FC DEBUT: 2012. PROV CAREER: SWD 2012 14-5-0-0-0-25. Lions 2013-14 10-5-0-0-0-25. Young Lions 2013-14 10-2-0-0-0-10. SUPER RUGBY: Lions 2014 3-0-0-0-0-0. Lions P/R 2013 2-2-0-0-0-10. REP HONOURS: SA U20 2009 5-2-0-0-0-10. FC RECORD: 44-16-0-0-0-80. RECORD IN 2014: (Lions SR, Lions, Young Lions) 21-6-0-0-0-30.
Hanekom, Pierre Francois (Marlow Agric. HS, Cradock & UFS) b 06/02/1989, Port Elizabeth. 1.86m. 120kg. Prop. FC DEBUT: 2012. PROV CAREER: Boland 2012-14 45-0-0-0-0-0. Sharks XV 2012 1-0-0-0-0-0. FC RECORD: 46-0-0-0-0-0. RECORD IN 2014 (Boland) 13-0-0-0-0-0.

Harris, Juan (Brok) (Bastion HS, Krugersdorp) b 22/02/85, Roodepoort. 1.83m. 113kg. Prop. FC DEBUT: 2006. PROV CAREER: WP 2006-14 120-15-0-0-0-75. SUPER RUGBY: Stormers 2007-14 93-2-0-0-0-10. FC RECORD: 213-17-0-0-0-85. RECORD IN 2014: (Stormers, WP) 20-1-0-0-0-5.
Hartnick, Lyndon Lee (Kairos HS, Johannesburg) b 08/07/86, Heidelberg. 1.90m. 97kg. Flanker. FC DEBUT: 2008. PROV CAREER: Border 2008 6-0-0-0-0-0. SWD 2010-14 68-9-0-0-0-45. FC RECORD: 74-9-0-0-0-45. RECORD IN 2014: (SWD) 12-0-0-0-0-0.
Hattingh, Grant Neil (Kingswood Coll., Grahamstown) b 03/10/1990, Johannesburg. 2.01m. 105kg. Lock. FC DEBUT: 2011. PROV CAREER: WP 2011-12 2-0-0-0-0-0. Blue Bulls 2012-14 29-2-0-0-0-10. SUPER RUGBY: Lions 2012 9-1-0-0-0-5. Bulls 2013-14 25-0-0-0-0-0. FC RECORD: 65-3-0-0-0-15. RECORD IN 2014: (Bulls, Blue Bulls) 24-2-0-0-0-10.
Haupt, Kurt Stanley (St Albans Coll., Pretoria & UP) b 17/01/1989, Johannesburg. 1.90m. 112kg. Hooker. FC DEBUT: 2013. PROV CAREER: Blue Bulls 2013 2-0-0-0-0-0. SWD 2014 12-3-0-0-0-15. FC RECORD: 14-3-0-0-0-15. RECORD IN 2014: (SWD) 12-3-0-0-0-15.
Hay, Wiehan (Jeugland HS, Kempton Park) b 02/02/1992, Kempton Park. 1.96m. 122kg. Lock. FC DEBUT: 2013. PROV CAREER: Sharks XV 2013 1-0-0-0-0-0. KZN 2014 1-0-0-0-0-0. FC RECORD: 2-0-0-0-0-0. RECORD IN 2014: (KZN) 1-0-0-0-0-0.
Hector, Brendan Roberto Eden (Unzon HS & NMMU) b 03/02/1993, Graaff-Reinett. 1.98m. 90kg. Lock. FC DEBUT: 2014. PROV CAREER: EP Kings 2014 2-0-0-0-0-0. FC RECORD: 2-0-0-0-0-0. RECORD IN 2014: (EP Kings) 2-0-0-0-0-0.
Hedin, Sven Erik (Merensky HS, Tzaneen) b 26/03/1984, Tzaneen. 1.87m. 96kg. Flank. FC DEBUT: 2014. PROV CAREER: Limpopo 2014 1-0-0-0-0-0. FC RECORD: 1-0-0-0-0-0. RECORD IN 2014: (Limpopo) 1-0-0-0-0-0.
Helberg, Gideon Gerhardus (Middelburg THS) b 27/09/1989, Lichtenburg. 1.87m. 91kg. Wing. FC DEBUT: 2010. PROV CAREER: Blue Bulls 2010 10-4-0-0-0-20. Lions 2012-13 18-5-0-0-0-25. Young Lions 2013-14 10-2-0-0-0-10. SUPER RUGBY: Bulls 2010 1-0-0-0-0-0. Lions P/R 2013 1-0-0-0-0-0. FC RECORD: 40-11-0-0-0-55. RECORD IN 2014: (Young Lions) 3-0-0-0-0-0.
Hendricks, Carlyle (Kyle) (Excelsior HS) b 12/12/86, Cape Town. 1.74m. 70kg. Wing. FC DEBUT: 2009. PROV CAREER: Valke 2009-14 79-34-19-10-0-238. FC RECORD: 79-34-19-10-0-238. RECORD IN 2014: (Valke) 18-6-3-0-0-36.
Hendricks, Cornal (Berg River HS, Wellington) b 18/04/88, Paarl. 1.88m. 85kg. Wing. FC DEBUT: 2008. PROV CAREER: Boland 2008-12 68-27-0-0-0-135. SUPER RUGBY: Cheetahs 2014 16-6-0-0-0-30. REP HONOURS: SA 2014 Tests: 11-5-0-0-0-25. Springbok XV 2014 1-0-0-0-0-0. SA Barbarians 2012 1-0-0-0-0-0. SA Sevens 2012-14. FC RECORD: 97-38-0-0-0-190. RECORD IN 2014 (SA, Springbok XV, Cheetahs SR, SA Sevens) 28-11-0-0-0-55.
Herbert, Colin (Goudveld HS, Welkom) b 19/03/1992, Welkom. 1.9m. 85kg. Flyhalf. FC DEBUT: 2012. PROV CAREER: Griffons 2012-14 16-1-4-1-0-16. MISC INFO: Son of former Free State and Griffons flyhalf Eric Herbert. FC RECORD: 16-1-4-1-0-16. RECORD IN 2014: (Griffons) 7-0-3-1-0-9.
Herbst, Wiehahn Jovan (Klerksdorp HS & Unisa) b 05/07/88, Klerksdorp. 1.80m. 110kg. Prop. FC DEBUT: 2009. PROV CAREER: KZN 2009-13 52-1-0-0-0-5. Sharks XV 2009-11 & 14 28-1-0-0-0-5. Sharks Inv XV 2009-10 2-0-0-0-0-0. SUPER RUGBY: Sharks 2010-14 40-0-0-0-0-0. REP HONOURS: SA U20 2008 4-0-0-0-0-0. FC RECORD:

126-2-0-0-0-10. RECORD IN 2014: (Sharks XV) 7-1-0-0-0-5.
Herne, Frank (Grey Coll., Bloemfontein & UOFS) b 31/10/1989, Ficksburg. 1.78m. 101kg. Hooker. FC DEBUT: 2011. PROV CAREER: EP Kings 2011-12 39-4-0-0-0-20. Pumas 2013-14 40-10-0-0-0-50. REP HONOURS: SA Kings 2011 3-0-0-0-0-0. SA Pres XV 2013 4-0-0-0-0-0. FC RECORD: 86-14-0-0-0-70. RECORD IN 2014: (Pumas) 19-2-0-0-0-10.
Hewitt, Brandan Benjamin b 15/09/1994. Flyhalf. FC DEBUT: 2014. PROV CAREER: Young Lions 2014 1-0-0-0-0-0. FC RECORD: 1-0-0-0-0-0. RECORD IN 2014: (Young Lions) 1-0-0-0-0-0.
Hewitt, Edwin Westley (Affies, Pretoria) b 28/03/1988, Pretoria. 1.94m. 115kg. Lock. FC DEBUT: 2010. PROV CAREER: Griquas 2010-13 32-1-0-0-0-5. SWD 2011 1-0-0-0-0-0. KZN 2013 9-0-0-0-0-0. Sharks XV 2014 8-0-0-0-0-0. SUPER RUGBY: Sharks 2013 3-0-0-0-0-0. FC RECORD: 53-1-0-0-0-5. RECORD IN 2014: (Sharks XV) 8-0-0-0-0-0.
Hlongwane, Nhlanhla (Louis Botha THS, Bloemfontein & UFS) b 28/06/1993, Petrus Steyn. 1.69m. 71kg. Scrumhalf. FC DEBUT: 2014. PROV CAREER: Free State XV 2014 1-0-0-0-0-0. FC RECORD: 1-0-0-0-0-0. RECORD IN 2014: (Free State XV) 1-0-0-0-0-0.
Hollenbach, Alwyn Wilhelm Cornelius Johannes (Grey Coll., Bloemfontein) b 14/06/85, Johannesburg. 1.90m. 95kg. Wing. FC DEBUT: 2005. PROV CAREER: Cheetahs 2005-07,09 41-11-0-0-0-55. Griquas 2008 2-0-0-0-0-0. Lions 2009 & 2011-12 & 14 35-8-0-0-0-40. Young Lions 2010-11 & 13-14 15-2-0-0-0-10. SUPER RUGBY: Cheetahs 2007 2-0-0-0-0-0. Lions 2011-12 & 14 21-2-0-0-0-10. FC RECORD: 116-23-0-0-0-115. RECORD IN 2014: (Lions SR, Lions, Young Lions) 11-1-0-0-0-5.
Hoffmann, Conrad Fritz (Paarl Boys' HS) b 09/11/87, Worcester. 1.81m. 79kg. Scrumhalf. FC DEBUT: 2007. PROV CAREER: WP 2007,09-10 44-7-4-8-0-67. KZN 2011 & 14 18-1-0-0-0-5. Sharks XV 2011-12 5-1-0-0-0-5. SUPER RUGBY: Stormers 2008 1-0-0-0-0-0. Sharks 2011 11-0-0-0-0-0. FC RECORD: 79-9-4-8-0-77. RECORD IN 2014: (KZN) 8-0-0-0-0-0.
Hope, Devlin (Bryanston HS, Johannesburg & UJ, UP) b 27/04/1990, Johannesburg. 1.80m. 94kg. Hooker. FC DEBUT: 2013. PROV CAREER: Valke 2013-14 12-2-0-0-0-10. FC RECORD: 12-2-0-0-0-10. RECORD IN 2014: (Valke) 11-2-0-0-0-10.
Horn, Joubert Prinsloo (Burgersdorp HS & Grey Coll., Bloemfontein & UFS) b 08/10/1988, Welkom. 1.95m. 100kg. Lock. FC DEBUT: 2010. PROV CAREER: Griffons 2010-12 30-2-0-0-0-10. Griquas 2013 5-0-0-0-0-0. Free State XV 2014 2-0-0-0-0-0. FC RECORD: 37-2-0-0-0-10. RECORD IN 2014: (Free State XV) 2-0-0-0-0-0.
Horne, Francis Henry (Frankie) (Huguenot HS, Wellington) b 24/02/1983, Port Elizabeth. 1.87m. 100kg. Flanker. FC DEBUT: 2005. PROV CAREER: Boland 2005-08 22-0-0-0-0-0. Rep. Honours: SA Sevens 2007-14. FC RECORD: 22-0-0-0-0-0. RECORD IN 2014: (SA Sevens).
Hougaard, Francois (Paul Roos Gym., Stellenbosch) b 06/04/88, Paarl. 1.79m. 92kg. Scrumhalf. FC DEBUT: 2007. PROV CAREER: WP 2007 3-0-0-0-0-0. Blue Bulls 2008-10 & 12 38-11-0-0-0-55. SUPER RUGBY: Bulls 2008-14 72-19-0-0-0-95. REP HONOURS: SA 2009-12 & 14 Tests: 35-5-0-0-0-25. Tour: 2009-10 3-0-0-0-0-0. Total: 38-5-0-0-0-25. SA U20 2008 3-0-0-0-0-0. S/Kings 2009 1-0-0-0-0-0. MISC INFO: PoY nominee 2011. YPoY nominee 2009, 2011. IRPA try of the year 2014 (vs All Blacks). FC RECORD: 155-35-0-0-0-180. RECORD IN 2014: (SA, Bulls) 24-2-0-0-0-10.
Howard, Patrick Benjamin (Michaelhouse HS, Balgowan) b 27/03/1992, Pietermaritzburg. 1.87m. 101kg. Centre. FC DEBUT: 2012. PROV CAREER: WP 2012-14 20-5-0-0-0-25. REP HONOURS: SA U20

2012 3-1-0-0-0-5. FC RECORD: 23-6-0-0-0-30. RECORD IN 2014: (WP) 6-2-0-0-0-10.
Huggett, Elandre (Premier HS, Johannesburg) b 05/10/1991, Cape Town. 1.76m. 93kg. Hooker. FC DEBUT: 2011. PROV CAREER: Cheetahs 2011-12 4-0-0-0-0-0. Free State XV 2012-13 12-2-0-0-0-10. Griffons 2013-14 15-2-0-0-0-10. FC RECORD: 31-4-0-0-0-20. RECORD IN 2014: (Griffons) 12-1-0-0-0-5.
Hugo, Abraham Pieter Marnus (Paarl Gym.) b 24/09/86, Paarl. 1.70m. 84kg. Scrumhalf. FC DEBUT: 2006. PROV CAREER: Boland 2006 & 08-09 & 2011 & 14 47-4-0-0-0-20. Griquas 2010-13 57-1-0-0-0-5. SUPER RUGBY: Cheetahs 2010 2-0-0-0-0-0. FC RECORD: 106-5-0-0-0-25. RECORD IN 2014: (Boland) 15-0-0-0-0-0.
Hugo, Daniel Pieter (Reniel) (Paul Roos Gym., Stellenbosch & US) b 19/07/1990, Belville. 1.97m. 112kg. Lock. FC DEBUT: 2011. PROV CAREER: WP 2011 2-0-0-0-0-0. Blue Bulls 2014 6-2-0-0-0-10. REP HONOURS: SA Univ 2013 1-0-0-0-0-0. FC RECORD: 9-2-0-0-0-10. RECORD IN 2014: (Blue Bulls) 6-2-0-0-0-10.
Hugo, Morne James (Worcester Gym., US & TUT) b 11/10/1991, Oudtshoorn. 1.79m. 86kg. Flyhalf. FC DEBUT: 2014. PROV CAREER: EP Kings 2014 2-0-0-0-0-0. Boland 2014 7-0-6-8-1-39. FC RECORD: 9-0-6-8-1-39. RECORD IN 2014: (EP Kings) 9-0-6-8-1-39.
Hunt, Steven Mark (Grey HS, PE & US) b 14/10/88, Port Elizabeth. 1.79m. 81kg. FC DEBUT: 2009. PROV CAREER: WP 2009 & 2011 4-0-0-0-0-0. Rep. Honours: SA Sevens 2010-14. FC RECORD: 4-0-0-0-0-0. RECORD IN 2014: (SA Sevens).
Huysamen, Andy Richard (Elsies River HS, Belville HTS & Schoonspruit HS, Malmesbury) b 16/02/1993, Elsies River. 1.7m. 82kg. Centre/Flyhalf. FC DEBUT: 2014. PROV CAREER: Limpopo 2014 7-0-4-3-0-17. FC RECORD: 7-0-4-3-0-17. RECORD IN 2014: (Limpopo) 7-0-4-3-0-17.
Immelman, Jacob Nicolaas Olivier (Grey Coll., Bloemfontei & UP) b 18/06/1993, Upington. 1.91m. 109kg. Flank. FC DEBUT: 2014. PROV CAREER: Free State XV 2014 1-0-0-0-0-0. FC RECORD: 1-0-0-0-0-0. RECORD IN 2014: (Free State XV) 1-0-0-0-0-0.
Isbell, Ruwellyn Miguel (Grey Coll., Bloemfontein) b 17/02/1993, Somerset East. 1-78m. 88kg. Wing. FC DEBUT: 2014. PROV CAREER: Pumas 2014 12-4-0-0-0-20. FC RECORD: 12-4-0-0-0-20. REP HONOURS: SA Sevens 2012. RECORD IN 2014: (Pumas) 12-4-0-0-0-20.
Ismaiel, Travis Keenan (Tygerberg HS, Cape Town & UP) b 02/06/1992, Cape Town. 1.83m. 92kg. Wing. FC DEBUT: 2012. PROV CAREER: Blue Bulls 2013-14 15-7-0-0-0-35. REP HONOURS: SA U20 2012 1-0-0-0-0-0. FC RECORD: 16-7-0-0-0-35. RECORD IN 2014: (Blue Bulls) 5-0-0-0-0-0.
Izaacs, Alcino Marchioni (Namib HS) b 16/11/1993, Windhoek. 1.89m. 84kg. Wing. FC DEBUT: 2014. PROV CAREER: Sharks XV 2014 7-0-0-0-0-0. FC RECORD: 7-0-0-0-0-0. RECORD IN 2014: (Sharks XV) 7-0-0-0-0-0.
Jacobs, Adri Justin (Schoonspruit HS, Malmesbury) b 08/07/1990, Stellenbosch. 1.80m. 93kg. Centre. FC DEBUT: 2010. PROV CAREER: Boland 2013 2-0-0-0-0-0. Leopards 2014 3-3-0-0-0-15. Leopards XV 2014 7-2-0-0-0-10. REP HONOURS: SA U20 2010 1-0-0-0-0-0. FC RECORD: 13-5-0-0-0-25. RECORD IN 2014: (Leopards, Leopards XV) 10-5-0-0-0-25.
Jacobs, Cameron Luciano (Framesby HS, Port Elizabeth & UFS) b 31/10/89, Port Elizabeth. 1.78m. 85kg. Wing. FC DEBUT: 2008. PROV CAREER: Griffons 2011-12 & 14 14-3-0-0-0-15. Cheetahs 2011 13-3-0-0-0-15. Free State XV 2012 & 14 4-0-0-0-0-0. Emerging Cheetahs 2011 1-0-0-0-0-0. SUPER RUGBY: Cheetahs 2012 9-0-0-0-0-0. REP HONOURS: SA Students 2008. FC RECORD: 42-6-0-0-0-30. RECORD IN

SEASON IN 2014

2014: (Griffons, Free State XV) 5-0-0-0-0-0.

Jacobs, Niell (Affies, Pretoria) b 30/06/88, Pretoria. 1.83m. 91kg. Flyhalf. FC DEBUT: 2009. PROV CAREER: Leopards 2009-11 14-0-6-5-1-30. Border 2012-14 35-3-1-2-0-23. MISC INFO: Twin brother of Ruan Jacobs. FC RECORD: 49-3-7-7-1-53. RECORD IN 2014: (Border) 4-0-0-1-0-3.

Jacobs, Ruan (Affies, Pretoria & NWU) b 30/06/88, Pretoria. 1.82m. 92kg. Centre. FC DEBUT: 2008. PROV CAREER: Cheetahs 2008-09 7-1-0-0-0-5. Leopards 2011 1-0-0-0-0-0. Border 2012-14 31-4-0-0-0-20. MISC INFO: Twin brother of Niell Jacobs. FC RECORD: 39-5-0-0-0-25. RECORD IN 2014: (Border) 8-0-0-0-0-0.

Jacobs, Willem Johannes (Lohan) (Affies, Pretoria) b 23/04/1991, Krugersdorp. 1.76m. 88kg. Scrumhalf. FC DEBUT: 2011. PROV CAREER: Blue Bulls 2011-14 23-2-0-0-0-10. REP HONOURS: SA U20 2010-11 6-0-0-0-0-0. FC RECORD: 29-2-0-0-0-10. RECORD IN 2014: (Blue Bulls) 8-2-0-0-0-10.

Jaer, Malcolm Adrian Emile (Brandwag HS, Uitenhage) b 29/06/1995, Uitenhage. 1.74m. 72kg. Fullback. FC DEBUT: 2014. PROV CAREER: EP Kings 2014 1-0-0-0-0-0. FC RECORD: 1-0-0-0-0-0. RECORD IN 2014: (EP Kings) 1-0-0-0-0-0.

James, Eldred Garth (Parkdene HS, George) b 22/04/1993, Swellendam. 1.82m. 77kg. Centre. FC DEBUT: 2013. PROV CAREER: SWD 2013-14 2-0-0-0-0-0. FC RECORD: 2-0-0-0-0-0. RECORD IN 2014: (SWD) 1-0-0-0-0-0.

Janke, Grant Donovan (Welkom HS) b 02/11/1990, Cape Town. 1.78m. 87kg. Wing. FC DEBUT: 2011. PROV CAREER: Griffons 2011-12 9-0-0-0-0-0. Leopards 2012 3-0-0-0-0-0. Lions 2013 1-0-0-0-0-0. Young Lions 2013 1-0-0-0-0-0. Valke 2014 10-2-0-0-0-10. FC RECORD: 24-2-0-0-0-10. RECORD IN 2014: (Valke) 10-2-0-0-0-10.

Janse van Rensburg, Koning Baird b 27/02/1989. Wing. FC DEBUT: 2014. PROV CAREER: Limpopo 2014 5-1-0-0-0-5. FC RECORD: 5-1-0-0-0-5. RECORD IN 2014: (Limpopo) 5-1-0-0-0-5.

Janse van Rensburg, Nicolaas Jacobus (Nico) (Affies, Pretoria) b 06/05/1994, Pretoria. 1.99m. 109kg. Lock. FC DEBUT: 2014. PROV CAREER: Blue Bulls 2014 13-0-0-0-0-0. SUPER RUGBY: Bulls 2014 1-0-0-0-0-0. REP HONOURS: SA U20 2014 5-0-0-0-0-0. FC RECORD: 19-0-0-0-0-0. RECORD IN 2014: (Bulls, Blue Bulls, SA U20) 19-0-0-0-0-0.

Janse van Rensburg, Rohan (Waterkloof HS, Pretoria) b 11/09/1994, Welkom. 1.86m. 100kg. Centre. FC DEBUT: 2013. PROV CAREER: Blue Bulls 2013-14 7-4-0-0-0-20. REP HONOURS: SA U20 2013-14 3-0-0-0-0-0. FC RECORD: 10-4-0-0-0-20. RECORD IN 2014: (Blue Bulls, SA U20) 2-0-0-0-0-0.

Janse van Rensburg, Ruan (Voortrekker HS, Bethlehem) b 31/03/1993, Bethlehem. 1.8m. 87kg. Scrumhalf. FC DEBUT: 2014. PROV CAREER: Young Lions 2014 2-0-0-0-0-0. FC RECORD: 2-0-0-0-0-0. RECORD IN 2014: (Young Lions) 2-0-0-0-0-0.

Jansen, Jaquin (Bergrivier HS, Wellington) b 27/05/86, Paarl. 1.75m. 83kg. Flyhalf. FC DEBUT: 2008. PROV CAREER: Boland 2008-13 66-21-60-39-0-342. Griquas 2014 11-0-6-6-0-30. REP HONOURS: SA Barbarians 2012 1-0-0-0-0-0. SA Pres XV 2013 2-0-0-0-0-0. FC RECORD: 80-21-66-45-0-372. RECORD IN 2014: (Griquas) 11-0-6-6-0-30.

Jansen, Rocco Reginald (Queens Coll., Queenstown) b 21/07/86, Queenstown) b 21/07/86, Queenstown. 1.79m. 88kg. Wing. FC DEBUT: 2007. PROV CAREER: Blue Bulls 2007-09 28-22-0-0-0-110. Blue Bulls XV 2007 1-1-0-0-0-5. Elephants 2009 5-6-0-0-0-30. Sharks Inv XV 2009 1-0-0-0-0-0. Griquas 2010-14 79-31-0-0-0-155. SUPER RUGBY: Cheetahs 2012 4-0-0-0-0-0. REP HONOURS: Emerging Springboks 2008 3-1-0-0-0-5. FC RECORD: 121-61-0-0-0-305. RECORD IN 2014: (Griquas) 14-3-0-0-0-15.

Jantjies, Altonio (Tony) (Menlopark HS, Pretoria) b 19/04/1992, Cape Town. 1.78m. 90kg. Flyhalf. FC DEBUT: 2012. PROV CAREER: Blue Bulls 2012-14 20-3-36-31-0-180. REP HONOURS: SA U20 2012 3-0-2-5-0-19. MISC INFO: Brother of Elton Jantjies. FC RECORD: 23-3-38-36-0-199. RECORD IN 2014: (Blue Bulls) 6-0-4-7-0-29.

Jantjies, Elton Thomas (Florida HS, Johannesburg & UJ) b 01/08/1990, Graaff Reinet. 1.76m. 84kg. Flyhalf. FC DEBUT: 2010. PROV CAREER: Golden Lions 2010-13 42-4-75-101-2-479. Young Lions 2010-11 & 14 3-0-3-2-0-12. SUPER RUGBY: Lions 2011-12 & 14 38-1-40-56-1-256. Lions P/R 2013 2-0-3-6-0-24. Stormers 2013 13-0-1-3-0-11. REP HONOURS: SA 2012 Tests: 2-0-0-2-0-6. 2010 Tour: 1-0-1-1-0-5. Total: 3-0-1-3-0-11. SA U20 2010 5-2-1-0-0-12. MISC INFO: YPoY 2011 and 2012 nominee. CC PoY 2012 nominee. MISC INFO: Brother of Tony Jantjies. FC RECORD: 106-7-124-171-3-800. RECORD IN 2014: (Lions SR, Young Lions) 12-1-9-5-0-38.

Jenkinson, John-Roy (Glenwood HS, Durban & NWU) b 26/03/1991, Worcester. 1.77m. 127kg. Prop. FC DEBUT: 2011. PROV CAREER: Leopards 2011-14 27-1-0-0-0-5. Cheetahs 2013 2-0-0-0-0-0. Leopards XV 2014 2-1-0-0-0-5. REP HONOURS: SA Students 2012 2-1-0-0-0-5. SA U20 2011 5-0-0-0-0-0. FC RECORD: 38-3-0-0-0-15. RECORD IN 2014: (Leopards, Leopards XV) 13-2-0-0-0-10.

Jenner, Dwayne (Dr. EG Jansen HS, Boksburg) b 17/11/1990, Benoni. 1.83m. 99kg. Wing. FC DEBUT: 2010. PROV CAREER: Border 2011-13 26-3-0-0-0-15. Sharks Inv XV 2010 1-1-0-0-0-5. EP Kings 2014 2-1-0-0-0-5. FC RECORD: 29-5-0-0-0-25. RECORD IN 2014: (EP Kings) 2-1-0-0-0-5.

Jho, Andile (Dale Coll., King William's Town & NMMU) b 21/04/1992, Kingwilliamstown. 1.73m. 83kg. Centre. FC DEBUT: 2013. PROV CAREER: EP Kings 2013-14 9-0-0-0-0-0. FC RECORD: 9-0-0-0-0-0. RECORD IN 2014: (EP Kings) 3-0-0-0-0-0.

Jinka, Dustin (Bishops HS, Rondebosch) b 28/04/1986, Cape Town. 1.76m. 82kg. Scrumhalf. FC DEBUT: 2010. PROV CAREER: Blue Bulls 2010-11 20-0-1-1-0-5. WP 2010 5-1-1-0-0-7. Griquas 2014 11-1-7-0-0-19. FC RECORD: 36-2-9-1-0-31. RECORD IN 2014: (Griquas) 11-1-7-0-0-19.

Jobo, Vincent Thabiso (KES, Johannesburg, UJ &UCT) b 01/02/1991, Krugersdorp. 1.86m. 104kg. Eighthman. FC DEBUT: 2013. PROV CAREER: WP 2013 1-0-0-0-0-0. Cheetahs 2014 4-0-0-0-0-0. FC RECORD: 5-0-0-0-0-0. RECORD IN 2014: (Cheetahs) 4-0-0-0-0-0.

Johannes, Reuben Benjamin (Paul Roos Gym., Stellenbosch & US) b 05/10/1990, Belville. 1.83m, 96kg, Flank. FC DEBUT: 2011. PROV CAREER: WP 2011-12 & 14 11-3-0-0-0-15. REP HONOURS: SA Sevens 2012-13. FC RECORD: 11-3-0-0-0-15. RECORD IN 2014: (WP) 4-0-0-0-0-0.

Johnson, Arno Marthinich b 15/11/1983. Flank. FC DEBUT: 2014. PROV CAREER: Limpopo 2014 3-0-0-0-0-0. FC RECORD: 3-0-0-0-0-0. RECORD IN 2014: (Limpopo) 3-0-0-0-0-0.

Johnson, Niyaas b 25/07/1993. Scrumhalf. FC DEBUT: 2014. PROV CAREER: Limpopo 2014 7-2-0-0-0-10. FC RECORD: 7-2-0-0-0-10. RECORD IN 2014: (Limpopo) 7-2-0-0-0-10.

Jonck, Juan-Pierre b 07/12/1991. Flank. FC DEBUT: 2014. PROV CAREER: Valke 2014 8-0-0-0-0-0. FC RECORD: 8-0-0-0-0-0. RECORD IN 2014: (Valke) 8-0-0-0-0-0.

Jones, Huw Richard Forbes (Milfield HS, UK) b 17/12/1993, Edinburgh. 1.86m. 91kg. Centre. FC DEBUT: 2014. PROV CAREER: WP 2014 2-1-0-0-0-5. FC RECORD: 2-1-0-0-0-5. RECORD IN 2014: (WP) 2-1-0-0-0-5.

Jonker, Jacobus Willem (JW) (Grey Coll., Bloemfontein) b 19/03/87,

Bloemfontein. 1.81m. 85kg. Centre. FC DEBUT: 2006. PROV CAREER: Cheetahs 2006-10 65-18-0-0-0-90. Griffons 2010 4-6-0-0-0-30. Pumas 2011-12 & 14 56-23-0-0-0-115. SUPER RUGBY: Cheetahs 2008-09 16-6-0-0-0-30. Lions 2014 11-0-0-0-0-0. REP HONOURS: SA Students 2007 1-0-0-0-0-0. SA Barbarians 2012 1-0-0-0-0-0. MISC INFO: CC First Div PoY 2012 nominee. FC RECORD: 154-53-0-0-0-265. RECORD IN 2014: (Lions SR, Pumas) 21-2-0-0-0-10.

Jonker, Johannes Gideon Andries (Hudson Park HS, East London) b 22/08/1994, East London. 1.84m. 118kg. Prop. FC DEBUT: 2014. PROV CAREER: Border 2014 11-2-0-0-0-10. FC RECORD: 11-2-0-0-0-10. RECORD IN 2014: (Border) 11-2-0-0-0-10.

Jordaan, Daniel Barend (Fochville HS & NWU) b 25/01/1991, Johannesburg. 1.96m. 104kg. Lock. FC DEBUT: 2012. PROV CAREER: Leopards 2012-14 7-0-0-0-0-0. Leopards XV 2014 2-0-0-0-0-0. FC RECORD: 9-0-0-0-0-0. RECORD IN 2014: (Leopards, Leopards XV) 7-0-0-0-0-0.

Jordaan, Daniel Niell (Grey Coll., Bloemfontein) b 13/01/1992, Newcastle. 1.90m. 103kg. Eighthman. FC DEBUT: 2013. PROV CAREER: Free State XV 2013 4-0-0-0-0-0. Griffons 2014 3-0-0-0-0-0. FC RECORD: 7-0-0-0-0-0. RECORD IN 2014: (Griffons) 3-0-0-0-0-0.

Jordaan, Gerhard Johan (Boland Agric., Wellington & US) b 10/04/1992, Kemptonpark. 1.8m. 83kg. Scrumhalf. FC DEBUT: 2014. PROV CAREER: WP 2014 1-0-0-0-0-0. FC RECORD: 1-0-0-0-0-0. RECORD IN 2014: (WP) 1-0-0-0-0-0.

Jordaan, Paul Abraham (Grey Coll., Bloemfontein) b 04/01/1992, Somerset East. 1.80m. 88kg. Centre. FC DEBUT: 2011. PROV CAREER: KZN 2012 & 14 19-6-0-0-0-30. Sharks XV 2011-12 3-1-0-0-0-5. SUPER RUGBY: Sharks 2012-14 30-5-0-0-0-25. Rep. Honours: SA U20 2011-12 8-1-0-0-0-5. SA Sevens 2010-11. FC RECORD: 60-13-0-0-0-65. RECORD IN 2014: (Sharks, KZN) 20-6-0-0-0-30.

Jordaan, Zandre (Paarl Boys' HS) b 24/09/87, Empangeni. 1.91m. 93kg. FC DEBUT: 2009. PROV CAREER: Boland 2009-14 74-23-0-0-0-115. WP 2009 4-2-0-0-0-10. REP HONOURS: SA Barbarians 2012 1-0-0-0-0-0. SA Pres XV 2013 2-1-0-0-0-5. FC RECORD: 81-26-0-0-0-130. RECORD IN 2014: (Boland) 8-2-0-0-0-10.

Kankowski, Ryan (St Andrew's Coll., Grahamstown) b 14/10/85, Port Elizabeth. 1.93m. 103kg. Eighthman. FC DEBUT: 2006. PROV CAREER: KZN 2006-11 59-16-0-0-0-80. Sharks XV 2009 & 12-13 3-0-0-0-0-0. SUPER RUGBY: Sharks 2007-14 98-18-0-0-0-90. REP HONOURS: SA 2007-12 Tests: 20-1-0-0-0-5. Tour: 2-0-0-0-0-0. Total: 22-1-0-0-0-5. SA Sevens 2006. MISC INFO: PoY nominee 2008. YPoY nominee 2008. Son of former EP, Border & Griquas wing Tino Kankowski. FC RECORD: 182-35-0-0-0-175. RECORD IN 2014: (Sharks) 16-0-0-0-0-0.

Karemaker, Leon (Bellville HS) b 18/05/85, Cape Town. 1.92m. 98kg. FC DEBUT: 2004. PROV CAREER: WP 2005-06 14-5-0-0-0-25. Griquas 2010-14 66-24-0-0-0-120. SUPER RUGBY: Cheetahs 2011 2-0-0-0-0-0. REP HONOURS: SA U21 2004 2-0-0-0-0-0. SA U19s 2003-2004. SA Schools 2002-03. CW WP 2003. FC RECORD: 84-29-0-0-0-145. RECORD IN 2014: (Griquas) 7-1-0-0-0-5.

Katzen, Joshua Mathew (Wynberg Boys' HS & UCT) b 07/06/1992, Cape Town. 1.81m. 95kg. Flank. FC DEBUT: 2013. PROV CAREER: WP 2013-14 3-0-0-0-0-0. FC RECORD: 3-0-0-0-0-0. RECORD IN 2014: (WP) 1-0-0-0-0-0.

Kebble, Oliver Ralph (Bishops HS, Rondebosch) b 18/06/1992, Durban. 1.91m. 124kg. Prop. FC DEBUT: 2012. PROV CAREER: WP 2012 & 14 5-0-0-0-0-0. Superrubgy: Stormers 2014 9-1-0-0-0-5. Rep honours: SA U20 2012 4-0-0-0-0-0. FC RECORD: 18-1-0-0-0-5. RECORD IN 2014: (Stormers, WP) 13-1-0-0-0-5.

Kebe, Ntando Lucky (Thubalethu HS, Fort Beaufort & UFH) b 19/08/1988, East London. 1.79m. 80kg. Scrumhalf. FC DEBUT: 2010. PROV CAREER: Border 2010-12 & 14 52-4-0-0-0-20. Boland 2013 21-1-0-0-0-5. Griquas 2014 2-1-0-0-0-5. REP HONOURS: SA Barbarians 2012 1-0-0-0-0-0. SA Pres XV 2013 4-0-0-0-0-0. FC RECORD: 80-6-0-0-0-30. RECORD IN 2014: (Griquas, Border) 12-1-0-0-0-5.

Kelly, Dwayne (Westville Boys' HS & NMMU) b 19/10/1991, Bloemfontein. 1.80m. 88kg. Scrumhalf. FC DEBUT: 2013. PROV CAREER: EP Kings 2013-14 18-1-1-0-0-7. SWD 2014 12-7-0-0-0-35. REP HONOURS: SA Univ 2013 1-0-0-0-0-0. FC RECORD: 31-8-1-0-0-42. RECORD IN 2014: (EP Kings, SWD) 18-8-1-0-0-42.

Kember, Reginald (RW) (Daniel Pienaar THS, Uitenhage) b 15/04/83, Adelaide. 1.87m. 105kg. Eighthman. FC DEBUT: 2006. PROV CAREER: Elephants 2006-07 30-5-0-0-0-25. Leopards 2008-11 51-7-0-0-0-35. Lions 2008 6-0-0-0-0-0. Pumas 2011-14 70-16-0-0-0-80. SUPER RUGBY: Lions 2008 1-0-0-0-0-0. REP HONOURS: Royal XV 2009 1-0-0-0-0-0. FC RECORD: 159-28-0-0-0-140. RECORD IN 2014: (Pumas) 12-0-0-0-0-0.

Kemp, Grant Dale (Wynberg Boys' HS, UCT & UP) b 31/10/1988, Cape Town. 1.87m. 119kg. Prop. FC DEBUT: 2012. PROV CAREER: SWD 2012-14 43-4-0-0-0-20. SUPER RUGBY: Southern Kings 2013 12-0-0-0-0-0. P/R 2013 1-0-0-0-0-0. FC RECORD: 56-4-0-0-0-20. RECORD IN 2014: (SWD) 19-0-0-0-0-0.

Kennedy, Michael (Kearsney Coll., Botha's Hill & UCT) b 12/01/1993, Durban. 1.79m. 100kg. Hooker. FC DEBUT: 2014. PROV CAREER: WP 2014 3-0-0-0-0-0. FC RECORD: 3-0-0-0-0-0. RECORD IN 2014: (WP) 3-0-0-0-0-0.

Kerrod, Simon b 25/08/1992. Prop. FC DEBUT: 2013. PROV CAREER: Sharks XV 2013 2-0-0-0-0-0. EP Kings 2014 5-1-0-0-0-5. Border 2014 1-0-0-0-0-0. FC RECORD: 8-1-0-0-0-5. RECORD IN 2014: (EP Kings, Border) 6-1-0-0-0-5.

Khan, Wayne (PW Botha HS, George) b 21/01/1991, Cape Town. 1.84m. 79kg. Hooker. FC DEBUT: 2011. PROV CAREER: Griffons 2011 3-0-0-0-0-0. SWD 2012-14 35-2-0-0-0-10. FC RECORD: 38-2-0-0-0-10. RECORD IN 2014: (SWD) 20-0-0-0-0-0.

Khoza, Caswell September (Southdowns HS, Centurion) b 01/09/1994, Nelspruit. 1.79m. 77kg. Wing. FC DEBUT: 2014. PROV CAREER: Young Lions 2014 4-1-0-0-0-5. FC RECORD: 4-1-0-0-0-5. RECORD IN 2014: (Young Lions) 4-1-0-0-0-5.

Killian, Michael (Muir Coll., Uitenhage) b 22/11/83, Uitenhage. 1.82m. 84kg. Wing. FC DEBUT: 2004. Prov career; EP Kings 2004-07 & 12-14 84-28-0-0-0-140. Lions 2008-11 45-21-0-0-0-105. Young Lions 2008-09 & 12 12-4-0-0-1-23. Lions XV 2008. SUPER RUGBY: Lions 2009-12 37-10-0-0-0-50. Southern Kings 2013 4-0-0-0-0-0. REP HONOURS: SA Students 2005,07 2-0-0-0-0-0. FC RECORD: 185-63-0-0-1-318. RECORD IN 2014: (EP Kings) 1-1-0-0-0-5.

King, Kalvano Xenito (Alexandria HS) b 10/01/1989, Grahamstown. 1.6m. 62kg. Scrumhalf. FC DEBUT: 2014. PROV CAREER: EP Kings 2014 1-0-0-0-0-0. FC RECORD: 1-0-0-0-0-0. RECORD IN 2014: (EP Kings) 1-0-0-0-0-0.

Kirchner, Zane (PW Botha Coll., George) b 16/06/84, George. 1.84m. 92kg. Fullback. FC DEBUT: 2003. PROV CAREER: Griquas 2003-04 & 06-07 58-9-32-22-0-175. Blue Bulls 2008-12 43-6-2-0-0-34. SUPER RUGBY: Bulls 2008-13 82-21-0-0-0-105. REP HONOURS: SA 2009-10 & 12-14 Tests: 29-5-0-0-0-25. Emerging Springboks 2009 1-0-0-0-0-0. CW SWD 2002. MISC INFO: VC PoY 2007. FC RECORD: 213-41-34-22-0-339. RECORD IN 2014: (SA) 1-0-0-0-0-0.

Kirkwood, Shane Monro (Marais Viljoen HS, Alberton) b 06/09/89, Alberton. 1.94m. 113kg. Lock. FC DEBUT: 2009. PROV CAREER: Valke

2013-14 25-4-0-0-0-20. Young Lions 2009 3-1-0-0-0-5. FC RECORD: 28-5-0-0-0-25. RECORD IN 2014: (Valke) 16-3-0-0-0-15.

Kirsten, Frederick Barend Christoffel (Frik) (Affies, Pretoria) b 18/08/88, Sandton. 1.93m. 118kg. Prop. FC DEBUT: 2008. PROV CAREER: Blue Bulls 2008-13 47-0-0-0-0-0. SUPER RUGBY: Bulls 2009 & 2012-14 34-0-0-0-0-0. REP HONOURS: SA 2013 no appearances. SA U20 2008 5-1-0-0-0-5. MISC INFO: Son of former Eastern Transvaal Flank Barend Kirsten. FC RECORD: 86-1-0-0-0-5. RECORD IN 2014: (Bulls) 3-0-0-0-0-0.

Kitshoff, Johannes Jakobus (Hanno) (Worcester Gym.) b 25/01/1984, George. 1.91m. 92kg. Flanker. FC DEBUT: 2012. PROV CAREER: Boland 2012-14 30-0-0-0-0-0. FC RECORD: 30-0-0-0-0-0. RECORD IN 2014: (Boland) 15-0-0-0-0-0.

Kitshoff, Rohan (Drostdy THS, Worcester) b 13/09/85, Windhoek. 1.81m. 95kg. Flank. FC DEBUT: 2007. PROV CAREER: Griquas 2007-10 59-12-0-0-0-60. WP 2011-14 33-13-0-0-0-65. SUPER RUGBY: Stormers 2013-14 2-0-0-0-0-0. MISC INFO: Represented Namibia at RWC 2011. FC RECORD: 94-25-0-0-0-125. RECORD IN 2014: (Stormers, WP) 12-6-0-0-0-30.

Kitshoff, Steven (Paul Roos Gym., Stellenbosch) b 10/02/1992, Somerset West. 1.83m. 114kg. Prop. FC DEBUT: 2011. PROV CAREER: WP 2011-13 32-1-0-0-0-5. SUPER RUGBY: Stormers 2011-14 45-0-0-0-0-0. REP HONOURS: SA U20 2012 5-1-0-0-0-5. FC RECORD: 82-2-0-0-0-10. RECORD IN 2014: (Stormers) 10-0-0-0-0-0.

Klaasen, Harlon Jason (Labori HS & Northlink Coll.) b 13/08/1993, Malmesbury. 1.86m. 83kg. Fullback. FC DEBUT: 2014. PROV CAREER: Boland 2014 3-2-0-0-0-10. FC RECORD: 3-2-0-0-0-10. RECORD IN 2014: (Boland) 3-2-0-0-0-10.

Kleinhans, Curtis (Stirling HS, East London & UFH) b 15/01/1992, East London. 1.78m. 87kg. Fullback. FC DEBUT: 2014. PROV CAREER: Border 2014 2-0-0-0-0-0. FC RECORD: 2-0-0-0-0-0. RECORD IN 2014: (Border) 2-0-0-0-0-0.

Kleinhans, Francois (Glenwood HS, Durban) b 07/01/1991, Parklands. 1.84m. 96kg. Flank. FC DEBUT: 2011. PROV CAREER: KZN 2011-12 & 14 11-0-0-0-0-0. Sharks XV 2011-14 26-3-0-0-0-15. REP HONOURS: SA U20 2011 3-1-0-0-0-5. FC RECORD: 40-4-0-0-0-20. RECORD IN 2014: (KZN, Sharks XV) 10-0-0-0-0-0.

Klopper, Marco (Voortrekker HS, Bethlehem & UFS) b 16/03/1993, Estcourt. 1.82m. 101kg. Hooker. FC DEBUT: 2014. PROV CAREER: Free State XV 2014 1-0-0-0-0-0. FC RECORD: 1-0-0-0-0-0. RECORD IN 2014: (Free State XV) 1-0-0-0-0-0.

Kloppers, Pieter Hugo (Worcester Gym. & US) b 14/10/1988, Worcester. 1.97m. 99kg. Lock. FC DEBUT: 2010. PROV CAREER: WP 2010 4-0-0-0-0-0. Lions 2013 4-0-0-0-0-0. Young Lions 2013-14 12-1-0-0-0-5. Griquas 2014 9-0-0-0-0-0. REP HONOURS: SA Students 2012 2-1-0-0-0-5. FC RECORD: 31-2-0-0-0-10. RECORD IN 2014: (Griquas, Young Lions) 17-1-0-0-0-5.

Knoetze, Naythan (Selborne Coll. & Hudson Park HS, East London) b 10/09/1994, King William's Town. 1.81m. 95kg. Eighthman. FC debut: 2014. PROV CAREER: Border 2014 1-0-0-0-0-0. FC RECORD: 1-0-0-0-0-0. RECORD IN 2014: (Border) 1-0-0-0-0-0.

Kobese, Bangihlombe (Dale Coll., King William's Town & UFH) b 19/01/1992, Mdantsane. 1.68m. 63kg. Scrumhalf. FC DEBUT: 2014. PROV CAREER: Border 2014 10-1-5-1-0-18. FC RECORD: 10-1-5-1-0-18. RECORD IN 2014: (Border) 10-1-5-1-0-18.

Koch, Vincent Philip (Hugenote HS, Springs) b 13/03/1990, Empangeni. 1.85m. 118kg. Prop. FC DEBUT: 2012. PROV CAREER: Blue Bulls 2012 3-1-0-0-0-5. Pumas 2012-14 46-7-0-0-0-35. REP HONOURS:

SA Pres XV 2013 2-0-0-0-0-0. FC RECORD: 51-8-0-0-0-40. RECORD IN 2014: (Pumas) 16-1-0-0-0-5.

Kohler, Thurlow Ashley (Paarl Boys' HS) b 04/06/1990, Paarl. 1.83m. 108kg. Hooker. FC DEBUT: 2011. PROV CAREER: Young Lions 2011 & 14 3-0-0-0-0-0. Golden Lions XV 2011 1-0-0-0-0-0. FC RECORD: 4-0-0-0-0-0. RECORD IN 2014: (Young Lions) 2-0-0-0-0-0.

Kok, Werner (Nelspruit HS) b 17/01/1993, Nelspruit. 1.79m. 88kg. Wing. REP HONOURS: SA Sevens 2013-14. RECORD IN 2014: (SA Sevens).

Kolbe, Cheslin (Brackenfell HS, Cape Town) b 28/10/1993, Kraaifontein. 1.7m. 69kg. Utility back. FC DEBUT: 2013. PROV CAREER: WP 2013-14 29-12-1-0-0-62. SUPER RUGBY: Stormers 2014 7-0-0-0-0-0. REP HONOURS: SA U20 2013 5-2-0-0-0-10. SA Sevens 2012-14. FC RECORD: 41-14-1-0-0-72. RECORD IN 2014: (Stormers, WP, SA sevens) 17-5-1-0-0-27.

Kolisi, Siya (Grey HS, PE) b 16/06/1991, Port Elizabeth. 1.86m. 96kg. Eighthman. FC DEBUT: 2011. PROV CAREER: WP 2011-14 29-7-0-0-0-35. SUPER RUGBY: Stormers 2012-14 44-4-0-0-0-20. REP HONOURS: SA 2013 Tests: 10-0-0-0-0-0. SA U20 2010-11 8-2-0-0-0-10. FC RECORD: 91-13-0-0-0-65. RECORD IN 2014: (Stormers, WP) 21-3-0-0-0-15.

Koster, Armandt (Pionier HS, Vryheid & UFS) b 20/01/1990, Vryheid. 1.92m. 105kg. Flanker. FC DEBUT: 2012. PROV CAREER: Griffons 2012-14 27-3-0-0-0-15. Free State XV 2012 2-0-0-0-0-0. FC RECORD: 29-3-0-0-0-15. RECORD IN 2014: (Griffons) 16-3-0-0-0-15.

Kotze, Jaun (Ben Vorster HS, Tzaneen) b 18/05/1992. 1.75m. 70kg. Flyhalf. FC DEBUT: 2011. PROV CAREER: Valke 2011-14 55-13-98-46-8-423. FC RECORD: 55-13-98-46-8-423. RECORD IN 2014: (Valke) 13-5-32-19-2-152.

Kotze, John-Ben (Johnny) (Bishops Coll., Cape Town) b 24/01/1993, Carltonville. 1.85m. 89kg. Centre. FC DEBUT: 2014. PROV CAREER: WP 2014 6-1-0-0-0-5. FC RECORD: 6-1-0-0-0-5. RECORD IN 2014: (WP) 6-1-0-0-0-5.

Kotze, Stephan Clyde (Grey Coll., Bloemfontein) b 21/01/1991, Kimberley. 1.88m. 119kg. Prop. FC DEBUT: 2011. PROV CAREER: Cheetahs 2011 3-0-0-0-0-0. Free State XV 2012 2-0-0-0-0-0. Pumas 2013-14 6-0-0-0-0-0. REP HONOURS: SA U20 2011 2-0-0-0-0-0. FC RECORD: 13-0-0-0-0-0. RECORD IN 2014: (Pumas) 1-0-0-0-0-0.

Koza, Luxolo (Muir Boys' HS, Uitenhage) b 18/09/1994, Uitenhage. 1.89m. 101kg. Flank. FC DEBUT: 2014. PROV CAREER: Griquas 2014 5-0-0-0-0-0. FC RECORD: 5-0-0-0-0-0. RECORD IN 2014: (Griquas) 5-0-0-0-0-0.

Krause, Gareth Edward (Dale Coll., King William's Town & UNISA) b 30/12/81, East London. 1.90m. 100kg. Flank. FC DEBUT: 2002. PROV CAREER: Border 2002-03,09,12-14 84-14-0-0-0-70. Griquas 2004-08 97-19-0-0-0-95. SUPER RUGBY: Cheetahs 7-0-0-0-0-0. REP HONOURS: SA Sevens 2004-05. FC RECORD: 188-33-0-0-0-165. RECORD IN 2014: (Border) 6-1-0-0-0-5.

Kriel, Daniel David (Maritzburg Coll.) b 15/02/1994, Cape Town. 1.93m. 103kg. Centre. FC DEBUT: 2014. REP HONOURS: SA U20 2014 4-0-0-0-0-0. FC RECORD: 4-0-0-0-0-0. RECORD IN 2014: (SA U20) 4-0-0-0-0-0.

Kriel, Jacobus Albertus (Jaco) (Standerton HS & UJ) b 21/08/1989, Standerton. 1.83m. 86kg. Flanker. FC DEBUT: 2010. PROV CAREER: Golden Lions 2010-14 35-16-0-0-0-80. Young Lions 2010-13 26-7-0-0-0-35. SUPER RUGBY: Lions 2011-12 & 14 23-3-0-0-0-15. P/R 2013 2-1-0-0-0-0. MISC INFO: VC PoY 2012 nominee. FC RECORD: 86-27-0-0-0-135. RECORD IN 2014: (Lions SR, Lions) 28-10-0-0-0-50.

Kriel, Jason (Dirkie Uys HS, Moorreesburg & UP) b 30/01/1990,

Moorreesburg. 1.90m. 102kg. Wing. FC DEBUT: 2013. PROV CAREER: Boland 2013-14 2-0-0-0-0-10. FC RECORD: 2-2-0-0-0-10. RECORD IN 2014: (Boland) 1-0-0-0-0-0.

Kriel, Jesse Andre (Maritzburg Coll. & UP) b 15/02/1994, Cape Town. 1.86m. 95kg. Fullback. FC DEBUT: 2013. PROV CAREER: Blue Bulls 2014 16-4-0-0-0-20. SUPER RUGBY: 2014 Bulls 1-0-0-0-0-0. REP HONOURS: SA U20 2013-14 9-7-0-0-0-35. FC RECORD: 26-11-0-0-0-55. RECORD IN 2014: (Bulls, Blue Bulls, SA U20) 22-9-0-0-0-45.

Kritzinger, Inus Michael (Wilgeriver HS, Frankfort & UFS) b 13/05/1989, Welkom. 1.76m. 83kg. Scrumhalf. FC DEBUT: 2011. PROV CAREER: Griffons 2011-14 22-7-5-0-0-45. Free State XV 2012 4-1-0-0-0-5. REP HONOURS: SA Pres XV 2013 1-0-0-0-0-0. FC RECORD: 27-8-5-0-0-50. RECORD IN 2014: (Griffons) 3-1-0-0-0-5.

Kruger, Marco (Nelspruit HS) b 20/08/1992, Nelspruit. 1.94m. 113kg. Lock. FC DEBUT: 2014. PROV CAREER: Pumas 2014 1-0-0-0-0-0. FC RECORD: 1-0-0-0-0-0. RECORD IN 2014: (Pumas) 1-0-0-0-0-0.

Kruger, Robert Albertus (Standerton HS & NWU) b 28/04/1988, Johannesburg. 1.94m. 106kg. FC DEBUT: 2009. PROV CAREER: Lions 2009-10 4-0-0-0-0-0. Young Lions 2009-11 5-1-0-0-0-5. Leopards 2011-14 36-2-0-0-0-10. Leopard XV 2013-14 13-2-0-0-0-10. SUPER RUGBY: Lions 2009-10 9-0-0-0-0-0. FC RECORD: 67-5-0-0-0-25. RECORD IN 2014: (Leopards, Leopard XV) 9-0-0-0-0-0.

Kruger, Rossouw (Boland Agric. HS, Paarl) b 03/05/1989, Cape Town. 121kg. Prop. FC DEBUT: 2010. PROV CAREER: Boland 2010-14 42-3-0-0-0-15. FC RECORD: 42-3-0-0-0-15. RECORD IN 2014: (Boland) 1-0-0-0-0-0.

Kruger, Victor Eric (Strand HS, Cape Town & NWU) b 19/01/1989, Welkom. 1.99m. 112kg. Lock. FC DEBUT: 2011. PROV CAREER: Leopards 2011-13 14-1-0-0-0-5. Griquas 2013 2-0-0-0-0-0. Boland 2014 10-2-0-0-0-10. FC RECORD: 26-3-0-0-0-15. RECORD IN 2014: (Boland) 10-2-0-0-0-10.

Kruger, Werner (Kempton Park HS) b 23/01/85, Kempton Park. 1.90m. 107kg. Prop. FC DEBUT: 2003. PROV CAREER: Blue Bulls 2003 & 05-07-14 123-7-0-0-0-35. Blue Bulls XV 2007 1-0-0-0-0-0. SUPER RUGBY: Bulls 2008-14 108-8-0-0-0-40. REP HONOURS: SA 2011-12 Tests: 4-0-0-0-0-0. Tour: 2010 1-0-0-0-0-0. Total: 5-0-0-0-0-0. Emerging Springboks 2009 1-0-0-0-0-0. SA U21 2005-06 6-0-0-0-0-0. FC RECORD: 244-15-0-0-0-75. RECORD IN 2014: (Bulls, Blue Bulls) 27-0-0-0-0-0.

Kuatu, Thierry Marcial Kounga (David) b 15/06/1994. 1.76m. Prop. FC DEBUT: 2014. PROV CAREER: Valke 2014 2-0-0-0-0-0. FC RECORD: 2-0-0-0-0-0. RECORD IN 2014: (Valke) 2-0-0-0-0-0.

Kubekha, Sandile Mlungisi (Kearsney Coll., Botha's Hill) b 03/07/1994, Durban. 1.76m. 86kg. Centre. FC DEBUT: 2014. PROV CAREER: Sharks XV 2014 5-0-0-0-0-0. FC RECORD: 5-0-0-0-0-0. RECORD IN 2014: (Sharks XV) 5-0-0-0-0-0.

Kyd, Blake Jonathan (Maritzburg Coll.) b 10/06/1988, Pietermaritzburg. 1.78m. 94kg. Prop. FC DEBUT: 2012. PROV CAREER: Border 2012-14 50-2-0-0-0-10. FC RECORD: 50-2-0-0-0-10. RECORD IN 2014: (Border) 17-0-0-0-0-0.

Labuschagne, Pieter Hermias Cornelius (Grey Coll., Bloemfontein & UFS) b 11/01/1989, Pretoria. 1.89m. 103kg. Flank. FC DEBUT: 2011. PROV CAREER: Cheetahs 2011-14 44-11-0-0-0-55. Free State XV 2012 2-0-0-0-0-0. Emerging Cheetahs 2011 1-0-0-0-0-0. SUPER RUGBY: Cheetahs 2012-14 27-2-0-0-0-10. FC RECORD: 74-13-0-0-0-65. RECORD IN 2014: (Cheetahs SR, Cheetahs) 13-1-0-0-0-5.

Labuschagne, Renier Lourens b 20/12/1991. Hooker. FC DEBUT: 2014. PROV CAREER: Limpopo 2014 2-0-0-0-0-0. FC RECORD: 2-0-0-0-0-0. RECORD IN 2014: (Limpopo) 2-0-0-0-0-0.

Ladendorf Ernst (Marais Viljoen HS, Alberton) b 05/02/1992, Alberton. 2.0m. 103kg. Flank. FC DEBUT: 2013. PROV CAREER: Border 2013 3-0-0-0-0-0. Valke 2014 12-0-0-0-0-0. FC RECORD: 15-0-0-0-0-0. RECORD IN 2014: (Valke) 12-0-0-0-0-0.

Lambie, Patrick Jonathan (Michaelhouse, Balgowan) b 17/10/90, Durban. 1.77m. 90kg. Flyhalf. FC DEBUT: 2009. PROV CAREER: KZN 2009-14 29-6-50-63-2-325. Sharks Inv XV 2009 1-0-1-1-0-5. SUPER RUGBY: Sharks 2010-14 56-9-69-129-1-573. REP HONOURS: SA 2010-14 Tests: 40-2-18-18-2-106. Tour: 1-0-0-0-0-0. Total: 41-2-18-18-2-106. SA U20 2010 5-4-17-9-0-75. British Barbarians 2013 1-0-4-0-0-8. MISC INFO: SARU PoY 2011 and 2012 nominee. SA Rugby YPoY 2011. MISC INFO: Son of former Natal utility back Ian Lambie. Grandson of Nic Labuschagne (England and Natal) and former President of the KZNRU. FC RECORD: 133-21-159-220-5-1092. RECORD IN 2014: (SA, Sharks, KZN) 15-2-10-22-2-102.

Landman, Rynard Jaco (Despatch HS) b 24/07/86, East London. 1.97m. 114kg. Lock. FC DEBUT: 2008. PROV CAREER: Leopards 2008-11 41-2-0-0-0-10. Boland 2011 13-4-0-0-0-20. Griquas 2012-14 26-8-0-0-0-40. SUPER RUGBY: Lions 2009 2-0-0-0-0-0. Cheetahs 2013-14 18-0-0-0-0-0. REP HONOURS: Royal XV 2009 1-0-0-0-0-0. FC RECORD: 101-14-0-0-0-70. RECORD IN 2014: (Cheetahs SR, Griquas) 7-1-0-0-0-5.

Language, Juan Michael (Framesby HS, Port Elizabeth) b 19/04/1989, Port Elizabeth. 1.83m. 97kg. Flank. FC DEBUT: 2014. PROV CAREER: Leopards 2014 8-6-0-0-0-30. FC RECORD: 8-6-0-0-0-30. RECORD IN 2014: (Leopards) 8-6-0-0-0-30.

Law, Duran Gavin (Ladysmith HS) b 21/02/1992, Ladysmith. 1.81m. 88kg. Flyhalf. FC DEBUT: 2014. PROV CAREER: Limpopo 2014 7-0-0-0-0-0. FC RECORD: 7-0-0-0-0-0. RECORD IN 2014: (Limpopo) 7-0-0-0-0-0.

Lawson, Richard James (Wynberg Boys' HS) b 20/10/86, Johannesburg. 1.83m. 87kg. Fullback. FC DEBUT: 2006. PROV CAREER: WP 2006-08 16-3-0-0-0-15. Griquas 2009-13 47-14-0-0-0-70. Boland 2014 8-2-0-0-0-10. REP HONOURS: Emerging Springboks 2008 3-0-0-0-0-0. FC RECORD: 74-19-0-0-0-95. RECORD IN 2014: (Boland) 8-2-0-0-0-10.

Lee, Nicolaas Jacobus (Affies, Pretoria & UFS) b 13/03/1994, Pretoria. 1.8m. 89kg. Centre. FC DEBUT: 2014. PROV CAREER: Free State XV 2014 8-6-0-0-0-30. FC RECORD: 8-6-0-0-0-30. RECORD IN 2014: (Free State XV) 8-6-0-0-0-30.

La Grange, Gideon (Doppies) (Port Natal HS & RAU) b 01/12/81, Sasolburg. 1.82m. 93kg. Centre. FC DEBUT: 2003. PROV CAREER: Lions 2003-04 & 06-11 92-24-0-0-0-120. Young Lions 2003-08 10-3-0-0-0-15. Griquas 2014 6-0-0-0-0-0. SUPER RUGBY: Cats 2003-06 17-1-0-0-0-5. Lions 2007-12 52-4-0-0-0-20. FC RECORD: 177-32-0-0-0-160. RECORD IN 2014: (Griquas) 6-0-0-0-0-0.

Le Roux, Abraham Jacobus (AJ) (Overkruin HS, Pretoria) b 12/12/1990, Pretoria. 1.80m. 108kg. Hooker. FC DEBUT: 2010. PROV CAREER: Blue Bulls 2010 2-0-0-0-0-0. Cheetahs 2012-14 11-1-0-0-0-5. Young Lions 2011-12 9-0-0-0-0-0. Golden Lions XV 2011 1-0-0-0-0-0. Griffons 2013-14 13-5-0-0-0-25. FC RECORD: 36-6-0-0-0-30. RECORD IN 2014: (Cheetahs, Griffons) 12-3-0-0-0-15.

Le Roux, Christo (Oakdale Agri. HS, Riversdale) b 28/03/85, Bloemfontein. 1.91m. 108kg. Eighthman. FC DEBUT: 2008. PROV CAREER: SWD 2008 15-3-0-0-0-15. Pumas 2009-14 98-15-0-0-0-75. SUPER RUGBY: Lions 2012 1-0-0-0-0-0. FC RECORD: 114-18-0-0-0-90. RECORD IN 2014: (Pumas) 1-1-0-0-0-5.

SEASON IN 2014

Le Roux, Grant (Flippie) (Vereeniging THS & NWU) b 13/01/86, Sasolburg. 1.97m. 110kg. Lock. FC DEBUT: 2009. PROV CAREER: Boland 2009-11 44-1-0-0-0-5. SWD 2012-14 48-3-0-0-0-15. FC RECORD: 92-4-0-0-0-20. RECORD IN 2014: (SWD) 16-0-0-0-0-0.

Le Roux, Hendrik Frederik (Erik) (Grey Coll., Bloemfontein & UFS) b 24/02/1988, Bloemfontein. 1.90m. 96kg. Eighthman. FC DEBUT: 2011. PROV CAREER: Griffons 2011-14 43-4-0-0-0-20. Cheetahs 2011 1-0-0-0-0-0. FC RECORD: 44-4-0-0-0-20. RECORD IN 2014: (Griffons) 14-2-0-0-0-10.

Le Roux, Willem Jacobus (Willie) (Paul Roos Gym., Stellenbosch) b 18/08/1989, Cape Town. 1.86m. 88kg. Flyhalf. FC DEBUT: 2010. PROV CAREER: Boland 2010-11 39-27-31-6-2-221. Griquas 2012-13 11-1-0-0-0-5. SUPER RUGBY: Cheetahs 2012-14 49-18-0-0-0-90. REP HONOURS: SA 2013-14 Tests: 25-7-0-0-0-35. Springbok XV 2014 1-1-0-0-0-5. British Barbarians 2013 1-0-0-0-0-0. MISC INFO: IRB PoY nominee 2014. PoY 2014 nominee. FC RECORD: 126-54-31-6-2-356. RECORD IN 2014: (SA, Springbok XV, Cheetahs SR) 30-9-0-0-0-45.

Lemley, Wayne (Daniel Pienaar HS, Uitenhage) b 15/05/1991, Uitenhage. 1.93m. 113kg. Prop. FC DEBUT: 2013. PROV CAREER: Border 2013-14 21-1-0-0-0-5. FC RECORD: 21-1-0-0-0-5. RECORD IN 2014: (Border) 14-1-0-0-0-5.

Lerm, Ruan Stephan (Dr. EG Jansen, Boksburg) b 25/03/1992, Kempton Park. 1.92m. 93kg. Eighthman. FC DEBUT: 2012. PROV CAREER: Young Lions 2012-14 17-6-0-0-0-30. Griquas 2014 8-1-0-0-0-5. FC RECORD: 25-7-0-0-0-35. RECORD IN 2014: (Griquas, Young Lions) 17-6-0-0-0-30.

Lewies, Joseph Stephanus Theuns (Stephan) (Eldoraigne HS, Pretoria) b 27/01/1992, Pretoria. 2m. 114kg. Lock. FC DEBUT: 2012. PROV CAREER: Sharks XV 2012-13 2-0-0-0-0-0. KZN 20213-14 14-1-0-0-0-5. SUPER RUGBY: Sharks 2014 17-0-0-0-0-0. REP HONOURS: SA 2014 Tests: 1-0-0-0-0-0. FC RECORD: 34-1-0-0-0-5. RECORD IN 2014: (SA, Sharks, KZN) 27-1-0-0-0-5.

Lewis, Clemen (Boland Agric. HS, Paarl) b 10/10/83. 1.75m. 90kg. Flank. FC DEBUT: 2006. PROV CAREER: Boland 2006-14 119-9-0-0-0-45. REP HONOURS: SA Barbarians 2012 1-0-0-0-0-0. FC RECORD: 120-9-0-0-0-45. RECORD IN 2014: (Boland) 17-2-0-0-0-10.

Lewis, Earl Cassidy (Atlantis HS, CPUT & UJ) b 15/07/1987, Darling. 1.78m. 84kg. Wing. FC DEBUT: 2008. PROV CAREER: Boland 2008 & 14 8-1-0-0-0-5. Lions 2009 2-0-0-0-0-0. Young Lions 2009 4-1-4-0-0-13. REP HONOURS: SA Students 2009 2-6-3-1-0-39. FC RECORD: 16-8-7-1-0-57. RECORD IN 2014: (Boland) 7-1-0-0-0-5.

Lewis, Jean-Paul (Paul Roos Gym., Stellenbosch & US) b 20/10/1983, Stellenbosch. 1.76m. 72kg. Centre. FC DEBUT: 2013. PROV CAREER: WP 2014 8-3-0-0-0-15. REP HONOURS: SA Univ 2013 1-3-0-0-0-15. FC RECORD: 9-6-0-0-0-30. RECORD IN 2014: (WP) 8-3-0-0-0-15.

Leyds, Dillyn Yullrich (Bishops Coll., Rondebosch & UCT) b 12/09/1982, Somerset West. 1.85m. 78kg. Flyhalf. FC DEBUT: 2012. PROV CAREER: WP 2013-14 4-0-1-1-0-5. REP HONOURS: SA U20 2012 4-0-0-0-0-0. FC RECORD: 8-0-1-1-0-5. RECORD IN 2014: (WP) 2-0-0-0-0-0.

Liebenberg, Armandt (Florida HS) b 18/12/1992, Springs. 1.93m. 95kg. Lock. FC DEBUT: 2011. PROV CAREER: Leopards 2011-12 13-0-0-0-0-0. Leopards XV 2014 7-2-0-0-0-10. FC RECORD: 20-2-0-0-0-10. RECORD IN 2014: (Leopards XV) 7-2-0-0-0-10.

Liebenberg, Christiaan Rudolph (Tiaan) (Grey Coll., Bloemfontein) b 18/12/81, Kimberley. 1.85m. 107kg. Hooker. FC DEBUT: 2002. PROV CAREER: KZN 2002 2-0-0-0-0-0. Griquas 2003-06 64-4-1-0-0-22. WP 2006-07,09-14 62-6-0-0-0-30. SUPER RUGBY: Cheetahs 2006 13-1-0-0-0-5. Stormers 2007-14 73-5-0-0-0-25. REP HONOURS: SA 2012 Tests: 5-0-0-0-0-0. SA 2007 Tour: 1-0-0-0-0-0. Total: 6-0-0-0-0-0. Emerging Springboks 2009 1-0-0-0-0-0. MISC INFO: Brother of FS hooker Hercu. Son of former GW & FS flyhalf & fullback Henning Liebenberg. FC RECORD: 221-16-1-0-0-82. RECORD IN 2014: (Stormers, WP) 7-0-0-0-0-0.

Liebenberg, Henru (Voortrekker HS, Bethlehem & UJ) b 19/10/1992, Bethlehem. 1.88m. 98kg. Flank. FC DEBUT: 2014. PROV CAREER: Griffons 2014 1-0-0-0-0-0. FC RECORD: 1-0-0-0-0-0. RECORD IN 2014: (Griffons) 1-0-0-0-0-0.

Liebenberg, Herculaas Johannes (Hercu) (Grey Coll., Bloemfontein) b 16/05/86, Bloemfontein. 1.78m. 104kg. Hooker. FC DEBUT: 2006. PROV CAREER: Cheetahs 2006-08 & 10-14 58-0-0-0-0-0. Elephants 2009 11-1-0-0-0-5. Griffons 2011 2-0-0-0-0-0. Emerging Cheetahs 2011 1-0-0-0-0-0. Free State XV 2013-14 11-0-0-0-0-0. SUPER RUGBY: Cheetahs 2012 6-0-0-0-0-0. MISC INFO: Brother of GW & WP hooker Tiaan. Son of former GW & FS flyhalf & fullback Henning Liebenberg. FC RECORD: 89-1-0-0-0-5. RECORD IN 2014: (Cheetahs, Free State XV) 5-0-0-0-0-0.

Liebenberg, RJ (Voortrekker HS, Bethlehem) b 11/12/1990, Bethlehem. 1.84m. 101kg. Flank. FC DEBUT: 2011. PROV CAREER: Golden Lions XV 2011 1-0-0-0-0-0. Griquas 2013-14 21-0-0-0-0-0. REP HONOURS: SA Univ 2013 1-0-0-0-0-0. FC RECORD: 23-0-0-0-0-0. RECORD IN 2014: (Griquas) 12-0-0-0-0-0.

Liebenberg, Willem Andries (Wiaan) (Drostdy HS, Worcester) b 31/08/1992, Belville. 1.89m. 100kg. Flanker. FC DEBUT: 2012. PROV CAREER: Blue Bulls 2012-14 34-12-0-0-0-60. SUPER RUGBY: Bulls 2014 1-0-0-0-0-0. REP HONOURS: SA U20 2012 (captain) 4-0-0-0-0-0. FC RECORD: 39-12-0-0-0-60. RECORD IN 2014: (Bulls, Blue Bulls) 17-2-0-0-0-10.

Liedeman, Evan b 15/08/1983. FC DEBUT: 2014. PROV CAREER: Boland 2014 2-0-0-0-0-0. FC RECORD: 2-0-0-0-0-0. RECORD IN 2014: (Boland) 2-0-0-0-0-0.

Lindsay, Cameron (Michaelhouse, Balgowan, US & NMMU) b 15/10/1991, Pretoria. 2m. 115kg. Lock. FC DEBUT: 2014. PROV CAREER: EP Kings 2014 7-1-0-0-0-5. FC RECORD: 7-1-0-0-0-5. RECORD IN 2014: (EP Kings) 7-1-0-0-0-5.

Lobberts, Hilton (New Orleans SS, Paarl) b 11/06/86, Paarl. 1.90m. 102kg. Flank. FC DEBUT: 2005. PROV CAREER: Blue Bulls 2006-08 37-5-0-0-0-25. Boland 2009-10 17-0-0-0-0-0. WP 2009 & 2011-12 34-3-0-0-0-15. Griquas 2013-14 18-1-0-0-0-5. SUPER RUGBY: Bulls 2007-08 7-0-0-0-0-0. Stormers 2009 5-0-0-0-0-0. Cheetahs 2014 1-0-0-0-0-0. REP HONOURS: SA 2006-07 Tests: 2-0-0-0-0-0. Tour: 2006,07 2-0-0-0-0-0. Total: 4-0-0-0-0-0. Emerging Springboks 2007 1-0-0-0-0-0. SA U21 2005-06 10-1-0-0-0-5. SA U19s 2004-05. FC RECORD: 134-10-0-0-0-50. RECORD IN 2014: (Cheetahs SR, Griquas) 15-1-0-0-0-5.

Lombard, Kyle (Paul Roos Gym., Stellenbosch) b 16/03/1993, Port Elizabeth. 1.76m. 87kg. Centre. FC DEBUT: 2014. PROV CAREER: WP 2014 6-1-0-0-0-5. FC RECORD: 6-1-0-0-0-5. RECORD IN 2014: (WP) 6-1-0-0-0-5.

Lourens, Werner (Wonderboom HS, Pretoria & TUT) b 26/06/1990, Pretoria. 1.99m. 118kg. Lock. FC DEBUT: 2014. PROV CAREER: Cheetahs 2014 3-0-0-0-0-0. Griffons 2014 8-0-0-0-0-0. FC RECORD: 11-0-0-0-0-0. RECORD IN 2014: (Cheetahs, Griffons) 11-0-0-0-0-0.

Louw, Lance b 28/06/1990. Wing. FC DEBUT: 2014. PROV CAREER: EP Kings 2014 3-0-0-0-0-0. FC RECORD: 3-0-0-0-0-0. RECORD IN 2014: (EP Kings) 3-0-0-0-0-0.

Louw, Louis-Francois Pickard (Francois) (Bishops, Rondebosch

b 15/06/85, Cape Town. 1.90m. 114kg. Flank. FC DEBUT: 2006. PROV CAREER: WP 2006-10 65-13-0-0-0-65. SUPER RUGBY: Stormers 2008-11 52-4-0-0-0-20. REP HONOURS: SA 2010-14 Tests: 34-5-0-0-0-25. Springbok XV 2014 1-0-0-0-0-0. British Barbarians 2013 1-0-0-0-0-0. MISC INFO: Grandson of former Springbok Jan Pickard. FC RECORD: 153-22-0-0-0-110. RECORD IN 2014: (SA, Springbok XV) 7-0-0-0-0-0.
Louw, Wilco Mario (HTS Drostdy, Worcester & UP) b 20/07/1994, Ceres. 1.85m. 130kg. Prop. FC DEBUT: 2014. REP HONOURS: SA U20 2014 5-0-0-0-0-0. FC RECORD: 5-0-0-0-0-0. RECORD IN 2014: (SA U20) 5-0-0-0-0-0.
Louw, Willem Johannes (Hans Strijdom HS, Naboomspruit) b 03/02/1988, Pietersburg. 1.93m. 119kg. Lock. FC DEBUT: 2013. PROV CAREER: Limpopo 2013-14 5-0-0-0-0-0. FC RECORD: 5-0-0-0-0-0. RECORD IN 2014: (Limpopo) 4-0-0-0-0-0.
Louw, Wilmaure Derrick (Carlton van Heerden HS, Upington) b 02/02/87, Upington. 1.83m. 86kg. Centre. FC DEBUT: 2009. PROV CAREER: Griquas 2009-12 63-11-0-0-0-55. Pumas 2013-14 32-1-0-0-0-5. SUPER RUGBY: Cheetahs 2010-11 6-0-0-0-0-0. REP HONOURS: SA Pres XV 2013 3-1-0-0-0-5. FC RECORD: 104-13-0-0-0-65. RECORD IN 2014: (Pumas) 8-0-0-0-0-0.
Luiters, Kevin (Grey Coll., Bloemfontein & UFS) b 02/07/1992, Port Elizabeth. 1.72m. 75kg. Scrumhalf. FC DEBUT: 2011. PROV CAREER: Cheetahs 2011 & 13 6-1-0-0-0-5. Free State XV 2012-13 6-0-0-0-0-0. EP Kings 2014 9-1-0-0-0-5. REP HONOURS: SA Sevens 2012-13. FC RECORD: 21-2-0-0-0-10. RECORD IN 2014: (EP Kings) 9-1-0-0-0-5.
Lusaseni, Luvuyiso (Selborne Coll., East London & Ethekwini Coll.) b 16/12/88, East London. 1.96m. 102kg. FC DEBUT: 2009. PROV CAREER: Sharks XV 2009-10 11-1-0-0-0-5. Griquas 2010 3-0-0-0-0-0. Leopards 2011-13 43-2-0-0-0-10. Leopard XV 2013 4-0-0-0-0-0. Lions 2014 6-0-0-0-0-0. SUPER RUGBY: Lions 2014 11-0-0-0-0-0. REP HONOURS: SA Barbarians 2012 1-0-0-0-0-0. SA U20 2008 1-0-0-0-0-0. SA Univ 2013 1-0-0-0-0-0. FC RECORD: 81-2-0-0-0-15. RECORD IN 2014: (Lions SR, Lions) 17-0-0-0-0-0.
Maarman, Tertius (Hentie Cilliers HS, Virginia) b 14/04/87, Port Elizabeth. 1.69m. 79kg. Utility back. FC DEBUT: 2008. PROV CAREER: Griffons 2008-14 89-28-5-0-0-150. FC RECORD: 89-28-5-0-0-150. RECORD IN 2014: (Griffons) 19-8-1-0-0-42.
Maart, Alvandre Graham (Breidbach HS. & Dale Coll., King William's Town) b 09/11/1985, King William's Town. 1.79m. 80kg. Scrumhalf. FC DEBUT: 2009. PROV CAREER: Valke 2009-10 12-1-0-0-0-5. Griffons 2012 1-0-0-0-0-0. Border 2014 1-0-0-0-0-0. FC RECORD: 14-1-0-0-0-5. RECORD IN 2014: (Border) 1-0-0-0-0-0.
Mabuza, Sikhumbuzo Thabo (Centurion HS) b 01/03/1994, Nelspruit. 1.82m. 90kg. Flank. FC DEBUT: 2014. PROV CAREER: Young Lions 2014 6-2-0-0-0-10. REP HONOURS: SA U20 2014 1-0-0-0-0-0. FC RECORD: 7-2-0-0-0-10. RECORD IN 2014: (Young Lions, SA U20) 7-2-0-0-0-10.
Mafela, Mashudu Cornelius (Merensky HS, Tzaneen & NWU) b 16/06/1991, Vierfontein, Limpopo. 1.83m. 118kg. Prop. FC DEBUT: 2014. PROV CAREER: Leopards 2014 6-0-0-0-0-0. FC RECORD: 6-0-0-0-0-0. RECORD IN 2014: (Leopards) 6-0-0-0-0-0.
Mahlo, Kefentse Seshego (Ben Vorster HS, Tzaneen & UP) b 31/03/1993, Tzaneen. 1.78m. 78kg. Wing. FC DEBUT: 2014. PROV CAREER: Blue Bulls 2014 3-1-0-0-0-5. FC RECORD: 3-1-0-0-0-5. RECORD IN 2014: (Blue Bulls) 3-1-0-0-0-5.
Mahuza, Sylvian (Outeniqua HS, George & NWU) b 29/07/1993, George. 1.78m. 80kg. Wing. FC DEBUT: 2013. PROV CAREER: Leopards 2013-14 14-15-0-0-0-75. REP HONOURS: SA U20 2013 no appearances. FC RECORD: 14-15-0-0-0-75. RECORD IN 2014: (Leopards) 11-14-0-0-0-70.
Majola, Khaya (Westville Boys' HS) b 13/03/1992, Kokstad. 1.85m. 98kg. Flanker. FC DEBUT: 2012. PROV CAREER: Sharks XV 2012-14 16-0-0-0-0-0. KZN 2014 5-0-0-0-0-0. REP HONOURS: SA U20 2012 1-0-0-0-0-0. FC RECORD: 22-0-0-0-0-0. RECORD IN 2014: (KZN, Sharks XV) 13-0-0-0-0-0.
Majola, Sonwabo Qengeba (Muir Coll., Uitenhage) b 20/03/1993, Uitenhage. 1.68m. 69kg. Scrumhalf. FC DEBUT: 2014. PROV CAREER: EP Kings 2014 3-1-0-0-0-5. FC RECORD: 3-1-0-0-0-5. RECORD IN 2014: (EP Kings) 3-1-0-0-0-5.
Makase, Michael b 20/01/1990. Wing. FC DEBUT: 2014. PROV CAREER: Border 2014 13-2-0-0-0-10. FC RECORD: 13-2-0-0-0-10. RECORD IN 2014: (Border) 13-2-0-0-0-10.
Maku, Bandise Grey (Dale Coll., King William's Town) b 24/06/86, King William's Town. 1.87m. 111kg. Hooker. FC DEBUT: 2006. PROV CAREER: Blue Bulls 2006-10 & 13-14 74-3-0-0-0-15. Lions 2011-12 23-1-0-0-0-5. SUPER RUGBY: Bulls 2008 & 10 & 14 21-0-0-0-0-0. Lions 2011 14-0-0-0-0-0. Southern Kings 2013 16-0-0-0-0-0. P/R 2013 2-0-0-0-0-0. REP HONOURS: SA 2010 Tests: 1-0-0-0-0-0. Tour: 2009-10 3-1-0-0-0-5. Total: 4-1-0-0-0-5. Emerging Springboks 2007,09 2-0-0-0-0-0. SA U21 2006 3-0-0-0-0-0. FC RECORD: 159-5-0-0-0-25. RECORD IN 2014: (Bulls, Blue Bulls) 7-0-0-0-0-0.
Malatji, Ditsepu Lloyd (Genl. Piet Joubert HS, Polokwane) b 12/11/1991. Polokwane. 1.72m. 78kg. Wing. FC DEBUT: 2014. PROV CAREER: Limpopo 2014 7-0-0-0-0-0. FC RECORD: 7-0-0-0-0-0. RECORD IN 2014: (Limpopo) 7-0-0-0-0-0.
Malherbe, Jozua Francois (Paarl Boys' HS) b 14/03/1991, Paarl. 1.90m. 124kg. Prop. FC DEBUT: 2011. PROV CAREER: WP 2011-14 34-0-0-0-0-0. SUPER RUGBY: Stormers 2011-14 41-2-0-0-0-10. REP HONOURS: SA 2012-14 Tests: 4-0-0-0-0-0. FC RECORD: 79-2-0-0-0-10. RECORD IN 2014: (SA, Stormers, WP) 12-2-0-0-0-10.
Mamojele, Thabo (Patriot HS, Witbank) b 29/07/86, Witbank. 1.95m. 104kg. Flank. FC DEBUT: 2007. PROV CAREER: KZN 2007 2-2-0-0-0-10. Valke 2008 5-0-0-0-0-0. Leopards 2009 & 2011 16-0-0-0-0-0. EP Kings 2012-13 16-2-0-0-0-10. Young Lions 2014 5-0-0-0-0-0. SUPER RUGBY: Southern Kings 2013 1-0-0-0-0-0. FC RECORD: 45-4-0-0-0-20. RECORD IN 2014: (Young Lions) 5-0-0-0-0-0.
Manentsa, Athenkosi (Khwazi Lomso HS, Port Elizabeth) b 20/05/1990, Kieskammahoek. 1.7m. 90kg. Eighthman. FC DEBUT: 2014. PROV CAREER: Border 2014 4-0-0-0-0-0. FC RECORD: 4-0-0-0-0-0. RECORD IN 2014: (Border) 4-0-0-0-0-0.
Mangweni, Siyabonga (Tiger) (Ntsonkotha SS, Lady Frere) b 20/06/80, Nxaruni. 1.87m. 80kg. Fullback. FC DEBUT: 2001. PROV CAREER: Border 2001-05 63-17-29-20-0-203. Griquas 2005-07 22-3-2-3-0-28. Blue Bulls 2008-10 46-15-0-0-1-78. EP Kings 2010-14 68-11-0-0-0-55. SUPER RUGBY: Stormers 2005 2-0-0-0-0-0. Cheetahs 2007 7-1-0-0-0-5. Bulls 2010 1-0-0-0-0-0. REP HONOURS: SA 'A' 2004 2-0-0-0-0-0. S/Kings 2009 1-0-0-0-0-0. FC RECORD: 212-47-31-23-1-369. RECORD IN 2014: (EP Kings) 3-1-0-0-0-5.
Manuel, Nathaniel Graham Phillip b 28/04/1990. FC DEBUT: 2014. PROV CAREER: Boland 2014 3-1-0-0-0-5. FC RECORD: 3-1-0-0-0-5. RECORD IN 2014: (Boland) 3-1-0-0-0-5.
Maphaga, Sinethemba (Isilamela HS & Cape Town Coll.) b 21/11/1989, Eastern Cape. 89kg. Centre. FC DEBUT: 2014. PROV CAREER: Limpopo 2014 7-1-0-0-0-5. FC RECORD: 7-1-0-0-0-5. RECORD IN 2014: (Limpopo) 7-1-0-0-0-5.
Maphimpi, Makazole (Jim Mvabaza HS) b 26/07/1990. 90kg.

Wing. FC DEBUT: 2014. PROV CAREER: Border 2014 17-5-0-0-0-25. FC RECORD: 17-5-0-0-0-25. RECORD IN 2014: (Border) 17-5-0-0-0-25.

Mapoe, Lionel Granton (Fichardtpark HS, Bloemfontein) b 13/07/88, Port Elizabeth. 1.82m. 84kg. Wing. FC DEBUT: 2008. PROV CAREER: Cheetahs 2008-09 12-6-0-0-0-30. Cheetahs XV 2010 1-0-0-0-0-0. Lions 2011-14 32-6-0-0-0-30. SUPER RUGBY: Cheetahs 2010 5-1-0-0-0-5. Lions 2011-12 & 14 33-8-0-0-0-40. Bulls 2013 12-2-0-0-0-10. REP HONOURS: SA 2012 no Tests. SA U20 2008 4-5-0-0-0-25. MISC INFO: YPOY Nominee 2009. FC RECORD: 99-28-0-0-0-140. RECORD IN 2014: (Lions SR, Lions) 22-7-0-0-0-35.

Marais, Brenvin Bradley (Weston HS, Vredenburg) b 15/01/1993, Vredenburg. 1.82m. 86kg. Centre. FC DEBUT: 2013. PROV CAREER: Griffons 2013-14 2-0-0-0-0-0. FC RECORD: 2-0-0-0-0-0. RECORD IN 2014: (Griffons) 1-0-0-0-0-0.

Marais, Charles Maclean (Paarl Boys' HS & UFS) b 29/08/1988, Paarl. 1.91m. 114kg. Prop. FC DEBUT: 2010. PROV CAREER: Cheetahs 2010-11 7-0-0-0-0-0. Free State XV 2012-13 8-0-0-0-0-0. Griffons 2012-13 6-1-0-0-0-5. Young Lions 2014 10-0-0-0-0-0. EP Kings 2014 4-0-0-0-0-0. SUPER RUGBY: Lions 2014 1-0-0-0-0-0. FC RECORD: 36-1-0-0-0-5. RECORD IN 2014: (Lions SR, Young Lions, EP Kings) 15-0-0-0-0-0.

Marais, Daniel Rudolf (Niel) (Grey Coll., Bloemfontein & UFS) b 21/01/1992, Bloemfontein. 1.81m. 97kg. Centre. FC DEBUT: 2013. PROV CAREER: Free State XV 2013-14 12-1-9-6-0-41 Griquas 2014 1-0-0-0-0-0. FC RECORD: 13-1-9-6-0-41. RECORD IN 2014: (Griquas, Free State XV) 7-1-9-6-0-41.

Marais, Franco Stephan (Transvalia HS, Vanderbijlpark) b 23/09/1992, Vereeniging. 1.86m. 94kg. Hooker. FC DEBUT: 2012. PROV CAREER: KZN 2012 & 14 5-0-0-0-0-0. Sharks XV 2013-14 15-1-0-0-0-5. SUPER RUGBY: Sharks 2014 1-0-0-0-0-0. SA U20 2012 1-0-0-0-0-0. FC RECORD: 22-1-0-0-0-5. RECORD IN 2014: (Sharks, KZN, Sharks XV) 12-0-0-0-0-0.

Marais, Peet Celliers (Welkom Gym.) b 31/10/1990, Welkom. 1.98m. 115kg. Lock. FC DEBUT: 2011. PROV CAREER: KZN 2011-13 18-0-0-0-0-0. Sharks XV 2011-14 31-1-0-0-0-5. REP HONOURS: SA U20 2010 2-0-0-0-0-0. MISC INFO: Brother of Jandre Marais. FC RECORD: 51-1-0-0-0-5. RECORD IN 2014: (Sharks XV) 8-1-0-0-0-5.

Marais, Renier Johannes (Grey HS, Port Elizabeth, Paul Roos Gym., Stellenbosch & US) b 18/06/1992, Queenstown. 1.81m. 107kg. Hooker. FC DEBUT: 2014. PROV CAREER: WP 2014 1-0-0-0-0-0. FC RECORD: 1-0-0-0-0-0. RECORD IN 2014: (WP) 1-0-0-0-0-0.

Marais, Sarel Petrus (Paarl Boys' HS) b 16/03/1989. 1.84m. 80kg. Wing. PROV CAREER: Leopards 2010 2-3-1-0-0-17. EP Kings 2011-12 36-18-4-0-0-98. KZN 2013-14 21-7-0-2-0-41. SUPER RUGBY: Southern Kings 2013 8-0-0-0-0-0. P/R 2013 2-0-0-0-0-0. Sharks 2014 18-0-0-1-0-3. REP HONOURS: SA Kings 2011 3-0-0-0-0-0. FC RECORD: 90-28-5-3-0-159. RECORD IN 2014: (Sharks, KZN) 28-3-0-3-0-24.

Marich, George (Afrikaans HS, Kroonstad) b 11/07/1992, Kroonstad. 1.83m. 120kg. Prop. FC DEBUT: 2014. PROV CAREER: Cheetahs 2014 8-0-0-0-0-0. FC RECORD: 8-0-0-0-0-0. RECORD IN 2014: (Cheetahs) 8-0-0-0-0-0.

Maritz, Hoffman Van Heerden (Voortrekker HS, Bethlehem) b 29/03/1989, Bethlehem. 1.85m. 93kg. Wing. FC DEBUT: 2011. PROV CAREER: Young Lions 2011 5-0-0-0-0-0. Leopards 2011-12 & 14 37-16-0-0-0-80. Leopard XV 2013 4-1-0-0-0-5. REP HONOURS: SA Barbarians 2012 1-0-0-0-0-0. SA Pres XV 2013 1-1-0-0-0-5. SA Univ 2013 1-0-0-0-0-0. FC RECORD: 49-18-0-0-0-90. RECORD IN 2014: (Leopards) 8-7-0-0-0-35.

Maritz, Neil Kobus (Paarl Boys' HS) b 22/02/1994, Worcester. 1.83m. 94kg. Centre. FC DEBUT: 2014. PROV CAREER: Sharks XV 2014 6-3-0-0-0-15. FC RECORD: 6-3-0-0-0-15. RECORD IN 2014: (Sharks XV) 6-3-0-0-0-15.

Maruping, Mosoeu Vincent (HTS Louis Botha, Bloemfontein) b 25/11/1993, Virginia. 1.92m. 90kg. Flank. FC DEBUT: 2014. PROV CAREER: Free State XV 2014 1-0-0-0-0-0. FC RECORD: 1-0-0-0-0-0. RECORD IN 2014: (Free State XV) 1-0-0-0-0-0.

Marutlulle, Edgar (Potchefstroom HS) b 20/12/87, Boksburg. 1.77m. 91kg. Hooker. FC DEBUT: 2007. PROV CAREER: Golden Lions 2010 13-1-0-0-0-5. Young Lions 2011-12 11-3-0-0-0-15. Leopards 2012-13 26-10-0-0-0-50. Leopard XV 2013-14 8-0-0-0-0-0. EP Kings 2014 8-0-0-0-0-0. SUPER RUGBY: Lions 2011 8-0-0-0-0-0. Southern Kings: 2013 4-0-0-0-0-0. REP HONOURS: SA Students 2007-09 4-0-0-0-0-0. FC RECORD: 82-14-0-0-0-70. RECORD IN 2014: (EP Kings, Leopard XV) 15-0-0-0-0-0.

Marx, Malcolm Justin (KES, Johannesburg) b 13/07/1994, Germiston. 1.88m. 119kg. Hooker. FC DEBUT: 2014. PROV CAREER: Lions 2014 1-0-0-0-0-0. Young Lions 2014 6-0-0-0-0-0. SUPER RUGBY: Lions 2014 2-0-0-0-0-0. REP HONOURS: SA U20 2014 1-1-0-0-0-5. FC RECORD: 10-1-0-0-0-5. RECORD IN 2014: (Lions SR, Lions, Young Lions, SA U20) 10-1-0-0-0-5.

Maseko, Sizophilo Sabelo (Ermelo HS & US) b 03/03/1991, Ermelo. 1.84m. 88kg. Wing. FC DEBUT: 2013. PROV CAREER: KZN 2013 4-1-0-0-0-5. Sharks XV 2013-14 15-7-0-0-0-35. FC RECORD: 19-8-0-0-0-40. RECORD IN 2014: (Sharks XV) 7-2-0-0-0-10.

Masemda, Malope Thusho (Polokwane HS) b 29/11/1991, Polokwane. 1.94m. 117kg. Eighthman. FC DEBUT: 2014. PROV CAREER: Limpopo 1-0-0-0-0-0. FC RECORD: 1-0-0-0-0-0. RECORD IN 2014: (Limpopo) 1-0-0-0-0-0.

Masimla, Godlen Herschelle Derrick (Hugenote HS, Wellington & UWC) b 11/08/1992, Wellington. 1.77m. 80kg. Scrumhalf. FC DEBUT: 2013. PROV CAREER: WP 2013-14 13-0-0-0-0-0. FC RECORD: 13-0-0-0-0-0. RECORD IN 2014: (WP) 4-0-0-0-0-0.

Mastriet, Sampie (Drostdy HS, Worcester) b 03/08/1990, Mairsdas. 1.80m. 84kg. Wing. FC DEBUT: 2011. PROV CAREER: Blue Bulls 2011-14 49-31-0-0-0-155. SUPER RUGBY: Bulls 2013-14 2-1-0-0-0-5. REP HONOURS: SA U20 2009-10 6-4-0-0-0-20. SA Sevens 2013-14. FC RECORD: 57-36-0-0-0-180. RECORD IN 2014: (Bulls, Blue Bulls, SA Sevens) 16-11-0-0-0-55.

Mateza, Sikhangele (Queens Coll., Queenstown & UFH) b 21/02/1986. 1.75m. 85kg. Scrumhalf. FC DEBUT: 2014. PROV CAREER: Border 2014 3-0-0-0-0-0. FC RECORD: 3-0-0-0-0-0. RECORD IN 2014: (Border) 3-0-0-0-0-0.

Matfield, Victor (Pietersburg HS & UP) b 11/05/77, Pietersburg. 2.01m. 110kg. Lock. FC DEBUT: 1997. PROV CAREER: Blue Bulls 1998 & 2001-02 & 04-05 & 08-10 52-5-0-0-0-25; Griquas 1999-2000 36-8-0-0-0-40. Blue Bulls XV 2-0-0-0-0-0. SUPER RUGBY: Cats 1999-2000 8-0-0-0-0-0; Bulls 2001-07 & 09-11 & 14 130-8-0-0-0-40. REP HONOURS: SA 2000-11 & 14 Tests 121-7-0-0-0-35, Tour 4-0-0-0-0-0, Total 125-7-0-0-0-35; SA U23s 2000 5-1-0-0-0-5; SA U21s 1997-98 8-1-0-0-0-5; Springbok XV 2014 1-0-0-0-0-0. SA 'A' 2002 1-0-0-0-0-0. S Hemisphere XV 2005 1-0-0-0-0-0. British Barbarians 2009 1-0-0-0-0-0. SA Academy 1995; CW Far North 1994-95. MISC INFO: PoY nominee 2005, 2006, 2007, 2009, 2011. IRB PoY nominee 2005. Holds SA record for most Tests as a lock - 121. Locked together with Bakkies Botha in 63 Tests (world record). FC RECORD: 370-30-0-0-0-150. RECORD IN 2014: (SA, Springbok XV, Bulls) 26-0-0-0-0-0.

SEASON IN 2014

Mathee, Rudi (Otto du Plessis HS, Port Elizabeth) b 25/02/86, Port Elizabeth. 1.95m. 108kg. Lock. FC DEBUT: 2006. PROV CAREER: Lions 2006-07 6-1-0-0-0-5. Leopards 2008-09 26-6-0-0-0-30. Cheetahs 2010 6-2-0-0-0-10. Griffons 2010 6-2-0-0-0-10. Pumas 2011-14 52-7-0-0-0-35. SUPER RUGBY: Lions 2014 5-0-0-0-0-0. REP HONOURS: SA Students 2007 1-1-0-0-0-5. Royal XV 2009 1-0-0-0-0-0. SA Barbarians 2012 1-0-0-0-0-0. MISC INFO: CC First Div PoY 2012 nominee. FC RECORD: 104-19-0-0-0-95. RECORD IN 2014: (Lions SR, Pumas) 7-3-0-0-0-15.

Mathonsi, Thulani Densel b 10/10/1983. Prop. FC DEBUT: 2013. PROV CAREER: Limpopo 2013-14 13-1-0-0-0-5. FC RECORD: 13-1-0-0-0-5. RECORD IN 2014: (Limpopo) 6-1-0-0-0-5.

Mbonambi, Mbongeni Theo (Bongi) (Voortrekker HS, Bethlehem, St Albans HS & TUT) b 07/01/1991, Bethlehem. 1.80m. 97kg. Hooker. FC DEBUT: 2012. PROV CAREER: Blue Bulls 2012-14 30-1-0-0-0-5. SUPER RUGBY: Bulls 2012 & 14 15-0-0-0-0-0. REP HONOURS: SA U20 2011 5-0-0-0-0-0. FC RECORD: 50-1-0-0-0-5. RECORD IN 2014: (Bulls, Blue Bulls) 24-1-0-0-0-5.

Mbotho, Vuyo (Lukhozi HS, Debenek). b 28/09/1988. Wing. FC DEBUT: 2010. PROV CAREER: Border 2010-12 26-7-0-0-0-35. Griffons 2013-14 34-6-0-0-0-30. FC RECORD: 60-13-0-0-0-65. RECORD IN 2014: (Griffons) 18-4-0-0-0-20.

Mbovane, Tshotsho (Paul Roos Gym., Stellenbosch) b 01/08/1992, Cape Town. 1.75m. 82kg. Wing. FC DEBUT: 2011. PROV CAREER: Leopards 2014 2-0-0-0-0-0. REP HONOURS: SA U20 2011-12 7-5-0-0-0-25. FC RECORD: 9-5-0-0-0-25. SA Sevens 2011-13. RECORD IN 2014: (Leopards) 2-0-0-0-0-0.

McDonald, Aubrey Neville (Winterberg Agric., Fort Beaufort & UJ) b 03/02/1968, Port Elizabeth. 1.83m. 87kg. Fullback. FC DEBUT: 2008. PROV CAREER: Blue Bulls 2008 1-0-0-0-0-0. Griffons 2013-14 26-5-0-0-0-25. FC RECORD: 27-5-0-0-0-25. RECORD IN 2014: (Griffons) 11-2-0-0-0-10.

McDonald, Shaun (Tygerberg HS, Cape Town) b 09/02/1989, Goodwood. 1.92m. 117kg. Flank. FC DEBUT: 2014. PROV CAREER: EP Kings 2014 5-0-0-0-0-0. FC RECORD: 5-0-0-0-0-0. RECORD IN 2014: (EP Kings) 5-0-0-0-0-0.

McLeod, Charl (Wonderboom HS, Pretoria) b 05/08/83, Johannesburg. 1.79m. 82kg. Scrumhalf. FC DEBUT: 2005. PROV CAREER: WP 2005-06 12-1-0-0-0-5. Lions 2007 6-3-0-0-0-15. Valke 2007 11-2-0-0-0-10. KZN 2008-13 59-12-0-0-0-60. Sharks XV 2008-10 19-7-0-0-0-35. Sharks Inv XV 2009-10 2-2-0-0-0-10. Lions XV 2007 1-0-0-0-0-0. SUPER RUGBY: Sharks 2009-14 73-5-0-0-0-25. REP HONOURS: SA 2011 Tests: 1-0-0-0-0-0. Tour 2010: 1-0-0-0-0-0. Total: 2-0-0-0-0-0. FC RECORD: 185-32-0-0-0-160. RECORD IN 2014: (Sharks) 18-0-0-0-0-0.

Mdaka, Siyabulela (George Campbell HS, Durban & NWU) b 14/02/1988, Umtata. 1.88m. 102kg. Flank. FC DEBUT: 2011. PROV CAREER: Leopards 2011 4-0-0-0-0-0. Border 2012-14 38-1-0-0-0-5. FC RECORD: 42-1-0-0-0-5. RECORD IN 2014: (Border) 18-0-0-0-0-0.

Mellet, Morne Melvin (Dr. EG Jansen HS, Boksburg) b 02/10/1988, Boksburg. 1.87m. 115kg. Prop. FC DEBUT: 2010. PROV CAREER: Blue Bulls 2010-14 26-2-0-0-0-10. SUPER RUGBY: Bulls 2013-14 24-0-0-0-0-0. REP HONOURS: SA U20 2009 5-0-0-0-0-0. FC RECORD: 55-2-0-0-0-10. RECORD IN 2014: (Bulls, Blue Bulls) 15-0-0-0-0-0.

Memese, Sinthamdile Amos (Ndzondelelo HS) b 22/02/1982, Somerset East. 1.8m. 100kg. Flank. FC DEBUT: 2013. PROV CAREER: Limpopo 2013-14 3-0-0-0-0-0. FC RECORD: 3-0-0-0-0-0. RECORD IN 2014: (Limpopo) 2-0-0-0-0-0.

Meslane, Dumisane Kelvin (Ithembelhle HS, Port Elizabeth) b 11/05/85, Port Elizabeth. 1.86m. 92kg. Flanker. FC DEBUT: 2008. PROV CAREER: Border 2008-10 42-7-0-0-0-35. SWD 2011-13 26-8-0-0-0-40. Boland 2014 10-0-0-0-0-0. FC RECORD: 78-15-0-0-0-75. RECORD IN 2014: (Boland) 10-0-0-0-0-0.

Meyer, Johan Gert (Queens Coll., Queenstown) b 26/02/1993, Port Elizabeth. 1.93m. 104kg. Eighthman. FC DEBUT: 2013. PROV CAREER: Sharks XV 2013-14 13-3-0-0-0-15. KZN 2014 5-0-0-0-0-0. FC RECORD: 18-3-0-0-0-15. RECORD IN 2014: (KZN, Sharks XV) 13-3-0-0-0-15.

Meyer, Thomas Leon b 20/01/1992. Scrumhalf. FC DEBUT: 2014. PROV CAREER: Leopards XV 2014 2-0-0-0-0-0. FC RECORD: 2-0-0-0-0-0. RECORD IN 2014: (Leopards XV) 2-0-0-0-0-0.

Meyer, Tian Carel (Westville HS) b 20/09/1988, Pietermaritzburg. 1.76m. 71kg. Scrumhalf/Centre. FC DEBUT: 2010. PROV CAREER: Pumas 2010-11 36-10-0-0-0-50. Sharks XV 2013 4-0-0-0-0-0. Lions 2013 6-0-0-0-0-0. Griquas 2014 24-8-0-0-0-40. SUPER RUGBY: Lions 2012 11-2-0-0-0-10. Cheetahs 2014 1-0-0-0-0-0. FC RECORD: 82-20-0-0-0-100. RECORD IN 2014: (Cheetahs SR, Griquas) 25-8-0-0-0-40.

Mgwadleka, Lithabile (Bisho HS & UFH) b 07/01/1991, Bisho. 1.8m. 86kg. Centre. FC DEBUT: 2014. PROV CAREER: Border 2014 12-2-0-0-0-10. FC RECORD: 12-2-0-0-0-10. RECORD IN 2014: (Border) 12-2-0-0-0-10.

Mhlongo, Stembiso Santo (Siyahomula HS, Wartburg & UP) b 13/05/1987, Pietermaritzburg. 2.01m. 112kg. Lock. FC DEBUT: 2013. PROV CAREER: Border 2013 9-1-0-0-0-5. Leopards 2014 2-1-0-0-0-5. Leopards XV 2014 6-2-0-0-0-10. FC RECORD: 17-4-0-0-0-20. RECORD IN 2014: (Leopards, Leopards XV) 8-3-0-0-0-15.

Mienie, Daniel Jacobus (Danie) (Merensky HS, Tzaneen) b 01/03/1991, Polokwane. 1.78m. 104kg. Prop. FC DEBUT: 2012. PROV CAREER: KZN 2013-14 9-0-0-0-0-0. Sharks XV 2012-14 15-0-0-0-0-0. SUPER RUGBY: Sharks 2013 1-0-0-0-0-0. FC RECORD: 25-0-0-0-0-0. RECORD IN 2014: (KZN, Sharks XV) 5-0-0-0-0-0.

Mienie, Shane b 25/02/1992. Prop. FC DEBUT: 2013. PROV CAREER: Limpopo 2013-14 6-0-0-0-0-0. FC RECORD: 6-0-0-0-0-0. RECORD IN 2014: (Limpopo) 3-0-0-0-0-0.

Minnie, Derick Johannes (Marais Viljoen HS, Alberton) b 29/10/86, Alberton. 1.86m. 95kg. Flank. FC DEBUT: 2006. PROV CAREER: Golden Lions 2006-14 70-22-0-0-0-110. Young Lions 2006-09 & 13 22-5-0-0-0-25. Lions XV 2007 1-0-0-0-0-0. SUPER RUGBY: Lions 2010-12 & 14 52-6-0-0-0-30. Lions P/R 2013 2-1-0-0-0-5. Sharks 2013 3-3-0-0-0-15. FC RECORD: 150-37-0-0-0-185. RECORD IN 2014: (Lions SR, Lions) 20-3-0-0-0-15.

Mkhabela, Mthokozisi Cyprial (Glenwood HS, Durban) b 15/10/1994, Empangeni. 1.68m. 73kg. Scrumhalf. FC DEBUT: 2014. REP HONOURS: SA U20 2014 1-0-0-0-0-0. FC RECORD: 1-0-0-0-0-0. RECORD IN 2014: (SA U20) 1-0-0-0-0-0.

Mkhafu, Khwezilokusa (Kwezi) (Lebogang HS, Welkom) b 17/06/1988, Engcobo. 1.77m. 97kg. Hooker. FC DEBUT: 2010. PROV CAREER: Border 2010-13 70-6-0-0-0-30. Boland 2014 18-1-0-0-0-5. REP HONOURS: SA Pres XV 2013 2-1-0-0-0-5. FC RECORD: 90-8-0-0-0-40. RECORD IN 2014: (Boland) 18-1-0-0-0-5.

Mkokeli, Thembani Moeren (Msobumvu HS) b 12/03/84, East London. 1.79m. 77kg. Flyhalf. FC DEBUT: 2003. PROV CAREER: Border 2003-06 & 08-12 & 14 105-18-0-1-0-93. REP HONOURS: SA U19 2003. SA Schools 2001-02. CW Border 2001-02. FC RECORD: 105-18-0-1-0-93. RECORD IN 2014: (Border) 15-3-0-0-0-15.

Mlondobozi, Nhlanhla Don (Ben Vorster HS, Tzaneen) b

25/01/1993, Limpopo. 1.77m. 80kg. Wing. FC DEBUT: 2014. PROV CAREER: Free State XV 2014 6-3-0-0-0-15. FC RECORD: 6-3-0-0-0-15. RECORD IN 2014: (Free State XV) 6-3-0-0-0-15.

Mnisi, Xolane Howard (Standerton HS & NMMU) b 13/07/1989, Elukwatini. 1.86m. 96kg. Centre. FC DEBUT: 2011. PROV CAREER: Sharks XV 2011 3-1-0-0-0-5. Griquas 2013-14 20-3-0-0-0-15. Lions 2014 12-2-0-0-0-10. SUPER RUGBY: Cheetahs 2013-14 3-0-0-0-0-0. REP HONOURS: SA Students 2012 1-0-0-0-0-0. SA Univ 2013 1-0-0-0-0-0. FC RECORD: 40-6-0-0-0-30. RECORD IN 2014: (Cheetahs SR, Lions, Griquas) 23-4-0-0-0-20.

Mntunjani, Bonga (Hlumani HS) b 07/04/1983, Komga. 1.92m. 92kg. Flank. FC DEBUT: 2006. PROV CAREER: Border 2006,09-11 & 14 40-4-0-0-0-20. FC RECORD: 40-4-0-0-0-20. RECORD IN 2014: (Border) 5-0-0-0-0-0.

Mohoje, Teboho Stephen (Louis Botha THS, Bloemfontein & UFS) b 03/08/1990, Qwa Qwa. 1.92m. 103kg. Lock. FC DEBUT: 2012. PROV CAREER: Griffons 2012-13 6-0-0-0-0-0. Cheetahs 2013-14 12-0-0-0-0-0. Free State XV 2013-14 7-3-0-0-0-15. SUPER RUGBY: Cheetahs 2014 10-1-0-0-0-5. REP HONOURS: SA 2014 Tests: 7-0-0-0-0-0. FC RECORD: 42-4-0-0-0-20. RECORD IN 2014: (SA, Cheetahs SR, Cheetahs, Free State XV) 20-2-0-0-0-10.

Molefe, Thabang (Kimberley Boys" HS & TUT) b 06/06/1984, Taung. 1.80m. 96kg. Centre. FC DEBUT: 2005. PROV CAREER: Blue Bulls 2005 5-1-0-0-0-5. Lions 2006-08 20-2-0-0-0-10. Lions XV 2007 1-0-0-0-0-0. Griffons 2009-12 48-14-0-0-0-70. Griquas 2009 & 14 3-1-0-0-0-5. REP HONOURS: SA U21 2005 4-0-0-0-0-0. SA Students 2005 1-0-0-0-0-0. MISC INFO: IRB U21 PoY nominee 2005. FC RECORD: 82-18-0-0-0-90. RECORD IN 2014: (Griquas) 1-1-0-0-0-5.

Momberg, Christiaan Jacobus (Jacques) (Waterkloof HS, Pretoria & UP) b 18/02/1991, Pretoria. 1.8m. 105kg. Hooker. FC DEBUT: 2012. PROV CAREER: Blue Bulls 2012 2-0-0-0-0-0. Pumas 2013-14 26-3-0-0-0-15. FC RECORD: 28-3-0-0-0-15. RECORD IN 2014: (Pumas) 9-1-0-0-0-5.

Mona, Khwezi Jongamazizi (Selborne Coll., East London) b 08/10/1992, East London. 1.81m. 112kg. Prop. FC DEBUT: 2014. PROV CAREER: Sharks XV 2014 4-0-0-0-0-0. FC RECORD: 4-0-0-0-0-0. RECORD IN 2014: (Sharks XV) 4-0-0-0-0-0.

Montgomery, Devin Sean (St Stithians Coll., Randburg & UW) b 02/09/1989, Johannesburg. 1.92m. 112kg. Flank. FC DEBUT: 2014. PROV CAREER: Griffons 2014 1-0-0-0-0-0. FC RECORD: 1-0-0-0-0-0. RECORD IN 2014: (Griffons) 1-0-0-0-0-0.

Morison, Chase Wayne (Selborne Coll., East London) b 37/11/1992, Germiston. 1.81m. 105kg. Prop. FC DEBUT: 2014. PROV CAREER: Free State XV 2014 4-0-0-0-0-0. FC RECORD: 4-0-0-0-0-0. RECORD IN 2014: (Free State XV) 4-0-0-0-0-0.

Mostert, Francois John (Franco) (Brits HS & UP) b 27/11/1990, Bloemfontein. 1.98m. 103kg. Lock. FC DEBUT: 2012. PROV CAREER: Blue Bulls 2012 12-2-0-0-0-10. Young Lions 2013 3-0-0-0-0-0. Lions 2014 12-4-0-0-0-20. SUPER RUGBY: Lions 2014 14-0-0-0-0-0. FC RECORD: 41-6-0-0-0-30. RECORD IN 2014: (Lions SR, Lions) 26-4-0-0-0-20.

Mostert, Juan-Pierre Francois (JP) (Brits HS & US) b 22/01/1988, Brits. 1.93m. 106kg. Flank. FC DEBUT: 2011. PROV CAREER: Pumas 2011-12 21-1-0-0-0-5. Valke 2012-14 37-11-0-0-0-55. FC RECORD: 58-12-0-0-0-60. RECORD IN 2014: (Valke) 17-3-0-0-0-15.

Mpafi, Mihlali (Hudson Park HS, East London & CUT) b 17/06/1992, East London. 1.78m. 94kg. Hooker. FC DEBUT: 2014. PROV CAREER: Border 2014 13-1-0-0-0-5. FC RECORD: 13-1-0-0-0-5. RECORD IN 2014: (Border) 13-1-0-0-0-5.

Msutwana, Siphumelele Nkosikhona Petros (Siphu) (Dale Coll., King William's Town) b 31/10/1993, Fort Beaufort. 1.73m. 85kg. Wing. FC DEBUT: 2014. PROV CAREER: EP Kings 2014 4-0-0-0-0-0. FC RECORD: 4-0-0-0-0-0. RECORD IN 2014: (EP Kings) 4-0-0-0-0-0.

Mtawarira, Tendai (Beast) (Peterhouse, Zimbabwe) b 01/07/85, Harare. 1.88m. 118kg. Prop. FC DEBUT: 2006. PROV CAREER: KZN 2006-13 37-3-0-0-0-15. Sharks XV 2006-08 & 12 9-0-0-0-0-0. Sharks Inv XV 2010 1-1-0-0-0-5. SUPER RUGBY: Sharks 2007-14 102-2-0-0-0-10-. REP HONOURS: SA 2008-14 Tests 64-2-0-0-0-10. 2010 Tour: 1-0-0-0-0-0. Total: 65-2-0-0-0-10. Springbok XV 2014 1-0-0-0-0-0. British Barbarians 2009 & 13 2-0-0-0-0-0. MISC INFO: PoY nominee 2008. YPoY nominee 2008. FC RECORD:217-8-0-0-0-40. RECORD IN 2014: (SA, Springbok XV, Sharks) 26-0-0-0-0-0.

Mtembu, Lubabalo Siphosethu (Dale Coll., King William's Town) b 09/12/1990, East London. 1.87m. Eighthman. FC DEBUT: 2011. PROV CAREER: Sharks XV 2011-14 18-4-0-0-0-20. KZN 2012-14 22-4-0-0-0-20. SUPER RUGBY: Sharks 2012-14 16-1-0-0-0-5. Rep. honours: SA U20 2010 4-0-0-0-0-0. SA Sevens 2010-11. FC RECORD: 60-9-0-0-0-45. RECORD IN 2014: (Sharks, KZN, Sharks XV) 22-3-0-0-0-15.

Mtyanda, Lubabalo (Cowan HS, Hilton) b 19/03/86, Port Elizabeth. 1.99m. 116kg. Lock. FC DEBUT: 2006. PROV CAREER: Elephants 2006 13-0-0-0-0-0. Lions 2007 4-0-0-0-0-0. SWD 2010-13 70-8-0-0-0-40. Pumas 2013-14 36-4-0-0-0-20. REP HONOURS: SA Pres XV 2013 4-0-0-0-0-0. FC RECORD: 127-12-0-0-0-60. RECORD IN 2014: (Pumas) 18-2-0-0-0-10.

Muir, Dean (Glenwood HS, Durban) b 06/02/1989, Durban. 1.81m. 102kg. Hooker. FC DEBUT: 2012. PROV CAREER: Border 2012-13 31-4-0-0-0-20. Valke 2014 6-0-0-0-0-0. FC RECORD: 37-4-0-0-0-20. RECORD IN 2014: (Valke) 6-0-0-0-0-0.

Muller, Bruce (Klerksdorp HS) b 24/02/1989, Klerksdorp. 1.76m. 116kg. Prop. FC DEBUT: 2012. PROV CAREER: Valke 2012-14 29-7-0-0-0-35. FC RECORD: 29-7-0-0-0-35. RECORD IN 2014: (Valke) 11-3-0-0-0-15.

Muller, Frederick Jacobus (Hugenote HS, Wellington & UWC) b 03/02/1990, Belville. 1.68m. 78kg. Scrumhalf. FC DEBUT: 2013. PROV CAREER: WP 2014 4-0-0-0-0-0. REP HONOURS: SA U20 2010 no appearances. SA Univ 2013 1-0-0-0-0-0. FC RECORD: 5-0-0-0-0-0. RECORD IN 2014: (WP) 4-0-0-0-0-0.

Muller, Martin Dirk (Bishops HS, Rondebosch & UCT) b 23/03/1988, Cape Town. 1.98m. 105kg. Lock. FC DEBUT: 2009. PROV CAREER: WP 2009-10 22-1-0-0-0-5. Griquas 2011-12 23-1-0-0-0-5. Lions 2014 10-1-0-0-0-5. Young Lions 2014 2-0-0-0-0-0. SUPER RUGBY: Stormers 2009 3-0-0-0-0-0. Cheetahs 2011 11-0-0-0-0-0. Lions 2014 5-0-0-0-0-0. REP HONOURS: SA Students 2009 2-0-0-0-0-0. SA U20 2008 5-1-0-0-0-5. FC RECORD: 83-4-0-0-0-20. RECORD IN 2014: (Lions SR, Lions, Young Lions) 17-1-0-0-0-5.

Muller, Ruan b 10/10/1985. Centre. FC DEBUT: 2013. PROV CAREER: Limpopo 2013-14 7-1-0-0-0-5. FC RECORD: 7-1-0-0-0-5. RECORD IN 2014: (Limpopo) 1-0-0-0-0-0.

Mulumba, Tyson b 03/04/1983, Prop. FC DEBUT: 2014. PROV CAREER: Young Lions 2014 1-0-0-0-0-0. FC RECORD: 1-0-0-0-0-0. RECORD IN 2014: (Young Lions) 1-0-0-0-0-0.

Murray, Waylon Michael (Westville Boys" HS) b 27/04/86, Durban. 1.90m. 105kg. Centre. FC DEBUT: 2005. PROV CAREER: KZN 2005-09 52-18-0-0-0-90. Sharks XV 2005-10 8-0-0-0-0-0. Golden Lions 2010-12 19-5-0-0-0-25. Blue Bulls 2013-14 14-2-0-0-0-10. EP Kings 2013 1-0-0-0-0-0. SUPER RUGBY: Sharks 2006-10 41-5-0-0-0-25. Lions 2011-12 14-3-0-0-0-15. Southern Kings 2013 7-0-0-0-0-0. P/R 2013

SEASON IN 2014

1-0-0-0-0-0. REP HONOURS: SA Tests: 2007 3-0-0-0-0-0. Tour: 1-0-0-0-0-0. Total: 4-0-0-0-0-0. SA U21 2006 5-3-0-0-0-15. FC RECORD: 166-36-0-0-0-180. RECORD IN 2014: (Blue Bulls) 8-2-0-0-0-10.

Mvovo, Lwazi Ncedo (Maria Louw HS, Queenstown) b 03/06/86, Umthatha. 1.81m. 92kg. Wing. FC DEBUT: 2007. PROV CAREER: KZN 2007-14 62-28-0-0-0-140. Sharks XV 2007-10 20-9-0-0-0-45. Sharks Inv XV 2009 1-0-0-0-0-0. SUPER RUGBY: Sharks 2010-14 70-19-0-0-0-95. REP HONOURS: SA 2010-12 & 14 Tests: 10-3-0-0-0-15. Tour: 1-0-0-0-0-0. Total: 11-3-0-0-0-15. Springbok XV 2014 1-0-0-0-0-0. FC RECORD: 165-59-0-0-0-295. RECORD IN 2014: (SA, Springbok XV, Sharks, KZN) 27-7-0-0-0-35.

Mxoli, Nqobisizwe Mimentle (Westville Boys' HS & UP) b 02/02/1994, Durban. 1.83m. 112kg. Prop. FC DEBUT: 2014. PROV CAREER: Blue Bulls 2014 1-0-0-0-0-0. REP HONOURS: SA U20 2014 no appearances. FC RECORD: 1-0-0-0-0-0. RECORD IN 2014: (Blue Bulls) 1-0-0-0-0-0.

Mxoli, Sangoni Mpumelelo (Durban HS & Univ. of KZN) b 08/01/85, Durban. 1.83m. 110kg. Prop. FC DEBUT: 2004. PROV CAREER: KZN 2005-07 21-0-0-0-0-0. Valke 2007 8-0-0-0-0-0. Blue Bulls 2008-09 8-0-0-0-0-0. EP Kings 2009-10 21-2-0-0-0-10. EP Inv XV 2010 1-0-0-0-0-0. Sharks XV 2014 4-0-0-0-0-0. REP HONOURS: Emerging Springboks 2007-08 3-0-0-0-0-0. SA U21 2004-06 15-4-0-0-0-20. SA U19 2003-04. SA Schools 2002-03. CW KZN 2002-03. FC RECORD: 81-6-0-0-0-30. RECORD IN 2014: (Sharks XV) 4-0-0-0-0-0.

Mxunyelwa, Buhle (Stirling HS, East London) b 25/06/86, East London. 1.87m. 129kg. Prop. FC DEBUT: 2008. PROV CAREER: Border 2008-09 & 14 28-2-0-0-0-10. E/Cape XV 2008 1-0-0-0-0-0. WP 2010 8-0-0-0-0-0. Leopards 2011-12 6-0-0-0-0-0. Leopard XV 2013 3-0-0-0-0-0. MISC INFO: Brother of Siya Mxunyelwa. FC RECORD: 46-2-0-0-0-10. RECORD IN 2014: (Border) 9-0-0-0-0-0.

Ndlela, Lindani Ntobela (Estcourt HS & George Campbell HS, Durban) b 06/09/1993, Durban. 1.65m. 85kg. Wing. FC DEBUT: 2014. PROV CAREER: Border 2014 4-3-0-0-0-15. FC RECORD: 4-3-0-0-0-15. RECORD IN 2014: (Border) 4-3-0-0-0-15.

Ndungane, Akona Zilindlovu (Hudson Park HS, East London) b 20/02/81, Umtata. 1.83m. 86kg. Wing. FC DEBUT: 2003. PROV CAREER: Elephants 2003 13-6-0-0-0-30. Border 2004-05 17-14-0-0-0-70. Blue Bulls 2005-06 & 08-14 71-30-0-0-0-150. SUPER RUGBY: Bulls 2005-09 & 11-14 108-33-0-0-0-165. REP HONOURS: SA 2006-07 Tests: 11-1-0-0-0-5. Tour: 2007 2-0-0-0-0-0. Total: 13-1-0-0-0-5. SA 'A' 2004 1-3-0-0-0-15. SA Sevens 2004. MISC INFO: Holds Border record for most CC tries in a season (10). Twin Brother of Natal Sharks wing Odwa Ndungane. FC RECORD: 223-87-0-0-0-435. RECORD IN 2014: (Bulls, Blue Bulls) 21-4-0-0-0-20.

Ndungane, Odwa Mzuzo (Hudson Park HS, East London & Eastern Cape Tech.) b 20/02/81, Umtata. 1.83m. 93kg. Wing. FC DEBUT: 2000. PROV CAREER: Border 2000-03 49-25-0-0-0-125. Blue Bulls 2004 2-0-0-0-0-0. KZN 2005-14 84-29-1-0-0-147. Sharks XV 2005-08 & 12 4-0-0-0-0-0. SUPER RUGBY: Bulls 2004 10-3-0-0-0-15. Sharks 2005-14 103-26-0-0-0-130. REP HONOURS: SA 2008-11 Tests: 9-2-0-0-0-10. Tour: 2009-10 3-1-0-0-0-5. Total: 12-3-0-0-0-15. SA 'A' 2004 2-2-0-0-0-10. Emerging Springboks 2007 2-0-0-0-0-0. SA U21 2002 1-0-0-0-0-0. MISC INFO: Twin brother of Springbok and Blue Bulls wing Akona Ndungane. FC RECORD: 269-88-1-0-0-442. RECORD IN 2014: (Sharks, KZN) 14-2-0-0-0-10.

Nel, Adriaan Ruhan (Brandwag HS, Benoni) b 17/05/1991. 1.92m. 88kg. Wing. FC DEBUT: 2012. PROV CAREER: Lions 2013 3-1-0-0-0-5. Young Lions 2012-14 7-4-0-0-0-20. FC RECORD: 10-5-0-0-0-25.

RECORD IN 2014: (Young Lions) 3-3-0-0-0-15.

Nel, Frederik Jean (Paarl Boys' HS & US) b 27/01/1993, Pretoria. 1.76m. 84kg. Scrumhalf. FC DEBUT: 2014. PROV CAREER: WP 2014 4-0-0-0-0-0. FC RECORD: 4-0-0-0-0-0. RECORD IN 2014: (WP) 4-0-0-0-0-0.

Nel, Japie (Goudveld HS, Welkom) b 20/11/82, Welkom. 1.90m. 105kg. Wing. FC DEBUT: 2005. PROV CAREER: Griffons 2005-07 & 2011-14 96-39-0-0-0-195. Leopards 2008-10 35-4-0-0-0-20. FC RECORD: 131-43-0-0-0-215. RECORD IN 2014: (Griffons) 17-9-0-0-0-45.

Nell, Darron Paul (Muir Coll., Uitenhage) b 08/03/80, Uitenhage. 1.94m. 108kg. Eighthman. FC DEBUT: 2002. PROV CAREER: Cheetahs 2002-08 66-11-0-0-0-55. EP Kings 2010-14 56-10-0-0-0-50. SUPER RUGBY: Cheetahs 2007-08 10-2-0-0-0-10. Southern Kings 2013 5-0-0-0-0-0. P/R 2013 2-0-0-0-0-0. REP HONOURS: SA Kings 2011 2-0-0-0-0-0. S/Kings 2009 1-0-0-0-0-0. FC RECORD: 142-23-0-0-0-115. RECORD IN 2014: (EP Kings) 6-1-0-0-0-5.

Nell, Ryan Desmond (Paarl Gym. & US) b 04/09/1990, Port Elizabeth. 1.91m. 95kg. Utility back. PROV CAREER: WP 2013 2-0-0-0-0-0. Blue Bulls 2014 9-2-0-0-0-10. REP HONOURS: SA Univ 2013 1-0-0-0-0-0. SA Sevens 2012. FC RECORD: 12-2-0-0-0-10. RECORD IN 2014: (Blue Bulls) 9-2-0-0-0-10.

Nelson, Norman Tsimba (Patensie HS) b 10/08/83, Patensie. 1.75m. 81kg. Wing. FC DEBUT: 2006. PROV CAREER: EP Kings 2006-08 & 10-13 92-56-0-0-0-280. E/Cape XV 2008 1-0-0-0-0-0. SWD 2009 20-15-1-0-0-77. Griffons 2013-14 23-14-0-0-0-70. REP HONOURS: SA Barbarians 2012 1-1-0-0-0-5. FC RECORD: 137-86-1-0-0-432. RECORD IN 2014: (Griffons) 18-11-0-0-0-55.

Nepgen, Jaco (Hangklip HS, Queenstown) b 03/01/86. 1.98m. 103kg. Lock. FC DEBUT: 2008. PROV CAREER: Griquas 2010-14 72-7-0-0-0-35. SWD 2011 1-0-0-0-0-0. REP HONOURS: SA Students 2008-09 3-1-0-0-0-5. FC RECORD: 76-8-0-0-0-40. RECORD IN 2014: (Griquas) 24-3-0-0-0-15.

Ngande, Siyamthanda b 11/07/1990. Prop. FC DEBUT: 2014. PROV CAREER: Border 2014 4-0-0-0-0-0. FC RECORD: 4-0-0-0-0-0. RECORD IN 2014: (Border) 4-0-0-0-0-0.

Ngcamu, Nhalanhla (Maritzburg Coll. & NWU) b 27/03/1992, Pietermaritzburg. 1.78m. 110kg. Prop. FC DEBUT: 2014. PROV CAREER: Leopards 2014 5-0-0-0-0-0. FC RECORD: 5-0-0-0-0-0. RECORD IN 2014: (Leopards) 5-0-0-0-0-0.

Ngcobo, Sandile Caleb (Stix) (Highlands North HS, Johannesburg & UJ) b 01/08/1989, Thembisa. Wing. FC DEBUT: 2012. PROV CAREER: Valke 2012-14 36-10-0-0-0-50. FC RECORD: 36-10-0-0-0-50. RECORD IN 2014: (Valke) 6-4-0-0-0-20.

Ngidi, Thulani Sphamandla (Nhlanhlayethu HS) b 11/01/1986, Durban. 1.74m. 111kg. Prop. FC DEBUT: 2010. PROV CAREER: Valke 2010-11 & 14 40-0-0-0-0-0. FC RECORD: 40-0-0-0-0-0. RECORD IN 2014: (Valke) 17-0-0-0-0-0.

Nhlapo, Sabelo (Highlands North Boys' HS, Johannesburg) b 17/12/88, Johannesburg. 1.90m. 116kg. Prop. FC DEBUT: 2009. PROV CAREER: Sharks XV 2009-11 20-0-0-0-0-0. Boland 2013 8-0-0-0-0-0. Pumas 2014 7-0-0-0-0-0. REP HONOURS: SA U20 2008 3-1-0-0-0-5. FC RECORD: 38-1-0-0-0-5. RECORD IN 2014: (Pumas) 7-0-0-0-0-0.

Niemand, Samuel Jacobus (SJ) (Klerksdorp HS & NWU) b 06/03/1991, Pretoria. 1.87m. 103kg. Eighthman. FC DEBUT: 2012. PROV CAREER: Leopards 2012-13 7-2-0-0-0-10. Leopards XV 2014 6-2-0-0-0-10. FC RECORD: 13-4-0-0-0-20. RECORD IN 2014: (Leopards XV) 6-2-0-0-0-10.

Niewoudt, Luan (Nico Malan HS, Humansdorp) b 17/04/1995,

SEASON IN 2014

Pretoria. 1.84m. 91kg. Centre. FC DEBUT: 2014. PROV CAREER: EP Kings 1-0-0-0-0-0. FC RECORD: 1-0-0-0-0-0. RECORD IN 2014: (EP Kings) 1-0-0-0-0-0.

Nkosi, Mondi Nicholas (George Campbell HS, Durban) b 09/10/1994, Ladysmith. 1.75m. 85kg. Fullback. FC DEBUT: 2014. PROV CAREER: Border 2014 2-0-0-0-0-0. FC RECORD: 2-0-0-0-0-0. RECORD IN 2014: (Border) 2-0-0-0-0-0.

Nkuna, Musa Phanuel (Ben Vorster HS, Tzaneen & TUT) b 08/03/1985, Tzaneen. 1.89m. 96kg. Lock. FC DEBUT: 2013. PROV CAREER: Limpopo 2013-14 9-0-0-0-0-0. FC RECORD: 9-0-0-0-0-0. RECORD IN 2014: (Limpopo) 5-0-0-0-0-0.

Nofemele, Siphosenkosi (Eyabantu HS & UFH) b 12/11/1989, Fort Beaufort. 1.6m. 75kg. Wing. FC DEBUT: 2014. PROV CAREER: Border 2014 9-3-0-0-0-15. FC RECORD: 9-3-0-0-0-15. RECORD IN 2014: (Border) 9-3-0-0-0-15.

Nofuma, Nkosikhana (Lebogang HS, CUT & UFH) b 29/04/1988, Qumbu. 1.9m. 95kg. Flank. FC DEBUT: 2014. PROV CAREER: Border 2014 14-0-0-0-0-0. FC RECORD: 14-0-0-0-0-0. RECORD IN 2014: (Border) 14-0-0-0-0-0.

Nokwe, Jongikhaya Lutric (Jongi) (Kwamfundo SS, Khayelitsha) b 30/12/81, Ngxalawe, Ciskei. 1.82m. 80kg. Wing. FC DEBUT: 2003. PROV CAREER: Boland 2003-07 55-33-0-0-0-165. Cheetahs 2008-10 35-26-0-0-0-130. Cheetahs XV 2010 1-0-0-0-0-0. Griffons 2011 1-0-0-0-0-0. EP Kings 2012 6-3-0-0-0-15. Valke 2013 14-6-0-0-0-30. Sharks XV 2014 1-1-0-0-0-5. SUPER RUGBY: Stormers 2006 6-2-0-0-0-10. Cheetahs 2008-10 30-15-0-0-0-75. REP HONOURS: SA 2008-09 Tests: 4-5-0-0-0-25. Tour: 2006,09 3-3-0-0-0-15. Total: 7-8-0-0-0-40. SA Sevens 2004-05. MISC INFO: YPoY 2005. FC RECORD: 156-94-0-0-0-470. RECORD IN 2014: (Sharks XV) 1-1-0-0-0-5.

Nomzanga, Lukhanyo Welcome (Forbes Grant HS) b 08/10/1987, King William's Town. 1.83m. 83kg. Flank. FC DEBUT: 2014. PROV CAREER: Border 2014 9-0-0-0-0-0. FC RECORD: 9-0-0-0-0-0. RECORD IN 2014: (Border) 9-0-0-0-0-0.

Nonkontwana, Abongile (Selborne Coll., East London & St. Albans Coll.) b 10/04/1995, Port Elizabeth. 1.96m. 107kg. Lock. FC DEBUT: 2014. REP HONOURS: SA U20 2014 2-0-0-0-0-0. FC RECORD: 2-0-0-0-0-0. RECORD IN 2014: (SA U20) 2-0-0-0-0-0.

Noordman, Mario (Harmony Sport Academy, Virginia & Welkom Gym.) b 21/06/1992, George. 1.61m. 77kg. Scrumhalf. FC DEBUT: 2014. PROV CAREER: Border 2014 8-1-1-0-0-7. FC RECORD: 8-1-1-0-0-7. RECORD IN 2014: (Border) 8-1-1-0-0-7.

Nortier, Gerhard Johan (Oudtshoorn HS & NWU) b 04/03/1989, George. 1.8m. 88kg. Flyhalf. FC DEBUT: 2012. PROV CAREER: Leopards 2012-13 15-2-2-1-0-17. Leopards XV 2014 7-1-22-9-1-79. FC RECORD: 22-3-24-10-1-96. RECORD IN 2014: (Leopards XV) 7-1-22-9-1-79.

Nortje, Oshwill (Hentie Cilliers HS, Virginia) b 03/12/1990, George. 1.65m. 67kg. Scrumhalf. FC DEBUT: 2011. PROV CAREER: Griffons 2011-14 40-6-0-0-0-30. FC RECORD: 40-6-0-0-0-30. RECORD IN 2014: (Griffons) 14-0-0-0-0-0.

Notshe, Sikhumbuzo (Wynberg Boys' HS) b 28/05/1993, King William's Town. 1.90m. 100kg. Eighthman. FC DEBUT: 2013. PROV CAREER: WP 2013-14 23-6-0-0-0-30. SUPER RUGBY: Stormers 2014 3-1-0-0-0-5. FC RECORD: 26-7-0-0-0-35. RECORD IN 2014: (Stormers, WP) 17-5-0-0-0-25.

November, Siyamthanda (Hentie Cilliers HS, Virginia, Port Rex HS & NWU) b 28/03/1992, Mthatha. 1.93m. 101kg. Lock. FC DEBUT: 2014. PROV CAREER: Leopards XV 2014 2-0-0-0-0-0. FC RECORD: 2-0-0-0-0-0. RECORD IN 2014: (Leopards XV) 2-0-0-0-0-0.

Ntshoko, Mayizukiswe b 27/03/1986. FC DEBUT: 2014. PROV CAREER: Griffons 2014 2-0-0-0-0-0. FC RECORD: 2-0-0-0-0-0. RECORD IN 2014: (Griffons) 2-0-0-0-0-0.

Ntubeni, Siyabonga (King Edward VII HS, Johannesburg) b 18/02/1991, East London. 1.77m. 92kg. Hooker. FC DEBUT: 2011. PROV CAREER: WP 2011-14 38-2-0-0-0-10. SUPER RUGBY: Stormers 2011-14 16-1-0-0-0-5. REP HONOURS: SA 2013 no appearances. FC RECORD: 54-3-0-0-0-15. RECORD IN 2014: (Stormers, WP) 11-2-0-0-0-10.

Nyakane, Trevor Ntando (Ben Vorster HS, Tzaneen) b 04/05/1989, Bushbuck Ridge. 1.78m. 109kg. Prop. FC DEBUT: 2010. PROV CAREER: Cheetahs 2010-14 38-2-0-0-0-10. Griffons 2011 1-0-0-0-0-0. Emerging Cheetahs 2011 1-0-0-0-0-0. SUPER RUGBY: Cheetahs 2012-14 42-3-0-0-0-15. REP HONOURS: SA Tests: 2013-14 13-1-0-0-0-5. FC RECORD: 93-6-0-0-0-30. RECORD IN 2014: (SA, Cheetahs SR, Cheetahs) 24-1-0-0-0-5.

Nyoka, Sinovuyo (Dale Coll., King William's Town) b 07/08/1990, King William's Town. 1.68m. 67kg. Scrumhalf. FC DEBUT: 2010. PROV CAREER: Border 2010-13 49-2-0-0-0-10. Valke 2014 1-0-0-0-0-0. Pumas 2014 10-0-0-0-0-0. REP HONOURS: SA Pres XV 2013 3-0-0-0-0-0. FC RECORD: 63-2-0-0-0-10. RECORD IN 2014: (Pumas, Valke) 11-0-0-0-0-0.

Oberholzer, Johan Christiaan (Jan Viljoen HS, Randfontein) b 14/11/1989, Krugersdorp. 1.78m. 92kg. Hooker. FC DEBUT: 2010. PROV CAREER: Leopards 2010-14 18-0-0-0-0-0. Leopard XV 2013-14 2-0-0-0-0-0. REP HONOURS: SA Univ 2013 1-0-0-0-0-0. FC RECORD: 21-0-0-0-0-0. RECORD IN 2014: (Leopards, Leopard XV) 11-0-0-0-0-0.

Obi, Luther Banks St Charles (St Benedicts Coll., Johannesburg) b 29/04/1993, Aba. 1.75m. 86kg. Wing. FC DEBUT: 2013. PROV CAREER: Leopards 2013-14 23-18-0-0-0-90. REP HONOURS: SA U 20 2013 5-4-0-0-0-20. FC RECORD: 28-22-0-0-0-110. RECORD IN 2014: (Leopards) 9-10-0-0-0-50.

O'Brien, Patrick Lloyd (Paul Roos Gym., Stellenbosch & US) b 25/12/1989, Durban. 1.89m. 109kg. Lock. FC DEBUT: 2013. PROV CAREER: Griquas 2013 9-0-0-0-0-0. WP 2014 1-0-0-0-0-0. FC RECORD: 10-0-0-0-0-0. RECORD IN 2014: (WP) 1-0-0-0-0-0.

Odendaal, Megiel Burger (Monument HS, Krugersdorp & UP) b 15/04/1993, Bloemfontein. 1.87m. 95kg. Centre. FC DEBUT: 2013. PROV CAREER: Blue Bulls 2013-14 17-5-0-0-0-25. FC RECORD: 17-5-0-0-0-25. RECORD IN 2014: (Blue Bulls) 16-5-0-0-0-25.

Odendaal, Willem Adriaan (Eldoraigne HS, Pretoria) b 11/07/1990, Pretoria. 1.83m. 92kg. Centre. FC DEBUT: 2010. PROV CAREER: Valke 2010-14 76-14-0-0-0-70. FC RECORD: 76-14-0-0-0-70. RECORD IN 2014: (Valke) 13-0-0-0-0-0.

Oelofse, Schalk Wentzel (Daniel Pienaar THS, Uitenhage & NMMU) b 02/11/1988, Port Elizabeth. 1.97m. 111kg. Lock. FC DEBUT: 2013. PROV CAREER: EP Kings 2013 1-0-0-0-0-0. SWD 2013-14 23-1-0-0-0-5. REP HONOURS: SA Univ 2013 1-0-0-0-0-0. FC RECORD: 25-1-0-0-0-5. RECORD IN 2014: (SWD) 12-0-0-0-0-0.

Olivier, Alwyn Manie b 10/02/1990. Fullback. FC DEBUT: 2014. PROV CAREER: Limpopo 2014 1-0-0-0-0-0. FC RECORD: 1-0-0-0-0-0. RECORD IN 2014: (Limpopo) 1-0-0-0-0-0.

Olivier, Brenden Hercules (Nico Malan HS, Humansdorp) b 19/03/1992, Kareedouw. 1.89m. 110kg. Prop. FC DEBUT: 2012. PROV CAREER: EP Kings 2012-14 20-0-0-0-0-0. FC RECORD: 20-0-0-0-0-0. RECORD IN 2014: (EP Kings) 3-0-0-0-0-0.

Olivier, Friedle (Dr Johan Jurgens HS, Springs) b 27/05/1992, Pretoria. 1.98m. 94kg. Flank. FC DEBUT: 2013. PROV CAREER: Valke

2013-14 21-2-0-0-0-10. FC RECORD: 21-2-0-0-0-10. RECORD IN 2014: (Valke) 12-1-0-0-0-5.
Olivier, Gerhardus Johannes (Grey Coll., Bloemfontein & UFS) b 17/02/1993, Ficksburg. 1.89m. 103kg. Eighthman. FC DEBUT: 2014. PROV CAREER: Free State XV 2014 2-0-0-0-0-0. FC RECORD: 2-0-0-0-0-0. RECORD IN 2014: (Free State XV) 2-0-0-0-0-0.
Olivier, Wynand (Affies, Pretoria) b 11/06/83, Welkom. 1.84m. 87kg. Centre. FC DEBUT: 2003. PROV CAREER: Blue Bulls 2003-06 & 08-11 72-26-0-0-0-130. SUPER RUGBY: Bulls 2005-13 110-29-0-0-0-145. REP HONOURS: SA 2006-07 & 09-12 & 14 Tests: 38-1-0-0-0-5. Tour: 4-0-0-0-0-0. Total: 42-1-0-0-0-5. SA XV 2006 1-0-0-0-0-0. SA U21 2004 5-2-0-0-0-10. MISC INFO: YPoY nominee 2005. FC RECORD: 230-58-0-0-0-290. RECORD IN 2014: (SA) 1-0-0-0-0-0.
Olivier, Wynand Sarel (Zwartkop HS, Centurion) b 16/07/1992, Pretoria. 1.81m. 90kg. Fullback. FC DEBUT: 2014. PROV CAREER: Leopards XV 2014 1-0-0-0-0-0. FC RECORD: 1-0-0-0-0-0. RECORD IN 2014: (Leopards XV) 1-0-0-0-0-0.
Oosthuizen, Caylib Rees (Oudtshoorn HS & UJ) b 01/09/1989, Cape Town. 1.86m. 114kg. Prop. FC DEBUT: 2011. PROV CAREER: Lions 2012 2-0-0-0-0-0. Young Lions 2011 2-0-0-0-0-0. Cheetahs 2013-14 8-0-0-0-0-0. Free State XV 2013 3-0-0-0-0-0. SUPER RUGBY: Lions 2012 6-1-0-0-0-5. Cheetahs 2014 16-0-0-0-0-0. REP HONOURS: SA U20 2009 5-0-0-0-0-0. FC RECORD: 42-1-0-0-0-5. RECORD IN 2014: (Cheetahs SR, Cheetahs) 21-0-0-0-0-0.
Oosthuizen, Coenraad Victor (Grey Coll., Bloemfontein) b 22/03/89, Potchefstroom. 1.83m. 127kg. Prop. FC DEBUT: 2008. PROV CAREER: Cheetahs 2008-14 55-11-0-0-0-55. Cheetahs XV 2010 1-0-0-0-0-0. SUPER RUGBY: Cheetahs 2010-14 66-8-0-0-0-40. REP HONOURS: SA Tests: 2012-14 21-3-0-0-0-15. 2010 Tour: 1-0-0-0-0-0. Total: 22-3-0-0-0-15. Springbok XV 2014 1-0-0-0-0-0. British Barbarians 2013 1-0-0-0-0-0. SA U20 2009 5-0-0-0-0-0. FC RECORD: 151-22-0-0-0-110. RECORD IN 2014: (SA, Springbok XV, Cheetahs SR, Cheetahs) 19-1-0-0-0-5.
Oosthuizen, Devin Andre (HTS John Vorster, Nigel) b 28/05/1988. 1.94m. 104kg. Flanker. FC DEBUT: 2010. PROV CAREER: Blue Bulls 2010 10-1-0-0-0-5. EP Kings 2010-14 58-10-0-0-0-50. SUPER RUGBY: Southern Kings 2013 9-0-0-0-0-0. P/R 2013 2-0-0-0-0-0. REP HONOURS: SA Kings 2011 3-0-0-0-0-0. FC RECORD: 82-11-0-0-0-55. RECORD IN 2014: (EP Kings) 6-0-0-0-0-0.
Oosthuizen, Ettienne (Bergsig HS, Rustenburg) b 22/12/1992, Klerksdorp. 1.98m. 120kg. Flanker. FC DEBUT: 2012. PROV CAREER: Lions 2012 3-0-0-0-0-0. Young Lions 2012 3-1-0-0-0-5. KZN 2014 11-0-0-0-0-0. SUPER RUGBY: Lions 2012 3-0-0-0-0-0. Sharks 2014 15-0-0-0-0-0. FC RECORD: 35-1-0-0-0-5. RECORD IN 2014: (Sharks, KZN) 26-0-0-0-0-0.
Oosthuizen, Jaco (Waterkloof HS, Pretoria) b 08/03/1990, Johannesburg. 1.85m. 97kg. Wing. FC DEBUT: 2012. PROV CAREER: Valke 2012-14 19-4-0-0-0-20. FC RECORD: 19-4-0-0-0-20. RECORD IN 2014: (Valke) 3-0-0-0-0-0.
Oosthuizen, Schalk Willem (Wolmaransstad HS & NWU) b 07/03/1990, Wolmaransstad. 1.88m. 91kg. Fullback. FC DEBUT: 2011. PROV CAREER: Leopards 2011 & 13 4-0-2-0-0-4. Leopards XV 2014 5-2-0-1-0-13. FC RECORD: 9-2-2-1-0-17. RECORD IN 2014: (Leopards XV) 5-2-0-1-0-13.
Orie, Marvin (Tygerberg HS, Parow) b 15/02/1993, Cape Town. 1.98m. 104kg. Lock. FC DEBUT: 2014. PROV CAREER: Blue Bulls 2014 6-0-0-0-0-0. SUPER RUGBY: Bulls 2014 2-0-0-0-0-0. REP HONOURS: SA U20 2012 no appearances. FC RECORD: 8-0-0-0-0-0. RECORD IN

2014: (Bulls, Blue Bulls) 8-0-0-0-0-0.
Paige, Rudy (Bastion HS, Krugersdorp & UJ) b 02/08/1989, Riversdal. 1.67m. 70kg. Scrumhalf. FC DEBUT: 2010. PROV CAREER: Lions 2011 2-0-0-0-0-0. Young Lions 2010-12 10-0-0-0-0-0. Blue Bulls 2012-14 33-2-0-0-0-10. SUPER RUGBY: Bulls 2013-14 7-0-0-0-0-0. REP HONOURS: SA Students 2012 2-0-0-0-0-0. SA U20 2009 4-0-0-0-0-0. FC RECORD: 58-2-0-0-0-10. RECORD IN 2014: (Bulls, Blue Bulls) 18-0-0-0-0-0.
Parks, Buran Joshua (Harmony Sports Academy, Virginia) b 27/06/1992, George. 1.80m. 85kg. Eighthman. FC DEBUT: 2011. PROV CAREER: SWD 2011-14 30-2-0-0-0-10. FC RECORD: 30-2-0-0-0-10. RECORD IN 2014: (SWD) 5-1-0-0-0-5.
Pati, Siyasonga b 04/04/1984. Wing. FC DEBUT: 2014. PROV CAREER: Border 2014 1-0-0-0-0-0. FC RECORD: 1-0-0-0-0-0. RECORD IN 2014: (Border) 1-0-0-0-0-0.
Paul, Tyler Warne (St Andrews Coll., Grahamstown & NMMU) b 20/01/1995, Duiwelskloof. 1.94m. 110kg. Lock. FC DEBUT: 2014. PROV CAREER: EP Kings 2014 3-0-0-0-0-0. FC RECORD: 3-0-0-0-0-0. RECORD IN 2014: (EP Kings) 3-0-0-0-0-0.
Pedro, Hentzwill Nowellen (George HS) b 21/07/1987, George. 1.86m. 80kg. Wing. FC DEBUT: 2013. PROV CAREER: SWD 2013-14 16-7-0-0-0-35. FC RECORD: 16-7-0-0-0-35. RECORD IN 2014: (SWD) 13-6-0-0-0-30.
Petersen, Sergeal (Grey HS, Port Elizabeth) b 01/08/1994, Port Elizabeth. 1.75m. 80kg. Wing. FC DEBUT: 2013. PROV CAREER: EP Kings 2013-14 5-1-0-0-0-5. SUPER RUGBY: Southern Kings 2013 8-4-0-0-0-20. REP HONOURS: SA U20 2014 5-3-0-0-0-15. FC RECORD: 18-8-0-0-0-40. RECORD IN 2014: (EP Kings, SA U20) 7-4-0-0-0-20.
Petzer, Adolf Quinten (Vereeniging HS & NWU) b 13/04/1984, Vereeniging. 1.89m. 123kg. Flank. FC DEBUT: 2011. PROV CAREER: SWD 2011-12 & 14 13-1-0-0-0-5. FC RECORD: 13-1-0-0-0-5. RECORD IN 2014: (SWD) 5-1-0-0-0-5.
Phunguzwa, Siphesihle Qhamani (Sipho) (Selborne Coll., East London) b 21/05/1993, Butterworth. 1.78m. 87kg. Flank. FC DEBUT: 2014. PROV CAREER: EP Kings 2014 6-1-0-0-0-5. FC RECORD: 6-1-0-0-0-5. RECORD IN 2014: (EP Kings) 6-1-0-0-0-5.
Pienaar, Jacob Arnoldus (Lichtenburg HS & NWU) b 19/09/1993, Barberton. 1.86m. 99kg. Centre. FC DEBUT: 2014. PROV CAREER: Leopards XV 2014 1-0-0-0-0-0. FC RECORD: 1-0-0-0-0-0. RECORD IN 2014: (Leopards XV) 1-0-0-0-0-0.
Pienaar, Ruan (Grey Coll., Bloemfontein) b 10/03/84, Bloemfontein. 1.86m. 92kg. Scrumhalf. FC DEBUT: 2004. PROV CAREER: Cheetahs 2004 9-2-1-0-0-12. KZN 2005-06 & 08-10 33-7-59-36-0-261. SUPER RUGBY: Sharks 2005-10 67-10-35-42-2-252. REP HONOURS: SA 2006-14 Tests: 80-8-22-17-0-135. Tour 2006,07, 09 5-0-1-7-0-23. Total: 85-8-23-24-1-158. Springbok XV 2014 1-0-0-0-0-0. British Barbarians 2011 1-0-1-0-0-2. SA U21 2004-05 10-1-3-0-0-11. SA U19 2003. SA Schools 2002. CW Free State 2002. MISC INFO: YPoY nominee 2005, Son of 1980-81 Springbok Gysie Pienaar. FC RECORD: 206-28-122-102-3-699. RECORD IN 2014: (SA, Springbok XV) 7-1-0-0-0-5.
Pienaar, Wynand Christo (Welkom Gym.) b 05/08/1989, Welkom. 1.86m. 95kg. Fullback. FC DEBUT: 2013. PROV CAREER: Boland 2013 6-1-0-0-0-5. Griffons 2014 18-5-6-0-0-37. FC RECORD: 24-6-6-0-0-42. RECORD IN 2014: (Griffons) 18-5-6-0-0-37.
Pietersen, Jon-Paul Roger (JP) (General Hertzog HS, Emalahleni) b 12/07/86, Stellenbosch. 1.91m. 103kg. Wing/Fullback. FC DEBUT: 2005. PROV CAREER: KZN 2005-06 & 08-12 42-17-0-0-0-85. SUPER RUGBY: Sharks 2006-14 112-34-0-0-0-170. REP HONOURS: SA 2006-14 Tests:

SEASON IN 2014

59-18-0-0-0-90. Tour: 2-0-0-0-0-0. Total: 61-18-0-0-0-90. Springbok XV 2014 1-0-0-0-0-0. SA U21 2006 5-2-0-0-0-10. Misc. info: YPoY nominee 2005, 2006. SARU PoY 2012 nominee. Super PoY 2012 nominee. SARPA PPoY 2012. FC RECORD: 221-71-0-0-0-355. RECORD IN 2014: (SA, Springbok XV, Sharks) 23-3-0-0-0-15.

Poley, Arno Pieter (Dr Malan HS, Meyerton) b 14/03/1991, Barberton. 1.94m. 95kg. Fullback. FC DEBUT: 2011. PROV CAREER: Valke 2011-14 54-4-2-0-1-27. FC RECORD: 54-4-2-0-1-27. RECORD IN 2014: (Valke) 11-1-1-0-0-7.

Pollard, Handre (Paarl Gym.) b 11/03/1994, Somerset West. 1.89m. 96kg. Flyhalf. FC DEBUT: 2012. PROV CAREER: Blue Bulls 2013-14 10-1-19-14-1-88. SUPER RUGBY: Bulls 2014 13-1-10-16-1-76. REP HONOURS: SA 2014 9-2-14-8-1-65. SA U20 2012-14 14-2-37-18-1-141. MISC INFO: PoY nominee 2014. FC RECORD: 46-6-80-56-4-370. RECORD IN 2014: (SA, Bulls, Blue Bulls, SA U20) 29-6-44-31-2-217.

Potgieter, Dewald Johan (Daniel Pienaar HTS, Uitenhage) b 22/02/87, Port Elizabeth. 1.90m. 98kg. Eighthman. FC DEBUT: 2007. PROV CAREER: Blue Bulls 2007-12 63-10-0-0-0-50. SUPER RUGBY: Bulls 2008-14 70-4-0-0-0-20. REP HONOURS: SA Tests: 2009-10 6-1-0-0-0-5. Tour: 2009 2-0-0-0-0-0. Total: 8-1-0-0-0-5. Emerging Springboks 2009 1-0-0-0-0-0. FC RECORD: 142-15-0-0-0-75. RECORD IN 2014: (Bulls) 3-0-0-0-0-0.

Potgieter, Jacques-Louis (Affies, Pretoria) b 02/09/84, Pretoria. 1.98m. 86kg. Flyhalf. FC DEBUT: 2005. PROV CAREER: Blue Bulls 2005-07 & 10 & 14 64-7-101-112-4-585. Griffons 2008 5-2-9-17-0-79. Cheetahs 2008-09 26-4-57-32-5-245. KZN 2011 4-0-0-0-0-0. Sharks XV 2011 2-0-6-3-0-21. SUPER RUGBY: Bulls 2007 & 10 & 14 29-3-15-35-3-159. Cheetahs 2008-09 17-1-19-13-1-85. Sharks 2011 10-1-2-6-0-27. FC RECORD: 157-18-209-218-13-1201. RECORD IN 2014: (Bulls, Blue Bulls) 23-1-29-65-3-267.

Pretorius, André Stefan (Dinamika HS, Alberton) b 29/12/78, Johannesburg. 1.76m. 90kg. Flyhalf. FC DEBUT: 1998. PROV CAREER: Lions 1999-06,09 45-7-120-72-15-536. Young Lions 2009 & 2011 6-0-9-13-1-60. KZN 2010 8-0-6-0-0-12. Leopards 2012 & 14 33-1-112-36-5-352. Leopard XV 2013 6-2-28-9-0-93. SUPER RUGBY: Cats 2002-06 47-10-74-95-5-498. Lions 2007 & 09 & 11 25-1-28-26-8-163. REP HONOURS: SA 2002-03& 05-07 Tests: 31-2-31-25-8-171. Tour: 2007 2-0-0-1-0-3. Total: 33-2-31-26-8-174. SA 'A' 2004 3-1-11-0-0-27. SA U23s 2001 2-2-2-0-0-14; SA Sevens 2000-01 (inc RWC 7s); SA U21s 1998 6-3-7-9-1-59; SA Barbarians 2001 1-0-0-0-0-0. MISC INFO: Holds Cats/Lions record for most career points (661), cons (102), pens (121), drop goals (13). SA 7s PoY 2001; Leading scorer U21s champs. 1999 (129 points) & 1998 (80 points). FC RECORD: 215-29-428-286-43-1988. RECORD IN 2014: (Leopards) 12-1-53-6-1-132.

Pretorius, Conway (Strand HS & Harmony Sport Academy, Virginia) b 04/07/1992, Pretoria. 1.9m. 108kg. Eighthman. FC DEBUT: 2014. PROV CAREER: Boland 2014 5-3-0-0-0-15. FC RECORD: 5-3-0-0-0-15. RECORD IN 2014: (Boland) 5-3-0-0-0-15.

Pretorius, Dewald Petrus (Stilfontein HS) b 29/11/86, Welkom. 1.86m. 96kg. Centre. FC DEBUT: 2007. PROV CAREER: Blue Bulls 2007 3-2-0-0-0-10. Valke 2008 & 14 19-4-0-0-0-20. Griquas 2009-10 20-10-0-0-0-50. Pumas 2011-14 40-9-0-0-0-45. FC RECORD: 82-25-0-0-0-125. RECORD IN 2014: (Pumas, Valke) 8-2-0-0-0-10.

Pretorius, Jerome (Voortrekker HS, Pietermaritzburg) b 22/03/1988, Boksburg. 1.81m. 85kg. Centre. FC DEBUT: 2010. PROV CAREER: Sharks XV 2010-11 18-7-0-0-0-35. Blue Bulls 2012 4-1-0-0-0-5. Pumas 2012-14 42-13-0-0-0-65. REP HONOURS: SA Pres XV 2013 3-0-0-0-0-0. FC RECORD: 67-21-0-0-0-105. RECORD IN 2014: (Pumas)

17-6-0-0-0-30.

Pretorius, Johannes Hendrik (Juan) (Klerksdorp HS) b 22/10/1987, Klerksdorp. 1.90m. 101kg. Flank. FC DEBUT: 2011. PROV CAREER: Leopards 2011-12 28-4-0-0-0-20. Border 2013 20-2-0-0-0-10. Valke 2014 5-0-0-0-0-0. FC RECORD: 53-6-0-0-0-30. RECORD IN 2014: (Valke) 5-0-0-0-0-0.

Pretorius, Johannes Willem (Brandwag HS, Benoni & UP) b 14/01/1992, Benoni. 1.74m. 80kg. Scrumhalf. FC DEBUT: 2014. PROV CAREER: Pumas 2014 1-1-3-0-0-11. FC RECORD: 1-1-3-0-0-11. RECORD IN 2014: (Pumas) 1-1-3-0-0-11.

Pretorius, Mark (Nelspruit HS) b 09/06/1992, Nelspruit. 1.76m. 102kg. Hooker. FC DEBUT: 2013. PROV CAREER: Young Lions 2013-14 6-0-0-0-0-0. SUPER RUGBY: Lions 2014 1-0-0-0-0-0. REP HONOURS: SA U20 2012 4-1-0-0-0-5. FC RECORD: 11-1-0-0-0-5. RECORD IN 2014: (Lions SR, Young Lions) 6-0-0-0-0-0.

Pretorius, Nicolaas (THS John Vorster, Nigel & UP) b 29/02/84, Pretoria. 1.84m. 119kg. Prop/Hooker. FC DEBUT: 2006. PROV CAREER: Griffons 2006 10-0-0-0-0-0. Valke 2007-08 & 12-14 62-1-0-0-0-5. Griquas 2013 1-0-0-0-0-0. FC RECORD: 73-1-0-0-0-5. RECORD IN 2014: (Valke) 9-0-0-0-0-0.

Pretorius, Sarel Johannes (Reitz HS) b 18/04/84, Reitz. 1.75m. 75kg. Scrumhalf. FC DEBUT: 2006. PROV CAREER: Valke 2006-07 37-16-0-0-0-80. Griquas 2007-11 65-25-0-0-0-125. Cheetahs 2012-14 32-14-0-0-0-70. Cheetahs XV 2010 1-0-0-0-0-0. SUPER RUGBY: Cheetahs 2009-11 & 13-14 66-22-0-0-0-110. REP HONOURS: Emerging Springboks 2008 3-0-0-0-0-0. Royal XV 2009 1-0-0-0-0-0. British Barbarians 2014 2-0-0-0-0-0. MISC INFO: Super PoY 2011. FC RECORD: 207-77-0-0-0-385. RECORD IN 2014: (Cheetahs SR, Cheetahs, British Barbarians) 25-10-0-0-0-50.

Pretorius, Ulrich De Beer (Marlow Agric., Cradock & NMMU) b 21/11/1988, Eliott. 1.85m. 110kg. Hooker. FC DEBUT: 2013. PROV CAREER: Boland 2013-14 30-8-0-0-0-40. FC RECORD: 30-8-0-0-0-40. RECORD IN 2014: (Boland) 14-2-0-0-0-10.

Pretorius, Walter b 23/04/1982. Lock. FC DEBUT: 2013. PROV CAREER: Limpopo 2013-14 7-0-0-0-0-0. FC RECORD: 7-0-0-0-0-0. RECORD IN 2014: (Limpopo) 5-0-0-0-0-0.

Prinsloo, Johannes Gerhardus (Boom) (Grey Coll.) b 12/03/1989, Bloemfontein. 1.87m. 95kg. Flanker. FC DEBUT: 2010. PROV CAREER: Cheetahs 2010-12 & 14 33-9-0-0-0-45. Emerging Cheetahs 2011 1-0-0-0-0-0. Free State XV 2013 3-5-0-0-0-25. SUPER RUGBY: Cheetahs 2012-14 27-5-0-0-0-25. Rep. honours: SA Sevens 2010-12. FC RECORD: 64-19-0-0-0-95. RECORD IN 2014: (Cheetahs SR, Cheetahs) 16-4-0-0-0-20.

Prinsloo, Johannes Gouws (Gouws) (Marlow Agric. HS, Cradock) b 19/07/1990, East London. 1.79m. 80kg. Fullback. FC DEBUT: 2011. PROV CAREER: KZN 2011-12 4-0-0-0-0-0. Sharks XV 2011-13 21-7-28-30-0-181. Griquas 2013-14 24-4-41-43-1-237. SUPER RUGBY: Cheetahs 2014 1-0-0-0-0-0. MISC INFO: VC PoY 2012 nominee. FC RECORD: 50-11-69-73-1-418. RECORD IN 2014: (Cheetahs SR, Griquas) 16-4-33-29-1-179

Putuma, Wandile (Port Rex HS) b 08/08/1990, East London. 1.92m. 92kg. Lock. FC DEBUT: 2014. PROV CAREER: Border 2014 17-2-0-0-0-10. FC RECORD: 17-2-0-0-0-10. RECORD IN 2014: (Border) 17-2-0-0-0-10.

Qinisile, Siphatho Liyabona (Selborne Coll., East London) b 07/01/1993, East London. 1.77m. 91kg. Hooker. FC DEBUT: 2014. PROV CAREER: Young Lions 2014 3-3-0-0-0-15. FC RECORD: 3-3-0-0-0-15. RECORD IN 2014: (Young Lions) 3-3-0-0-0-15.

SEASON IN 2014

Radyn, Tiaan (Boland Agric. HS, Paarl) b 22/03/1991, Cape Town. 1.84m. 90kg. Flyhalf. FC DEBUT: 2014. PROV CAREER: Boland 2014 2-1-0-0-0-5. FC RECORD: 2-1-0-0-0-5. RECORD IN 2014: (Boland) 2-1-0-0-0-5.

Ralarala, Lundi Sinclair (Cradock HS & UFH) b 18/02/1990, Cradock. 1.82m. 84kg. Centre. FC DEBUT: 2014. PROV CAREER: Border 2014 12-5-0-0-0-25. FC RECORD: 12-5-0-0-0-25. RECORD IN 2014: (Border) 12-5-0-0-0-25.

Raubenheimer, Davon (Pacaltsdorp SS) b 16/07/1984, Knysna. 1.94m. 92kg. Flank. FC DEBUT: 2005. PROV CAREER: SWD 2005-08 & 14 72-5-0-0-0-25. Griquas 2009-11 56-4-0-0-0-20. Cheetahs 2012-13 16-0-0-0-0-0. Free State XV 2012-13 6-0-0-0-0-0. Griffons 2013 5-0-0-0-0-0. SUPER RUGBY: Cheetahs 2010-12 20-2-0-0-0-10. REP HONOURS: SA Tour: 2009 2-0-0-0-0-0. Emerging Springboks 2008 2-0-0-0-0-0. Royal XV 2009 1-0-0-0-0-0. SA U21 2005 3-0-0-0-0-0. FC RECORD: 183-11-0-0-0-55. RECORD IN 2014: (SWD) 12-0-0-0-0-0.

Raubenheimer, Shaun (George Hill HS, George) b 10/11/83, George. 1.80m. 94kg. Flanker. FC DEBUT: 2008. PROV CAREER: Border 2008 15-2-0-0-0-10. SWD 2009-10 & 12-14 72-26-0-0-0-130. Griffons 2011 13-2-0-0-0-10. REP HONOURS: SA Barbarians 2012 1-0-0-0-0-0. FC RECORD: 101-30-0-0-0-150. RECORD IN 2014: (SWD) 13-6-0-0-0-30.

Rautenbach, Neil (Paarl Boys' HS & UCT) b 17/05/1991, Cape Town. 1.78m. 101kg. Hooker. FC DEBUT: 2012. PROV CAREER: WP 2014 10-0-0-0-0-0. REP HONOURS: SA Students 2012 2-0-0-0-0-0. FC RECORD: 12-0-0-0-0-0. RECORD IN 2014: (WP) 10-0-0-0-0-0.

Redelinghuys, Julian (Monument HS, Krugersdorp) b 11/09/89, Pretoria. 1.76m. 100kg. Prop. FC DEBUT: 2009. PROV CAREER: KZN 2009 & 2011-12 9-0-0-0-0-0. Sharks XV 2010-11 8-0-0-0-0-0. Lions 2013-14 9-0-0-0-0-0. Young Lions 2013 4-1-0-0-0-5. SUPER RUGBY: Lions 2014 15-0-0-0-0-0. Lions P/R 2013 2-0-0-0-0-0. REP HONOURS: SA 2014 Tests: 2-0-0-0-0-0. SA U20 2009 4-0-0-0-0-0. FC RECORD: 53-1-0-0-0-5. RECORD IN 2014: (SA, Lions SR, Lions) 23-0-0-0-0-0.

Reinach, Jacobus Meyer (Cobus) (Grey Coll., Bloemfontein) b 07/02/1990, Bloemfontein. 1.75m. 83kg. Scrumhalf. FC DEBUT: 2011. PROV CAREER: KZN 2011-14 27-4-0-0-0-20. Sharks XV 2011-12 19-4-0-0-0-20. REP HONOURS: SA 2014 Tests: 6-2-0-0-0-10. SUPER RUGBY: Sharks 2012-14 26-7-0-0-0-35. MISC INFO: Son of former Springbok Jaco Reinach. FC RECORD: 78-17-0-0-0-85. RECORD IN 2014: (SA, Sharks, KZN) 19-8-0-0-0-40.

Rennie, Bryce Mark (Hudson Park HS, East London) b 22/01/1994, East London. 1.77m. 93kg. Hooker. FC DEBUT: 2014. PROV CAREER: Border 2014 4-0-0-0-0-0. FC RECORD: 4-0-0-0-0-0. RECORD IN 2014: (Border) 4-0-0-0-0-0.

Reynolds, Theunis Johannes (Monument HS, Krugersdorp) b 19/02/1993, Pretoria. 1.84m. 91kg. Hooker. FC DEBUT: 2014. PROV CAREER: Young Lions 2014 1-0-0-0-0-0. FC RECORD: 1-0-0-0-0-0. RECORD IN 2014: (Young Lions) 1-0-0-0-0-0.

Rhodes, Michael Kenworthy (Michaelhouse, Balgowan) b 19/12/87, Durban. 1.97m. 110kg. Lock. FC DEBUT: 2007. PROV CAREER: KZN 2009-10 19-1-0-0-0-5. Sharks XV 2008-10 18-5-0-0-0-25. Sharks Inv XV 2007 & 10 2-1-0-0-0-5. Lions 2011-12 21-5-0-0-0-25. Young Lions 2011 1-0-0-0-0-0. WP 2013-14 22-5-0-0-0-25. SUPER RUGBY: Lions 2011 11-2-0-0-0-10. Stormers 2013-14 17-1-0-0-0-5. REP HONOURS: British Barbarian 2014 1-1-0-0-0-5. FC RECORD: 112-21-0-0-0-105. RECORD IN 2014: (Stormers, WP, British Barbarians) 26-3-0-0-0-15.

Rhoode, Deroy Elizandro (Groot Brak HS, Mossel Bay) b 28/10/88. 1.6m. 64kg. FC DEBUT: 2009. PROV CAREER: SWD 2009-14 60-4-13-3-0-55. Boland 2014 5-0-0-0-0-0. FC RECORD: 65-4-13-3-0-55. RECORD IN 2014: (SWD, Boland) 12-0-1-0-0-2.

Rhule, Raymond Kofi (Louis Botha THS, Bloemfontein & UFS) b 06/11/1992, Accra (Ghana). 1.78m. 78kg. Wing. FC DEBUT: 2012. PROV CAREER: Cheetahs 2012-14 31-18-0-0-0-90. Free State XV 2012 1-0-0-0-0-0. SUPER RUGBY: Cheetahs 2013-14 26-7-0-0-0-35. MISC INFO: YPoY 2012 nominee. CC PoY 2012 nominee. REP HONOURS: SA 2012 no Tests. SA U20 2012 3-2-0-0-0-10. FC RECORD: 61-27-0-0-0-135. RECORD IN 2014: (Cheetahs SR, Cheetahs) 18-5-0-0-0-25.

Richards, Mark (Michaelhouse HS, Balgowan) b 09/09/1989, Springs. 1.75m. 81kg. Wing. FC DEBUT: 2010. PROV CAREER: KZN 2011 4-1-0-0-0-5. Sharks XV 2010-11 16-6-0-0-0-30. Sharks Inv XV 2010 1-1-0-0-0-5. Lions 2014 8-0-0-0-0-0. Rep. honours: SA Sevens 2010-14. FC RECORD: 29-8-0-0-0-40. RECORD IN 2014: (Lions, SA Sevens) 8-0-0-0-0-0.

Richardson, Christopher James (Oakdale HS, Riversdale & Outeniqua HS, George) b 26/01/1993, George. 1.82m. 103kg. Hooker. FC DEBUT: 2014. PROV CAREER: Valke 2014 6-1-0-0-0-5. FC RECORD: 6-1-0-0-0-5. RECORD IN 2014: (Valke) 6-1-0-0-0-5.

Richter, Anrich (Dr EG Jansen HS, Boksburg) b 30/05/1991, Kempton Park. 78kg. Scrumhalf. FC DEBUT: 2011. PROV CAREER: Valke 2011-14 62-23-0-0-0-115. FC RECORD: 62-23-0-0-0-115. RECORD IN 2014: (Valke) 19-8-0-0-0-40.

Rick, Shannon Michael Kendrick (Dale Coll., King William's Town) b 21/10/1988, East London. 1.78m. 86kg. Scrumhalf. FC DEBUT: 2011. PROV CAREER: SWD 2011 1-0-0-0-0-0. Griquas 2011 3-0-0-0-0-0. Sharks XV 2012 & 14 5-0-0-0-0-0. Border 2013 18-2-0-0-0-10. FC RECORD: 27-2-0-0-0-10. RECORD IN 2014: (Sharks XV) 4-0-0-0-0-0.

Roberts, Adrian Duncan (Rosendal HS, Cape Town) b 08/04/1992, Cape Town. 1.79m. 79kg. Flyhalf. FC DEBUT: 2014. PROV CAREER: WP 2014 2-1-1-0-0-7. FC RECORD: 2-1-1-0-0-7. RECORD IN 2014: (WP) 2-1-1-0-0-7.

Roberts, Cheslyn Dean (John Ramsey HS, Cape Town) b 10/04/1990, Cape Town. 1.76m. 91kg. Wing. FC DEBUT: 2013. PROV CAREER: Boland 2013-14 15-2-0-0-0-10. FC RECORD: 15-2-0-0-0-10. RECORD IN 2014: (Boland) 4-1-0-0-0-5.

Roberts, Daniel Cornelius (PW Botha Coll., George) b 20/01/1992, Riversdal. 1.85m. 73kg. Fullback. FC DEBUT: 2013. PROV CAREER: SWD 2013-14 27-6-0-0-0-30. FC RECORD: 27-6-0-0-0-30. RECORD IN 2014: (SWD) 17-6-0-0-0-30.

Roberts, Willem Andries Stephanus (Steph) (Grey Coll., Bloemfontein) b 20/03/85, Bloemfontein. 1.80m. 108kg. Prop. FC DEBUT: 2005. PROV CAREER: Cheetahs 2005-07 15-0-0-0-0-0. Griquas 2008-14 132-4-0-0-0-20. REP HONOURS: Royal XV 2009 1-0-0-0-0-0. SA Students 2007 1-0-0-0-0-0. FC RECORD: 149-4-0-0-0-20. RECORD IN 2014: (Griquas) 21-0-0-0-0-0.

Robertse, Francois (George Campbell HS, Durban) b 03/03/1989, Durban. 1.97m. 118kg. Lock. FC DEBUT: 2014. PROV CAREER: Leopards 2014 7-3-0-0-0-15. FC RECORD: 7-3-0-0-0-15. RECORD IN 2014: (Leopards) 7-3-0-0-0-15.

Robinson, Sean Jack (Waterkloof HS, Pretoria) b 02/11/1993, Pretoria. 1.81m. 85kg. Wing. FC DEBUT: 2013. PROV CAREER: Sharks XV 2013-14 5-1-0-0-0-5. SUPER RUGBY: Sharks 2013 3-0-0-0-0-0. FC RECORD: 8-1-0-0-0-5. RECORD IN 2014: (Sharks XV) 4-0-0-0-0-0.

Roelfse, Heinrich Rashid (George HS) b 25/01/1990, Mossel Bay. 1.86m. 110kg. Prop. FC DEBUT: 2012. PROV CAREER: Griffons 2012-14 33-0-0-0-0-0. FC RECORD: 33-0-0-0-0-0. RECORD IN 2014: (Griffons) 19-0-0-0-0-0.

SEASON IN 2014

Roos, Juan-Claude (Waterkloof HS, Pretoria) b 12/09/1990, Witbank. 1.83m. 94kg. Flyhalf. FC DEBUT: 2011. PROV CAREER: Blue Bulls 2011 1-0-0-0-1-3. Pumas 2011-14 47-3-105-89-1-495. Valke 2013 1-0-1-1-0-5. REP HONOURS: SA Barbarians 2012 1-0-4-1-0-11. FC RECORD: 50-3-110-91-2-514. RECORD IN 2014: (Pumas) 17-1-27-26-0-137.

Ross, Jonathan Montague (Jono) (St Stithians Coll., Randburg) b 27/10/1990, Sandton. 1.88m. 107kg. Flank. FC DEBUT: 2011. PROV CAREER: Blue Bulls 2011-14 33-2-0-0-0-10. SUPER RUGBY: Bulls 2013-14 19-4-0-0-0-20. FC RECORD: 52-6-0-0-0-30. RECORD IN 2014: (Bulls, Blue Bulls) 26-4-0-0-0-20.

Roux, Jacobus Stephanus (Bees) (Marlow Agricultural, Cradock) b 09/12/81, Upington. 1.86m. 115kg. Forward. FC DEBUT: 2005. PROV CAREER: Leopards 2005-06 41-1-0-0-0-5. Griquas 2007-09 31-1-0-0-0-5. Blue Bulls 2010 7-0-0-0-0-0. Lions 2013 2-0-0-0-0-0. Young Lions 2014 1-0-0-0-0-0. Cheetahs 2014 1-0-0-0-0-0. SUPER RUGBY: Cheetahs 2008-09 17-0-0-0-0-0. Bulls 2010 14-0-0-0-0-0. REP HONOURS: Royal XV 2009 1-0-0-0-0-0. FC RECORD: 115-2-0-0-0-10. RECORD IN 2014: (Cheetahs, Young Lions) 2-0-0-0-0-0.

Rust, Hendri Christian (Oakdale HS, Riversdale) b 07/04/1992, Malmesbury. 1.83m. 83kg. Fullback. FC DEBUT: 2014. PROV CAREER: Boland 2014 15-5-8-4-0-53. FC RECORD: 15-5-8-4-0-53. RECORD IN 2014: (Boland) 15-5-8-4-0-53.

Sadie, Johann (Paarl Gym. & US) b 23/01/1989, Malmesbury. 1.88m. 88kg. Wing. FC DEBUT: 2010. PROV CAREER: WP 2010-11 24-12-0-0-0-60. Blue Bulls 2012 3-0-0-0-0-0. Cheetahs 2013 11-3-0-0-0-15. SUPER RUGBY: Stormers 2011 7-2-0-0-0-10. Bulls 2012 10-0-0-0-0-0. Cheetahs 2013-14 33-6-0-0-0-30. REP HONOURS: SA U20 2009 4-1-0-0-0-5. FC RECORD: 92-24-0-0-0-120. RECORD IN 2014: (Cheetahs SR) 16-1-0-0-0-5.

Sampson, Marcello Edward Dennis (Wynberg Boys' HS & UWC) b 27/03/1987, Cape Town. 1.83m. 85kg. Wing. FC DEBUT: 2011. PROV CAREER: EP Kings 2011-13 37-19-0-0-0-95. Pumas 2014 3-0-0-0-0-0. SUPER RUGBY: Southern Kings 2013 13-0-0-0-0-0. P/R 2013 1-1-0-0-0-5. REP HONOURS: SA Kings 2011 1-0-0-0-0-0. FC RECORD: 55-20-0-0-0-100. RECORD IN 2014: (Pumas) 3-0-0-0-0-0.

Samuels, Juwell Phill (Wesbank HS, Malmesbury) b 01/06/1987, Darling. 1.61m. 64kg. FC DEBUT: 2009. PROV CAREER: Boland 2009 & 12 & 14 10-1-0-0-0-5. FC RECORD: 10-1-0-0-0-5. RECORD IN 2014: (Boland) 2-0-0-0-0-0.

Sass, Edwin (Tygerberg HS, Cape Town) b 07/02/1993, Ceres. 1.83m. 90kg. Centre. FC DEBUT: 2014. PROV CAREER: Boland 2014 10-0-0-0-0-0. FC RECORD: 10-0-0-0-0-0. RECORD IN 2014: (Boland) 10-0-0-0-0-0.

Scharneck, Henri Ashton (HTS Vereeniging & NWU) b 13/09/1989, Vereeniging. 1.91m. 114kg. Prop. FC DEBUT: 2011. PROV CAREER: Leopards 2011 1-0-0-0-0-0. Leopards XV 2014 2-0-0-0-0-0. FC RECORD: 3-0-0-0-0-0. RECORD IN 2014: (Leopards XV) 2-0-0-0-0-0.

Scheepers, Jacobus Nicolaas (Nico) (Nico Malan HS, Humansdorp & UFS) b 27/02/1990, Port Elizabeth. 1.86m. 90kg. Wing. FC DEBUT: 2011. PROV CAREER: Cheetahs 2011-12 16-3-17-27-0-130. Free State XV 2012-13 8-3-12-5-0-54. Emerging Cheetahs 2011 1-0-0-0-0-0. Griquas 2013-14 14-2-20-17-0-101. SUPER RUGBY: Cheetahs 2012 3-0-0-0-0-0. REP HONOURS: SA U20 2010 4-1-0-0-0-5. FC RECORD: 46-9-49-49-0-290. RECORD IN 2014: (Griquas) 7-1-15-5-0-50.

Schickerling, John Dave (JD) (Paarl Gym.) b 09/05/1995, Calvinia. 2.02m. 108kg. Lock. FC DEBUT: 2014. PROV CAREER: WP 2014 1-0-0-0-0-0. REP HONOURS: SA U20 2014 5-0-0-0-0-0. FC RECORD: 6-0-0-0-0-0. RECORD IN 2014: (WP, SA U20) 6-0-0-0-0-0.

Schmidt, Marais (Krugersdorp HS) b 23/04/1992, Sandton. 1.83m. 83kg. Flyhalf. FC DEBUT: 2011. PROV CAREER: Young Lions 2012-14 8-1-10-7-0-46. Golden Lions XV 2011 1-0-2-2-0-10. Griquas 2014 6-0-1-1-0-5. REP HONOURS: SA U20 2012 1-0-0-0-0-0. FC RECORD: 16-1-13-10-0-61. RECORD IN 2014: (Griquas, Young Lions) 8-0-1-1-0-5.

Schoeman, Christian Francois (Tian) (John Vorster HTS, Nigel & UP) b 23/09/1991, Pretoria. 1.82m. 89kg. Flyhalf. FC DEBUT: 2014. PROV CAREER: Blue Bulls 2014 7-1-18-9-0-68. FC RECORD: 7-1-18-9-0-68. RECORD IN 2014: (Blue Bulls) 7-1-18-9-0-68.

Schoeman, Danie Burger (Boland Agric. HS, Paarl) b 26/09/1988, Paarl. 1.90m. 105kg. Eighthman. FC DEBUT: 2010. PROV CAREER: Griquas 2010-14 55-10-0-0-0-50. Griffons 2011-12 3-2-0-0-0-10. FC RECORD: 58-12-0-0-0-60. RECORD IN 2014: (Griquas) 18-5-0-0-0-25.

Schoeman, Juan Louw (Affies, Pretoria) b 18/09/1991, Pretoria. 1.87m. 105kg. Prop. FC DEBUT: 2011. PROV CAREER: Blue Bulls 2011 & 14 9-0-0-0-0-0. REP HONOURS: SA U20 2011 3-0-0-0-0-0. FC RECORD: 12-0-0-0-0-0. RECORD IN 2014: (Blue Bulls) 7-0-0-0-0-0.

Schoeman, Marnus (Waterkloof HS, Pretoria) b 09/02/89, Edenvale. 1.78m. 95kg. FC DEBUT: 2009. PROV CAREER: Blue Bulls 2009 & 2011 12-3-0-0-0-15. Griquas 2011-14 65-42-0-0-0-210. REP HONOURS: SA U20 2009 5-0-0-0-0-0. FC RECORD: 82-45-0-0-0-225. RECORD IN 2014: (Griquas) 24-17-0-0-0-85.

Schoeman, Paul (Marlow Agric., Cradock) b 19/12/1992, Cradock. 1.90m. 97kg. Eighthman. FC DEBUT: 2013. PROV CAREER: EP Kings 2013-14 19-5-0-0-0-25. FC RECORD: 19-5-0-0-0-25. RECORD IN 2014: (EP Kings) 11-3-0-0-0-15.

Schoeman, Pierre (Affies, Pretoria & UP) b 07/05/1994, Nelspruit. 1.84m. 118kg. Prop. FC DEBUT: 2014. PROV CAREER: Blue Bulls 2014 2-0-0-0-0-0. REP HONOURS: SA U20 2014 5-1-0-0-0-5. FC RECORD: 7-1-0-0-0-5. RECORD IN 2014: (Blue Bulls, SA U20) 7-1-0-0-0-5.

Schoeman, Renier (Walla) (Ben Viljoen HS, Groblersdal) b 27/05/83, Potgieterus. 1.90m 128kg. Prop. FC DEBUT: 2005. PROV CAREER: Pumas 2005 3-0-0-0-0-0. Leopards 2007-08 7-0-0-0-0-0. Griquas 2007 2-0-0-0-0-0. SWD 2009 6-0-0-0-0-0. Border 2011-14 41-0-0-0-0-0. FC RECORD: 59-0-0-0-0-0. RECORD IN 2014 (Border) 1-0-0-0-0-0

Scholtz, Pieter Ernst (Diamantveld HS, Kimberley) b 20/03/1994, Pretoria. 1.87m. 120kg. Prop. FC DEBUT: 2014. PROV CAREER: Young Lions 2014 1-0-0-0-0-0. FC RECORD: 1-0-0-0-0-0. RECORD IN 2014: (Young Lions) 1-0-0-0-0-0.

Schonert, Nicholas Peter (Nic) (Maritzburg Coll.) b 20/09/1991, Durban. 1.89m. 118kg. Prop. FC DEBUT: 2012. PROV CAREER: Sharks XV 2012 1-0-0-0-0-0. Griquas 2013 14-0-0-0-0-0. Free State XV 2014 3-0-0-0-0-0. REP HONOURS: SA U20 2011 5-0-0-0-0-0. FC RECORD: 23-0-0-0-0-0. RECORD IN 2014: (Free State XV) 3-0-0-0-0-0.

Schoor, Wade Walter (Labori HS, Paarl & CPUT) b 22/10/1992, Paarl. 1.94m. 104kg. Lock. FC DEBUT: 2014. PROV CAREER: Limpopo 2014 5-0-0-0-0-0. FC RECORD: 5-0-0-0-0-0. RECORD IN 2014: (Limpopo) 5-0-0-0-0-0.

Schreuder, Louis (Paarl Gym.) b 25/04/1990, Paarl. 1.84m. 82kg. Wing. FC DEBUT: 2010. PROV CAREER: WP 2010-14 54-3-0-0-0-15. SUPER RUGBY: Stormers 2011-14 39-1-0-0-0-5. REP HONOURS: SA 2013 no appearances. SA U20 2010 5-0-0-0-0-0. FC RECORD: 98-4-0-0-0-20. RECORD IN 2014: (Stormers, WP) 22-0-0-0-0-0.

Schroeder, Ricky Darryl (Paul Roos Gym., Stellenbosch & UCT) b 05/01/1991, Worcester. 1.68m. 77kg. Scrumhalf. FC DEBUT: 2012. PROV CAREER: WP 2012-13 7-0-0-0-0-0. Boland 2013 10-0-0-0-0-0. Lions 2014 4-0-0-0-0-0. Young Lions 2014 10-0-0-0-0-0. FC RECORD: 31-0-0-0-0-0. RECORD IN 2014: (Lions, Young Lions) 14-0-0-0-0-0.

Schutte, Andries Stefanus (Hoogenhout HS) b 18/01/1994,

Secunda. 1.88m. 117kg. Prop. FC DEBUT: 2014. PROV CAREER: Valke 2014 5-0-0-0-0-0. FC RECORD: 5-0-0-0-0-0. RECORD IN 2014: (Valke) 5-0-0-0-0-0.
Scott, Ashwin Robert (Parkdene HS, George) b 02/06/85. 1.74m. 80kg. Wing. FC DEBUT: 2004. PROV CAREER: SWD 2004-08 & 14 43-12-0-0-1-63. Pumas 2009-14 51-14-0-0-0-70. Griffons 2013 2-0-0-0-0-0. REP HONOURS: SA Schools 2003. CW SWD 2003. FC RECORD: 96-26-0-0-1-133. RECORD IN 2014: (Pumas, SWD) 5-4-0-0-0-20.
Sibeko, Anele (Vubimzibuko HS) b 23/11/1987, Queenstown. 1.9m. 90kg. Lock. FC DEBUT: 2014. PROV CAREER: Border 2014 1-0-0-0-0-0. FC RECORD: 1-0-0-0-0-0. RECORD IN 2014: (Border) 1-0-0-0-0-0.
Seerane, Johannes (Joe) (Merensky HS, Tzaneen & NWU) b 30/03/1987, Ackonhoek. 1.72m. 85kg. FC DEBUT: 2011. PROV CAREER: Leopards 2011 1-1-0-0-0-5. Border 2012-14 12-6-0-0-0-30. REP HONOURS: SA Students 2012 2-1-0-0-0-5. SA Pres XV 2013 1-0-0-0-0-0. FC record 16-8-0-0-0-40. RECORD IN 2014: (Border) 2-0-0-0-0-0.
Sekekete, Victor Kutlwano (Queens HS, Sandton) b 28/01/1994, Johannesburg. 1.95m. 99kg. Flank. FC DEBUT: 2014. REP HONOURS: SA U20 2014 1-0-0-0-0-0. FC RECORD: 1-0-0-0-0-0. RECORD IN 2014: (SA U20) 1-0-0-0-0-0.
Senatla, Seabelo Mohanoe (Riebeeckstad HS & CUT) b 10/02/1993, Welkom. 1.86m. 76kg. Wing. FC DEBUT: 2013. PROV CAREER: WP 2014 6-3-0-0-0-15. SUPER RUGBY: Stormers 2014 2-0-0-0-0-0. REP HONOURS: SA U20 2013 5-7-0-0-0-35. SA Sevens 2013-14. FC RECORD: 13-10-0-0-0-50. RECORD IN 2014: (Stormers, WP, SA Sevens) 8-3-0-0-0-15.
September, Chriswill Bradley (Drostdy HS, Worcester) b 30/06/1994, Worcester. 1.72m. 69kg. Scrumhalf. FC DEBUT: 2014. PROV CAREER: Leopards XV 2014 2-0-0-0-0-0. FC RECORD: 2-0-0-0-0-0. RECORD IN 2014: (Leopards XV) 2-0-0-0-0-0.
September, Franzel Julio (Bergrivier HS, Wellington) b 06/06/86, Paarl. 1.80m. 100kg. FC DEBUT: 2009. PROV CAREER: SWD 2009 1-0-0-0-0-0. Boland 2010-14 80-29-0-0-0-145. FC RECORD: 80-29-0-0-0-145. RECORD IN 2014: (Boland) 15-5-0-0-0-25.
Serfontein, Jan Lodewyk (Grey HS, PE/ Grey Coll. Bloem) b 15/04/1993, Port Elizabeth. 1.87m. 97kg. Centre. FC DEBUT: 2012. PROV CAREER: Blue Bulls 2012-13 11-4-0-0-0-20. SUPER RUGBY: Bulls 2013-14 28-5-0-0-0-25. MISC INFO: VC PoY 2012 nominee. SA U20 PoY 2012. IRB U/20 PoY. Brother of Willem Serfontein. Son of former EP No. 8 Jan Serfontein. REP HONOURS: SA Tests: 2013-14 20-2-0-0-0-10. SA U20 2012 5-4-0-0-0-20. FC RECORD: 64-15-0-0-0-75. RECORD IN 2014: (SA, Bulls) 27-4-0-0-0-20.
Serfontein, Willem Jacob (Framesby HS, Port Elizabeth & Unisa) b 16/09/88, Port Elizabeth. 1.95m. 112kg. Lock. FC DEBUT: 2009. PROV CAREER: Blue Bulls 2009 8-1-0-0-0-5. Pumas 2010-13 62-1-0-0-0-5. Griquas 2014 10-1-0-0-0-5. SUPER RUGBY: Cheetahs 2014 3-0-0-0-0-0. REP HONOURS: SA Barbarians 2012 1-0-0-0-0-0. MISC INFO: Brother of Jan Serfontein. Son of former EP No. 8 Jan Serfontein. FC RECORD: 84-3-0-0-0-15. RECORD IN 2014: (Cheetahs SR, Griquas) 13-1-0-0-0-5.
Shabangu, Simphiwe Brian (Glenwood HS, Durban) b 11/04/1988, Durban. 1.73m. 96kg. Flanker. FC DEBUT: 2012. PROV CAREER: Border 2012-13 26-4-0-0-0-20. Valke 2014 1-0-0-0-0-0. Pumas 2014 5-1-0-0-0-5. REP HONOURS: SA Pres XV 2013 3-0-0-0-0-0. FC RECORD: 35-5-0-0-0-25. RECORD IN 2014: (Pumas, Valke) 6-1-0-0-0-5.
Short, Basil Gordon (Standerton HS & UP) b 19/05/1991, Vryheid. 1.89m. 116kg. Prop. FC DEBUT: 2012. PROV CAREER: Blue Bulls 2012-14 18-2-0-0-0-10. FC RECORD: 18-2-0-0-0-10. RECORD IN 2014: (Blue Bulls) 9-0-0-0-0-0.
Sibiya, Pule (WH de Klerk HS, Witbank) b 26/10/1993, Pretoria. 1.88m. 78kg. Wing. FC DEBUT: 2014. PROV CAREER: Pumas 2014 1-1-0-0-0-5. FC RECORD: 1-1-0-0-0-5. RECORD IN 2014: (Pumas) 1-1-0-0-0-5.
Siebert, Robert Steven (Steelpoort HS) b 09/02/1990, Bloemfontein. 1.78m. 76kg. Centre. FC DEBUT: 2014. PROV CAREER: Limpopo 2014 7-0-0-0-0-0. FC RECORD: 7-0-0-0-0-0. RECORD IN 2014: (Limpopo) 7-0-0-0-0-0.
Sisita, Frans Leonardo (Sand du Plessis HS, Bloemfontein & CUT) b 06/08/1990, Vryburg. 1.86m. 103kg. Wing. FC DEBUT: 2013. PROV CAREER: Griffons 2013-14 10-1-0-0-0-5. Griquas 2014 1-0-0-0-0-0. FC RECORD: 11-1-0-0-0-5. RECORD IN 2014: (Griffons, Griquas) 10-1-0-0-0-5.
Sithole, Sibusiso Camagu Thokazani (Varsity Coll.) b 14/06/1990, Queenstown. 1.78m. 90kg. Wing/Centre. FC DEBUT: 2010. PROV CAREER: KZN 2011-12 & 14 30-8-0-0-0-40. Sharks XV 2010-13 20-12-0-0-0-60. SUPER RUGBY: Sharks 2013-14 18-2-0-0-0-10. Rep. honours: SA U20 2010 3-4-0-0-0-20. SA Sevens 2010-11 & 13. FC RECORD: 71-26-0-0-0-130. RECORD IN 2014: (Sharks, KZN) 27-6-0-0-0-30.
Sithole, Simphiwe Martin (Ikusaselethu SS, Mtubatuba) b 03/02/1984, Pietermaritzburg. 1.81m. 95kg. Flanker. FC DEBUT: 2005. Prov. career: Pumas 2008-11 37-6-0-0-0-30. Griffons 2011-14 55-19-0-0-0-95. Rep. honours: SA U21 2005 1-0-0-0-0-0. SA Barbarians 2012 1-0-0-0-0-0. CW Pumas 2001-02. FC RECORD: 94-25-0-0-0-125. Record in 2014 (Griffons) 17-5-0-0-0-25.
Sithole, Sithembiso Mfundo Siphesihle (Westville Boys' HS & UCT) b 31/03/1993, Durban. 1.79m. 104kg. Prop. FC DEBUT: 2013. PROV CAREER: WP 2014 3-0-0-0-0-0. SUPER RUGBY: Stormers 2014 3-0-0-0-0-0. REP HONOURS: SA U20 2013 4-0-0-0-0-0. FC RECORD: 10-0-0-0-0-0. RECORD IN 2014: (Stormers, WP) 6-0-0-0-0-0.
Skorbinski, Alfred Henry (Framesby HS, Port Elizabeth & NWU) b 25/09/1990, Port Elizabeth. 1.84m. 93kg. Centre. FC DEBUT: 2011. PROV CAREER: Leopards 2011-13 18-3-0-0-0-15. Leopard XV 2013 2-1-0-0-0-5. Pumas 2014 8-3-0-0-0-15. FC RECORD: 28-7-0-0-0-35. RECORD IN 2014: (Pumas) 8-3-0-0-0-15.
Skosan, Courtnall Douglas (Brackenfell HS, Cape Town) b 24/07/1991, Cape Town. 1.83m. 90kg. Wing. FC DEBUT: 2011. PROV CAREER: Blue Bulls 2011-13 12-7-0-0-0-35. Lions 2014 9-1-0-0-0-5. Young Lions 2014 1-0-0-0-0-0. SUPER RUGBY: Lions 2014 10-4-0-0-0-20. REP HONOURS: SA U20 2011 3-1-0-0-0-5. FC RECORD: 35-13-0-0-0-65. RECORD IN 2014: (Lions SR, Lions, Young Lions) 20-5-0-0-0-25.
Skosana, Mthangala Brian JR (St Andrews Coll., Grahamstown) b 05/12/1991, Johannesburg. 1.80m. 89kg. Wing. FC DEBUT: 2013. PROV CAREER: EP Kings 2013-14 19-3-0-0-0-15. SWD 2014 11-6-0-0-0-30. FC RECORD: 30-9-0-0-0-45. RECORD IN 2014: (EP Kings, SWD) 18-8-0-0-0-40.
Small-Smith, William Thomas (Grey Coll., Bloemfontein) b 31/03/1992, Johannesburg. 1.84m. 91kg. Centre. FC DEBUT: 2011. PROV CAREER: Blue Bulls 2011 & 13-14 16-6-0-0-0-30. SUPER RUGBY: Bulls 2014 7-1-0-0-0-5. Rep. Honours: SA U20 2012 3-2-0-0-0-10. SA Sevens 2011-12. FC RECORD: 26-9-0-0-0-45. RECORD IN 2014: (Bulls, Blue Bulls) 17-4-0-0-0-20.
Smart, Duwayne Enslin (George HS) b 08/09/87, George. 1.70m. 72kg. Wing. FC DEBUT: 2008. PROV CAREER: SWD 2008 & 2011 & 14 17-11-0-0-0-55. Pumas 2009-10 7-2-0-0-0-10. Boland 2014 5-1-0-0-0-5. FC RECORD: 29-14-0-0-0-70. RECORD IN 2014: (SWD,

Boland) 9-6-0-0-0-30.

Smid, Rayn (Rondebosch HS) b 26/03/1992, Cape Town. 1.93m. 107kg. Eighthman. FC DEBUT: 2013. PROV CAREER: WP 2013-14 15-7-0-0-0-35. FC RECORD: 15-7-0-0-0-35. RECORD IN 2014: (WP) 5-5-0-0-0-25.

Smit, Adriaan Jacobus (Riaan) (THS Springs) b 28/04/84, Springs. 1.78m. 85kg. Fullback. FC DEBUT: 2006. PROV CAREER: Leopards 2006,09 7-2-7-6-0-42. Pumas 2007 15-5-14-12-0-89. Valke 2008 11-3-9-3-0-42. Griffons 2010 2-0-4-2-0-14. Cheetahs 2010-13 35-10-20-19-0-147. Free State XV 2012-14 10-3-23-9-1-91. Emerging Cheetahs 2011 1-1-2-3-0-18. SUPER RUGBY: Cheetahs 2011-14 25-3-11-23-0-106. FC RECORD: 106-27-90-77-1-549. RECORD IN 2014: (Cheetahs SR, Free State XV) 5-2-12-6-0-52.

Smit, Dillon (Middelburg HS) b 11/12/1992, Bethal. 1.75m. 83kg. Scrumhalf. FC DEBUT: 2013. PROV CAREER: Border 2013 5-0-0-0-0-0. Leopards 2014 10-6-0-0-0-30. Leopards XV 2014 1-0-0-0-0-0. FC RECORD: 16-6-0-0-0-30. RECORD IN 2014: (Leopards, Leopards XV) 11-6-0-0-0-30.

Smit, Roelof Andries (Hangklip HS, Queenstown) b 11/01/1993, Queenstown. 1.90m. 90kg. Flank. FC DEBUT: 2013. PROV CAREER: Blue Bulls 2013-14 7-3-0-0-0-15. SUPER RUGBY: Bulls 2014 2-0-0-0-0-0. REP HONOURS: SA U20 2013 4-0-0-0-0-0. FC RECORD: 13-3-0-0-0-15. RECORD IN 2014: (Bulls, Blue Bulls) 6-1-0-0-0-5.

Smith, Albertus Stephanus (Kwagga) (HTS Middelburg) b 11/06/1993, Lydenburg. 1.80m. 80kg. Flank. FC DEBUT: 2013. PROV CAREER: Lions 2014 10-3-0-0-0-15. REP HONOURS: SA U20 2013 3-2-0-0-0-10. SA Sevens 2014. FC RECORD: 13-5-0-0-0-25. RECORD IN 2014: (Lions, SA Sevens) 10-3-0-0-0-15.

Smith, Dylan Thomas (KES, Johannesburg) b 26/02/1994, Durban. 1.81m. 102kg. Prop. FC DEBUT: 2014. PROV CAREER: Young Lions 2014 8-0-0-0-0-0. FC RECORD: 8-0-0-0-0-0. RECORD IN 2014: (Young Lions) 8-0-0-0-0-0.

Smith, Gerhardus Phillipus Johannes (Gerrit) (FH Odendaal HS, Pretoria & UP & NMMU) b 12/02/88, Pretoria. 1.79m. 91kg. Centre. FC DEBUT: 2009. PROV CAREER: Valke 2009 1-0-0-0-0-0. SWD 2013-14 21-3-11-2-0-43. FC RECORD: 22-3-11-2-0-43. RECORD IN 2014: (SWD) 9-0-0-0-0-0.

Smith, Johan (Joe) (Volkskool Potchefstroom) b 02/12/1991, Fochville. 1.83m. 99kg. Hooker. FC DEBUT: 2012. PROV CAREER: Leopards 2012-14 15-0-0-0-0-0. Leopard XV 2013 3-1-0-0-0-5. FC RECORD: 18-1-0-0-0-5. RECORD IN 2014: (Leopards) 6-0-0-0-0-0.

Smith, Juanne Hugo (Juan) (JBM Hertzog HS) b 30/07/81, Bloemfontein. 1.94m. 106kg. Eighthman/flank. FC DEBUT: 2002. PROV CAREER: Cheetahs 2002 & 04-05 & 08 & 10 41-8-0-0-0-40. Cheetahs XV 2010 11-0-0-0-0-0. SUPER RUGBY: Cats 2003-05 32-11-0-0-0-55. Cheetahs 2006-11 47-7-0-0-0-35. REP HONOURS: SA 2003 & 05-10 & 14 Tests: 70-12-0-0-0-60. Tour: 2-0-0-0-0-0. Total: 72-12-0-0-0-60. SA 'A' 2003 1-0-0-0-0-0. SA U21 2002 5-3-0-0-0-15. MISC INFO: PoY nominee 2003, 2007. FC RECORD: 199-41-0-0-0-205. RECORD IN 2014: (SA) 1-0-0-0-0-0.

Smith, Juan-Philip (Queens Coll., Queenstown & UP) b 30/03/1994, Bloemhof. 1.87m. 91kg. Scrumhalf. FC DEBUT: 2014. REP HONOURS: SA U20 2014 5-0-0-0-0-0. FC RECORD: 5-0-0-0-0-0. RECORD IN 2014: (SA U20) 5-0-0-0-0-0.

Smith, Rhyno Christo (Paarl Boys' HS & NWU) b 11/02/1993, Paarl. 1.72m. 75kg. Fullback. FC DEBUT: 2014. PROV CAREER: Leopards 2014 4-3-5-0-0-25. FC RECORD: 4-3-5-0-0-25. RECORD IN 2014: (Leopards) 4-3-5-0-0-25.

Smith, Sarel Johannes Petrus (Pieter) (Grey Coll., Bloemfontein & NWU) b 21/07/1993, Klerksdorp. 1.7m. 84kg. Scrumhalf. FC DEBUT: 2014. PROV CAREER: Leopards XV 2014 2-0-0-0-0-0. FC RECORD: 2-0-0-0-0-0. RECORD IN 2014: (Leopards XV) 2-0-0-0-0-0.

Smith, Wayven Leandre (Brandwag HS, Uitenhage) b 05/08/1992, Uitenhage. 1.8m. 81kg. Flank. FC DEBUT: 2014. PROV CAREER: Free State XV 2014 6-3-0-0-0-15. FC RECORD: 6-3-0-0-0-15. RECORD IN 2014: (Free State XV) 6-3-0-0-0-15.

Snell, Dilen Christo-Lee (Hillcrest HS) b 13/04/1993, Mossel Bay. 1.78m. 79kg. Centre. FC DEBUT: 2014. PROV CAREER: SWD 2014 2-0-0-0-0-0. FC RECORD: 2-0-0-0-0-0. RECORD IN 2014: (SWD) 2-0-0-0-0-0.

Snyman, Brendon Michael (Pietersburg HS) b 21/08/84, Pietersburg. 122kg. Forward. FC DEBUT: 2005. PROV CAREER: SWD 2005 16-1-0-0-0-5. Griquas 2006-09 67-9-0-0-0-45. EP Kings 2009-10 10-0-0-0-0-0. EP Inv XV 2010 1-0-0-0-0-0. Leopards 2011-13 46-5-0-0-0-25. Leopard XV 2013-14 14-0-0-0-0-0. REP HONOURS: SA Pres XV 2013 4-0-0-0-0-0. FC RECORD: 158-15-0-0-0-75. RECORD IN 2014: (Leopard XV) 7-0-0-0-0-0.

Snyman, Earl-Jivan (Outeniqua HS, George & UFS) b 23/05/1989, Ashton. 1.77m. 89kg. Centre. FC DEBUT: 2011. PROV CAREER: Griffons 2011 2-0-0-0-0-0. Free State XV 2014 3-0-0-0-0-0. FC RECORD: 5-0-0-0-0-0. RECORD IN 2014: (Free State XV) 3-0-0-0-0-0.

Snyman, Johannes Jurgens (Hannes) (AHS, Kroonstad) b 29/03/1989, Kroonstad. 1.86m. 90kg. Hooker. FC DEBUT: 2010. PROV CAREER: Griffons 2011-12 & 14 30-1-0-0-0-5. Sharks XV 2010 3-0-0-0-0-0. FC RECORD: 33-1-0-0-0-5. RECORD IN 2014: (Griffons) 7-0-0-0-0-0.

Snyman, Jacobus Phillipus (Jaco) (Schweizer Reneke HS) b 09/06/86, Schweizer Reneke. 1.75m. 78kg. Scrumhalf. FC DEBUT: 2007. PROV CAREER: Lions 2007-08 4-0-0-0-0-0. Valke 2009-14 58-8-0-0-0-40. FC RECORD: 62-8-0-0-0-40. RECORD IN 2014: (Valke) 12-0-0-0-0-0.

Snyman, Phillipus Albertus Borman (Phillip) (Grey Coll., Bloemfontein) b 26/03/87, Bloemfontein. 1.88m. 95kg. Centre. FC DEBUT: 2008. PROV CAREER: Griffons 2008-09 6-0-0-0-0-0. Cheetahs 2008-12 59-19-0-0-0-95. Emerging Cheetahs 2011 1-0-0-0-0-0. SUPER RUGBY: Cheetahs 2011-12 20-1-0-0-0-5. REP HONOURS: SA Sevens 2008 & 12-14. FC RECORD: 86-20-0-0-0-100. RECORD IN 2014: (SA Sevens).

Sofisa, Mzuvukile Gift (Mzu) (Grey HS, Port Elizabeth) b 06/04/1993, Port Elizabeth. 1.81m. 110kg. Prop. FC DEBUT: 2014. PROV CAREER: EP Kings 2014 5-0-0-0-0-0. FC RECORD: 5-0-0-0-0-0. RECORD IN 2014: (EP Kings) 5-0-0-0-0-0.

Solomon, Chad (Paul Roos Gym., Stellenbosch & UCT) b 23/02/1994, Belville. 1.79m. 100kg. Hooker. FC DEBUT: 2014. PROV CAREER: WP 2014 2-0-0-0-0-0. FC RECORD: 2-0-0-0-0-0. RECORD IN 2014: (WP) 2-0-0-0-0-0.

Sonkosi, Kuhle (Westering HS) b 23/08/1992, East London. 1.85m. 96kg. Eighthman. FC DEBUT: 2014. PROV CAREER: EP Kings 2014 2-1-0-0-0-5. FC RECORD: 2-1-0-0-0-5. RECORD IN 2014: (EP Kings) 2-1-0-0-0-5.

Soyizwapi, Siviwe Sonwabile (Dale Coll., King William's Town) b 07/12/1992, Mthatha. 1.72m. 75kg. Wing. FC DEBUT: 2012. PROV CAREER: EP Kings 2012-14 21-6-0-0-0-30. SUPER RUGBY: Southern Kings 2013 6-0-0-0-0-0. FC RECORD: 27-6-0-0-0-30. RECORD IN 2014: (EP Kings) 12-2-0-0-0-10.

Speckman, Rosco Shane (Mary Waters HS, Grahamstown) b 28/04/1989, Grahamstown. 1.66m. 70kg. Wing. FC DEBUT: 2010. PROV

SEASON IN 2014

CAREER: KZN 2012 1-0-0-0-0-0. Sharks XV 2010-12 13-5-0-0-0-25. Pumas 2013-14 34-24-0-0-0-120. REP HONOURS: SA Pres XV 2013 3-1-0-0-0-5. SA Sevens 2014. FC RECORD: 51-30-0-0-0-150. RECORD IN 2014: (Pumas, SA Sevens) 9-1-0-0-0-5.

Spies, Frederik Albertus (Frikkie) (AHS, Kroonstad). b 08/02/85, Odendaalsrus. 1.96m. 109kg. Lock. FC DEBUT: 2005. PROV CAREER: Lions 2005,07 7-0-0-0-0-0. Cheetahs 2006 6-0-0-0-0-0. Boland 2008-09 22-0-0-0-0-0. Griquas 2010-12 36-4-0-0-0-20. Pumas 2014 8-1-0-0-0-5. FC RECORD: 79-5-0-0-0-25. RECORD IN 2014: (Pumas) 8-1-0-0-0-5.

Spies, Pierre Johan (Affies, Pretoria) b 08/06/1985, Pretoria. 1.94m. 108kg. Loose Forward. FC DEBUT: 2005. PROV CAREER: Blue Bulls 2005-06 & 08-10 17-4-0-0-0-20. SUPER RUGBY: Bulls 2005-14 103-25-0-0-0-125. REP HONOURS: SA 2006-13 Tests: 53-7-0-0-0-35. SA U21 2006 4-3-0-0-0-15. SA Students 2005 1-1-0-0-0-5. MISC INFO: SA record of 48 Tests as a No. 8. YPoY 2006. Son of former N-Tvl and Transvaal wing and Springbok Athlete Pierre Spies. FC RECORD: 178-40-0-0-0-200. RECORD IN 2014: (Bulls) 1-0-0-0-0-0.

Stander, Jan Hendrik (Jannie) (Monument HS, Krugersdorp) b 21/04/1993, Phalaborwa. 1.96m. 107kg. Lock. FC DEBUT: 2013. PROV CAREER: Young Lions 2013-14 4-0-0-0-0-0. REP HONOURS: SA U20 2013 no appearances. FC RECORD: 4-0-0-0-0-0. RECORD IN 2014: (Young Lions) 1-0-0-0-0-0.

Stander, Johannes Hendrik (Janneman) (Oakdale Agric. HS, Riversdale) b 08/09/1993, George. 1.88m. 94kg. Flank. FC DEBUT: 2013. PROV CAREER: Young Lions 2013 1-0-0-0-0-0. SWD 2014 8-1-0-0-0-5. FC RECORD: 9-1-0-0-0-5. RECORD IN 2014: (SWD) 8-1-0-0-0-5.

Stander, Joshua Trevor (Queens Coll., Queenstown & UP) b 01/01/1994, Cradock. 1.83m. 89kg. Flyhalf. FC DEBUT: 2014. PROV CAREER: Blue Bulls 2014 5-1-8-0-0-21. FC RECORD: 5-1-8-0-0-21. RECORD IN 2014: (Blue Bulls) 5-1-8-0-0-21.

Steenkamp, Cornelius Jacobus (Corné) (Ermelo HS) b 20/02/82, Ermelo. 1.80m. 94kg. Flank. FC DEBUT: 2005. PROV CAREER: Pumas 2005-11 & 13-14 159-34-0-0-0-170. FC RECORD: 159-34-0-0-0-170. RECORD IN 2014: (Pumas) 18-6-0-0-0-30.

Steenkamp, Gurthrö Garth (Paarl Boys' HS & UFS) b 12/06/81, Paarl. 1.89m. 122kg. Prop. FC DEBUT: 2001. PROV CAREER: Cheetahs 2002-04 42-2-0-0-0-10. Blue Bulls 2005 & 08-10 24-5-0-0-0-25. SUPER RUGBY: Cats 2004 10-1-0-0-0-5. Bulls 2005,07-11 60-1-0-0-0-5. REP HONOURS: SA Tests: 2004-05, 07-14 53-6-0-0-0-30. Tour: 2007, 09 2-0-0-0-0-0. Total: 55-6-0-0-0-30. Springbok XV 2014 1-0-0-0-0-0. SA U21s 2001-02 8-1-0-0-0-5; CW WP 1998-99. FC RECORD: 200-16-0-0-0-80. RECORD IN 2014: (SA, Springbok XV) 5-0-0-0-0-0.

Steenkamp, Michiel de Kock (Paarl Boys' HS & Stellenbosch Univ.) b 16/02/87, Calvinia. 1.97m. 106kg. Lock. FC DEBUT: 2009. PROV CAREER: WP 2009-13 62-1-0-0-0-5. SUPER RUGBY: Stormers 2010-14 49-0-0-0-0-0. Misc. info: Brother of Wilhelm Steenkamp. FC RECORD: 111-1-0-0-0-5. RECORD IN 2014: (Stormers, WP) 2-0-0-0-0-0.

Stegmann, Gideon Johannes (Deon) (Grey Coll., Bloemfontein) b 22/03/86, Cradock. 1.81m. 99kg. Flank. FC DEBUT: 2007. PROV CAREER: Blue Bulls 2007-12 & 14 67-12-0-0-0-60. SUPER RUGBY: Bulls 2008-14 79-6-0-0-0-30. REP HONOURS: SA 2010-11 Tests: 6-0-0-0-0-0. FC RECORD: 152-18-0-0-0-90. RECORD IN 2014: (Bulls, Blue Bulls) 14-5-0-0-0-25.

Stemmet, Pieter Franz (Paul Roos Gym., Stellenbosch) b 18/02/1992, Paarl. 1.84m. 115kg. Prop. FC DEBUT: 2012. PROV CAREER: WP 2012 1-1-0-0-0-5. EP Kings 2013-14 6-1-0-0-0-5. FC RECORD: 7-2-0-0-0-10. RECORD IN 2014: (EP Kings) 5-1-0-0-0-5.

Stevens, Kevin Bruce (Grey Coll., Bloemfontein) b 30/01/87, Virginia. 1.86m. 112kg. FC DEBUT: 2009. PROV CAREER: Cheetahs 2007 & 2009 & 14 11-0-0-0-0-0. Griffons 2009-14 73-3-0-0-0-15. Griquas 2011 1-0-0-0-0-0. Free State XV 2014 8-1-0-0-0-5. SUPER RUGBY: Cheetahs 2014 1-0-0-0-0-0. FC RECORD: 94-4-0-0-0-20. RECORD IN 2014: (Cheetahs SR, Cheetahs, Griffons, Free State XV) 15-1-0-0-0-5.

Stevens, Matthew John Hamilton (Kearsney Coll) b 01/10/1982, Durban. 1.87m. 126kg. Prop. SA FC DEBUT: 2014. SA PROV CAREER: KZN 2014 8-0-0-0-0-0. SA FC RECORD: 8-0-0-0-0-0. REP HONOURS: England 2004-11. British & Irish Lions 2013. IRB World Cup 2007 & 11. RECORD IN 2014: (KZN) 8-0-0-0-0-0.

Stevens, Wayne (Grey Coll., Bloemfontein) b 17/05/88. 1.85m. 86kg. Centre. FC DEBUT: 2008. PROV CAREER: Cheetahs 2009-10 10-1-0-0-0-5. EP Kings 2010-13 56-13-0-0-0-65. Griquas 2014 21-1-0-0-0-5. REP HONOURS: SA Students 2008 1-0-0-0-0-0. SA Kings 2011 3-0-0-0-0-0. SA Barbarians 2012 1-0-0-0-0-0. FC RECORD: 92-15-0-0-0-75. RECORD IN 2014: (Griquas) 21-1-0-0-0-5.

Steyl, Heinrich Diederick (Boland Agric. HS, Paarl & US) b 06/07/1990, Belville. 1.80m. 82kg. Fullback. FC DEBUT: 2011. PROV CAREER: WP 2011 2-0-0-0-0-0. Blue Bulls 2013 2-0-0-0-0-0. Pumas 2014 3-0-0-0-0-0. FC RECORD: 7-0-0-0-0-0. RECORD IN 2014: (Pumas) 3-0-0-0-0-0.

Steyn, Francois Philippus Lodewyk (Frans) (Grey Coll., Bloemfontein) b 14/05/87, Aliwal North. 1.91m. 110kg. Utility back. FC DEBUT: 2006. PROV CAREER: KZN 2006 & 08 & 13 20-4-12-6-1-65. SUPER RUGBY: Sharks 2007-09 & 12-14 68-4-23-53-8-249. REP HONOURS: SA 2006-12 Tests: 53-10-5-21-3-132. Tour: 2-0-3-1-0-9. Total: 55-10-8-22-3-141. Springbok XV 2014 1-0-0-0-0-0. SA U19 2005-06. British Barbarians 2008 1-0-0-0-0-0. MISC INFO: YPoY 2007. U19 PoY 2006. YPOY Nominee 2009. IRB POY Nominee 2009. FC RECORD: 145-18-43-81-12-455. RECORD IN 2014: (Springbok XV, Sharks) 19-0-16-43-1-164.

Steyn, Morné (Sand du Plessis HS, Bloemfontein) b 11/07/84, Bellville. 1.84m. 91kg. Flyhalf. FC DEBUT: 2003. PROV CAREER: Blue Bulls 2003-10 & 12 95-26-180-106-11-841. SUPER RUGBY: Bulls 2005-13 123-13-242-275-25-1449. REP HONOURS: SA 2009-14 Tests: 59-8-99-142-8-688. Springbok XV 2014 1-0-2-3-0-13. SA 'A' 2004 1-0-1-0-0-2. SA U21 2005 5-3-17-7-1-73. British Barbarians 2009 1-0-0-1-0-3. CW Free State 2001-2002. MISC INFO: YPoY nominee 2005. Holds SA record for most penalty goals by a player in a test (8 vs. New Zealand in 2009). Holds SA record for most penalty goals in a season (40 in 2010). Holds SA record for most test matches as a flyhalf (57, also one at fullback and one at centre). Holds Bulls Super record for most cons in a season (38) and a career (242). Holds Bulls record for most penalties in a season (57) and a career (275). Holds Bulls record for most drop goals in a match (4), in a season (11) and a career (25). Holds Bulls and SA record for most points in a Super career (1449). SA S14 POY 2009. POY Nominee 2009. FC RECORD: 285-50-541-534-45-3069. RECORD IN 2014: (SA, Springbok XV) 6-0-13-13-0-65.

Steyn, Nicolaas Phillipus Jacobus (Nicky) (Welkom Gym.) b 02/08/85, Kroonstad. 1.90m. 101kg. Loose Forward. FC DEBUT: 2006. PROV CAREER: Cheetahs 2006-08 19-12-0-0-0-60. Griffons 2008-14 106-46-0-0-0-230. REP HONOURS: SA Barbarians 2012 1-0-0-0-0-0. FC RECORD: 126-58-0-0-0-290. RECORD IN 2014: (Griffons) 18-8-0-0-0-40.

Strauss, Jan Adriaan (Grey Coll., Bloemfontein) b 18/11/85, Bloemfontein. 1.84m. 102kg. Hooker. FC DEBUT: 2005. PROV CAREER: Blue Bulls 2005-06 22-3-0-0-0-15. Cheetahs 2007-13 56-9-0-0-0-45.

SEASON IN 2014

SUPER RUGBY: Bulls 2006 8-0-0-0-0-0. Cheetahs 2007-14 97-8-0-0-0-40. REP HONOURS: SA 2008-10 & 12-14 Tests: 44-5-0-0-0-25. Tour: 2-0-0-0-0-0. Total: 46-5-0-0-0-25. British Barbarians 2011 1-0-0-0-0-0. SA U21 2005-06 8-2-0-0-0-10. SA U19 2004. SA Schools 2003. CW Free State 2003. MISC INFO: Holds Cheetahs Super rugby record for most matches in a career (97). Cousin of Andries (SA 2010) and Richardt Strauss (Ireland 2012-2014). FC RECORD: 238-27-0-0-0-135. RECORD IN 2014: (SA, Cheetahs SR, Cheetahs) 27-0-0-0-0-0.

Strydom, Louis Isias (Welkom THS) b 21/10/80, Welkom. 1.78m. 72kg. Flyhalf. FC DEBUT: 2001. PROV CAREER: Griffons 2001-03 & 13-14 45-5-62-74-3-380. Blue Bulls 2003-04 23-3-59-23-0-202. Valke 2005-06 42-3-70-83-6-422. Lions 2007-08 24-1-20-23-2-120. Lions XV 2007-08 2-1-5-0-0-15. Cheetahs 2009-11 44-1-81-68-1-374. EP Kings 2011 12-1-23-18-1-108. SUPER RUGBY: Lions 2007-08 12-0-4-18-0-62. Cheetahs 2010 1-0-1-0-0-2. REP HONOURS: SA Kings 2011 3-1-5-10-0-45. FC RECORD: 208-16-330-317-13-1730. RECORD IN 2014: (Griffons) 12-0-17-15-2-85.

Strydom, Willem Johannes (Affies, Pretoria) b 26/11/1993, Vereeniging. 1.73m. 70kg. Fullback. REP HONOURS: SA Sevens 2013-14. RECORD IN 2014: (SA Sevens).

Swanepoel, Jacobus Christoffel Entienne (Tygerberg HS, Cape Town) b 09/03/93, Sasolburg. 1.91m. 126kg. Prop. FC DEBUT: 2014. PROV CAREER: WP 2014 6-0-0-0-0-0. FC RECORD: 6-0-0-0-0-0. RECORD IN 2014: (WP) 6-0-0-0-0-0.

Swart, Clinton Ryno (Standerton HS & UP) b 06/09/1992, Standerton. 1.84m. 91kg. Flyhalf. FC DEBUT: 2014. PROV CAREER: Valke 2014 4-0-0-0-1-3. FC RECORD: 4-0-0-0-1-3. RECORD IN 2014: (Valke) 4-0-0-0-1-3.

Swart, Henro-Pierre (HP) (Framesby HS, Port Elizabeth & NWU) b 17/03/1989, Port Elizabeth. 1.89m. 108kg. Eighthman. FC DEBUT: 2012. PROV CAREER: Leopards 2012-14 24-4-0-0-0-20. Leopard XV 2013 4-1-0-0-0-5. FC RECORD: 28-5-0-0-0-25. RECORD IN 2014: (Leopards) 11-2-0-0-0-10.

Swart, Malherbe (Volkskool Potchefstroom) b 27/03/1991, Klerksdorp. 1.79m. 68kg. Scrumhalf. FC DEBUT: 2013. PROV CAREER: Leopard XV 2013-14 8-1-0-0-0-5. FC RECORD: 8-1-0-0-0-5. RECORD IN 2014: (Leopard XV) 5-0-0-0-0-0.

Swiel, Tomothy Gregory (Bishops Coll., Rondebosch) b 04/06/1993, Taunton. 1.80m. 85kg. Fullback. FC DEBUT: 2013. PROV CAREER: WP 2013 9-2-3-0-1-19. KZN 2014 3-0-0-0-0-0. Sharks XV 2014 5-2-11-7-0-53. SUPER RUGBY: Sharks 2014 6-0-4-10-0-38. FC RECORD: 23-4-18-17-1-110. RECORD IN 2014: (Sharks, KZN, Sharks XV) 14-2-15-17-0-91.

Sykes, Steven Robert (Marlow HS, Cradock) b 05/08/84, Middelburg, Cape. 1.97m. 106kg. Lock. FC DEBUT: 2005. PROV CAREER: KZN 2005-10 & 12 88-5-0-0-0-25. Sharks XV 2005-08 21-0-0-0-0-0. EP Kings 2013-14 12-3-0-0-0-15. SUPER RUGBY: Sharks 2007-12 69-9-0-0-0-45. Southern Kings 2013 13-1-0-0-0-5. P/R 2013 2-1-0-0-0-5. REP HONOURS: Emerging Springboks 2009 1-0-0-0-0-0. FC RECORD: 206-19-0-0-0-95. RECORD IN 2014: (EP Kings) 6-0-0-0-0-0.

Tagicakibau, Sailosi Wing. SA FC DEBUT: 2014. SUPER RUGBY: Stormers 2014 10-1-0-0-0-5. SA FC RECORD: 10-1-0-0-0-5. REP HONOURS: Samoa. RECORD IN 2014: (Stormers) 10-1-0-0-0-5.

Taljaard, Etienne (Jim Fouche HS, Bloemfontein) b 21/07/1993, Cape Town. 1.8m. 90kg. Wing. FC DEBUT: 2014. PROV CAREER: Valke 2014 6-2-0-0-0-10. FC RECORD: 6-2-0-0-0-10. RECORD IN 2014: (Valke) 6-2-0-0-0-10.

Taljard, Jeffrey John (Hudson Park HS, East London) b 22/04/87, East London. 1.81m. 90kg. Utility back. FC DEBUT: 2008. PROV CAREER: Border 2008-10 & 14 37-7-28-35-0-196. E/Cape XV 2008 2-0-0-0-0-0. SWD 2011-13 51-10-19-11-0-121. FC RECORD: 90-17-47-46-0-317. RECORD IN 2014: (Border) 4-1-5-7-0-36.

Tambwera, Lenience (Churchill Boys' HS) b 02/01/1993, Harare. 1.8m. 89kg. Flyhalf. FC DEBUT: 2014. PROV CAREER: Valke 2014 1-0-0-0-0-0. FC RECORD: 1-0-0-0-0-0. RECORD IN 2014: (Valke) 1-0-0-0-0-0.

Taute, Jacob Johannes (Jaco) (Monument HS, Krugersdorp) b 21/03/91, Springs. 1.87m. 95kg. Fullback. FC DEBUT: 2009. PROV CAREER: Lions 2009-12 31-13-0-1-0-68. Young Lions 2010 3-0-2-0-0-4. WP 2014 9-2-0-0-0-10. SUPER RUGBY: Lions 2010-12 31-9-0-2-0-51. Stormers 2013-14 18-1-0-0-1-8. REP HONOURS: SA 2012 Tests: 3-0-0-0-0-0. SA U20 2010-11 7-4-0-0-0-20. MISC INFO: YPoY nominee 2011. FC RECORD: 102-29-2-3-1-161. RECORD IN 2014 (Stormers, WP) 23-3-0-0-1-18.

Taylor, Jacques (Glenwood HS, Durban) b 05/01/1993, Pretoria. 1.8m. 100kg. Hooker. FC DEBUT: 2014. PROV CAREER: Sharks XV 2014 1-0-0-0-0-0. FC RECORD: 1-0-0-0-0-0. RECORD IN 2014: (Sharks XV) 1-0-0-0-0-0.

Tecklenburg, Warwick John (Uplands Coll., White River) b 22/01/1987, Nelspruit. 1.88m. 102kg. Flank. FC DEBUT: 2011. PROV CAREER: Blue Bulls 2011-12 22-4-0-0-0-20. Lions 2013-14 23-3-0-0-0-15. Young Lions 2013 7-1-0-0-0-5. SUPER RUGBY: Lions 2014 13-2-0-0-0-10. Lions P/R 2013 2-0-0-0-0-0. FC RECORD: 67-10-0-0-0-50. RECORD IN 2014: (Lions SR, Lions) 25-4-0-0-0-20.

Terblanche, De-Jay (Knysna HS) b 25/06/85, Knysna. 1.89m. 124kg. Prop. FC DEBUT: 2008. PROV CAREER: Pumas 2008-14 122-7-0-0-0-35. FC RECORD: 122-7-0-0-0-35. RECORD IN 2014: (Pumas) 19-1-0-0-0-5.

Thomas, Egnatius Elmo Chestney b 20/03/1985. Fullback. FC DEBUT: 2014. PROV CAREER: Limpopo 2014 6-0-0-0-0-0. FC RECORD: 6-0-0-0-0-0. RECORD IN 2014 (Limpopo) 6-0-0-0-0-0.

Tinise, Odwa (Ndzondelelo HS, Port Elizabeth) b 22/08/1987, Port Elizabeth. 1.67m. 81kg. Hooker. FC DEBUT: 2014. PROV CAREER: Limpopo 2014 2-0-0-0-0-0. FC RECORD: 2-0-0-0-0-0. RECORD IN 2014: (Limpopo) 2-0-0-0-0-0.

Tladi, Thabo Godfrey (Bokamoso HS, Polokwane) b 27/11/1985, Polokwane. 1.89m. 98kg. Eighthman. FC DEBUT: 2014. PROV CAREER: Limpopo 2014 1-0-0-0-0-0. FC RECORD: 1-0-0-0-0-0. RECORD IN 2014: (Limpopo) 1-0-0-0-0-0.

Tobias, Sidney (Paul Roos Gym., Stellenbosch) b 20/03/1989, Caledon. 1.75m. 93kg. Hooker. FC DEBUT: 2010. PROV CAREER: WP 2010-12 22-2-0-0-0-10. SWD 2012 13-0-0-0-0-0. Blue Bulls 2013-14 8-1-0-0-0-5. MISC INFO: Son of former Springbok Errol Tobias. FC RECORD: 43-3-0-0-0-15. RECORD IN 2014: (Blue Bulls) 7-1-0-0-0-5.

Tom, Siphosethu (Grey Coll., Port Elizabeth) b 12/02/1992, Port Elizabeth. 1.74m. 85kg. Wing. FC DEBUT: 2012. PROV CAREER: Free State XV 2012-14 7-2-0-0-0-10. FC RECORD: 7-2-0-0-0-10. RECORD IN 2014: (Free State XV) 1-0-0-0-0-0.

Torrens, Sergio Lorenzo (Belville South HS) b 29/01/1990, Bishop Lavis. 1.8m. 78kg. Centre. FC DEBUT: 2014. PROV CAREER: Leopards 2014 10-1-0-0-0-5. Leopards XV 2014 7-0-0-0-0-0. FC RECORD: 17-1-0-0-0-5. RECORD IN 2014: (Leopards, Leopards XV) 17-1-0-0-0-5.

Tossel, George de la Rey (Middelburg THS & NWU) b 05/03/1988, Pretoria. 1.93m. 105kg. Fullback. FC DEBUT: 2011. PROV CAREER: Leopards 2011-14 41-15-2-2-0-85. Leopard XV 2013-14 14-9-1-0-0-47. FC RECORD: 55-24-3-2-0-132. RECORD IN 2014: (Leopards, Leopard XV) 17-15-1-0-0-77.

SEASON IN 2014

Trytsman, Albert Meyer (Brandwag HS, Uitenhage) b 05/11/1987, Knysna. 1.86m. 95kg. Centre. FC DEBUT: 2013. PROV CAREER: Boland 2013-14 19-3-0-0-0-15. FC RECORD: 19-3-0-0-0-15. RECORD IN 2014: (Boland) 16-2-0-0-0-10.

Tshibidi, Claude Kalombo (Potchefstroom Boys' HS) b 31/03/1993, Tembisa. 1.90m. 92kg. Flank. FC debut: 2013. PROV CAREER: Young Lions 2013 2-0-0-0-0-0. EP Kings 2014 1-1-0-0-0-5. FC RECORD: 3-1-0-0-0-5. RECORD IN 2014: (EP Kings) 1-1-0-0-0-5.

Ulengo, Jamba Isaac (Jim Fouche HS, Bloemfontein & UFS) b 07/01/1990, Vryburg. 1.85m. 88kg. Wing. FC DEBUT: 2012. PROV CAREER: Free State XV 2012 1-0-0-0-0-0. Blue Bulls 2014 1-0-0-0-0-0. SA Sevens 2012-14. FC RECORD: 2-0-0-0-0-0. RECORD IN 2014: (Blue Bulls, SA Sevens) 1-0-0-0-0-0.

Ungerer, Stefan (Maritzburg Coll.) b 23/11/1993, Pietermaritzburg. 1.85m. 88kg. Scrumhalf. FC DEBUT: 2013. PROV CAREER: Sharks XV 2013-14 7-0-0-0-0-0. SUPER RUGBY: Sharks 2014 4-1-0-0-0-5. REP HONOURS: SA U20 2013 4-1-0-0-0-5. FC RECORD: 15-2-0-0-0-10. RECORD IN 2014: (Sharks, Sharks XV) 7-1-0-0-0-5.

Uys, BG (Paarl Gym.) b 20/06/88. 1.90m. 113kg. Prop. FC DEBUT: 2008. PROV CAREER: Leopards 2010-13 61-8-0-0-0-40. Leopard XV 2013 5-1-0-0-0-5. EP Kings 2014 5-0-0-0-0-0. REP HONOURS: SA Students 2008-09 3-1-0-0-0-5. SA Barbarians 2012 1-0-0-0-0-0. FC RECORD: 75-10-0-0-0-50. RECORD IN 2014: (EP Kings) 5-0-0-0-0-0.

Uys, Francois Jacobus (Dr EG Jansen, Boksburg) b 12/03/86, Springs. 1.91m. 103kg. Flank. FC DEBUT: 2006. PROV CAREER: Lions 2006-08 24-5-0-0-0-25. Cheetahs 2009-14 68-8-0-0-0-40. Griffons 2008 & 10 & 12 14-1-0-0-0-5. Lions XV 2008 1-0-0-0-0-0. Emerging Cheetahs 2011 1-0-0-0-0-0. Free State XV 2012 5-1-0-0-0-5. SUPER RUGBY: Cheetahs 2009 & 2011-14 49-1-0-0-0-5. REP HONOURS: SA U19 2005. FC RECORD: 162-16-0-0-0-80. RECORD IN 2014: (Cheetahs SR, Cheetahs) 26-2-0-0-0-10.

Uys, Jan-Frederik (Paul Roos Gym., Stellenbosch) b 03/01/1994, Potchefstroom. 1.99m. 114kg. Lock. FC DEBUT: 2014. PROV CAREER: WP 2014 8-0-0-0-0-0. FC RECORD: 8-0-0-0-0-0. RECORD IN 2014: (WP) 8-0-0-0-0-0.

Uys, Petrus Johannes Jacobus (PJ) (Monument HS, Krugersdorp) b 05/12/1990, Krugersdorp. 1.95m. 107kg. Flank. FC DEBUT: 2014. PROV CAREER: Leopards 2014 3-0-0-0-0-0. FC RECORD: 3-0-0-0-0-0. RECORD IN 2014: (Leopards) 3-0-0-0-0-0.

Uys, Wiehan. Lock. FC DEBUT: 2013. PROV CAREER: Limpopo 2013-14 10-0-0-0-0-0. FC RECORD: 10-0-0-0-0-0. RECORD IN 2014: (Limpopo) 6-0-0-0-0-0.

Van Aswegen, Gary Jacques (Standerton HS & US) b 18/02/1990, Pretoria. 1.76m. 83kg. Flyhalf. FC DEBUT: 2010. PROV CAREER: WP 2010-14 20-1-25-21-2-124. EP Kings 2014 8-0-9-4-0-30. SUPER RUGBY: Stormers 2011-13 15-0-3-7-1-30. FC DEBUT: 2006. FC RECORD: 43-1-37-32-3-184. RECORD IN 2014: (WP, EP Kings) 15-1-18-9-0-68.

Van der Hoogt, Nico Johan (Ben Vorster HS, Tzaneen & UJ) b 19/02/1991, Pretoria. 1.95m. 105kg. Flanker. FC DEBUT: 2012. PROV CAREER: Young Lions 2012 2-0-0-0-0-0. Griffons 2014 7-1-0-0-0-5. FC RECORD: 9-1-0-0-0-5. RECORD IN 2014: (Griffons) 7-1-0-0-0-5.

Van der Linde, Christoffel Johannes (CJ) (Grey Coll., Bloemfontein) b 27/08/80, Welkom. 1.90m. 123kg. Prop. FC DEBUT: 2000. PROV CAREER: Cheetahs 2002-05 & 10 49-6-0-0-0-30. Lions 2011-13 18-0-0-0-0-0. EP Kings 2014 7-0-0-0-0-0. SUPER RUGBY: Cats 2004-05 19-1-0-0-0-5. Cheetahs 2006-08 19-2-0-0-0-10. Stormers 2011 11-0-0-0-0-0. Lions 2012 7-0-0-0-0-0. REP HONOURS: SA 2002 & 2004-12 Tests: 75-4-0-0-0-20. Tour: 2006,07,09,10 5-0-0-0-0-0.

Total: 78-4-0-0-0-20. SA U21s 2000-01 8-0-0-0-0-0; SA U19s 1999; SA Schools 1998; CW Cheetahs 1998. FC RECORD: 218-13-0-0-0-65. RECORD IN 2014: (EP Kings) 7-0-0-0-0-0.

Van der Merwe, Armand Hendrik Petrus (Akker) (Outeniqua HS, George & NWU) b 17/06/1991, Vanderbijlpark. 1.78m 106kg. Hooker. FC DEBUT: 2013. PROV CAREER: Leopards 2013-14 11-0-0-0-0-0. Leopard XV 2013 6-2-0-0-0-10. Lions 2014 12-3-0-0-0-15. SUPER RUGBY: Lions 2014 7-1-0-0-0-5. FC RECORD: 36-6-0-0-0-30. RECORD IN 2014: (Lions SR, Lions, Leopards) 21-4-0-0-0-20.

Van der Merwe, Daniel Joubert (Wilgerivier HS, Frankfort) b 24/01/1989, Frankfort. 1.83m. 119kg. Prop. FC DEBUT: 2010. PROV CAREER: Young Lions 2010 1-0-0-0-0-0. Griffons 2012-14 31-3-0-0-0-15. FC RECORD: 32-3-0-0-0-15. RECORD IN 2014: (Griffons) 13-1-0-0-0-5.

Van der Merwe, Daniel Malan (Standerton HS & NWU) b 21/09/1988, Potchefstroom. 1.77m. 85kg. Fullback. FC DEBUT: 2012. PROV CAREER: Leopards 2012 5-1-0-0-0-5. Leopards XV 2014 2-1-0-0-0-5. FC RECORD: 7-2-0-0-0-10. RECORD IN 2014: (Leopards XV) 2-1-0-0-0-5.

Van der Merwe, Duhan (Outeniqua HS, George) b 04/06/1994, George. 1.94m. 96kg. Wing. FC DEBUT: 2014. REP HONOURS: SA U20 2014 2-0-0-0-0-0. FC RECORD: 2-0-0-0-0-0. RECORD IN 2014: (SA U20) 2-0-0-0-0-0.

Van der Merwe, Franco (Hartswater HS) b 15/03/83, Paarl. 1.99m. 107kg. Lock/Flank. FC DEBUT: 2004. PROV CAREER: Leopards 2004-06 58-8-0-0-0-40. Lions 2006-13 100-10-0-0-0-50. Lions XV 2007-08 2-0-0-0-0-0. Young Lions 2009 2-0-0-0-0-0. SUPER RUGBY: Lions 2007-12 & 14 83-7-0-0-0-35. Lions P/R 2013 2-0-0-0-0-0. Sharks 2013 16-0-0-0-0-0. REP HONOURS: SA 2012-13 Tests: 1-0-0-0-0-0. Emerging Springboks 2009 1-0-0-0-0-0. SA U21 2004 3-0-0-0-0-0. FC RECORD: 268-25-0-0-0-125. RECORD IN 2014: (Lions SR) 8-0-0-0-0-0.

Van der Merwe, Frans Jacobus (Franco) (Grey Coll., Bloemfontein & UFS) b 16/12/1989, Bloemfontein. 1.94m. 118kg. Prop. FC DEBUT: 2013. PROV CAREER: Free State XV 2013 2-0-0-0-0-0. Griffons 2014 5-0-0-0-0-0. FC RECORD: 7-0-0-0-0-0. RECORD IN 2014: (Griffons) 5-0-0-0-0-0.

Van der Merwe, Marcel (Paarl Boys' HS) b 24/10/1990, Welkom. 1.89m. 121kg. Prop. FC DEBUT: 2011. PROV CAREER: Cheetahs 2011-12 32-13-0-0-0-65. Emerging Cheetahs 2011 1-0-0-0-0-0. Free State XV 2012 6-4-0-0-0-20. Blue Bulls 2013-14 13-1-0-0-0-5. SUPER RUGBY: Cheetahs 2012 3-0-0-0-0-0. Bulls 2014 16-2-0-0-0-10. REP HONOURS: SA 2014 Tests: 5-0-0-0-0-0. SA U20 2010 5-2-0-0-0-10. FC RECORD: 81-22-0-0-0-110. RECORD IN 2014: (SA, Bulls, Blue Bulls) 26-2-0-0-0-10.

Van der Merwe, Phillip Rudolph (Flip) (Grey Coll., Bloemfontein) b 03/06/85, Potchefstroom. 1.99m. 117kg. Lock. FC DEBUT: 2006. PROV CAREER: Cheetahs 2006-09 37-2-0-0-0-10. Griffons 2007 1-0-0-0-0-0. Blue Bulls 2009-12 36-5-0-0-0-25. SUPER RUGBY: Cheetahs 2007-09 6-1-0-0-0-5. Bulls 2010-14 66-2-0-0-0-10. REP HONOURS: SA 2010-14 Tests: 35-1-0-0-0-5. Tour: 1-0-0-0-0-0. Total: 36-1-0-0-0-5. Springbok XV 2014 1-0-0-0-0-0. SA Students 2007 1-0-0-0-0-0. MISC INFO: Son of Springbok Flippie van der Merwe. Brother of Francois van der Merwe (WP). FC RECORD: 184-11-0-0-0-55. RECORD IN 2014: (SA, Springbok XV, Bulls) 11-0-0-0-0-0.

Van der Merwe, Schalk Willem (Duineveld HS, Upington & Grey Coll., Bloemfontein) b 04/12/1990, Tzaneen. 1.84m. 104kg. Prop. FC DEBUT: 2011. PROV CAREER: Cheetahs 2011-13 15-2-0-0-0-10. Emerging Cheetahs 2011 1-0-0-0-0-0. Griffons 2013 5-1-0-0-0-5.

SEASON IN 2014

Lions 2014 11-2-0-0-0-10. SUPER RUGBY: Lions 2014 15-0-0-0-0-0. FC RECORD: 47-5-0-0-0-25. RECORD IN 2014: (Lions SR, Lions) 26-2-0-0-0-10.

Van der Spuy, Michael George (Grey Coll., Bloemfontein & US) b 20/02/1991, Bethlehem. 1.80m. 86kg. Flyhalf. FC DEBUT: 2011. PROV CAREER: WP 2011-14 36-7-0-0-0-35. SUPER RUGBY: Stormers 2014 4-0-0-0-0-0. FC RECORD: 40-7-0-0-0-35. RECORD IN 2014: (Stormers, WP) 16-2-0-0-0-10.

Van der Walt, Andre Jacobus (Marlow Agric. HS, Cradock) b 10/07/1989, Middelburg. 1.79m. 82kg. Scrumhalf. FC DEBUT: 2012. PROV CAREER: Free State XV 2012-13 13-0-0-0-0-0. Griffons 2014 3-0-0-0-0-0. FC RECORD: 16-0-0-0-0-0. RECORD IN 2014: (Griffons) 3-0-0-0-0-0.

Van der Walt, Andries Petrus (Peet) (Outeniqua HS, George) b 19/09/1991, Kimberley. 1.94m. 103kg. Flank. FC DEBUT: 2013. PROV CAREER: Leopards 2013 12-0-0-0-0-0. Leopard XV 2013 5-0-0-0-0-0. SWD 2014 8-0-0-0-0-0. FC RECORD: 25-0-0-0-0-0. RECORD IN 2014: (SWD) 8-0-0-0-0-0.

Van der Walt, Christoffel Philippus (Philip) (Adelaide Gym. & UFS) b 14/07/1989, Adelaide. 1.94m. 105kg. Eighthman. FC DEBUT: 2010. PROV CAREER: Cheetahs 2010-13 31-4-0-0-0-20. Griffons 2011 1-1-0-0-0-5. SUPER RUGBY: Cheetahs 2010-14 49-5-0-0-0-25. FC RECORD: 81-10-0-0-0-50. RECORD IN 2014: (Cheetahs SR) 8-2-0-0-0-10.

Van der Walt, Jaco (Monument HS, Krugersdorp) b 01/02/1994, Randfontein. 1.82m. 84kg. Flyhalf. FC DEBUT: 2014. PROV CAREER: Lions 2014 10-1-7-3-1-31. FC RECORD: 10-1-7-3-1-31. RECORD IN 2014: (Lions) 10-1-7-3-1-31.

Van der Walt, Petrus Willem (Wimpie) (Nelspruit HS) b 06/01/1989, Brits. 1.87m. 102kg. Flanker. FC DEBUT: 2010. PROV CAREER: WP 2010-11 17-5-0-0-0-25. EP Kings 2012 17-3-0-0-0-15. Blue Bulls 2014 5-2-0-0-0-10. SUPER RUGBY: Southern Kings 2013 15-6-0-0-0-30. P/R 2013 2-0-0-0-0-0. Bulls 2014 4-0-0-0-0-0. FC RECORD: 60-16-0-0-0-80. RECORD IN 2014: (Bulls, Blue Bulls) 9-2-0-0-0-10.

Van der Watt, Vian (Florida HS) b 18/11/1992, Springs. 1.68m. 77kg. Scrumhalf. FC DEBUT: 2011. PROV CAREER: Golden Lions XV 2011 1-0-0-0-0-0. Young Lions 2012-13 3-2-0-0-0-10. Leopards 2014 6-0-0-0-0-0. SUPER RUGBY: Lions P/R 2013 1-0-0-0-0-0. REP HONOURS: SA U20 2012 5-2-0-0-0-10. FC RECORD: 16-4-0-0-0-20. RECORD IN 2014: (Leopards) 6-0-0-0-0-0.

Van der Westhuizen, Dandre (Affies, Pretoria) b 06/11/1991, Pretoria. 1.86m. 114kg. Prop. FC DEBUT: 2011. PROV CAREER: Blue Bulls 2011 2-0-0-0-0-0. Valke 2012-14 27-0-0-0-0-0. FC RECORD: 29-0-0-0-0-0. RECORD IN 2014: (Valke) 13-0-0-0-0-0.

Van der Westhuizen, Dayan Leslie (Centurion HS) b 05/04/1994, Newton. 1.82m. 118kg. Prop. FC DEBUT: 2014. REP HONOURS: SA U20 2014 5-0-0-0-0-0. FC RECORD: 5-0-0-0-0-0. RECORD IN 2014: (SA U20) 5-0-0-0-0-0.

Van der Westhuizen, Ewald (Voortrekker HS, Pietermaritzburg & UJ) b 03/04/1990, Ladysmith. 1.82m. 114kg. Prop. FC DEBUT: 2013. PROV CAREER: Griquas 2013-14 21-3-0-0-0-15. FC RECORD: 21-3-0-0-0-15. RECORD IN 2014: (Griquas) 20-3-0-0-0-15.

Van der Westhuyzen, Dane Robert (St Andrews Coll., Grahamstown) b 16/08/1992, Queenstown. 1.80m. 95kg. Hooker. FC DEBUT: 2013. PROV CAREER: EP Kings 2013-14 14-0-0-0-0-0. FC RECORD: 14-0-0-0-0-0. RECORD IN 2014: (EP Kings) 4-0-0-0-0-0.

Van Breda, Scott (Rondebosch HS) b 12/12/1991. Fullback/Wing. FC DEBUT: 2012. PROV CAREER: EP Kings 2012-14 49-10-42-51-0-287. SUPER RUGBY: Southern Kings 2013 1-0-0-0-0-0. P/R 2013 1-1-2-3-0-18. FC RECORD: 51-11-44-54-0-305. RECORD IN 2014: (EP Kings) 10-2-8-6-0-44.

Van Coller, Drew (Waterkloof HS, Pretoria) b 09/02/87, Johannesburg. 1.87m. 116kg. Prop. FC DEBUT: 2008. PROV CAREER: Cheetahs 2008 8-0-0-0-0-0. Griquas 2009 2-0-0-0-0-0. Pumas 2012-14 28-2-0-0-0-10. FC RECORD: 38-2-0-0-0-10. RECORD IN 2014: (Pumas) 6-0-0-0-0-0.

Van Dyk, Nicolaas Johannes John (Maks) (Paarl Boys' HS) b 21/01/1992, Johannesburg. 1.86m. 118kg. Prop. FC DEBUT: 2012. PROV CAREER: Sharks XV 2012-13 10-0-0-0-0-0. Griquas 2014 14-1-0-0-0-5. SUPER RUGBY: Cheetahs 2014 11-0-0-0-0-0. REP HONOURS: SA U20 2012 4-0-0-0-0-0. FC RECORD: 39-1-0-0-0-5. RECORD IN 2014: (Cheetahs SR, Griquas) 25-1-0-0-0-5.

Van Eeden, Marco-Pieter (Ermelo HS) b 11/04/1989, Ermelo. 1.91m. 104kg. Eighthman. FC DEBUT: 2012. PROV CAREER: Pumas 2012 1-0-0-0-0-0. Valke 2013-14 20-1-0-0-0-5. FC RECORD: 21-1-0-0-0-5. RECORD IN 2014: (Valke) 3-0-0-0-0-0.

Van Heerden, Pieter Schalk (Waterkloof HS, Pretoria) b 31/01/1992, Thabazimbi. 1.98m. 100kg. Lock. FC DEBUT: 2012. PROV CAREER: Blue Bulls 2012-14 12-0-0-0-0-0. Leopards 2014 4-0-0-0-0-0. MISC INFO: Son of former Springbok Moaner van Heerden and brother of former Springbok Wikus van Heerden. FC RECORD: 16-0-0-0-0-0. RECORD IN 2014: (Blue Bulls, Leopards) 12-0-0-0-0-0.

Van Jaarsveld, Torsten George (Hendrik Verwoerd HS, Pretoria) b 30/06/87, Windhoek. 1.75m. 89kg. Hooker. FC DEBUT: 2008. PROV CAREER: Pumas 2008-12 73-8-0-0-0-40. Free State XV 2013-14 8-0-0-0-0-0. Cheetahs 2014 10-0-0-0-0-0. SUPER RUGBY: Cheetahs 2014 5-1-0-0-0-5. REP HONOURS: SA Barbarians 2012 1-0-0-0-0-0. FC RECORD: 97-9-0-0-0-45. RECORD IN 2014: (Cheetahs SR, Cheetahs, Free State XV) 21-1-0-0-0-5.

Van Niekerk, Angelo Gordon (Poena) (Schoonspruit HS, Malmesbury) b 11/12/1988, Atlantis. 1.78m. 88kg. Flyhalf. FC DEBUT: 2014. PROV CAREER: Boland 2014 2-0-0-0-0-0. FC RECORD: 2-0-0-0-0-0. RECORD IN 2014: (Boland) 2-0-0-0-0-0.

Van Niekerk, Johan Andreas (Daniel Pienaar HTS, Uitenhage & UFS) b 19/01/1989, Colesberg. 1.85m. 125kg. Prop. FC DEBUT: 2014. PROV CAREER: Free State XV 2014 2-0-0-0-0-0. FC RECORD: 2-0-0-0-0-0. RECORD IN 2014: (Free State XV) 2-0-0-0-0-0.

Van Niekerk, Johannes Lambrechts (Janru) (Paarl Boys' HS) b 05/11/82, Worcester. 1.82m. 110kg. Prop. FC DEBUT: 2006. PROV CAREER: Boland 2006-11 106-5-0-0-0-25. Griquas 2012-14 36-5-0-0-0-25. REP HONOURS: Emerging Springboks 2008 3-0-0-0-0-0. FC RECORD: 145-10-0-0-0-50. RECORD IN 2014: (Griquas) 14-1-0-0-0-5.

Van Rensburg, Andries Gideon (Deon) (Potchefstroom THS) b 24/01/82, Potchefstroom. 1.78m. 92kg. Centre. FC DEBUT: 2004. PROV CAREER: Leopards 2004-09 92-44-0-0-0-220. Golden Lions 2010-12 27-10-0-0-0-50. Young Lions 2013 6-4-0-0-0-20. SUPER RUGBY: Lions 2009-12 & 14 54-4-0-0-0-20. P/R 2013 1-0-0-0-0-0. REP HONOURS: Emerging Springboks 2009 1-0-0-0-0-0. Royal XV 2009 1-0-0-0-0-0. FC RECORD: 182-62-0-0-0-310. RECORD IN 2014: (Lions SR) 13-1-0-0-0-5.

Van Rooyen, Jacques (Pretoria North HS & UP, TUT) b 24/10/1986, Pretoria. 1.86m. 122kg. Prop. FC DEBUT: 2013. PROV CAREER: Lions 2013-14 21-2-0-0-0-10. Young Lions 2013-14 10-0-0-0-0-0. SUPER RUGBY: Lions 2014 6-0-0-0-0-0. FC RECORD: 37-2-0-0-0-10. RECORD IN 2014: (Lions SR, Lions, Young Lions) 20-0-0-0-0-0.

Van Rooyen, Reynier (Rob Ferreira HS, White River) b 25/04/1990,

Nelspruit. 1.72m. 74kg. Scrumhalf. FC DEBUT: 2012. PROV CAREER: EP Kings 2012 5-0-0-0-0-0. Pumas 2013-14 32-3-0-0-0-15. FC RECORD: 37-3-0-0-0-15. RECORD IN 2014: (Pumas) 19-2-0-0-0-10.

Van Rooyen, Rudi (Affies, Pretoria) b 05/01/1992, Pretoria. 1.84m. 79kg. Scrumhalf. FC DEBUT: 2012. PROV CAREER: Blue Bulls 2012 & 14 4-0-0-0-0-0. Griquas 2014 3-0-0-0-0-0. FC RECORD: 7-0-0-0-0-0. RECORD IN 2014: (Blue Bulls, Griquas) 4-0-0-0-0-0.

Van Schoor, Chevandre Conwin (Klein Nederburg HS, Paarl) b 28/09/1992, Paarl. 80kg. Wing. FC DEBUT: 2014. PROV CAREER: WP 2014 2-0-0-0-0-0. Boland 2014 3-0-0-0-0-0. FC RECORD: 5-0-0-0-0-0. RECORD IN 2014: (WP, Boland) 5-0-0-0-0-0.

Van Staden, Justin (Merensky HS, Tzaneen) b 03/06/1990, Tzaneen. 1.79m. 86kg. Centre. FC DEBUT: 2010. PROV CAREER: Blue Bulls 2010 1-0-0-0-0-0. EP Kings 2012 7-0-6-18-1-66. SWD 2013 12-1-25-26-2-139. Pumas 2014 16-3-17-23-0-118. REP HONOURS: SA Univ 2013 1-0-5-0-0-10. FC RECORD: 37-4-53-67-3-333. RECORD IN 2014: (Pumas) 16-3-17-23-0-118.

Van Tonder, Andrew Stephen (Dr Malan HS, Meyerton & Dr EG Jansen, Boksburg) b 24/05/1993, Meyerton. 1.85m. 98kg. Flank. FC DEBUT: 2014. PROV CAREER: Valke 2014 9-1-0-0-0-5. FC RECORD: 9-1-0-0-0-5. RECORD IN 2014: (Valke) 9-1-0-0-0-5.

Van Tonder, Jaco (Outeniqua HS, George) b 07/04/1991, Cape Town. 1.86m. 95kg. Centre. FC DEBUT: 2012. PROV CAREER: Sharks XV 2012-14 12-3-1-2-0-23. KZN 2013-14 7-0-0-0-0-0. SUPER RUGBY: Sharks 2013-14 3-0-0-0-0-0. FC RECORD: 18-2-0-0-0-10. RECORD IN 2014: (Sharks, KZN, Sharks XV) 7-1-1-2-0-13.

Van Vuuren, Elric (Despatch HS) b 08/04/85, Port Elizabeth. 1.83m. 95kg. Fullback. FC DEBUT: 2006. PROV CAREER: Elephants 2006 & 08 24-7-0-0-0-35. Border 2007 10-1-4-3-0-22. SWD 2011-14 47-15-92-53-0-418. SUPER RUGBY: Southern Kings 2013 2-0-0-0-0-0. FC RECORD: 83-23-96-56-0-475. RECORD IN 2014: (SWD) 16-1-26-16-0-105.

Van Vuuren, Jurie George (Oakdale Agric. HS, Riversdale) b 07/06/1993, Ladybrand. 1.92m. 100kg. Lock. FC DEBUT: 2014. PROV CAREER: WP 2014 2-0-0-0-0-0. SUPER RUGBY: Stormers 2014 5-0-0-0-0-0. FC RECORD: 7-0-0-0-0-0. RECORD IN 2014: (Stormers, WP) 7-0-0-0-0-0.

Van Vuuren, Michael Thomas (Grey HS, Port Elizabeth) b 28/09/1991, East London. 1.86m. 108kg. Hooker. FC DEBUT: 2011. PROV CAREER: Cheetahs 2011 9-0-0-0-0-0. Emerging Cheetahs 2011 1-0-0-0-0-0. Free State XV 2012 6-1-0-0-0-5. EP Kings 2014 4-1-0-0-0-5. REP HONOURS: SA U20 2011 5-0-0-0-0-0. FC RECORD: 25-2-0-0-0-10. RECORD IN 2014: (EP Kings) 4-1-0-0-0-5.

Van Wyk, Andrew Justerine Deometrie (Diamantveld HS, Kimberley & NWU) b 04/08/1989, Prieska. 1.77m. 85kg. Wing. FC DEBUT: 2011. PROV CAREER: Leopards 2011-12 8-0-0-0-0-0. Leopard XV 2013 4-0-0-0-0-0. Border 2013 12-5-0-0-0-25. Valke 2014 19-4-0-0-0-20. FC RECORD: 43-9-0-0-0-45. RECORD IN 2014: (Valke) 19-4-0-0-0-20.

Van Wyk, Arno (Boland Agric., Paarl & UP) b 19/05/1994, Parow. 1.84m. 105kg. Hooker. FC DEBUT: 2014. PROV CAREER: Blue Bulls 2014 2-1-0-0-0-5. REP HONOURS: SA U20 2014 no appearances. FC RECORD: 2-1-0-0-0-5. RECORD IN 2014: (Blue Bulls, SA U20) 2-1-0-0-0-5.

Van Wyk, Coenraad George (Coenie) (Paul Roos Gym., Stellenbosch) b 08/01/88, Belville. 1.83m. 80kg. FC DEBUT: 2009. PROV CAREER: WP 2009 5-0-1-0-0-2. Griquas 2010 3-2-7-1-0-27. Pumas 2011-14 73-32-35-21-0-293. SUPER RUGBY: Lions 2014 8-1-0-0-0-5. REP HONOURS: SA Barbarians 2012 1-0-0-0-0-0. SA Pres XV 2013 3-0-0-0-0-0. FC RECORD: 93-35-43-22-0-327. RECORD IN 2014: (Lions SR, Pumas) 17-1-0-1-0-8.

Van Wyk, Christo Jacques (Brackenfell HS, Cape Town) b 04/10/88, Louis Leipoldt. 1.88m. 144kg. FC DEBUT: 2009. PROV CAREER: Boland 2009 5-0-0-0-0-0. WP 2014 4-1-0-0-0-5. FC RECORD: 9-1-0-0-0-5. RECORD IN 2014: (WP) 4-1-0-0-0-5.

Van Wyk, Hendrik Jacobus (Hencus) (Nylstroom HS) b 02/03/1992, Nigel. 1.83m. 116kg. Prop. FC DEBUT: 2011. PROV CAREER: Blue Bulls 2011 & 13-14 16-4-0-0-0-20. SUPER RUGBY: Bulls 2013 1-0-0-0-0-0. FC RECORD: 17-4-0-0-0-20. RECORD IN 2014: (Blue Bulls) 11-3-0-0-0-15.

Van Wyk, Jacobus Petrus (Kobus) (Paarl Gym.) b 22/01/1992, Nababeep. 1.90m. 94kg. Wing. FC DEBUT: 2012. PROV CAREER: WP 2013-14 16-8-0-0-0-40. SUPER RUGBY: Stormers 2014 10-2-0-0-0-10. REP HONOURS: SA U20 2012 1-0-0-0-0-0. FC RECORD: 27-10-0-0-0-50. RECORD IN 2014: (Stormers, WP) 21-7-0-0-0-35.

Van Wyk, Rynardt Ian (Merensky HS, Tzaneen) b 06/03/1991, Rustenburg. 1.88m. 97kg. Prop. FC DEBUT: 2012. PROV CAREER: Border 2012-14 38-8-0-0-0-40. FC RECORD: 38-8-0-0-0-40. RECORD IN 2014: (Border) 11-4-0-0-0-20.

Van Zyl, Anton (Rondebosch Boys' HS & US) b 23/02/1980, Cape Town. 1.97m. 114kg. Lock. FC DEBUT: 2002. PROV CAREER: WP 2002,09-11 & 14 46-2-0-0-0-10. Lions 2006-08 45-3-0-0-0-15. SUPER RUGBY: Lions 2007-09 30-1-0-0-0-5. Stormers 2010-11 23-1-0-0-0-5. REP HONOURS: British Barbarians 2010 1-0-0-0-0-0. MISC INFO: Son of former Natal lock Mike van Zyl. FC RECORD: 145-7-0-0-0-35. RECORD IN 2014: (WP) 1-0-0-0-0-0.

Van Zyl, Christopher Machiel (Chris) (Rondebosch HS & US) b 12/07/1986, Cape Town. 1.97m. 112kg. Lock. FC DEBUT: 2013. PROV CAREER: Lions 2013-14 8-0-0-0-0-0. Young Lions 2013-14 10-0-0-0-0-0. FC RECORD: 18-0-0-0-0-0. RECORD IN 2014: (Lions, Young Lions) 8-0-0-0-0-0.

Van Zyl, Kayle Deon (Nico Malan HS, Humansdorp & NMMU) b 10/12/1991, Johannesburg. 1.85m. 88kg. Scrumhalf. FC DEBUT: 2013. PROV CAREER: EP Kings 2013-14 18-3-7-2-0-35. FC RECORD: 18-3-7-2-0-35. RECORD IN 2014: (EP Kings) 3-0-1-1-0-5.

Van Zyl, Petrus Erasmus (Pieter) (Grey Coll., Bloemfontein & UFS) b 14/09/1989, Pretoria. 1.74m. 81kg. Scrumhalf. FC DEBUT: 2010. PROV CAREER: Cheetahs 2010-13 31-6-0-0-0-30. Emerging Cheetahs 2011 1-0-0-0-0-0. Blue Bulls 2014 11-1-0-0-0-5. SUPER RUGBY: Cheetahs 2012-13 32-5-0-0-0-25. Bulls 2014 12-0-0-0-0-0. REP HONOURS: SA 2013 Tests: 2-0-0-0-0-0. FC RECORD: 89-12-0-0-0-60. RECORD IN 2014: (Bulls, Blue Bulls) 23-1-0-0-0-5.

Van Zyl, Philippus Jacobus (PJ) (Bergsig HS, Rustenburg) b 23/04/1988, Rustenburg. 1.93m. 91kg. Flank. FC DEBUT: 2011. PROV CAREER: Boland 2011-14 65-10-0-0-0-50. FC RECORD: 65-10-0-0-0-50. RECORD IN 2014: (Boland) 7-0-0-0-0-0.

Velleman, Cyril John (CJ) (Grey HS, Port Elizabeth & NMMU) b 24/02/1995, Somerset East. 1.78m. 90kg. Flank. FC DEBUT: 2014. PROV CAREER: EP Kings 2014 3-0-0-0-0-0. FC RECORD: 3-0-0-0-0-0. RECORD IN 2014: (EP Kings) 3-0-0-0-0-0.

Venter, Anver (Oudtshoorn HS) b 01/02/1990, Aliwal North. 1.86m. 80kg. Wing. FC DEBUT: 2013. PROV CAREER: SWD 2013-14 10-2-0-0-0-10. FC RECORD: 10-2-0-0-0-10. RECORD IN 2014: (SWD) 9-1-0-0-0-5.

Venter, Benjamin Christoffel Gerhardus (Ben) (Henneman HS) b 15/05/1987, Johannesburg. 1.97m. 116kg. Lock. FC DEBUT: 2010. PROV CAREER: Border 2010-12 32-3-0-0-0-15. Griquas 2010 1-0-0-0-0-0. Boland 2013-14 21-0-0-0-0-0. FC RECORD: 54-3-0-0-0-15. RECORD

IN 2014: (Boland) 3-0-0-0-0-0.
Venter, Elardus Desederus (Merensky HS, Tzaneen & NWU) b 26/03/1990, Nelspruit. 1.85m. 123kg. Prop. FC DEBUT: 2013. PROV CAREER: Leopards 2013 10-0-0-0-0-0. Leopard XV 2014 9-0-0-0-0-0. FC RECORD: 19-0-0-0-0-0. RECORD IN 2014: (Leopard XV) 4-0-0-0-0-0.
Venter, Hanco Charles (Monument HS, Krugersdorp) b 07/01/1993, Witbank. 1.76m. 82kg. Scrumhalf. FC DEBUT: 2012. PROV CAREER: Sharks XV 2012-14 14-2-0-0-0-10. KZN 2014 3-0-0-0-0-0. REP HONOURS: SA U20 2013 3-0-0-0-0-0. FC RECORD: 20-2-0-0-0-10. RECORD IN 2014: (KZN, Sharks XV) 10-1-0-0-0-5.
Venter, Hendrik Petrus (Henco) (Grey Coll., Bloemfontein & UFS) b 27/03/1992, Bloemfontein. 1.93m. 107kg. Lock. FC DEBUT: 2012. PROV CAREER: Cheetahs 2012 & 14 10-0-0-0-0-0. Free State XV 2014 2-0-0-0-0-0. SUPER RUGBY: Cheetahs 2014 1-0-0-0-0-0. MISC INFO: Nephew of former Springbok Ruben Kruger. FC RECORD: 13-0-0-0-0-0. RECORD IN 2014: (Cheetahs SR, Cheetahs, Free State XV) 12-0-0-0-0-0.
Venter, Jacobus Francois (Grey Coll., Bloemfontein & UP) b 19/04/1991, Bloemfontein. 1.85m. 91kg. Centre. FC DEBUT: 2011. PROV CAREER: Blue Bulls 2011-13 43-12-0-0-0-60. Cheetahs 2014 9-2-0-0-0-10. SUPER RUGBY: Bulls 2012-13 11-0-0-0-0-0. Cheetahs 2014 5-1-0-0-0-5. REP HONOURS: SA U20 2010-11 9-7-0-0-0-35. FC RECORD: 77-22-0-0-0-110. RECORD IN 2014: (Cheetahs SR, Cheetahs) 14-3-0-0-0-15.
Venter, Ruan Christov (Monument HS, Krugersdorp) b 11/05/1992, Rustenburg. 1.98m. 108kg. Lock. FC DEBUT: 2011. PROV CAREER: Lions 2013 2-0-0-0-0-0. Young Lions 2014 1-0-0-0-0-0. Pumas 2014 2-0-0-0-0-0. Leopards 2014 11-0-0-0-0-0. REP HONOURS: SA U20 2011 2-0-0-0-0-0. FC RECORD: 18-0-0-0-0-0. RECORD IN 2014: (Pumas, Leopards, Young Lions) 14-0-0-0-0-0.
Venter, Ruan Jurgens b 20/04/1989. Prop. FC DEBUT: 2014. PROV CAREER: Limpopo 2014 6-0-0-0-0-0. FC RECORD: 6-0-0-0-0-0. RECORD IN 2014: (Limpopo) 6-0-0-0-0-0.
Venter, Shaun Harold (Affies, Pretoria) b 16/03/87, Witbank. 1.80m. 80kg. Scrumhalf. FC DEBUT: 2007. PROV CAREER: Pumas 2007-13 105-28-0-0-0-140. Cheetahs 2014 8-0-0-0-0-0. SUPER RUGBY: Southern Kings 2013 16-2-0-0-0-10. P/R 2013 2-0-0-0-0-0. Cheetahs 2014 14-0-0-0-0-0. REP HONOURS: SA Barbarians 2012 1-2-0-0-0-10. SA Sevens 2009. FC RECORD: 146-32-0-0-0-160. RECORD IN 2014: (Cheetahs SR, Cheetahs) 22-0-0-0-0-0.
Venton, Leslie b 01/12/1988. Hooker. FC DEBUT: 2014. PROV CAREER: Limpopo 2014 1-0-0-0-0-0. FC RECORD: 1-0-0-0-0-0. RECORD IN 2014: (Limpopo) 1-0-0-0-0-0.
Vermaak, Alistair Fernando (Hillside HS & Hentie Cilliers HS, Virginia) b 28/04/1989, Port Elizabeth. 1.79m. 108kg. Prop. FC DEBUT: 2011. PROV CAREER: WP 2011-12 & 14 25-1-0-0-0-5. Boland 2013 3-0-0-0-0-0. SUPER RUGBY: Stormers 2014 6-0-0-0-0-0. REP HONOURS: SA Univ 2013 1-0-0-0-0-0. FC RECORD: 35-1-0-0-0-5. RECORD IN 2014: (Stormers, WP) 24-0-0-0-0-0.
Vermaak, Jacobus Cornelius (Jacques) (Volkskool Potchefstroom) b 17/09/1991, Potchefstroom. 1.78m. 95kg. Hooker. FC DEBUT: 2013. PROV CAREER: Leopards 2013-14 15-1-0-0-0-5. Leopard XV 2013-14 10-4-0-0-0-20. FC RECORD: 25-5-0-0-0-25. RECORD IN 2014: (Leopards, Leopard XV) 14-3-0-0-0-15.
Vermaak, Ruan (Monument Park HS, Kraaifontein & US) b 18/02/1991, Cape Town. 1.95m. 105kg. Lock. FC DEBUT: 2014. PROV CAREER: WP 2014 1-0-0-0-0-0. FC RECORD: 1-0-0-0-0-0. RECORD IN 2014: (WP) 1-0-0-0-0-0.

Vermeulen, Daniel Johannes (Duane) (Nelspruit HS) b 03/07/86, Nelspruit. 1.92m. 90kg. Flank. FC DEBUT: 2005. PROV CAREER: Pumas 2005-06 26-4-0-0-0-20. Cheetahs 2007-08 28-2-0-0-0-10. WP 2009-10 & 12-13 38-7-0-0-0-35. SUPER RUGBY: Cheetahs 2007-08 20-3-0-0-0-15. Stormers 2009-14 78-3-0-0-0-15. REP HONOURS: SA 2012-14 Tests: 29-2-0-0-0-10. Springbok XV 2014 1-0-0-0-0-0. Emerging Springboks 2009 1-0-0-0-0-0. British Barbarians 2013 1-1-0-0-0-5. MISC INFO: Super PoY nominee 2011. IRB PoY 2014 nominee. PoY nominee 2014. FC RECORD: 222-22-0-0-0-110. RECORD IN 2014: (SA, Springbok XV, Stormers) 30-2-0-0-0-10.
Vermeulen, Johannes Frederick (Jacques) (Paarl Gym.) b 08/02/1995, Paarl. 1.94m. 107kg. Flank. FC DEBUT: 2014. REP HONOURS: SA U20 2014 4-0-0-0-0-0. FC RECORD: 4-0-0-0-0-0. RECORD IN 2014: (SA U20) 4-0-0-0-0-0.
Vermeulen, Petrus Jacobus (PJ) (Northern Cape HS, Kimberley) b 03/03/87, De Aar. 1.82m. 86kg. Centre. FC DEBUT: 2007. PROV CAREER: WP 2007-09 26-6-0-0-0-30. Boland 2009-11 39-6-0-0-0-30. Griquas 2012-14 37-8-1-0-0-42. FC RECORD: 102-20-1-0-0-102. RECORD IN 2014: (Griquas) 16-3-0-0-0-15.
Vermeulen, Petrus Van der Walt (Waltie) (Grey Coll., Bloemfontein & UFS) b 11/11/88. 1.99m. 108kg. Lock. FC DEBUT: 2008. PROV CAREER: Cheetahs 2009-14 46-0-0-0-0-0. Free State XV 2012-14 11-0-0-0-0-0. Cheetahs XV 2010 1-0-0-0-0-0. SUPER RUGBY: Cheetahs 2010-14 26-1-0-0-0-5. REP HONOURS: SA Students 2008 1-0-0-0-0-0. FC RECORD: 85-1-0-0-0-5. RECORD IN 2014: (Cheetahs SR, Cheetahs, Free State XV) 12-0-0-0-0-0.
Verwey, Tobie Jacques (Middelburg HS) b 09/12/89, Middelburg. 1.94m. 91kg. Flank. FC DEBUT: 2009. PROV CAREER: Pumas 2009 4-0-0-0-0-0. Blue Bulls 2012-13 2-0-0-0-0-0. Valke 2013-14 29-7-0-0-0-35. FC RECORD: 35-7-0-0-0-35. RECORD IN 2014: (Valke) 17-7-0-0-0-35.
Viljoen, EW (Grey Coll., Bloemfontein) b 09/05/1995, Bloemfontein. 1.92m. 100kg. Fullback/Wing. FC DEBUT: 2014. PROV CAREER: WP 2014 2-0-0-0-0-0. FC RECORD: 2-0-0-0-0-0. RECORD IN 2014: (WP) 2-0-0-0-0-0.
Visagie, Callie-Theron (Paarl Boys' HS & US) b 09/07/1988, Paarl. 1.89m. 103kg. Hooker. FC DEBUT: 2010. PROV CAREER: WP 2010 9-0-0-0-0-0. Lions 2012 10-0-0-0-0-0. Young Lions 2013 1-0-0-0-0-0. Blue Bulls 2013-14 13-1-0-0-0-5. SUPER RUGBY: Lions 2012 16-0-0-0-0-0. Bulls 2013-14 22-2-0-0-0-10. FC RECORD: 71-3-0-0-0-15. RECORD IN 2014: (Bulls, Blue Bulls) 24-2-0-0-0-10.
Visagie, Gerrit Jacobus (Jaco) (Augsburg HS, Clanwilliam & UP) b 08/07/1992, Cape Town. 1.88m. 98kg. Hooker. FC DEBUT: 2013. PROV CAREER: Blue Bulls 2013-14 8-0-0-0-0-0. FC RECORD: 8-0-0-0-0-0. RECORD IN 2014: (Blue Bulls) 4-0-0-0-0-0.
Visser, Petrus Jurgen (Paarl Gym.) b 13/09/89, Paarl. 1.91m. 88kg. Flyhalf. FC DEBUT: 2009. PROV CAREER: WP 2009-10 8-1-9-4-1-38. Blue Bulls 2011-14 39-7-2-5-0-54. SUPER RUGBY: Bulls 2013-14 25-2-0-1-0-13. FC RECORD: 72-10-11-10-1-105. RECORD IN 2014: (Bulls, Blue Bulls) 16-1-0-1-0-8.
Visser, Wickus Thomas (Riebeeck Rand HS, Randfontein) b 07/10/1981, Randfontein. 1.75m. 96kg. Hooker. FC DEBUT: 2014. PROV CAREER: Limpopo 2014 1-0-0-0-0-0. FC RECORD: 1-0-0-0-0-0. RECORD IN 2014: (Limpopo) 1-0-0-0-0-0.
Volmink, Anthonie Alfred (HTS Bredasdorp) b 10/02/90, Bredasdorp. 1.80m. 85kg. Wing. FC DEBUT: 2009. PROV CAREER: Boland 2009 2-1-0-0-0-5. Lions 2012-13 16-9-0-0-0-45. Young Lions 2012-14 18-20-1-0-0-102. SUPER RUGBY: Lions 2012 & 14 10-1-0-0-0-5. P/R

2013 2-0-0-0-0-0. FC RECORD: 48-31-1-0-0-157. RECORD IN 2014: (Lions SR, Young Lions) 10-2-0-0-0-10.

Vorster, Harold William (Frans du Toit HS, Phalaborwa) b 11/10/1993, Phalaborwa. 1.86m. 92kg. Centre. FC DEBUT: 2012. PROV CAREER: Young Lions 2012-14 11-1-0-0-0-5. Lions 2014 6-0-0-0-0-0. FC RECORD: 17-1-0-0-0-5. RECORD IN 2014: (Lions, Young Lions) 11-0-0-0-0-0.

Vorster, Petrus Johannes Hendrik (Peet) (Waterkloof HS, Pretoria) b 04/04/1989, Roodepoort. 1.90m. 116kg. Prop. FC DEBUT: 2011. PROV CAREER: Boland 2011 4-0-0-0-0-0. Limpopo 2014 4-0-0-0-0-0. Valke 2014 5-1-0-0-0-5. FC RECORD: 13-1-0-0-0-5. RECORD IN 2014: (Valke, Limpopo) 9-1-0-0-0-5.

Vosloo, Johannes Arnoldus (Grey Coll., Bloemfontein) b 11/09/1994, Bloemfontein. 1.78m. 80kg. Scrumhalf. FC DEBUT: 2014. PROV CAREER: Sharks XV 2014 1-0-0-0-0-0. FC RECORD: 1-0-0-0-0-0. RECORD IN 2014: (Sharks XV) 1-0-0-0-0-0.

Vulindlu, Luzuko (Durban HS) b 14/11/87, Grahamstown. 1.83m. 98kg. Centre. FC DEBUT: 2008. PROV CAREER: KZN 2009-10 6-1-0-0-0-5. Sharks XV 2008-11 13-2-0-0-0-10. Sharks Inv XV 2009 1-0-0-0-0-0. Griquas 2012-13 11-2-0-0-0-10. SWD 2013-14 9-1-0-0-0-5. SUPER RUGBY: Sharks 2009 9-1-0-0-0-5. REP HONOURS: Emerging Springboks 2009 1-0-0-0-0-0. FC RECORD: 50-7-0-0-0-35. RECORD IN 2014: (SWD) 6-1-0-0-0-5.

Wagman, Clinton Andrew (Florida HS) b 05/10/1990, George. 1.79m. 78kg. Wing. FC DEBUT: 2011. PROV CAREER: SWD 2011-14 51-14-0-0-0-70. FC RECORD: 51-14-0-0-0-70. RECORD IN 2014: (SWD) 8-2-0-0-0-10.

Waka, Lolo Yanga (Forbes Grant SS, King William's Town NWU & UJ) b 23/12/1986, King William's Town. 1.8m. 86kg. Wing. FC DEBUT: 2007. PROV CAREER: Border 2007,09 & 13-14 28-10-0-0-0-50. Griquas 2012 3-1-0-0-0-5. REP HONOURS: Emerging Springboks 2008 1-1-0-0-0-5. FC RECORD: 32-12-0-0-0-60. RECORD IN 2014: (Border) 6-2-0-0-0-10.

Watermeyer, Stefan (Waterkloof HS, Pretoria) b 03/06/88, Nelspruit. 1.85m. 95kg. FC DEBUT: 2007. PROV CAREER: Blue Bulls 2008-11 55-20-9-2-0-124. Blue Bulls XV 2007 1-0-0-0-0-0. Griquas 2012 3-0-0-0-0-0. Pumas 2013-14 33-13-0-0-0-65. SUPER RUGBY: Bulls 2010 1-0-0-0-0-0. Lions 2014 13-2-0-0-0-10. REP HONOURS: SA Pres XV 2013 3-0-0-0-0-0. SA U20 2008 4-4-0-0-0-20. FC RECORD: 113-39-9-2-0-219. RECORD IN 2014: (Lions SR, Pumas) 22-6-0-0-0-30.

Watson, Luke Asher (Grey HS, Port Elizabeth) b 26/10/83, Port Elizabeth. 1.84m. 97kg. Flank. FC DEBUT: 2002. PROV CAREER: EP Kings 2002 & 2011-14 29-25-0-0-0-125. KZN 2003-04 19-2-0-0-0-10. WP 2005-09 48-26-0-0-0-130. SUPER RUGBY: Sharks 2003-04 20-1-0-0-0-5. Stormers 2005-09 62-10-0-0-0-50. Southern Kings 2013 6-2-0-0-0-10. REP HONOURS: SA 2007-08 Tests: 10-0-0-0-0-0. SA U21 2004 (captain) 2-1-1-0-0-7. SA Kings 2011 2-0-0-0-0-0. WP XV 2006. SA Sevens 2002. SA U19 2002 (captain). SA Schools 2001 (captain). CW EP 2001. MISC INFO: YPoY nominee 2004. S14 PoY 2006. CC First Div PoY 2012 nominee. Son of former Eastern Free State & EP winger and current President of the EP Rugby Union Cheeky Watson. FC RECORD: 199-67-1-0-0-337. RECORD IN 2014: (EP Kings) 2-1-0-0-0-5.

Watts, Elgar Graeme (Klein Nederberg HS, Paarl) b 24/09/85, Paarl. 1.81m. 84kg. Flyhalf. FC DEBUT: 2008. PROV CAREER: Boland 2008-09 & 2011-12 75-21-101-45-1-445. Pumas 2010 22-10-17-9-0-111. Cheetahs 2013-14 13-5-10-10-0-75. Free State XV 2013 2-0-3-1-0-9. SUPER RUGBY: Cheetahs 2013-14 19-1-17-16-0-87. REP HONOURS: SA Barbarians 2012 1-0-3-0-0-6. Misc: First Division POY 2011. FC RECORD: 132-37-151-81-1-733. RECORD IN 2014: (Cheetahs SR, Cheetahs) 15-2-12-9-0-61.

Wegner, Carl August (Grey Coll., Bloemfontein & CUT) b 07/02/1991, Ficksburg. 2.01m. 117kg. Lock. FC debut: 2012. PROV CAREER: Cheetahs 2012 & 14 8-0-0-0-0-0. SUPER RUGBY: Cheetahs 2014 2-0-0-0-0-0. REP HONOURS: SA U20 2011 2-0-0-0-0-0. MISC INFO: Son of former Free State and Eastern Free State hooker Callie Wegner. FC RECORD: 12-0-0-0-0-0. RECORD IN 2014: (Cheetahs SR, Cheetahs) 5-0-0-0-0-0.

Wehr, Wendal Peter (Worcester SS, Boland Coll. & UJ) b 27/12/87, Worcester. 1.88m. 96kg. Flank. FC DEBUT: 2008. PROV CAREER: Boland 2008-09 16-2-0-0-0-10. Leopards 2012 2-0-0-0-0-0. Griquas 2014 1-0-0-0-0-0. FC RECORD: 19-2-0-0-0-10. RECORD IN 2014: (Griquas) 1-0-0-0-0-0.

Welemu, Lindokuhle b 29/04/1991. Lock. FC DEBUT: 2014. PROV CAREER: Border 2014 11-0-0-0-0-0. FC RECORD: 11-0-0-0-0-0. RECORD IN 2014: (Border) 11-0-0-0-0-0.

Welgemoed, Rhyk (Framesby HS, Port Elizabeth) b 21/12/1990, Port Elizabeth. 1.91m. 90kg. Eighthman. FC DEBUT: 2013. PROV CAREER: Leopards 2013-14 13-3-0-0-0-15. Leopard XV 2013 7-4-0-0-0-20. FC RECORD: 20-7-0-0-0-35. RECORD IN 2014: (Leopards) 11-3-0-0-0-15.

Weller-Blaber, Dennis Harold (Labori HS, Paarl & CUT) b 26/07/1986, Wynberg. 1.87m. 101kg. Centre. FC DEBUT: 2014. PROV CAREER: Limpopo 2014 2-0-0-0-0-0. FC RECORD: 2-0-0-0-0-0. RECORD IN 2014: (Limpopo) 2-0-0-0-0-0.

Wentzel, Marco Van Zyl (Outeniqua HS, George & UNISA) b 05/05/79, George. 2.00m. 103kg. Lock. FC DEBUT: 1998. PROV CAREER: SWD 1998-99 4-0-0-0-0-0. Pumas 2000-02 29-3-0-0-0-15. Cheetahs 2003-05 26-4-0-0-0-20. Boland 2006 7-1-0-0-0-5. KZN 2013-14 14-1-0-0-0-5. Sharks XV 2014 4-0-0-0-0-0. Super 12: Bulls 2001-02 16-0-0-0-0-0. Cats 2003 10-0-0-0-0-0. REP HONOURS: SA 2002 Tests: 2-0-0-0-0-0. SA U23s 2001 4-2-0-0-0-10. S/Kings 2009 1-0-0-0-0-0. British Barbarians 2013 2-0-0-0-0-0. CW SWD 1996-97. MISC INFO: Treviso (Italy) 2005/06. FC RECORD: 120-11-0-0-0-55. RECORD IN 2014: (KZN, Sharks XV) 13-0-0-0-0-0.

Wepener, Frederik Willem (Willie) (Helpmekaar HS, Johannesburg) b 02/04/81, Newcastle. 1.80m. 106kg. Hooker. FC DEBUT: 2002. PROV CAREER: Lions 2002-04 & 06-09 & 13-14 43-7-0-0-0-35. Young Lions 2002-08 14-1-0-0-0-5. Leopards 2004 15-2-0-0-0-10. Lions XV 2008 1-0-0-0-0-0. Griquas 2005-06 34-4-0-0-0-20. Blue Bulls 2011-13 25-1-0-0-0-5. SUPER RUGBY: Cats 2006 2-0-0-0-0-0. Lions 2007-09 & 14 46-2-0-0-0-10. Bulls 2012-13 23-1-0-0-0-5. FC RECORD: 203-18-0-0-0-90. RECORD IN 2014: (Lions SR, Lions) 11-1-0-0-0-5.

Wessels, Petrus Johannes (Johan) (AHS Kroonstad & UFS) b 29/11/88, Vredefort. 1.85m. 103kg. Flank. FC DEBUT: 2009. PROV CAREER: Cheetahs 2009-11 39-4-0-0-0-20. Griffons 2010 8-0-0-0-0-0. Free State XV 2012 2-0-0-0-0-0. Leopards 2014 3-0-0-0-0-0. SUPER RUGBY: Cheetahs 2011 4-0-0-0-0-0. FC RECORD: 56-4-0-0-0-20. RECORD IN 2014: (Leopards) 3-0-0-0-0-0.

Wessels, Stephanus Petrus (Jan Kriel HS) b 09/11/1992, Paarl. 1.84m. 100kg. Prop. FC DEBUT: 2014. PROV CAREER: Boland 2014 2-0-0-0-0-0. FC RECORD: 2-0-0-0-0-0. RECORD IN 2014: (Boland) 2-0-0-0-0-0.

Westraadt, Simon (Grey HS, Port Elizabeth) b 31/03/86, Port Elizabeth. 1.76m. 107kg. Hooker. FC DEBUT: 2007. PROV CAREER: WP 2007-08 6-0-0-0-0-0. Griquas 2009-14 68-10-0-0-0-50. FC RECORD: 74-10-0-0-0-50. RECORD IN 2014: (Griquas) 14-1-0-0-0-5.

Whitehead, George Alexander (Grey Coll., Bloemfontein) b 17/03/89, Bloemfontein. 1.85m. 80kg. FC DEBUT: 2009. PROV CAREER:

SEASON IN 2014

Cheetahs 2009-10 9-1-2-3-0-18. EP Kings 2011-14 45-8-61-28-1-249. SUPER RUGBY: Southern Kings 2013 15-2-6-3-0-31. P/R 2013 2-0-0-0-0-0. FC RECORD: 71-11-69-34-1-298. RECORD IN 2014: (EP Kings) 6-0-2-1-1-10.

Whitehead, Tim (Grey HS, Port Elizabeth & UCT) b30/05/88. 1.86m. 88kg. Centre. FC DEBUT: 2009. PROV CAREER: WP 2010-11 23-2-0-0-0-10. KZN 2012-13 14-1-0-0-0-5. EP Kings 2014 8-2-0-0-0-10. SUPER RUGBY: Stormers 2010 10-0-0-0-0-0. Sharks 2012 15-1-0-0-0-5. REP HONOURS: SA Students 2009 2-1-0-0-0-5. FC RECORD: 72-7-0-0-0-35. RECORD IN 2014: (EP Kings) 8-2-0-0-0-10.

Whiteley, Warren Roger (Glenwood HS, Durban) b 18/09/87, Durban. 1.92m. 97kg. Flank. FC DEBUT: 2008. PROV CAREER: Sharks XV 2008-09 13-4-0-0-0-20. Elephants 2009 5-1-0-0-0-5. Golden Lions 2010-14 47-6-0-0-0-30. Young Lions 2010 & 13 11-4-0-0-0-20. SUPER RUGBY: Lions 2011-12 & 14 36-5-0-0-0-25. P/R 2013 2-0-0-0-0-0. REP HONOURS: SA 2014 Tests: 2-0-0-0-0-0. SA Sevens 2013-14. FC RECORD: 116-20-0-0-0-100. RECORD IN 2014: (SA, Lions SR, Lions, SA Sevens) 23-3-0-0-0-15.

Willemse, Chaney (Hexriver Valley HS) b 14/02/1993, De Doorns. 1.86m. 86kg. Flank. FC DEBUT: 2014. PROV CAREER: Boland 2014 6-0-0-0-0-0. FC RECORD: 6-0-0-0-0-0. RECORD IN 2014: (Boland) 6-0-0-0-0-0.

Willemse, Michael Evan (Grey HS, Port Elizabeth & UCT) b 14/02/1993, Cape Town. 1.85m. 104kg. Hooker. FC DEBUT: 2013. PROV CAREER: WP 2013-14 10-1-0-0-0-5. SUPER RUGBY: Stormers 2014 1-0-0-0-0-0. REP HONOURS: SA U20 2013 5-2-0-0-0-10. FC RECORD: 16-3-0-0-0-15. RECORD IN 2014: (Stormers, WP) 5-0-0-0-0-0.

Willemse, Paul (Monument HS, Krugersdorp) b 13/11/1992, Pretoria. 2.00m. 127kg. Lock. FC DEBUT: 2012. PROV CAREER: Lions 2012 1-0-0-0-0-0. Young Lions 2012 5-2-0-0-0-10. Blue Bulls 2013-14 23-3-0-0-0-15. SUPER RUGBY: Lions 2012 1-0-0-0-0-0. Bulls 2013-14 20-3-0-0-0-15. REP HONOURS: SA U20 2012 5-2-0-0-0-10. FC RECORD: 55-10-0-0-0-50. RECORD IN 2014: (Bulls, Blue Bulls) 26-3-0-0-0-15.

Willemse, Stefan (Paarl Gym. & NMMU) b 12/04/1992, Paarl. 1.94m. 114kg. Flank. FC DEBUT: 2013. PROV CAREER: EP Kings 2013-14 27-8-0-0-0-40. FC RECORD: 27-8-0-0-0-40. RECORD IN 2014: (EP Kings) 11-0-0-0-0-0.

Williams, Cheswin b 22/09/1987. 79kg. Wing. FC DEBUT: 2012. PROV CAREER: Boland 2012-14 29-6-1-4-0-44. FC RECORD: 29-6-1-4-0-44. RECORD IN 2014: (Boland) 7-2-0-0-0-10.

Williams, Devon Frank (Paarl Boys' HS) b 16/04/1992, Stellenbosch. 1.74m. 73kg. Wing. FC DEBUT: 2013. PROV CAREER: WP 2013-14 16-11-0-0-0-55. SUPER RUGBY: Stormers 2013 3-1-0-0-0-5. FC RECORD: 19-12-0-0-0-60. RECORD IN 2014: (Stormers, WP) 11-10-0-0-0-50.

Williams, Heimar (Affies, Pretoria & Unisa) b 02/09/1991, Krugersdorp. 1.80m. 93kg. Centre. FC DEBUT: 2011. PROV CAREER: Sharks XV 2011-14 24-2-0-0-0-10. KZN 2013-14 12-4-0-0-0-20. SUPER RUGBY: Sharks 2014 10-0-0-0-0-0. FC RECORD: 46-6-0-0-0-30. RECORD IN 2014: (Sharks, KZN, Sharks XV) 14-0-0-0-0-0.

Williams, Kurshwill (Oudtshoorn HS) b 05/06/1993, George. 1.6m. 70kg. Scrumhalf. FC DEBUT: 2013. PROV CAREER: Young Lions 2013 3-0-0-0-0-0. Leopards 2014 4-0-0-0-0-0. REP HONOURS: SA U20 2013 1-0-0-0-0-0. FC RECORD: 8-0-0-0-0-0. RECORD IN 2014: (Leopards) 4-0-0-0-0-0.

Williams, Marlyn Earl (Paulus Joubert HS) b 09/01/1993, Paarl. 1.95m. 105kg. Lock. FC DEBUT: 2014. PROV CAREER: Valke 2014 18-1-0-0-0-5. FC RECORD: 18-1-0-0-0-5. RECORD IN 2014: (Valke) 18-1-0-0-0-5.

Willis, Vainon Shanon (Waterkloof HS, Pretoria) b 11/10/1988, Cape Town. 1.83m. 85kg. Wing. FC DEBUT: 2009. PROV CAREER: Blue Bulls 2009-10 & 13 12-3-0-0-0-15. Pumas 2010 9-2-0-0-0-10. Leopards 2011-12 27-3-0-0-0-15. Boland 2012 3-2-0-0-0-10. Young Lions 2014 9-2-0-0-0-10. REP HONOURS: SA U20 2008 4-1-0-0-0-5. FC RECORD: 64-13-0-0-0-65. RECORD IN 2014: (Young Lions) 9-2-0-0-0-10.

Wright, Cameron Robin (Hilton Coll. & UKZN) b 20/04/1994, Westville. 1.81m. 92kg. Scrumhalf. FC DEBUT: 2014. PROV CAREER: KZN 2014 10-0-0-0-0-0. FC RECORD: 10-0-0-0-0-0. RECORD IN 2014: (KZN) 10-0-0-0-0-0.

Xakalashe, Yonga (Gwaba HS) b 16/08/1983, East London. 103kg. Prop. FC DEBUT: 2014. PROV CAREER: Border 2014 16-1-0-0-0-5. FC RECORD: 16-1-0-0-0-5. RECORD IN 2014: (Border) 16-1-0-0-0-5.

Xoli, Lihleli Tandokuhle (Kingswood Coll., Grahamstown & UCT) b 28/02/1993, Port Elizabeth. 1.89m. 88kg. Wing. FC DEBUT: 2014. PROV CAREER: WP 2014 2-0-0-0-0-0. FC RECORD: 2-0-0-0-0-0. RECORD IN 2014: (WP) 2-0-0-0-0-0.

Zaayman, Stephan (Framesby HS, Port Elizabeth & NMMU) b 18/06/1993, Middelburg, MP. 1.96m. 100kg. Flank. FC DEBUT: 2013. PROV CAREER: EP Kings 2013-14 5-0-0-0-0-0. FC RECORD: 5-0-0-0-0-0. RECORD IN 2014: (EP Kings) 3-0-0-0-0-0.

Zana, Eric Sydney (Outeniqua HS, George) b 25/03/1987, George. 1.76m. 70kg. Flyhalf. FC DEBUT: 2010. PROV CAREER: SWD 2010-11 23-0-1-8-0-26. Boland 2012-14 41-12-41-22-1-211. FC RECORD: 64-12-42-30-1-237. RECORD IN 2014: (Boland) 16-7-22-14-1-124.

Zeilinga, Frederik Johannes (Fred) (Glenwood HS, Durban) b 11/12/1992. Ladysmith. 1.75m. 82kg. Flyhalf. FC DEBUT: 2011. PROV CAREER: KZN 2013-14 18-2-19-41-3-180. Sharks XV 2011-14 22-3-39-34-0-195. SUPER RUGBY: Sharks 2013-14 4-1-2-7-0-30. FC RECORD: 44-6-60-82-3-396. RECORD IN 2014: (Sharks, KZN, Sharks XV) 14-1-17-38-0-153.

Zito, Mzwanele Richman (Solomon Mahlangu HS & Bol Coll.) b 23/11/1988, Uitenhage. 1.95m. 108kg. Lock. FC DEBUT: 2013. PROV CAREER: EP Kings 2013 1-0-0-0-0-0. SWD 2013-14 31-6-0-0-0-30. FC RECORD: 32-6-0-0-0-30. RECORD IN 2014: (SWD) 19-4-0-0-0-20.

Zono, Oliver (Eyabantu HS & UFH) b 26/11/1991, Fort Beaufort. 1.75m. 78kg. Flyhalf. FC DEBUT: 2014. PROV CAREER: Border 2014 9-1-0-0-0-5. FC RECORD: 9-1-0-0-0-5. RECORD IN 2014: (Border) 9-1-0-0-0-5.

SEASON IN 2014

Notable Obituaries

By Paul Dobson (for all obituaries, see pages 630-640)

Tinus Linee (1969-2014)
Crash-tackling WP, Stormers & Springbok centre
TINUS Linee first made himself known at the Craven Week in Paarl in 1987. He was playing for Western Province League and their first match was against powerful Northern Transvaal, but Linee was in the midfield. Say Tinus Linee and you say Tackling. He tackled the Northern Transvalers, fed by an abundance of possession, so that they battled for their victory.

He was back at Craven Week in 1988, this time in a centre partnership with Chester Williams. That year they lost all three of their matches but to strong teams, including Free State, who had future Springbok centres Pieter Müller and Heinrich Fuls in their side. Linee and Williams tackled and tackled and were the wonder of the week. Right throughout his playing career Linee was renowned for his tackling, and it took him a long way. After leaving Paul Joubert in Paarl, Linee joined the army and became an instructor. He played for Defence, which was a strong club then, and made his provincial debut in 1992. He played 112 matches for WP from 1992-2001 – a popular warrior at Newlands along with his great friend Williams. Linee tackled, for sure, but he had skills beyond that – a strong centre, capable of offloading in the tackle before such a skill became as popular as it is today.

In 1993 he toured the UK with the SA Barbarians and became a Springbok, touring Australia. He played five matches but no Tests, and scored a try in their victory over Sydney. In 1994 he was again chosen, for the tour to Wales, Scotland and Ireland, Kitch Christie's first involvement with the Springboks. Linee played four times and scored a try against Wales A but did not make the Test side.

Dougie Dyers, the great player, coach and administrator, who was involved in Linee's career from under-13 on, said on hearing the news of his death: "Tinus was a great role model for our young players. He showed how it was possible to come from humble beginnings to the top of the game through talent and courage."

Linee eventually left the army and was employed by WPRFU. In 2013 he was diagnosed with motor neuron disease, a horrible, all-encompassing condition. He suffered greatly. Joost van der Westhuizen is the most prominent sufferer of the disease. Rugby did its best to help Linee, including financially.

❖ *Marthinus Linee was born in Paarl on 23 August 1969. He died at his home in Paarl in the night of 2 November 2014, survived by his former wife and present wife, Diana, and her two sons. Apart from his tackling he will be remembered as the most friendly of men, always smiling broadly. There was great sorrow at the brave man's death and an upwelling of sympathy for his family.*

Abie Malan (1935-2014)
Former Springbok captain, selector & manager
ABIE Malan, rugby man and farmer, died from complications following knee replacement surgery. His death came as a shock.

Malan did many things in rugby: he played for and captained the Springboks, became a national selector, and managed the Springboks on an overseas tour, a strong, decisive but genial man. His achievements came a long way from his birthplace, Kenhardt in the Northern Cape, a small town in a sheep-farming area about 190 kilometres from Upington. While still at Hoërskool Kenhardt, Malan played for the town team and for the Oranje Sub-Union. School finished, he went to Stellenbosch in 1954 and remained a Matie for the rest of his life. His last visit was to Ian Kirkpatrick's funeral when he made the long journey from Upington by bus – just to be there for his team-mate's send-off.

In 1955, Malan, a hooker with the attributes of a tough loose forward, played for Maties, was in the Southern Universities team that lost 20-17 to the touring Lions, and made his debut for WP for whom he played till 1960. After that he moved to Vereeniging and played for Transvaal from 1961-65.

At 22 he made his Springbok debut against France. In 1960 he played in three Tests against the All Blacks and toured with the Springboks on their Grand Slam tour to the UK, Ireland and France. It was then that he hurt the knee that was finally operated on in 2014.

Despite his injured knee and the arrival of a replacement, Malan played on in five more matches, including the Tests against Scotland and France. In 1962 he played in three Tests against the Lions and then in 1963 captained the Springboks in the first, second and fourth Tests against a great Wallaby side. He was captain again against Wales in 1964 and then went under Dawie de Villiers on the 1965 tour to Australasia when the Springboks won just one Test out of six. Malan played in two in Australia and the first two in New Zealand. In all he played in 18 Tests, a large number for those times, and in 26 tour matches for the Springboks. He was South Africa's 29th Test captain.

Playing days over, Abie was a Transvaal selector and team manager, then a national selector and in 1992 the manager of the Springbok team that came out of isolation. The Springboks won one of those five Tests and for the manager the French part of their end-of-year tour, which included nine matches, it was a difficult experience indeed. After that Malan went back to his Orange River oasis and farmed.

In 2014, Waratahs and Wallaby prop, Benn Robinson, returned Abie's 1963 playing jersey to its owner from his opponent, Jim Miller, with whom he had swapped at the time.

❖ *Gabriël Frederick Malan, usually called Abe or Abie, was born on 18 November 1935. He died unexpectedly on 23 October 2014, survived by wife Anna, son David (Abie's father's name), daughters Lizmari and Annalee and seven grandchildren.*

Vuyisa Qunta (1949-2014)
Pioneering rugby historian

VUYISA Qunta was a special man. He suffered and bore no rancour. No matter how dire things were, his gentle sense of humour remained. He propagated black awareness, but not to the exclusion of those of a paler hue. And he loved rugby and its players. His knowledge of the game and its history was vast, his turn of phrase refreshing.

Qunta was born in Langa where his father was the principal of Langa High, founded in 1937, which Vuyisa attended before going to Fort Hare in Alice, where many great African leaders increased their knowledge. It was there that Grant Khomo learnt to play rugby and later went on to captain the very first African Springboks in 1950.

At Fort Hare, Qunta was an elegant fullback and got to know many of the great men of African rugby. At the university he also became an activist; his particular passion was the Black Conscious Movement, founded by Steve Biko. He threw in his lot not with the ANC but with AZAPO, the Azanian People's Organisation. Comrade Qunta joined their military wing. His political activities got him expelled from the university and, for a period, he became an exile in Australia. By then he was married to Christine. He worked as a labourer while his wife read law at the University of New South Wales.

His attitude to the military side of the struggle was typical of the gentle man. He said: "While war is a very tough business, if it is a war of liberation it needs compassion. When you fight a people's war, you fight it very hard with strong bones but you keep a soft glove."

They returned to South Africa and Qunta's interest in rugby did not wane. He wrote about it often and made important contributions to two books – *112 Years of Springbok Rugby* and *The Badge*. Both embraced all groups within South African rugby. Qunta also worked for the Department of Sport & Recreation. He maintained his house – originally his father's house – in Langa but spent much of his time in Pretoria.

Asked in 2013 how he would like to be remembered, Qunta said: "Firstly, as a person seeking to create an atmosphere of fairness and peace. I am endowed with a big capacity for affection and real deep compassion. I think this is what has driven my patriotism. I would like to be remembered as someone who gave a lot to heal and grow my country, my community and my family, in that order."

❖ *Vuyisa Qunta was born in Langa, a suburb of Cape Town, in January 1949. After falling seriously ill, he spent a month in One Military Hospital in Pretoria and a week after the amputation of his right leg, he died, on 26 August 2014, survived by Christine and their daughters Yolisa and Nzinga.*

REFEREES

Jonker hangs up his whistle

Recruitment continues to be a challenge

By Paul Dobson & Frikkie van Rensburg

FOR 45-year-old Marius Jonker, 2014 signalled the end of the road as far as onfield refereeing was concerned.

His illustrious career ended with a match in Windhoek between Namibia and Germany, his 25th Test match. The only South African referees who have refereed more Tests are Jonathan Kaplan, Craig Joubert, Mark Lawrence and André Watson. Possibly the highlights of his Test career were Australia vs New Zealand, two Calcutta Cup matches, New Zealand vs Scotland and France, and Ireland vs Australia.

Besides the Tests there were numerous Super Rugby and Currie Cup matches. Jonker has been a familiar figure on the rugby fields, with his accurate, calm and good-humoured way of refereeing. Now there is no more refereeing in the big time, at least not on the field. The 2014 season saw Jonker get a taste of playing TMO and he hopes to be more involved in that in the future, a Test referee who has become a TMO, as Shaun Veldsman has done.

Recruiting and keeping referees continues to be a problem in the climate of criticism and even abuse that persists in South Africa. The worst case in 2014 was in Pretoria where the referee, Marais van Zyl, a member of the Blue Bulls Referees' Society, was assaulted in the carpark after his match at Tuine RFC and ended up in ICU. But great efforts have been made to recruit young referees, starting at school level and using the opportunity of shadowing a top referee on match day. A shortage of referees is now a global problem.

TEST REFEREES IN 2014:
Craig Joubert: Ireland vs Scotland, England vs Ireland, Australia vs France, New Zealand vs Australia and Australia vs New Zealand in Bledisloe Cup matches, Argentina vs New Zealand, USA vs New Zealand, Wales vs Australia, Italy vs Argentina.
Jaco Peyper: France vs Italy, New Zealand vs England, Japan vs Italy, Australia vs New Zealand, Barbarians vs Australia, England vs Samoa.
Stuart Berry: USA vs Canada, Canada vs Namibia.
Lourens van der Merwe: Kenya vs Zimbabwe, Zimbabwe vs Madagascar
Marius Jonker: Namibia vs Germany.
Jaco Kotze: Lesotho vs Swaziland.
Marlize Jordaan: Italy vs England, Spain vs France, Samoa vs Kazhakstan (Women's World Cup).

REFEREES

As fas as other referees are concerned, Deon van Blommestein was a TMO for three Tests in Argentina when the Pumas played Scotland, New Zealand and Australia. Marius van der Westhuizen went to New Zealand for the Junior World Championship. He refereed there, and he, Rodney Bonaparte and Quinton Immelman refereed age-group friendlies when Argentina, England, France and Wales came to South Africa. Again South African referees were prominent on the IRB's World Sevens Series, namely Ben Crouse, Rasta Rasivhenge, Marius van der Westhuizen.

A new move in 2014 saw Jaco van Heerden off to France for two matches, one in Pro D2, which is the second division of professional rugby in France, and one in the Top 14, the great Paris derby between Stade Francais and Racing-Metro. During 2015's Currie Cup season, France will send an exchange referee to South Africa for two matches.

REFEREES IN FINALS:

Super Rugby: Craig Joubert **Currie Cup:** Craig Joubert **Vodacom Cup:** Jaco van Heerden **Under-21:** Lesego Legoete **Under-19:** Rodney Bonaparte **Community Cup:** Quinton Immelman **Varsity Cup:** Marius van der Westhuizen and Cwengile Jadezweni **Varsity Shield:** Quinton Immelman **Varsity Young Guns:** Lesego Legoete **Koshuis Final:** Francois Pretorius **Final Match Craven Week:** Oregopotse Rametsi **Final Match Academy Week:** AJ Jacobs **Final Match Grant Khomo Week:** Ruhan Meiring

SA REFEREES' AWARDS:

Honorary Life Membership: Gabriel Pappas **Referees' Referee of the Year:** Craig Joubert
Most improved Referee of the Year: Quinton Immelman
Referee with Exceptional Performance in 2014: Jaco van Heerden
Ratel Awards: Marius van der Westhuizen, Willie Vos, Stuart Berry, Kobus Wessels

PANELS IN 2014:

Super Rugby (chosen by SANZAR):
Stuart Berry, Jason Jaftha, Craig Joubert, Jaco Peyper, Lourens an der Merwe, Marius van der Westhuizen

Elite:
Stuart Berry, Christie du Preez, Jason Jaftha, Marius Jonker, Craig Joubert, Lesego Legoete, Jaco Peyper, Rasta Rasivhenge, Marius van der Westhuizen, Lourens van der Merwe, Jaco van Heerden

National:
Rodney Bonaparte (Eastern Province), Ben Crouse (Blue Bulls),Gerrie de Bruin (Blue Bulls), Daniel Fortuin (Western Province), Stephan Geldenhuys (Blue Bulls), Quinton Immelman (Western Province), Cwengile Jadezweni (Western Province), Lusanda Jam (Border), Tiaan Jonker (Golden Lions),Jaco Kotze (Free State), Sindile Mayende (Border),Eduan Nel (Golden Lions), Tahla Ntshakaza (Golden Lions), Francois Pretorius (Western Province), Jaco Pretorius (Valke), Lihan Pretorius (Valke), Oregopotse Rametsi (Leopards), Archie Sehlako (Natal)

Women's:
Aimee Barrett (Western Province), Larentia Fred (South Western Districts), Marlize Jordaan (Free State), Ashleigh Murray (Golden Lions), Henchalla Oerson (Boland), Elizna Wilsnagh (Valke)

Assistant Referees:
Stefan Breytenbach (Pumas), Francois de Bruin (Griquas), Linston Manuels (Boland), Sieg van Staden (Valke), Marc van Zyl (Western Province), Cobus Wessels (Blue Bulls)

TMOs:
Johan Greeff (Blue Bulls), Marius Jonker (KwaZulu-Natal), Deon van Blommestein (Western Province), Shaun Veldsman (Boland), Willie Vos (Golden Lions)

REFEREES

PERFORMANCE REVIEWERS:
National:
Mark Lawrence, Neville Heilbron, Keith Hendricks (Boland), Jacques Hugo (Eastern Province), Dennis Immelman (Western Province), Pierre Oelofse (Valke), Willie Roos (Valke), Deon van Blommestein (Western Province), Banks Yantolo (Border)

Regional:
Eska Claasen (South Western Districts), Theuns Janse van Vuuren (Golden Lions), Allan O'Connell (Natal), Kim Smit (Pumas), Mngqibisa Thuso (Western Province), Pieter White (Blue Bulls)

COACHES
National:
Mark Lawrence, Balie Swart, Deon van Blommestein, Johan Zurich

Academy:
Manager: Eugene Daniels, Sieg van Staden, Jamiel Panday

Peer Coaches:
Craig Joubert, Jaco Peyper

Timekeepers:
Albert Mocke (Free State), Gabriel Pappas, Kat Swanepoel (Griquas), Pieter van der Merwe (Golden Lions)

Test Referees

1. **Griffin, John** – 1 Test 1891: SA vs BI (1).
2. **Frames, Percy Ross** – 1 Test 1891: SA vs BI (2).
3. **Castens, Herbert Hayton** (HH or Fatty) – 1 Test 1891: SA vs BI (3).
4. **Kemsley, Henry Rickon** – 1 Test 1896: SA vs BI (1).
5. **Beves, Gordon** – 1 Test 1896: SA vs BI (2).
6. **Bisset, William Molteno** (Bill) – 1 Test 1896: SA vs BI (3).
7. **Richards, Alfred Renfrew** (Alf) – 1 Test 1896: SA vs BI (4).
8. **Donaldson, William Patrick** (Bill) – 1 Test 1903: SA vs BI (1).
9. **Day, Percy Ware** – 1 Test 1903: SA vs BI (2).
10. **Anderson, John Henry** (Biddy) – 1 Test 1903: SA vs BI (3).
11. **Stanton, Reginald William** (Reg) – 3 Tests 1910: SA vs BI (1,2,3).
12. **Oakley, Lionel David** – 1 Test 1924: SA vs BI (1).
13. **Neser, Vivian Herbert** (Boet or Knoppies) – 9 Tests 1924: SA vs BI (2). 1928: SA vs NZ (1,2,3,4). 1933: SA vs A (1,2,3,5).
14. **Millar, William Alexander** (Billy) – 2 Tests 1924: SA vs BI (3,4).
15. **Van der Horst, Alexander Wilhelm Archibald** (Alex) – 1 Test 1933: SA vs A (4).
16. **Horak, Adriaan Marthinus** (Att) – 1 Test 1938: SA vs BI (1).
17. **Strasheim, Johannes Jacobus** (Johnny) – 1 Test 1938: SA vs BI (2).
18. **Pretorius, Nicolaas Francois** (Nic) – 1 Test 1938: SA vs BI (3).
19. **Hofmeyr, Edwin William Neilson** (Eddie) – 4 Tests 1949: SA vs NZ (1,3). 1961: SA vs A (2). 1963: SA vs A (1).
20. **Burmeister, Ralph Douglas** – 8 Tests 1949: SA vs NZ (2,4). 1953: SA vs A (1). 1955: SA vs BI (1,3). 1960: SA vs NZ (3,4). 1961: SA vs A (1).
21. **Ackermann, Chrisman Joël** (Chris) – 4 Tests 1953: SA vs A (2,3). 1955: SA vs BI (4). 1958: F (2).
22. **Louw, Lambertus Petrus Johannes** (Lammie) – 1 Test 1953: SA vs A (4).
23. **Slabber, Michael John** (Mike) – 2 Tests 1955: SA vs BI (2). 1960: SA vs NZ (2).
24. **Strasheim, Erdam Albert** (Bertie) – 7 Tests 1958: SA vs F (1). 1960: SA vs S; SA vs NZ (1). 1962: SA vs BI (1,3). 1964: SA vs F. 1967: SA vs F (1). 1968: SA vs BI (4).
25. **Calitz, Pieter Melt Hertzog** (Piet) – 1 Test 1961: SA vs I.
26. **Carlson, Kenneth Robert Victor** (Ken) – 1 Test 1962: SA vs BI (2).
27. **Myburgh, Pieter Abraham** (Toy) – 4 Tests 1962: SA vs BI (4). 1963: SA vs A (2,3,4).
28. **Engelbrecht, Gert Kotzé** (Kallie) – 1 Test 1964: SA vs W.
29. **Baise, Max** – 7 Tests 1967: SA vs F (2,3). 1968: SA vs BI (1,3). 1969: SA vs A (2). 1974: SA vs BI (1,4).
30. **Robbertse, Pieter** (Piet) – 4 Tests 1967: SA vs F (4). 1969: SA vs A (1). 1970: SA vs NZ (1,3).
31. **Schoeman, Johannes Petrus Jacobus** (Hansie) – 1 Test 1968: SA vs BI (2).
32. **Baise, Solomon Louis** (Solly) – 1 Test 1969: SA vs A (3).
33. **De Bruyn, Casparus Johannes** (Cas) – 3 Tests 1969: SA vs A (4). 1974: SA vs BI (2,3).
34. **Malan, Wynand Charl** – 3 Tests 1970: SA vs NZ (2). 1971: SA vs F (1,2).
35. **Woolley, Thomas Herbert** (Bert) – 1 Test 1970: SA vs NZ (4).
36. **Moolman, Justus de Jager** (Justus) – 1 Test 1972: SA vs E.
37. **Gourlay, Ian Watson** (Ian) – 1 Test 1976: SA vs NZ (1).
38. **Bezuidenhout, Gert Peter** (Gert) – 3 Tests 1976: SA vs NZ (2,3,4).
39. **Gouws, Johannes Stephanus**

REFEREES

(Johan) - 1 Test 1977: SA vs World XV.

40 **Strydom, Stefanus** (Steve) - 11 Tests 1979: Arg vs A (1 & 2). 1980: Arg vs WT; U vs Par; Braz vs Par; U vs Chile; 1982: SA vs S Am (1). 1985: S vs I; F vs W. 1986: F vs NZ (2 & 3).

41 **Muller, Frans** (Fransie) - 3 Tests 1982: SA vs S Am (2). 1988: S vs F; F vs I.

42 **Coetzer, Gerrit** (Gerrit) - 1 Test 1988: Uru vs Arg.

43 **Burger, Frederick** (Freek) - 10 Tests 1989: F vs A (1,2). 1990: S vs Arg. 1992: S vs F; F vs I; Arg vs F (1,2). 1993: S vs NZ; E vs NZ. 1994: HK vs PNG.

44 **Adams, Albert Louie** (Albert) - 4 Tests 1991: US vs F (1,2); Nam vs Z (1,2).

45 **Rogers, Ian** (Ian) - 10 Tests 1993: Z vs W (1); Arab Gulf vs Ken; Ken vs Nam. 1994: C vs F; C vs W; A vs It (1,2). 1995: E vs WS (2); [I vs W (2)]. 1997: Arg vs E (1). 1998 Tun vs Z.

46 **Anderson, Ian Charles** (Ian) - 3 Tests 1993: Z vs W (2); Nam vs Arab Gulf; Z vs Arab Gulf.

47 **Neethling, Stefanus Johannes** (Stef) - 3 Tests 1993: IC vs Mor. 1994: E vs R. 1995: [I vs J].

48 **Henning, Willem Taljaardt Stopforth** (Tappe) - 12 Tests 1995: S vs WS. 1996: NZ vs WS; E vs Arg. 1997: S vs A. 1998: T vs Sam. 1999: U vs P. 2000: Sam vs It. 2001: E vs F; A vs NZ (2). 2002: NZ vs I (2); W vs NZ. 2004: Fiji vs Sam.

49 **Watson, André Jacobus** (André) - 27 Tests 1996: A vs C. 1997: I vs F; E vs A (2). 1998: I vs S; A vs E (1); A vs S (1); F vs A. 1999: W vs E; A vs I (1,2); [E vs It; A vs US; A vs F-RWC-FINAL]. 2000: Arg vs I; A vs NZ (1); E vs A. 2001: A vs BI (1); I vs NZ. 2002: F vs E; A vs NZ (2). 2003: I vs F; NZ vs F (1); [I vs Arg; NZ vs W; E vs A (2) RWC-FINAL]. 2004: A vs PI; Andorra vs Nor.

50 **Spannenberg, Carl Moses** (Carl) - 6 Tests 1996: It vs W (2). 1997: T vs Z; Ken vs Arab Gulf. 1998: Nam vs Z; U vs US. 2000: Z vs Nam.

51 **Kaplan, Jonathan Isaac** (Jonathan) - 70 Tests 1996: Z vs Nam. 1997: Bots vs Arab Gulf; Arg vs E (2). 1998: Fiji vs T; G vs R. 2000: It vs S; NZ vs A (2); F vs NZ. 2001: It vs I; A vs BI (2); W vs I. 2002: NZ vs A (1); E vs NZ; Russ vs Sp. 2003: I vs E; NZ vs A (2); [I vs R; S vs US; E vs Sam; F vs I]. 2004: NZ vs E (1); A vs NZ (2); F vs Arg. 2005: I vs E; S vs W; T vs Fiji; NZ vs BI (3); I vs NZ. 2006: NZ vs I; NZ vs A; I vs W; S vs F. 2007: E vs F; It vs I; A vs W; SA vs Nam; E vs USA; Sam vs T. C vs J; S vs It; F vs E. 2008: I vs It; S vs E; NZ vs E; Ken vs Uga; A vs NZ; Fr vs Arg; W vs NZ. 2009: W vs E, S vs I, Fj vs Sam; Fj vs J; A vs NZ (1); I vs A; E vs NZ. 2010: W vs F; I vs S; NZ vs W; Z vs Bots; Z vs Mad; NZ vs A; F vs Arg. 2011: W vs I; [T vs Can; E vs Geor; Can vs Jap; I vs It]; A vs W. 2013: Nam vs Z; Nam vs Ken.

52 **Schoonwinkel, Arnold Jacobus** (Arrie) - 1 Test 1997: T vs Nam.

53 **Meuwesen, Johannes Coenraad** (Johann) - 5 Tests 1994: Neth vs Czech Rep. 1995: SA vs WS. 1996: SA vs Fj. 1997: Tun vs Ken. 1998: Z vs W.

54 **Lawrence, Steven Mark** (Mark) – 30 Tests 2000: Fiji vs It. 2001: It vs Nam; F vs Fiji. 2002: It vs E; US vs Chile; S vs Fiji. 2003: A vs W; F vs E (2). 2004: W vs It; A vs S (2); SA VS NZ (2R). 2005: E vs It; E vs Sam. 2007: Ug vs Nam. 2008: E vs I; F vs W; A vs NZ; NZ vs A; I vs NZ. 2009: E vs It; F vs W; A vs NZ (3); Tun vs Nam. 2010: E vs I; Ken vs Ug; A vs NZ; U vs Rom; I vs Arg. 2011: Can vs USA; USA vs Can.

55 **Turner, Daniel Andrew** (Andy) - 9 Tests 2000: Nam vs Z. 2001: US vs E; It vs Fiji. 2002: Nam vs Tun; S vs R. 2003: Kor vs T; W vs R. 2004: It vs E; C vs F.

56 **Daniels, Eugene Clive** (Eugene) - 5 Tests 2001: Nam vs Z; Mad vs Ken; Ug vs Bots. 2004: Bots vs Swazi; Nam vs Mor.

57 **Mzomba, Louis** (Louis) - 10 Tests 2001: Swazi vs Mad. 2002: Ug vs Z; Ug vs Cam. 2003: Ug vs Zam; Ug vs Ken; Mad vs Z; Swazi vs Bots; Bots vs Ken. 2006: Ken vs Tun. 2007: IC v Ken.

58 **Katzenellenbogen, Michael Labe** (Michael) - 2 Tests 2002: Nam vs Mad. 2003: Ug vs Z.

59 **Joubert, Craig** (Craig) - 55 Tests 2003: Nam vs Ug. 2005: US vs Wal; Tga vs Sam. 2006: Tga vs Fji; Ur vs Chile, It vs Arg. 2007: Fra vs Sco; NZ vs Fra. 2008: Eng vs Wal; Aus vs NZ, Fra vs Aus. 2009: Ire vs Eng; Nam vs IC; NZ vs Aus (1); NZ vs Aus (3); Wal vs NZ. 2010: Ire vs Wal; Zim vs Ken; Aus vs NZ; Eng vs Aus. 2011: Eng vs It; Fra vs Wal; NZ vs Aus; Ire vs Fra; [Ire vs USA; Fra vs Can; Ire vs Rus; Eng vs Sco; Ire vs Wal; Aus vs NZ-RWC-SEMI; NZ vs Fra-RWC-FINAL]. 2012: Ire vs It; Wal vs Fra; Mexico vs Jamaica; Aus vs Wal (1); Aus vs Wal (3); Arg vs Aus; Aus vs NZ; Wal vs NZ. 2013: Eng vs Fra; Sco vs Wal; Sam vs It; Aus vs B & I (2); Aus vs NZ; NZ vs Aus; Eng vs NZ. 2014: Ire vs Sco; Eng vs Ire; Aus vs Fra; Arg vs NZ; Aus vs NZ; USA vs NZ; Wal vs Aus; It vs Arg.

60 **Veldsman, Shaun Ivan** (Shaun) - 3 Tests 2003: Nam vs Sam; Arg vs C. 2004: Nam vs Ken.

61 **Roos, Hendrik Willem** (Willie) - 9 Tests 2004: Bots vs Tanz. 2005: Zam vs Senegal. 2006: Nam vs Ken; Ug vs Mad. 2007: Sam vs Tga; Mad vs IC; Ug vs Mad. 2008: Jpn vs Tga; Ug vs Ken.

62 **Fortuin, Jerome Christopher** (JC) - 3 Tests 2005: Ken vs Mad; Zim vs Ug. 2006: Ug vs IC.

63 **Jonker, Marius** (Marius) - 28 Tests 2005: Ug vs Z; Mauritius vs Burkina Faso. 2006: Fiji vs It; It vs Can; I vs Aus. 2007: E vs S; A vs NZ; It vs P; Fj vs J; S vs NZ. 2008: W vs F; A vs F; E vs A. 2009: E vs S; NZ vs F; Ug vs Ken; I vs Fj; Nam vs Tun. 2010: S vs E; Z vs Ug; I vs NZ. 2011: Fj vs T; Fj vs Sam; A vs Sam. 2012: Nam vs Zim; Nam vs Sp. 2014 (2): U vs Ken; Nam vs Ger.

64 **Legoete, Lesego** (Pro) - 5 Tests 2008: R vs U; Nam vs Zim. 2009: Ug vs Tun. 2013: Ug vs Ken; Mada vs Ug.

65 **Peyper, Jaco** (Jaco) - 19 Tests 2011: Ken vs Zim; Nig vs Maur. 2012: Ug vs Ken; A vs S; Fj vs Sco; Sam vs Sco; Arg vs NZ; Rom vs Jpn; Ire vs Arg. 2013: Sco vs It; NZ vs Aus; Arg vs NZ; Fra vs NZ; Sco vs Aus. 2014: Fra vs It; NZ vs Eng; Jpn vs It; Aus vs NZ; Eng vs Sam.

66 **Van der Merwe, Lourens** (Lourens) – 8 Tests 2012: Ug vs Ken; Ken vs Ug; Rom vs Rus; It vs Aus. 2013: Jpn vs Wal; Zim vs Mada; Ken vs Zim; Geor vs Can.

67 **Japhta, Jason Jamaine** (Jason) – 1 Test 2012: Sp vs Zim.

68 **Berry, Stuart** (Stuart) – 4 Tests 2013: Jpn vs Aus. 2014: USA vs Can; Can vs Nam; Rom vs Jpn.

69 **Kotze, Jaco** (Jaco) – 1 Test 2014: Les vs Swazi.

70 **Geldenhuys, Stephan** (Stephan) – 1 Test 2014: Swazi vs Les.

REFEREES

SOUTH AFRICAN REFEREES IN FIRST-CLASS RUGBY - 2014

REFEREE	International	Super Rugby	Currie Cup Premier Division, Qualifiers & First Division	Vodacom Cup	Other First-Class	Total
Federico Anselmi (Argentina)	–	–	2	2	–	4
Stuart Berry	3	5	5	1	–	14
Rodney Bonaparte	–	–	–	4	–	4
Ben Crouse	–	–	10	3	–	13
Gerrie de Bruin	–	–	–	2	–	2
Christie du Preez	–	–	3	4	–	7
Daniel Fortuin	–	–	–	1	–	1
Stephan Geldenhuys	1	–	–	4	–	5
Quinton Immelman	–	–	7	6	–	13
Cwengile Jadwezweni	–	–	–	1	–	1
Marius Jonker	2	–	7	2	–	11
Craig Joubert	8	15	7	1	–	31
Jaco Kotze	1	–	–	2	–	3
Lesego Legoete	–	–	11	5	–	16
Eduan Nel	–	–	–	1	–	1
Tahla Ntshakaza	–	–	–	4	–	4
Jaco Peyper	5	14	6	1	Barbarians vs Australia	27
Francois Pretorius	–	–	–	3	–	3
Oregopotse Rametsi	–	–	–	2	–	2
Rasta Rasivhenge	–	–	6	2	–	8
Archie Sehlako	–	–	–	1	–	1
Juan Sylvestre (Argentina)	–	–	–	2	–	2
Lourens van der Merwe	–	2	4	1	EP Kings vs Wales	8
Marius van der Westhuizen	–	4	7	3	–	14
Jaco van Heerden	–	–	7	5	–	12
Shaun Veldsman	–	–	–	1	–	1
26 Referees	20	40	82	64	3	209

INTERNATIONAL MATCHES PLAYED IN 2014*

*This list of 233 matches excludes 46 RWC Qualifying matches played during 2014. See Rugby World Cup section for separate list.

DATE	HOME	RESULT	AWAY	VENUE
01/02/2014	Wales	23-15	Italy	Cardiff
01/02/2014	France	26-24	England	Paris
02/02/2014	Ireland	28-6	Scotland	Dublin
08/02/2014	Ireland	26-3	Wales	Dublin
08/02/2014	Scotland	0-20	England	Murrayfield
09/02/2014	France	30-10	Italy	Paris
21/02/2014	Wales	27-6	France	Cardiff
22/02/2014	Italy	20-21	Scotland	Roma
22/02/2014	England	13-10	Ireland	Twickenham
08/03/2014	Ireland	46-7	Italy	Dublin
08/03/2014	Scotland	17-19	France	Murrayfield
09/03/2014	England	29-18	Wales	Twickenham
15/03/2014	Italy	11-52	England	Roma
15/03/2014	Wales	51-3	Scotland	Cardiff
15/03/2014	France	20-22	Ireland	Paris
29/03/2014	Andorra	23-13	Serbia-Montenegro	Andorra-la-Vella
05/04/2014	Poland	12-21	Moldova	Siedlce
05/04/2014	Germany	76-12	Czech Republic	Heidelburg
05/04/2014	Malta	10-33	Netherlands	Paola
12/04/2014	Moldova	28-8	Ukraine	Chisinau
12/04/2014	Netherlands	45-13	Croatia	Amsterdam
12/04/2014	Switzerland	14-29	Malta	Winterthur
12/04/2014	Israel	20-16	Andorra	Netanya
12/04/2014	Serbia-Montenegro	19-33	Denmark	Belgrade
12/04/2014	Hungary	23-12	Austria	Esztergom
12/04/2014	Slovenia	43-17	Bulgaria	Ljubliana
19/04/2014	Croatia	25-21	Lithuania	Zagreb
19/04/2014	Bosnia Herzegovina	43-0	Norway	Zenica
23/04/2014	United Arab Emirates	13-30	Singapore	Dubai
26/04/2014	Ukraine	29-28	Poland	Lvov
26/04/2014	Czech Republic	37-19	Moldova	Prague
26/04/2014	Sweden	20-45	Germany	Stockholm
26/04/2014	Lithuania	24-18	Switzerland	Siauliai
26/04/2014	Latvia	29-22	Israel	Riga
26/04/2014	Bulgaria	15-46	Cyprus	Sofia
26/04/2014	Greece	8-52	Luxembourg	Thessaloniki
26/04/2014	Paraguay	10-34	Uruguay	Asuncion
26/04/2014	Brazil	24-16	Chile	Sao Paulo
26/04/2014	Mexico	56-9	Bermuda	Huixquilucan
03/05/2014	Denmark	9-16	Latvia	Odense
03/05/2014	Austria	20-8	Slovenia	Vienna
03/05/2014	Brazil	9-34	Uruguay	Bento Goncalves
03/05/2014	Chile	22-18	Paraguay	Concepcion
10/05/2014	Kazakhstan	37-8	Chinese Taipei	Hong Kong
10/05/2014	Norway	45-23	Greece	Tonsberg
10/05/2014	Luxembourg	27-7	Finland	Luxembourg
10/05/2014	USA South	33-6	Bermuda	Atlanta
10/05/2014	Curacao	56-7	St Lucia	Sint Michiel

INTERNATIONAL MATCHES PLAYED IN 2014*

DATE	HOME	RESULT	AWAY	VENUE
10/05/2014	Uruguay	55-13	Chile	Montevideo
10/05/2014	Paraguay	31-24	Brazil	Asuncion
17/05/2014	Cyprus	46-13	Hungary	Paphos
17/05/2014	Barbados	19-48	Guyana	Bridgetown
17/05/2014	Bahamas	18-33	Mexico	Nassau
17/05/2014	British Virgin Isles	22-24	St Vincent & Grenadines	Road Town, Tortola
17/05/2014	Jamaica	10-6	Turks & Caicos Islands	Kingston
17/05/2014	Uruguay	9-65	Argentina	Paysandu
20/05/2014	Malaysia	43-22	Iran	Doha
20/05/2014	Qatar	24-11	Thanet Wanderers	Doha
23/05/2014	Thanet Wanderers	23-26	Iran	Doha
23/05/2014	Qatar	22-31	Malaysia	Doha
24/05/2014	Trinidad & Tobago	34-5	Barbados	Port of Spain
25/05/2014	Chile	12-73	Argentina	Santiago
29/05/2014	Laos	10-48	Guam	Vientiane
29/05/2014	Indonesia	6-10	China	Vientiane
30/05/2014	Japan	33-14	Samoa	Tokyo
31/05/2014	Laos	10-11	Indonesia	Vientiane
31/05/2014	Guam	10-41	China	Vientiane
31/05/2014	Finland	29-25	Bosnia Herzegovina	Turku
31/05/2014	Turks & Caicos Islands	11-13	Bahamas	Providenciales
03/06/2014	Rwanda	15-6	Burundi	Kigali
07/06/2014	Rwanda	5-9	DR Congo	Kigali
07/06/2014	Bosnia Herzegovina	12-26	Austria	Tesanj
07/06/2014	Bermuda	3-24	Cayman Islands	Devonshire, Hamilton
07/06/2014	Guyana	15-8	Trinidad & Tobago	Georgetown
07/06/2014	Jamaica	8-34	Mexico	Ewarton
07/06/2014	Canada	25-34	Japan	Vancouver
07/06/2014	Samoa	18-18	Tonga	Apia
07/06/2014	Australia	50-23	France	Brisbane
07/06/2014	United States	6-24	Scotland	Houston
07/06/2014	New Zealand	20-15	England	Auckland
07/06/2014	Fiji	25-14	Italy	Suva
07/06/2014	Argentina	17-29	Ireland	Resistencia
08/06/2014	St Vincent & Grenadines	12-19	Curacao	Kingstown
08/06/2014	British Virgin Isles	18-29	St Lucia	Road Town, Tortola
10/06/2014	Tunisia	22-14	Senegal	Tunis
10/06/2014	Ivory Coast	22-19	Uganda	Tunis
13/06/2014	Emerging Ireland	66-0	Russia	Bucharest
13/06/2014	Romania	34-16	Uruguay	Bucharest
14/06/2014	Tunisia	26-6	Ivory Coast	Tunis
14/06/2014	Uganda	31-32	Senegal	Tunis
14/06/2014	Cayman Islands	30-34	USA South	George Town
14/06/2014	United States	29-37	Japan	Carson, USA
14/06/2014	Fiji	45-17	Tonga	Lautoka
14/06/2014	Georgia	23-13	Spain	Tbilisi
14/06/2014	Emerging Italy	20-45	Argentina Jaguars	Tbilisi
14/06/2014	Australia	6-0	France	Melbourne

INTERNATIONAL MATCHES

DATE	HOME	RESULT	AWAY	VENUE
14/06/2014	New Zealand	28-27	England	Dunedin
14/06/2014	Canada	17-19	Scotland	Toronto
14/06/2014	South Africa	38-16	Wales	Durban
14/06/2014	Samoa	15-0	Italy	Apia
14/06/2014	Argentina	17-23	Ireland	Tucuman
15/06/2014	Botswana	87-0	Swaziland	Gaborone
15/06/2014	South Africa XV	61-17	Mauritius	Gaborone
15/06/2014	Niger	20-30	Zambia	Gaborone
17/06/2014	Brunei	13-38	Mongolia	Bandar Seri Begawan
18/06/2014	Botswana	9-54	South Africa XV	Gaborone
18/06/2014	Niger	61-10	Swaziland	Gaborone
18/06/2014	Zambia	17-67	Mauritius	Gaborone
18/06/2014	Emerging Ireland	51-3	Uruguay	Bucharest
18/06/2014	Romania	20-18	Russia	Bucharest
18/06/2014	Georgia	16-26	Argentina Jaguares	Tbilisi
18/06/2014	Emerging Italy	37-0	Spain	Tbilisi
19/06/2014	India	17-23	Uzbekistan	Lahore
19/06/2014	Pakistan	3-17	Lebanon	Lahore
19/06/2014	Cambodia	5-49	Mongolia	Bandar Seri Begawan
20/06/2014	Argentina	19-21	Scotland	Cordoba
21/06/2014	Brunei	20-25	Cambodia	Bandar Seri Begawan
21/06/2014	Botswana	66-14	Zambia	Gaborone
21/06/2014	Mauritius	134-0	Swaziland	Gaborone
21/06/2014	South Africa XV	86-10	Niger	Gaborone
21/06/2014	Latvia	10-16	Croatia	Rida
21/06/2014	Curacao	42-12	British Virgin Isles	Sint Michiel
21/06/2014	St Lucia	26-22	St Vincent & Grenadines	Castries
21/06/2014	United States	38-35	Canada	Sacramento
21/06/2014	Fiji	13-18	Samoa	Suva
21/06/2014	Australia	39-13	France	Sydney
21/06/2014	New Zealand	36-13	England	Hamilton
21/06/2014	South Africa	31-30	Wales	Nelspruit
21/06/2014	Japan	26-23	Italy	Tokyo
22/06/2014	Pakistan	7-25	India	Lahore
22/06/2014	Uzbekistan	19-20	Lebanon	Lahore
22/06/2014	Romania	10-31	Emerging Ireland	Bucharest
22/06/2014	Russia	6-13	Uruguay	Bucharest
22/06/2014	Georgia	34-10	Emerging Italy	Tbilisi
22/06/2014	Argentina Jaguares	41-7	Spain	Tbilisi
28/06/2014	Mexico	96-0	Turks & Caicos Islands	Mexico City
28/06/2014	Bahamas	17-10	Jamaica	Nassau
28/06/2014	USA South	27-30	Guyana	Atlanta
28/06/2014	South Africa	55-6	Scotland	Port Elizabeth
11/07/2014	Peru	45-0	Ecuador	Chiclayo
12/07/2014	Uganda	21-14	Kenya	Kampala
13/07/2014	Peru	36-8	Ecuador	Chiclayo
19/07/2014	Kenya	34-0	Uganda	Kasarani, Nairobi
16/08/2014	Australia	12-12	New Zealand	Sydney

INTERNATIONAL MATCHES

DATE	HOME	RESULT	AWAY	VENUE
16/08/2014	South Africa	13-6	Argentina	Pretoria
23/08/2014	New Zealand	51-20	Australia	Auckland
23/08/2014	Argentina	31-33	South Africa	Salta
31/08/2014	Venezuela	33-28	Peru	Antioquia
31/08/2014	Colombia	112-0	Ecuador	Antioquia
03/09/2014	Ecuador	3-68	Venezuela	Antioquia
03/09/2014	Colombia	56-6	Peru	Antioquia
06/09/2014	Poland	29-17	Sweden	Warsaw
06/09/2014	Ecuador	17-24	Peru	Antioquia
06/09/2014	Colombia	27-10	Venezuela	Antioquia
06/09/2014	Australia	24-23	South Africa	Perth
06/09/2014	New Zealand	28-9	Argentina	Napier
13/09/2014	Australia	32-25	Argentina	Gold Coast
13/09/2014	New Zealand	14-10	South Africa	Wellington
20/09/2014	Curacao	0-29	Barbados	Willemstad
27/09/2014	South Africa	28-10	Australia	Cape Town
27/09/2014	Argentina	13-34	New Zealand	Buenos Aires
04/10/2014	Finland	32-10	Norway	Helsinki
04/10/2014	Bosnia Herzegovina	59-12	Bulgaria	Zenica
04/10/2014	Estonia	59-12	Belarus	Tallin
04/10/2014	South Africa	27-25	New Zealand	Johannesburg
04/10/2014	Argentina	21-17	Australia	Mendoza
05/10/2014	Guatemala	23-17	El Salvador	Panama
05/10/2014	Panama	10-18	Costa Rica	Panama
08/10/2014	Panama	19-24	Guatemala	Panama
08/10/2014	Costa Rica	14-25	El Salvador	Panama
11/10/2014	Austria	29-27	Denmark	Vienna
11/10/2014	Panama	3-29	El Salvador	Panama
11/10/2014	Costa Rica	22-17	Guatemala	Panama
18/10/2014	Poland	9-8	Netherlands	Warsaw
18/10/2014	Sweden	0-45	Ukraine	Enkoping
18/10/2014	Andorra	15-34	Lithuania	Andorra-la-Vella
18/10/2014	Slovenia	48-3	Serbia-Montenegro	Ljubliana
18/10/2014	Norway	20-12	Finland	Oslo
18/10/2014	Australia	28-29	New Zealand	Brisbane
25/10/2014	Israel	18-29	Switzerland	Netanya
25/10/2014	Lithuania	38-29	Hungary	Siauliai
25/10/2014	Serbia-Montenegro	0-36	Luxembourg	Belgrade
25/10/2014	Denmark	10-16	Slovenia	Odense
25/10/2014	Turkey	25-34	Bosnia Herzegovina	Edirne
25/10/2014	Thailand	33-16	Malaysia	Bangkok
28/10/2014	Thailand	12-29	Malaysia	Bangkok
29/10/2014	Namibia	58-20	Germany	Windhoek
01/11/2014	Switzerland	14-27	Czech Republic	Nyon
01/11/2014	Malta	31-26	Croatia	Paola
01/11/2014	Cyprus	30-10	Andorra	Paphos
01/11/2014	Bulgaria	26-19	Turkey	Pernik
01/11/2014	United States	6-74	New Zealand	Chicago

INTERNATIONAL RUGBY IN 2014

INTERNATIONAL MATCHES

DATE	HOME	RESULT	AWAY	VENUE
02/11/2014	Hungary	14-16	Latvia	Esztergom
07/11/2014	Canada	17-13	Namibia	Colwyn Bay
08/11/2014	Moldova	29-15	Ukraine	Chisinau
08/11/2014	Czech Republic	27-13	Malta	Prague
08/11/2014	Croatia	31-20	Israel	Split
08/11/2014	Luxembourg	18-13	Austria	Luxembourg
08/11/2014	Ireland	29-15	South Africa	Dublin
08/11/2014	England	21-24	New Zealand	Twickenham
08/11/2014	Scotland	41-31	Argentina	Murrayfield
08/11/2014	Wales	28-33	Australia	Cardiff
08/11/2014	France	40-15	Fiji	Marseille
08/11/2014	Georgia	9-23	Tonga	Vake, Tbilisi
08/11/2014	Italy	24-13	Samoa	Ascoli Piceno
08/11/2014	Romania	17-27	United States	Bucharest
08/11/2014	Hong Kong	10-31	Russia	Hong Kong
14/11/2014	Italy	18-20	Argentina	Genova
14/11/2014	Samoa	23-13	Canada	Vannes
15/11/2014	Moldova	48-25	Poland	Chisinau
15/11/2014	Belgium	25-10	Ukraine	Namur
15/11/2014	Latvia	39-20	Cyprus	Riga
15/11/2014	England	28-31	South Africa	Twickenham
15/11/2014	Scotland	16-24	New Zealand	Murrayfield
15/11/2014	Wales	17-13	Fiji	Cardiff
15/11/2014	France	29-26	Australia	Paris
15/11/2014	Tonga	40-12	United States	Gloucester
15/11/2014	Romania	13-18	Japan	Bucharest
15/11/2014	Hong Kong	27-39	Russia	Hong Kong
16/11/2014	Ireland	49-7	Georgia	Dublin
21/11/2014	Fiji	20-14	United States	Vannes
22/11/2014	Moldova	57-8	Sweden	Chisinau
22/11/2014	Ireland	26-23	Australia	Dublin
22/11/2014	England	28-9	Samoa	Twickenham
22/11/2014	Scotland	37-12	Tonga	Kilmarnock
22/11/2014	Italy	6-22	South Africa	Padova
22/11/2014	Wales	16-34	New Zealand	Cardiff
22/11/2014	France	13-18	Argentina	Paris
22/11/2014	Portugal	29-20	Namibia	Lisbon
22/11/2014	Romania	18-9	Canada	Bucharest
23/11/2014	Georgia	35-24	Japan	Vake, Tbilisi
29/11/2014	England	26-17	Australia	Twickenham
29/11/2014	Wales	12-6	South Africa	Cardiff

INTERNATIONAL RUGBY IN 2014

South Africans Capped by Other Countries – 1896-2014

Compiled by Stuart Farmer
† *Indicates also played for South Africa.*

Abbott, SRD (Stuart) - England - 9 Tests - 2003-2006
Abendanon, NJ (Nick) - England - 2 tests - 2007
†Allan, J (John) - Scotland - 9 Tests - 1990-1991
Alexander, M (Matt) - USA - 25 Tests - 1995-1998
Anderson HJ (Henry) - Ireland - 4 Tests - 1903-1906
Antoni, JA (Giovani) - Italy - 2 Tests - 2001
Appleford, GN (Geoff) - England - 1 Test - 2002
Badenhorst, RS (Skipper) - Namibia - 2 Tests - 2007
Barnard, J (Barries) - Namibia - 22 Tests - 1990-1993
Barritt, BM (Brad) - England - 22 Tests - 2013-2014
Bell, PJD (Patrick) - USA - 7 Tests - 2006
Binikos, A (Andrew) - Cyprus -
Black, BH (Brian) - England - 10 Tests - 1930-1933
Blom, A (André) - USA - 13 Tests - 1998-2000
Blom, ML (Morne) - Namibia - 15 Tests - 2011-2014
Botes, LW (Lu-Wayne) - Namibia - 9 Tests 2006-2007
Botes, WT (Tobias) - Italy - 22 Tests 2012-2014
Botha, MJ (Mouritz) - England - 10 Tests - 2011-2012
Bothma, R (Renaldo) - Namibia - 3 Tests - 2014
Bouwer, AC (Arthur) - Namibia - 10 Tests - 2012-2014
Breytenbach, CL (Conrad) - Russia - 2 Tests - 2002
Brooks, FG (Freddie) - England - 1 Test - 1906
Buchanan, JCR (Rankin) - Scotland - 16 Tests - 1921-1925
Buitendag, A (Basie) - Namibia - 22 Tests - 1990-1993
Catterall, BW (Brenton) - Zimbabwe - 7 Tests - 1991-1998
Catt, MJ (Mike) - England (75 Tests), Lions (1 Test) - 1994-2007
Chistolini, D (Dario) - Italy - 5 Tests - 2014
Claassen, AD (Antonie) - France - 6 Tests - 2013-2014

Constable R (Ryan) - Australia - 1 Test - 1994
Cuttitta, M (Marcello) - Italy - 54 Tests - 1987-1999
Cuttitta, M (Massimo) - Italy - 69 Tests - 1990-2000
Dalzell, K (Kevin) - USA - 42 Tests - 1996-2003
Dames, HDP (Danie) - Namibia - 8 Tests - 2011-2013
Davey, J (Jas) - England - 2 Tests - 1908-1909
Davies, MJ (Mickey) - Wales - 2 Tests - 1939
Davies, S (Shaun) - USA - 1 Test - 2013
De Jager, B (Benjamin) - Italy - 1 Test - 2006
De Jong, MG (Mike) - USA - 9 Tests - 1990-1991
De Marigny, JR (Roland) - Italy - 19 Tests - 2004-2007
De Villiers, P (Pieter) - France - 69 Tests - 1999-2007
Del Fava, CA (Carlo) - Italy - 54 Tests - 2004-2011
Diack, RJE (Robbie) - Ireland - 2 Tests - 2014
Dickson, WM (Mike) - Scotland - 7 Tests - 1912-1913
Dingley, J (Jon) - Hong Kong - 21 Tests - 1994-1998
Dirksen, CW (Cornelius) - USA - 2 Tests - 2012
Downes, GT (Graham) - USA - 1 Test - 1992
Duncan, DD (Denoon) - Scotland - 4 Tests - 1920
Ehrentraut, M (Michael) - Germany - 3 Tests - 1995-1998
Elgie, MK (Kim) - Scotland - 8 Tests - 1954-1955
Eloff, PT (Phillip) - USA - 35 Tests - 2000-2007
Engels, JB (Jaco) - Namibia - 8 Tests - 2013-2014
Erasmus, DJ (Danie) - Australia - 2 Tests - 1923
Erasmus, J (Jaco) - Italy - 3 Tests - 2008
Erskine, CE (Chad) - USA - 10 Tests - 2007-2008
Evans, IR (Ian) - Wales - 33 Tests - 2006-2014
Forrest, JGS (John) - Scotland - 3 Tests - 1938
Fourie, CH (Hendre) - England - 8 Tests - 2010-2011
Francis, TES (Tim) - England - 4 Tests - 1926

Franken, HH (Henk) - Namibia - 3 Tests - 2011-2012
Freakes, HD (Hubert) - England - 3 Tests - 1938-1939
†Gage, JH (Jack) - Ireland - 4 Tests - 1926-1927
Gagiano, JR (JJ) - USA - 14 Tests - 2008-2011
Geldenhuys, Q (Quintin) - Italy - 52 Tests - 2009-2014
Goedeke, F (Frank) - Germany - 4 Tests - 1999-2001
Gouws, J (Jurie) - USA - 8 caps - 2003-2004
Grobler, J (Juan) - USA - 33 caps - 1996-2002
Hauck, A (Alexander) - Germany - 6 Tests - 2009-2010
Hall, S (Steven) - France - 2 Tests - 2002
Hands, RHM (Reg) - England - 2 Tests - 1910
Harris, SW (Stan) - England (2 Tests) Lions (2 Tests) - 1920-1924
Hauck, A (Alexander) - Germany - 6 Tests - 2009-2010
Hawkins, M (Matt) - USA - 1 Test - 2010
Heatlie, BH (Fairy) - Argentina - 1 Test - 1910
Henderson, JH (Chick) - Scotland - 9 Tests - 1953-1954
Hendriks, JHF (Tenk) - Russia - 7 Tests - 2002
Herring, RW (Rob) - Ireland - 1 Test - 2014
Hindson, RE (Ro) - Canada - 31 Tests - 1973-1990
Hofmeyr, MB (Murray) - England - 3 Tests - 1950
Holmes, T (Tyrone) - Scotland - 1 Test - 2014
Hopley, FJV (John) - England - 3 Tests - 1907-1908
Horak, MJ (Michael) - England - 1 Test - 2002
Human, P (Petrus) - Namibia - 2 Tests - 2012
Jantjies, R (Riaan) - Namibia - 15 Tests - 1994-2000
Jeffery, D (Doug) - Namibia - 1 Test - 1990
Jones, IC (Ian) - Wales - 1 Test - 1968
Jordaan, PJ (Pieter) - Germany - 12 Tests - 2011-2014
Keyter, JC (Jason) - USA - 17 Tests - 2000-2003
Klerck, GS (Gerhard) - USA - 8 Tests - 2003-2004
Kockott, RM (Rory) - France - 3 Tests - 2014
Kotze, DM (Dan) - France - 1 Test - 2013
Krige, JA (Jannie) - England - 1 Test - 1920
Kumbier, KR (Karl) - Germany - 6 Tests - 1998-2000

INTERNATIONAL RUGBY IN 2014

Labuschagne, NA (Nick) - England - 5 Tests - 1953-1955
Lentz, O (Owen) - USA - 8 Tests - 2006-2007
Le Roux, B (Bernard) - France - 11 Tests - 2013-2014
Le Roux, JE (Jacques) - Portugal - 13 Tests - 2011-2014
Le Roux, RP (Ryan) - Spain - 4 Tests 2011-2012
Liebenberg, B (Brian) - France - 12 Tests - 2003-2005
Lipman, S (Sean) - USA - 9 Tests - 1988-1991
London, CJ (Chad) - USA - 1 Test - 2014
Losper, SJ (Sarel) - Namibia - 18 Tests - 1990-1991
Lupini, E (Tito) - Italy - 11 Tests - 1987-1989
Luscombe, HN (Hal) - Wales - 16 Tests - 2003-2007
Macdonald, DSM (Don) - Scotland - 7 Tests - 1977-1978
MacDonald, JS (Jimmy) - Scotland - 5 Tests - 1903-1905
Marinos, AWN (Andy) - Wales - 8 Tests - 2002-2003
Maritz, WM (Willem) - Namibia - 8 Tests - 1990-1991
Marshall, KW (Kenneth) - Scotland - 8 Tests - 1934-1937
Matsushima, K (Kotaro) - Japan - 6 Tests - 2014
McCowat, RH (Harold) - Scotland - 1 Test - 1905
McMillan, KHD (Keith) - Scotland - 4 Tests - 1953
Mehrtens, AP (Andrew) - New Zealand - 70 Tests - 1995-2004
Melck, RJG (Justin) - Germany - 1 Test - 2014
†**Mellish, FW** (Frank) - England - 6 Tests - 1920-1921
Melville, E (Eric) - France - 6 Tests - 1990-1991
Meyer, EA (Eden) - Namibia - 21 Tests - 1991-1996
Meyer, JM (Johannes) - Namibia - 16 Tests - 2003-2007
Milton, HC (Cecil) - England - 1 Test - 1906
Milton, JG (Jumbo) - England - 5 Tests - 1904-1907
Mulligan, PJ (Patrick) - Australia - 1 Test - 1925
Mullins, RC (Cuthbert) - British Isles - 2 Tests - 1896
Newman, SC (Syd) - England - 3 Tests - 1947-1948
Newton-Thompson, JO (Ossie) - England - 2 Tests - 1947
Nieuwenhuis, J (Jacques) - Namibia - 23 Tests 2006-2011
O'Cuinneagain, D (Dion) - Ireland - 19 Tests - 1998-2000
†**Oosthuizen, LT** (Theo) - Namibia - 7 Tests - 1990
Openshaw, WE (William) - England - 1 Test - 1879
Osler, FL (Frank) - Scotland - 2 Tests - 1911
Owen-Smith, HG (Tuppy) - England - 10 Tests - 1934-1937
Peens, G (Gert) - Italy - 23 Tests - 2002-2006
Pieters, W (Werner) - Russia - 2 Tests - 2002
Pieterse, W (Werner) - Russia - 7 Tests - 2002
Pocock, DW (David) - Australia - 45 Tests - 2008-2012
Poppmeier, M (Michael) - Germany - 6 Tests - 2009-2010
Praschma, P (Paul) - Germany - 2 Tests - 1998
Pretorius, A (Andries) - Wales - 2 Tests - 2013
Proudfoot, MC (Matthew) - Scotland - 4 Tests - 1998-2003
Rathbone, C (Clyde) - Australia - 26 Tests - 2004-2006
Rawlinson, GP (Greg) - New Zealand - 4 Tests 2006-2007
Reid, RE (Roland) - Scotland - 2 Tests - 2001
Robertsen, JR (John) - Canada - 9 Tests - 1985-1991
Rosenblum, ME (Myer) - Australia - 4 Tests - 1928
Roxburgh, JR (Jim) - Australia - 9 Tests - 1968-1970
Schulze, MR (Mark) - Germany - 16 Tests - 1996-2000
Scriba, HM (Hans) - Germany - 4 Tests - 1997-1998
Small, HD (Harry) - England - 4 Tests - 1950
Smit, H (Heinrich) - Namibia - 6 Tests - 2014
Smith, C (Collen) - Namibia - 4 Tests - 2012
Spedding, SL (Scott) - France - 3 Tests - 2014
Stevens, MJH (Matt) - England - 44 Tests - 2004-2012
†**Stewart, JC** (Christian) - Canada - 14 Tests - 1991-1995
Steyn, SSL (Stephen) - Scotland - 2 Tests - 1911-1912
Stickling, C (Conrad) - Portugal - 5 Tests - 2010
†**Strauss, CP** (Tiaan) - Australia - 11 Tests - 1999
Strauss, CR (Richardt) - Ireland - 6 Tests - 2013-2014
Theron, JP (Diumpie) - Namibia - 8 Tests - 1997-1999
Thomas, RM (Rhys) - Wales - 7 Tests - 2006-2009
Tonks, GA (Greig) - Scotland - 1 Test - 2013
Trenkel, N (Nick) - Canada - 1 Test - 2007
Van der Bergh, H (Henri) - Portugal - 4 Tests - 2003
Van der Merwe, AP (Arra) - Namibia - 19 Tests - 1990-1992
Van der Merwe, D (Danie) - Namibia - 1 Test - 1990
Van der Merwe, DTH - Canada - 32 Tests - 2006-2014
Van der Merwe, HJ (Hendrik) - Germany - 2 Tests - 2014
Van Heerden, A (Andries) - France - 2 Tests - 1992
Van Ryneveld, CB (Clive) - England - 4 Tests - 1949
Van Zyl, CC (Cornelius) - Italy - 8 Tests - 2011-2012
Van Zyl, WP (Piet) - Namibia - 18 Tests - 2007-2011
Van Zyl, R (Riaan) - USA - 13 Tests - 2003-2004
Vickerman, DJ (Dan) - Australia - 63 Tests - 2002-2011
Viljoen, F (Francois) - USA - 16 Tests - 2004-2006
Visser, W (Wim) - Italy - 22 Tests - 1999-2002
Volschenk, R (Bloues) - Russia - 9 Tests - 2002
Waters, FHH (Fraser) - England - 3 Tests - 2001-2004
White-Cooper, WRS (Steve) - England - 2 Tests - 2001
Williamson, RH (Rupert) - England - 5 Tests - 1908-1909
Wilson, AW (Andy) - Scotland - 1 Test - 2005
Wilson, DS (Tug) - England - 8 Tests - 1952-1955
Zaayman, C (Christian) - Namibia - 12 Tests - 1997-1999

Opinion: The State of the Game

By Craig Ray

WITH just months to go until Rugby World Cup 2015, global custodians of the game have much to ponder to ensure that the sport continues to grow and prosper in a demanding commercial world.

With careers, livelihoods, titles and sponsorships on the line, it is becoming increasingly vital that rugby sorts out the standard of officiating at the all levels, but particularly in the Test arena, to draw new audiences and retain the current one.

In many ways rugby has never been more popular in certain parts of the world but in other places, such as Australia, the morass of laws and their inconsistent application is driving people away from the sport. At its core, rugby is a simple sport but with bigger and stronger athletes, better coaching and a saturation of analytical tools to study opponents, officials are under increasingly severe pressure.

Officiating professionally is a mammoth task for any referee but consistency in the application of the laws has been one of the stumbling blocks in the game. Coaches, meanwhile, cannot voice their concerns publicly but privately they have become increasingly exasperated at avoidable errors and seemingly random decisions.

The use of the television match official (TMO) in theory should have assisted in coming to the correct decision almost all of the time, but it hasn't because it isn't applied consistently. The All Blacks' coaching staff were within their rights to be upset after their wonderful clash against the Springboks at Ellis Park. Pressure from television producers, who repeatedly broadcast an illegal tackle by Liam Messam on Schalk Burger, eventually forced referee Wayne Barnes to ask for a review when he otherwise would have played on. He awarded the home team a penalty that won the game.

It was the correct decision but how it was reached was incorrect. Television production companies should not be taking the lead but rather following requests from the officials.

Earlier in the year, the Springbok No. 8 Duane Vermeulen was penalised for an illegal tackle on Australia's prop, James Slipper. It was an entirely legal hit, as numerous TV replays showed, but referee George Clancy nevertheless awarded a penalty. All he had to do was view a replay, which, unfathomably, he chose not to do.

Against Wales in Cardiff, Springbok wing Cornal Hendricks was yellow-carded for playing Wales fullback Leigh Halfpenny in the air. Referee John Lacey felt Hendricks had infringed when it was clear both players had simultaneously leapt for the ball. The fact that Halfpenny reached the ball first shouldn't have come into the equation. Viewing replays in super-slow-motion does not help the cause. Earlier in the match, lock Eben Etzebeth also contested a high ball against Halfpenny and again the fullback was flattened in a marginal contest. Lacey only penalised Etzebeth but if there were consistency, the second-rower should have also received a yellow card.

Springbok coach Heyneke Meyer, careful not to criticise the officials directly, did ponder whether it was worth even trying to challenge a kick-chase fairly if no contest would be allowed. Scrums also remain a grey area and referees are struggling to give clear and consistent rulings. New Wallaby coach Michael Cheika suggested that referees went into matches with preconceived ideas about which team had the better scrum and blew accordingly. Numerous tweaks to the laws as well as changes to the engagement sequence have been tried and tested but rugby seems no closer to finding a consistent way to apply its laws.

That's due to a combination of the technicalities of scrumming, the skulduggery of players and referees' ability to adequately understand that aspect of the game. In a World Cup where penalties can be the difference between winning the title or heading home on an early flight, the scrum will be a focal point.

Another area of the game that needs urgent addressing is the breakdown. There is no clear pattern and the game is often dictated not by skill alone, but by the team that best adapts to refereeing 'interpretations'.

And that's precisely the difficulty for coaches, players and fans because officials and lawmakers have allowed this situation to blossom. Laws should be a simple case of right and wrong, but in rugby they are grey because referees 'interpret' decisions. As a consequence, players and coaches have to spend as much time studying the referee to glean an understanding of how the official might react to a certain part of the game. It's an untenable situation.

The laws of the game are confusing fans, players and coaches alike, says the author.

As for the game itself, the ball is now in play for longer and the Springboks have reacted by gradually changing their approach to playing. Against Australia at Newlands the ball was 'alive' for 44 minutes – an unheard of amount compared to an average of 35 minutes. As a consequence of this trend players require a different kind of fitness.

More cardiovascular and endurance training is already in vogue as players are shedding hitherto fashionable bulk. Schalk Burger returned from his medically-enforced hiatus about 5kg lighter in 2014, while Bakkies Botha's fighting weight was around 6kg less that it was between 2007 and 2010. Both were visibly more mobile as a result.

In terms of tactics, while the game is still territory-based and there is a high percentage of kicking from hand, opponents tend to kick the ball out less against the Springboks, knowing that the South African lineout is a great weapon. Meyer has recognised that opponents will shy away from playing to his team's strengths. So he's been working hard on improving skills in areas such as contestable and tactical kicking and perfecting the 'pressure and suffocate' game, as he puts it.

As always the World Cup, especially in England in autumn, is unlikely to be won by a team employing free-scoring running rugby; instead success at the tournament will demand quality set pieces, strong defence, intelligent and accurate kicking encompassing all the associated skills of contesting, positioning, timing, courage and discipline and, of course, some plain old good luck.

'Even today I'm still overcome...'

Twenty years later, Morné du Plessis looks back at 1995

Interview by Stephen Nell

WHILE he will go down as one of the great Springbok captains, Morné du Plessis may well be remembered most fondly for his role as manager of the team that won the World Cup in 1995.

As a close confidant of the coach, Kitch Christie, mentor to the players and ambassador for South African rugby, Du Plessis' contribution was immense.

Two decades down the line, from his seat as managing director of the Sports Science Institute of South Africa, he could still vividly recall the great moments and reflect fondly on the enormity of a remarkable episode in the Rainbow Nation's history.

Do you still think about it often?
There are little memories that pop up every now and then when I see one of the players. It could be Joost van der Westhuizen and the challenge of motor neuron disease that he's dealing with so proudly, Joel Stransky on television or Francois Pienaar. I still think about it, but as with everything life moves on.

What about the final itself?
It was stressful and not a game we enjoyed. Someone recently asked me about a scene where I sat looking worried while the rest of the bench was cheering after Joel's winning drop goal, and I said there had still been another three minutes left to play! The game ended when Joost knocked the ball on after a scrum feed.

It's the aftermath that we really remember – the scenes in the streets. It was almost dreamlike and unbelievable. There was a lot of concern that we were very late for the official dinner, but we couldn't move. We struggled to get to our hotel. The guys had a post-match gathering there and then we couldn't get out of the hotel again.

What have your impressions been of the way the various characters have developed since?
If you go through the team they have, by and large, all been successful. I would like to be able to ask each player what the most valuable aspect of the World Cup was to him personally. I'm sure everyone will say it was just to be part of something so unique in terms of nation-building. I don't think anyone had such an opportunity before then or have had subsequently.

With no disrespect to John Smit's fantastic winning team of 2007, their success was achieved outside the country. I was in Paris and the Champs Elysees looked like downtown Johannesburg with all the green and gold, but it wasn't in South Africa.

Do you think South African rugby missed an opportunity to grow the game among the broader population in the aftermath of the 1995 World Cup?
I don't think one should over-romanticise things. While there is no doubt that it had an amazing effect on the nation and showed that we can put our differences aside to work

The infamous Haka confrontation between Kobus Wiese and Jonah Lomu ahead of the 1995 World Cup final.

towards a single objective, it wasn't a solution to our challenges. It was, after all, a rugby match and aside from that about Nelson Mandela. If you look at the success Madiba had in building the nation from the World Cup, then you can say it was huge. But could we have got more people to play rugby, did we make mistakes and what were they? I don't know.

We had fluctuations of leadership. The complication of Dr Louis Luyt's relationship with Madiba, and the end of his reign (as president of the then South African Rugby Football Union), as well as Brian van Rooyen's term (as Saru president) weren't circumstances conducive to doing the core business of rugby.

Did you see professionalism on the horizon in the immediate aftermath of the 1995 World Cup? How did that change the landscape for South African rugby?

It was on the cards. Even prior to the World Cup we had agreed with Dr Luyt that there would be some financial recognition through a trust if the players were successful. It was a stipend rather than serious money. But the world was marching towards that inevitability. The battle between Kerry Packer and Rupert Murdoch for content rights turned the ignition key. The rest is history.

It was nice that during the tournament the team was, by and large, completely focused on the job at hand and there wasn't talk about money. But that came into play five minutes after the final whistle.

I think professionalism has been great for rugby. It has made the game more attractive because the players are better conditioned. The only potential loser was the club environment, which is why there are so many attempts at reviving it through competitions. Even amateur clubs are now semi-professional. The game has changed and there is no way of stopping it.

Did you foresee Francois Pienaar being so successful beyond his playing career?

Francois would have been successful even if he hadn't captained the Springboks at the World Cup. He's ambitious, driven, has an open mind and is great with people. With the greatest respect to him, the captaincy didn't hamper his progress. He has used it well and with dignity. Francois hasn't put a foot wrong and has contributed through his MAD-foundation.

When the guys were expecting a huge motivational speech from Kitch and I at our final team talk, all we said was that we had managed to get there, that we were proud of them, that they had made a difference to the way people perceived one another, and that that was enough. Whatever happened in the final would happen. I think the guys were quite surprised that we had such a low-key approach to it. The point being that Francois then started his foundation and called it Make A Difference (MAD).

A number of other guys have all been involved in some way promoting a cause. Hopefully that spirit was fostered during the World Cup and stemmed from a feeling that we owed the nation something.

What are your iconic memories from the World Cup?

Funnily enough it was not a rugby moment. I was last out of the tunnel at the final after the players had already lined up for the anthems and as I walked out I just heard the cheering and chanting of "Nelson, Nelson, Nelson". Even today I'm still overcome by that moment – hearing a predominantly white crowd of over 60,000 chanting that, and seeing Madiba smiling and loving it.

The other great moment was Newlands on the opening day. It was South Africa at its best – the weather, the game and the people. There was a joy I had seldom experienced. It was the first time I had known rugby players to go out onto the field before kick-off to walk around and meet the crowd. It was so joyous and a celebration of a new country.

Those two moments, and perhaps also the first singing of the national anthem, stand out. The guys knew the words of the anthem and it had a significant impact.

The Springboks sing the national anthem with Nelson Mandela looking on.

Twickenham – fitting venue for RWC final

All roads lead to 'Cabbage Patch' in 2015

By Dan Retief

AUCKLAND, Sydney, Paris, Cardiff or Cape Town… the signposts in all the major rugby cities of the world will this year point to Twickenham, incongruously referred to as the 'Cabbage Patch', 'Headquarters' or simply 'HQ'.

Situated in Richmond-upon-Thames, home to the rich and famous in south-west London, Twickenham has come a long way since the land on which the original stadium was built was used to grow cabbages. Today it is the headquarters of rugby's oldest founding body, the RFU, and will be the hub of the eighth Rugby World Cup tournament.

England will play all but one of their Pool A matches at 'Twickers' while two quarter-finals, both semi-finals and the Final on Saturday, October 31, will be staged at what today is a fine 82 000-seater stadium served by all manner of public transport systems.

The aim of every competing nation in 2015 will be to make sure they get to Twickenham. For the Springboks, they must aim to 'be there' on Saturday 17 October, signifying that they would have topped Pool B to qualify for the quarter-finals.

Win their match in the last eight and the next key date will be a week later, Saturday 24 October, for the semi-finals, in which they are seeded to meet the All Blacks, followed by the Final on Saturday 31 October.

On the face of it, it sounds simple. As Jake White said when the Springboks went all the way in France in 2007, "You have to win seven Tests in a row to win the World Cup."

Upsets often occur – as they did in '07 for France and New Zealand and in virtually all the other championships – but coaches cannot factor in the interventions of fate. As Peter de Villiers was fond of saying, they can but "control the controllables".

For the Springboks that means topping their pool by beating Samoa, Scotland, Japan and the USA and successfully negotiating a draw that does not see them getting to 'Headquarters' until more than a month after arriving in England. (South Africa will play in Brighton, Birmingham, Newcastle and the Olympic Stadium in London before setting foot on the hallowed turf of Twickenham.)

Although the Springboks are on a run of five successive wins at Twickenham – over England dating back to 2006 – the ground nevertheless holds some bad memories for the men in green and gold.

It was there in 2002, as a precursor to Australia's World Cup in 2003, that they suffered their worst-ever defeat, 53-3 against Martin Johnson's soon-to-be world champions, to go with a horror story in 1999.

Under Nick Mallett the Springboks, as defending champions, had reached the semi-final of the '99 RWC thanks to Jannie de Beer's world record five dropped goals against

Joost van der Westhuizen's try against England in 1999 is largely overshadowed by Jannie de Beer's five drop goals!

England in the quarter-finals at the Stade de France.

South Africa were up against the Wallabies and in a see-sawing match that went to extra time it was level-pegging with seven minutes left to play of the second period of additional time.

It seemed the Springboks were getting on top but then, from an awkward angle to the right of the field and 45 metres from the posts, Aussie flyhalf Stephen Larkham decided to try a drop. In the 2000 *SA Rugby Annual* it was described as "an ungainly looking action resulting in a surprisingly clean strike which sent the ball soaring over the cross-bar".

It was the death-knell for the Springboks and few remember that Matthew Burke nailed the last of his eight penalties to give the Wallabies a 27-21 win – taking them to their second Final in Britain; a week later in the new Millennium Stadium in Cardiff.

Such are the cruel twists of fate. South Africa had won the World Cup at their first attempt in 1995 thanks to Joel Stransky's dropped goal and Jannie de Beer had shepherded them into the semis with his goals in the quarters but they fell to the one and only Test match drop of Larkham's career.

That there was magic in the Twickenham air was confirmed the next day when France staged one of the greatest comebacks in the annals of rugby to beat the All Blacks 43-31. With Jonah Lomu running rampant New Zealand built a lead of 14 points just after half-time and it seemed they would cruise to victory.

But the French, who had been exhorted to "start a revolution" by 1998 FIFA World Cup football winners Franck Leboeuf and Didier Deschamps, did just that and from the 46th minute to the 59th the Tricolores garnered 26 unanswered points to go from 10-24 to 36-24.

The turnaround started almost unobtrusively as Christophe Lamaison kicked two penalties and a drop but then came tries by Christophe Dominici, Richard Dourthe and Philippe Bernat-Salles which left the All Blacks in tatters.

Jeff Wilson got a consolation try for New Zealand near the end but it hardly mattered as the French marched to Cardiff thanks to their astonishing victory.

The famous golden lion that stands atop the West gate at Twickenham had looked down on World Cup action eight years previously when England hosted the second tournament. In 1991 the emphasis was on 'World' and the RFU officials strove to create an all-inclusive element.

Thus the quarter-finals were held in Edinburgh, Paris, Dublin and Lille; the semi-finals at Lansdowne Road and Murrayfield; the play-off for third at Cardiff Arms Park with only the finale at Twickenham.

As would also be the case in South Africa in 1995 it was decreed that the host nation would play the defending champions in the opening game and it would be an off-key start for England as they lost 18-12 to New Zealand.

But, displaying the grit that years later would again be evident in France in 2007, Will Carling's men revealed the old bulldog spirit to fight through to the final the hard way.

In their quarter-final England beat France away in Paris, 19-10, in what would be the great Serge Blanco's last match for his country, and then travelled to Murrayfield to edge out Scotland 9-6 in their semi-final; this time breaking the heart of Gavin Hastings who fluffed a penalty from right in front.

The other side of the draw contained the powerhouses of the southern hemisphere – an All Black side that had come into the tournament on the back of a long undefeated run, and a terrific generation of Wallabies.

Coached by Bob Dwyer, the Wallabies, containing the likes of David Campese, Nick Farr-Jones, Michael Lynagh, Tim Horan and a young John Eales, prepared to the nth degree and played a unique brand of rugby.

In the semi-final the Wallabies were up against the all-conquering New Zealanders but a nightmare which would recur for the All Blacks in later tournaments was spawned as the Australians ran out comfortable victors, 16-6.

Campese, who had scored two tries in the quarter-final, weighed in with an improbable try as he ran a diagonal line from right to left across the All Blacks' backline. It seemed he would pass to a team-mate cutting back to straighten the thrust but instead the winger, who these days resides in Durban, confounded the All Blacks by going all the way to score far out.

Thus Twickenham's first final was between the home side, England, and Australia.

Having plodded their way through the tournament on the backs of their forwards, and allied to plenty of kicking, England made what was later seen as crucial error by deciding to run the ball at the Wallabies.

Tactically it made sense but England could not pull off the execution and in a tense match Australia prevailed 12-6 as the strain of the final inverted pre-match expectations of the Wallabies striking a blow for the running game.

Instead the only try came by way of Aussie props Tony Daly and Ewen McKenzie being driven over the line in typical England fashion. It was unclear who had scored but the try was later entered into the history books as belonging to Daly.

Twickenham will thus join Auckland's Eden Park as the only stadiums to present two World Cup Finals.

Namibia do the impossible to deny Zimbabwe World Cup ticket

Welwitschias to face All Blacks in first match of England 2015

By Ken Borland

RESTORING Namibian rugby to its former health was the key project for union president Bradley Basson and chief executive Sybrand de Beer in 2014 and their success off the field was mirrored on the park by coach Danie Vermeulen steering the side to World Cup qualification.

On 6 July in the Africa Cup CAR Division 1 qualifier in Antananarivo, Namibia scored an emphatic 89-10 victory over Madagascar to sneak ahead of Zimbabwe and Kenya on points difference and into their fifth successive World Cup, where they will take on the mighty All Blacks as well as Argentina, Tonga and Georgia in Pool C.

Just eight days earlier, Namibia's campaign looked set to end in tears as a shock 29-22 defeat at the hands of Kenya left their hopes of qualifying for the 2015 World Cup hanging by the slimmest of threads. But by 5pm on 6 July, the Namibian rugby team were crying tears of joy at the Mahamasina Stadium as their extraordinary victory over the hosts had booked their spot in England 2015.

Following that opening-day loss – just their second against the East Africans since 2006 – results had fallen Namibia's way to keep their hopes alive. The Welwitschias beat Zimbabwe 24-20 to stay in contention, while their fellow Southern Africans did them a favour by overcoming Kenya 28-10 on the final day. Crucially, neither Zimbabwe nor Kenya managed to get a bonus point in that match, which left Namibia needing to beat Madagascar by 53 points to qualify for the finals of the global showpiece.

"We were down in the dumps up to the last day, but we just believed until the very end. We had the will to keep on fighting until our last breath, until all 15 of us had to be carried off the field if necessary," flank Tinus du Plessis said after the triumph.

For Zimbabwe, who showed encouraging improvement through the year, there was a second chance in the form of the repechage, but they went down 23-15 to Russia in Krasnoyarsk and their race was run. Director of rugby Liam Middleton left for Canada shortly thereafter and by mid-November there was yet to be a taker to replace him. But the Sables enjoyed something of a renaissance in 2014, boosted by the presence of former Natal Sharks and Lions Super Rugby flyhalf Guy Cronjé.

Kenya will look back on their year with some frustration as they struggled with consistency. They managed to beat Namibia, but lost to Zimbabwe; they lost 21-14 to Uganda, only to beat the same team 34-0 the following weekend.

They will need to develop more consistency – which will come with playing more often – if they are to follow their Sevens team up the world rankings. Under the guidance of former Western Province loose forward Jerome Paarwater, they also competed in the Vodacom Cup, which was a valuable exercise for them.

They will also need to clear their team of doping allegations that were made by a Kenyan governmental task force.

While playing enough internationals is always a challenge for the African sides, Namibia have been able to fill their calendar ahead of the World Cup, playing Germany, Canada, the French Barbarians and Portugal after returning from their Madagascan triumph.

The last three games were on an invaluable year-end tour to Europe, giving the Welwitschias the chance to experience Northern Hemisphere conditions ahead of the World Cup and test their depth.

WP's Rohan Kitshoff adds experience to Namibia's cause.

Namibia also hope to be invited to the IRB Nations Cup in Romania as African champions, which could result in another four matches, while home Tests against Zimbabwe and Kenya are also planned for 2015.

The Namibian Rugby Union also successfully negotiated with their South African counterparts to ensure their participation in the Vodacom Cup in the first half of 2015.

Germany were comfortably beaten, 58-20, in Windhoek, in a match that marked Free State Cheetahs hooker Torsten van Jaarsveld's first game in Namibian colours.

Coach Vermeulen was able to call on a dozen overseas-based players through the year, with Pumas flank Renaldo Bothma (recently signed by the Sharks) outstanding in the World Cup qualifier in Madagascar, while Jacques Burger, the stoical grafter of the Saracens loose trio, played for Namibia for the first time since September 2011 when he led the team against Canada at Colwyn Bay in northern Wales.

Fullback Chrysander Botha, who played Super Rugby for the Lions and was then signed by the Exeter Chiefs, was one of the stars of the backline before his year ended with a broken leg in the 17-13 loss to Canada. The likes of flank Rohan Kitshoff and prop Jaco Engels, both stalwarts of the South African domestic scene, also added experience and quality to the Welwitschias.

The dissent which plagued Namibian rugby around the time of the previous World Cup is now also in the past.

"Rugby in Namibia was quite badly hit in 2011 when the exco resigned and technically we were insolvent. But the latest financial statements have been declared clean and passed without any qualifications and there is good governance and the basic foundation in place. We are now back to concentrating on rugby," De Beer said.

The plaudits kept coming for Namibia when they were named sports team of the year, Vermeulen won coach of the year and De Beer administrator of the year at the Namibian Sports Commission's annual awards.

To add to the feel-good factor, their Under-19 team won the Confederation of African Rugby's tournament hosted in Windhoek in September to qualify for the IRB Junior Trophy competition in Portugal in 2015.

SPRINGBOKS AT THE RUGBY WORLD CUP 1995-2011*

*Alphabetical listing of all 108 Springboks who have played in RWC, from #1 Andre Joubert to #108 Chiliboy Ralepelle

NO.	Name	Union	Tournament	M	T	C	P	D	PTS
101	Alberts, WS (Willem)	KwaZulu-Natal	2011	5	0	0	0	0	0
12	Andrews, MG (Mark)	KwaZulu-Natal	1995, 1999	9	1	0	0	0	5
103	Aplon, GG (Gio)	Western Province	2011	1	2	0	0	0	10
62	Bands, RE (Richard)	Blue Bulls	2003	4	1	0	0	0	5
54	Barry, D (De Wet)	Western Province	2003	4	0	0	0	0	0
75	Bezuidenhout, CJ (Christo)	Mpumalanga	2003	3	0	0	0	0	0
70	Boome, CS (Selborne)	Western Province	2003	3	0	0	0	0	0
85	Botha, BJ (BJ)	KwaZulu-Natal	2007	4	0	0	0	0	0
94	Botha, G van G (Gary)	Blue Bulls	2007	1	0	0	0	0	0
61	Botha, JP (Bakkies)	Blue Bulls	2003, 2007, 2011	14	3	0	0	0	15
22	Brink, RA (Robby)	Western Province	1995	2	0	0	0	0	0
99	Brussow, HW (Heinrich)	Free State	2011	5	0	0	0	0	0
77	Burger, SWP (Schalk)	Western Province	2003, 2007, 2011	13	2	0	0	0	10
63	Coetzee, D (Danie)	Blue Bulls	2003	4	0	0	0	0	0
14	Dalton, J (James)	Golden Lions	1995	2	0	0	0	0	0
33	De Beer, JH (Jannie)	Free State	1999	5	0	17	15	6	97
104	De Jongh, JL (Juan)	Western Province	2011	2	2	0	0	0	10
68	De Kock, NA (Neil)	Western Province	2003	4	1	0	0	0	5
79	De Villiers, (Jean)	Western Province	2007, 2011	4	0	0	0	0	0
55	Delport, GM (Thinus)	Valke	2003	4	1	0	0	0	5
28	Drotske, AE (Naka)	Free State	1995, 1999	7	0	0	0	0	0
84	Du Plessis, BW (Bismarck)	KwaZulu-Natal	2007, 2011	9	0	0	0	0	0
96	Du Plessis, JN (Jannie)	Free State, KwaZulu-Natal	2007, 2011	6	0	0	0	0	0
82	Du Preez, PF (Fourie)	Blue Bulls	2007, 2011	11	2	0	0	0	10
15	Du Randt, JP (Os)	Free State	1995, 1999, 2007	16	0	0	0	0	0
36	Erasmus, J (Rassie)	Golden Lions	1999	5	0	0	0	0	0
31	Fleck, RF (Robbie)	Western Province	1999	5	2	0	0	0	10
53	Fourie, J (Jaque)	Golden Lions, WP	2003, 2007, 2011	15	9	0	0	0	45
49	Garvey, AC (Adrian)	KwaZulu-Natal	1999	1	0	0	0	0	0
51	Greeff, WW (Werner)	Western Province	2003	2	1	0	0	0	5
80	Habana, BG (Bryan)	Blue Bulls, WP	2007, 2011	11	10	0	0	0	50
5	Hendriks, P (Pieter)	Golden Lions	1995	3	1	0	0	0	5
50	Honiball, HW (Henry)	KwaZulu-Natal	1999	2	0	1	3	0	11
66	Hougaard, DJ (Derick)	Blue Bulls	2003	5	2	10	5	1	48
102	Hougaard, F (Francois)	Blue Bulls	2011	5	3	0	0	0	15
25	Hurter, MH (Marius)	Blue Bulls	1995	2	0	0	0	0	0
81	James, AD (Butch)	KwaZulu-Natal/Golden Lions	2007, 2011	7	1	2	0	0	9
88	Januarie, ER (Ricky)	Golden Lions	2007	2	0	0	0	0	0
17	Johnson, GK (Gavin)	Golden Lions	1995	3	0	4	5	0	23
1	Joubert, AJ (Andre)	KwaZulu-Natal	1995	5	0	0	0	0	0
43	Julies, W (Wayne)	Boland/Blue Bulls	1999, 2007	2	0	0	0	0	0
30	Kayser, DJ (Deon)	Eastern Province	1999	5	2	0	0	0	10

SPRINGBOKS AT THE RUGBY WORLD CUP 1995-2011

NO.	Name	Union	Tournament	M	T	C	P	D	PTS
56	Koen, LJ (Louis)	Golden Lions	2003	4	0	7	2	0	20
74	Krige, CPJ (Corne)	Western Province	2003	3	0	0	0	0	0
9	Kruger, RJ (Ruben)	Blue Bulls	1995, 1999	7	1	0	0	0	5
105	Lambie, PJ (Patrick)	KwaZulu-Natal	2011	4	0	0	0	0	0
39	Le Roux, A-H (Ollie)	KwaZulu-Natal	1999	6	1	0	0	0	5
4	Le Roux, HP (Hennie)	Golden Lions	1995	6	0	0	0	0	0
47	Leonard, A (Anton)	South Western Districts	1999	1	1	0	0	0	5
67	Loubscher, RIP (Ricardo)	KwaZulu-Natal	2003	2	0	0	0	0	0
106	Louw, L-FP (Francois)	Bath, England	2011	3	0	0	0	0	0
45	Malotana, K (Kaya)	Border	1999	1	0	0	0	0	0
60	Matfield, V (Victor)	Blue Bulls	2003, 2007, 2011	14	0	0	0	0	0
29	Montgomery, PC (Percy)	WP/KwaZulu-Natal	1999, 2007	12	2	22	17	2	111
100	Mtawarira, T (Beast)	KwaZulu-Natal	2011	4	1	0	0	0	5
3	Mulder, JC (Japie)	Golden Lions	1995	4	0	0	0	0	0
86	Muller, GJ (Johann)	KZN/Ulster, Ireland	2007, 2011	5	0	0	0	0	0
73	Muller, GP (Jorrie)	Golden Lions	2003	4	1	0	0	0	5
44	Muller, PG (Pieter)	KwaZulu-Natal	1999	4	1	0	0	0	5
95	Ndungane, AZ (Akona)	Blue Bulls	2007	1	0	0	0	0	0
107	Ndungane, OM (Odwa)	KwaZulu-Natal	2011	1	0	0	0	0	0
93	Olivier, W (Wynand)	Blue Bulls	2007	3	0	0	0	0	0
23	Otto, K (Krynauw)	Blue Bulls	1995, 1999	9	0	0	0	0	0
16	Pagel, GL (Garry)	Western Province	1995	4	0	0	0	0	0
41	Paulse, BJ (Breyton)	Western Province	1999, 2003	4	1	0	0	0	5
10	Pienaar, JF (Francois)	Golden Lions	1995	5	0	0	0	0	0
92	Pienaar, R (Ruan)	KZN/Ulster, Ireland	2007, 2011	6	2	6	0	0	22
78	Pietersen, J-PR (JP)	KwaZulu-Natal	2007, 2011	11	4	0	0	0	20
89	Pretorius, AS (André)	Golden Lions	2007	5	0	1	0	0	2
108	Ralepelle, MC (Chiliboy)	Blue Bulls	2011	1	0	0	0	0	0
71	Rautenbach, SJ (Faan)	Western Province	2003	4	0	0	0	0	0
21	Richter, AJ (Adriaan)	Blue Bulls	1995	3	4	0	0	0	20
26	Rossouw, C le C (Chris)	Golden Lions/KZN	1995, 1999	6	1	0	0	0	5
58	Rossouw, DJ (Danie)	Blue Bulls	2003, 2007, 2011	15	6	0	0	0	30
32	Rossouw, PWG (Pieter)	Western Province	1999	4	1	0	0	0	5
20	Roux, JP (Johan)	Golden Lions	1995	3	0	0	0	0	0
76	Santon, D (Dale)	South Western Districts	2003	1	0	0	0	0	0
18	Scholtz, CP (Christiaan)	Golden Lions	1995	3	0	0	0	0	0
69	Scholtz, H (Hendro)	Free State	2003	2	1	0	0	0	5
64	Sephaka, LD (Lawrence)	Golden Lions	2003	3	0	0	0	0	0
34	Skinstad, RB (Bob)	Western Province/KZN	1999, 2007	9	2	0	0	0	10
2	Small, JT (James)	KwaZulu-Natal	1995	4	0	0	0	0	0
65	Smit, JW (John)	KwaZulu-Natal	2003, 2007, 2011	17	1	0	0	0	5
57	Smith, JH (Juan)	Free State	2003, 2007	11	5	0	0	0	25

SPRINGBOKS AT THE RUGBY WORLD CUP 1995-2011

NO.	Name	Union	Tournament	M	T	C	P	D	PTS
98	Spies, PJ (Pierre)	Blue Bulls	2011	5	0	0	0	0	0
91	Steenkamp, GG (Gurthro)	Blue Bulls	2007, 2011	7	1	0	0	0	5
90	Steyn, FPL (Francois)	KZN/Racing Metro, France	2007, 2011	11	4	0	6	0	38
97	Steyn, M (Morne)	Blue Bulls	2011	5	2	14	7	1	62
8	Straeuli, RAW (Rudolf)	Golden Lions	1995	3	0	0	0	0	0
6	Stransky, JT (Joel)	Western Province	1995	5	1	4	13	3	61
11	Strydom, JJ (Hannes)	Golden Lions	1995	4	0	0	0	0	0
46	Swanepoel, W (Werner)	Golden Lions	1999	2	1	0	0	0	5
13	Swart, IS de V (Balie)	Golden Lions	1995	4	0	0	0	0	0
42	Terblanche, CS (Stefan)	KwaZulu-Natal	1999, 2003	5	0	0	0	0	0
37	Van den Berg, PA (Albert)	Griqualand West/KZN	1999, 2007	7	2	0	0	0	10
83	Van der Linde, CJ (CJ)	Free State/Golden Lions	2007, 2011	7	1	0	0	0	5
7	Van der Westhuizen, JH (Joost)	Blue Bulls	1995, 1999, 2003	15	6	0	0	0	30
72	Van der Westhuyzen, JNB (Jaco)	Blue Bulls	2003	3	1	0	0	0	5
48	Van Heerden, FJ (Fritz)	Western Province	1999	1	0	0	0	0	0
87	Van Heerden, JL (Wikus)	Blue Bulls	2007	6	0	0	0	0	0
59	Van Niekerk, JC (Joe)	Golden Lions	2003	4	3	0	0	0	15
35	Venter, AG (Andre)	Free State	1999	5	1	0	0	0	5
19	Venter, B (Brendan)	Free State	1995, 1999	6	1	0	0	0	5
38	Visagie, IJ (Cobus)	Western Province	1999	5	0	0	0	0	0
40	Vos, AN (Andre)	Golden Lions	1999	5	2	0	0	0	10
24	Wiese, JJ (Kobus)	Golden Lions	1995	5	0	0	0	0	0
52	Willemse, AK (Ashwin)	Golden Lions	2003, 2007	5	1	0	0	0	5
27	Williams, CM (Chester)	Western Province	1995	3	4	0	0	0	20
	Penalty try		1999, 2011	0	2	0	0	0	10
				569	115	88	73	13	1009

‹ DID YOU KNOW? ›

Amazingly the Springboks of 1906, 1931 and 1951 all defeated Oxford University by 24 points to 3 at the Iffley Road ground in Oxford.

Tournament Records

TEAM RECORDS

Best performance		AUSTRALIA - Winners in 1991 & 1999
		SOUTH AFRICA - Winners in 1995 & 2007
		NEW ZEALAND - Winners in 1987 & 2011
Biggest win	142	Australia vs Namibia, 2003 (142-0)
Most points in a match	145	New Zealand vs Japan, 1995 (145-17)
Most tries in a match	22	Australia vs Namibia, 2003 (22-0)
Most conversions in a match	20	New Zealand vs Japan, 1995 (20)
Most penalty goals in a match	8	Scotland vs Tonga, 1995
	8	France vs Ireland, 1995
	8	Argentina vs Samoa, 1999
	8	Australia vs South Africa, 1999
Most drop goals in a match	5	South Africa vs England, 1999
Most points in a tournament	361	New Zealand in 2003 (7 matches)
Most points conceded in a tournament	310	Namibia in 2003 (4 matches)
Most tries in a tournament	52	New Zealand in 2003 (7 matches)
Most tries conceded in a tournament	47	Namibia in 2003 (4 matches)
Most conversions in a tournament	40	New Zealand in 2003 (7 matches)
Most penalty goals in a tournament	32	Argentina in 1999 (5 matches)
Most drop goals in a tournament	8	South Africa in 1999 (6 matches)
	8	England in 2003 (7 matches)
Penalty tries for	6	Argentina
Penalty tries against	6	Samoa
Yellow cards in previous tournaments	9	Tonga
Red Cards in previous tournaments	3	Canada
Highest attendance	82 957	Australia vs England, 2003 (Stadium Australia, Sydney)
Most consecutive wins	12	Australia (3/10/1999 - 15/11/2003)
Most consecutive losses	15	Namibia (1/10/1999 - 26/9/2011)

INDIVIDUAL RECORDS

Most points in a match	45	SD (Simon) Culhane (NZ) vs Japan, 1995
Most tries in a match	6	MCG (Marc) Ellis (NZ) vs Japan, 1995
Most conversions in a match	20	SD (Simon) Culhane (NZ) vs Japan, 1995
Most penalty goals in a match	8	AG (Gavin) Hastings (Scotland) vs Tonga, 1995
	8	T (Thierry) Lacroix (France) vs Ireland, 1995
	8	G (Gonzalo) Quesada (Arg) vs Samoa, 1999
Most drop goals in a match	5	JH (Jannie) de Beer (SA) vs England, 1999
Most points in a tournament	126	GJ (Grant) Fox (NZ) in 1987

RUGBY WORLD CUP

Most tries in a tournament	8	JT (Jonah) Lomu (NZ) in 1995
	8	BG (Bryan) Habana (SA) in 2007
Most conversions in a tournament	30	GJ (Grant) Fox (NZ) in 1987
Most penalty goals in a tournament	31	G (Gonzalo) Quesada (Arg) in 1999
Most drop goals in a tournament	8	JP (Jonny) Wilkinson (England) in 2003
Most appearances	22	J (Jason) Leonard (England) between 1991-2003
Youngest appearance	19y 8d	T (Thretton) Palamo (USA) vs South Africa, 2007
Oldest appearance	40y 26d	D (Diego) Ormaechea (Uruguay) vs South Africa, 1999
Most matches as captain	11	WDC (Will) Carling (England) 1991-1995
	11	R (Raphael) Ibanez (France) 1999-2007
	11	MO (Martin) Johnson (England) 1999-2003
	11	JW (John) Smit (South Africa) 2003-2011
Most tournaments	5	BP (Brian) Lima (Samoa) 1991-2007
Most points in a career	277	JP (Jonny) Wilkinson (England) 1999-2011
Most tries in a career	15	JT (Jonah) Lomu (NZ) 1995-1999
Most conversions in a career	39	AG (Gavin) Hastings (Scotland) 1987-1995
Most penalty goals in a career	58	JP (Jonny) Wilkinson (England) 1999-2011
Most drop goals in a career	14	JP (Jonny) Wilkinson (England) 1999-2011

TEAM RECORDS FOR SOUTH AFRICA

Best performance		Winner 1995 & 2007
Biggest win	87	vs Namibia, 2011 (87-0)
Biggest defeat	20	vs New Zealand, 2003 (9-29)
Most points in a match	87	vs Namibia, 2011 (87-0)
Most points conceded in a match	29	vs Scotland, 1999 (46-29)
	29	vs New Zealand, 2003 (9-29)
Most tries in a match	12	vs Uruguay, 2003 (72-6)
	12	vs Namibia, 2011 (87-0)
Most tries conceded in a match	3	vs New Zealand, 2003 (0-3)
	3	vs Tonga, 2007 (4-3)
Most conversions in a match	12	vs Namibia, 2011
Most penalty goals in a match	6	vs Australia, 1999
Most drop goals in a match	5	vs England, 1999
Most points in a tournament	278	2007 (7 matches)
Most points conceded in a tournament	101	1999 (6 matches)
Most tries in a tournament	33	2007 (7 matches)
Most tries conceded in a tournament	9	2007 (7 matches)
Most conversions in a tournament	25	2007 (7 matches)
Most penalty goals in a tournament	21	2007 (7 matches)
Most drop goals in a tournament	8	1999 (6 matches)
Penalty tries for	1	vs Spain, 1999
	1	vs Namibia, 2011

RUGBY WORLD CUP

Penalty tries against	–	
Highest attendance	80 430	vs England, 2007 (Stade de France, Paris)
Most consecutive wins	11	9/9/ 2007 - 30/9/2011
Most consecutive losses	1	30/10/1999, 18/10/2003, 8/11/2003 & 9/10/2011

INDIVIDUAL RECORDS FOR SOUTH AFRICA

Most points in a match	34	JH (Jannie) de Beer vs England, 1999
Most tries in a match	4	CM (Chester) Williams vs Samoa, 1995
		BG (Bryan) Habana vs Samoa, 2007
Most conversions in a match	6	JH (Jannie) de Beer vs Spain, 1999
	6	PC (Percy) Montgomery vs USA, 2007
	6	R (Ruan) Pienaar vs Namibia, 2011
	6	M (Morne) steyn vs Namibia, 2011
Most penalty goals in a match	6	JH (Jannie) de Beer vs Australia, 1999
Most drop goals in a match	5	JH (Jannie) de Beer vs England, 1999
Most points in a tournament	105	PC (Percy) Montgomery, 2007 (7 matches)
Most tries in a tournament	8	BG (Bryan) Habana, 2007 (7 matches)
Most conversions in a tournament	22	PC (Percy) Montgomery, 2007 (7 matches)
Most penalty goals in a tournament	17	PC (Percy) Montgomery, 2007 (7 matches)
Most drop goals in a tournament	6	JH (Jannie) de Beer, 1999 (5 matches)
Most appearances	17	JW (John) Smit between 2003-2011
Youngest appearance	20y 118d	FPL (Francois) Steyn (SA vs Samoa, 2007)
Oldest appearance	35y 151d	JP (Os) du Randt (SA vs England, 2007)
Most matches as a captain	11	JW (John) Smit between 2003-2011
Most tournaments	3	JH (Joost) van der Wersthuizen - 1995, 1999, 2003
	3	JP (Os) du Randt - 1995, 1999, 2007
	3	JP (Bakkies) Botha - 2003, 2007, 2011
	3	SWP (Schalk) Burger - 2003, 2007, 2011
	3	J (Jaque) Fourie - 2003, 2007, 2011
	3	V (Victor) Matfield - 2003, 2007, 2011
	3	DJ (Danie) Rossouw - 2003, 2007, 2011
	3	JW (John) Smit - 2003, 2007, 2011
Most points in a career	111	PC (Percy) Montgomery 1999-2007
Most tries in a career	10	BG (Bryan) Habana 2007-2011
Most conversions in a career	22	PC (Percy) Montgomery 1999-2007
Most penalty goals in a career	17	PC (Percy) Montgomery 1999-2007
Most drop goals in a career	6	JH (Jannie) de Beer in 1999
Yellow cards in previous tournaments	5	H (Hendro) Scholtz vs Georgia, 2003
		FPL (Francois) Steyn vs Tonga, 2007
		BG (Bryan) Habana vs Tonga, 2007
		JH (Juan) Smith vs Argentina, 2007
		JW (John) Smit vs Samoa, 2011
Red cards in previous tournaments	2	J (James) Dalton vs Canada, 1995
		B (Brendan) Venter vs Uruguay, 1999

RUGBY WORLD CUP 2015 QUALIFYING MATCHES

Date	Team 1	Score	Score	Team 2	Venue
24/03/2012	Mexico	68	14	Jamaica	La Ibero Santa Fe
07/04/2012	Jamaica	19	18	Cayman Islands	Kingston
07/04/2012	St Vincent and Grenadines	3	34	Barbados	Kingstown
15/04/2012	Philippines	37	20	Singapore	Manila
15/04/2012	Sri Lanka	36	8	Chinese Taipei	Manila
18/04/2012	Philippines	34	12	Chinese Taipei	Manila
18/04/2012	Sri Lanka	35	10	Singapore	Manila
21/04/2012	Barbados	51	0	St Vincent and Grenadines	Bridgetown
21/04/2012	Cayman Islands	46	13	Mexico	Grand Caymans
21/04/2012	Chinese Taipei	49	31	Singapore	Manila
21/04/2012	Philippines	28	18	Sri Lanka	Manila
26/05/2012	Cayman Islands	27	7	Bahamas	Grand Caymans
30/05/2012	Guam	38	17	Indonesia	Royal Selangor Club, Kuala Lumpur
30/05/2012	India	34	5	Pakistan	Royal Selangor Club, Kuala Lumpur
31/05/2012	Malaysia	89	0	China	Royal Selangor Club, Kuala Lumpur
31/05/2012	Thailand	37	17	Iran	Royal Selangor Club, Kuala Lumpur
01/06/2012	Guam	16	18	India	Royal Selangor Club, Kuala Lumpur
01/06/2012	Indonesia	13	7	Pakistan	Royal Selangor Club, Kuala Lumpur
02/06/2012	Iran	52	3	China	Royal Selangor Club, Kuala Lumpur
02/06/2012	Malaysia	19	22	Thailand	Royal Selangor Club, Kuala Lumpur
02/06/2012	Trinidad and Tobago	0	20	Guyana	Georgetown
09/06/2012	Bahamas	8	16	Bermuda	Nassau
23/06/2012	Bermuda	18	0	Guyana	Hamilton, Devonshire
04/07/2012	Madagascar	35	28	Morocco	Mahamasina Stadium, Antananarive
04/07/2012	Senegal	18	20	Namibia	Mahamasina Stadium, Antananarive
08/07/2012	Madagascar	57	54	Namibia	Mahamasina Stadium, Antananarive
08/07/2012	Senegal	26	23	Morocco	Mahamasina Stadium, Antananarive
09/07/2012	Tunisia	14	30	Zimbabwe	Jammal
09/07/2012	Uganda	21	19	Kenya	Jammal
14/07/2012	Thailand	42	19	India	Pattaya
14/07/2012	Tunisia	24	31	Kenya	Jammal
14/07/2012	Zimbabwe	22	18	Uganda	Jammal
22/07/2012	Mauritius	26	22	Nigeria	Gaberone
22/07/2012	Zambia	15	23	Botswana	Gaberone
25/07/2012	Ivory Coast	29	17	Nigeria	Gaberone
28/07/2012	Botswana	25	14	Mauritius	Gaberone
28/07/2012	Ivory Coast	24	18	Zambia	Gaberone
09/09/2012	Paraguay	54	17	Colombia	Valencia, Venezuela
09/09/2012	Venezuela	28	17	Peru	Valencia, Venezuela
15/09/2012	Colombia	49	9	Peru	Valencia, Venezuela
15/09/2012	Venezuela	8	73	Paraguay	Valencia, Venezuela
03/11/2012	Latvia	27	15	Denmark	University Riga
03/11/2012	Malta	34	17	Lithuania	Hibernians Ground, Paola
03/11/2012	Norway	11	9	Bosnia and Herzegovina	Bergen
03/11/2012	Poland	22	13	Germany	Gdansk
03/11/2012	Serbia and Montenegro	23	26	Andorra	Belgrade
03/11/2012	Switzerland	29	20	Croatia	Nyon
10/11/2012	Czech Republic	18	22	Sweden	Prague
10/11/2012	Lithuania	16	24	Netherlands	Central Stadium, Siauliai

RUGBY WORLD CUP 2015 QUALIFYING MATCHES

Date	Home	Score	Score	Away	Venue
10/11/2012	Luxembourg	15	8	Norway	Stade Josy Barthel, Luxembourg
17/11/2012	Germany	32	14	Moldova	Fritz Grunebaum Stadium, Heidelburg
17/11/2012	Greece	22	17	Bosnia and Herzegovina	Thessaloniki
17/11/2012	Netherlands	24	7	Switzerland	National Rugby Centre, Amsterdam
17/11/2012	Ukraine	42	15	Czech Republic	Dnepropetrovsk
08/12/2012	Cyprus	49	8	Slovenia	Paphiako Stadium, Paphos
02/02/2013	Belgium	13	17	Georgia	Stade Roi Baudouin, Brussels
02/02/2013	Portugal	13	19	Romania	University, Lisbon
02/02/2013	Russia	13	9	Spain	Sochi
09/02/2013	Belgium	21	21	Spain	Stade Roi Baudouin, Brussels
09/02/2013	Georgia	25	12	Portugal	Tbilisi
09/02/2013	Romania	29	14	Russia	Arcul de Triumf, Bucharest
23/02/2013	Portugal	18	12	Belgium	Lisbon
23/02/2013	Romania	25	15	Spain	Gijon
23/02/2013	Russia	9	23	Georgia	Sotchi
09/03/2013	Czech Republic	8	27	Germany	Prague
09/03/2013	Georgia	61	18	Spain	Tbilisi
09/03/2013	Romania	32	14	Belgium	Brussels
09/03/2013	Russia	31	23	Portugal	Coimbra
16/03/2013	Moldova	37	12	Czech Republic	Chisinau
16/03/2013	Romania	9	9	Georgia	Bucharest
16/03/2013	Russia	43	32	Belgium	Sochi
16/03/2013	Spain	9	9	Portugal	Estadio Nacional Universidad Complutense, Madrid
30/03/2013	Andorra	11	22	Latvia	Andorra la Vella
30/03/2013	Greece	11	13	Finland	Athens
30/03/2013	Ukraine	12	13	Poland	Gdynia
31/03/2013	Chinese Taipei	8	39	Sri Lanka	Colombo
31/03/2013	Kazakhstan	10	33	Thailand	Colombo
03/04/2013	Chinese Taipei	10	42	Kazakhstan	Colombo
03/04/2013	Thailand	7	45	Sri Lanka	Colombo
06/04/2013	Austria	10	11	Hungary	Vienna
06/04/2013	Chinese Taipei	52	23	Thailand	Colombo
06/04/2013	Germany	73	17	Sweden	Hamburg
06/04/2013	Israel	17	15	Latvia	Wingate Institute, Netanya
06/04/2013	Malta	10	19	Switzerland	Hibernians Ground, Paola
06/04/2013	Slovenia	14	20	Bulgaria	Sofia
06/04/2013	Sri Lanka	49	18	Kazakhstan	Race Course Ground, Colombo
07/04/2013	Moldova	38	18	Ukraine	Odessa
13/04/2013	Bosnia and Herzegovina	33	23	Luxembourg	Tesanj
13/04/2013	Denmark	38	0	Serbia and Montenegro	Odense
13/04/2013	Greece	21	14	Norway	Athens
13/04/2013	Lithuania	21	37	Switzerland	Nyon
13/04/2013	Netherlands	48	10	Malta	National Rugby Centre, Amsterdam
13/04/2013	Poland	20	24	Moldova	Chisinau
20/04/2013	Bosnia and Herzegovina	19	5	Finland	Zenica
20/04/2013	Croatia	24	29	Netherlands	Zagreb
20/04/2013	Hong Kong	53	7	United Arab Emirates	Hong Kong Football Club Ground, Hong Kong
20/04/2013	Israel	46	3	Denmark	Wingate Institute, Netanya
20/04/2013	Japan	121	0	Philippines	Fukuoka

RUGBY WORLD CUP 2015 QUALIFYING MATCHES

Date	Home	Score		Away	Venue
20/04/2013	Luxembourg	20	7	Greece	Stade Josy Barthel, Luxembourg
20/04/2013	Slovenia	22	20	Austria	Ljubliana
26/04/2013	United Arab Emirates	10	75	Korea	Al Ain
27/04/2013	Chile	38	22	Brazil	Temuco
27/04/2013	Hong Kong	0	38	Japan	Hong Kong Football Club Ground, Hong Kong
27/04/2013	Lithuania	15	14	Croatia	Vilnius
27/04/2013	Uruguay	18	29	Argentina	Charrua Stadium, Montevideo
01/05/2013	Argentina	85	10	Chile	Charrua Stadium, Montevideo
01/05/2013	Uruguay	58	7	Brazil	Charrua Stadium, Montevideo
04/05/2013	Argentina	83	0	Brazil	Charrua Stadium, Montevideo
04/05/2013	Japan	64	5	Korea	Tokyo
04/05/2013	Philippines	20	59	Hong Kong	Manila
04/05/2013	Uruguay	23	9	Chile	Charrua Stadium, Montevideo
05/05/2013	Luxembourg	22	10	Slovenia	Stade Josy Barthel, Luxembourg
10/05/2013	United Arab Emirates	3	93	Japan	Dubai
11/05/2013	Philippines	19	62	Korea	Ansan
18/05/2013	Korea	43	22	Hong Kong	Ansan
18/05/2013	Philippines	24	8	United Arab Emirates	Manila
01/06/2013	Senegal	12	35	Namibia	Stade Iba Mar Doip
01/06/2013	Sweden	19	11	Poland	Enkoping
01/06/2013	Tunisia	43	12	Botswana	Stade Iba Mar Doip
15/06/2013	Botswana	5	41	Senegal	Stade Iba Mar Doip
15/06/2013	Namibia	45	13	Tunisia	Stade Iba Mar Doip
06/07/2013	Cook Islands	38	5	Tahiti	Port Moresby
06/07/2013	Papua New Guinea	29	22	Solomon Islands	Port Moresby
09/07/2013	Cook Islands	39	12	Solomon Islands	Port Moresby
09/07/2013	Tahiti	32	39	Papua New Guinea	Port Moresby
10/07/2013	Madagascar	18	38	Zimbabwe	Mahamasina Stadium, Antananarive
10/07/2013	Uganda	11	52	Kenya	Antananarive
13/07/2013	Cook Islands	37	31	Papua New Guinea	Port Moresby
13/07/2013	Solomon Islands	23	22	Tahiti	Port Moresby
14/07/2013	Madagascar	48	32	Uganda	Mahamasina Stadium, Antananarive
14/07/2013	Zimbabwe	17	29	Kenya	Mahamasina Stadium, Antananarive
17/08/2013	United States of America	9	27	Canada	Charleston
24/08/2013	Canada	13	11	United States of America	Toronto
07/09/2013	Poland	30	9	Sweden	Warsaw
05/10/2013	Luxembourg	12	26	Israel	Stade Josy Barthel, Luxembourg
12/10/2013	Poland	30	10	Czech Republic	Warsaw
19/10/2013	Sweden	11	17	Czech Republic	Enkoping
26/10/2013	Israel	8	52	Netherlands	Wingate Institute, Netanya
26/10/2013	Ukraine	16	28	Germany	Metalist Stadium, Komsomolsk
02/11/2013	Ukraine	35	11	Sweden	Kiev
08/11/2013	Namibia	35	26	Zimbabwe	Windhoek
09/11/2013	Germany	43	13	Poland	Berlin
09/11/2013	Moldova	50	20	Sweden	Chisinau
12/11/2013	Zimbabwe	29	14	Kenya	Windhoek
16/11/2013	Czech Republic	10	17	Ukraine	Zlin
16/11/2013	Moldova	30	15	Germany	Chisinau
16/11/2013	Namibia	55	35	Kenya	Windhoek

RUGBY WORLD CUP 2015 QUALIFYING MATCHES

Date	Home			Away	Venue
01/02/2014	Georgia	35	0	Belgium	Avchala Stadium, Tbilisi
01/02/2014	Romania	24	0	Portugal	Cluj Arena, Cluj
01/02/2014	Spain	25	28	Russia	Estadio Nacional Universidad Complutense, Madrid
08/02/2014	Portugal	9	34	Georgia	Estadio Universitario, Lisbon
08/02/2014	Russia	3	34	Romania	Molnia Hotel, Tuapse
08/02/2014	Spain	11	6	Belgium	Estadio Nacional Universidad Complutense, Madrid
22/02/2014	Belgium	6	19	Portugal	Stade Roi Baudouin, Brussels
22/02/2014	Georgia	36	10	Russia	Dinamo Arena, Tbilisi
22/02/2014	Romania	32	6	Spain	Cluj Arena, Cluj
08/03/2014	Romania	29	10	Belgium	Stadionul Mihail Naca, Constanta
08/03/2014	Russia	34	18	Portugal	Sochi
08/03/2014	Spain	17	24	Georgia	Estadio Nacional Universidad Complutense, Madrid
15/03/2014	Belgium	20	34	Russia	Stade Roi Baudouin, Brussels
15/03/2014	Georgia	22	9	Romania	Mikheil Meskhi Stadium, Tbilisi
15/03/2014	Portugal	24	28	Spain	Estadio Universitario, Lisbon
22/03/2014	Uruguay	27	27	United States of America	Charrua Stadium, Montevideo
29/03/2014	United States of America	32	13	Uruguay	Fifth Third Bank Stadium, Atlanta
05/04/2014	Germany	76	12	Czech Republic	Fritz Grunebaum Stadium, Heidelburg
05/04/2014	Poland	12	21	Moldova	Siedlce
12/04/2014	Moldova	28	8	Ukraine	Chisinau
26/04/2014	Czech Republic	37	19	Moldova	Prague
26/04/2014	Hong Kong	108	0	Philippines	Hong Kong Football Club Ground, Hong Kong
26/04/2014	Korea	59	3	Sri Lanka	Incheon Munhak Stadium, Incheon
26/04/2014	Sweden	20	45	Germany	Enkoping
26/04/2014	Ukraine	29	28	Poland	Lvov
03/05/2014	Philippines	10	99	Japan	Eagle's Nest Stadium, Silangan
03/05/2014	Sri Lanka	10	41	Hong Kong	Race Course Ground, Colombo
10/05/2014	Hong Kong	39	6	Korea	Hong Kong Football Club Ground, Hong Kong
10/05/2014	Japan	132	10	Sri Lanka	Nagoya Municipal Mizuho Park Rugby Ground, Nagoya
10/05/2014	Netherlands	7	17	Germany	National Rugby Centre, Amsterdam
17/05/2014	Korea	5	62	Japan	Incheon Munhak Stadium, Incheon
17/05/2014	Sri Lanka	25	26	Philippines	Race Course Ground, Colombo
24/05/2014	Germany	20	31	Russia	Wolfgang-Meyer-Sportanlage, Hamburg
24/05/2014	Philippines	22	52	Korea	Eagle's Nest Stadium, Silangan
25/05/2014	Japan	49	8	Hong Kong	National Olympic Stadium, Tokyo
28/06/2014	Fiji	108	6	Cook Islands	Churchill Park, Suva
28/06/2014	Kenya	29	22	Namibia	Mahamasina Stadium, Antananarive
28/06/2014	Madagascar	22	57	Zimbabwe	Mahamasina Stadium, Antananarive
02/07/2014	Madagascar	0	34	Kenya	Mahamasina Stadium, Antananarive
02/07/2014	Namibia	24	20	Zimbabwe	Mahamasina Stadium, Antananarive
06/07/2014	Kenya	10	28	Zimbabwe	Mahamasina Stadium, Antananarive
06/07/2014	Madagascar	10	89	Namibia	Mahamasina Stadium, Antananarive
02/08/2014	Russia	23	15	Zimbabwe	Central Stadium, Krasnoyarsk
02/08/2014	Uruguay	28	3	Hong Kong	Charrua Stadium, Montevideo
27/09/2014	Russia	22	21	Uruguay	Central Stadium, Krasnoyarsk
11/10/2014	Uruguay	36	27	Russia	Charrua Stadium, Montevideo

De Villiers injury spoils season

All Black win the highlight, defeat to Ireland & Wales the lowlights

By Stephen Nell, Springbok Team Correspondent

IN A year in which the Springboks scaled the heights of an epic victory over the All Blacks, it feels most inappropriate that the lasting memory is that of skipper Jean de Villiers being stretchered off at the Millennium Stadium in Cardiff.

Coupled with the deflating 12-6 defeat to Wales, it put a very different slant on a season that would otherwise have been considered a success.

The Springboks showed they were a team on the up by running the All Blacks close in Wellington before toppling them at Ellis Park in Johannesburg. All the pointers were there that South Africa had the potential to rival New Zealand as the world's best team in the foreseeable future.

In fairness, the Springboks had to rally for great escapes from the jaws of defeat against Wales in Nelspruit and Argentina in Salta, but notwithstanding those iffy performances it also spoke of impressive resolve and mental toughness.

While the loss to Wales raised some doubts about South Africa's readiness for the 2015 World Cup, there was plenty to celebrate.

The return to the international fold of Schalk Burger and Victor Matfield were triumphs against the odds.

Prior to the season's first Test against Wales in Durban, both had last been capped in the World Cup quarter-final defeat to Australia in 2011. Matfield had retired then, while Burger missed the 2012 and 2013 international seasons due a combination of injury and serious illness.

Having stared down death in the shape of bacterial meningitis, Burger made a return to the Green and Gold in the victory over the World XV at Newlands before resuming his Test career as a substitute for Willem Alberts in Durban.

Matfield went as far as making his Test comeback as captain after a knee injury ruled De Villiers out of the June internationals.

It was the first of many times the Springboks had to absorb the blow of losing key personnel. The absence of the likes of openside flank Francois Louw and scrumhalf Fourie du Preez, for example, was tangibly felt during a largely forgettable November tour.

THE SPRINGBOKS IN 2014

Kieran Read charges into Duane Vermeulen. The battle between these two No. 8s was worth the admission price alone.

But at the same time doors opened. Handré Pollard made his Test debut against Scotland in Port Elizabeth and by the end of the season coach Heyneke Meyer could reflect on the incredible flyhalf depth at his disposal.

Patrick Lambie, as substitute for Pollard, proved a match-winner in the home victories over the Wallabies and All Blacks. His decisive penalty from 55 metres out in the latter match was arguably the best moment of the Springbok season.

But for the biggest hero of the day few would have looked beyond No 8 Duane Vermeulen, who was named man of the match after playing through the pain barrier with sore ribs. He was immense throughout the year.

That inspirational story, together with Lambie's coming of age and the rise of players such as Pollard, scrumhalf Cubus Reinach, centre Jan Serfontein and wing Cornal Hendricks, made it a generally pleasing year.

Meyer was in addition able to reflect on expanded front-row depth after Coenie Oosthuizen played with authority at tighthead prop in the northern hemisphere. Loosehead prop Trevor Nyakane also gave a good scrumming account of himself against Italy's revered tighthead, Martin Castrogiovanni.

The match that demonstrated South Africa still had a long way to go was the 29-15 defeat to Ireland in Dublin. The Springboks were cavalier as they set about trying to break down the Irish with ball in hand rather than build the proverbial innings in wet conditions. Coming on the back of the win over the All Blacks, it was a sobering moment. South Africa were taught a lesson in tactical kicking and struggled to assert themselves at the breakdowns on their November tour. Barring the victory over England at Twickenham, the Springboks could not come to grips with the messy nature of the rucks in the northern hemisphere.

It was a tour that exposed a soft underbelly where prior to the journey South Africans thought their team carried a six-pack.

Patrick Lambie, as he did against the All Blacks at Ellis Park, slots the winning points against England at Twickenham.

Similarly, the Springboks' mental constitution remains an enigma. They lost after being favourites against Ireland and the old backs-to-the-wall scenario brought the best out of them against the English. The following week they lumbered to victory against Italy before going down to Wales.

So, in the final analysis, one's perspective on the season might depend on whether you prefer to see the glass as half-full or half-empty.

The Springboks had the world's best team in their sights, but were themselves exposed as incomplete and in the process their captain was injured to the point of requiring reconstruction of the anterior and posterior cruciate ligaments around his knee.

Come the end of the year, Meyer nevertheless felt he had most boxes ticked. The fundamentals of the Springboks' game were solid enough. They still had a dominant setpiece, which he felt needed to be complemented by a better kicking game.

He will most likely have experienced personnel available to shore up some of the glaring deficiencies that were exposed in November. Keep in mind too that the team that lost to Wales was shorn of a number of players that would otherwise probably have made the match-day 23: Jannie du Plessis (tighthead prop), Louw, Burger, Alberts (all loose forwards), Du Preez, Ruan Pienaar (both scrumhalves), and Bryan Habana and JP Pietersen (wings).

There was also the continued absence of the mercurial Frans Steyn, who through personal circumstances did not see his way open to playing for the Springboks.

Perhaps then it would be more appropriate to take a largely positive view of the Springboks' season. They won nine out of 13 Tests and the last one against Wales, arranged outside the International Rugby Board's international window, was a bridge too far for tired minds and battered bodies.

More than any defeat, it was the injury to De Villiers that hurt and at the time of going to print we could do no more than hope against hope that he would be fit come the World Cup.

THE SPRINGBOKS IN 2014

TEST RESULTS & SCORERS

Played	Won	Lost	Drawn	Points for	Points against	Tries For	Tries Against
13	9	4	0	332	237	38	19

Date	Venue	Opponent	Result	Score	Tries	Referee	Scorers
14 Jun	Growth-Point Kings Park, Durban	Wales	WON	38-16	5-1	R Poite	T: Habana (2), Vermeulen, Le Roux, Hendricks. C: Steyn (5). P: Steyn.
21 Jun	Mbombela Stadium, Nelspruit	Wales	WON	31-30	4-3	SR Walsh	T: Penalty tries (2), Hendricks, Le Roux. C: Steyn (4). P: Steyn.
28 Jun	Nelson Mandela Bay Stadium, Port Elizabeth	Scotland	WON	55-6	8-0	G Jackson	T: Mvovo (2), Coetzee (2), De Jager (2), Pietersen, Le Roux. C: Pollard (5), Boshoff. P: Pollard.
16 Aug	Loftus Versfeld, Pretoria	Argentina	WON	13-6	1-0	J Lacey	T: Pienaar. C: Pollard. P: Pollard, Steyn.
23 Aug	Estadio Padre Ernesto Martearena, Salta	Argentina	WON	33-31	3-3	SR Walsh	T: Habana, Hendricks, Coetzee. C: Steyn (2), Pollard. P: Pollard (3), Steyn.
6 Sep	Patersons Stadium, Perth	Australia	Lost	23-24	1-2	G Clancy	T: Hendricks. P: Steyn (6).
13 Sep	Westpac Stadium, Wellington	New Zealand	Lost	10-14	1-1	J Garces	T: Hendricks. C: Pollard. P: Pollard.
27 Sep	Newlands, Cape Town	Australia	WON	28-10	4-1	N Owens	T: De Villiers (2), Coetzee, Lambie. C: Lambie. P: Pollard. DG: Lambie.
4 Oct	Ellis Park, Johannesburg	New Zealand	WON	27-25	3-3	W Barnes	T: Pollard (2), Hougaard. C: Pollard (3). P: Pollard, Lambie.
8 Nov	Aviva Stadium, Dublin	Ireland	Lost	15-29	2-2	R Poite	T: Coetzee, Pietersen. C: Pollard. P: Pollard.
15 Nov	Twickenham, London	England	WON	31-28	3-3	SR Walsh	T: Serfontein, Burger, Reinach. C: Lambie (2). P: Lambie (3). DG: Lambie.
22 Nov	Stadio Euganeo, Padova	Italy	WON	22-6	3-0	J Garces	T: Oosthuizen, Reinach, Habana. C: Pollard (2). P: Lambie.
29 Nov	Millennium Stadium, Cardiff	Wales	Lost	6-12	0-0	J Lacey	P: Lambie (2).

THE SPRINGBOKS IN 2014

TEST APPEARANCES & POINTS

PLAYER	Wal 1	Wal 2	Scot 1	Arg 1	Arg 2	Aus 1	NZ 1	Aus 2	NZ 2	Ire	Eng	Ita	Wal 3	Apps	T	C	P	DG	Pts
WJ le Roux	15	15	15	15	15	15	15	15	15	15	15	15R	15	13	3	–	–	–	15
C Hendricks	14	14	14	14	14	14	14	14	14	14	x	–	14	11	5	–	–	–	25
JP-R Pietersen	13	13	13	–	–	–	–	11R	14R	14R	14	14	–	8	2	–	–	–	10
JL Serfontein	12	12	12	x	–	13	13	13	13	13	13	13	13	11	1	–	–	–	5
BG Habana	11	11	–	11	11	11	11	11	11	11	11	11	–	11	4	–	–	–	20
M Steyn	10	10	–	10R	10R	10	–	–	–	–	–	–	–	5	–	11	10	–	52
PF du Preez	9	9	9	–	–	–	–	–	–	–	–	–	–	3	–	–	–	–	0
DJ Vermeulen	8	8	8	8	8	8	8	8	8	8	8	8	8	13	1	–	–	–	5
WS Alberts	7	7	–	–	–	–	–	–	–	–	–	–	–	2	–	–	–	–	0
L-FP Louw	6	6	–	6	6	6	6	–	–	–	–	–	–	6	–	–	–	–	0
V Matfield	5c	5c	5c	–	–	5	5	5	5	5	5	5	5	11	–	–	–	–	0
JP Botha	4	–	–	4	4R	–	8R	4R	4R	4R	–	–	–	7	–	–	–	–	0
JN du Plessis	3	3	3	3	3	3	3	3	3	3	3	–	–	11	–	–	–	–	0
BW du Plessis	2	2	2	2	2	2R	2R	2R	2	2	2R	2R	2	13	–	–	–	–	0
GG Steenkamp	1	1R	–	–	1	–	–	–	–	–	–	1R	–	4	–	–	–	–	0
SB Brits	2R	2R	–	–	–	–	–	–	–	–	–	–	–	2	–	–	–	–	0
T Mtawarira	1R	1	–	1	1R	1	1	1	1	1	1	–	1	11	–	–	–	–	0
CV Oosthuizen	3R	3R	1	–	–	–	–	–	3R	3R	3	3	–	7	1	–	–	–	5
L de Jager	5R	4R	4	5	5	4R	4R	–	–	–	4R	4R	–	9	2	–	–	–	10
SWP Burger	6R	7R	7	–	–	–	7R	7R	7R	7	–	–	–	7	1	–	–	–	5
R Pienaar	22R	10R	–	9	9	9	9	–	–	–	–	–	–	6	1	–	–	–	5
JL Goosen	10R	–	–	–	–	–	–	–	–	–	15	–	–	2	–	–	–	–	0
LN Mvovo	11R	x	11	–	x	–	–	–	–	–	–	–	11	3	2	–	–	–	10
PR van der Merwe	–	4	–	–	–	–	–	–	–	–	–	–	–	1	–	–	–	–	0
W Olivier	–	12R	–	–	–	–	–	–	–	–	–	–	–	1	–	–	–	–	0
H Pollard	–	–	10	10	10	–	10	10	10	10	x	10R	10R	9	2	14	8	1	65
MC Coetzee	–	–	6	7	7R	7	7	6	6	6	6	6	–	11	5	–	–	–	25
Z Kirchner	–	–	15R	–	–	–	–	–	–	–	–	–	–	1	–	–	–	–	0
F Hougaard	–	–	9R	x	9R	x	9	9	9	x	9R	9R	9R	8	1	–	–	–	5
M van der Merwe	–	–	1R	–	–	3R	3R	3R	3R	–	–	–	–	5	–	–	–	–	0
JA Strauss	–	–	2R	2R	2R	2	2	2	2R	2R	2	2	2R	11	–	–	–	–	0
TS Mohoje	–	–	8R	x	–	–	–	7	7	7	7R	7	7	7	–	–	–	–	0
JST Lewies	–	–	5R	–	–	–	–	–	–	–	–	–	–	1	–	–	–	–	0
TN Nyakane	–	–	3R	1R	–	1R	1R	1R	1R	1R	1	–	1R	10	–	–	–	–	0
ML Boshoff	–	–	10R	–	–	–	–	–	–	–	–	–	–	1	–	1	–	–	2
D de Allende	–	–	–	13	13	x	x	–	–	–	–	–	12R	3	–	–	–	–	0
J de Villiers	–	–	–	12c	12c	12c	12c	12c	12c	12c	12c	12c	12c	10	2	–	–	–	10
E Etzebeth	–	–	–	4R	4	4	4	4	4	4	4	4	4	10	–	–	–	–	0
JF Malherbe	–	–	–	3R	3R	–	–	–	–	–	–	–	–	2	–	–	–	–	0
JH Smith	–	–	–	–	7	–	–	–	–	–	–	–	–	1	–	–	–	–	0
PJ Lambie	–	–	–	–	–	6R	15R	10R	10R	10R	10	10	10	8	1	3	7	2	38
WR Whiteley	–	–	–	–	–	22R	6R	–	–	–	–	–	–	2	–	–	–	–	0
JM Reinach	–	–	–	–	–	–	9R	9R	9R	9	9	9	9	6	2	–	–	–	10
N Carr	–	–	–	–	–	–	–	–	–	–	7R	7	7	3	–	–	–	–	0
J Redelinghuys	–	–	–	–	–	–	–	–	–	–	–	3R	3R	2	–	–	–	–	0
Penalty tries	–	–	–	–	–	–	–	–	–	–	–	–	–	–	2	–	–	–	10
45 players took the field in a Test match in 2014														**288**	**38**	**29**	**25**	**3**	**332**

THE SPRINGBOKS IN 2014

TEST PLAYERS IN 2014 - CAREER STATS

PLAYER	Union/Club	Date of birth	Height	Weight	Career Tests	Career Tries	Career Conv.	Career Pen	Career DG	Pts
WS Alberts	KwaZulu-Natal	11/05/1984	1,92	120	32	7	0	0	0	25
ML Boshoff	Golden Lions	11/01/1989	1,79	87	1	0	1	0	0	2
JP Botha	Toulon, France	22/09/1979	2,02	122	85	7	0	0	0	35
SB Brits	Saracens, UK	16/05/1981	1,82	100	7	0	0	0	0	0
SWP Burger	Suntory Sungoliath, Japan	13/04/1983	1,93	110	75	14	0	0	0	70
N Carr	Western Province	04/04/1991	1,84	103	2	0	0	0	0	0
MC Coetzee	KwaZulu-Natal	08/05/1991	1,91	106	26	6	0	0	0	30
D de Allende	Western Province	25/11/1991	1,89	104	3	0	0	0	0	0
L de Jager	Free State	17/12/1992	2,05	125	9	2	0	0	0	10
J de Villiers	Western Province	24/02/1981	1,90	100	106	27	0	0	0	135
BW du Plessis	KwaZulu-Natal	22/05/1984	1,89	112	70	9	0	0	0	45
JN du Plessis	KwaZulu-Natal	16/11/1982	1,88	120	62	1	0	0	0	5
PF du Preez	Suntory Goliath, Japan	24/03/1982	1,82	91	70	15	0	0	0	75
E Etzebeth	Western Province	29/10/1991	2,03	117	33	0	0	0	0	0
JL Goosen	Racing Metro, France	27/07/1992	1,85	85	6	0	1	2	0	8
BG Habana	Toulon, France	12/06/1983	1,80	94	106	57	0	0	0	285
C Hendricks	Free State	18/04/1988	1,89	90	11	5	0	0	0	25
F Hougaard	Blue Bulls	06/04/1988	1,79	91	35	5	0	0	0	25
Z Kirchner	Leinster, Ireland	16/06/1984	1,84	92	29	5	0	0	0	25
PJ Lambie	KwaZulu-Natal	17/10/1990	1,78	87	40	2	18	18	2	106
WJ Le Roux	Griqualand West	18/08/1989	1,86	88	25	7	0	0	0	35
JST Lewies	KwaZulu-Natal	27/01/1992	2,00	114	1	0	0	0	0	0
L-FP Louw	Bath, England	15/06/1985	1,90	114	34	5	0	0	0	25
JF Malherbe	Western Province	14/03/1991	1,90	120	4	0	0	0	0	0
V Matfield	Blue Bulls	11/05/1977	2,00	108	121	7	0	0	0	35
TS Mohoje	Free State	03/08/1990	1,93	106	7	0	0	0	0	0
T Mtawarira	KwaZulu-Natal	01/08/1985	1,83	115	64	2	0	0	0	10
LN Mvovo	KwaZulu-Natal	03/06/1986	1,85	94	10	3	0	0	0	15
TN Nyakane	Free State	04/05/1989	1,78	109	13	1	0	0	0	5
W Olivier	Montpellier, France	11/06/1983	1,86	94	38	1	0	0	0	5
CV Oosthuizen	Free State	22/03/1989	1,81	127	21	3	0	0	0	15
R Pienaar	Ulster, Ireland	10/03/1984	1,87	92	80	8	22	17	0	135
J-PR Pietersen	Panasonic Wild Knights, Japan	12/07/1986	1,90	106	59	18	0	0	0	90
H Pollard	Blue Bulls	11/03/1994	1,89	97	9	2	14	8	1	65
J Redelinghuys	Golden Lions	11/09/1989	1,76	100	2	0	0	0	0	0
JM Reinach	KwaZulu-Natal	07/02/1990	1,75	84	6	2	0	0	0	10
JL Serfontein	Blue Bulls	15/04/1993	1,87	97	20	2	0	0	0	10
JH Smith	Toulon, France	30/07/1981	1,96	110	70	12	0	0	0	60
GG Steenkamp	Toulouse, France	12/06/1981	1,89	122	53	6	0	0	0	30
M Steyn	Stade Francais, France	11/07/1984	1,84	91	59	8	99	142	8	688
JA Strauss	Free State	18/11/1985	1,84	114	44	5	0	0	0	25
M van der Merwe	Blue Bulls	24/10/1990	1,88	128	4	0	0	0	0	0
PR van der Merwe	Blue Bulls	03/06/1985	1,98	120	35	1	0	0	0	5
DJ Vermeulen	Western Province	03/07/1986	1,93	108	29	2	0	0	0	10
WR Whiteley	Golden Lions	18/09/1987	1,92	97	2	0	0	0	0	0
45 Players					257	155	187	11	2179	

Bold letters denotes new Springbok.

CASTLE LAGER INCOMING TOUR

Incoming Tours

Date	Match	Venue	Referee
7 Jun	South Africa 47 World XV 13	Newlands, Cape Town	George Clancy (Ireland)
10 Jun	Eastern Province 12 Wales 34	Nelson Mandela Bay Stadium, PE	Lourens van der Merwe (South Africa)
14 Jun	South Africa 38 Wales 16	Kings Park, Durban	Roman Poite (France)
21 Jun	South Africa 31 Wales 30	Mbombela Stadium, Nelspruit	Steve R Walsh (Australia)
28 Jun	South Africa 55 Scotland 6	Nelson Mandela Bay Stadium, PE	Glen Jackson (New Zealand)

The Springbok old guard of Fourie du Preez and Victor Matfield made their return to international rugby in 2014.

CASTLE LAGER INCOMING TOUR

South Africa 38 Wales 16
(Half-time 28-9)

14 June, Growth-Point Kings Park, Durban (37 812). Referee: R Poite (France)

SOUTH AFRICA

Tries: Habana (2), Vermeulen, Le Roux, Hendricks. Conversions: Steyn (5). Penalty: Steyn.

WJ le Roux (LN Mvovo, 70), C Hendricks, JP-R Pietersen, JL Serfontein, BG Habana, M Steyn (J Goosen, 70/R Pienaar, 74), PF du Preez, DJ Vermeulen, WS Alberts (SWP Burger, 58), L-FP Louw, V Matfield (capt), JP Botha (L de Jager, 41), JN du Plessis (CV Oosthuizen, 59), BW du Plessis (SB Brits, 70), GG Steenkamp (T Mtawarira, 45).

TEST DEBUTS: C Hendricks [Springbok # 855], L de Jager [Springbok #856].

NOTES: V Matfield played in his 111th Test (equalled JW Smit's SA record). Equalled JN Ackermann's record for oldest Springbok at 37 years & 34 days. Oldest Springbok captain ever. GG Steenkamp played in his 50th Test.

WALES

Try: Cuthbert. Conversion: Hook. Penalty goal: Biggar. Drop Goal: Biggar (2).

LB Williams (MJ Morgan, 56), ACG Cuthbert, JJV Davies, JH Roberts, GP North, DR Biggar (JW Hook, 65), WM Phillips (G Davies, 56), TT Faletau, AC Shingler (J Turnbull, 56), DJ Lydiate, AW Jones (capt), LC Charteris (IR Evans, 56), AR Jones (S Lee, 32), KJ Owens (M Rees, 59), GD Jenkins (P James, 59).

TEST DEBUTS: G Davies, MJ Morgan. YELLOW CARD: JH Roberts (13-23). NOTES: AR Jones played in his 100th Test (Wales 95, British & Irish Lions 5)

THERE WERE remarkable performances by Willie le Roux and Francois Louw, while the Springboks' comfortable 38-16 victory over Wales in Durban also marked the return to Test rugby of evergreen stalwarts Victor Matfield and Schalk Burger.

Had it not been so easy for the Springboks in the first half – they notched their fourth try a few minutes before half-time – the scoreline might have been bigger.

They led 28-9 at the break and increased that stranglehold to 38-9 before effectively marking time for a half an hour as opposed to displaying the urgency to inflict humiliation on the Welsh.

Fullback Le Roux provided the attacking spark as he crafted two tries for wing Bryan Habana with a superbly weighted chip kick and a show-and-go dummy respectively; he also made the scoring pass to energetic Test debutant Cornal Hendricks.

For good measure Le Roux also scored one himself by gathering his own dab over the top after the roll of the ball had flummoxed Wales fullback Liam Williams.

South Africa's other try was scored by No 8 Duane Vermeulen after they had put the ball in the corner from a penalty and produced a variation on their usual driving maul.

The Springboks were helped in no small measure by a contentious call between referee Romain Poite and television match official Graham Hughes to sin-bin the visitors' inside centre, Jamie Roberts, for playing Le Roux in the air in the 13th minute.

Vermeulen scored his try and Habana his second in Roberts' absence as the hosts stretched their lead from 7-3 to 21-3.

Willie le Roux with his Man of the Match award.

Matfield led South Africa in regular skipper Jean de Villiers' absence and the 37-year-old lock's performance in the lineouts and general play belied his age.

Burger, having cheated death in hospital – he contracted bacterial meningitis the year before – also made an emotional and high-tempo return to Test rugby as a flank replacement for Willem Alberts.

While Le Roux's performance was, on the face of it, the most outstanding one, the statistics point to a phenomenal contribution by openside flank Louw.

He won three turnovers on defence and made 13 tackles, of which one was 'positive', meaning he drove an opponent back, and the other 12 'dominant'.

Louw also managed to slow Wales's possession 15 times and in 13 of those instances he was the second man to the breakdown – in other words, the first after the tackle had been made. On top of that he cleaned 41 rucks on attack. Quite simply, he was everywhere.

These statistics – the most industrious yet by a Springbok during Heyneke Meyer's coaching tenure – were achieved with the ball in play for a mere 39 minutes and 13 seconds.

Aside from a purposeful start in which flyhalf Dan Biggar slotted an early drop goal, Wales were awful. This was highlighted by a schoolboy error that saw Biggar passing the ball forward off the ground to substitute scrumhalf Gareth Davies with the tryline at their mercy. It was all the more criminal given Davies' superb break in the build-up.

Jan Serfontein, playing inside centre for South Africa, had done superbly well to scythe down Biggar with a cover tackle.

Wales did manage a moment of inspiration with a long-range try scored by right wing Alex Cuthbert from a counter-attack 11 minutes before the end, but by then the horse had bolted.

SCORING SEQUENCE

Min	Action	Score
3	Biggar drop goal	0-3
7	Habana try, Steyn conversion	7-3
16	Vermeulen try, Steyn conversion	14-3
20	Biggar drop goal	14-6
21	Habana try, Steyn conversion	21-6
38	Le Roux try, Steyn conversion	28-6
40	Biggar penalty	28-9
45	Steyn penalty	31-9
52	Hendricks try, Steyn conversion	38-9
69	Cuthbert try, Hook conversion	38-16

CASTLE LAGER INCOMING TOUR

South Africa 31 Wales 30
(Half-time 14-17)

21 June, Mbombela Stadium, Nelspruit (25 424). Referee: SR Walsh (Australia)

SOUTH AFRICA

Tries: Penalty tries (2), Hendricks, Le Roux. Conversions: Steyn (4). Penalty: Steyn.

WJ le Roux, C Hendricks, JP-R Pietersen, JL Serfontein (W Olivier, 74), BG Habana, M Steyn (R Pienaar, 23-29), PF du Preez, DJ Vermeulen, WS Alberts (SWP Burger, 25), L-FP Louw, V Matfield (capt), PR van der Merwe (L de Jager, 46-50), JN du Plessis (CV Oosthuizen, 58), BW du Plessis (SB Brits, 66), T Mtawarira (GG Steenkamp, 66).

UNUSED SUB: *LN Mvovo.* **YELLOW CARD:** *PR van der Merwe (58-68).*

WALES

Tries: Roberts, Cuthbert, Owens. Conversions: Biggar (3). Penalties: Biggar (3).

LB Williams, ACG Cuthbert, JJV Davies, JH Roberts, GP North, DR Biggar, WM Phillips, TT Faletau, J Turnbull, DJ Lydiate, AW Jones (capt), LC Charteris (J Ball, 74), S Lee (AR Jarvis, 52), KJ Owens (M Rees, 74), GD Jenkins (P James, 74). Unused subs: DT Baker, G Davies, JW Hook, MJ Morgan.

YELLOW CARD: *LC Charteris (30-40), DR Biggar (32-43)*

THE SPRINGBOKS stared disaster in the face before two tries inside the final 10 minutes secured a lucky 31-30 victory at the Mbombela Stadium.

Notwithstanding their poor performance, South Africa's tremendous fightback from 30-17 down demonstrated immense character.

The clincher was a penalty try in the 78th minute. Cornal Hendricks, playing like a man possessed on the right wing, was shoulder-charged into touch by Wales fullback Liam Williams as he reached for the right-hand corner.

Had Williams made a legal tackle, he would have left Morné Steyn with a difficult touchline conversion attempt. The Springbok flyhalf, however, was able to convert from in front of the posts.

There were some nervous moments at the death as Wales held onto possession until the second minute of added time, when flyhalf Dan Biggar hurriedly attempted a drop goal. He missed to leave local fans breathing an enormous sigh of relief but at the same time marvelling at the fightback they had witnessed.

Earlier, it was as if the Springboks hadn't pitched mentally after the previous week's comfortable victory. Wales, on the other hand, were a team determined to win. With a little more composure and belief, they might have pulled it off, although it must be said that they also enjoyed a large slice of luck when hooker Kenneth Owens' converted try in the 46th minute saw them establish a 24-14 lead.

Owens appeared to knock the ball on, but it was ruled otherwise after a conference between referee Steve Walsh, who was watching the stadium screen, and television match official Glenn Newman.

By then the Springboks had already staged a rally in the final 10 minutes of the first

Willem Alberts, Francois Louw, Duane Vermeulen and Schalk Burger celebrate the series victory over Wales.

half to come back from a 17-0 deficit – after just 23 minutes – to pull back to within three points at half-time.

South Africa got the first of their two penalty tries after Wales had continuously resorted to illegal play to stop the driving maul. Lock Luke Charteris was yellow-carded in the 30th minute and Biggar joined him in the sin-bin two minutes after that as the visitors resorted to desperate defensive measures.

Biggar's creative touches had earlier been crucial in paving the way for tries by their Lions duo of inside centre Jamie Roberts and right wing Alex Cuthbert.

The Springboks immediately made their two-man advantage count from the kick-off and fullback Willie le Roux threw a crucial long pass to Pietersen before collecting the ball again in the middle of the pitch. He then floated laterally across the field to flummox the defence before making a scoring pass to Hendricks.

But the first half-hour of the second half yielded only anxiety, which was magnified by a yellow card to lock Flip van der Merwe for foul play from a kick-off in the 58th minute. Wales could however manage no more than the Biggar penalty that increased their lead to 30-17 during the bruiser's absence.

Staring down the barrel, the Springboks set about casting their magic.

Le Roux finished off in the 72nd minute after South Africa produced an inspired spell of attacking play – a team transformed from the one that was uncharacteristically peeling off tackles in the first half.

Then followed the final flurry that led to the decisive penalty try – late, but great!

SCORING SEQUENCE

Min	Action	Score
13	Biggar missed penalty	0-0
13	Biggar penalty	0-3
17	Steyn missed penalty	0-3
19	Roberts try, Biggar conversion	0-10
22	Cuthbert try, Biggar conversion	0-17
32	Penalty try, Steyn conversion	7-17
34	Hendricks try, Steyn conversion	14-17
46	Owens try, Biggar conversion	14-24
55	Steyn penalty	17-24
57	Biggar penalty	17-27
66	Biggar penalty	17-30
72	Le Roux try, Steyn conversion	24-30
78	Penalty try, Steyn conversion	31-30

CASTLE LAGER INCOMING TOUR

South Africa 55 Scotland 6
(Half-time 19-6)

---

28 June, Nelson Mandela Bay Stadium, Port Elizabeth (40 973). Referee: G Jackson (NZ)

SOUTH AFRICA
Tries: De Jager (2), Mvovo (2), Coetzee (2), Pietersen, Le Roux. Conversions: Pollard (5). Penalties: Pollard, Boshoff.

WJ le Roux (Z Kirchner 22-28, 76), C Hendricks, JP-R Pietersen, JL Serfontein, LN Mvovo, H Pollard (ML Boshoff, 71), PF du Preez (F Hougaard, 29), DJ Vermeulen (TS Mohoje, 67), SWP Burger, MC Coetzee, V Matfield (capt, JST Lewies, 71), L de Jager, JN du Plessis (TN Nyakane, 71), BW du Plessis (JA Strauss, 55), CV Oosthuizen (M van der Merwe, 50).

TEST DEBUTS: H Pollard [Springbok # 857], M van der Merwe [# 858], TS Mohoje [# 859], JST Lewies [# 860], ML Boshoff [# 861]

SCOTLAND
Penalties: Weir (2).

SW Hogg (PE Murchie, 71), SD Maitland (DJ Fife, 54), NJ de Luca, P Horne, TSF Seymour, D Weir, HB Pyrgos (GJ Hart, 76), A Ashe, CC Fusaro (T Holmes, 51), RJ Harley (T Holmes, 53-63), GS Gilchrist (capt), TJM Swinson (JD Gray, 61), GDS Cross (EA Murray, 53), RW Ford (K Bryce, 61), AG Dickinson (MJ Low, 78).

TEST DEBUT: A Ashe, T Holmes. **YELLOW CARD:** TJM Swinson (51-61)

SOUTH AFRICA's comfortable 55-6 victory over an under-strength Scotland team will quickly be forgotten for the rugby, but may well go down as a significant day as it eased Handré Pollard into Test rugby.

It was a bold selection by Heyneke Meyer after the previous week's great escape against Wales, especially as the 20-year-old flyhalf would not have Fourie du Preez and Jean de Villiers either side of him to provide guidance.

Instead, the sometimes flaky Ruan Pienaar started at scrumhalf with Du Preez tied to Suntory Sungoliath in Japan, while youngster Jan Serfontein continued at inside centre in place of the injured De Villiers.

But any doubts about Pollard's ability to step into the big leagues were soon eradicated. He provided a clue as to what was to come later in the match, and indeed the season, when he attacked the advantage line with little more than two minutes played.

His distribution skills also played a big role in the crafting of South Africa's second and third tries, scored by fullback Willie le Roux and left wing Lwazi Mvovo respectively.

Le Roux's came off second-phase ball after South Africa had kicked for touch from a penalty. The ball travelled through the hands with Pollard attacking the line and timing his pass superbly to pave the way for the touchdown.

For Mvovo's try, Pollard threw a delightful cut-out pass to right wing JP Pietersen, who broke the line and grubbered. Mvovo chased down the kick and finished.

With those tries added to an earlier one by flank Marcell Coetzee, who eventually drove over after the Springboks had relentlessly plugged away, the lead was 19-3 with just 17 minutes played.

Perhaps it happened all too easy because it took the Springboks until the 12th min-

Handre Pollard makes his Test debut against Scotland.

ute of the second half to score their next try – Coetzee's second after a rolling maul.

South Africa had added no more than a penalty in the preceding 30-odd minutes, but importantly administered a dosage of slow poison.

Coetzee's second try was the catalyst for the floodgates to open. First, Pietersen finished in the corner in the 57th minute as the Springboks piled on the pressure, Mvovo then added an intercept try in the 62nd and there were two more by lock Lood de Jager.

The No 4 lock's first was a delightful effort after he collected an off-load by Coetzee, who had pounced on the ball after Scotland scrumhalf Henry Pergos had failed to field a high kick by Pienaar's replacement, Francois Hougaard.

De Jager added his second from a scoring pass by Hougaard after South Africa had been handed the initiative thanks to a poorly-judged kick by Scotland flyhalf Duncan Weir. Mvovo initiated the attack after gathering the ball.

Marnitz Boshoff, who had meanwhile also made his Test debut as a replacement for Pollard, converted to bring up the final score.

Sharks lock Stephan Lewies, Bulls prop Marcel van der Merwe and Cheetahs flank Teboho Mohoje also made their Test debuts as they were sent on in place of Victor Matfield, Coenie Oosthuizen and Duane Vermeulen respectively.

It was one of those occasions that afforded Meyer the opportunity to run the rule over a few players, with Pollard, Van der Merwe and Mohoje all going on to make good contributions in the Castle Rugby Championship.

SCORING SEQUENCE

Min	Action	Score
4	Coetzee try, Pollard conversion	7-0
8	Weir penalty	7-3
11	Le Roux try, Pollard conversion	14-3
17	Mvovo try, Pollard missed conversion	19-3
37	Weir penalty	19-6
45	Pollard penalty	22-6
52	Coetzee try, Pollard conversion	29-6
57	Pietersen try, Pollard missed conv.	34-6
62	Mvovo try, Pollard conversion	41-6
65	De Jager try, Pollard conversion	48-6
78	De Jager try, Boshoff conversion	55-6

SOUTH AFRICA APPEARANCES & POINTS

Player	Date of birth	Height	Weight	Union/Club	Wales	Wales	Scotland	Apps	T	C	P	DG	Pts
WJ (Willie) le Roux	18/08/1989	1,86	88	Free State	15	15	15	3	3	–	–	–	15
C (Cornal) Hendricks	18/04/1988	1,89	90	Free State	14	14	14	3	2	–	–	–	10
JP-R (JP) Pietersen	12/07/1986	1,90	106	KZN	13	13	13	3	1	–	–	–	5
JL (Jan) Serfontein	15/04/1993	1,87	97	Blue Bulls	12	12	12	3	–	–	–	–	0
BG (Bryan) Habana	12/06/1983	1,79	94	Toulon (Fra)	11	11	–	2	2	–	–	–	10
M (Morné) Steyn	11/07/1984	1,86	91	Stade Francais (Fra)	10	10	–	2	–	9	2	–	24
PF (Fourie) du Preez	24/03/182	1,82	91	Suntory Goliath (Jap)	9	9	9	3	–	–	–	–	0
DJ (Duane) Vermeulen	03/07/1986	1,93	108	Western Province	8	8	8	3	1	–	–	–	5
WS (Willem) Alberts	05/11/1984	1,91	119	KZN	7	7	–	2	–	–	–	–	0
L-FP (Francois) Louw	15/06/1985	1,90	114	Bath (Eng)	6	6	–	2	–	–	–	–	0
V (Victor) Matfield	11/05/1977	2,00	108	Blue Bulls	5c	5c	5c	3	–	–	–	–	0
JP (Bakkies) Botha	22/09/1979	2,02	122	Toulon (Fra)	4	–	–	1	–	–	–	–	0
JN (Jannie) du Plessis	16/11/1982	1,87	119	KZN	3	3	3	3	–	–	–	–	0
BW (Bismarck) du Plessis	22/05/1984	1,89	113	KZN	2	2	2	3	–	–	–	–	0
GG (Gurthro) Steenkamp	12/06/1981	1,89	122	Toulouse (Fra)	1	1R	–	2	–	–	–	–	0
SB (Schalk) Brits	16/05/1981	1,82	100	Saracens (Eng)	2R	2R	–	2	–	–	–	–	0
T (Tendai) Mtawarira	01/07/1985	1,83	115	KZN	1R	1	–	2	–	–	–	–	0
CV (Coenie) Oosthuizen	22/03/1989	1,83	127	Free State	3R	3R	1	3	–	–	–	–	0
L (Lood) de Jager	17/12/1992	2,05	125	Free State	5R	4R	4	3	2	–	–	–	10
SWP (Schalk) Burger	11/04/1983	1,93	110	Western Province	6R	7R	7	3	–	–	–	–	0
R (Ruan) Pienaar	10/03/1984	1,86	92	Ulster (N Ire)	22R	10R	–	2	–	–	–	–	0
JL (Johan) Goosen	27/07/1992	1,85	85	Free State	10R	–	–	1	–	–	–	–	0
LN (Lwazi) Mvovo	03/06/1986	1,81	92	KZN	11R	x	11	2	2	–	–	–	10
PR (Flip) van der Merwe	03/06/1985	1,99	120	Blue Bulls	–	4	–	1	–	–	–	–	0
W (Wynand) Olivier	11/06/1983	1,86	94	Montpellier (Fra)	–	12R	–	1	–	–	–	–	0
H (Handre) Pollard	11/03/1994	1,89	97	Blue Bulls	–	–	10	1	–	5	1	–	0
MC (Marcell) Coetzee	08/05/1991	1,90	106	KZN	–	–	6	1	–	–	–	–	0
Z (Zane) Kirchner	16/06/1984	1,84	92	Leinster (Ire)	–	–	15R	1	–	–	–	–	0
F (Francois) Hougaard	06/04/1988	1,79	91	Blue Bulls	–	–	9R	1	–	–	–	–	0
M (Marcel) van der Merwe	24/10/1990	1,88	128	Blue Bulls	–	–	1R	1	–	–	–	–	0
JA (Adriaan) Strauss	18/11/1985	1,84	111	Free State	–	–	2R	1	–	–	–	–	0
TS (Teboho) Mohoje	03/08/1990	1,93	106	Free State	–	–	8R	1	–	–	–	–	0
JST (Stephan) Lewies	27/01/1992	2,00	114	KZN	–	–	5R	1	–	–	–	–	0
TN (Trevor) Nyakane	04/05/1989	1,78	109	Free State	–	–	3R	1	–	–	–	–	0
ML (Marnitz) Boshoff	11/01/1989	1,79	87	Golden Lions	–	–	10R	1	–	1	–	–	0
Penalty tries	–	–	–	–	–	–	–	–	2	–	–	–	10
35 Players								68	17	15	3	0	124

WALES APPEARANCES & POINTS

	Date of birth	Height	Weight	Club	EP	SA 1	SA 2	Apps	T	C	P	DG	Pts
MJ (Matthew) Morgan	23/04/1992	1,73	75	Ospreys	15	15R	x	2	–	–	–	–	0
ACH (Alex) Cuthbert	05/04/1990	1,98	103	Cardiff	14	14	14	3	3	–	–	–	15
C (Cory) Allen	11/02/1993	1,93	100	Cardiff	13	–	–	1	1	–	–	–	5
S (Steven) Shingler	20/06/1991	1,90	88	Scarlets	12	–	–	1	–	–	–	–	0
J (Jordan) Williams	20/09/1993	1,73	81	Scarlets	11	–	–	1	–	–	–	–	0
JW (James) Hook	27/06/1985	1,83	96	Perpignan (Fra)	10	10R	x	2	1	4	1	–	16
R (Rhodri) Williams	05/05/1993	1,76	84	Scarlets	9	–	–	1	–	–	–	–	0
D (Dan) Baker	06/07/1992	1,88	114	Ospreys	8	–	x	1	–	–	–	–	0
J (Josh) Turnbull	12/03/1988	1,93	99	Scarlets	7	7R	7	3	1	–	–	–	5
DJ (Dan) Lydiate	18/12/1987	1,93	114	Racing Metro (Fra)	6c	6	6	3	–	–	–	–	0
IR (Ian) Evans	04/10/1984	2,04	116	Ospreys	5	4R	–	2	–	–	–	–	0
J (Jake) Ball	21/06/1991	2,00	121	Scarlets	4	–	4R	2	–	–	–	–	0
RP (Rhodri) Jones	23/12/1991	1,91	116	Scarlets	3	–	–	1	–	–	–	–	0
SJ (Scott) Baldwin	12/07/1988	1,90	114	Ospreys	2	–	–	1	–	–	–	–	0
P (Paul) James	13/05/1982	1,86	115	Bath (Eng)	1	1R	1R	3	–	–	–	–	0
M (Matthew) Rees	09/12/1980	1,83	108	Cardiff	2R	2R	2R	3	–	–	–	–	0
A (Aaron) Jarvis	20/05/1986	1,83	117	Ospreys	1R	–	3R	2	–	–	–	–	0
S (Samson) Lee	30/11/1992	1,80	115	Scarlets	3R	3R	3	3	–	–	–	–	0
LC (Luke) Charteris	09/03/1983	2,06	125	Perpignan (Fra)	4R	4	4	3	–	–	–	–	0
AC (Aaron) Shingler	07/08/1987	1,96	105	Scarlets	6R	7	–	2	–	–	–	–	0
G (Gareth) Davies	18/08/1990	1,78	85	Scarlets	14R	9R	x	2	1	–	–	–	5
GP (George) North	13/04/1992	1,92	109	Northampton (Eng)	x	11	11	2	–	–	–	–	0
LB (Liam) Williams	09/04/1991	1,88	86	Scarlets	x	15	15	2	–	–	–	–	0
JJV (Jonathan) Davies	05/04/1988	186	105	Scarlets	–	13	13	2	–	–	–	–	0
JH (Jamie) Roberts	08/11/1986	1,93	110	Racing Metro (Fra)	–	12	12	2	1	–	–	–	5
DR (Dan) Biggar	16/10/1989	1,88	89	Ospreys	–	10	10	2	–	3	4	2	24
WM (Mike) Phillips	29/08/1982	1,91	101	Racing Metro (Fra)	–	9	9	2	–	–	–	–	0
TT (Toby) Faletau	12/11/1990	1,88	110	Newport Gwent Dragons	–	8	8	2	–	–	–	–	0
A-W (Alun-Wyn) Jones	19/09/1985	1,96	12	Ospreys	–	5c	5c	2	–	–	–	–	0
AR (Adam) Jones	08/03/1981	1,83	122	Ospreys	–	3	–	1	–	–	–	–	0
KJ (Ken) Owens	03/01/1987	1,86	109	Scarlets	–	2	2	2	1	–	–	–	5
GD (Gethin) Jenkins	17/11/1980	1,88	121	Cardiff	–	1	1	2	–	–	–	–	0
32 Players								63	9	7	5	2	80

Head Coach: Warren Gatland **Assistant Coaches:** Rob Howley, Robin McBryde & Shaun Edwards **Skills Coach:** Neil Jenkins **Team Manager:** Alan Phillips **Strength & Conditioning:** Adam Beard & John Asby **Doctor:** Dr Geoff Davies **Physio:** Mark Davies **Performance Analysis:** Rhys Long, Rhodri Brown & Andrew Hughes **Equipment Support:** John Rowlands **Media Manager:** Luke Broadley **Medical Manager:** Prav Mathema **Sport Scientist:** Ryan Chambers **Nutritionist:** John Williams **Soft Tissue Therapist:** Angela Rickard **Player Welfare:** Andy McCann

CASTLE LAGER INCOMING TOUR

SCOTLAND APPEARANCES & POINTS

PLAYER	Date of birth	Height	Weight	Club	SA	Apps	T	C	P	DG	Pts
SW (Stuart) Hogg	24/06/1992	1,83	87	Glasgow	15	1	–	–	–	–	0
SD (Sean) Maitland	14/09/1988	1,87	98	Glasgow	14	1	–	–	–	–	0
NJ (Nick) de Luca	01/02/1984	1,83	93	Biarritz (Fra)	13	1	–	–	–	–	0
P (Peter) Horne	05/10/1989	1,83	90	Glasgow	12	1	–	–	–	–	0
TSF (Tommy) Seymour	01/07/1988	1,83	94	Glasgow	11	1	–	–	–	–	0
D (Duncan) Weir	10/05/1991	1,76	90	Glasgow	10	1	–	–	2	–	6
HB (Henry) Pyrgos	09/07/1989	1,78	80	Glasgow	9	1	–	–	–	–	0
A (Adam) Ashe	24/07/1993	1,93	105	Glasgow	8	1	–	–	–	–	0
CC (Chris) Fusaro	21/07/1989	1,80	95	Glasgow	7	1	–	–	–	–	0
RJ (Rob) Harley	26/05/1990	1,98	107	Glasgow	6	1	–	–	–	–	0
GS (Grant) Gilchrist	09/08/1990	2,03	120	Edinburgh	5c	1	–	–	–	–	0
TJM (Tim) Swinson	17/02/1987	1,93	111	Glasgow	4	1	–	–	–	–	0
GDS (Geoff) Cross	11/12/1982	1,83	116	Edinburgh	3	1	–	–	–	–	0
RW (Ross) Ford	23/04/1984	1,85	114	Edinburgh	2	1	–	–	–	–	0
AG (Alasdair) Dickinson	11/09/1983	1,85	107	Sale (Eng)	1	1	–	–	–	–	0
K (Kevin) Bryce	07/09/1988	1,85	101	Glasgow	2R	1	–	–	–	–	0
MJ (Moray) Low	28/11/1984	1,88	122	Glasgow	1R	1	–	–	–	–	0
EA (Euan) Murray	07/08/1980	1,88	115	Worcester (Eng)	3R	1	–	–	–	–	0
JD (Jonny) Gray	14/03/1994	1,98	119	Glasgow	4R	1	–	–	–	–	0
T (Tyrone) Holmes	15/04/1986	1,85	100	Glasgow	7R	1	–	–	–	–	0
GJ (Grayson) Hart	19/06/1988	1,85	91	Edinburgh	9R	1	–	–	–	–	0
DJ (Dougie) Fife	08/08/1990	1,87	95	Edinburgh	14R	1	–	–	–	–	0
(PE) Peter Murchie	07/01/1986	1,91	93	Glasgow	15R	1	–	–	–	–	0
P (Pat) MacArthur	27/04/1987	1,83	99	Glasgow	–	–	–	–	–	–	0
J (Jon) Welsh	13/10/1986	1,85	112	Glasgow	–	–	–	–	–	–	0
RJH (Ruaridh) Jackson	12/02/1988	1,83	86	Glasgow	–	–	–	–	–	–	0
AJ (Alex) Dunbar	23/04/1990	1,87	100	Glasgow	–	–	–	–	–	–	0
27 Players (of which 23 appeared in the Test vs South Africa)						23	0	0	2	0	6

Head Coach: Vern Cotter **Director of Rugby:** Scott Johnson
Assistant Coaches: Jonathan Humphreys, Massimo Cuttita & Duncan Hodge
Team Manager: Gavin Scott **Strength & Conditioning:** Neill Potts & James Walkinshaw
Doctor: Dr James Robson **Physio:** Paul McGinley & Stuart Paterson
Video Analyst: Robert Holdsworth **Baggage master:** John Pennycuick
Media Manager: Graham Law

CASTLE LAGER RUGBY CHAMPIONSHIP

Rugby Championship

Date	Venue				
16 Aug	ANZ Stadium, Sydney	Australia	12	New Zealand	12
16 Aug	Loftus Versfeld, Pretoria	South Africa	13	Argentina	6
23 Aug	Eden Park, Auckland	New Zealand	51	Australia	20
23 Aug	Estadio Padre Ernesto Martearena, Salta	Argentina	31	South Africa	33
6 Sep	McLean Park, Napier	New Zealand	28	Argentina	9
6 Sep	Patersons Stadium, Perth	Australia	24	South Africa	23
13 Sep	Westpac Stadium, Wellington	New Zealand	14	South Africa	10
13 Sep	Cbus Super Stadium, Gold Coast	Australia	32	Argentina	25
27 Sep	Newlands, Cape Town	South Africa	28	Australia	10
27 Sep	Estadio Ciudad de la Plata, La Plata	Argentina	13	New Zealand	34
4 Oct	Ellis Park, Johannesburg	South Africa	27	New Zealand	25
4 Oct	Estadio Malvinas Argentinas, Mendoza	Argentina	21	Australia	17

LOG

Team	P	W	L	D	PF	PA	PD	TF	TA	BP	PTS
New Zealand	6	4	1	1	164	91	73	18	7	4	22
South Africa	6	4	2	0	134	110	24	13	10	3	19
Australia	6	2	3	1	115	160	-45	10	16	1	11
Argentina	6	1	5	0	105	157	-52	9	17	3	7

Note: BP = Bonus point

The Springboks finally get one over the All Blacks.

CASTLE LAGER RUGBY CHAMPIONSHIP

South Africa 13 Argentina 6
(Half-time 10-6)

17 August, Loftus Versfeld, Pretoria, (30 453). Referee: John Lacey (Ireland)

SOUTH AFRICA
Try: Pienaar. Conversion: Pollard. Penalties: Pollard, Steyn.

WJ Le Roux, C Hendricks, D de Allende, J de Villiers (Capt), BG Habana, H Pollard (M Steyn, 46), R Pienaar, DJ Vermeulen, MC Coetzee, L-F Louw, L de Jager, JP Botha (E Etzebeth, 41), JN du Plessis (JF Malherbe, 67), BW du Plessis (JA Strauss, 56), T Mtawarira (TN Nyakane, 79).

UNUSED SUBS: TS Mohoje, F Hougaard, JL Serfontein. *TEST DEBUT:* D de Allende [Springbok #862].
CHAMPIONSHIP DEBUTS: C Hendricks, D de Allende, H Pollard, L de Jager, JF Malherbe.
Note: J de Villiers played in his 45th Rugby Championship match for a new SA record.

ARGENTINA
Penalties: Sanchez (2).

J Tuculet, H Agulla (LP Gonzalez Amorosino, 61), MT Bosch, S Gonzales Iglesias, M Montero, FN Sanchez (J de la Fuente, 65), M Landajo (TM Cubelli, 41), JM Leguizamon, JM Fernandez Lobbe, PN Matera (LV Senatore, 58), T Lavanini (M Alemanno, 75), MT Galarza, R Herrera (FN Tetaz Chaparo, 61), A Creevy (Capt), MI Ayerza (L Noguera Paz, 78). Unused sub: ME Cortese.
CHAMPIONSHIP DEBUTS: J Tuculet, M Montero, S Gonzalez Iglesias, J de la Fuente, M Alemanno, R Herrera, FN Tetaz Chaparo, L Noguera Paz.

SOMETIMES you just have to take the win without reflecting on the performance and South Africa's 13-6 victory over Argentina at a rain-soaked Loftus Versfeld fell neatly into that category.

The Springboks started superbly, with scrumhalf Ruan Pienaar finishing after a surge down the blindside in which he combined nicely with right wing Cornal Hendricks. Flyhalf Handré Pollard converted expertly and the nerves were duly settled.

But a torrential downpour instantly changed the dynamic of the game, which ended up being a messy, error-ridden affair in which neither side was able to construct much.

Both sides added six points after Pienaar's early score and the Springboks ended up desperately defending their goal-line before the Pumas knocked on and referee John Lacey's final whistle poured cold water on the very distinct possibility of a draw.

For coach Heyneke Meyer the unseasonal, monsoon-like conditions brought about a very unsatisfying turn of events.

A home fixture against Argentina would, under normal circumstances, be regarded as an opportunity for a bonus-point victory. The Springboks, after all, had thrashed their opponents 73-13 in the corresponding fixture in 2013.

It was not the mature performance Meyer would have hoped for from his side in the difficult conditions. But a reflection thereon also needs to take into consideration that Meyer experimented with Lood de Jager, normally a front-of-the-lineout second-rower, as a No 5 lock, while also fielding inexperienced players in crucial backline spots in Pollard and outside centre Damian de Allende.

The conditions deprived Meyer of the opportunity to build properly on Pollard's confidence following his impressive debut against Scotland. De Allende, for his part,

CASTLE LAGER RUGBY CHAMPIONSHIP

Damian de Allende made his Test debut in monsoon-like conditions at Loftus Versfeld.

could not get his hands on the ball in favourable positions.

Pollard had a bit of a nightmare in the first half, twice booting the ball directly out from restarts and making a few other errors that hamstrung the home side.

He was replaced by Morné Steyn in the 46th minute and, but for a kick that was charged down by Pumas substitute wing Lucas Gonzalez Amorosino, the veteran brought a much-needed steady head.

While just deserving of their victory, South Africa had their fair share of luck as well. Flyhalf Nicolas Sanchez broke impressively for Argentina in the 18th minute but his pass was knocked on by left wing Manuel Montero, who might otherwise have had a sprint for the corner.

Argentina forced the Springbok scrum into submission early on but Lacey was wise to their illegal tricks, which might have fooled a less observant match official. South Africa's inability to win clean lineout possession however meant that Meyer could not reflect positively on their performance in the set phases.

The Springboks' biggest heroes were openside flank Francois Louw and fullback Willie le Roux. Louw competed superbly at the breakdown while Le Roux showed that he can be as safe at the back as he can be potent on attack.

The home side would probably have made sure of victory earlier had skipper Jean de Villiers not decided for the ball to be kicked into the corner in the 64th minute instead of asking Steyn to slot an easy penalty.

But with victory ultimately secured it mattered little.

It was as ugly a win as you can get, but as the tired old adage goes: a win is a win!

SCORING SEQUENCE

Min	Action	Score
2	Pienaar try, Pollard conversion	7-0
6	Bosch missed penalty	7-0
8	Sanchez penalty	7-3
17	Pollard penalty	10-3
42	Sanchez penalty	10-6
50	Steyn penalty	13-6

CASTLE LAGER RUGBY CHAMPIONSHIP

Argentina 31 South Africa 33
(Half-time 13-16)

23 August, Estadio Padre Ernesto Martearena, Salta (17 000). Referee: SR Walsh (Australia)

ARGENTINA
Tries: Montero, Cubelli, Tuculet. Conversions: Sanchez (2). Penalty goals: Sanchez (2), Bosch. Drop Goal: Hernandez.

J Tuculet, LP Gonzalez Amorosino, MT Bosch, JM Hernandez, M Montero (H Agulla, 77), FN Sanchez (J de la Fuente, 78), M Landajo (TM Cubelli, 34), JM Leguizamon, JM Fernandez Lobbe, PN Matera (LV Senatore, 36), T Lavanini (M Alemanno, 70), MT Galarza, R Herrera (FN Tetaz Chaparo, 68), A Creevy (Capt, ME Cortese, 81), MI Ayerza (B Postioglioni, 78).

Note: *MI Ayerza's 50th Test for Argentina. Championship debut: B Postiglioni*

SOUTH AFRICA
Tries: Habana, Hendricks, Coetzee. Conversions: Steyn (2), Pollard. Penalty goals: Pollard (3), Steyn.

WJ Le Roux, C Hendricks, D de Allende, J de Villiers (Capt), BG Habana, H Pollard (M Steyn, 56), R Pienaar (F Hougaard, 61), DJ Vermeulen, JH Smith (MC Coetzee, 52), L-F Louw, L de Jager, E Etzebeth (JP Botha, 70), JN du Plessis (JF Malherbe, 46/JN du Plessis, 79), BW du Plessis (JA Strauss, 52), GG Steenkamp (T Mtawarira, 46). **UNUSED SUB:** *LN Mvovo.*

Note: *JH Smith's first Test since 27 November 2010.*

HAVING already staged a great escape against Wales in Nelspruit, the Springboks pushed the corners of the envelope by overturning a 12-point deficit to defeat Argentina 33-31 in round two.

It was an undeserved victory born out of immense character, with the contributions of impact players Marcell Coetzee, Morné Steyn and Adriaan Strauss a crucial ingredient. And, of course, there was luck. Lots of it.

Coetzee had replaced a ponderous Juan Smith, who was making an emotional return to Test rugby after years on the sidelines, on the flank in the 52nd minute and immediately got South Africa the go forward they so desperately sought.

Steyn, for his part, kept a cool head by slotting three pressure kicks – conversions of Cornal Hendricks' and Coetzee's tries, as well as the penalty that clinched the result three minutes from time.

Argentina deserved more. They mauled South Africa in virtually every scrum and gave them the runaround with a high-tempo game in which the point of attack was frequently switched.

South Africa led 16-13 at half-time only because of a try against the run of play in the 32nd minute. The Pumas had lost the ball on attack and scrumhalf Ruan Pienaar kicked it through before wing Bryan Habana finished.

Perhaps the Springboks had expected Argentina's traditional approach of trench warfare. But the Pumas mixed their game up nicely and won the physical battle handsomely by forcing numerous scrum penalties. Their dominance extended to opposition feeds, which robbed the visitors of attacking momentum.

Apart from the one scrum penalty awarded in their favour in the 21st minute, the

South African pack only stood steady for the first time with barely 10 minutes remaining.

By then coach Heyneke Meyer had rung the changes in the front row. Tendai Mtawarira, Adriaan Strauss and Frans Malherbe had been sent on to replace the out-of-sorts unit of Gurthrö Steenkamp and the Du Plessis brothers, Jannie and Bismarck.

Jannie du Plessis had to return for the injured Malherbe late on and South African nerves were frayed as the teams packed down for a scrum in line with the posts in the dying moments. Another penalty and Argentina would probably have clinched it. But the Springboks held their nerve.

Earlier, the Argentines had used their platform from first phase and their general physical dominance to good effect.

Left wing Manuel Montero finished a sustained assault in the 26th minute, replacement scrumhalf Tomas Cubelli likewise in the 44th minute, while fullback Joaquin Tuculet rounded off in the corner after clean scrum possession in the 51st.

The latter try made the score 25-16 and when flyhalf Nicolas Sanchez added another penalty in the 55th minute, the situation looked dire for South Africa.

But enter Steyn and the Springboks suddenly had a steady head at flyhalf, where the promising Handré Pollard had only just earned his third cap.

Strauss and Coetzee had also entered the equation immediately after Tuculet's try and upped the pace for the struggling South Africans.

Hendricks finished in the corner in the 60th minute before Coetzee dotted down from a rolling maul in the 69th to edge the Springboks into a 30-28 lead.

But the anxiety would extend beyond that as a penalty by centre Marcelo Bosch seven minutes from time gave the Pumas a 31-30 lead. It's then that the South African spirit again came through, with a final foray into Pumas territory yielding a breakdown penalty.

Enter Steyn to add the finishing touch to a remarkable match, albeit an unremarkable Springbok performance.

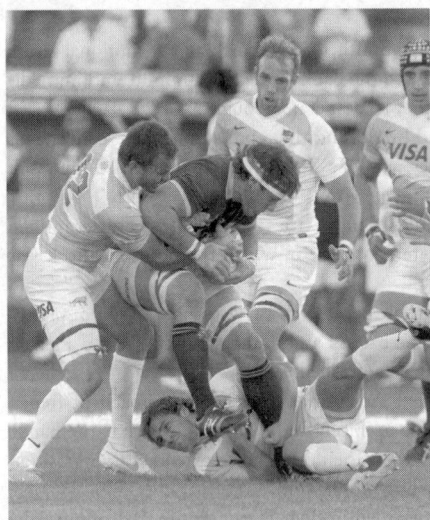

Marcell Coetzee on the charge against Argentina.

SCORING SEQUENCE

Min	Action	Score
4	Sanchez penalty	3-0
7	Sanchez missed penalty	3-0
11	Pollard penalty	3-3
13	Hernandez drop goal	6-3
23	Pollard penalty	6-6
26	Montero try, Sanchez conversion	13-6
30	Pollard penalty	13-9
32	Habana try, Pollard conversion	13-16
39	Sanchez missed penalty	13-16
47	Cubelli try, Sanchez conversion	20-16
51	Tuculet try, Sanchez missed conv.	25-16
56	Sanchez penalty	28-16
60	Hendricks try, Steyn conversion	28-23
65	Sanchez missed drop goal	28-23
69	Coetzee try, Steyn conversion	28-30
74	Bosch penalty	31-30
77	Steyn penalty	31-33

CASTLE LAGER RUGBY CHAMPIONSHIP

Australia 24 South Africa 23
(Half-time 11-14)

6 September, Patersons Stadium, Perth (25 718). Referee: George Clancy (Ireland)

AUSTRALIA
Tries: Folau, Horne. Conversion: Foley. Penalties: Foley (4).

I Folau, AP Ashley-Cooper, RTRN Kuridrani, MP Toomua (KJ Beale, 73), RG Horne, BT Foley, NJ Phipps, WL Palu (S Higginbotham, 60), M Hooper (Capt), SM Fardy (M Hodgson, 70), RA Simmons, STG Carter (JE Horwill, 60), SM Kepu, (BE Alexander, 67), JE Hanson, JA Slipper (PJM Cowan, 53). **UNUSED SUBS:** NW White, JW Mann-Rea.

SOUTH AFRICA
Try: Hendricks. Penalties: Steyn (6).

WJ Le Roux, C Hendricks, JL Serfontein, J de Villiers (Capt), BG Habana, M Steyn, R Pienaar, DJ Vermeulen, MC Coetzee, L-F Louw (PJ Lambie, 69*/WR Whiteley, 79**) V Matfield, E Etzebeth (L de Jager, 73), JN du Plessis (M van der Merwe, 67), JA Strauss (BW du Plessis, 61), T Mtawarira (TN Nyakane, 69). **UNUSED SUBS:** F Hougaard, D de Allende. **YELLOW CARD:** BG Habana (66-79).

* Lambie to 15, Le Roux to 11. ** Whiteley to 6. **TEST DEBUT:** WR Whiteley [Springbok #863]. **CHAMPIONSHIP DEBUT:** WR Whiteley.

Note: *BG Habana's 100th Test for SA.*

HAD they taken control of their destiny, the Springboks would have been well within their rights to claim the moral high ground over referee George Clancy after a heartbreaking 24-23 defeat to the Wallabies at the Patersons Stadium.

Unfortunately, however, they had only themselves to blame. Having weathered a storm by securing a penalty close to their line minutes before the end, South Africa needed to just kick the ball out, secure the lineout and hold onto possession until the final whistle.

However, the usually reliable Morné Steyn was over-ambitious with his kick, handing Australia the opportunity for a counter-attack from broken play that ended in wing Rob Horne scoring a try. Flyhalf Bernard Foley held his nerve for the conversion that edged the Wallabies home.

Had wing Bryan Habana not been unfairly yellow-carded by Clancy in the 66th minute, the Boks would have had all hands on deck to defend the surge. Crucially, he would have been allowed to return to play had Steyn's kick been out.

The Springboks still had a last-gasp straw to clutch at – a kick-off that they might win back if it was adequately contestable. But the kick didn't travel the required 10 metres and the Wallabies were able to wind down the clock.

Clancy's clangers were substantial. Whilst the high nature of Habana's tackle justified a penalty that would have kept the Springboks under pressure, there was no excuse for the decision to punish No 8 Duane Vermeulen for a perfectly legitimate one on Aussie prop James Slipper in the 27th minute.

It allowed Foley to lift the flags and pull the Wallabies back to a three-point deficit at 14-11. By then the visitors had methodically worked their way towards gaining the upper hand after a shocking start. They conceded possession from the kick-off, which led to Wal-

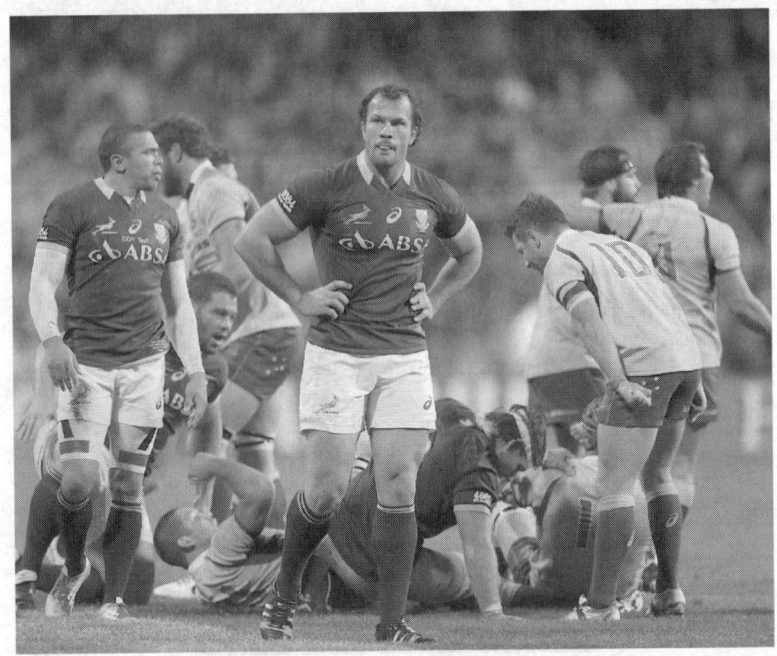

Bismarck du Plessis experienced a mediocre season by his high standards.

laby fullback Israel Folau finishing to give the home side a 5-0 lead.

Not long after that, flyhalf Steyn struck a penalty to reduce the deficit to two points before right wing Cornal Hendricks finished after some slick build-up play involving fullback Willie le Roux and the centre pairing of Jean de Villiers and Jan Serfontein.

Foley drew the Wallabies level at 8-8 in the 17th minute, but then followed a period in which South Africa gained a firm grip and edged into a 14-8 lead courtesy of two Steyn penalties. It's fair, therefore, to say that Clancy's controversial call on Vermeulen played a big part in halting their momentum.

While Foley again drew the Wallabies level at 14-14 early in the second half, the Springboks gained a firm grip in the ensuing 20 minutes by winning the territorial battle. Steyn added three penalties and a 23-14 lead with 17 minutes left should have been enough to see them through.

Clancy, however, made the controversial call on Habana and Australia laid siege to the Springboks' tryline.

South Africa defended bravely and physically. Just when it looked to have been enough, Steyn made the crucial blunder that led to the Wallabies clinching an undeserved victory.

SCORING SEQUENCE

Min	Action	Score
2	Folau try, Foley missed conversion	5-0
6	Steyn penalty	5-3
13	Hendricks try, Steyn missed conversion	5-8
17	Foley penalty	8-8
19	Steyn penalty	8-11
25	Steyn penalty	8-14
28	Foley penalty	11-14
42	Foley penalty	14-14
45	Steyn penalty	14-17
48	Steyn penalty	14-20
63	Steyn penalty	14-23
69	Foley penalty	17-23
78	Horne try, Foley conversion	24-23

CASTLE LAGER RUGBY CHAMPIONSHIP

New Zealand 14 South Africa 10
(Half-time 6-7)

---

13 September, Westpac Stadium, Wellington (35 747). Referee: Jerome Garces (France)

NEW ZEALAND
Try: McCaw. Penalties: Cruden (2), Barrett.

IJA Dagg, BR Smith, CG Smith, MA Nonu (CS Jane, 41), SJ Savea, AW Cruden (BJ Barrett, 59), AL Smith, KJ Read, RH McCaw (Capt), DS Luatua (SJ Cane, 51), JI Thrush (P Tuipoluto, 78), BA Retallick, OT Franks (BJ Franks, 59), DS Coles (KF Mealamu, 72), WWV Crockett (JPT Moody, 59).

UNUSED SUB: *TTR Perenara.* **CHAMPIONSHIP DEBUT:** *P Tuipoluto.*

SOUTH AFRICA
Try: Hendricks. Conversion: Pollard. Drop Goal: Pollard.

WJ Le Roux (PJ Lambie, 72), C Hendricks, JL Serfontein, J de Villiers (Capt), BG Habana, H Pollard, R Pienaar (F Hougaard, 36), DJ Vermeulen, MC Coetzee, L-F Louw (WR Whiteley, 48), V Matfield, E Etzebeth (L de Jager, 72), JN du Plessis (M van der Merwe, 78), JA Strauss (BW du Plessis, 55), T Mtawarira (TN Nyakane, 67).

Notes: *J de Villiers' 100th Test for SA. BG Habana's 100th Test as a wing for SA.*

THE Springboks came desperately close to recording a famous win over the All Blacks on the South Island, but ultimately failed to convert a late siege into points and suffered an agonising defeat.

Lood de Jager, on as a lock replacement for Eben Etzebeth, was forced into touch metres from the All Black tryline before the home team secured the lineout and hacked the ball into touch, to the great relief of the crowd at the Westpac Stadium.

South Africa needed only to score a try to clinch a victory and they very much had the upper hand when New Zealand were penalised for a side entry at a maul in the 74th minute.

Rather than ask flyhalf Handré Pollard to draw the Springboks to within a point, skipper Jean de Villiers ordered a kick into touch. The All Blacks transgressed in an effort to stop the maul and did so again after De Villiers had issued the same instruction.

However, at the third attempt, South Africa's lineout possession was untidy, which deprived them of the opportunity to clinch the Test with a rolling maul. They then conceded a scrum in the 78th minute when replacement flank Warren Whiteley strayed into De Jager's way to be ruled accidentally off-side.

It offered New Zealand an opportunity to relieve the pressure but the drama didn't end there. The Springbok scrum flexed its muscles, prompting referee Jerome Garces to award South Africa the put-in.

An uninspired attack down the blindside, however, yielded little reward. No 8 Duane Vermeulen should, like Joe van Niekerk at Ellis Park a decade earlier, have insisted on a quick heel to allow for a quick pick-up at the base and a hard, straightening run that would have drawn the blindside wing and put wing Cornal Hendricks clear.

But what should have been a simple move, given the space available on the short

CASTLE LAGER RUGBY CHAMPIONSHIP

All Black captain Richie McCaw addresses Springbok skipper Jean de Villiers on the occasion of his 100th Test.

side, turned into a laboured and lateral attempt to score which ended with De Jager being forced into touch. The All Blacks nearly made a hash of winning the throw-in, but crucially secured the ball.

In fairness, it was a deserved victory. While down 7-6 at the break, New Zealand had played the better rugby and enjoyed significant territorial advantage. South Africa stayed in the game through offensive defence.

While spending most of the first half boxing off the ropes, the Springboks produced an inspired bit of attacking play for a try, which Pollard crafted with an inside pass to twinkle-toed wing Hendricks.

Pollard's performance, in fact, proved that the gifted 20-year-old had the temperament for world rugby's ultimate Test.

The decisive moment in the match was a remarkable bit of skill by All Black No 8 Kieran Read. Despite the attentions of skipper Jean de Villiers, who, at 1.90 metres is no slouch in the air, Read plucked a cross-kick by flyhalf Aaron Cruden from under De Villiers' nose and delayed his off-load until skipper Richie McCaw was on hand to finish with an old-fashioned dive in the corner.

It was so sublime that it almost defined this great All Black side.

Read's opposite number, Vermeulen, was equally influential but in a different way as he frustrated the All Blacks with superb breakdown skills in a fierce physical battle.

South Africa also delivered in the scrums and had the better of the lineouts until Meyer decided to substitute hooker Adriaan Strauss with Bismarck du Plessis for the last 25 minutes. It was an understandable move given Du Plessis' potential impact, but with that the lineout battle was turned on its head.

New Zealand, in fairness, also delivered under pressure. There was Read's moment of magic but by and large this was a result secured in the trenches.

SCORING SEQUENCE

Min	Action	Score
11	Cruden penalty	3-0
16	Hendricks try, Pollard conversion	3-7
24	Cruden penalty	6-7
40	Cruden missed penalty	6-7
47	McCaw try, Cruden missed conversion	11-7
56	Pollard drop goal	11-10
63	Pollard missed penalty	11-10
67	Barrett penalty	14-10

CASTLE LAGER RUGBY CHAMPIONSHIP

South Africa 28 Australia 10
(Half-time 5-10)

28 September, Newlands, Cape Town (44 955). Referee: Nigel Owens (Wales)

SOUTH AFRICA

Tries: De Villiers (2), Coetzee, Lambie. Conversion: Lambie. Penalties: Pollard. Drop Goal: Lambie.

WJ Le Roux, C Hendricks, JL Serfontein, J de Villiers (Capt), BG Habana (JP-R Pietersen, 27-38, 41), H Pollard (P Lambie, 59), F Hougaard (JM Reinach, 77), DJ Vermeulen (JP Botha, 62)*, TS Mohoje (SWP Burger, 55), MC Coetzee, V Matfield, E Etzebeth, JN du Plessis (M van der Merwe, 66), JA Strauss (BW du Plessis, 59), T Mtawarira (TN Nyakane, 70).

* Botha to lock, Matfield to flank. **TEST DEBUT:** *JM Reinach [Springbok #864].* **CHAMPIONSHIP DEBUT:** *JM Reinach.*

AUSTRALIA

Try: Ashley-Cooper. Conversion: Foley. Penalty goal: Foley.

I Folau, AP Ashley-Cooper, RTRN Kuridrani, MP Toomua (KJ Beale, 55), JM Tomane (RG Horne, 67), BT Foley, NJ Phipps, BJ McCalman (S Higginbotham, 59), M Hooper (Capt), SM Fardy, RA Simmons (JE Horwill, 41), STG Carter, SM Kepu (BE Alexander, 70), SM Faingaa (JE Hanson, 62) JA Slipper (BA Robinson, 66).

UNUSED SUB: *NW White.*

SPRINGBOK coach Heyneke Meyer's masterful use of his substitute bench paved the way for a remarkable victory over the Wallabies at Newlands.

The Springboks were still trailing 10-8 when replacement flyhalf Patrick Lambie slotted a drop goal in the 70th minute.

By then Australia had been struggling to cope with a relentless onslaught and the Springboks added three tries – two by captain Jean de Villiers and another by Lambie in the final eight minutes.

Lambie was sent on in the 59th minute for an out-of-sorts Handré Pollard and apart from a try in which he beat four mesmerised Aussies, he also brought a measure of tactical control with his boot.

Of equal value were the contributions of Schalk Burger and Bismarck du Plessis after they had been sent on – for flank Teboho Mohoje and hooker Adriaan Strauss respectively.

Burger, in his 25 minutes on the field, carried the ball a remarkable 15 times, while Du Plessis provided physical impetus and twice off-loaded in the tackle, the second of which was the scoring pass for De Villiers' first try.

Bakkies Botha was an effective lock replacement, while props Marcel van der Merwe and Trevor Nyakane also upped the ante.

JP Pietersen had his first taste of action in the 27th minute when left wing Bryan Habana was tested for concussion and, after his initial 11-minute spell, played out the entire second half.

Even replacement scrumhalf Cobus Reinach joined the party after being sent on in the 77th minute, breaking superbly in the build-up to De Villiers' second try.

It was an emotional moment for the quick-as-lightning Reinach as his late father,

The Springboks retained the Mandela Challenge Plate with victory over Australia at Newlands.

Jaco, a former national 400 metres record holder and one of the fastest Springboks of all time, had made his Test debut at the same ground against the New Zealand Cavaliers 28 years earlier, in 1986.

To put the Springboks' dominance late in the match in perspective: Australia made 82 of their 278 tackles in the final 10 minutes. South Africa made 178 tackles, while also dominating territory (57%) and possession (58%).

Between them Burger, Lambie, Du Plessis, Botha, Van der Merwe and Nyakane had to make just 10 tackles after their entry, while they produced 34 ball carries.

Remarkably, the ball was in play for 44 minutes and 49 seconds – that statistic very seldom touches on 40 – which was probably the result of South Africa's ability to carry the ball through countless phases. By way of example: there had been 28 phases in the build-up to Lambie's drop goal.

It must be noted however that the Springboks didn't have it all their own way in the first hour. They led 5-0 courtesy of a try by flank Marcel Coetzee off the back of a driving maul, but 15 minutes later the Aussies were 10-5 up courtesy of a penalty by flyhalf Bernard Foley and right wing Adam Ashley-Cooper's corner-flag converted try.

Much of the Springboks' troubles stemmed from confusion in their attacking play, which was ineffectively spearheaded by fullback Willie le Roux.

Perhaps it was because Le Roux had been so brilliant earlier in the year that the Springboks appeared to have developed an over-reliance on him. Time and again the home side's plays with the ball in hand broke down.

The forwards were nevertheless doing a good job softening the Aussies up and once Meyer started ringing the changes the visitors could offer little to no resistance.

SCORING SEQUENCE

Min	Action	Score
9	Foley missed penalty	0-0
12	Coetzee try, Pollard missed conv.	5-0
25	Foley penalty	5-3
26	Ashley-Cooper try, Foley conv.	5-10
44	Pollard penalty	8-10
70	Lambie drop goal	11-10
72	De Villiers try, Lambie missed conv.	16-10
79	Lambie try, Lambie missed conv.	21-10
81	De Villiers try, Lambie conv.	28-10

CASTLE LAGER RUGBY CHAMPIONSHIP

South Africa 27 New Zealand 25
(Half-time 21-13)

4 October, Ellis Park, Johannesburg (61 261). Referee: Wayne Barnes (England)

SOUTH AFRICA
Tries: Pollard (2), Hougaard. Conversions: Pollard (3). Penalties: Pollard, Lambie.

WJ Le Roux, C Hendricks (J-PR Pietersen, 58), JL Serfontein, J de Villiers (Capt), BG Habana, H Pollard (P Lambie, 63), F Hougaard (JM Reinach, 66), DJ Vermeulen, TS Mohoje (SWP Burger, 50), MC Coetzee, V Matfield, E Etzebeth (JP Botha, 63), JN du Plessis (M van der Merwe, 63), BW du Plessis (JA Strauss, 52), T Mtawarira (TN Nyakane, 72).

Note: *50th Test for J de Villiers in the Rugby Championship (SA Record).*

NEW ZEALAND
Tries: BR Smith, Coles, Fekitoa. Conversions: Barrett (2). Penalties: Barrett (2).

IJA Dagg, BR Smith, CG Smith (RS Crotty, 73), M Fekitoa, SJ Savea, BJ Barrett, AL Smith (T Kerr-Barlow, 66/CR Slade, 75), KJ Read, RH McCaw (Capt), J Kaino (DS Luatua, 61), SL Whitelock, JI Thrush (LJ Messam, 49), OT Franks (CC Faumuina, 58), KF Mealamu (DS Coles, 49), J Moody (BJ Franks, 41).

WITH the Rugby World Cup around the corner, it was imperative that the Springboks beat the All Blacks in 2014 and the manner in which they did it at Ellis Park inspired much confidence.

It ultimately came down to a late, sweet strike of 55 metres from the boot of replacement flyhalf Patrick Lambie to give the Springboks their 27-25 victory. The ball sailed majestically over the crossbar one minute before full-time.

The scenes were of unbridled joy – among the players, coaching staff and the famously passionate Ellis Park fans. For South Africa it was a victory of great significance. They had stood toe to toe with New Zealand, and won.

As befitting a side playing at their spiritual home, the Springboks found their rhythm early and impressively set about beating the All Blacks at their own game.

Trailing 3-0 after a penalty by All Black flyhalf Beauden Barrett, the Springboks launched an impressive counter-attack that ended with scrumhalf Francois Hougaard diving over – albeit rather unmajestically – under the posts.

Jean de Villiers, who was inspirational both as captain and as a player in midfield, grubbered expertly and right wing Cornal Hendricks gathered the ball before passing inside to Jan Serfontein.

De Villiers' centre partner was brought down, but he popped the ball to Hougaard, who tore away and finally beat All Black skipper Richie McCaw's despairing tackle to finish. Flyhalf Handré Pollard converted and the Springboks were 7-3 up in the 12th minute. Pollard then confirmed his status as one of world rugby's finest prospects.

The Springboks moved the ball from a lineout, with Habana beating fullback Israel Dagg in a surge into the visitors' 22-metre area. A handful of phases ensued before Pollard took the ball beautifully to the line and, like Hougaard, finished under the posts.

CASTLE LAGER RUGBY CHAMPIONSHIP

Patrick Lambie celebrates his match-winning penalty against the All Blacks at Ellis Park.

Pollard's awareness was superb, as he had spotted a gap between heavies Joe Moody and Sam Whitelock.

With a touch under 30 minute played, the Springboks were up 14-6!

New Zealand, however, showed their class when centre Malakai Fekitoa finished a sweeping attacking move under the posts. Remarkably it all started from a retreating scrum, which forced the Kiwis to initiate the attack down the blind side.

Pollard then scored his second try just before half-time, receiving the ball at pace from Hougaard in the All Blacks' 22-metre area and cutting inside. He beat the halfback pairing of Aaron Smith and Barrett on his way.

It was 21-13 at half-time and less than seven minutes into the second half Pollard made it 24-13.

However, the All Blacks showed their pedigree by laying siege to the Springbok line. Right wing Ben Smith, and then substitute hooker Dane Coles, both finished to edge the visitors into a 25-24 lead.

The restart offered respite as South Africa managed to regain the territorial advantage they had long since surrendered.

With the match at a knife's edge, flank Liam Messam lost his cool for a split second and struck Schalk Burger with a stiff arm. Lambie stepped up and etched his name into folklore.

Yet there were unsung Springbok heroes aplenty, none more so than No 8 Duane Vermeulen, who turned in a man-of-the-match performance in spite of struggling with painful ribs in the build-up to the match.

It was that spirit that encapsulated the Springboks' desire.

SCORING SEQUENCE

Min	Action	Score
6	Pollard missed penalty	0-0
9	Barrett penalty	0-3
11	Hougaard try, Pollard conversion	7-3
23	Barrett penalty	7-6
27	Pollard try, Pollard conversion	14-6
33	Fekitoa try, Barrett conversion	14-13
40	Pollard try, Pollard conversion	21-13
47	Pollard penalty	24-13
65	B Smith try, Barrett conversion	24-20
70	Coles try, Barrett missed conversion	24-25
79	Lambie penalty	27-25

CASTLE LAGER RUGBY CHAMPIONSHIP

ALL SCORERS

PLAYER	Country	Apps	T	C	P	DG	Pts
FN Sanchez	Argentina	6	0	5	14	0	52
H Pollard	South Africa	5	2	6	6	1	43
BT Foley	Australia	6	0	5	11	0	43
AW Cruden	New Zealand	3	0	5	9	0	37
BJ Barrett	New Zealand	6	0	6	6	0	30
M Steyn	South Africa	3	0	2	8	0	28
KJ Beale	Australia	5	0	2	6	0	22
SJ Savea	New Zealand	6	4	0	0	0	20
C Hendricks	South Africa	6	3	0	0	0	15
M Hooper	Australia	6	3	0	0	0	15
RH McCaw	New Zealand	6	3	0	0	0	15
PJ Lambie	South Africa	4	1	1	1	1	13
BR Smith	New Zealand	6	2	0	0	0	10
I Folau	Australia	6	2	0	0	0	10
J de Villiers	South Africa	6	2	0	0	0	10
J Tuculet	Argentina	6	2	0	0	0	10
M Montero	Argentina	4	2	0	0	0	10
MC Coetzee	South Africa	6	2	0	0	0	10
MT Bosch	Argentina	6	1	0	1	0	8
AL Smith	New Zealand	6	1	1	0	0	7
AP Ashley-Cooper	Australia	5	1	0	0	0	5
BG Habana	South Africa	6	1	0	0	0	5
DS Coles	New Zealand	5	1	0	0	0	5
F Hougaard	South Africa	4	1	0	0	0	5
H Agulla	Argentina	5	1	0	0	0	5
IJA Dagg	New Zealand	4	1	0	0	0	5
JJ Imhoff	Argentina	4	1	0	0	0	5
KJ Read	New Zealand	6	1	0	0	0	5
LV Senatore	Argentina	6	1	0	0	0	5
LJ Messam	New Zealand	3	1	0	0	0	5
M Fekitoa	New Zealand	4	1	0	0	0	5
PJ Betham	Australia	1	1	0	0	0	5
RG Horne	Australia	6	1	0	0	0	5
R Pienaar	South Africa	4	1	0	0	0	5
S Higginbotham	Australia	6	1	0	0	0	5
DS Luatua	New Zealand	3	1	0	0	0	5
RTRN Kuridarani	Australia	5	1	0	0	0	5
TTR Perenara	New Zealand	3	1	0	0	0	5
TM Cubelli	Argentina	6	1	0	0	0	5
CR Slade	New Zealand	3	0	1	1	0	5
Penalty try	New Zealand	0	1	0	0	0	5
JM Hernandez	Argentina	5	0	0	0	1	3
S Gonzales Iglesia	Argentina	3	0	1	0	0	2
		205	50	35	63	3	518

CASTLE LAGER RUGBY CHAMPIONSHIP

SOUTH AFRICA APPEARANCES & POINTS

PLAYER	Date of birth	Height	Weight	Union/Club	Arg 1	Arg 2	Aus 1	NZ 1	Aus 2	NZ 2	Apps	T	C	P	DG	Pts
WJ (Willie) Le Roux	18/08/1989	1,86	88	Free State	15	15	15	15	15	15	6	-	-	-	-	0
C (Cornal) Hendricks	18/08/1988	1,89	90	Free State	14	14	14	14	14	14	6	3	-	-	-	15
D (Damian) de Allende	25/11/1991	1,89	104	WP¹	13	13	x	x	-	-	2	-	-	-	-	0
J (Jean) de Villiers (c)	24/02/1981	1,90	100	WP¹	12c	12c	12c	12c	12c	12c	6	2	-	-	-	10
BG (Bryan) Habana	12/06/1983	1,79	94	Toulon²	11	11	11	11	11	11	6	1	-	-	-	5
H (Handre) Pollard	11/03/1994	1,89	97	Blue Bulls	10	10	-	10	10	10	5	2	6	6	1	43
R (Ruan) Pienaar	10/03/1984	1,86	92	Ulster³	9	9	9	9	-	-	4	1	-	-	-	5
DJ (Duane) Vermeulen	03/07/1986	1,92	90	WP¹	8	8	8	8	8	8	6	-	-	-	-	0
MC (Marcell) Coetzee	08/05/1991	1,90	106	KZN	7	7R	7	7	6	6	6	2	-	-	-	10
L-FP (Francois) Louw	15/06/1985	1,90	114	Bath (Eng)	6	6	6	6	-	-	4	-	-	-	-	0
L (Lood) de Jager	17/12/1992	2,05	125	Free State	5	5	4R	4R	-	-	4	-	-	-	-	0
JP (Bakkies) Botha	22/09/1979	2,02	122	Toulon²	4	4R	-	-	8R	4R	4	-	-	-	-	0
JN (Jannie) du Plessis	16/11/1982	1,87	119	KZN	3	3	3	3	3	3	6	-	-	-	-	0
BW (Bismarck) du Plessis	22/05/1984	1,89	113	KZN	2	2	2R	2R	2R	2	6	-	-	-	-	0
T (Tendai) Mtawarira	01/07/1985	1,83	115	KZN	1	1R	1	1	1	1	6	-	-	-	-	0
JA (Adriaan) Strauss	18/11/1985	1,84	111	Free State	2R	2R	2	2	2	2R	6	-	-	-	-	0
TN (Trevor) Nyakane	04/05/1989	1,78	109	Free State	1R	-	1R	1R	1R	1R	5	-	-	-	-	0
JF (Frans) Malherbe	14/03/1991	1,90	122	WP¹	3R	3R	-	-	-	-	2	-	-	-	-	0
E (Eben) Etzebeth	29/10/1991	2,03	117	WP¹	4R	4	4	4	4	4	6	-	-	-	-	0
TS (Teboho) Mohoje	03/08/1990	1,93	106	Free State	x	-	-	-	7	7	2	-	-	-	-	0
F (Francois) Hougaard	06/08/1988	1,79	91	Blue Bulls	x	9R	x	9R	9	9	4	1	-	-	-	5
M (Morné) Steyn	11/07/1984	1,86	91	Stade Francais²	10R	10R	10	-	-	-	3	-	2	8	-	28
JL (Jan) Serfontein	15/04/1993	1,87	97	Blue Bulls	x	-	13	13	13	13	4	-	-	-	-	0
JH (Juan) Smith	30/07/1980	1,96	110	Toulon²	-	7	-	-	-	-	1	-	-	-	-	0
GG (Gurthro) Steenkamp	12/06/1981	1,89	124	Toulouse²	-	1	-	-	-	-	1	-	-	-	-	0
LN (Lwazi) Mvovo	03/06/1986	1,85	94	KZN	-	x	-	-	-	-	0	-	-	-	-	0
V (Victor) Matfield	11/05/1977	2,00	108	Blue Bulls	-	-	5	5	5	5	4	-	-	-	-	0
M (Marcel) van der Merwe	24/10/1990	1,88	128	Blue Bulls	-	-	3R	3R	3R	3R	4	-	-	-	-	0
PJ (Patrick) Lambie	17/10/1990	1,78	87	KZN	-	-	6R	15R	10R	10R	4	1	1	1	1	13
WR (Warren) Whiteley	18/09/1987	1,92	97	Golden Lions	-	-	22R	6R	-	-	2	-	-	-	-	0
J-P R (JP) Pietersen	12/07/1986	1,90	106	Knights⁴	-	-	-	-	11R	14R	2	-	-	-	-	0
SWP (Schalk) Burger	13/04/1983	1,93	110	WP¹	-	-	-	-	7R	7R	2	-	-	-	-	0
JM (Cobus) Reinach	07/02/1990	1,75	84	KZN	-	-	-	-	9R	9R	2	-	-	-	-	0
33 Players (of which 32 made a Championship appearance)											131	13	9	15	2	134

Note: C = Captain, 1 = Western Province, 2 = France, 3 = Northern Ireland, 4 = Panasonic Wild Knights (Japan).

Head Coach: Heyneke Meyer **Forwards Coach:** Johan van Graan **Backs Coach:** Ricardo Loubscher
Fitness Coach: Basil Carzis **Defence Coach:** John McFarland **Team Manager:** Ian Schwartz
Team Doctor: Dr Craig Roberts **Physiotherapist:** Vivian Verwant **Masseuse:** Daliah Hurwitz
Operational Head: Charles Wessels **PR and Admin:** Annelee Murray **Logistics:** JJ Fredericks
Technical Analyst: Albé Visser **Communications Manager:** De Jongh Borchardt
Kicking Consultant: Louis Koen **Scrum Consultant:** Pieter de Villiers **Performance analyst:** Chean Roux **Physiotherapist:** Rene Naylor **Breakdown Consultant:** Richie Gray

CASTLE LAGER RUGBY CHAMPIONSHIP

NEW ZEALAND APPEARANCES & POINTS

PLAYER	Date of birth	Height	Weight	Province	Aus	Aus	Arg	SA	Arg	SA	Apps	T	C	P	DG	Pts
BR (Ben) Smith	01/06/1986	1,86	93	Otago	15	15	14	14	14	14	6	2	–	–	–	10
CS (Cory) Jane	08/02/1983	1,83	89	Wellington	14	14	–	12R	x	–	3	–	–	–	–	0
M (Malakai) Fekitoa	10/05/1992	1,87	99	Auckland	13	12R	x	–	12	12	4	1	–	–	–	5
MA (Ma'a) Nonu	21/05/1982	1,82	107	Wellington	12	–	12	12	–	–	3	–	–	–	–	0
SJ (Julian) Savea	07/08/1990	1,92	103	Wellington	11	11	11	11	11	11	6	4	–	–	–	20
AW (Aaron) Cruden	08/01/1989	1,78	83	Manawatu	10	10	–	10	–	–	3	–	5	9	–	37
AL (Aaron) Smith	21/11/1988	1,71	83	Manawatu	9	9	9	9	9	9	6	1	1	–	–	7
KJ (Kieran) Read	26/10/1985	1,93	110	Canterbury	8	8	8	8	8	8	6	1	–	–	–	5
RH (Richie) McCaw (C)	31/12/1980	1,87	107	Canterbury	7c	7c	7c	7c	7c	7c	6	3	–	–	–	15
J (Jerome) Kaino	06/04/1983	1,95	109	Auckland	6	–	–	–	6	6	3	–	–	–	–	0
SL (Sam) Whitelock	12/10/1988	2,02	116	Canterbury	5	5	5	–	5	5	5	–	–	–	–	0
BA (Brodie) Retallick	31/05/1991	2,04	117	Bay of Plenty	4	4	4	4	4	–	5	–	–	–	–	0
OT (Owen) Franks	23/12/1987	1,85	118	Canterbury	3	3	3	3	3	3	6	–	–	–	–	0
DS (Dane) Coles	12/10/1986	1,84	103	Wellington	2	2	2	2	–	2R	5	1	–	–	–	5
WWV (Wyatt) Crockett	24/01/1983	1,93	116	Canterbury	1	1	1	1	1	–	5	–	–	–	–	0
KF (Keven) Mealamu	20/03/1979	1,81	118	Auckland	2R	2R	2R	2R	2	2	6	–	–	–	–	0
BJ (Ben) Franks	27/03/1984	1,83	116	Hawke's Bay	1R	1R	3R	3R	3R	1R	6	–	–	–	–	0
JPT (Joe) Moody	18/09/1988	1,87	112	Canterbury	3R	–	1R	1R	1R	1	5	–	–	–	–	0
DS (Steven) Luatua	29/04/1991	1,96	110	Auckland	x	6R	–	6	–	6R	3	1	–	–	–	5
SJ (Sam) Cane	13/01/1992	1,89	104	Bay of Plenty	6R	4R	6R	6R	7R	–	5	–	–	–	–	0
TTR (TJ) Perenara	23/01/1993	1,84	94	Wellington	x	10R	9R	x	9R	–	3	1	–	–	–	5
BJ (Beauden) Barrett	27/05/1991	1,87	90	Taranaki	10R	14R	10	10R	10	10	6	–	6	6	–	30
RS (Ryan) Crotty	23/09/1988	1,81	92	Canterbury	12R	12	–	–	–	13R	3	–	–	–	–	0
CG (Conrad) Smith	12/10/1981	1,86	95	Wellington	–	13	13	13	13	13	5	–	–	–	–	0
LJ (Liam) Messam	25/03/1984	1,90	108	Waikato	–	6	6	–	–	4R	3	1	–	–	–	5
CC (Charlie) Faumuina	24/12/1986	1,84	128	Auckland	–	3R	–	–	–	3R	2	–	–	–	–	0
IJA (Israel) Dagg	06/06/1988	1,86	94	Hawke's Bay	–	–	15	15	15	15	4	1	–	–	–	5
JI (Jeremy) Thrush	19/04/1985	1,98	109	Wellington	–	–	5R	5	4R	4	4	–	–	–	–	0
CR (Colin) Slade	10/10/1987	1,83	90	Canterbury	–	–	10R	–	13R	21R	3	–	1	1	–	5
P (Patrick) Tuipuloto	23/01/1993	1,98	120	Auckland	–	–	–	5R	–	–	1	–	–	–	–	0
N (Nathan) Harris	08/03/1992	1,85	105	Bay of Plenty	–	–	–	–	2R	–	1	–	–	–	–	0
TNJ (Tewita) Kerr-Barlow	15/08/1990	1,87	89	Waikato	–	–	–	–	–	9R	1	–	–	–	–	0
Penalty try											1	–	–	–	–	5
32 Players											**133**	**18**	**13**	**16**	**0**	**164**

Note: C = Captain

Head Coach: Steve Hansen **Manager:** Darren Shand **Assistant Manager:** Gilbert Enoka
Assistant Coach: Ian Foster **Forwards Coach:** Mike Cron **Analyst:** Aussie McLean
Kicking coach: Mick Byrne **Selector:** Grant Fox **Doctor:** Dr Tony Page
Physiotherapist: Peter Gallagher **Manual Therapist:** George Duncan
Strength & Conditioning: Dr Nic Gill **Performance Analyst:** Alistair Rogers
Logistics: Chalky Carr **Media Manager:** Joe Locke **Nutritionist:** Katrina Darry
Executive Assistant: Bianca Thiel

AUSTRALIA APPEARANCES & POINTS

PLAYER	Date of birth	Height	Weight	Province	NZ	NZ	SA	Arg	SA	Arg	Apps	T	C	P	DG	Pts
I (Israel) Folau	03/04/1989	1,93	103	NSW	15	15	15	15	15	15	6	2	–	–	–	10
PJ (Pat) McCabe	21/03/1988	1,85	94	ACT	14	14	–	–	–	–	2	–	–	–	–	0
AP (Adam) Ashley-Cooper	27/03/1984	1,82	98	NSW	13	13	14	–	14	14	5	1	–	–	–	5
MP (Matt) To'omua	02/01/1990	1,82	89	ACT	12	12	12	12	12	12	6	–	–	–	–	0
RG (Rob) Horne	04/09/1989	1,86	92	NSW	11	11	11	11	11R	11R	6	1	–	–	–	5
KJ (Kurtley) Beale	06/01/1989	1,84	90	NSW	10	10	12R	12R	12R	–	5	–	2	6	–	22
NW (Nic) White	13/06/1990	1,73	82	ACT	9	9	9R	9R	x	9R	5	–	–	–	–	0
WL (Wycliff) Palu	27/07/1982	1,94	116	NSW	8	8	8	–	–	–	3	–	–	–	–	0
MK (Michael) Hooper (c)	29/10/1991	1,82	97	NSW	7c	7c	7c	7c	7c	7c	6	3	–	–	–	15
SM (Scott) Fardy	05/07/1984	1,98	110	ACT	6	6	6	6	6	6	6	–	–	–	–	0
RA (Rob) Simmons	19/04/1989	2,00	115	Queensland	5	5	5	5	5	–	5	–	–	–	–	0
SGT (Sam) Carter	10/09/1989	2,00	110	ACT	4	4	4	4	4	4	6	–	–	–	–	0
SM (Sekope) Kepu	05/02/1986	1,88	125	NSW	3	3	3	3	3	3	6	–	–	–	–	0
NL (Nathan) Charles	09/01/1989	1,83	106	Force	2	2	–	–	–	–	2	–	–	–	–	0
JA (James) Slipper	06/06/1989	1,85	113	Queensland	1	1	1	1	1	1	6	–	–	–	–	0
JE (James) Hanson	15/09/1988	1,83	104	Queensland	x	2R	2	2R	2R	–	4	–	–	–	–	0
PJM (Pek) Cowan	02/06/1986	1,85	115	Force	1R	x	1R	1R	–	–	3	–	–	–	–	0
BE (Ben) Alexander	13/11/1984	1,89	117	ACT	3R	3R	3R	3R	3R	3R	6	–	–	–	–	0
WRJ (Will) Skelton	03/05/1992	2,03	135	NSW	8R	4R	–	–	–	5R	3	–	–	–	–	0
S (Scott) Higginbotham	05/09/1986	1,95	110	Rebels	6R	8R	8R	6R	8R	8	6	1	–	–	–	5
NJ (Nick) Phipps	09/01/1989	1,80	87	NSW	9R	9R	9	9	9	9	6	–	–	–	–	0
BT (Bernard) Foley	08/09/1989	1,80	85	NSW	10R	10R	10	10	10	10	6	–	5	11	–	43
RTRN (Tevita) Kuridrani	31/03/1991	1,96	102	ACT	x	13R	13	13	13	13	5	1	–	–	–	5
JE (James) Horwill	29/05/1985	2,00	115	Queensland	–	–	4R	4R	5R	5	4	–	–	–	–	0
M (Matthew) Hodgson	25/06/1981	1,84	100	Force	–	–	6R	8R	–	x	2	–	–	–	–	0
JW (Josh) Mann-Rea	19/02/1981	1,81	105	ACT	–	–	x	–	–	2R	1	–	–	–	–	0
PJJ (Peter) Betham	06/01/1989	1,91	98	NSW	–	–	–	14	–	–	1	1	–	–	–	5
BJ (Ben) McCalman	09/01/1989	1,80	85	Victoria	–	–	–	8	8	–	2	–	–	–	–	0
SUT (Tatafu) Polota-Nau	26/07/1985	1,81	115	NSW	–	–	–	2	–	–	1	–	–	–	–	0
SM (Saia) Fainga'a	02/02/1987	1,87	108	Queensland	–	–	–	–	2	2	2	–	–	–	–	0
JM (Joe) Tomane	02/02/1990	1,90	102	ACT	–	–	–	–	11	11	2	–	–	–	–	0
BA (Benn) Robinson	19/07/1984	1,83	113	NSW	–	–	–	–	1R	1R	2	–	–	–	–	0
JW (Jake) Schatz	25/07/1990	1,92	109	Queensland	–	–	–	–	–	8R	1	–	–	–	–	0
33 Players											132	10	7	17	0	115

Note: C = Captain

Head Coach: Ewen McKenzie **Attack Coach:** Jim McKay **Forwards Coach:** Andrew Blades
Coaching Assistant: Nick Scrivener **Strength & Conditioning:** Scott Murphy
Manager: Bob Egerton **Logistics Manager:** Matt Sheppard **Doctor:** Dr Angus Bathgate
Head Physiotherapist: Andrew Ryan **Sports Medicine Co-ordinator:** Ed Fitzgerald
Analyst: Cathal Garvey **Media Manager:** Brendon Altadonna **Physiotherapist:** Kieran Cleary
Performance Assistance: Matt Lieschke

CASTLE LAGER RUGBY CHAMPIONSHIP

ARGENTINA APPEARANCES & POINTS

PLAYER	Date of birth	Height	Weight	Club	SA	SA	NZ	Aus	NZ	Aus	Apps	T	C	P	DG	Pts
J (Joaquin) Tuculet	08/08/1989	1,84	86	Unattached	15	15	15	15	15	15	6	2	–	–	–	10
H (Horacio) Agulla	22/10/1984	1,81	92	Bath[1]	14	11R	14	–	13R	13	5	1	–	–	–	5
MT (Marcello) Bosch	07/01/1984	1,86	92	Saracens[1]	13	13	13	13	13	13R	6	1	–	1	–	8
S Gonzalez Iglesias	16/06/1988	1,78	85	Alumni	12	–	10R	–	12R	–	3	–	1	–	–	2
M (Manuel) Montero	21/11/1991	1,93	100	Pucara	11	11	–	11	11	–	4	2	–	–	–	10
FN (Nicolas) Sánchez	26/10/1988	1,77	83	Toulon[2]	10	10	10	10	10	10	6	–	5	14	–	52
M (Martin) Landajo	14/06/1988	1,71	81	Club Atletico	9	9	9	9	9R	9	6	–	–	–	–	0
J-M Leguizamón	06/06/1983	1,90	104	Lyon[2]	8	8	6	6	–	–	4	–	–	–	–	0
J-M Fernández Lobbe	19/11/1981	1,91	106	Toulon[2]	7	7	7	7	7	–	5	–	–	–	–	0
PN (Pablo) Matera	18/07/1993	1,93	99	Leicester[3]	6	6	–	–	–	–	2	–	–	–	–	0
T (Tomas) Lavanini	22/01/1993	2,00	118	Racing Metro[2]	5	5	5	–	5	5	5	–	–	–	–	0
M (Mariano) Galarza	12/11/1986	2,03	111	Gloucester[1]	4	4	4	4	4	4	6	–	–	–	–	0
R (Ramiro) Herrera	14/02/1989	1,90	125	Castres[2]	3	3	3	3	3	3R	6	–	–	–	–	0
A (Agustin) Creevy	15/03/1985	1,81	110	Worcester[1]	2c	2c	2c	2c	2c	2c	6	–	–	–	–	0
MI (Marcos) Ayerza	12/01/1983	1,86	114	Leicester[1]	1	1	1	1	1	1	6	–	–	–	–	0
ME (Matias) Cortese	01/10/1985	1,83	107	Liceo Naval	x	2R	2R	2R	2R	x	4	–	–	–	–	0
L (Lucas) Noguera Paz	10/05/1993	1,78	107	Lince	1R	–	1R	–	1R	–	3	–	–	–	–	0
FN Tetaz Chaparro	06/11/1989	1,93	115	Lyon[2]	3R	3R	3R	3R	3R	3	6	–	–	–	–	0
M (Matias) Alemanno	05/12/1991	1,98	108	Tablada	5R	5R	4R	5	5R	5R	6	–	–	–	–	0
LV (Leonardo) Senatore	13/05/1984	1,91	106	Worcester[1]	6R	6R	8	8	8	8	6	1	–	–	–	5
TM (Tomás) Cubelli	12/06/1989	1,77	81	Belgrano	9R	9R	9R	9R	9	9R	6	1	–	–	–	5
J (Jeronimo) de la Fuente	24/02/1991	1,83	93	Duendes	15R	10R	–	12R	–	15R	4	–	–	–	–	0
LP González Amorosino	11/02/1985	1,85	93	Cardiff[3]	14R	14	11	11R	–	11	5	–	–	–	–	0
J-M Hernández	07/08/1982	1,87	94	Toulon[2]	–	12	12	12	12	12	5	–	–	–	1	3
B (Bruno) Postiglioni	08/04/1987	1,83	95	La Plata	–	1R	–	1R	–	1R	3	–	–	–	–	0
J-J (Juan) Imhoff	11/05/1988	1,85	90	Racing Metro[2]	–	–	14R	14	14	14	4	1	–	–	–	5
R (Rodrigo) Baez	08/02/1989	1,90	86	Liceo Naval	–	–	8R	6R	8R	6	4	–	–	–	–	0
B (Benjamin) Macome	10/01/1986	1,90	106	Bayonne[2]	–	–	–	8R	6	7	3	–	–	–	–	0
J (Javier) Ortega Desio	14/06/1990	1,93	100	Parana	–	–	–	–	–	7R	1	–	–	–	–	0
29 Players											**136**	**9**	**6**	**15**	**1**	**105**

Note: C = Captain, 1 = In England, 2 = In France, 3 = In Wales

---

Team President: Carlos Barbieri **Head Coach:** Daniel Hourcade
Assistant Coaches: Emiliano Bergamaschi, Raul Perez, Pablo Bouza & Germán Fernández
Team Manager: Rodrigo Jimenez Salice **Doctor:** Dr Guillermo Botto
Media Manager: Rafael Laría **Physiotherapists:** Christian Barrea & Lucas Toro
Bagage Master: Jorge Ruarte **Video Analyst:** Daniel Pérez **Logistics Manager:** Jose Santamarina
Trainer: Gonzalo Santos

CASTLE LAGER RUGBY CHAMPIONSHIP

Australia 12 New Zealand 12 (half-time 6-9)

August 17, ANZ Stadium, Sydney (68 627). Referee: Jaco Peyper (South Africa)
AUSTRALIA *Penalty goals: Beale (4).*
I Folau, PJ McCabe, AP Ashley-Cooper, MP Toomua, RG Horne, KJ Beale (BT Foley, 71), NW White (NJ Phipps, 67), WL Palu (WRJ Skelton, 71), M Hooper (Capt), SM Fardy (S Higginbotham, 67), RA Simmons, STG Carter, SM Kepu (BE Alexander, 79), NL Charles, JA Slipper (PJM Cowan, 71).
UNUSED SUBS: JE Hanson, RTRN Kuridrani. **CHAMPIONSHIP DEBUTS:** *STG Carter, NL Charles, PJM Cowan, WRJ Skelton.*
NEW ZEALAND *Penalty goals: Cruden (4).*
BR Smith, CS Jane, M Fekitoa, MA Nonu (RS Crotty, 57), SJ Savea, AW Cruden (BJ Barrett, 64), AL Smith, KJ Read, RH McCaw (Capt), J Kaino (BJ Franks, 39-48; SJ Cane, 70), SL Whitelock, BA Retallick, OT Franks (JPT Moody, 71), DS Coles (KF Mealamu, 49), WWV Crockett (BJ Franks, 48).
UNUSED SUBS: DS Luatua, TTR Perenara. **TEST DEBUT:** *JPT Moody.* **CHAMPIONSHIP DEBUTS:** *M Fekitoa, JPT Moody*
YELLOW CARD: *WWV Crockett (39-48)*
Notes: RH McCaw – 50th Rugby Championship Test (RC record);
150th Test between Australia & New Zealand since 1903

New Zealand 51 Australia 20 (half-time 23-6)

August 23, Eden Park, Auckland (48 211). Referee: Romain Poite (France)
NEW ZEALAND – *T: McCaw (2), Savea, Read, Luatua, Penalty try. C: Cruden (5), A Smith. P: Cruden (3).*
BR Smith, CS Jane (BJ Barrett, 46), CG Smith, RS Crotty (M Fekitoa, 41), SJ Savea, AW Cruden (TTR Perenara, 76), BJ Barrett, AL Smith, KJ Read, RH McCaw (Capt), LJ Messam (DS Luatua, 63), SL Whitelock, BA Rettallick (SJ Cane, 72), OT Franks (CC Faumuina, 60), DS Coles (KF Mealamu, 66), WWV Crockett (BJ Franks, 60). **YELLOW CARD:** *RH McCaw (13-24), BJ Franks (77-80)*
Note: CS Jane's 50th Test for New Zealand.
AUSTRALIA – *T: Folau, Hooper. C: Beale (2). P: Beale (2).*
I Folau, PJ McCabe, AP Ashley-Cooper (RTRN Kuridrani, 60), MP Toomua (BT Foley, 55), RG Horne, KJ Beale, NW White (NJ Phipps, 52), WL Palu (S Higginbotham, 55), M Hooper (Capt), SM Fardy (WRJ Skelton, 64), RA Simmons, STG Carter, SM Kepu (BE Alexander, 63), NL Charles (JE Hanson, 32), JA Slipper.
UNUSED SUBS: PJM Cowan. **YELLOW CARD:** *RA Simmons (23-33).* **CHAMPIONSHIP DEBUT:** *JE Hanson.*

New Zealand 28 Argentina 9 (half-time 13-6)

September 6, McLean Park, Napier (22 164). Referee: Pascal Gauzere (France)
NEW ZEALAND – *T: Savea (2), Messam, A Smith. C: Slade. P: Barrett, Slade.*
IJA Dagg, BR Smith, CG Smith, MA Nonu, SJ Savea, BJ Barrett (CR Slade, 56), AL Smith (TTR Perenara, 74), KJ Read, RH McCaw (Capt), LJ Messam (SJ Cane, 43), SL Whitelock (JI Thrush, 26), BA Retallick, OT Franks (BJ Franks, 65), DS Coles (KF Mealamu, 65), WWV Crockett (JPT Moody, 59).
UNUSED SUB: M Fekitoa.
ARGENTINA – *P: Sanchez (3).*
J Tuculet, H Agulla (JJ Imhoff, 66), LP Gonzalez Amorosino, MT Bosch, JM Hernandez, LP Gonzales Amorosino, FN Sanchez (S Gonzales Iglesias, 74), M Landajo (TM Cubelli, 54), LV Senatore (R Baez, 68), JM Fernandez Lobbe, JM Leguizamon, T Lavanini, MT Galarza (M Alemanno, 74), R Herrera (FN Tetaz Chaparo, 65), A Creevy (Capt, ME Cortese, 74), MI Ayerza (L Noguera Paz, 65).
CHAMPIONSHIP DEBUT: *R Baez*

CASTLE LAGER RUGBY CHAMPIONSHIP

Australia 32 Argentina 25 (half-time 14-7)

September 13, Cbus Super Stadium, Gold Coast (14 281). Referee: Glen Jackson (New Zealand)
AUSTRALIA - *T: Hooper (2), Betham. C: Foley. P: Foley (5).*
I Folau, PJJ Betham, RTRN Kuridrani, MP Toomua (KJ Beale, 53), RG Horne, BT Foley, NJ Phipps, BJ McCalman (M Hodgson, 70), M Hooper (Capt), SM Fardy (S Higginbotham, 50), RA Simmons, STG Carter (JE Horwill, 62), SM Kepu (BE Alexander, 58), SUT Polota-Nau (JE Hanson, 41), JA Slipper (PJM Cowan, 50). **UNUSED SUB:** *NW White.* **CHAMPIONSHIP DEBUT:** *PJJ Betham*
ARGENTINA - *T: Montero, Bosch, Tuculet. C: Sanchez (2). P: Sanchez (2).*
J Tuculet, JJ Imhoff, MT Bosch, JM Hernandez (J de la Fuente, 50), M Montero (LP Gonzales Amorosino, 78), FN Sanchez, M Landajo (TM Cubelli, 56), LV Senatore (B Macome, 36), JM Fernandez Lobbe, JM Leguizamon (R Baez, 50), M Afemanno, MT Galarza, R Herrera (FN Tetaz Chaparo, 60), A Creevy (Capt, ME Cortese, 74), MI Ayerza (B Postiglioni, 50-58, 68).

Argentina 13 New Zealand 34 (half-time 6-20)

September 27, Estadio Ciudad, La Plata (37 000). Referee: Craig Joubert (South Africa)
ARGENTINA - *T: Aguila. C: Gonzales Iglesias. P: Sanchez (2).*
J Tuculet, JJ Imhoff, MT Bosch (H Aguila, 69), JM Hernandez (S Gonzalez Iglesias, 59), M Montero, FN Sanchez, TM Cubelli (M Landajo, 53) LV Senatore (R Baez, 59), JM Fernandez Lobbe, B Macome, T Lavanini, MT Galarza (M Alemanno, 53), R Herrera (FN Tetaz Chaparo, 53), A Creevy (Capt, ME Cortese, 70), MI Ayerza (L Noguera Paz, 64).
NEW ZEALAND - *T: B Smith, Savea, Dagg, Perenara. C: Barrett (4). P: Barrett (2).*
IJA Dagg, BR Smith, CG Smith (CR Slade, 72), M Fekitoa, SJ Savea, BJ Barrett, AL Smith (TTR Perenara, 65), KJ Read, RH McCaw (Capt/SJ Cane, 65), J Kaino, SL Whitelock, BA Retallick (JI Thrush, 53), OT Franks (BJ Franks, 59), KF Mealamu (N Harris, 72), WWV Crockett (JPT Moody, 1-13, 53).
UNUSED SUB: *CS Jane.* **TESTS AND CHAMPIONSHIP DEBUT:** *N Harris*

Argentina 21 Australia 17 (half-time 8-14)

October 4, Estadio Malvinas Argentinas, Mendoza (26 000). Referee: Nigel Owens (Wales)
ARGENTINA - *T: Senatore, Imhoff. C: Sanchez. P: Sanchez (3).*
J Tuculet (J de la Fuente, 75), JJ Imhoff, H Aguila (MT Bosch, 69), JM Hernandez, LP Gonzales Amorosino, FN Sanchez, M Landajo (TM Cubelli, 58), LV Senatore, B Macome (J Ortega Desio, 14), R Baez, T Lavanini, MT Galarza (M Alemanno, 74), FN Tetaz Chaparo (R Herrera, 64), A Creevy (Capt), MI Ayerza (B Postiglioni, 67). **UNUSED SUB:** *ME Cortese.* **CHAMPIONSHIP DEBUT:** *J Ortega Desio*
AUSTRALIA - *T: Kuridrani, Higginbotham. C: Foley (2). P: Foley.*
I Folau, AP Ashley-Cooper, RTRN Kuridrani, MP Toomua (RG Horne, 31), JM Tomane, BT Foley, NJ Phipps (NW White, 64), S Higginbotham (J Schatz, 58), M Hooper (Capt), SM Fardy, JE Horwill (WRJ Skelton, 67), STG Carter, SM Kepu (BE Alexander, 61), SM Faingaa (JW Mann-Rea, 71) JA Slipper (BA Robinson, 58). **UNUSED SUB:** *M Hodgson.* **YELLOW CARD:** *Phipps (43-54), Hooper (74-80).*
TEST AND CHAMPIONSHIP DEBUT: *JW Mann-Rea, JW Schatz.*

Tournament Records
(Incorporating old Tri-Nations records)

CHAMPIONS

1996	New Zealand	2003	New Zealand	2010	New Zealand
1997	New Zealand	**2004**	**SOUTH AFRICA**	2011	Australia
1998	**SOUTH AFRICA**	2005	New Zealand	2012	New Zealand
1999	New Zealand	2006	New Zealand	2013	New Zealand
2000	Australia	2007	New Zealand	2014	New Zealand
2001	Australia	2008	New Zealand		
2002	New Zealand	**2009**	**SOUTH AFRICA**		

MATCH RECORDS

Most points by a team
73-13	South Africa vs Argentina	17/08/2013	Johannesburg

Biggest winning margin
60	South Africa vs Argentina	17/08/2013	Johannesburg

Most points away from home
54	New Zealand vs Argentina	29/09/2012	La Plata
54	Australia vs Argentina	05/10/2013	Rosario

Most tries by a team
8	South Africa vs Australia	23/08/1997	Pretoria
8	South Africa vs Australia	30/08/2008	Johannesburg

Most points by a player
31	M Steyn (1t, 1c, 8p), SA vs NZ	01/08/2009	Durban

Most tries by a player
4	JL Nokwe, SA vs Australia	30/08/2008	Johannesburg

Most conversions by a player
8	M Steyn, SA vs Argentina	17/08/2013	Johannesburg

Most penalty goals by a player
9	AP Mehrtens, NZ vs Australia	24/07/1999	Auckland

Most drop goals by a player
2	JH de Beer, SA vs NZ	19/07/1997	Johannesburg

[**MOST TOURNAMENT CAREER TRIES** **18** *BG Habana* South Africa

CASTLE LAGER RUGBY CHAMPIONSHIP

SEASON RECORDS BY THE TEAM

Most points
| 203 | South Africa | 2013 |

Most points conceded
| 224 | Argentina | 2013 |

Most tries
| 24 | New Zealand | 2013 |

Most tries conceded
| 25 | Argentina | 2013 |

Most log points
| 28 | New Zealand | 2013 |

SEASON RECORDS BY A PLAYER

Most points
| 99 | DW Carter | New Zealand | 2006 |

Most tries
| 8 | BR Smith | New Zealand | 2013 |

Most conversions
| 17 | M Steyn | South Africa | 2013 |

Most penalty goals
| 23 | M Steyn | South Africa | 2009 |

Most drop goals
| 3 | M Steyn | South Africa | 2009 |

MOST PENALTY GOALS IN A SEASON BY A PLAYER — 23 — M Steyn, South Africa

CAREER RECORDS

Most points
		App	T	C	P	D	Pts
DW Carter	New Zealand	39	6	72	115	4	531

Most tries
| 18 | BG Habana | South Africa |

Most conversions
| 72 | DW Carter | New Zealand |

Most penalty goals
| 115 | DW Carter | New Zealand |

Most drop goals
| 4 | AS Pretorius | South Africa |

Most appearances
| 55 | RH McCaw | New Zealand |

Most matches as a captain
| 44 | RH McCaw | New Zealand |

More than 30 wins
| 45 | RH McCaw | New Zealand |

END-OF-YEAR-TOUR to Ireland, England, Italy & Wales

TOURING SQUAD APPEARANCES & POINTS

Player	Date of birth	Height	Weight	Union/Club	Ireland	England	Italy	Wales	Apps	T	C	P	DG	Pts
WJ (Willie) le Roux	18/08/1989	1,86	88	Free State	15	15	15R	15	4	0	0	0	0	0
C (Cornal) Hendricks	18/04/1988	1,89	90	Free State	14	x	-	14	2	0	0	0	0	0
JL (Jan) Serfontein	15/04/1993	1,87	97	Blue Bulls	13	13	13	13	4	1	0	0	0	5
J (Jean) de Villiers	24/02/1981	1,90	100	Western Province	12c	12c	12c	12c	4	0	0	0	0	0
BG (Bryan) Habana	12/06/1983	1,79	94	Toulon, France	11	11	11	-	3	1	0	0	0	5
H (Handre) Pollard	11/03/1994	1,89	97	Blue Bulls	10	x	10R	10R	3	0	3	1	0	9
F (Francois) Hougaard	06/04/1988	1,79	91	Blue Bulls	9	x	9R	9R	3	0	0	0	0	0
DJ (Duane) Vermeulen	03/07/1986	1,92	90	Western Province	8	8	8	8	4	0	0	0	0	0
TS (Teboho) Mohoje	03/08/1990	1,93	106	Free State	7	7R	7	7	4	0	0	0	0	0
MC (Marcell) Coetzee	08/05/1991	1,90	106	KwaZulu-Natal	6	6	6	6	4	1	0	0	0	5
V (Victor) Matfield	11/05/1977	2,00	108	Blue Bulls	5	5	5	5	4	0	0	0	0	0
E (Eben) Etzebeth	29/10/1991	2,03	117	Western Province	4	4	4	4	4	0	0	0	0	0
JN (Jannie) du Plessis ***	16/11/1982	1,88	120	KwaZulu-Natal	3	3	-	-	2	0	0	0	0	0
BW (Bismarck) du Plessis	22/05/1984	1,89	113	KwaZulu-Natal	2	2R	2R	2	4	0	0	0	0	0
T (Tendai) Mtawarira	01/07/1985	1,88	118	KwaZulu-Natal	1	1R	-	1	3	0	0	0	0	0
JA (Adriaan) Strauss	18/11/1985	1,84	111	Free State	2R	2	2	2R	4	0	0	0	0	0
TN (Trevor) Nyakane	04/05/1989	1,78	109	Free State	1R	1R	1	1R	4	0	0	0	0	0
CV (Coenie) Oosthuizen	22/03/1989	1,81	127	Free State	3R	3R	3	3	4	1	0	0	0	5
JP (Bakkies) Botha	22/09/1979	2,02	122	Toulon, France	4R	4R	-	-	2	0	0	0	0	0
SWP (Schalk) Burger	13/04/1983	1,93	110	Suntory Sungoliath[1]	7R	7	-	-	2	1	0	0	0	5
JM (Cobus) Reinach	07/02/1990	1,76	100	KwaZulu-Natal	9R	9	9	9	4	2	0	0	0	10
PJ (Patrick) Lambie	17/10/1990	1,77	87	KwaZulu-Natal	10R	10	10	10	4	0	2	6	1	25
J-PR (JP) Pietersen	12/07/1986	1,91	103	Panasonic[2]	14R	14	14	-	3	1	0	0	0	5
JL (Johan) Goosen	27/07/1992	1,85	85	Racing Metro, France	-	-	15	-	1	0	0	0	0	0
N (Nizaam) Carr	04/04/1991	1,84	103	Western Province	-	-	7R	7R	2	0	0	0	0	0
J (Julian) Redelinghuys	11/09/1989	1,76	100	Golden Lions	-	-	3R	3R	2	0	0	0	0	0
L (Lood) de Jager	17/12/1992	2,05	125	Free State	-	-	4R	4R	2	0	0	0	0	0
GG (Gurthro) Steenkamp	12/06/1981	1,89	122	Toulouse, France	-	-	1R	-	1	0	0	0	0	0
LN (Lwazi) Mvovo	03/06/1986	1,85	94	KwaZulu-Natal	-	-	-	11	1	0	0	0	0	0
D (Damian) de Allende	25/11/1991	1,89	104	Western Province	-	-	-	12R	1	0	0	0	0	0

Note: C = Captain, 1 = Japan, 2 = Panasonic Wild Knights (Japan).

SPRINGBOKS WHO TOURED BUT DID NOT PLAY

Player	Date of birth	Height	Weight	Union/Club	Ireland	England	Italy	Wales	Apps	T	C	P	DG	Pts
ML (Marnitz) Boshoff ****	11/01/1989	1,79	87	Golden Lions	-	-	-	-	0	0	0	0	0	0
R (Ruan) Pienaar *	10/03/1984	1,87	92	Ulster, Ireland	-	-	-	-	0	0	0	0	0	0
M (Morne) Steyn	11/07/1984	1,84	91	Stade Francais, France	-	-	-	-	0	0	0	0	0	0
J Vermaak *	01/01/1985	1,75	82	Toulouse, France	-	-	-	-	0	0	0	0	0	0
WR Whiteley	18/09/1987	1,92	97	Golden Lions	-	-	-	-	0	0	0	0	0	0

END-OF-YEAR-TOUR to Ireland, England, Italy & Wales

TOURING SQUAD APPEARANCES & POINTS

	Date of birth	Height	Weight	Union/Club	Ireland	England	Italy	Wales	Apps	T	C	P	DG	Pts
NON-SPRINGBOKS WHO TOURED & DID NOT PLAY														
RL (Robbie) Coetzee **	02/05/1989	1,85	105	Golden Lions	-	-	-	-	0	0	0	0	0	0
R (Ross) Cronje *****	26/07/1989	1,80	88	Golden Lions	-	-	-	-	0	0	0	0	0	0
RM (Ruan) Dreyer ***	16/09/1990	1,86	110	Golden Lions	-	-	-	-	0	0	0	0	0	0
JA (Jaco) Kriel	21/08/1989	1,84	97	Golden Lions	-	-	-	-	0	0	0	0	0	0
S (Siya) Ntubeni **	18/02/1991	1,77	102	Western Province	-	-	-	-	0	0	0	0	0	0
R (Rudy) Paige ****	02/08/1989	1,69	82	Blue Bulls	-	-	-	-	0	0	0	0	0	0
SM (Seabelo) Senatla ******	10/02/1993	1,86	76	Western Province	-	-	-	-	0	0	0	0	0	0
42 Players									89	8	5	7	1	74

(of which 35 players are Springboks)
(of which 30 made a Test appearance on tour)
(of which 12 did not play any matches on tour)
(of which 7 – Coetzee, Cronje, Dreyer, Kriel, Ntubeni, Paige, Senatla – are not Springboks until such time as they may take the field in a Test match in the future)

* Pienaar replaced by Vermaak, who did not play on tour.
** Coetzee replaced by Ntubeni, who did not play on tour.
*** JN du Plessis replaced by Dreyer, who did not play on tour.
**** Boshoff and Paige joined the squad as cover for the last Test, but did not play.
***** Cronje joined the squad when Paige got injured.
****** Senatla departed home before the last Test, to join the Springbok Sevens team.

Head Coach: Heyneke Meyer **Forwards Coach:** Johan van Graan **Backs Coach:** Ricardo Loubscher
Fitness Coach: Basil Carzis **Defence Coach:** John McFarland **Team Manager:** Ian Schwartz
Team Doctor: Dr Craig Roberts **Physiotherapist:** Vivian Verwant **Masseuse:** Daliah Hurwitz
Operational Head: Charles Wessels **PR and Admin:** Annelee Murray **Logistics:** JJ Fredericks
Technical Analyst: Albé Visser **Communications Manager:** De Jongh Borchardt
Kicking Consultant: Louis Koen **Scrum Consultant:** Pieter de Villiers **Performance analyst:** Chean Roux **Physiotherapist:** Rene Naylor **Breakdown Consultant:** Richie Gray

END-OF-YEAR-TOUR to Ireland, England, Italy & Wales

Ireland 29 South Africa 15
(half-time 6-3)

8 November, Aviva Stadium, Dublin (51 100). Referee: Romain Poite (France)

IRELAND

Tries: Ruddock, Bowe. Conversions: Sexton (2). Penalties: Sexton (4), Madigan.

RDJ Kearney (FA Jones, 74), TJ Bowe, JB Payne (EGE Reddan, 78), R Henshaw, S Zebo, JJ Sexton (I Madigan, 74), C Murray, JPR Heaslip, R Ruddock, P O'Mahony (T O'Donnell, 71), PJ O'Connell (Captain), D Toner (MPA McCarthy, 74), MA Ross (RL Ah You, 74), S Cronin (CR Strauss, 58), JC McGrath (D Kilcoyne, 74).

TEST DEBUT: JB Payne

SOUTH AFRICA

Tries: Coetzee, Pietersen. Conversion: Pollard. Penalties: Pollard.

WJ Le Roux, C Hendricks (J-PR Pietersen, 49), JL Serfontein, J de Villiers (capt), BG Habana, H Pollard (PJ Lambie, 67), F Hougaard (JM Reinach, 57), DJ Vermeulen, TS Nohoje (SWP Burger, 47), MC Coetzee (BW du Plessis, 72-77), V Matfield, E Etzebeth (JP Botha, 65), JN du Plessis (CV Oosthuizen, 71), BW du Plessis (JA Strauss, 51), T Mtawarira (TN Nyakane, 68).

YELLOW CARD: JA Strauss (67-77)

HAVING beaten New Zealand in their last outing, the Springboks were probably still walking on air as they headed into the Test against Ireland at the Aviva Stadium in Dublin.

However, they were brought down to earth with an almighty thud, in spite of spending much time in Ireland's 22-metre area. What separated Ireland from the Springboks was simply that they took their opportunities. Flyhalf Jonny Sexton was the hero of the day, striking four penalties and two conversions, as well as giving Ireland tactical direction.

For South Africa it was a strange defeat. They dominated territory to the tune of 63% and possession 55%. They got themselves into Ireland's 22-metre area five times alone in the first half, while skipper Jean de Villiers also turned down three kickable penalties at goal. On top of that, South Africa dominated the scrums and won all their lineouts while also pinching a few of Ireland's.

So what went wrong?

Firstly, the Springboks struggled for quick ball from the rucks and scrumhalf Francois Hougaard played the proverbial shocker by twice knocking on the ball behind the oven during the forays into Ireland's red zone. De Villiers was also cavalier in his decision-making. The field was wet after a heavy downpour before kick-off and the conditions begged a conservative approach in terms of taking kickable penalties. Ireland grew in confidence each time they defended their line and also came up with an innovative strategy to stop the Springboks' lineout drives. At one stage they held back instead of binding and consequently were entitled to come around and grab the ball-carrier after the Springboks had transferred the ball to the back of the maul.

After all that, the first half yielded only three points for the Springboks through fly-

END-OF-YEAR-TOUR to Ireland, England, Italy & Wales

Jan Serfontein is smothered by Irish defence.

half Handré Pollard's penalty shortly before half-time. South Africa, however, addressed their technical deficiency at the mauls and a lineout drive yielded a try for flank Marcell Coetzee that brought them back to 10-13 with a little over 20 minutes left.

It should have been the cue for the Springboks to push home.

Even after Sexton had increased Ireland's lead to six points, one got the impression the momentum was very much with the Springboks. But the wheels came off when replacement hooker Adriaan Strauss was sin-binned for challenging Ireland fullback Rob Kearney in the air. Losing their hooker proved calamitous for the Springboks. Ireland pushed home their advantage with another penalty by Sexton and a try by right wing Tommy Bowe. It was 26-10 with seven minutes left and there would be no great escape for the Springboks as there was earlier in the season against Argentina and Wales.

Ian Madigan, on for Sexton, added one more penalty two minutes from time. The Springboks managed a consolation try through right wing JP Pietersen, but to even call it that much is stretching the truth.

If anything, this was a savage disappointment. The Springboks had, after all, conquered the world's best team in their last match, but perhaps that was the problem.

Complacency, poor decision-making and execution had conspired against them. Ireland, of course, deserve immense credit, but more than anything the Springboks had beaten themselves.

SCORING SEQUENCE

Min	Action	Score
9	Sexton penalty	3-0
17	Pollard missed penalty	3-0
24	Sexton penalty	6-0
38	Pollard penalty	6-3
42	Ruddock try, Sexton conversion	13-3
57	Coetzee try, Pollard conversion	13-10
63	Sexton penalty	16-10
71	Sexton penalty	19-10
72	Bowe try, Sexton conversion	26-10
78	Madigan penalty	29-10
80	Pietersen try, Lambie missed conversion	29-15

END-OF-YEAR-TOUR to Ireland, England, Italy & Wales

England 28 South Africa 31
(half-time 6-13)

15 November, Twickenham, London (82 125). Referee: Steve R Walsh (Australia)

ENGLAND

Tries: Wilson, Morgan, Barritt. Conversions: Farrell (2). Penalties: Farrell (2), Ford.

MN Brown, AKC Watson, BM Barritt, KO Eastmond, JJ May, OA Farrell (GT Ford, 64), DS Care (BR Youngs, 64), VML Vunipola (BJ Morgan, 44), CDC Robshaw (Captain), TA Wood (RW Webber, 61-71), CL Lawes, DMJ Attwood (GEJ Kruis, 67), DG Wilson (K Brooks, 73), DM Hartley (R Webber, 71), JWG Marler (MJ Mullan, 67). **UNUSED SUB:** MXG Yarde. **YELLOW CARD:** DM Hartley (61-71).

Note: DS Care played in his 50th Test for England.

SOUTH AFRICA

Tries: Serfontein, Reinach, Burger. Conversions: Lambie (2). Penalties: Lambie (3). Drop Goal: Lambie

WJ Le Roux, J-PR Pietersen, JL Serfontein, J de Villiers (capt), BG Habana, PJ Lambie, JM Reinach, DJ Vermeulen, SWP Burger (TS Mohoje, 78), MC Coetzee, V Matfield, E Etzebeth (JP Botha, 65), JN du Plessis (CV Oosthuizen, 64), JA Strauss (BW du Plessis, 60), T Mtawarira (TN Nyakane, 75). **UNUSED SUBS:** F Hougaard, H Pollard, C Hendricks. **YELLOW CARD:** V Matfield (44-54).

Note: SWP Burger scored his 12th Test try as a flanker (New SA Record)

THE old adage that there is nothing as dangerous as a wounded Springbok rang true as England were yet again brought down a notch by South Africa at Twickenham.

While the scoreline of 31-28 suggests it was close, South Africa's supremacy was only briefly in doubt after lock Victor Matfield had been yellow-carded early in the second half.

The one-man advantage allowed England to score twice from rolling mauls, drawing them back from 6-20 to 20-all. Suddenly, in a game which the Springboks had dominated prior to that, *Swing Low Sweet Chariot* was bellowed loud enough to be heard from Richmond to Baker Street.

But this was just the scenario the Springboks needed to demonstrate their maturity. Even before Matfield's return, they had managed to regain the lead with a try by outstanding flank Schalk Burger following a rolling maul.

For the Springboks it was a frustration to have even found themselves in that position to begin with. They led 13-6 at half-time after an outstanding defensive effort and then increased the lead by seven points in the first minute of the second half.

Flyhalf Pat Lambie's chip over the English defensive line was caught by fullback Willie le Roux, who off-loaded to scrumhalf Cobus Reinach to score.

In the first half the Springboks had returned to their traditional template after being guilty of playing too much rugby in the previous week's heavy defeat to Ireland. England ran predictable lines in carrying the ball up and time and again were picked off with South African offensive defence.

An intercept try by centre Jan Serfontein in the 16th minute was crucial. It made the

END-OF-YEAR-TOUR to Ireland, England, Italy & Wales

Schalk Burger was back to his irrepressible self against England.

score 10-0 to South Africa and left England chasing the game.

For all their efforts, the home side's advantage of 73% territory and 56% possession in the first half had yielded only three points through a penalty by flyhalf Owen Farrell.

The rolling-maul tries by tighthead prop David Wilson and loose-forward replacement Ben Morgan, which brought England level, added an exciting dynamic.

But at the same time it allowed the Springboks to walk away with more satisfaction after closing out the game in the final 15 minutes.

With Burger's try having given the tourists a 25-20 lead, Lambie added another penalty to edge the Springboks eight points ahead with 13 minutes left. George Ford, who had replaced Farrell, reduced the deficit to five again shortly thereafter before the visitors turned the screws. Lambie positioned himself for a superbly worked drop goal four minutes from time to edge the Springboks into a decisive 31-23 lead. England pulled back with a try from centre Brad Barritt in the 79th minute, but it was a classic case of too little, too late.

Apart from the maturity to close out the game, the Springboks could also take satisfaction from the way that Reinach had excelled in his first start. But it was the old faithfuls that mostly crafted this victory. Burger and his loose-forward partners, Duane Vermeulen and Marcell Coetzee, together with skipper Jean de Villiers, were immense on defence.

It was ultimately a tactical masterclass, which took South Africa's unbeaten run in matches against England to 12.

SCORING SEQUENCE

Min	Action	Score
11	Lambie penalty	0-3
16	Serfontein try, Lambie conversion	0-10
28	Farrell penalty	3-10
33	Lambie penalty	3-13
36	Farrell penalty	6-13
38	Lambie missed penalty	6-13
41	Reinach try, Lambie conversion	6-20
45	Wilson try, Farrell conversion	13-20
48	Morgan try, Farrell conversion	20-20
54	Burger try, Lambie missed conversion	20-25
67	Lambie penalty	20-28
68	Ford penalty	23-28
76	Lambie drop goal	23-31
79	Barritt try, Ford missed conversion	28-31

END-OF-YEAR-TOUR to Ireland, England, Italy & Wales

Italy 6 South Africa 22
(half-time 6-8)

22 November, Stadio Euganeo, Padova (24 500). Referee: Jerome Garces (France)

ITALY
Penalties: Hamona (2).

A Masi, L Sarto (G Toniolatti, 78), M Campagnaro, LER Morisi, LJ McLean, KJ Haimona (L Orquera, 76), E Gori (G Palazanni, 66), SM Parisse (Captain), SN Vunisa, A Zanni (F Minto, 41), RJ Furno (M Bortolami, 71), Q Geldenhuys, ML Castrogiovanni (D Chistolini, 64), LL Ghiraldini (A Manici, 64), M Aguero (A de Marchi, 35). *TEST DEBUT: SN Vunisa*

SOUTH AFRICA
Tries: Oosthuizen, Reinach, Habana. Conversions: Pollard (2). Penalties: Lambie.

JL Goosen (WJ Le Roux, 58), J-PR Pietersen, JL Serfontein, J de Villiers (capt), BG Habana, PJ Lambie (H Pollard, 57), JM Reinach (F Hougaard, 61), DJ Vermeulen, TS Mohoje (N Carr, 57), MC Coetzee, V Matfield, E Etzebeth (L de Jager, 71), CV Oosthuizen (J Redelinghuys, 61), JA Strauss (BW du Plessis, 51), TN Nyakane (GG Steenkamp, 57). *TEST DEBUT: N Carr (#865), J Redelinghuys (#866)*

SOUTH Africa's 22-6 victory over Italy in Padova may be remembered fondly, if only because of a dream debut for Nizaam Carr and some impressive scrumming that revealed depth in the front-row department.

The rugby was entirely forgettable and the Springboks made a meal of imposing themselves on vastly inferior opponents. Enter Carr as replacement for flank Teboho Mohoje in the 57th minute. With the Springboks struggling to break down the Azzurri, the Western Province loose forward ran a delightful line and cut through before offloading to scrumhalf Cobus Reinach for the try. With the conversion the tourists were up 15-6 and had finally managed to put some distance between themselves and a pugnacious home side. Prior to that, Italy had succeeded in dragging the Springboks down to their level. Credit the home side with defending ferociously and being highly competitive at the breakdowns, even if they were sometimes guilty of illegal play. Is it not against the laws of the game to pull a scrumhalf into the rucks and to slap the ball out of an opponent's hand? It matters not because the Springboks won, even if they waited for the stroke of full-time to twist the dagger with a try from left wing Bryan Habana.

Willie le Roux, who had replaced Johan Goosen following the latter's experimental selection at fullback, provided the spark for the final touchdown by initiating a counter-attack.

The Springboks contributed to their own struggles with a dysfunctional lineout, which on three occasions led to them surrendering attacking positions. On another day they might have built an innings by mauling their way over.

Surprisingly, it was at the scrums where the Springboks made it a difficult day for the Azzurri. Trevor Nyakane, who started at loosehead so that Tendai Mtawarira could

END-OF-YEAR-TOUR to Ireland, England, Italy & Wales

Nizaam Carr enjoyed a dream debut off the bench for South Africa.

take a breather, more than held his own against the revered Italian tighthead Martin Castrogiovanni. In addition, Coenie Oosthuizen had an impressive scrumming outing in the No 3 jersey after many an expert had expressed the view that he was suited only to the position occupied by Nyakane.

Oosthuizen's work-rate was also exceptional. Apart from scoring the Springboks' first try, he won three internal awards after the match – one for exceptional service to the team and the others respectively for registering the highest tackle count and cleaning the most rucks. Who knows what might have happened had Nyakane and Oosthuizen not embraced the challenge with such aplomb?

Flyhalf Patrick Lambie also deserves some plaudits, even if the Springboks' inaccuracy undid much of his good work. He got superb distance on his line kicks and also attacked the advantage line with vigour. On Italy's side No 8 Sergio Parisse was his usual brilliant self, standing head and shoulders above generally average team-mates who punched above their collective weight. Their efforts were rewarded with a standing ovation after the final whistle. For the Springboks it was mission accomplished, even if it was achieved in underwhelming fashion.

Veteran lock Bakkies Botha, who had secretly turned down the opportunity to start the Test, announced his retirement from international rugby immediately at its conclusion.

SCORING SEQUENCE

Min	Action	Score
1	Hamona missed penalty	0-0
12	Hamona penalty	3-0
16	Lambie penalty	3-3
22	Oosthuizen try,	
	Lambie missed conversion	3-8
40	Hamona penalty	6-8
57	Hamona missed penalty	6-8
59	Reinach try, Pollard conversion	6-15
80	Habana try, Pollard conversion	6-22

END-OF-YEAR-TOUR to Ireland, England, Italy & Wales

Wales 12 South Africa 6
(half-time 3-3)

29 November, Millennium Stadium (58 235). Referee: John Lacey (Ireland)

WALES
Penalties: Halfpenny (4).

SL Halfpenny (MS Williams, 67), ACG Cuthbert, JJV Davies, JH Roberts, LB Williams, DR Biggar, R Webb, TT Faletau, SK Warburton (Captain), DJ Lydiate, A-W Jones, JD Ball, S Lee, SJ Baldwin, GD Jenkins (AR Jarvis, 75). Unused subs: E Phillips, AR Jones, LC Charteris, J King, WM Phillips, R Priestland.

SOUTH AFRICA
Penalties: Lambie (2).

WJ Le Roux, C Hendricks, JL Serfontein, J de Villiers (capt, D de Allende, 57)*, LN Mvovo, PJ Lambie (H Pollard, 57), JM Reinach (F Hougaard, 62), DJ Vermeulen, TS Mohoje (N Carr, 54), MC Coetzee, V Matfield, E Etzebeth (L de Jager, 69), CV Oosthuizen (J Redelinghuys, 70), BW du Plessis (JA Strauss, 51), T Mtawarira (TN Nyakane, 54).

YELLOW CARD: *Cornal Hendricks (63-75). *Serfontein to 12, De Allende to 13.*

THE Springboks' season-ending Test against Wales proved a bridge too far as they went down 12-6 on the back of a performance that suggested they already had one foot on the plane home.

Much worse than the defeat, however, was the serious knee injury suffered by captain Jean de Villiers. Play was suspended for several minutes as paramedics prepared to stretcher him from the field. The incident occurred in the 57th minute after Wales fullback Leigh Halfpenny had struck his fourth penalty. If that wasn't a devastating enough blow for the Springboks, right wing Cornal Hendricks was sin-binned six minutes later for supposedly playing Halfpenny in the air.

It appeared to be a perfectly legitimate contest for a high ball, but as the Springbok motto goes: 'The referee is always right.' The only problem is that the referee's infinite wisdom in this instance just about sounded the death knell. All credit to the Springboks for holding on bravely under siege without conceding a penalty. But panic had also set in. Francois Hougaard, for example, inexplicably tapped a penalty and kicked the ball directly into touch, while Willie le Roux knocked on right in front of the Springboks' tryline.

They were rattled and failed to make the most of one last opportunity. Handré Pollard, who had replaced Patrick Lambie, failed to find touch in the corner to set up a potential lineout drive, although the ball was fortuitously knocked dead by Welsh hands in an attempt to keep it in.

Sadly South Africa made a mess of the attacking scrum and Wales could relieve the pressure. In truth, it would have been a miscarriage of justice had the Springboks managed to get out of jail. Wales, in spite of their limitations, appeared to want it more. The home side dominated territory and possession in the opening 30 minutes, with the Springboks happy to pick off the big ball-carriers who ran predictable lines. In boxing

END-OF-YEAR-TOUR to Ireland, England, Italy & Wales

Eben Etzebeth drives strongly in an ultimately losing cause against Wales.

terms, Wales were winning the bout on points, but the danger was also there that they would leave themselves open to the sucker punch.

South Africa had a good spell in the final 10 minutes of the first half, but failed to make the most of it. Lambie missed with a penalty in line with the posts, albeit from far out, in the 31st minute and lock Eben Etzebeth was heroically cut down by Halfpenny after charging clean through two minutes later. Then, three minutes later, the Springboks knocked the ball on a few phases after winning a tighthead at a scrum in Wales' 22-metre area. South Africa also decided to forego the opportunity of a three-pointer at the end of the first half in an attempt to score through a lineout drive, but again the ball was fumbled, which meant the score was 3-3 at the break.

One would have thought the Springboks might kick on after taking Wales' best punches, but they were strangely off-colour after the restart in spite of Lambie having responded in kind to Halfpenny's second penalty. The Springboks, who had mostly dominated at set-piece, were pushed into submission at a scrum in the 56th minute and the chants of 'Wales, Wales, Wales!' consequently resounded inside the stadium.

De Villiers' sad exit followed immediately after Halfpenny's fourth penalty and from then on the Springboks simply disappeared into a black hole.

SCORING SEQUENCE

Min	Action	Score
4	Halfpenny penalty	3-0
10	Lambie penalty	3-3
15	Halfpenny missed penalty	3-3
31	Lambie missed penalty	3-3
48	Halfpenny penalty	6-3
50	Lambie penalty	6-6
53	Halfpenny penalty	9-6
57	Halfpenny penalty	12-6

South Africa's Internationals 1891-2014

A complete list of all 866 players to have played Test rugby for South Africa, with Springbok number.

Springbok #324 **Ackermann, DSP** (Dawie) b 03/06/1930 d 01/01/1970 - WP - 8 Tests (3 - 1T) 19 matches (27 - 9T) *1955: BI2, 3, 4. 1956: A1, 2, NZ1, 3. 1958: F2.*

632 **Ackermann, JN** (Johan) b 03/06/1970 - NTvl - 13 Tests (-) 15 matches (-) *1996: Fj, A1, NZ1, A2. 2001: F2(R), It1, NZ1(R), A1. 2006: I, E1, 2. 2007: Sm1, A2. 2007: tour of UK - no tests*

805 **Adams, HJ** (Heinie) b 29/05/1980 - BB - No Tests - 2 matches (-) *Toured F, It, I & E. 2009.*

853 **Adriaanse, LC** (Lourens) b 05/02/1988 - GW - 1 Test (-) 1 match (-) *2013: Rugby Championship squad - no tests, F(R).*

658 **Aitken, AD** (Andrew) b 10/06/1968 - WP - 7 Tests (-) 9 matches (-) *1997: F2(R), E. 1998: I2(R), W1(R), NZ1, 2(R), A2(R).*

822 **Alberts, WS** (Willem) b 05/11/1984 - KZN - 32 Tests (35 - 7T) 33 matches (35 - 7T) *2010: W2(R), S(t+R), E(R). 2011: NZ2, [W(R), Fj(R), Nam, Sm(t+R)A3(t+R).]. 2012: E1, 2, Arg1, 2, A1, NZ1, A2, NZ2, I, S, E4. 2013: Sam, Arg1, Arg2, A1, NZ1, A2, NZ2, W, S, F. 2014: W1, W2.*

179 **Albertyn, PK** (Pierre) b 27/05/1897 d 07/03/1973 - SWD - 4 Tests (3 - 1T) 4 matches (3 - 1T) *1924:BI1*, 2*, 3*, 4*.*

673 **Alcock, CD** (Chad) b 09/01/1973 - EP - No Tests - 4 matches (5 - 1T) *Toured BI & I. 1998.*

13 **Alexander, FA** (Fred) b 30/12/1870 d 20/04/1937 - GW - 2 Tests (-) 2 matches (-) *1891: BI1, 2.*

594 **Allan, J** (John) b 25/11/1963 - Natal - 13 Tests (-) 25 matches (30 - 6T) *1993: A1(R), Arg1, 2(R). 1994: E1, 2, NZ1, 2, 3. 1996: Fj, A1, NZ1, A2, NZ2.*

355 **Allen, PB** (Peter) b 10/04/1930 d 22/01/1998 - EP - 1 Test (-) 1 match (-) *1960: S.*

121 **Allport, PH** (Percy) b 24/03/1885 d 01/01/1959 - WP - 2 Tests (3 - 1T) 2 matches (3 - 1T) *1910:BI2, 3.*

31 **Anderson, JH** (Biddy) b 26/04/1874 d 11/03/1926 - WP - 3 Tests (-) 3 matches (-) *1896:BI1, 3, 4.*

89 **Anderson, JW** (Joe) b 31/12/1881 d 02/11/1953 - WP - 1 Test (-) 1 match (-) *1903:BI3.*

47 **Andrew, JB** (Ben) b 15/05/1870 d 09/04/1911 - Tvl - 1 Test (-) 1 match (-) *1896:BI2.*

759 **Andrews, EP** (Eddie) b 18/03/1977 - WP - 23 Tests (-) 23 matches (-) *2004: I1, 2, W1(t+R), PI, NZ1, A1, NZ2, A2, W2, I3, E. 2005: F1, A2, NZ2(t), Arg(R), F3(R). 2006: S1, 2, F, A1(R), NZ1(t). 2007:A2(R), NZ2(R).*

574 **Andrews, KS** (Keith) b 03/05/1962 - WP - 9 Tests (-) 31 matches (-) *1992: E. 1993: F1, 2, A1(R), 2, 3, Arg1(R), 2. 1994: NZ3.*

602 **Andrews, MG** (Mark) b 21/02/1972 - Natal - 77 Tests (60 - 12T) 90 matches (60 - 12T) *1993: tour of Arg - no tests. 1994:E2, NZ1, 2, 3, Arg1, 2, S, W. 1995:WS1, [A, WS2, F, NZ], W, It, E. 1996:Fj, A1, NZ1, A2, NZ2, 3, 4, 5, Arg1, 2, F1, 2, W. 1997:T(R), BI1, 2, NZ1, A1, NZ2, A2, It, F1, 2, E, S. 1998:I1, 2, W1, E1, A1, NZ1, 2, A2, W2, S, I3, E2. 1999:NZ1, 2(R), A2(R), [S, U, E, A3, NZ3]. 2000:A2, NZ2, A3, Arg, I, W, E3. 2001:F1, 2, It1, NZ1, A1, 2, NZ2, F3, E.*

358 **Antelme, JGM** (Mike) b 23/04/1934 - Tvl - 5 Tests (-) 25 matches (45 - 15T) *1960:NZ1, 2, 3, 4. 1961:F.*

816 **Aplon, GG** (Gio) b 06/10/1982 - WP - 17 Tests (25 - 5T) 18 matches (25 - 5T) *2010:W1, F, It1, 2, NZ1(R), 2(R), A1, NZ3, A3(R), I, W2, S, E. 2011:A1, 2.[Nam.]. 2012:E3. 2013: Tour of W, S & F - no Tests.*

243 **Apsey, JT** (John) b 16/04/1911 d 12/11/1987 - WP - 3 Tests (-) 3 matches (-) *1933:A4, 5. 1938:BI2.*

76 **Ashley, S** (Syd) b 23/02/1880 d 20/01/1959 - WP - 1 Test (-) 1 match (-) *1903:BI2.*

32 **Aston, FTD** (Ferdy) b 18/09/1871 d 15/10/1926 - Tvl - 4 Tests (-) 4 matches (-) *1896:BI1*, 2*, 3*, 4.*

576 **Atherton, S** (Steve) b 17/03/1965 - Natal - 8 Tests (-) 23 matches (5 - 1T) *1992: tour of F & E - no tests. 1993:Arg1, 2. 1994:E1, 2, NZ1, 2, 3. 1996:NZ2.*

178 **Aucamp, J** (Hans) b 27/10/1898 d 14/03/1970 - WTvl - 2 Tests (3 - 1T) 2 matches (3 - 1T) *1924:BI1, 2.*

376 **Baard, AP** (Attie) b 17/05/1933 - 01/05/2009 - WP - 1 Test (-) 13 matches (9 - 3T) *1960:I.*

246 **Babrow, L** (Louis) b 24/04/1915 d

26/01/2004 - WP - 5 Tests (9 - 3T) 16 matches (42 - 14T) *1937:A1, 2, NZ1, 2, 3.*

712 **Badenhorst, AJ** (Adri) b 18/07/1978 - WP - No Tests - 1 match (-) *Toured E. 2000.*

610 **Badenhorst, C** (Chris) b 12/12/1965 - OFS - 2 Tests (10 - 2T) 12 matches (45 - 9T) *1994: tours of NZ and S & W - no tests. 1994: Arg2. 1995:WS1(R).*

745 **Bands, RE** (Richard) b 25/03/1974 - BB - 11 Tests (10 - 2T) 11 matches (10 - 2T) *2003: S1, 2, Arg(R), A1, NZ1, A2, NZ2, [U, E, Sm(R), NZ3(R)].*

538 **Barnard, AS** (Anton) b 07/04/1958 - EP - 4 Tests (-) 4 matches (-) *1984: S.Am&Sp1, 2. 1986: NZC1, 2.*

399 **Barnard, JH** (Jannie) b 29/01/1945 d 21/02/1985 - Tvl - 5 Tests (-) 18 matches (21 - 7T) *1965: S, A1, 2, NZ3, 4.*

442 **Barnard, RW** (Robbie) b 26/11/1941 d 20/10/2013 - Tvl - 1 Test (-) 10 matches (9 - 3T) *1969-70: tour of UK - no tests. 1970:NZ2(R). 1971: tour of A - no tests.*

285 **Barnard, WHM** (Willem) b 07/08/1923 d 13/06/2012 - NTvl - 2 Tests (-) 14 matches (3 - 1T) *1949:NZ4. 1951:W.*

690 **Barry, D** (De Wet) b 24/06/1978 - WP - 39 Tests (15 - 3T) 41 matches (20 - 4T) *2000: C, E1, 2, A1(R), NZ1, A2. 2001: F1, 2, US(R). 2002: W2, Arg, Sm, NZ1, A1, NZ2, A2. 2003: A1, NZ1, A2, [U, E, Sm, NZ3]. 2004: PI, NZ1, A1, NZ2, A2, W2, I3, E, Arg(t). 2005: F1, 2, A1, NZ2, W(R), F3(R). 2006: F.*

63 **Barry, J** (Joe) b 16/03/1876 d 29/03/1961 - WP - 3 Tests (3 - 1T) 3 matches (3 - 1T) *1903: BI1, 2, 3.*

545 **Bartmann, WJ** (Wahl) b 13/06/1963 - Tvl - 8 Tests (-) 15 matches (5 - 1T) *1986: NZC1, 2, 3, 4. 1992: NZ, A, F1, 2.*

817 **Basson, BA** (Bjorn) b 11/02/1987 - GW - 11 Tests (15 - 3T) 11 matches (15 - 3T) *2010: W1(R), It1(R), I, W2. 2011: A1, NZ1. 2013: It, S, Sam, Arg1, Arg2.*

661 **Basson, WW** (Wium) b 23/10/1975 d 22/04/2001 - BB - No Tests - 2 matches (-) *Toured It, F, E & S. 1997.*

252 **Bastard, WE** (Ebbo) b 10/12/1912 d 14/02/1949 - Natal - 6 Tests (6 - 2T) 18 matches (15 - 5T) *1937: A1, NZ1, 2, 3. 1938: BI1, 3.*

438 **Bates, AJ** (Albie) b 18/04/1941 - WTvl - 4 Tests (-) 18 matches (3 - 1T) *1969: E. 1970: NZ1, 2. 1971: tour of A - no tests. 1972: E.*

468 **Bayvel, PCR** (Paul) b 28/03/1949 - Tvl - 10 Tests (-) 13 matches (-) *1974: BI2, 4, F1, 2. 1975: F1, 2. 1976: NZ1, 2, 3, 4.*

524 **Beck, JJ (**Colin) b 27/03/1959 - WP - 3 Tests (4 - 1T) 12 matches (35 - 5T, 3C, 2P, 1D) *1981: NZ2(R), 3(R), US.*

387 **Bedford, TP** (Tommy) b 08/02/1942 - Natal - 25 Tests (3 - 1T) 48 matches (12 - 4T) *1963: A1, 2, 3, 4. 1964: W, F. 1965: I, A1, 2. 1968: BI1, 2, 3, 4, F1, 2. 1969: A1, 2*, 3*, 4, S*, E. 1970: I, W. 1971: F1, 2. 1971: tour of A - no tests.*

795 **Bekker, A** (Andries) b 05/12/1983 - WP - 29 Tests (5 - 1T) 31 matches (5 - 1T) *2008: W1, 2(R), It(R), NZ1(R), 2(t+R), A1(t+R), Arg(R), NZ3, A2, 3, W3(R), S(R), E(R). 2009: BI1(R), 2(R), NZ2(R), A1(R), 2(R), F(t+R), It, I. 2010: It2, NZ1(R), 2(R). 2012:Arg1, 2, NZ1(t+R), A2, NZ2.*

527 **Bekker, HJ** (Hennie) b 12/09/1952 - WP - 2 Tests (4 - 1T) 10 matches (16 - 4T) *1981: NZ1, 3.*

298 **Bekker, HPJ** (Jaap) b 11/02/1925 d 06/08/1999 - NTvl - 15 Tests (3 - 1T) 39 matches (12 - 4T) *1952: E, F. 1953: A1, 2, 3, 4. 1955: BI2, 3, 4. 1956: A1, 2, NZ1, 2, 3, 4.*

353 **Bekker, MJ** (Martiens) b 03/05/1930 d 10/11/1971 - NTvl - 1 Test (-) 1 match (-) *1960: S.*

308 **Bekker, RP** (Dolph) b 15/12/1926 d 17/06/2012 - NTvl - 2 Tests (3 - 1T) 2 matches (3 - 1T) *1953: A3, 4.*

639 **Bekker, S** (Schutte) b 21/10/1971 - NTvl - 1 Test (-) 3 matches (15 - 3T) *1996: tour of Arg, F & W - no tests. 1997: A2(t).*

640 **Bennett, RG** (Russell) b 27/11/1971 - Border - 6 Tests (10 - 2T) 10 matches (25 - 5T) *1996: tour of Arg, F & W - no tests. 1997: T(R), BI1(R), 3, NZ1, A1, NZ2.*

228 **Bergh, WF v R v O** (Ferdie) b 02/11/1906 d 28/05/1973 - SWD - 17 Tests (21 - 7T) 41 matches (42 - 14T) *1931: W, I. 1932: E, S. 1933: A1, 2, 3, 4, 5. 1937: A1, 2, NZ1, 2, 3. 1938: BI1, 2, 3.*

485 **Bestbier, A** (André) b 31/03/1946 - OFS - 1 Test (-) 5 matches (-) *1974: F2(R).*

186 **Bester, JJN** (Jack) b 02/03/1898 d 27/10/1943 - WP - 2 Tests (3 - 1T) 2 matches (3 - 1T) *1924: BI2, 4.*

247 **Bester, JLA** (Johnny) b 25/12/1917 d 14/05/1977 - WP - 2 Tests (6 - 2T) 14 matches (30 - 10T) *1937: tour of A & NZ - no tests. 1938: BI2, 3.*

49 **Beswick, AM** (Allan) b 30/06/1870 d 06/09/1908 - Border - 3 Tests (-) 3 matches (-) *1896: BI2, 3, 4.*

383 **Bezuidenhout, CE** (Chris) b 13/10/1937 d ??/??/2002 - NTvl - 3 Tests (-) 3 matches (-) *1962: BI2, 3, 4.*

SPRINGBOKS

751 **Bezuidenhout, CJ** (Christo) b 14/05/1970 - Mpu - 4 Tests (-) 4 matches (-) *2003: NZ2(R), [E, Sm, NZ3].*

457 **Bezuidenhout, NSE** (Niek) b 04/08/1950 - NTvl - 9 Tests (-) 13 matches (-) *1972: E. 1974: BI2, 3, 4, F1, 2. 1975: F1, 2. 1977: WT.*

225 **Bierman, JN** (Nic) b 13/02/1910 d 08/06/1977 - Tvl - 1 Test (-) 14 matches (18 - 6T) *1931: I.*

8 **Bisset, WM** (William) b 11/09/1867 d 23/02/1958 - WP - 2 Tests (-) 2 matches (-) *1891: BI1, 3.*

494 **Blair, R** (Robbie) b 03/06/1953 - WP - 1 Test (21 - 3C, 5P) 1 match (21 - 3C, 5P) *1977: WT.*

747 **Bobo, G** (Gcobani) b 12/09/1979 - GL - 6 Tests (-) 6 matches (-) *2003:S2(R), Arg, A1(R), NZ2. 2004: S(R). 2008:It.*

670 **Boome, CS** (Selborne) b 16/05/1975 - WP - 20 Tests (10 - 2T) 25 matches (15 - 3T) *1998: tour of UK & I - no tests. 1999: It1, 2, W, NZ1(R), A1, NZ2, A2. 2000: C, E1, 2. 2003: S1(R), 2(R), Arg(R), A1(R), NZ1(R), A2, NZ2(R), [U(R), G, NZ3(R)].*

467 **Bosch, GR** (Gerald) b 12/05/1949 - Tvl - 9 Tests (89 - 7C, 23P, 2D) 14 matches (132 - 15C, 31P, 3D) *1974: BI2, F1, 2. 1975: F1, 2. 1976: NZ1, 2, 3, 4.*

861 **Boshoff, ML** (Marnitz) b 11/01/1989 - GL - 1 Test (2 -1C) 1 match (2 - 1C) *2014: S(R).*

771 **Bosman, HM** (Meyer) b 19/04/1985 - FS - 3 Tests (7 - 2C, 1P) 6 matches (7 - 2C, 1P) *2005: W, F3. 2006: A1(R). 2009: tour of UK - no tests.*

185 **Bosman, NJS** (Nico) b 06/10/1902 d ??/??/1990 - Tvl - 3 Tests (-) 3 matches (-) *1924: BI2, 3, 4.*

843 **Botha, AF** (Arno) b 26/10/1991 - BB - 2 Tests (-) 2 matches (-) *2012: Toured I, S & E. - no tests. 2013: It, S.*

778 **Botha, BJ** (BJ) b 04/01/1980 - KZN - 25 Tests (5 - 1T) 26 matches (5 - 1T) *2006: NZ2(R), 3, A3, I(R), E1, 2. 2007: E1, Sm1, A1, NZ1, N(R), S(t+R), [Sm(R), E3, T(R), US.]. 2008: W2. 2009: It(R), I. 2010: W1, F, It2(R), NZ1(R), 2(R), A1.*

522 **Botha, DS** (Darius) b 26/06/1955 - NTvl - 1 Test (-) 8 matches (12 - 3T) *1981: NZ1.*

770 **Botha, GvG** (Gary) b 12/10/1981 - BB - 12 Tests (-) 14 matches (-) *2005:A3(R), F3(R). 2006: tour of UK - no tests. 2007: E1(R), 2(R), Sm1(R), A1(R), NZ1, A2, NZ2(R), N, S, [T.].*

502 **Botha, HE** (Naas) b 27/02/1958 - NTvl - 28 Tests (312 - 2T, 50C, 50P, 18D) 40 matches (485 - 6T, 91C, 66P, 27D) *1980: S.Am1, 2, BI1, 2, 3, 4, S.Am3, 4, F. 1981: I1, 2, NZ1, 2, 3, US. 1982: S.Am1, 2. 1986: NZC1*, 2*, 3*, 4*. 1989: WT1, 2. 1992: NZ*, A*, F1*, 2*, E*.*

90 **Botha, JA** (John) b 19/11/1879 d 08/12/1920 - Tvl - 1 Test (-) 1 match (-) *1903: BI3.*

733 **Botha, JP** (Bakkies) b 22/09/1979 - BB - 85 Tests (35 - 7T) 86 matches (40 - 8T) *2002: F. 2003: S1, 2, A1, NZ1, A2(R), [U, E, G, Sm, NZ3]. 2004: I1, PI, NZ1, A1, NZ2, A2, W2, I3, E, S, Arg. 2005: A1, 2, 3, NZ1, A4, NZ2, Arg, W, F3. 2007: E1, 2, A1, NZ1, N, S.[Sm, E3, T, US(R), Fiji, Arg, E4.]. W. 2008: W1, 2, It, NZ1, 2, A1, Arg, W3, S, E. 2009: BI1, 2, NZ1, 2, A1, 2, 3, NZ3, F, It. 2010: It1, 2, NZ1, I, W2, S, E. 2011: A2, NZ2, [Fj, N.]. 2013: S2, F(R). 2014: W1, Arg1, Arg2(R), A2(R), NZ2(R), I(R), E(R).*

374 **Botha, JPF** (Hannes) b 11/05/1937 d 30/08/2011 - NTvl - 3 Tests (-) 10 matches (9 - 3T) *1960-61: tour of UK - no tests. 1962: BI2, 3, 4.*

412 **Botha, PH** (Piet) b 13/09/1935 - Tvl - 2 Tests (-) 11 matches (3 - 1T) *1965: A1, 2.*

4 **Boyes, HC** (Harry) b 12/03/1868 d 26/10/1892 - GW - 2 Tests (-) 2 matches (-) *1891: BI1, 2.*

149 **Braine, JS** (Jack) b 01/05/1891 d 25/10/1940 - GW - No Tests - 11 matches (-) *Toured BI, I & F. 1912/13.*

204 **Brand, GH** (Gerry) b 08/10/1906 d 04/02/1996 - WP - 16 Tests (55 - 13 C, 7P, 2D) 46 matches (293 - 2T, 100C, 25P, 3D) *1928: NZ2, 3. 1931: W, I. 1932: E, S. 1933: A1, 2, 3, 4, 5. 1937: A1, 2, NZ2, 3. 1938: BI1.*

39 **Bredenkamp, MJ** (Mike) b 02/05/1873 d 22/12/1940 - GW - 2 Tests (-) 2 matches (-) *1896: BI1, 3.*

547 **Breedt, JC** (Jannie) b 04/06/1959 - Tvl - 8 Tests (-) 8 matches (-) *1986: NZC1, 2, 3, 4. 1989: WT1*, 2*. 1992: NZ, A.*

268 **Brewis, JD (**Hannes) b 15/06/1920 d 09/09/2007 - NTvl - 10 Tests (18 - 1T, 5D) 19 matches (36 - 6T, 6D) *1949: NZ1, 2, 3, 4. 1951: S, I, W. 1952: E, F. 1953: A1.*

313 **Briers, TPD** (Theuns) b 11/07/1929 - WP - 7 Tests (15 - 5T) 12 matches (27 - 9T) *1955: BI1, 2, 3, 4. 1956: NZ2, 3, 4.*

104 **Brink, DJ** (Koei) b 07/11/1882 d 29/10/1970 - WP - 3 Tests (-) 18 matches (9 - 3T) *1906: S, W, E.*

626 **Brink, RA** (Robby) b 21/07/1971 - WP - 2 Tests (-) 2 matches (-) *1995: [R, C].*

799 **Brits, SB** (Schalk) b 16/05/1981 - WP - 5 Tests (-) 5 matches (-) *2008: It(R), NZ2(R), A1. 2012: S(R), E4(R).*

760 **Britz, GJJ** (Gerrie) b 14/04/1978 - FS - 13

Tests (-) 14 matches (-) *2004: I1(R), 2(R), W1(R), PI, A1, NZ2, A2(R), I3(t), S(t+R), Arg(R). 2005: U. 2006: E2(R). 2007: NZ2(R).*

725 **Britz, WK** (Warren) b 07/11/1973 - Natal - 1 Test (-) 1 match (-) *2002: W1.*

244 **Broodryk, JA** (Tallie) b 11/04/1910 d 22/10/1993 - Tvl - No Tests - 6 matches (22 - 6T, 1D) *Toured A & NZ. 1937.*

100 **Brooks, D** (Cocky) b 22/09/1881 d 14/11/1962 - Border - 1 Test (-) 11 matches (3 - 1T) *1906: S.*

655 **Brosnihan, WG** (Warren) b 28/12/1971 - GL - 6 Tests (5 - 1T) 10 matches (10 - 2T) *1997: A2. 2000: NZ1(t+R), A2(t+R), NZ2(R), A3(R), E3(R).*

74 **Brown, CB** (Charlie) b 29/01/1878 d 18/06/1944 - WP - 3 Tests (-) 3 matches (-) *1903: BI1, 2, 3.*

801 **Brüssow, HW** (Heinrich) b 21/07/1986 - FS - 20 Tests (5 - 1T) 20 matches (5 - 1T) *2008: E(R). 2009: BI1, 2(R), 3, NZ1, 2, A1, 2, 3, NZ3, F, It, I. 2011: A2, NZ2, [W, Fj, N(R), Sm, A3.].*

407 **Brynard, GS** (Gertjie) b 21/10/1938 - WP - 7 Tests (6 - 2T) 21 matches (42 - 14T) *1965: A1, NZ1, 2, 3, 4. 1968: BI3, 4.*

287 **Buchler, JU** (Johnny) b 07/04/1930 - Tvl - 10 Tests (8 - 1C, 1P, 1D) 26 matches (26 - 4C, 5P, 1D) *1951: S, I, W. 1952: E, F. 1953: A1, 2, 3, 4. 1956: A2.*

837 **Burden, CB** (Craig) b 13/05/1985 - KZN - No Tests - No matches *Rugby Championship Squad 2012*

108 **Burdett, AF** (Adam) b 20/08/1882 d 04/11/1918 - WP - 2 Tests (-) 11 matches (6 - 2T) *1906: S, I.*

552 **Burger, JM** (Kobus) b 31/03/1964 - WP - 2 Tests (-) 2 matches (-) *1989: WT1, 2.*

511 **Burger, MB** (Thys) b 10/11/1954 - NTvl - 3 Tests (8 - 2T) 13 matches (52 - 13 T) *1980: BI2(R), S.Am3. 1981: US(R).*

535 **Burger, SWP** (Schalk) b 06/10/1955 - WP - 6 Tests (-) 6 matches (-) *1984: E1, 2. 1986: NZC1, 2, 3, 4.*

754 **Burger, SWP** (Schalk) b 13/04/1983 - WP - 75 Tests (70 - 14T) 75 matches (70 - 14T) *2003: [G(R), Sm(R), NZ3(R)]. 2004: I1, 2, W1, PI, NZ1, A1, NZ2, A2, W2, I3, E. 2005: F1, 2, A1, 2(R), 3(R), NZ1, A4, NZ2, Arg(R), W, F3. 2006: S1, 2. 2007: E1, 2, A1, NZ1, N, S, [Sm, US, Fiji, Arg, E4.], W. 2008: It(R), NZ1, 2, A1, NZ3, A2, 3, W3, S, E. 2009: BI2, A2(R), 2(R), NZ3, F, I. 2010: F, It2, NZ1, 2, A1, NZ3, A2, 3. 2011: [W, Fj, N, Sm, A3.]. 2014: W1(R), W2(R), S, A2(R), NZ(R), I(R), E.*

99 **Burger, WAG** (Bingo) b 12/08/1883 d 08/08/1963 - Border - 4 Tests (-) 23 matches (3 - 1T) *1906: S, I, W. 1910: BI2.*

91 **Burmeister, ARD** (Arthur) b 01/05/1885 d 25/05/1952 - WP - No Tests - 10 matches (-) *Toured BI, I & F. 1906/07.*

395 **Carelse, G** (Gawie) b 21/07/1941 d 03/08/2002 - EP - 14 Tests (-) 30 matches (5 - 1T, 1C) *1964: W, F. 1965: I, S. 1967: F1, 2, 3. 1968: F1, 2. 1969: A1, 2, 3, 4, S.*

456 **Carlson, RA** (Ray) b 02/10/1948 - WP - 1 Test (-) 1 match (-) *1972: E.*

83 **Carolin, HW** (Paddy) b 10/04/1881 d 15/03/1967 - WP - 3 Tests (-) 18 matches (73 - 6T, 15C, 3P, 4D) *1903: BI3. 1906: S*, I.*

865 **Carr, N** (Nizaam) b 04/04/1991 - WP - 2 Tests (-) 2 matches (-) *2014: It(R), W3(R).*

734 **Carstens, PD** (Deon) b 03/06/1979 - Natal - 9 Tests (-) 10 matches (-) *2002: S, E. 2006: E1(t+R), 2(R). 2007: E1, 2(t+R), Sm1(R). 2009: BI1(R), 3(t).*

9 **Castens, HH** (Herbert) b 23/11/1864 d 18/10/1929 - WP - 1 Test (-) 1 match (-) *1891: BI1*.*

768 **Chavhanga, T** (Tonderai) b 24/12/1983 - WP - 4 Tests (30 - 6T) 4 matches (30 - 6T) *2005: U. 2007: NZ2(R). 2008: W1, 2.*

28 **Chignell, TW** (Charlie) b 28/04/1866 d 17/10/1952 - WP - 1 Test (-) 1 match (-) *1891: BI3.*

384 **Cilliers, GD** (Gert) b 28/07/1940 d 26/01/1986 - OFS - 3 Tests (3 - 1T) 6 matches (3 - 1T) *1963: A1, 3, 4. 1965: tour of I & S - no tests.*

637 **Cilliers, NV** (Vlok) b 26/03/1968 - WP - 1 Test (-) 1 match (-) *1996: NZ3(t).*

835 **Cilliers, PM** (Pat) b 03/03/1987 - GL - 6 Tests (-) 6 matches (-) *2012: Arg1(t+R), 2(R), A1(t+R), 2(R), I(R), E4(R).*

319 **Claassen, JT** (Johan) b 23/09/1929 - WTvl - 28 Tests (10 - 2T, 2C) 56 matches (16 - 4T, 2C) *1955: BI1, 2, 3, 4. 1956: A1, 2, NZ1, 2, 3, 4. 1958: F1*, 2*. 1960: S, NZ1, 2, 3, W, I. 1961: E, S, F, I*, A1*, 2*. 1962: BI1*, 2*, 3*, 4*.*

519 **Claassen, W** (Wynand) b 16/01/1951 - Natal - 7 Tests (-) 13 matches (8 - 2T) *1981: I1*, 2*, NZ2*, 3*, US*. 1982: S.Am 1*, 2*.*

611 **Claassens, JP** (Jannie) b 30/06/1969 - NTvl - No Tests - 8 matches (15 - 3T)   *Toured NZ. 1994 and W, S & I. 1994.*

765 **Claassens, M** (Michael) b 28/10/1982 - FS - 8 Tests (-) 8 matches (-) *2004: W2(R), S(R), Arg(R). 2005: Arg(R), W, F3. 2007: A2(R), NZ2(R).*

SPRINGBOKS

240 **Clark, WHG** (Ginger) b 22/09/1906 d 20/09/1999 - Tvl - 1 Test (-) 1 match (-) *1933: A3.*

157 **Clarkson, WA** (Wally) b 08/07/1896 d 03/06/1973 - Natal - 3 Tests (-) 11 matches (9 - 3T) *1921: NZ1, 2. 1924: BI1.*

61 **Cloete, HA** (Patats) b 15/06/1873 d 29/03/1959 - WP - 1 Test (-) 1 match (-) *1896: BI4.*

441 **Cockrell, CH** (Charlie) b 10/01/1939 - WP - 3 Tests (-) 10 matches (-) *1969: S. 1970: I, W.*

486 **Cockrell, RJ** (Robert) b 04/04/1950 d 26/05/2000 - WP - 11 Tests (4 - 1T) 25 matches (8 - 2T) *1974: F1, 2. 1975: F1, 2. 1976: NZ1, 2. 1977: WT. 1980: tour of Sam – no tests. 1981: NZ1, 2(R), 3, US.*

513 **Cocks, TMD** (Tim) b 29/09/1952 - Natal - No Tests - 3 matches (8 - 2T) *Toured S.Am. 1980.*

730 **Coetzee, D** (Danie) b 02/09/1977 - BB - 15 Tests (5 - 1T) 15 matches (5 - 1T) *2002: Sm. 2003: S1, 2, Arg, A1, NZ1, A2, NZ2, [U, E, Sm(R), NZ3(R)]. 2004: S(R), Arg(R). 2006: A1(R).*

463 **Coetzee, JHH** (Boland) b 20/01/1945 - WP - 6 Tests (-) 6 matches (-) *1974: BI1. 1975: F2(R). 1976: NZ1, 2, 3, 4.*

831 **Coetzee, MC** (Marcell) b 08/05/1991 - KZN - 26 Tests (30 - 6T) 26 matches (30 - 6T) *2012: E1, 2, 3, Arg1, 2, A1, NZ1(R), A2(R), NZ2(t+R), I(R), S(R), E4(R). 2013: It(R), Sam, S2(R). S, Arg1, A1, NZ1, A2, NZ2, I, E.It, W3.*

724 **Conradie, JHJ** (Bolla) b 24/02/1978 - WP - 18 Tests (13 - 2T, 1D) 18 matches (13 - 2T, 1D) *2002: W1, 2, Arg(R), Sm, NZ1, A1, NZ2(R), A2(R), S, E. 2004: W1(R), PI, NZ2, A2. 2005:Arg. 2008:W1, 2(R), NZ1(R).*

404 **Conradie, SC** (Faan) b 27/06/1942 d 21/10/1992 - WP - No Tests - No matches *Toured I & S. 1965.*

41 **Cope, DG** (Davie) b 14/08/1877 d 16/08/1898 - Tvl - 1 Test (2 - 1C) 1 match (2 - 1C) *1896: BI2.*

53 **Cotty, WAH** (Bill) b 24/02/1875 d 06/09/1928 - GW - 1 Test (-) 1 match (-) *1896: BI3.*

81 **Crampton, G** (George) b 30/03/1875 d 27/12/1946 - GW - 1 Test (-) 1 match (-) *1903:BI2.*

219 **Craven, DH** (Danie) b 11/10/1910 d 04/01/1993 - WP - 16 Tests (6 - 2T) 38 matches (24 - 8T) *1931: W, I. 1932: S. 1933: A1, 2, 3, 4, 5. 1937: A1, 2, NZ1*, 2, 3. 1938: BI1*, 2*, 3*.*

406 **Cronjé, CJC** (Kerneels) b 16/04/1940 d 13/05/2009 - ETvl - No Tests - No matches *Toured A & NZ. 1965.*

750 **Cronjé, G** (Geo) b 23/07/1980 - BB - 3 Tests (-) 3 matches (-) *2003: NZ. 2004: I2(R), W1(R).*

758 **Cronjé, J** (Jacques) b 04/08/1982 - BB - 32 Tests (20 - 4T) 33 matches (25 - 5T) *2004: I1, 2, W1, PI, NZ1, A1, NZ2(R), A2(t+R), S(t+R), Arg. 2005: U, F1, 2, A1, 3, NZ1(R), 2(t), Arg, W, F3. 2006: S2(R), F(R), A1(t+R), NZ1, A2, NZ2, A3(R), I(R), E1. 2007: A2(R), NZ2, N.*

447 **Cronje, PA** (Peter) b 21/09/1949 - Tvl - 7 Tests (10 - 3T) 15 matches (16 - 5T) *1971: F1, 2, A1, 2, 3. 1974: BI3, 4.*

144 **Cronjé, SN** (Fanie) b 24/04/1886 d 20/09/1972 - Tvl - No Tests - 7 matches (3 - 1T) *Toured BI, I & F. 1912/13.*

51 **Crosby, JH** (Jim) b 03/07/1873 d 25/02/1960 - Tvl - 1 Test (-) 1 match (-) *1896: BI2.*

116 **Crosby, NJ** (Nic) b 21/08/1883 d 14/07/1938 - Tvl - 2 Tests (-) 2 matches (-) *1910: BI1, 3.*

78 **Currie, C** (Clem) b 21/10/1880 d 12/10/1937 - GW - 1 Test (-) 1 match (-) *1903: BI2.*

235 **D'Alton, G** (George) b 17/08/1908 d 22/11/1975 - WP - 1 Test (-) 1 match (-) *1933: A1.*

614 **Dalton, J** (James) b 16/08/1972 - Tvl - 43 Tests (25 - 5T) 58 matches (25 - 5T) *1994: tour of NZ and W & S – no tests. 1994: Arg1(R). 1995:[A, C], W, It, E. 1996: NZ2(R), 3, Arg1, 2, F1, 2, W. 1997: T(R), BI3, NZ2, A2, It, F1, 2, E, S. 1998: I1, 2, W1, E1, A1, NZ1, 2, A2, W2, S, I3, E2. 2002: W1, 2, Arg, NZ1, A1, NZ2, A2, F, E.*

197 **Daneel, GM** (George) b 29/08/1904 d 19/10/2004 - WP - 8 Tests (6 - 2T) 20 matches (9 - 3T) *1928: NZ1, 2, 3, 4. 1931: W, I. 1932:E, S.*

102 **Daneel, HJ** (Pinkie) b 04/05/1882 d 07/01/1947 - WP - 4 Tests (-) 15 matches (3 - 1T) *1906: S, I, W, E.*

823 **Daniel, KR** (Keegan) b 05/03/1985 - KZN - 5 Tests (-) 6 matches (-) *2010: I(R). 2012: E1(R), 2(R), Arg1, 2(R).*

302 **Dannhauser, G** (Gert) b 16/04/1918 d 07/10/1983 - Tvl - No Tests - 12 matches (-) *Toured BI, I & F. 1951/52.*

706 **Davids, Q** (Quinton) b 17/08/1975 - WP - 9 Tests (-) 13 matches (-) *2000: tour to Arg & UK – no tests. 2002: W2, Arg(R), Sm(R). 2003: Arg. 2004:I1(R), 2, W1, PI(t+R), NZ1(R).*

700 **Davidson, CD** (Craig) b 23/02/1977 - Natal - 5 Tests (10 - 2T) 8 matches (10 - 2T) *2000: tour of Arg & UK – no tests. 2002: W2(R), Arg. 2003: Arg, NZ1(R), A2.*

119 **Davison, PM** (Max) b 05/06/1885 d 14/11/1931 - EP - 1 Test (-) 1 match (-) *1910: BI1.*

862 **De Allende, D** (Damian) b 25/11/1991 - WP - 3 Tests (-) 3 matches (-) *2014: Arg1, Arg2, W3(R).*

653 **De Beer, JH** (Jannie) b 22/04/1971 - FS - 13 Tests (181 - 2T, 33C, 27P, 8D) 14 matches (188 - 3T, 34C, 27P, 8D) *1997: BI3, NZ1, A1, NZ2, A2, F2(R), S. 1999: A2, [S, Sp, U, E, A3].*

475 **De Bruyn, J** (Johan) b 12/10/1948 - OFS - 1 Test (-) 4 matches (-) *1974: BI3. 1974: tour of F - no tests.*

856 **De Jager, L** (Lood) b 17/12/1992 - FS - 9 Tests (10 -2T) 9 matches (10-2T) *2014: W1(R), W2(R), S, Arg1, Arg2, A1(R), NZ(R), It(R), W3(R).*

205 **De Jongh, HPK** (Manus) b 10/10/1902 d 05/09/1974 - WP - 1 Test (3 - 1T) 1 match (3 - 1T) *1928:NZ3.*

806 **De Jongh, JL** (Juan) b 15/04/1988 - WP - 14 Tests (15 - 3T) 16 matches (20 - 4T) *2009: tour of UK - no tests. 2010: W1, F(R), It1(R), 2, A1(R), NZ3. 2011: A1, NZ1, [Fj(R), N(R).]. 2012: A2(R), NZ2(R), S, E4. 2013: Championship Squad - no tests*

440 **De Klerk, IJ** (Sakkie) b 28/10/1938 - Tvl - 3 Tests (-) 9 matches (-) *1969: E. 1970: I, W.*

464 **De Klerk, KBH** (Kevin) b 06/06/1950 - Tvl - 13 Tests (-) 18 matches (4 - 1T) *1974: BI1, 2, 3(R). 1974: tour of F - no tests. 1975: F1, 2. 1976: NZ2(R), 3, 4. 1980: S.Am1, 2, BI2. 1981: I1, 2.*

16 **De Kock, AN** (Arthur) b 11/01/1866 d 06/07/1957 - GW - 1 Test (-) 1 match (-) *1891: BI2.*

722 **De Kock, D** (Deon) b 11/05/1975 - GF - 2 Tests (-) 2 matches (-) *2001: It2(R), US.*

160 **De Kock, JS** (Sas) b 17/08/1896 d 04/11/1972 - WP - 2 Tests (-) 7 matches (6 - 2T) *1921: NZ3. 1924: BI3.*

717 **De Kock, NA** (Neil) b 20/11/1978 - WP - 10 Tests (10 - 2T) 10 matches (10 - 2T) *2001: It1. 2002: Sm(R), NZ1(R), 2, A2, F. 2003: [U(R), G, Sm(R), NZ3(R)].*

75 **De Melker, SC** (Syd) b 31/03/1884 d 01/11/1953 - GW - 2 Tests (-) 14 matches (9 - 3T) *1903: BI2. 1906: E.*

334 **De Nysschen, CJ** (Chris) b 31/01/1936 - Natal - No Tests - 10 matches (3 - 1T) *Toured A & NZ. 1956.*

112 **De Villiers, DI** (Dirkie) b 20/07/1889 d 01/10/1958 - Tvl - 3 Tests (3 - 1T) 3 matches (3 - 1T) *1910: BI1, 2, 3.*

382 **De Villiers, DJ** (Dawie) b 10/07/1940 - WP - 25 Tests (9 - 3T) 53 matches (29 - 5T, 4C, 2P) *1962: BI2, 3. 1965: I, NZ1*, 3*, 4*. 1967: F1*, 2*, 3*, 4*. 1968: BI1*, 2*, 3*, 4*, F1*, 2*. 1969: A1*, 4*,* E*. *1970: I*, W*, NZ1*, 2*, 3*, 4*.*

95 **De Villiers, HA** (Boy) b 05/01/1883 d 09/11/1944 - WP - 3 Tests (-) 18 matches (22 - 6T, 1D) *1906: S, W, E.*

418 **De Villiers, HO** (HO) b 10/03/1945 - WP - 14 Tests (26 - 7C, 4P) 29 matches (80 - 2T, 22C, 10P) *1967: F1, 2, 3, 4. 1968: F1, 2. 1969: A1, 2, 3, 4, S, E. 1970: I, W.*

151 **De Villiers, IB** (IB) b 10/03/1892 d 09/01/1966 - Tvl - No Tests - 10 matches (35 - 10C, 5P) *Toured A & NZ. 1921.*

735 **De Villiers, J** (Jean) b 24/02/1981 - WP - 106 Tests (135 - 27T) 106 matches (135 - 27T) *2002: F. 2004: PI, NZ1, A1, NZ2, A2, W2(R), E. 2005: U, F1, 2, A1, 2, 3, NZ1, A4, NZ2, Arg, W, F3. 2006: S1, NZ2, 3, A3, I, E1, 2. 2007: E1, 2, A1, NZ1, N, [Sm.]. 2008: W1, 2, It, NZ1, 2, A1Arg, NZ3, A2, 3, W3, S, E. 2009: BI1, 2, NZ1, 2, A1, 2, 3, NZ3, I. 2010: F(t+R), It1, 2, NZ1, 2, 3, A2, 3, I, W2, S, E. 2011:A2, NZ2, [W, Sm(R), A3.]. 2012: E1*, 2*, 3*, Arg1*, 2*, A1*, NZ1*, A2*, NZ2*, I*, S*, E4*. 2013: It*, S*, Sam*, Arg1*, Arg2*, A1*, NZ1*, A2*, NZ2*, W*, S*, F*. 2014: Arg1*, Arg2*, A1*, NZ1*, A2*, NZ2*, I*, E*, It*, W3*.*

195 **De Villiers, P du P** (Pierie) b 14/06/1905 d 14/11/1975 - WP - 8 Tests (-) 28 matches (6 - 2T) *1928: NZ1, 3, 4. 1932: E. 1933: A4. 1937: A1, 2, NZ1.*

400 **De Vos, DJJ** (Dirkie) b 08/04/1941 d 12/02/2011 - WP - 3 Tests (-) 18 matches (9 - 3T) *1965: S. 1969: A3, S. 1971: tour of A - no tests.*

423 **De Waal, AN** (Albie) b 04/02/1942 - WP - 4 Tests (-) 4 matches (-) *1967: F1, 2, 3, 4.*

60 **De Waal, PJ** (Paul) b 02/06/1875 d 18/05/1945 - WP - 1 Test (-) 1 match (-) *1896: BI4.*

429 **De Wet, AE** (André) b 01/08/1946 - WP - 3 Tests (-) 11 matches (-) *1969: A3, 4, E.*

261 **De Wet, PJ** (Piet) b 12/03/1917 d 18/10/1968 - WP - 3 Tests (-) 3 matches (-) *1938: BI1, 2, 3.*

335 **De Wilzem, CJ** (Chris) b 14/10/1932 d 02/03/2006 - OFS - No Tests - 16 matches (3 - 1T) *Toured A & NZ. 1956.*

145 **Delaney, ETA** (Ned) b 12/06/1892 d 18/10/1918 - GW - No Tests - 13 matches (-) *Toured BI, I & F. 1912/13.*

662 **Delport, GM** (Thinus) b 02/02/1975 - GL - 18 Tests (15 - 3T) 20 matches (15 - 3T) *1997: tour of It, F, E & S - no tests. 2000: C(R), E1(t+R), A1, NZ1, A2, NZ2, A3, Arg, I, W. 2001: F2, It1. 2003: A1, NZ2, [U, E, Sm, NZ3].*

297 **Delport, WH** (Willa) b 05/11/1920 d 14/10/1984 - EP - 9 Tests (6 - 2T) 21 matches

(12 - 4T) *1951: S, I, W. 1952: E, F. 1953: A1, 2, 3, 4.*

50 **Devenish, CE** (Charles) b 13/01/1874 d 11/01/1922 - GW - 1 Test (-) 1 match (-) *1896: BI2.*

10 **Devenish, GE** (Tiger) b 27/07/1870 d 23/03/1930 - Tvl - 1 Test (-) 1 match (-) *1891: BI1.*

45 **Devenish, G St L** (Long George) b 11/05/1871 d 01/02/1943 - Tvl - 1 Test (-) 1 match (-) *1896: BI2.*

189 **Devine, D** (Dauncie) b 20/03/1904 d 22/09/1965 - Tvl - 2 Tests (-) 2 matches (-) *1924: BI3. 1928: NZ2.*

814 **Deysel, JR** (Jean) b 05/03/1985 - KZN - 4 Tests (-) 6 matches (-) *2009: It(R). 2011: A1(R), NZ1, A2(R).*

300 **Dinkelmann, EE** (Ernst) b 14/05/1927 d 22/10/2010 - NTvl - 6 Tests (6 - 2T) 21 matches (9 - 3T) *1951:S, I. 1952: E, F. 1953: A1, 2.*

597 **Dirks, CA** (Chris) b 23/05/1967 - Tvl - No Tests - 2 matches (10 - 2T)   *Toured Arg. 1993.*

393 **Dirksen, CW** (Corra) b 22/01/1938 - NTvl - 10 Tests (9 - 3T) 11 matches (9 - 3T) *1963: A4. 1964: W. 1965: I, S. 1967: F1, 2, 3, 4. 1968: BI1, 2.*

713 **Dixon, PJ** (Pieter) b 17/10/1977 - WP - No Tests - 1 match (-) *Toured E. 2000.*

762 **Dlulane, VT** (Tim) b 05/06/1981 - Mpu - 1 Test (-) 1 match (-) *2004: W2(R).*

67 **Dobbin, FJ** (Uncle) b 10/10/1879 d 05/02/1950 - GW - 9 Tests (3 - 1T) 36 matches (21 - 7T) *1903: BI1, 2. 1906: S, W, E. 1910: BI1. 1912: S*, I, W.*

202 **Dobie, JAR** (John) b 04/08/1905 d 12/08/1989 - Tvl - 1 Test (-) 1 match (-) *1928: NZ2.*

230 **Dold, JB** (Jack) b 03/01/1902 d 17/09/1968 - EP - No Tests - 10 matches (3 - 1T) *Toured BI & I. 1931/32.*

54 **Dormehl, PJ** (Pieter) b 04/11/1872 d 01/09/1958 - WP - 2 Tests (-) 2 matches (-) *1896: BI3, 4.*

40 **Douglass, FW** (Frank) b 15/07/1875 d Post 1920 - EP - 1 Test (-) 1 match (-) *1896: BI1.*

601 **Drotské, AE** (Naka) b 15/03/1971 - OFS - 26 Tests (15 - 3T) 34 matches (20 - 4T) *1993: Arg(2). 1995: [WS2(R)]. 1996: A1(R). 1997: T, BI1, 2, 3(R), NZ1, A1, NZ2(R). 1998: I2(R), W1(R), I3(R). 1999: It1, 2, W, NZ1, A1, NZ2, A2, [S, Sp(R), U, E, A3, NZ3].*

321 **Dryburgh, RG** (Roy) b 01/11/1929 d 10/05/2000 - WP - 8 Tests (28 - 3T, 5C, 3P) 20 matches (116 - 15T, 13C, 15P) *1955: BI2, 3, 4.*

1956: A2, NZ1, 4. 1960: NZ1*, 2*.

787 **Du Plessis, BW** (Bismarck) b 22/05/1984 - KZN - 70 Tests (45 - 9T) 72 matches (45 - 9T) *2007: A2(t+R), NZ2, N(R), S(R), [Sm(R), E3(R), US(R), Arg(R), E4(t).], W(R). 2008: W1(R), 2(R), It, NZ1(R), 2, Arg, NZ3, A2, 3, W3, S. 2009: BI1, 2, 3(R), NZ1, 2, A1, 2, 3, NZ3, F, I(R). 2010: I, W2, S, E. 2011: A2(R), NZ2, [W(R), Fj(R), Sm, A3(R).]. 2012: E1, 2, 3, Arg1. 2013: S(R), Sam(R), Arg1(R), Arg2(R), A1, NZ1, A2(R), NZ2, W, S(R), F. 2014: W1, W2, S, Arg1, Arg2, A1(R), NZ1(R), A2(R), NZ2, I, E(R), It(R), W3.*

523 **Du Plessis, CJ** (Carel) b 24/06/1960 - WP - 12 Tests (16 - 4T) 22 matches (40 - 10T) *1981: tour of NZ & USA - no tests. 1982: S.Am1, 2. 1984: E1, 2, S.Am&Sp1, 2. 1986: NZC1, 2, 3, 4. 1989: WT1, 2.*

496 **Du Plessis, DC** (Daan) b 09/08/1948 - NTvl - 2 Tests (-) 2 matches (-) *1977: WT. 1980: S.Am2.*

275 **Du Plessis, F** (Felix) b 24/11/1919 d 01/05/1978 - Tvl - 3 Tests (-) 3 matches (-) *1949: NZ1*, 2*, 3*.*

788 **Du Plessis, JN** (Jannie) b 16/11/1982 - FS - 62 Tests (5 - 1T) 64 matches (5 - 1T) *2007: A2, NZ2, [Fiji, Arg(t+R).], W. 2008:A3(R), E. 2009:NZ1(t), 2(R), A1(R), 2(R), NZ3(R). 2009: tour of UK - no tests 2010: W1(R), F(R), It1, 2, NZ1, 3, A2, 3, I, W2, S, E. 2011: A2, NZ2, [W, Fj, Sm, A3.]. 2012: E1, 2, 3, Arg1, 2, A1, NZ1, A2, NZ2, I, S, E4. 2013: It, S, Sam, Arg1, Arg2, A1, NZ1, A2, NZ2. 2014: W1, W2, S, Arg1, Arg2, A1, NZ1, A2, NZ2, I, E.*

455 **Du Plessis, M** (Morné) b 21/10/1949 - WP - 22 Tests (12 - 3T) 32 matches (18 - 5T) *1971: A1, 2, 3. 1974:BI1, 2, F1, 2. 1975: F1*, 2*. 1976:NZ1*, 2*, 3*, 4*. 1977: WT*. 1980: S.Am1*, 2*, BI1*, 2*, 3*, 4*, S.Am4*, F*.*

537 **Du Plessis, MJ** (Michael) b 04/11/1958 - WP - 8 Tests (7 - 1T, 1D) 8 matches (7 - 1T, 1D) *1984: S.Am&Sp1, 2. 1986: NZC1, 2, 3, 4. 1989: WT1, 2.*

166 **Du Plessis, NJ** (Nic) b 04/12/1894 d 10/08/1949 - WTvl - 5 Tests (-) 20 matches (-) *1921:NZ2, 3. 1924:BI1, 2, 3.*

458 **Du Plessis, PG** (Piet) b 23/07/1947 - NTvl - 1 Test (-) 1 match (-) *1972: E.*

503 **Du Plessis, TD** (Tommy) b 29/06/1953 - NTvl - 2 Tests (4 - 1T) 5 matches (12 - 3T) *1980: S.Am1, 2. 1980: tour of S.Am - no tests.*

500 **Du Plessis, W** (Willie) b 04/09/1955 - WP - 14 Tests (12 - 3T) 20 matches (28 - 7T) *1980: S.Am1, 2, BI1, 2, 3, 4, S.Am3, 4, F. 1981: NZ1, 2, 3. 1982: S.Am1, 2.*

317 **Du Plooy, AJJ** (Amos) b 31/05/1921 d 17/05/1980 - EP - 1 Test (-) 1 match (-) *1955: BI1.*

375 **Du Preez, FCH** (Frik) b 28/11/1935 - NTvl - 38 Tests (11 - 1T, 1C, 2P) 87 matches (87 - 12T, 15C, 7P) *1961: E, S, A1, 2. 1962: BI1, 2, 3, 4. 1963: A1. 1964: W, F. 1965: tour of I & S – no tests. 1965: A1, 2, NZ1, 2, 3, 4. 1967: F4. 1968: BI1, 2, 3, 4, F1, 2. 1969: A1, 2, S. 1970: I, W, NZ1, 2, 3, 4. 1971: F1, 2, A1, 2, 3.*

701 **Du Preez, GJD** (Delarey) b 12/06/1975 - GL - 2 Tests (5 - 1T) 5 matches (10 - 2T) *2000: tour of Arg & UK – no tests. 2002: Sm(R), A1(R).*

327 **Du Preez, JGH** (Jan) b 06/10/1930 - WP - 1 Test (-) 6 matches (15 - 5T) *1956: NZ1.*

757 **Du Preez, PF** (Fourie) b 24/03/1982 - BB - 70 Tests (75 - 15T) 70 matches (75 - 15T) *2004: I1, 2, W1, PI(R), NZ1, A1, NZ2(R), A2(R), W2, I3, E, S, Arg. 2005: U(R), F1, 2(R), A1(R)2(R), 3, NZ1(R), A4(R). 2006: S1, 2, F, A1(R), NZ1, A2, NZ2, 3, A3. 2007: N, S, [Sm, E3, US, Fiji, Arg, E4.]. 2008: Arg(R), NZ3, A2, 3, 3. 2009: BI1, 2, 3, NZ1, 2, A1, 2, 3, NZ3, F, It, I. 2011: A2, NZ2, [W, Fj, N(R), Sm, A3.]. 2013: Arg1(R), A2, NZ2, W, S. 2014: W1, W2, S.*

562 **Du Preez, RJ** (Robert) b 19/07/1963 - Natal - 7 Tests (-) 15 matches (45 - 9T) *1992: NZ, A. 1993: F1, 2, A1, 2, 3.*

792 **Du Preez, WH** (Wian) b 30/10/1982 - FS - 1 Test (-) 2 matches (-) *2007: tour of UK – no tests. 2009: It.*

281 **Du Rand, JA** (Salty) b 16/01/1926 d 27/02/1979 - Rhodesia - 21 Tests (12 - 4T) 47 matches (27 - 9T) *1949: NZ2, 3. 1951: S, I, W. 1952: E, F. 1953: A1, 2, 3, 4. 1955: BI1, 2, 3, 4. 1956: A1, 2, NZ1*, 2, 3, 4.*

619 **Du Randt, JP** (Os) b 08/09/1972 - OFS - 80 Tests (25 - 5T) 85 matches (25 - 5T) *1994: Arg1, 2, S, W. 1995: WS1, [A, WS2, F, NZ]. 1996: Fj, A1, NZ1, A2, NZ2, 3, 4. 1997: T, BI1, 2, 3, NZ1, A1, NZ2, A2, It, F1, 2, E, S. 1999: NZ1, A1, NZ2, A2, [S, Sp(R), U, E, A3, NZ3]. 2004: I1, 2, W1, PI, NZ1, A1, NZ2, A2, W2, I3, E, S(R), Arg(R). 2005: U(R), F1, A1, NZ1, A4, NZ2, Arg, W(R), F3. 2006: S1, 2, F, A1, NZ1, A2, NZ2, 3, A3. 2007: Sm1, NZ1, N, S, [Sm, E3, US, Fj, Arg, E4.].*

208 **Du Toit, AF** (AF) b 12/05/1899 d 09/09/1988 - WP - 2 Tests (-) 2 matches (-) *1928: NZ3, 4.*

253 **Du Toit, BA** (Ben) b 10/11/1912 d 25/01/1989 - Tvl - 3 Tests (3 - 1T) 10 matches (9 - 3T) *1937: tour of A & NZ – no tests. 1938: BI1, 2, 3.*

667 **Du Toit, GS** (Gaffie) b 24/03/1976 - GW - 14 Tests (108 - 5T, 25C, 11P) 23 matches (153 - 10T, 29C, 15P) *1998: I1. 1999: It1, 2, W(R), NZ1, 2. 2004: I1, W1(R), A1(R), S(R), Arg. 2006: S1(R), 2(R), F(R).*

279 **Du Toit, PA** (Fonnie) b 13/03/1920 d 21/07/2001 - NTvl - 8 Tests (6 - 2T) 25 matches (9 - 3T) *1949: NZ2, 3, 4. 1951: S, I, W. 1952: E, F.*

516 **Du Toit, PG** (Hempies) b 23/08/1953 - WP - 5 Tests (-) 16 matches (8 - 2T) *1981: NZ1. 1982: S.Am1, 2. 1982: tour of S.Am – nio tests. 1984: E1, 2.*

332 **Du Toit, PS** (Piet) b 09/10/1935 d 26/02/1997 - WP - 14 Tests (-) 49 matches (9 - 3T) *1956: tour of A & NZ – no tests. 1958: F1, 2. 1960: NZ1, 2, 3, 4, W, I. 1961: E, S, F, I, A1, 2.*

854 **Du Toit, PS** (Pieter-Steph) b 20/08/1992 - KZN - 2 Tests (-) 2 matches (-) *2013: W(R), F(R).*

220 **Du Toit, SR** (Schalk) b 08/08/1902 d 18/11/1965 - WP - No Tests - 12 matches (3 - 1T) *Toured BI & I. 1931/32.*

1 **Duff, BR** (Ben) b 16/10/1867 d 25/06/1943 - WP - 3 Tests (-) 3 matches (-) *1891: BI1, 2, 3.*

194 **Duffy, BAA** (Bernie) b 17/11/1905 d 16/03/1958 - Border - 1 Test (-) 1 match (-) *1928: NZ1.*

430 **Durand, PJ** (Paul) b 21/01/1946 d 01/09/1988 - WTvl - No Tests - 2 matches (-) *Toured BI & I. 1969/70.*

265 **Duvenage, FP** (Floors) b 06/11/1917 d 16/09/1999 - GW - 2 Tests (-) 2 matches (-) *1949: NZ1, 3.*

499 **Edwards, P** (Pierre) b 23/05/1953 - NTvl - 2 Tests (-) 2 matches (-) *1980: S.Am1, 2.*

415 **Ellis, JH** (Jan) b 05/01/1942 d 08/02/2013 - SWA - 38 Tests (21 - 7T) 74 matches (97 - 32T) *1965: NZ1, 2, 3, 4. 1967: F1, 2, 3, 4. 1968: BI1, 2, 3, 4, F1, 2. 1969: A1, 2, 3, 4, S. 1970: I, W, NZ1, 2, 3, 4. 1971: F1, 2, A1, 2, 3. 1972: E. 1974: BI1, 2, 3, 4, F1, 2. 1976: NZ1.*

165 **Ellis, MC** (Mervyn) b 16/09/1892 d 24/03/1959 - Tvl - 6 Tests (-) 20 matches (3 - 1T) *1921: NZ2, 3. 1924: BI1, 2, 3, 4.*

656 **Els, WW** (Braam) b 01/11/1971 - FS - 1 Test (-) 3 matches (-) *1997: A2(R).*

836 **Engelbrecht, JJ** (JJ) b 22/02/1989 - BB - 12 Tests (20 - 4T) 12 matches (20 - 4T) *2012: Arg1(R). 2013: It, S, Sam, Arg1, Arg2, A1, NZ1, A2, NZ2, W(R), S(R).*

347 **Engelbrecht, JP** (Jannie) b 10/11/1938 - WP - 33 Tests (24 - 8T) 67 matches (132 - 44T) *1960: S, W, I. 1961: E, S, F, A1, 2. 1962: BI2, 3, 4. 1963: A2, 3. 1964: W, F. 1965: I, S, A1, 2, NZ1, 2, 3, 4. 1967: F1, 2, 3, 4. 1968: BI1, 2, F1, 2. 1969:*

A1, 2.

549 Erasmus, FS (Frans) b 19/06/1959 d 07/03/1998 - NTvl - 3 Tests (-) 3 matches (-) *1986: NZC3, 4. 1989: WT2.*

649 Erasmus, J (Rassie) b 05/11/1972 - FS - 36 Tests (35 - 7T) 39 matches (35 - 7T) *1996: tour of Arg, F & W - no tests. 1997: BI3, A2, It, F1, 2, S. 1998: I1, 2, W1, E1, A1, NZ2, A2, W2, S, I3, E2. 1999: It1, 2, W, A1*, NZ2, A2, [S, U, E, A3, NZ3]. 2000: C, E1, A1, NZ1, 2, A3. 2001: F1, 2.*

692 Esterhuizen, G (Grant) b 28/04/1976 - GL - 7 Tests (-) 7 matches (-) *2000: NZ1(R), 2, A3, Arg, I, W(R), E3(t).*

58 Etlinger, TE (Tommy) b 07/09/1872 d 23/02/1953 - WP - 1 Test (-) 1 match (-) *1896: BI4.*

833 Etzebeth, E (Eben) b 29/10/1991 - WP - 33 Tests (-) 33 matches (-) *2012: E1, 2, 3, Arg1, 2, A1, 2, NZ2, I, S, E4. 2013: It, S, Sam, Arg1, Arg2, A1, NZ1, A2, NZ2, W, S(R), F. 2014: Arg2(R), Arg2, A1, NZ1, A2, NZ2, I, E, It, W3.*

543 Ferreira, C (Christo) b 28/08/1960 - OFS - 2 Tests (-) 2 matches (-) *1986: NZC1, 2.*

540 Ferreira, PS (Kulu) b 17/03/1959 - WP - 2 Tests (4 - 1T) 2 matches (4 - 1T) *1984: S.Am & Sp1, 2.*

84 Ferris, HH (Hugh) b 06/12/1877 d 17/07/1929 - Tvl - 1 Test (-) 1 match (-) *1903: BI3.*

674 Fleck, RF (Robbie) b 17/07/1975 - WP - 31 Tests (50 - 10T) 36 matches (65 - 13T) *1998: tour of UK & I - no tests. 1999: It1, 2, NZ1(R), A1, NZ2(R), A2, [S, U, E, A3, NZ3]. 2000: C, E1, 2, A1, NZ1, A2, NZ2, A3, Arg, I, W, E3. 2001: F1(R), 2, It1, NZ1, A1, 2. 2002: S, E.*

784 Floors, L (Kabamba) b 15/11/1980 - FS - 1 Test (-) 1 match (-) *2006: E2.*

42 Forbes, HH (Spanner) b 02/01/1873 d 17/09/1955 - Tvl - 1 Test (-) 1 match (-) *1896: BI2.*

229 Forrest, HM (Skaap) b 17/11/1907 d 26/01/1989 - Tvl - No Tests - 7 matches (-) *Toured BI & I. 1931/32.*

780 Fortuin, BA (Bevin) b 06/02/1979 - FS - 2 Tests (-) 3 matches (-) *2006: I. 2007: A2.*

481 Fourie, C (Tossie) b 01/08/1950 - d 05/05/1997 - EP - 4 Tests (10 - 1T, 2P) 9 matches (14 - 2T, 2P) *1974: F1, 2. 1975: F1, 2.*

752 Fourie, J (Jaque) b 04/03/1983 - GL - 72 Tests (160 - 32T) 72 matches (160 - 32T) *2003: [U, G, Sm(R), NZ3(R)]. 2004: I2, E(R), S, Arg. 2005: U(R), F2(R), A1(R), 2, 3, NZ1, A4, NZ2, Arg, W, F3. 2006: S1, A1, NZ1, A2, NZ2, 3, A3. 2007: Sm1(R), A1, NZ1, N, S, [Sm, E3, US, Fiji,* *Arg, E4.], W. 2008: Arg(R), W3(R), S(R), E(R). 2009: BI1(R), 2(R), 3, NZ1, 2, A1, 2, 3, NZ3, F, It, I. 2010: W1, F, It2, NZ1, 2, A1, 2, 3. 2011: A2, NZ2, [W, Fj, N, Sm, A3.]. 2013: W, S, F.*

476 Fourie, TT (Polla) b 10/07/1945 - SETvl - 1 Test (-) 5 matches (12 - 3T) *1974: BI3. 1974: tour of F - no tests.*

339 Fourie, WL (Loftie) b 23/07/1936 d 23/07/2001 - SWA - 2 Tests (3 - 1T) 2 matches (3 - 1T) *1958: F1, 2.*

148 Francis, JAJ (Joe) b 24/01/1889 d 20/12/1924 - Tvl - 5 Tests (6 - 2T) 19 matches (9 - 3T) *1912: S, I, W. 1913: E, F.*

218 Francis, MG (Tiny) b 26/08/1907 d 02/08/1961 - OFS - No Tests - 8 matches (18 - 1T, 4C, 1P, 1D) *Toured BI & I. 1931/32.*

469 Frederickson, CA (Dave) b 17/08/1950 - Tvl - 3 Tests (-) 3 matches (-) *1974: BI2. 1980: S.Am1, 2.*

68 Frew, A (Alex) b 24/10/1877 d 29/04/1947 - Tvl - 1 Test (3 - 1T) 1 match (3 - 1T) *1903: BI1*.*

492 Froneman, DC (Dirk) b 14/04/1954 - OFS - 1 Test (-) 1 match (-) *1977: WT.*

234 Froneman, IL (Fronie) b 18/12/1907 d 11/08/1984 - Border - 1 Test (-) 1 match (-) *1933: A1.*

294 Fry, DJ (Dennis) b 25/02/1926 d 25/02/2003 - WP - No Tests - 17 matches (12 - 4T) *Toured BI, I & F. 1951/52.*

303 Fry, SP (Stephen) b 14/07/1924 d 29/06/2002 - WP - 13 Tests (-) 28 matches (9 - 3T) *1951: S, I, W. 1952: E, F. 1953: A1, 2, 3, 4. 1955: BI1*, 2*, 3*, 4*.*

567 Fuls, HT (Heinrich) b 08/03/1971 - Tvl - 8 Tests (-) 21 matches (5 - 1T) *1992: NZ(R). 1992: tour of F & E - no tests. 1993: F1, 2, A1, 2, 3, Arg1, 2.*

710 Fynn, EE (Etienne) b 14/12/1972 - Natal - 2 Tests (-) 4 matches (-) *2000: tour of Arg & UK - no tests. 2001: F1, It1(R).*

638 Fyvie, WS (Wayne) b 28/03/1972 - Natal - 3 Tests (-) 8 matches (10 - 2T) *1996: NZ4(t), 5(R), Arg2(R).*

233 Gage, JH (Jack) b 02/04/1907 d 30/06/1989 - OFS - 1 Test (-) 1 match (-) *1933: A1.*

348 Gainsford, JL (John) b 04/08/1938 - WP - 33 Tests (24 - 8T) 71 matches (93 - 31T) *1960: S, NZ1, 2, 3, 4, W, I. 1961: E, S, F, A1, 2. 1962: BI1, 2, 3, 4. 1963: A1, 2, 3, 4. 1964: W, F. 1965: I, S, A1, 2, NZ1, 2, 3, 4. 1967: F1, 2, 3.*

645 Garvey, AC (Adrian) b 25/06/1968 - Natal - 28 Tests (20 - 4T) 28 matches (20 - 4T) *1996: Arg1, 2, F1, 2, W. 1997: T, BI1, 2, 3(R), A1(t), It,*

F1, 2, E, S. 1998: I1, 2, W1, E1, A1, NZ1, 2, A2, W2, S, I3, E2. 1999: [Sp].

282 **Geel, PJ** (Flip) b 07/02/1914 d 12/06/1971 - OFS - 1 Test (-) 1 match (-) *1949: NZ3.*

227 **Geere, V** (Manie) b 09/09/1905 d 25/10/1989 - Tvl - 5 Tests (-) 17 matches (-) *1931-32 tour of UK - no tests. 1933: A1, 2, 3, 4, 5.*

270 **Geffin, AO** (Okey) b 28/05/1921 d 16/10/2004 - Tvl - 7 Tests (48 - 9C, 10P) 17 matches (121 - 1T, 26C, 22P) *1949: NZ1, 2, 3, 4. 1951: S, I, W.*

564 **Geldenhuys, A** (Adri) b 11/07/1964 - EP - 4 Tests (-) 11 matches (-) *1992: NZ, A, F1, 2.*

528 **Geldenhuys, SB** (Burger) b 18/05/1956 - NTvl - 7 Tests (4 - 1T) 15 matches (20 - 5T) *1981: NZ2, 3, US. 1982: S.Am1, 2. 1989: WT1, 2.*

316 **Gentles, TA** (Tommy) b 31/05/1934 d 29/06/2011 - WP - 6 Tests (-) 18 matches (9 - 3T) *1955: BI1, 2, 4. 1956: NZ2, 3. 1958: F2.*

283 **Geraghty, EM** (Carrots) b 20/04/1927 - Border - 1 Test (-) 1 match (-) *1949: NZ4.*

514 **Gerber, DM** (Danie) b 14/04/1958 - EP - 24 Tests (82 - 19T, 1C) 35 matches (120 - 28T, 1C) *1980: S.Am3, 4, F. 1981: I1, 2, NZ1, 2, 3, US. 1982: S.Am1, 2. 1984: E1, 2, S.Am&Sp1, 2. 1986: NZC1, 2, 3, 4. 1992: NZ, A, F1, 2, E.*

709 **Gerber, HJ** (Hendrik) b 12/04/1976 - WP - 2 Tests (-) 6 matches (-) *2000: tour of Arg & UK - no tests. 2003: S1, 2.*

337 **Gerber, MC** (Mickey) b 12/10/1935 d 07/10/2005 - EP - 3 Tests (8 - 4C) 3 matches (8 - 4C) *1958: F1, 2. 1960: S.*

351 **Gericke, FW** (Mannetjies) b 08/06/1933 d 22/10/2010 - Tvl - 1 Test (3 - 1T) 1 match (3 - 1T) *1960: S.*

465 **Germishuys, JS** (Gerrie) b 29/10/1949 - OFS - 20 Tests (48 - 12T) 29 matches (76 - 19T) *1974: BI2. 1976: NZ1, 2, 3, 4. 1977: WT. 1980: S.Am1, 2, BI1, 2, 3, 4, S.Am3, 4, F. 1981: I1, 2, NZ2, 3, US.*

77 **Gibbs, EAH** (Bertie) b 25/08/1878 d 29/12/1952 - GW - 1 Test (-) 1 match (-) *1903: BI2.*

641 **Gillingham, JW** (Joe) b 27/02/1974 - GL - No Tests - 7 matches (5 - 1T) *Toured Arg, F & W. 1996 and It, F, E & S. 1997.*

413 **Goosen, CP** (Piet) b 03/02/1937 - d 06/06/1991 - OFS - 1 Test (-) 13 matches (3 - 1T) *1965: NZ2.*

839 **Goosen, JL** (Johan) b 27/07/1992 - FS - 6 Tests (8 - 1C, 2P) 6 matches (8 - 1C, 2P) *2012: A1(R), NZ1(R), A2, NZ2. 2013: Tour of W, S & F - no tests. 2014: W1(R), It.*

37 **Gorton, HC** (Hubert) b 28/10/1871 d 11/01/1900 - Tvl - 1 Test (-) 1 match (-) *1896: BI1.*

424 **Gould, RL** (Rodney) b 10/08/1942 - Natal - 4 Tests (3 - 1D) 7 matches (3 - 1D) *1968: BI1, 2, 3, 4. 1968: tour to F - no tests.*

789 **Grant, PJ** (Peter) b 15/08/1984 - WP - 5 Tests (-) 5 matches (-) *2007: A2(R), NZ2(R). 2008: W1(t+R), It(R), A1(R).*

215 **Gray, BG** (Geoff) b 28/07/1909 d 04/08/1989 - WP - 4 Tests (-) 13 matches (12 - 4T) *1931: W. 1932: E, S. 1933: A5.*

729 **Greeff, WW** (Werner) b 14/07/1977 - WP - 11 Tests (31 - 4T, 4C, 1D) 11 matches (31 - 4T, 4C, 1D) *2002: Arg(R), Sm, NZ1, A1, NZ2, A2, F, S, E. 2003: [U, G].*

379 **Greenwood, CM** (Colin) b 25/01/1936 d 03/10/1998 - WP - 1 Test (6 - 2T) 1 match (6 - 2T) *1961: I.*

829 **Greyling, MD** (Dean) b 01/01/1986 - BB - 3 Tests (-) 3 matches (-) *2011: A1, NZ1. 2012: NZ1(R).*

422 **Greyling, PJF** (Piet) b 16/05/1942 - OFS - 25 Tests (15 - 5T) 43 matches (18 - 6T) *1967: F1, 2, 3, 4. 1968: BI1, F1, 2. 1969: A1, 2, 3, 4, S, E. 1970: I, W, NZ1, 2, 3, 4. 1971: F1, 2, A1, 2, 3. 1972: E*.*

478 **Grobler, CJ** (Kleintjie) b 24/08/1944 d 29/09/1999 - OFS - 3 Tests (4 - 1T) 7 matches (12 - 3T) *1974: BI4. 1974: tour of F - no tests. 1975: F1, 2.*

431 **Grobler, RN** (Rysmier) b 14/11/1946 d 26/05/1971 - NTvl - No Tests - 10 matches (9 - 3T) *Toured BI & I. 1969/70.*

5 **Guthrie, FEH** (Frank) b 03/11/1869 d 19/06/1954 - WP - 3 Tests (-) 3 matches (-) *1891: BI1, 3. 1896: BI1.*

766 **Habana, BG** (Bryan) b 12/06/1983 - GL - 106 Tests (285 - 57T) 108 matches (285 - 57T) *2004: E(R), S, Arg. 2005: U, F1, 2, A1, 2, 3, NZ1, A4, NZ2, Arg, W, F3. 2006: S2, F, A1, NZ1, A2, NZ2, 3, I, E1, 2. 2007: E1, 2, S, [Sm, E3, T(R), US, Fiji, Arg, E4.], W. 2008: W1, 2, It, NZ1, A1, NZ3, W3, S, E. 2009: BI1, 2, NZ1, 2, A1, 2, 3, NZ3, F, It, I. 2010: F, It1, 2, NZ1, 2, A1, NZ3, A2, 3, I, W2. 2011: A2, NZ2, [W, N, Sm, A3.]. 2012: E1, 2, 3, Arg1, 2, A1, NZ1.A2, NZ2. 2013: It, S, Sam, Arg1, Arg2, A1, NZ1, A2, NZ2, W, S, F. 2014: W1, W2, Arg1, Arg2, A1, NZ1, A2, NZ2, I, E, It.*

113 **Hahn, CHL** (Cocky) b 07/01/1886 - d 27/09/1948 - Tvl - 3 Tests (3 - 1T) 3 matches (3 - 1T) *1910: BI1, 2, 3.*

714 **Hall, DB** (Dean) b 02/09/1977 - GL - 13 Tests (20 - 4T) 13 matches (20 - 4T) *2001: F1, 2, NZ1, A1, 2, NZ2, It2, E, US. 2002: Sm, NZ1, 2, A2.*

720 **Halstead, TM** (Trevor) b 17/06/1976 - Natal - 6 Tests (15 - 3T) 6 matches (15 - 3T) *2001: F3, It2, E, US(R). 2003: S1, 2.*

15 **Hamilton, GH** (George) b 30/04/1863 d 07/08/1901 - EP - 1 Test (-) 1 match (-) *1891: BI1.*

333 **Hanekom, M v d S** (Melt) b 27/07/1931 d 1997/1998 - Boland - No Tests - 9 matches (9 - 3T) *Toured A & NZ. 1956.*

809 **Hargreaves, AJ** (Alistair) b 29/04/1986 - KZN - 4 Tests (-) 7 matches (-) *2009: tour of UK - no tests. 2010: W1(R), It1(R). 2010: tour of UK - no tests. 2011: A1, NZ1.*

251 **Harris, TA** (Tony) b 27/08/1916 d 07/03/1993 - Tvl - 5 Tests (3 - 1T) 13 matches (16 - 4T, 1D) *1937: NZ2, 3. 1938: BI1, 2, 3.*

24 **Hartley, AJ** (Jack) b 18/08/1873 d 15/05/1923 - WP - 1 Test (-) 1 match (-) *1891: BI3.*

568 **Hattingh, H** (Drikus) b 21/02/1968 - NTvl - 5 Tests (-) 17 matches (20 - 4T) *1992: A(R), F2(R), E. 1994: Arg1, 2. 1994: tour of W & S - no tests.*

239 **Hattingh, LB** (Lappies) b 01/09/1903 d 16/10/1974 - OFS - 1 Test (-) 1 match (-) *1933: A2.*

623 **Hattingh, SJ** (Ian) b 31/10/1964 - Tvl - No Tests - 7 matches (10 - 2T)   *Toured W, S & I. 1994.*

22 **Heatlie, BH** (Fairy) b 25/04/1872 d 19/08/1951 - WP - 6 Tests (6 - 3C) 6 matches (6 - 3C) *1891: BI2, 3. 1896: BI1, 4*. 1903: BI1, 3*.*

855 **Hendricks, C** (Cornal) b 18/04/1988 - FS - 11 Tests (25 - 3T) 11 matches (25 - 5T) *2014: W1, W2, S, Arg1, Arg2, A1, NZ1, A2, NZ2, I, W3.*

657 **Hendricks, M** (McNeil) b 10/07/1973 - Boland - 2 Tests (5 - 1T) 4 matches (5 - 1T) *1997: tour of It, F, E & S - no tests. 1998: I2(R), W1(R).*

559 **Hendriks, P** (Pieter) b 13/04/1970 - Tvl - 14 Tests (10 - 2T) 23 matches (30 - 6T) *1992: NZ, A. 1992: tour of F & E - no tests. 1994: S, W. 1995: [A, R, C]. 1996: A1, NZ1, A2, NZ2, 3, 4, 5.*

57 **Hepburn, TB** (Tommy) b 14/02/1872 d 13/09/1933 - WP - 1 Test (2 - 1C) 1 match (2 - 1C) *1896: BI4.*

521 **Heunis, JW** (Johan) b 26/01/1958 - NTvl - 14 Tests (41 - 2T, 6C, 7P) 24 matches (72 - 3T, 9C, 14P) *1981: NZ3(R), US. 1982: S.Am1, 2. 1984: E1, 2, S.Am&Sp1, 2. 1986: NZC1, 2, 3, 4. 1989: WT1, 2.*

372 **Hill, RA** (Ronnie) b 20/12/1934 d 06/01/2011 - Rhodesia - 7 Tests (-) 21 matches (18 - 6T) *1960: W, I. 1961: I, A1, 2. 1962: BI4. 1963: A3.*

575 **Hills, WG** (Willie) b 26/01/1962 - NTvl - 6 Tests (-) 13 matches (-) *1992: F1, 2, E. 1993: F1, 2, A1.*

96 **Hirsch, JG** (Jack) b 20/02/1883 d 26/02/1958 - EP - 2 Tests (-) 18 matches (37 - 11T, 1D) *1906: I. 1910: BI1.*

86 **Hobson, TEC** (Tommy) b 26/03/1881 d 02/09/1937 - WP - 1 Test (-) 1 match (-) *1903: BI3.*

307 **Hoffman, RS** (Steve) b 02/12/1931 d 15/05/1986 - Boland - 1 Test (-) 1 match (-) *1953: A3.*

248 **Hofmeyr, SR** (Koffie) b 23/08/1912 d 06/01/1975 - WP - No Tests - 11 matches (17 - 3T, 2D) *Toured A & NZ. 1937.*

352 **Holton, DN** (Dougie) b 28/09/1932 d 12/04/1994 - EP - 1 Test (-) 4 matches (-) *1960: S. 1960-61: tour of UK - no tests.*

590 **Honiball, HW** (Henry) b 01/12/1965 - Natal - 35 Tests (156 - 1T, 38C, 25P) 45 matches (191 - 1T, 45C, 32P) *1993: A3(R), Arg2. 1995: WS1(R). 1996: Fj, A1, NZ5, Arg1, 2, F1, 2, W. 1997: T, BI1, 2, 3(R), NZ1(R), A1(R), NZ2, A2, It, F1, 2, E. 1998: W1(R), E1, A1, NZ1, 2, A2, W2, S, I3, E2. 1999: [A3(R), NZ3].*

356 **Hopwood, DJ** (Doug) b 03/06/1934 d 10/01/2002 - WP - 22 Tests (15 - 5T) 53 matches (45 - 15T) *1960: S, NZ3, 4, W. 1961: E, S, F, I, A1, 2. 1962: BI1, 2, 3, 4. 1963: A1, 2, 4. 1964: W, F. 1965: S, NZ3, 4.*

753 **Hougaard, DJ** (Derick) b 04/01/1983 - BB - 8 Tests (69 - 2T, 13C, 10P, 1D) 8 matches (69 - 2T, 13C, 10P, 1D) *2003: [U(R), E(R), G, Sm, NZ3]. 2007: Sm1, A2, NZ2.*

807 **Hougaard, F** (Francois) b 06/04/1988 - BB - 35 Tests (25 - 5T) 38 matches (25 - 5T) *2009: It(R). 2010: A1(R), NZ3, A2, 3, W2(R), S, E(t). 2011: A2(t), NZ2(R), [W(R), Fj(R), N, Sm(R), A3(R).]. 2012: E1, 2, 3, Arg1, 2, A1, NZ1, A2, NZ2, I, S, E4. 2014: S(R), Arg2(R), NZ1(R), A2, NZ2, I, It(R), W3(R).*

330 **Howe, BF** (Pee-Wee) b 30/08/1932 d 22/04/2010 - Border - 2 Tests (3 - 1T) 18 matches (9 - 3T) *1956: NZ1, 4.*

118 **Howe-Browne, NRFG** (Noel) b 24/12/1884 d 03/04/1943 - WP - 3 Tests (-) 3 matches (-) *1910: BI1, 2, 3.*

555 **Hugo, DP** (Niel) b 11/11/1958 - WP - 2 Tests (-) 2 matches (-) *1989: WT1, 2.*

726 **Human, DCF** (Daan) b 03/04/1976 - WP - 4 Tests (-) 4 matches (-) *2002: W1, 2, Arg(R), Sm(R).*

627 **Hurter, MH** (Marius) b 08/10/1970 - NTvl - 13 Tests (-) 18 matches (5 - 1T) *1995: [R, C], W. 1996: Fj, A1, NZ1, 2, 3, 4, 5. 1997: NZ1, 2, A2.*

139 **Immelman, JH** (Jack) b 02/08/1888 d 21/07/1960 - WP - 1 Test (-) 13 matches (3 - 1T) *1913: F.*

97 **Jackson, DC** (Mary) b 21/04/1885 d 17/09/1976 - WP - 3 Tests (-) 17 matches (29 - 7T, 4C) *1906: I, W, E.*

80 **Jackson, JS** (Jack) b 01/10/1878 d 30/06/1954 - WP - 1 Test (-) 1 match (-) *1903: BI2.*

721 **Jacobs, AA** (Adrian) b 14/08/1980 - GF - 34 Tests (35 - 7T) 35 matches (35 - 7T) *2001: It2(R), US. 2002: W1(R), Arg, Sm(R), NZ1(t+R), A1(R), F, S, E(R). 2008: W1, 2, NZ1, 2, Arg, NZ3, A2, 3, W3, S, E. 2009: BI1, 2, NZ2(R), A1(R), 2(R), 3(R), NZ3(R), F, It. 2010: I(R), E(R). 2011: A1(R), NZ1.*

715 **James, AD** (Butch) b 08/01/1979 - Natal - 42 Tests (154 - 3T, 26C, 28P, 1D) 43 matches (159 - 3T, 27C, 29P, 1D) *2001: F1, 2, NZ1, A1, 2, NZ2. 2002: F(R), S, E. 2006: NZ1, A2, NZ2, 3(R), E1. 2007: E1, 2, A1, NZ1, N, S, [Sm, E3, US, Fiji, Arg, E4.]. 2008: W1, 2, NZ1, 2, A1, Arg, NZ3, A2, 3. 2010: It1, 2(R), NZ1(R), A1(R), 2(R). 2011: A2, [W(R).].*

847 **Janse van Rensburg, JC** (JC) b 09/01/1986 - GL - No Tests - No matches *Toured I, S & E. 2012.*

436 **Janse van Rensburg, MC** (Martin) b 29/12/1944 - Natal - No Tests - 6 matches (10 - 2C, 2P) *Toured BI & I. 1969/70.*

518 **Jansen, E** (Eben) b 05/06/1954 - OFS - 1 Test (-) 11 matches (16 - 4T) *1980: tour of S.Am - no tests. 1981: NZ1.*

444 **Jansen, JS** (Joggie) b 05/02/1948 - OFS - 10 Tests (3 - 1T) 15 matches (18 - 6T) *1970: NZ1, 2, 3, 4. 1971: F1, 2, A1, 2, 3. 1972: E.*

414 **Janson, A** (Andrew) b 29/05/1935 d 2007 - WP - No Tests - 11 matches (24 - 8T) *Toured A & NZ. 1965.*

716 **Jantjes, CA** (Conrad) b 24/03/1980 - GL - 24 Tests (22 - 4T, C) 25 matches (22 - 4T, C) *2001: It1, A1, 2, NZ2, F3, It2, E, US. 2005: Arg, W. 2007: W(R). 2008: W1, 2, It, NZ1, 2(R), A1, Arg, NZ3(R), A2, 3, W3, S, E.*

819 **Jantjies, ET** (Elton) b 01/08/1990 - GL - 2 Tests (6 - 2P) 3 matches (11 - 1C, 3P) *2010: tour of UK - no tests. 2012: A2(R), NZ2(R). 2012: tour of UK - no tests.*

769 **Januarie, ER** (Ricky) b 01/02/1982 - GL - 47 Tests (25 - 5T) 50 matches (25 - 5T) *2005: U, F2, A1, 2, 3(R), NZ1, A4, NZ2. 2006: S1(R), 2(R), F(R), A1, I, E1, 2. 2007: E1, 2, Sm1, N(R), [Sm(R), T.], W. 2008: W2, It, NZ1, 2, A1, Arg, NZ3(R), A2(R), 3(R), W3(R), S, E. 2009: BI1(R), NZ1(R), 2(R), A1(R), 2(R), NZ3(R). 2010: W1, F,*

It1, 2, NZ1, 2, 3(R).

254 **Jennings, CB** (CB) b 16/08/1914 d 02/10/1989 - Border - 1 Test (-) 11 matches (9 - 3T) *1937: NZ1.*

439 **Jennings, MW** (Mike) b 21/12/1946 - Boland - No Tests - 10 matches (6 - 2T) *Toured BI & I. 1969/70.*

377 **Johns, RG** (Bobby) b 21/02/1934 d 01/07/1990 - WP - No Tests - 1 match (-) *Toured BI, I & F. 1960/61.*

810 **Johnson, AF** (Ashley) b 16/05/1986 - FS - 3 Tests (-) 5 matches (-) *2009: tour of UK - no tests. 2011: A1, NZ1(R), 2(t+R).*

604 **Johnson, GK** (Gavin) b 17/10/1966 - Tvl - 7 Tests (86 - 5T, 14C, 11P) 17 matches (173 - 9T, 25C, 26P) *1993:Arg2. 1994: NZ3, Arg1. 1994: tour of W & - no tests. 1995: WS1, [R, C, WS2].*

291 **Johnstone, PGA** (Paul) b 30/06/1930 d 22/04/1996 - WP - 9 Tests (11 - 2T, 1C, 1P) 35 matches (68 - 14T, 7C, 4P) *1951:S, I, W. 1952: E, F. 1956: A1, NZ1, 2, 4.*

62 **Jones, CH** (Charlie) b 24/03/1880 d 06/03/1908 - Tvl - 2 Tests (-) 2 matches (-) *1903: BI1, 2.*

30 **Jones, PST** (Percy) b 13/09/1876 d 08/03/1954 - WP - 3 Tests (3 - 1T) 3 matches (3 - 1T) *1896: BI1, 3, 4.*

742 **Jordaan, N** (Norman) b 03/04/1975 - BB - 1 Test (-) 1 match (-) *2002: E(R).*

271 **Jordaan, RP** (Jorrie) b 13/07/1920 d 22/09/1998 - NTvl - 4 Tests (-) 4 matches (-) *1949: NZ1, 2, 3, 4.*

557 **Joubert, AJ** (André) b 15/04/1964 - OFS - 34 Tests (115 - 10T, 7C, 17P) 49 matches (258 - 18T, 39C, 30P) *1989: WT1(R). 1993: A3, Arg1. 1994: E1, 2, NZ1, 2(R), 3, Arg2, S, W. 1995: [A, C, WS2, F, NZ], W, It, E. 1996: Fj, A1, NZ1, 3, 4, 5, Arg1, 2, F1, 2, W. 1997: T, BI1, 2, A2.*

711 **Joubert, MC** (Marius) b 10/07/1979 - Boland - 30 Tests (45 - 9T) 31 matches (45 - 9T) *2000: tour of Arg & UK - no tests. 2001: NZ1. 2002: W1, 2, Arg(R), Sm, NZ1, A1, NZ2, A2, F(R). 2003: S2, Arg, A1. 2004: I1, 2, W1, PI, NZ1, A1, NZ2, A2, W2, I3, E, S, Arg. 2005: U, F1, 2, A1.*

110 **Joubert, SJ** (Steve) b 08/04/1887 - d 27/03/1939 - WP - 3 Tests (8 - 1T, 1C, 1P) 6 matches (20 - 1T, 4C, 2P, 1D) *1906: I, W, E.*

689 **Julies, W** (Wayne) b 23/10/1978 - Boland - 11 Tests (10 - 2T) 12 matches (10 - 2T) *1999: [Sp]. 2004: I1, 2, W1, S, Arg. 2005: A2(R), 3(t). 2005: tour of Arg & UK. 2006: F(R). 2007: Sm1, [T.]. 2007: tour of UK - no tests.*

509 **Kahts, WJH** (Willie) b 20/02/1947 - NTvl - 11 Tests (4 - 1T) 15 matches (12 - 3T) *1980:*

BI1, 2, 3, S.Am3, 4, F. 1981: I1, 2, NZ2. 1982: S.Am1, 2.

344 **Kaminer, J** (Joe) b 25/01/1934 - Tvl - 1 Test (-) 1 match (-) *1958: F2.*

791 **Kankowski, R** (Ryan) b 14/10/1985 - KZN - 20 Tests (5 - 1T) 22 matches (5 - 1T) *2007: W. 2008: W2(R), It, A1(R), W3(R), S(R), E(R). 2009: BI3, NZ3(R), F, It. 2010: W1(R), It1(R), NZ2(R), A1, 3(R), S. 2011: A1(R), NZ1(R). 2012: E3(R).*

675 **Kayser, DJ** (Deon) b 03/07/1970 - EP - 13 Tests (25 - 5T) 21 matches (30 - 6T) *1998: tour of UK & I - no tests. 1999: It2(R), A1(R), NZ2, A2, [S, Sp(R), U, E, A3]. 2001: It1(R), NZ1(R), A2(R), NZ2(R).*

599 **Kebble, GR** (Guy) b 02/05/1966 - Natal - 4 Tests (-) 12 matches (5 - 1T) *1993: Arg1, 2. 1994: NZ1(R), 2.*

288 **Keevy, AC** (Jakkals) b 12/11/1917 d 09/02/1990 - ETvl - No Tests - 13 matches (10 - 2C, 2P) *Toured BI, I & F. 1951/52.*

55 **Kelly, EW** (Ted) b 23/10/1869 d 11/03/1949 - GW - 1 Test (-) 1 match (-) *1896: BI3.*

669 **Kempson, RB** (Robbie) b 23/02/1974 - Natal - 37 Tests (5 - 1T) 38 matches (5 - 1T) *1998: I2(R), W1, E1, A1, NZ1, 2, A2, W2, S, I3, E2. 1999: It1, 2, W. 2000: C, E1, 2, A1, NZ1, A2, 3, Arg, I, W, E3. 2001: F1, 2(R), NZ1, A1, 2, NZ2. 2003: S1(R), 2(R), Arg, A1(R), NZ1(R), A2.*

286 **Kenyon, BJ** (Basil) b 19/05/1918 d 09/05/1996 - Border - 1 Test (-) 6 matches (13 - 2T, 2C, 1P) *1949: NZ4*. 1951-52: tour of UK - no tests.*

226 **Kipling, HG** (Bert) b 24/12/1903 d 13/09/1981 - GW - 9 Tests (-) 24 matches (-) *1931: W, I. 1932: E, S. 1933: A1, 2, 3, 4, 5.*

804 **Kirchner, Z** (Zane) b 16/06/1984 - BB - 29 Tests (25 - 5T) 29 matches (25 - 5T) *2009: BI3, F, It, I. 2010: W1(R), F, It1, NZ1, 2, A1, I, W2(R), S, E. 2012: E1, Arg1, 2, A1, NZ1, A2, NZ2, I, S, E4. 2013: A1, NZ1, A2, NZ2. 2014: S(R)*

306 **Kirkpatrick, AI** (Ian) b 25/07/1930 d 18/11/2012 - GW - 13 Tests (-) 43 matches (18 - 6T) *1953: A2. 1956: NZ2. 1958: F1. 1960: S, NZ1, 2, 3, 4, W, I. 1961: E, S, F.*

143 **Knight, AS** (Saturday) b 16/12/1885 d 01/07/1946 - Tvl - 5 Tests (-) 18 matches (3 - 1T) *1912: S, I, W. 1913: E, F.*

553 **Knoetze, F** (Faffa) b 18/01/1963 - WP - 2 Tests (4 - 1T) 8 matches (14 - 3T) *1989: WT1, 2.*

280 **Koch, AC** (Chris) b 21/09/1927 d 21/03/1986 - Boland - 22 Tests (15 - 5T) 46 matches (33 - 11T) *1949: NZ2, 3, 4. 1951: S, I, W. 1952: E, F. 1953: A1, 2, 4. 1955: BI1, 2, 3, 4. 1956: A1, NZ2, 3. 1958: F1, 2. 1960: NZ1, 2.*

274 **Koch, HV** (Bubbles) b 13/06/1921 d 02/11/2003 - WP - 4 Tests (-) 4 matches (-) *1949: NZ1, 2, 3, 4.*

693 **Koen, LJ** (Louis) b 07/07/1975 - GL - 15 Tests (145 - 23C, 31P, 2D) 15 matches (145 - 23C, 31P, 2D) *2000: A1. 2001: It2, E, US. 2003: S1, 2, Arg, A1, NZ1, A2, NZ2, [U, E, Sm(R), NZ3(R)].*

851 **Kolisi, S** (Siya) b 16/06/1991 - WP - 10 Tests (-) 10 matches (-) *2013: S(R), Sam(R), Arg1(R), Arg2(R), A1(R), NZ1(R), A2(R), NZ2(R), W(R), F(R).*

420 **Kotzé, GJM** (Gert) b 12/08/1940 - WP - 4 Tests (-) 4 matches (-) *1967: F1, 2, 3, 4.*

487 **Krantz, EFW** (Edrich) b 10/08/1954 - OFS - 2 Tests (4 - 1T) 11 matches (48 - 12T) *1976: NZ1. 1980: tour of S.Am - no tests. 1981: I1. 1981: tour of NZ & USA - no tests.*

676 **Krige, CPJ** (Corné) b 21/03/1975 - WP - 39 Tests (10 - 2T) 43 matches (15 - 3T) *1998: tour of UK & I - no tests. 1999: It2*, W, NZ1. 2000: C(R), E1(R), 2, A1(R), NZ1, A2, NZ2, A3, Arg, I, W, E3. 2001: F2, It1(R), A1(t+R), It2(R), E(R). 2002: W2, Arg*, Sm*, NZ1*, A1*, NZ2*, A2*, F*, S*, E*. 2003: Arg*, A1*, NZ1*, A2*, NZ2*.[E*, Sm*, NZ3*].*

64 **Krige, JD** (Japie) b 05/07/1879 d 14/01/1961 - WP - 5 Tests (3 - 1T) 13 matches (12 - 4T) *1903: BI1, 3. 1906: S, I, W.*

136 **Krige, WA** (Willie) b 02/12/1887 d 20/08/1961 - WP - No Tests - 9 matches (10 - 2T, 1D) *Toured BI, I & F. 1912/13.*

477 **Kritzinger, JL** (Klippies) b 01/03/1948 - Tvl - 7 Tests (4 - 1T) 12 matches (4 - 1T) *1974: BI3, 4, F1, 2. 1975: F1, 2. 1976: NZ4.*

318 **Kroon, CM** (Colin) b 22/02/1931 d 13/11/1981 - EP - 1 Test (-) 1 match (-) *1955: BI1.*

550 **Kruger, PE** (Piet) b 11/04/1958 - Tvl - 2 Tests (-) 2 matches (-) *1986: NZC3, 4.*

832 **Kruger, PJJ** (Juandré) b 06/09/1985 - BB - 17 Tests (-) 17 matches (-) *2012: E1, 2, 3, A1, NZ1, I, S, E4. 2013: It, S, Sam(R), Arg1, Arg2, A1(R), NZ1(R), A2(R), NZ2 (R).*

596 **Kruger, RJ** (Ruben) b 30/03/1970 d 27/01/2010 - OFS - 36 Tests (35 - 7T) 56 matches (105 - 21T) *1993: tour of A - no tests. 1993: Arg1, 2. 1994: tour of NZ - no tests. 1994: S, W. 1995: WS1, [A, R, WS2, F, NZ], W, It, E. 1996: Fj, A1, NZ1, A2, NZ2, 3, 4, 5, Arg1, 2, F1, 2, W. 1997: T, BI1, 2, NZ1, A1, NZ2. 1999: NZ2, A2(R), [Sp, NZ3(R)].*

169 **Krüger, TL** (Theuns) b 17/06/1896 d 06/07/1957 - Tvl - 8 Tests (-) 21 matches (6 - 2T) *1921: NZ1, 2. 1924: BI1, 2, 3, 4. 1928:*

NZ1, 2.

828 Kruger, W (Werner) b 23/01/1985 - BB - 4 Tests (-) 5 matches (-) *2010: tour of UK - no tests. 2011:A1, NZ1. 2012: E2(R), 3(R).*

364 Kuhn, SP (Fanie) b 12/06/1935 d 22/01/2014 - Tvl - 19 Tests (-) 37 matches (-) *1960: NZ3, 4, W, I. 1961: E, S, F, I, A1, 2. 1962: BI1, 2, 3, 4. 1963: A1, 2, 3. 1965: I, S.*

191 La Grange, JB (Paul) b 25/05/1897 d 23/05/1971 - WP - 2 Tests (-) 2 matches (-) *1924: BI3, 4.*

694 Labuschagne, JJ (Jannes) b 16/04/1976 - GL - 11 Tests (-) 11 matches (-) *2000: NZ1(R). 2002: W1, 2, Arg, NZ1, A1, NZ2, A2, F, S, E.*

820 Lambie, PJ (Patrick) b 17/10/1990 -KZN - 40 Tests (106 - 2T, 18C, 18P 2D) 41 matches (100 - 2T, 18C, 18P, 2D) *2010: I(R), W2(R), S(R), E(R). 2011: A1(R), NZ1, 2, [Fj, N, Sm, A3.]. 2012: E1(R), 2, A1, NZ1(R), A2(R), NZ2(R), I, S, E4. 2013: It(R), S(R), Sam(R), Arg1(R), Arg2(R), A1(R), NZ1(R), A2(R), NZ2(R), W, S, F(R). 2014: A1(R), NZ1(R), A2(R), NZ2(R), I(R), E, It, W3.*

46 Larard, A (Alf) b 30/12/1870 d 15/08/1936 - Tvl - 2 Tests (3 - 1T) 2 matches (3 - 1T) *1896: BI2, 4.*

266 Lategan, MT (Tjol) b 29/09/1925 - WP - 11 Tests (9 - 3T) 26 matches (15 - 5T) *1949: NZ1, 2, 3, 4. 1951: S, I, W. 1952: E, F. 1953: A1, 2.*

620 Laubscher, TG (Tommie) b 08/10/1963 d 26/05/2007 - WP - 6 Tests (-) 12 matches (-) *1994: Arg1, 2, S, W. 1995: It, E.*

396 Lawless, MJ (Mike) b 17/09/1941 - WP - 4 Tests (-) 15 matches (12 - 1T, 1P, 2D) *1964: F. 1969: E(R). 1970: I, W.*

245 Lawton, AD (Dandy) b 21/08/1911 d 06/05/1967 - WP - No Tests - 5 matches (24 - 8T) *Toured A & NZ. 1937.*

600 Le Roux, A-H (Ollie) b 10/05/1973 - OFS - 54 Tests (5 - 1T) 68 matches (25 - 5T) *1993: tour of Arg - no tests. 1994:E1. 1994: tour of NZ - no tests. 1998: I1, 2, W1(R), E1(R), A1(R), NZ1(R), 2(R), A2(R), W2(R), S(R), I3(R), E2(t+R). 1999: It1(R), 2(R), W(R), NZ1(R), A1(R), NZ2(R), A2(R), [S(R), Sp, U(t+R), E(R), A3(R), NZ3(R)]. 2000: E1(t+R), 2(R), A1(R), 2(R), NZ2, A3(R), Arg(R), I(t), W(R), E3(R). 2001: F1(R), 2, It1, NZ1(R), A1(R), 2(R), NZ2(R), F3, It2, E, US(R). 2002: W1(R), 2(R), Arg, NZ1(R), A1(R), NZ2(R), A2(R).*

572 Le Roux, HP (Hennie) b 10/07/1967 - Tvl - 27 Tests (34 - 4T, 1C, 4P) 51 matches (90 - 12T, 6C, 6P) *1992: tour of F &E - no tests. 1993: F1, 2.*

1993: tour of A & Arg - no tests. 1994: E1, 2, NZ1, 2, 3, Arg2, S, W. 1995: WS1, [A, R, C(R), WS2, F, NZ], W, It, E. 1996: Fj, NZ2, Arg1, 2, F1, 2, W.

608 Le Roux, JHS (Johan) b 15/11/1961 - Tvl - 3 Tests (-) 7 matches (-) *1994: E2, NZ1, 2.*

94 Le Roux, JSR (Japie) b 21/08/1882 d 04/03/1949 - WP - No Tests - 9 matches (30 - 10T) *Toured BI, I & F. 1906/07.*

510 Le Roux, M (Martiens) b 30/03/1951 d 14/10/2006 - OFS - 8 Tests (-) 12 matches (4 - 1T) *1980: BI1, 2, 3, 4, S.Am3, 4, F. 1981: I1.*

103 Le Roux, PA (Pietie) b 22/01/1885 d 11/07/1954 - WP - 3 Tests (-) 16 matches (11 - 3T, 1C) *1906: I, W, E.*

848 Le Roux, WJ (Willie) b 18/08/1989 - GW - 25 Tests (35 - 7T) 25 matches (35 - 7T) *2013: It, S, Sam, Arg1, Arg2, A1, NZ1, A2, NZ2, W(R), S, F. 2014: W1, W2, S, Arg1, Arg2, A1, NZ1, A2, NZ2, I, E, It, W3.*

146 Ledger, SH (Sep) b 29/04/1889 d 30/01/1918 - GW - 4 Tests (3 - 1T) 15 matches (3 - 1T) *1912: S, I. 1913:E, F.*

688 Leonard, A (Anton) b 31/05/1974 - SWD - 2 Tests (5 - 1T) 2 matches (5 - 1T) *1999: A1, [Sp].*

860 Lewies, JST (Stephan) b 27/01/1992 - KZN - 1 Test (-) 1 match (-) *2014: S(R)*

794 Liebenberg, CR (Tiaan) b 18/12/1981 - WP - 5 Tests (-) 6 matches (-) *2007: tour of UK - no tests. 2012: Arg2(R), A1(R), NZ1(R), A2(R), NZ2(R).*

591 Linee, M (Tinus) b 23/08/1969 d 03/11/2014 - WP - No Tests - 9 matches (10 - 2T) *Toured A. 1993 and W, S & I. 1994.*

12 Little, EM (Edward) b 01/11/1864 d ??/05/1945 - GW - 2 Tests (-) 2 matches (-) *1891: BI1, 3.*

781 Lobberts, H (Hilton) b 11/06/1986 - BB - 2 Tests (-) 4 matches (-) *2006: E1(R). 2007: NZ2(R).*

326 Lochner, GP (Butch) b 01/02/1931 d 27/08/2010 - WP - 9 Tests (6 - 2T) 22 matches (15 - 5T) *1955: BI3. 1956: A1, 2, NZ1, 2, 3, 4. 1958: F1, 2.*

249 Lochner, GP (Flappie) b 11/01/1914 d 30/01/1996 - EP - 3 Tests (3 - 1T) 12 matches (27 - 9T) *1937: NZ3. 1938: BI1, 2.*

360 Lockyear, RJ (Dick) b 26/06/1931 d 03/03/1988 - GW - 6 Tests (20 - 4C, 4P) 20 matches (97 - 32C, 11P) *1960: NZ1, 2, 3, 4, I. 1961: F.*

127 Lombard, AC (Antonie) b 06/12/1885 d 22/02/1960 - EP - 1 Test (-) 1 match (-) *1910: BI2.*

736 **Lombard, F** (Friedhelm) b 04/03/1979 - FS - 2 Tests (-) 2 matches (-) *2002: S, E.*

588 **Lötter, D** (Deon) b 10/11/1957 - Tvl - 3 Tests (-) 7 matches (5 - 1T) *1993: F2, A1, 2.*

255 **Lotz, JW** (Jan) b 26/08/1910 d 13/08/1986 - Tvl - 8 Tests (3 - 1T) 26 matches (6 - 2T) *1937: A1, 2, NZ1, 2, 3. 1938: BI1, 2, 3.*

697 **Loubscher, RIP** (Ricardo) b 11/06/1974 - EP - 4 Tests (-) 7 matches (-) *2000: tour of Arg & UK - no tests. 2002: W1. 2003: S1, [U(R), G].*

85 **Loubser, JA** (Bob) b 06/08/1884 d 07/12/1962 - WP - 7 Tests (9 - 3T) 23 matches (66 - 22T) *1903: BI3. 1906: S, I, W, E. 1910: BI1, 2.*

425 **Lourens, MJ** (Thys) b 15/05/1943 - NTvl - 3 Tests (3 - 1T) 11 matches (12 - 4T) *1968: BI2, 3, 4. 1968: tour to F - no tests. 1971: tour to A - no tests.*

704 **Louw, FH** (Hottie) b 02/03/1976 - WP - 3 Tests (-) 7 matches (-) *2000: tour of Arg & UK - no tests. 2002: W2(R), Arg, Sm.*

11 **Louw, JS** (Japie) b 30/08/1867 d 17/08/1936 - Tvl - 3 Tests (-) 3 matches (-) *1891: BI1, 2, 3.*

147 **Louw, LH** (Louis) b 23/06/1884 d 13/09/1968 - WP - No Tests - 12 matches (3 - 1T) *Toured BI, I & F. 1912/13.*

815 **Louw, L-FP** (Francois) b 15/06/1985 - WP - 34 Tests (25 - 5T) 34 matches (25 - 5T) *2010: W1, F, It1, 2, NZ1, 2, 3(R). 2011: [Fj(t), N(t+R), A3(R).]. 2012: A1(R), NZ1, A2, NZ2, I, S, E4. 2013: It, Sam, Arg1, Arg2, A1, NZ1, A2, NZ2, W, S, F. 2014: W1, W2, Arg1, Arg2, A1, NZ1.*

454 **Louw, MJ** (Martiens) b 20/04/1938 d 12/10/2013 - Tvl - 2 Tests (-) 9 matches (-) *1971: A2, 3.*

207 **Louw, MM** (Boy) b 21/02/1906 d 03/05/1988 - WP - 18 Tests (3 - 1T) 49 matches (18 - 6T) *1928: NZ3, 4. 1931: W, I. 1932: E, S. 1933: A1, 2, 3, 4, 5. 1937: A1, 2, NZ2, 3. 1938: BI1, 2, 3.*

505 **Louw, RJ** (Rob) b 26/03/1955 - WP - 19 Tests (20 - 5T) 28 matches (44 - 11T) *1980: S.Am1, 2, BI1, 2, 3, 4, S.Am3, 4, F. 1981: I1, 2, NZ1, 3. 1982: S.Am1, 2. 1984: E1, 2, S.Am&Sp1, 2.*

222 **Louw, SC** (Fanie) b 16/09/1909 d 13/07/1940 - WP - 12 Tests (6 - 2T) 30 matches (24 - 8T) *1931-32 tour of UK - no tests. 1933: A1, 2, 3, 4, 5. 1937: A1, NZ1, 2, 3. 1938: BI1, 2, 3.*

650 **Lubbe, JMF** (Edrich) b 29/07/1969 - GW - 2 Tests (17 - 7C, 1P) 2 matches (17 - 7C, 1P) *1997: T, BI1.*

114 **Luyt, FP** (Freddie) b 26/02/1888 d 06/06/1965 - WP - 7 Tests (8 - 2T, 1C) 21 matches (27 - 5T, 6C) *1910: BI1, 2, 3. 1912: S, I, W. 1913: E.*

150 **Luyt, JD** (John) b 06/12/1884 d 03/10/1964 - EP - 4 Tests (-) 19 matches (3 - 1T) *1912: S, W. 1913: E, F.*

122 **Luyt, RR** (Dick) b 16/04/1886 d 14/01/1967 - WP - 7 Tests (3 - 1T) 21 matches (28 - 8T, 1D) *1910: BI2, 3. 1912: S, I, W. 1913: E, F.*

29 **Lyons, DJ** (Dykie) b 03/08/1873 d 01/05/1921 - EP - 1 Test (-) 1 match (-) *1896: BI1.*

236 **Lyster, PJ** (Pat) b 31/05/1913 d 25/07/2002 - Natal - 3 Tests (-) 11 matches (39 - 13T) *1933: A2, 5. 1937: NZ1.*

409 **MacDonald, AW** (Andy) b 27/08/1934 d 18/08/1987 - Rhodesia - 5 Tests (-) 17 matches (3 - 1T) *1965: A1, NZ1, 2, 3, 4.*

470 **MacDonald, DA** (Dugald) b 20/01/1950 - WP - 1 Test (-) 1 match (-) *1974: BI2.*

811 **Maku, BG** (Bandise) b 24/06/1986 - BB - 1 Test (-) 4 matches (5 - 1T) *2009: tour of UK - no tests. 2010:It1(R). 2010: tour of UK - no tests.*

361 **Malan, AS** (Avril) b 09/04/1937 - Tvl - 16 Tests (-) 36 matches (3 - 1T) *1960: NZ1, 2, 3*, 4*, W*, I*. 1961: E*, S*, F*. 1962: BI1. 1963: A1, 2, 3*. 1964: W. 1965: I*, S*.*

556 **Malan, AW** (Adolf) b 06/09/1961 - NTvl - 7 Tests (-) 11 matches (-)   *1989:WT1, 2. 1992:NZ, A, F1, 2, E.*

512 **Malan, E** (Ewoud) b 04/07/1953 - NTvl - 2 Tests (-) 2 matches (-) *1980: BI3(R), 4.*

345 **Malan, GF** (Abie) b 18/11/1935 d 23/10/2014 - WP - 18 Tests (3 - 1T) 44 matches (9 - 3T) *1958: F2. 1960: NZ1, 3, 4. 1961: E, S, F. 1962: BI1, 2, 3. 1963: A1*, 2*, 4*. 1964: W*. 1965: A1, 2, NZ1, 2.*

284 **Malan, P** (Piet) b 13/02/1919 - Tvl - 1 Test (-) 1 match (-) *1949: NZ4.*

841 **Malherbe, JF** (Frans) b 14/03/1991 - WP - 4 Tests (-) 4 matches (-) *2012: Rugby Championship Squad - no tests. 2013: W, S. 2014: Arg1(R), Arg2(R).*

541 **Mallett, NVH** (Nick) b 30/10/1956 - WP - 2 Tests (4 - 1T) 2 matches (4 - 1T) *1984: S.Am&Sp1, 2.*

687 **Malotana, K** (Kaya) b 30/01/1976 - Border - 1 Test (-) 1 match (-) *1999: [Sp].*

708 **Manana, TD** (Thando) b 16/10/1977 - GW - No Tests - 3 matches (-) *Toured Arg, I, W & E. 2000.*

398 **Mans, WJ** (Wynand) b 21/02/1942 - WP - 2 Tests (5 - 1T, 1C) 19 matches (123 - 14T, 30C, 6P, 1D) *1965: I, S. 1965: tour of A & NZ - no tests.*

844 **Mapoe, LG** (Lionel) b 13/07/1988 - GL -

No Tests - No matches *Toured I, S & E. 2012.*

685 **Marais, CF** (Charl) b 02/09/1970 - WP - 12 Tests (5 - 1T) 15 matches (5 - 1T) *1999: It1(R), 2(R). 2000: C, E1, 2, A1, NZ1, A2, NZ2, A3, Arg(R), W(R).*

264 **Marais, FP** (Buks) b 13/12/1927 d 12/12/1996 - Boland - 5 Tests (10 - 1T, 2C, 1P) 18 matches (40 - 11T, 2C, 1P) *1949: NZ1, 2. 1951: S. 1953: A1, 2.*

390 **Marais, JFK** (Hannes) b 21/09/1941 - WP - 35 Tests (3 - 1T) 75 matches (38 - 12T) *1963: A3. 1964: W, F. 1965: I, S, A2. 1968: BI1, 2, 3, 4, F1, 2. 1969: S, E, A1, 2, 3, 4. 1970: I, W, NZ1, 2, 3, 4. 1971: F1*, 2*, A1*, 2*, 3*. 1974: BI1*, 2*, 3*, 4*, F1*, 2*.*

529 **Marais, JH** (Johan) b 28/05/1959 - NTvl - No Tests - 5 matches (4 - 1T) *Toured NZ & USA. 1981.*

98 **Maré, DS** (Dietlof) b 02/07/1885 d 14/10/1913 - Tvl - 1 Test (-) 11 matches (31 - 2T, 11C, 1P) *1906: S.*

677 **Markram, RL** (Robert) b 15/09/1975 d 06/07/2001 - GW - No Tests - 4 matches (-) *Toured BI & I. 1998.*

92 **Marsberg, AFW** (Artie) b 24/09/1883 d 15/01/1942 - GW - 3 Tests (-) 18 matches (15 - 5T) *1906: S, W, E.*

111 **Marsberg, PA** (Archie) b 01/10/1885 d 23/10/1962 - GW - 1 Test (-) 1 match (-) *1910: BI1.*

598 **Martens, HJ** (Hentie) b 29/10/1971 - OFS - No Tests - 3 matches (5 - 1T) *Toured Arg. 1993.*

82 **Martheze, WC** (Rajah) b 29/11/1877 d 16/02/1912 - GW - 3 Tests (-) 16 matches (18 - 6T) *1903: BI2. 1906: I, W.*

256 **Martin, HJ** (Kalfie) b 10/06/1910 d 20/10/2000 - Tvl - 1 Test (-) 16 matches (9 - 3T) *1937: A2.*

705 **Matfield, V** (Victor) b 11/05/1977 - GW - 121 Tests (35 - 7T) 125 matches (35 - 7T) *2000: tour of Arg & UK - no tests. 2001: It1(R), NZ1, A2, NZ2, F3, It2, E, US. 2002: W1, Sm, NZ1, A1, NZ2(R). 2003: S1, 2, Arg, A1, NZ1, A2, NZ2, [U, E, Sm, NZ3]. 2004: I1, 2, W1, NZ2, A2, W2, I3, E, S, Arg. 2005: F1, 2, A1, 2, 3, NZ1, A4, NZ2, Arg, W, F3. 2006: S1, 2, F, A1, NZ1, A2, NZ2, 3, A3. 2007: E1, 2, A1, NZ1*, N*, S*, [Sm, E3, T(R), US, Fiji, Arg, E4.]. 2008: W1(R), 2, It*, NZ1, 2*, A1*, Arg*, NZ3*, A2*, 3*, W3, S, E. 2009: BI1, 2, 3, NZ1, 2, A1, 2, 3, NZ3, F, It(R), I. 2010: W1, F, It1*, NZ1, 2, A1, NZ3, A2, 3, I*, W2*, S*, E*. 2011: A2, NZ2*, [W, Sm*, A3.]. 2014: W1, W2, S, A1, NZ1, A2, NZ2, I, E, It, W3.*

443 **McCallum, ID** (Ian) b 30/07/1944 - WP - 11 Tests (62 - 10C, 14P) 17 matches (134 - 2T, 28C, 24P) *1970: NZ1, 2, 3, 4. 1971: F1, 2, A1, 2, 3. 1974: BI1, 2.*

462 **McCallum, RJ** (Roy) b 12/04/1946 - WP - 1 Test (-) 5 matches (4 - 1T) *1974: BI1. 1974: tour of F - no tests.*

138 **McCulloch, JD** (John) b 11/04/1885 d 23/04/1953 - GW - 2 Tests (-) 11 matches (3 - 1T) *1913: E, F.*

565 **McDonald, I** (Ian) b 22/02/1968 - Tvl - 6 Tests (-) 18 matches (25 - 5T) *1992: NZ, A. 1992: tour of F & E - no tests. 1993: F1, A3. 1994: E2. 1995: WS1(R).*

223 **McDonald, JAJ** (André) b 17/02/1909 - d 13/07/1991 - WP - 4 Tests (-) 15 matches (15 - 5T) *1931: W, I. 1932: E, S.*

69 **McEwan, WMC** (Willie) b 24/10/1875 d 04/04/1934 - Tvl - 2 Tests (-) 2 matches (-) *1903: BI1, 3.*

134 **McHardy, EE** (Boetie) b 11/06/1890 d 13/12/1959 - OFS - 5 Tests (18 - 6T) 17 matches (60 - 20T) *1912: S, I, W. 1913: E, F.*

27 **McKendrick, JA** (Jim) b 27/07/1870 d 01/01/1895 - WP - 1 Test (-) 1 match (-) *1891: BI3.*

826 **McLeod, C** (Charl) b 05/08/1983 - KZN - 1 Test (-) 2 matches (-) *2010: tour of UK - no tests. 2011: NZ1(R).*

131 **Meintjes, JJ** (Cooper) b 05/05/1887 d 30/01/1970 - GW - No Tests - 4 matches (-) *Toured BI, I & F. 1912/13.*

612 **Meiring, FA** (FA) b 24/08/1967 - NTvl - No Tests - 7 matches (10 - 2T) *Toured NZ. 1994.*

48 **Mellet, TB** (Tom) b 29/08/1871 d 29/07/1943 - GW - 1 Test (-) 1 match (-) *1896: BI2.*

172 **Mellish, FW** (Frank) b 26/03/1897 d 21/08/1965 - WP - 6 Tests (-) 15 matches (-) *1921: NZ1, 3. 1924: BI1, 2, 3, 4.*

427 **Menter, MA** (Alan) b 03/10/1941 - NTvl - No Tests - 2 matches (-) *Toured F. 1968.*

756 **Mentz, H** (Henno) b 25/09/1979 - Natal - 2 Tests (-) 2 matches (-) *2004: I1, W1(R).*

14 **Merry, GA** (George) b 03/03/1869 d 02/05/1917 - EP - 1 Test (-) 1 match (-) *1891: BI1.*

79 **Metcalf, HD** (Henry) b 20/04/1878 d 03/03/1966 - Border - 1 Test (-) 1 match (-) *1903: BI2.*

159 **Meyer, C du P** (Charlie) b 14/01/1897 d 31/05/1980 - WP - 3 Tests (-) 15 matches (27 - 9T) *1921: NZ1, 2, 3.*

38 **Meyer, PJ** (PJ) b ??/05/1873 d 27/07/1919 - GW - 1 Test (-) 1 match (-) *1896: BI1.*

663 **Meyer, W** (Willie) b 06/11/1967 - FS - 26

Tests (5 - 1T) 31 matches (10 - 2T) *1997: S(R). 1999: It2, NZ1(R), A1(R). 2000: C(R), E1, NZ1(R), 2(R), Arg, I, W, E3. 2001: F1(R), 2, It1, F3(R), It2, E, US(t+R). 2002: W1, 2, Arg, NZ1, 2, A2, F.*

168 Michau, JM (Baby) b 14/08/1890 d 20/06/1945 - Tvl - 1 Test (-) 10 matches (-) *1921: NZ1.*

162 Michau, JP (Mannetjies) b 06/10/1900 d 22/05/1960 - WP - 3 Tests (-) 16 matches (6 - 2T) *1921: NZ1, 2, 3.*

109 Millar, WA (Billy) b 06/11/1883 d 18/03/1949 - WP - 6 Tests (6 - 2T) 37 matches (15 - 5T) *1906: E. 1910: BI2*, 3*. 1912: I*, W*. 1913: F*.*

123 Mills, WJ (Wally) b 16/06/1891 d 23/02/1975 - WP - 1 Test (3 - 1T) 13 matches (30 - 10T) *1910: BI2. 1912-13 tour of UK - No Tests*

859 Mohoje, TS (Teboho) b 03/08/1990 - FS - 7 Tests (-) 7 matches (-) *2014: S(R), A2, NZ2, I, E(R), It, W3.*

125 Moll, TM (Toby) b 20/07/1890 d 14/07/1916 - Tvl - 1 Test (-) 1 match (-) *1910: BI2.*

651 Montgomery, PC (Percy) b 15/03/1974 - WP - 102 Tests (893 - 25T, 153C, 148P, 6D) 104 matches (906 - 26T, 157C, 148P, 6D) *1997: BI2, 3, NZ1, A1, NZ2, A2, F1, 2, E, S. 1998: I1, 2, W1, E1, A1, NZ1, 2, A2, W2, S, I3, E2. 1999: It1, 2, W, NZ1, A1, NZ2, A2, [S, U, E, A3, NZ3]. 2000: C, E1, 2, A1, NZ1, A2(R), Arg, I, W, E3. 2001: F1, 2(t), It1, NZ1, F3(R), It2(R). 2004: I2, W1, PI, NZ1, A1, NZ2, A2, W2, I3, E, S. 2005: U, F1, 2, A1, 2, 3, NZ1, A4, NZ2, Arg, W, F3. 2006: S1, 2, F, A1, NZ1, A2, NZ2. 2007: E1, 2, Sm1(R), A1, NZ1, N, S, [Sm, E3, T(R), US, Fiji, Arg, E4.]. 2008: W1(R), 2(R), NZ1(R), 2, Arg(R), NZ3, A2(R), 3(R).*

328 Montini, PE (Pat) b 15/06/1929 d 26/08/2008 - WP - 2 Tests (-) 11 matches (6 - 1T, 1D) *1956: A1, 2.*

498 Moolman, LC (Louis) b 21/01/1951 d 10/02/2006 - NTvl - 24 Tests (-) 31 matches (12 - 3T) *1977: WT. 1980: S.Am1, 2, BI1, 2, 3, 4, S.Am3, 4, F. 1981: I1, 2, NZ1, 2, 3, US. 1982: S.Am1, 2. 1984: S.Am&Sp1, 2. 1986: NZC1, 2, 3, 4.*

501 Mordt, RH (Ray) b 15/02/1957 - Zimbabwe - 18 Tests (48 - 12T) 25 matches (88 - 22T) *1980: S.Am1, 2, BI1, 2, 3, 4, S.Am3, 4, F. 1981: I2, NZ1, 2, 3, US. 1982: S.Am1, 2. 1984: S.Am&Sp1, 2.*

106 Morkel, DFT (Dougie) b 26/10/1885 d 20/02/1950 - Tvl - 9 Tests (38 - 3T, 7C, 5P) 40 matches (137 - 8T, 37C, 13P) *1906: I, E. 1910: BI1*, 3. 1912: S, I, W. 1913: E*, F.*

66 Morkel, DJA (Andrew) b 04/08/1882 d 14/06/1965 - Tvl - 1 Test (-) 2 matches (-) *1903:BI1. 1906 tour of UK - no tests*

173 Morkel, HJL (Harry) b 08/12/1888 d 16/07/1956 - WP - 1 Test (-) 13 matches (6 - 2T) *1921: NZ1.*

155 Morkel, HW (Henry) b 14/07/1894 d 25/12/1969 - WP - 2 Tests (-) 9 matches (18 - 6T) *1921: NZ1, 2.*

171 Morkel, JA (Royal) b 30/04/1894 d 22/10/1926 - WP - 2 Tests (-) 13 matches (9 - 2T, 1D) *1921: NZ2, 3.*

137 Morkel, JWH (Jacky) b 13/11/1890 d 15/05/1916 - WP - 5 Tests (16 - 4T, 2C) 18 matches (34 - 6T, 4C, 2D) *1912: S, I, W. 1913: E, F.*

130 Morkel, PG (Gerhard) b 15/10/1888 d 05/09/1963 - WP - 8 Tests (16 - 6C, 1D) 33 matches (79 - 33C, 3P, 1D) *1912: S, I, W. 1913: E, F. 1921: NZ1, 2, 3.*

211 Morkel, PK (PK) b 01/07/1905 d 24/07/1993 - WP - 1 Test (-) 1 match (-) *1928: NZ4.*

128 Morkel, WH (Boy) b 02/01/1885 d 06/02/1955 - WP - 9 Tests (6 - 2T) 31 matches (21 - 7T) *1910: BI3. 1912: S, I, W. 1913:E, F. 1921: NZ1*, 2*, 3*.*

105 Morkel, WS (Sommie) b 26/09/1879 d 11/07/1921 - Tvl - 4 Tests (-) 16 matches (3 - 1T) *1906: S, I, W, E.*

267 Moss, C (Cecil) b 12/02/1925 - Natal - 4 Tests (-) 4 matches (-) *1949: NZ1, 2, 3, 4.*

830 Mostert, G (Gerhard) b 04/10/1984 - KZN - 2 Tests (-) 2 matches (-) *2011: NZ1, A2(R).*

176 Mostert, PJ (Phil) b 30/10/1898 d 03/10/1972 - WP - 14 Tests (6 - 1T, 1D) 40 matches (18 - 5T, 1D) *1921: NZ1, 2, 3. 1924: BI1, 2, 4. 1928: NZ1*, 2*, 3*, 4*. 1931: W, I. 1932: E, S.*

682 Moyle, BS (Brent) b 31/03/1974 - GF - No Tests - 1 match (-) *Toured BI & I. 1998.*

797 Mtawarira, T (Tendai) b 01/08/1985 - KZN - 64 Tests (10 - 2T) 65 matches (10 - 2T) *2008: W2, It, A1(R), Arg, NZ3, A2, 3, W3, S, E. 2009: BI1, 2, 3, NZ1, 2, A1, 2, 3, NZ3, F, It(R), I. 2010: I, W2, S, E. 2011: A2, NZ2(R), [W, Fj(R), N(R), Sm.]. 2012: E1, 2, 3, Arg1, 2, A1, NZ1, A2, NZ2. 2012: tour of UK - no tests. 2013: It, S, Sam, Arg1, Arg2, A1, NZ1, A2, NZ2, W, S(R), F. 2014: W1(R), W2, Arg1, Arg2(R), A1, NZ1, A2, NZ2, I, E, W3.*

642 Muir, DJ (Dick) b 20/03/1965 - Natal - 5 Tests (10 - 2T) 10 matches (20 - 4T) *1996: tour* *of Arg, F & W – no tests. 1997: It, F1, 2, E, S.*

796 Mujati, BV (Brian) b 28/09/1984 – WP – 12 Tests (–) 12 matches (–) *2008: W1, It(R), NZ1(R), 2(t), A1(R), Arg(R), NZ3(R), A2(R), 3, W3(t), S(R), E(R).*

405 Mulder, CG (Boet) b 21/05/1939 – ETvl – No Tests – 13 matches (20 – 7C, 2P) *Toured A & NZ. 1965.*

617 Mulder, JC (Japie) b 18/10/1969 – Tvl – 34 Tests (30 – 6T) 43 matches (45 – 9T) *1994: NZ2, 3, S, W. 1995: WS1, [A, WS2, F, NZ], W, It, E. 1996: Fj, A1, NZ1, A2, NZ2, 5, Arg1, 2, F1, 2, W. 1997: T, BI1. 1999: It1(R), 2, W, NZ1. 2000: C(R), A1, E3. 2001: F1, It1.*

428 Müller, GH (Gert) b 10/05/1948 – WP – 14 Tests (12 – 4T) 20 matches (45 – 15T) *1969: A3, 4, S. 1970: W, NZ1, 2, 3, 4. 1971: F1, 2. 1971: tour of A – no tests. 1972: E. 1974: BI1, 3, 4.*

773 Muller, GJ (Johan) b 01/06/1980 – KZN – 24 Tests (–) 26 matches (–) *2006: S1(R), NZ1(R), A2, NZ2, 3, A3, I(R), E1, 2. 2007: E1(R), 2(R), Sm1(R), A1(R), NZ1(R), A2, NZ2*, N(R), [Sm(R), E3(R), Fiji(t+R), Arg(t+R).], W. 2009: BI3. 2011: [W(R).].*

748 Müller, GP (Jorrie) b 03/01/1981 – GL – 6 Tests (5 – 1T) 6 matches (5 – 1T) *2003: A2, NZ2, [E, G(R), Sam, NZ3].*

551 Müller, HL (Helgard) b 01/06/1963 – OFS – 2 Tests (–) 5 matches (–) *1986: NZC4(R). 1989: WT1(R).*

277 Muller, HSV (Hennie) b 26/03/1922 d 26/04/1977 – Tvl – 13 Tests (16 – 3T, 2C, 1P) 28 matches (28 – 4T, 5C, 2P) *1949: NZ1, 2, 3, 4. 1951: S*, I*, W*. 1952: E*, F*. 1953: A1*, 2*, 3*, 4*.*

563 Müller, LJJ (Lood) b 05/07/1959 – Natal – 2 Tests (–) 2 matches (–) *1992: NZ, A.*

560 Müller, PG (Pieter) b 05/05/1969 – Natal – 33 Tests (15 – 3T) 52 matches (50 – 10T) *1992: NZ, A, F1, 2, E. 1993: F1, 2, A1, 2, 3, Arg1, 2. 1994: E1, 2, NZ1, S, W. 1998: I1, 2, W1, E1, A1, NZ1, 2, A2. 1999: It1, W, NZ1, A1, [Sp, E, A3, NZ3].*

785 Murray, WM (Waylon) b 27/04/1986 – KZN – 3 Tests (–) 4 matches (–) *2007: Sm1, A2, NZ2.*

821 Mvovo, LN (Lwazi) b 03/06/1986 – KZN – 10 Tests (15 – 3T) 11 matches (15 – 3T) *2010: S, E. 2011: A1, NZ1. 2012: Arg1, 2, A1(R). 2012: tour of UK – no tests. 2014: W1(R), S, W3.*

305 Myburgh, B (Ben) b 17/06/1919 d 30/10/1984 – ETvl – No Tests – 17 matches (12 – 4T) *Toured BI, I & F. 1951/52.*

34 Myburgh, FR (Francis) b 20/07/1871 d 30/11/1929 – EP – 1 Test (–) 1 match (–) *1896: BI1.*

371 Myburgh, JL (Mof) b 24/08/1936 d 15/06/2012 – NTvl – 18 Tests (–) 57 matches (9 – 3T) *1960-61: tour of UK – no tests. 1962: BI1. 1963: A4. 1964: W, F. 1968: BI1, 2, 3, F1, 2. 1969: A1, 2, 3, 4, E. 1970: I, W, NZ3, 4.*

182 Myburgh, WH (Champion) b 10/10/1897 d 14/03/1979 – WTvl – 1 Test (–) 1 match (–) *1924: BI1.*

394 Naudé, JP (Tiny) b 02/11/1936 d 28/12/2006 – WP – 14 Tests (47 – 2T, 4C, 11P) 28 matches (90 – 6T, 9C, 18P) *1963: A4. 1965: A1, 2, NZ1, 3, 4. 1967: F1, 2, 3, 4. 1968: BI1, 2, 3, 4. 1968: tour of F – no tests.*

774 Ndungane, AZ (Akona) b 20/02/1981 – BB – 11 Tests (5 – 1T) 13 matches (5 – 1T) *2006: A1, 2, NZ2, 3, A3, E1, 2. 2007: E2, N(R), [US.], W(R).*

798 Ndungane, OM (Odwa) b 20/02/1981 – KZN – 9 Tests (10 – 2T) 12 matches (15 – 3T) *2008: It, NZ1, A3. 2008: tour of UK – no tests. 2009: BI3, A3, NZ3. 2009: tour of UK – no tests. 2010: W1. 2010: tour of UK – no tests. 2011: NZ1(R), [Fj.].*

401 Neethling, JB (Tiny) b 06/07/1939 d 03/04/2009 – WP – 8 Tests (–) 23 matches (3 – 1T) *1965: tour of I & S – no tests. 1967: F1, 2, 3, 4. 1968: BI4. 1968: tour of F – no tests. 1969: S. 1970: NZ1, 2.*

101 Neill, WA (William) b 30/12/1882 d 03/02/1947 – Border – No Tests – 4 matches (–) *Toured BI, I & F. 1906/07.*

362 Nel, JA (Lofty) b 11/08/1935 – Tvl – 11 Tests (–) 24 matches (18 – 6T) *1960: NZ1, 2. 1963: A1, 2. 1965: A2, NZ1, 2, 3, 4. 1970: NZ3, 4.*

329 Nel, JJ (Jeremy) b 21/09/1934 – WP – 8 Tests (3 – 1T) 23 matches (32 – 9T, 1C, 1P) *1956: A1, 2, NZ1, 2, 3, 4. 1958: F1, 2.*

72 Nel, PARO (PO) b 17/04/1877 d 23/07/1928 – Tvl – 3 Tests (–) 3 matches (–) *1903: BI1, 2, 3.*

199 Nel, PJ (Flip) b 17/06/1902 d 12/02/1984 – Natal – 16 Tests (3 – 1T) 46 matches (6 – 2T) *1928: NZ1, 2, 3, 4. 1931: W, I. 1932: E, S. 1933: A1*, 3*, 4*, 5*. 1937: A1*, 2*, NZ2*, 3*.*

238 Nijkamp, JL (Joe) b 16/10/1904 d 03/04/1969 – Tvl – 1 Test (–) 1 match (–) *1933: A2.*

369 Nimb, CF (Charlie) b 06/09/1938 d 15/06/2004 – WP – 1 Test (9 – 3C, 1P) 6 matches (20 – 2T, 4C, 2P) *1960-61: tour of UK – no tests. 1961: I.*

679 Nkumane, SO (Owen) b 10/08/1975 – GL – No Tests – 4 matches (–) *Toured BI & I. 1998.*

767 Nokwe, JL (Jongi) b 30/12/1981 – Boland – 4 Tests (25 – 5T) 7 matches (40 – 8T) *2004: tour of UK – no test. 2008: Arg, A2, 3. 2008: tour of UK –*

no tests. 2009: BI3. 2009: tour of UK - no tests.
408 **Nomis, SH** (Syd) b 15/11/1941 - Tvl - 25 Tests (18 - 6T) 54 matches (45 - 15T) *1965: tour of A & NZ - no tests. 1967: F4. 1968: BI1, 2, 3, 4, F1, 2. 1969: A1, 2, 3, 4, S, E. 1970: I, W, NZ1, 2, 3, 4. 1971: F1, 2, A1, 2, 3. 1972: E.*
850 **Nyakane, TN** (Trevor) b 04/05/1989 - FS - 13 Tests (5 - 1T) 13 matches (5 - 1T) *2013: It(R), S(R), Sam(R). 2014: S(R), Arg1(R), A1(R), NZ1(R), A2(R), NZ2(R), I(R), E(R), It, W3.*
289 **Ochse, JK** (Chum) b 09/02/1925 d 13/07/1996 - WP - 7 Tests (9 - 3T) 22 matches (48 - 16T) *1951: I, W. 1952: E, F. 1953: A1, 2, 4.*
295 **Oelofse, JSA** (Hansie) b 16/12/1926 d 31/05/1978 - Tvl - 4 Tests (6 - 2T) 13 matches (12 - 4T) *1951-52: tour of UK - no tests. 1953: A1, 2, 3, 4.*
209 **Oliver, JF** (John) b 17/05/1897 d ??/??/1980 - Tvl - 2 Tests (-) 2 matches (-) *1928: NZ3, 4.*
417 **Olivier, E** (Eben) b 10/04/1944 - WP - 16 Tests (15 - 5T) 34 matches (30 - 10T) *1965: tour of A & NZ - no tests. 1967: F1, 2, 3, 4. 1968: BI1, 2, 3, 4, F1, 2. 1969:A1, 2, 3, 4, S, E.*
570 **Olivier, J** (Jacques) b 13/11/1968 - NTvl - 17 Tests (15 - 3T) 34 matches (65 - 13T) *1992: F1, 2, E. 1993: F1, 2, A1, 2, 3, Arg1. 1994: tour of W & S - no tests. 1995: W, It(R), E. 1996: Arg1, 2, F1, 2, W.*
174 **Olivier, JS** (Fien) b 27/05/1897 d 08/06/1980 - WP - No Tests - 13 matches (2 - 1C) *Toured A & NZ. 1921.*
772 **Olivier, W** (Wynand) b 11/06/1983 - BB - 38 Tests (5 - 1T) 42 matches (5 - 1T) *2006: S1(R), 2, F, A1, NZ1, A2, NZ2(R), 3, A3, I(R), E1, 2. 2007: E1, E2, NZ1(R), A2, NZ2, [E3(R), T, Arg(R).], W(R). 2009: BI3, NZ1(R), 2(R), F(R), It(R), I. 2010: F, It2(R), NZ1, 2, A1. 2011:A1, NZ1(R). 2012: E1(t), 2(R), 3. 2014: S(R).*
33 **Olver, E** (Ernest) b 27/07/1874 d 12/06/1943 - EP - 1 Test (-) 1 match (-) *1896: BI1.*
824 **Oosthuizen, CV** (Coenie) b 22/03/1989 - FS - 21 Tests (15 - 3T) 22 matches (15 - 3T) *2010: tour of UK - no tests. 2012: E1(R), NZ2(R). 2013: It(R), S(R), Sam(R), Arg1(R), Arg2(R), A1(R), NZ1(R), A2(R), NZ2(R), W(R), S(R), F. 2014: W1(R), W2(R), S, I(R), E(R), It, W3.*
460 **Oosthuizen, JJ** (Johan) b 04/07/1951 - WP - 9 Tests (8 - 2T) 14 matches (23 - 5T, 1D) *1974: BI1, F1, 2. 1975: F1, 2. 1976: NZ1, 2, 3, 4.*
646 **Oosthuizen, LT** (Theo) b 24/02/1964 - GW - No Tests - 4 matches (15 - 3T) *Toured Arg, F & W. 1996.*
520 **Oosthuizen, OW** (Okkie) b 01/04/1955 - NTvl - 9 Tests (4 - 1T) 14 matches (12 - 3T)

1981: I1(R), 2, NZ2, 3, US. 1982: S.Am1, 2. 1984: E1, 2.
571 **Oosthuysen, DE** (Deon) b 04/12/1963 - NTvl - No Tests - 12 matches (20 - 4T) *Toured F & E. 1992 and A. 1993.*
181 **Osler, BL** (Bennie) b 23/11/1901 d 24/04/1962 - WP - 17 Tests (46 - 2T, 6C, 4P, 4D) 30 matches (108 - 7T, 17C, 7P, 8D) *1924: BI1, 2, 3, 4. 1928: NZ1, 2, 3, 4. 1931: W*, I*. 1932: E*, S*. 1933: A1, 2*, 3, 4, 5.*
193 **Osler, SG** (Sharkey) b 31/01/1907 d 16/04/1980 - WP - 1 Test (-) 1 match (-) *1928: NZ1.*
615 **Otto, K** (Krynauw) b 08/10/1971 - NTvl - 38 Tests (5 - 1T) 51 matches (30 - 6T) *1994: tours of NZ and W & S - no tests. 1995:[R, C(R), WS2(R)]. 1996: tours of A - no tests. 1997: BI3, NZ1, A1, NZ2, It, F1, 2, E, S. 1998: I1, 2, W1, E1, A1, NZ1, 2, A2, W2, S, I3, E2. 1999: It1, W, NZ1, A1, [S(R), Sp, U, E, A3, NZ3]. 2000: C, E1, 2, A1.*
359 **Oxlee, K** (Keith) b 17/12/1934 d 31/08/1998 - Natal - 19 Tests (88 - 5T, 14C, 14P, 1D) 48 matches (201 - 11T, 45C, 23P, 3D) *1960: NZ1, 2, 3, 4, W, I. 1961: S, A1, 2. 1962: BI1, 2, 3, 4. 1963: A1, 2, 4. 1964: W. 1965: tour of I & S - no tests. 1965: NZ1, 2.*
628 **Pagel, GL** (Garry) b 17/09/1966 - WP - 5 Tests (-) 8 matches (-) *1995: [A(R), R, C, NZ(R)]. 1996: NZ5(R).*
411 **Parker, WH** (Hambly) b 13/04/1934 d 19/09/2014 - EP - 2 Tests (-) 14 matches (-) *1965: A1, 2.*
73 **Partridge, JEC** (Birdie) b 13/06/1879 d 01/07/1965 - Tvl - 1 Test (-) 1 match (-) *1903: BI1.*
698 **Passens, GA** (Gavin) b 18/05/1976 - Mpu - No Tests - 3 matches (10 - 2T) *Toured Arg, I, W & E. 2000.*
647 **Paulse, BJ** (Breyton) b 25/04/1976 - WP - 64 Tests (130 - 26T) 74 matches (195 - 39T) *1996: tour of Arg, F & W - no tests. 1999: It1, 2, NZ1, A1, 2(R), [S(R), Sp, NZ3]. 2000: C, E1, 2, A1, NZ1, A2, NZ2, A3, Arg, W, E3. 2001: F1, 2, It1, NZ1, A1, 2, NZ2, F3, It2, E. 2002: W1, 2, Arg, Sm(R), A1, NZ2, A2, F, S, E. 2003: [G]. 2004: I1, 2, W1, PI, NZ1, A1, NZ2, A2, W2, I3, E. 2005: A2, 3, NZ1, A4, F3. 2006: S1, 2, A1(R), NZ1, 3(R), A3(R). 2007: A2, NZ2.*
183 **Payn, C** (Bill) b 09/08/1893 d 31/10/1959 - Natal - 2 Tests (-) 2 matches (-) *1924: BI1, 2.*
341 **Pelser, HJM** (Martin) b 23/03/1934 - Tvl - 11 Tests (6 - 2T) 26 matches (18 - 6T) *1958: F1. 1960: NZ1, 2, 3, 4, W, I. 1961: F, I, A1, 2.*
331 **Pfaff, BD** (Brian) b 02/03/1930 d

08/05/1998 - WP - 1 Test (-) 5 matches (6 - 2T) *1956: A1.*
301 **Pickard, JAJ** (Jan) b 25/12/1927 d 30/05/1998 - WP - 4 Tests (-) 34 matches (19 - 5T, 2C) *1951-52: tour of UK - no tests. 1953: A3, 4. 1956: NZ2. 1958: F2.*
584 **Pienaar, JF** (Francois) b 02/01/1967 - Tvl - 29 Tests (15 - 3T) 40 matches (20 - 4T) *1993: F1*, 2*, A1*, 2*, 3*, Arg1*, 2*. 1994: E1*, 2*, NZ2*, 3*, Arg1*, 2*, S*, W*. 1995: WS1*, [A*, C*, WS2*, F*, NZ*], W*, It*, E*. 1996: Fj*, A1*, NZ1*, A2*, NZ2*.*
779 **Pienaar, R** (Ruan) b 10/03/1984 - KZN - 80 Tests (135 - 8T, 22C, 17P) 84 matches (158 - 8T, 23C, 24P) *2006: NZ2(R), 3(R), A3(R), I(t), E1(R). 2007: E1(R), 2(R), Sm1(R), A1, NZ1, A2, NZ2, N(R), S(R), [E3(t+R), T, US(R), Arg(R).], W. 2008: W1(R), It(R), NZ2(R), A1(R), 3(R), W3, S, E. 2009: BI1, 2, 3(R), NZ1, A1(R), 2, 3, It(R), I(R). 2010: W1, F(R), It1(R), 2(R), NZ1(R), 2(R), A1, I, W2, S(R), E. 2011: A1, NZ1, [Fj(R), N(R).]. 2012: E1(R), 2(R), 3(R), Arg1(R), 2(R), A1, NZ1, A2, NZ2, I, S, E4. 2013: It(R), S, Sam, Arg1, Arg2, A1, NZ1NZ2(R), W(R), S(R), F. 2014: W1(R), W2(R), Arg1, Arg2, A2, NZ2.*
164 **Pienaar, TB** (Theo) b 23/11/1888 d 14/11/1960 - WP - No Tests - 10 matches (-) *Toured A & NZ. 1921.*
506 **Pienaar, ZMJ** (Gysie) b 21/12/1954 - OFS - 13 Tests (14 - 2T, 2P) 21 matches (59 - 6T, 10C, 4P, 1D) *1980: S.Am2(R), BI1, 2, 3, 4, S.Am3, 4, F. 1981: I1, 2, NZ1, 2, 3.*
793 **Pieterse, BH** (Barend) b 23/01/1979 - FS - No Tests (-) 1 match (5 - 1T) *Toured I & E. 2007.*
775 **Pietersen, J-PR** (JP) b 12/07/1986 - KZN - 59 Tests (90 - 18T) 61 matches (90 - 18T) *2006: A3 2006: tour of UK - no tests. . 2007: Sm1, A1, NZ1, A2, NZ2, N, S, [Sm, E3, T, US(R), Fiji, Arg, E4.], W. 2008: NZ2, A1, Arg, NZ3, A2, W3, S, E. 2009: BI1, 2, NZ1, 2, A1, 2, F, It, I. 2010: NZ3, A2, 3. 2011: A2, NZ2, [W, Fj, Sm, A3.]. 2012: E1, 2, 3, I, S, E4. 2013: W, S, F. 2014: W1, W2, S, A2(R), NZ2(R), I(R), E, It.*
421 **Pitzer, G** (Gys) b 08/07/1939 - NTvl - 12 Tests (-) 16 matches (-) *1967: F1, 2, 3, 4. 1968: BI1, 2, 3, 4, F1, 2. 1969: A3, 4. 1969-70: tour to UK - no tests.*
857 **Pollard, H** (Handre) b 11/03/1994 - BB - 9 Tests (65 -2T, 14C, 8P, 1D) 9 matches (65 - 2T, 14C, 8P, 1D) *2014: S, Arg1, Arg2, NZ1, A2, NZ2, I, It(R), W3(R).*
461 **Pope, CF** (Chris) b 30/09/1952 - WP - 9 Tests (4 - 1T) 13 matches (4 - 1T) *1974: BI1, 2, 3, 4. 1974: tour of F - no tests. 1975: F1, 2. 1976:*

NZ2, 3, 4.
812 **Potgieter, DJ** (Dewald) b 22/02/1987 - BB - 6 Tests (5 - 1T) 8 matches (5 - 1T) *2009: I(t). 2010: W1, F(R), It1, 2(R), A1(R).*
200 **Potgieter, HJ** (Hennie) b 24/10/1903 d 11/11/1957 - OFS - 2 Tests (-) 2 matches (-) *1928: NZ1, 2.*
493 **Potgieter, HL** (Hermanus) b 11/01/1953 - OFS - 1 Test (4 - 1T) 1 match (4 - 1T) *1977: WT.*
435 **Potgieter, R** (Ronnie) b 18/11/1943 - NTvl - No Tests - 6 matches (-) *Toured BI & I. 1969/70.*
834 **Potgieter, UJ** (Jacques) b 24/04/1986 - BB - 3 Tests (-) 3 matches (-) *2012: E3, Arg1(R), 2.*
531 **Povey, SA** (Shaun) b 09/08/1954 - WP - No Tests - 2 matches (-) *Toured NZ & USA. 1981.*
52 **Powell, AW** (Bertie) b 18/07/1873 d 11/09/1948 - GW - 1 Test (-) 1 match (-) *1896: BI3.*
17 **Powell, JM** (Jackie) b 12/12/1871 d 19/12/1955 - GW - 4 Tests (-) 4 matches (-) *1891: BI2. 1896: BI3. 1903: BI1, 2*.*
504 **Prentis, RB** (Richard) b 27/02/1947 - Tvl - 11 Tests (-) 14 matches (-) *1980: S.Am1, 2, BI1, 2, 3, 4, S.Am3, 4, F. 1981: I1, 2.*
723 **Pretorius, AS** (André) b 29/12/1978 - GL - 31 Tests (171 - 2T, 31C, 25P, 8D) 33 matches (174 - 2T, 31C, 26P, 8D) *2002: W1, 2, Arg, Sm, NZ1, A1, NZ2, F, S(R), E. 2003: NZ1(R), A2. 2005: A2, 3, NZ1, A4, NZ2, Arg. 2006: NZ2(R), 3, A3, I, E1(t+R), 2. 2007: S(R), [Sm(R), E3(R), T, US(R), Arg(R).], W.*
782 **Pretorius, JC** (Jaco) b 10/12/1979 - GL - 2 Tests (-) 3 matches (-) *2006: I. 2007: NZ2.*
198 **Pretorius, NF** (Nick) b 10/12/1904 d 19/02/1990 - Tvl - 4 Tests (-) 4 matches (-) *1928: NZ1, 2, 3, 4.*
577 **Pretorius, PIL** (Piet) b 17/08/1964 - NTvl - No Tests - 6 matches (-) *Toured F & E. 1992.*
392 **Prinsloo, J** (Poens) b 11/10/1935 - NTvl - 1 Test (-) 1 match (-) *1963: A3.*
338 **Prinsloo, JC** (Jan) b 28/01/1935 d 28/07/1966 - Tvl - 2 Tests (-) 2 matches (-) *1958: F1, 2.*
192 **Prinsloo, JP** (Boet) b 14/10/1905 d 04/10/1968 - Tvl - 1 Test (-) 1 match (-) *1928: NZ1.*
622 **Putt, KB** (Kevin) b 28/07/1965 - Natal - No Tests - 11 matches (15 - 3T) *Toured W, S & I. 1994 and Arg, F & W. 1996.*
386 **Putter, DJ** (Dick) b 13/02/1937 d 31/10/2002 - WTvl - 3 Tests (-) 3 matches (-) *1963: A1, 2, 4.*
71 **Raaff, JWE** (Klondyke) b 10/03/1879 d

SPRINGBOKS

13/07/1949 - GW - 6 Tests (3 - 1T) 20 matches (12 - 4T) *1903: BI1, 2. 1906: S, W, E. 1910: BI1.*

776 **Ralepelle, MC** (Chiliboy) b 11/09/1986 - BB - 22 Tests (5 - 1T) 24 matches (5 - 1T) *2006: NZ2(R), E2(R). 2008: E(t+R). 2009: BI3, NZ1(R), 2(R), A2(R), NZ3(R). 2009: tour of UK - no tests. 2010: W1(R), F(R), It1, 2(R), NZ1(R), 2(R), A1(R), 2(R), 3(R), W2(R). 2011: A1(R), NZ1(R), [N(R).]. 2012: tour of UK - no tests. 2013: It(R).*

488 **Ras, WJ de W** (De Wet) b 28/01/1954 - OFS - 2 Tests (-) 5 matches (69 - 4T, 25C, 1P) 1976: NZ1(R). *1980: S.Am2(R). 1980: tour of S.Am - no tests.*

813 **Raubenheimer, D** (Davon) b 16/07/1984 - GW - No Tests - 2 matches (-) *Toured F, It, I & E. 2009.*

728 **Rautenbach, SJ** (Faan) b 22/02/1976 - WP - 14 Tests (5 - 1T) 14 matches (5 - 1T) *2002: W1(R), 2(t+R), Arg(R), Sm, NZ1(R), A1, NZ2(R), A2(R). 2003: [U(R), G, Sm, NZ3]. 2004: W1, NZ1(R).*

866 **Redelinghuys, J** (Julian) b 11/09/1989 - GL - 2 Tests (-) 2 matches (-) *2014: It(R), W3(R),*

569 **Reece-Edwards, HM** (Hugh) b 05/01/1961 - Natal - 3 Tests (-) 12 matches (103 - 3T, 23C, 14P) *1992: F1, 2. 1993: A2.*

87 **Reid, A** (Oupa) b 23/11/1878 d 18/05/1952 - WP - 1 Test (3 - 1T) 1 match (3 - 1T) *1903: BI3.*

242 **Reid, BC** (Bunny) b 12/07/1910 d 11/09/1976 - Border - 1 Test (-) 1 match (-) *1933: A4.*

107 **Reid, HG** (Bert) b 19/12/1881 - d 30/05/1944 - Tvl - No Tests - 14 matches (6 - 2T) *Toured BI, I & F. 1906/07.*

542 **Reinach, J** (Jaco) b 01/01/1962 d 21/01/1997 - OFS - 4 Tests (8 - 2T) 4 matches (8 - 2T) *1986: NZC1, 2, 3, 4.*

864 **Reinach, JM** (Cobus) b 07/02/1990 - KZN - 6 Tests (10-2T) 6 matches (10-2T) *2014: A2(R), NZ2(R), I(R), E, It.W3.*

310 **Rens, IJ** (Natie) b 19/07/1929 d 19/12/1989 - Tvl - 2 Tests (19 - 5C, 2P, 1D) 2 matches (19 - 5C, 2P, 1D) *1953: A3, 4.*

320 **Retief, DF** (Daan) b 28/06/1925 d 22/09/2010 - NTvl - 9 Tests (12 - 4T) 21 matches (36 - 12T) *1955: BI1, 2, 4. 1956: A1, 2, NZ1, 2, 3, 4.*

129 **Reyneke, HJ** (Koot) b 19/01/1882 d 22/03/1970 - WP - 1 Test (3 - 1T) 1 match (3 - 1T) *1910: BI3.*

845 **Rhule, RK** (Raymond) b 06/11/1992 - FS - No Tests - No matches *Toured I, S & E. 2012.*

6 **Richards, AR** (Alf) b 14/12/1867 d 09/01/1904 - WP - 3 Tests (-) 3 matches (-) *1891: BI1, 2, 3*.*

580 **Richter, AJ** (Adriaan) b 10/05/1966 - NTvl - 10 Tests (20 - 4T) 29 matches (55 - 11T) *1992: F1, 2, E. 1993: tour of A - no tests. 1994: E2, NZ1, 2, 3. 1995: [R*, C, WS2(R)].*

388 **Riley, NM** (Norman) b 25/02/1939 - ETvl - 1 Test (-) 1 match (-) *1963: A3.*

117 **Riordan, CA** (Cliff) b 24/12/1885 d 07/02/1958 - Tvl - 2 Tests (-) 2 matches (-) *1910: BI1, 2.*

573 **Roberts, H** (Harry) b 03/12/1960 - Tvl - No Tests - 6 matches (5 - 1T) *Toured F & E. 1992.*

480 **Robertson, IW** (Ian) b 28/04/1950 - Rhodesia - 5 Tests (3 - 1D) 10 matches (21 - 3T, 1P, 2D) *1974: F1, 2. 1976: NZ1, 2, 4.*

554 **Rodgers, PH** (Heinrich) b 23/06/1962 - NTvl - 5 Tests (-) 12 matches (-) *1989: WT1, 2. 1992: NZ, F1, 2.*

534 **Rogers, CD** (Chris) b 10/10/1956 - Tvl - 4 Tests (-) 4 matches (-) *1984: E1, 2, S.Am&Sp1, 2.*

126 **Roos, GD** (Gideon) b 20/07/1890 d 08/03/1920 - WP - 2 Tests (3 - 1T) 2 matches (3 - 1T) *1910: BI2, 3.*

88 **Roos, PJ** (Paul) b 30/10/1880 d 22/09/1948 - WP - 4 Tests (-) 22 matches (5 - 1T, 1C) *1903: BI3. 1906: I*, W*, E*.*

802 **Rose, EE** (Earl) b 12/01/1984 - GL - No Tests - 2 matches (-) *Toured BI, 2008 and E, F, It & I, 2009.*

322 **Rosenberg, W** (Wilf) b 18/06/1934 - Tvl - 5 Tests (6 - 2T) 9 matches (6 - 2T) *1955: BI2, 3, 4. 1956: NZ3. 1958: F1.*

699 **Rossouw, C** (Chris) b 14/11/1976 - WP - No Tests - 4 matches (-) *Toured Arg, I, W & E. 2000.*

624 **Rossouw, C le C** (Chris) b 14/09/1969 - Tvl - 9 Tests (10 - 2T) 10 matches (10 - 2T) *1995: WS1, [R, WS2, F, NZ]. 1999: NZ2(R), A2(R), [Sp, NZ3(R)].*

309 **Rossouw, DH** (Daantjie) b 05/09/1930 d 28/01/2010 - WP - 2 Tests (3 - 1T) 2 matches (3 - 1T) *1953: A3, 4.*

755 **Rossouw, DJ** (Danie) b 05/06/1978 - BB - 63 Tests (50 - 10T) 67 matches (55 - 11T) *2003: [U, G, Sm(R), NZ3]. 2004: E(R), S, Arg. 2005: U, F1, 2, A1, W(R), F3(R). 2006: S1, 2, F, A1, I, E1, 2. 2007: E1, Sm1, A1(R), NZ1, S, [Sm, E3, T, Fiji, Arg, E4.]. 2008: W1(t+R), NZ3(R), A3(R), S(R), E. 2009: BI1(R), 2(R), NZ1(R), 2(R), A1(R), 3(R), NZ3(R), F(R), It, I. 2010: W1, F, NZ1(R), 2, A1, NZ3(t+R), A2(R), 3. 2011: A1, NZ1, A2, NZ2(t+R), [W, Fj, N, Sm, A3.].*

SPRINGBOKS

578 **Rossouw, PB** (Botha) b 03/11/1969 - WTvl - No Tests - 2 matches (5 - 1T) *Toured F & E. 1992.*

652 **Rossouw, PWG** (Pieter) b 03/12/1971 - WP - 43 Tests (105 - 21T) 43 matches,(105 - 21T) *1997: BI2, 3, NZ1, A1, NZ2(R), A2(R), It, F1, 2, E, S. 1998: I1, 2, W1, E1, A1, NZ1, 2, A2, W2, S, I3, E2. 1999: It1, W, NZ1, A1(R), NZ2, A2, [S, U, E, A3]. 2000: C, E1, 2, A2, Arg(R), I, W. 2001: F3, US. 2003: Arg.*

206 **Rousseau, WP** (Willie) b 11/08/1906 d 28/12/1996 - WP - 2 Tests (-) 2 matches (-) *1928: NZ3, 4.*

367 **Roux, F du T** (Mannetjies) b 12/04/1939 - WP - 27 Tests (18 - 6T) 56 matches (39 - 13T) *1960: W. 1961: A1, 2. 1962: BI1, 2, 3, 4. 1963: A2. 1965: A1, 2, NZ1, 2, 3, 4. 1968: BI3, 4, F1, 2. 1969: A1, 2, 3, 4. 1970: I, NZ1, 2, 3, 4.*

607 **Roux, JP** (Johan) b 25/02/1969 - Tvl - 12 Tests (10 - 2T) 17 matches (20 - 4T) *1994: E2, NZ1, 2, 3, Arg1. 1995: [R, C, F(R)]. 1996: A1(R), NZ1, A2, NZ3.*

426 **Roux, OA** (Tonie) b 22/02/1947 - NTvl - 7 Tests (-) 31 matches (15 - 4T, 1D) *1968: tour of F – no tests. 1969: S, E. 1970: I, W. 1971: tour of A – no tests. 1972: E. 1974: BI3, 4.*

737 **Roux, WG** (Wessel) b 01/10/1976 - Blue Bulls - 3 Tests (-) 3 matches (-) *2002: F(R), S, E.*

727 **Russell, RB** (Brent) b 05/03/1980 - Mpu - 23 Tests (40 - 8T) 23 matches (40 - 8T) *2002: W1(R), 2, Arg, A1(R), NZ2(R), A2, F, E(R). 2003: Arg(R), A1(R), NZ1, A2(R). 2004 :I2(t+R), W1, NZ1(R), W2(R), Arg(R). 2005: U(R), F2(R), A1(t), Arg(R), W(R). 2006: F.*

44 **Samuels, TA** (Theo) b 21/07/1873 d 16/11/1896 - GW - 3 Tests (6 - 2T) 3 matches (6 - 2T) *1896: BI2, 3, 4.*

666 **Santon, D** (Dale) b 18/08/1969 - Boland - 4 Tests (-) 5 matches (-) *1997: tour of It, F, E & S – no tests. 2003: A1(R), NZ1(R), A2(t), [G(R)].*

449 **Sauermann, JT** (Theo) b 16/11/1944 d 13/06/2014 - Tvl - 5 Tests (-) 11 matches (-) *1971: F1, 2, A1. 1972: E. 1974: BI1.*

290 **Saunders, MJ** (Cowboy) b 26/11/1927 d 17/05/2006 - Border - No Tests - 14 matches (33 - 11T) *Toured BI, I & F. 1951/52.*

472 **Schlebusch, JJJ** (Jan) b 05/05/1949 - OFS - 3 Tests (-) 3 matches (-) *1974: BI3, 4. 1975: F2.*

346 **Schmidt, LU** (Louis) b 06/02/1936 d 23/01/1999 - NTvl - 2 Tests (-) 2 matches (-) *1958: F2. 1962: BI2.*

544 **Schmidt, UL** (Uli) b 10/07/1961 - NTvl - 17 Tests (9 - 2T) 25 matches (29 - 6T) *1986: NZC1, 2, 3, 4. 1989: WT1, 2. 1992: NZ, A. 1993: F1, 2, A1, 2, 3. 1994: Arg1, 2, S, W.*

391 **Schoeman, J** (Haas) b 15/03/1940 d 01/01/2006 - WP - 7 Tests (-) 23 matches (15 - 5T) *1963: A3, 4. 1965: I, S, A1, NZ1, 2.*

618 **Scholtz, CP** (Christiaan) b 22/10/1970 - Tvl - 4 Tests (-) 4 matches (-) *1994: Arg1. 1995: [R, C, WS2].*

732 **Scholtz, H** (Hendro) b 22/03/1979 - FS - 5 Tests (5 - 1T) 5 matches (5 - 1T) *2002: A1(R), NZ2(R), A2(R). 2003: [U(R), G].*

177 **Scholtz, H** (Tokkie) b 29/08/1892 d 08/04/1959 - WP - 2 Tests (-) 15 matches (-) *1921: NZ1, 2.*

582 **Schutte, PJW** (Phillip) b 07/10/1969 - NTvl - 2 Tests (-) 8 matches (-) *1992: tour of F & E – no tests. 1994: S, W.*

36 **Scott, PA** (Paul) b 26/10/1872 d (unknown) - Tvl - 4 Tests (-) 4 matches (-) *1896: BI1, 2, 3, 4.*

156 **Sendin, WD** (Billy) b 04/10/1895 d 16/07/1977 - GW - 1 Test (3 - 1T) 9 matches (18 - 6T) *1921: NZ2.*

702 **Sephaka, LD** (Lawrence) b 08/08/1978 - GF - 24 Tests (-) 29 matches (-) *2000: tour of Arg & UK – no tests. 2001: US. 2002: Sm, NZ1, A1, NZ2, A2, F. 2003: S1, 2, A1, NZ1, A2(t+R), NZ2, [U, E(t+R), G]. 2005: F2, A1, 2(R), W. 2006: S1(R), NZ3(t+R), A3(R), I.*

508 **Serfontein, DJ** (Divan) b 03/08/1954 - WP - 19 Tests (12 - 3T) 26 matches (16 - 4T) *1980: BI1, 2, 3, 4, S.Am3, 4, F. 1981: I1, 2, NZ1, 2, 3, US. 1982: S.Am1, 2. 1984: E1, 2, S.Am&Sp1*, 2*.*

849 **Serfontein, JL** (Jan) b 15/04/1992 - Blue Bulls - 20 Tests (10 - 2T) 20 matches (10 - 2T) *2013: It(R), S(R), Sam(R)Arg1(R), Arg2(R), A1(R), NZ1(R), A2(R), NZ2(R). 2014: W1, W2, S, A1, NZ1, A2, NZ2, I, E, It, W3.*

19 **Shand, R** (Bob) b 27/08/1866 d 01/03/1934 - GW - 2 Tests (-) 2 matches (-) *1891: BI2, 3.*

613 **Sherrell, LR** (Lance) b 09/02/1966 - NTvl - No Tests - 6 matches (31 - 3T, 5C, 2P) *Toured NZ. 1994.*

257 **Sherriff, AR** (Roger) b 17/03/1913 d 04/12/1951 - Tvl - 3 Tests (-) 6 matches (3 - 1T) *1927: tour of A & NZ – no tests. 1938: BI1, 2, 3.*

761 **Shimange, MH** (Hanyani) b 17/04/1978 - FS - 9 Tests (-) 9 matches (-) *2004: W1(R), NZ2(R), A2(R), W2(R). 2005: U(R), A1(R), 2(R), Arg(R). 2006: S1(R).*

140 **Shum, EH** (Baby) b 17/08/1886 d 27/06/1952 - Tvl - 1 Test (-) 15 matches (6 - 2T) *1913: E.*

175 **Siedle, LB** (Jack) b 01/07/1891 d 07/11/1962 - Natal - No Tests - 1 match (-) *Toured A & NZ. 1921.*

292 **Sinclair, DJ** (Des) b 14/07/1927 d 29/04/1996 - Tvl - 4 Tests (-) 17 matches (15 - 5T) *1951-52: tour of UK - no tests. 1955: BI1, 2, 3, 4.*

70 **Sinclair, JH** (Jimmy) b 16/10/1876 d 23/02/1913 - Tvl - 1 Test (-) 1 match (-) *1903: BI1.*

343 **Skene, AL** (Alan) b 02/10/1932 d 13/08/2001 - WP - 1 Test (-) 1 match (-) *1958: F2.*

659 **Skinstad, RB** (Bob) b 03/07/1976 - WP - 42 Tests (55 - 11T) 47 matches (70 - 14T) *1997: E(t). 1998: W1(R), E1(t), NZ1(R), 2(R), A2(R), W2(R), S, I3, E2. 1999: [S, Sp(R), U, E, A3]. 2001: F1(R), 2(R), It1*, NZ1*, A1*, 2*, NZ2*, F3*, It2*, E*. 2002: W1*, 2*, Arg, Sm, NZ1, A1, NZ2, A2. 2003: Arg(R). 2007: E2(t+R), Sm1, NZ1, A2*[E3(R), T*, US(R), Arg(R).].*

416 **Slabber, LJ** (Louis) b 05/03/1935 d 11/05/2003 - OFS - No Tests - 7 matches (9 - 3T) *Toured A & NZ. 1965.*

188 **Slater, JT** (Jack) b 16/04/1901 d 16/02/1986 - EP - 3 Tests (6 - 2T) 3 matches (6 - 2T) *1924:BI3, 4. 1928: NZ1.*

546 **Smal, GP** (Gert) b 27/12/1961 - WP - 6 Tests (4 - 1T) 6 matches (4 - 1T) *1986: NZC1, 2, 3, 4. 1989: WT1, 2.*

561 **Small, JT** (James) b 10/02/1969 - Tvl - 47 Tests (100 - 20T) 60 matches (135 - 27T) *1992: NZ, A, F1, 2, E. 1993: F1, 2, A1, 2, 3, Arg1, 2. 1994: E1, 2, NZ1, 2, 3(t), Arg1. 1995: WS1, [A, R, F, NZ], W, It, E(R). 1996: Fj, A1, NZ1, A2, NZ2, Arg1, 2, F1, 2, W. 1997: T, BI1, NZ1(R), A1(R), NZ2, A2, It, F1, 2, E, S.*

583 **Smit, FC** (FC) b 13/08/1966 - WP - 1 Test (-) 4 matches (-) *1992: E.*

691 **Smit, JW** (John) b 03/04/1978 - Natal - 111 Tests (40 - 8T) 112 matches (40 - 8T) *2000: C(t), A1(R), NZ1(t+R), A2(R), NZ2(R), A3(R), Arg, I, W, E3. 2001: F1, 2, It1, NZ1(R), A1(R), 2(R), NZ2(R), F3(R), It2, E, US(R). 2003: [U(R), E(t+R), G*, Sm, NZ3]. 2004: I1*, 2*, W1*, PI*, NZ1*, A1*, NZ2*, A2*, W2*, I3*, E*, S*, Arg*. 2005: U*, F1*, 2*, A1*, 2*, 3*, NZ1*, A4*, NZ2*, Arg*, W*, F3*. 2006: S1*, 2*, F*, A1*, NZ1*, A2*, NZ2*, 3*, A3*, I*, E1*, 2*. 2007: E1*, 2*, Sm1*, A1*, [Sm*, E3*, T(R), US*, Fiji*, Arg*, E4*.], W*. 2008: W1*, 2*, NZ1*, W3*, S*, E*. 2009: BI1*, 2*, 3*, NZ1*, 2*, A1*, A2*, A3*, NZ3*, F*, It*, I*. 2010: W1*, F*, It2*, NZ1*, 2*, A1*, NZ3*, A2*, 3*. 2011: A1*, NZ1*, A2*, NZ2(R), [W*, Fj*, N*, Sm(R), A3*.].*

660 **Smit, PL** (Philip) b 27/07/1973 - GW - No Tests - 5 matches (-) *Toured It, F, E & S. 1997 and BI & I. 1998.*

389 **Smith, CM** (Nelie) b 08/05/1934 - OFS - 7 Tests (12 - 1T, 3P) 19 matches (21 - 4T, 3P) *1963: A3, 4. 1964: W, F*. 1965: A1*, 2*, NZ2*.*

23 **Smith, CW** (Toski) b 09/04/1871 d 28/02/1934 - GW - 3 Tests (-) 3 matches (-) *1891: BI2. 1896: BI2, 3.*

507 **Smith, DJ** (David) b 09/11/1957 - Zimbabwe - 4 Tests (-) 4 matches (-) *1980: BI1, 2, 3, 4.*

21 **Smith, DW** (Dan) b 08/04/1869 d 27/02/1926 - GW - 1 Test (-) 1 match (-) *1891: BI2.*

262 **Smith, GAC** (George) b 31/08/1916 d 23/03/1978 - EP - 1 Test (-) 1 match (-) *1938: BI3.*

746 **Smith, JH** (Juan) b 30/07/1981 - FS - 70 Tests (60 - 12T) 72 matches (60 - 12T) *2003: S1(R), 2(R), A1, NZ1, A2, NZ2, [U, E, Sm, NZ3]. 2004: W2. 2005: U(R), F2(R), A2, 3, NZ1, A4, NZ2, Arg, W, F3. 2006: S1, 2, F, A1, NZ1, A2, I, E2. 2007: E1, 2, A1, N, S, [Sm, E3, T(R), US, Fiji, Arg, E4.], W. 2008: W1, 2, It, NZ1, 2, A1, Arg, NZ3, A2, 3, W3, S. 2009: BI1, 2, 3, NZ1, 2, A1, 2, 3. 2010: NZ3, A2, 3, I, W2, S, E. 2014: Arg2.*

643 **Smith, PF** (Franco) b 29/07/1972 - GW - 9 Tests (23 - 2T, 2C, 3P) 18 matches (85 - 5T, 21C, 6P) *1996: tour of Arg, F & W - no tests. 1997: S(R). 1998: I1(t), 2, W1, NZ1(R), 2(R), A2(R), W2. 1999: NZ2.*

241 **Smollan, FC** (Fred) b 20/08/1908 d 02/08/1998 - Tvl - 3 Tests (-) 3 matches (-) *1933: A3, 4, 5.*

18 **Snedden, RCD** (Bob) b 20/03/1867 d 03/04/1931 - GW - 1 Test (-) 1 match (-) *1891: BI2*.*

636 **Snyman, AH** (André) b 02/02/1974 - NTvl - 38 Tests (50 - 10T) 42 matches (60 - 12T) *1996: NZ3, 4, Arg2(R), W(R). 1997: T, BI1, 2, 3, NZ1, A1, NZ2, A2, It, F1, 2, E, S. 1998: I1, 2, W1, E1, A1, NZ1, 2, A2, W2, S, I3, E2. 1999: NZ2. 2001: NZ2, F3, US. 2002: W1. 2003: S1, NZ1. 2006: S1, 2.*

453 **Snyman, DSL** (Dawie) b 05/07/1949 - WP - 10 Tests (24 - 1T, 1C, 4P, 2D) 22 matches (86 - 7T, 13C, 8P, 4D) *1971: tour of A - no tests. 1972: E. 1974: BI1, 2(R), F1, 2. 1975: F1, 2. 1976: NZ2, 3. 1977: WT.*

466 **Snyman, JCP** (Jackie) b 14/04/1948 - OFS - 3 Tests (18 - 6P) 7 matches (29 - 4C, 6P, 1D) *1974: BI2, 3, 4. 1974: tour of F - no tests.*

473 **Sonnekus, GHH** (Gerrie) b 01/02/1953 -

OFS - 3 Tests (4 - 1T) 3 matches (4 - 1T) *1974: BI3. 1984: E1, 2.*

731 **Sowerby, RS** (Shaun) b 01/07/1978 - Natal - 1 Test (-) 1 match (-) *2002: Sm(R).*

446 **Spies, JJ** (Johan) b 08/05/1945 - NTvl - 4 Tests (-) 11 matches (-) *1970: NZ1, 2, 3, 4. 1971: tour of A - no tests.*

777 **Spies, PJ** (Pierre) b 08/06/1985 - BB - 53 Tests (35 - 7T) 53 matches (35 - 7T) *2006: A1, NZ2, 3, A3, I, E1. 2007: E1(R), 2, A1. 2008: W1, 2, A1, Arg, NZ3, A2, 3, W3, S, E. 2009: BI1, 2, 3(R), NZ1, 2, A1, 2, 3, NZ3. 2010: F, It1, 2, NZ1, 2, A1, NZ3, A2, 3, I, W2, E. 2011: A2, NZ2, [W, Fj, N, Sm, A3.]. 2012: E1, 2, 3. 2013: It, S, Sam.*

479 **Stander, JCJ** (Rampie) b 25/12/1944 d 28/08/1980 - OFS - 5 Tests (-) 8 matches (4 - 1T) *1974: BI4(R). 1974: tour of F - no tests. 1976: NZ1, 2, 3, 4.*

482 **Stapelberg, WP** (Willem) b 29/01/1947 - NTvl - 2 Tests (8 - 2T) 6 matches (12 - 3T) *1974: F1, 2.*

336 **Starke, JJ** (James) b 16/05/1931 - WP - 1 Test (-) 8 matches (3 - 1T) *1956: NZ4.*

180 **Starke, KT** (Kenny) b 18/06/1900 d 03/01/1982 - WP - 4 Tests (13 - 3T, 1D) 4 matches (13 - 3T, 1D) *1924: BI1, 2, 3, 4.*

342 **Steenekamp, J** (Johan) b 02/09/1935 d 16/08/2007 - Tvl - 1 Test (-) 1 match (-) *1958: F1.*

764 **Steenkamp, GG** (Gurthro) b 12/06/1981 - FS - 53 Tests (30 - 6T) 55 matches (30 - 6T) *2004: S, Arg. 2005: U, F2(R), A2, 3, NZ1(R), A4(R). 2007: E1(R), 2, A1, [T, Fiji(R).]. 2008: W1, 2(R), NZ1, 2, A1, W3(R), S(R). 2009: BI1(R), 3(R). 2009: tour of UK - no tests. 2010: F, It1, 2, NZ1, 2, A1, NZ3, A2, 3. 2011: A2(R), NZ2, [W(R), Fj, N, Sm(R), A3.]. 2012: S, E4. 2013: Arg1(R), Arg2(R), A1(R), NZ1(R), A2(R), NZ2(R), W(R), S, F(R). 2014: W1, W2(R), Arg2, It(R).*

93 **Stegmann, AC** (Anton) b 25/08/1883 d 23/01/1972 - WP - 2 Tests (3 - 1T) 16 matches (54 - 18T) *1906: S, I.*

825 **Stegmann, GJ** (Deon) b 22/03/1986 - BB - 6 Tests (-) 6 matches (-) *2010: I, W2, S, E. 2011: A1, NZ1.*

132 **Stegmann, JA** (Jan) b 21/06/1887 d 07/12/1984 - Tvl - 5 Tests (15 - 5T) 16 matches (39 - 13T) *1912: S, I, W. 1913: E, F.*

350 **Stewart, DA** (Dave) b 14/07/1935 - WP - 11 Tests (9 - 1T, 2P) 30 matches (25 - 5T, 2C, 2P) *1960: S. 1961: E, S, F, I. 1963: A1, 3, 4. 1964: W, F. 1965: I.*

678 **Stewart, JC** (Christian) b 17/10/1966 - WP - 3 Tests (-) 5 matches (-) *1998: S, I3, E2.*

783 **Steyn, FPL** (Francois) b 14/05/1987 - KZN - 53 Tests (132 - 10T, 5C, 21P, 3D) 55 matches (141 - 10T, 8C, 22P, 3D) *2006: I, E1, 2. 2007: E1(R), 2(R), Sm1, A1(R), NZ1(R), S, [Sm(R), E3, T(R), US, Fiji, Arg, E4.], W. 2008: W2(R), It, NZ1(R), 2(R), A1NZ3(R), A2(R), W3(R), S(R), E(R). 2009: BI1, 2, 3(R), NZ1, 2, A1, 2(R), 3(R), NZ3. 2010: W1, A2, 3, W2, S, E. 2011: A2, [W, Fj, N, Sm.]. 2012: E1, 2, Arg1, 2, A1, NZ1.*

803 **Steyn, M** (Morné) b 11/07/1984 - BB - 59 Tests (688 - 8T, 99C, 142P, 8D) 59 matches (688 - 8T, 99C, 142P, 8D) *2009: BI1(t+R), 2(R), 3, NZ1(R), 2, A1, 2, 3, NZ3, F, It, I. 2010: F, It1, 2, NZ1, 2, A1, NZ3, A2, 3, I, W2, S, E. 2011: A1, NZ1, A2(R), NZ2, [W, Fj, N, Sm, A3.]. 2012: E1, 2, 3, Arg1, A1, NZ1, S(R). 2013: It, S, Sam, Arg1, Arg2, A1, NZ1, A2, NZ2, W, S(R), F. 2014: W1, W2, Arg1(R), Arg2(R), A1.*

489 **Stofberg, MTS** (Theuns) b 06/06/1955 - OFS - 21 Tests (24 - 6T) 29 matches (36 - 9T) *1976: NZ2, 3. 1977: WT. 1980: S.Am1, 2, BI1, 2, 3, 4, S.Am3*, 4, F. 1981: I1, 2, NZ1*, 2, US. 1982: S.Am1, 2. 1984: E1*, 2*.*

224 **Strachan, LC** (Louis) b 12/09/1907 d 04/03/1985 - Tvl - 10 Tests (-) 38 matches (18 - 6T) *1932: E, S. 1937: A1, 2, NZ1, 2, 3. 1938: BI1, 2, 3.*

616 **Straeuli, RAW** (Rudolf) b 20/08/1963 - Tvl - 10 Tests (20 - 4T) 23 matches (45 - 9T) *1994: NZ1, Arg1, 2, S, W. 1995: WS1, [A, WS2, NZ(R)], E(R).*

592 **Stransky, JT** (Joel) b 16/07/1967 - Natal - 22 Tests (240 - 6T, 30C, 47P, 3D) 36 matches (329 - 9T, 55C, 55P, 3D) *1993: A1, 2, 3, Arg1. 1994: Arg1, 2. 1994: tour of W & S - no tests. 1995: WS1, [A, R(t), C, F, NZ], W, It, E. 1996: Fj(R), NZ1, A2, NZ2, 3, 4, 5(R).*

827 **Strauss, AJ** (Andries) b 05/03/1984 - FS - No Tests - 1 match (-) *Toured BI & I. 2010.*

579 **Strauss, CP** (Tiaan) b 28/06/1965 - WP - 15 Tests (20 - 4T) 37 matches (55 - 11T) *1992: F1, 2, E. 1993: F1, 2, A1, 2, 3, Arg1, 2. 1994: E1, NZ1*, 2, Arg1, 2. 1994: tour of W & S - no tests.*

539 **Strauss, JA** (Attie) b 02/09/1959 - WP - 2 Tests (-) 2 matches (-) *1984: S.Am&Sp1, 2.*

800 **Strauss, JA** (Adriaan) b 18/11/1985 - FS - 44 Tests (25 - 5T) 46 matches (25 - 5T) *2008: A1(R), Arg(R), NZ3(R), A2(R), 3(R). 2009: F(R), It. 2010: S(R), E(R). 2012: E1(R), 2(R), 3(R), Arg1(R), 2, A1, NZ1, A2, NZ2, I, S, E4. 2013: It, S, Sam, Arg1, Arg2, A1(R), NZ1(R), A2, NZ2(R), W(R), S, F(R). 2014: S(R), Arg1(R), Arg2(R), A1, NZ1, A2, NZ2(R), I(R), E, It, W3(R).*

490 **Strauss, JHP** (Johan) b 27/09/1951 - Tvl - 3 Tests (-) 3 matches (-) *1976: NZ3, 4. 1980: S.Am1.*

158 **Strauss, SSF** (Sarel) b 24/11/1891 d 06/02/1946 - GW - 1 Test (-) 12 matches (23 - 5T, 2D) *1921: NZ3.*

325 **Strydom, CF** (Popeye) b 20/01/1932 d 31/03/2001 - OFS - 6 Tests (-) 17 matches (3 - 1T) *1955: BI3. 1956: A1, 2, NZ1, 4. 1958: F1.*

586 **Strydom, JJ** (Hannes) b 13/07/1965 - Tvl - 21 Tests (5 - 1T) 31 matches (10 - 2T) *1993: F2, A1, 2, 3, Arg1, 2. 1994: E. 1995: [A, C, F, NZ]. 1996: A2(R), NZ2(R), 3, 4, W(R). 1997: T, BI1, 2, 3, A2.*

276 **Strydom, LJ** (Ou-Boet) b 27/10/1921 d 11/05/2003 - NTvl - 2 Tests (-) 2 matches (-) *1949: NZ1, 2.*

566 **Styger, JJ** (Johan) b 31/01/1962 - OFS - 7 Tests (-) 18 matches (-) *1992: NZ(R), A, F1, 2, E. 1993: F2(R), A3(R).*

403 **Suter, MR** (Snowy) b 14/12/1939 - Natal - 2 Tests (-) 4 matches (3 - 1T) *1965: I, S.*

654 **Swanepoel, W** (Werner) b 15/04/1973 - FS - 20 Tests (25 - 5T) 25 matches (30 - 6T) *1997: BI3(R), A2(R), F1(R), 2, E, S. 1998: I2(R), W1(R), E2(R). 1999: It1, 2(R), W, A1, [Sp, NZ3(t)]. 2000: A1, NZ1, A2, NZ2, A3.*

452 **Swanson, PS** (Peter) b 26/12/1946 d 26/10/2003 - Tvl - No Tests - 4 matches (5 - 1T, 1C) *Toured A. 1971.*

595 **Swart, IS de V** (Balie) b 18/05/1964 - Tvl - 16 Tests (-) 31 matches (-) *1993: A1, 2, 3, Arg1. 1994: E1, 2, NZ1, 3, Arg2(R). 1994: tour of W & S - no tests. 1995: WS1, [A, WS2, F, NZ], W. 1996: A2.*

630 **Swart, J** (Justin) b 23/07/1972 - WP - 10 Tests (5 - 1T) 13 matches (15 - 3T) *1996: Fj, NZ1(R), A2, NZ2, 3, 4, 5. 1997: BI3(R), It, S(R).*

312 **Swart, JJN** (Sias) b 29/07/1934 d 18/01/1993 - SWA - 1 Test (3 - 1T) 1 match (3 - 1T) *1955: BI1.*

43 **Taberer, WS** (Bill) b 11/04/1872 d 10/02/1938 - GW - 1 Test (-) 1 match (-) *1896: BI2.*

842 **Taute, JJ** (Jaco) b 21/03/1991 - GL - 3 Tests (-) 3 matches (-) *2012: A2, NZ2, I.*

380 **Taylor, OB** (Ormy) b 05/06/1937 - Natal - 1 Test (-) 1 match (-) *1962: BI1.*

603 **Teichmann, GH** (Gary) b 09/01/1967 - Natal - 42 Tests (30 - 6T) 52 matches (35 - 7T) *1993: tour of Arg - no tests. 1995: W. 1996: Fj, A1, NZ1, A2, NZ2, 3*, 4*, 5*, Arg1*, 2*, F1*, 2*, W*. 1997: T*, BI1*, 2*, 3*, NZ1*, A1*, NZ2*, A2*, It*, F1*, 2*, E*, S*. 1998: I1*, 2*, W1*, E1*, A1*, NZ1*, 2*, A2*, W2*, S*, I3*, E2*. 1999: It1*, W*, NZ1*.*

668 **Terblanche, CS** (Stefan) b 02/07/1975 - Boland - 37 Tests (95 - 19T) 41 matches (115 - 23T) *1998: I1, 2, W1, E1, A1, NZ1, 2, A2, W2, S, I3, E2. 1999: It1(R), 2, W, A1, NZ2(R), [Sp, E(t), A3(R), NZ3]. 2000: E3. 2002: W1, 2, Arg, Sm, NZ1, A1, 2(R). 2003: S1, 2, Arg, A1, NZ1, A2, NZ2, [G].*

633 **Theron, DF** (Dawie) b 15/09/1966 - GW - 13 Tests (-) 15 matches (-) *1996: A2(R), NZ2(R), 5, Arg1, 2, F1, 2, W. 1997: BI2(R), 3, NZ1(R), A1, NZ2(R).*

749 **Theron, JT** (Gus) b 10/01/1975 - WP - No Tests - No matches *Toured Aus & NZ. 2003.*

56 **Theunissen, DJ** (Danie) b 12/07/1869 d 19/03/1964 - GW - 1 Test (-) 1 match (-) *1896: BI3.*

142 **Thompson, G** (Tommy) b 04/10/1886 d 20/06/1916 - WP - 3 Tests (-) 15 matches (-) *1912: S, I, W.*

648 **Thomson, JRD** (Jeremy) b 24/06/1967 - Natal - No Tests - 4 matches (5 - 1T) *Toured Arg, F & W. 1996.*

161 **Tindall, JC** (Jackie) b 26/03/1900 d 03/05/1946 - WP - 5 Tests (-) 27 matches (3 - 1T) *1921: Tour of A & NZ - no tests. 1924: BI1. 1928: NZ1, 2, 3, 4. 1931-32 tour of UK - no tests.*

515 **Tobias, EG** (Errol) b 18/03/1950 - Boland - 6 Tests (22 - 1T, 3C, 4P) 15 matches (65 - 5T, 15C, 5P) *1980: tour of S.Am - no tests. 1981: I1, 2. 1981: tour of NZ & USA - no tests. 1984: E1, 2, S.Am&Sp1, 2.*

201 **Toe, NS** (Jacko) b 11/03/1904 d 01/05/1965 - Natal - 1 Test (-) 1 match (-) *1928: NZ2.*

163 **Townsend, WH** (Taffy) b 12/03/1896 d 27/01/1943 - Natal - 1 Test (-) 11 matches (3 - 1T) *1921: NZ1.*

20 **Trenery, WE** (Wilfred) b 21/09/1867 d 23/08/1905 - GW - 1 Test (-) 1 match (-) *1891: BI2.*

635 **Tromp, H** (Henry) b 29/12/1966 - NTvl - 4 Tests (-) 8 matches (5 - 1T) *1996: NZ3, 4, Arg2(R), F1(R).*

581 **Truscott, JA** (Andries) b 22/07/1968 - NTvl - No Tests - 4 matches (-) *Toured F & E. 1992.*

187 **Truter, DR** (Pally) b 19/04/1897 d 21/11/1962 - WP - 2 Tests (-) 2 matches (-) *1924: BI2, 4.*

385 **Truter, JT** (Trix) b 05/06/1939 - Natal - 3 Tests (3 - 1T) 16 matches (33 - 11T) *1963: A1. 1964: F. 1965: A2.*

680 **Trytsman, JW** (Johnny) b 29/07/1971 - WP - No Tests - 4 matches (-) *Toured BI & I. 1998.*

232 **Turner, FG** (Freddy) b 18/03/1914 d

SPRINGBOKS

12/09/2003 - EP - 11 Tests (29 - 4T, 4C, 3P) 24 matches (131 - 18T, 26C, 7P, 1D) *1933: A1, 2, 3. 1937: A1, 2, NZ1, 2, 3. 1938: BI1, 2, 3.*

349 **Twigge, RJ** (Robert) b 24/07/1936 - NTvl - 1 Test (-) 1 match (-) *1960: S.*

763 **Tyibilika, S** (Solly) b 23/06/1979 d 13/11/2011 - KZN - 8 Tests (15 - 3T) 8 matches (15 - 3T) *2004: S, Arg. 2005: U, A2, Arg. 2006: NZ1, A2, NZ2.*

315 **Ulyate, CA** (Clive) b 11/12/1933 - Tvl - 7 Tests (6 - 1T, 1D) 16 matches (12 - 2T, 2D) *1955: BI1, 2, 3, 4. 1956: NZ1, 2, 3.*

370 **Uys, P de W** (Piet) b 10/12/1937 d 12/12/2009 - NTvl - 12 Tests (-) 29 matches (12 - 4T) *1960: W. 1961: E, S, I, A1, 2. 1962: BI1, 4. 1963: A1, 2. 1968: tour of F - no tests. 1969: A1(R), 2.*

738 **Uys, PJ** (Pierre) b 05/02/1976 - Mpu - 1 Test (-) 1 match (-) *2002: S.*

525 **Van Aswegen, HJ** (Henning) b 11/02/1955 - WP - 2 Tests (-) 10 matches (-) *1981: NZ1. 1982: S.Am2(R).*

718 **Van Biljon, L** (Lukas) b 16/03/1976 - Natal - 13 Tests (5 - 1T) 13 matches (5 - 1T) *2001: It1(R), NZ1, A1, 2, NZ2, F3, It2(R), E(R), US. 2002: F(R), S, E(R). 2003: NZ2(R).*

59 **Van Broekhuizen, HD** (Broekie) b 17/06/1872 d 04/08/1953 - WP - 1 Test (-) 1 match (-) *1896: BI4.*

2 **Van Buuren, MCWE** (Mosey) b 12/08/1865 d 03/10/1951 - Tvl - 1 Test (-) 1 match (-) *1891: BI1.*

250 **Van de Vyver, DF** (Vandie) b 14/12/1909 d 18/03/1977 - WP - 1 Test (-) 14 matches (12 - 4T) *1937: A2.*

484 **Van den Berg, DS** (Derek) b 02/01/1946 - Natal - 4 Tests (-) 7 matches (-) *1974: tour of F - no tests. 1975: F1, 2. 1976: NZ1, 2.*

258 **Van den Berg, MA** (Mauritz) b 09/05/1909 d 09/04/1948 - WP - 4 Tests (-) 18 matches (15 - 5T) *1937: A1, NZ1, 2, 3.*

684 **Van den Berg, PA** (Albert) b 26/01/1974 - GW - 51 Tests (20 - 4T) 55 matches (30 - 6T) *1999: It1(R), 2, NZ2, A2, [S, U(R), E(R), A3(R), NZ3(R)]. 2000: E1(t+R), A1, NZ1, A2, NZ2(R), A3(t+R), Arg, I, W, E3. 2001: F1(R), 2, A2(R), NZ2(R), US. 2004: NZ1. 2005: U, F1, 2, A1(R), 2(R), 3(R), 4(R), Arg(R), F3(R). 2006: S2(R), A1(R), NZ1, A2(R), NZ2(R), A3(R), I, E1(R), 2(R). 2007: Sm1, A2(R), NZ2, N(t+R), S(R), [T, US.], W(R).*

621 **Van den Bergh, E** (Elandré) b 09/12/1966 - EP - 1 Test (-) 8 matches (5 - 1T) *1994: Arg2(t+R).*

133 **Van der Hoff, AD** (Apie) b 24/09/1888 d 09/03/1970 - Tvl - No Tests - 9 matches (30 - 10T) *Toured BI, I & F. 1912/13.*

629 **Van der Linde, A** (Toks) b 30/12/1969 - WP - 7 Tests (-) 18 matches (10 - 2T) *1995: It, E. 1996: Arg1(R), 2(R), F1(R), W(R). 2001: F3(R).*

741 **Van der Linde, CJ** (CJ) b 27/08/1980 - FS - 75 Tests (20 - 4T) 80 matches (20 - 4T) *2002: S(R), E(R). 2004: I1(R), 2(R), PI(R), A1(R), NZ2(t+R), A2(R), W2(R), I3(R), E(t+R), S, Arg. 2005: U, F1(R), 2, A1(R), 3, NZ1, A4, NZ2, Arg, W, F3. 2006: S2(R), F(R), A1, NZ1, A2, NZ2, I, E1, 2. 2007: E1(R), 2, A1(R), NZ1(R), A2, NZ2, N, S, [Sm, E3(R), T, US(R), Arg, E4.], W. 2008: W1(t+R), It, NZ1, 2, A1, Arg, NZ3, A2. 2009: F(R), I(t). 2010: W1, It1(R), NZ2, A1(t+R), NZ3(R), A2(R), 3(R), I(R), W2(R), S(R), E(R). 2011: A1(t+R), NZ1(R), 2(R), [N.]. 2012: I, S(R).*

323 **Van der Merwe, AJ** (Bertus) b 14/07/1929 d 23/11/1971 - Boland - 12 Tests (-) 26 matches (3 - 1T) *1955: BI2, 3, 4. 1956: A1, 2, NZ1, 2, 3, 4. 1958: F1. 1960: S, NZ2.*

221 **Van der Merwe, AV** (Alvi) b 14/09/1908 d 18/09/1986 - WP - 1 Test (-) 13 matches (6 - 2T) *1931: W.*

273 **Van der Merwe, BS** (Fiks) b 02/01/1917 d 11/07/2005 - NTvl - 1 Test (-) 1 match (-) *1949: NZ1.*

703 **Van der Merwe, CP** (Carel) b 05/10/1971 - Boland - No Tests - 4 matches (-) *Toured Arg, I, W & E. 2000.*

846 **Van der Merwe, F** (Franco) b 15/03/1983 - GL - 1 Test (-) 1 match (-) *2012 - Tour of I, S & E. - no tests. 2013: NZ2(R)*

365 **Van der Merwe, HS** (Stompie) b 24/08/1936 d 04/06/1988 - NTvl - 5 Tests (-) 17 matches (6 - 2T) *1960: NZ4. 1960-61: tour of UK - no tests. 1963: A2, 3, 4. 1964: F.*

790 **Van der Merwe, HS** (Heinke) b 03/05/1985 - GL - 4 Tests (-) 7 matches (-) *2007: W(t+R). 2009: tour of UK - no tests. 2012: I(R), S(R), E4(R).*

433 **Van der Merwe, JP** (JP) b 07/12/1947 - WP - 1 Test (-) 12 matches (9 - 3T) *1970: W.*

858 **Van der Merwe, M** (Marcel) b 24/10/1990 - BB - 5 Tests (-) 5 matches (-) *2014: S(R), A1(R), NZ1(R), A2(R), NZ2(R).*

526 **Van der Merwe, PR** (Flippie) b 08/07/1957 - SWD - 6 Tests (-) 12 matches (-) *1981: NZ2, 3, US. 1986: NZC1, 2. 1989: WT1.*

818 **Van der Merwe, PR** (Flip) b 03/06/1985 - BB - 35 Tests (5 - 1T) 36 matches (5 - 1T) *2010: F(R), It2(R), A1(R), NZ3, A2, 3(R), I(R), W2(R), S(R), E(R). 2011: A1. 2012: E1(R), 2(R), 3(R),*

Arg1(R), 2(R), A1(R), NZ1, A2(R), NZ2(R), I(R), S(R), E4(R). 2013: It(R), S(R), Sam, Arg1(R), Arg2(R), A1, NZ1, A2, W, S, F. 2014: W2.

299 **Van der Ryst, FE** (Franz) b 17/10/1920 d 21/02/1981 - Tvl - No Tests - 14 matches (-) *Toured BI, I & F. 1951/52.*

263 **Van der Schyff, JH** (Jack) b 11/06/1928 d 02/12/2001 - GW - 5 Tests (10 - 2C, 2P) 5 matches (10 - 2C, 2P) *1949: NZ1, 2, 3, 4. 1955: BI1.*

434 **Van der Schyff, PJ** (Johan) b 19/01/1942 - WTvl - No Tests - 2 matches (-) *Toured BI & I. 1969/70.*

432 **Van der Watt, AE** (Andy) b 10/10/1946 - WP - 3 Tests (-) 22 matches (42 - 14T) *1969: S(R), E. 1970: I. 1971: tour of A – no tests.*

203 **Van der Westhuizen, JC** (JC) b 22/11/1905 d 08/07/2003 - WP - 4 Tests (3 - 1T) 19 matches (25 - 7T, 1D) *1928: NZ2, 3, 4. 1931: I.*

609 **Van der Westhuizen, JF** (Cabous) b 11/01/1965 - Natal - No Tests - 11 matches (10 - 2T) *Toured NZ 1994 and W, S & I. 1994.*

593 **Van der Westhuizen, JH** (Joost) b 20/02/1971 - NTvl - 89 Tests (190 - 38T) 111 matches (280 - 56T) *1993: tour of A – no tests. 1993: Arg1, 2. 1994: E1, 2(R) 1994: tour of NZ – no tests. 1994: Arg2, S, W. 1995: WS1, [A, C(R), WS2, F, NZ], W, It, E. 1996: Fj, A1, 2(R), NZ2, 3, (R), 4, 5, Arg1, 2, F1, 2, W. 1997: T, BI1, 2, 3, NZ1, A1, NZ2, A2, It, F1. 1998: I1, 2, W1, E1, A1, NZ1, 2, A2, W2, S, I3, E2. 1999: NZ2*, A2*, [S*, Sp(R), U*, E*, A3*, NZ3*]. 2000: C, E1, 2, A1(R), NZ1(R), A2(R), Arg, I, W, E3. 2001: F1, 2, It1(R), NZ1, A1, 2, NZ2, F3, It2, E, US(R). 2003: S1*, S2*, A1, NZ1, A2(R), NZ2, [U*, E, Sm, NZ3].*

213 **Van der Westhuizen, JH** (Ponie) b 04/11/1909 d 05/03/1995 - WP - 3 Tests (-) 16 matches (45 - 12T, 1C, 2D) *1931: I. 1932: E, S.*

696 **Van der Westhuyzen, JNB** (Jaco) b 06/04/1978 - Mpu - 32 Tests (51 - 5T, 7C, 1P, 3D) 32 matches (51 - 5T, 7C, 1P, 3D) *2000: NZ2(R). 2001: It1(R). 2003: S1(R), 2, Arg, A1, [E, Sm, NZ3]. 2004: I1, 2, W1, PI, NZ1, A1, NZ2, A2, W2, I3, E, S, Arg. 2005: U, F1, 2, A1, 4(R), NZ2(R). 2006: S1, 2, F, A1.*

437 **Van Deventer, PI** (Piet) b 06/06/1946 d 14/03/2013- GW - No Tests - 12 matches (12 - 4T) *Toured BI & I. 1969/70.*

184 **Van Druten, NJV** (Jack) b 12/06/1898 d 16/01/1989 - Tvl - 8 Tests (6 - 2T) 8 matches (6 - 2T) *1924: BI1, 2, 3, 4. 1928: NZ1, 2, 3, 4.*

152 **Van Heerden, AJ** (Attie) b 10/03/1898 d 14/10/1965 - Tvl - 2 Tests (3 - 1T) 17 matches (42 - 14T) *1921: NZ1, 3.*

606 **Van Heerden, FJ** (Fritz) b 29/06/1970 - WP - 14 Tests (5 - 1T) 26 matches (5 - 1T) *1994: E1, 2(R), NZ3. 1995: It, E. 1996: NZ5(R), Arg1(R), 2(R). 1997: T, BI2(t+R), 3(R), NZ1(R), 2(R). 1999: [Sp].*

474 **Van Heerden, JL** (Moaner) b 18/07/1951 - NTvl - 17 Tests (4 - 1T) 23 matches (4 - 1T) *1974: BI3, 4, F1, 2. 1975: F1, 2. 1976: NZ1, 2, 3, 4. 1977: WT. 1980: BI1, 3, 4, S.Am3, 4, F.*

744 **Van Heerden, JL** (Wikus) b 25/02/1979 - GL - 14 Tests (5 - 1T) 16 matches (10 - 2T) *2003: S1, 2, A1, NZ1, A2(t). 2005: tour of Arg & UK – no tests. 2006: tour of UK – no tests. 2007: A2, NZ2, S(R), [Sm(R), E3, T, US, Fiji(R), E4(R).].*

272 **Van Jaarsveld, CJ** (Hoppy) b 21/02/1917 d 08/12/1980 - Tvl - 1 Test (-) 1 match (-) *1949: NZ1.*

354 **Van Jaarsveldt, DC** (Des) b 31/03/1929 - Rhodesia - 1 Test (3 - 1T) 1 match (3 - 1T) *1960: S*.*

368 **Van Niekerk, BB** (Bennie) b 01/12/1937 b 21/08/2000 - OFS - No Tests - 5 matches (3 - 1T) *Toured BI, I & F. 1960/61.*

210 **Van Niekerk, JA** (Jock) b 01/06/1907 d 19/04/1983 - WP - 1 Test (-) 2 matches (-) *1928: NZ4. 1931-32 tour of UK – no tests*

719 **Van Niekerk, JC** (Joe) b 14/05/1980 - GL - 52 Tests (50 - 10T) 52 matches (50 - 10T) *2001: NZ1(R), A1(R), NZ2(t+R), F3(R), It2, US. 2002: W1(R), 2(R), Arg(R), Sm, NZ1, A1, NZ2, A2, F, S, E. 2003: A2, NZ2, [U, E, G, Sm]. 2004: NZ1(R), A1(t), NZ2, A2, W2, I3, E, S, Arg(R). 2005: U(R), F2(R), A1(R), 2, 3, NZ1, A4, NZ2. 2006: S1, 2, F, A1, NZ1(R), A2(R). 2008: It(R), NZ1, 2, Arg(R), A2(R). 2010: W1.*

259 **Van Reenen, GL** (George) b 29/03/1914 d 12/11/1967 - WP - 2 Tests (6 - 2T) 11 matches (24 - 8T) *1937: A2, NZ1.*

26 **Van Renen, CG** (Charlie) b 23/08/1868 d 20/07/1942 - WP - 3 Tests (-) 3 matches (-) *1891: BI3. 1896: BI1, 4.*

65 **Van Renen, WA** (Willie) b 29/08/1880 d 17/02/1942 - WP - 2 Tests (-) 2 matches (-) *1903: BI1, 3.*

558 **Van Rensburg, JTJ** (Theo) b 26/05/1967 - Tvl - 7 Tests (40 - 2C, 12P) 22 matches (182 - 7T, 21C, 34P, 1D) *1992: NZ, A, E. 1993: F1, 2, A1. 1994: NZ2.*

167 **Van Rooyen, GW** (Tank) b 09/12/1892 d 21/09/1942 - Tvl - 2 Tests (-) 13 matches (3 - 1T) *1921: NZ2, 3.*

124 **Van Ryneveld, RCB** (Clive) b 07/07/1891 d 25/08/1969 - WP - 2 Tests (-) 2 matches (-) *1910: BI2, 3.*

SPRINGBOKS

631 **Van Schalkwyk, D** (Danie) b 01/02/1975 - NTvl - 8 Tests (10 - 2T) 8 matches (10 - 2T) *1996: Fj(R), NZ1, 2, 3. 1997: BI2, 3, NZ1, A1.*

278 **Van Schoor, RAM** (Ryk) b 03/12/1921 d 22/03/2009 - Rhodesia - 12 Tests (6 - 2T) 23 matches (21 - 7T) *1949: NZ2, 3, 4. 1951: S, I, W. 1952: E, F. 1953: A1, 2, 3, 4.*

483 **Van Staden, JA** (André) b 15/12/1945 - NTvl - No Tests - 3 matches (-) *Toured F. 1974.*

671 **Van Straaten, AJJ** (Braam) b 28/09/1971 - GF - 21 Tests (221 - 2T, 23C, 55P) 27 matches (294 - 5T, 46C, 59P) *1998: tour of UK & I - no tests. 1999: It2(R), W, NZ1(R), A1. 2000: C, E1, 2, NZ1, A2, NZ2, A3, Arg(R), I(R), W, E3. 2001: A1, 2, NZ2, F3, It2, E.*

314 **Van Vollenhoven, KT** (Tom) b 29/04/1935 - NTvl - 7 Tests (15 - 4T, 1D) 23 matches (63 - 20T, 1D) *1955: BI1, 2, 3, 4. 1956: A1, 2, NZ3.*

141 **Van Vuuren, TFJ** (Tom) b 09/07/1889 d 07/07/1947 - EP - 5 Tests (-) 17 matches (6 - 2T) *1912: S, I, W. 1913: E, F.*

304 **Van Wyk, CJ** (Basie) b 05/11/1923 d 29/08/2002 - Tvl - 10 Tests (18 - 6T) 23 matches (24 - 8T) *1951: S, I, W. 1952: E, F. 1953: A1, 2, 3, 4. 1955: BI1. 1956: tour of A & NZ - no tests*

445 **Van Wyk, JFB** (Piston) b 21/12/1943 - NTvl - 15 Tests (-) 19 matches (-) *1970: NZ1, 2, 3, 4. 1971: F1, 2, A1, 2, 3. 1972: E. 1974: BI1, 3, 4. 1976: NZ3, 4.*

196 **Van Wyk, SP** (SP) b 12/01/1901 d 22/01/1978 - WP - 2 Tests (-) 2 matches (-) *1928: NZ1, 2.*

378 **Van Zyl, BP** (Ben-Piet) b 01/08/1935 d 10/03/1973 - WP - 1 Test (6 - 2T) 5 matches (12 - 4T) *1960-61: tour of UK - no tests. 1961: I.*

410 **Van Zyl, CGP** (Sakkie) b 01/07/1932 - OFS - 4 Tests (-) 16 matches (6 - 2T) *1965: NZ1, 2, 3, 4.*

665 **Van Zyl, DJ** (Dan) b 08/01/1971 - Mpu - 1 Test (-) 7 matches (10 - 2C, 2P) *1997: tour of It, F, E & S - no tests. 2000: E(R).*

340 **Van Zyl, GH** (Hugo) b 20/08/1932 d 08/05/2007 - WP - 17 Tests (12 - 4T) 35 matches (27 - 9T) *1958: F1. 1960: S, NZ1, 2, 3, 4, W, I. 1961: E, S, F, I, A1, 2. 1962: BI1, 3, 4.*

357 **Van Zyl, HJ** (Hennie) b 31/01/1936 - Tvl - 10 Tests (18 - 6T) 24 matches (54 - 18T) *1960: NZ1, 2, 3, 4, I. 1961: E, S, I, A1, 2.*

852 **Van Zyl, PE** (Piet) b 14/09/1989 - FS - 2 Tests (-) 2 matches (-) *2013: S(R), Sam(R).*

373 **Van Zyl, PJ** (Piet) b 23/07/1933 d 28/05/1988 - Boland - 1 Test (-) 17 matches (3 - 1T) *1960-61: tour of UK - no tests. 1961: I.*

190 **Vanderplank, BE** (BV) b 29/04/1894 d 22/12/1990 - Natal - 2 Tests (-) 2 matches (-) *1924: BI3, 4.*

497 **Veldsman, PE** (Piet) b 11/03/1952 - WP - 1 Test (-) 1 match (-) *1977: WT.*

634 **Venter, AG** (André) b 14/11/1970 - FS - 66 Tests (45 - 9T) 70 matches (50 - 10T) *1996: NZ3, 4, 5, Arg1, 2, F1, 2, W. 1997: T, BI1, 2, 3, NZ1, A1, NZ2, It, F1, 2, E, S. 1998: I1, 2, W1, E1, A1, NZ1, 2, A2, W2, S(R), I3(R), E2(R). 1999: It1, 2(R), W(R), NZ1, A1, NZ2, A2, [S, U, E, A3, NZ3]. 2000: C, E1, 2, A1, NZ1, A2, NZ2, A3, Arg, I, W, E3. 2001: F1, It1, NZ1, A1, 2, NZ2, F3(R), It2(R), E(t+R), US(R).*

695 **Venter, AJ** (AJ) b 29/07/1973 - Natal - 25 Tests (-) 28 matches (-) *2000: W(R), E3(R). 2001: F3, It2, E, US. 2002: W1, 2, Arg, NZ1(R), 2, A2, F, S(R), E. 2003: Arg. 2004: PI, NZ1, A1, NZ2(R), A2, I3, E. 2006: NZ3, A3.*

605 **Venter, B** (Brendan) b 29/12/1969 - OFS - 17 Tests (10 - 2T) 26 matches (30 - 6T) *1994: E1, 2, NZ1, 2, 3, Arg1, 2. 1994: tour of W & S - no tests. 1995: [R, C, WS2(R), NZ(R)]. 1996: A1, NZ1, A2. 1999: A2, [S, U].*

214 **Venter, FD** (Floors) b 13/04/1909 d ??/??/1992 - Tvl - 3 Tests (-) 14 matches (24 - 8T) *1931: W. 1932: S. 1933: A3.*

672 **Venter, SL** (Lourens) b 25/06/1976 - GW - No Tests - 4 matches (15 - 3T) *Toured BI & I. 1998.*

838 **Vermaak, J** (Jano) b 01/01/1985 - BB - 3 Tests (0 - 0) 3 matches (0 - 0) *2012: Rugby Championship Squad - no tests. 2013: It, A1(R), NZ1(R), tour of W, S & F - no tests.*

840 **Vermeulen, DJ** (Duane) b 03/07/1986 - WP - 29 Tests (10 - 2T) 29 matches (10 - 2T) *2012: A1, NZ1, A2, NZ2, I, S, E4. 2013: Arg1, Arg2, A1, NZ1, A2, NZ 2, W, S, F. 2014: W1, W2, S, Arg1, Arg2, A1, NZ1, A2, NZ2, I, E, It, W3.*

25 **Versfeld, C** (Hasie) b 24/09/1866 d 06/01/1942 - WP - 1 Test (-) 1 match (-) *1891: BI3.*

7 **Versfeld, M** (Oupa) b 15/05/1860 d 01/09/1931 - WP - 3 Tests (-) 3 matches (-) *1891: BI1, 2, 3.*

3 **Vigne, JT** (Chubb) b 23/12/1868 d 09/04/1955 - Tvl - 3 Tests (-) 3 matches (-) *1891: BI1, 2, 3.*

448 **Viljoen, JF** (Joggie) b 14/05/1945 - GW - 6 Tests (6 - 2T) 10 matches (12 - 4T) *1971: F1, 2, A1, 2, 3. 1972: E.*

644 **Viljoen, R** (Joggie) b 22/07/1976 - WP - No Tests - 3 matches (-) *Toured Arg, F & W. 1996.*

808 **Viljoen, R** (Riaan) b 04/01/1983 - GW - No Tests - 2 matches (-) *Toured F, It, I & E. 2009.*

451 **Viljoen, JT** (Hannes) b 21/04/1943 - Natal - 3 Tests (6 - 2T) 10 matches (48 - 16T) *1971: A1, 2, 3.*

532 **Villet, JV** (John) b 03/11/1954 - WP - 2 Tests (-) 2 matches (-) *1984: E1, 2.*

530 **Visagie, GP** (Gawie) b 31/03/1955 d 19/11/2014 - Natal - No Tests - 3 matches (8 - 2T) *Toured NZ & USA. 1981.*

683 **Visagie, IJ** (Cobus) b 31/10/1973 - WP - 29 Tests (-) 29 matches (-) *1999: It1, W, NZ1, A1, NZ2, A2, [S, U, E, A3, NZ3]. 2000: C, E2, A1, NZ1, A2, NZ2, A3. 2001: NZ1, A1, 2, NZ2, F3, It2(R), E(t+R), US. 2003: S1(R), 2(R), Arg.*

419 **Visagie, PJ** (Piet) b 16/04/1943 - GW - 25 Tests (130 - 6T, 20C, 19P, 5D) 44 matches (240 - 8T, 36C, 40P, 8D) *1967: F1, 2, 3, 4. 1968: BI1, 2, 3, 4, F1, 2. 1969: A1, 2, 3, 4, S, E. 1970: NZ1, 2, 3, 4. 1971: F1, 2, A1, 2, 3.*

536 **Visagie, RG** (Rudi) b 27/06/1959 - OFS - 5 Tests (-) 9 matches (5 - 1T) *1984: E1, 2, S.Am&Sp1, 2. 1993: F1. 1993: tour of A no tests.*

517 **Visser, J de V** (De Villiers) b 26/11/1958 - WP - 2 Tests (-) 12 matches (16 - 4T) *1980: tour of S.Am – no tests. 1981: NZ2, US.*

625 **Visser, M** (Mornay) b 30/03/1969 - WP - 1 Test (-) 1 match (-) *1995: WS1(R).*

237 **Visser, PJ** (Paul) b 25/12/1903 d 25/04/1963 - Tvl - 1 Test (-) 1 match (-) *1933: A2.*

293 **Vivier, SS** (Basie) b 01/03/1927 d 18/10/2009 - OFS - 5 Tests (11 - 4C, 1P) 31 matches (165 - 5T, 45C, 17P, 3D) *1951-52: tour of UK – no tests. 1956: A1*, 2*, NZ2*, 3*, 4*.*

471 **Vogel, ML** (Leon) b 22/10/1949 - OFS - 1 Test (-) 1 match (-) *1974: BI2(R).*

686 **Von Hoesslin, DJB** (Dave) b 10/05/1975 - GW - 5 Tests (10 - 2T) 5 matches (10 - 2T) *1999: It1(R), 2, W(R), NZ1, A1(R).*

681 **Vos, AN** (André) b 09/01/1975 - GL - 33 Tests (25 - 5T) 38 matches (30 - 6T) *1998: tour of UK & I – no tests. 1999: It1(t+R), 2, NZ1(R), 2(R), A2, [S(R), Sp*, E(R), A3(R), NZ3]. 2000: C*, E1*, 2*, A1*, NZ1*, A2*, NZ2*, A3*, Arg*, I*, W*, E3*. 2001: F1*, 2*, It1, NZ1, A1, 2, NZ2, F3, It2, E, US*.*

491 **Wagenaar, C** (Christo) b 11/03/1952 - NTvl - 1 Test (-) 1 match (-) *1977: WT.*

269 **Wahl, JJ** (Ballie) b 10/07/1920 d 25/06/1978 - WP - 1 Test (-) 1 match (-) *1949: NZ1.*

170 **Walker, AP** (Alf) b 08/05/1893 d 17/07/1971 - Natal - 6 Tests (-) 14 matches (-) *1921: NZ1, 3. 1924: BI1, 2, 3, 4.*

311 **Walker, HN** (Harry) b 01/07/1928 d 05/08/2008 - OFS - 4 Tests (-) 19 matches (-) *1953: A3. 1956: A2, NZ1, 4.*

115 **Walker, HW** (Henry) b 22/02/1884 d 21/08/1951 - Tvl - 3 Tests (-) 3 matches (-) *1910: BI1, 2, 3.*

397 **Walton, DC** (Don) b 05/04/1939 - Natal - 8 Tests (-) 31 matches (12 - 4T) *1964: F. 1965: I, S, NZ3, 4. 1968: tour of F – no tests. 1969: A1, 2, E.*

739 **Wannenburg, PJ** (Pedrie) b 02/01/1981 - BB - 20 Tests (15 - 3T) 20 matches (15 - 3T) *2002: F(R), E. 2003: S1, 2, Arg, A1(t+R), NZ1(R). 2004: I1, 2, W1, PI(R). 2006: S1(R), F, NZ2(R), 3, A3. 2007: Sm1(R), NZ1(R), A2, NZ2.*

216 **Waring, FW** (Franky) b 07/11/1908 d 24/01/2000 - WP - 7 Tests (6 - 2T) 19 matches (12 - 4T) *1931: I. 1932: E. 1933: A1, 2, 3, 4, 5.*

707 **Wasserman, JG** (Johan) b 29/07/1977 - SWD - No Tests - 4 matches (5 - 1T) *Toured Arg, I, W & E. 2000*

786 **Watson, LA** (Luke) b 26/10/1983 - WP - 10 Tests (-) 10 matches (-) *2007: Sm1. 2008: W1, 2, It, NZ1(R), 2(R), Arg, NZ3(R), A2(R), 3(t+R).*

260 **Watt, HH** (Howard) b 01/03/1911 d 18/08/2005 - WP - No Tests - 7 matches (9 - 3T) *Toured A & NZ. 1937.*

154 **Weepner, JS** (Jackie) b 16/01/1896 b 14/12/1965 - WP - No Tests - 9 matches (6 - 2T) *Toured A & NZ. 1921.*

587 **Wegner, GN** (Nico) b 03/12/1968 - WP - 4 Tests (-) 12 matches (-) *1993: F2, A1, 2, 3.*

366 **Wentzel, GJ** (Giepie) b 28/02/1938 d 01/07/1996 - EP - No Tests - 12 matches (37 - 2T, 14C, 1P) *Toured BI, I & F. 1960/61.*

740 **Wentzel, M v Z** (Marco) b 05/05/1979 - Mpu - 2 Tests (-) 2 matches (-) *2002: F(R), S.*

664 **Wessels, JC** (Boeta) b 30/06/1973 - GW - No Tests - 1 match (-) *Toured It, F, E & S. 1997.*

35 **Wessels, JJ** (Scraps) b 13/09/1874 d 06/04/1929 - WP - 3 Tests (-) 3 matches (-) *1896: BI1, 2, 3.*

402 **Wessels, JW** (John) b 14/05/1935 d 22/01/2006 - OFS - No Tests - 2 matches (-) *Toured I & S. 1965.*

296 **Wessels, PW** (Piet) b 11/02/1926 d 24/08/1997 - OFS - No Tests - 14 matches (-) *Toured BI, I & F. 1951/52.*

459 **Whipp, PJM** (Peter) b 22/09/1950 - WP - 8 Tests (4 - 1T) 10 matches (4 - 1T) *1974: BI1, 2. 1974: tour of F – no tests. 1975: F1. 1976: NZ1, 3, 4. 1980: S.Am1, 2.*

217 **White, J** (Jimmy) b 20/05/1911 d 03/07/1997 - Border - 10 Tests (10 - 2T, 1D) 26 matches (23 - 5T, 2D) *1931: W. 1933: A1, 2, 3, 4, 5. 1937: A1, 2, NZ1, 2.*

863 **Whiteley, WR** (Warren) b 18/09/1987 - GL - 2 Tests (-) 2 matches (-) *2014: A1(R), NZ1(R).*

585 **Wiese, JJ** (Kobus) b 16/05/1964 - Tvl - 18 Tests (5 - 1T) 32 matches (15 - 3T) *1993: tour of A - no tests. 1994: tours of NZ, W & S - no tests. 1993: F1. 1995: WS1, [R, C, WS2, F, NZ], W, It, E. 1996: NZ3(R), 4(R), 5, Arg1, 2, F1, 2, W.*

743 **Willemse, AK** (Ashwin) b 08/09/1981 - GL - 19 Tests (20 - 4T) 20 matches (25 - 5T) *2003: S1, 2, NZ1, A2, NZ2, [U, E, Sm, NZ3]. 2004: W2, I3. 2007: E1, 2(R), Sm1, A1, NZ1, N, S(R), [T.].*

120 **Williams, AE** (Arthur) b 01/07/1879 d 21/07/1930 - GW - 1 Test (-) 1 match (-) *1910: BI1.*

533 **Williams, AP** (Avril) b 10/02/1961 - WP - 2 Tests (-) 2 matches (-) *1984: E1, 2.*

589 **Williams, CM** (Chester) b 08/08/1970 - WP - 27 Tests (70 - 14T) 47 matches (135 - 27T) *1993: tour of A - no tests. 1993: Arg2. 1994: E1, 2, NZ1, 2, 3, Arg1, 2, S, W. 1995: WS1, [WS2, F, NZ], It, E. 1998: A1(t), NZ1(t). 2000: C(R), E1(t), 2(R), A1(R), NZ2, A3, Arg, I, W(R).*

231 **Williams, DO** (Dai) b 16/06/1913 d 24/12/1975 - WP - 8 Tests (15 - 5T) 18 matches (51 - 17T) *1931-32 tour of UK - no tests. 1937: A1, 2, NZ1, 2, 3. 1938: BI1, 2, 3.*

450 **Williams, JG** (John) b 29/10/1946 - NTvl - 13 Tests (-) 24 matches (3 - 1T) *1971: F1, 2, A1, 2, 3. 1972: E. 1974: BI1, 2, 4, F1, 2. 1976: NZ1, 2.*

363 **Wilson, LG** (Lionel) b 25/05/1933 - WP - 27 Tests (6 - 2D) 58 matches (19 - 3T, 2C, 2D) *1960: NZ3, 4, W, I. 1961: E, F, I, A1, 2. 1962: BI1, 2, 3, 4. 1963: A1, 2, 3, 4. 1964: W, F. 1965: I, S, A1, 2, NZ1, 2, 3, 4.*

495 **Wolmarans, BJ** (Barry) b 22/02/1953 - OFS - 1 Test (4 - 1T) 7 matches (4 - 1T) *1977: WT. 1981: tour of NZ & USA - no tests.*

135 **Wrentmore, GM** (Bai) b 20/02/1893 d 16/08/1953 - WP - No Tests - 9 matches (27 - 3T, 5C, 2D) *Toured BI, I & F. 1912/13.*

548 **Wright, GD** (Garth) b 09/09/1963 - EP - 7 Tests (4 - 1T) 12 matches (4 - 1T) *1986: NZC3, 4. 1989: WT1, 2. 1992: F1, 2, E.*

381 **Wyness, MRK** (Wang) b 23/01/1937 d 06/11/2011 - WP - 5 Tests (3 - 1T) 5 matches (3 - 1T) *1962: BI1, 2, 3, 4. 1963: A2.*

153 **Zeller, WC** (Bill) b 18/07/1894 d 27/07/1969 - Natal - 2 Tests (-) 14 matches (39 - 13T) *1921: NZ2, 3.*

212 **Zimerman, M** (Morris) b 08/06/1911 - d 09/01/1992 - WP - 4 Tests (3 - 1T) 18 matches (42 - 14T) *1931: W, I. 1932: E, S.*

PROVINCIAL REPRESENTATION

South Africa's 866 International Players have come from 15 provincial unions as follows:

Western Province	259
Golden Lions (former Transvaal)	164
Blue Bulls (former Northern Transvaal)	109
Free State (former Orange Free State)	83
KwaZulu-Natal (former Natal)	79
Griqualand West	63
Eastern Province	34
Border	16
Boland	15
Valke (former Eastern Transvaal)	10
Mpumalanga (former South Eastern Transvaal)	9
Leopards (former Western Transvaal)	9
Rhodesia	8
South Western Districts	5
South West Africa	3
TOTAL	866

SOUTH AFRICA TEST RESULTS 1891 – 2014

OPPONENTS	PLAYED	WON	LOST	DRAWN	% WON	PF	PA	SOUTH AFRICA T	C	P	D	OPPONENTS T	C	P	D
Argentina	19	18	0	1	95%	728	361	88	69	49	1	33	26	46	2
Australia	80	45	34	1	56%	1552	1391	184	106	173	19	142	89	174	12
British & Irish Lions	46	23	17	6	50%	600	516	95	48	52	7	68	30	59	14
Canada	2	2	0	0	100%	71	18	10	6	3	0	2	1	0	0
England	37	23	12	2	62%	780	592	72	49	100	14	42	27	106	7
Fiji	3	3	0	0	100%	129	41	16	11	9	0	4	3	2	0
France	39	22	11	6	56%	783	578	89	60	93	7	51	28	81	19
Georgia	1	1	0	0	100%	46	19	7	4	1	0	1	1	0	0
Ireland	22	16	5	1	73%	432	277	62	33	34	5	26	16	41	0
Italy	12	12	0	0	100%	599	145	82	66	19	0	12	8	22	1
Namibia	2	2	0	0	100%	192	13	27	24	3	0	1	1	2	0
New Zealand	89	35	51	3	39%	1392	1718	137	90	175	29	177	106	203	20
New Zealand Cavaliers	4	3	1	0	75%	96	62	7	7	15	0	5	3	11	0
Pacific Islands	1	1	0	0	100%	38	24	4	4	4	0	2	2	0	0
Romania	1	1	0	0	100%	21	8	2	1	3	0	1	0	1	0
Scotland	25	20	5	0	80%	652	270	83	58	50	3	27	20	32	1
South America	6	5	1	0	83%	156	86	22	16	6	0	7	5	13	0
South America & Spain	2	2	0	0	100%	54	28	9	3	4	0	3	2	4	0
Spain	1	1	0	0	100%	47	3	7	6	0	0	0	0	1	0
Tonga	2	2	0	0	100%	104	35	16	9	2	0	4	3	3	0
USA	3	3	0	0	100%	145	42	23	16	0	0	4	1	0	0
Uruguay	3	3	0	0	100%	245	12	38	23	2	0	0	0	4	0
Wales	30	27	2	1	90%	814	440	101	70	61	2	32	18	66	1
Western Samoa/Samoa	8	8	0	0	100%	385	93	53	36	15	2	12	6	7	2
World Teams (recognised Tests)	3	3	0	0	100%	87	59	11	5	10	1	9	7	3	0
	441	281	139	21	63,7%	10148	6831	1245	819	886	100	667	403	896	88

SPRINGBOKS

Records

COMPARATIVE WIN RATIO vs MAJOR RIVALS*

	Played	Won	Win%
New Zealand	526	402	76,4%
SOUTH AFRICA	441	281	63,7%
France	709	388	54,7%
Argentina	389	210	54,0%
England	680	364	53,5%
Wales	667	342	51,3%
Australia	577	293	50,8%
Ireland	641	273	42,6%
Scotland	640	271	42,3%

*as at 30/11/2014

TEST MATCHES BY DECADE

	Played	Won	Lost	Drawn	Win %	Prog. win %
1891-1900	7	1	6	0	14,3%	14,3%
1901-1910	10	5	2	3	50%	35,3%
1911-1920	5	5	0	0	100%	50%
1921-1930	11	6	3	2	54,5%	51,5%
1931-1940	17	13	4	0	76,5%	60,0%
1941-1950	4	4	0	0	100%	63,0%
1951-1960	28	18	8	2	64,3%	63,4%
1961-1970	46	26	14	6	56,5%	60,9%
1971-1980	28	20	6	2	71,4%	62,8%
1981-1990	18	14	4	0	77,8%	64,4%
1991-2000	94	60	32	2	63,8%	64,2%
2001-2010	127	78	47	2	61,4%	63,3%
2011-2020	46	31	13	2	67,4%	63,7%
	441	281	139	21		

SPRINGBOKS

SOUTH AFRICA'S TESTS & TOUR MATCHES

Test No.	Tour Match	Date	Venue	Opponent	Captain	Result	PF	PA
1		30/07/1891	Port Elizabeth	BRITISH ISLES	HH Castens	Lost	0	4
2		29/08/1891	Kimberley	BRITISH ISLES	RCD Snedden	Lost	0	3
3		05/09/1891	Cape Town	BRITISH ISLES	AR Richards	Lost	0	4
4		30/07/1896	Port Elizabeth	BRITISH ISLES	FTD Aston	Lost	0	8
5		22/08/1896	Johannesburg	BRITISH ISLES	FTD Aston	Lost	8	17
6		29/08/1896	Kimberley	BRITISH ISLES	FTD Aston	Lost	3	9
7		05/09/1896	Cape Town	BRITISH ISLES	BH Heatlie	Won	5	0
8		26/08/1903	Johannesburg	BRITISH ISLES	A Frew	Drew	10	10
9		05/09/1903	Kimberley	BRITISH ISLES	JM Powell	Drew	0	0
10		12/09/1903	Cape Town	BRITISH ISLES	BH Heatlie	Won	8	0
	1	27/09/1906	Northampton	East Midlands	PJ Roos	Won	37	0
	2	29/09/1906	Leicester	Midland Counties	PJ Roos	Won	29	0
	3	03/10/1906	Blackheath	Kent	PJ Roos	Won	21	0
	4	06/10/1906	West Hartlepool	Durham	PJ Roos	Won	22	4
	5	10/10/1906	Newcastle	Northumberland	PJ Roos	Won	44	0
	6	13/10/1906	Leeds	Yorkshire	PJ Roos	Won	34	0
	7	17/10/1906	Plymouth	Devon	PJ Roos	Won	22	6
	8	20/10/1906	Taunton	Somerset	WAG Burger	Won	14	0
	9	24/10/1906	Richmond	Middlesex	PJ Roos	Won	9	0
	10	27/10/1906	Newport	Newport	PJ Roos	Won	8	0
	11	31/10/1906	Cardiff	Glamorgan	PJ Roos	Won	6	3
	12	03/11/1906	Gloucester	Gloucestershire	HW Carolin	Won	23	0
	13	07/11/1906	Oxford	Oxford University	PJ Roos	Won	24	3
	14	10/11/1906	Cambridge	Cambridge University	FJ Dobbin	Won	29	0
	15	13/11/1906	Hawick	South of Scotland	HW Carolin	Won	32	5
11		17/11/1906	Glasgow	SCOTLAND	HW Carolin	Lost	0	6
	16	20/11/1906	Aberdeen	North of Scotland	FJ Dobbin	Won	35	3
12		24/11/1906	Belfast	IRELAND	PJ Roos	Won	15	12
	17	27/11/1906	Dublin	Dublin University	HW Carolin	Won	28	3
13		01/12/1906	Swansea	WALES	PJ Roos	Won	11	0
14		08/12/1906	London	ENGLAND	PJ Roos	Drew	3	3
	18	12/12/1906	Manchester	Lancashire	PJ Roos	Won	11	8
	19	15/12/1906	Carlisle	Cumberland	PJ Roos	Won	21	0
	20	19/12/1906	Richmond	Surrey	PJ Roos	Won	33	0
	21	22/12/1906	Redruth	Cornwall	PJ Roos	Won	9	3
	22	26/12/1906	Newport	Monmouthshire	PJ Roos	Won	17	0
	23	29/12/1906	Llanelli	Llanelli	PJ Roos	Won	16	3
	24	01/01/1907	Cardiff	Cardiff	PJ Roos	Lost	0	17
15		06/08/1910	Johannesburg	BRITISH ISLES	DFT Morkel	Won	14	10
16		27/08/1910	Port Elizabeth	BRITISH ISLES	WA Millar	Lost	3	8
17		03/09/1910	Cape Town	BRITISH ISLES	WA Millar	Won	21	5
	25	03/10/1912	Bath	Somerset	WA Millar	Won	24	3
	26	05/10/1912	Exeter	Devon	WA Millar	Won	8	0
	27	10/10/1912	Redruth	Cornwall	DFT Morkel	Won	15	3
	28	12/10/1912	Newport	Monmouthshire	WA Millar	Won	16	0
	29	17/10/1912	Cardiff	Glamorgan	WA Millar	Won	35	3
	30	19/10/1912	Llanelli	Llanelli	FJ Dobbin	Won	8	7
	31	24/10/1912	Newport	Newport	WA Millar	Lost	3	9
	32	26/10/1912	Blackheath	London	WA Millar	Won	12	8
	33	30/10/1912	Portsmouth	United Services	WA Millar	Won	18	16

SPRINGBOKS

SOUTH AFRICA'S TESTS & TOUR MATCHES

Test No.	Tour Match	Date	Venue	Opponent	Captain	Result	PF	PA
	34	02/11/1912	Northampton	East Midlands	WA Millar	Won	14	5
	35	06/11/1912	Oxford	Oxford University	WA Millar	Won	6	0
	36	09/11/1912	Leicester	Midland Counties	WA Millar	Won	25	3
	37	14/11/1912	Cambridge	Cambridge University	DFT Morkel	Won	24	0
	38	16/11/1912	Twickenham	London	WA Millar	Lost	8	10
	39	20/11/1912	Newcastle	North of England	DFT Morkel	Won	17	0
18		23/11/1912	Edinburgh	SCOTLAND	FJ Dobbin	Won	16	0
	40	27/11/1912	Glasgow	West of Scotland	WA Millar	Won	38	3
19		30/11/1912	Dublin	IRELAND	WA Millar	Won	38	0
	41	04/12/1912	Belfast	Ulster	WA Millar	Won	19	0
	42	07/12/1912	Birkenhead	North of England	DFT Morkel	Won	21	8
20		14/12/1912	Cardiff	WALES	WA Millar	Won	3	0
	43	19/12/1912	Neath	Neath	WA Millar	Won	8	3
	44	21/12/1912	Cardiff	Cardiff	WA Millar	Won	7	6
	45	26/12/1912	Swansea	Swansea	WA Millar	Lost	0	3
	46	28/12/1912	Bristol	Gloucestershire	DFT Morkel	Won	11	0
21		04/01/1913	Twickenham	ENGLAND	DFT Morkel	Won	9	3
22		11/01/1913	Bordeaux	FRANCE	WA Millar	Won	38	5
	47	25/06/1921	Sydney	New South Wales	TB Pienaar	Won	25	10
	48	27/06/1921	Sydney	New South Wales	TB Pienaar	Won	16	11
	49	02/07/1921	Sydney	New South Wales	WH Morkel	Won	28	9
	50	06/07/1921	Sydney	Metropolitan	WH Morkel	Won	14	8
	51	13/07/1921	Wanganui	Wanganui	TB Pienaar	Won	11	6
	52	16/07/1921	New Plymouth	Taranaki	WH Morkel	Drew	0	0
	53	20/07/1921	Masterton	Wairarapa-Bush	TB Pienaar	Won	18	3
	54	23/07/1921	Wellington	Wellington	TB Pienaar	Won	8	3
	55	27/07/1921	Greymouth	West Coast - Buller	HJL Morkel	Won	33	3
	56	30/07/1921	Christchurch	Canterbury	TB Pienaar	Lost	4	6
	57	03/08/1921	Timaru	South Canterbury	WH Morkel	Won	34	3
	58	06/08/1921	Invercargill	Southland	TB Pienaar	Won	12	0
	59	10/08/1921	Dunedin	Otago	WH Morkel	Won	11	3
23		13/08/1921	Dunedin	NEW ZEALAND	WH Morkel	Lost	5	13
	60	17/08/1921	Palmerston N.	Manawatu-Horowhenua	TB Pienaar	Won	3	0
	61	20/08/1921	Auckland	Auckland - North Auckland	TL Krüger	Won	24	8
	62	24/08/1921	Rotorua	Bay of Plenty	TL Krüger	Won	17	9
24		27/08/1921	Auckland	NEW ZEALAND	WH Morkel	Won	9	5
	63	31/08/1921	Hamilton	Waikato	TB Pienaar	Won	6	0
	64	03/09/1921	Napier	Hawkes Bay - Poverty Bay	TB Pienaar	Won	14	8
	65	07/09/1921	Napier	New Zealand Maoris	WH Morkel	Won	9	8
	66	10/09/1921	Nelson	Nelson, Marlborough & Golden Bay - Motueka	JP Michau	Won	26	3
25		17/09/1921	Wellington	NEW ZEALAND	WH Morkel	Drew	0	0
26		16/08/1924	Durban	BRITISH ISLES	PK Albertyn	Won	7	3
27		23/08/1924	Johannesburg	BRITISH ISLES	PK Albertyn	Won	17	0
28		13/09/1924	Port Elizabeth	BRITISH ISLES	PK Albertyn	Drew	3	3
29		20/09/1924	Cape Town	BRITISH ISLES	PK Albertyn	Won	16	9
30		30/06/1928	Durban	NEW ZEALAND	PJ Mostert	Won	17	0
31		21/07/1928	Johannesburg	NEW ZEALAND	PJ Mostert	Lost	6	7
32		18/08/1928	Port Elizabeth	NEW ZEALAND	PJ Mostert	Won	11	6
33		01/09/1928	Cape Town	NEW ZEALAND	PJ Mostert	Lost	5	13

SPRINGBOKS

SOUTH AFRICA'S TESTS & TOUR MATCHES

Test No.	Tour Match	Date	Venue	Opponent	Captain	Result	PF	PA
	67	03/10/1931	Bristol	Gloucestershire & Somerset	BL Osler	Won	14	3
	68	08/10/1931	Newport	Newport	BL Osler	Won	15	3
	69	10/10/1931	Swansea	Swansea	JC van der Westhuizen	Won	10	3
	70	14/10/1931	Abertillery	Abertillery & Cross Keys	BL Osler	Won	10	9
	71	17/10/1931	Twickenham	London	BL Osler	Won	30	3
	72	21/10/1931	Birmingham	Midland Counties	Phil Mostert	Won	13	3
	73	24/10/1931	Sunderland	Durham & Northumberland	JC van der Westhuizen	Won	41	0
	74	28/10/1931	Glasgow	Glasgow	JC van der Westhuizen	Won	21	13
	75	31/10/1931	Melrose	South of Scotland	MM Louw	Drew	0	0
	76	04/11/1931	Cambridge	Cambridge University	BL Osler	Won	21	9
	77	07/11/1931	Twickenham	Combined Services	BL Osler	Won	23	0
	78	12/11/1931	Oxford	Oxford University	BL Osler	Won	24	3
	79	14/11/1931	Leicester	Midland Counties	JC van der Westhuizen	Lost	21	30
	80	18/11/1931	Devonport	Devon & Cornwall	BL Osler	Drew	3	3
	81	21/11/1931	Cardiff	Cardiff	BL Osler	Won	13	5
	82	24/11/1931	Llanelli	Llanelli	MM Louw	Won	9	0
	83	28/11/1931	Neath	Neath & Aberavon	BL Osler	Won	8	3
34		05/12/1931	Swansea	WALES	BL Osler	Won	8	3
	84	09/12/1931	Liverpool	Lancashire & Cheshire	BL Osler	Won	20	9
	85	12/12/1931	Belfast	Ulster	Unknown	Won	30	3
35		19/12/1931	Dublin	IRELAND	BL Osler	Won	8	3
	86	26/12/1931	Twickenham	London	BL Osler	Won	16	8
36		02/01/1932	Twickenham	ENGLAND	BL Osler	Won	7	0
	87	06/01/1932	Workington	Yorkshire & Cumberland	BL Osler	Won	27	5
	88	09/01/1932	Aberdeen	North of Scotland	JC van der Westhuizen	Won	9	0
37		16/01/1932	Edinburgh	SCOTLAND	BL Osler	Won	6	3
38		08/07/1933	Cape Town	AUSTRALIA	PJ Nel	Won	17	3
39		22/07/1933	Durban	AUSTRALIA	BL Osler	Lost	6	21
40		12/08/1933	Johannesburg	AUSTRALIA	PJ Nel	Won	12	3
41		26/08/1933	Port Elizabeth	AUSTRALIA	PJ Nel	Won	11	0
42		02/09/1933	Bloemfontein	AUSTRALIA	PJ Nel	Lost	4	15
	89	12/06/1937	Melbourne	Victoria	PJ Nel	Won	45	11
	90	16/06/1937	Orange	Combined Western Districts	GH Brand	Won	63	0
	91	19/06/1937	Sydney	New South Wales	PJ Nel	Lost	6	17
43		26/06/1937	Sydney	AUSTRALIA	PJ Nel	Won	9	5
	92	30/06/1937	Newcastle	Newcastle	PJ Nel	Won	58	8
	93	03/07/1937	Brisbane	Australian XV	PJ Nel	Won	36	3
	94	07/07/1937	Toowoomba	Toowoomba	PJ Nel	Won	60	0
	95	10/07/1937	Brisbane	Queensland	PJ Nel	Won	39	4
44		17/07/1937	Sydney	AUSTRALIA	PJ Nel	Won	26	17
	96	24/07/1937	Auckland	Auckland	PJ Nel	Won	19	5
	97	28/07/1937	Hamilton	Waikato-King Country-Thames Valley	PJ Nel	Won	6	3
	98	31/07/1937	New Plymouth	Taranaki	PJ Nel	Won	17	3
	99	04/08/1937	Palmerston N.	Manawatu	PJ Nel	Won	39	3
	100	07/08/1937	Wellington	Wellington	GH Brand	Won	29	0
45		14/08/1937	Wellington	NEW ZEALAND	DH Craven	Lost	7	13
	101	18/08/1937	Blenheim	Nelson-Golden Bay-Motueka-Marlborough	PJ Nel	Won	22	0

SPRINGBOKS

SOUTH AFRICA'S TESTS & TOUR MATCHES

Test No.	Tour Match	Date	Venue	Opponent	Captain	Result	PF	PA
	102	21/08/1937	Christchurch	Canterbury	PJ Nel	Won	23	8
	103	25/08/1937	Greymouth	West Coast-Buller	PJ Nel	Won	31	6
	104	28/08/1937	Timaru	South Canterbury	PJ Nel	Won	43	6
46		04/09/1937	Christchurch	NEW ZEALAND	PJ Nel	Won	13	6
	105	08/09/1937	Invercargill	Southland	PJ Nel	Won	30	17
	106	11/09/1937	Dunedin	Otago	DH Craven	Won	47	7
	107	15/09/1937	Napier	Hawke's Bay	PJ Nel	Won	21	12
	108	18/09/1937	Gisborne	Poverty Bay-Bay of Plenty-East Coast	PJ Nel	Won	33	3
47		25/09/1937	Auckland	NEW ZEALAND	PJ Nel	Won	17	6
	109	29/09/1937	Whangarei	North Auckland	PJ Nel	Won	14	6
48		06/08/1938	Johannesburg	BRITISH ISLES	DH Craven	Won	26	12
49		03/09/1938	Port Elizabeth	BRITISH ISLES	DH Craven	Won	19	3
50		10/09/1938	Cape Town	BRITISH ISLES	DH Craven	Lost	16	21
51		16/07/1949	Cape Town	NEW ZEALAND	F du Plessis	Won	15	11
52		13/08/1949	Johannesburg	NEW ZEALAND	F du Plessis	Won	12	6
53		03/09/1949	Durban	NEW ZEALAND	F du Plessis	Won	9	3
54		17/09/1949	Port Elizabeth	NEW ZEALAND	BJ Kenyon	Won	11	8
	110	10/10/1951	Bournemouth	South Eastern Counties	BJ Kenyon	Won	31	6
	111	13/10/1951	Plymouth	South Western Counties	HSV Muller	Won	17	8
	112	18/10/1951	Pontypool	Pontypool & Newbridge	BJ Kenyon	Won	15	6
	113	20/10/1951	Cardiff	Cardiff	HSV Muller	Won	11	9
	114	23/10/1951	Llanelli	Llanelli	BJ Kenyon	Won	20	11
	115	27/10/1951	Liverpool	North Western Counties	BJ Kenyon	Won	16	9
	116	31/10/1951	Glasgow	Glasgow & Edinburgh	HSV Muller	Won	43	11
	117	03/11/1951	Newcastle	North Eastern Counties	BJ Kenyon	Won	19	8
	118	08/11/1951	Cambridge	Cambridge University	HSV Muller	Won	30	0
	119	10/11/1951	Twickenham	London Counties	HSV Muller	Lost	9	11
	120	15/11/1951	Oxford	Oxford University	HSV Muller	Won	24	3
	121	17/11/1951	Port Talbot	Neath & Aberavon	HSV Muller	Won	22	0
55		24/11/1951	Edinburgh	SCOTLAND	HSV Muller	Won	44	0
	122	28/11/1951	Aberdeen	North of Scotland	JA du Rand	Won	14	3
	123	01/12/1951	Belfast	Ulster	HSV Muller	Won	27	5
56		08/12/1951	Dublin	IRELAND	HSV Muller	Won	17	5
	124	11/12/1951	Limerick	Munster	PA du Toit	Won	11	6
	125	15/12/1951	Swansea	Swansea	HSV Muller	Won	11	3
57		22/12/1951	Cardiff	WALES	HSV Muller	Won	6	3
	126	26/12/1951	Twickenham	Combined Services	SP Fry	Won	24	8
	127	29/12/1951	Leicester	Midland Counties	B Myburgh	Won	3	0
58		05/01/1952	Twickenham	ENGLAND	HSV Muller	Won	8	3
	128	10/01/1952	Newport	Newport	HSV Muller	Won	12	6
	129	12/01/1952	Bristol	Western Counties	PA du Toit	Won	16	5
	130	16/01/1952	Coventry	Midland Counties	PA du Toit	Won	19	8
	131	19/01/1952	Hawick	South of Scotland	HSV Muller	Won	13	3
	132	26/01/1952	Cardiff	Barbarians	HSV Muller	Won	17	3
	133	02/02/1952	Lyon	South Eastern France	HSV Muller	Won	9	3
	134	07/02/1952	Bordeaux	South Western France	SP Fry	Won	20	12
	135	09/02/1952	Toulouse	France 'B'	HSV Muller	Won	9	6
59		16/02/1952	Paris	FRANCE	HSV Muller	Won	25	3
60		22/08/1953	Johannesburg	AUSTRALIA	HSV Muller	Won	25	3

SPRINGBOKS

SOUTH AFRICA'S TESTS & TOUR MATCHES

Test No.	Tour Match	Date	Venue	Opponent	Captain	Result	PF	PA
61		05/09/1953	Cape Town	AUSTRALIA	HSV Muller	Lost	14	18
62		19/09/1953	Durban	AUSTRALIA	HSV Muller	Won	18	8
63		26/09/1953	Port Elizabeth	AUSTRALIA	HSV Muller	Won	22	9
64		06/08/1955	Johannesburg	BRITISH ISLES	SP Fry	Lost	22	23
65		20/08/1955	Cape Town	BRITISH ISLES	SP Fry	Won	25	9
66		03/09/1955	Pretoria	BRITISH ISLES	SP Fry	Lost	6	9
67		24/09/1955	Port Elizabeth	BRITISH ISLES	SP Fry	Won	22	8
	136	15/05/1956	Canberra	Australian Capital Territories	SS Vivier	Won	41	6
	137	19/05/1956	Sydney	New South Wales	SS Vivier	Won	29	9
	138	22/05/1956	Tamworth	New South Wales Country	JAJ Pickard	Won	15	8
68		26/05/1956	Sydney	AUSTRALIA	SS Vivier	Won	9	0
	139	29/05/1956	Brisbane	Queensland	SS Vivier	Won	47	3
69		02/06/1956	Brisbane	AUSTRALIA	SS Vivier	Won	9	0
	140	09/06/1956	Hamilton	Waikato	JAJ Pickard	Lost	10	14
	141	13/06/1956	Whangarei	North Auckland	SS Vivier	Won	3	0
	142	16/06/1956	Auckland	Auckland	SS Vivier	Won	6	3
	143	20/06/1956	Palmerston N.	Manawatu-Horowhenua	AC Koch	Won	14	3
	144	23/06/1956	Wellington	Wellington	JA du Rand	Won	8	6
	145	27/06/1956	Gisborne	Poverty Bay-East Coast	JA du Rand	Won	22	0
	146	30/06/1956	Napier	Hawke's Bay	JA du Rand	Won	20	8
	147	04/07/1956	Nelson	Nelson, Marlborough & Golden Bay - Motueka	JA du Rand	Won	41	3
	148	07/07/1956	Dunedin	Otago	JA du Rand	Won	14	9
70		14/07/1956	Dunedin	NEW ZEALAND	JA du Rand	Lost	6	10
	149	18/07/1956	Timaru	S Canterbury, Mid Canterbury & North Otago	JAJ Pickard	Won	20	8
	150	21/07/1956	Christchurch	Canterbury	JA du Rand	Lost	6	9
	151	25/07/1956	Westport	West Coast-Buller	SS Vivier	Won	27	6
	152	28/07/1956	Invercargill	Southland	JA du Rand	Won	23	12
	153	31/07/1956	Masterton	Wairarapa-Bush	SS Vivier	Won	19	8
71		04/08/1956	Wellington	NEW ZEALAND	SS Vivier	Won	8	3
	154	08/08/1956	Wanganui	Wanganui-King Country	SS Vivier	Won	36	16
	155	11/08/1956	New Plymouth	Taranaki	SS Vivier	Drew	3	3
72		18/08/1956	Christchurch	NEW ZEALAND	SS Vivier	Lost	10	17
	156	22/08/1956	Wellington	New Zealand Universities	SS Vivier	Lost	15	22
	157	25/08/1956	Auckland	New Zealand Maoris	SS Vivier	Won	37	0
	158	28/08/1956	Rotorua	Bay of Plenty-Thames Valley-Counties	SS Vivier	Won	17	6
73		01/09/1956	Auckland	NEW ZEALAND	SS Vivier	Lost	5	11
74		26/07/1958	Cape Town	FRANCE	JT Claasen	Drew	3	3
75		16/08/1958	Johannesburg	FRANCE	JT Claasen	Lost	5	9
76		30/04/1960	Port Elizabeth	SCOTLAND	DC van Jaarsveld	Won	18	10
77		25/06/1960	Johannesburg	NEW ZEALAND	RG Dryburgh	Won	13	0
78		23/07/1960	Cape Town	NEW ZEALAND	RG Dryburgh	Lost	3	11
79		13/08/1960	Bloemfontein	NEW ZEALAND	AS Malan	Drew	11	11
80		27/08/1960	Port Elizabeth	NEW ZEALAND	AS Malan	Won	8	3
	159	22/10/1960	Hove	Southern Counties	AS Malan	Won	29	9
	160	26/10/1960	Oxford	Oxford University	RJ Lockyear	Won	24	5
	161	29/10/1960	Cardiff	Cardiff	AS Malan	Won	13	0
	162	02/11/1960	Pontypool	Pontypool & Cross Keys	JT Claasen	Won	30	3

SPRINGBOKS

SOUTH AFRICA'S TESTS & TOUR MATCHES

Test No.	Tour Match	Date	Venue	Opponent	Captain	Result	PF	PA
	163	05/11/1960	Leicester	Midland Counties	RJ Lockyear	Drew	3	3
	164	09/11/1960	Cambridge	Cambridge University	AS Malan	Won	12	0
	165	12/11/1960	Twickenham	London Counties	AS Malan	Won	20	3
	166	16/11/1960	Glasgow	Glasgow & Edinburgh	JT Claasen	Won	16	11
	167	19/11/1960	Hawick	South of Scotland	AS Malan	Won	19	3
	168	23/11/1960	Manchester	North Western Counties	JT Claasen	Won	11	0
	169	26/11/1960	Swansea	Swansea	RJ Lockyear	Won	19	3
	170	29/11/1960	Ebbw Vale	Ebbw Vale & Abertillery	AS Malan	Won	3	0
81		03/12/1960	Cardiff	WALES	AS Malan	Won	3	0
	171	07/12/1960	Camborne	South Western Counties	AS Malan	Won	21	9
	172	10/12/1960	Gloucester	Western Counties	AS Malan	Won	42	0
	173	13/12/1960	Llanelli	Llanelli	AS Malan	Won	21	0
82		17/12/1960	Dublin	IRELAND	AS Malan	Won	8	3
	174	21/12/1960	Cork	Munster	JT Claasen	Won	9	3
	175	26/12/1960	Twickenham	Combined Services	AS Malan	Won	14	5
	176	28/12/1960	Birmingham	Midland Couties	AS Malan	Won	16	5
	177	31/12/1960	Gosforth	North Eastern Counties	JT Claasen	Won	21	9
	178	03/01/1961	Bournemouth	South Eastern Counties	AS Malan	Won	24	0
83		07/01/1961	Twickenham	ENGLAND	AS Malan	Won	5	0
	179	11/01/1961	Newport	Newport	AS Malan	Won	3	0
	180	14/01/1961	Neath	Neath & Aberavon	AS Malan	Won	25	5
84		21/01/1961	Edinburgh	SCOTLAND	AS Malan	Won	12	5
	181	25/01/1961	Aberdeen	North of Scotland	AS Malan	Won	22	9
	182	28/01/1961	Belfast	Ulster	JT Claasen	Won	19	6
	183	01/02/1961	Dublin	Leinster	AS Malan	Won	12	5
	184	04/02/1961	Cardiff	Barbarians	AS Malan	Lost	0	6
	185	08/02/1961	Bordeaux	South Western France	RJ Lockyear	Won	29	3
	186	11/02/1961	Toulouse	France 'B'	RJ Lockyear	Won	26	10
	187	14/02/1961	Bayonne	Coast of Basque	AS Malan	Won	36	9
85		18/02/1961	Paris	FRANCE	AS Malan	Drew	0	0
86		13/05/1961	Cape Town	IRELAND	JT Claasen	Won	24	8
87		05/08/1961	Johannesburg	AUSTRALIA	JT Claasen	Won	28	3
88		12/08/1961	Port Elizabeth	AUSTRALIA	JT Claasen	Won	23	11
89		23/06/1962	Johannesburg	BRITISH ISLES	JT Claasen	Drew	3	3
90		21/07/1962	Durban	BRITISH ISLES	JT Claasen	Won	3	0
91		04/08/1962	Cape Town	BRITISH ISLES	JT Claasen	Won	8	3
92		25/08/1962	Bloemfontein	BRITISH ISLES	JT Claasen	Won	34	14
93		13/07/1963	Pretoria	AUSTRALIA	GF Malan	Won	14	3
94		10/08/1963	Cape Town	AUSTRALIA	GF Malan	Lost	5	9
95		24/08/1963	Johannesburg	AUSTRALIA	AS Malan	Lost	9	11
96		07/09/1963	Port Elizabeth	AUSTRALIA	GF Malan	Won	22	6
97		23/05/1964	Durban	WALES	GF Malan	Won	24	3
98		25/07/1964	Springs	FRANCE	CM Smith	Lost	6	8
	188	03/04/1965	Belfast	Combined Provinces (Ireland)	AS Malan	Drew	8	8
	189	06/04/1965	Limerick	Combined Universities, Past & Present	AS Malan	Lost	10	12
99		10/04/1965	Dublin	IRELAND	AS Malan	Lost	6	9
	190	13/04/1965	Hawick	Scottish Districts XV	DJ de Villiers	Lost	8	16
100		17/04/1965	Edinburgh	SCOTLAND	AS Malan	Lost	5	8
	191	10/06/1965	Perth	Western Australia	DJ de Villiers	Won	60	0

SPRINGBOKS

SOUTH AFRICA'S TESTS & TOUR MATCHES

Test No.	Tour Match	Date	Venue	Opponent	Captain	Result	PF	PA
	192	12/06/1965	Melbourne	Victoria	CM Smith	Won	52	6
	193	14/06/1965	Sydney	New South Wales	DJ de Villiers	Lost	3	12
101		19/06/1965	Sydney	AUSTRALIA	CM Smith	Lost	11	18
	194	22/06/1965	Brisbane	Queensland	CM Smith	Won	50	5
102		26/06/1965	Brisbane	AUSTRALIA	CM Smith	Lost	8	12
	195	30/06/1965	Gisborne	Poverty Bay - East Coast	CM Smith	Won	32	3
	196	03/07/1965	Wellington	Wellington	CM Smith	Lost	6	23
	197	07/07/1965	Palmerston N.	Manawatu-Horowhenua	DJ de Villiers	Won	30	8
	198	10/07/1965	Dunedin	Otago	DJ de Villiers	Won	8	6
	199	14/07/1965	Christchurch	New Zealand Juniors	CM Smith	Won	23	3
	200	17/07/1965	New Plymouth	Taranaki	DJ de Villiers	Won	11	3
	201	21/07/1965	Invercargill	Southland	CM Smith	Won	19	6
	202	24/07/1965	Christchurch	Canterbury	DJ de Villiers	Won	6	5
	203	27/07/1965	Greymouth	West Coast-Buller	CM Smith	Won	11	0
103		31/07/1965	Wellington	NEW ZEALAND	DJ de Villiers	Lost	3	6
	204	04/08/1965	Wanganui	Wanganui-King Country	DJ de Villiers	Won	24	19
	205	07/08/1965	Hamilton	Waikato	CM Smith	Won	26	13
	206	11/08/1965	Whangarei	North Auckland	CM Smith	Won	14	11
	207	14/08/1965	Auckland	Auckland	DJ de Villiers	Lost	14	15
	208	17/08/1965	Blenheim	Marlborough, Nelson & Golden Bay- Motueka	CM Smith	Won	45	6
104		21/08/1965	Dunedin	NEW ZEALAND	CM Smith	Lost	0	13
	209	25/08/1965	Timaru	S Canterbury, Mid Canterbury & North Otago	DJ de Villiers	Won	28	13
	210	28/08/1965	Wellington	New Zealand Maoris	DJ de Villiers	Won	9	3
	211	31/08/1965	Masterton	Wairarapa-Bush	CM Smith	Won	36	0
105		04/09/1965	Christchurch	NEW ZEALAND	DJ de Villiers	Won	19	16
	212	08/09/1965	Auckland	New Zealand Universities	CM Smith	Won	55	11
	213	11/09/1965	Napier	Hawke's Bay	DJ de Villiers	Won	30	12
	214	14/09/1965	Rotorua	Bay of Plenty-Counties-Thames Valley	DJ de Villiers	Won	33	17
106		18/09/1965	Auckland	NEW ZEALAND	DJ de Villiers	Lost	3	20
107		15/07/1967	Durban	FRANCE	DJ de Villiers	Won	26	3
108		22/07/1967	Bloemfontein	FRANCE	DJ de Villiers	Won	16	3
109		29/07/1967	Johannesburg	FRANCE	DJ de Villiers	Lost	14	19
110		12/08/1967	Cape Town	FRANCE	DJ de Villiers	Drew	6	6
111		08/06/1968	Pretoria	BRITISH ISLES	DJ de Villiers	Won	25	20
112		22/06/1968	Port Elizabeth	BRITISH ISLES	DJ de Villiers	Drew	6	6
113		13/07/1968	Cape Town	BRITISH ISLES	DJ de Villiers	Won	11	6
114		27/07/1968	Johannesburg	BRITISH ISLES	DJ de Villiers	Won	19	6
	215	29/10/1968	Toulon	Littoral-Provence	DJ de Villiers	Won	24	3
	216	02/11/1968	Lyon	South Eastern France	TP Bedford	Won	3	0
	217	05/11/1968	Clermont-Ferrand	Auvergne-Limousin	DJ de Villiers	Won	26	9
115		09/11/1968	Bordeaux	FRANCE	DJ de Villiers	Won	12	9
	218	11/11/1968	Toulouse	South Western France	TP Bedford	Lost	3	11
116		16/11/1968	Paris	FRANCE	DJ de Villiers	Won	16	11
117		02/08/1969	Johannesburg	AUSTRALIA	DJ de Villiers	Won	30	11
118		16/08/1969	Durban	AUSTRALIA	TP Bedford	Won	16	9
119		06/09/1969	Cape Town	AUSTRALIA	TP Bedford	Won	11	3
120		20/09/1969	Bloemfontein	AUSTRALIA	DJ de Villiers	Won	19	8

SPRINGBOKS

SOUTH AFRICA'S TESTS & TOUR MATCHES

Test No.	Tour Match	Date	Venue	Opponent	Captain	Result	PF	PA
	219	05/11/1969	Twickenham	Oxford University	DJ de Villiers	Lost	3	6
	220	08/11/1969	Leicester	Midland Counties (E)	TP Bedford	Won	11	9
	221	12/11/1969	Newport	Newport	DJ de Villiers	Lost	6	11
	222	15/11/1969	Swansea	Swansea	DJ de Villiers	Won	12	0
	223	19/11/1969	Ebbw Vale	Gwent	JFK Marais	Lost	8	14
	224	22/11/1969	Twickenham	London Counties	DJ de Villiers	Won	22	6
	225	26/11/1969	Manchester	North Western Counties	DJ de Villiers	Won	12	9
	226	02/12/1969	Aberdeen	North & Midlands of Scotland	DJ de Villiers	Won	37	3
121		06/12/1969	Edinburgh	SCOTLAND	TP Bedford	Lost	3	6
	227	10/12/1969	Aberavon	Aberavon & Neath	TP Bedford	Won	27	0
	228	13/12/1969	Cardiff	Cardiff	DJ de Villiers	Won	17	3
	229	16/12/1969	Aldershot	Combined Services	JFK Marais	Won	14	6
122		20/12/1969	Twickenham	ENGLAND	DJ de Villiers	Lost	8	11
	230	27/12/1969	Exeter	South Western Counties	DJ de Villiers	Won	9	6
	231	31/12/1969	Bristol	Western Counties	TP Bedford	Drew	3	3
	232	03/01/1970	Gosforth	North Eastern Counties	DJ de Villiers	Won	24	11
	233	06/01/1970	Coventry	Midland Counties (W)	TP Bedford	Won	21	6
123		10/01/1970	Dublin	IRELAND	DJ de Villiers	Drew	8	8
	234	14/01/1970	Limerick	Munster	DJ de Villiers	Won	25	9
	235	17/01/1970	Galashiels	South of Scotland	TP Bedford	Drew	3	3
	236	20/01/1970	Llanelli	Llanelli	DJ de Villiers	Won	10	9
124		24/01/1970	Cardiff	WALES	DJ de Villiers	Drew	6	6
	237	28/01/1970	Gloucester	Southern Counties	TP Bedford	Won	13	0
	238	31/01/1970	Twickenham	Barbarians	DJ de Villiers	Won	21	12
125		25/07/1970	Pretoria	NEW ZEALAND	DJ de Villiers	Won	17	6
126		08/08/1970	Cape Town	NEW ZEALAND	DJ de Villiers	Lost	8	9
127		29/08/1970	Port Elizabeth	NEW ZEALAND	DJ de Villiers	Won	14	3
128		12/09/1970	Johannesburg	NEW ZEALAND	DJ de Villiers	Won	20	17
129		12/06/1971	Bloemfontein	FRANCE	JFK Marais	Won	22	9
130		19/06/1971	Durban	FRANCE	JFK Marais	Drew	8	8
	239	26/06/1971	Perth	Western Australia	JFK Marais	Won	44	18
	240	30/06/1971	Adelaide	South Australia	TP Bedford	Won	43	0
	241	03/07/1971	Melbourne	Victoria	JFK Marais	Won	50	0
	242	06/07/1971	Sydney	Sydney	JFK Marais	Won	21	12
	243	10/07/1971	Sydney	New South Wales	JFK Marais	Won	25	3
	244	13/07/1971	Orange	New South Wales Country	PJF Greyling	Won	19	3
131		17/07/1971	Sydney	AUSTRALIA	JFK Marais	Won	19	11
	245	21/07/1971	Canberra	Australian Capital Territories	JFK Marais	Won	34	3
	246	24/07/1971	Brisbane	Queensland	JFK Marais	Won	33	14
	247	27/07/1971	Brisbane	Junior Wallabies	JFK Marais	Won	31	12
132		31/07/1971	Brisbane	AUSTRALIA	JFK Marais	Won	14	6
	248	03/08/1971	Toowoomba	Queensland Country	PJF Greyling	Won	45	14
133		07/08/1971	Sydney	AUSTRALIA	JFK Marais	Won	18	6
134		03/06/1972	Johannesburg	ENGLAND	PJF Greyling	Lost	9	18
135		08/06/1974	Cape Town	BRITISH ISLES	JFK Marais	Lost	3	12
136		22/06/1974	Pretoria	BRITISH ISLES	JFK Marais	Lost	9	28
137		13/07/1974	Port Elizabeth	BRITISH ISLES	JFK Marais	Lost	9	26
138		27/07/1974	Johannesburg	BRITISH ISLES	JFK Marais	Drew	13	13
	249	06/11/1974	Nice	South Eastern France	JFK Marais	Won	10	7

SPRINGBOKS

SOUTH AFRICA'S TESTS & TOUR MATCHES

Test No.	Tour Match	Date	Venue	Opponent	Captain	Result	PF	PA
	250	09/11/1974	Lyon	North Eastern France	DSL Snyman	Won	25	12
	251	13/11/1974	Agen	South Western France	JFK Marais	Won	16	3
	252	16/11/1974	Tarbes	Second Division Clubs	JFK Marais	Won	36	4
	253	20/11/1974	Clermont-Ferrand	Central France	DSL Snyman	Won	29	10
139		23/11/1974	Toulouse	FRANCE	JFK Marais	Won	13	4
	254	27/11/1974	Angoulême	Western France	JCP Snyman	Lost	4	7
140		30/11/1974	Paris	FRANCE	JFK Marais	Won	10	8
	255	04/12/1974	Reims	Northern France	JFK Marais	Won	27	19
141		21/06/1975	Bloemfontein	FRANCE	M du Plessis	Won	38	25
142		28/06/1975	Pretoria	FRANCE	M du Plessis	Won	33	18
143		24/07/1976	Durban	NEW ZEALAND	M du Plessis	Won	16	7
144		14/08/1976	Bloemfontein	NEW ZEALAND	M du Plessis	Lost	9	15
145		04/09/1976	Cape Town	NEW ZEALAND	M du Plessis	Won	15	10
146		18/09/1976	Johannesburg	NEW ZEALAND	M du Plessis	Won	15	14
147		27/08/1977	Pretoria	WORLD TEAM	M du Plessis	Won	45	24
148		26/04/1980	Johannesburg	SOUTH AMERICA	M du Plessis	Won	24	9
149		03/05/1980	Durban	SOUTH AMERICA	M du Plessis	Won	18	9
150		31/05/1980	Cape Town	BRITISH ISLES	M du Plessis	Won	26	22
151		14/06/1980	Bloemfontein	BRITISH ISLES	M du Plessis	Won	26	19
152		28/06/1980	Port Elizabeth	BRITISH ISLES	M du Plessis	Won	12	10
153		12/07/1980	Pretoria	BRITISH ISLES	M du Plessis	Lost	13	17
	256	09/10/1980	Asunción	Paraguay Invitation XV	RB Prentiss	Won	84	6
	257	11/10/1980	Asunción	South America Invitation XV	MTS Stofberg	Won	79	18
	258	14/10/1980	Montevideo	British Schools Old Boys	MTS Stofberg	Won	83	13
154		18/10/1980	Montevideo	SOUTH AMERICA	MTS Stofberg	Won	22	13
	259	21/10/1980	Santiago	Chile Invitation XV	M du Plessis	Won	78	12
155		25/10/1980	Santiago	SOUTH AMERICA	M du Plessis	Won	30	16
156		08/11/1980	Pretoria	FRANCE	M du Plessis	Won	37	15
157		30/05/1981	Cape Town	IRELAND	W Claassen	Won	23	15
158		06/06/1981	Durban	IRELAND	W Claassen	Won	12	10
	260	22/07/1981	Gisborne	Poverty Bay	E Jansen	Won	24	6
	261	29/07/1981	New Plymouth	Taranaki	W Claassen	Won	34	9
	262	01/08/1981	Palmerston N.	Manawatu	MTS Stofberg	Won	31	19
	263	05/08/1981	Wanganui	Wanganui	W Claassen	Won	45	9
	264	08/08/1981	Invercargill	Southland	MTS Stofberg	Won	22	6
	265	11/08/1981	Dunedin	Otago	W Claassen	Won	17	13
159		15/08/1981	Christchurch	NEW ZEALAND	MTS Stofberg	Lost	9	14
	266	22/08/1981	Nelson	Nelson Bays	W Claassen	Won	83	0
	267	25/08/1981	Napier	New Zealand Maoris	DJ Serfontein	Drew	12	12
160		29/08/1981	Wellington	NEW ZEALAND	W Claassen	Won	24	12
	268	02/09/1981	Rotorua	Bay of Plenty	MTS Stofberg	Won	29	24
	269	05/09/1981	Auckland	Auckland	W Claassen	Won	39	12
	270	08/09/1981	Whangarei	North Auckland	E Jansen	Won	19	10
161		12/09/1981	Auckland	NEW ZEALAND	W Claassen	Lost	22	25
	271	19/09/1981	Wisconsin	Midwest	MTS Stofberg	Won	46	12
	272	22/09/1981	New York	Eastern	W Claassen	Won	41	0
162		25/09/1981	New York	USA	W Claassen	Won	38	7
163		27/03/1982	Pretoria	SOUTH AMERICA	W Claassen	Won	50	18
164		03/04/1982	Bloemfontein	SOUTH AMERICA	W Claassen	Lost	12	21
165		02/06/1984	Port Elizabeth	ENGLAND	MTS Stofberg	Won	33	15

SPRINGBOKS

SOUTH AFRICA'S TESTS & TOUR MATCHES

Test No.	Tour Match	Date	Venue	Opponent	Captain	Result	PF	PA
166		09/06/1984	Johannesburg	ENGLAND	MTS Stofberg	Won	35	9
167		20/10/1984	Pretoria	S AMERICA & SPAIN	DJ Serfontein	Won	32	15
168		27/10/1984	Cape Town	S AMERICA & SPAIN	DJ Serfontein	Won	22	13
169		10/05/1986	Cape Town	NZ CAVALIERS	HE Botha	Won	21	15
170		17/05/1986	Durban	NZ CAVALIERS	HE Botha	Lost	18	19
171		24/05/1986	Pretoria	NZ CAVALIERS	HE Botha	Won	33	18
172		31/05/1986	Johannesburg	NZ CAVALIERS	HE Botha	Won	24	10
173		26/08/1989	Cape Town	WORLD TEAM	JC Breedt	Won	20	19
174		02/09/1989	Johannesburg	WORLD TEAM	JC Breedt	Won	22	16
175		15/08/1992	Johannesburg	NEW ZEALAND	HE Botha	Lost	24	27
176		22/08/1992	Cape Town	AUSTRALIA	HE Botha	Lost	3	26
	273	03/10/1992	Bordeaux	French Selection	HE Botha	Lost	17	24
	274	07/10/1992	Pau	Aquitaine XV	WJ Bartmann	Won	29	22
	275	10/10/1992	Toulouse	Midi-Pyrénées XV	HE Botha	Won	18	15
	276	13/10/1992	Marseilles	Provence-Côte D'Azur XV	RJ du Preez	Won	41	12
177		17/10/1992	Lyon	FRANCE	HE Botha	Won	20	15
	277	20/10/1992	Béziers	Languedoc XV	RJ du Preez	Won	36	15
178		24/10/1992	Paris	FRANCE	HE Botha	Lost	16	29
	278	28/10/1992	Tours	French Universities	RJ du Preez	Lost	13	18
	279	31/10/1992	Lille	French Barbarians	HE Botha	Lost	20	25
	280	04/11/1992	Leicester	Midland Division	HE Botha	Won	32	9
	281	07/11/1992	Bristol	England 'B'	HE Botha	Won	20	16
	282	10/11/1992	Leeds	Northern Division	RJ du Preez	Won	19	3
179		14/11/1992	Twickenham	ENGLAND	HE Botha	Lost	16	33
180		26/06/1993	Durban	FRANCE	JF Pienaar	Drew	20	20
181		03/07/1993	Johannesburg	FRANCE	JF Pienaar	Lost	17	18
	283	14/07/1993	Perth	Western Australia	JF Pienaar	Won	71	8
	284	17/07/1993	Adelaide	South Australian Invitation XV	CP Strauss	Won	90	3
	285	21/07/1993	Melbourne	Victoria	AH Richter	Won	78	3
	286	24/07/1993	Sydney	New South Wales	JF Pienaar	Lost	28	29
	287	27/07/1993	Orange	New South Wales Country	AH Richter	Won	41	7
182		31/07/1993	Sydney	AUSTRALIA	JF Pienaar	Won	19	12
	288	04/08/1993	Canberra	Australian Capital Territories	AH Richter	Won	57	10
	289	08/08/1993	Brisbane	Queensland	JF Pienaar	Won	17	3
	290	11/08/1993	Mackay	Queensland Country	AH Richter	Won	63	5
183		14/08/1993	Brisbane	AUSTRALIA	JF Pienaar	Lost	20	28
	291	18/08/1993	Sydney	Sydney	AH Richter	Won	31	20
184		21/08/1993	Sydney	AUSTRALIA	JF Pienaar	Lost	12	19
	292	27/10/1993	Cordoba	Provincial XV	CP Strauss	Won	55	37
	293	30/10/1993	Buenos Aires	Buenos Aires XV	WJ Bartmann	Lost	27	28
	294	03/11/1993	Tucumán	Tucumán	CP Strauss	Won	40	12
185		06/11/1993	Buenos Aires	ARGENTINA	JF Pienaar	Won	29	26
	295	09/11/1993	Rosario	Provincial XV	WJ Bartmann	Won	40	26
186		13/11/1993	Buenos Aires	ARGENTINA	JF Pienaar	Won	52	23
187		04/06/1994	Pretoria	ENGLAND	JF Pienaar	Lost	15	32
188		11/06/1994	Cape Town	ENGLAND	JF Pienaar	Won	27	9
	296	23/06/1994	Taupo	King Country	JF Pienaar	Won	46	10
	297	25/06/1994	Pukekohe	Counties	WJ Bartmann	Won	37	26
	298	28/06/1994	Wellington	Wellington	JF Pienaar	Won	36	26
	299	02/07/1994	Invercargill	Southland	AH Richter	Won	51	15

SPRINGBOKS

SOUTH AFRICA'S TESTS & TOUR MATCHES

Test No.	Tour Match	Date	Venue	Opponent	Captain	Result	PF	PA
	300	05/07/1994	Timaru	Hanan Shield Districts	CP Strauss	Won	67	19
189		09/07/1994	Dunedin	NEW ZEALAND	CP Strauss	Lost	14	22
	301	13/07/1994	New Plymouth	Taranaki	RAW Straeuli	Won	16	12
	302	16/07/1994	Hamilton	Waikato	CP Strauss	Won	38	17
	303	19/07/1994	Palmerston N.	Manawatu	JF Pienaar	Won	47	21
190		23/07/1994	Wellington	NEW ZEALAND	JF Pienaar	Lost	9	13
	304	27/07/1994	Dunedin	Otago	CP Strauss	Lost	12	19
	305	30/07/1994	Christchurch	Canterbury	JF Pienaar	Won	21	11
	306	02/08/1994	Rotorua	Bay of Plenty	CP Strauss	Won	33	12
191		06/08/1994	Auckland	NEW ZEALAND	JF Pienaar	Drew	18	18
192		08/10/1994	Port Elizabeth	ARGENTINA	JF Pienaar	Won	42	22
193		15/10/1994	Johannesburg	ARGENTINA	JF Pienaar	Won	46	26
	307	22/10/1994	Cardiff	Cardiff	RAW Straeuli	Won	11	6
	308	26/10/1994	Newport	Wales 'A'	RAW Straeuli	Won	25	13
	309	29/10/1994	Llanelli	Llanelli	JF Pienaar	Won	30	12
	310	02/11/1994	Neath	Neath	CP Strauss	Won	16	13
	311	05/11/1994	Swansea	Swansea	JF Pienaar	Won	78	7
	312	09/11/1994	Melrose	Scotland 'A'	CP Strauss	Lost	15	17
	313	12/11/1994	Glasgow	Scottish Combined Districts	JF Pienaar	Won	33	6
	314	15/11/1994	Aberdeen	Scottish Select	CP Strauss	Won	35	10
194		19/11/1994	Edinburgh	SCOTLAND	JF Pienaar	Won	34	10
	315	22/11/1994	Pontypridd	Pontypridd	CP Strauss	Won	9	3
195		26/11/1994	Cardiff	WALES	JF Pienaar	Won	20	12
	316	29/11/1994	Belfast	Combined Provinces	RAW Straeuli	Won	54	19
	317	03/12/1994	Dublin	Barbarians	JF Pienaar	Lost	15	23
196		13/04/1995	Johannesburg	WESTERN SAMOA	JF Pienaar	Won	60	8
197		25/05/1995	Cape Town	AUSTRALIA	JF Pienaar	Won	27	18
198		30/05/1995	Cape Town	ROMANIA	AJ Richter	Won	21	8
199		03/06/1995	Port Elizabeth	CANADA	JF Pienaar	Won	20	0
200		10/06/1995	Johannesburg	WESTERN SAMOA	JF Pienaar	Won	42	14
201		17/06/1995	Durban	FRANCE	JF Pienaar	Won	19	15
202		24/06/1995	Johannesburg	NEW ZEALAND	JF Pienaar	Won	15	12
203		02/09/1995	Johannesburg	WALES	JF Pienaar	Won	40	11
204		12/11/1995	Rome	ITALY	JF Pienaar	Won	40	21
205		18/11/1995	Twickenham	ENGLAND	JF Pienaar	Won	24	14
206		02/07/1996	Pretoria	FIJI	JF Pienaar	Won	43	18
207		13/07/1996	Sydney	AUSTRALIA	JF Pienaar	Lost	16	21
208		20/07/1996	Christchurch	NEW ZEALAND	JF Pienaar	Lost	11	15
209		03/08/1996	Bloemfontein	AUSTRALIA	JF Pienaar	Won	25	19
210		10/08/1996	Cape Town	NEW ZEALAND	JF Pienaar	Lost	18	29
211		17/08/1996	Durban	NEW ZEALAND	GH Teichmann	Lost	19	23
212		24/08/1996	Pretoria	NEW ZEALAND	GH Teichmann	Lost	26	33
213		31/08/1996	Johannesburg	NEW ZEALAND	GH Teichmann	Won	32	22
	318	05/11/1996	Rosario	Rosario	WS Fyvie	Won	45	36
214		09/11/1996	Buenos Aires	ARGENTINA	GH Teichmann	Won	46	15
	319	12/11/1996	Mendoza	Mendoza	WS Fyvie	Won	89	19
215		16/11/1996	Buenos Aires	ARGENTINA	GH Teichmann	Won	44	21
	320	23/11/1996	Brive	French Barbarians	WS Fyvie	Lost	22	30
	321	26/11/1996	Lyon	South East Selection	WS Fyvie	Won	36	20
216		30/11/1996	Bordeaux	FRANCE	GH Teichmann	Won	22	12

SPRINGBOKS

SOUTH AFRICA'S TESTS & TOUR MATCHES

Test No.	Tour Match	Date	Venue	Opponent	Captain	Result	PF	PA
	322	03/12/1996	Lille	French Universities	WS Fyvie	Lost	13	20
217		07/12/1996	Paris	FRANCE	GH Teichmann	Won	13	12
218		15/12/1996	Cardiff	WALES	GH Teichmann	Won	37	20
219		10/06/1997	Cape Town	TONGA	GH Teichmann	Won	74	10
220		21/06/1997	Cape Town	BRITISH ISLES	GH Teichmann	Lost	16	25
221		28/06/1997	Durban	BRITISH ISLES	GH Teichmann	Lost	15	18
222		05/07/1997	Johannesburg	BRITISH ISLES	GH Teichmann	Won	35	16
223		19/07/1997	Johannesburg	NEW ZEALAND	GH Teichmann	Lost	32	35
224		02/08/1997	Brisbane	AUSTRALIA	GH Teichmann	Lost	20	32
225		09/08/1997	Auckland	NEW ZEALAND	GH Teichmann	Lost	35	55
226		23/08/1997	Pretoria	AUSTRALIA	GH Teichmann	Won	61	22
227		08/11/1997	Bologna	ITALY	GH Teichmann	Won	62	31
	323	11/11/1997	Biarritz	French Barbarians	AD Aitken	Lost	22	40
228		15/11/1997	Lyon	FRANCE	GH Teichmann	Won	36	32
	324	18/11/1997	Toulon	France 'A'	AD Aitken	Lost	7	21
229		22/11/1997	Paris	FRANCE	GH Teichmann	Won	52	10
230		29/11/1997	Twickenham	ENGLAND	GH Teichmann	Won	29	11
231		06/12/1997	Edinburgh	SCOTLAND	GH Teichmann	Won	68	10
232		13/06/1998	Bloemfontein	IRELAND	GH Teichmann	Won	37	13
233		20/06/1998	Pretoria	IRELAND	GH Teichmann	Won	33	0
234		27/06/1998	Pretoria	WALES	GH Teichmann	Won	96	13
235		04/07/1998	Cape Town	ENGLAND	GH Teichmann	Won	18	0
236		18/07/1998	Perth	AUSTRALIA	GH Teichmann	Won	14	13
237		25/07/1998	Wellington	NEW ZEALAND	GH Teichmann	Won	13	3
238		15/08/1998	Durban	NEW ZEALAND	GH Teichmann	Won	24	23
239		22/08/1998	Johannesburg	AUSTRALIA	GH Teichmann	Won	29	15
	325	10/11/1998	Firhill	Glasgow Caledonians	RB Skinstad	Won	62	9
240		14/11/1998	London	WALES	GH Teichmann	Won	28	20
	326	17/11/1998	Edinburgh	Edinburgh Reivers	RB Skinstad	Won	49	3
241		21/11/1998	Edinburgh	SCOTLAND	GH Teichmann	Won	35	10
	327	24/11/1998	Cork	Combined Provinces	AN Vos	Won	32	5
242		28/11/1998	Dublin	IRELAND	GH Teichmann	Won	27	13
	328	01/12/1998	Belfast	Ireland 'A'	AN Vos	Won	50	19
243		05/12/1998	Twickenham	ENGLAND	GH Teichmann	Lost	7	13
244		12/06/1999	Port Elizabeth	ITALY	GH Teichmann	Won	74	3
245		19/06/1999	Durban	ITALY	CPJ Krige	Won	101	0
246		26/06/1999	Cardiff	WALES	GH Teichmann	Lost	19	29
247		10/07/1999	Dunedin	NEW ZEALAND	GH Teichmann	Lost	0	28
248		17/07/1999	Brisbane	AUSTRALIA	J Erasmus	Lost	6	32
249		07/08/1999	Pretoria	NEW ZEALAND	JH van der Westhuizen	Lost	18	34
250		14/08/1999	Cape Town	AUSTRALIA	JH van der Westhuizen	Won	10	9
251		03/10/1999	Edinburgh	SCOTLAND	JH van der Westhuizen	Won	46	29
252		10/10/1999	Edinburgh	SPAIN	AN Vos	Won	47	3
253		15/10/1999	Glasgow	URUGUAY	JH van der Westhuizen	Won	39	3
254		24/10/1999	Paris	ENGLAND	JH van der Westhuizen	Won	44	21
255		30/10/1999	London	AUSTRALIA	JH van der Westhuizen	Lost	21	27
256		04/11/1999	Cardiff	NEW ZEALAND	JH van der Westhuizen	Won	22	18
257		10/06/2000	East London	CANADA	AN Vos	Won	51	18
258		17/06/2000	Pretoria	ENGLAND	AN Vos	Won	18	13
259		24/06/2000	Bloemfontein	ENGLAND	AN Vos	Lost	22	27

SPRINGBOKS

SOUTH AFRICA'S TESTS & TOUR MATCHES

Test No.	Tour Match	Date	Venue	Opponent	Captain	Result	PF	PA
260		08/07/2000	Melbourne	AUSTRALIA	AN Vos	Lost	23	44
261		22/07/2000	Christchurch	NEW ZEALAND	AN Vos	Lost	12	25
262		29/07/2000	Sydney	AUSTRALIA	AN Vos	Lost	6	26
263		19/08/2000	Johannesburg	NEW ZEALAND	AN Vos	Won	46	40
264		26/08/2000	Durban	AUSTRALIA	AN Vos	Lost	18	19
	329	08/11/2000	Tucuman	Argentina 'A'	DJ van Zyl	Won	32	21
265		12/11/2000	Buenos Aires	ARGENTINA	AN Vos	Won	37	33
	330	15/11/2000	Limerick	Ireland 'A'	A-H le Roux	Lost	11	28
266		19/11/2000	Dublin	IRELAND	AN Vos	Won	28	18
	331	22/11/2000	Cardiff	Wales 'A'	DJ van Zyl	Won	34	15
267		26/11/2000	Cardiff	WALES	AN Vos	Won	23	13
	332	28/11/2000	Worcester	England National Divisions XV	V Matfield	Lost	30	35
268		02/12/2000	Twickenham	ENGLAND	AN Vos	Lost	17	25
	333	09/12/2000	Cardiff	Barbarians	AN Vos	Won	41	31
269		16/06/2001	Johannesburg	FRANCE	AN Vos	Lost	23	32
270		23/06/2001	Durban	FRANCE	AN Vos	Won	20	15
271		30/06/2001	Port Elizabeth	ITALY	RB Skinstad	Won	60	14
272		21/07/2001	Cape Town	NEW ZEALAND	RB Skinstad	Lost	3	12
273		28/07/2001	Pretoria	AUSTRALIA	RB Skinstad	Won	20	15
274		18/08/2001	Perth	AUSTRALIA	RB Skinstad	Drew	14	14
275		25/08/2001	Auckland	NEW ZEALAND	RB Skinstad	Lost	15	26
276		10/11/2001	Paris	FRANCE	RB Skinstad	Lost	10	20
277		17/11/2001	Genoa	ITALY	RB Skinstad	Won	54	26
278		24/11/2001	London	ENGLAND	RB Skinstad	Lost	9	29
279		01/12/2001	Houston	USA	AN Vos	Won	43	20
280		08/06/2002	Bloemfontein	WALES	RB Skinstad	Won	34	19
281		15/06/2002	Cape Town	WALES	RB Skinstad	Won	19	8
282		29/06/2002	Springs	ARGENTINA	CPJ Krige	Won	49	29
283		06/07/2002	Pretoria	SAMOA	CPJ Krige	Won	60	18
284		20/07/2002	Wellington	NEW ZEALAND	CPJ Krige	Lost	20	41
285		27/07/2002	Brisbane	AUSTRALIA	CPJ Krige	Lost	27	38
286		10/08/2002	Durban	NEW ZEALAND	CPJ Krige	Lost	23	30
287		17/08/2002	Johannesburg	AUSTRALIA	CPJ Krige	Won	33	31
288		09/11/2002	Marseilles	FRANCE	CPJ Krige	Lost	10	30
289		16/11/2002	Edinburgh	SCOTLAND	CPJ Krige	Lost	6	21
290		23/11/2002	London	ENGLAND	CPJ Krige	Lost	3	53
291		07/06/2003	Durban	SCOTLAND	JH van der Westhuizen	Won	29	25
292		14/06/2003	Johannesburg	SCOTLAND	JH van der Westhuizen	Won	28	19
293		28/06/2003	Port Elizabeth	ARGENTINA	CPJ Krige	Won	26	25
294		12/07/2003	Cape Town	AUSTRALIA	CPJ Krige	Won	26	22
295		19/07/2003	Pretoria	NEW ZEALAND	CPJ Krige	Lost	16	52
296		02/08/2003	Brisbane	AUSTRALIA	CPJ Krige	Lost	9	29
297		09/08/2003	Dunedin	NEW ZEALAND	CPJ Krige	Lost	11	19
298		11/10/2003	Perth	URUGUAY	JH van der Westhuizen	Won	72	6
299		18/10/2003	Perth	ENGLAND	CPJ Krige	Lost	6	25
300		24/10/2003	Sydney	GEORGIA	JW Smit	Won	46	19
301		01/11/2003	Brisbane	SAMOA	CPJ Krige	Won	60	10
302		08/11/2003	Melbourne	NEW ZEALAND	CPJ Krige	Lost	9	29
303		12/06/2004	Bloemfontein	IRELAND	JW Smit	Won	31	17
304		19/06/2004	Cape Town	IRELAND	JW Smit	Won	26	17

SPRINGBOKS

SOUTH AFRICA'S TESTS & TOUR MATCHES

Test No.	Tour Match	Date	Venue	Opponent	Captain	Result	PF	PA
305		26/06/2004	Pretoria	WALES	JW Smit	Won	53	18
306		17/07/2004	Gosford	PACIFIC ISLANDS	JW Smit	Won	38	24
307		24/07/2004	Christchurch	NEW ZEALAND	JW Smit	Lost	21	23
308		31/07/2004	Perth	AUSTRALIA	JW Smit	Lost	26	30
309		14/08/2004	Johannesburg	NEW ZEALAND	JW Smit	Won	40	26
310		21/08/2004	Durban	AUSTRALIA	JW Smit	Won	23	19
311		06/11/2004	Cardiff	WALES	JW Smit	Won	38	36
312		13/11/2004	Dublin	IRELAND	JW Smit	Lost	12	17
313		20/11/2004	London	ENGLAND	JW Smit	Lost	16	32
314		27/11/2004	Edinburgh	SCOTLAND	JW Smit	Won	45	10
315		04/12/2004	Buenos Aires	ARGENTINA	JW Smit	Won	39	7
316		11/06/2005	East London	URUGUAY	JW Smit	Won	134	3
317		18/06/2005	Durban	FRANCE	JW Smit	Drew	30	30
318		25/06/2005	Port Elizabeth	FRANCE	JW Smit	Won	27	13
319		09/07/2005	Sydney	AUSTRALIA	JW Smit	Lost	12	30
320		23/07/2005	Johannesburg	AUSTRALIA	JW Smit	Won	33	20
321		30/07/2005	Pretoria	AUSTRALIA	JW Smit	Won	22	16
322		06/08/2005	Cape Town	NEW ZEALAND	JW Smit	Won	22	16
323		20/08/2005	Perth	AUSTRALIA	JW Smit	Won	22	19
324		27/08/2005	Dunedin	NEW ZEALAND	JW Smit	Lost	27	31
325		05/11/2005	Buenos Aires	ARGENTINA	JW Smit	Won	34	23
326		19/11/2005	Cardiff	WALES	JW Smit	Won	33	16
327		26/11/2005	Paris	FRANCE	JW Smit	Lost	20	26
328		10/06/2006	Durban	SCOTLAND	JW Smit	Won	36	16
329		17/06/2006	Port Elizabeth	SCOTLAND	JW Smit	Won	29	15
330		24/06/2006	Cape Town	FRANCE	JW Smit	Lost	26	36
331		15/07/2006	Brisbane	AUSTRALIA	JW Smit	Lost	0	49
332		22/07/2006	Wellington	NEW ZEALAND	JW Smit	Lost	17	35
333		05/08/2006	Sydney	AUSTRALIA	JW Smit	Lost	18	20
334		26/08/2006	Pretoria	NEW ZEALAND	JW Smit	Lost	26	45
335		02/09/2006	Rustenburg	NEW ZEALAND	JW Smit	Won	21	20
336		09/09/2006	Johannesburg	AUSTRALIA	JW Smit	Won	24	16
337		11/11/2006	Dublin	IRELAND	JW Smit	Lost	15	32
338		18/11/2006	London	ENGLAND	JW Smit	Lost	21	23
339		25/11/2006	London	ENGLAND	JW Smit	Won	25	14
	334	03/12/2006	Leicester	World XV	GvG Botha	Won	32	7
340		26/05/2007	Bloemfontein	ENGLAND	JW Smit	Won	58	10
341		02/06/2007	Pretoria	ENGLAND	JW Smit	Won	55	22
342		09/06/2007	Johannesburg	SAMOA	JW Smit	Won	35	8
343		16/06/2007	Cape Town	AUSTRALIA	JW Smit	Won	22	19
344		23/06/2007	Durban	NEW ZEALAND	V Matfield	Lost	21	26
345		07/07/2007	Sydney	AUSTRALIA	RB Skinstad	Lost	17	25
346		14/07/2007	Christchurch	NEW ZEALAND	GJ Muller	Lost	6	33
347		15/08/2007	Cape Town	NAMIBIA	V Matfield	Won	105	13
	335	21/08/2007	Galway	Connacht	RB Skinstad	Won	18	3
348		25/08/2007	Edinburgh	SCOTLAND	V Matfield	Won	27	3
349		09/09/2007	Paris	SAMOA	JW Smit	Won	59	7
350		14/09/2007	St Denis	ENGLAND	JW Smit	Won	36	0
351		22/09/2007	Lens	TONGA	RB Skinstad	Won	30	25
352		30/09/2007	Montpellier	USA	JW Smit	Won	64	15

SPRINGBOKS

SOUTH AFRICA'S TESTS & TOUR MATCHES

Test No.	Tour Match	Date	Venue	Opponent	Captain	Result	PF	PA
353		07/10/2007	Marseilles	FIJI	JW Smit	Won	37	20
354		14/10/2007	St Denis	ARGENTINA	JW Smit	Won	37	13
355		20/10/2007	St Denis	ENGLAND	JW Smit	Won	15	6
356		24/11/2007	Cardiff	WALES	JW Smit	Won	34	12
	336	01/12/2007	London	Barbarians	GJ Muller	Lost	5	22
357		07/06/2008	Bloemfontein	WALES	JW Smit	Won	43	17
358		14/06/2008	Pretoria	WALES	JW Smit	Won	37	21
359		21/06/2008	Cape Town	ITALY	V Matfield	Won	26	0
360		05/07/2008	Wellington	NEW ZEALAND	JW Smit	Lost	8	19
361		12/07/2008	Dunedin	NEW ZEALAND	V Matfield	Won	30	28
362		19/07/2008	Perth	AUSTRALIA	V Matfield	Lost	9	16
363		09/08/2008	Johannesburg	ARGENTINA	V Matfield	Won	63	9
364		16/08/2008	Cape Town	NEW ZEALAND	V Matfield	Lost	0	19
365		23/08/2008	Durban	AUSTRALIA	V Matfield	Lost	15	27
366		30/08/2008	Johannesburg	AUSTRALIA	V Matfield	Won	53	8
367		08/11/2008	Cardiff	WALES	JW Smit	Won	20	15
368		15/11/2008	Edinburgh	SCOTLAND	JW Smit	Won	14	10
369		22/11/2008	London	ENGLAND	JW Smit	Won	42	6
370		20/06/2009	Durban	BRITISH ISLES	JW Smit	Won	26	21
371		27/06/2009	Pretoria	BRITISH ISLES	JW Smit	Won	28	25
372		04/07/2009	Johannesburg	BRITISH ISLES	JW Smit	Lost	9	28
373		25/07/2009	Bloemfontein	NEW ZEALAND	JW Smit	Won	28	19
374		01/08/2009	Durban	NEW ZEALAND	JW Smit	Won	31	19
375		08/08/2009	Cape Town	AUSTRALIA	JW Smit	Won	29	17
376		29/08/2009	Perth	AUSTRALIA	JW Smit	Won	32	25
377		05/09/2009	Brisbane	AUSTRALIA	JW Smit	Lost	6	21
378		12/09/2009	Hamilton	NEW ZEALAND	JW Smit	Won	32	29
	337	06/11/2009	Leicester	Leicester Tigers	MC Ralepelle	Lost	17	22
379		13/11/2009	Toulouse	FRANCE	JW Smit	Lost	13	20
	338	17/11/2009	London	Saracens	DJ Potgieter	Lost	23	24
380		21/11/2009	Florence	ITALY	JW Smit	Won	32	10
381		28/11/2009	Dublin	IRELAND	JW Smit	Lost	10	15
382		05/06/2010	Cardiff	WALES	JW Smit	Won	34	31
383		12/06/2010	Cape Town	FRANCE	JW Smit	Won	42	17
384		19/06/2010	Witbank	ITALY	V Matfield	Won	29	13
385		26/06/2010	East London	ITALY	JW Smit	Won	55	11
386		10/07/2010	Auckland	NEW ZEALAND	JW Smit	Lost	12	32
387		17/07/2010	Wellington	NEW ZEALAND	JW Smit	Lost	17	31
388		24/07/2010	Brisbane	AUSTRALIA	JW Smit	Lost	13	30
389		21/08/2010	Johannesburg	NEW ZEALAND	JW Smit	Lost	22	29
390		28/08/2010	Pretoria	AUSTRALIA	JW Smit	Won	44	31
391		04/09/2010	Bloemfontein	AUSTRALIA	JW Smit	Lost	39	41
392		06/11/2010	Dublin	IRELAND	V Matfield	Won	23	21
393		13/11/2010	Cardiff	WALES	V Matfield	Won	29	25
394		20/11/2010	Edinburgh	SCOTLAND	V Matfield	Lost	17	21
395		27/11/2010	London	ENGLAND	V Matfield	Won	21	11
	339	04/12/2010	London	Barbarians	JH Smith	Lost	20	26
396		23/07/2011	Sydney	AUSTRALIA	JW Smit	Lost	20	39
397		30/07/2011	Wellington	NEW ZEALAND	JW Smit	Lost	7	40
398		13/08/2011	Durban	AUSTRALIA	JW Smit	Lost	9	14

South Africa vs World XV (Newlands, Cape Town, 7 June 2014)

South Africa vs Wales (Mbombela Stadium, Nelspruit, 21 June 2014)

South Africa vs Wales (Kings Park, Durban, 14 June 2014)

South Africa vs Scotland (Nelson Mandela Bay Stadium, Port Elizabeth, 28 June 2014)

South Africa vs Argentina (Loftus Versfeld, Pretoria, 16 August 2014)

Argentina vs South Africa (Salta, 23 August 2014)

Australia vs South Africa (Patersons Stadium, Perth, 6 September 2014)

New Zealand vs South Africa (Westpac Stadium, Wellington, 13 September 2014)

South Africa vs Australia (Newlands, Cape Town, 27 September 2014)

South Africa vs New Zealand (Ellis Park, Johannesburg, 4 October 2014)

Ireland vs South Africa (Aviva Stadium, Dublin, 8 November 2014)

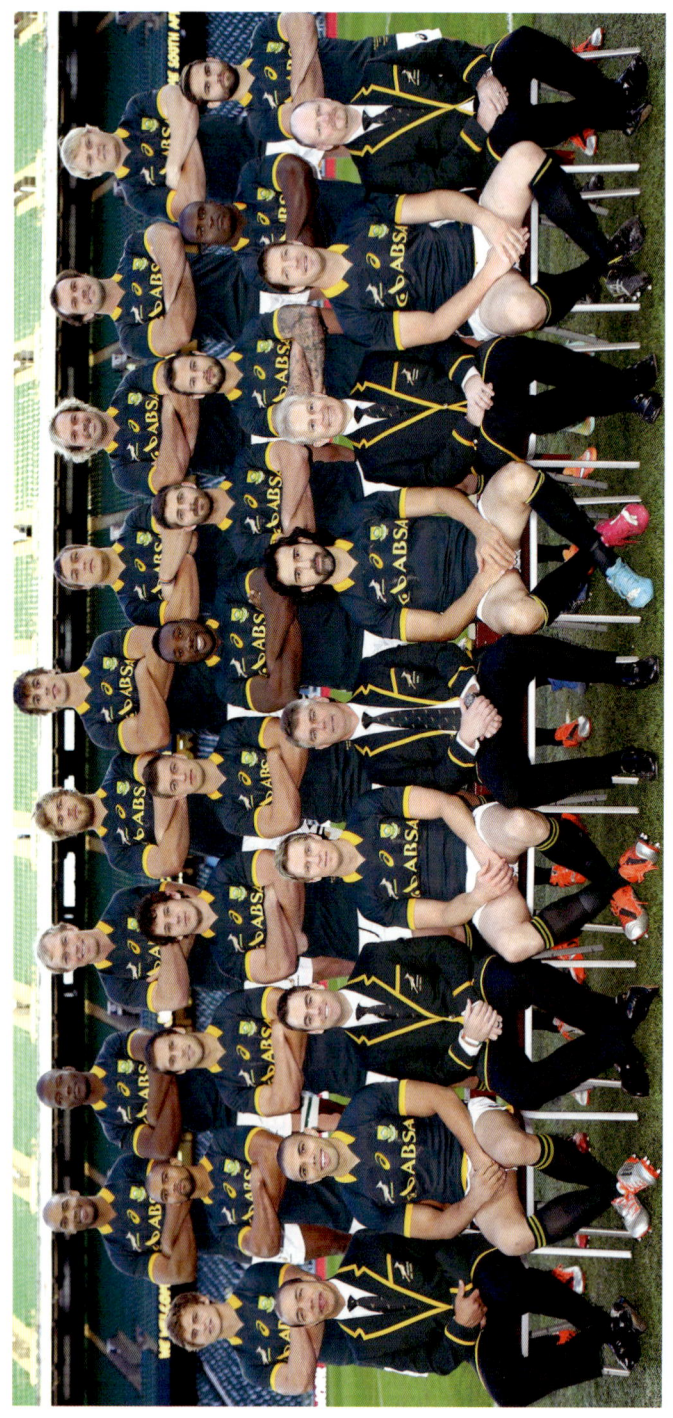

England vs South Africa (Twickenham, London, 15 November 2014)

Italy vs South Africa (Padova, 22 November 2014)

Wales vs South Africa (Millennium Stadium, Cardiff: 29 November 2014)

The Annual's best action photo of 2014: Francois Hougaard breaks away for a try vs New Zealand at Ellis Park.

Springbok Sevens: Commonwealth Games Gold Medal winners.

The Springbok Sevens team celebrates victory in the Las Vegas leg of the world series.

Springbok Women to the Women's Rugby World Cup in France.

South Africa's Under-20 team who competed at the Junior World Championships in New Zealand.

South African Schools 2014.

Eastern Province's Under18 Coca-Cola Craven Week squad, who made history in 2014.

Boland's victorious LSEN Youth Weeks squad.

Western Province's Under-18 Academy Week squad.

Western Province's Under-16 Grant Khomo Week squad.

Western Province's Under-13 Coca-Cola Craven Week squad.

2014 Absa Currie Cup winners DHL Western Province.

2014 Absa First Division winners the Griffons.

2014 Absa Under-21 champions the Vodacom Blue Bulls.

2014 Absa Under-19 champions DHL Western Province.

2014 Cell C Community Cup national club champions Roustenburg Impala.

2014 FNB Varsity Cup champions University of Cape Town.

RUGBY WORLD CUP 2015 TRAVEL PACKAGES AVAILABLE

Follow the green and gold whilst they blaze through to the UK taking on the best. Lose yourself in the sheer ferocity of the Springboks and watch these momentous matches first hand whilst the Springboks charge for their third Rugby World Cup win.

RUGBY WORLD CUP 2015 TRAVEL PACKAGES AVAILABLE NOW
SA Rugby Travel proudly brings you Rugby World Cup 2015 Travel Packages. Visit our website to view our exciting range of unique SA Rugby Travel packages for the Rugby World Cup 2015 Tournament!

+27 (0) 21 525 2515
www.sarugbytravel.com

SOUTH AFRICA'S TESTS & TOUR MATCHES

Test No.	Tour Match	Date	Venue	Opponent	Captain	Result	PF	PA
399		20/08/2011	Port Elizabeth	NEW ZEALAND	V Matfield	Won	18	5
400		11/09/2011	Wellington	WALES	JW Smit	Won	17	16
401		17/09/2011	Wellington	FIJI	JW Smit	Won	49	3
402		22/09/2011	Albany	NAMIBIA	JW Smit	Won	87	0
403		30/09/2011	Albany	SAMOA	V Matfield	Won	13	5
404		09/10/2011	Wellington	AUSTRALIA	JW Smit	Lost	9	11
405		09/06/2012	Durban	ENGLAND	J de Villiers	Won	22	17
406		16/06/2012	Johannesburg	ENGLAND	J de Villiers	Won	36	27
407		23/06/2012	Port Elizabeth	ENGLAND	J de Villiers	Drawn	14	14
408		18/08/2012	Cape Town	ARGENTINA	J de Villiers	Won	27	6
409		25/08/2012	Mendoza	ARGENTINA	J de Villiers	Drawn	16	16
410		08/09/2012	Perth	AUSTRALIA	J de Villiers	Lost	19	26
411		15/09/2012	Dunedin	NEW ZEALAND	J de Villiers	Lost	11	21
412		29/09/2012	Pretoria	AUSTRALIA	J de Villiers	Won	31	8
413		06/10/2012	Johannesburg	NEW ZEALAND	J de Villiers	Lost	16	32
414		10/11/2012	Dublin	IRELAND	J de Villiers	Won	16	12
415		17/11/2012	Edinburgh	SCOTLAND	J de Villiers	Won	21	10
416		24/11/2012	London	ENGLAND	J de Villiers	Won	16	15
417		08/06/2013	Durban	ITALY	J de Villiers	Won	44	10
418		15/06/2013	Nelspruit	SCOTLAND	J de Villiers	Won	30	17
419		22/06/2013	Pretoria	SAMOA	J de Villiers	Won	56	23
420		17/08/2013	Johannesburg	ARGENTINA	J de Villiers	Won	73	13
421		24/08/2013	Mendoza	ARGENTINA	J de Villiers	Won	22	17
422		07/09/2013	Brisbane	AUSTRALIA	J de Villiers	Won	38	12
423		14/09/2013	Auckland	NEW ZEALAND	J de Villiers	Lost	15	29
424		28/09/2013	Cape Town	AUSTRALIA	J de Villiers	Won	28	8
425		05/10/2013	Johannesburg	NEW ZEALAND	J de Villiers	Lost	27	38
426		09/11/2013	Cardiff	WALES	J de Villiers	Won	24	15
427		17/11/2013	Edinburgh	SCOTLAND	J de Villiers	Won	28	0
428		23/11/2013	Paris	FRANCE	J de Villiers	Won	19	10
429		14/06/2014	Durban	WALES	V Matfield	Won	38	16
430		21/06/2014	Nelspruit	WALES	V Matfield	Won	31	30
431		28/06/2014	Port Elizabeth	SCOTLAND	V Matfield	Won	55	6
432		16/08/2014	Pretoria	ARGENTINA	J de Villiers	Won	13	6
433		23/08/2014	Salta	ARGENTINA	J de Villiers	Won	33	31
434		06/09/2014	Perth	AUSTRALIA	J de Villiers	Lost	23	24
435		13/09/2014	Wellington	NEW ZEALAND	J de Villiers	Lost	10	14
436		27/09/2014	Cape Town	AUSTRALIA	J de Villiers	Won	28	10
437		04/10/2014	Johannesburg	NEW ZEALAND	J de Villiers	Won	27	25
438		08/11/2014	Dublin	IRELAND	J de Villiers	Lost	15	29
439		15/11/2014	London	ENGLAND	J de Villiers	Won	31	28
440		22/11/2014	Padova	ITALY	J de Villiers	Won	22	6
441		29/11/2014	Cardiff	WALES	J de Villiers	Lost	6	12
						TEST	10148	6831
						TOUR	8268	2758
						TOTAL	18416	9589

SPRINGBOKS

TEST RESULTS BY OPPONENT

ARGENTINA

Played 19 - Won 18 - Lost 0 - Drawn 1
PF 728 - PA 361

Year	Winner	Score	Venue
1993	South Africa	29-26	Buenos Aires
1993	South Africa	52-23	Buenos Aires
1994	South Africa	42-22	Port Elizabeth
1994	South Africa	46-26	Johannesburg
1996	South Africa	46-15	Buenos Aires
1996	South Africa	44-21	Buenos Aires
2000	South Africa	37-33	Buenos Aires
2002	South Africa	49-29	Springs
2003	South Africa	26-25	Port Elizabeth
2004	South Africa	39-7	Buenos Aires
2005	South Africa	34-23	Buenos Aires
2007	South Africa	37-13	Paris
2008	South Africa	63-9	Johannesburg
2012	South Africa	27-6	Cape Town
2012	Drawn	16-16	Mendoza
2013	South Africa	73-13	Johannesburg
2013	South Africa	22-17	Mendoza
2014	South Africa	13-6	Pretoria
2014	South Africa	33-31	Salta

AUSTRALIA

Played 80 - Won 45 - Lost 34 - Drawn 34
PF - 1552 - PA 1391

Year	Winner	Score	Venue
1933	South Africa	17-3	Cape Town
1933	Australia	6-21	Durban
1933	South Africa	12-3	Johannesburg
1933	South Africa	11-0	Port Elizabeth
1933	Australia	4-15	Bloemfontein
1937	South Africa	9-5	Sydney
1937	South Africa	26-17	Sydney
1953	South Africa	25-3	Johannesburg
1953	Australia	14-18	Cape Town
1953	South Africa	18-8	Durban
1953	South Africa	22-9	Port Elizabeth
1956	South Africa	9-0	Sydney
1956	South Africa	9-0	Brisbane
1961	South Africa	28-3	Johannesburg
1961	South Africa	23-11	Port Elizabeth
1963	South Africa	14-3	Pretoria
1963	Australia	5-9	Cape Town
1963	Australia	9-11	Johannesburg
1963	South Africa	22-6	Port Elizabeth
1965	Australia	11-18	Sydney
1965	Australia	8-12	Brisbane
1969	South Africa	30-11	Johannesburg
1969	South Africa	16-9	Durban
1969	South Africa	11-3	Cape Town
1969	South Africa	19-8	Bloemfontein
1971	South Africa	19-11	Sydney
1971	South Africa	14-6	Brisbane
1971	South Africa	18-6	Sydney
1992	Australia	3-26	Cape Town
1993	South Africa	19-12	Sydney
1993	Australia	20-28	Brisbane
1993	Australia	12-19	Sydney
1995	South Africa	27-18	Cape Town
1996	Australia	16-21	Sydney
1996	South Africa	25-19	Bloemfontein
1997	Australia	20-32	Brisbane
1997	South Africa	61-22	Pretoria
1998	South Africa	14-13	Perth
1998	South Africa	29-15	Johannesburg
1999	Australia	6-32	Brisbane
1999	South Africa	10-9	Cape Town
1999	Australia	21-27	London
2000	Australia	23-44	Melbourne
2000	Australia	6-26	Sydney
2000	Australia	18-19	Durban
2001	South Africa	20-15	Pretoria
2001	Drawn	14-14	Perth
2002	Australia	27-38	Brisbane
2002	South Africa	33-31	Johannesburg
2003	South Africa	26-22	Cape Town
2003	Australia	9-29	Brisbane
2004	Australia	26-30	Perth
2004	South Africa	23-19	Durban
2005	Australia	12-30	Sydney
2005	South Africa	33-20	Johannesburg
2005	South Africa	22-16	Pretoria
2005	South Africa	22-19	Perth
2006	Australia	0-49	Brisbane
2006	Australia	18-20	Sydney
2006	South Africa	24-16	Johannesburg
2007	South Africa	22-19	Cape Town
2007	Australia	17-25	Sydney
2008	Australia	9-16	Perth
2008	Australia	15-27	Durban
2008	South Africa	53-8	Johannesburg
2009	South Africa	29-17	Cape Town
2009	South Africa	32-25	Perth
2009	Australia	6-21	Brisbane
2010	Australia	13-30	Brisbane
2010	South Africa	44-31	Pretoria
2010	Australia	39-41	Bloemfontein
2011	Australia	20-39	Sydney
2011	Australia	9-14	Durban
2011	Australia	9-11	Wellington

SPRINGBOKS

TEST RESULTS BY OPPONENT

Year	Winner	Score	Venue
2012	Australia	19-26	Perth
2012	South Africa	31-8	Pretoria
2013	South Africa	38-12	Brisbane
2013	South Africa	28-8	Cape Town
2014	Australia	24-23	Perth
2014	South Africa	28-10	Cape Town

BRITISH ISLES
Played 46 – Won 23 – Lost 17 – Drawn 6
PF 600 – PA 516

Year	Winner	Score	Venue
1891	British Isles	0-4	Port Elizabeth
1891	British Isles	0-3	Kimberley
1891	British Isles	0-4	Cape Town
1896	British Isles	0-8	Port Elizabeth
1896	British Isles	8-17	Johannesburg
1896	British Isles	3-9	Kimberley
1896	South Africa	5-0	Cape Town
1903	Drawn	10-10	Johannesburg
1903	Drawn	0-0	Kimberley
1903	South Africa	8-0	Cape Town
1910	South Africa	14-10	Johannesburg
1910	British Isles	3-8	Port Elizabeth
1910	South Africa	21-5	Cape Town
1924	South Africa	7-3	Durban
1924	South Africa	17-0	Johannesburg
1924	Drawn	3-3	Port Elizabeth
1924	South Africa	16-9	Cape Town
1938	South Africa	26-12	Johannesburg
1938	South Africa	19-3	Port Elizabeth
1938	British Isles	16-21	Cape Town
1955	British Isles	22-23	Johannesburg
1955	South Africa	25-9	Cape Town
1955	British Isles	6-9	Pretoria
1955	South Africa	22-8	Port Elizabeth
1962	Drawn	3-3	Johannesburg
1962	South Africa	3-0	Durban
1962	South Africa	8-3	Cape Town
1962	South Africa	34-14	Bloemfontein
1968	South Africa	25-20	Pretoria
1968	Drawn	6-6	Port Elizabeth
1968	South Africa	11-6	Cape Town
1968	South Africa	19-6	Johannesburg
1974	British Isles	3-12	Cape Town
1974	British Isles	9-28	Pretoria
1974	British Isles	9-26	Port Elizabeth
1974	Drawn	13-13	Johannesburg
1980	South Africa	26-22	Cape Town
1980	South Africa	26-19	Bloemfontein
1980	South Africa	12-10	Port Elizabeth
1980	British Isles	13-17	Pretoria
1997	British Isles	16-25	Cape Town
1997	British Isles	15-18	Durban
1997	South Africa	35-16	Johannesburg
2009	South Africa	26-21	Durban
2009	South Africa	28-25	Pretoria
2009	British Isles	9-28	Johannesburg

CANADA
Played 2 – Won 2 – Lost 0 – Drawn 0
PF 71 – PA 18

Year	Winner	Score	Venue
1995	South Africa	20-0	Port Elizabeth
2000	South Africa	51-18	East London

ENGLAND
Played 37 – Won 23 – Lost 12 – Drawn 2
PF 780 – PA 592

Year	Winner	Score	Venue
1906	Drawn	3-3	Crystal Palace
1913	South Africa	9-3	Twickenham
1932	South Africa	7-0	Twickenham
1952	South Africa	8-3	Twickenham
1961	South Africa	5-0	Twickenham
1969	England	8-11	Twickenham
1972	England	9-18	Johannesburg
1984	South Africa	33-15	Port Elizabeth
1984	South Africa	35-9	Johannesburg
1992	England	16-33	Twickenham
1994	England	15-32	Pretoria
1994	South Africa	27-9	Cape Town
1995	South Africa	24-14	Twickenham
1997	South Africa	29-11	Twickenham
1998	South Africa	18-0	Cape Town
1998	England	7-13	Twickenham
1999	South Africa	44-21	Paris
2000	South Africa	18-13	Pretoria
2000	England	22-27	Bloemfontein
2000	England	17-25	Twickenham
2001	England	9-29	Twickenham
2002	England	3-53	Twickenham
2003	England	6-25	Perth
2004	England	16-32	Twickenham
2006	England	21-23	Twickenham
2006	South Africa	25-14	Twickenham
2007	South Africa	58-10	Bloemfontein
2007	South Africa	55-22	Pretoria
2007	South Africa	36-0	Paris
2007	South Africa	15-6	Paris
2008	South Africa	42-6	Twickenham
2010	South Africa	21-11	Twickenham
2012	South Africa	22-17	Durban

SPRINGBOKS

TEST RESULTS BY OPPONENT

Year	Winner	Score	Venue
2012	South Africa	36-27	Johannesburg
2012	Drawn	14-14	Port Elizabeth
2012	South Africa	16-15	Twickenham
2014	South Africa	31-28	London

FIJI
Played 3 - Won 3 - Lost 0 - Drawn 0
PF 129 - PA 41

Year	Winner	Score	Venue
1996	South Africa	43-18	Pretoria
2007	South Africa	37-20	Marseille
2011	South Africa	49-3	Wellington

FRANCE
Played 39 - Won 22 - Lost 11 - Drawn 6
PF 783 - PA 578

Year	Winner	Score	Venue
1913	South Africa	38-5	Bordeaux
1952	South Africa	25-3	Paris
1958	Drawn	3-3	Cape Town
1958	France	5-9	Johannesburg
1961	Drawn	0-0	Paris
1964	France	6-8	Springs
1967	South Africa	26-3	Durban
1967	South Africa	16-3	Bloemfontein
1967	France	14-19	Johannesburg
1967	Drawn	6-6	Cape Town
1968	South Africa	12-9	Bordeaux
1968	South Africa	16-11	Paris
1971	South Africa	22-9	Bloemfontein
1971	Drawn	8-8	Durban
1974	South Africa	13-4	Toulouse
1974	South Africa	10-8	Paris
1975	South Africa	38-25	Bloemfontein
1975	South Africa	33-18	Pretoria
1980	South Africa	37-15	Pretoria
1992	South Africa	20-15	Lyon
1992	France	16-29	Paris
1993	Drawn	20-20	Durban
1993	France	17-18	Johannesburg
1995	South Africa	19-15	Durban
1996	South Africa	22-12	Bordeaux
1996	South Africa	13-12	Paris
1997	South Africa	36-32	Lyon
1997	South Africa	52-10	Paris
2001	France	23-32	Johannesburg
2001	South Africa	20-15	Durban
2001	France	10-20	Paris
2002	France	10-30	Marseilles
2005	Drawn	30-30	Durban
2005	South Africa	27-13	Port Elizabeth
2005	France	20-26	Paris
2006	France	26-36	Cape Town
2009	France	13-20	Toulouse
2010	South Africa	42-17	Cape Town
2013	South Africa	19-10	Paris

GEORGIA
Played 1 - Won 1 - Lost 0 - Drawn 0
PF 46 - PA 19

Year	Winner	Score	Venue
2003	South Africa	46-19	Sydney

IRELAND
Played 22 - Won 16 - Lost 5 - Drawn 1
PF 432 - PA 277

Year	Winner	Score	Venue
1906	South Africa	15-12	Belfast
1912	South Africa	38-0	Dublin
1931	South Africa	8-3	Dublin
1951	South Africa	17-5	Dublin
1960	South Africa	8-3	Dublin
1961	South Africa	24-8	Cape Town
1965	Ireland	6-9	Dublin
1970	Drawn	8-8	Dublin
1981	South Africa	23-15	Cape Town
1981	South Africa	12-10	Durban
1998	South Africa	37-13	Bloemfontein
1998	South Africa	33-0	Pretoria
1998	South Africa	27-13	Dublin
2000	South Africa	28-18	Dublin
2004	South Africa	31-17	Bloemfontein
2004	South Africa	26-17	Cape Town
2004	Ireland	12-17	Dublin
2006	Ireland	15-32	Dublin
2009	Ireland	10-15	Dublin
2010	South Africa	23-21	Dublin
2012	South Africa	16-12	Dublin
2014	Ireland	29-15	Dublin

ITALY
Played 12 - Won 12 - Lost 0 - Drawn 0
PF 599 - PA 145

Year	Winner	Score	Venue
1995	South Africa	40-21	Rome
1997	South Africa	62-31	Bologna
1999	South Africa	74-3	Port Elizabeth
1999	South Africa	101-0	Durban
2001	South Africa	60-14	Port Elizabeth
2001	South Africa	54-26	Genoa
2008	South Africa	26-0	Cape Town
2009	South Africa	32-10	Udine

SPRINGBOKS

TEST RESULTS BY OPPONENT

Year	Winner	Score	Venue
2010	South Africa	29-13	Witbank
2010	South Africa	55-11	East London
2013	South Africa	44-10	Durban
2014	South Africa	22-06	Padova

NAMIBIA
Played 2 - Won 2 - Lost 0 - Drawn 0
PF 192 - PA 13

Year	Winner	Score	Venue
2007	South Africa	105-13	Cape Town
2011	South Africa	87-0	Albany

NEW ZEALAND
Played 89 - Won 35 - Lost 51 - Drawn 3
PF 1392 - PA 1718

Year	Winner	Score	Venue
1921	New Zealand	5-13	Dunedin
1921	South Africa	9-5	Auckland
1921	Drawn	0-0	Wellington
1928	South Africa	17-0	Durban
1928	New Zealand	6-7	Johannesburg
1928	South Africa	11-6	Port Elizabeth
1928	New Zealand	5-13	Cape Town
1937	New Zealand	7-13	Wellington
1937	South Africa	13-6	Christchurch
1937	South Africa	17-6	Auckland
1949	South Africa	15-11	Cape Town
1949	South Africa	12-6	Johannesburg
1949	South Africa	9-3	Durban
1949	South Africa	11-8	Port Elizabeth
1956	New Zealand	6-10	Dunedin
1956	South Africa	8-3	Wellington
1956	New Zealand	10-17	Christchurch
1956	New Zealand	5-11	Auckland
1960	South Africa	13-0	Johannesburg
1960	New Zealand	3-11	Cape Town
1960	Drawn	11-11	Bloemfontein
1960	South Africa	8-3	Port Elizabeth
1965	New Zealand	3-6	Wellington
1965	New Zealand	0-13	Dunedin
1965	South Africa	19-16	Christchurch
1965	New Zealand	3-20	Auckland
1970	South Africa	17-6	Pretoria
1970	New Zealand	8-9	Cape Town
1970	South Africa	14-3	Port Elizabeth
1970	South Africa	20-17	Johannesburg
1976	South Africa	16-7	Durban
1976	New Zealand	9-15	Bloemfontein
1976	South Africa	15-10	Cape Town
1976	South Africa	15-14	Johannesburg
1981	New Zealand	9-14	Christchurch
1981	South Africa	24-12	Wellington
1981	New Zealand	22-25	Auckland
1992	New Zealand	24-27	Johannesburg
1994	New Zealand	14-22	Dunedin
1994	New Zealand	9-13	Wellington
1994	Drawn	18-18	Auckland
1995	South Africa	15-12	Johannesburg
1996	New Zealand	11-15	Christchurch
1996	New Zealand	18-29	Cape Town
1996	New Zealand	19-23	Durban
1996	New Zealand	26-33	Pretoria
1996	South Africa	32-22	Johannesburg
1997	New Zealand	32-35	Johannesburg
1997	New Zealand	35-55	Auckland
1998	South Africa	13-3	Wellington
1998	South Africa	24-23	Durban
1999	New Zealand	0-28	Dunedin
1999	New Zealand	18-34	Pretoria
1999	South Africa	22-18	Cardiff
2000	New Zealand	12-25	Christchurch
2000	South Africa	46-40	Johannesburg
2001	New Zealand	3-12	Cape Town
2001	New Zealand	15-26	Auckland
2002	New Zealand	20-41	Wellington
2002	New Zealand	23-30	Durban
2003	New Zealand	16-52	Pretoria
2003	New Zealand	11-19	Dunedin
2003	New Zealand	9-29	Melbourne
2004	New Zealand	21-23	Christchurch
2004	South Africa	40-26	Johannesburg
2005	South Africa	22-16	Cape Town
2005	New Zealand	27-31	Dunedin
2006	New Zealand	17-35	Wellington
2006	New Zealand	26-45	Pretoria
2006	South Africa	21-20	Rustenburg
2007	New Zealand	21-26	Durban
2007	New Zealand	6-33	Christchurch
2008	New Zealand	8-19	Wellington
2008	South Africa	30-28	Dunedin
2008	New Zealand	0-19	Cape Town
2009	South Africa	28-19	Bloemfontein
2009	South Africa	31-19	Durban
2009	South Africa	32-29	Hamilton
2010	New Zealand	12-32	Auckland
2010	New Zealand	17-31	Wellington
2010	New Zealand	22-29	Johannesburg
2011	New Zealand	7-40	Wellington
2011	South Africa	18-5	Port Elizabeth
2012	New Zealand	11-21	Dunedin
2012	New Zealand	16-32	Johannesburg
2013	New Zealand	15-29	Auckland

SPRINGBOKS

TEST RESULTS BY OPPONENT

Year	Winner	Score	Venue
2013	New Zealand	27-38	Johannesburg
2014	New Zealand	14-10	Wellington
2014	South Africa	27-25	Johannesburg

NEW ZEALAND CAVALIERS
Played 4 - Won 3 - Lost 1 - Drawn 0
PF 96 - PA 62

Year	Winner	Score	Venue
1986	South Africa	21-15	Cape Town
1986	NZ Cavaliers	18-19	Durban
1986	South Africa	33-18	Pretoria
1986	South Africa	24-10	Johannesburg

PACIFIC ISLANDS
Played 1 - Won 1 - Lost 0 - Drawn 0
PF 38 - PA 24

Year	Winner	Score	Venue
2004	South Africa	38-24	Gosford

ROMANIA
Played 1 - Won 1 - Lost 0 - Drawn 0
PF 21 - PA 8

Year	Winner	Score	Venue
1995	South Africa	21-8	Cape Town

SAMOA
Played 8 - Won 8 - Lost 0 - Drawn 0
PF 385 - PA 93

Year	Winner	Score	Venue
1995	South Africa	60-8	Johannesburg
1995	South Africa	42-14	Johannesburg
2002	South Africa	60-18	Pretoria
2003	South Africa	60-10	Brisbane
2007	South Africa	35-8	Johannesburg
2007	South Africa	59-7	Paris
2011	South Africa	13-5	Albany
2013	South Africa	56-23	Pretoria

SCOTLAND
Played 25 - Won 20 - Lost 5 - Drawn 0
PF 652 - PA 270

Year	Winner	Score	Venue
1906	Scotland	0-6	Glasgow
1912	South Africa	16-0	Edinburgh
1932	South Africa	6-3	Edinburgh
1951	South Africa	44-0	Edinburgh
1960	South Africa	18-10	Port Elizabeth
1961	South Africa	12-5	Edinburgh
1965	Scotland	5-8	Edinburgh
1969	Scotland	3-6	Edinburgh
1994	South Africa	34-10	Edinburgh
1997	South Africa	68-10	Edinburgh
1998	South Africa	35-10	Edinburgh
1999	South Africa	46-29	Edinburgh
2002	Scotland	6-21	Edinburgh
2003	South Africa	29-25	Durban
2003	South Africa	28-19	Johannesburg
2004	South Africa	45-10	Edinburgh
2006	South Africa	36-16	Durban
2006	South Africa	29-15	Port Elizabeth
2007	South Africa	27-3	Edinburgh
2008	South Africa	14-10	Edinburgh
2010	Scotland	17-21	Edinburgh
2012	South Africa	21-10	Edinburgh
2013	South Africa	30-17	Nelspruit
2013	South Africa	28-0	Edinburgh
2014	South Africa	55-6	Port Elizabeth

SOUTH AMERICA
(*indicates includes Spain)
Played 8 - Won 7 - Lost 1 - Drawn 0
PF 210 - PA 114

Year	Winner	Score	Venue
1980	South Africa	24-9	Johannesburg
1980	South Africa	18-9	Durban
1980	South Africa	22-13	Montevideo
1980	South Africa	30-16	Santiago
1982	South Africa	50-18	Pretoria
1982	South America	12-21	Bloemfontein
1984*	South Africa	32-15	Pretoria
1984*	South Africa	22-13	Cape Town

SPAIN
Played 1 - Won 1 - Lost 0 - Drawn 0
PF 47 - PA 3

Year	Winner	Score	Venue
1999	South Africa	47-3	Edinburgh

TONGA
Played 2 - Won 2 - Lost 0 - Drawn 0
PF 104 - PA 35

Year	Winner	Score	Venue
1997	South Africa	74-10	Cape Town
2007	South Africa	30-25	Lens

UNITED STATES OF AMERICA
Played 3 - Won 3 - Lost 0 - Drawn 0
PF 145 - PA 42

Year	Winner	Score	Venue
1981	South Africa	38-7	Glenville
2001	South Africa	43-20	Houston
2007	South Africa	64-15	Montpellier

SPRINGBOKS

TEST RESULTS BY OPPONENT

URUGUAY
Played 3 - Won 3 - Lost 0 - Drawn 0
PF 245 - PA 12

Year	Winner	Score	Venue
1999	South Africa	39-3	Glasgow
2003	South Africa	72-6	Perth
2005	South Africa	134-3	East London

WALES
Played 30 - Won 27 - Lost 2 - Drawn 1
PF 814 - PA 440

Year	Winner	Score	Venue
1906	South Africa	11-0	Swansea
1912	South Africa	3-0	Cardiff
1931	South Africa	8-3	Swansea
1951	South Africa	6-3	Cardiff
1960	South Africa	3-0	Cardiff
1964	South Africa	24-3	Durban
1970	Drawn	6-6	Cardiff
1994	South Africa	20-12	Cardiff
1995	South Africa	40-11	Johannesburg
1996	South Africa	37-20	Cardiff
1998	South Africa	96-13	Pretoria
1998	South Africa	28-20	Wembley
1999	Wales	19-29	Cardiff
2000	South Africa	23-13	Cardiff
2002	South Africa	34-19	Bloemfontein
2002	South Africa	19-8	Cape Town
2004	South Africa	53-18	Pretoria
2004	South Africa	38-36	Cardiff
2005	South Africa	33-16	Cardiff
2007	South Africa	34-12	Cardiff
2008	South Africa	43-17	Bloemfontein
2008	South Africa	37-21	Pretoria
2008	South Africa	20-15	Cardiff
2010	South Africa	34-31	Cardiff
2010	South Africa	29-25	Cardiff
2011	South Africa	17-16	Wellington, NZ
2013	South Africa	24-15	Cardiff
2014	South Africa	38-16	Durban
2014	South Africa	31-30	Nelspruit
2014	Wales	12-6	Cardiff

WORLD TEAMS
Played 3 - Won 3 - Lost 0 - Drawn 0
PF 87 - PA 59

Year	Winner	Score	Venue
1977	South Africa	45-24	Pretoria
1989	South Africa	20-19	Cape Town
1989	South Africa	22-16	Johannesburg

Handré Pollard dives over against New Zealand at Ellis Park in 2014.

SPRINGBOKS

South African Test Records

MATCH RECORDS

Highest score (on SA soil)
134-3	vs Uruguay	East London	2005

Highest score (abroad)
87-0	vs Namibia	Albany	2011

Biggest winning margin (SA)
131	vs Uruguay (134-3)	East London	2005

Biggest winning margin (abroad)
87	vs Namibia (87-0)	Albany	2011

Most tries scored (SA)
15	vs Italy	Durban	1999
15	vs Wales	Pretoria	1998
15	vs Namibia	Cape Town	2007

Most tries scored (abroad)
12	vs Uruguay	Perth	2003
12	vs Namibia	Albany	2011

Most points conceded (SA)
52-16	vs New Zealand	Pretoria	2003

Most points conceded (abroad)
55-35	vs New Zealand	Auckland	1997

Biggest defeats (SA)
36	New Zealand (16-52)	Pretoria	2003

Biggest defeats (abroad)
50	England (3-53)	Twickenham	2002

[**MOST POINTS BY A PLAYER IN A MATCH** **35** *PC Montgomery vs Namibia 2007*]

Most points by a player (SA)
35	PC Montgomery vs Namibia (1t, 12c, 2p)	Cape Town	2007

Most points by a player (abroad)
34	JH de Beer vs England (2c, 5p, 5dg)	Paris	1999

Most tries by a player (SA)
6	T Chavhanga vs Uruguay	East London	2005

Most tries by a player (abroad)
4	PWG Rossouw vs France	Paris	1997
4	BG Habana vs Samoa	Paris	2007

Most conversions by a player (SA)
12	PC Montgomery vs Namibia	Cape Town	2007

SOUTH AFRICAN TEST RECORDS

Most conversions by a player (abroad)
| 8 | PC Montgomery vs Scotland | Edinburgh | 1997 |

Most penalty goals by a player (SA)
| 8 | M Steyn vs New Zealand | Durban | 2009 |

Most penalty goals by a player (abroad)
| 6 | JH de Beer vs Australia | Twickenham | 1999 |
| 6 | M Steyn vs Australia | Perth | 2014 |

Most drop goals by a player (SA)
| 3 | HE Botha vs South America | Durban | 1980 |
| 3 | HE Botha vs Ireland | Durban | 1981 |

Most drop goals by a player (abroad)
| 5 | JH de Beer vs England | Paris | 1999 |

Scored all points in a Test (SA)
| 31* | M Steyn vs New Zealand | Durban | 2009 |

World record

Scored all points in a Test (abroad)
| 21 | JH de Beer vs Australia | Twickenham | 1999 |

Scored in all four ways in a Test
22	JT Stransky (22 pts - 1t, 1c, 4p, 1dg) vs Australia	1995
18	AS Pretorius (18 pts - 1t, 2c, 2p, 1dg) vs New Zealand	2002
21	DJ Hougaard (21 pts - 1t, 5c, 1p, 1dg) vs Samoa	2003

Most points by a player against SA (SA)
27	CR Andrew, England (1t, 2c, 5p, 1d)	Pretoria	1994
27	JP Wilkinson, England (8p, 1d)	Bloemfontein	2000
27	G Merceron, France (1t, 2c, 6p)	Johannesburg	2001

Most points by a player against SA (abroad)
| 29 | SA Mortlock, Australia (2t, 2c, 5p) | Melbourne | 2000 |

Most tries by a player against SA (SA)
| 2 | 16 times by 14 players |

Most tries by a player against SA (abroad)
| 2 | 22 times by 20 players |

Most conversions by a player against SA (SA)
4	A Cameron (British Isles)	Johannesburg	1955
4	PE McLean (World Team)	Pretoria	1977
4	AP Mehrtens (New Zealand)	Johannesburg	2000
4	CJ Spencer (New Zealand)	Pretoria	2003
4	DW Carter (New Zealand)	Pretoria	2006
4	MJ Giteau (Australia)	Pretoria	2010
4	MJ Giteau (Australia)	Bloemfontein	2010

Most conversions by a player against SA (abroad)
| 5 | SA Mortlock (Australia) | Brisbane | 2006 |

Most penalty goals by a player against SA (SA)
| 8 | JP Wilkinson (England) | Bloemfontein | 2000 |

Most penalty goals by a player against SA (abroad)
| 8 | MC Burke (Australia) | Twickenham | 1999 |

SOUTH AFRICAN TEST RECORDS

Most drop goals by a player against SA (SA)

2	G Camberabero (France)	Johannesburg	1967
2	P Bennett (British Isles)	Port Elizabeth	1974
2	DR Biggar (Wales)	Durban	2014

Most drop goals by a player against SA (abroad)

2	JP Wilkinson (England)	Perth	2003

SEASON RECORDS
BY THE TEAM

Most points
658   17 Tests   38.7 per game   2007

Most tries
81   17 Tests   4.8 per game   2007

Most conversions
62   17 Tests   3.7 per game   2007

Most penalty goals
46   14 Tests   3.3 per game   2010

Most drop goals
8   13 Tests   1999

Most consecutive wins
17   23 Aug 1997 – 28 Nov 1998

Most consecutive defeats
7   25 July 1964 – 21 Aug 1965

Most consecutive matches without scoring a try
4   1891–1896 & 1972–1974

BY A PLAYER

Most points
219   PC Montgomery in 14 Tests (5t, 52c, 30p)   2007

Most tries
13   BG Habana in 11 Tests   2007

Most conversions
52   PC Montgomery in 14 Tests   2007

Most penalty goals
40   M Steyn in 13 Tests   2010

Most drop goals
6   HE Botha in 9 Tests   1980
6   JH de Beer in 6 Tests   1999

CAREER RECORDS

Most Test match appearances
121   V Matfield   2001-2014

Most appearances in all Springbok matches
125   V Matfield   2001-2014

Most points in Test matches
893   PC Montgomery (102 Tests)   1997-2008

Most points in all Springbok matches
906   PC Montgomery (104 matches)   1997-2008

Most tries in Test matches
57   BG Habana (106 Tests)   2004-2014

Most tries in all Springbok matches
57   BG Habana (108 matches)   2004-2014

Most conversions in Test matches
153   PC Montgomery (102 Tests)   1997-2008

Most conversions in all Springbok matches
157   PC Montgomery (104 matches)   1997-2008

Most penalty goals in Test matches
148   PC Montgomery (102 Tests)   1997-2008

Most penalty goals in all Springbok matches
148   PC Montgomery (104 matches)   1997-2008

Most drop goals in Test matches
18   HE Botha (28 Tests)   1980-1992

Most drop goals in all Springbok matches
27   HE Botha (40 matches)   1980-1992

Most Test match appearances against SA
30   GM Gregan (Australia)   1994-2007

Most points in Tests against SA
245   DW Carter (New Zealand) (18 Tests)   2003-2013

Most tries in Tests against SA
10   CM Cullen (New Zealand) (15 Tests)   1996-2002

Most conversions in Tests against SA
31   DW Carter (New Zealand) (18 Tests)   2003-2013

Most penalty goals in Tests against SA
54   DW Carter (New Zealand) (18 Tests)   2003-2013

Most drop goals in Tests against SA
4   AP Mehrtens (New Zealand) (16 Tests)   1995-2004

SOUTH AFRICAN TEST RECORDS

MISCELLANEOUS RECORDS

Most Test match appearances in each position (starting XV)

Fullback	PC Montgomery [1]	87
Wing	BG Habana [2]	105
Centre	J de Villiers [3]	91
Flyhalf	M Steyn [4]	57
Scrumhalf	JH van der Westhuizen [5]	87
Prop	JP du Randt	80
Hooker	JW Smit [6]	96
Lock	V Matfield	121
Flank	SWP Burger [7]	73
Eighthman	PJ Spies [8]	48
Captain	JW Smit	83

1 Also made nine appearances as a centre, five as flyhalf and one as wing.
2 Also made one appearance as a centre.
3 Also made fifteen appearance as a wing.
4 Also made one appearance as a fullback and one as a centre.
5 Also made two appearances as a replacement wing.
6 Also made two appearances as a replacement prop and thirteen as a prop in the starting 15.
7 Also made two appearances as No 8.
8 Also made four appearances as a flank and one as wing.

Most consecutive Test match appearances by position

Fullback	PC Montgomery (1997-1999)	24
Wing	PWG Rossouw (1997-1999)	24
Centre	J de Villiers (2011-2013)	25
Flyhalf	BL Osler (1924-1933)	17
	HE Botha (1980-1982)	17
	JNB van der Westhuyzen (2004-2005)	17
Scrumhalf	PF du Preez (2004-2006)	21
Prop	A-H le Roux (1998-1999)	25
Hooker	JW Smit (2003-2007)	46
Lock	V Matfield (2008-2010)	28
Flank	RJ Kruger (1995-1997)	22
Eighthman	GH Teichmann (1996-1999)	39
Captain	JW Smit (2004-2007)	43

Most consecutive Test match appearances

	Player	Years
46	JW Smit (hooker)	2003-2007
39	GH Teichmann (eighthman)	1996-1999
30	M Steyn (Flyhalf/fullback)	2010-2012
28	V Matfield (lock)	2008-2010
26	AH Snyman (centre/wing)	1996-1998
26	AN Vos (eighthman/flank)	1999-2001
25	J de Villiers (centre)	2011-2013

SOUTH AFRICAN TEST RECORDS

Most Test match tries in each position

Position	Tries	Player	Tests
Fullback	18	PC Montgomery	*87 Tests
Wing	57	BG Habana	*105 Tests
Centre	28	J Fourie	*61 Tests
Flyhalf	8	M Steyn	*57 Tests
Scrumhalf	38	JH van der Westhuizen	*87 Tests
Prop	6	GG Steenkamp	53 Tests
Hooker	9	BW du Plessis	70 Tests
Lock	12	MG Andrews	*75 Tests
Flank	11	SWP Burger	*71 Tests
	11	JH Smith	*60 Tests
Eighthman	7	PJ Spies	*48 Tests

*Excludes tests played in other positions

Longest international career

Seasons	Player	Duration
14 seasons	V Matfield (2001-2014)	13 years, 152 days
14 seasons	JP du Randt (1994-2007)	13 years, 12 days
13 seasons	HE Botha (1980-1992)	12 years, 202 days
13 seasons	DM Gerber (1980-1992)	12 years, 27 days
13 seasons	J de Villiers (2002-2014)	12 years, 20 days
13 seasons	BH Heatlie (1891-1903)	12 years, 14 days
13 seasons	JM Powell (1891-1903)	12 years, 7 days
13 seasons	JP Botha (2002-2014)	12 years, 6 days

Most Test matches as a substitute — Total tests

43		A-H le Roux	54
39		R Pienaar	80

Most Test matches as an unused substitute — Total tests

22	W Swanepoel	20

Oldest living Springboks*

P Malan	b 13/02/1919	95 years, 290 days
C Moss	b 12/02/1925	89 years, 291 days
MT Lategan	b 29/09/1925	89 years, 62 days

* as at 30/11/2014

Oldest deceased Springboks

GM Daneel	b 29/08/1904 d 19/10/2004	100 years 51 days
JC van der Westhuizen	b 22/11/1905 d 08/07/2003	97 years 228 days
JA Stegmann	b 21/06/1887 d 07/12/1984	97 years 169 days

SOUTH AFRICAN TEST RECORDS

Most appearances as a Test match combination (starting XV)

Fullback/wings	PC Montgomery, CS Terblanche & PWG Rossouw (1998-1999)	13
Centre pair	J de Villiers & J Fourie (2005-2013)	29
Halfbacks	JH van der Westhuizen & HW Honiball (1993-1999)	24
Locks	V Matfield & JP Botha (2003-2011)	63*
Front row	T Mtawarira, BW du Plessis, JN du Plessis (2010-2014)	16
Loose forwards	AG Venter, RJ Kruger & GH Teichmann (1996-1997)	14
	AG Venter, J Erasmus & GH Teichmann (1997-1999)	14

*World record

Springboks sent off in Tests (8)

Player	Opponent	Referee	Venue	Date
JT Small	vs Australia	EF Morrison (England)	Brisbane	1993
J Dalton	vs Canada	DTM McHugh (Ireland)	Port Elizabeth	1995
AG Venter	vs New Zealand	WD Bevan (Wales)	Auckland	1997
B Venter	vs Uruguay	PL Marshall (Australia)	Glasgow	1999
MC Joubert	vs Australia	PD O'Brien (New Zealand)	Johannesburg	2002
JJ Labuschagne	vs England	PD O'Brien (New Zealand)	Twickenham	2002
PC Montgomery*	vs Wales	SJ Dickinson (Australia)	Cardiff	2005
BW du Plessis **	vs New Zealand	R Poite (France)	Auckland	2013

*Montgomery's first yellow card was subsequently dismissed by a disciplinary commission and his red card rescinded. ** Du Plessis first yellow card was subsequently dismissed by a disciplinary commission and his red card rescinded.

Players sent off in Tests against South Africa (5)

Player	Team	Referee	Venue	Date
R Snow	Canada	DTM McHugh (Ireland)	Port Elizabeth	1995
GL Rees	Canada	DTM McHugh (Ireland)	Port Elizabeth	1995
GR Jenkins	Wales	J Dumé (France)	Johannesburg	1995
PW Williams	Samoa	N Owens (Wales)	Albany	2011
AT Tuilagi	Samoa	P Gauzere (France)	Pretoria	2013

International referees in South African Test matches

Tests	Referee	Country	SA Won	SA Lost	Drawn	% Wins
18	SR Walsh	NZ/Australia	14	1	3	78%

Highest winning percentage as a Springbok (20 or more Tests)

	Played	Won	Lost	Drawn	% Wins
AC Garvey	28	24	4	0	86%

Lowest winning percentage as a Springbok (20 or more Tests)

	Played	Won	Lost	Drawn	% Wins
AJJ van Straaten	21	9	11	1	43%

SOUTH AFRICAN TEST RECORDS

TEST CAPTAINS

	Captain	Test as Captain (Total tests)	Debut as captain	Debut match
1	HH Castens - Prop, Western Province	1 (1)	1891	British Isles 1st test
2	RCD Snedden - Prop, Griqualand West	1 (1)	1891	British Isles 2nd test
3	AR Richards - Flyhalf, Western Province	1 (3)	1891	British Isles 3rd test
4	FTD Aston - Centre & wing, Transvaal	3 (4)	1896	British Isles 1st test
5	BH Heatlie - Prop & lock, Western Province	2 (6)	1896	British Isles 4th test
6	A Frew - Prop, Transvaal	1 (1)	1903	British Isles 1st test
7	JM Powell - Flyhalf, Griqualand West	1 (4)	1903	British Isles 2nd test
8	HW Carolin - Flyhalf, Western Province	1 (3)	1906	Scotland
9	PJ Roos - Prop, Western Province	3 (4)	1906	Ireland
10	DFT Morkel - Prop, Transvaal	2 (9)	1910	British Isles 1st test
11	WA Millar - No. 8 & flank, Western Province	5 (6)	1910	British Isles 2nd test
12	FJ Dobbin - Scrumhalf, Griqualand West	1 (9)	1912	Scotland
13	TB Pienaar - Prop, Western Province	0 (0)	1921	Did not play in tests
14	WH Morkel - No. 8, Transvaal	3 (9)	1921	New Zealand 1st test
15	PK Albertyn - Centre, South Western Districts	4 (4)	1924	British Isles 1st test
16	PJ Mostert - Prop & hooker, Western Province	4 (14)	1928	New Zealand 1st test
17	BL Osler - Flyhalf, Western Province	5 (17)	1931	Wales
18	PJ Nel - Lock & prop, Natal	8 (16)	1933	Australia 1st test
19	DH Craven - Flyhalf & scrumhalf, Eastern Province	4 (16)	1937	New Zealand 1st test
20	F du Plessis - Lock, Transvaal	3 (3)	1949	New Zealand 1st test
21	BJ Kenyon - Flank, Border	1 (1)	1949	New Zealand 4th test
22	HSV Muller - No. 8, Transvaal	9 (13)	1951	Scotland
23	SP Fry - Flank, Western Province	4 (13)	1955	British Isles 1st test
24	SS Viviers - Fullback & flyhalf	5 (5)	1956	Australia 1st test
25	JA du Rand - Lock, Northern Transvaal	1 (21)	1956	New Zealand 1st test
26	JT Claassen - Lock, Western Transvaal	9 (28)	1958	France 1st test
27	DC van Jaarsveldt - Flank, Rhodesia	1 (1)	1960	Scotland
28	RG Dryburgh - Fullback, Natal	2 (8)	1960	New Zealand 1st test
29	AS Malan - Lock, Transvaal	10 (16)	1960	New Zealand 3rd test
30	GF Malan - Hooker, Transvaal	4 (18)	1963	Australia 1st test
31	CM Smith - Scrumhalf, Orange Free State	4 (7)	1964	France
32	DJ de Villiers - Scrumhalf, Western Province	22 (25)	1965	New Zealand 1st test
33	TP Bedford - No. 8, Natal	3 (25)	1969	Australia 2nd test
34	JFK Marais - Prop, Eastern Province	11 (35)	1971	France 1st test
36	M du Plessis - No. 8, Western Province	15 (22)	1975	France 1st test
37	MTS Stofberg - Flank, Northern Transvaal	4 (21)	1980	South America 1st test
38	W Claassen - No. 8, Natal	7 (7)	1981	Ireland 1st test
39	DJ Serfontein - Scrumhalf, Western Province	2 (19)	1984	South America & Sp. 1st test
40	HE Botha - Flyhalf, Northern Transvaal	9 (28)	1986	NZ Cavaliers 1st test
41	JC Breedt - No. 8, Transvaal	2 (8)	1989	World Team 1st test
42	JF Pienaar - Flank & No. 8, Transvaal	29 (29)	1993	France 1st test
43	CP Strauss - Flank, Western Province	1 (15)	1994	New Zealand 1st test
44	AJ Richter - No. 8, Northern Transvaal	1 (10)	1995	Romania
45	GH Teichmann - No. 8, Natal	36 (42)	1996	New Zealand 1st test

SOUTH AFRICAN TEST RECORDS

TEST CAPTAINS

	Captain	Test as Captain (Total tests)	Debut as captain	Debut match
46	CPJ Krige - Flank, Western Province	18 (39)	1999	Italy 2nd test
47	J Erasmus - Flank, Golden Lions	1 (36)	1999	Australia 1st test
48	JH van der Westhuizen - Scrumhalf, Blue Bulls	10 (89)	1999	New Zealand 2nd test
49	AN Vos - No. 8, Golden Lions	16 (33)	1999	Spain
50	RB Skinstad - No. 8, Western Province	12 (42)	2001	Italy
51	JW Smit - Hooker, Natal	83 (111)	2003	Georgia
52	V Matfield - Lock, Blue Bulls	20 (121)	2007	New Zealand 1st test
53	GJ Muller - Lock, Natal	1 (24)	2007	New Zealand 2nd test
54	J de Villiers - Centre, Western Province	34 (106)	2012	England 1st test

WINNING PERCENTAGES OF SPRINGBOK CAPTAINS (10 OR MORE TESTS)

	Player	M	W	D	L	PF	PA
86,67%	M du Plessis	15	13	0	2	357	230
80%	JH van der Westhuizen	10	8	0	2	329	191
75%	V Matfield	20	15	0	5	623	302
72,22%	GH Teichmann	36	26	0	10	1228	661
67,64%	J de Villiers	34	23	4	7	783	506

Percentage of Springbok points scored during a Test career

	Player	Player points	Springbok points
50,73%	HE Botha	312	615
43,59%	M Steyn	688	1578

Percentage of Springbok tries scored during a Test career

	Player	Tries	Springbok tries
26,76%	DM Gerber	19	71
17,98%	BG Habana	57	317

Springbok relationships

Father & son	Twelve sets	Last J Reinach & JM Reinach	1986 & 2014
Three brothers	Three sets	Last W, CJ & MJ du Plessis	1980-1982, 1981-1989 & 1984-1989
Two brothers	Thirty two sets	Last AK & OM Ndungane	2008

Brothers in tests (since World War II)

Twice	HPJ & RP Bekker	1953
Once	ID & RJ McCallum	1974
Once	DSL & JCP Snyman	1974
Once	HE & DS Botha	1981
Twice	CJ & W du Plessis	1982
Eight times	CJ & MJ du Plessis	1984-1989
Twice	G & J Cronjé	2004
Forty two times	JN & BW du Plessis	2007-2014

SOUTH AFRICAN TEST RECORDS

Tallest, shortest, heaviest, lightest

Tallest	A Bekker	2.08m (6ft 10in)
Shortest	TA Gentles	1.60m (5ft 3in)
Heaviest	RG Visagie	138kgs (21st 8lbs)
Lightest	WD Sendin	60kgs (9st 6lbs)

Youngest Springboks on Test debut

18 Years, 18 days	AJ Hartley	British Isles (3rd Test)	1891
19 Years, 8 days	DG Cope	British Isles (2nd Test)	1896
19 Years, 37 days	JA Loubser	British Isles (3rd Test)	1903
19 Years, 51 days	RCB van Ryneveld	British Isles (2nd Test)	1910
19 Years, 72 days	WJ Mills	British Isles (2nd Test)	1910
19 Years, 112 days	FG Turner	Australia (1st Test)	1933
19 Years, 126 days	BH Heatlie	British Isles (2nd Test)	1891
19 Years, 158 days	SC de Melker	British Isles (2nd Test)	1903

Oldest Springboks in final test

37 Years, 202 days	V Matfield	Wales (3rd Test)	2014
37 Years, 34 days	JN Ackermann	Australia (2nd Test)	2007
36 Years, 258 days	WH Morkel	New Zealand (3rd Test)	1921
35 Years, 277 days	D Lötter	Australia (2nd Test)	1993
35 Years, 252 days	FCH du Preez	Australia (3rd Test)	1971
35 Years, 130 days	LC Moolman	NZ Cavaliers (4th Test)	1986

Least and most experienced Springbok starting XVs since 1992

115 Caps - vs. Italy, Durban, 1999: PC Montgomery (23); BJ Paulse (1), RF Fleck (1), JC Mulder (26), CS Terblanche (13); GS du Toit (2), DNB von Hoesslin (1); AN Vos (1), J Erasmus (18), CPJ Krige (0), CS Boome (1), PA van den Berg (1), W Meyer (1), AE Drotské (14), RB Kempson (12).

836 Caps - vs. Australia, Wellington, 2011: P Lambie (10); J-PR Pietersen (41), J Fourie (68), J de Villiers (71), BG Habana (73); M Steyn (33), PF du Preez (61); PJ Spies (46), SWP Burger (67), HW Brüssow (19), V Matfield (109), DJ Rossouw (62), JN du Plessis (29), JW Smit (110), GG Steenkamp (37). *(This is the most experienced side of all time)*

SPRINGBOK COACHES SINCE 1992

	First & Last Test	P	W	L	D	PF	PA	Diff	TF	TA	Win %
JG Williams	Aug 92 - Nov 92	5	1	4	0	79	130	-51	7	14	20,00%
GHH Sonnekus	Did not take up appointment	-	-	-	-	-	-	-	-	-	-
IB McIntosh	June 93 - Aug 94	12	4	6	2	252	240	12	25	14	33,33%
GM Christie	Oct 94 - Nov 95	14	14	0	0	450	191	259	54	16	100,00%
AT Markgraaff	July 96 - Dec 96	13	8	5	0	352	260	92	38	21	61,54%
CJ du Plessis	June 97 - Aug 97	8	3	5	0	288	213	75	39	22	37,50%
NVH Mallett	Nov 97 - Aug 00	38	27	11	0	1251	678	573	152	49	71,05%
HJ Viljoen	Nov 00 - Dec 01	15	8	6	1	376	312	64	38	18	53,33%
RAW Straeuli	Jun 02 - Nov 03	23	12	11	0	622	598	24	71	61	52,17%
JA White	Jun 04 - Dec 07	54	36	17	1	1740	1097	643	194	110	66,67%
P de Villiers	Jun 08 - Oct 11	48	30	18	0	1262	921	341	126	87	62,50%
H Meyer	Jun 12 -	37	26	9	2	981	633	348	108	54	70,27%
South Africa's record since 1992		267	169	92	6	7653	5273	2380	852	466	63,29%

SOUTH AFRICAN TEST RECORDS

SPRINGBOKS BY STADIUM - HOME

		P	W	L	D	PF	PA	TF	TA	Avg. score	%Win
Rustenburg	Royal Bafokeng Sports Palace	1	1	0	0	21	20	2	2	21-20	100%
East London	Border Rugby Stadium	3	3	0	0	240	32	36	3	80-11	100%
Johannesburg	Wanderers (New)	1	1	0	0	24	9	3	1	24-09	100%
Witbank	Puma Stadium	1	1	0	0	29	13	4	1	29-13	100%
Nelspruit	Mbombela Stadium	2	2	0	0	61	47	7	5	30-24	100%
Port Elizabeth	Boet Erasmus Stadium	16	14	1	1	423	182	49	17	26-11	88%
Durban	Kingsmead	5	4	1	0	57	35	7	7	11-07	80%
Pretoria	Loftus Versfeld	33	25	8	0	1085	656	131	65	33-20	76%
Bloemfontein	Free State Stadium	18	13	4	1	504	307	57	28	28-17	72%
Johannesburg	Ellis Park	46	32	12	2	1211	744	151	69	26-16	70%
Cape Town	Newlands	51	35	14	2	994	611	129	65	19-12	69%
Port Elizabeth	Nelson Mandela Bay Stadium	3	2	0	1	87	25	9	2	29-08	67%
Durban	Kings Park	30	19	8	3	724	471	74	41	24-16	63%
Port Elizabeth	Crusader Ground	10	6	3	1	102	57	18	15	11-06	60%
Johannesburg	Wanderers (Old)	4	2	1	1	49	37	12	7	12-09	50%
Springs	PAM Brink Stadium	2	1	1	0	55	37	7	3	28-19	50%
Johannesburg	FNB Stadium	3	1	2	0	111	74	11	8	37-25	33%
Bloemfontein	Springbok Park	1	0	1	0	4	15	0	3	04-15	0%
Kimberley	Eclectic Ground	1	0	1	0	0	3	0	0	00-03	0%
Kimberley	KAC Ground	2	0	1	1	3	9	1	1	02-05	0%
		233	162	58	13	5784	3384	708	343	25-14	70%

SPRINGBOKS BY STADIUM - AWAY

		P	W	L	D	PF	PA	TF	TA	Avg. score	%Win
Padova	Stadio Euganeo	1	1	0	0	22	6	3	0	22-06	100%
Gosford, Australia	Advocate Express	1	1	0	0	38	24	4	4	38-24	100%
Belfast	Balmoral Ground	1	1	0	0	15	12	4	3	15-12	100%
Bologna	Stadio Dall'Ara	1	1	0	0	62	31	9	3	62-31	100%
Bordeaux	Route de Médoc, Le Bouscat	1	1	0	0	38	5	9	1	38-05	100%
Bordeaux	Municipal Stadium	1	1	0	0	12	9	0	3	12-09	100%
Bordeaux	Parc Lescure	1	1	0	0	22	12	2	0	22-12	100%
Brisbane	Exhibition Ground	2	2	0	0	23	6	5	0	12-03	100%
Buenos Aires	Ferro Carril Oeste Stadium	4	4	0	0	171	85	24	8	43-22	100%
Buenos Aires	River Plate Stadium	1	1	0	0	37	33	5	3	37-33	100%
Buenos Aires	Velez Sarsfield Stadium	2	2	0	0	73	30	8	4	37-15	100%
Edinburgh	Inverleith	1	1	0	0	16	0	4	0	16-00	100%
Genoa	Luigi Ferraris Stadium	1	1	0	0	54	26	8	2	54-26	100%
Glenville, New York	Owl Creek Polo Field	1	1	0	0	38	7	8	1	38-07	100%
Houston, Texas	Robertson Stadium	1	1	0	0	43	20	6	1	43-20	100%
Lens	Stade Felix Bollaert	1	1	0	0	30	25	4	3	30-25	100%
London	Wembley Stadium	1	1	0	0	28	20	3	1	28-20	100%
Lyon	Stade Gerland	2	2	0	0	56	47	7	5	28-24	100%
Montevideo	Wanderers Club	1	1	0	0	22	13	3	2	22-13	100%
Montpellier	Stade de la Mosson	1	1	0	0	64	15	9	2	64-15	100%
Rome	Olympic Stadium	1	1	0	0	40	21	4	2	40-21	100%

SPRINGBOKS BY STADIUM – AWAY

		P	W	L	D	PF	PA	TF	TA	Avg. score	% Win
Santiago	Prince of Wales Country Club	1	1	0	0	30	16	6	2	30-16	100%
Swansea	St Helen's	2	2	0	0	19	3	5	1	10-02	100%
Hamilton	Waikato Stadium	1	1	0	0	32	29	2	2	32-29	100%
Udine	Stadio Friuli	1	1	0	0	32	10	4	1	32-10	100%
Albany	North Harbour Stadium	2	2	0	0	100	5	13	1	50-03	100%
Salta	Estadio Padre Ernesto Martearena	1	1	0	0	33	31	3	3	33-31	100%
Sydney	Sydney Cricket Ground	6	5	1	0	92	57	18	8	15-10	83%
Cardiff [1]	Millennium Stadium	17	14	2	1	357	263	38	18	21-15	82%
Paris	Parc des Princes	5	4	1	0	150	66	18	6	30-13	80%
Edinburgh	Murrayfield	17	13	4	0	458	159	63	14	27-09	76%
Paris	Stade de France	7	5	2	0	181	96	13	6	26-14	71%
Paris	Colombes Stadium	3	2	0	1	41	14	9	1	41-14	67%
Dublin	Lansdowne Road/Aviva Stadium	13	8	4	1	221	170	33	15	17-13	62%
London	Twickenham	20	11	9	0	335	351	30	29	17-18	55%
Toulouse	Municipal Stadium	2	1	1	0	26	24	2	2	13-12	50%
Sydney	Aussie Stadium	4	2	2	0	93	71	13	4	23-18	50%
Marseille	Stade Velodrome	2	1	1	0	47	50	6	4	24-25	50%
Glasgow	Hampden Park	2	1	1	0	39	9	5	2	20-05	50%
Mendoza	Malvinas Argentinas Stadium	2	1	0	1	38	33	2	3	19-17	50%
Wellington	Athletic Park	7	3	3	1	64	50	5	6	09-07	43%
Perth	Patersons Stadium	10	4	5	1	237	198	25	18	24-20	40%
Christchurch	Jade Stadium	8	2	6	0	101	149	13	17	13-19	25%
Wellington	Westpac Stadium	9	2	7	0	154	210	17	21	17-23	22%
Brisbane [2]	Suncorp Stadium	9	2	7	0	160	227	19	21	18-25	22%
Auckland	Eden Park	10	2	7	1	151	227	19	26	15-23	20%
Dunedin	Carisbrook	8	1	7	0	93	164	9	18	12-21	13%
Brisbane	Ballymore	1	0	1	0	20	28	2	3	20-28	0%
Brisbane	The Gabba	1	0	1	0	27	38	4	4	27-38	0%
Melbourne	Telstra Dome	2	0	2	0	32	73	3	8	16-37	0%
Sydney	Telstra Stadium	5	0	5	0	73	140	6	17	15-28	0%
London	Crystal Palace	1	0	0	1	3	3	1	1	03-03	0%
Dublin	Croke Park	1	0	1	0	10	15	1	0	10-15	0%
Dunedin	Forsyth Barr Stadium	1	0	1	0	11	21	1	2	11-21	0%
		208	119	81	8	4364	3447	537	332	21-16	57%

1 Includes records of the original Cardiff Arms Park on the Millennium Stadium site.
2 Includes one match at Lang Park on which site the Suncorp Stadium was developed.

England dash SA's hopes in thriller

Cold comfort for precocious Pollard

THERE's little doubt Handré Pollard would have happily traded his silver world junior player of the year trophy for a winner's gold medal after a nailbiting IRB Junior World Championship (JWC) final at Eden Park, Auckland that saw nemesis England edge South Africa by a single point.

Pollard was named player of the tournament shortly after the Junior Springboks lost 21-20 at the spiritual home of New Zealand rugby. Precocious as he is, few would have bet that, within the space of a few months, the 20-year-old Pollard would be scoring two tries against the All Blacks in a performance at Ellis Park that would cement his place as South Africa's number-one flyhalf.

Pollard, who would make his Test debut against Scotland just a week after the Eden Park final, was the second South African to win the award after Jan Serfontein. Fittingly, Serfontein was Pollard's team-mate not only when South Africa won the JWC on home soil in 2012, but also when the Springboks beat the All Blacks 27-25 in the final round of the Castle Rugby Championships on the first weekend of October.

IRB Chairman Bernard Lapasset said: "It is always a difficult task to select a winner, especially when all the candidates have performed so impressively during a spectacular Championship, but Handré Pollard is a deserved recipient of the prestigious IRB Junior Player of the Year award.

"His superb marshalling at flyhalf has been an eye-catching feature of the Junior Springboks' passage to the final and Pollard has performed throughout with great poise, control and adventure."

That Pollard was outstanding throughout cannot be doubted. It can also be argued that, painful as a one-point defeat in a final might have been, were it not for Pollard, coach Dawie Theron's charges might not have reached the final at all. Such was the 'Pollard effect'.

South Africa notched wins over Scotland and Samoa en route to the final but it was their two victories over hosts New Zealand – once in the Pools and then in the semi-finals – which made a silver-medal finish that much easier to bear.

Any South African team who achieves back-to-back victories over an All Blacks

Handré Pollard followed in the footsteps of his current Springbok team-mate, Jan Serfontein.

team – whether senior or junior – in New Zealand deserve only the highest praise, irrespective of the results of other matches.

Ironically, it was a fortuitous logistical arrangement that Theron believed helped his team to their double, with South Africa and New Zealand holed up in the same hotel for the duration of the JWC.

"The players could deal with them face to face every day, and the manner in which the guys handled it, with maturity, is praiseworthy," said Theron. "We are all friends off the field anyway in rugby, and it was probably two of the most titanic battles ever fought at junior level – against New Zealand in New Zealand and with all that backing that they had. I was just so proud of the guys."

Theron hinted, quite understandably, that the twin victories over New Zealand, plus a bruising encounter against Samoa, eventually took its toll on his players in the final.

"Perhaps it was the mental fatigue, and we didn't show the same patience that we did against New Zealand," he said. "We lost a vital ball that we knocked on from an attacking scrum and if we had scored there, it would have been 17-3 for us and it would've been a different ball game."

Looking to 2015, Theron said nine players of his squad were eligible for the next JWC in Italy, including the Du Preez twins, Dan and Jean-Luc, Joseph Dweba and the highly-rated Western Province duo of Jacques Vermeulen and JD Schickerling.

"Overall, we lost one of nine matches this year. Unfortunately, that was the JWC final and it was by a single point against the defending world champions. Although we fell just short of our goal, South Africans can be very proud of the effort, conduct and commitment of these youngsters," said Theron.

Both sides started the final nervously and, with the scores at 3-3, centre Jesse Kriel ran onto a deft Pollard chip to score. But England capitalised on South African errors, slotting a penalty before wing Nathan Earle went over to give them an 11-10 half-time lead.

The second half started well for England as flyhalf Billy Burns kicked another penalty to stretch the lead to four points.

Pollard replied with a penalty but a powerful maul by England secured a second try when Joel Conlon went over under a heap of bodies. The successful conversion made it 21-13 and the Junior Boks faced a test of their resolve – not to mention endurance.

A second try to Kriel, converted by Pollard, gave South Africa a chance to grab the win. The flyhalf came close with a drop goal attempt, but it was England who held their nerve.

South Africa might not have won gold, but in Pollard they have certainly unearthed a rare diamond.

LOG

Pool A	P	W	D	L	PF	PA	TF	TA	BP	PTS
England	3	3	0	0	118	43	15	4	2	14
Australia	3	2	0	1	89	58	11	7	2	10
Italy	3	1	0	2	35	118	2	15	0	4
Argentina	3	0	0	3	59	82	5	7	2	2
Pool B										
Ireland	3	2	0	1	86	40	10	4	3	11
Wales	3	2	0	1	82	57	10	7	1	9
France	3	2	0	1	59	31	7	3	1	9
Fiji	3	0	0	3	24	123	4	17	0	0
Pool C										
South Africa	3	3	0	0	115	37	16	5	2	14
New Zealand	3	2	0	1	126	52	18	7	2	10
Samoa	3	1	0	2	47	87	6	13	0	4
Scotland	3	0	0	3	30	142	5	20	0	0

Note: BP = Bonus point

FINAL POSITIONS

1 England 2 South Africa 3 New Zealand 4 Ireland 5 Australia 6 France 7 Wales 8 Samoa 9 Argentina 10 Scotland 11 Italy 12 Fiji

MATCH DETAILS

South Africa 61 Scotland 5 (halftime 14-5)

June 2. QBE Stadium, Albany, Auckland. Referee: Jaquin Montes (Uruguay)

SOUTH AFRICA - *Tries: J Kriel (2), Greeff (2), Davis, Marx, Schoeman, Petersen, Gelant. Conversions: Pollard (7), Du Plessis.*

Gelant, Greeff, J Kriel, Esterhuizen *(Janse van Rensburg, 55)*, Petersen, Pollard *(capt, Du Plessis, 76)*, Mkhabela *(Smith, 69)*, Davis, Brink *(Du Preez, 67)*, Vermeulen, Janse van Rensburg, Nonkontwana *(Schickerling, 53)*, Louw *(Van der Weshuizen, 70)*, Marx, Schoeman *(Du Toit, 70)*. *NOT USED: Els*

SCOTLAND - *Try: Farndale.*

Ruairidh Young, Jamie Farndale, Christopher Dean, Neil Herron, Damien Hoyland *(Sam Pecquer, 36)*, Ben Chalmers *(Rory Hutchinson, 48)*, Alex Glashan *(Ben Vellacot, 62)*, Magnus Bradbury *(Gabriel Carroll, 67)*, Tommy Spinks *(capt.)*, Neil Irvine-Hess, Lewis Carmichael, Andy Cramond *(Glen Young, 55)*, Darcy Rae *(Zander Fagerson, 41)*, Sam James *(James Malcolm, 48)*, Jock Cosgrove *(Phil Cringle, 58)*.

JUNIOR SPRINGBOKS

South Africa 33 New Zealand 24 (halftime 14-17)
June 6. QBE Stadium, Albany, Auckland. Referee: Alexandre Ruiz (France)
S AFRICA - *Tries: Pollard, J Kriel, Greeff, Gelant. Conversions: Pollard (2). Penalties: Pollard (3).*
Gelant, Greeff, J Kriel, D Kriel *(Du Plessis, 63)*, Petersen, Pollard *(capt)*, Smith, Davis, Brink *(Nonkontwana, 75)*, Du Preez *(Sekekete, 25)*, Janse van Rensburg, Schickerling, Van der Weshuizen *(Louw, 63)*, Els *(Dweba, 79)*, Du Toit *(Schoemam, 63)*. *NOT USED: Mkhabela, Van der Merwe.*
NEW ZEALAND - *Tries: Li (3). Cons: Hickey (2), Mo'unga. Pen: Hickey.*
Damian McKenzie, Vincent Tavae-Aso, Anton Lienert-Brown, Jackson Garden-Bachop *(Tauasosi Tuimavave, 72)*, Tevita Li, Simon Hickey *(capt, Richard Mo'unga, 72)*, Mitchell Drummomd *(Josh Renton, 72)*, Matt Peni *(Kyle Harris, 61)*, Lachlan Boshier, Tom Sanders, Geoffrey Cridge, James Tucker *(YC, 79)*, Tau Koloamatangi *(Tim Cadwallader, 72)*, Hame Faiva *(James O'Reilly, 57)*, Atunaisa Moli *(Scott Mellow, 72)*. *NOT USED: Josh Dickson.*

Jesse Kriel celebrates his try in the first match against New Zealand.

South Africa 21 Samoa 8 (halftime 7-8)
June 10. ECO Light Stadium, Pukekohe. Referee: Ben O'Keefe (New Zealand)
SOUTH AFRICA - *Tries: Davis, Esterhuizen, Petersen. Conversions: Pollard (3).*
J Kriel *(Gelant, 74)*, Petersen, D Kriel, Esterhuizen, Van der Merwe, Pollard *(capt)*, Smith, Davis, Vermeulen, Mabuza *(Brink, 45)*, Janse van Rensburg, Schickerling, Louw *(Van der Westhuizen, 74)*, Els, Schoeman. *NOT USED: Dweba, Mxoli, Sekekete, Mkhabela, Du Plessis.*
SAMOA - *Try: Apa.*
Luteru Laulala, Harry Luteru, Joseph Ikenasio, Nathanial Apa *(YC, 47)*, Nu'u Nu'u, William Talaitane Mu, Mark Talaese *(Emil Pittman)*, Richard Mariota, Henry Stowers *(capt)*, Sootala Fa'aso'o, Cameron Skelton *(Joe Lee, 74)*, Jotham Wrampling, Etimani Sului *(Andrew Lemalu, 63)*, Leif Schwenke *(Ieremia Mataena, 59)*, Feretii Saaga. *NOT USED: Louis Kapteni, Ezra Meleises, Johan Fagasua, Aujuso Tuitama.*

JUNIOR SPRINGBOKS

South Africa 32 New Zealand 25 (halftime 10-15) (Semi-Final)
June 15, QBE Stadium, Albany, Auckland. Referee: Federico Anselmi (Argentina)
S AFRICA - *Tries: Esterhuizen, Petersen, Pollard, Els. Conversions: Pollard (3). Penalties: Pollard (2).*
Gelant, Greeff *(D Kriel, 37)*, J Kriel, Esterhuizen *(YC, 29)*, Petersen, Pollard *(capt)*, Smith, Davis, Brink, Vermeulen, Janse van Rensburg, Schickerling, Van der Westhuizen *(Louw, 65)*, Els, Du Toit *(Schoeman, 68)*. NOT USED: Dweba, Nonkontwana, Sekekete, Mkhabela, Du Plessis.
NEW ZEALAND - *Tries: Faiva, Li, Tavae-Aso. Con: McKenzie (2). Pens: McKenzie (2).*
Damian McKenzie, Vincent Tavae-Aso, Anton Lienert-Brown *(capt)*, TJ Faiane *(Kaveinga Finau, 61)*, Tevita Li, Richard Mo'unga, Mitchell Drummomd *(Josh Renton, 57)*, Tom Sanders, Lachlan Boshier, Kyle Harris *(Matt Peni, 57)*, Geoffrey Cridge, James Tucker *(Troy Callander, 74)*, Tau Koloamatangi *(Tim Cadwallader, 68)*, Hame Faiva *(James O'Reilly, 68)*, Atunaisa Moli. NOT USED: Scott Mellow, David Kaetau Havili.

South Africa 20 England 21 (halftime 21-26) (Final)
June 20, Eden Park, Auckland. Referee: Ben O'Keefe (New Zealand).
SOUTH AFRICA - *Tries: J Kriel (2). Conversions: Pollard (2). Penalties: Pollard (2).*
Gelant, D Kriel, J Kriel, Esterhuizen *(Van der Merwe, 53)*, Petersen, Pollard *(capt)*, Smith, Davis, Brink, Vermeulen *(Du Preez, 46)*, Janse van Rensburg, Schickerling, Van der Westhuizen *(Louw, 46)*, Els *(Dweba, 49)*, Du Toit *(Schoeman, 62)*. UNUSED SUBS: Sekekete, Mkhabela, Du Plessis.
ENGLAND - *Tries: Conlon, Earle. Conversion: Burns. Penalties: Burns (2), Morris.*
Aaron Morris, Howard Packman, Nic Tompkins, Harry Sloan, Nathan Earle, Billy Burns, Henry Taylor, James Chisholm, Gus Jones (Joel Conlon, 41), Ross Moriarty, Charlie Ewels, Maro Itoje (capt), Paul Hill, Tom Woostencroft (Jack Walker, Danny Hobbs-Awoyeni (Alex Lundberg, 70). Unused subs: Biyi Alo, Hayden Thompson-Stringer, Callum Brayley, Sam Olver, Henry Purdy.

RESULTS

June 02
Argentina	17	Australia	36
Wales	48	Fiji	19
South Africa	61	Scotland	5
France	19	Ireland	13
England	63	Italy	3
New Zealand	48	Samoa	12

June 06
Scotland	18	Samoa	27
Argentina	26	Italy	29
France	37	Fiji	5
England	38	Australia	24
Wales	21	Ireland	35
New Zealand	24	South Africa	33

June 10
Ireland	38	Fiji	0
Australia	29	Italy	3
Wales	13	France	3
England	17	Argentina	16
Samoa	8	South Africa	21
New Zealand	54	Scotland	7

June 15
9th place Semi Final
Argentina	38	Fiji	12
Italy	18	Scotland	21

5th place Semi Final
Australia	53	Samoa	16
Wales	18	France	19

Semi Finals
England	42	Ireland	15
South Africa	32	New Zealand	25

JUNIOR SPRINGBOKS

June 20

11th Place Play-Off

| Fiji | 17 | Italy | 22 |

9th Place Play-Off

| Argentina | 41 | Scotland | 21 |

7th Place Play-Off

| Wales | 20 | Samoa | 3 |

5th Place Play-Off

| France | 27 | Australia | 34 |

3rd Place Play-Off

| New Zealand | 45 | Ireland | 23 |

Final

| England | 21 | South Africa | 20 |

LEADING SCORERS

POINTS

Patricio Fernandez	Argentina	73
Handre Pollard	South Africa	65
Andrew Kellaway	Australia	50
Jake McIntyre	Australia	47
Billy Burns	England	42
Angus O'Brien	Wales	40
Ross Byrne	Ireland	38
Tevita Li	New Zealand	35
Filipo Buscema	Italy	32
Nathan Earle	England	30

TRIES

Andrew Kelaway	Australia	10
Tevita Li	New Zealand	7
Nathan Earle	England	6
James Benjamin	Wales	5
Jesse Kriel	South Africa	5
Gus Jones	England	4
Nathaniel Apa	Samoa	3
Lloyd Greeff	South Africa	3
Sergeal Petersen	South Africa	3
Garry Ringrose	Ireland	3

SOUTH AFRICA AT THE IRB JUNIOR WORLD CHAMPIONSHIPS *

Year	Event	Place	Captain	Coach
2008	New Zealand in Wales	3rd	Gerrit-Jan van Velze	Eric Sauls
2009	New Zealand in Japan	3rd	Robert Ebersohn	Eric Sauls
2010	New Zealand in Argentina	3rd	CJ Stander	Eric Sauls
2011	New Zealand in Italy	5th	Arno Botha	Dawie Theron
2012	South Africa in South Africa	1st	Wiaan Liebenberg	Dawie Theron
2013	England in France	3rd	Ruan Steenkamp	Dawie Theron
2014	England in New Zealand	2nd	Handre Pollard	Dawie Theron

This tournament replaced the separate Under 19 & Under 21 IRB Junior World Championships.

IRB JUNIOR PLAYERS OF THE YEAR

2008	Luke Braid (New Zealand)		2012	Jan Serfontein (South Africa)
2009	Aaron Cruden (New Zealand)		2013	Sam Davies (Wales)
2010	Julian Savea (New Zealand)		2014	Handre Pollard (South Africa)
2011	George Ford (England)			

❰ DID YOU KNOW? ❱

Theo Samuels of Griqualand West scored South Africa's first-ever Test points. A late replacement, Samuels scored a try in the second Test of the 1896 series against the British Isles, then grabbed another later on in the match.

SQUAD

	Position	Date of Birth	Height (cm)	Weight	Union
BACKS					
WW (Warrick) Gelant	Fullback	20/05/1994	179	86	Blue Bulls
LD (Lloyd) Greeff	Wing	03/01/1994	194	105	Leopards
S (Sergeal) Petersen	Wing	01/08/1994	175	80	Eastern Province
D (Duhan) van der Merwe	Wing	04/06/1995	194	96	Blue Bulls
JA (Jesse) Kriel	Centre	15/02/1994	186	95	Blue Bulls
DD (Dan) Kriel	Centre	15/02/1994	193	103	Blue Bulls
AP (Andre) Esterhuizen	Centre	30/03/1994	191	106	KwaZulu-Natal
R (Rohan) Janse van Rensburg	Centre	11/09/1994	186	100	Blue Bulls
H (Handre) Pollard (capt.)	Flyhalf	11/03/1994	189	96	Blue Bulls
J-L (Jean-Luc) du Plessis	Flyhalf	07/05/1994	179	87	KwaZulu-Natal
MC (Mthokozisi) Mkhabela	Scrumhalf	10/10/1994	168	73	Free State
JP (Juan-Philip) Smith	Scrumhalf	30/03/1994	187	91	Blue Bulls
FORWARDS					
A (Aidon) Davis	No. 8	29/04/1994	189	102	Eastern Province
CJ (Cyle) Brink	Flanker	16/01/1994	183	112	Golden Lions
JF (Jacques) Vermeulen	Flanker	08/02/1995	194	107	Western Province
J-L (Jean-Luc) du Preez	Flanker	05/08/1994	193	110	KwaZulu-Natal
ST (Thabo) Mabuza	Flanker	01/02/1994	184	90	Golden Lions
VK (Victor) Sekekete	Flanker	28/01/1994	195	99	Golden Lions
NJ (Nico) Janse van Rensburg	Lock	06/05/1994	200	109	Blue Bulls
A (Abongile) Nonkontwana	Lock	10/04/1994	193	107	Blue Bulls
JD (JD) Schickerling	Lock	09/05/1994	202	108	Western Province
P (Pierre) Schoeman	Prop	07/05/1994	183	116	Blue Bulls
TJ (Thomas) du Toit	Prop	05/05/1995	189	130	KwaZulu-Natal
WM (Wilco) Louw	Prop	20/07/1994	185	130	Blue Bulls
NM (Mox) Mxoli	Prop	02/02/1994	183	112	Blue Bulls
DL (Dayan) van der Westhuizen	Prop	05/04/1994	182	118	Blue Bulls
MJ (Malcolm) Marx	Hooker	13/07/1994	188	119	Golden Lions
J (Joseph) Dweba	Hooker	25/10/1994	172	103	Free State
CW (Corniel) Els	Hooker	19/01/1994	183	102	Blue Bulls
A (Arno) van Wyk	Hooker	19/05/1994	184	105	Blue Bulls

Notes:

- D (Daniel) du Preez (KwaZulu-Natal) & DV (Duncan) Matthews (Blue Bulls) were originally selected but both had to withdraw because of injury. They were replaced by JF (Jacques) Vermeulen (WP) & R (Rohan) Janse van Rensburg (Blue Bulls) respectively.
- Janse van Rensburg sustained an injury during the tournament and was replaced by D (Duhan) van der Merwe (Blue Bulls).
- MJ (Malcolm) Marx (Golden Lions) sustained an injury during the tournament and was replaced by A (Arno) van Wyk (Blue Bulls).

JUNIOR SPRINGBOKS

APPEARANCES & POINTS

	Scotland	NZ	Samoa	NZ	England	Apps	T	C	P	DG	PTS
Warrick Gelant	15	15	15R	15	15	5	2	–	–	–	10
Lloyd Greeff	14	14	–	14	–	3	3	–	–	–	15
Jesse Kriel	13	13	15	13	13	5	5	–	–	–	25
Andre Esterhuizen	12	–	12	12	12	4	2	–	–	–	10
Sergeal Petersen	11	11	14	11	11	5	3	–	–	–	15
Handre Pollard	10c	10c	10c	10c	10c	5	2	17	7	–	65
Mthokozisi Mkhabela	9	x	x	x	x	1	–	–	–	–	0
Aidon Davis	8	8	8	8	8	5	2	–	–	–	10
Cyle Brink	7	7	6R	7	7	5	–	–	–	–	0
Jacques Vermeulen	6	–	7	6	6	4	–	–	–	–	0
Nico Janse van Rensburg	5	5	5	5	5	5	–	–	–	–	0
Abongile Nonkontwana	4	7R	–	x	–	2	–	–	–	–	0
Wilco Louw	3	3R	3	3R	3R	5	–	–	–	–	0
Malcolm Marx	2	–	–	–	–	1	1	–	–	–	5
Pierre Schoeman	1	1R	1	1R	1R	5	1	–	–	–	5
Corniel Els	x	2	2	2	2	4	1	–	–	–	5
Dayan van der Westhuizen	3R	3	3R	3	3	5	–	–	–	–	0
Thomas du Toit	1R	1	–	1	1	4	–	–	–	–	0
JD Schickerling	4R	4	4	4	4	5	–	–	–	–	0
Jean-Luc du Preez	7R	6	–	–	6R	3	–	–	–	–	0
JP Smith	9R	9	9	9	9	5	–	–	–	–	0
Jean-Luc du Plessis	15R	12R	x	x	x	2	–	1	–	–	2
Rohan Janse van Rensburg	12R	–	–	–	–	1	–	–	–	–	0
Dan Kriel	–	12	13	14R	14	4	–	–	–	–	0
Victor Sekekete	–	6R	x	x	x	1	–	–	–	–	0
Joseph Dweba	–	2R	–	x	2R	2	–	–	–	–	0
Duhan van der Merwe	–	x	11	–	12R	2	–	–	–	–	0
Thabo Mabuza	–	–	6	–	–	1	–	–	–	–	0
Mox Mxoli	–	–	x	–	–	0	–	–	–	–	0
Arno van Wyk	–	–	–	–	–	0	–	–	–	–	–
30 PLAYERS							22	18	7	0	167

Head Coach: Dawie Theron **Assistant coaches:** Deon Davids & Nazeem Adams
Physiotherapist: Aneurin Robyn **Doctor:** Jerome Mampane **Video Analyst:** Norman Laker
Team Manager: Yusuf Jackson **Strength & Conditioning:** Warren Adams
Media Manager: Rayaan Adriaanse **Defence Coach:** Jacques Nienaber

JUNIOR SPRINGBOKS

SA Under-20 2008-2014

† Indicates became a Springbok

Adendorff, S (Shaun) - BB - 2012
Afrika, CS (Cecil) - Grif - 2008
Badenhorst, WHB (Brummer) - WP - 2010
Bali, M (Mlungisi) - BB - 2010
Bantjes, HJ (Henri) - BB - 2008
Barry, C (Craig) - WP - 2011
Beerwinkel, A (Andrew) - BB - 2013
Beyers, U (Ulrich) - BB - 2011
Blommetjies, C (Clayton) - BB - 2009
Booysen, FCF (Fabian) - GL - 2012
† Botha, AF (Arno) - BB - 2011
Botha, R (Ruan) - GL - 2012
Botha, ZW (Zane) - BB - 2009
Brink, CJ (Cyle) - GL - 2014
Brummer, F (Francois) - BB - 2008, 2009
Bullbring, DJ (David) - GL - 2009
Carr, N (Nizaam) - WP - 2011
Chikukwa, TA (Tendayi) - BB - 2009
Coetzee, M (Marne) - BB - 2013
Cook, JG (Jean) - FS - 2011
Cooper, KL (Kyle) - KZN - 2009
Cronjé, L (Lionel) - FS - 2009
Cronjé, R (Ross) - KZN - 2009
Davis, A (Aidon) - EP - 2013, 2014
De Bruin, L (Luan) - FS - 2013
De Chaves, SJ (Sebastian) - GL - 2010
Dell, AME (Allan) - KZN - 2012
Dippenaar, SC (Stephan) - BB - 2008
Dreyer, RM (Ruan) - GL - 2010
Du Rand, CW (Wessel) - GL - 2010
Du Toit, F (Francois) - GL - 2010
Du Toit, OJJ (Jacques) - FS - 2013
† Du Toit, PS (Pieter-Steph) - KZN - 2012
Du Toit, TJ (Thomas) - KZN - 2014
Duvenage, DO (Dewaldt) - Bol - 2008
Du Plessis, J-L (Jean-Luc) - KZN - 2014
Du Plessis, WHJ (Jacques) - BB - 2013
Du Preez, BBN (Branco) - BB - 2010
Du Preez, CG (Cornell) - Leop - 2011
Du Preez, J-L (Jean-Luc) - KZN - 2014
Du Preez, RJ (Rob) - KZN - 2013
Dweba, J (Joseph) - FS - 2014
Ebersohn, JM (Sias) - FS - 2008, 2009
Ebersohn, RT (Robert) - FS - 2008, 2009
Els, CW (Corniel) - BB - 2014
Elstadt, R (Rynhardt) - WP - 2009
Esterhuizen, AP (Andre) - KZN - 2014
† Etzebeth, E (Eben) - WP - 2011
Fourie, C (Corné) - BB - 2008
Geduld, JG (Justin) - WP - 2013
Gelant, WW (Warrick) - BB - 2014
† Goosen, JL (Johan) - FS - 2011
Greeff, LD (Lloyd) - Leop - 2014
Griesel, AJ (Abrie) - BB - 2012
Hadebe, MS (Monde) - KZN - 2010
Hammond, D (Dean) - WP - 2012
Hanekom, NJ (Nicolaas) - WP - 2009
Hartzenberg, Y (Yaasir) - WP - 2009
Howard, PB (Patrick) - WP - 2012

Herbst, IP (Irne) - BB - 2013
Herbst, WJ (Wiehan) - Leop - 2008
Hess, CN (Cornell) - BB - 2008
† Hougaard, F (Francois) - BB - 2008
Ismaiel, TK (Travis) - BB - 2012
Jacobs, AJ (Adri) - BB - 2010
Jacobs, WJ (Lohan) - BB - 2010, 2011
Janse van Rensburg, Nico - BB - 2014
Janse van Rensburg, Rohan - BB - 2013, 2014
Jantjies, A (Tony) - BB - 2012
† Jantjies, ET (Elton) - GL - 2010
Jenkinson, JR (John-Roy) - Leop - 2011
Jordaan, PA (Paul) - KZN - 2011, 2012
Kebble, O (Oliver) - WP - 2012
Kirsten, FBC (Frik) - BB - 2008
Kirsten, JC (Jannes) - BB - 2013
Kitshoff, S (Steven) - WP - 2012
Kleinhans, F (Francois) - KZN - 2011
Kolbe, C (Cheslin) - WP - 2013
† Kolisi, S (Siya) - WP - 2010, 2011
Koster, RN (Nick) - WP - 2008
Kotze, SC (Stephan) - FS - 2011
Kriel, DD (Dan) - BB - 2014
Kriel, JA (Jesse) - BB - 2013, 2014
† Lambie, PJ (Patrick) - KZN - 2010
Leyds, DY (Dillyn) - WP - 2012
Liebenberg, WA (Wian) - BB - 2012
Louw, WM (Wilco) - BB - 2014
Lusaseni, L (Luyvuyiso) - KZN - 2008
Mabuza, ST (Thabo) - GL - 2014
Majola, K (Khaya) - KZN - 2012
† Mapoe, L (Lionel) - FS - 2008
Marais, FS (Franco) - KZN - 2012
Marais, JA (Jandré) - KZN - 2009
Marais, PC (Peet) - KZN - 2010
Marole, T (Thiliphatu) - KZN - 2008
Martinus, DR (Devon) - GL - 2013
Marx, MJ (Malcolm) - GL - 2014
Mastriet, S (Sampie) - BB - 2009, 2010
Mbonambi, M (Mbongeni) - BB - 2013
Mbovane, T (Tshotso) - WP - 2011, 2012
Mellett, MM (Morné) BB - 2009
Mjekevu, WG (Wandile) - GL - 2010, 2011
Mkhabela, MC (Mthokozi) - FS - 2014
Moolman, BJ (Bradley) - BB - 2011
Mtembu, LS (Lubabalo) - KZN - 2010
Muller, FJ (Freddie) - WP - 2010
Muller, MD (Martin) - WP - 2008
Mxoli, NM (Mox) - BB - 2014
Nhlapo, S (Sabelo) - KZN - 2008
Nonkontwana, A (Abongile) - BB - 2014
Obi, LBS (Luther) - Leopards - 2014
Okafor, K (Kene) - KZN - 2009, 2010
Oosthuizen, CR (Caylib) - GL - 2009
† Oosthuizen, CV (Coenie) - FS - 2009
Orie, M (Marvin) - BB - 2012
Paige, R (Rudy) - GL - 2009
Petersen, S (Sergeal) - EP - 2014
Pietersen, WJ (Wilton) - FS 2008

Pollard, H (Handre) - WP, BB - 2012, 2013, 2014
Pretorius, M (Mark) - GL - 2012
Rademan, PJ (Pieter) - FS - 2011
Redelinghuys, J (Julian) - KZN - 2009
Rossouw, JJ (Jean-Jacques) - WP - 2008
† Ruhle, RK (Raymond) - FS - 2012
Sadie, J (Johann) - WP - 2009
Scheepers, JN (Nico) - FS - 2010
Schickerling, JD (JD) - WP - 2014
Schmidt, D (Marais) - GL - 2012
Schoeman, JL (Juan) - BB - 2011
Schoeman, M (Marnus) - BB - 2009
Schoeman, P (Pierre) - BB - 2014
Schonert. NP (Nic) - KZN - 2011
Schreuder, L (Louis) - WP - 2010
Seabela OT (Omphile) - BB - 2008, 2009
Sekekete, VK (Victor) - GL - 2012
Senatla, Seabelo - FS - 2013
† Serfontein, JL (Jan) - BB - 2012
Sithole, SMS (Sithembiso) - KZN - 2013
Sithole, ST (Sibusiso) - KZN - 2010
Skosan, CD (Courtnal) - BB - 2011
Small-Smith, WT (William) - BB - 2012
Smit, RA (Roelof) - BB - 2013
Smith, AS (Kwagga) - GL - 2013
Smith, JP (Juan-Pierre) - BB - 2014
Stander, CJ (CJ) - BB - 2009, 2010
Stander, JH (Jannie) - GL - 2013
Steenkamp, R (Ruan) - BB - 2013
Steyn, AJ (Braam) - KZN - 2012
Swanepoel, AE (Dries) - BB - 2013
† Taute, JJ (Jaco) - GL - 2010, 2011
Thomas, JN (Jason) - BB - 2012
Ungerer, S (Stefan) - KZN - 2013
Van den Heever, GJ (Gerhard) - BB - 2009
Van der Merwe, D (Duhan) - BB - 2014
Van der Merwe, M (Marcel) - FS - 2010
Van der Walt, HS (Fanie) - FS - 2010
Van der Watt, V (Vian) - GL - 2012
Van der Westhuizen, DL (Dayan) - BB - 2014
Van Deventer, JC (Johan) - GL - 2010
Van Dyk, NJJ (Nico) - KZN - 2012
Van Velze, G-J (Gerrit-Jan) - BB - 2008
Van Vuuren, MT (Michael) - FS - 2011
Van Vuuren, P-W (PW) - FS - 2008
Van Wyk, A (Arno) - BB - 2014
Van Wyk, JP (Kobus) - WP - 2012
Vermeulen, JF (Jacques) - WP - 2014
Venter, HC (Hanco) - KZN - 2013
Venter, JF (Francois) - BB - 2010, 2011
Venter, RC (Ruan) - GL - 2011
Visser, D (Dennis) - BB - 2013
Watermeyer, S (Stefan) - BB - 2008
Wegner, C (Carl) - FS - 2011
Welthagen, JJ (Johnny) - Leop - 2011
Willemse, ME (Michael) - BB - 2013
Wiillemse, P (Paul) - GL - 2012
Williams, K (Percy) - GL - 2013
Willis, VS (Vainon) Willis - BB - 2008

Winning year for Sevens Boks

Commonwealth gold caps off first year of Powell era

By JJ Harmse & Gideon Nieman

THE Springboks Sevens team started the 2013/2014 HSBC Sevens World Series with a new coaching staff following the mutual decision by SARU and head coach Paul Treu to part ways. Former players Neil Powell and Vuyo Zangqa were appointed coach and assistant coach respectively and jumped into the deep end of the pool immediately to prepare the squad for the opening tournament in Gold Coast, Australia.

That said, the Blitzboks did well in making the semi-finals, but did suffer a record 49-0 loss to England in the bronze play-off as everything went wrong in their final match.

There was more turbulence to come once they landed back in South Africa as Zangqa resigned and joined Treu as part of the Kenya set-up.

Powell landed on his feet though and guided the South Africans to the final of their next tournament, the Emirates Dubai Sevens where they lost to Fiji.

The series then moved to Nelson Mandela Bay Stadium in Port Elizabeth, but the passing of Nelson Mandela three days before kick-off almost resulted in the cancellation of the tournament.

It was played in the memory of the great Madiba and South Africa responded magnificently by winning only their second home tournament (the other was in 2008 in George). Under immense emotional pressure and massive national expectation, the hosts outplayed New Zealand in a stunning second-half performance to win the final and help the country along the road to healing from their pain.

Fast forward six weeks to Las Vegas and it became clear that the Madiba magic was still worth a lucky charm. The Springboks outlasted New Zealand once again, winning the USA 7s 14-7 to take top spot on the log.

The Kiwis did strike back a week later however as they won their home tournament in Wellington by beating the Springboks 21-0 in driving rain.

All was not lost as the series moved to Japan. The South Africans managed a courtesy visit to new apparel sponsor Asics before reaching their fifth final in a row in Tokyo. They came up short against Fiji, losing 33-26 in the final, but looked set for a strong push for the overall series title.

SPRINGBOK SEVENS

The Springbok Sevens team won gold convincingly at the Commonwealth Games.

The wheels came off, for no apparent reason, in Hong Kong a week later. Some unexpected defeats resulted in the team not making it into the top eight for the first time in six tournaments and, to add injury to insult, regular captain Kyle Brown cried off with an injury.

With both the Scotland and England leg having being won in the past, the team had plenty of reasons to still be confident of securing only a second series title, but it was not to be.

A determined effort by the hosts saw Scotland edge the Blitzboks 12-7 in the quarter-finals of the Cup in Glasgow and with New Zealand winning the tournament they also snatched the series title for under the noses of the South Africans.

The series ended with a whimper as South Africa limped out of the London tournament as well. They lost to New Zealand in the quarters, but still secured an overall second place in the series.

For Powell it was a promising start to his tenure as boss and to cap the progress of the side, the likes of Seabelo Sebaltla, Werner Kok, Kwagga Smith and Justin Geduld grew into championship players. Not to mention Frankie Horne, who finished the season on 59 consecutive HSBC World Series tournaments.

The team also took part in the Commonwealth Games under the colours of SAS-COC and romped to the gold medal to cap off a memorable year. The team was strengthened by the return of Kyle Brown, Cornal Hendriks, Cecil Afrika and Warren Whiteley. Bryan Habana and Schalk Brits were initially included in the training squad as both were keen to participate in the Games, but both had to withdraw due to it falling outside the Test window agreed to with European clubs.

SA results: *bt Trinidad & Tobago 36-0; bt Cook Islands 50-0; bt Kenya 20-0; bt Scotland 35-12 (QF); bt Samoa 35-7 (SF); bt New Zealand 17-12 (Final & Gold Medal).*

TOURNAMENT 1: Gold Coast, Australia, 12-13 October 2013
SA results: *bt France 29-5, bt Spain 38-7; bt England 22-14; bt Wales 28-21 (QF Cup); lost Australia 19-24 (SF Cup); lost England 0-47 (3rd place).*

TOURNAMENT 2: Dubai, 29-30 November 2013
SA results: *bt Argentina 17-7; bt Russia 34-5; bt Samoa 26-5; bt Kenya 21-12 (QF Cup); bt England 26-12 (SF Cup); lost Fiji (Final Cup).*

TOURNAMENT 3: Nelson Mandela Bay, South Africa 7-8 December 2013
SA results: *bt Canada 24-7; bt Spain 38-0; bt Kenya 27-7; bt Portugal 45-0 (QF Cup); bt Argentina 31-0 (SF Cup); bt New Zealand 17-14 (Final Cup).*

TOURNAMENT 4: Las Vegas, USA, 24-26 January 2014
SA results: *bt Wales 43-0; bt Canada 29-0; bt Kenya 19-7; bt Argentina 36-0 (QF Cup); bt Samoa 14-0 (SF Cup); bt New Zealand 14-7 (Final Cup).*

TOURNAMENT 5: Wellington, New Zealand, 7-8 February 2014
SA results: *bt Wales 26-0; bt Portugal 27-5; lost England 5-19; bt Australia 10-0 (QF Cup); bt Fiji 10-0 (SF Cup); lost 0-21 New Zealand (Final Cup).*

TOURNAMENT 6: Tokyo, Japan, 22-24 March 2014
SA results: *bt Kenya 26-12; bt Japan 33-5; bt Argentina 28-12; bt USA 17-12 (QF Cup); bt England 17-0 (SF Cup); lost Fiji 26-33 (Final Cup).*

TOURNAMENT 7: Hong Kong, China, 30-31 March 2014
SA results: *bt France 31-7; bt Spain 22-14; lost Australia 7-10; lost England 7-14 (QF Cup); bt USA 24-19 (SF Plate); bt Wales 19-14 (Final Plate).*

TOURNAMENT 8: Glasgow, Scotland, 3-4 May 2014
SA results: *bt Portugal 38-0; bt Samoa 40-0; lost New Zealand 5-19; lost Scotland 7-12 (QF Cup); lost Kenya 7-14 (SF Plate).*

TOURNAMENT 9: London, England, 10-11 May 2014
SA results: *bt Portugal 43-7; bt France 47-7; bt Scotland 26-12; lost New Zealand 5-32 (QF Cup); bt Samoa 24-17 (SF Plate); bt Kenya 38-14 (Final Plate).*

IRB SEVENS WORLD SERIES 2013-14
(Only top 15 countries listed)

Team	AUS	DUB	SA	USA	NZ	JAP	HK	SCO	LON	Pts
New Zealand	22	17	19	19	22	15	22	22	22	180
South Africa	15	19	22	22	19	19	13	10	13	152
Fiji	13	22	13	8	17	22	17	17	15	144
England	17	15	8	13	15	17	19	13	17	134
Australia	19	8	7	12	13	13	15	10	19	116
Canada	7	5	2	17	12	10	10	19	8	90
Kenya	12	10	10	7	8	10	3	12	12	84
Samoa	10	5	17	15	10	2	5	5	10	79
Argentina	5	13	15	10	10	3	5	7	7	75
France	8	3	12	10	5	5	7	8	10	68
Wales	10	12	5	5	5	8	123	3	5	65
Scotland	5	10	3	5	7	7	8	15	1	61
United States	3	1	5	3	3	12	10	1	3	41
Portugal	2	7	10	1	1	1	2	1	1	26
Spain	1	2	1	2	2	1	1	5	5	20

SPRINGBOK SEVENS

SA SEVENS PLAYERS 2013-14

Player	Union	AUS	DUB	SA	USA	NZ	JAP	HK	SCO	LON	CG
Dry, C (Chris)	SARU	x	x	x	x	x	x	x	x	x	x
Snyman, P (Phillip)	SARU	x	x	x	x	x	x	x	x	x	–
Horne, F (Frankie)	SARU	x	x	x	x	x	x	x	x(c)	x(c)	x
Ulengo, J (Jamba)	SARU	x	x	–	–	x	x	x	x	x	–
Hendriks, C (Cornal)	Free State Cheetahs	x	–	–	–	–	–	–	–	–	x
Brown, K (Kyle)	SARU	x(c)	x(c)	x(c)	x(c)	x(c)	x(c)	x(c)	–	–	x(c)
Mastriet, S (Sampie)	Blue Bulls	x	x	x	x	–	–	–	–	–	–
Dippenaar, S (Stephan)	SARU	x	x	x	x	x	x	x	x	–	–
Geduld, J (Justin)	SARU	x	x	x	x	x	x	x	x	x	x
Afrika, C (Cecil)	SARU	x	x	x	x	–	x	–	–	x	x
Richards, M (Mark)	SARU	x	x	–	–	–	–	–	x	x	x
Hunt, S (Steven)	SARU	x	–	x	–	–	x	–	–	–	–
Kok, W (Werner)	SARU	–	x	x	x	x	x	x	x	x	x
Du Preez, B (Branco)	SARU	x	x	x	x	x	x	x	x	x	x
Kolbe, C (Cheslin)	Western Province	–	x	x	–	–	–	–	–	–	–
Smith, A (Kwagga) *	SARU	–	–	x	x	–	x	x	x	x	x
Specman, R (Rosco) *	Pumas	–	–	–	x	–	–	–	–	–	–
Senatla, S (Seabelo)	SARU	–	–	x	x	–	x	x	x	–	–
Adendorff, S (Shaun)	Blue Bulls	–	–	–	–	–	–	–	x	x	–
Strydom WJ (WJ)	Blue Bulls	–	–	–	–	–	–	–	–	x	–
Whitely, W (Warren)	Golden Lions	–	–	–	–	–	–	–	–	–	x

*New caps

SA Sevens Internationals 1993-2014

† indicates 15-a-side Springbok

Adams, Bl (Bennie) (WP) – 04 HK, Sing, Bor, Lon, Dub, SA.
Adendorff, S (Shaun) (Blue Bulls) 14 Sco, Lon.
Afrika, CS (Cecil) (Griffons) 09 WG, 09 Dub, SA, 10 NZ, USA, Aus, HK, Lon, Sco, CG; 10 Dub, SA; 11 USA; HK; Aus: Lon; Sco, 11 Aus, SA, 12 NZ, USA, HK; Aus; SA;,13 Jap; Lon; RWC, 13 Aus, Dub, SA, 14 USA, NZ, HK, CG.
Alberts, N (Nico) (WP) – 01 Wel.
†Aplon, GG (Gio) (WP) 06 Wel, LA, Par, Lon 07 Lon, Sco 08 Lon, Sco, 08 Dub, SA, 09 NZ, USA, Lon, Sco, RWC.
April, C (Chelton) (WP) – 96 HK.
Arnold, P (Peet) (N Tvl) – 96 Dub; 98 Arg, Ur, Viña .
†Badenhorst, C (Chris) (FS)* – 93 HK, RWC; 96 Ur.
Basson, S (Stefan) (WP) – 04 HK, Sing, Bor, Lon. 05 Sing, Lon, Par, RWC, WG, Dub, SA, 06 Wel, LA, Par, Lon, CG, Dub, SA, 07 HK, Aus, 08 lon, Sco.
Benjamin, RS (Ryno) (Boland) 05 Sing, Lon, Par, WG, 06 Par, Lon, Dub, SA, 07 HK, Aus, 08 Dub, SA, 09 NZ, USA, HK, Aus, Lon, Sco, RWC, WG,) (Dub, 10 NZ, USA, Aus, HK, Lon, Sco, CG; 13 RWC.
Blom, J (Jandré) (FS) 05 Dub, SA, 06 HK, Sing 07 Wel, USA.
Blommetjies, C (Clayton) (SARU) 12 Sco, Lon.

†Bobo, G (Gcobani) (Lions) - 99 SA; 01 Lon, Car, Jap, 07 Wel, USA, HK, Aus, Lon (c); Sco (c).
Bock, AG (Alshaun) (Bol) – 03 HK.
†Boome, CS (Selborne) (WP) – 98 Arg, Ur, Viña .
Botha, B (Bernardo) (Golden Lions) 10 CG; 10 Dub; SA; 11 NZ; USA; HK, 11 Aus, Dub, SA, 12 NZ, USA, HK, Jap; SA;,13 Lon; WG.
Bouwer, G (Graeme) (NTvl) – 96 Dub; 97 RWC; 98 HK; 99 Fiji*, HK.
Bowles, J (Jovan) (Sharks) 06 Dub, SA, 07 Lon, Sco.
Brand, J (Janneman) (WP) – 96 Ur, HK.
Breytenbach, C (Conrad) (NTvl) – 96 HK.
Brink, HM (Helgard) (FS) - 99 Par, Dub, SA; 00 NZ, Fiji, Aus, HK, Jap, Fr, Dur, Dub; 01 RWC, HK, Sha, KL, Tok, Lon, Car, Jap, Dub, Dur; 02 San, Arg, Bris, Wel, Sing, KL, Bris.
Brink, S (Stephen) (FS) – 96 Ur, HK, Dub (c); 97 RWC; 98 Arg (c), Ur (c), Viña (c).
†Britz, GJJ (Gerrie) (FS) – 01 Dub, Dur, San, Arg.
†Britz, WK (Warren) (Sharks) - 99 Par, Dub, SA; 00 Ur, Arg, NZ, Fiji, Aus, HK, Jap, Fr, Dur, Dub; 01 RWC.
Brown, K (Kyle) (WP) 08 Dub, SA, 09 NZ, USA, HK, Aus, Lon, Sco, RWC, WG, 09 Dub, SA, 10 NZ, USA, Aus (c), HK (c); 10 Dub (c); SA (c) ; 11 NZ (c); USA (c); HK (c); Aus (c); Lon (c); Sco (c), 11 Aus (c), Dub (c), SA (c), 12 NZ (c), USA (c), HK

(c), Jap (c), Sco (c), Lon (c); Aus (c); SA (c);,13 RWC (c); WG (c), 13 Aus (c), Dub (c), SA (c), 14 USA (c), NZ (c), Jap (c), HK (c), CG (c).
†Brüssow, HW (Heinrich) (FS) 06 HK, Sing.
Burger, PB (Phillip) (FS) 06 Wel, LA, Par, Lon, CG, Dub, SA, 12 Sco, Lon.
Calitz, JP (Johan) (Leopards) - 99 Arg, San, Fiji, HK, Tok, Par; 00 HK, Tok*, Dur, Dub; 01 Wel, HK, Sha, KL, Tok, Lon, Car, Jap.
†Chavhanga, T (Tonderai) (Free State) – 03 Dub, SA
†Cilliers, NV (Vlok) (WP) – 93 HK; 94 HK; 96 Dub; 98 HK.
†Claassens, JP (Jannie) (NTvl)* - 93 HK, RWC; 96 HK, Dub.
Coeries, DB (Darryl) (SWD Eagles) - 02 Dub, SA; 03 Bris, NZ, HK.
Coetzee, F (Fielies) (Falcons) - 99 Arg, San.
Coetzee, R (Rudi) (Lions) - 02 Dub, SA; 03 Car, Lon.
†Conradie , JHJ (Bolla) (WP) – 99 Dub, SA; 00 NZ, Fiji, Aus.
Dames, A (Archer) (Pumas) - 99 Par.
Damons, O (Ossie) (Griffons) 05 Lon, Par.
Dazel, RL (Renfred) (Boland) 05 WG, Dub, SA, 06 Wel, LA, HK, Sing, CG, SA, 07 Wel, USA, Dub, SA, 08 Wel, USA, HK, Aus 08 Dub, SA, 09 Nz, USA, HK, Aus, Lon, Sco, RWC, WG,

SPRINGBOK SEVENS

10 Lon, Sco, CG, 10 Dub; 11 NZ; USA, 11 Aus, Dub, 12 USA, Jap.
†De Jongh, JL (Juan) (WP) 08 Wel.
Delport, PS (Paul) (WP) – 03 Dub, 04 Wel, LA 06 Par, Lon, 08 Dub, Sa, 09 Nz, USA, Sco, RWC, WG, 09 Dub (c), SA (c), CG (c); 10 SA; 11 NZ; HK; Aus; Lon; Sco, 11 Aus, Dub, SA, 12 NZ, HK; Aus; Dub; SA; '13 NZ; USA; HK; Sco.
De Marigny, MRD (Marc) (Sharks) – 03 Bris, NZ, HK, Car, Lon, Dub (c), SA (c),04 Wel, LA, HK (c), Sing (c), Bor (c), Lon (c) Dub.
Demas, D (Danwel) (WP) – 03 Dub, SA, 04 Wel, LA, HK, Sing, Bor ,Lon, 05 Sing, Lon, Par, RWC, WG, Dub, SA, 06 Par, CG, Dub, SA, 07 Dub, SA, 08 Lon, Sco.
†De Villiers, J (Jean) (WP) – 02 San, Arg, Bris, Wel, Bei, HK, Sing, KL, Lon, Car, CG.
Dippenaar, D. (Dirk) (SARU) 12 Jap
Dippenaar, S. (Stephan) (SARU) 12 NZ, USA, HK, Jap, Sco; Aus; Dub; SA;,13 NZ; USA; HK; Jap; Sco; Lon; RWC; WG, 13 Aus, Dub, 14 USA, NZ, Jap, HK.
†Dirks, CA (Chris) (Tvl)* – 94 HK.
Dry, C. (Chris) (SARU contracted) 10 Aus, HK, Lon, Sco; 11 NZ; USA; HK; Aus; Lon; Sco; 11 Aus, Dub, SA, 12 NZ, USA, HK, Jap, Sco, Lon, Dub ; SA ; '13 NZ ; USA ; HK ; Jap ; Sco ; RWC, 13 Aus, Dub, SA, 14 USA, NZ, Jap, HK, Sco, Lon, CG.
Du Plessis, M (Malan) (Bol) – 03 HK.
Du Plooy, JP (JP) (Lions) – 98 Arg, Ur, Viña .
Du Preez, B (Branco) (Blue Bulls) 10 NZ, USA, Aus, HK; 10 dub; SA; 11 NZ; USA; HK; Aus: Lon; Sco, 11 Dub, SA, 12 NZ, USA, HK, Jap, Sco, Lon ; Aus ; '13 USA ; HK ; Jap ; RWC, 13 Dub, SA, 14 USA, NZ, Jap, HK, Sco, Lon, CG.
†Du Toit, GS (Gaffie) (GW) – 98 CG; 02 CG.
Ebersohn, RT (Robert) (Free State) 08 HK, Aus, 08 Dub, SA, 09 NZ, USA, HK, Aus, Lon, RWC, 11 Aus, Dub.
Engelbrecht, G (Gerrie) (Griffons) – 00 Ur, Arg, NZ, Fiji, Aus, HK, Jap; 01 Wel.
Engelbrecht, J (Jacques) (SARU). 10 SA.
Engelbrecht, P (Pieter) (SARU) 10 Dub; SA; 11 NZ; USA; Aus; 13 NZ; USA; Sco; Lon.
Engelbrecht, P. (Petrus) (SARU) 12 HK, Jap, Sco, Lon
†Esterhuizen, G (Grant) (Lions) – 03 NZ.
Eyre, NJ (Nicolas) (Lions) – 03 NZ, 04 bor, Lon.
Fihlani, IZ (Ian) (Bulldogs) – 01 Wel; 02 Bei, HK, Sing, KL, Lon, Car, Dub, SA; 03 HK, Car, Lon.
†Floors, L (Lucas) (SWD Eagles) — 03 Dub, SA, 04 HK, Sing, Bor 05 Dub 06 Dub (c), SA 07 SA, 08 Lon, Sco.
Foote, KW (Kevin) (Natal) – 02 Dub; 03 Bris, NZ, HK, Car, Lon, 04 Wel (c), LA(c).
Fourie, AJ (Andries) (EP) – 99 Arg, San, Fiji, HK, Par (c), Dub, SA; 00 Ur, Arg, NZ (c), Fiji (c), Aus (c), HK (c), Jap (c), Fr (c), Dur, Dub; 01 Wel, HK, Sha, KL, Tok, Lon, Car.
Fourie, DA (Deon) (Western Province) 07 Lon, Sco.

Fowles, JJ (Josh) (Bulldogs) - 02 Sing, KL.
Francis, E (Eugene) (WP) – 02 Bris, Wel, Bei, HK, Sing, KL, Lon, Car; 03 Bris, NZ, HK, Car, Lon 03 Dub, SA, 04 Wel, LA,
Fredericks, ER (Eddie) (NW) – 99 Par; 00 NZ, Fiji, Aus.04 Dub, SA, 05 Wel, LA, Lon, Par, RWC.
Frolick, S (Shandre) (WP) 05 Wel, LA 06 Dub.
Geduld, J (Justin) (SARU) 13 NZ; HK; Jap; Sco, 13 Aus, Dub, SA, 14 USA, NZ, Jap, HK, Sco, Lon, CG.
†Gerber, HJ (Hendrik) (WP) – 98 Arg, Ur, Viña , CG.
†Gillingham, JW (Joe) (Lions) – 98 Arg, Ur, Viña , CG.
Grobler, D (??) – 99 Fiji, HK.*
†Habana, BG (Bryan) (Lions) — 04 Wel, LA.
Haupt, PJ (Hannru) (FS) – 03 Bris, NZ.
Heidtmann, DM (Dale) (Bulldogs) - 01 Wel, Dub, Dur; 02 San, Arg, Bris, Wel, Bei, HK, Sing, KL, Lon, Car, CG, 03 Dub, SA, 04 Wel, LA, HK, Sing, Bor, Lon, SA
Helberg, D. (Deon) (Blue Bulls) 09 Dub, SA.
†Hendriks, C. (Cornal) (SARU) 11 SA, 12 NZ, USA, HK, Jap, Sco, Lon; Aus; Dub; SA; ,13 NZ; USA; HK; Jap; Sco; Lon; RWC; 13 Aus, 14 CG.
†Honiball, HW (Henry) (Natal) 94 HK.
Horne, FH (Frankie) (SARU contract) 07 Dub, SA, 08 Wel, USA, HK, Aus, Lon, Sco, 08 Dub, SA, 09 NZ, USA, HK, Aus, Lon, Sco, RWC, WG, 09 Dub, SA 10 NZ, USA, Aus,HK, Lon, Sco; 10 Dub; SA; 11 NZ; USA; HK; Aus;Lon; Sco, 11 Aus, Dub, SA, 12 NZ, USA, HK, Jap, Sco, Lon; Aus; Dub; SA (c);,13 NZ (c); USA (c); HK (c); Jap (c); Sco (c); Lon (c); 13 Aus,Dub, SA, 14 USA, NZ, Jap, HK, Sco (c), Lon (c), CG.
Houtshamer, J (Juan) (Falcons) – 00 HK, Jap.
Hulme, A (Alten) (BB) – 03 HK.
Human, WA (Wylie) (FS) – 00 HK, Jap, Fr.
Hunt, S (Steven) (WP) 10 NZ, USA, Aus; 10 SA ; 11 NZ; USA; Lon; Sco, 11 Aus, SA, 12 NZ, USA, Sco, Lon; Aus; Dub; '13 HK; Jap; Sco; WG, 13 Aus, SA, 14 Jap.
Isbell, R (Ruwellyn) (SARU) '12 Aus; Dub; SA; '13 WG
Jackson, KL (Lesley) (Boland) 04 Dub, SA 04 RWC 05 SA,06 HK, Sing.
†Jacobs, AA (Adi) (Falcons) – 00 HK, Tok.*
Jacobsz, SPE (Barry) (SWD Eagles) - 01 Jap.
†Jantjes, CA (Conrad) (Lions) – 99 Dub, SA; 00 Ur, Arg, NZ, Fiji, Aus, HK, Jap, Fr; 01 HK, Sha; 02 CG, Dub; 03 Car, Lon.
Johannes, R (Reuben) (SARU) '12 Aus; '13 WG
Joka, W (Wonga) (Elephants) – 00 NZ, Fiji, Aus.
Jonker, J (Jacques) (FS) – 95 HK.
Jonker, JW ("JW") (SARU contracted) 09 Dub, SA, 10 Aus, HK.
Jordaan, P. (Paul) (SARU). 11 NZ; USA; HK.
†Joubert, AJ (André) (Natal) – 93 HK (c), RWC (c); 94 HK (c).

Juries, FM (Fabian) (EP) – 00 Dur, Dub; 01 Wel, HK, Sha, KL, Tok, Lon, Car, Jap, Dub, Dur; 02 San, Arg, Bris, Wel, CG; 03 Car, Lon, 03 Dub, Sa, 04 Wel, LA, HK, Sing, Bor, Lon, 05 Wel, LA, Sing, Lon, Par, RWC, WG, SA, 06 Wel (c), LA (c), HK, Sing, CG, 07 Dub, SA, 08 Wel, USA, HK, Aus, Lon, Sco, 10 Lon, Sco.
†Kankowski, R (Ryan) (KZNI) 06 Wel, LA, HK, Sing, CG.
†Kayser, DJ (Deon) (EP) – 98 HK, CG.
Kok, W (Werner) (SARU) 13 Lon; WG, 13 Dub, SA,14 USA, NZ, Jap, HK, Sco, Lon, CG.
Kolbe, C (Cheslin) (SARU) 12 Lon; SA; ,13 NZ; USA 13 Dub, SA.
Krause, GE (Gareth) (GW) 04 Dub, SA, 05 Wel, LA, RWC.
Kriese, D (Dieter) (Natal) – 93 HK, RWC; 95 HK.
Kruger, CR (Chris) (FS) – 98 Arg; 99 San.
†Kruger, RJ (Ruben) (FS) – 93 HK, RWC; 94 HK.
Kruger, HJ (Jorrie) (FS) – 96 Dub; 98 Arg, Ur, Viña .
Kruger, O. (Okkie) (Blue Bulls) 10 CG
Kuün, GWF (Derick) (Blue Bulls) 05 Wel, LA,
†Loubscher, RIP (Ricardo) (EP) – 99 Arg, San; 00 Fr; 01 RWC.
Luiters, K (Kevin) (Free State Cheetahs) '12 Dub
Mapoe, LG (Lionel) (Cheetahs) 09 USA, HK, Aus, RWC.
Maritz, H (Hoffman) (Cheetahs) 10 NZ, USA, Aus, HK, Lon, Sco.
Markow, A (Tony) (EP) – 95 HK.
Masina, M (Mac) (Lions) – 99 Dub; 00 Ur, Arg, Dur, Dub; 02 Bris, Wel.
Mastriet, S. (Sampie) (Blue Bulls) 10 Aus, HK; 13 RWC, 13 Aus, Dub, SA, 14 USA, NZ.
Mbiyozo, MM (Mpho) (Western Province) 06 Dub, 07 Wel, USA, HK, Aus, Lon, Sco, 07 Dub, 07 SA, 08 Wel, USA, HK, Aus, Lon, Sco 08 Dub, SA, 09 NZ, USA (c), HK, Aus, Lon, Sco, RWC (c), WG;09 Dub; Sa; 10 NZ; USA; Aus; HK; Lon; Sco.
Mbovane, T. (Tshotsho) (SARU). 11 HK; Aus; '12 Aus; Dub; SA; '13 NZ; USA; HK; Jap; Lon.
McBean, BJH (Baldwin) (Griquas) 07 Wel, USA, 07 Dub, SA.
Mdaka, TLP (Thobela) (Border) – 00 NZ, Fiji, Aus, HK, Jap, Fr, Dur, Dub; 01 Wel, Dub 05 Wel, LA, Sing, Lon, Par, RWC, WG, Dub,06 Wel, LA, HK, Sing, Par, Lon, CG, Dub, SA 07 HK, Aus 08 Wel, USA.
Mentz, MJ ("MJ") (Griquas) 07 Lon, Sco 07 Dub, SA, 08 Wel, USA, HK, Aus, Lon, Sco, 09 Dub, SA, 10 HK, Lon, Sco, CG; 10 Dub; 11 Aus.
Minnaar, C (Chase (SARU contract) 09 HK, Aus, Lon, WG; 09 Dub; SA; 10 NZ, USa, Aus, HK, Lon, Sc, CG, 11 Aus, Dub, SA.
Mofu, Z (Zolani) 05 WG, Dub, SA, 06 Wel, LA, CG.
Mokuena, J (Jonathan) (Leopards) 05 Lon, Par, WG, Dub, SA, 06 Wel, LA, HK, Sing, Par, Lon, CG, Dub(c), SA (c) 07 Wel (c), USA (c), H K

SPRINGBOK SEVENS

(c), Aus (c) 07 Dub, 08 Wel, USA, HK, Aus, Sco.
Mostert, H (Herman) (WP) - 99 Fiji, HK, Par; 00 NZ, Fiji, Aus, HK, Jap, Fr, Dur, Dub; 01 Wel, HK, Sha, KL, Tok, Lon, Car.
Mtembu, L. (Lubabalo) (Sharks) 10 CG; 10 Dub; 11 NZ; USA.
†Müller, GP (Jorrie) (Lions) - 01 HK, Sha, KL, Tok, Dur; 02 San, Arg, Bris, Wel, Lon, Car, CG, SA.
Munn, W (Wayne) (SWD Eagles) - 99 Fiji*, 99 HK.
†Muir, D (Dick) (Natal) - 93 RWC; 95 HK.
†Ndungane, AZ (Akona) (Bulldogs) — 04 Hk, Sing, Bor, Lon
Nell, R (Ryan) (SARU) 12 Sco.
Nelson, NT (Norman) (SARU contract) 08 Lon, Sco.
Noble, DC (Dusty) (Sharks) 06 Dub, SA, 07 HK, Aus, Lon, Sco.
Noble, HG (Howard) (Sharks) 07 Wel, USA, HK, Aus, 09 NZ, USA, Aus.
†Nokwe, JL (Jongi) (Boland) 04 SA, 05 Sing.
Nqoro, M (Milo) (Sharks) 08 SA.
O'Cuinneagan, D (Dion) (WP) - 93 HK, 93 RWC; 95 HK (c); 96 Ur (c), 96HK (c).
† Olivier, J (Jacques) (NtVl) – 93 HK, RWC; 97 RWC; 99 Arg (c), San (c), Dub (c); 00 Ur (c), Arg (c), Dur, Dub; 01 HK, Sha, KL, Tok, Lon, Car, Jap.
†Oosthuysen, DE (Deon) (Lions) - 99 San.
†Paulse, BJ (Breyton) (WP)* - 96 Ur, HK; 98 Arg, Ur, Viña; 01 RWC.
Payne, L (Shaun) (Natal) - 95 HK; 97 RWC; 98 Ur, Viña .
Penrose, N (Neil) (WP) - 98 HK.
Petersen, PB (Patrick) (WP) - 00 Fr.
Philander, D (Daniel) (WP) - 01 Jap.
Pietersen, JC (Johan) (WP) 04 Dub, SA.
Pietersen, WJ (Wilton) (WP) 08 HK, Aus.
Pitout, AC (Anton) (FS) - 01 Dub, Dur; 02 San, Arg, Bris, Wel, Bei, HK, Sing, KL, Lon, Car, CG, 04 Dub.
Plumtree, J (John) (Natal) - 94 HK; 95 HK.
Potgieter, R (Riaan) (EP) - 95 HK.
Potgieter, SP (Sarel) (WP) 06 HK, Sing, Par, Lon.
Powell, JD (Neil) (FS) - 01 Dur; 02 San, Arg, Bei, HK, Lon, Car, CG, Dub, SA, 07 Dub (c), SA (c), 08 Wel (c), USA (c), HK (c), Aus (c), Lon (c), Sco (c), 09 HK, Aus, Lon, Sco, RWC, WG, 09 Dub, 10 Lon, Sco, CG; 11 USA; HK; Aus; Lon; Sco, 12 Lon
Pretorius, A (Abrie) (GW) - 96 Ur.
†Pretorius, AS (André) (Lions) – 00 Dur, Dub; 01 RWC, Wel, KL, Tok, Lon, Car.
†Pretorius, JC (Jaco) (Lions) - 02 Dub, 02 SA; 03 Bris (c), NZ (c), HK(c), Car , Lon 04 Dub, SA (c), 05 Wel (c), LA (c),Sing (c),Lon (c), Par (c),RWC (c),Dub (c),SA (c) 06 HK (c),Sing (c), Par (c), Lon (c), CG (c).
Prinsloo, B (Boom) (FS) 10 CG; 10 Dub; SA; 11 NZ; HK; Aus; Lon; Sco, 11 Aus, Dub, SA, 12 NZ, USA, HK, Jap.
†Putt, KB (Kevin) (Natal) - 95 HK
Raats, W (Wemer) (WP) - 98 HK, CG.

Rafferty, AC (Ashwell) (FS) - 99 Par.
Rees, G (Grant) (Sharks) 07 Wel, USA.
Richards, M. (Mark) (SARU) 10 Dub; SA; 11 Lon; Sco, 11 Aus, Dub, SA, 12 NZ, USA ; 13 WG, 13 Aus, 14 Sco, Lon, CG.
†Richter, AJ (Adriaan) (WP) – 94 HK.
†Rose, EE (Earl) (WP) – 03 Bris, NZ, Car, Lon, Dub, SA, 04 Wel, LA.
†Rossouw, PWG (Pieter) (WP) - 96 Dub; 97 RWC; 98 CG.
†Russell, RB (Brent) (Pumas) - 01 Dur; 02 San, Arg, Bris, Wel, Bei, HK, Sing, KL, SA. 03 SA.
Saayman, JIA (Izak) (Eagles) 05 SA.
Schoeman, MW (Marius) (Pumas) - 01 HK, Sha, KL, Tok, Lon, Car, Jap; 02 Bei, HK, Sing, KL, Lon, Car, Dub, SA; 03 Bris, NZ, HK, Car, Lon, Dub, SA, 04 Wel, LA, Lon, 05 Sing, Lon, Par, RWC, WG (c) 06 SA, 07 Wel, USA, HK, Aus, Lon, Sco. 07 SA, 08 Wel, USA, 08 Dub, 09 Sco, WG, 09 SA, 10 NZ, USA.
Seconds, ER (Egon) (WP) – 01 Dub, Dur; 02 Bei, HK, Sing, KL, Lon, Car, CG 05 Dub.
Senatla, S (Seabelo) (SARU) 13 NZ; USA; HK; Jap; Sco; RWC; WG 14 USA, Jap, HK, Sco, Lon, CG.
Sithole, S (Sibusiso) (Sharks) 10 CG; 10 Dub; SA; 11 HK; Aus; Lon: Sco; 13 RWC.
Siwundla, O. (Oginga) (Golden Lions) 04 Dub, SA
†Skinstad, RB (Bob) (WP) – 96 Dub, 97 RWC, 98 CG, 01 RWC.
Small-Smith, W. (William) (SARU). 11 Lon; Sco, 11 Dub, 12 USA, Jap.
Smith, A (Kwagga) (SARU) 13 SA, 14 NZ, Jap, HK, Sco, Lon, CG.
Smith, LA (Luke) (Natal) - 95 HK.
†Smit, PL (Philip) (GW) - 98 Ur, Viña .
Smith, RF (Rodger) (GW) - 98 HK; 99 Mar, San, Fiji (c), HK (c), Dub, SA; 00 Ur, Arg, Par; 01 RWC; 02 Dub, SA; 03 Bris.
†Snyman, AH (André) (NtVl) - 97 RWC.
Snyman, PAB (Phillip) (Cheetahs) 08 Dub, SA, 09 NZ, USA, HK, Lon, Sco, RWC, WG; '12 Dub; SA; '13 NZ; USA; HK; Jap; Sco; Lon; RWC, 13 Aus, Dub, Sa, 14 NZ, Jap, HK, Sco, Lon.
Specman, R (Rosco) (Pumas) 14 USA.
Stevens, J (Jeffrey) (Boland) - 96 Dub; 97 RWC; 98 CG, 99 Arg, San, Fiji, HK, Tok, Par, Dub, SA; 00 Ur, Arg, NZ, Fiji, Aus, HK, Jap, Fr.
Stick, M (Mzwandile) (Elephants) – 04 HK, Sing, Bor, Lon.Dub, 05 Wel, LA,Sing, RWC, WG, Dub, SA, 06 Wel, LA, HK, Sing, CG, 07 Wel, USA, HK, Aus, Lon, Sco 07 Dub, 08 USA, HK, Aus, 08 Dub (c), SA (c), 09 NZ (c), HK (c), Aus (c), lon (c), Sco (c), WG (c), 09 Dub, SA, 10 NZ (c), USA (c), Lon (c), Sco (c)
†Strauss, AJ (Andries) (Sharks) 07 Lon, Sco.
Strydom, DH (Dirkie) (NtVl) - 96 Dub; 98 HK; 99 Arg, San, Fiji, Tok, Dub, SA; 00 Ur, Arg, NZ, Fiji, Aus, Fr, Dur, Dub
Strydom, W J (Willem-Johannes) (SARU) 13 Sco; Lon; WG, 14 Lon.
Treu, PM (Paul) (SWD Eagles) - 99 Fiji*, HK,

Dub, SA; 00 Ur, Arg, Dur, Dub; 01 RWC, Wel, HK, Sha, KL, Tok, Lon, Car, Jap, Dub, Dur; 02 San, Arg, Bris, Wel, Bei, HK, Sing, KL, Lon, Car, CG, Dub (c), SA (c).
Truter, HJ (Hendrik) (FS) - 94 HK.
Ulengo, J (Jamba) (SARU) 12 Sco, Lon; 13 HK; Jap; Sco; Lon; WG, 13 Aus, Dub, 14 NZ, Jap, HK, Sco, Lon.
Van den Heever, LM (Leon) (Bol) - 02 Dub, SA, 03 Bris, NZ
Van der Merwe, SM (Schalk) (Golden Lions) 05 Wel, LA, Sing, Lon, Par, RWC, WG, Dub, SA, 06 Wel, LA, Par, Lon, CG, Dub, SA, 07 Wel, USA, HK, Aus, Lon, Sco , 07 Dub, SA, 08 Wel, USA, HK, Aus, Lon, Sco.
Van der Walt, P (Phillip) (Cheetahs) 10 NZ, USA.
†Van der Westhuizen, JH (Joost) (NTvl) - 93 HK, RWC; 94 HK; 97 RWC (c).
Van Heerden, W (Wayne) (EP) - 01 RWC, Wel, HK, Sha, KL, Tok, Lon, Car, Jap, Dub; 02 Lon, Car, CG, 03 Dub, SA, 04 Wel, LA, HK, Sing, Bor, Lon Dub, SA, 05 Wel, LA.
†Van Niekerk, JC (Joe) (Lions) - 01 HK, Sha, KL, Tok, Lon, Car.
Van Rensburg, JM (José) (GW) - 02 Dub, SA; 03 Bris, NZ, HK, Car, Lon, Dub, SA, 04 Wel, LA, HK, Sing, Bor, Lon. Dub, SA, 05 Wel, LA, Sing, Lon, Par.
Van Schalkwyk, J (Jaco) (FS) - 03 HK, Car, Lon, SA, 04 HK, Sing, 04 Dub,SA.
Van Wyk, JH (Jan-Harm) (WP) - 98 Arg, Ur, Viña; 01 Dub; 02 San, Arg, Bris, Wel, Beij, HK.
Van Zyl, R (Riaan) (WP) - 96 Ur, HK.
†Venter AG (André) (FS) - 96 Ur, HK; 97 RWC; 98 CG.
†Venter, AJ (AJ) (FS) - 98 Arg, Ur, Viña .
Venter, J (Hannes) (Blue Bulls) - 99 Arg, San, Dub, SA; 00 Ur, Arg.
Venter, N (Nico) (Bor) - 98 HK.
Venter, S. (Shaun) (SARU contracted) 09 SA.
Verhoeven, AG (Antonius) (Bol) - 02 San, Arg, Bris, Wel, 06 Wel, LA, HK, Sing, Par, Lon, CG, 07 Wel, USA.
†Vermaak, J (Jano) (Golden Lions) 05 Wel, LA, RWC.
Verster, E (Eben) (WP) - 99 Par.
†Watson, LA (Luke) (Elephants) – 02 CG.
†Whitely, W (Warren) (Golden Lions) '12 Dub; SA; '13 NZ, USA, 14 CG.
†Willemse, AK (Ashwin) (Bol) - 01 Dub, Dur.
†Williams, CM (Chester) (WP) - 93 RWC; 94 HK; 98 Arg, Ur, Viña , HK (c), CG (c); 99 SA; 00 Ur, Arg; 01 RWC.
Winter, RG (Russell) (Lions) - 98 HK, CG.
Witbooi, N (Nigel) (WP) - 96 Ur, HK.
Zangqa, V (Vuyo) (Border) 07 HK, Aus, Lon, Sco, 07 Dub, SA, 08 Wel, USA, HK, Aus, Lon, Sco, 08 Dub, SA, 09 NZ, USA, HK, Aus, Lon, Sco, RWC.

unconfirmed

SA WOMEN

World Cup to forget

Sevens the silver lining in landmark year

By Zeena Isaacs

THE 2014 women's rugby season will be remembered as one of the most significant for especially the Springbok women's sevens team. Apart from being awarded professional contracts for the first time, they also gained qualification for the IRB Women's Sevens World Series, again for the first time.

The season, however, was less memorable for the Springbok Women's 15-a-side team, who had a disappointing IRB Women's Rugby World Cup campaign in France, winning only one of their five matches.

The Sevens team, in contrast, had a memorable year with 15 players receiving contracts early in the season, while on the field things also looked promising. The team, which spent the first half of the year at their training base in Port Elizabeth, defended their Confederation of African Rugby title in Kenya, registered a third-place finish in the Hong Kong Invitational and finished fourth in the IRB Women's World Series qualifier, also in the Chinese city.

The latter, which featured victories against France and the Netherlands, earned them a place among the core teams on the 2014/2015 IRB Women's World Series, as well as a chance to qualify for the 2016 Olympic Games. The top four teams on the log table at the end of the season will qualify automatically for Rio.

The first leg of the 2014/2015 series took place in December in Dubai, while the other five tournaments will be hosted in Brazil, the USA, Canada, England and the Netherlands from February to May 2015.

The 15-a-side team, meanwhile, had a busy year with two World Cup trial matches at Newlands and Ellis Park, followed by a warm-up tour to the UK and France late in June and the World Cup in August at the French Rugby Federation headquarters in Marcoussis, outside of Paris.

The trial matches between the Springbok Women's XV and the Women's Interprovincial XV teams assisted coach Lawrence Sephaka in the selection process ahead of the World Cup. And to his delight the team performed well by registering a 45-7 victory in Cape Town and an 87-12 win in Johannesburg.

With a clear idea about which players were the best, Sephaka named a 25-mem-

In 2014, the Springbok Women could not improve on their 10th-place finish in the 2010 World Cup.

ber squad for their World Cup warm-up tour, which featured two matches against the Nomads at the Lensbury Club in Teddington and Wasps Football Club in London respectively, as well as a Test against France in Marcoussis.

The team won the clashes against the Nomads 20-5 and 32-24, but went down 46-8 against a strong French outfit in the final match on the tour.

The team returned to South Africa where they had a two-week holding camp in Cape Town to fine-tune their preparations ahead of the World Cup. But despite their good preparation, which featured several training sessions with the SARU Mobi-Unit and two training matches against the Stellenbosch Academy Under-19 boys' team, they battled to make their presence felt at the tournament. The vast World Cup experience within the squad also did little to boost their performance.

While the team showed good signs on attack throughout the tournament, their Achilles heel was their inability to convert their chances into points, while their defence also let them down.

The Springboks opened their campaign with a 26-3 defeat to Australia before going down 55-3 to France and 35-3 to. They bounced back against Samoa in their first seeding match by registering a narrow 25-24 victory, which secured them a spot in the ninth- and tenth-place play-off. This kept alive their hopes of registering their best finish yet in the tournament.

These hopes, however, were dashed as the team suffered a 36-0 defeat to Spain in their final game, a result which ensured a 10th-place finish, just as they did at the 2010 World Cup in London.

WOMEN'S RUGBY

RUGBY WORLD CUP WARM-UP TOUR

Date	Opponent	Venue	Result	Score	Scorers
28 Jun	Nomads	Lensbury Club, Teddington, UK	WON	20-5	T: Gadu, Brown, Cant. C: Cant. P: Kinsey.
1 Jul	Nomads	Wasps FC, London, UK	WON	32-24	T: Gadu, Geldenhuys, Ngxatu, Grain, Vazi, Momoti,. C: Cant.
4 Jul	France	Marcoussis, Paris, France	LOST	8-46	T: Jordaan. P: Cant.

WARM-UP TOUR APPEARANCES & POINTS

PLAYER	Nomads	Nomads	France	Apps	T	C	P	DG	Pts
Cindy Cant	15	x	15	2	1	2	1	–	12
Veroeshka Grain	14	13	13	3	1	–	–	–	5
Benele Makwezela	13	12	–	2	–	–	–	–	0
Lorinda Brown	12	x	12	2	1	–	–	–	5
Phumeza Gadu	11	11	11	3	2	–	–	–	10
Zenay Jordaan	10	x	10	2	1	–	–	–	5
Tayla Kinsey	9	x	9R	2	–	–	1	–	3
Shona-Lee Weston	8	x	6R	2	–	–	–	–	0
Vuyowetha Vazi	7	7	7	3	1	–	–	–	5
Lamla Momoti	6c	8c	8c	3	1	–	–	–	5
Cindy Booi	5	x	5	2	–	–	–	–	0
Celeste Adonis	4	x	5R	2	–	–	–	–	0
Portia Jonga	3	x	3	2	–	–	–	–	0
Denita Wentzel	2	x	2R	2	–	–	–	–	0
Asithandile Ntoyanto	1	x	3R	2	–	–	–	–	0
Thantaswa Macingwana	x	2	2	2	–	–	–	–	0
Cebisa Kula	x	1	1R	2	–	–	–	–	0
Nwabisa Ngxatu	x	3	1	2	1	–	–	–	5
Noma Faleni	x	4	4	2	–	–	–	–	0
Rachelle Geldenhuys	x	6	6	2	1	–	–	–	5
Fundiswa Plaatjie	x	9	9	2	–	–	–	–	0
Siviwe Basweni	x	15	15R	2	–	–	–	–	0
Nosiphiwo Goda	x	14	14	2	–	–	–	–	0
Andrea Mentoor	x	5	–	1	–	–	–	–	0
Zandile Nojoko	x	10	10R	2	–	–	–	–	0
25 Players				53	10	2	2	0	60

‹ DID YOU KNOW? ›

The late Ettienne Botha of the Blue Bulls has scored more tries (4) in Currie Cup Finals than any other player.

Women's Rugby World Cup 2014

RESULTS & SCORERS

Date	Venue	Opponent	Result	Score	Referee	Scorers
01/08/2014	Marcoussis 1, Paris	Australia	Lost	3-26	L Berard (USA)	P: Kinsey.
05/08/2014	Marcoussis 1, Paris	France	Lost	3-55	A Perrett (Aus)	P: Jordaan.
09.08.2014	Marcoussis 2, Paris	Wales	Lost	3-35	J Beard (NZ)	P: Nojoko.
13/08/2014	Marcoussis 1, Paris	Samoa	WON	25-24	A Nievas (Spain)	T: Geldenhuys, Graim, Nojoko. C: Jordaan (2). P: Jordaan (2).
17/08/2014	Marcoussis 1, Paris	Spain	Lost	0-36	J Beard (NZ)	

LEADING SCORERS

POINTS

70	Emily Scarratt	England	40	Niamh Briggs	Ireland
61	Magali Harvey	Canada	39	Ashleigh Hewson	Australia
45	Kelly Brazier	New Zealand	35	Bella Milo	Samoa

TRIES

6	Shakira Baker	New Zealand	4	Magali Harvey	Canada
6	Selica Winiata	New Zealand	4	Huriana Manuel	New Zealand
5	Honey Hireme	New Zealand	4	Marlie Packer	England
4	Tricia Brown	Australia	4	Kay Wilson	England
4	Sioned Harries	Wales			

RESULTS

August 1

New Zealand	79	Kazakhstan	5	Wales	35	South Africa	3
Canada	31	Spain	7	New Zealand	34	USA	3
Australia	26	South Africa	3	Australia	3	France	17
USA	17	Ireland	23				

August 13

9th place Semi Final

England	65	Samoa	3
France	26	Wales	0

South Africa	25	Samoa	24
Spain	18	Kazakhstan	5

August 5

5th place Semi Final

USA	47	Kazakhstan	7	New Zealand	63	Wales	7
Australia	25	Wales	3	Australia	20	USA	23

Semi Finals

England	45	Spain	5	Ireland	7	England	40
Canada	42	Samoa	7	France	16	Canada	18
New Zealand	14	Ireland	17				
France	55	South Africa	3				

August 17

11th Place Play-Off

August 9

Ireland	40	Kazakhstan	5	Samoa	31	Kazakhstan	0

9th Place Play-Off

Spain	41	Samoa	5
England	13	Canada	13

Spain	36	South Africa	0

SA WOMEN

7th Place Play-Off				3rd Place Play-Off			
Australia	30	Wales	3	Ireland	18	France	25
5th Place Play-Off				Final			
New Zealand	55	USA	5	England	21	Canada	9

LOG

Pool A	P	W	D	L	PF	PA	TF	TA	BP	PTS
England	3	2	1	0	123	21	17	3	2	12
Canada	3	2	1	0	86	25	12	3	2	12
Spain	3	1	0	2	51	81	8	11	1	5
Samoa	3	0	0	3	15	148	2	22	0	0
Pool B	P	W	D	L	PF	PA	TF	TA	BP	PTS
Ireland	3	3	0	0	80	36	10	4	1	13
New Zealand	3	2	0	1	127	25	20	3	3	11
USA	3	1	0	2	67	64	10	9	2	6
Kazakhstan	3	0	0	3	17	166	3	27	0	0
Pool C	P	W	D	L	PF	PA	TF	TA	BP	PTS
France	3	3	0	0	98	6	15	0	2	14
Australia	3	2	0	1	54	23	6	2	0	8
Wales	3	1	0	2	38	54	4	7	1	5
South Africa	3	0	0	3	9	116	0	16	0	0

Note: BP = Bonus point

FINAL POSITIONS

1 England 2 Canada 3 France 4 Ireland 5 New Zealand 6 USA
7 Australia 8 Wales 9 Spain 10 South Africa 11 Samoa 12 Kazakhstan

PREVIOUS CHAMPIONS & SA PERFORMANCES, CAPTAINS & COACHES

1991	USA in Wales	–		
1994	England in Scotland	–		
1998	New Zealand in Holland	–		
2002	New Zealand in Spain	–		
2006	New Zealand in Canada	8th	Nomsebenzi Tsotsobe	David Dobela
2010	New Zealand in England	10th	Mandisa Williams	Denver Wannies
2014	England in France	10th	Mandisa Williams	Lawrence Sephaka

‹ DID YOU KNOW? ›

Thys Lourens, at 35 years & 138 days, is the oldest winning captain in a Currie Cup Final (Northern Transvaal, 1978).

SPRINGBOK WOMEN - WORLD CUP APPEARANCES & POINTS

PLAYER	Australia	France	Wales	Samoa	Spain	Apps	T	C	P	DG	Pts
Cindy Cant	15	14R	15	15	15R	5	–	–	–	–	0
Veroeshka Grain	14	14	x	14R	13	4	1	–	–	–	5
Benele Makwezela	13	13	–	–	–	2	–	–	–	–	0
Lorinda Brown	12	12	12	12	12	5	–	–	–	–	0
Phumeza Gadu	11	11	11	x	14R	4	–	–	–	–	0
Zenay Jordaan	10	10c	13c	13c	10c	5	–	2	3	–	13
Tayla Kinsey	9	9R	15R	x	x	3	–	–	1	–	3
Mandisa Williams	8c	–	–	–	–	1	–	–	–	–	0
Vuyowetha Vazi	7	7	7R	6R	6	5	–	–	–	–	0
Rachelle Geldenhuys	6	7R	6	6	–	4	1	–	–	–	5
Cindy Booi	5	5	5	4R	5	5	–	–	–	–	0
Celeste Adonis	4	4	4	4	4	5	–	–	–	–	0
Cebisa Kula	3	3	3	3R	3R	5	–	–	–	–	0
Denita Wentzel	2	2	2	2	x	4	–	–	–	–	0
Asithandile Ntoyanto	1	1R	–	–	–	2	–	–	–	–	0
Thantaswa Macingwana	2R	–	2R	2R	2	4	–	–	–	–	0
Nwbisa Ngxatu	1R	8R	1	1	1	5	–	–	–	–	0
Andrea Mentoor	7R	4R	7	–	–	3	–	–	–	–	0
Shona-Lee Weston	6R	8	x	7	4R	4	–	–	–	–	0
Fundiswa Plaatjie	9R	9	9	9	9	5	–	–	–	–	0
Zandile Nojoko	10R	11R	10	10	15	5	1	–	1	–	8
Siviwe Basweni	15R	15	14	14	14	5	–	–	–	–	0
Lamla Momoti	⊠	6	8	8	8	4	–	–	–	–	0
Portia Jonga	⊠	1	4R	3	3	4	–	–	–	–	0
Sinazo Nobele	⊠	–	11R	11	11	3	–	–	–	–	0
Noma Mayongo	⊠	–	–	5	7	2	–	–	–	–	0
Siphosethu Tshingana	–	–	–	–	10R	1	–	–	–	–	0
27 Players						104	3	2	5	0	34

SA WOMEN

SPRINGBOK WOMEN - WORLD CUP SQUAD

	Position	Date of Birth	Height (m)	Weight	Union
BACKS					
Siviwe Basweni	Fullback	17/10/1990	1,66	60	Border
Cindy Cant	Fullback	09/10/1982	1,66	62	Blue Bulls
Phumeza Gadu	Wing	21/06/1985	1,56	60	Eastern Province
Veroeshka Grain	Wing	11/12/1990	1,65	60	Western Province
Sinazo Nobele	Wing	05/10/1988	1,63	57	Border
Lorinda Brown	Centre	16/12/1983	1,61	65	Eastern Province
Benele Makwezela	Centre	16/01/1986	1,66	66	Western Province
Zandile Nojoko	Flyhalf	01/07/1986	1,80	65	Eastern Province
Zenay Jordaan	Flyhalf	04/04/1991	1,57	57	Eastern Province
Tayla Kinsey	Scrumhalf	05/09/1993	1,63	60	KwaZulu-Natal
Siphosethu Tshingana	Scrumhalf	12/10/1987	1,40	56	Eastern Province
Fundiswa Plaatjie	Scrumhalf	12/04/1985	1,55	70	Border
FORWARDS					
Mandisa Williams (Capt)	No 8	11/08/1984	1,71	82	Border
Shona-Leah Weston	No 8	25/11/1991	1,72	63	Blue Bulls
Nombulelo Mayongo	Flanker	26/05/1985	1,58	69	Free State
Lamla Momoti	Flanker	27/03/1985	1,67	68	Border
Rachelle Geldenhuys	Flanker	20/10/1987	1,65	67	Blue Bulls
Vuyolwethu Vazi	Flanker	11/07/1987	1,64	68	Blue Bulls
Nolusindiso Booi	Lock	29/06/1985	1,72	76	Border
Andrea Mentoor	Lock	21/01/1987	1,67	75	Western Province
Celeste Adonis	Lock	07/06/1992	1,75	81	Western Province
Nwabisa Ngxatu	Hooker	25/10/1983	1,69	77	Border
Asithandile Ntoyanto	Prop	06/05/1991	1,74	94	Border
Portia Jonga	Prop	24/04/1973	1,65	104	Eastern Province
Cebisa Kula	Prop	19/05/1981	1,66	86	Eastern Province
Thantaswa Macingwane	Hooker	13/01/1994	1,66	87	Border
Denita Wentzel	Hooker	31/03/1990	1,66	66	Western Province
27 Players					

Head Coach: Lawrence Sephaka **Assistant coach:** Renfred Dazel
Manager: Nomsebenzi Tsotsobe **Biokineticist:** Heyno Kraft
Physio: Dr Tanushree Pillay **Doctor:** Dr Jerome Mampame
Communications: Zeena Isaacs

SA WOMEN

Women's Provincial Rugby

RESULTS AND LOGS

Inter Provincial Women A1

Date	Result	Venue
Apr 25	South Western Districts 8, Border 37	Outeniqua Park, George
Apr 26	KwaZulu-Natal 7, Blue Bulls 35	KP2, Kings Park, Durban
Apr 26	Eastern Province 15, Western Province 12	Central Grounds, Uitenhage
May 10	Western Province 55, South Western Districts 3	City Park, Cape Town
May 10	Border 43, KwaZulu-Natal 3	BCM Stadium, East London
May 10	Blue Bulls 24, Eastern Province 26	Loftus Versfeld, Pretoria
May 24	KwaZulu-Natal 10, Eastern Province 13	Sugar Ray Xulu Stadium, Clermont
May 24	Border 34, Western Province 3	BCM Stadium, East London
May 24	South Western Districts 5, Blue Bulls 59	Bridgton Sport Grounds, Oudtshoorn
Jun 07	Western Province 34, KwaZulu-Natal 7	City Park, Cape Town
Jun 07	Blue Bulls 10, Border 31	Loftus B, Pretoria
Jun 07	Eastern Province 66, South Western Districts 7	Humansdorp Country Club
Jun 14	KwaZulu-Natal 31, South Western Districts 15	Harlequins RC, Durban
Jun 14	Western Province 5, Blue Bulls 8	Theo Marais Park, Milnerton
Jun 14	Border 54, Eastern Province 10	BCM Stadium, East London

SEMI-FINALS

Date	Result	Venue
Sep 19	Border 22, Western Province 7	BCM Stadium, East London
Sep 20	Eastern Province 5, Blue Bulls 08	Central Grounds, Uitenhage

FINAL

Date	Result	Venue
Sep 27	Border 32, Blue Bulls 14	BCM Stadium, East London

LOG

Section A1	P	W	L	D	PF	PA	PD	TF	TA	BP	PTS
Border	5	5	0	0	199	34	165	33	4	5	25
Eastern Province	5	4	1	0	130	107	23	19	16	2	18
Blue Bulls	5	3	2	0	136	74	62	18	12	3	15
Western Province	5	2	3	0	109	67	42	17	9	4	12
KwaZulu-Natal	5	1	4	0	58	140	-82	7	22	2	6
South Western Districts	5	0	5	0	38	248	-210	6	37	0	0

WOMEN'S RUGBY

Inter Provincial Women A2

Date	Match	Venue
Jul 04	Golden Lions 25, Griffons 32	Ellis Park, Johannesburg
Jul 12	Golden Lions 10, Free State 39	Ellis Park, Johannesburg
Jul 12	Griffons 5, Boland 29	North West Stadium, Welkom
Jul 19	Boland 34, Golden Lions 07	Boland Stadium, Wellington
Jul 19	Free State 74, Griffons 15	Old Greys Club, Bloemfontein
Jul 26	Boland 14, Free State 26	Boland Stadium, Wellington

FINAL

Date	Match	Venue
Sep 27	Free State 34, Boland 0	BCM Stadium, East London

LOG

Section A2	P	W	L	D	PF	PA	PD	TF	TA	BP	PTS
Free State	3	3	0	0	139	39	100	23	6	3	15
Boland	3	2	1	0	77	38	39	13	6	2	10
Griffons	3	1	2	0	52	128	-76	8	22	1	5
Golden Lions	3	0	3	0	42	105	-63	8	18	2	2

Inter Provincial Women B

Date	Match	Venue
Jul 05	Blue Bulls Limpopo 10, Griquas 25	Seshego Stadium, Seshego
Jul 05	Mpumalanga 26, Valke 15	Nelspruit Rugby Club, Nelspruit
Jul 12	Leopards 19, Mpumalanga 5	Profert Olën Park, Potchefstroom
Jul 19	Griquas 10, Valke 5	Nababeep Stadium, Springbok
Jul 19	Blue Bulls Limpopo 17, Leopards 59	Seshego Stadium, Seshego
Jul 25	Leopards 48, Griquas 18	Profert Olën Park, Potchefstroom
Jul 26	Mpumalanga 70, Blue Bulls Limpopo 15	Sakhile Stadium, Standerton

SEMI-FINALS

Date	Match	Venue
Aug 02	Griquas 25, Mpumalanga 43	Nababeep Stadium, Springbok
Aug 02	Valke 19, Leopards 64	Barnard Stadium, Kempton Park

FINAL

Date	Match	Venue
Sep 27	Leopards 34, Mpumalanga 17	BCM Stadium, East London

LOG

Section B	P	W	L	D	PF	PA	PD	TF	TA	BP	PTS
Leopards	4	4	0	0	190	59	131	33	10	3	19
Mpumalanga	4	3	1	0	144	74	70	24	13	3	15
Griquas	4	2	2	0	78	106	-28	8	16	1	9
Valke	3	0	3	0	39	100	-61	7	16	0	1
Blue Bulls Limpopo	3	0	3	0	42	154	-112	6	23	0	0

England do the junior double

SA Schools handed first series defeat in four years

ENGLAND reinforced their dominance over South Africa at junior level when their Under-18 side handed the SA Schools team their first defeat in four years in August's four-nation U18 series that also involved France and Wales.

England's 30-22 victory at Paul Roos Gymnasium's Markötter Stadium in Stellenbosch came two months after their U20 team edged the Junior Springboks by a point at Eden Park in Auckland to hang onto their IRB Junior World Championship crown.

The big difference between the teams was England's ability to convert their point-scoring chances into points, while the hosts paid the price for mistakes at crucial moments.

For South Africa, the series, which grows in popularity with each passing year and in 2014 also involved an Italy U18 team that played three local invitation sides, was nevertheless a memorable and constructive one. They beat their Welsh counterparts 40-15 at Outeniqua Park in George after handing the French juniors a 28-13 defeat in the opening match at Cape Town's City Park.

"Our objectives with this series is to afford our best under-18 players with international playing opportunities," said SARU CEO, Jurie Roux. "One of the benefits of this is that we will identify the players who have impressed for possible further representation in our national structures, be it for the Junior Boks, Springbok Sevens or ultimately the Springboks."

England dominated territory and possession in the first 25 minutes of the series decider and they used most of their try-scoring chances. Tries from wing Roti Segan and lock Joe Batley gave the visitors a 14-0 lead before fullback Curwin Bosch reduced the deficit with a penalty. But England's impressive attacking play saw them score a third try, to centre Max Clarke, who forced his way through two defenders to stretch their lead to 16 points. SA Schools wing Keanu Vers scored a vital try for the hosts four minutes before half-time to make it 19-8.

A fourth England try wasn't long in coming, however, flanker Sam Underhill sprinting clear shortly after the break to restore the 16-point buffer.

Not to be outdone, Vers hit back with his second touchdown to make it 24-15 after which England flyhalf Rory Jennings added three points in the 55th minute to make it

Andell Loubser played right wing for SA Schools in all three series matches.

a 12-point game heading into the final quarter. SA Schools clawed their way back into the match in the last 10 minutes when centre JT Jackson scored their third try following a fantastic run by Vers – who else?

Bosch converted to reduce the gap to 27-22 with six minutes to go. The hosts' momentum was stalled when England kicked another penalty to edge beyond the seven-point barrier, and while Vers had a chance to manufacture a late try it was the boys in white who held on for a famous win.

SA SCHOOLS - RESULTS & SCORERS

Date	Venue	Opponent	Result	Score	Referee	Scorers
15 Aug	City Park Stadium, Cape Town	France	WON	28-13	Robert Price	T: Loubser (2), Willemse, Smit. C: Bosch (4).
19 Aug	Outeniqua Park, George	Wales	WON	40-15	Jamie Leahy	T: Fortuin, Papier, Bezuidenhout, Jackson. C: De Beer (4). P: De Beer (4).
23 Aug	Markotter Stadium, Stellenbosch	England	LOST	22-30	Robert Price	T: Vers (2), Jackson. C: Bosch (2). P: Bosch.

Other results:

15 Aug	City Park Stadium, Cape Town	WP U/18 45 Italy U/18 12
15 Aug	City Park Stadium, Cape Town	England U/18 24 Wales U/18 21
19 Aug	Outeniqua Park, George	SWD U/18 21 Italy 38
19 Aug	Outeniqua Park, George	England U/18 23 France U/18 6
23 Aug	Markotter Stadium, Stellenbosch	SARU Ac XV 48 Italy U/18 29
23 Aug	Markotter Stadium, Stellenbosch	France U/18 9 Wales U/18 10

SA SCHOOLS

APPEARANCES & POINTS

PLAYER	School	Union	France	Wales	England	Apps	T	C	P	DG	Pts
EN (Eduan) Keyter	Affies, Pretoria	Blue Bulls	15	–	10R	2	–	–	–	–	0
AA (Andel) Loubser	Menlo Park, Pretoria	Blue Bulls	14	14	14	3	2	–	–	–	10
BJ (Barend) Smit	HTS, Middelburg	Mpumalanga	13	15c	–	2	1	–	–	–	5
JT (JT) Jackson	Oakdale Agric., Riversdale	SWD	12	12	12	3	2	–	–	–	10
J (Jerry) Danquah	Queen's College, Queenstown	Border	11	–	12R	2	–	–	–	–	0
CD (Curwin) Bosch	Grey High, Port Elizabeth	EP	10	15R	15	3	–	6	1	–	15
M (Marco) Jansen van Vuren	Transvalia, Vanderbijlpark	Valke	9	9R	9	3	–	–	–	–	0
AJ (Jaco) Coetzee	Glenwood, Durban	KZN	8c	–	–	1	–	–	–	–	0
TV (Victor) Maruping	Louis Botha, Bloemfontein	Free State	7	7R	x	2	–	–	–	–	0
E (Edmund) Rheeder	HS Klerksdorp, Klerksdorp	Leopards	6	8	8	3	–	–	–	–	0
E le R (Eduard) Zandberg	Oakdale Agric., Riversdale	SWD	5	5	5c	3	–	–	–	–	0
J (Jaco) Willemse	Paarl Gymnasium, Paarl	WP	4	–	–	1	1	–	–	–	5
IM (Ignatius) Prinsloo	Grey College, Bloemfontein	Free State	3	3R	3R	3	–	–	–	–	0
J-H (Jan-Henning) Campher	Garsfontein, Pretoria	Blue Bulls	2	2R	2	3	–	–	–	–	0
N (Ngonidzashe) Chidoma	Northwood, Durban	KZN	1	–	1R	2	–	–	–	–	0
Le R (Le Roux) Baard	Outeniqua, George	SWD	2R	2	2R	3	–	–	–	–	0
L (Lupumlo) Mguca	Daniel Pienaar, Uitenhage	EP	1R	1	1	3	–	–	–	–	0
SM (Sarel) Smith	Eldoraigne, Centurion	Blue Bulls	3R	3	3	3	–	–	–	–	0
AB (Aston) Fortuin	Southdown Coll., Centurion	Blue Bulls	4R	4	4	3	1	–	–	–	5
JH (Cobus) Wiese	HS Upington, Upington	Griquas (CD)	8R	7	7R	3	–	–	–	–	0
EC (Embrose) Papier	Garsfontein, Pretoria	Blue Bulls	9R	9	9R	3	1	–	–	–	5
MH (Tinus) de Beer	Waterkloof, Pretoria	Blue Bulls	x	10	10	2	–	4	4	–	20
KA (Keanu) Vers	Grey High, Port Elizabeth	EP	x	11	11	2	2	–	–	–	10
H (Heino) Bezuidenhout	Daniel Pienaar, Uitenhage	EP	–	13	13	2	1	–	–	–	5
HA (Arnold) Gerber	Menlo Park, Pretoria	Blue Bulls	–	6	6	2	–	–	–	–	0
M (Nazo) Nkala	Welkom Gymnasium	Griffons	–	14R	–	1	–	–	–	–	0
KM (Kenny) van Niekerk	Glenwood, Durban	KZN	–	1R	–	1	–	–	–	–	0
JS (Junior) Pokomela	Grey High, Port Elizabeth	EP	–	x	7	1	–	–	–	–	0
28 Players						65	11	10	5	0	90

Note: M (Morne) Joubert (Glenwood High, Durban, KZN) and MMT (Michael) Kumbirai (St Alban's Coll., Blue Bulls) were originally chosen but did not take the field due to injury. They were replaced by H (Heino) Bezuidenhout and KM (Kenny) van Niekerk respectively.

Coach: Hein Kriek (WP)

SA Schools Players 1974-2014

† Indicates became senior Springbok (15-man code).
* Indicates SA Schools captain (in second year if played for two years)

Adams, Tythan – (Paul Roos Gym) – WP - 2008
Afrika, Cecil - (Harmony Sport) - Griffons - 2006
Alberts, Nicolaas - (Affies, Pretoria) - BB - 1996
†Alcock, Chad - (Alexander Road) - EP - 1991
Alexander, Enwill - (Stellenberg) - WP - 2002
Anderson, Severin - (Westering) - EP – 1978
April, Garth – (Bergrivier) – Boland - 2008
April, Randall – (Bergrivier) - Boland - 2004
Arends, Neil – (McCarthy, Uitenhage) - EP – 1999
Arendse, Riaan – (Brandwag, Uitenhage) - (EP) - 2007
Arlow, Wium – (Nelspruit) - Mpu – 2002
Baard, Le Roux (Outeniqua) – SWD – 2014
Bakkes, Luther – (Diamantveld) - GW – 1989
Bali, Mlungisi – (St Alban's) – BB – 2008
Bannink, Wimpie – (Hans Strijdom) - Far North - 1992
Barker, Michael (DHS) - Natal – 1978
Barnard, Jan-Hendrik - (Menlopark) - BB - 1988
Barnard, Kierie - (Volkskool, Potchefstroom) - Leopards - 1981
Barnard, Lee - (King Edward VII) - GL - 1974-75
Barnies, Francois - (Parow HS) - WP - 2000
Baronet, Dennis - (Glenwood) - Natal - 1985
Barrett, Brett - (Kingswood Coll) - EP - 1991
¹Barritt, Bradley - (Kearsney Coll) - Natal – 2004
Bartle, Grant - (Middelburg THS) - Mpu - 1995
†Bartmann, Wahl - (Florida) - GL – 1981
Bartmann, Leon - (Florida) - GL – 1978
Basson, JP - (Boland Agric.) - WP - 1994-95
Basson, Stefan - (Boland Agric.) - WP – 2000
Beerwinkel, Andrew – (Porterville) - Boland - 2011
Bennett, Richard - (Dale Coll.) - Border - 1992
Beukes, Chris - (DHS) - Natal – 1990
Bezuidenhout, Heino - (Daniel Pienaar) – EP – 2014
Bezuidenhout, Riaan – (Framesby) - EP – 1984
Bitterhout, Leroy – (Klein Nederb) – Boland – 2010
Bitzi, Anrich – (Grey Coll.) – FS – 2010
Blignaut, Robert – (Muir Coll.) - EP – 1978
†Bobo, Gcobani – (Dale Coll.) - Border - 1996
Böhmer, Manfred – (Ermelo) - Mpu – 1998
Bolofo, Moeka – (Louis Botha) - Free State - 2007
Bolus, Robert – (Bishops) - WP - 1974-75

Bonthuys, John - (Abbots Coll.) - WP - 1974-75
Bosch, Curwin – (Grey HS) – EP - 2014
Bosch, Jan - (Helpmekaar) - GL – 1991
†Boshoff, Marnitz – (Nelspruit) – Mpu – 2007
†Botha, Bakkies – (Vereeniging THS) - Valke – 1998
Bothma,* Rikus – (Paarl Gym) – WP – 2013
Botes, Bennie - (Affies, Pretoria) - BB - 1991
Botha, Calla - (DF Malan) - GL - 1979
Botha, Ettienne - (John Vorster, Nigel) - Valke - 1997
†Botha, Gary - (Overkruin) - BB - 1998-99
Botha, Justin - (Monument) - GL - 2006
Botha, Leon - (Grey Coll.) - FS – 1981
Botha, Ruan – (Jeugland) – Valke - 2010
Botha, Wimpie - (Queen's Coll.) - Border - 1998
Breedt, Johan - (Wonderboom) - BB - 1993
Breedt, Nico - (Kearsney Coll.) - Natal - 1998
Brink, Stephen - (Sentraal) - FS - 1991-92
†Brits, Schalk - (Paul Roos Gym.) - WP – 1999
Britz, Conraad - (Oakdale Agric) - SWD – 2005
Britz, Riaan – (Grey Coll.) - FS – 2009
Bronkhorst, Stephan - (Randburg) - GL - 1992
Brown, Dick - (Pearson) - EP - 1986
Brown, John - (Hentie Cilliers) - NFS - 1999
†Brussouw, Heinrich - (Grey Coll) - FS - 2004
Buckle, Albertus - (Boland Agric) - Boland - 2001
†Burger, Kobus - (Paarl Gym.) - WP - 1980-81
Burger, Altus - (Ermelo) - Mpu - 1982-83
Burton-Moore, Mark - (Bishops) - WP - 1978
Bushney, Marais - (Roodepoort) - GL – 1989
Caldo, Kobus - (Oakdale Agric) - SWD - 1998-99
Campbell-McGeachy, Walter - (Pietersburg) - Far North - 1994-95
Campher, Connie - (Potchefstroom THS) - Leopards - 1985
Campher, Fanie - (Wolmaransstad THS) - Stellaland - 1974-75
Campher, Jan-Henning - (Garsfontein) – BB – 2014
†Carr, Nizaam – (Bishops) – WP - 2009
†Carstens, Deon - (Boland Agric) - WP - 1997
Carswell, Michael - (Grey HS) - EP - 1984
Carty, Shane - (King Edward VII) - GL - 1974-75
Cattrell,* Brenton - (Maritzburg Coll) - Natal - 1987
Cawood, Mark - (Wynberg BH) - WP - 1974-75
Celliers,* Norman - (Ermelo) - Mpu – 1991
Chadwick, Dale – (Westville) - KwaZulu Natal – 2007
Chidoma, Ngonidzashe – (Northwood) – KZN - 2014

Claassen, Andrew - (Andrew Rabie) - EP - 1988
Clancy, Sean - (Selborne Coll) - Border – 1995
Cloete, Chris – (Selborne Coll) – Border - 2009
Cloete, Hannes – (Jim Fouché) - FS – 1995
Cloete, Jan – (Waterkloof) - BB - 1996
Coetzee, Deon – (Helpmekaar) - GL – 1979
Coetzee, Eduard - (Affies, Pretoria) - BB - 1997
Coetzee, Jaco – (Ellisras) - Far North – 1988
Coetzee,* Jaco – (Glenwood) – KZN - 2014
Coetzee, Jannie - (Bloemfontein THS) - FS – 1982
Coetzee, Marne – (Waterkloof) – BB – 2011
Coetzer, Jacques - (Middelburg THS) - Mpu – 1996
†Conradie, Bolla - (Kasselsvlei) - WP - 1996-97
Cook, Jean – (Grey Coll) – FS - 2009
Cooper, Barney - (Paarl Gym) - WP - 1986
Cooper, John - (Soa Bras Mosselbaai) - SWD - 1998
Coyle-Meybery,* Craig - (Dale Coll) - Border - 1983-84
Craven, Jean - (Grey Coll) - FS – 1990
Cronjé, Frans - (Grey Coll) - FS – 1985
†Cronjé, Jacques - (John Vorster THS) - BB - 2000
Croy, Ricardo - (Paarl Gym.) - WP - 2004
Daffue, Hendrik - (Grey Coll) - FS - 1980
Daffue, Willem - (Grey Coll) - FS – 1977
Damens, Leneve – (Grey Coll) – FS – 2011
Dames, Arno - (Framesby) - EP - 1990
Dames, Rudi - (Vereeniging THS) - Valke – 1999
Daniller, Hennie - (Paarl Gym) - WP – 2002
Danquah, Jerry – (Queen's Coll) – Border - 2014
Davel, Chris - (Ermelo) - Mpu – 1985
Davis, Aidon – (Daniel Pienaar) – EP – 2012
De Beer,* Conrad - (Grey Coll) - FS – 1981
De Beer, Thinus – (Waterkloof) - BB
De Bruin, Michael – (Nelspruit) - Mpu - 2001
De Bruyn, Corné - (Worcester) - Boland - 1994
De Coning,* Basil – (Kingswood Coll) - EP - 1990
De Haas, Pieter - (Grey Coll) - FS – 1986
De Jager, Bruce - (Bishops) - WP - 1994
De Jager, Wilhelm - (Ermelo) - Mpu - 2002
De Kock, Jason - (Hugenote HS) - Valke - 1996
De Kock, Zander - (Vereeniging THS) - Valke - 2005
De Nobrega, Paul - (Worcester) - Boland - 1984
De Ru, Ian - (Marais Viljoen THS) - GL – 1989
†De Villiers, Jean - (Paarl Gym) - WP Acad. - 1999

SA SCHOOLS

De Waal, Adriaan - (Paarl BH) - WP Acad. – 1995
Dell, Allan – (Queen's Coll) – Border - 2010
Delport,* Paul - (SACS) - WP - 2001-02
Delport, Marius - (Zwartkop) - BB - 2003
Derksen, Chris - (Grey Coll) - FS - 1993
Diedericks, Ernest - (Scottsville) - WP - 1994
†Dixon,* Pieter - (Maritzburg Coll) - Natal - 1995
Dreyer, Hano - (Winterberg Agric) - NEC - 1995
†Drotské, Naka - (Grey Coll) - FS - 1989
†Du Plessis, Carel - (Paarl BH) - WP - 1978
†Du Plessis, Bismarck - (Grey Coll) - FS - 2001-02
Du Plessis, Charl - (Kroonstad Agric) - NFS - 1978
Du Plessis, Daniel - (Paul Roos Gym) - WP – 2013
Du Plessis, Jacques – (Ermelo) - Mpu - 2011
Du Plessis, Johan - (Sand du Plessis) - FS – 1985
Du Plessis, JP – (Paul Roos Gym) – WP – 2009
Du Plessis, Morné - (Waterkloof) - BB - 2011
Du Plessis, Neil - (Selborne Coll) - Border - 1984
Du Plessis, Pierre - (Port Natal) - Natal - 1987
†Du Preez, Delarey - (Hangklip) - Border - 1994
Du Preez, André - (Oudtshoorn THS) - SWD – 1974
Du Preez, Daniel – (Kearsney) – KZN - 2012-13
Du Preez, Fransie - (EG Jansen) - GL – 1985
Du Preez, Jean-Luc – (Kearsney) – KZN – 2012-13
Du Preez, Philip – (Monument) - GL - 2011
†Du Preez, Wian - (Grey Coll) - FS - 1999-00
†Du Randt, Os - (Piet Retief) - NEC - 1990
Du Toit, Dawie - (Vereeniging THS) - GL - 1974-75
Du Toit, Dawie - (Monument) - GL - 1992-93
Du Toit, Franna – (Grey Coll) – FS – 2008
Du Toit, Jaco - (Paarl Gym) - WP – 1999
Du Toit, Thomas - (Paarl BH) - WP – 2013
Duvenhage, Braam - (HSS Hugenote) - Valke - 1982
Duvenhage, Stoffel - (Middelburg THS) - Mpu – 2004
Dwebe, Joseph – (Florida) – GL – 2013
Ebersöhn, Robert – (Grey Coll) - Free State - 2007
Edgar, David - (Michaelhouse) - Natal - 2001
Ehrentraut,* Michael - (Bishops) - WP – 1989
Eksteen, Ryno – (Affies, Pretoria) – BB - 2012
Ellerd, Rialoo – (Jacobsdal) - Griquas - 2005
†Els, Braam - (AHS, Kroonstad) - NFS - 1990
Els,* Anton - (DHS du Plessis) - EP - 1975
Engelbrecht, Andries - (Volkskool) - Leopards - 1981
Engelbrecht,* Fanus - (Rob Ferreira Witrivier) - Mpu - 1983
Engelbrecht,* Frankel – (Paarl Gym) - WP - 1986
Engelbrecht, Johan - (Paul Roos Gym) - WP - 1986
Engelbrecht, Morné - (Rustenburg) - Leopards - 1994
Erasmus, Greyling - (Ermelo) - Mpu - 2000
Erasmus, Kerneels - (Frikkie Meyer) - Far North - 1982
Erlank, Karel - (Klerksdorp) - Leopards - 1979
Erwee,* Jurie - (Grey Coll) - FS - 1980
Espag,* Jaco - (Witbank THS) - Mpu - 1984-85
Esterhuizen, Francois – (Overberg) – Boland - 2012
Faas, Chuma – (Grey HS) – EP – 2008
Faku, Zolani – (Grey HS) – SA Acad (EP) - 2009
Farmer, Steven - (Kasselsvlei) - WP - 2001
Fenwick, Alex - (Grey Coll) - FS - 1990-91
Fenwick, Kobie - (Grey Coll) - FS – 1975
Ferreira, Andries – (AHS, Pretoria) – BB - 2008
†Ferreira, Christo - (Welkom Gym) - NFS - 1978
Ferreira, Freddie - (Brandwag) - EP - 1980
Ferreira, Marthinus – (Florida) - GL - 2000
Ferreira, Schalk - (Paul Roos Gym) - WP - 2002
Feurer, Lee - (Bishops) - WP – 1988
Fisher, Tyler – (Westville) – KZN - 2011
Fitchet, Christo - (Kirkwood) - EP - 1975
Flanagan, Sean - (Westville) - Natal - 1999
Forslara, Vuyani – (Grens HS) - Border – 1999
Fortuin, Aston (Southdowns Coll) — BB - 2014
Fortuin, Sean - (Bellville South HS) - WP – 1999
Fouche, Neethling - (Grey Coll) – FS - 2010
Fourie, Andries - (Framesby) - EP - 1990
Fourie, Dawie - (Kroonstad Agric) - NFS - 1978-79
Fourie, Kenneth - (Port Shepstone) - Natal - 1994
Fourie, Nel - (Ermelo) - Mpu - 2000
Fourie, Stompie - (Grey Coll) - FS - 1984
Frolick, Shandré – (Worcester Gym.) - Boland - 2004
Froneman, Stephan - (Montana) - BB - 1995
Fullard, Neil - (Paarl BH) - WP - 2000
†Fynn, Etienne - (St Charles) - Natal - 1990
Gage, Shaun - (DHS) - Natal - 1985
Galant, Warrick – (Outeniqua) – SWD – 2012-13
Geldenhuys, Jan - (Grey Coll) - FS - 1974-75
Genis, James - (DF Malan) - WP – 1977
Gerber, Arnold - (Menlo Park) – BB - 2014
†Gerber,* Danie - (Despatch) - EP - 1975-77
†Gerber, Hendrik - (Nico Malan) - EP - 1993-94
Gericke, Jaco - (Port Elizabeth THS) - EP – 1988
Gericke, Neethling – (Oakdale Agric) – SWD – 2008
Gibbs, Herchelle - (Bishops) - WP - 1992
Giezing, Kalf - (Grey Coll) - FS - 1983
†Gillingham, Joe - (Alberton) - GL – 1992
Glover, Shaun - (Maritzburg Coll) - Natal - 1985
Goedeke, Frank – (Carter) - Natal - 1990
Goedeke, Udo - (Maritzburg Coll) - Natal - 1987
†Goosen, Johan – (Grey Coll) – FS - 2010
Goosen, Niel - (Waterkloof) - BB - 1997
Goosen, Gregory - (Kearsney Coll) - Natal - 2001
Gouws, Scheepers – (Grey Coll) - FS - 1981
Gqoba, Andisa – (Hudson Park) - Border - 2003
†Grant, Peter - (Maritzburg Coll) - Natal - 2002
Greyling, Gert - (Sand du Plessis) - FS - 2003
Griesel, Jannie – (Verwoerdburg) - BB - 1987
Gronum, Antonie – (Oakdale Agric) - SWD - 2003
Grobler, Gerbrand - (Grey Coll) - FS - 1981
Grobler, Jacques - (FH Odendaal) - BB - 1990
Grobler, Lukas - (Hugenote HS) - Valke - 1981
Gwavu, Vincent - (Daniël Pienaar - Uitenhage) - EP - 2005
*Hall, Stephen - (Dale Coll) - Border - 1991
Hammer, Ernst - (Fakkel) - GL - 1993
Hancke, Wim - (Linden) - GL - 1974-75
Hankinson, Rob - (Michaelhouse) - Natal - 1974-75
†Hargreaves,* Alistair - (Durban HS) - Natal – 2004
Hartzenberg, Vaasir - (Paarl BHS) - WP - 2006
Hearne, Ashlyn - (Hottentots Holland) - WP - 2000
†Hendriks, Pieter - (Standerton) - Mpu - 1988
Hendriks, Braam - (Sandveld) - NFS – 1993
Herbst, Irne – (Waterkloof) - BB – 2011
Hermanus, Grant - (Paarl Gym) - WP – 2013
Hess, Cornel - (Affies Pretoria) - BB - 2006-07
Heuer, Merrick - (Queen's Coll) - Border - 1988
Heunis, Nico - (Dirkie Uys) - Boland - 1994
Heydenrich,* Johan - (Standerton) - Mpu - 1982
Hickson, André - (Bosmansdam) - WP - 1985
Hill, Jaydon – (Glenwood) - Natal – 2002
Hlongwane, Nhlanhla – (Louis Botha) – FS (2011)
Hollenbach, Alwyn - (Grey Coll) - FS - 2003
Hopkins, Clifford – (Kearsney Coll) - Natal - 1979
Hopp, Dean - (Kairos SS) - SWD - 2000
†Hougaard, Derick - (Boland Agric) - Boland - 2001
Hough, André - (Framesby) - EP - 1988
Hugo, Jan-Harm - (Ermelo) - Mpu - 1997
Hugo, Werner - (Paarl BH) - WP - 1993
Hulme,* Altenstädt - (Voortrekker, CT) - WP – 1999
Human, Dewald – (Outeniqua) – SWD - 2013
Human, Gerhard – (Despatch) – EP – 1977
Ingles, Warren - (Alexander Road) - EP – 1987
†Jacobs, Adrian - (Scottsville) - WP - 1998
Jacobs, Divan - (Ermelo) - Mpu - 2001
Jacobs, Jaco - (Grey Coll) - FS – 1987
Jackson JT - (Oakdale) – SWD - 2014
Jaer, Malcolm – (Brandway) – EP - 2013
Jamieson, Craig – (Maritzburg Coll) - Natal – 1979
Jankowitz, Anton - (Hilton Coll) - Natal – 1989
Janse van Rensburg, Nicholaas – (AHS, Pretoria) – BB – 2012
Janse van Rensburg, Rohan – (Affies, Pretoria) – BB – 2012

SA SCHOOLS

Janse van Vuuren, Marco – (Transvalia) – Valke – 2013-14
†Jantjes, Conrad – (CBS Boksburg) - Valke – 1997
†Jantjies, Elton – (Florida HS) – GL – 2008
Jantjies, Tony – (Menlo Park) – BB – 2009
†Januarie, Enrico - (Weston HS) – Boland – 2000
Jho, Andile (Dale Coll) – Border – 2009-10
Job, Izak – (Pres. Steyn Bloemfontein) - FS - 1998
†John'son, Ashley - (Paarl Gym.) - WP - 2004
John'son, Nicolas – (Selborne Coll) – Border - 1998
John'ston, Gordon - (Paarl BH) – WP – 1999
Jooste, Morné – (The Settlers) – WP - 2005
Jordaan, Hennie – (Menlopark) – BB – 1980
Jordaan, Paul – (Grey Coll) – FS - 2010
Joubert, Jan-Hendrik - (Oakdale Agric) - SWD – 2001
Joubert, Morné (Glenwood) – KZN – 2014
Joubert, Riaan - (Grey Coll) – FS – 1978
Joubert, Wilhelm – (Overkruin) – BB – 1982
Juries, Christopher – (Kingswood Coll) - EP - 2005
Kalonji, Kadima – (Pretoria THS) – BB - 1998
Kankowski, Tino – (PJ Olivier) – EP - 1977
Kaplan, Kevin – (Kimberley THS) - GW – 1980
Kapp, Divan - (Middelburg THS) - Mpu — 2005
Kapp, Neil – (Outeniqua) – SWD – 2008
Karemaker, Leon – (Bellville) - WP - 2003
Kasselman, Chris - (Sandveld) – NFS – 1979-80
Kelly, Richard - (Maritzburg Coll) - Natal - 1996
Kemp,* Scott – (Hudson Park) - Border - 1991-92
†Kempson, Robert - (Queen's Coll) - Border – 1992
Keyter, Eduan (Affies, Pretoria) – BB - 2014
Khubeka, Sandile – (Kearsney) – KZN - 2012
King, Kelvano – (Alexandria) – Eastern Province - 2007
Kirsten, Frik - (Affies Pretoria) – BB – 2006
Kitshoff, Steven – (Paul Roos) – WP - 2010
Kleinenberg, Mark – (Selborne Coll) - Border - 1974-75
Klopper, Chris – (Die Burger) - GL - 1978
Knoetze, Frederick - (Framesby) – EP – 1982
Kobese, Bangihlonbe – (Dale Coll) – Border -- 2009
Koch, Agie - (Paul Roos Gym) - WP - 1974-75
Koch, Hendrik - (Rustenburg) - Leopards – 1978
Koegelenberg, Gideon – (Hugenote) – Boland - 2012
†Koen, Louis - (Paarl Gym) - WP - 1993-94
Koen, Barabas – (Ermelo) – Mpu – 1991
†Kolisi, Siyamthanda – (Grey HS) – EP – 2008-09
Köster, Nick - (Bishops) - WP - 2006-07
Kotze, Christo – (Dirkie Uys) - Boland - 1977-78
Kotze, Divan – (Waterkloof) – BB – 2006
Kotze, Stephanus – (Grey Coll) – FS - 2009
Koyana, Ncedo - (Selborne Coll) – Border – 2003

Kramer, Ruan – (Grey Coll) – FS - 2013
Krause, Piet - (Sasolburg THS) - Vaal Triangle – 1991
Kriel, Jesse – (Maritzburg Coll) – KZN - 2012
†Krige,* Corné - (Paarl BH) – WP – 1993
†Kruger,* Ruben - (Grey Coll) – FS - 1987-88
Kruger, Bertus – (Die Burger) - GL - 1989
Kruger, Ernst – (Jeugland) - GL – 1974-75
Kruger, Kobus – (Middelburg THS) - Mpu - 1996
Kruger, Morné – (Monument) – GL - 2001
Kruger, Warren – (SACS) - WP - 1974-75
Kuttel, Peter – (Bishops) - WP – 1983
Kumbirai, Michael (St Alban's Coll) – BB - 2014
Kuün, Derick – (Affies, Pretoria) – BB – 2002
†Lambie, Patrick – (Michaelhouse) – Natal – 2007-08
Lanning, Andrew – (Bishops) – WP – 1989
Laubscher, Michael – (Tygerberg) – WP - 1974-75
Laufs, Gerhard – (Alberton) - GL – 1992
Le Grange, Anton – (Despatch) – EP – 1975
Le Maitre, Eugene – (Marais Viljoen) – GL - 2011
Le Marque,* Derek – (Glenwood) – Natal - 1979
†Le Roux, Ollie – (Grey Coll) – FS - 1991
Le Roux,* Chris – (Waterkloof) – BB - 1996-97
Le Roux, Kobus - (Boland Agric) - WP - 1995
Le Roux, Stephan – (Brits/Waterkloof) - BB - 1993-94
Lehmann, Helmut – (Paarl Gym) – WP - 2008
Lewis, Marlon – (Bertram) – EP - 2004-05
Lewis, Jean-Paul – (Paul Roos) – WP – 2010-11
Liebenberg, Christo – (Roodepoort) - GL – 1986
Liebenberg, Wiaan – (Drostdy THS) – Boland - 2010
Lightfoot, Wessel - (Diamantveld) - GW – 1981
Linde, Jurie – (Affies, Pretoria) – BB – 2012-13
Linde, Nico - (Grey Coll) – FS - 1990
Linde, Rob - (Maritzburg Coll) – Natal – 1997
Lindeque, Piet – (Grey Coll) – FS – 2009
Lindsay, Paul - (Maritzburg Coll) – Natal - 1975-77
†Lobberts, Hilton – (N. Orleans Paarl) - Boland - 2004
Loest, Gary – (Queen's Coll) – Border - 1985-86
†Lombard, Friedrich - (Frankfort) – NFS – 1997
Loubser, Andell – (Menlo Park) – BB - 2014
Loubser, Pieter - (Paarl BH/Bishops) – WP - 1975-76
Louw, Coenie - (Dirkie Uys) - Boland – 1995
†Louw, Hottie - (Boland Agric) - WP - 1994
Louw,* Pieter - (Paarl BH) – WP – 2003
Louw, Wilco – (Drostdy) – Boland - 2012
Luiters, Kevin – (Grey Coll) – FS - 2010

Lusaseni, Luvuyo - (Selborne Coll) – Border – 2006
Mabuza, Thabo – (Centurion) - Blue Bulls – 2011-12
Maherry, Chet - (Grey Coll) – FS - 1985-86
Mahlangu, Daniel - (Oosterland Secunda) - Mpu – 1999
Majola, Khaya – (Westville) – KZN – 2010
Malan, Remu – (Outeniqua) – SWD - 2013
Malgas, Warren – (PW Botha) – SWD – 2003
†Malherbe, Frans – (Paarl BH) – WP – 2009
†Mallett, Nick - (St Andrew's) - EP - 1974-75
Malton, Shaun – (Glenwood) – KZN – 2008
Manuel, David - (Waterkloof) - BB – 1997-98
Manuel, Rodrique - (Ben. Heigths) - WP - 1996
Marais, Abrie - (Grey Coll) - FS – 1977
Marais, Gert - (Grey Coll) – FS – 1983
Marothodi, Ompile - (Pretoria BHS) - BB -2007
Martyn, Angus – (Michaelhouse) – Natal – 1998
Maruping, Victor (Louis Botha THS) – FS - 2014
Marutlulle, Edgar - (Potch, BHS) – Leopards - 2004-05
Marx, Malcolm – (King Edward VII) – GL - 2012
Maseko, Sizo – (Ermelo) – Mpu - 2009
Mashele, Ntokozo – (Nelspruit) - Mpu – 2006
Masina, Sibi – (Standerton) – Mpu – 2007
Masuga, Tshepo – (Monument) - GL – 2006
Matthysen, John - (Sand du Plessis) - FS - 1974-75
Mbonambi, Bongi – (St Alban's) – BB – 2009
Mbovane, Tshotso – (Paul Roos) – WP - 2010
McAlister, Daniel - (Selborne Coll) – Border - 1991
McCann, Warren – (Jeppe BH) – GL – 1985
[S]McDonald, Aubrey - (Winterberg HS - Fort Beaufort) - EP – 2005
[S]McDonald, Aubrey – (Waterkloof HS) – BB - 2006
[6]McDonald, Barry - (Adelaide Gym) - NEC - 1996
[6]McDonald, Barry – (Waterkloof) – BB - 1997
McIntyre, Mark – (Grey Coll) – FS – 1989
†Meiring, FA – (Gill Coll) – NEC - 1986
Mentz, Kosie - (Paarl Gym) – WP - 1988
Mentz, MJ – (Ermelo) – Mpu - 2000
Meyer, Altus – (Vredenburg HS) – Boland - 1997
Meyer, Clinton – (Maritzburg Coll) – Natal - 1989
Meyer, Pieter - (Waterkloof) – BB - 2005
Meyer, Renier – (Wessel Maree) – NFS – 1998
Mguca, Lupumlo – (Daniel Pienaar) – EP - 2014
Mhlobiso, Luvuyo - (Daniel Pienaar) – EP - 2004
Michaels, Devan – (Kasselsvlei) - WP – 2001
Micklewood, Christopher (Westville) -

SA SCHOOLS

Natal - 2005
Miller, Greg - (Grey Coll) - EP - 1991
Mills, David - (Maritzburg Coll) - Natal - 1978
Milton, Cliff - (Affies, Pretoria) - BB - 2001-02
Mjekevu, Wandile - (King Edward VII) – GL – 2008
Mkize, Njabula — (Westville) – KZN - 2008
Mkokeli, Tembani – (Msobomvu) – Border - 2001-02
Molapo, Matjikinyane – (Ben Vorster) – Limpopo BB - 2012
Moller, JD - (Paarl BH) - WP - 2000
†**Montgomery, Percy** - (SACS) - WP - 1992-93
Moolman, Hansie – (Ermelo) – Mpu – 2005
Mostert, Juan-Pierre - (Brits) - Leopards - 2006
Mthula, Petros - (Glenwood) - Natal - 2001
Moyle-Meyberry,* Craig – (Dale) - Border– 1983-84
Mtimka, Lonwaba – (Dale Coll) – Border – 1999
Mtsi, Thabani – (Selborne Coll) – Border - 2013
†**Müller, Helgard** - (Grey Coll) - FS - 1981-82
†**Müller, Pieter** - (Grey Coll) - FS - 1987-88
†**Müller, Jorrie** - (Monument) - GL - 1999
Muller, Lourens - (Hartbeespoort) - BB - 1993
Muller, Rudi - (Potch. Gym) - Leopards - 1993
Munn, Wayne - (Maritzburg Coll) - Natal - 1994
Mxoli, Sangoni - (Durban OB) - Natal - 2003
Myburgh, Jaco - (Paarl BH) - WP - 1996
Myburgh, Pieter - (Paul Roos Gym.) - WP - 2004
Myburgh, Stefan - (Paul Roos Gym) - WP - 1996
Naudé, Dawie - (David Ross) - NEC – 1986
Nche, Ox — (Louis Botha THS) – FS – 2012-13
Neethling, Sydwhill - (Worcester Gym) - Boland - 2000
Nel, Boeta - (Bloemfontein THS) - FS - 1979-80
Nel, Johan - (Wolmaranstad) - Stellaland - 1987
Nel, Leon - (Nelspruit) - Mpu - 1982
Nel, Pieter - (Patriot, Witbank) - Mpu - 1983
Nell, Jacques - (Grey Coll) - FS - 1977
Ngoro, Mlindazwe – (St John's) – Border CD - 2006
Nieuwenhuys, Jacques - (Monument) - GL - 1984
Ngonyoza, Mtobeli - (Oscar Mpetha) - WP - 2003
Nkala, Nazo (Welkom Gym) – Griffons - 2014
Nkosi, Malungisa (Giant) - (St Stithians) - GL - 2005
Nonkontwana, Abongile – (St Alban's) – BB- 2012-13
North, Andrew - (Bishops) - WP - 1989
Nortjé, Danie - (Jan Viljoen) - GL - 1976
Notshe, Sikhumbuzo - (Wynberg BH) – WP

– 2010-11
Ntubeni, Siyabonga – (King Edward VII) – GL – 2009
Ntunja,* Kaunda - (Dale Coll) - Border - 1999-2000
Nyoka, Sinovuyo – (Dale Coll) – Border - 2008
²**O'Cuinneagain, Dion** - (Rondebosch BH) - WP - 1989-90
O'Neill, Pieter - (Despatch) - EP - 1988-89
Oberholster, Johan - (Vereeniging THS) - Valke – 1998
Oberholzer, Johan – (Jan Viljoen) – Golden Lions - 2007
Oberholzer, Lourens – (Linden) - GL – 1982
Ockafor, Kene — (Kearsney Coll) – Natal - 2007
Oelschig, Noël - (Grey Coll) - FS – 1997
Olckers, Riaan - (Affies, Pretoria) - BB – 1995
Olivier, HJ - (Kroonstad) - NFS – 1995
†**Oosthuizen, Coenie** – (Grey Coll) – FS - 2007
Oosthuizen. Josephus – (Grey Coll) – FS - 2005
Oosthuizen, JR - (Grey Coll) - FS - 1992
Oosthuizen,* Willie - (Helpmekaar) – GL – 1976
Paige, Rudy,* - (Bastion) - Golden Lions - 2007
Palmer, Shaun - (Middelburg THS) - Mpu – 1986
Papier, Embrose – (Garsfontein) — BB - 2014
Penzhorn, Adrian - (Maritzburg Coll) - Natal - 2002
Petersen, Patrick - (Florida) - WP – 1995
Petersen, Sergeal – (Grey HS) – EP – 2012
Phillips, Justin — (Waterkloof) — BB — 2012-13
†**Pienaar, Francois** - (Patriot Witbank) - Mpu - 1985
Pienaar, Andries - (Paarl BH) - WP - 1975
Pienaar,* Bernard - (Paarl Gym) - WP - 1974-75
Pienaar, Pieter - (Paarl BH) - Boland - 2001
Pienaar, Roelof – (Grey Coll) – Free State - 2007
†**Pienaar, Ruan** - (Grey Coll) - FS - 2002
Pieterse, Koen - (Grey Coll) - FS - 1980
Pietersen, Ricardo - (Groot Brak) - SWD - 1999
Plaatjies, Jeremy – (Outeniqua) – SWD - 2001
Plaatjies,* Sean - (Brandwag, Uitenhage) - EP – 1996
Pokomela, Junior – (Grey HS) – EP - 2014
†**Pollard, Handré** – (Paarl Gym) – WP – 2012
Poni, Onke - (Selborne) - Border - 2002
†**Potgieter,* Dewald** (Daniël Pienaar – Uitenhage) – EP - 2005
Pretorius, Christo - (Paarl Gym) - WP - 1996
Pretorius, Herman - (Grey Coll) - FS - 2004
Pretorius, Flippie - (De Wet Nel THS) - NFS - 1979
Pretorius, Johannes - (Hentie Cilliers) - NFS - 1984

Pretorius, Riaan - (Ben Viljoen, Groblersdal) - Mpu - 1994
Pretorius, Wynand - (Sand du Plessis) - FS - 1975-76
Prinsloo, Carlo - (Paarl Gym.) - WP – 2004
Prinsloo, Ig (Grey Coll) – FS – 2014
Prinsloo, Jamie - (John Vorster THS) - BB - 1975
Prinsloo, Michael - (Ficksburg THS) - EFS - 1977
Radebe, Colin - (Secunda HS) - Mpu – 2000
Rademan, Pieter* – (Grey Coll) – FS – 2009
†**Ralepelle, Chiliboy** - (Pretoria BHS) - BB - 2002-03
Rampeta, Refuoe (Louis Botha THS) – FS - 2013
³**Rathbone, Clyde** - (Kingsway High) - Natal - 1999
†**Rautenbach, Faan** - (Kroonstad Agric) - NFS - 1993-94
Rautenbach, George - (Paul Roos Gym) - WP - 1974-75
†**Redelinghuys, Julian** - (Monument) - GL – 2006-07
Reid, Grant - (Maritzburg Coll) - Natal - 1987
†**Reinach, Jaco** - (Grey Coll) - FS - 1979-80
Reingold, Jeremy — (Constantia) – WP - 1985
Rich, Rockey - (Kearsney Coll) - Natal - 1975
Richardson, Craig - (Despatch) - EP - 1986
Richardson, Michael - (Despatch) - EP - 1989
Richter, Jan - (Grey Coll) - FS - 1977
Richter, Toppie - (Grey Coll) - FS – 1977
Ries, Alfred - (Monument) - GL - 2006
Robberts, Steph - (Grey Coll) - FS - 2003
Robinson, Sean — (Waterkloof) – BB - 2011
Roodt, Hendrik - (Lichtenburg HS) - Leopards - 2005
†**Rose, Earl** - (Strand) - WP - 2002
Rose, Jody - (Paul Roos Gym) - WP - 2003
†**Rossouw, Chris** – (Hugenote HS) - Valke - 1987
Rossouw, Francois - (Middelburg) - Mpu – 1986
Rossouw,* Jean-Jacques - (Paarl Gym) - BB - 2006
Rossouw, Johan - (Durbanville) - WP – 1977
Roux, Daan - (Lichtenburg) - Stellaland - 1974-75
Roux, Paul - (Paul Roos Gym) - WP - 2000
Ruiters, Marlin - (Greyn Coll) - EP - 2006
Saaiman, Willem – (Menlopark) - BB - 1991
Saayman, Daniel - (Daniel Pienaar THS) - EP - 1992
Sadie, Ian - (Grey Coll) - FS - 1979
Scheepers, Eben - (Grey Coll) - FS - 1983
Schnetler, Fredrick – (Glenwood) – KZN - 2009
Schickerling, Adriaan - (Boland Agric) - Boland – 1984
Schickerling, JD — (Paarl Gym) — WP – 2012
Schoeman, Barry – (Verwoerdburg) - BB - 1975
Schoeman, Marnus - (Waterkloof) – BB – 2006-07
Schoeman,* Pierre — (Affies, Pretoria) -

SA SCHOOLS

BB – 2011-12
†Scholtz, Hendro - (Voortrekker, Bethlehem) - NFS – 1997
Schurmann, Deon - (Eldoraigne) - BB – 1984
Schwartz, Lean – (Waterkloof) – BB – 2009
Scott, Ashwin - (Parkdene) - SWD - 2003
Scriba, Hans - (Outeniqua) – SWD - 1983
Searson, Paul - (Bishops) - WP – 1989
Senekal, Dawie - (Abbot's Coll) - WP – 1988
ᴬSerfontein,* Jan – (Otto du Plessis) - EP - 1976-78
ᴬ†Serfontein, Jan – (Grey Coll) – FS – 2011
Rheeder, Edmund - (Klerksdorp) – Leopards – 2014
Siegelaar, Alastair - (Paul Roos Gym.) - WP – 2004
Sihunu, Akhona – (Dale Coll) – Border - 2012
Sitole, Martin – (Embalenthele) - Mpu - 2001-02
Sithole, Sibusiso – (Queen's Coll) - Border - 2008
Skeate, Ross - (SACS) - WP - 2000
†Skinstad, Bob - (Hilton Coll) - Natal – 1994
Skosana, Brian – (St Andrew's) – EP CD - 2009
Slabbert, Henk - (Potch. Gym) - Leopards - 1980
†Small, James – (Greenside) - GL – 1987
Small-Smith,* William – (Grey Coll) – FS - 2010
Smit,* Barend – (Middelburg THS) – Mpu - 2014
Smit, Chris - (Grey Coll) - FS - 1979
†Smit, John - (Pretoria BHS) - BB – 1996
Smith, André – (Paarl Gym.) - WP - 2005
†Smith, David – (Hamilton, Rhodesia) - Rhodesia - 1975-76
Smith, Headley – (Gey Coll) – FS
Smith, Philip – (Hangklip) – Border – 1975
Smith, Ruan – (Paarl Gym) – WP – 2008
Smith, Sarel-Marco – (Eldoraigne) – BB - 2014
Snyman, Earl – (Outeniqua) – SWD - 2007
Snyman, Johan – (Outeniqua) - SWD – 2004
Snyman, RG – (Affies, Pretoria) – BB - 2013
Snyman, Tiaan – (Affies, Pretoria) - BB - 1997-98
Sofoko, Jerry - (Pretoria THS) - BB - 2002
Sogidashe, Luvo – (Kama) - Border – 2002
Solomon, Chad – (Paul Roos Gym) – WP - 2012
Sonnekus, Pieter - (Bloemfontein THS) - FS - 1980
†Sowerby, Shaun – (Sasolburg) - Vaal Triangle - 1996
Spamer, Pieter - (Pietersburg) - Limpopo BB - 2003
Sparks, Bradley - (Selborne Coll) - Border - 1998
Squires, Brandon - (Maritzburg Coll) - Natal – 2002
Stampu, Yondela – (St Alban's) – BB – 2007
Stander,* Chris – (Oakdale Agric) – SWD - 2008
Steenkamp, Buks - (Grey Coll) - FS - 1985-86
Steenkamp, Corrie - (Vereeniging THS) - Valke - 1997
Steenkamp, Wilhelm – (Paarl BH) - WP - 2003
Steenkamp, Pieta - (Grey Coll) - FS – 1990
Steenkamp,* Ruan – (Monument) - GL - 2011
Steenkamp, Virgulle – (Excelsior Belhar) - WP - 1997
Steenkamp, Willie – (Grey Coll) - FS - 2000
†Stegmann, Deon – (Grey Coll) - FS - 2004
Stevens, Jeffrey – (Breërivier) - Boland - 1995-96
Stevens, Kees – (Grey Coll) - FS - 1983
Stevenson, Jacques - (Ermelo) - Mpu -1989
Stewart, Clayton - (Strand HS) - WP - 2006
Stewart, Errol - (Westville) - Natal - 1987
Steyn, Christo - (Bloemfontein THS) - FS – 1976
Steyn, Francois - (Affies, Pretoria) – BB - 2013
Steyn, Jacques - (Andrew Rabie) - EP - 1995
Stoop, Ockert - (John Vorster, Nigel) - Valke - 1974-75
†Stransky, Joel - (Maritzburg Coll) - Natal - 1984
†Strauss, Adriaan - (Grey Coll) - FS - 2003
Strauss, Johan - (Kearsney Coll) - Natal - 2004
ᴬStrauss, Richardt - (Grey Coll) - FS - 2003
Strydom, Emil-Jan - (Grey Coll) - FS – 1986
Swanepoel, Dries – (Grey Coll) – FS - 2011
†Swanepoel, Werner – (Grey Coll) - FS – 1991
†Swart, Justin - (Paul Roos Gym) - WP - 1991
Swart, Hakkies - (Drostdy THS) - Boland - 1988
Swart, Johan - (Paarl Gym) - WP - 1982
†Swart, Balie - (Paarl Gym) - WP - 1983
Swartbooi, Dewey - (Worcester Gym) - Boland – 2000
Swiel, Timothy (Bishops) – WP - 2011
Swiegers, Gielie - (Monument) - GL - 1984
Taute, Jaco - (Klerksdorp) - Leopards - 1989
Temple, Stephan – (Pretoria Boys' High) - BB - 1993
Theron, Danie - (Kimberley THS) - GW - 1980
Theron, Gerrie - (Rustenburg) - Leopards - 1994-95
Theron, Jannie - (Sand du Plessis) - FS - 1987
Theron, Pieter - (Grey Coll) - FS - 1975
Thomas, Gray - (Volkskool) - Leopards – 1984
Thomas, Jason – (Muir Coll) – EP – 2010
Thomson, Brandon – (Ermelo) – Mpu - 2013
†Thompson, Jeremy – (Maritzburg Coll) - Natal - 1986
Thompson, Malcolm - (Maritzburg Coll) - Natal - 1974-75
Tile, Mandilakhe - (Dale Coll) - Border – 2005
Toerien, PJ - (Garsfontein) – BB - 2013
Tom, Siyabonga – (Glenwood) – KZN - 2011
Topkin, Gareth – (Rondebosch) – WP - 2008
†Truscott, Andries – (Grey Coll) - FS – 1986
Uys, Petrus – (Monument) – GL - 2008
Van Buuren, Albertus – (Hoopstad) - NFS - 1992
Van Coller, Stephan - (Volkskool) - Leopards - 1981
†Van der Linde, CJ - (Grey Coll) - FS - 1998
Van der Linden, Lallie - (Pretoria-Noord) - BB - 1974-75
Van der Merwe, Bennie - (Paarl BH) - WP - 1979-80
Van der Merwe, Danie - (Mariental) - SWA – 1980
Van der Merwe, Duhan – (Outeniqua) – SWD – 2012-13
Van der Merwe, Gert - (DF Malan) - WP - 1976
Van der Merwe, Jaco - (Bishops) - WP - 1983
Van der Merwe, Joepie – (Grey Coll) - FS - 1979-80
Van der Merwe, Marinus – (Standerton) – Pumas - 2010
†Van der Merwe, Flip - (Grey Coll) - FS - 2003
Van der Merwe, Pikkie - (Helpmekaar) - GL - 1978
Van der Mescht, JP - (Daniel Pienaar) - EP - 1993
Van der Schyff, Jonathan - (Monument) - GL - 2001
Van der Walt, CP - (Piet Potgieter) - Far North - 1981
Van der Walt, Danie - (Ermelo) - Mpu - 1989
Van der Walt, James - (Ermelo) - Mpu – 1997
Van der Walt, Jaco – (Monument) – GL - 2011
Van der Walt, Kobus - (Affies, Pretoria) - BB - 1999
Van der Walt, Nardus – (Affies, Pretoria) – BB - 2010
Van der Walt, Nicky – (Ermelo) - Mpu - 1993
Vd Westhuizen, Chrisjan – (Menlopark) - BB – 1995
Vd Westhuizen, Dayan – (Centurion) – BB - 2012
Vd Westhuizen, Richard - (Vryburger) - GL - 1976
Vd Westhuizen, Roedolf - (Affies, Pretoria) - BB - 2000
†Vd Westhuyzen, Jaco - (Ben Viljoen) - Mpu - 1996
Van Genderen, Jan – (Monument) - GL - 1978
Van Genderen, Kolie - (Monument) - GL - 1980
Van Heerden, Frans - (Langenhoven) - BB – 1975
Van Heerden, Schalk – (Affies, Pretoria)

SA SCHOOLS

– BB - 2010
Van Heerden, Wayne - (Brandwag, Uit.) - EP - 1997-98
Van Heerden, Wickus - (Voortrekkerhoogte) - BB - 1982
†**Van Niekerk, Joe** - (King Edward VII) - GL - 1997-98
Van Niekerk, Ernst - (Paarl Gym) - WP – 1986
Van Niekerk, Kenneth – (Glenwood) – KZN - 2014
Van Niekerk, Niekie – (De Wet Nel THS) – NFS - 1985
Van Rensburg, Charl - (Queen's Coll) - Border - 1992
Van Rensburg, Robbie - (Affies, Pretoria) - BB - 1998
Van Rooyen, Leon - (Estcourt) - Natal - 1987
Van Rooyen, Nico - (Rustenburg) - Leopards – 1981
Van Rooyen, Rudi – (Affies, Pretoria) – BB – 2010
Van Vuuren, Coenraad – (Nelspruit) – Mpu – 2013
Van Vuuren, Kosie - (AHS, Kroonstad) - NFS – 1994
Van Rooyen, Marchand – (Jan Viljoen) - Golden Lions - 2007
Van Vuuren, Pieter-Willem - (Grey Coll) - FS - 2006
Van Vuuren, Rodney - (AHS, Kroonstad) - NFS - 1983
Van Westing, Carl - (Marais Viljoen THS) - GL - 1992
Van Wyk, Cobus - (Schoonspruit) - Leopards – 1976
Van Wyk, William – (Paarl Gym) – WP - 2009
Van Zyl, Jaco - (JG Meiring) - WP - 1994
Van Zyl, Willem-Petrus - (Paarl BH) - WP - 1997

Venske, Herman - (Vanderbijlpark) - GL - 1979
†**Venter, Brendan** - (Monument) - GL - 1987
[7]**Venter, André** – (Grey Coll) - FS - 1990-91
[7]**Venter, André** - (Monument) - GL - 1989
Venter, Deon - (Affies, Pretoria) - BB – 2001
Venter, Francois – (Grey Coll) – FS - 2008
Venter, Hugo - (Grey Coll) – FS – 1991
Venter, Jano – (Middelburg THS) – Mpu - 2012
Venter, Ruan – (Monument) – GL - 2010
Verhoeven, Antonius - (Charlie Hofmeyer) - Boland - 1995
†**Vermaak, Jano** - (Vereeniging THS) - Valke - 2003
Vermeulen, Gielie - (Paul Roos Gym) - WP – 1983
Vermeulen, Jacques – (Paarl Gym) – WP - 2013
Vermeulen, PJ – (Noordkaap HS) – Griquas - 2005
Vermeulen, Riaan - (Grey Coll) – FS – 2002
Vers, Keanu (Grey HS) – EP - 2014
Viljoen, EW – (Grey Coll) – FS – 2013
Viljoen, Gert - (De Wet Nel THS) - NFS - 1980
Viljoen, Harry - (Florida) - GL - 1976-77
†**Viljoen, Roelof** - (Joggie) – (Framesby) - EP - 1993-94
Visagie, Johan - (Potchefstroom THS) - Leopards - 1974
Visagie, Ronnie - (Rob Ferreira, Witrivier) - Mpu - 1983-84
†**Visser, De Villiers** - (Voortrekker, CT) - WP - 1976
†**Visser, Mornay** - (Paarl Gym) - WP - 1988
Visser, Jacques - (Paarl Gym) - WP - 1982
Volschenk, Johan - (Oakdale Agric.) - SWD - 2004
†**Von Hoesslin, David** - (Bishops) - WP - 1993
Vundla, Tshipiso – (St Alban's) – BB - 2000
Wagenstroom, Frank - (Tygerberg) -

WP - 2003
Wait, Clayton - (Pearson) - EP - 1989
Walker, Robert - (St John's) - GL - 1981
Walters, Clint – (Woodridge) - EP – 1993
Walters, Rowan – (Upington HS) – Griquas - 2005
Wannenburg, Callie – (Oakdale Agric) - SWD - 2001
†**Wannenburg, Pedrie** - (Oakdale Agric) - SWD – 1999
Watermeyer, Stefan – (Waterkloof) – BB – 2005-06
†**Watson,** * **Luke** - (Grey Coll) - EP - 2001
Weideman, Greyling - (Drostdy THS) - Boland - 1996
Weitz, Gerhard - (Grey Coll) – FS – 1974-75
Wenger, Charl – (Grey Coll) – FS – 2009
White, Bruce - (Maritzburg Coll) - Natal - 1974-75
Whitfield, Brendon – (Selborne Coll) - Border - 1994
Wiese, Cornel - (Paarl Gym) - WP League – 1988
Wiese, Kobus – (Upington) – Griquas - 2014
Wiggins, Deon – (Hugenote) - Boland - 1988
Willemse, Coenie – (Hendrik Verwoerd) - BB – 1982
Willemse, Jaco - (Paarl Gym) – WP – 2014
Willemse, Martin – (Sandveld) - NFS - 1993
Williams, Jerome – (Middelande Sec.) - EP – 2004
Williams, Percey – (Oudtshoorn) – SWD - 2011
Willis, Vainon – (Waterkloof) - BB - 2006
Wilson, Warren – (Maritzburg Coll) - Natal - 1987
Wolmarans, Jan - (Wonderboom) - BB - 1982
Zaltsman, Neil – (Northlands) - Natal – 1985
Zandberg, * **Eduan** (Outeniqua) – SWD - 2014
Zass, Leolin – (Hermanus) – Boland - 2013

1 Appeared for England at full international level 2 Appeared for Ireland at full international level. 3 Appeared for Australia at full international level. 4 Appeared for France at full international level. 5, 6 & 7 Earned SA Schools caps from two different provinces. 8 Jan (snr) and Jan (jnr) Serfontein are the first father-son combination to have represented the SA Schools team. 9 Appeared for Ireland at full international level.

Five SA Schools players gained senior national colours in other sports than rugby: Warren McCann, Jaco Reinach, Herrman Venske (athletics); and Errol Stewart and Herschelle Gibbs (cricket). Two SA School players later coached the Springbok team: Harry Viljoen and Nick Mallett

PROVINCIAL REPRESENTATION

Western Province	123	Griquas	7
Free State	107	Far North/Limpopo BB	7
Blue Bulls	95	North Eastern Cape/EP CD	6
KwaZulu-Natal	70	Stellaland	3
Golden Lions	61	Vaal Triangle	2
Eastern Province	59	WP Academy	2
Mpumalanga	48	Griquas CD	1
Border	33	WP League	1
South Western Districts	30	Border CD	1
Boland	29	Zimbabwe (Rhodesia)	1
Griffons	22	Namibia (South West Africa)	1
North West	19	SA Academy (EP)	1
Valke	16		

South African First-Class Records

MATCH RECORDS

Highest score by a team
163 Lowveld vs Transkei (163-10) 1994

Biggest win by a team
158 Golden Lions vs Limpopo BB (161-3) 2013

Most tries by a team
26 Lowveld vs Transkei (163-10) 1994

Most tries by a player
9 AA Volmink, Golden Lions vs Lim BB 2013

Most conversions by a player
20 WJ de W Ras, Free State vs EOFS 1977

Most penalty goals by a player
9 JH Kruger, N-Transvaal vs WP 1996
9 E Herbert, NFS vs Valke 1997
9 E Herbert, Griffons vs Pumas 2001
9 DJ Hougaard, Blue Bulls vs WP 2002
9 PC Montgomery, SA XV vs World XV 2006
9 ET Jantjies, Lions vs Cheetahs 2012

Most drop goals by a player
5 HE Botha, N-Transvaal vs Natal 1992
5 JH de Beer, SA vs England 1999

SEASON RECORDS

Most points by a team
1434 Free State 1996

Most tries by a team
191 Free State 1996

Most points by a player
528 NB Scholtz, WP 1988

Most tries by a player
35 P Hendriks, Transvaal 1992

CAREER RECORDS

Most points by a player
3781 HE Botha (N-Tvl, SA) 1977-1995

Most tries by a player
173 C Badenhorst (FS, SA) 1986-1999

Most conversions by a player
669 HE Botha (N-Tvl, SA) 1977-1995

Most penalties by a player
710 E Herbert (NFS, FS) 1986-2001

Most drop goals by a player
210 HE Botha (N-Tvl, SA) 1977-1995

Most appearances in a single position
159 HM Reece Edwards Fullback
221 C Badenhorst Wing
225 HL Muller Centre
205 E Herbert Flyhalf
162 E Hare Scrumhalf
154 AWA van Wyk No. 8
183 SB Geldenhuys Flank
191 WH Lessing Lock
177 CJ Botha Prop
157 T van der Walt Hooker

Most matches as a provincial captain
129 E Hare 1989-1986

Fastest to 100 games
3 years, 240 days CJ Kapp (SWD) 1997-2000

Youngest player to 100 games
24 years, 339 days P Hendriks (Transvaal) 18/03/1995

Played for seven provinces
J-P Joubert NFS, SWD, Bol, GW, BB, FS, GL
R Geldenhuys Bor, Pum, GL, Bol, Griff, FS, EP

More than 300 first-class matches *
370 V Matfield (BB, GW, Cats, Bulls, SA)
344 CS Terblanche (Bol, KZN, Sharks, SA)
343 A-H le Roux (FS, KZN, Cheetahs, SA)
338 PA van den Berg (Vaal Triangle, GW, KZN, SA)
328 JW Smit (KZN, Sharks, SA)

* for South African teams only

Blue Bulls Records

MATCH RECORDS

Biggest win	147-8	vs South Western Districts (CC) (Currie Cup Record)	Polokwane	1996
Heaviest defeat	13-57	vs Transvaal (CC)	Johannesburg	1994
Highest score	147	vs South Western Districts (147-8, CC)	Polokwane	1996
Most points conceded	64	vs Wellington Hurricanes (32-64)	New Plymouth	1997
Most tries	23	vs SWD (147-8, CC) (Currie Cup Record)	Polokwane	1996
Most points by a player	40	CP Steyn vs SWD Eagles (CC)	Pretoria	2000
Most tries by a player	7	J Olivier vs SWD (CC) (Currie Cup Record)	Polokwane	1996
Most conversions by a player	14	LR Sherrell vs SWD (CC) (Currie Cup Record)	Polokwane	1996
	15	W du Plessis vs Limpopo (VC)	Lephalele	2013
Most penalties by a player	9	JH Kruger vs Western Province (CC) (SA Record)	Pretoria	1996
	9	DJ Hougaard vs Western Province (CC) (SA Record)	Pretoria	2002
Most drop goals by a player	5	HE Botha vs Natal (CC Record)	Pretoria	1992

SEASON RECORDS

Most team points	1193	28 matches	1996
Most team points in Currie Cup	783	13 matches	1997
Most points by a player	361	CP Steyn	1999
Most Currie Cup points	268	JW Heunis (Currie Cup Record)	1989
Most team tries	142	28 matches	2004
Most tries by a player	25	PJ Spies	1975
Most Currie Cup tries by a player	18	E Botha	2004

CAREER RECORDS

Most appearances	184	SB Geldenhuys	1977-1989
Most points	2511	HE Botha (179 matches)	1977-1992
Most tries	85	DE Oosthuysen (140 matches)	1986-1994

HONOURS

ABSA Currie Cup	1946, 1956, 1968, 1969, 1971 (shared), 1973, 1974, 1975, 1977, 1978, 1979 (shared), 1980, 1981, 1987, 1988, 1989 (shared), 1991, 1998, 2002, 2003, 2004, 2006 (shared), 2009.
Lion Cup	1985, 1990, 1991
Bankfin Cup	2000
Vodacom Cup	2001, 2008, 2009

FIRST-CLASS RUGBY

Eastern Province Records

MATCH RECORDS

Biggest win	110-17	vs Welwitschias (Namibia)	2001
Biggest Currie Cup win	63-7	vs Griffons	2013
Heaviest defeat	12-80	vs Griqualand West	1998
Heaviest Currie Cup defeat	3-65	vs Northern Transvaal	1984
Highest score	110	vs Welwitschias (Namibia) (110-17)	2001
Most points conceded	80	vs Griqualand West (12-80)	1998
Most tries	16	vs Welwitschias (Namibia) (110-17)	2001
Most Currie Cup tries	11	vs Griffons (67-26)	2011
Most points by a player	38	HP le Roux vs Eastern Transvaal	1991
Most Currie Cup points by a player	29	AP Kruger vs North West	1996
Most tries by a player	5	FW Knoetze vs Stellaland	1991
	5	FG Crous vs Western Transvaal	1994
	5	N Nelson vs Valke (Currie Cup, First Div.)	2010

SEASON RECORDS

Most team points	875	27 matches	2012
Most Currie Cup points by team	611	18 matches	2012
Most points by a player	282	AP Kruger	1996
Most Currie Cup points by a player	153	B Hennessey	2002
Most team tries	103	24 matches	2003
	103	27 matches	2012
Most Currie Cup tries by team	76	18 matches	2012
Most tries by a player	14	M Van Vuuren	1994
	14	H Pedro	1998
	14	FM Juries	2003
Most Currie Cup tries by a player	13	H Pedro	1998
	13	L Watson	2012

CAREER RECORDS

Most appearances	173	BC Pinnock	1993-2002
Most points	1126	GC van Zyl	1981-1988
Most Currie Cup points	755	GC van Zyl	1981-1988
Most tries	56	NT Nelson	2006-2013

HONOURS

Vodacom Shield	2002
First Division	2010, 2012

Free State Records

MATCH RECORDS

Biggest win	132-3	vs Eastern Orange Free State	1977
Biggest Currie Cup win	106-0	vs Northern Free State	1997
Heaviest defeat	0-50	vs Eastern Province (Currie Cup)	1993
Highest score	132	vs Eastern Orange Free State (132-3)	1977
Highest Currie Cup score	113	vs South Western Districts (113-11)	1996
Most points conceded	64	vs Griqualand West (17-64)	1998
Most tries	23	vs Eastern Orange Free State (132-3)	1977
Most Currie Cup tries	17	vs South Western Districts (113-11)	1996
Most points by a player	48	WJ de W Ras vs Eastern Orange Free State	1977
Most Currie Cup points by player	46	JH de Beer vs Northern Free State	1977
Most tries by a player	6	HL Potgieter vs Eastern Orange Free State	1977
Most Currie Cup tries by a player	4	On seven occasions	
Most conversions by a player	20	WJ de W Ras vs Eastern Orange Free State (SA Record)	1977
Most Currie Cup conversions	14	JH de Beer vs Northern Free State	1977
Most penalties by a player	8	AF Fourie vs Griqualand West (Currie Cup)	1997

SEASON RECORDS

Most team points	1434	31 matches (SA Record)	1996
Most Currie Cup points by team	703	15 matches	1997
Most points by a player	460	MJ Smith	1996
Most Currie Cup points by player	230	K Tsimba	2003
Most team tries	191	31 matches (SA Record)	1996
Most Currie Cup tries by team	91	15 matches	1997
Most tries by a player	24	J-H van Wyk	1996
Most Currie Cup tries by a player	16	J-H van Wyk	1997

CAREER RECORDS

Most appearances	245	HL Müller (SA Record)	1983-1998
Most Currie Cup appearances	142	HL Müller	1983-1998
Most points	1707	WJ de W Ras	1974-1986
Most Currie Cup points	1101	WJ de W Ras	1974-1986
Most tries	136	C Badenhorst	1986-1999
Most Currie Cup tries	65	C Badenhorst	1986-1999

HONOURS

ABSA Currie Cup	1976, 2005, 2006 (shared), 2007
Lion Cup	1983
Bankfin Nite Series	1996
Vodacom Cup	2000

Golden Lions Records

MATCH RECORDS

Biggest win	116-10	vs South Eastern Transvaal	1993
Biggest Currie Cup win	99-9	vs Far North	1973
	104-14	vs SWD	2003
Heaviest defeat	10-74	vs British Lions	2009
Heaviest Currie Cup defeat	5-59	vs Free State	2006
Highest score	116	vs South Eastern Transvaal (116-10)	1993
Most points conceded	74	vs British Lions (10-74)	2009
Most tries	18	vs Madrid XV (96-6)	1979
Most Currie Cup tries	16	vs Far North (99-9)	1973
Most points by a player	40	L Barnard vs North East Cape	1979
Most CC points by a player	36	GR Bosch vs Far North	1973
Most tries by a player	6	SA Smit vs Orange Free State	1941
Most Currie Cup tries by a player	4	On seven occasions (most recently by GM Delport vs Griffons 1997)	
Most conversions by a player	16	L Barnard vs North East Cape	1979
Most Currie Cup conversions	13	GR Bosch vs Far North	1973
Most penalties by a player	7	On five occasions in Currie Cup	
Most drop goals by a player	3	GR Bosch vs Eastern Transvaal (CC, 1972) & vs WP (CC, 1974)	
	3	JC Robbie vs Eastern Province (1987)	1987
	3	AS Pretorius vs Griquas (CC)	2005

SEASON RECORDS

Most team points	1390	33 matches	1999
Most team points in Currie Cup	580	14 matches	1997
Most points by a player	414	J Engelbrecht	1999
Most CC points by a player	263	GE Lawless	1996
Most team tries	181	33 matches	1999
Most team tries in Currie Cup	74	14 matches	1997
Most tries by a player	23	P Hendriks	1994
Most Currie Cup tries by a player	14	JA van der Walt	1996

CAREER RECORDS

Most appearances	153	HP le Roux	1992-2000
Most Currie Cup appearances	108	PJJ Grobbelaar	2003-2012
Most points	896	GR Bosch	1972-1978
Most Currie Cup points	521	GR Bosch	1972-1978
Most tries	89	P Hendriks	1990-1997
Most Currie Cup tries	38	P Hendriks	1990-1997

HONOURS

ABSA Currie Cup	1922, 1939, 1950, 1952, 1971 (shared), 1972, 1993, 1994, 1999, 2011
Lion Cup	1986, 1987, 1992, 1993, 1994
Super 10	1993
Vodacom Cup	1999, 2002, 2003, 2004, 2013

Griqualand West Records

MATCH RECORDS

Biggest win	94-0	vs South Western Districts Federation	1978
Biggest win (Currie Cup)	87-14	vs Border	1998
	80-07	vs Cavaliers	2009
Heaviest defeat	3-75	vs Western Province	1985
Heaviest defeat (Currie Cup)	7-78	vs Natal Sharks	2002
Highest score	94	vs South Western Districts Federation (94-0)	1978
Highest score (Currie Cup)	87	vs Border (87-14)	1998
Most points conceded	75	vs Western Province	1985
Most points conceded (CC)	78	vs Natal Sharks (7-78)	2002
	78	vs Western Province (31-78)	2004
Most tries	18	vs South Western Districts Federation	1978
Most tries (Currie Cup)	14	vs Griffons (84-12)	2002
Most points by a player	42	IP Olivier vs Griffons	2009
Most points by a player (CC)	33	PJ Visagie vs Rhodesia	1968
Most tries by a player	7	J Jonker vs Namibia	1996
Most tries by a player (CC)	4	D Prins vs Eastern Province	1978
	4	J Nicholas vs North West	1998
	4	BA Basson vs Sharks	2010
Most conversions by a player (CC)	11	JC Wessels vs Border	1998

SEASON RECORDS

Most team points	1428	32 matches	1998
Most team points (Currie Cup)	489	14 matches	1998
Most points by a player	361	GS du Toit	1998
Most points by a player (CC)	173	IP Olivier	2010
Most team tries	210	32 matches	1998
Most team tries (Currie Cup)	86	21 matches	2003
Most tries by a player	29	BA Basson	2010
Most tries by a player (CC)	21	BA Basson	2010
Most conversions by a player	98	GS du Toit	1998
Most drop goals by a player	7	GS du Toit	1998

CAREER RECORDS

Most appearances	161	AWA van Wyk	1984-1995
Most appearances (Currie Cup)	69	D Prins	1979-1987
Most consecutive games	97	P Smith	1963-1973
Most matches as captain	66	AWA van Wyk	1989-1994
Most points	719	JMF Lubbe	1995-2001
Most points (Currie Cup)	440	CS Erasmus	1977-1985
Most tries	61	J Nicholas	1998-2002
Most tries (Currie Cup)	37	D Prins	1979-1987
Most conversions by a player	133	JMF Lubbe	1995-2001
Most penalties by a player	91	JMF Lubbe	1995-2001
Most drop goals by a player	15	PJ Visagie	1964-1974
Most drop goals by a player (CC)	8	PJ Visagie	1964-1974

HONOURS

Bankfin Currie Cup	1899, 1911, 1970
Vodacom Cup	1998, 2005, 2007, 2009

KwaZulu-Natal RU Records

MATCH RECORDS

Biggest win	90-9	vs South Eastern Transvaal (Currie Cup)	1996
Heaviest defeat	6-62	vs Northern Transvaal	1991
Heaviest Currie Cup defeat	0-52	vs Western Province	1932
Highest score	90	vs South Eastern Transvaal (Currie Cup) (90-9)	1996
Most points conceded	62	vs Northern Transvaal (6-62)	1991
Most tries	15	vs Northern Natal (78-0)	1990
Most Currie Cup tries	13	vs South Eastern Transvaal (90-9)	1996
Most points by a player	50	GK Lawless vs Otago Highlanders	1997
Most Currie Cup points by a player	38	HW Honiball vs Boland	1996
Most tries by a player	4	By 11 players - most recently by JP Pietersen vs Leopards	2005
Most conversions by a player	11	HW Honiball vs South Eastern Transvaal (Currie Cup)	1996
Most penalties by a player	8	GS du Toit vs Western Province (Currie Cup)	2001
Most drop goals by a player	4	WJ de W Ras vs Western Province (Currie Cup)	1979

SEASON RECORDS

Most team points	1348	30 matches	1996
Most Currie Cup points by team	792	15 matches	1996
Most points by a player	304	JT Stransky	1990
Most Currie Cup points by a player	205	P Lambie	2010
Most team tries	184	30 matches	1996
Most Currie Cup tries by team	112	15 matches	1996
Most tries by a player	28	JF van der Westhuizen	1993
Most Currie Cup tries by a player	13	JF van der Westhuizen	1996
	13	J Joubert	1996
	13	H Mentz	2005

CAREER RECORDS

Most appearances	165	HM Reece-Edwards	1982-1995
	165	S Atherton	1988-2000
Most points	1114	HM Reece-Edwards	1982-1995
Most tries	90	JF van der Westhuizen	1992-1998

HONOURS

ABSA Currie Cup	1990, 1992, 1995, 1996, 2008, 2010, 2013

Mpumalanga RU Records

MATCH RECORDS

Biggest win	154-0	vs Limpopo Blue Bulls	2013
Biggest Currie Cup win	111-14	vs Vodacom Eagles	2001
Heaviest defeat	10-116	vs Transvaal	1993
Heaviest Currie Cup defeat	9-90	vs Natal	1996
Highest score	154	vs Limpopo Blue Bulls (154-0)	2013
Most points conceded	116	vs Transvaal (10-116)	1993
Most tries	22	vs Limpopo Blue Bulls	2013
Most Currie Cup tries	16	vs Vodacom Eagles (111-14)	2001
Most points by a player	37	J Benade vs Lowveld	1995
	37	CP Steyn vs Vodacom Cheetahs (Currie Cup)	2003
Most tries by a player	5	D Pretorius vs South Western Districts Federation	1978
Most Currie Cup tries by a player	4	A Fourie vs North West	1998

SEASON RECORDS

Most team points	1283	28 matches	2013
Most Currie Cup points by team	758	18 matches	2013
Most points by a player	353	C Bezuidenhout	2013
Most Currie Cup points by a player	225	C Bezuidenhout	2013
Most team tries	163	28 matches	2013
Most Currie Cup tries by team	92	18 matches	2013
Most tries by a player	24	A Kettledas	2009
Most Currie Cup tries by a player	18	A Kettledas	2009

CAREER RECORDS

Most appearances	183	FJ Rossouw	1991-2000
Most points	869	JH Muller	1973-1985
Most tries	57	K Grobler	1979-1990

HONOURS

ABSA Currie Cup (First Division)   2005, 2009, 2013

Western Province Records

MATCH RECORDS

Biggest win	151-3	vs Eastern Transvaal	1995
Biggest win (Currie Cup)	107-23	vs South Western Districts	1996
Heaviest defeat	18-58	vs Pumas	2002
Heaviest defeat (Currie Cup)	13-50	vs Lions	2002
Highest score	151	vs Eastern Transvaal (151-3)	1995
Highest score (Currie Cup)	107	vs South Western Districts (107-23)	1996
Moist points conceded	62	vs Griqualand West (26-62)	1998
Moist points conceded (Currie Cup)	66	vs Transvaal	1992
Most tries	23	vs Easten Transvaal (151-3)	1995
Most tries (Currie Cup)	17	vs South Western Districts (107-23)	1996
Most points by a player	46	JT Stransky vs Eastern Transvaal	1995
Most points by a player (Currie Cup)	33	C Rossouw vs Blue Bulls	2003
Most tries by a player	6	S Berridge vs Eastern Transvaal	1995
Most tries by a player (Currie Cup)	5	J Swart vs Northern Free State	1996
	5	BJ Paulse vs Falcons	1997
	5	ER Seconds vs Griquas	2004
	5	A Bekker vs Valke	2008
Most conversions by a player	18	JT Stransky vs Eastern Transvaal	1995
Most conversions by a player (Currie Cup)	11	LJ Koen vs South Western Districts	1996
Most penalties by a player (Currie Cup)	7	LR Sherrell vs Northern Transvaal	1991
	7	NV Cilliers vs Transvaal	1993
	7	C Rossouw vs Falcons	2001
	7	AJJ van Straaten vs Cheetahs	2001
Most drop goals by a player (Currie Cup)	4	L Rodriguez vs Griqualand West	1950

SEASON RECORDS

Most team points	1357	31 matches	1997
Most team points (Currie Cup)	619	15 matches	1997
Most points by a player	391	NB Scholtz	1988
Most points by a player (Currie Cup)	227	NB Scholtz	1988
Most team tries	182	31 matches	1997
Most team tries (Currie Cup)	84	15 matches	1997
Most tries by a player	25	CJ du Plessis	1989
	25	J Swart	1997
Most tries by a player (Currie Cup)	19	CJ du Plessis	1989
Most conversions by a player	80	NB Scholtz	1989
Most penalties by a player	73	LR Sherrell	1991
Most drop goals by a player	5	NV Cilliers	1997

CAREER RECORDS

Most appearances	156	CP Strauss	1986-1995
Most points	1570	NB Scholtz (116 matches)	1982-1989
Most points (Currie Cup)	992	NB Scholtz	1982-1989
Most tries	95	NJ Burger	1982-1991
Most tries (Currie Cup)	70	BJ Paulse	1996-2007
Most conversions by a player	293	NB Scholtz	1982-1989
Most penalties by a player	256	NB Scholtz	1982-1989
Most drop goals by a player	12	NB Scholtz	1982-1989

HONOURS

Currie Cup
1889, 1892, 1894, 1895, 1897, 1898, 1904, 1906, 1908, 1914, 1920, 1925, 1927, 1929, 1932, (shared), 1934 (shared), 1936, 1947, 1954, 1959, 1964, 1966, 1979 (shared), 1982, 1983, 1984, 1985, 1986, 1989 (shared), 1997, 2000, 2001, 2012, 2014

Vodacom Cup
2012

Lion Cup
1984, 1988, 1989

Bankfin Nite Series
1997

Boland Records

MATCH RECORDS

Biggest win	96-5	vs Zimbabwe	1996
Biggest win (Currie Cup)	65-5	vs Mpumalanga	2007
Heaviest defeat	8-96	vs Western Province	1993
	3-91	vs Free State Cheetahs (Currie Cup)	2007
Highest score	96	vs Zimbabwe (96-5)	1996
Highest score (Currie Cup)	79	vs Valke (79-26)	2012
Most points conceded	96	vs Western Province (8-96)	1993
Most points conceded (Currie Cup)	91	vs Free State Cheetahs	2007
Most tries	15	vs Zimbabwe	1996
Most tries (Currie Cup)	12	vs Valke	2012
Most points by a player	34	F Horn vs South Western Districts	1996
Most points by a player (Currie Cup)	25	P O'Neill vs Northern Free State	1997
Most tries by a player (Currie Cup)	6	FP Marais vs North Eastern Districts	1952

SEASON RECORDS

Most team points	956	24 matches	2001
Most team points (Currie Cup)	566	12 matches	2011
Most points by a player	355	F Horn	1996
Most points by a player (Currie Cup)	197	EG Watts	2011
Most team tries	137	24 matches	2001
Most team tries (Currie Cup)	75	12 matches	2011
Most tries by a player	20	CS Terblanche	1997
Most tries by a player (Currie Cup)	16	RS Benjamin	2006

CAREER RECORDS

Most appearances	154	N Papier	2001-2012
Most points	524	P O'Neill	1996-2002
Most tries	82	JI Daniels	1998-2008

HONOURS

Currie Cup First Division	2001, 2003, 2004, 2006, 2011
Vodacom Shield	2004

Border Records

MATCH RECORDS

Biggest win	85-3	vs Zimbabwe	1996
Biggest Currie Cup win	56-23	vs Northern Free State	1997
Heaviest defeat	15-103	vs Leopards (Currie Cup)	2014
	9-84	vs Griqualand West (Vodacom Cup)	2011
Highest score	85	vs Zimbabwe (85-3)	1996
Most points conceded	103	vs Leopards (15-103)	2014
Most tries	15	vs Zimbabwe (85-3)	1996
Most Currie Cup tries	8	vs Northern Free State (56-23)	1997
Most points by a player	31	L Basson vs Valke	2010
Most Currie Cup points by player	31	L Basson vs Valke	2010
Most tries by a player	4	A Stephenson vs Far North	1976
	4	RG Bennett vs Zimbabwe	1996

SEASON RECORDS

Most team points	778	27 matches	1996
Most Currie Cup points by team	332	12 matches	2004
Most points by a player	299	M Flutey	1995
Most Currie Cup points by player	125	R Gerber	2004
Most team tries	101	27 matches	1996
Most Currie Cup tries by team	42	14 matches	2012
Most tries by a player	20	RG Bennett	1996
Most Currie Cup tries by a player	10	A Ndungane	2004

CAREER RECORDS

Most appearances	183	W Weyer	1988-2000
Most points	672	GK Miller	1996-2001
Most tries	44	A Alexander	

HONOURS

ABSA Currie Cup	1932 (shared), 1934 (shared)
Vodacom Shield	2003

Griffons Records

MATCH RECORDS

Biggest win	72-12	vs Stellaland	1992
Biggest win (Currie Cup)	74-6	vs Eastern Orange Free State	1988
Heaviest defeat	8-91	vs Free State	1995
Heaviest defeat (Currie Cup)	0-106	vs Free State Cheetahs	1997
Highest score	72	vs Stellaland (72-12)	1992
Highest score (Currie Cup)	74	vs Eastern Orange Free State (74-6)	1988
Moist points conceded	91	vs Free State (8-91)	1995
Moist points conceded (Currie Cup)	106	vs Free State Cheetahs (0-106)	1997
Most tries	11	vs Stellaland (72-12)	1992
Most tries (Currie Cup)	12	vs Eastern Orange Free State (74-6)	1988
Most points by a player	36	E Herbert vs Stellaland	1992
Most points by a player (Currie Cup)	36	E Herbert vs Falcons	1997
Most tries by a player (Currie Cup)	5	P Maritz vs SE Tvl	1982
Most conversions by a player	11	E Herbert vs Stellaland	1992
Most conversions by a player (Currie Cup)	10	E Herbert vs EOFS	1988
Most penalties by a player	9	E Herbert vs Pumas	2001
Most penalties by a player (Currie Cup)	9	E Herbert vs Falcons	1997
Most drop goals by a player (Currie Cup)	3	E Herbert vs FS Cheetahs	2000

SEASON RECORDS

Most team points	657	24 matches	2001
Most team points (Currie Cup)	506	15 matches	2012
Most points by a player	263	E Herbert	2001
Most points by a player (Currie Cup)	195	E Herbert	1988
Most team tries	86	21 matches	2012
Most team tries (Currie Cup)	68	15 matches	2012
Most tries by a player	14	O Damons	2004
Most tries by a player (Currie Cup)	8	GA Passens	1999
	8	MP Goosen	2005
	8	CS Afrika	2008
	8	J Nel	2013
Most conversions by a player	43	E Herbert	2001
Most penalties by a player	56	E Herbert	2001
Most drop goals by a player	10	E Herbert	1988

CAREER RECORDS

Most appearances	205	E Herbert	1986-2001
Most consecutive games	102	A Gerber	1979-1985
Most matches as captain	95	JJ Jerling	1989-1997
Most points	2608	E Herbert	1986-2001
Most tries	46	NPJ Steyn	2008-2014
Most conversions by a player	331	E Herbert	1986-2001
Most penalties by a player	544	E Herbert	1986-2001
Most drop goals by a player	66	E Herbert	1986-2001

HONOURS

Paul Roos Trophy	1970
Vodacom Shield	2001
Bankfin Cup	2008, 2014

Leopards Records

MATCH RECORDS

Biggest win	80-3	vs Niteroi, Brasilia	1993
Biggest win (Currie Cup)	103-9	vs Eastern Orange Free State	1988
Heaviest defeat	12-98	vs Transvaal	1996
Heaviest defeat (Currie Cup)	21-92	vs Blue Bulls	2011
Highest score	83	vs Uruguay (83-10)	1994
Highest score (Currie Cup)	103	vs Eastern Orange Free State (103-9)	1988
Moist points conceded	98	vs Transvaal (12-98)	1996
Moist points conceded (Currie Cup)	92	vs Blue Bulls (21-92)	2011
Most tries (Currie Cup)	18	vs Eastern Orange Free State	1988
Most points by a player	41	D Basson vs Namibia	1994
Most points by a player (Currie Cup)	31	T Marais vs Eastern Orange Free State	1988
	31	IP Olivier vs Pumas	2005
Most tries by a player	5	T Van Niekerk vs Eastern Transvaal	1965
Most tries by a player (Currie Cup)	5	A Kettledas vs SWD Eagles	2012

SEASON RECORDS

Most points by a player	368	D Basson	1994
Most points by a player (Currie Cup)	204	C Durand	2008
Most tries by a player	25	CR Lloyd	2006
Most tries by a player (Currie Cup)	19	CR Lloyd	2006

CAREER RECORDS

Most appearances	191	WH (Werner) Lessing	1998-2007
Most matches as captain	129	E Hare	1989-1996
Most points	1183	D Basson	1991-1998
Most points (Currie Cup)	703	T Marais	1980-1988
Most tries	48	CR (Colin) Lloyd	2004-2011

SWD Records

MATCH RECORDS

Biggest win	102-0	vs Transkei	1995
Biggest win (Currie Cup)	102-0	vs Griffons	1999
Heaviest defeat	0-97	vs British Lions	1974
Heaviest defeat (Currie Cup)	8-147	vs Northern Transvaal	1996
Highest score	105	vs Transkei (105-8)	1994
Highest score (Currie Cup)	102	vs Griffons (102-0)	1999
Most points conceded	97	vs British Lions (0-97)	1974
Most points conceded (Currie Cup)	147	vs Northern Transvaal (8-147)	1996
Most tries	16	vs Transkei (102-0)	1995
Most tries (Currie Cup)	16	vs Griffons (102-0)	1999
Most points by a player	28	AJJ Van Straaten	1997
Most points by a player (Currie Cup)	29	CR Van As vs Leopards	2002
Most tries by a player	4	G Cilliers vs North Eastern Districts	1965
	4	F Amsterdam vs Northern Natal	1992
Most tries by a player (Currie Cup)	4	MG Joubert vs Valke	2009

SEASON RECORDS

Most team points	943	29 matches	1998
Most team points (Currie Cup)	493	15 matches	2013
Most points by a player	252	AJJ Van Straaten	1997
Most points by a player (Currie Cup)	173	CR Van As	2002
Most team tries	132	29 matches	1998
Most team tries (Currie Cup)	79	21 matches	2003
Most tries by a player	20	AG Bock	2013
Most tries by a player (Currie Cup)	17	AG Bock	2013

CAREER RECORDS

Most appearances	191	C Botha	1993-2011
Most points	638	CR Van As	2000-2004
Most points (Currie Cup)	480	CR Van As	2000-2004
Most tries	53	DB Coeries	1998-2005
Most conversions by a player	134	CR Van As	2000-2004
Most penalties by a player	105	CR Van As	2000-2004

HONOURS

Bankfin Cup	2002
ABSA Cup (First Division)	2007

Valke Records

MATCH RECORDS

Biggest win	109-0	vs Vagabonds	1998
Biggest Currie Cup win	65-15	vs North West	1999
Heaviest defeat	3-151	vs Western Province	1995
Heaviest Currie Cup defeat	14-95	vs Pumas	2009
Highest score	109	vs Vagabonds (109-0)	1998
Most points conceded	151	vs Western Province (3-151)	1995
Most points conceded (CC)	95	vs Pumas (14-95)	2009
Most tries	17	vs Vagabonds	1998
Most Currie Cup tries	11	vs Griquas	2001
	11	vs Griffons	2003
Most points by a player	33	A de Kock vs Eastern Orange Free State	1994
	33	A de Kock vs Namibia	1995
Most Currie Cup points by a player	27	G Peens vs Border	1997
Most tries by a player	4	C van Zyl vs North West Cape	1980
	4	P Hiten vs Curda	1986
	4	D Nortje vs Eastern Orange Free State	1989
	4	W Geyer vs Northern Free State	1998
	4	W Geyer vs Blue Bulls	1998
	4	J Houtsamer vs Mighty Elephants	2001
	4	LD Lubbe vs Griffons	2003
	4	G Mbangeni vs Leopards	2004
	4	JP Mostert vs Limpopo	2013

SEASON RECORDS

Most team points	884	35 matches	1998
Most Currie Cup points by team	393	14 matches	2012
Most points by a player	277	J Viljoen	1996
Most Currie Cup points by a player	158	Louis Strydom	2005
Most team tries	118	35 matches	1998
Most Currie Cup tries by team	56	14 matches	2012
Most tries by a player	22	W Geyer	1998
Most Currie Cup tries by a player	10	LD Lubbe	1989
	10	E Botha	2001

CAREER RECORDS

Most appearances	158	E Rossouw	1997-2004
Most points	732	H Labuschagne	
Most tries	55	L Lubbe	

HONOURS

Vodacom Cup	2006

Marnitz Boshoff was the leading point-scorer in South African first-class rugby in 2014, with 281 points.

Sharks forever the bridesmaids

Player drain set to dilute SA challenge even further

By John Bishop, Sunday Tribune

THE South African franchises, in their own special way, made a pig's ear of their 2014 Vodacom Super Rugby campaigns and even the Cell C Sharks, in advancing to the semi-finals, fell frustratingly short of their target yet again.

The southern hemisphere franchise tournament stretched interminably over seven months but did produce a rousing final and deserved champions in the New South Wales Waratahs, the most dedicated attacking team amongst the 15 competing sides.

The Sharks set the pace for most of the way and were never challenged as conference leaders as the other four South African sides found themselves unable to move up from the bottom half of the log.

But, in both failing to convert a strong start into a home semi-final and in playing rigid, inhibited rugby, the Sharks were again denied. It was their eighth semi-final since 1996 – the most by any South African province or franchise – to go with their four finals. Forever the bridesmaids.

The Absa Currie Cup champions, with depth in every area and a World Cup-winning coach in Jake White, were quickly out of the blocks. But the loss to injury of Springbok flyhalf Pat Lambie in the fifth game forced a shift in emphasis with the prodigious boot of Frans Steyn pivotal to a more conservative approach.

The statistics tell the story. They picked up try-scoring bonus points in two of their first three outings (when Lambie was still pulling the strings) but then failed to score four tries in any of their remaining 13 league games.

The Sharks were highly effective in defence, conceding the fewest number of tries (22), but scored just 29 of their own with the Vodacom Bulls (28) the only team with a worse attacking record. The Sharks' heroes were among the younger players: opportunistic scrumhalf Cobus Reinach (son of 1986 Springbok, the late Jaco Reinach), the perservering Marcell Coetzee and lock Stephan Lewies, whose toiling efforts would be rewarded with an unexpected Test debut during the June international break.

The Sharks' conservative, territory-driven game was both the strength and weakness of the team. Their highs came when their powerful pack played with intensity and there

Cobus Reinach clears the ball during the Sharks' win over the Crusaders in Christchurch.

was purpose to their tactical kicking. But when the forwards failed to fire, and their kick-chase game lacked accuracy, there was no Plan B and they suffered ugly defeats.

What was galling was that they beat both finalists: first the Waratahs (32-10) in Durban and then, with 14 men, the Crusaders (30-25) in Christchurch. Three wins on their Antipodean tour saw the Sharks on a seemingly inevitable high road to the final. But it changed almost overnight and, to paraphrase White, they found themselves on the low road after their home loss to a young, depleted DHL Stormers side and then the "dirt road" when they were beaten by the 14th-placed Toyota Cheetahs.

These two unexpected losses to struggling South African opponents in their last three league games, and the paucity of try-scoring bonus points, left the Sharks one log point adrift of nailing down a home semi-final. Instead they travelled and were mugged 38-6 by the vengeful Crusaders in the Christchurch play-off.

It was a winter of discontent for the ninth-placed Bulls and coach Frans Ludeke blamed it all on erratic form.

"Consistency is what cost us this season and the games we should have won, we lost," he said.

Ironically, in terms of results anyway, consistency was not a problem. The Bulls were unbeaten at home but their camouflage away strip proved so effective that they disappeared on foreign fields and failed to win a single game on the road.

For much of their campaign they appeared to be marking time, notching up encouraging victories in front of their home support at Loftus, only to take a step backwards with defeat away from home.

One of their better displays came in a bonus-point win (44-23) over the Brumbies, while they also beat all the other South African franchises at Loftus. But away from home they kept making the same mistakes, with poor execution costing them possession. The closing weeks were particularly painful as they lost to the Lions (32-21) and the Stormers

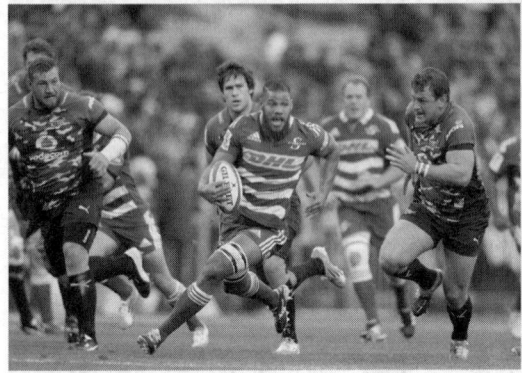

Nizaam Carr's form for the Stormers and Western Province was rewarded when he won a Test cap on tour with the Springboks in November.

(16-0) to drop out of play-off contention.

The Bulls have lost a host of players to foreign clubs while injuries to loose forwards Arno Botha, Pierre Spies and Deon Stegmann were particularly damaging. Their selection also came under fire with coach Ludeke persisting with a back-row trio of big ball-carriers that failed to gel as a unit, while his regular front row was the most heavily penalised in the competition.

Itinerant flyhalf Jacques-Louis Potgieter proved effective at pivot but there were grumblings that the 20-year-old Handré Pollard, who would be established as the Springboks' starting No. 10 by the start of the Castle Rugby Championship, would have added a fresh dimension to the Bulls' back play.

The one success story was the return of evergreen lock Victor Matfield from retirement and he made an immediate impression while young Springbok centre Jan Serfontein was the pick of their backline players.

The Stormers were ravaged by injury with all five of their first-choice tight forwards missing most of the campaign, with the result that they never enjoyed any continuity or cohesion. A poor start and a dismal overseas tour ended their play-off aspirations as early as the seventh round.

Coach Allister Coetzee said their horrific run of injuries was a major factor but also believed the last-minute loss to the Crusaders in Christchurch was decisive.

"I think a win in the Crusaders game could have turned our season around," he lamented.

The mid-year signing of Gert Smal as director of rugby offered a change of direction, and the Stormers finally found some attacking spark but it was far too late and they finished 11th on the log.

Still, they had their moments late in the season, beating the log-leading Sharks 21-19 with a young, watered-down team in Durban and whitewashing the Bulls 16-0 in their next game at Newlands. This resurgence would culminate in Western Province winning the Currie Cup only a few months later.

Emerging centre Damian de Allende, hit by injury, played only half the season, and in a losing team, but that was enough to win a Test cap in June.

Their back row remained effective with Nizaam Carr, who would tour with the Springboks at year-end, and the overplayed Duane Vermeulen battling valiantly, while there was an encouraging return to the big-time for fit-again veteran Schalk Burger.

The energetic MTN Lions, after spending 2013 in the rugby wilderness and short of high-profile players, did emerge from the season with some credit even if they finished 12th on the log.

They responded positively to the exhortations of captain Warren Whiteley, a rangy number eight in the Gary Teichmann mould who would become a Test Springbok during the Rugby Championship, and coach Johan Ackermann and surprised many by winning a record (for them) seven games. The downing of the Stormers and Bulls was particularly satisfying and they ended their season on the highest possible note by running in eight tries and thumping the Cheetahs 60-25.

They were less impressive on the road and a sequence of six successive defeats cost them any chance of challenging for a play-off spot. Ackermann paid tribute to the players' determination and this never-say-die attitude was a feature of their rugby throughout the campaign.

"There were mistakes but if you ask players to play with commitment, passion and pride, and they put in the work, then you can't ask for more," he said.

The Lions played high-tempo, ambitious rugby, their largely unknown front-rowers scrummed superbly and flyhalf Marnitz Boshoff enjoyed an excellent campaign, his efforts enough for a Springbok Test cap as a substitute against Scotland.

The enigmatic Cheetahs, who had many bright moments on attack but no defence, fell away badly after their 2013 play-off success. They leaked an embarrassing 527 points in the season (an average of 33 per match) and finished 14th.

Their porous defence resulted in them losing games they should have won. They scored 37 tries but conceded a whopping 58 and swung from the highs of a bonus-point victory over the Stormers (35-22) and upsetting both the Brumbies and Sharks to a crushing 35-point loss to the Lions.

They had the individual talents – seven Cheetahs were in the Test match squad against Scotland – but the team's cohesion and organisation on defence were lacking while the talented but injury-hit Johan Goosen battled with consistent form at flyhalf.

Springbok fullback Willie le Roux was superb on attack while wing Cornal Hendricks and lock Lood de Jager were good enough in a losing cause to earn Test selection.

Naka Drotské will again be in charge of the team in 2015 but he was sent to the UK during the Currie Cup season to study new coaching techniques. Finding an effective defensive structure will most likely be at the top of his agenda.

It was, generally, a forgettable Super Rugby season for South Africans. The Lions emerged with a satisfied smile but there was little joy for the Bulls, Stormers and Cheetahs. The Sharks certainly deserve credit for reaching the semi-finals, but in coming up just short after months of promise and expectation, there was that familiar hollow feeling of what might, could or should have been.

The end of the Super Rugby season brought an exodus of South Africans to overseas clubs and the increasing player drain of both experienced campaigners and emerging talent is being felt by all the franchises. Bringing the Super Rugby trophy back to South Africa is becoming more difficult with each passing year.

❮ DID YOU KNOW? ❯

'Mr Rugby', Danie Craven, was a jack-of-all-trades. He played 16 Tests, of which 12 were at scrumhalf, two at flyhalf and one at centre. He also played one Test - his 10th - in the forwards, at No 8, against Australia in Sydney.

VODACOM SUPER RUGBY

LOG

Team	P	W	L	D	PF	PA	PD	TF	TA	B7	B4	BP	Pts
Waratahs	16	12	4	0	481	272	209	55	24	1	9	10	58
Crusaders	16	11	5	0	445	322	123	41	36	3	4	7	51
SHARKS	16	11	5	0	406	293	113	29	22	4	2	6	50
Brumbies	16	10	6	0	412	378	34	53	39	1	4	5	45
Chiefs	16	8	6	2	384	378	6	48	39	3	5	8	44
Highlanders	16	8	8	0	401	442	-41	39	52	5	5	10	42
Hurricanes	16	8	8	0	439	374	65	49	36	3	6	9	41
Force	16	9	7	0	343	393	-50	37	40	1	3	4	40
BULLS	16	7	8	1	365	335	30	28	29	5	3	8	38
Blues	16	7	9	0	419	395	24	46	43	3	6	9	37
STORMERS	16	7	9	0	290	326	-36	30	29	2	2	4	32
LIONS	16	7	9	0	367	413	-46	31	46	1	2	3	31
Reds	16	5	11	0	374	493	-119	42	52	4	4	8	28
CHEETAHS	16	4	11	1	372	527	-155	38	59	3	3	6	24
Rebels	16	4	12	0	303	460	-157	29	49	4	1	5	21

Note: B7 = Losing Bonus, B4 = Try Bonus

LEADING SCORERS

60 POINTS OR MORE

	TEAM	T	C	P	DG	Pts
Bernard Foley	Waratahs	6	45	44	0	252
Beauden Barrett	Hurricanes	5	32	40	0	209
Colin Slade	Crusaders	4	20	46	0	198
Marnitz Boshoff	Lions	0	18	43	8	189
Lima Sopoaga	Highlanders	2	27	38	0	178
Francois Steyn	Sharks	0	16	43	1	164
Jason Woodward	Rebels	3	15	33	0	144
Jacques-Louis Potgieter	Bulls	1	14	34	3	144
Johan Goosen	Cheetahs	1	21	30	2	143
Simon Hickey	Blues	0	20	28	0	124
Quade Cooper	Reds	2	22	21	1	120
Sias Ebersohn	Force	1	17	25	1	117
Nic White	Brumbies	2	17	22	0	110
Aaron Cruden	Chiefs	1	21	19	0	104
Gareth Anscombe	Chiefs	3	9	17	0	84
Handre Pollard	Bulls	1	10	16	1	76
Christian Lealiifano	Brumbies	0	12	15	0	69
Mike Harris	Reds	3	11	10	0	67
Israel Folau	Waratahs	12	0	0	0	60
Nemani Nadolo	Crusaders	12	0	0	0	60

VODACOM SUPER RUGBY

6 TRIES OR MORE

12	Israel Folau	Waratahs	7	Malakai Fekitoa	Highlanders
12	Nemani Nadolo	Crusaders	7	Nick Cummins	Force
8	Kurtley Beale	Waratahs	7	Tim Nanai-Williams	Chiefs
8	Jesse Mogg	Brumbies	6	Bernard Foley	Waratahs
8	George Moala	Blues	6	Cobus Reinach	Sharks
8	Robbie Coleman	Brumbies	6	Cornal Hendricks	Cheetahs
7	Matt Toomua	Brumbies	6	Lionel Mapoe	Lions
7	Johnny McNicholl	Crusaders	6	Matthew Hodgson	Force
7	Julian Savea	Hurricanes	6	Beauden Barrett	Hurricanes

PLAY-OFF RESULTS

PLAY-OFF: Brumbies 32 Chiefs 30 (halftime 22-10)
GIO Stadium, Canberra, Saturday 19 July. Referee: Craig Joubert (SA)
Brumbies: *Tries: Butler, Mogg, White, Coleman. Conversions: Lealiifano (3). Penalties: Lealiifano (2).*
Chiefs: *Tries: Aki, Anscombe, Kerr-Barlow, Nanai-Williams. Conversions: Cruden (2). Penalties: Cruden (2).*

PLAY-OFF: Sharks 31 Highlanders 27 (halftime 13-17)
Growth-Point Kings Park, Durban, Saturday 19 July. Referee: Steve R Walsh (Aus)
Sharks: *Tries: B du Plessis, Coetzee, Chavhanga. Conversions: Steyn (2). Penalties: Steyn (4).*
Highlanders: *Tries: Hames, Fekitoa, Burleigh. Conversions: Sopoaga (3). Penalties: Sopoaga (2).*

SEMI-FINAL: Crusaders 38 Sharks 6 (halftime 16-6)
AMI Stadium, Christchurch, Saturday 26 July. Referee: Glen Jackson (NZ)
Crusaders: *Tries: McNicholl, Read, Todd, Nadolo, Heinz. Conversions: Carter (2). Penalties: Carter (3).*
Sharks: *Penalties: Lambie (2).*

SEMI-FINAL: Waratahs 26 Brumbies 8 (halftime 11-8)
Allianz Stadium, Sydney, Saturday 26 July. Referee: Jaco Peyper (SA)
Waratahs: *Tries: Alofa, Foley, Beale. Conversion: Foley. Penalties: Foley (3).*
Brumbies: *Try: Speight. Penalty: Lealiifano.*

FINAL: Waratahs 33 Crusaders 32 (halftime 20-13)
ANZ Stadium, Sydney, Saturday 2 August. Referee: Craig Joubert (SA)
Waratahs: *Tries: Ashley-Cooper (2). Conversion: Foley. Penalties: Foley (7).*
Israel Folau, Alofa Alofa *(Peter Betham, 75)*, Adam Ashley-Cooper, Kurtley Beale, Rob Horne, Bernard Foley, Nick Phipps *(Brendan McKibbin, 77)*, Wycliff Palu *(Will Skelton, 20-26)*, Michael Hooper *(capt.)*, Stephen Hoiles *(Mitch Chapman, 65)*, Kane Douglas, Jacques Potgieter *(Will Skelton, 50)*, Sekope Kepu *(Paddy Ryan, 66)*, Tatafu Polota-Nau *(Tola Latu, 43)*, Benn Robinson.
UNUSED SUBS: *Jeremy Tilse, Pat McCutcheon*
Crusaders: *Tries: Todd, Nadolo. Conversions: Carter, Slade. Penalties: Slade (6).*
Israel Dagg, Kieron Fonotia *(Johnny McNicholl, 65)*, Ryan Crotty, Dan Carter *(Tom Taylor, 31)*, Nemani Nadolo, Colin Slade, Andy Ellis *(Willi Heinz, 73)*, Kieran Read *(capt.)*, Matt Todd, Richie McCaw, Sam Whitelock, Dominic Bird *(Jimmy Tupou, 65)*, Owen Franks, Corey Flynn *(Ben Funnell, 65)*, Wyatt Crockett *(Joe Moody, 57 / Nepo Laulala, 65)*. UNUSED SUB: *Jordan Taufua*.

VODACOM SUPER RUGBY

POSITIONS LOG

	1996	1997	1998	1999	2000	2001	2002	2003	2004	2005
Crusaders	12th	6th	**2nd**	4th	2nd	10th	**1st**	2nd	2nd	**1st**
ACT Brumbies	5th	2nd	10th	5th	1st	**1st**	3rd	4th	**1st**	5th
NSW Waratahs	7th	9th	6th	8th	9th	8th	2nd	5th	8th	2nd
Blues	**2nd**	**1st**	1st	9th	6th	11th	6th	**1st**	5th	7th
Natal/Sharks	4th	4th	3rd	7th	12th	2nd	10th	11th	7th	12th
Northern Transvaal/Bulls	3rd	8th	11th	12th	11th	12th	12th	6th	6th	3rd
Chiefs	6th	11th	7th	6th	10th	6th	8th	10th	4th	6th
Western Province/Stormers	11th	-	9th	2nd	5th	7th	7th	9th	3rd	9th
Hurricanes	9th	3rd	8th	10th	8th	9th	9th	3rd	11th	4th
Queensland Reds	1st	10th	5th	1st	7th	4th	5th	8th	10th	10th
Highlanders	8th	12th	4th	3rd	3rd	5th	4th	7th	9th	8th
Free State/Cheetahs	-	7th	-	-	-	-	-	-	-	-
Western Force	-	-	-	-	-	-	-	-	-	-
Cats/Lions	10th	5th	12th	11th	4th	3rd	11th	12th	12th	11th
Melbourne Rebels	-	-	-	-	-	-	-	-	-	-
Southern Kings	-	-	-	-	-	-	-	-	-	-

Bold type indicates champion

WIN PERCENTAGE LOG

Team	P	W	L	D	PF	PA
Crusaders	268	180	82	6	7920	5817
ACT Brumbies	255	149	101	5	6840	5680
Blues	250	139	107	4	6852	6002
NSW Waratahs	249	134	111	4	6354	5482
Sharks	254	131	116	7	6311	6005
Stormers	234	120	109	5	5303	5336
Chiefs	247	125	115	7	6329	6265
Hurricanes	245	123	117	5	6313	6221
Bulls	250	123	119	8	6497	6631
Queensland Reds	246	120	121	5	5658	6088
Highlanders	245	109	134	2	5840	6299
Western Force	129	45	77	7	2581	3197
Cheetahs	141	46	92	3	3215	3993
Lions	225	59	161	5	4942	6948
Melbourne Rebels	64	16	48	0	1328	2060
Southern Kings	16	3	12	1	298	564
	3318	1622	1622	74	82581	82588

❰ DID YOU KNOW? ❱

Flyhalf Hansie Brewis holds the South African record of kicking drop goals in four successive Tests, namely the final match of the 1949 All Black series and thereafter against Scotland, Ireland and Wales on the 1951-2 tour.

VODACOM SUPER RUGBY

POSITIONS LOG

2006	2007	2008	2009	2010	2011	2012	2013	2014	Play-offs	Semi-finals	Finals	Total	Champions	Avg. Pos
1st	3rd	1st	4th	4th	3rd	4th	4th	2nd	3	16	11	30	7	3,57
6th	5th	9th	7th	6th	13th	7th	3rd	4th	2	8	5	15	2	5,10
3rd	13th	2nd	5th	3rd	5th	11th	9th	1st	1	6	3	10	1	6,15
8th	4th	6th	9th	7th	4th	12th	10th	10th	1	6	4	11	3	6,26
5th	1st	3rd	6th	9th	6th	6th	8th	3rd	3	8	4	15	-	6,26
4th	2nd	10th	1st	1st	7th	5th	2nd	9th	2	7	3	12	3	6,36
7th	6th	7th	2nd	11th	10th	2nd	1st	5th	1	4	3	8	2	6,57
11th	10th	5th	10th	2nd	2nd	1st	7th	11th	-	5	1	6	-	6,72
2nd	8th	4th	3rd	8th	9th	8th	11th	7th	-	6	1	7	-	7,00
12th	14th	12th	13th	5th	1st	3rd	5th	13th	2	4	1	7	1	7,26
9th	9th	11th	11th	12th	8th	9th	14th	6th	1	4	1	6	-	8,00
10th	11th	13th	14th	10th	11th	10th	6th	14th	1	-	-	1	-	10,60
14th	7th	8th	8th	13th	12th	14th	13th	8th	-	-	-	0	-	10,77
13th	12th	14th	12th	14th	14th	15th	-	12th	-	2	-	2	-	10,94
-	-	-	-	15th	13th	12th	15th	-	-	-	-	0	-	13,75
-	-	-	-	-	-	15th	-	-	-	-	-	0	-	15,00

WIN PERCENTAGE LOG

PD	TF	TA	B7	B4	Pts	Win rate
2103	862	617	31	92	751	67.16%
1160	804	583	40	90	670	58.43%
850	817	646	46	96	666	55.60%
872	714	574	49	80	640	53.82%
306	685	639	51	68	617	51.57%
-33	542	552	43	47	555	51.28%
64	707	689	49	72	593	50.61%
92	719	677	34	79	609	50.20%
-134	679	747	37	65	560	49.20%
-430	610	670	47	58	559	48.78%
-459	621	719	51	51	553	44.49%
-616	264	354	30	17	241	34.88%
-778	340	450	32	23	233	32.62%
-2006	511	811	48	44	358	26.22%
-732	140	246	16	10	85	25.00%
-266	27	69	0	2	2	18.75%
-7	9042	9043	604	894	7692	

❰ DID YOU KNOW? ❱

Frik du Preez and Jan Ellis, with 38 Tests apiece, jointly held the record for the most Springbok Test appearances for 21 years until James Small won his 39th cap on 19 July 1997 against the All Blacks at Ellis Park.

Records

CHAMPIONS

Year	Champion	Year	Champion	Year	Champion
1996	Blues	2003	Blues	2010	Bulls
1997	Blues	2004	Brumbies	2011	Reds
1998	Crusaders	2005	Crusaders	2012	Chiefs
1999	Crusaders	2006	Crusaders	2013	Chiefs
2000	Crusaders	2007	Bulls	2014	Waratahs
2001	Brumbies	2008	Crusaders		
2002	Crusaders	2009	Bulls		

RESULTS OF FINALS

Year	Winner	Score	Loser	Score	Venue
1996	Blues	45	Sharks	21	Auckland
1997	Blues	23	Brumbies	7	Auckland
1998	Blues	13	Crusaders	20	Auckland
1999	Highlanders	19	Crusaders	24	Dunedin
2000	Brumbies	19	Crusaders	20	Canberra
2001	Brumbies	36	Sharks	6	Canberra
2002	Crusaders	31	Brumbies	13	Christchurch
2003	Blues	21	Crusaders	17	Auckland
2004	Brumbies	47	Crusaders	38	Canberra
2005	Crusaders	35	Waratahs	25	Christchurch
2006	Crusaders	19	Hurricanes	12	Christchurch
2007	Sharks	19	Bulls	20	Durban
2008	Crusaders	20	Waratahs	12	Christchurch
2009	Bulls	61	Chiefs	17	Pretoria
2010	Bulls	25	Stormers	17	Soweto
2011	Reds	18	Crusaders	13	Brisbane
2012	Chiefs	37	Sharks	6	Hamilton
2013	Chiefs	27	Brumbies	33	Hamilton
2014	Waratahs	33	Crusaders	32	Sydney

MATCH RECORDS

Most points scored by a team - ALL

| 96-19 | Crusaders vs New South Wales | Christchurch | 2002 |

Most points scored by a South African team

| 92-3 | Bulls vs Queensland | Pretoria | 2007 |

Biggest winning margin by a team - ALL

| 89 | Bulls vs Queensland (92-3) | Pretoria | 2007 |

Most tries scored by a team - ALL

| 14 | Crusaders vs New South Wales (96-19) | Christchurch | 2002 |

Most tries scored by a South African team

| 13 | Bulls vs Queensland (92-3) | Pretoria | 2007 |

VODACOM SUPER RUGBY

Most points scored by a player - ALL

50	GE Lawless (4t, 9c, 4p) Natal vs Highlanders	1997

Most tries scored by a player - ALL

4	JWC Roff, ACT Brumbies vs Natal	1996
4	GE Lawless, Natal vs Highlanders	1997
4	CS Terblanche, Sharks vs Chiefs	1998
4	J Vidiri, Blues vs Bulls	2000
4	DC Howlett, Blues vs Hurricanes	2002
4	M Muliaina, Blues vs Bulls	2002
4	CS Ralph, Crusaders vs NSW Waratahs	2002
4	SW Sivivatu, Chiefs vs Blues	2009
4	DA Mitchell, Waratahs vs Lions	2010
4	SD Maitland, Crusaders vs Brumbies	2011
4	AT Tikoroituma, Chiefs vs Blues	2012

Most conversions by a player - ALL

13	AP Mehrtens, Crusaders vs Waratahs	2002

Most conversions by a South African player

11	DJ Hougaard, Vodacom Bulls vs Queensland Reds	2007

Most penalties by a player - ALL

9	ET Jantjies, Lions vs Cheetahs	2012

Most drop drop goals by a player - ALL

4	M Steyn, Bulls vs Crusaders	2009

SEASON RECORDS

Most points scored by a player - ALL

		Team	Season	T	C	P	DG
263	M Steyn	Bulls	2010	5	38	51	3
252	BT Foley	NSW	2014	6	45	46	0
251	AW Cruden	Chiefs	2012	3	43	50	0
240	M Steyn	Bulls	2013	2	32	57	1
228	QS Cooper	Reds	2011	5	31	43	4
221	DW Carter	Crusaders	2006	5	38	37	3
216	M Steyn	Bulls	2011	0	33	46	4
209	BJ Barrett	Hurricanes	2014	5	32	40	0
206	AP Mehrtens	Crusaders	1998	5	23	41	4
201	DW Carter	Crusaders	2004	6	27	39	0

Most tries by a player - ALL

15	JWC Roff	ACT Brumbies	1997
15	RL Gear	Crusaders	2005
13	JT Small	Natal	1996
13	AM Walker	ACT Brumbies	2000
12	AJ Joubert	Natal	1996
12	JF Umaga	Hurricanes	1997
12	RQ Randle	Chiefs	2002
12	DC Howlett	Blues	2003
12	JP Pietersen	Sharks	2007
12	I Folau	NSW	2014
12	N Nadolo	Crusaders	2014

VODACOM SUPER RUGBY

Most conversions by a player - ALL

51	JWC Roff	ACT Brumbies	2004
45	BT Foley	NSW	2014
43	AW Cruden	Chiefs	2012
39	SA Mortlock	ACT Brumbies	2000
38	DW Carter	Crusaders	2006
38	M Steyn	Bulls	2010
37	DW Carter	Crusaders	2005
36	SR Donald	Crusaders	2009
35	JWC Roff	ACT Brumbies	2003

Most penalties by a player - ALL

58	CP Lealiifano	Brumbies	2013
57	M Steyn	Bulls	2013
51	M Steyn	Bulls	2010
50	AW Cruden	Chiefs	2012
47	JD O'Connor	Western Force	2011
46	M Steyn	Bulls	2011
46	CR Slade	Crusaders	2014
44	JC Pietersen	Stormers	2013
44	BT Foley	NSW	2014

Most drop goals by a player - ALL

11	M Steyn	Bulls	2009
8	ML Boshoff	Lions	2014
7	LJ Koen	Bulls	2003
6	AS Pretorius	Lions	2009

TEAM RECORDS

Most points in a log season - ALL

481	Waratahs	2014

Most points in a log season - SA TEAMS

436	Sharks *(16 matches)*	2012

Most points in all matches - ALL

541	Crusaders *(13 matches)*	2005

Most points in all matches - SA TEAMS

498	Sharks *(19 matches)*	2012

Most points conceded - ALL

590	Southern Kings	2013

Most log points - ALL

66	Reds	2011
66	Stormers	2012
66	Chiefs	2013

Fewest log points - ALL

4	Bulls	2002

Fewest log points to reach semi-finals - ALL

30	Sharks	1997
31	Brumbies	2003

Most tries in a log season - ALL

61	Crusaders	2005

Most tries in a log season - SA TEAMS

47	Natal	1996

Most tries in all matches - ALL

71	Crusaders	2005

Most tries in all matches - SA TEAMS

56	Natal	1996

Fewest tries scored - ALL

13	Lions	2007
15	Blues	1999
15	Queensland Reds	2007

Most tries conceded - ALL

74	Melbourne Rebels	2011

Most tries conceded - SA TEAMS

72	Lions	2010

Most wins in a log season - ALL

14	Stormers	2013
13	Reds	2011

Fewest wins in a season - ALL

0	Lions	2010
0	Bulls	2002

CAREER RECORDS

Most points by a player - ALL

	Player	Team	Matches	Tries	Cons	Pens	DG
1581	DW Carter	Crusaders	128	33	264	285	11
1431	M Steyn	Bulls	123	13	242	275	25
1036	SA Mortlock	ACT Brumbies	142	55	162	146	–
990	AP Mehrtens	Crusaders	87	13	134	202	17
959	MC Burke	NSW Waratahs	79	24	160	173	–
942	TE Brown	Highl/Sharks/Stormers	107	5	148	199	8
866	PJ Grant	Stormers	104	10	126	188	0
857	SR Donald	Chiefs	85	19	150	153	1
751	MJ Giteau	Brumbies/Force	104	33	113	117	3
728	QS Cooper	Reds	100	21	106	130	7

Most tries by a player - ALL

59	DC Howlett	Hurricanes/Highlanders/Blues
58	CS Ralph	Chiefs/Crusaders
57	JWC Roff	ACT Brumbies
56	CM Cullen	Hurricanes
56	BG Habana	Bulls/Stormers
55	SA Mortlock	ACT Brumbies
48	JF Umaga	Hurricanes/Chiefs
48	MA Nonu	Hurricanes/Blues/High
43	J Vidiri	Blues
42	LR MacDonald	Crusaders
42	SW Sivivatu	Chiefs

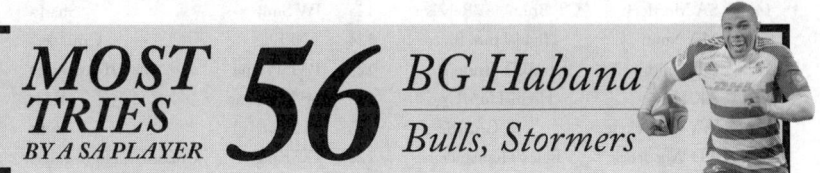

MOST TRIES BY A SA PLAYER — 56 — BG Habana — Bulls, Stormers

Most conversions by a player - ALL

264	DW Carter	Crusaders
242	M Steyn	Bulls
162	SA Mortlock	ACT Brumbies/Rebels
160	MC Burke	NSW Waratahs
150	SR Donald	Chiefs
147	TE Brown	Highlanders/Sharks/Stormers
134	AP Mehrtens	Crusaders
126	PJ Grant	Stormers
123	DE Holwell	Hurricanes/Blues
121	CS Spencer	Blues/Lions

VODACOM SUPER RUGBY

Most penalties by a player - ALL

285	DW Carter	Crusaders
275	M Steyn	Bulls
202	AP Mehrtens	Crusaders
199	TE Brown	Highl./Sharks/Stormers
188	PJ Grant	Stormers
173	MC Burke	NSW Waratahs
153	SR Donald	Chiefs
144	SA Mortlock	ACT Brumbies
138	DE Holwell	Hurricanes/Blues

Most drop goals by a player - ALL

25	M Steyn	Bulls
17	AP Mehrtens	Crusaders
13	AS Pretorius	Cats/Lions
11	LJ Koen	Bulls
11	DW Carter	Crusaders
10	DJ Hougaard	Bulls
9	BS Barnes	Reds/Waratahs
8	TE Brown	Highlanders/Sharks
8	ML Boshoff	Lions
6	AJD Mauger	Crusaders

100 appearances by a player - ALL

162	NC Sharpe	Reds/Force	127	BJ Robinson	Waratahs
162	KF Mealamu	Blues/Chiefs	126	A Ashley-Cooper	Waratahs/Brumbies
150	CR Flynn	Crusaders	125	AJ Venter	Cats/Sharks/Stormers
146	SA Mortlock	ACT Brumbies/Rebels	125	JW Smit	Sharks
144	MA Nonu	Highl/Hurr/Blues	124	AM Ellis	Crusaders
142	GB Smith	ACT Brumbies	124	PAT Weepu	Blues/Hurricanes
141	AK Hore	Highl/Hurr/Crus	123	SP Hardman	Reds
140	WVV Crockett	Crusaders	123	M Steyn	Bulls
139	TD Woodcock	Blues/Highlanders	122	CC King	Crusaders, Highlanders
138	V Matfield	Cats/Bulls	122	CS Terblanche	Sharks
136	CS Ralph	Chiefs/Crusaders/Reds	121	AKE Baxter	NSW Waratahs
136	GM Gregan	ACT Brumbies	120	BW du Plessis	Sharks
132	PR Waugh	NSW Waratahs	120	SUT Polota-Nau	Waratahs
132	JN du Plessis	Sharks/Cheetahs	119	GS Holmes	Reds
131	GM Somerville	Crusaders/Rebels	118	BG Habana	Bulls/Stormers
131	ST Moore	Brumbies/Reds	118	NJ Henderson	Rebels/Force/ACT
130	RH McCaw	Crusaders	117	AJ Williams	Blues/Crusaders
129	RD Thorne	Crusaders	116	SJ Larkham	ACT Brumbies
129	LJ Messam	Chiefs	116	DJ Rossouw	Bulls
128	JF Umaga	Hurricanes/Chiefs	115	LJ Botes	Sharks
128	DW Carter	Crusaders	113	TD Latimer	Chiefs
127	AD Oliver	Highlanders	113	MJ Hodgson	Force
127	LR MacDonald	Crusaders/Chiefs	113	JA Paul	ACT Brumbies

VODACOM SUPER RUGBY

113	BJ Franks	Hurricanes/Crusaders		106	SNG Staniforth	Waratahs/Force
113	PJ Wannenburg	Bulls		105	JW Marshall	Crusaders
113	AA Jacobs	Cats/Bulls/Sharks		105	J de Villiers	Stormers
113	OM Ndungane	Bulls/Sharks		105	WL Palu	Waratahs
112	PF du Preez	Bulls		105	JA Strauss	Cheetahs/Bulls
112	J-PR Pietersen	Sharks		104	DC Howlett	Highlanders/Blues
111	MJ Dunning	NSW Waratahs/Force		104	MJ Giteau	Brumbies/Force
111	A Mitchell	Reds/Force/NSW		104	JM Muliaina	Chiefs/Blues
111	BC Thorn	Highlanders/Crusaders		104	A Bekker	Stormers
110	CR Jack	Crusaders		104	AL Freier	Rebels/Brum/NSW
110	W Olivier	Bulls		104	J Vermaak	Bulls/Lions/Cats
110	CG Smith	Hurricanes		104	KR Daniel	Sharks
109	CE Latham	Waratahs/Reds		104	PJ Grant	Stormers
109	JE Horwill	Reds		103	JA Collins	Blues/Chiefs
108	W Kruger	Bulls		103	MD Chisholm	ACT Brumbies
108	HM Bosman	Cheetahs/Sharks		103	WS Alberts	Sharks/Lions
108	QJ Cowan	Highlanders		103	PJ Spies	Bulls
108	A-H Le Roux	Sharks/Cheetahs		102	PA van den Berg	Cats/Sharks
108	CJ Spencer	Blues/Lions		102	HE Gear	Highlanders/Hurricanes
108	AS Mathewson	Force/Blues		102	T Mtawarira	Sharks
108	AZ Ndungane	Bulls		101	R So'oialo	Hurricanes
108	KJ Read	Crusaders		101	IF Afoa	Blues
107	CJ Whitaker	NSW Waratahs		101	NS Tialata	Hurricanes
107	TE Brown	Highl./Stormers/Sharks		100	DJ Lyons	Waratahs
107	MA Gerrard	Rebels/Brum/NSW		100	WK Young	ACT Brumbies
106	SM Faingaa	Reds/Brumbies		100	JP Botha	Bulls
106	BJ Cannon	Waratahs/Force		100	KJ Beale	Waratahs
106	AKE Baxter	NSW Waratahs		100	QS Cooper	Reds

Tallest player ever

2.08m	Andries Bekker	Stormers

❰ DID YOU KNOW? ❱

Northern Transvaal scrumhalf Piet Uys was the first player to play for the Springboks as a substitute, when he replaced captain Dawie de Villiers, who had dislocated his shoulder, on 2 August 1969 against Australia at Ellis Park.

Vodacom Bulls

Ground: Loftus Versfeld **Capacity:** 50 000 **Address:** Kirkness Street, Sunnyside, Pretoria, 0132
Telephone number: 012-420 0700 **Website:** www.vodacombulls.co.za
Colours: Navy fading from chest to hem. Herringbone design under arm and sides. Navy collar with faded sleeves. Navy shorts with herringbone insert.
Coach: Frans Ludeke **Captain:** Flip van der Merwe **CEO:** Barend van Graan
Chairman: John Newbury **President:** Louis Nel

Head Coach: Frans Ludeke **Assistant Coach (Backline):** Pieter Rossouw
Forwards/Attack Coach: Victor Matfield **Assistant Coach (Defence):** Pine Pienaar
Assistant Coach (Scrum): Wessel Roux **Team Manager:** Tim Dlulane
Kicking Coach: Vlok Cilliers **Strength and Conditioning:** Andre Volsteedt
Conditioning and Rehabilitation: Stephen Plummer **Team Doctor:** Dr Org Strauss
Physiotherapist: Roneé Eksteen & Karabo Morokane **Kit Manager:** Andries Kabinde
Masseuse: Elzanne van Coller **Analyst:** John-William Meyer
Mental Life Coach: Dr Jannie Botha

VODACOM SUPER RUGBY

'96*	'97*	'98	'99	'00	'01	'02	'03	'04	'05	'06	'07	'08	'09	'10	'11	'12	'13	'14
3rd	8th	11th	12th	11th	12th	12th	6th	6th	3rd	4th	2nd	10th	1st	1st	7th	5th	2nd	9th

Played	Won	Lost	Drawn	Points for	Points against	Tries for	Tries against
16	7	8	1	365	335	28	29

Date	Venue	Opponent	Result	Score	Referee	Scorers
15 Feb	Durban	Sharks	LOST	16-31	J Peyper	T: Ross. C: Pollard. P: Fouche (2). DG: Fouche.
21 Feb	Bloemfontein	Cheetahs	LOST	9-15	S Berry	P: Pollard (2), Fouche.
1 Mar	Pretoria	Lions	WON	25-17	C Pollock	T: Serfontein. C: J-L Potgieter. P: J-L Potgieter (5). DG: J-L Potgieter.
8 Mar	Pretoria	Blues	WON	38-22	A Lees	T: J-L Potgieter, Ross, Serfontein, M van der Merwe. C: J-L Potgieter (2), Pollard. P: J-L Potgieter (3). DG: J-L Potgieter.
22 Mar	Pretoria	Sharks	WON	23-19	M Fraser	T: Du Plessis, JJ Engelbrecht. C: J-L Potgieter (2). P: J-L Potgieter, Pollard. DG: J-L Potgieter.
29 Mar	Pretoria	Chiefs	DREW	34-34	C Joubert	T: Basson, Stegmann, Penalty try. C: J-L Potgieter (2). P: J-L Potgieter (5)
5 Apr	Napier	Hurricanes	LOST	20-25	SR Walsh	T: Visser, Pollard. C: J-L Potgieter, Pollard. P: J-L Potgieter (2).
11 Apr	Dunedin	Highlanders	LOST	20-27	R Hoffman	T: Basson, M van der Merwe. C: J-L Potgieter (2). P: J-L Potgieter (2).
19 Apr	Sydney	Waratahs	LOST	12-19	R Hoffman	P: J-L Potgieter (3), Pollard.
26 Apr	Perth	Force	LOST	9-15	A Gardner	P: J-L Potgieter (2), Pollard.
3 May	Pretoria	Cheetahs	WON	26-21	M vd Westhuizen	T: Willemse, Visagie. C: Pollard (2). P: Pollard (2), J-L Potgieter, Visser.
10 May	Pretoria	Stormers	WON	28-12	C Joubert	T: Ndungane. C: Pollard. P: Pollard (5), J-L Potgieter. DG: Pollard.
23 May	Pretoria	Brumbies	WON	44-23	C Joubert	T: Ross (2), Serfontein, Basson. C: J-L Potgieter (2), Pollard. P: J-L Potgieter (6).
31 May	Johannesburg	Lions	LOST	21-32	C Joubert	T: Small-Smith, Du Plessis. C: J-L Potgieter. P: J-L Potgieter.
5 Jul	Cape Town	Stormers	LOST	0-16	C Joubert	
11 Jul	Pretoria	Rebels	WON	40-7	R Hoffman	T: Willemse (2), Greyling, Hougaard. C: Pollard (3), J-L Potgieter. P: Pollard (4).

Note: ■ = *Champion*, * *Played as Northern Transvaal*

‹ DID YOU KNOW? ›

South Africa's first-ever 'blood bin' replacement was wing James Small, when he came on for Gavin Johnson between the 32nd and 37th minutes against New Zealand at Eden Park on 6 August 1994.

VODACOM SUPER RUGBY

2014 SQUAD

PLAYER	Union	Debut	BULLS CAREER M	T	C	P	DG	Pts	Debut	SUPER RUGBY CAREER M	T	C	P	DG	Pts
BA (Bjorn) Basson	BB	2011	62	23	–	–	–	115	2009	71	29	–	–	–	145
U (Ulrich) Beyers	BB	2013	10	–	–	–	–	0	2013	10	–	–	–	–	0
WHJ (Jacques) du Plessis	BB	2013	15	2	–	–	–	10	2013	15	2	–	–	–	10
JJ (Jacques) Engelbrecht	BB	2014	13	–	–	–	–	0	2013	28	1	–	–	–	5
JJ (JJ) Engelbrecht	BB	2012	49	8	–	–	–	40	2012	49	8	–	–	–	40
LD van Z (Louis) Fouche	BB	2012	23	2	5	8	1	47	2012	23	2	5	8	1	47
MD (Dean) Greyling	BB	2008	54	5	–	–	–	25	2008	54	5	–	–	–	25
GN (Grant) Hattingh	BB	2013	25	–	–	–	–	0	2012	34	1	–	–	–	5
F (Francois) Hougaard	BB	2008	72	19	–	–	–	95	2008	72	19	–	–	–	95
NJ (Nico) Janse van Rensburg	BB	2014	1	–	–	–	–	0	2014	1	–	–	–	–	0
FBC (Frik) Kirsten	BB	2009	34	–	–	–	–	0	2009	34	–	–	–	–	0
JA (Jesse) Kriel	BB	2014	1	–	–	–	–	0	2014	1	–	–	–	–	0
W (Werner) Kruger	BB	2008	108	8	–	–	–	40	2008	108	8	–	–	–	40
WA (Wiaan) Liebenberg	BB	2014	1	–	–	–	–	0	2014	1	–	–	–	–	0
BG (Bandise) Maku	BB	2008	21	–	–	–	–	0	2008	51	–	–	–	–	0
S (Sampie) Mastriet	BB	2013	2	1	–	–	–	5	2013	2	1	–	–	–	5
V (Victor) Matfield	BB	2001	130	8	–	–	–	40	1999	138	8	–	–	–	40
MT (Bongi) Mbonambi	BB	2012	15	–	–	–	–	0	2012	15	–	–	–	–	0
MM (Morne) Mellett	BB	2013	24	–	–	–	–	0	2013	24	–	–	–	–	0
AZ (Akona) Ndungane	BB	2005	108	33	–	–	–	165	2005	108	33	–	–	–	165
M (Marvin) Orie	BB	2014	2	–	–	–	–	0	2014	2	–	–	–	–	0
R (Rudy) Paige	BB	2013	7	–	–	–	–	0	2013	7	–	–	–	–	0
H (Handre) Pollard	BB	2014	13	1	10	16	1	76	2014	13	1	10	16	1	76
DJ (Dewald) Potgieter	BB	2008	70	4	–	–	–	20	2008	70	4	–	–	–	20
J-L (Jacques-Louis) Potgieter	BB	2007	29	3	15	35	3	159	2007	56	5	36	54	4	271
JM (Jono) Ross	BB	2013	19	4	–	–	–	20	2013	19	4	–	–	–	20
JL (Jan) Serfontein	BB	2013	28	5	–	–	–	25	2013	28	5	–	–	–	25
WT (William) Small-Smith	BB	2014	7	1	–	–	–	5	2014	7	1	–	–	–	5
RA (Roelof) Smit	BB	2014	2	–	–	–	–	0	2014	2	–	–	–	–	0
PJ (Pierre) Spies	BB	2005	103	25	–	–	–	125	2005	103	25	–	–	–	125
GJ (Deon) Stegmann	BB	2008	79	6	–	–	–	30	2008	79	6	–	–	–	30
M (Marcel) van der Merwe	BB	2014	16	2	–	–	–	10	2012	19	2	–	–	–	10
PR (Flip) van der Merwe	BB	2010	66	2	–	–	–	10	2007	72	3	–	–	–	15
PW (Wimpie) van der Walt	BB	2014	4	–	–	–	–	0	2013	19	6	–	–	–	30
PE (Piet) van Zyl	BB	2014	12	–	–	–	–	0	2012	44	5	–	–	–	25
C-T (Callie) Visagie	BB	2013	22	2	–	–	–	10	2012	38	2	–	–	–	10
PJ (Jurgen) Visser	BB	2013	25	2	–	1	–	13	2013	25	2	–	1	–	13
P (Paul) Willemse	BB	2013	20	3	–	–	–	15	2012	21	3	–	–	–	15
TOTALS			1292	169	30	60	5	1100		1463	191	51	79	6	1312

Note: BB = Blue Bulls

APPEARANCES & POINTS

PLAYER	Sharks	Cheetahs	Lions	Blues	Sharks	Chiefs	Hurricanes	Highlanders	Waratahs	Force	Cheetahs	Brumbies	Lions	Stormers	Rebels	Apps	T	C	P	D/G	Pts
Visser	15	15	15	15	15	15	15	–	15	15	15	15	15	–	15	14	1	–	1	–	8
Ndungane	14	14	14	14	–	14	14	–	–	14	14	14	14	14	–	12	1	–	–	–	5
Engelbrecht, JJ	13	13	13	13	13	13	13	13	13	13R	13	13	13	13	13	16	1	–	–	–	5
Serfontein	12	12	12	12	12	12	12	12	12	12	12	12	12	12	12	16	3	–	–	–	15
Basson	11	11	11	11	11	11	11	14	14	11	11	11	11	11	14	16	3	–	–	–	15
Fouche	10	10	–	–	–	–	–	–	–	–	–	x	–	–	2	–	–	3	1	12
Hougaard	9	9	9	9	9	9	9	11	11	9	9	9	9	9	11	16	1	–	–	–	5
Spies	8c	–	–	–	–	–	–	–	–	–	–	–	–	–	–	1	–	–	–	–	0
Du Plessis	7	7	7	7	7	7	6R	7	7	7	7	7	7	–	–	14	2	–	–	–	10
Ross	6	6	6	8	6R	6R	–	6	6	6	6	6	6	6	7	15	4	–	–	–	20
Van der Merwe, F	5	4c	4c	4c	–	–	5c	4c	4c	–	–	4c	4c	–	–	9	–	–	–	–	0
Willemse	4	–	4R	4R	4	4	4	4R	4R	4	4	4R	8R	4	4	15	3	–	–	–	15
Kruger	3	3	3R	3	3	3	3	3	3	3R	3R	3	3R	3	3R	16	–	–	–	–	0
Visagie	2	2	2	2	2	2	2	2	2	–	2	2	2	2	2R	15	1	–	–	–	5
Greyling	1	1	1	1	1	1	1	1	1	1	1	1	1	1	1R	16	1	–	–	–	5
Mbonambi	2R	x	2R	2R	2R	x	2R	2R	2	2R	2R	2R	2R	2R	–	13	–	–	–	–	0
Kirsten	3R	3R	3	–	–	–	–	–	–	–	–	–	–	–	–	3	–	–	–	–	0
Matfield	4R	5R	5	5	5c	5c	–	5	5	5c	5c	5c	5	–	5c	5c	14	–	–	–	–	0
Engelbrecht, J	8R	8	8R	6R	–	–	8	8R	6R	x	7R	7R	7R	8	7	8	13	–	–	–	–	0
Van Zyl	9R	9R	x	14R	14R	11R	14R	9	9	–	–	–	14R	14R	14R	9	12	–	–	–	–	0
Pollard	10R	10R	x	10R	10R	10R	10R	x	10R	10R	10	10	10R	–	10	10	13	1	10	16	1	76
Beyers	x	14R	x	12R	x	12R	15R	12R	15	x	–	–	15R	–	15	–	8	–	–	–	–	0
Van der Merwe, M	1R	1R	1R	1R	1R	3R	23R	1R	3R	3R	3R	3	3	3R	3	3R	3	16	2	–	–	–	10
Hattingh	–	5	8	–	5R	4R	7R	8	8	8	8	8	5	8	–	13	–	–	–	–	0
Liebenberg	–	8R	–	–	–	–	–	–	–	–	–	–	–	–	–	1	–	–	–	–	0
Potgieter, J-L	–	–	10	10	10	10	10	10	10	10R	10R	10	10	10R	10R	14	1	14	34	3	144
Stegmann	–	–	–	6	6	6	6	–	–	–	–	–	–	–	–	4	1	–	–	–	5
Mellett	–	–	–	3R	1R	1R	x	1R	1R	1R	1R	1R	1R	1R	1R	1	12	–	–	–	–	0
Mastriet	–	–	–	–	14	–	–	–	–	–	–	–	–	–	–	1	–	–	–	–	0
Potgieter, D	–	–	–	–	8	8	7	–	–	–	–	–	–	–	–	3	–	–	–	–	0
Small-Smith	–	–	–	–	–	–	15R	13R	–	13	11R	–	13R	13R	13R	7	1	–	–	–	5
Paige	–	–	–	–	–	–	9R	11R	x	14R	–	–	–	–	–	3	–	–	–	–	0
Maku	–	–	–	–	–	–	2R	–	–	–	–	–	–	–	2	2	–	–	–	–	0
Van der Walt	–	–	–	–	–	–	6R	6R	6R	–	5R	–	–	–	–	4	–	–	–	–	0
Smit	–	–	–	–	–	–	–	–	–	–	–	7R	6	–	–	2	–	–	–	–	0
Orie	–	–	–	–	–	–	–	–	–	–	–	–	5R	5R	–	2	–	–	–	–	0
Janse van Rensburg	–	–	–	–	–	–	–	–	–	–	–	–	–	6R	–	1	–	–	–	–	0
Kriel	–	–	–	–	–	–	–	–	–	–	–	–	–	9R	–	1	–	–	–	–	0
Penalty try	–	–	–	–	–	–	–	–	–	–	–	–	–	–	–	1	–	–	–	5
38 Players																355	28	24	54	5	365

Records

MATCH RECORDS

Biggest win	89	vs Queensland Reds (92-3)	Pretoria	2007
Heaviest defeat	64	vs ACT Brumbies (9-73)	Canberra	1999
Highest score	92	vs Queensland Reds (92-3)	Pretoria	2007
Most points conceded	75	vs Crusaders (25-75)	Christchurch	2000
Most tries	13	vs Queensland Reds (92-3)	Pretoria	2007
Most tries conceded	11	vs Crusaders (25-75)	Christchurch	2000
Most points by a player	39	JH Kruger (1t 5c 8p) vs H'landers	Pretoria	1996
Most tries by a player	3	AJ Richter vs Blues	Pretoria	1997
	3	PF du Preez vs Cats	Pretoria	2004
	3	W Olivier vs Rebels	Pretoria	2011
Most conversions by a player	11	DJ Hougaard vs Queensland Reds	Pretoria	2007
Most penalties by a player	8	JH Kruger vs Highlanders	Pretoria	1996
	8	DJ Hougaard vs Crusaders	Pretoria	2007
Most drop goals by a player	4	M Steyn vs Crusaders	Pretoria	2009

SEASON RECORDS

Most team points	500	from 15 matches	2010
Most points by a player	263	M Steyn	2010
Most team tries	52	from 17 matches	2012
Most tries by a player	10	BA Basson	2012
Most conversions by a player	38	M Steyn	2010
	38	M Steyn	2012
Most penalties by a player	57	M Steyn	2013
Most drop goals by a player	11	M Steyn	2009

CAREER RECORDS

Most appearances	130	V Matfield	2001-2014
Most points	1449	M Steyn	2005-2013
Most tries	37	BG Habana	2005-2009
Most conversions	242	M Steyn	2005-2013
Most penalties	275	M Steyn	2005-2013
Most drop goals	25	M Steyn	2005-2013

Toyota Cheetahs

Ground: Free State Stadium **Capacity:** 46 000 **Address:** Att Horak Ave, Bloemfontein
Telephone: 051-407 1700 **Colours:** White jersey with an orange collar and russet orange and Biscay bay detail. White shorts, russet orange socks **Website:** www.fscheetahs.co.za
Coach: Naka Drotské **Captain:** Adriaan Strauss **Manager:** Eugene van Wyk
CEO: Harold Verster **Chairman:** Randal September

Head Coach: Naka Drotské **Assistant coaches:** Hawies Fourie & Oersond Gorgonzola
Forwards & Scrum Coach: Os du Randt **Strength & Conditioning:** Niel du Plessis
Video analyst: Charl Strydom **Manager:** Eugene van Wyk **Doctor:** Dr Ferdie Wesso
Physiotherapist: JP du Toit **Kit Manager:** Sakkie Wessels **Media officer:** Ronel Pienaar
Defence coach: Michael Horak

VODACOM SUPER RUGBY

| '96 | '97 7th | '98 | '99 | '00 | '01 | '02 | '03 | '04 | '05 | '06 10th | '07 11th | '08 13th | '09 14th | '10 10th | '11 11th | '12 10th | '13 6th | '14 14th |

Played	Won	Lost	Drawn	Points for	Points against	Tries for	Tries against
16	4	11	1	372	527	38	59

Date	Venue	Opponent	Result	Score	Referee	Scorers
15 Feb	Bloemfontein	Lions	LOST	20-21	C Joubert	T: Rhule, C: Goosen (2). P: Goosen, Watts.
21 Feb	Bloemfontein	Bulls	WON	15-9	S Berry	P: Goosen (4). DG: Goosen.
28 Feb	Melbourne	Rebels	LOST	14-35	A Gardner	T: Cook, Barnes. C: Goosen (2).
7 Mar	Brisbane	Reds	LOST	33-43	G Williamson	T: Prinsloo, Watts, F Venter. C: Goosen (2), Watts. P: Goosen (4).
15 Mar	Wellington	Hurricanes	LOST	27-60	A Gardner	T: Le Roux, Van der Walt, Uys. C: Goosen (3). P: Goosen (2).
22 Mar	Auckland	Blues	LOST	30-40	F Pastrana	T: Prinsloo, Hendricks, Daniller. C: Watts (2), Goosen. P: Goosen (2), Watts.
5 Apr	Bloemfontein	Chiefs	DREW	43-43	C Joubert	T: Pretorius (2), Prinsloo, Benjamin. C: Goosen (4). P: Goosen (5).
12 Apr	Bloemfontein	Crusaders	LOST	31-52	G Jackson	T: Hendricks, Pretorius, Mohoje, Le Roux. C: Watts (4). P: Watts.
19 Apr	Durban	Sharks	LOST	8-19	J Peyper	T: Benjamin. P: Watts.
26 Apr	Bloemfontein	Stormers	WON	35-22	C Joubert	T: Hendricks, Daniller, Benjamin, Nyakane, Le Roux. C: Watts (2). P: Watts (2)
3 May	Pretoria	Bulls	LOST	21-26	M vd Westhuizen	T: Sadie, Rhule. C: Watts. P: Watts (2), Goosen.
10 May	Bloemfontein	Force	LOST	16-23	C Pollock	T: Prinsloo. C: Goosen. P: Goosen (3).
17 May	Bloemfontein	Brumbies	WON	27-21	M vd Westhuizen	T: Le Roux, Goosen. C: Goosen. P: Goosen (4). DG: Goosen.
24 May	Cape Town	Stormers	LOST	0-33	S Berry	
5 Jul	Bloemfontein	Sharks	WON	27-20	R Hoffman	T: De Jager, Van der Walt, Van Jaarsveld. C: Goosen (3), P: Goosen (2).
12 Jul	Johannesburg	Lions	LOST	25-60	M vd Westhuizen	T: Hendricks (2), Le Roux. C: Goosen (2). P: Goosen (2).

‹ DID YOU KNOW? ›

Toks van der Linde was the Springboks' first-ever tactical substitution when he came on for Dawie Theron in the 62nd minute against Argentina in Buenos Aires on 9 November 1996, in a 46-15 victory.

VODACOM SUPER RUGBY

2014 SQUAD

PLAYER	Union	Debut	CHEETAHS CAREER						Debut	SUPER RUGBY CAREER					
			M	T	C	P	DG	Pts		M	T	C	P	DG	Pts
RJ (Ryno) Barnes	GW	2010	34	1	–	–	–	5	2010	34	1	–	–	–	5
RS (Ryno) Benjamin	FS	2011	41	10	–	–	–	50	2006	64	14	–	–	–	70
R (Renier) Botha	FS	–	0	–	–	–	–	0	–	–	–	–	–	–	0
HW (Heinrich) Brüssow	FS	2007	76	6	–	–	–	30	2007	76	6	–	–	–	30
JG (Jean) Cook	FS	2014	13	1	–	–	–	5	2013	14	2	–	–	–	10
HJ (Hennie) Daniller	FS	2008	90	9	–	–	–	45	2004	97	9	–	–	–	45
L (Luan) de Bruin	FS	2014	1	–	–	–	–	0	2014	1	–	–	–	–	0
L (Lodewyk) de Jager	FS	2013	28	1	–	–	–	5	2013	28	1	–	–	–	5
PR (Rossouw) de Klerk	FS	2014	7	–	–	–	–	0	2010	21	–	–	–	–	0
AS (Andries) Ferreira	FS	2014	6	–	–	–	–	0	2014	20	1	–	–	–	5
JL (Johan) Goosen	FS	2012	27	4	46	70	3	331	2012	27	4	46	70	3	331
CFK (Carel) Greeff	GW	2014	1	–	–	–	–	0	2014	1	–	–	–	–	0
C (Cornal) Hendricks	FS	2014	16	6	–	–	–	30	2014	16	6	–	–	–	30
PHC (Pieter) Labuschagne	FS	2012	27	2	–	–	–	10	2012	27	2	–	–	–	10
RJ (Rynard) Landman	GW	2013	18	–	–	–	–	0	2013	18	–	–	–	–	0
WJ (Willie) le Roux	FS	2012	49	18	–	–	–	90	2012	49	18	–	–	–	90
H (Hilton) Lobberts	GW	2014	1	–	–	–	–	0	2007	13	–	–	–	–	0
TC (Tian) Meyer	GW	2014	1	–	–	–	–	0	2012	12	2	–	–	–	10
XH (Howard) Mnisi	GW	2013	3	–	–	–	–	0	2013	3	–	–	–	–	0
TS (Oupa) Mohoje	FS	2014	10	1	–	–	–	5	2014	10	1	–	–	–	5
TN (Trevor) Nyakane	FS	2012	42	3	–	–	–	15	2012	42	3	–	–	–	15
CR (Caylib) Oosthuizen	FS	2014	16	–	–	–	–	0	2012	22	1	–	–	–	5
CV (Coenie) Oosthuizen	FS	2010	66	8	–	–	–	40	2010	66	8	–	–	–	40
SJ (Sarel) Pretorius	FS	2009	66	22	–	–	–	110	2009	80	24	–	–	–	120
JG (Gouws) Prinsloo	GW	2014	1	–	–	–	–	0	2014	1	–	–	–	–	0
JGP (Boom) Prinsloo	FS	2012	27	5	–	–	–	25	2012	27	5	–	–	–	25
RK (Raymond) Rhule	FS	2013	26	7	–	–	–	35	2013	26	7	–	–	–	35
J (Johann) Sadie	FS	2013	33	6	–	–	–	30	2011	50	8	–	–	–	40
WJ (Willem) Serfontein	GW	2014	3	–	–	–	–	0	2014	3	–	–	–	–	0
AJ (Riaan) Smit	FS	2011	25	3	11	23	–	106	2011	25	3	11	23	–	106
KB (Kevin) Stevens	FS	2014	1	–	–	–	–	0	2014	1	–	–	–	–	0
JA (Adriaan) Strauss	FS	2007	97	8	–	–	–	40	2006	105	8	–	–	–	40
FJ (Francois) Uys	FS	2009	49	1	–	–	–	5	2009	49	1	–	–	–	5
CP (Philip) van der Walt	FS	2010	49	5	–	–	–	25	2010	49	5	–	–	–	25
NJJ (Maks) van Dyk	GW	2014	11	–	–	–	–	0	2014	11	–	–	–	–	0
TG (Torsten) van Jaarsveld	FS	2014	5	1	–	–	–	5	2014	5	1	–	–	–	5
JF (Francois) Venter	FS	2014	5	1	–	–	–	5	2012	16	1	–	–	–	5
HP (Henco) Venter	FS	2014	1	–	–	–	–	0	2014	1	–	–	–	–	0
SH (Shaun) Venter	FS	2014	14	–	–	–	–	0	2013	30	2	–	–	–	10
PV (Waltie) Vermeulen	FS	2010	26	1	–	–	–	5	2010	26	1	–	–	–	5
EG (Elgar) Watts	FS	2013	19	1	17	16	–	87	2013	19	1	17	16	–	87
CA (Carl) Wegner	FS	2014	1	–	–	–	–	0	2014	1	–	–	–	–	0
TOTALS			991	120	57	93	3	1139		1132	144	57	93	3	1122

Note: FS = Free State, GW = Griqualand West

VODACOM SUPER RUGBY

APPEARANCES & POINTS

PLAYER	Lions	Bulls	Rebels	Reds	Hurricanes	Blues	Chiefs	Crusaders	Sharks	Stormers	Bulls	Force	Brumbies	Stormers	Sharks	Lions	Apps	T	C	P	DG	Pts
Le Roux	15	15	15	11	15	15	15	15	11	11	11	11	11	11	15	15	16	5	–	–	–	25
Hendricks	14	14	14	14R	14	14	14	14	14	14R	14R	14R	14	14	14	14	16	6	–	–	–	30
Sadie	13	13	13	13	13	13	13	13	13	13	13	13	13	13	13	13	16	1	–	–	–	5
Venter, F	12	12	12	12	12	–	–	–	–	–	–	–	–	–	–	–	5	1	–	–	–	5
Rhule	11	11	11	–	11	–	–	–	x	14	14	14	–	–	11	11	9	2	–	–	–	10
Goosen	10	10	10	10	10	10	10	10	–	–	10R	10	10	10	10	10	14	1	21	30	2	143
Venter, S	9	9	9	9	13R	x	9R	9R	x	9R	9R	9R	9	9	9R	9R	14	–	–	–	–	0
Van der Walt	8	8	8	8	8	8	–	–	–	–	–	–	–	–	8	8	8	2	–	–	–	10
Labuschagne	7	7	7	7	7	7R	7	7	–	–	–	–	–	–	–	–	8	–	–	–	–	0
Prinsloo, Boom	6	6	6	6	6	6	6	6	8	8	8	8	8	8	–	–	14	4	–	–	–	20
Uys	5	5	5	5	5	5	5	5	5	5	5	5	5	5	5	5	16	1	–	–	–	5
De Jager	4	4	4	4	4	4	4	4	–	–	–	–	–	–	4	4	11	1	–	–	–	5
Oosthuizen, Coenie	3	3	3	–	–	–	–	–	–	3R	3	3	3	3	–	3	9	–	–	–	–	0
Strauss	2c	2c	2c	2c	2c	2c	2c	2c	2c	2c	2c	2c	2c	2c	2c	2c	16	1	–	–	–	5
Oosthuizen, Caylib	1	1	1	1	1	1	1R	1R	1	1	1	1	1	1	1R	1	16	1	–	–	–	5
Barnes	x	x	7R	x	2R	x	x	6R	8R	–	–	–	–	–	–	–	4	1	–	–	–	5
Nyakane	1R	1R	1R	1R	1R	1R	1	1	1R	1R	1R	1R	1R	1R	1	–	15	1	–	–	–	5
Van Dyk	3R	x	x	3	3	3	3	3	3	3	3	3R	x	3R	–	–	11	–	–	–	–	0
Landman	4R	4R	4R	6R	–	–	–	–	x	–	–	–	–	–	–	–	4	–	–	–	–	0
Cook	6R	6R	6R	7R	7R	7	8	8	7	7	7	–	–	–	6R	6R	13	1	–	–	–	5
Pretorius	9R	x	9R	9R	9	9	9	9	9	9	9	9	–	–	9	9	13	3	–	–	–	15
Watts	10R	x	10R	10R	12R	10R	x	10R	10	10	10	15R	15R	15R	x	10R	13	1	10	8	–	49
Benjamin	14R	–	–	14	–	12	12	12	12	12	12	12	12	12	12	12	13	3	–	–	–	15
Daniller	–	x	11R	15	15R	11	11	11	15	15	15	15	15	15	15R	11R	14	2	–	–	–	10
De Klerk	–	–	–	3R	3R	3R	3R	3R	3R	–	–	–	–	–	–	–	7	–	–	–	–	0
Ferreira	–	–	–	–	4R	x	4R	8R	4R	4	4	–	–	–	–	–	6	–	–	–	–	0
Mnisi	–	–	–	–	–	x	12R	12R	–	–	–	–	–	–	–	–	2	–	–	–	–	0
Mohoje	–	–	–	–	–	8R	7R	7R	4R	7R	7	7	7	7	7	7	10	1	–	–	–	5
Brussow	–	–	–	–	–	–	6	6	6	6	6	6	–	–	–	–	6	–	–	–	–	0
Smit	–	–	–	–	–	–	x	10R	–	–	–	x	–	–	–	–	1	–	–	–	–	0
Van Jaarsveld	–	–	–	–	–	–	–	–	8R	8R	x	x	2R	6	6	–	5	1	–	–	–	5
Vermeulen	–	–	–	–	–	–	–	–	7R	–	4	4R	–	–	–	–	3	–	–	–	–	0
Serfontein	–	–	–	–	–	–	–	–	–	4R	4	4	–	–	–	–	3	–	–	–	–	0
Greeff	–	–	–	–	–	–	–	–	–	x	x	8R	–	–	–	–	1	–	–	–	–	0
Botha	–	–	–	–	–	–	–	–	–	–	x	–	–	–	–	–	0	–	–	–	–	0
Lobberts	–	–	–	–	–	–	–	–	–	–	–	–	4R	–	–	–	1	–	–	–	–	0
Meyer	–	–	–	–	–	–	–	–	–	–	–	–	9R	–	–	–	1	–	–	–	–	0
Prinsloo, Gouws	–	–	–	–	–	–	–	–	–	–	–	–	10R	–	–	–	1	–	–	–	–	0
Venter, H	–	–	–	–	–	–	–	–	–	–	–	–	–	x	19R	–	1	–	–	–	–	0
Wegner	–	–	–	–	–	–	–	–	–	–	–	–	–	5R	5R	–	2	–	–	–	–	0
De Bruin	–	–	–	–	–	–	–	–	–	–	–	–	–	x	3R	–	1	–	–	–	–	0
Stevens	–	–	–	–	–	–	–	–	–	–	–	–	–	–	1R	–	1	–	–	–	–	0
42 Players (of which 41 made an appearance during 2014)																	340	38	31	38	2	372

Note: ■ = *Yellow card*

Records

MATCH RECORDS

Biggest win	49	vs Lions (59-10)	Welkom	2010
Heaviest defeat	46	vs Brumbies (15-61)	Canberra	2010
Highest score	59	vs Lions (59-10)	Welkom	2010
Most points conceded	61	vs Brumbies (15-61)	Canberra	2010
Most tries	9	vs Lions (59-10)	Welkom	2010
Most tries conceded	9	vs Brumbies (15-61)	Canberra	2010
Most points by a player	26	HM Bosman vs Stormers	Cape Town	2006
Most tries by a player	3	SJ Pretorius vs Hurricanes	Bloemfontein	2011
	3	R Viljoen vs Lions	Johannesburg	2011
	3	RS Benjamin vs Stormers	Bloemfontein	2011
Most conversions by a player	7	JH de Beer vs Highlanders	Invercargill	1997
Most penalties by a player	8	HM Bosman vs Stormers	Cape Town	2006
Most drop goals by a player	2	JM Ebersohn vs Hurricanes	Bloemfontein	2011
	2	R Viljoen vs Brumbies	Bloemfontein	2011

SEASON RECORDS

Most team points	435	in 16 games	2011
Most points by a player	179	JM Ebersohn	2011
Most team tries	44	in 16 games	2011
Most tries by a player	9	SJ Pretorius	2011
Most conversions by a player	32	JM Ebersohn	2011
Most penalties by a player	33	JM Ebersohn	2011
Most drop goals by a player	2	IP Olivier	2010
	2	JM Ebersohn	2011
	2	R Viljoen	2011

CAREER RECORDS

Most appearances	97	JA Strauss	2007-2014
Most points	331	JL Goosen	2012-2014
Most tries	22	SJ Pretorius	2009-2014
Most conversions	46	JL Goosen	2012-2014
Most penalties	70	JL Goosen	2012-2014
Most drop goals	2	IP Olivier	2009-2010
	2	JM Ebersohn	2010-2011
	2	R Viljoen	2010-2011

VODACOM SUPER RUGBY

Lions

Ground: Coca-Cola Park (previously Ellis Park) **Capacity:** 62 300
Address: South Office Block, Johannesburg Stadium, 124 Van Beek Street, Doornfontein 2094
Telephone number: 011-402 2960 **Colours:** White and red trim jersey, black shorts and black socks
Website: www.lionsrugby.co.za **Captain:** Warren Whiteley **Coach:** Johan Ackermann
CEO: Rudolf Straeuli **President:** Kevin de Klerk

Head Coach: Johan Ackermann **Assistant Coach:** Swys de Bruin
Forward coach: Johan Ackermann **Team Manager:** Mustapha Boomgaard
Performance Analyst: JP Ferreira **Strength & Conditioning:** Ivan van Rooyen
Doctor: Dr Rob Collins **Physiotherapist:** David van Wyk
Assistant Team Manager: Johane Singwane **Media officer:** Tarryn Steenekamp

VODACOM SUPER RUGBY

'96¹	'96²	'98	'99	'00	'01	'02	'03	'04	'05	'06	'07	'08	'09	'10	'11	'12	'13	'14
10th	5th	12th	11th	4th	3rd	11th	12th	12th	11th	13th	12th	14th	12th	13th	14th	15th		12th

Played	Won	Lost	Drawn	Points for	Points against	Tries for	Tries against
16	7	9	0	367	413	31	46

Date	Venue	Opponent	Result	Score	Referee	Scorers
15 Feb	Bloemfontein	Cheetahs	WON	21-20	C Joubert	P: Boshoff (6). DG: Boshoff.
22 Feb	Johannesburg	Stormers	WON	34-10	J Peyper	T: Watermeyer. C: Boshoff. P: Boshoff (6). DG: Boshoff (3).
1 Mar	Pretoria	Bulls	LOST	17-25	C Pollock	T: Watermeyer, Wepener. C: Boshoff (2). P: Boshoff.
7 Mar	Durban	Sharks	LOST	23-37	J Peyper	T: De Klerk, Van Rensburg. C: Boshoff (2). P: Boshoff (3).
15 Mar	Johannesburg	Blues	WON	39-36	S Berry	T: De Klerk, Van Wyk, Skosan. C: Boshoff (3). P: Boshoff (4). DG: Boshoff (2).
22 Mar	Johannesburg	Reds	WON	23-20	S Berry	T: Skosan, Mapoe. C: Boshoff (2). P: Boshoff (3).
5 Apr	Johannesburg	Crusaders	LOST	7-28	M vd westhuizen	T: Mapoe. C: Boshoff.
12 Apr	Johannesburg	Sharks	LOST	12-25	C Joubert	P: Boshoff (4).
19 Apr	Cape Town	Stormers	LOST	3-18	S Berry	P: Boshoff.
3 May	Hamilton	Chiefs	LOST	8-38	C Pollock	T: Skosan. P: Jantjies.
10 May	Dunedin	Highlanders	LOST	22-23	A Gardner	T: Skosan, De Klerk, Mapoe, A van der Merwe. C: Boshoff.
18 May	Sydney	Waratahs	LOST	13-41	N Briant	T: Kriel. C: Boshoff. P: Boshoff (2).
24 May	Perth	Force	LOST	19-29	SR Walsh	T: Jantjies. C: Boshoff. P: Boshoff (4).
31 May	Johannesburg	Bulls	WON	32-21	C Joubert	T: Hollenbach, Tecklenburg. C: Boshoff. P: Boshoff (4). DG: Boshoff.
4 Jul	Johannesburg	Rebels	WON	34-17	J Peyper	T: Volmink, Whiteley, Tecklenburg. C: Boshoff (2). P; Boshoff (5).
12 Jul	Johannesburg	Cheetahs	WON	60-25	M vd westhuizen	T: Mapoe (3), A Coetzee, Fourie, R Coetzee, Cronje, Whiteley. C: Jantjies (7). P: Jantjies (2).

Note: *1 = As Transvaal, 2 = As Golden Lions.*

⟨ DID YOU KNOW? ⟩

In the second Test against South America on 3 May 1980 at Kings Park in Durban, there were four Du Plessis' in the team. Willie (centre), Tommy (scrumhalf), Daan (prop) and Morné (No 8). They were not related!

VODACOM SUPER RUGBY

2014 SQUAD

PLAYER	Union	Debut	LIONS CAREER M	T	C	P	DG	Pts	Debut	SUPER RUGBY CAREER M	T	C	P	DG	Pts
ML (Marnitz) Boshoff	GL	2014	16	–	18	43	8	189	2014	16	–	18	43	8	189
CA (Chrysander) Botha	GL	2014	9	–	–	–	–	0	2014	9	–	–	–	–	0
WS (Willie) Britz	GL	2014	13	–	–	–	–	0	2014	13	–	–	–	–	0
A (Andries) Coetzee	GL	2012	15	1	–	–	1	8	2012	16	1	–	–	1	8
RL (Robbie) Coetzee	GL	2014	14	1	–	–	–	5	2014	14	1	–	–	–	5
RJ (Ruan) Combrinck	GL	2012	13	–	–	1	–	3	2012	13	–	–	1	–	3
R (Ross) Cronje	GL	2012	22	1	–	–	–	5	2009	23	1	–	–	–	5
F (Faf) de Klerk	Pum	2014	16	3	–	–	–	15	2014	16	3	–	–	–	15
AS (Stephan) de Wit	GL	2014	2	–	–	–	–	0	2014	2	–	–	–	–	0
RM (Ruan) Dreyer	GL	2012	19	1	–	–	–	5	2012	19	1	–	–	–	5
C (Corne) Fourie	Pum	2014	12	1	–	–	–	5	2014	12	1	–	–	–	5
NJ (Stokkies) Hanekom	GL	2014	3	–	–	–	–	0	2014	3	–	–	–	–	0
AWCJ (Alwyn) Hollenbach	GL	2011	21	2	–	–	–	10	2007	23	2	–	–	–	10
ET (Elton) Jantjies	GL	2011	38	1	40	56	1	256	2011	51	1	41	59	1	267
JW (JW) Jonker	Pum	2014	11	–	–	–	–	0	2008	27	6	–	–	–	30
JA (Jaco) Kriel	GL	2011	23	3	–	–	–	15	2011	23	3	–	–	–	15
L (Luvuyiso) Lusaseni	GL	2014	11	–	–	–	–	0	2014	11	–	–	–	–	0
LG (Lionel) Mapoe	GL	2011	33	8	–	–	–	40	2010	50	11	–	–	–	55
CM (Charles) Marais	GL	2014	1	–	–	–	–	0	2014	1	–	–	–	–	0
MJ (Malcolm) Marx	GL	2014	2	–	–	–	–	0	2014	2	–	–	–	–	0
R (Rudi) Mathee	Pum	2014	5	–	–	–	–	0	2014	5	–	–	–	–	0
DJ (Derick) Minnie	GL	2010	52	6	–	–	–	30	2010	55	9	–	–	–	45
FJ (Franco) Mostert	GL	2014	14	–	–	–	–	0	2014	14	–	–	–	–	0
MD (Martin) Muller	GL	2014	5	–	–	–	–	0	2014	19	–	–	–	–	0
M (Mark) Pretorius	GL	2014	1	–	–	–	–	0	2014	1	–	–	–	–	0
J (Julian) Redelinghuys	GL	2014	15	–	–	–	–	0	2014	15	–	–	–	–	0
CD (Courtnall) Skosan	GL	2014	10	4	–	–	–	20	2014	10	4	–	–	–	20
WJ (Warwick) Tecklenburg	GL	2014	13	2	–	–	–	10	2014	13	2	–	–	–	10
AHP (Armand) van der Merwe	Leo	2014	7	1	–	–	–	5	2014	7	1	–	–	–	5
F (Franco) van der Merwe	GL	2007	83	7	–	–	–	35	2007	99	7	–	–	–	35
SW (Schalk) van der Merwe	GL	2014	15	–	–	–	–	0	2014	15	–	–	–	–	0
AG (Deon) van Rensburg	GL	2009	54	4	–	–	–	20	2009	54	4	–	–	–	20
J (Jacques) van Rooyen	GL	2014	6	–	–	–	–	0	2014	6	–	–	–	–	0
CG (Coenie) van Wyk	Pum	2014	8	1	–	–	–	5	2014	8	1	–	–	–	5
AA (Anthony) Volmink	GL	2012	10	1	–	–	–	5	2012	10	1	–	–	–	5
S (Stefan) Watermeyer	Pum	2014	13	2	–	–	–	10	2014	13	2	–	–	–	10
FW (Willie) Wepener	GL	2007	46	2	–	–	–	10	2006	71	3	–	–	–	15
WR (Warren) Whiteley	GL	2011	36	5	–	–	–	25	2011	36	5	–	–	–	25
TOTALS			687	57	58	100	10	731		795	70	59	103	10	807

Note: GL = Golden Lions, Pum = Pumas, Leo = Leopards

APPEARANCES & POINTS

PLAYER	Cheetahs	Stormers	Bulls	Sharks	Blues	Reds	Crusaders	Sharks	Stormers	Chiefs	Highlanders	Waratahs	Force	Bulls	Rebels	Cheetahs	Apps	T	C	P	DG	Pts
Botha	15	15	15	11	–	–	–	15	15	15	15	–	11	–	–		9	–	–	–	–	0
Van Rensburg	14	14	14	13	13	13	14	14	–	14	–	14	13	11R	14	–	13	1	–	–	–	5
Mapoe	13	–	–	–	–	13R	13	13	13	13	13	13	–	–	14R	14	10	6	–	–	–	30
Watermeyer	12	13	12	12	12	12	12	12	12	12	12	12	12R	–	–	–	13	2	–	–	–	10
Combrinck	11	11	11	14	14R	15R	–	–	–	–	–	–	–	–	–	–	6	–	–	–	–	0
Boshoff	10	10	10	15	10	10	10	10	10	15R	10	10	10	10	10	12R	16	–	18	43	8	189
De Klerk	9	9	9	9	9	9	9	9	9R	9	9	9	9R	9R	9R	9R	16	3	–	–	–	15
Whiteley	8c	8c	8c	8c	8c	8c	8c	8c	–	8c	8c	8c	8c	8c	8c	8c	15	2	–	–	–	10
Minnie	7	7	–	–	–	–	6	7c	7	7	7	–	6R	6R	6R		10	–	–	–	–	0
Kriel	6	6	6	6	6	6	8R	6	6	6	6	6	6	6	6		16	1	–	–	–	5
Van der Merwe, F	5	5	5	5	5	5	–	–	–	–	–	–	–	–	5	5	8	–	–	–	–	0
Mostert	4	4	4	4	4	4	5	5	5	5	–	–	5	5	4	4	14	–	–	–	–	0
Redelinghuys	3	3	3	3	3	3	3	3	3	3	3	3	3R	–	3	3	15	–	–	–	–	0
Coetzee, R	2	2	2	2R	2	–	–	2R	2	2	2	2	2R	2	2	2	14	1	–	–	–	5
Van der Merwe, S	1	1	1	1	1	1	1	1	1	1	1	1	–	1	1	1	15	–	–	–	–	0
Wepener	2R	2R	2R	2	2R	2	2	2	–	–	–	–	–	–	–	–	8	1	–	–	–	5
Van Rooyen	1R	1R	1R	–	–	–	–	–	1R	3R	–	1R	–	–	–	–	6	–	–	–	–	0
Dreyer	3R	3R	3R	3R	3R	3R	3R	3R	3R	–	3R	3	3	3R	3R		15	–	–	–	–	0
Britz	4R	–	6R	6R	7	7	7	7	8	6R	–	–	4R	4R	5R	7R	13	–	–	–	–	0
Tecklenburg	6R	7R	7	7	6R	–	6R	–	8R	–	7R	7R	7	7	7	7	13	2	–	–	–	10
Cronje	9R	9R	9R	9R	9R	9R	9R	9R	9	9R	9R	9R	9	9	9	9	16	1	–	–	–	5
Hollenbach	11R	12	–	–	–	–	14R	–	–	–	–	12	12	12	12		7	1	–	–	–	5
Van Wyk	x	14R	15R	10R	15	15	–	–	–	–	–	–	15	15	15	–	8	1	–	–	–	5
Jonker	–	12R	13	11R	14	14	11R	–	12R	14R	15R	11	14	–	–	–	11	–	–	–	–	0
Lusaseni	–	4R	4R	4R	4R	5R	4R	4R	4	5R	4	4	–	–	–	–	11	–	–	–	–	0
Skosan	–	–	14R	–	11	11	11	14	11	14	–	–	14	–	15R		10	4	–	–	–	20
Jantjies	–	–	–	10	x	–	15R	15R	10R	10	10R	15R	2R	15R	11R	10	11	1	7	3	–	28
Fourie	–	–	–	1R	1R	1R	1R	1R	–	1R	1R	1	1R	1R	1R		12	1	–	–	–	5
Pretorius	–	–	–	–	–	2R	–	–	–	–	–	–	–	–	–	–	1	–	–	–	–	0
De Wit	–	–	–	–	–	6R	–	–	–	–	–	6R	–	–	–	–	2	–	–	–	–	0
Coetzee, A	–	–	–	–	–	15	15	–	–	–	–	–	–	–	15		3	1	–	–	–	5
Muller	–	–	–	–	–	–	4	4	–	4	5	5	–	–	–	–	5	–	–	–	–	0
Marx	–	–	–	–	–	–	2	2R	–	–	–	–	–	–	–	–	2	–	–	–	–	0
Volmink	–	–	–	–	–	–	11	–	11	13R	11	–	11	11	–	–	6	1	–	–	–	5
Mathee	–	–	–	–	–	–	4R	–	4R	4R	4	4	–	–	–	–	5	–	–	–	–	0
Van der Merwe, A	–	–	–	–	–	–	–	2R	2R	2R	2	2R	2R	2R	–	–	7	1	–	–	–	5
Hanekom	–	–	–	–	–	–	–	–	–	–	–	–	13	13	13		3	–	–	–	–	0
Marais	–	–	–	–	–	–	–	–	–	–	–	3R	–	–	–		1	–	–	–	–	0
38 Players																	**366**	**31**	**25**	**46**	**8**	**367**

Note: ■ = Yellow card

Records

MATCH RECORDS

Biggest win	50	vs Chiefs (53-3)	Bloemfontein	2000
Heaviest defeat	64	vs ACT Brumbies (0-64)	Canberra	2000
Highest score	65	vs Chiefs (65-72)	Johannesburg	2010
Most points conceded	72	vs Chiefs (65-72)	Johannesburg	2010
Most tries	9	vs Chiefs (65-72)	Johannesburg	2010
Most tries conceded	10	vs ACT Brumbies (16-64)	Canberra	2002
Most points by a player	32	GK Johnson vs Highlanders	Johannesburg	1997
Most tries by a player	3	JA van der Walt vs Bulls	Pretoria	1998
	3	JA van der Walt vs Stormers	Johannesburg	1998
	3	C Stoltz vs Crusaders	Nelson	1999
	3	G Bobo vs Bulls	Pretoria	2002
	3	GJJ Britz vs Bulls	Pretoria	2004
	3	J Fourie vs Blues	Johannesburg	2006
	3	H Mentz vs Reds	Brisbane	2009
	3	WG Mjekevu vs Chiefs	Johannesburg	2010
Most conversions by a player	7	CJN Fourie vs Bulls	Pretoria	2004
Most penalties by a player	9	ET Jantjies vs Cheetahs	Johannesburg	2012
Most drop goals by a player	2	GS du Toit vs Stormers	Cape Town	1999
	2	AS Pretorius vs Waratahs	Johannesburg	2009

SEASON RECORDS

Most team points	351	in 16 matches	2011
Most points by a player	157	LJ Koen	2001
Most team tries	37	in 11 matches	1999
Most tries by a player	9	JA van der Walt	1998
Most conversions by a player	22	AS Pretorius	2009
Most penalties by a player	36	LJ Koen	2001
Most drop goals by a player	6	AS Pretorius	2009

CAREER RECORDS

Most appearances	94	PJJ Grobbelaar	2004-2012
Most points	661	AS Pretorius	2002-2011
Most tries	24	J Fourie	2003-2009
Most conversions	102	AS Pretorius	2002-2011
Most penalties	121	AS Pretorius	2002-2011
Most drop goals	11	AS Pretorius	2002-2009

VODACOM SUPER RUGBY

Cell C Sharks

Ground: Growth-Point Kings Park **Capacity:** 52 000 **Address:** Isaiah Ntshangane Road, Durban
Telephone Number: 031-308 8400 **Colours:** Grey jersey with black and white trim, blacks shorts and socks **Website:** www.sharksrugby.co.za
Head Coach: Jake White **Captain:** Bismarck du Plessis **CEO:** John Smit
Chairman: Stephan Saad

Head Coach: Jake White **Forwards Coach:** Paul Anthony **Backline Coach:** Sean Everitt
Technical analyst: Brad MacLeod-Henderson **Manager:** Trevor Barnes
Doctor: Alan Kourie **Physiotherapist:** Deane Macquet **Physiotherapist:** James Fleming
Strength & Conditioning: Mark Steele **Biokineticist:** Jimmy Wright
Admin manager: Piet Strydom **Masseur:** Robert Russell **Media officer:** Novashni Chetty

VODACOM SUPER RUGBY

'96	'97	'98	'99	'00	'01	'02	'03	'04	'05	'06	'07	'08	'09	'10	'11	'12	'13	'14
4th	4th	3rd	7th	12th	2nd	10th	11th	7th	12th	5th	1st	3rd	6th	9th	6th	6th	8th	3rd

Played	Won	Lost	Drawn	Points for	Points against	Tries for	Tries against
18	12	6	0	443	358	32	30

Date	Venue	Opponent	Result	Score	Referee	Scorers
15 Feb	Durban	Bulls	WON	31-16	J Peyper	T: Jordaan, Reinach, Ndungane, Lambie. C: Lambie. P: Lambie (3).
22 Feb	Durban	Hurricanes	WON	27-9	A Lees	T: Mvovo, Alberts. C: Lambie. P: Lambie (5).
7 Mar	Durban	Lions	WON	37-23	J Peyper	T: Reinach, Coetzee, Ndungane, Jordaan. C: Steyn (4). P: Steyn (3).
15 Mar	Durban	Reds	WON	35-20	L v/d Merwe	T: Alberts, Chadwick. C: Lambie (2). P: Lambie (5), Steyn.
22 Mar	Pretoria	Bulls	LOST	19-23	M Fraser	T: Alberts. C: Swiel. P: Steyn (4).
29 Mar	Durban	Waratahs	WON	32-10	M Fraser	T: Coetzee, Daniel. C: Zeilinga (2). P: Zeilinga (5). Steyn.
12 Apr	Johannesburg	Lions	WON	25-12	C Joubert	T: Mvovo. C: Steyn. P: Steyn (4), Zeilinga (2).
19 Apr	Durban	Cheetahs	WON	19-08	J Peyper	T: Deysel. C: Steyn. P: Steyn (3), Swiel.
26 Apr	Durban	Highlanders	LOST	18-34	J Peyper	P: Swiel (6).
2 May	Melbourne	Reds	WON	22-16	A Lees	T: Pietersen. C: Steyn. P: Steyn (5).
10 May	Canberra	Brumbies	LOST	9-16	G Jackson	P: Steyn (3)
17 May	Christchurch	Crusaders	WON	30-25	R Hoffman	T: Reinach, Cooper, Sithole. C: Steyn: (2), Swiel. P: Steyn (2), Swiel.
23 May	Albany	Blues	WON	29-23	N Briant	T: Reinach, B du Plessis. C: Steyn (2). P: Steyn (3), Marais. DG: Steyn.
31 May	Durban	Stormers	LOST	19-21	J Peyper	T: Reinach. C: Steyn. P: Steyn (4).
5 Jul	Bloemfontein	Sharks	LOST	20-27	R Hoffman	T: B du Plessis, Reinach. C: Swiel (2). P: Swiel (2).
12 Jul	Cape Town	Stormers	WON	34-10	J Peyper	T: Jordaan, Sithole, Ungerer. C: Steyn (2). P: Steyn (5).

PLAY-OFFS

19 Jul	Durban	Highlanders	WON	31-27	SR Walsh	T: B du Plessis, Coetzee, Chavhanga. C: Steyn (2). P: Steyn (4).

SEMI-FINAL

26 Jul	Christchurch	Crusaders	LOST	6-38	G Jackson	P: Lambie (2).

> **‹ DID YOU KNOW? ›**
> In the Test against Ireland on 13 May 1961 at Newlands, Cape Town, there were four van Zyls in the team, namely Hennie and Ben-Piet on the wing, Hugo on the flank and Piet at lock. They were not related!

2014 SQUAD

PLAYER	Union	Debut	SHARKS CAREER M	T	C	P	DG	Pts	Debut	SUPER RUGBY CAREER M	T	C	P	DG	Pts
LC (Lourens) Adriaanse	KZN	2014	18	–	–	–	–	0	2011	48	–	–	–	–	0
WS (Willem) Alberts	KZN	2010	66	8	–	–	–	40	2007	103	12	–	–	–	60
LJ (Jacques) Botes	KZN	2005	115	27	–	–	–	135	2005	115	27	–	–	–	135
A (Anton) Bresler	KZN	2011	42	1	–	–	–	5	2011	42	1	–	–	–	5
DM (Dale) Chadwick	KZN	2012	26	1	–	–	–	5	2012	26	1	–	–	–	5
T (Tonderai) Chavhanga	KZN	2014	5	1	–	–	–	5	2004	53	17	–	–	–	85
M (Marcell) Coetzee	KZN	2011	54	8	–	–	–	40	2011	54	8	–	–	–	40
KL (Kyle) Cooper	KZN	2012	30	2	–	–	–	10	2012	30	2	–	–	–	10
KR (Keegan) Daniel	KZN	2006	105	16	–	–	–	80	2006	105	16	–	–	–	80
JR (Jean) Deysel	KZN	2008	67	1	–	–	–	5	2008	67	1	–	–	–	5
BW (Bismarck) du Plessis	KZN	2005	120	17	–	–	–	85	2005	120	17	–	–	–	85
JN (Jannie) du Plessis	KZN	2008	106	–	–	–	–	0	2006	132	–	–	–	–	0
PS (Pieter-Steph) du Toit	KZN	2012	22	–	–	–	–	0	2012	22	–	–	–	–	0
TJ (Thomas) du Toit	KZN	2014	4	–	–	–	–	0	2014	4	–	–	–	–	0
AP (Andre) Esterhuizen	KZN	2014	1	–	–	–	–	0	2014	1	–	–	–	–	0
WJ (Wiehahn) Herbst	KZN	2010	40	–	–	–	–	0	2010	40	–	–	–	–	0
PA (Paul) Jordaan	KZN	2012	30	5	–	–	–	25	2012	30	5	–	–	–	25
R (Ryan) Kankowski	KZN	2007	98	18	–	–	–	90	2007	98	18	–	–	–	90
P (Patrick) Lambie	KZN	2010	56	9	69	129	1	573	2010	56	9	69	129	1	573
JST (Joseph) Lewies	KZN	2014	17	–	–	–	–	0	2014	17	–	–	–	–	0
FS (Franco) Marais	KZN	2014	1	–	–	–	–	0	2014	1	–	–	–	–	0
SP (SP) Marais	KZN	2014	18	–	–	1	–	3	2013	26	–	–	1	–	3
C (Charl) McLeod	KZN	2008	73	5	–	–	–	25	2008	73	5	–	–	–	25
T (Tendai) Mtawarira	KZN	2007	102	2	–	–	–	10	2007	102	2	–	–	–	10
LS (Lubabalo) Mtembu	KZN	2012	16	1	–	–	–	5	2012	16	1	–	–	–	5
LN (Lwazi) Mvovo	KZN	2010	70	19	–	–	–	95	2010	70	19	–	–	–	95
OM (Odwa) Ndungane	KZN	2005	103	26	–	–	–	130	2004	113	29	–	–	–	145
E (Etienne) Oosthuizen	KZN	2014	15	–	–	–	–	0	2012	21	–	–	–	–	0
J-P R (JP) Pietersen	KZN	2006	112	34	–	–	–	170	2006	112	34	–	–	–	170
JM (Cobus) Reinach	KZN	2012	26	7	–	–	–	35	2012	26	7	–	–	–	35
SCT (S'bura) Sithole	KZN	2013	18	2	–	–	–	10	2013	18	2	–	–	–	10
FPL (Francois) Steyn	KZN	2007	68	4	23	53	8	249	2007	68	4	23	53	8	249
TG (Tim) Swiel	KZN	2014	6	–	4	10	–	38	2014	6	–	4	10	–	38
J (Jaco) van Tonder	KZN	2013	3	–	–	–	–	0	2013	3	–	–	–	–	0
S (Stefan) Ungerer	KZN	2014	4	1	–	–	–	5	2014	4	1	–	–	–	5
H (Heimar) Williams	KZN	2014	10	–	–	–	–	0	2014	10	–	–	–	–	0
FJ (Fred) Zeilinga	KZN	2013	4	1	2	7	–	30	2013	4	1	2	7	–	30
TOTALS			1671	216	96	193	9	1903		1836	239	96	193	9	2018

Note: KZN = KwaZulu-Natal

VODACOM SUPER RUGBY

APPEARANCES & POINTS

PLAYER	Bulls	Hurricanes	Lions	Reds	Bulls	Waratahs	Lions	Cheetahs	Highlanders	Rebels	Brumbies	Crusaders	Blues	Stormers	Cheetahs	Stormers	Highlanders	Crusaders	Apps	T	C	P	DG	Pts
Marais	15	15	15	15	15	14R	14R	11R	11R	13R	14R	15	15	15	15	15	15	15	18	–	–	1	–	3
Ndungane	14	14	14	–	–	14R	14	–	–	14	14	–	–	–	11R	–	–	–	8	2	–	–	–	10
Jordaan	13	13	13	–	–	–	–	13	13	12	12	12	12	12	–	12	12	13	12	3	–	–	–	15
Steyn	12	12	10	12	12	12	12	12	12	10	10	10	10	10	12	10	10	12	18	–	16	43	1	164
Mvovo	11	11	11	11	11	15	15	15	15	15	15	11	11	11	11	11	11	11	18	2	–	–	–	10
Lambie	10	10	–	10	10	–	–	–	–	–	–	–	–	–	–	–	14R	10	6	1	4	15	–	58
Reinach	9	9	9	9	9	–	–	–	–	x	9	9	9	9	9	–	9	9	12	6	–	–	–	30
Kankowski	8	8	8	8	8	8	8	8R	8R	8	8	x	7R	5R	–	8	8	8	16	–	–	–	–	0
Alberts	7	7	7	7	7	4	4	4	7	4	4	8	8	8	4R	7	7	4	18	3	–	–	–	15
Coetzee	6	6	6	6	6	6	6	6	6	–	–	–	6	6	6	6	6	–	15	3	–	–	–	15
Du Toit	5	5	5	–	–	–	–	–	–	–	–	–	–	–	–	–	–	–	3	–	–	–	–	0
Bresler	4	4	4	4	4	–	–	–	–	–	–	–	4	4	4	–	–	–	8	–	–	–	–	0
Du Plessis, J	3	3	3	3	3	3	3	3	3	3	3	3	3	3R	3	3	3	3	18	–	–	–	–	0
Du Plessis, B	2c	2c	2c	2c	2c	2c	2c	–	2c	2c	2c	2c	2c	2R	2c	2c	2c	2c	17	3	–	–	–	15
Mtawarira	1	1	1	1	1	1	1	1	1	1	1	1	1	1	–	–	–	–	14	–	–	–	–	0
Cooper	x	2R	x	2R	2R	2R	2R	2	x	x	2R	x	2R	2	2R	2R	2R	–	13	1	–	–	–	5
Chadwick	x	1R	1R	1R	1R	1R	1R	1R	1R	1R	1R	1R	1R	1	–	1R	1R	–	16	1	–	–	–	5
Adriaanse	3R	3R	3R	3R	3R	3R	3R	3R	3R	3R	3R	3R	3R	3	3R	3R	3R	–	18	–	–	–	–	0
Lewies	4R	4R	4R	5	5	5	5	5	5	5	5	5	5	5	5	5	–	5	17	–	–	–	–	0
Deysel	7R	7R	7R	–	–	7	7	7	–	7	7	7	–	–	7c	8R	4R	7	13	1	–	–	–	5
McLeod	9R	9R	9R	9R	9R	9	9	9	9c	9	9R	9R	9R	9R	9R	9	9R	9R	18	–	–	–	–	0
Williams	10R	x	12	12R	–	12R	10R	14R	10R	12	12R	x	x	12R	–	–	–	–	10	–	–	–	–	0
Sithole	x	14R	14R	13	13	13	13	13	11	–	13	13	13	13	14	14	14	15R	16	2	–	–	–	10
Zeilinga	–	–	x	–	–	10	10	–	–	x	–	–	–	–	–	10R	–	–	3	–	2	7	–	25
Pietersen	–	–	–	14	14	11	11	–	14	11	11	14	14	14	13	13	13	14	14	1	–	–	–	5
Van Tonder	–	–	–	15R	–	–	–	14	–	–	–	–	–	–	–	–	–	–	2	–	–	–	–	0
Oosthuizen	–	–	–	4R	4R	20R	4R	4R	4	4R	5R	4	4	4	8R	4R	5	7R	15	–	–	–	–	0
Mthembu	–	–	–	7R	5R	–	–	–	4R	–	8R	6	7	7	8	–	x	6R	9	–	–	–	–	0
Swiel	–	–	–	–	10R	–	–	10	10	–	–	10R	x	23R	10	–	–	–	6	–	4	10	–	38
Esterhuizen	–	–	–	–	22R	–	–	–	–	–	–	–	–	–	–	–	–	–	1	–	–	–	–	0
Daniel	–	–	–	–	–	8R	8R	8	8	6R	6	6R	6R	4R	–	–	–	–	9	1	–	–	–	5
Ungerer	–	–	–	–	–	9R	9R	x	9R	–	–	–	–	–	9R	–	–	–	4	1	–	–	–	5
Chavhanga	–	–	–	–	–	–	–	11	–	–	–	–	–	14R	13R	11R	14R	5	1	–	–	–	5
Marais	–	–	–	–	–	–	–	2R	–	–	–	–	–	–	–	–	–	–	1	–	–	–	–	0
Botes	–	–	–	–	–	–	–	–	–	–	6	–	–	–	–	–	–	–	1	–	–	–	–	0
Du Toit	–	–	–	–	–	–	–	–	–	–	–	–	–	1R	1	1	1	–	4	–	–	–	–	0
Herbst	–	–	–	–	–	–	–	–	–	–	–	–	–	1R	–	–	–	–	1	–	–	–	–	0
37 Players																			**397**	**32**	**26**	**76**	**1**	**443**

Note: ▨ = *Yellow card,* ■ = *Red card*

VODACOM SUPER RUGBY

Records

MATCH RECORDS

Biggest win	57	vs Rebels (64-7)	Durban	2013
Heaviest defeat	43	vs Crusaders (34-77)	Christchurch	2005
Highest score	75	vs Highlanders (75-43)	Durban	1997
Most points conceded	77	vs Crusaders (34-77)	Christchurch	2005
Most tries	10	vs Rebels (64-7)	Durban	2013
Most tries conceded	11	vs Crusaders (34-77)	Christchurch	2005
Most points by a player (Natal)	50	GE Lawless (4t, 9c, 4p) vs Highlanders	Durban	1997
Most points by a player (Sharks)	28	P Lambie (1t, 1c, 7p) vs Highlanders	Durban	2012
Most tries by a player (Natal)	4	GE Lawless vs Highlanders	Durban	1997
Most tries by a player (Sharks)	4	CS Terblanche vs Chiefs	Port Elizabeth	1998
Most conversions by a player	9	GE Lawless vs Highlanders	Durban	1997
Most penalties by a player	7	GE Lawless vs NSW Waratahs	Durban	1997
	7	PJ Lambie vs Highlanders	Durban	2012
	7	PJ Lambie vs Crusaders	Durban	2013
Most drop goals by a player	2	FPL Steyn vs Blues	Albany	2007
	2	F Michalak vs Stormers	Cape Town	2012

SEASON RECORDS

Most team points	498	in 19 matches	2012
Most points by a player	193	P Lambie	2011
Most team tries	56	in 13 matches	1996
Most tries by a player (Natal)	13	JT Small	1996
Most tries by a player (Sharks)	12	J-PR Pietersen	2007
Most conversions by a player	28	P Lambie	2011
Most penalties by a player	43	PJ Lambie	2013
Most drop goals by a player	4	FPL Steyn	2007

CAREER RECORDS

Most appearances	125	JW Smit	1999-2010
Most points	573	PJ Lambie	2010-2014
Most tries	35	CS Terblanche	1998-2011
Most conversions	69	PJ Lambie	2010-2014
Most penalties	129	PJ Lambie	2010-2014
Most drop goals	8	FPL Steyn	2007-2014

DHL Stormers

Ground: Newlands Rugby Stadium **Capacity:** 49 000
Address: 11 Boundary Road, Newlands, Cape Town **Telephone Number:** 021-659 4500
Colours: Navy blue jersey, shorts and socks **Website:** www.iamastormer.com
Coach: Allister Coetzee **Captain:** Jean de Villiers
CEO: Rob Wagner **Chairman:** Sam Dube **President:** Thelo Wakefield

Head Coach: Allister Coetzee **Assistant Coaches:** Robbie Fleck & Matthew Proudfoot
Defence Coach: Jacques Nienaber **Doctor:** Dr Arthur Williams
Strength & Conditioning: Stephan du Toit **Kicking Coach:** Greg Hechter
Physiotherapist: Wayne Hector **Masseur:** Greg Daniels **Media Officer:** Howard Kahn
Video Analyst: Human Kriek **Manager:** Chippie Solomon

VODACOM SUPER RUGBY

'96 11th	'97	'98 9th	'99 2nd	'00 5th	'01 7th	'02 7th	'03 9th	'04 3rd	'05 9th	'06 11th	'07 10th	'08 5th	'09 10th	'10 2nd	'11 2nd	'12 1st	'13 7th	'14 11th

Played	Won	Lost	Drawn	Points for	Points against	Tries for	Tries against
16	7	9	0	290	326	30	29

Date	Venue	Opponent	Result	Score	Referee	Scorers
22 Feb	Johannesburg	Lions	LOST	10-34	J Peyper	T: Ntubeni. C: Catrakilis. P: Catrakilis.
28 Feb	Cape Town	Hurricanes	WON	19-18	SR Walsh	T: Fourie. C: Catrakilis. P: Catrakilis (4).
7 Mar	Christchurch	Crusaders	LOST	13-14	R Hoffman	T: De Allende. C: Catrakilis. P: Catrakilis (2).
14 Mar	Hamilton	Chiefs	LOST	20-36	C Joubert	T: Aplon, Carr. C: Grant (2). P: Catrakilis (2).
22 Mar	Canberra	Brumbies	LOST	15-25	G Jackson	T: Vermeulen, De Jongh. C: Grant. P: Grant.
29 Mar	Brisbane	Reds	LOST	17-22	C Pollock	T: De Allende, Notshe. C: Grant, Catrakilis. P: Grant.
5 Apr	Cape Town	Waratahs	LOST	11-22	G Jackson	T: Van Wyk. P: Grant (2).
19 Apr	Cape Town	Lions	WON	18-3	S Berry	T: De Allende, Carr. C: Grant. P: Catrakilis, Grant.
26 Apr	Bloemfontein	Cheetahs	LOST	22-35	C Joubert	T: Williams, De Villiers, Carr. C: Grant, Coleman. P: Grant.
3 May	Cape Town	Highlanders	WON	29-28	C Joubert	T: Malherbe (2), De Allende, Kebble. C: Coleman (3). P: Grant.
10 May	Pretoria	Bulls	LOST	12-28	C Joubert	T: Coleman, de Jongh. C: Coleman.
17 May	Cape Town	Force	WON	24-8	C Pollock	T: De Jongh, Botha, Penalty try. C: Grant (3). P: Grant.
24 May	Cape Town	Cheetahs	WON	33-0	S Berry	T: Fourie, Van Wyk, Tagicakibau, Kolisi. C: Coleman, Grant. P: Coleman (2), Grant.
31 May	Durban	Sharks	WON	21-19	J Peyper	P: Coleman (4), Catrakilis (2). DG: Taute
5 Jul	Cape Town	Bulls	WON	16-0	C Joubert	T: Taute. C: Coleman. P: Coleman (3).
12 Jul	Cape Town	Sharks	LOST	10-34	J Peyper	T: Carr. C: Coleman. P: Coleman.

Note: * = *Western Province*

⟨ DID YOU KNOW? ⟩

When Jannie du Plessis made his debut vs Australia in 2007, he became the 11th Du Plessis to play for South Africa. The previous record was held by the famous Morkel family, of which 10 played for SA from 1903-28.

2014 SQUAD

PLAYER	Union	STORMERS CAREER Debut	M	T	C	P	DG	Pts	SUPER RUGBY CAREER Debut	M	T	C	P	DG	Pts
GG (Gio) Aplon	WP	2007	84	17	–	1	1	91	2007	84	17	–	1	1	91
R (Ruan) Botha	WP	2014	12	1	–	–	–	5	2014	17	1	–	–	–	5
SWP (Schalk) Burger	WP	2004	97	7	–	–	–	35	2004	97	7	–	–	–	35
M (Manuel) Carizza	WP	2014	5	–	–	–	–	0	2014	5	–	–	–	–	0
N (Nizaam) Carr	WP	2012	37	4	–	–	–	20	2012	37	4	–	–	–	20
D (Demetri) Catrakilis	WP	2014	8	–	4	12	–	44	2013	22	–	18	49	1	186
PM (Pat) Cilliers	WP	2013	23	–	–	–	–	0	2007	54	1	–	–	–	5
SH (Stephan) Coetzee	WP	2014	7	–	–	–	–	0	2014	7	–	–	–	–	0
KK (Kurt) Coleman	WP	2011	15	2	12	16	0	51	2011	15	2	12	16	0	82
D (Damian) de Allende	WP	2013	28	4	–	–	–	20	2013	28	4	–	–	–	20
JL (Juan) de Jongh	WP	2010	69	12	–	–	–	60	2010	69	12	–	–	–	60
J (Jean) de Villiers	WP	2005	105	28	–	–	–	140	2005	105	28	–	–	–	140
MC (Martin) Dreyer	Bol	2014	5	–	–	–	–	0	2014	5	–	–	–	–	0
R (Ryno) Eksteen	WP	2014	1	–	–	–	–	0	2014	1	–	–	–	–	0
R (Rynhardt) Elstadt	WP	2011	39	–	–	–	–	0	2011	39	–	–	–	–	0
DA (Deon) Fourie	WP	2008	84	12	–	–	–	60	2008	84	12	–	–	–	60
D (Dylon) Frylinck	WP	2014	1	–	–	–	–	0	2014	1	–	–	–	–	0
MG (Tazz) Fuzani	WP	–	0	–	–	–	–	0	–	0	–	–	–	–	0
PJ (Peter) Grant	WP	2006	104	10	126	188	0	866	2006	104	10	126	188	0	866
NJ (Nick) Groom	WP	2011	27	1	–	–	–	5	2011	27	1	–	–	–	5
J (Brok) Harris	WP	2007	93	2	–	–	–	10	2007	93	2	–	–	–	10
OR (Oliver) Kebble	WP	2014	9	1	–	–	–	5	2014	9	1	–	–	–	5
R (Rohan) Kitshoff	WP	2013	2	–	–	–	–	0	2013	2	–	–	–	–	0
S (Steven) Kitshoff	WP	2011	45	–	–	–	–	0	2011	45	–	–	–	–	0
J (Jean) Kleyn	WP	2014	4	–	–	–	–	0	2014	4	–	–	–	–	0
C (Cheslin) Kolbe	WP	2014	7	–	–	–	–	0	2014	7	–	–	–	–	0
S (Siya) Kolisi	WP	2012	44	4	–	–	–	20	2012	44	4	–	–	–	20
CR (Tiaan) Liebenberg	WP	2007	73	5	–	–	–	25	2006	86	6	–	–	–	30
JF (Frans) Malherbe	WP	2011	41	2	–	–	–	10	2011	41	2	–	–	–	10
S (Sikhumbuzo) Notshe	WP	2014	3	1	–	–	–	5	2014	3	1	–	–	–	5
S (Siya) Ntubeni	WP	2011	16	1	–	–	–	5	2011	16	1	–	–	–	5
MK (Michael) Rhodes	WP	2013	17	1	–	–	–	5	2011	28	3	–	–	–	15
L (Louis) Schreuder	WP	2011	39	1	–	–	–	5	2011	39	1	–	–	–	5
SM (Seabelo) Senatla	WP	2014	2	–	–	–	–	0	2014	2	–	–	–	–	0
SMS (Sti) Sithole	WP	2014	3	–	–	–	–	0	2014	3	–	–	–	–	0
M De K (De Kock) Steenkamp	WP	2010	49	–	–	–	–	0	2010	49	–	–	–	–	0
S (Sailosi) Tagicakibau	WP	2014	10	1	–	–	–	5	2005	17	2	–	–	–	10
JJ (Jaco) Taute	WP	2013	18	1	–	–	1	8	2010	49	10	–	2	1	59
JG (Jurie) Van Vuuren	WP	2014	5	–	–	–	–	0	2014	5	–	–	–	–	0
JP (Kobus) van Wyk	WP	2014	10	2	–	–	–	10	2014	10	2	–	–	–	10
MG (Michael) Van der Spuy	WP	2014	4	–	–	–	–	0	2014	4	–	–	–	–	0
AF (Allistair) Vermaak	WP	2014	6	–	–	–	–	0	2014	6	–	–	–	–	0
DJ (Duane) Vermeulen	WP	2009	78	3	–	–	–	15	2007	98	6	–	–	–	30
ME (Michael) Willemse	WP	2014	1	–	–	–	–	0	2014	1	–	–	–	–	0
DF (Devon) Williams	WP	2014	3	1	–	–	–	5	2014	3	1	–	–	–	5
Totals			1333	123	142	217	2	1530		1465	140	156	256	3	1794

Note: WP = DHL Western Province, Bol = Boland Cavaliers

VODACOM SUPER RUGBY

APPEARANCES & POINTS

PLAYER	Lions	Hurricanes	Crusaders	Chiefs	Brumbies	Reds	Waratahs	Lions	Cheetahs	Highlanders	Bulls	Force	Cheetahs	Sharks	Bulls	Sharks	Apps	T	C	P	DG	Pts
Aplon	15	11	11	11	15	15	–	–	–	–	–	–	–	–	14	14	8	1	–	–	–	5
Van Wyk	14	14	14	14	14	–	14	–	11R	11	–	14	14	–	–	–	10	2	–	–	–	10
Van der Spuy	13	–	–	–	–	14R	–	–	–	12R	20R	–	–	–	–	–	4	–	–	–	–	0
De Villiers	12c	13c	13c	13c	13c	12c	–	12c	12c	12c	–	–	–	–	–	–	9	1	–	–	–	5
De Allende	11	12	12	12	12	14	12	14	14	14	14	12	12	12	–	–	14	4	–	–	–	20
Catrakilis	10	10	10	10	x	10R	15R	10	–	–	–	–	10R	–	–	–	8	–	4	12	–	44
Schreuder	9	9	9R	9R	9R	9	9	9R	9R	9R	–	–	–	–	9R	9R	12	–	–	–	–	0
Vermeulen	8	8	8	8	8	8	8c	8	8	8	8	8c	8	8c	8	8	16	1	–	–	–	5
Burger	7	–	7	7	–	–	–	7R	7	7c	–	7c	–	7c	7c	–	9	–	–	–	–	0
Kolisi	6	7	–	6R	7	7	7	7	7	7R	7R	7	7R	7	8R	8R	15	1	–	–	–	5
Carizza	5	5	–	–	–	–	–	–	–	–	–	–	5R	6R	5R	–	5	–	–	–	–	0
Elstadt	4	4	–	–	–	–	–	–	–	–	–	–	–	–	–	–	2	–	–	–	–	0
Malherbe	3	3	3	–	3	3	3	3	3	–	–	–	–	–	–	–	9	2	–	–	–	10
Ntubeni	2	2	2	–	–	–	–	–	2	2	–	–	–	–	–	–	5	1	–	–	–	5
Kitshoff, S	1	1	1	1	1	1	1	1	1	1	–	–	–	–	–	–	10	–	–	–	–	0
Fourie	7R	6	6	6	6	2	2	2	2	2R	4R	2	2	–	2	–	14	2	–	–	–	10
Kebble	1R	x	1R	1R	1R	1R	1R	–	1R	1R	–	1R	–	–	–	–	9	1	–	–	–	5
Cilliers	3R	3R	3R	–	–	–	–	3R	–	–	3	3	3	3	3	3	10	–	–	–	–	0
Rhodes	5R	5R	4	–	5	5	5	5	5	5	–	4	4	4	4	–	14	–	–	–	–	0
Carr	6R	7R	7R	4R	7R	6	6	6	6	6	6	6	6	6	6	–	16	4	–	–	–	20
Groom	9R	9R	9	9	9	9R	9R	9	9	9	9	9	9	9	9	–	16	–	–	–	–	0
Coleman	10R	x	–	–	–	–	–	10R	10	10	10R	10	10	10	10	–	9	1	8	10	–	51
Eksteen	13R	x	–	–	–	–	–	–	–	–	–	–	–	–	–	–	1	–	–	–	–	0
Taute	–	15	15	15	–	15R	15	10R	15	15	15	15	15	15	15	–	14	1	–	–	1	8
Liebenberg	–	2R	2R	2	2	–	–	–	–	–	–	–	–	–	2R	2	6	–	–	–	–	0
Steenkamp	–	–	5	5	–	–	–	–	–	–	–	–	–	–	–	–	2	–	–	–	–	0
Tagicakibau	–	–	15R	15R	11	11	11	11	–	–	–	–	14R	11	13	13	10	1	–	–	–	5
Grant	–	–	10R	10R	10	10	10	15	10	10R	12	10	10R	12R	13R	10R	14	–	10	9	–	47
Botha	–	–	x	4	4	–	4	4	4	4	5	5	5	5	5	5	12	1	–	–	–	5
Harris	–	–	–	3	3R	3R	3R	3R	3R	3R	1	1	–	–	–	–	9	–	–	–	–	0
Coetzee	–	–	–	x	x	2R	2R	x	2R	–	2R	x	2R	2	–	2R	7	–	–	–	–	0
Dreyer	–	–	–	3R	–	–	–	–	–	–	x	17R	3R	x	3R	3R	5	–	–	–	–	0
Van Vuuren	–	–	–	–	4R	4	–	4R	4R	4R	–	–	–	–	–	–	5	–	–	–	–	0
De Jongh	–	–	–	11R	13	13	13	13	13	13	13	13	13	13	12	12	12	3	–	–	–	15
Notshe	–	–	–	4R	4R	7R	–	–	–	–	–	–	–	–	–	–	3	1	–	–	–	5
Fuzani	–	–	–	–	x	x	–	–	–	–	–	–	–	–	–	–	0	–	–	–	–	0
Williams	–	–	–	–	–	–	11R	11	–	13R	–	–	–	–	–	–	3	1	–	–	–	5
Kolbe	–	–	–	–	–	–	–	–	11R	11	11	11	14	11	11	–	7	–	–	–	–	0
Kleyn	–	–	–	–	–	–	–	–	4	7R	5R	4R	–	–	–	–	4	–	–	–	–	0
Vermaak	–	–	–	–	–	–	–	–	1R	1R	1	1	1	1	–	–	6	–	–	–	–	0
Frylinck	–	–	–	–	–	–	–	–	x	x	9R	x	–	–	–	–	1	–	–	–	–	0
Kitshoff, R	–	–	–	–	–	–	–	–	–	–	6R	–	–	–	–	–	1	–	–	–	–	0
Willemse	–	–	–	–	–	–	–	–	–	–	–	–	2R	–	–	–	1	–	–	–	–	0
Sithole	–	–	–	–	–	–	–	–	–	–	–	–	1R	1R	1R	–	3	–	–	–	–	0
Senatla	–	–	–	–	–	–	–	–	–	–	–	–	–	–	11R	15R	2	–	–	–	–	0
Penalty try	–	–	–	–	–	–	–	–	–	–	–	–	–	–	–	–	–	1	–	–	–	5

38 Players (of which 37 made an appearance during the season) — 352 30 22 31 1 290

Records

MATCH RECORDS

Biggest win	38	vs Lions (56-18)	Cape Town	2009
Heaviest defeat	61	vs Bulls (14-75)	Pretoira	2005
Highest score	56	vs Lions (56-18)	Cape Town	2009
Most points conceded	75	vs Bulls (14-75)	Pretoria	2005
Most tries	8	vs Blues (51-23)	Auckland	2004
	8	vs Lions (56-18)	Cape Town	2009
Most tries conceded	11	vs Blues (28-74)	Auckland	1998
Most points by a player	28	AJJ van Straaten (1t 4c 5p) vs Hurricanes	Cape Town	2000
Most tries by a player	3	BJ Paulse vs Bulls	Pretoria	2001
	3	PWG Rossouw vs Chiefs	Hamilton	2002
Most conversions by a player	6	PJ Grant vs W Force	Cape Town	2011
Most penalties by a player	7	JT Stransky vs Transvaal	Johannesburg	1996
	7	AJJ van Straaten vs Bulls	Pretoria	1999
	7	PJ Grant vs Crusaders	Cape Town	2010
	7	PJ Grant vs Cheetahs	Cape Town	2011
Most drop goals by a player	2	PC Montgomery vs Cats	Johannesburg	2000

SEASON RECORDS

Most team points	410	in 17 matches	2011
Most points by a player	170	JC Pietersen	2013
Most team tries	39	in 15 matches	2010
Most tries by a player	11	PWG Rossouw	2002
Most conversions by a player	23	AJJ van Straaten	2000
Most penalties by a player	44	JC Pietersen	2013
Most drop goals by a player	2	PC Montgomery	2000

CAREER RECORDS

Most appearances	105	A Bekker	2005-2013
	105	J de Villiers	2005-2014
Most points	866	PJ Grant	2006-2014
Most tries	35	BJ Paulse	1998-2007
Most conversions	126	PJ Grant	2006-2014
Most penalties	188	PJ Grant	2006-2014
Most drop goals	2	PC Montgomery	1996-2002

Blues

Ground: Eden Park **Capacity:** 42 500 **Address:** Walters Road, Mount Eden, Auckland
Telephone number: +64 9 815 4850 **Colours:** Blue with navy sleeves and white piping, blue shorts and socks **Website:** www.theblues.co.nz
Captain: Luke Braid **CEO:** Michael Redman **Chairman:** Tony Carter
Coach: Sir John Kirwan

Head Coach: Sir John Kirwan **Assistant Coach:** Grant Doorey **Assistant Coach:** Mick Byrne
Assistant Coach: Sir Graham Henry **Assistant Coach:** Nick White
Strength & Conditioning: Wally Rifle **Doctor:** Dr Stephen Kara
Physiotherapist: Mark Plummer **Analyst:** Troy Webber **Manager:** Richard Fry
Media officer: James Rigby **Mental Skills:** Ica Nacewa

VODACOM SUPER RUGBY

'96	'97	'98	'99	'00	'01	'02	'03	'04	'05	'06	'07	'08	'09	'10	'11	'12	'13	'14
2nd	1st	1st	9th	6th	11th	6th	1st	5th	7th	8th	4th	6th	9th	7th	4th	12th	10th	10th

Played	Won	Lost	Drawn	Points for	Points against	Tries for	Tries against
16	7	9	0	419	395	46	43

Date	Venue	Opponent	Result	Score	Referee	Scorers
22 Feb	Dunedin	Highlanders	LOST	21-29	G Williamson	T: F Saili, Ta'avao, Tuipulotu. C: Noakes (3).
29 Feb	Auckland	Crusaders	WON	35-24	M Fraser	T: Halai, Moala, Willison, Li. C: Hickey (3). P: Hickey (3).
8 Mar	Pretoria	Bulls	LOST	22-38	A Lees	T: Ahki. C: Hickey. P: Hickey (5).
15 Mar	Johannesburg	Lions	LOST	36-39	S Berry	T: Marshall, Hall, Piutau, Halai, Moala. C: Noakes (2), Hickey (2). P: Noakes.
22 Mar	Auckland	Cheetahs	WON	40-30	F Pastrana	T: Moala, Luatua, Li, Woodcock. C: Hickey (4). P: Hickey (4).
29 Mar	Auckland	Highlanders	WON	30-12	SR Walsh	T: Piutau, Moala, Nonu. C: Hickey (3). P: Hickey (3).
4 Apr	Canberra	Brumbies	LOST	9-26	R Hoffman	P: Hickey (3).
18 Apr	Wellington	Hurricanes	LOST	20-39	N Briant	T: Moala, Penalty try. C: Noakes, Marshall. P: Noakes, Marshall.
25 Apr	Auckland	Waratahs	WON	21-13	C Pollock	T: F Saili, Visinia. C: Hickey. P: Hickey (3).
2 May	Auckland	Reds	WON	44-14	N Briant	T: Hall, West, Willison, Visinia, Donnelly. C: Hickey (4), West. P: Hickey (3).
9 May	New Plymouth	Chiefs	LOST	20-32	M Fraser	T: Moala, Visinia. C: Hickey, West. P: Hickey (2).
23 May	Albany	Sharks	LOST	23-29	N Briant	T: Braid, Li. C: Hickey. West. P: Hickey (2), West.
31 May	Auckland	Hurricanes	WON	37-24	G Williamson	T: Moala, Kaino, Visinia, Tuipulotu, Penalty try. C: West (3). P: West (2).
28 Jun	Perth	Force	WON	40-14	R Hoffman	T: Faumuina, West, Visinia, Braid, Nonu, Ahki. C: West (5)
5 Jul	Christchurch	Crusaders	LOST	13-21	G Jackson	T: Halai. C: West. P: West (2).
11 Jul	Auckland	Chiefs	LOST	8-11	G Jackson	T: Moala. P: West.

Note: ■ = *Champion*

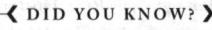

‹ DID YOU KNOW? ›

When the Springboks beat Wales 38-36 on 6 November 2004 at the Millennium Stadium in Cardiff, there were six players named Jones in the Wales starting line-up: Stephen, Duncan, Steve, Adam, Dafydd and Ryan.

2014 SQUAD

PLAYER	Date of Birth	Height	Weight	M	T	C	P	DG	Pts
PJ (Pita) Ahki	24/09/1992	1,80	95	9	2	–	–	–	10
KS (Kane) Barrett	16/04/1990	1,94	111	3	–	–	–	–	0
LG (Luke) Braid	05/101988	1,85	101	70	8	–	–	–	40
TJS (Tom) Donnelly	01/10/1981	2,00	118	98	4	–	–	–	20
CC (Charlie) Faumuina	24/12/1986	1,86	128	61	3	–	–	–	15
J (Jamison) Gibson-Park	23/02/1992	1,76	80	13	1	–	–	–	5
F (Frank) Halai	06/03/1988	1,95	105	31	13	–	–	–	65
BD (Bryn) Hall	03/02/1993	1,83	89	17	3	–	–	–	15
SC (Simon) Hickey	12/01/1994	1,74	83	10	–	20	28	–	124
J (Jeome) Kaino	06/04/1983	1,96	109	95	5	–	–	–	25
T (Tevita) Li	23/03/1995	1,82	94	8	3	–	–	–	15
DS (Steven) Luatua	29/04/1991	1,96	115	36	5	–	–	–	25
TR (Tom) McCartney	06/09/1985	1,85	109	63	2	–	–	–	10
JM (Jordan) Manihera	08/05/1993	1,95	113	2	–	–	–	–	0
B (Benji) Marshall	25/02/1985	1,82	93	6	1	1	1	–	10
KF (Keven) Mealamu	20/03/1979	1,81	108	162	10	–	–	–	50
G (George) Moala	05/11/1990	1,83	104	28	10	–	–	–	50
L (Liaki) Moli	04/01/1990	1,98	114	24	1	–	–	–	5
AN (Albert) Nikoro	07/08/1992	1,84	99	5	–	–	1	–	3
CM (Chris) Noakes	21/07/1985	1,81	88	28	2	34	32	–	182
MA (Ma'a) Nonu	21/05/1982	1,82	105	144	48	–	–	–	240
BR (Brendon) O'Connor	11/09/1989	1,86	100	27	–	–	–	–	0
JW (James) Parsons	27/11/1986	1,85	105	35	2	–	–	–	10
CT (Charles) Piutau	31/10/1991	1,86	95	41	8	–	–	–	40
SMJ (Sam) Prattley	16/01/1990	1,96	115	14	–	–	–	–	0
F (Francis) Saili	16/02/1991	1,78	99	28	5	–	–	–	25
P (Peter) Saili	04/01/1988	1,88	111	71	4	–	–	–	20
A (Angus) Ta'avo	22/03/1990	1,94	125	37	2	–	–	–	10
HS (Hayden) Triggs	22/02/1982	2,01	107	51	2	–	–	–	10
P (Patrick) Tuipulotu	23/01/1993	1,98	120	13	2	–	–	–	10
AOHM (Ofa) Tu'ungafasi	19/04/1992	1,95	129	12	–	–	–	–	0
L (Lolagi) Visinia	17/01/1993	1,94	99	10	5	–	–	–	25
PAT (Piri) Weepu	07/09/1983	1,78	96	124	6	51	57	–	303
IT (Ihaia) West	16/01/1992	1,75	84	7	2	12	6	–	52
JDK (Jackson) Willison	05/09/1988	1,83	94	60	9	–	–	–	45
TD (Tony) Woodcock	27/01/1981	1,84	118	129	10	–	–	–	50
TOTALS				1572	178	118	125	0	1509

APPEARANCES & POINTS

PLAYER	Highlanders	Crusaders	Bulls	Lions	Cheetahs	Highlanders	Brumbies	Hurricanes	Waratahs	Reds	Chiefs	Sharks	Hurricanes	Force	Crusaders	Chiefs	Apps	T	C	P	DG	Pts
Piutau	15	15	15	11	15	15	15	15	15	15	–	–	–	–	11	15	13	2	–	–	–	10
Halai	14	14	14	14	14	14	14R	14	14	14	14	14	14	14	–	–	15	3	–	–	–	15
Willison	13	12	12	12R	12	13	–	12	–	13	–	–	–	–	–	x	8	2	–	–	–	10
Saili, F	12	–	–	–	–	14R	13	13	–	–	–	–	12R	11R	13		7	2	–	–	–	10
Moala	11	13	13	13	13	11	13	14	–	13R	13	–	11	11	14R	14R	14	8	–	–	–	40
Noakes	10	–	x	10	–	–	10	–	–	–	–	–	–	–	–	–	3	–	6	2	–	18
Weepu	9	9	9	9	9	–	–	9R	9R	9R	–	9R	9R	–	–	–	10	–	–	–	–	0
Saili, P	8	8	8	–	8	–	–	–	8	6	–	6	6	8R	7R	7R	11	–	–	–	–	0
Braid	7c	7c	7c	7c	7c	7c	7R	7c	7c	–	7c	7c	7c	7c	–	–	13	2	–	–	–	10
Luatua	6	6	6	8	6	8	8	6	8R	8R	6	6R	6R	6	6	6	16	1	–	–	–	5
Donnelly	5	5	5	5	5	x	–	5	5	5	5	5	5	5	5	5	14	1	–	–	–	5
Moli	4	4R	4	4R	4	4	5R	–	–	–	–	–	–	–	–	–	8	–	–	–	–	0
Faumuina	3	3	3	3	3	3	3	3	3	3	3	3	3	3	3	3	16	1	–	–	–	5
Parsons	2	2	2	2	2	2R	2R	2R	2R	2R	x	2R	2R	2R	2R	2R	15	–	–	–	–	0
Tu'ungafasi	1	–	–	–	1R	1R	–	–	1R	–	–	–	1R	18R	3R	x	7	–	–	–	–	0
McCartney	7R	–	2R	x	2R	2	2	–	–	–	–	–	–	–	–	–	5	–	–	–	–	0
Prattley	1R	1	1R	1R	–	–	1R	1R	1R	–	x	1R	–	–	1R	1	10	–	–	–	–	0
Ta'avao	3R	3R	3R	3R	3R	3R	3R	3R	3R	3R	3R	3R	3R	3R	–	3R	15	1	–	–	–	5
Tuipulotu	4R	4	4R	4	–	–	–	4	4	4	4	4	4	4	4	4	13	2	–	–	–	10
O'Connor	5R	5R	8R	6	–	5R	7	4R	–	7	7	–	–	–	–	7	10	–	–	–	–	0
Hall	9R	9R	9R	9R	9R	9	9	9	9	9	9	9	9	9	9	9	16	2	–	–	–	10
Marshall	13R	x	–	15	11R	14R	11R	10R	–	–	–	–	–	–	–	–	6	1	1	1	–	10
Li	14R	11	11	–	11	–	11	–	–	–	–	11	–	15R	–	11	8	3	–	–	–	15
Hickey	–	10	10	10R	10	10	10	–	10	10	10	10	x	–	–	–	10	–	20	28	–	124
Mealamu	–	2R	–	–	–	–	2	2	2c	2c	2	2	2	2	2	2c	10	–	–	–	–	0
Woodcock	–	1R	1	1	1	1	1	1	1	1	1	1	1	1	–	–	14	1	–	–	–	5
Ahki	–	x	12R	12	–	13R	–	–	7R	–	15R	13	13	13	13	–	9	2	–	–	–	10
Manihera	–	–	–	6R	–	–	5R	–	–	–	–	–	–	–	–	–	2	–	–	–	–	0
Nonu	–	–	–	13R	12	12	–	12	12	12	12	12	12	12	12	12	11	2	–	–	–	10
Kaino	–	–	–	5R	6	6c	8	6	8	8	8	8	8	8	8	8	12	1	–	–	–	5
Triggs	–	–	–	4R	5	5	–	5R	5R	5R	5R	5R	5R	5R	5R	5R	11	–	–	–	–	0
Takulua	–	–	–	–	x	x	–	–	–	–	–	–	–	–	–	–	0	–	–	–	–	0
Visinia	–	–	–	–	–	–	11	11	11	11	15	15	15	15	15	14	9	5	–	–	–	25
Gibson-Park	–	–	–	–	–	–	9R	–	–	–	x	–	–	9R	x		2	–	–	–	–	0
West	–	–	–	–	–	–	–	x	12R	10R	10R	10	10	10	10		7	2	12	6	–	52
Barrett	–	–	–	–	–	–	–	–	–	–	x	–	–	–	–	–	0	–	–	–	–	0
Nikoro	–	–	–	–	–	–	–	–	–	–	x	15R	–	–	–	–	1	–	–	–	–	0
Penalty try	–	–	–	–	–	–	–	–	–	–	–	–	–	–	–	–	–	2	–	–	–	10
37 Players (of which 35 players made an appearance during the season)																	351	46	39	37	0	419

Note: ▓ = *Yellow card*

Records

CHAMPIONS: 1996, 1997, 2003

MATCH RECORDS

Biggest win	53	vs Hurricanes (60-7)	Wellington	2002
Heaviest defeat	47	vs Crusaders (12-59)	Christchurch	2012
Highest score	74	vs Stormers (74-28)	Auckland	1998
Most points conceded	63	vs Chiefs (34-63)	Hamilton	2009
Most tries	11	vs Stormers (74-28)	Auckland	1998
Most tries conceded	9	vs Chiefs (34-63)	Hamilton	2009
Most points by a player	29	GW Anscombe (2t, 2c, 5p) vs Bulls	Pretoria	2012
Most tries by a player	4	J Vidiri vs Bulls	Auckland	2000
	4	DC Howlett vs Hurricanes	Wellington	2002
	4	JM Muliaina vs Bulls	Auckland	2002
Most conversions by a player	7	AR Cashmore vs Stormers	Auckland	1998
	7	AR Cashmore vs Bulls	Auckland	2000
	7	CJ Spencer vs Bulls	Auckland	2002
Most penalties by a player	6	AR Cashmore vs Chiefs	Auckland	1998
	6	AR Cashmore vs Hurricanes	Auckland	1999
	6	JA Arlidge vs Bulls	Auckland	2001
	6	SA Brett vs Bulls	Auckland	2010
	6	C Noakes vs Stormers	Albany	2013
Most drop goals by a player	1	on eleven occasions		

SEASON RECORDS

Most team points	513	in 13 matches	1997
Most points by a player	180	AR Cashmore	1998
Most team tries	70	in 13 matches	1996
Most tries by a player	12	DC Howlett	2003
Most conversions by a player	34	AR Cashmore	1998
Most penalties by a player	34	AR Cashmore	1999
Most drop goals by a player	2	O Ai'i	2000
	2	SA Brett	2010

CAREER RECORDS

Most appearances	151	KF Mealamu	2000-2014
Most points	619	AR Cashmore	1996-2000
Most tries	55	DC Howlett	1999-2007
Most conversions	120	CJ Spencer	1996-2005
Most penalties	114	AR Cashmore	1996-2000
Most drop goals	3	CJ Spencer	1996-2005

VODACOM SUPER RUGBY

Chiefs

Ground: Waikato Stadium **Capacity:** 25 000 **Address:** Seddon Road, Hamilton
Telephone number: +64 7 839 5675 **Colours:** Black jersey with red and yellow panels.
Black shorts and socks **Website:** www.chiefs.co.nz
Coach: Dave Rennie **Captain:** Aaron Cruden & Liam Messam
CEO: Andrew Flexman **Chairman:** Dallas Fisher

Head Coach: Dave Rennie **Assistant Coaches:** Wayne Smith, Tom Coventry & Andrew Strawbridge
Strength & Conditioning Coach: Phil Healey **Video Analyst:** Regan Hall
Doctor: Dr Kevin Bell **Physiotherapist:** Paul Cameron **Manager:** Stewart Williams
Media officer: Kylie Sousa **Kit Manager:** Don Shergold **Masseur:** Dale McLunie
Sports Dietician: Dane Baker

336 SA RUGBY ANNUAL 2015 *www.sarugby.co.za*

VODACOM SUPER RUGBY

'96 6th	'97 11th	'98 7th	'99 6th	'00 10th	'01 6th	'02 8th	'03 10th	'04 4th	'05 6th	'06 7th	'07 6th	'08 7th	'09 2nd	'10 11th	'11 10th	'12 2nd	'13 1st	'14 5th

Played	Won	Lost	Drawn	Points for	Points against	Tries for	Tries against
17	8	7	2	414	410	48	39

Date	Venue	Opponent	Result	Score	Referee	Scorers
21 Feb	Christchurch	Crusaders	WON	18-10	C Pollock	T: Fruean, Lowe. C: Cruden. P: Cruden (2).
1 Mar	Hamilton	Highlanders	WON	21-19	R Hoffman	T: Nanai-Williams, Messam, Ngatai. C: Cruden (3).
14 Mar	Hamilton	Stormers	WON	36-20	C Joubert	T: Lowe, Latimer, Kerr-Barlow, Koloamatangani, T Marshall. C: Cruden (4). P: Cruden.
22 Mar	Perth	Force	LOST	15-18	L v/d Merwe	P: Cruden (4), Anscombe.
29 Mar	Pretoria	Bulls	DREW	34-34	C Joubert	T: Cruden, Anscombe, Messam, Symons, Muliaina. C: Anscombe (2), Cruden. P: Cruden.
5 Apr	Bloemfontein	Cheetahs	DREW	43-43	C Joubert	T: Tikoroituma (2), Pulu (2), Nanai-Williams (2). C: Cruden (5). P: Cruden.
12 Apr	Hamilton	Rebels	WON	22-16	M O'Brien	T: FitzGerald. C: Anscombe. P: Anscombe (5).
19 Apr	Hamilton	Crusaders	LOST	17-18	G Williamson	T: T Marshall. P: Anscombe (4).
25 Apr	Canberra	Brumbies	LOST	23-41	SR Walsh	T: Weber, Hohneck. C: Horrell (2). P: Anscombe (3).
3 May	Hamilton	Lions	WON	38-8	C Pollock	T: Aki, Ngatai, Anscombe, Manu, Latimer, Nanai-Williams. C: Anscombe (3). Horrell.
9 May	New Plymouth	Blues	WON	32-20	M Fraser	T: Tameifuna (2), Nanai-Williams, T Marshall. C: Anscombe (3). P: Anscombe (2).
24 May	Wellington	Hurricanes	LOST	8-45	A Gardner	T: Squire. P: Anscombe
31 May	New Plymouth	Waratahs	LOST	17-33	C Pollock	T: Aki (2). C: Cruden (2). P: Cruden
27 Jun	Dunedin	Highlanders	LOST	25-29	G Williamson	T: Sweeney, Hohneck, Nanai-Williams. C: Cruden (2). P: Cruden, Anscombe.
4 Jul	Hamilton	Hurricanes	WON	24-16	N Briant	T: Retallick, MacKintosh. C: Cruden. P: Cruden (4).
11 Jul	Auckland	Blues	WON	11-8	G Jackson	T: Messam. P: Cruden (2).
PLAY-OFFS						
19 Jul	Canberra	Brumbies	LOST	30-32	C Joubert	T: Aki, Anscombe, Kerr-Barlow, Nanai-Williams. C: Cruden (2). P: Cruden (2).

Note: ■ = Champion

〈 DID YOU KNOW? 〉

Two men named John Botha played lock for the Springboks a century apart. The first, lesser-known Botha played in the 3rd Test vs Britain in 1903 while, 99 years later, in 2002, John 'Bakkies' Botha made his debut!

VODACOM SUPER RUGBY

2014 SQUAD

PLAYER	Date of Birth	Height	Weight	M	T	C	P	DG	Pts
BTP (Ben) Afeaki	12/01/1988	1,93	127	36	1	–	–	–	5
B (Bundee) Aki	07/04/1990	1,82	92	25	10	–	–	–	50
GW (Gareth) Anscombe	10/05/1991	1,84	90	37	10	52	65	1	352
NB (Nick) Barrett	01/11/1988	1,84	116	1					0
SJ (Sam) Cane	13/01/1992	1,84	104	50	3	–	–	–	15
NJ (Nick) Crosswell	03/04/1986	1,95	110	42	–	–	–	–	0
AW (Aaron) Cruden	08/01/1989	1,78	85	73	10	92	123	–	603
RA (Ross) Filipo	14/04/1979	1,98	114	50	8	–	–	–	40
MJ (Michael) FitzGerald	03/02/1987	1,97	114	43	1	–	–	–	5
R (Robbie) Freuan	13/07/1988	1,90	108	66	16				80
NP (Nathan) Harris	08/03/1992	1,86	110	12					0
JW (Josh) Hohneck	06/01/1986	1,90	118	18	2		–		10
AA (Andrew) Horrell	18/07/1986	1,82	93	35	2	4	–	–	18
TNJ (Tawera) Kerr-Barlow	15/08/1990	1,87	90	56	6				30
TMPM (Tevita) Koloamatangi	07/09/1988	1,89	106	5	1				5
TD (Tanerau) Latimer	06/05/1986	1,86	101	113	9	–	–	–	45
AR (Anton) Lienert-Brown	16/04/1995	1,85	94	3					0
JFR (James) Lowe	08/07/1992	1,87	103	10	2				10
JL (Jamie) MacKintosh	20/02/1985	1,93	130	84	3				15
P (Pauliasi) Manu	23/12/1987	1,84	115	34	1	–	–	–	5
R (Rhys) Marshall	12/10/1992	1,84	104	18	1	–	–	–	5
TG (Tom) Marshall	05/07/1990	1,83	94	57	9				45
LJ (Liam) Messam	25/03/1984	1,90	108	130	27	–	–	–	135
JM (Mils) Muliaina	31/07/1980	1,83	93	110	30	1			152
TT (Tim) Nanai-Williams	12/06/1989	1,82	87	68	23	1	2	–	123
CJ (Charlie) Ngatai	17/08/1990	1,86	97	32	6	–	–	–	30
JM (Jordan) Payne	25/03/1993	1,87	95	2					0
AW (Augustin) Pulu	04/01/1990	1,80	93	35	3	–	–	–	15
BA (Brodie) Retallick	31/05/1991	2,04	117	57	3	–	–	–	15
MM (Mahonri) Schwalger	15/09/1979	1,80	107	68	–	–	–	–	0
LIJ (Liam) Squire	20/03/1991	1,95	112	10	1				5
DWH (Dwayne) Sweeney	08/08/1984	1,80	105	69	10	3			56
MJ (Matt) Symons	04/08/1989	2,00	117	14	1				5
BVC (Ben) Tameifuna	30/08/1991	1,82	137	50	10	–	–	–	40
KG (Kane) Thompson	09/01/1982	1,96	112	33	2				10
AT (Asaeli) Tikoiorutuma	24/06/1986	1,87	92	45	13	–	–	–	65
BM (Brad) Weber	17/01/1991	1,72	72	7	1				5
TOTALS				1598	225	153	190	1	1994

APPEARANCES & POINTS

PLAYER	Crusaders	Highlanders	Stormers	Force	Bulls	Cheetahs	Rebels	Crusaders	Brumbies	Lions	Blues	Hurricanes	Waratahs	Highlanders	Hurricanes	Blues	Brumbies	Apps	T	C	P	DG	Pts
Muliaina	15	15	–	14	15	12R	11	–	–	–	–	–	–	–	–	–	–	6	1	–	–	–	5
Nanai-Williams	14	14	14	13	14R	14	14	14	14	15	13	15	13	13R	13	13	13	17	7	–	–	–	35
Fruean	13	13	13R	–	–	–	–	–	–	–	–	–	13	–	–	–	–	4	1	–	–	–	5
Ngatai	12	12	13	–	–	–	–	–	13	–	13	–	–	12	–	–	–	6	2	–	–	–	10
Tikoirutuma	11	11	22R	11	11	11	–	–	11	–	–	11	11	–	14	14	14	12	2	–	–	–	10
Cruden	10c	10c	10c	10c	10c	–	–	–	–	12R	10c	10c	10c	10c	10c	–	10c	12	1	21	19	–	104
Pulu	9	–	–	9R	9R	9	9	9R	9	–	–	–	–	9	9R	9R	9R	11	2	–	–	–	10
Thompson	8	–	–	4R	8	4R	8	–	–	–	4R	–	–	–	–	–	–	6	–	–	–	–	0
Koloamatangi	7	x	8R	–	–	–	–	6R	–	–	–	–	7R	x	7R	x	–	5	1	–	–	–	5
Messam	6	8	6	6	6	8	8R	6c	8c	8c	8c	8c	6	6	6	6	6	17	3	–	–	–	15
Retallick	5	–	5	5	5	5	5c	5	5	5	5	5	5	5	5	5	5	16	1	–	–	–	5
FitzGerald	4	4	4R	4	5R	6	4	4	–	8R	4	4	4R	4	4	4	4	16	1	–	–	–	5
Tameifuna	3	3	3	3	3	3	3	3	3	3R	3	3	3	3	3	3	3	17	2	–	–	–	10
Marshall, R	2	2R	2R	2R	2	2	2	2	–	–	–	–	–	2R	–	–	–	9	–	–	–	–	0
MacKintosh	1	1R	1	1	1R	1R	1	1R	1R	1R	1R	1R	1	1R	1	1	1	17	1	–	–	–	5
Harris	7R	–	–	–	2R	2R	2R	2R	2	2	2	2	2R	–	2R	2R	–	12	–	–	–	–	0
Manu	1R	1	1R	1R	1	1	1R	1	1	1	1	1	1R	1	1R	1R	1R	17	1	–	–	–	5
Afeaki	3R	–	–	–	–	–	–	–	–	–	–	–	–	–	–	–	–	1	–	–	–	–	0
Symons	7R	5	4	–	4	4	–	4R	4R	4R	4R	–	4	5R	4R	4R	4R	14	1	–	–	–	5
Crosswell	8R	6	–	–	–	–	–	6	–	–	–	–	–	–	–	–	–	3	–	–	–	–	0
Weber	9R	9R	9R	–	–	–	–	9R	9R	x	9R	9R	–	–	–	–	–	7	1	–	–	–	5
Horrell	12R	13R	–	14R	13	13	13	13	13	10R	12R	–	12	–	–	–	–	11	–	3	–	–	6
Lowe	15R	15R	11	–	–	–	12R	11	11	–	–	11R	11	11	11	–	–	10	2	–	–	–	10
Kerr-Barlow	–	9	9	9	9	9R	9R	9	–	9	9	9	9	9R	9	9	9	15	2	–	–	–	10
Latimer	–	7	7	8R	7	6R	6	7	–	6	6	6	8R	7	7	7	7	15	2	–	–	–	10
Schwalger	–	2	2	2	2R	–	–	2	2R	2R	2R	2R	–	2	2	2	2	13	–	–	–	–	0
Squire	–	6R	8	8	–	–	–	8	–	x	6R	8	8	8	8	8	8	10	1	–	–	–	5
Hohneck	–	3R	3R	3R	3R	3R	3R	3R	3R	3	3R	3R	7R	3R	–	–	–	13	2	–	–	–	10
Anscombe	–	–	15	15	15R	15	10	10	10	10	10	11R	15	–	x	15R	11R	14	3	9	17	–	84
Marshall, T	–	–	12	12	12	12	12	15	15	15	12	15	11R	15	11	15	15R	15	3	–	–	–	15
Cane	–	–	–	7	8R	7	7	8R	7	7	7	7	7	–	–	–	–	10	–	–	–	–	0
Lienert-Brown	–	–	–	x	14	13R	x	12R	–	–	x	–	–	–	–	–	–	3	–	–	–	–	0
Aki	–	–	–	–	–	12	12	12	13R	12	12	12R	12	12R	12	12	–	11	4	–	–	–	20
Payne	–	–	–	–	11R	11	–	–	–	–	–	–	–	–	–	–	–	2	–	–	–	–	0
Filipo	–	–	–	–	4R	–	4	4	–	–	–	–	–	–	–	–	–	3	–	–	–	–	0
Sweeney	–	–	–	–	–	x	10R	14	14	14	14	14	–	11R	15	–	–	8	1	–	–	–	5
Barrett	–	–	–	–	–	–	–	–	–	–	–	–	–	x	x	3R	–	1	–	–	–	–	0
37 Players																		**379**	**48**	**33**	**36**	**0**	**414**

Records

CHAMPIONS: 2012, 2013

MATCH RECORDS

Biggest win	42	vs Cheetahs (45-3)	Hamilton	2013
Heaviest defeat	50	vs Cats (3-53)	Bloemfontein	2000
Highest score	72	vs Lions (72-65)	Johannesburg	2010
Most points conceded	65	vs Lions (72-65)	Johannesburg	2010
Most tries	9	vs Western Force (64-36)	Hamilton	2007
	9	vs Blues (63-34)	Hamilton	2009
	9	vs Lions (72-65)	Johannesburg	2010
Most tries conceded	9	vs Lions (72-65)	Johannesburg	2010
Most points by a player	32	SR Donald (1t, 9c, 3p) vs Lions	Johannesburg	2010
Most tries by a player	4	SW Sivivatu vs Blues	Hamilton	2009
	4	AT Tikoirotuma vs Blues	Albany	2012
Most conversions by a player	9	SR Donald vs Lions	Johannesburg	2010
Most penalties by a player	6	GW Jackson vs Queensland Reds	Rotorua	2001
	6	SR Donald vs Crusaders	Christchurch	2007
Most drop goals by a player	1	on eight occasions		

SEASON RECORDS

Most team points	369	in 15 matches	2009
Most points by a player	251	AW Cruden	2012
Most team tries	53	in 18 matches	2012
Most tries by a player	12	RQ Randle	2002
Most conversions by a player	43	AW Cruden	2012
Most penalties by a player	50	AW Cruden	2012
Most drop goals by a player	2	ID Foster	1996

CAREER RECORDS

Most appearances	130	LJ Messam	2006-2014
Most points	857	SR Donald	2005-2011
Most tries	42	SW Sivivatu	2003-2011
Most conversions	150	SR Donald	2005-2011
Most penalties	153	SR Donald	2005-2011
Most drop goals	2	ID Foster	1996-1998
	2	GW Jackson	1999-2004

Crusaders

Ground: AMI Stadium **Capacity:** 39 000 **Address:** 30 Stevens Street, Christchurch
Telephone: + 64 3 379 8300 **Colours:** Red jersey with black side panels. Black shorts and black socks **Website:** www.crusaders.co.nz
Coach: Todd Blackadder **Captain:** Kieran Read **CEO:** Hamish Riach
Chairman: Murray Ellis

Head Coach: Todd Blackadder **Assistant Coaches:** Dave Hewett, Aaron Mauger & Tabai Matson
High Performance Leader: Richard Smith **Analyst:** Jamie Hamilton
Logistics: John Miles **Doctor:** Deb Robinson **Physiotherapist:** John Roche
Manager: Angus Gardiner **Media officer:** Juliet Calder
Strength & Conditioning: Mark Drury

VODACOM SUPER RUGBY

'96	'97	'98	'99	'00	'01	'02	'03	'04	'05	'06	'07	'08	'09	'10	'11	'12	'13	'14
12th	6th	2nd	4th	2nd	10th	1st	2nd	2nd	1st	1st	3rd	1st	4th	4th	3rd	4th	4th	2nd

Played	Won	Lost	Drawn	Points for	Points against	Tries for	Tries against
18	12	6	0	515	361	48	38

Date	Venue	Opponent	Result	Score	Referee	Scorers
21 Feb	Christchurch	Chiefs	LOST	10-18	C Pollock	T: S Whitelock. C: T Taylor. P: T Taylor.
28 Feb	Auckland	Blues	LOST	24-35	M Fraser	T: Slade, Flynn, Crotty. C: Taylor (3). P: Taylor.
8 Mar	Christchurch	Stormers	WON	14-13	R Hoffman	T: Fonotia. P: Taylor (3).
14 Mar	Melbourne	Rebels	WON	25-19	J Leckie	T: Funnell. C: Taylor. P: Taylor (6).
28 Mar	Christchurch	Hurricanes	LOST	26-29	N Briant	T: McNicholl (2), Slade. C: Taylor. P: Taylor (3).
5 Apr	Johannesburg	Lions	WON	28-7	M vd Westhuizen	T: Ellis, Fonotia, Crotty. C: Slade, Bleyendaal. P: Slade (2), Dagg.
12 Apr	Bloemfontein	Cheetahs	WON	52-31	G Jackson	T: Nadolo (3), Slade, Dagg, T Taylor. C: Slade (4), Bleyendaal. P: Slade (4)
19 Apr	Hamilton	Chiefs	WON	18-17	G Williamson	P: Slade (6).
3 May	Christchurch	Brumbies	WON	40-20	G Jackson	T: McNicholl, L Whitelock, Nadolo. C: Slade, Heinz. P: Slade (7)
11 May	Brisbane	Reds	WON	57-29	J Peyper	T: McNicholl (2), Nadolo (2), L Whitelock, Crockett. C: Slade (6). P: Slade (5).
17 May	Christchurch	Sharks	LOST	25-30	R Hoffman	T: Slade. C: Slade. P: Slade (6).
24 May	Dunedin	Highlanders	WON	32-30	G Jackson	T: Taufua, Nadolo, Laulala, Perry. C: Slade (3). P: Slade (2).
30 May	Christchurch	Force	WON	30-7	M Fraser	T: Penalty tries (2), McNicholl. C: Slade (3). P: Slade (3).
28 Jun	Wellington	Hurricanes	LOST	9-16	M Fraser	P: Slade (3).
5 Jul	Christchurch	Blues	WON	21-13	G Jackson	T: Nadolo (2). C: Carter. P: Slade (2), Carter.
12 Jul	Christchurch	Highlanders	WON	34-8	C Joubert	T: Todd (2), Flynn, Nadolo. C: Carter. P: Carter (4).
SEMI-FINAL						
26 Jul	Christchurch	Sharks	WON	38-6	G Jackson	T: McNicholl, Read, Todd, Nadolo, Heinz. C: Carter (2). P: Carter (3).
FINAL						
2 Aug	Sydney	Waratahs	LOST	32-33	C Joubert	T: Todd, Nadolo. C: Carter, Slade. P: Slade (6).

Note: ■ = *Champion*

⟨ DID YOU KNOW? ⟩

In 1906 the Springbok selectors confused the two Marsbergs who were playing for Griquas – wing Artie and fullback Archie – and promptly chose Artie as fullback for the tour to the British Isles instead of his brother Archie!

2014 SQUAD

PLAYER	Date of Birth	Height	Weight	M	T	C	P	DG	Pts
S (Scott) Barrett	20/11/1993	1,97	108	1	–	–	–	–	0
DJ (Dominic) Bird	09/04/1991	2,06	112	26	–	–	–	–	0
T (Tyler) Bleyendaal	31/05/1990	1,85	96	20	2	10	27	–	111
DW (Dan) Carter	05/03/1982	1,78	94	128	33	264	285	11	1581
WWW (Wyatt) Crockett	24/01/1983	1,93	116	140	13	–	–	–	65
RS (Ryan) Crotty	23/09/1988	1,81	91	81	12	–	–	–	60
IJA (Israel) Dagg	06/06/1988	1,86	96	84	25	18	21	–	221
M (Mitchell) Drummond	15/12/1994	1,80	84	1	–	–	–	–	0
AM (Andy) Ellis	21/02/1984	1,82	89	125	21	–	–	3	114
CR (Corey) Flynn	05/01/1981	1,84	108	150	20	–	–	–	100
KT (Kieron) Fonotia	02/02/1988	1,86	108	10	2	–	–	–	10
OT (Owen) Franks	23/12/1987	1,85	118	93	2	–	–	–	10
BCJ (Ben) Funnell	06/06/1990	1,80	105	33	1	–	–	–	5
WA (Willi) Heinz	24/11/1986	1,79	93	56	4	1	–	–	22
NE (Nepo) Laulala	06/11/1991	1,84	116	15	1	–	–	–	5
R (Reynold) Lee-Lo	20/02/1986	1,81	96	17	1	–	–	–	5
D (David) Lienert-Brown	09/02/1993	1,85	106	2	–	–	–	–	0
RH (Richie) McCaw	31/12/1980	1,87	108	131	26	–	–	–	130
JZ (Johnny) McNicholl	24/09/1990	1,85	96	21	8	–	–	–	40
J (Joe) Moody	18/09/1988	1,88	112	21	–	–	–	–	0
N (Nemani) Nadolo	06/01/1991	1,96	125	14	12	–	–	–	60
TG (Tim) Perry	01/08/1988	1,88	116	16	1	–	–	–	5
KJ (Kieran) Read	26/10/1985	1,93	110	108	17	–	–	–	85
L (Luke) Romano	13/05/1987	1,98	110	53	5	–	–	–	25
CR (Colin) Slade	10/10/1987	1,83	90	64	8	60	89	1	430
J (Jordan) Taufua	29/01/1992	1,82	100	19	1	–	–	–	5
C (Codie) Taylor	31/03/1991	1,83	106	5	–	–	–	–	0
TJ (Tom) Taylor	11/03/1989	1,83	90	41	3	25	65	–	260
R (Rob) Thompson	06/11/1991	1,84	116	2	–	–	–	–	0
MB (Matt) Todd	24/03/1988	1,85	104	65	12	–	–	–	60
NH (Nafi) Tuitavake	21/01/1989	1,80	95	9	–	–	–	–	0
J (Jimmy) Tupou	08/08/1992	1,96	109	14	–	–	–	–	0
AJ (Adam) Whitelock	17/04/1987	1,85	95	55	7	–	–	–	35
GB (George) Whitelock	30/03/1986	1,90	106	85	8	–	–	–	40
LC (Luke) Whitelock	29/01/1991	1,90	104	42	5	–	–	–	25
SL (Sam) Whitelock	12/10/1988	2,02	116	76	3	–	–	–	15
TOTALS				1823	253	378	487	15	3524

APPEARANCES & POINTS

PLAYER	Chiefs	Blues	Stormers	Rebels	Hurricanes	Lions	Cheetahs	Chiefs	Brumbies	Reds	Sharks	Highlanders	Force	Hurricanes	Blues	Highlanders	Sharks	Waratahs	Apps	T	C	P	DG	Pts
Dagg	15	11R	11	15	15	15	15	15	15	15	–	15	15	–	15	15	15	15	16	1	–	1	–	8
McNicholl	14	–	14	11	11	14	14	14	14	14	14	14	14	14	10R	11R	14R	14R	17	7	–	–	–	35
Lee-Lo	13	13	13	–	–	–	–	13	13	–	–	–	–	–	–	–	–	–	5	–	–	–	–	0
Crotty	12	12	12	13	13	12c	12	12	12c	12c	12c	12c	12	12c	13	13	13	13	18	2	–	–	–	10
Tuitavake	11	11	–	14	14	–	–	22R	11R	x	11R	11R	11	–	–	–	–	–	9	–	–	–	–	0
Blyendaal	10	–	x	–	–	10R	10R	x	–	15R	x	–	–	–	–	–	–	–	4	–	2	–	–	4
Ellis	9	9	9R	9	9	9	9R	9R	9	9R	9	9	9	9	9	9	9	9	18	1	–	–	–	5
Whitelock, L	8	–	6	6	6	8	–	8R	8	8	8	8	6R	8	8R	8R	–	–	14	2	–	–	–	10
McCaw	7c	7	–	–	–	–	–	6	7	7	7	7	–	–	–	–	6	6	9	–	–	–	–	0
Whitelock, G	6	6	–	–	6	6	–	6R	6R	6R	–	–	–	–	–	–	–	–	7	–	–	–	–	0
Bird	5	5	x	5R	4R	4	4	4	–	4	4	4	4	4	4	4	4	4	16	–	–	–	–	0
Whitelock, S	4	4	5	5	5	5	5	5	5	5	5	5	5	–	5	5	5	5	17	1	–	–	–	5
Franks	3	3	3	3	3	3	3R	3	3	3	3R	3R	3R	3	3	3	3	3	18	–	–	–	–	0
Flynn	2	2	2	–	–	2R	2	2	2R	2	2	2R	2R	2	2R	2R	2	2	16	2	–	–	–	10
Perry	1	1	1R	1R	–	–	–	1R	1R	1R	x	1	1	–	–	–	–	–	9	1	–	–	–	5
Funnell	x	2R	2R	2	2	2	2R	2R	2	2R	2R	2	2	2R	2	2	2R	2R	17	1	–	–	–	5
Crockett	1R	1R	1	1	1	1	1	1	1	1	1	1R	1R	1	1	1	1	1	18	1	–	–	–	5
Laulala	x	3R	3R	3R	3R	3R	3	x	3R	3R	x	3	3	3	3R	3R	3R	17R	15	1	–	–	–	5
Romano	5R	5R	4	4	4	–	–	–	4R	4	–	–	–	–	–	–	–	–	7	–	–	–	–	0
Todd	6R	7R	7	7	7	7	7	7	7	–	–	–	–	7	7	7	7	7	14	4	–	–	–	20
Heinz	9R	9R	9	–	–	9R	9	9	10R	9R	9	14R	9R	9R	9R	9R	9R	9R	16	1	1	–	–	7
Taylor, T	10R	10	10	12	12	x	13R	13R	–	15	13	13	15	14R	10R	13R	12R	–	16	1	6	14	–	59
Thompson	x	14	–	–	–	–	–	–	–	–	–	–	11R	–	–	–	–	–	2	–	–	–	–	0
Slade	–	15	15	10	10	10	10	10	10	10	10	10	10	10	10	10	10	10	17	4	20	46	–	198
Read	–	8c	8c	8c	8c	–	8c	8c	–	–	–	8c	6R	8c	8c	8c	8c	8c	12	1	–	–	–	5
Whitelock, A	–	x	–	–	–	–	x	–	–	–	12R	15R	–	–	–	–	–	–	2	–	–	–	–	0
Fonotia	–	–	13R	13R	x	13	13	–	13	–	–	–	13	14	14	14	14	14	10	2	–	–	–	10
Taufua	–	–	x	6R	8R	8R	6R	6	7R	6	6	6	6	6	6	6	8R	x	14	1	–	–	–	5
Nadolo	–	–	–	15R	14R	11	11	11	11	11	11	11	11	–	11	11	11	11	14	12	–	–	–	60
Taylor, C	–	–	–	2R	2R	–	–	–	–	–	–	–	–	–	–	–	–	–	2	–	–	–	–	0
Drummond	–	–	–	11R	x	–	–	–	–	–	–	–	–	–	–	–	–	–	1	–	–	–	–	0
Lienert-Brown	–	–	–	–	x	1R	1R	–	–	–	–	–	–	–	–	–	–	–	2	–	–	–	–	0
Tupou	–	–	–	–	–	4R	4R	6R	–	4R	4R	4R	4R	4R	5	4R	4R	4R	12	–	–	–	–	0
Carter	–	–	–	–	–	–	–	–	–	–	–	–	10R	12	12	12	12	–	5	–	5	8	–	34
Moody	–	–	–	–	–	–	–	–	–	–	–	–	1R	1R	1R	1R	1R	–	5	–	–	–	–	0
Barrett	–	–	–	–	–	–	–	–	–	–	–	–	5R	–	–	–	–	–	1	–	–	–	–	0
Penalty tries	–	–	–	–	–	–	–	–	–	–	–	–	–	–	–	–	–	–	–	2	–	–	–	10
36 Players																			395	48	34	69	0	515

Note: ▪ = Yellow card

Records

CHAMPIONS: 1998, 1999, 2000, 2002, 2005, 2006, 2008

MATCH RECORDS

Biggest win	77	vs NSW Waratahs (96-19)	Christchurch	2002
Heaviest defeat	36	vs Queensland Reds (16-52)	Brisbane	1996
Highest score	96	vs NSW Waratahs (96-19)	Christchurch	2002
Most points conceded	58	vs Natal (26-58)	Durban	1996
Most tries	14	vs NSW Waratahs (96-19)	Christchurch	2002
Most tries conceded	8	vs Natal (26-58)	Durban	1996
Most points by a player	31	TJ Taylor (1t, 1c, 8p) vs Stormers	Christchurch	2012
Most tries by a player	4	CS Ralph vs NSW Waratahs	Christchurch	2002
	4	SD Maitland vs Brumbies	Nelson	2011
Most conversions by a player	13	AP Mehrtens vs NSW Waratahs	Christchurch	2002
Most penalties by a player	8	TJ Taylor vs Stormers	Christchurch	2012
Most drop goals by a player	3	AP Mehrtens vs Highlanders	Christchurch	1998

SEASON RECORDS

Most team points	541	from 13 matches	2005
Most points by a player	221	DW Carter	2006
Most team tries	71	from 13 matches	2005
Most tries by a player	15	RL Gear	2005
Most conversions by a player	37	DW Carter	2005
Most penalties by a player	43	AP Mehrtens	1999
Most drop goals by a player	4	AP Mehrtens	1998, 1999, 2002

CAREER RECORDS

Most appearances	150	CR Flynn	2002-2014
Most points	1581	DW Carter	2003-2014
Most tries	52	CS Ralph	1999-2008
Most conversions	264	DW Carter	2003-2014
Most penalties	285	DW Carter	2003-2014
Most drop goals	17	AP Mehrtens	1996-2005

‹ DID YOU KNOW? ›
Brothers Bert & Jock Kipling played for Griquas. Jock was a good utility forward and Bert was a hooker. The selectors intended selecting Jock but chose Bert by mistake for the 1931-32 tour to the UK! He played for SA until 1933.

Highlanders

Ground: Forsyth Barr Stadium **Capacity:** 30 000 **Address:** 130 Anzac Ave, Dunedin
Telephone number: +64 3 446 4010 **Colours:** Blue jersey with gold stripes. Blue shorts and socks
Website: www.thehighlanders.co.nz **Captain:** Ben Smith & Nasi Manu
General Manager: Roger Clark **Chairman:** Ross Laidlaw

Head Coach: Jamie Joseph **Assistant Coaches:** Scott McLeod, Jon Preston & Tony Brown
Administrator: Diane Ede **Conditioning Coach:** Andrew Beardmore
Physiotherapist: Adam Letts **Video Analyst:** Andy Watts **Doctor:** Dr Greg MacLeod
Sports Dietician: Dr Kirsty Fairbairn **Manager:** Graham Purvis **Media officer:** Amanda Gould
Commercial Manager: Mike Kerr **Scrum Coach:** Kees Meeuws **Kit Manager:** Neville Ives

VODACOM SUPER RUGBY

'96	'97	'98	'99	'00	'01	'02	'03	'04	'05	'06	'07	'08	'09	'10	'11	'12	'13	'14
8th	12th	4th	3rd	3rd	5th	4th	7th	9th	8th	9th	9th	11th	11th	12th	8th	9th	14th	6th

Played	Won	Lost	Drawn	Points for	Points against	Tries for	Tries against
17	8	9	0	428	473	42	55

Date	Venue	Opponent	Result	Score	Referee	Scorers
22 Feb	Dunedin	Blues	WON	29-21	G Williamson	T: A Smith, Fekitoa, B Smith, Osborne. C: Sopoaga (3). P: Sopoaga.
1 Mar	Hamilton	Chiefs	LOST	19-21	R Hoffman	T: Hardie. C: Sopoaga. P: Sopoaga (4).
15 Mar	Dunedin	Force	LOST	29-31	G Jackson	T: Parker, Fekitoa, Treeby. C: Sopoaga. P: Sopoaga (4).
21 Mar	Dunedin	Hurricanes	WON	35-31	N Briant	T: Osborne, Burleigh. C: Sopoaga (2). P: Sopoaga (7).
29 Mar	Auckland	Blues	LOST	12-30	SR Walsh	P: Sopoaga (4).
4 Apr	Dunedin	Rebels	WON	33-30	C Pollock	T: A Smith, B Smith, Christie. C: Sopoaga (3). P: Sopoaga (4).
11 Apr	Dunedin	Bulls	WON	27-20	R Hoffman	T: Evans, Sopoaga, Fekitoa. C: Sopoaga (3). P: Sopoaga (2).
25 Apr	Durban	Sharks	WON	34-18	J Peyper	T: A Smith, Fekitoa, Buckman, Christie. C: Sopoaga (4). P: Sopoaga (2).
3 May	Cape Town	Stormers	LOST	28-29	C Joubert	T: A Smith, B Smith, Fekitoa, Renata. C: Sopoaga (2), Renata (2).
10 May	Dunedin	Lions	WON	23-22	A Gardner	T: Buckman (2), Evans. C: Parker. P: Parker. DG: Parker.
16 May	Wellington	Hurricanes	WON	18-16	J Peyper	P: Parker (5). DG: Parker.
24 May	Dunedin	Crusaders	LOST	30-32	G Jackson	T: B Smith, Robinson, Fekitoa, Osborne. C: Parker, Sopoaga. P: Parker, Sopoaga
30 May	Brisbane	Reds	LOST	31-38	A Lees	T: Sopoaga, Osborne, Buckman, Tanaka. C: Sopoaga (2), Parker (2). P: Parker.
27 Jun	Dunedin	Chiefs	WON	29-25	G Williamson	T: B Smith, Osborne. C: Sopoaga (2). P: Sopoaga (4), Parker.
6 Jul	Sydney	Waratahs	LOST	16-44	SR Walsh	T: Burleigh. C: Parker. P: Sopoaga (3).
12 Jul PLAY-OFF	Christchurch	Crusaders	LOST	8-34	C Joubert	T: Buckman. P: Parker.
19 Jul	Durban	Sharks	LOST	27-31	SR Walsh	T: Hames, Fekitoa, Burleigh. C: Sopoaga (3). P: Sopoaga (2).

❮ DID YOU KNOW? ❯
South Africa's very first Test, in 1891, took place on a Thursday - the only logical explanation being that in those days Saturday was a working day and it was thought they might get more spectators on a Thursday.

2014 SQUAD

PLAYER	Date of Birth	Height	Weight	M	T	C	P	DG	Pts
LW (Lee) Allan	13/09/1991	1,90	103	2	–	–	–	–	0
SG (Sam) Anmderson-Heather	15/02/1988	1,84	104	1					0
KT (Kurt) Baker	07/10/1988	1,83	94	7	2	–	–	–	10
JJG (Josh) Bekhuis	26/04/1986	2,00	111	82	2				10
RJ (Richard) Buckman	27/05/1989	1,84	95	21	5				25
PD (Phil) Burleigh	22/10/1986	1,81	92	36	6	–	–	–	30
S (Shane) Christie	23/07/1985	1,84	107	17	2				10
LJ (Liam) Coltman	25/01/1990	1,85	109	27	–	–	–	–	0
MD (Matias) Diaz	16/02/1993	1,87	115	8					0
EC (Elliot) Dixon	04/09/1989	1,95	110	31	2	–	–	–	10
JWC (Jason) Emery	21/09/1993	1,73	88	14	1	–	–	–	5
GO (Gareth) Evans	05/08/1991	1,90	107	11	2	–	–	–	10
M (Malikai) Fekitoa	10/05/1992	1,87	99	17	7				35
SLM (Ma'afu) Fia	22/01/1989	1,80	114	36	–	–	–	–	0
TS (Tom) Franklin	11/08/1990	2,00	113	8					0
KS (Kane) Hames	28/08/1988	1,78	113	16	1				5
JI (John) Hardie	27/07/1988	1,83	103	44	2	–	–	–	10
JMRA (Jarrad) Hoeata	12/12/1983	1,95	115	58	1				5
TJ (TJ) Ioane	09/05/1989	1,82	104	18	–	–	–	–	0
CC (Chris) King	30/04/1981	1,86	118	123	7	–	–	–	35
JP (Juan) Koen	17/10/1983	1,83	116	3					0
LT (Nasi) Manu	15/08/1988	1,89	112	66	2	–	–	–	10
CW (Craig) Millar	29/10/1990	1,85	110	4					0
BT (Brayden) Mitchell	24/01/1989	1,83	104	12	–	–	–	–	0
PJJ (Patrick) Osborne	14/06/1987	1,89	105	20	7				35
HJ (Hayden) Parker	19/11/1990	1,75	80	21	1	9	18	2	83
TWK (Trent) Renata	13/05/1988	1,80	90	10	3	2	–	–	19
GP (Ged) Robinson	20/06/1983	1,78	104	66	8				40
AL (Aaron) Smith	21/11/1988	1,71	83	61	11	–	–	–	55
BR (Ben) Smith	01/06/1986	1,90	92	72	21	–	–	–	105
LZ (Lima) Sopoaga	03/02/1991	1,75	91	31	3	38	57	–	178
WTN (Winston) Stanley	11/02/1989	1,84	95	26	4				20
F (Fumiaki) Tanaka	03/01/1985	1,63	75	26	2	–	–	–	10
BC (Brad) Thorn	03/02/1975	1,95	112	111	12	–	–	–	60
S (Shaun) Treeby	26/01/1989	1,75	85	41	6	–	–	–	30
JT (Joe) Wheeler	20/10/1987	2,00	111	30	–	–	–	–	0
TOTALS				1177	120	49	75	2	845

VODACOM SUPER RUGBY

APPEARANCES & POINTS

PLAYER	Blues	Chiefs	Force	Hurricanes	Blues	Rebels	Bulls	Sharks	Stormers	Lions	Hurricanes	Crusaders	Reds	Chiefs	Waratahs	Crusaders	Sharks	Apps	T	C	P	DG	Pts
Smith, B	15c	15c	15c	15	15	15	15c	15c	15c	15	15c	15c	15	15	15	–	15c	16	5	–	–	–	25
Buckman	14	14	14	14	14	14	14	14	14	14	14	14	14	14	14	14	14	17	5	–	–	–	25
Fekitoa	13	11	13	13	13	13	13	13	13	13	13	13	13	13	13	13	13	17	7	–	–	–	35
Treeby	12	12	12	12R	12R	12	12	12	12	–	12	12	12	12	12	12	–	15	1	–	–	–	5
Osborne	11	–	–	11	11	–	11	11	–	–	–	11	11	11	11	11	11	11	5	–	–	–	25
Sopoaga	10	10	10	10	10	10	10	10	10	–	10	10	10	10	10R	10	–	15	2	27	38	–	178
Smith, A	9	9	9	9	9	9	9	9	9	9	9	9	9	9	9	9	9	17	4	–	–	–	20
Manu	8	8	8	8c	8c	8c	6R	8	8	8c	8	8	8c	8c	8c	8c	8	17	–	–	–	–	0
Christie	7	7R	7	7	7	7	7	7	8R	–	7	7	7	7	7	7	7	16	2	–	–	–	10
Evans	6	6	–	–	6	6	6R	–	7R	6R	6R	6	–	–	7R	6R	–	11	2	–	–	–	10
Hoeata	5	4	4	4R	5	4	4R	4	4R	–	4	4	4	–	–	–	4	13	–	–	–	–	0
Thorn	4	–	–	4	4	–	4	–	–	–	–	–	–	–	–	–	–	4	–	–	–	–	0
King	3	3	3	3R	3	1	3	3	3	1	–	3	3R	3R	3	3	3	16	–	–	–	–	0
Coltman	2	2	2	2	2R	2	2	2	2	2R	2	–	2	–	–	2	2R	14	–	–	–	–	0
Hames	1	1	1	1	1	–	1	1	1	3R	1	1	1	1	1	1	1	16	1	–	–	–	5
Robinson	2R	–	2R	2R	2	2R	2R	2R	–	2	2R	2	2R	2R	2R	2R	2	15	1	–	–	–	5
Fia	3R	–	–	3	3R	3	1R	3R	1R	3	3	3R	3	3	–	–	–	12	–	–	–	–	0
Millar	x	1R	x	–	1R	3R	x	1R	–	–	–	–	–	–	–	–	–	4	–	–	–	–	0
Bekhuis	4R	4R	4R	–	–	4R	–	4R	4	4	–	–	–	4R	5R	4R	5R	11	–	–	–	–	0
Ioane	5R	–	–	6R	6R	7R	–	–	8R	–	–	–	–	–	–	–	–	5	–	–	–	–	0
Tanaka	x	9R	9R	9R	9R	9R	9R	9R	x	x	x	9R	9R	9R	9R	x	–	12	1	–	–	–	5
Parker	10R	–	10R	10R	10R	–	–	–	10	10	10R	10R	10R	10R	10	–	–	11	1	5	10	2	51
Burleigh	11R	–	12R	12	12	–	–	12R	12	12R	12	12R	12R	12R	12R	12R	12	13	3	–	–	–	15
Stanley	–	13	–	–	–	–	–	–	–	–	–	–	–	–	–	–	–	1	–	–	–	–	0
Hardie	–	7	6	–	–	–	8R	7R	7	7	–	–	–	–	–	–	–	6	1	–	–	–	5
Wheeler	–	5	5	5	4R	5	5	5	5	5	5	5	5	5	5	5	5	16	–	–	–	–	0
Dixon	–	6R	6R	6	6	8R	6	6	6	6	6	4R	6	6	6	6	6	16	–	–	–	–	0
Renata	–	14R	–	–	–	x	11R	11R	11	12R	x	–	–	–	15	11R	–	7	1	2	–	–	9
Mitchell	–	2R	–	–	–	–	–	2R	–	–	–	–	2	2	–	–	–	4	–	–	–	–	0
Diaz	–	3R	x	3R	–	1R	–	x	1R	3R	x	18R	x	3R	3R	x	–	8	–	–	–	–	0
Baker	–	–	11	–	11	–	–	–	–	–	–	–	–	–	–	–	–	2	–	–	–	–	0
Emery	–	–	–	–	–	–	10R	11	11	–	–	–	–	–	–	–	–	3	–	–	–	–	0
Franklin	–	–	–	–	–	–	4R	4R	4R	5R	4	4	4	4R	–	–	–	8	–	–	–	–	0
Seiuli	–	–	–	–	–	–	–	–	x	–	–	–	–	–	–	–	–	0	–	–	–	–	0
Anderson-Heather	–	–	–	–	–	–	–	–	–	2R	–	–	–	–	–	–	–	1	–	–	–	–	0
Allan	–	–	–	–	–	–	–	–	–	–	–	6R	7R	–	–	–	–	2	–	–	–	–	0
Koen	–	–	–	–	–	–	–	–	–	–	–	17R	1R	3R	–	–	–	3	–	–	–	–	0

37 Players (of which 36 players made an appearance during the season)   375   42   34   48   2   428

Records

MATCH RECORDS

Biggest win	42	vs Bulls (65-23)	Invercargill	1999
Heaviest defeat	44	vs ACT Brumbies (26-70)	Canberra	1996
Highest score	65	vs Bulls (65-23)	Invercargill	1999
Most points conceded	75	vs Sharks (43-75)	Durban	1997
Most tries	9	vs Bulls (65-23)	Invercargill	1999
Most tries conceded	9	vs ACT Brumbies (26-70)	Canberra	1996
Most points by a player	28	BA Blair vs Sharks	Durban	2005
Most tries by a player	3	TM Vaega vs Western Province	Cape Town	1996
	3	DC Howlett vs Chiefs	Hamilton	1997
	3	JW Wilson vs Stormers	Cape Town	1998
	3	JC Stanley vs Stormers	Cape Town	1998
	3	TR Nicholas vs Bulls	Pretoria	2002
	3	BA Blair vs Sharks	Durban	2005
	3	IJA Dagg vs Bulls	Pretoria	2010
	3	AJ Thomson vs Rebels	Invercargill	2012
	3	KI Poki vs Cheetahs	Invercargill	2013
Most conversions by a player	7	TE Brown vs Bulls	Invercargill	1999
Most penalties by a player	8	WC Walker vs Chiefs	Hamilton	2003
Most drop goals by a player	1	on 18 occasions		

SEASON RECORDS

Most team points	374	from 12 matches	1998
	374	from 16 matches	2013
Most points by a player	178	LZ Sopoaga	2014
Most team tries	42	from 17 matches	2014
Most tries by a player	10	JW Wilson	1998
Most conversions by a player	27	LZ Sopoaga	2014
Most penalties by a player	38	LZ Sopoaga	2014
Most drop goals by a player	2	SD Culhane	1996
	2	BJ Laney	1999
	2	NJ Evans	2005
	2	HJ Parker	2014

CAREER RECORDS

Most appearances	127	AD Oliver	1996-2007
Most points	857	TE Brown	1996-2011
Most tries	35	JW Wilson	1996-2002
Most conversions	137	TE Brown	1996-2011
Most penalties	180	TE Brown	1996-2011
Most drop goals	5	TE Brown	1996-2011

Hurricanes

Ground: Westpac Stadium **Capacity:** 34 500 **Address:** Waterloo Quay, Wellington
Telephone number: + 64 4 389 0020 **Colours:** Yellow jersey with black piping, black shorts and socks **Website:** www.hurricanes.co.nz
Coach: Mark Hammett **Captain:** Conrad Smith **CEO:** James te Puni
Chairman: Brian Roche

Head Coach: Mark Hammett **Assistant Coach:** Alama Ieremia **Scrum Coach:** Dan Cron
Conditioning Coaches: David Gray & Paul Downes **Doctor:** Dr Theo Dorfling
Technical Advisor: Richard Watt **Physiotherapists:** Cam Shaw & Lee Van Santos
Manager: Tony Ward **Media Officer:** Hannah Fleming
Skills Coach: Clark Laidlaw **Masseur:** Paul Minehan

VODACOM SUPER RUGBY

'96	'97	'98	'99	'00	'01	'02	'03	'04	'05	'06	'07	'08	'09	'10	'11	'12	'13	'14
9th	3rd	8th	10th	8th	9th	9th	3rd	11th	4th	2nd	8th	4th	3rd	8th	9th	8th	11th	7th

Played	Won	Lost	Drawn	Points for	Points against	Tries for	Tries against
16	8	8	0	439	374	49	36

Date	Venue	Opponent	Result	Score	Referee	Scorers
28 Feb	Cape Town	Stormers	LOST	18-19	SR Walsh	T: J Savea, Jane. C: Barrett. P: Barrett (2).
7 Mar	Wellington	Brumbies	LOST	21-29	C Joubert	T: Thomson, Perenara. C: Barrett. P: Barrett (3).
15 Mar	Wellington	Cheetahs	WON	60-27	A Gardner	T: Barrett (2), Leiua, Smylie, Smith, Coles, Marshall, Thrush, Proctor. C: Barrett (5), Banks. P: Barrett.
21 Mar	Dunedin	Highlanders	LOST	31-35	N Briant	T: Barrett (2), Franks. C: Barrett (2). P: Barrett (4).
28 Mar	Christchurch	Crusaders	WON	29-26	N Briant	T: Leiua, Levave, J Savea, Perenara. C: Barrett (3). P: Barrett.
5 Apr	Napier	Bulls	WON	25-20	SR Walsh	T: Taylor. C: Barrett. P: Barrett (6).
18 Apr	Wellington	Blues	WON	39-20	N Briant	T: Leiua, Smith, J Savea, Matu'u, Perenara. C: Barrett (4). P: Barrett (2).
26 Apr	Wellington	Reds	WON	35-21	M Fraser	T: Jane (3), A Savea, Perenara. C: Barrett (2). P: Barrett (2).
3 May	Sydney	Waratahs	LOST	30-39	SR Walsh	T: Barrett, Toomaga-Allen, J Savea. C: Barrett (3). P: Barrett (3).
9 May	Melbourne	Rebels	WON	25-15	M O'Brien	T: Smith. C: Barrett. P: Barrett (6).
16 May	Wellington	Highlanders	LOST	16-18	J Peyper	T: Perenara. C: Taylor. P: Barrett (2), Taylor.
24 May	Wellington	Chiefs	WON	45-8	A Gardner	T: J Savea (2), Taylor, Franks, Shields, Lam. C: Barrett (6). P: Barrett.
31 May	Auckland	Blues	LOST	24-37	G Williamson	T: Levave (2), J Savea, A Savea. C: Barrett (2).
28 Jun	Wellington	Crusaders	WON	16-9	M Fraser	T: Thomson (2). Barrett (2).
4 Jul	Hamilton	Chiefs	LOST	16-24	N Briant	T: Parkes. C: Barrett. P: Barrett (3).

‹ DID YOU KNOW? ›
Natal fullback Tim Cocks (1980-81) & scrumhalf Kevin Putt (1994) each sat on the Springbok bench eight times without ever taking the field to win a Test cap. Both however at least played for the Springboks on overseas tours.

VODACOM SUPER RUGBY

2014 SQUAD

PLAYER	Date of Birth	Height	Weight	M	T	C	P	DG	Pts
MH (Mark) Abbott	20/02/1990	1,98	112	2	–	–	–	–	0
M (Marty) Banks	19/09/1989	1,90	90	5	–	1	1	–	5
BJ (Beauden) Barrett	27/05/1991	1,87	92	52	9	96	119	–	594
TES (Tim) Bateman	03/06/1987	1,83	91	72	6	–	–	–	30
JP (James) Broadhurst	01/12/1987	2,03	122	56	2	–	–	–	10
DS (Dane) Coles	12/10/1986	1,84	103	68	6	–	–	–	30
AL (Ash) Dixon	01/09/1988	1,82	102	15	3	–	–	–	15
BM (Brendon) Edmonds	28/11/1990	1,83	112	1	–	–	–	–	0
CI (Chris) Eves	11/12/1987	1,87	123	11	–	–	–	–	0
BJ (Ben) Franks	27/03/1984	1,84	118	112	6	–	–	–	30
R (Reg) Goodes	04/04/1992	1,84	112	30	1	–	–	–	5
BJA (Billy) Guyton	17/03/1990	1,87	91	1	–	–	–	–	0
AJ (Adam) Hill	19/10/1986	1,91	104	4	–	–	–	–	0
CS (Cory) Jane	08/02/1983	1,83	89	82	21	–	–	–	105
J (Jack) Lam	18/11/1987	1,88	103	53	3	–	–	–	15
A (Alapati) Leiua	21/09/1988	1,85	96	49	9	–	–	–	45
FJ (Faifile) Levave	15/01/1986	1,92	110	79	9	–	–	–	45
JR (James) Marshall	07/12/1988	1,83	90	12	1	–	–	–	5
M (Motu) Matu'u	30/04/1987	1,84	108	33	3	–	–	–	15
HW (Hadleigh) Parkes	05/10/1987	1,87	101	24	3	–	–	–	15
TJ (TJ) Perenara	23/01/1993	1,84	94	45	19	–	–	–	95
M (Matt) Proctor	26/10/1992	1,80	90	13	2	–	–	–	10
MJ (Mark) Reddish	03/03/1985	1,96	112	30	–	–	–	–	0
A (Ardie) Savea	14/10/1993	1,92	103	17	2	–	–	–	10
SJ (Julian) Savea	07/08/1990	1,92	103	56	24	–	–	–	120
JE (John) Schwalger	28/09/1983	1,87	122	84	3	–	–	–	15
BDF (Brad) Shields	02/04/1991	1,93	111	35	4	–	–	–	20
CG (Conrad) Smith	12/10/1981	1,86	95	110	21	–	–	–	105
CB (Chris) Smylie	22/03/1982	1,80	91	68	4	–	–	–	20
AS (Andre) Taylor	11/01/1988	1,78	93	54	16	2	1	–	87
BN (Blade) Thomson	04/12/1990	1,98	106	14	3	–	–	–	15
JI (Jeremy) Thrush	19/04/1985	1,98	115	95	9	–	–	–	45
J (Jeffrey) Toomaga-Allen	19/11/1990	1,92	125	41	3	–	–	–	15
C (Cardiff) Vaega	23/09/1991	1,82	102	1	–	–	–	–	0
VVJ (Victor) Vito	27/03/1987	1,93	109	69	8	–	–	–	40
TOTALS				1493	200	99	121	0	1561

VODACOM SUPER RUGBY

APPEARANCES & POINTS

PLAYER	Sharks	Stormers	Brumbies	Cheetahs	Highlanders	Crusaders	Bulls	Blues	Reds	Waratahs	Rebels	Highlanders	Chiefs	Blues	Crusaders	Chiefs	Apps	T	C	P	DG	Pts
Banks	15	15	15R	10R	15	x	x	–	–	–	–	–	–	–	–	–	5	–	1	1	–	5
Jane	14	14	14	–	–	14	14	14	14	14	14	14	14	14	14	14	13	4	–	–	–	20
Smith	13c	13c	13c	13c	13c	13c	13c	13c	13c	13c	13c	13c	13c	13c	–	–	14	3	–	–	–	15
Parkes	12	12	–	12	12	–	x	–	–	–	–	–	–	12R	12	6	1	–	–	–	5
Savea, J	11	11	11	11	11	11	11	11	11	11	11	11	11	11	11	11	16	7	–	–	–	35
Barrett	10	10	10	10	10	10	10	10	10	10	10	10	10	10	10	10	16	5	32	40	–	209
Perenara	9	9	9	9R	9	9	9	9	9	9	9	9	9	9	9	9	16	5	–	–	–	25
Thomson	8	8	8	8	–	8	5R	8R	5R	5R	5R	5R	–	–	5	5	13	3	–	–	–	15
Lam	7	7	7	8R	6	7	7	7	7	7	7R	7	7	7	8R	6	16	1	–	–	–	5
Levave	6	6	–	6	8	6	6	6	6	6	6	6	6	6	–	–	13	3	–	–	–	15
Abbott	5	–	–	–	4R	–	–	–	–	–	–	–	–	–	–	–	2	–	–	–	–	0
Thrush	4	4	4	4	–	4	4	4	4	4	4	4	4	4	4c	4c	15	1	–	–	–	5
Toomaga-Allen	3	3R	3R	3	3	3	3	3	3	3	3R	3	3	3	3	3	16	1	–	–	–	5
Coles	2	2	2	2	2	2	2	2	2	2	2	–	2	2	2	2	15	1	–	–	–	5
Franks	1	1	1	1	1	1	1	–	1	1	3	1	1	–	1	1	14	2	–	–	–	10
Matu'u	2R	2R	2R	2R	–	–	–	2R	2R	2R	2R	2	–	2R	2R	–	11	1	–	–	–	5
Eves	1R	x	1R	3R	1R	x	x	1R	3R	x	1R	x	3R	1R	3R	3R	11	–	–	–	–	0
Schwalger	3R	3	3	–	1R	3R	3R	–	–	–	–	–	–	–	–	–	6	–	–	–	–	0
Reddish	5R	5	5	5	5	4	5R	–	–	–	–	–	–	–	–	–	6	–	–	–	–	0
Hill	6R	–	6	–	6R	–	–	–	–	–	–	–	–	–	–	6R	4	–	–	–	–	0
Smylie	9R	9R	9R	9	–	–	–	9R	9R	–	–	x	9R	9R	9R	9R	10	1	–	–	–	5
Leiua	11R	x	12R	14	14	14	12	12	12	12	12	10R	12	12	12	–	14	3	–	–	–	15
Marshall	x	x	15	15	–	–	–	–	–	–	–	–	–	14R	x	11R	4	–	–	–	–	0
Broadhurst	–	5R	5R	5R	5	5	5	5	5	5	5	5	5	5	6R	8R	15	–	–	–	–	0
Savea, A	–	6R	6R	7	7	8R	–	7R	7R	4R	7	7R	7R	7R	7	7	14	2	–	–	–	10
Vaega	–	–	12	–	–	–	–	–	–	–	–	–	–	–	–	x	1	–	–	–	–	0
Proctor	–	–	–	12R	12R	x	–	15R	15R	15R	x	–	15R	15	15	15	9	1	–	–	–	5
Taylor	–	–	–	–	15R	15	15	15	15	15	15	15	15	–	–	–	9	2	1	1	–	15
Dixon	–	–	–	–	2R	2R	2R	–	–	–	–	2R	2R	–	–	2R	6	–	–	–	–	0
Guyton	–	–	–	–	x	x	x	–	–	9R	x	–	–	–	–	–	1	–	–	–	–	0
Bateman	–	–	–	–	–	12	–	12R	11R	14R	12R	12	13R	11R	13	13	10	–	–	–	–	0
Vito	–	–	–	–	–	–	8	8	8	8	8	8	8	8	8	–	9	–	–	–	–	0
Goodes	–	–	–	–	–	–	1R	1	1R	1R	1	1R	1R	1	2R	1R	10	–	–	–	–	0
Shields	–	–	–	–	–	–	8R	–	–	–	–	6R	5R	5R	6	8	6	1	–	–	–	5
Edmonds	–	–	–	–	–	–	3R	–	–	–	–	–	x	–	–	–	1	–	–	–	–	0
35 Players																	347	49	34	42	0	439

Note: ▪ = Yellow card

Records

MATCH RECORDS

Biggest win	49	vs Brumbies (56-7)	Wellington	2009
Heaviest defeat	53	vs Blues (7-60)	Wellington	2002
Highest score	64	vs Northern Transvaal (64-32)	New Plymouth	1997
	66	vs Melbourne Rebels (66-24)	Wellington	2012
Most points conceded	60	vs Blues (7-60)	Wellington	2002
Most tries	9	vs Highlanders (60-34)	Wellington	1997
	9	vs Melbourne Rebels (66-24)	Wellington	2012
	9	vs Cheetahs (60-27)	Wellington	2014
Most tries conceded	8	vs Blues (7-60)	Wellington	2002
Most points by a player	30	DE Holwell (1t, 2c, 7p) vs Highlanders	Napier	2001
Most tries by a player	3	JF Umaga vs Northern Transvaal	New Plymouth	1997
	3	JF Umaga vs Highlanders	Wellington	1997
	3	CM Cullen vs Free State	Wellington	1997
	3	JD O'Halloran vs Blues	Wellington	1998
	3	JF Umaga vs Queensland Reds	New Plymouth	2000
	3	MA Nonu vs ACT Brumbies	Wellington	2005
	3	AK Hore vs Chiefs	Wellington	2006
	3	HE Gear vs Reds	Wellington	2010
	3	TJ Perenara vs Force	Perth	2012
	3	SJ Savea vs Melbourne Rebels	Wellington	2012
	3	CS Jane vs Reds	Wellington	2014
Most conversions by a player	9	BJ Barrett vs Melbourne Rebels	Wellington	2012
Most penalties by a player	7	JB Cameron vs Blues	Palmerston North	1996
	7	DE Holwell vs Highlanders	Napier	2001
Most drop goals by a player	1	By three players		

SEASON RECORDS

Most team points	489	from 16 matches	2012
Most points by a player	209	BJ Barrett	2014
Most team tries	58	from 16 matches	2012
Most tries by a player	12	JF Umaga	1997
Most conversions by a player	35	BJ Barrett	2012
Most penalties by a player	40	BJ Barrett	2013
Most drop goals by a player	1	By three players	

CAREER RECORDS

Most appearances	122	JF Umaga	1996-2007
Most points	676	DE Holwell	1998-2006
Most tries	56	CM Cullen	1996-2003
Most conversions	118	DE Holwell	1998-2006
Most penalties	135	DE Holwell	1998-2006
Most drop goals	1	By three players	

ACT Brumbies

Ground: Canberra Stadium **Capacity:** 27 000 **Address:** Battye St, Bruce ACT
Telephone number: +61 2 6260 8588 **Colours:** Navy blue jersey with gold trim and white sides, navy shorts and socks **Website:** www.brumbies.com.au **Director of Rugby:** Laurie Fisher
Head Coach: Stephen Larkham **Captain:** Ben Mowen **CEO:** Simon Chester
Charmain: Sean Hammond **President:** Geoff Larkham

Director of Rugby: Laurie Fisher **Head Coach:** Stephen Larkham **Defence Coach:** Dan McKellar
Kicking Coach: Damien Hill **Team Manager:** Tony Thorpe **Asst Manager:** Sam Irwin
Strength & Conditioning: Damien Marsh **Performance Analyst:** Warrick Harrington
Doctor: Dr Kate Gazzard **Physiotherapist:** Hamish Macauley
Media officer: Elliott Woods

VODACOM SUPER RUGBY

'96	'97	'98	'99	'00	'01	'02	'03	'04	'05	'06	'07	'08	'09	'10	'11	'12	'13	'14
5th	2nd	10th	5th	1st	1st	3rd	4th	1st	5th	6th	5th	9th	7th	6th	13th	7th	3rd	4th

Played	Won	Lost	Drawn	Points for	Points against	Tries for	Tries against
18	11	7	0	452	437	54	42

Date	Venue	Opponent	Result	Score	Referee	Scorers
22 Feb	Canberra	Reds	LOST	17-27	J Leckie	T: Mogg. P: Mogg (3), White.
1 Mar	Perth	Force	WON	27-14	N Briant	T: Mogg, Fardy, Coleman. C: White (3). P: White (2)
7 Mar	Wellington	Hurricanes	WON	29-21	C Joubert	T: Mogg, McCaffrey, Coleman, Kuridrani. C: White (3). P: White
15 Mar	Canberra	Waratahs	WON	28-23	J Peyper	T: Mogg, White, Kuridrani. C: White (2). P: White (3)
22 Mar	Canberra	Stormers	WON	25-15	G Jackson	T: Coleman (2), Penalty try. C: White (2). P: White (2)
28 Mar	Melbourne	Rebels	LOST	24-32	J Peyper	T: Mogg, Coleman, Penalty try. C: White (2), Toomua. P: White
4 Apr	Canberra	Blues	WON	26-9	R Hoffman	T: McCabe (2), Coleman. C: White. P: White (2), Lealiifano
11 Apr	Brisbane	Reds	WON	23-20	SR Walsh	T: Tomane, Fardy. C: White (2). P: White (3)
25 Apr	Canberra	Chiefs	WON	41-23	SR Walsh	T: Toomua (2), Kuridrani (2), Tomane. C: White, Lealiifano, P: White (2), Lealiifano (2)
3 May	Christchurch	Crusaders	LOST	20-40	G Jackson	T: McCabe, Moore. C: Lealiifano, Toomua. P: White (2)
10 May	Canberra	Sharks	WON	16-9	G Jackson	T: Carter. C: Lealiifano. P: Lealiifano (3).
17 May	Bloemfontein	Cheetahs	LOST	21-27	M vd Westhuizen	T: Coleman, Moore. C: White. P: White (3).
23 May	Pretoria	Bulls	LOST	23-44	C Joubert	T: Mowen, Speight, Kuridrani. C: Lealiifano P: Lealiifano (2).
31 May	Canberra	Rebels	WON	37-10	SR Walsh	T: Toomua (2), McCabe, Carter, Sio, Power. C: Lealiifano (2). P: Laeliifano.
28 Jun	Sydney	Waratahs	LOST	8-39	SR Walsh	T: Mogg. P: Lealiifano
11 Jul	Canberra	Force	WON	47-25	SR Walsh	T: Toomua (3), Speight, Mogg, Tomane, McVerry. C: Lealiifano (3). P: Lealiifano(2).

PLAY-OFF

Date	Venue	Opponent	Result	Score	Referee	Scorers
19 Jul	Canberra	Chiefs	WON	32-30	C Joubert	T: Butler, Mogg, White, Coleman. C: Lealiifano (3). P: Lealiifano (2)

SEMI-FINAL

Date	Venue	Opponent	Result	Score	Referee	Scorers
26 Jul	Sydney	Waratahs	LOST	8-26	J Peyper	T: Speight. P: Lealiifano.

Note: ■ = Champion

2014 SQUAD

PLAYER	Date of Birth	Height	Weight	M	T	C	P	DG	Pts
A (Allan) Ala'alatoa	28/01/1994	1,82	120	2	–	–	–	–	0
BE (Ben) Alexander	14/11/1988	1,88	116	99	16	–	–	–	80
FM (Fotu) Auelua	29/01/1984	1,89	115	33	1	–	–	–	5
JM (Jarrad) Butler	20/07/1991	1,86	106	30	1	–	–	–	5
S (Sam) Carter	10/09/1989	2,00	110	50	4	–	–	–	20
RJ (Robbie) Coleman	03/08/1990	1,79	83	52	15	–	–	–	75
L (Lionel) Cronje	25/05/1989	1,84	92	10	–	4	8	–	32
M (Michael) Dowsett	23/03/1992	1,82	85	6	–	–	–	–	0
SM (Scott) Fardy	05/07/1984	1,98	113	48	5	–	–	–	25
C (Conrad) Hoffman	09/11/1987	1,81	82	17	–	–	–	–	0
LR (Luke) Holmes	14/10/1983	1,84	105	35	1	–	–	–	5
R (Rodney) Iona	17/08/1991	1,77	89	1	–	–	–	–	0
RTRN (Tevita) Kuridrani	31/03/1991	1,96	102	43	9	–	–	–	45
CP (Christian) Lealiifano	25/09/1991	1,80	89	83	12	51	98	2	465
JW (John) Mann-Rea	19/02/1981	1,81	105	11	–	–	–	–	0
P (Pat) McCabe	21/03/1988	1,85	90	76	10	–	–	–	50
L (Lachlan) McCaffrey	17/03/1990	1,94	108	16	1	–	–	–	5
MT (Tom) McVerry	30/06/1980	1,90	106	47	1	–	–	–	5
JD (Jesse) Mogg	08/06/1989	1,87	90	50	18	1	14	–	134
ST (Stephen) Moore	20/01/1983	1,90	112	131	9	–	–	–	45
BSC (Ben) Mowen	12/01/1984	1,95	106	93	8	–	–	–	40
RA (Ruaidhri) Murphy	05/07/1987	1,87	119	29	1	–	–	–	5
DW (David) Pocock	23/04/1988	1,83	101	74	8	–	–	–	40
LW (Leon) Power	27/02/1986	2,00	116	20	–	–	–	–	0
C (Clyde) Rathbone	23/07/1981	1,80	97	66	18	–	–	–	90
S (Siliva) Siliva	11/12/1991	1,78	113	16	1	–	–	–	5
ST (Scott) Sio	16/10/1991	1,87	116	36	2	–	–	–	10
J (Jordan) Smiler	19/06/1985	1,91	102	15	–	–	–	–	0
A (Andrew) Smith	10/01/1985	1,93	105	52	6	–	–	–	30
J-P (Jean-Pierre) Smith	24/01/1990	1,88	124	12	–	–	–	–	0
R-H (Ruan) Smith	24/01/1990	1,87	125	26	–	–	–	–	0
HV (Henry) Speight	24/03/1988	1,86	97	57	22	–	–	–	110
T (Thomas) Staniforth	13/08/1994	1,97	107	1	–	–	–	–	0
JM (Joe) Tomane	02/02/1990	1,90	102	42	11	–	–	–	55
MP (Matt) Toomua	03/01/1994	1,83	88	64	12	4	–	1	77
WJ (Jack) Whetton	05/05/1992	2,00	114	6	–	–	–	–	0
NW (Nic) White	13/06/1990	1,76	84	52	5	17	30	–	149
TOTALS				1501	192	60	120	3	1607

VODACOM SUPER RUGBY

APPEARANCES & POINTS

PLAYER	Reds	Force	Hurricanes	Waratahs	Stormers	Rebels	Blues	Reds	Chiefs	Crusaders	Sharks	Cheetahs	Bulls	Rebels	Waratahs	Force	Chiefs	Waratahs	Apps	T	C	P	DG	Pts
Mogg	15	15	15	15	15	15	15	15	15	15	15	15	11R	15	15	15	15		18	8	–	3	–	49
Speight	14	14	14	14	–	–	–	–	–	14	14	14	14	14	14	–	–		11	3	–	–	–	15
Smith, A	13	12R	12R	14R	13	–	15R	12R	11R	14R	13R	15R	14R	10R	–	–	–		13	–	–	–	–	0
McCabe	12	12	12	12	12	12	12	12	15R	15R	14R	11R	11R	15	–	15R	15R	15R	17	4	–	–	–	20
Tomane	11	–	–	–	14	14	14	14	14	–	14	–	–	–	–	11R	11R	14R	11	3	–	–	–	15
Toomua	10	10	10	10	10	10	10	10	10	10	10	10	10	10	–	10	10	10	17	7	2	–	–	39
White	9	9	9	9	9	9	9	9	9	9	9	9	9	9	9	9	9	9	18	2	17	22	–	110
Butler	8	8	7	7	7	7	7	7	7	7	7	7	7	7	7	7	7	7	18	1	–	–	–	5
Pocock	7	7	–	–	–	–	–	–	–	–	–	–	–	–	–	–	–	–	2	–	–	–	–	0
Mowen	6c	6c	8c	8c	8c	8c	8c	8c	8c	8c	8c	8c	8c	8c	8c	8c	8c	8c	18	1	–	–	–	5
Carter	5	5	5	5	5	5	–	5	5	5	5	5	–	–	5	5	5		16	2	–	–	–	10
Fardy	4	4	6	6	4	4	4	4	4	4	4	6	4	4	6	6	6		18	2	–	–	–	10
Alexander	3	3	3	3	3	3	3	3	3	3	3	3R	3	3	3	3	3	3	18	–	–	–	–	0
Moore	2	2	2	2	2	2	–	2	2	2	2	2	2	–	–	–	–	–	13	2	–	–	–	10
Sio	1	1	1	1	–	–	–	1	1	1	1	1	1	1	1	1	1	1	15	1	–	–	–	5
Smith, R-H	1R	7R	3R	3R	–	3R	3R	3R	1R	3R	–	1R	3R	3	3R	1R	1R	1R	16	–	–	–	–	0
Siliva	2R	2R	–	2R	2R	2	–	–	–	–	–	–	–	–	–	–	–	–	5	–	–	–	–	0
Murphy	3R	1R	–	1R	1R	1R	–	–	1R	–	–	–	2	2R	2R	2R	–		10	–	–	–	–	0
Power	5R	8R	4	4	–	–	–	–	–	–	4	8R	5	4	4	4	–		10	1	–	–	–	5
McCaffrey	8R	5R	4R	4R	7R	6R	6R	6R	–	–	–	–	–	–	–	–	–	–	8	1	–	–	–	5
Hoffmann	9R	9R	–	–	9R	9R	–	–	–	9R	–	–	–	–	–	–	–	–	5	–	–	–	–	0
Kuridrani	13R	13	13	13	–	13	13	13	13	13	13	13	13	13	13	13	13		17	5	–	–	–	25
Coleman	–	11	11	11	11	11	11	11	11	11	11	11	–	12	–	11	11		15	8	–	–	–	40
Cronje	–	13R	10R	–	–	–	–	–	–	–	–	–	22R	–	–	–	–		3	–	–	–	–	0
Smith, J-P	–	–	1R	1R	1	1	1	1R	3R	–	3R	1R	1R	1R	3R	–	–		12	–	–	–	–	0
Mann-Rea	–	–	2R	–	–	–	2R	–	2R	2R	–	2R	2R	–	2	2	2		9	–	–	–	–	0
Smiler	–	–	7R	7R	6	6	6	6	6	6	6R	–	–	6R	6	–	–		11	–	–	–	–	0
Whetton	–	–	–	–	6R	–	5R	5R	5R	5R	–	–	–	–	5R	–	–		6	–	–	–	–	0
Lealiifano	–	–	–	12R	10R	11R	12	12	12	12	12	12	10	12	12	12	–		13	–	12	15	–	69
Staniforth	–	–	–	–	–	–	5	–	–	–	–	–	–	–	–	–	–	–	1	–	–	–	–	0
McVerry	–	–	–	–	–	–	6R	6R	–	6R	7R	–	–	7R	–	–	7R		6	1	–	–	–	5
Dowsett	–	–	–	–	–	–	9R	9R	–	–	–	9R	9R	9R	–	9R	–		6	–	–	–	–	0
Auelua	–	–	–	–	–	–	–	–	6	6	4R	–	6R	4R	4R	4R	–		8	–	–	–	–	0
Rathbone	–	–	–	–	–	–	–	–	–	–	–	11	11	–	–	–	–		3	–	–	–	–	0
Iona	–	–	–	–	–	–	–	–	–	–	–	–	13R	–	–	–	–		1	–	–	–	–	0
Holmes	–	–	–	–	–	–	–	–	–	–	–	–	2R	–	–	–	–		1	–	–	–	–	0
Ala'alatoa	–	–	–	–	–	–	–	–	–	–	–	–	–	–	–	3R	3R		2	–	–	–	–	0
Penalty tries																			–	2	–	–	–	10
37 Players																			391	54	31	40	0	452

Note: ▨ = *Yellow card*

Records

CHAMPIONS: 2001, 2004

MATCH RECORDS

Biggest win	64	vs Bulls (73-9)	Canberra	1999
	64	vs Cats (64-0)	Canberra	2000
Heaviest defeat	49	vs Hurricanes (7-56)	Wellington	2009
Highest score	73	vs Bulls (73-9)	Canberra	1999
Most points conceded	56	vs Hurricanes (7-56)	Wellington	2009
Most tries	10	vs Bulls (73-9)	Canberra	1999
	10	vs Cats (64-16)	Canberra	2002
	10	vs Cats (68-28)	Canberra	2004
Most tries conceded	8	vs Hurricanes (7-56)	Wellington	2009
Most points by a player	25	SA Mortlock (1t 4c 4p) vs Stormers	Canberra	2001
	25	JWC Roff (1t 7c 2p) vs Chiefs	Canberra	2003
Most tries by a player	4	JWC Roff vs Sharks	Manuka	1996
Most conversions by a player	9	JWC Roff vs Cats	Canberra	2004
Most penalties by a player	6	J Huxley vs Highlanders	Canberra	2002
Most drop goals by a player	1	on 21 occasions		

SEASON RECORDS

Most team points	487	in 13 matches	2004
Most points by a player	233	CP Lealiifano	2013
Most team tries	67	in 13 matches	2004
Most tries by a player	15	JWC Roff	1997
Most conversions by a player	51	JWC Roff	2004
Most penalties by a player	57	CP Lealiifano	2013
Most drop goals by a player	2	GM Gregan	2001
	2	SJ Larkham	2001 & 2002
	2	CP Lealiifano	2009

CAREER RECORDS

Most appearances	142	GB Smith	2000-2013
Most points	1019	SA Mortlock	1998-2010
Most tries	57	JWC Roff	1996-2004
Most conversions	161	SA Mortlock	1998-2010
Most penalties	144	SA Mortlock	1998-2010
Most drop goals	5	SJ Larkham	

VODACOM SUPER RUGBY

Melbourne Rebels

Ground: AAMI Park, Melbourne **Capacity:** 30 000 **Address:** Visy Park Gate, Level 2, Royal Parade, Carlton North **Telephone number:** + 61 3 9221 0700
Colours: Dark blue jersey with white and red trim. Dark blue shorts with white trim. Dark blue socks with white band. **Website:** wwwmelbournerebels.com.au
Head Coach: Tony McGahan **Captain:** Scott Higginbotham **CEO:** Rob Clarke
Chairman: Jonathan Ling **President:** Gary Grey

Head Coach: Tony McGahan **Assistant Coaches:** Sean Hedger & Matt Cockbain
Head Conditioning Coach: Zane Leonard **Video Analyst:** Eion Toolan
Doctor: Dr Asheer Singh **Physiotherapist:** David Rundle **Asst Physiotherapist:** Paul Percy
Media Officer: Adam Freier **Manager:** Scott Harrison
Logistics Manager: Mark Rowe **Nutritionist:** Alison Garth

VODACOM SUPER RUGBY

| '96 | '97 | '98 | '99 | '00 | '01 | '02 | '03 | '04 | '05 | '06 | '07 | '08 | '09 | '10 | '11 15th | '12 13th | '13 12th | '14 15th |

Played	Won	Lost	Drawn	Points for	Points against	Tries for	Tries against
16	4	12	0	303	460	29	49

Date	Venue	Opponent	Result	Score	Referee	Scorers
28 Feb	Melbourne	Cheetahs	WON	35-14	A Gardner	T: Higginbotham, Burgess, Mitchell, Woodward, Hegarty. C: Hegarty (2). P: Roberts. DG: Roberts.
8 Mar	Perth	Force	LOST	7-32	N Briant	T: Veainu. C: Hegarty.
14 Mar	Melbourne	Crusaders	LOST	19-25	J Leckie	T: Fuglistaller. C: Hegarty. P: Hegarty, Woodward (3).
21 Mar	Sydney	Waratahs	LOST	8-32	J Peyper	T: Higginbotham. P: Hegarty.
28 Mar	Melbourne	Brumbies	WON	32-24	J Peyper	T: Inman, Woodward. C: Woodward (2). P: Woodward (6).
4 Apr	Dunedin	Highlanders	LOST	30-33	C Pollock	T: Fuglistaller, Woodward, Roberts. C: Woodward (3). P: Woodward (3).
12 Apr	Hamilton	Chiefs	LOST	16-22	M O'Brien	T: Horie. C: Woodward. P: Woodward (3).
18 Apr	Melbourne	Force	WON	22-16	A Lees	T: Higginbotham. C: Woodward. P: Woodward (5).
2 May	Melbourne	Sharks	LOST	16-22	A Lees	T: Leafa. C: Woodward. P: Woodward (3).
9 May	Melbourne	Hurricanes	LOST	15-25	M O'Brien	T: Ellison, Hegarty. C: Woodward. P: Woodward.
17 May	Brisbane	Reds	WON	30-27	SR Walsh	T: Kingston, Burgess (2). C: Woodward (3). P: Woodward (3).
23 May	Melbourne	Waratahs	LOST	19-41	R Hoffman	T: Veainu. C: Woodward. P: Woodward (4).
31 May	Canberra	Brumbies	LOST	10-37	SR Walsh	T: Higginbotham. C: Woodward. P: Woodward.
27 Jun	Melbourne	Reds	LOST	20-36	A Gardner	T: Inman, Burgess, Hegarty. C: Woodward. P: Woodward.
4 Jul	Johannesburg	Lions	LOST	17-34	J Peyper	T: English, Faingaa. C: Debreczeni (2). P: Debreczeni.
11 Jul	Pretoria	Bulls	LOST	7-40	R Hoffman	T: Debreczeni. C: Debreczeni.

‹ DID YOU KNOW? ›

On 23 July 1921 a monk played for Wellington against the Springboks under an assumed name. An ordained priest, Reverend Father Paul Kane, named as Paul Markham in the team sheet, played the whole game in an 8-3 defeat.

2014 SQUAD

PLAYER	Date of Birth	Height	Weight	M	T	C	P	DG	Pts
CD (Cruze) Ah Nau	10/08/1990	1,81	117	11	–	–	–	–	0
P (Paul) Alo-Emile	22/12/1991	1,80	120	35	1	–	–	–	5
L (Luke) Burgess	20/08/1983	1,80	83	73	8	–	–	–	40
JM (Jack) Debreczeni	06/06/1993	1,92	100	5	1	3	1	–	14
TE (Tamati) Ellison	01/04/1983	1,84	95	92	14	–	–	–	70
TAJ (Tom) English	08/03/1991	1,88	96	25	6	–	–	–	30
CG (Colby) Faingaa	31/03/1991	1,83	100	50	2	–	–	–	10
LLA (Lalakai) Foketi	22/12/1994	1,86	101	2	–	–	–	–	0
P (Steve) Fualau	03/08/1982	1,89	117	2	–	–	–	–	0
SA (Scott) Fuglistaller	16/04/1987	1,83	101	33	3	–	–	–	15
BS (Bryce) Hegarty	28/08/1992	1,85	90	20	5	4	2	–	39
S (Scott) Higginbotham	05/09/1986	1,95	102	94	26	–	–	–	130
JM (Josh) Holmes	06/01/1987	1,87	94	57	1	–	–	–	5
S (Shota) Horie	21/01/1986	1,80	104	19	1	–	–	–	5
MBW (Mitch) Inman	24/10/1988	1,91	102	62	5	–	–	–	25
SK (Sam) Jefferies	20/05/1992	2,00	114	1	–	–	–	–	0
LM (Luke) Jones	02/04/1991	2,01	108	47	–	–	–	–	0
TJ (Tom) Kingston	19/06/1991	1,90	89	41	7	–	–	–	35
MAP (Max) Lahiff	09/12/1989	1,85	117	8	–	–	–	–	0
PJ (Pat) Leafa	16/03/1989	1,81	108	17	1	–	–	–	5
SP (Sean) McMahon	18/06/1994	1,85	91	13	–	–	–	–	0
BIP (Ben) Meehan	21/01/1993	1,78	85	7	–	–	–	–	0
LV (Lachlan) Mitchell	30/09/1977	1,82	94	48	7	–	–	–	35
CD (Cadeyrn) Neville	09/11/1988	2,02	120	39	3	–	–	–	15
HW (Hugh) Pyle	21/09/1988	2,01	118	57	9	–	–	–	45
JT (Jordy) Reid	03/10/1991	1,85	107	12	–	–	–	–	0
AT (Angus) Roberts	17/12/1990	1,85	92	15	2	–	1	1	16
AV (Alex) Rokobaro	06/10/1989	1,83	91	4	–	–	–	–	0
M (Male) Sau	13/10/1987	1,84	98	8	–	–	–	–	0
TJ (Toby) Smith	10/10/1988	1,90	112	50	3	–	–	–	15
NR (Nick) Stirzaker	08/03/1991	1,79	80	23	–	–	–	–	0
L (Lopeti) Timani	28/09/1990	1,93	116	21	–	–	–	–	0
KTP (Telusa) Veainu	26/12/1990	1,80	83	14	3	–	–	–	15
LS (Laurie) Weeks	05/04/1986	1,81	114	75	1	–	–	–	5
JC (Jason) Woodward	17/05/1990	1,88	82	26	6	27	42	–	210
TOTALS				1106	115	7	4	1	784

APPEARANCES & POINTS

PLAYER	Cheetahs	Force	Crusaders	Waratahs	Brumbies	Highlanders	Chiefs	Force	Sharks	Hurricanes	Reds	Waratahs	Brumbies	Reds	Lions	Bulls	Apps	T	C	P	DG	Pts
Woodward	15	15	15	–	15	15	15	15	15	15	15	15	15	14	14R	–	14	3	15	33	–	144
Mitchell	14	11	14	14	–	–	–	–	–	–	–	–	–	–	–	–	4	1	–	–	–	5
Ellison	13	13	13	13	13	13	13	13	13	13	–	13	13	13	13	13	15	1	–	–	–	5
Inman	12	12	12	12	12	12	12	12	12	12	12	12	12	12	12	12	16	2	–	–	–	10
English	11	–	11	11	11	11	11	11	11	11	11	13	11	11	11	11	15	1	–	–	–	5
Hegarty	10	10R	10	10	10	10	10	10	10	10	10	10	10	10	10	–	15	3	4	2	–	29
Burgess	9	·9	9	9	9R	9R	9R	9R	9	9	9	–	–	9	9	9	14	4	–	–	–	20
Higginbotham	8c	8c	8c	8c	8c	8c	8c	8c	8c	8c	8c	8c	8c	8c	8c	–	15	4	–	–	–	20
Fuglistaller	7	–	7	7	7	7	7	7	7	7	7	7	7	6R	7	7c	15	2	–	–	–	10
McMahon	6	6	6	6	7R	6	7R	7R	6R	7R	7R	7R	–	6	–	–	13	–	–	–	–	0
Jones	5	5R	5	5	5	5	5	5	5	5	5	5	5	5	5	6	16	–	–	–	–	0
Pyle	4	4	4	4	4	4	4	4R	–	x	4R	4R	4R	4R	4	4	14	–	–	–	–	0
Weeks	3	3R	3	–	3	3	3	3	3	3	3	–	3	3	3	3	14	–	–	–	–	0
Leafa	2	2	2	2	2	2R	2R	2R	2R	2	2	2	2	2	2R	2R	16	1	–	–	–	5
Smith	1	1R	1	1	–	1	1	1	–	–	1	1	1	1	1	1	13	–	–	–	–	0
Fualau	2R	–	–	–	–	–	–	–	x	x	–	–	–	–	–	–	1	–	–	–	–	0
Lahiff	1R	1	1R	1R	1	–	–	–	1R	1R	–	3R	–	–	–	–	8	–	–	–	–	0
Alo-Emile	3R	3	3R	3	3R	x	3R	3R	3R	3R	3R	3	3R	3R	3R	3R	15	–	–	–	–	0
Neville	5R	5	5R	5R	x	5R	4R	4	4	4	4	4	4	4	4R	5	15	–	–	–	–	0
Faingaa	7R	7	6R	6R	6	–	6	6	6	6	6	6	6	7	6	8	15	1	–	–	–	5
Meehan	9R	9R	9R	9R	–	–	–	–	–	x	9R	9	9	–	–	–	7	–	–	–	–	0
Roberts	10R	10	15R	15	13R	10R	x	9R	x	–	–	–	–	–	–	–	7	1	–	1	1	11
Kingston	14R	14	–	14R	14	–	x	11R	11R	11R	14	11	14R	15R	14	–	12	1	–	–	–	5
Horie	–	2R	2R	2R	2R	2	2	2	2	2R	–	–	2R	2R	2	2	13	1	–	–	–	5
Timani	–	7R	–	–	–	–	–	–	–	–	–	–	–	–	–	5R	2	–	–	–	–	0
Veainu	–	14R	14R	–	–	–	–	–	–	13R	13	–	x	13R	15	–	6	2	–	–	–	10
Ah-Nau	–	–	–	3R	1R	3R	x	1R	1	1	1R	1R	x	1R	1R	1R	11	–	–	–	–	0
Sa'u	–	–	–	12R	14R	14	14	14	14	14	–	–	14	–	–	–	8	–	–	–	–	0
Stirzaker	–	–	–	–	9	9	9	9	9R	–	–	–	–	9R	9R	9R	8	–	–	–	–	0
Reid	–	–	–	–	–	x	–	–	–	–	–	7R	–	7R	6R	–	3	–	–	–	–	0
Rokobaro	–	–	–	–	–	x	–	–	–	–	–	–	–	–	–	14	1	–	–	–	–	0
Debreczeni	–	–	–	–	–	–	–	–	–	x	15R	13R	15	15	15	10	5	1	3	1	–	14
Holmes	–	–	–	–	–	–	–	–	–	x	9R	–	–	–	–	–	1	–	–	–	–	0
Foketi	–	–	–	–	–	–	–	–	–	–	–	13R	–	–	–	13R	2	–	–	–	–	0
Jeffries	–	–	–	–	–	–	–	–	–	–	–	–	–	–	–	7R	1	–	–	–	–	0
35 Players																	**350**	**29**	**22**	**37**	**1**	**303**

Note: ▪ = *Yellow card*

Records

MATCH RECORDS

Biggest win	21	vs Cheetahs (35-14)	Melbourne	2014
Heaviest defeat	57	vs Sharks (7-64)	Durban	2013
Highest score	42	vs Hurricanes (42-25)	Melbourne	2011
Most points conceded	66	vs Hurricanes (24-66)	Wellington	2012
Most tries	6	vs Hurricanes (42-25)	Melbourne	2011
Most tries conceded	10	vs Sharks (7-64)	Durban	2013
Most points by a player	27	JC Woodward vs Brumbies	Melbourne	2014
Most tries by a player	2	AM Campbell vs Hurricanes	Melbourne	2011
	2	KC Vuna vs Bulls	Melbourne	2012
	2	NJ Phipps vs Crusaders	Melbourne	2012
	2	C Neville vs Western Force	Perth	2012
	2	KC Vuna vs Hurricanes	Wellington	2012
	2	HW Pyle vs Lions	Johannesburg	2012
	2	J Woodward vs Force	Perth	2013
	2	HW Pyle vs Chiefs	Melbourne	2013
	2	M Inman vs Blues	Auckland	2013
	2	T English vs Waratahs	Melbourne	2013
	2	B Hegarty vs Highlanders	Melbourne	2013
	2	KC Vuna vs Highlanders	Melbourne	2013
	2	T English vs Highlanders	Melbourne	2013
Most conversions by a player	5	KJ Beale vs Bulls	Melbourne	2012
Most penalties by a player	6	DJ Cipriani vs Brumbies	Melbourne	2011
	6	JC Woodward vs Brumbies	Melbourne	2014
Most drop goals by a player	1	AT Roberts vs Cheetahs	Melbourne	2014

SEASON RECORDS

Most team points	382	from 16 matches	2013
Most points by a player	116	JD O'Connor	2013
Most team tries	44	from 16 matches	2013
Most tries by a player	7	KC Vuna	2012
Most conversions by a player	21	JD O'Connor	2013
Most penalties by a player	33	JC Woodward	2014
Most drop goals by a player	1	AT Roberts	2014

CAREER RECORDS

Most appearances	57	HW Pyle	2011-2014
Most points	210	JC Woodward	2013-2014
Most tries	13	KC Vuna	2011-2013
Most conversions	27	JD O'Connor	2012-2013
Most penalties	44	JD O'Connor	2012-2013
Most drop goals	1	AT Roberts	2014

VODACOM SUPER RUGBY

NSW Waratahs

Ground: Sydney Football Stadium **Capacity:** 44 000 **Address:** Driver Avenue, Moore Park
Telephone number: + 61 2 8354 3300 **Colours:** Sky blue jersey with navy collar, navy shorts and sky blue socks **Website:** www.waratahs.com.au
Coach: Michael Cheika **Captain:** Dave Dennis **CEO:** Jason Allen
Chairman: Roger Davis

Head Coach: Michael Cheika **Assistant Coaches:** Nathan Grey & Daryl Gibson
High Performance Analyst: Anthony Wakeling **Doctor:** Dr Sharron Flahive
Match-Day Doctor: Dr Luke Inman **Physiotherapist:** Kieran Cleary
Physiotherapist: Alex Hill **Strength & Conditioning:** Haydn Masters & Tom Tombleson
Manager: Sam Cashman **Media Officer:** Russel Fairfax

VODACOM SUPER RUGBY

'96	'97	'98	'99	'00	'01	'02	'03	'04	'05	'06	'07	'08	'09	'10	'11	'12	'13	'14
7th	9th	6th	8th	9th	8th	2nd	5th	8th	2nd	3rd	13th	2nd	5th	3rd	5th	11th	9th	**1st**

Played	Won	Lost	Drawn	Points for	Points against	Tries for	Tries against
18	14	4	0	540	312	60	23

Date	Venue	Opponent	Result	Score	Referee	Scorers
23 Feb	Sydney	Force	WON	43-21	R Hoffman	T: Folau (3), Beale, Douglas, Alofa. C: Foley (5). P: Foley.
1 Mar	Sydney	Reds	WON	32-5	G Jackson	T: Folau (2), Betham, Beale. C: Foley (3). P: Foley (2).
15 Mar	Canberra	Brumbies	LOST	23-28	J Peyper	T: Hooper, Folau. C: Foley (2). P: Foley (3)
21 Mar	Sydney	Rebels	WON	32-8	J Peyper	T: Folau (2), Betham, Alofa. C: Foley (3). P: Foley (2)
29 Mar	Durban	Sharks	LOST	10-32	M Fraser	T: Foley. C: Foley. P: Foley.
5 Apr	Cape Town	Stormers	WON	22-11	G Jackson	T: Phipps. C: Foley. P: Foley (3), Beale (2).
12 Apr	Perth	Force	LOST	16-28	A Gardner	T: Beale. C: Foley. P: Foley, Beale (2).
19 Apr	Sydney	Bulls	WON	19-12	R Hoffman	T: Folau. C: Foley. P: Foley (4).
25 Apr	Auckland	Blues	LOST	13-21	C Pollock	T: Potgieter. C: Foley. P: Foley (2).
3 May	Sydney	Hurricanes	WON	39-30	SR Walsh	T: Hoiles, Horne, Carraro, Dennis, Foley. C: Foley (4). P: Foley (2).
18 May	Sydney	Lions	WON	41-13	N Briant	T: Horne (2), Beale, Foley, Ashley-Cooper. C: Foley (5), P: Foley (2).
23 May	Melbourne	Rebels	WON	41-19	R Hoffman	T: Horne, Hooper, Beale, Folau, McKibbin, Ashley-Cooper. C: Foley. P: Foley (3).
31 May	New Plymouth	Chiefs	WON	33-17	C Pollock	T: Folau, Dennis, Foley. C: Foley (3). P: Foley (3), Beale.
28 Jun	Sydney	Brumbies	WON	39-8	SR Walsh	T: Alofa (2), Palu, Foley, Robinson. C: Foley (4). P: Foley, Beale.
6 Jul	Sydney	Highlanders	WON	44-16	SR Walsh	T: Naiyaravoro, Kepu, Horne, Phipps, Potgieter, Folau. C: Foley (4). P: Foley (2).
12 Jul	Brisbane	Reds	WON	34-3	M Fraser	T: Beale (2), Phipps, Lance. C: Foley (4). P: Foley (2)

SEMI-FINAL

Date	Venue	Opponent	Result	Score	Referee	Scorers
26 Jul	Sydney	Brumbies	WON	26-8	J Peyper	T: Beale, Foley, Alofa. C: Foley. P: Foley (3).

FINAL

Date	Venue	Opponent	Result	Score	Referee	Scorers
2 Aug	Sydney	Crusaders	WON	33-32	C Joubert	T: Ashley-Cooper (2). C: Foley. P: Foley (7).

Note: ■ = Champion

2014 SQUAD

PLAYER	Date of Birth	Height	Weight	M	T	C	P	DG	Pts
M (Michael) Alaalatoa	28/08/1991	1,89	135	1	–	–	–	–	0
AS (Alofa) Alofa	12/03/1991	1,85	94	15	5	–	–	–	25
AP (Adam) Ashley-Cooper	28/03/1984	1,83	96	126	22	–	–	1	113
KJ (Kurtley) Beale	06/01/1989	1,84	90	100	24	74	66	–	475
PJJ (Peter) Betham	06/01/1989	1,91	98	30	8	–	–	–	40
MJ (Matt) Carraro	04/08/1984	1,85	93	25	1	–	–	–	5
MJ (Mitchell) Chapman	15/03/1983	1,97	110	86	5	–	–	–	25
JC (Cam) Crawford	14/11/1988	1,93	98	13	8	–	–	–	40
DA (Dave) Dennis	01/10/1986	1,92	104	75	9	–	–	–	45
KP (Kane) Douglas	01/06/1989	2,01	115	76	2	–	–	–	10
I (Israel) Folau	03/04/1989	1,93	103	28	20	–	–	–	100
BT (Bernard) Foley	08/09/1989	1,80	85	48	14	49	48	–	318
TTT (Tala) Gray	28/02/1990	1,94	114	1	–	–	–	–	0
SA (Stephen) Hoiles	13/10/1981	1,90	105	46	3	–	–	–	15
MK (Michael) Hooper	29/10/1991	1,82	97	64	10	–	–	–	50
RG (Rob) Horne	15/08/1989	1,85	83	74	16	–	–	–	80
SM (Sekope) Kepu	05/02/1986	1,88	115	79	2	–	–	–	10
JB (Jonno) Lance	27/06/1990	1,83	92	30	2	–	–	1	13
S (Tolo) Latu	23/02/1993	1,78	110	14	–	–	–	–	0
PJ (Pat) McCutcheon	24/06/1987	1,87	100	32	1	–	–	–	5
B (Brendan) McKibbin	19/09/1985	1,75	86	64	2	41	52	–	248
TT (Taqule) Naiyaravoro	07/12/1991	1,94	123	5	1	–	–	–	5
WL (Wycliff) Palu	27/07/1982	1,93	118	105	13	–	–	–	65
NJ (Nick) Phipps	09/01/1989	1,80	87	65	9	–	–	–	45
SUT (Tatafu) Polota-Nau	26/07/1985	1,80	110	120	12	–	–	–	60
UJ (Jacques) Potgieter	24/04/1986	1,94	115	41	6	–	–	–	30
HE (Hugh) Roach	11/09/1992	1,78	105	2	–	–	–	–	0
BA (Benn) Robinson	19/07/1984	1,83	109	127	7	–	–	–	35
PJ (Paddy) Ryan	09/08/1986	1,91	120	45	2	–	–	–	10
WRJ (Will) Skelton	05/03/1992	2,03	135	24	–	–	–	–	0
JD (Jeremy) Tilse	06/02/1986	1,94	117	35	–	–	–	–	0
TOTALS				1596	204	164	166	2	1867

VODACOM SUPER RUGBY

APPEARANCES & POINTS

PLAYER	Force	Reds	Brumbies	Rebels	Sharks	Stormers	Force	Bulls	Blues	Hurricanes	Lions	Rebels	Chiefs	Brumbies	Highlanders	Reds	Brumbies	Crusaders	Apps	T	C	P	DG	Pts
Folau	15	15	15	15	–	–	–	15	15	15	15	15	15	15	15	–	15	15	14	12	–	–	–	60
Alofa	14	14	14	14	11R	14	–	–	14R	14R	14	14	14	14	14	14	14	14	15	5	–	–	–	25
Ashley-Cooper	13	13	13	13	13	13	13	13	13	13	13	13	13	13	13	13	13	13	18	4	–	–	–	20
Beale	12	12	12	12	12	15	12	12	12	12	12	12	12	12	12	12	12	12	18	8	–	6	–	58
Betham	11	11	11	11	11	11	–	–	–	–	–	–	–	–	–	–	–	14R	7	2	–	–	–	10
Foley	10	10	10	10	10	10	10	10	10	10	10	10	10	10	10	10	10	10	18	6	45	44	–	252
Phipps	9	9	9	9	9	9	9	9	9	9	9	9	9	9	9	9	9	9	18	3	–	–	–	15
Palu	8	8	8	4R	8	–	–	–	4R	8	8	8	8	8	8	8	8	8	15	1	–	–	–	5
Hooper	7	7c	7	7	7	7	7	7	7	7	7	7	7	7	7c	7c	7c	7c	18	2	–	–	–	10
Dennis	6	–	6c	8c	6c	8c	8c	8c	8c	6c	6c	6c	6c	6c	6c	–	–	–	13	2	–	–	–	10
Douglas	5	5	5	5	5	5	5	5	4	5	5	5	5	5	5	5	5	5	18	1	–	–	–	5
Skelton	4	4R	4R	4	8R	4	4	4	4	5R	4	4R	4R	4R	5R	4	5R	4R	18	–	–	–	–	0
Ryan	3	3	3	3	3	3R	3R	3R	3R	3R	3	3	3	3	1R	1R	–	3R	3R	17	–	–	–	–	0
Polatu-Nau	2	2	2	2	2	2	2	2	2	2	2	2	2	2	2	2	2	2	18	–	–	–	–	0
Robinson	1	1	1	3R	1	1	1	1	1	1	1	1	1	1	1	1	1	1	18	1	–	–	–	5
Latu	2R	2R	2R	2R	2R	2R	x	2R	2R	2R	–	–	–	2R	2R	2R	2R	2R	14	–	–	–	–	0
Tilse	3R	1R	x	18R	1R	1R	1R	1R	1R	x	1R	1R	x	3R	18R	1R	1R	x	14	–	–	–	–	0
Kepu	1R	3R	3R	1	3	3	3	3	3	3R	3R	3R	3R	3	3	3	3	3	18	1	–	–	–	5
Potgieter	4R	4	4	6	4	6	6	6	6	5	5R	4	4	4	4R	4	4	4	18	2	–	–	–	10
Hoiles	6R	6	6R	6R	–	4R	4R	4R	–	8R	6R	8R	8R	6R	6	6	6	6	16	1	–	–	–	5
McKibbin	9R	9R	9R	9R	9R	9R	9R	9R	9R	9R	9R	9R	9R	9R	9R	14R	9R	9R	18	1	–	–	–	5
Horne	13R	15R	x	14R	14	–	11	11	11	11	11	11	11	11	11	–	11	11	15	5	–	–	–	25
Carraro	14R	14R	14R	15R	14R	14R	14R	12R	14R	14	14	13R	14R	–	–	–	–	–	13	1	–	–	–	5
McCutcheon	–	8R	–	–	4R	6R	x	6R	6R	–	–	–	–	–	8R	8R	8R	x	8	–	–	–	–	0
Lance	–	–	–	–	15	12	15	x	13R	12R	–	10R	13R	10R	–	15	–	–	9	1	–	–	–	5
Crawford	–	–	–	–	11R	14	14	14	–	–	–	–	–	–	11	–	–	–	5	–	–	–	–	0
Gray	–	–	–	–	–	–	6R	–	–	–	–	–	–	–	–	–	–	–	1	–	–	–	–	0
Roach	–	–	–	–	–	–	–	–	–	–	2R	2R	x	–	–	–	–	–	2	–	–	–	–	0
Naiyaravoro	–	–	–	–	–	–	–	–	13R	–	–	14R	12R	15R	14R	–	–	–	5	1	–	–	–	5
Chapman	–	–	–	–	–	–	–	–	–	–	–	–	–	4R	5R	4R	6R	–	4	–	–	–	–	0
Alaalatoa	–	–	–	–	–	–	–	–	–	–	–	–	–	–	3R	–	–	–	1	–	–	–	–	0
31 Players																			**404**	**60**	**45**	**50**	**0**	**540**

Note: ▪ = *Yellow card*

Records

CHAMPIONS: 2014

MATCH RECORDS

Biggest win	62	vs Kings (72-10)	Port Elizabeth	2013
Heaviest defeat	77	vs Crusaders (19-96)	Christchurch	2002
Highest score	73	vs Lions (73-12)	Sydney	2010
Most points conceded	96	vs Crusaders (19-96)	Christchurch	2002
Most tries	11	vs Lions (73-12)	Sydney	2010
	11	vs Kings (72-10)	Port Elizabeth	2013
Most tries conceded	14	vs Crusaders (19-96)	Christchurch	2002
Most points by a player	34	P Hewat (3t 2c 5p) vs Bulls	Sydney	2005
Most tries by a player	4	DA Mitchell vs Lions	Sydney	2010
	3	A Murdoch vs Hurricanes	Sydney	1996
	3	MC Burke vs Northern Transvaal	Sydney	1997
	3	S Taupeaafe vs Sharks	Sydney	1998
	3	SNG Staniforth vs Chiefs	Rotorua	2002
	3	P Hewat vs Bulls	Sydney	2005
	3	JC Crawford vs Kings	Port Elizabeth	2013
Most conversions by a player	9	BS Barnes	Sydney	2010
Most penalties by a player	7	MC Burke vs Blues	Sydney	2001
Most drop goals by a player	1	on eight occasions		

SEASON RECORDS

Most team points	540	from 18 matches	2014
Most points by a player	252	BT Foley	2014
Most team tries	60	from 18 matches	2014
Most tries by a player	12	I Folau	2014
Most conversions by a player	45	BT Foley	2014
Most penalties by a player	44	BT Foley	2014
Most drop goals by a player	3	BS Barnes	2010

CAREER RECORDS

Most appearances	132	PR Waugh	2000-2011
Most points	959	MC Burke	1996-2004
Most tries	29	LD Tuqiri	2003-2009
Most conversions	160	MC Burke	1996-2004
Most penalties	173	MC Burke	1996-2004
Most drop goals	3	KJ Beale	2007-2014
	3	BS Barnes	2010-2013

Queensland Reds

Ground: Suncorp Stadium **Address:** Castlemaine Street, Milton
Telephone: + 61 7 3354 9333 **Capacity:** 52 000 **Colours:** Cardinal red jersey, socks and shorts
Website: www.redsrugby.com.au **Coach:** Richard Graham
Captain: James Horwill **CEO:** Jim Carmichael **Chairman:** Rod McCall
President: Tony Shaw

Head Coach: Richard Graham **Assistant Coaches:** Nick Stiles, Steve Meehan & Peter Wilkins
Doctor: Dr Abhi Varshney **Physiotherapist:** Nathan Carlos
Manager: Sam Cordingley **Media officer:** Tom Kennedy **Video Analyst:** Michael Todd
Therapist: Heather Arthy **Conditioning Coach:** Oliver Richardson
Logistics Manager: Michael Atkinson

VODACOM SUPER RUGBY

'96	'97	'98	'99	'00	'01	'02	'03	'04	'05	'06	'07	'08	'09	'10	'11	'12	'13	'14
1st	10th	5th	1st	7th	4th	5th	8th	10th	10th	12th	14th	12th	13th	5th	**1st**	3rd	5th	13th

Played	Won	Lost	Drawn	Points for	Points against	Tries for	Tries against
16	5	11	0	374	493	42	52

Date	Venue	Opponent	Result	Score	Referee	Scorers
22 Feb	Canberra	Brumbies	WON	27-17	J Leckie	T: Turner, Feauai-Sautia, Toua. C: Cooper (3). P: Cooper (2).
1 Mar	Sydney	Waratahs	LOST	5-32	G Jackson	T: Turner.
7 Mar	Brisbane	Cheetahs	WON	43-33	G Williamson	T: Davies, Hanson, Feauai-Sautia (2). C: Cooper (3). P: Cooper (4). PT.
15 Mar	Durban	Sharks	LOST	20-35	L vd Merwe	T: Genia, Harris. C: Cooper (2). P: Cooper (2).
22 Mar	Johannesburg	Lions	LOST	20-23	S Berry	T: Cooper (2). C: Cooper (2). P: Cooper (2).
29 Mar	Brisbane	Stormers	WON	22-17	C Pollock	T: Simmons. C: Cooper. P: Cooper (4). DG: Cooper.
5 Apr	Brisbane	Force	LOST	29-32	G Williamson	T: Slipper, Tapuai. C: Cooper (2). P: Harris (4), Cooper.
11 Apr	Brisbane	Brumbies	LOST	20-23	SR Walsh	T: Quirk, Robinson. C: Cooper (2). P: Cooper (2).
26 Apr	Welington	Hurricanes	LOST	21-35	M Fraser	T: Hanson, Lucas. C: Cooper. P: Cooper (3).
2 May	Auckland	Blues	LOST	14-44	N Briant	T: Horwill, Daley. C: Cooper (2).
11 May	Brisbane	Crusaders	LOST	29-57	J Peyper	T: Davies, Simmons, Taulagi, Shipperley. C: Cooper (3). P: Cooper.
17 May	Brisbane	Rebels	LOST	27-30	SR Walsh	T: Harris, Holmes, Lucas. C: Harris (2), Cooper. P: Harris (2)
30 May	Brisbane	Highlanders	WON	38-31	A Lees	T: Davies, Schatz, Shipperley, Browning (2). C: Harris (4), Genia. P: Harris.
27 Jun	Melbourne	Rebels	WON	36-20	A Gardner	T: Davies, Frisby (2), Harris, Turner (2). C: Harris (3).
5 Jul	Perth	Force	LOST	20-30	A Gardner	T: Kerevi, Anae. C: Harris (2). P: Harris (2).
12 Jul	Brisbane	Waratahs	LOST	3-34	M Fraser	P: Harris.

Note: ■ = *Champion*

〈 DID YOU KNOW? 〉

The honour of scoring South Africa's 1,000th Test try belongs to wing JP Pietersen when he dotted down against Fiji in the 2007 Rugby World Cup in France.

2014 SQUAD

PLAYER	Date of Birth	Height	Weight	M	T	C	P	DG	Pts
A (Albert) Anae	21/06/1989	1,85	114	27	–	–	–	–	0
C (Curtis) Browning	30/10/1993	1,88	106	11	2	–	–	–	10
TE (Tim) Buchanan	20/4/1988	1,94	109	1	–	–	–	–	0
QS (Quade) Cooper	05/04/1988	1,85	83	100	21	106	130	7	728
BP (Ben) Daley	27/06/1988	1,83	106	68	2	–	–	–	10
RW (Rod) Davies	18/05/1989	1,80	88	58	19	–	–	–	95
AS (Anthony) Fainga'a	02/02/1987	1,78	88	73	5	–	–	–	25
SM (Saia) Fainga'a	02/02/1987	1,87	100	107	8	–	–	–	40
C (Chris) Feauai-Sautia	17/11/1993	1,81	88	23	6	–	–	–	30
NH (Nick) Frisby	29/10/1992	1,85	80	26	5	–	–	–	25
ST (Scott) Gale	24/10/1994	1,85	86	2	–	–	–	–	0
SW (Will) Genia	17/01/1988	1,75	82	99	17	2	1	–	92
LB (Liam) Gill	08/06/1992	1,83	96	50	5	–	–	–	25
JE (James) Hanson	15/09/1988	1,80	100	66	7	–	–	–	35
MJ (Mike) Harris	08/07/1988	1,86	96	45	6	41	51	1	268
GS (Greg) Holmes	11/06/1983	1,83	110	119	7	–	–	–	35
JE (James) Horwill	29/05/1985	2,01	113	103	7	–	–	–	35
SM (Sam) Johnson	19/06/1993	1,84	100	2	–	–	–	–	0
BJ (Ben) Lucas	30/12/1987	1,80	79	73	7	5	7	–	66
SV (Samu) Kerevi	27/09/1993	1,86	108	4	1	–	–	–	5
CJ (Chris) Kuridrani	12/12/1991	1,89	99	1	–	–	–	–	0
D (David) McDuling	07/04/1989	1,96	115	5	–	–	–	–	0
ECT (Ed) O'Donoghue	26/06/1982	1,98	112	48	–	–	–	–	0
J (Jono) Owen	01/11/1986	1,88	120	29	–	–	–	–	0
J (Jonah) Placid	14/05/1995	1,83	96	1	–	–	–	–	0
EC (Ed) Quirk	28/08/1991	1,91	106	39	1	–	–	–	5
BS (Beau) Robinson	15/08/1986	1,81	97	74	2	–	–	–	10
JW (Jake) Schatz	25/07/1990	1,90	104	65	5	–	–	–	25
DP (Dom) Shipperley	04/01/1991	1,86	94	45	13	–	–	–	65
JA (James) Slipper	06/06/1989	1,85	113	65	4	–	–	–	20
RA (Rob) Simmons	19/04/1989	2,00	118	81	3	–	–	–	15
BNL (Ben) Tapuai	19/01/1989	1,78	95	56	8	–	–	–	40
JJ (Jamie) Taulagi	18/06/1993	1,80	90	8	1	–	–	–	5
AM (Aidan) Toua	19/01/1990	1,81	89	10	1	–	–	–	5
L (Lachie) Turner	11/05/1987	1,89	94	79	29	–	–	–	145
TOTALS				1663	192	154	189	8	1859

APPEARANCES & POINTS

PLAYER	Brumbies	Waratahs	Cheetahs	Sharks	Lions	Stormers	Force	Brumbies	Hurricanes	Blues	Crusaders	Rebels	Highlanders	Rebels	Force	Waratahs	Apps	T	C	P	DG	Pts
Toua	15	15	15	15	15	–	–	–	–	–	–	–	–	–	–	–	5	1	–	–	–	5
Turner	14	14	–	11	11	15	–	–	–	–	–	–	–	11R	11	11	9	4	–	–	–	20
Tapuai	13	13	13R	12R	13	13	13	13	13	13	13	13	13	13	12	12	16	1	–	–	–	5
Harris	12	–	12	12	12	12	12	–	12	15	15	15	15	15	15	15	14	3	11	10	–	67
Shipperley	11	11	11	14R	15R	11	–	–	–	–	14	14	11	11	–	–	10	2	–	–	–	10
Cooper	10	10	10	10	10	10	10	10	10	10	10	10	–	–	–	–	12	2	22	21	1	120
Genia	9	9	9	9	9	9	9	9	9	9	9	9	9	–	–	–	13	1	1	–	–	7
Schatz	8	8	8	8	8	8	8	8	8	8	8	8	8	8	8	8	16	1	–	–	–	5
Gill	7	7	7	7	7	–	–	–	7	–	–	7R	6R	–	6R	–	9	–	–	–	–	0
Quirk	6	6	6	6	6	6	6	6	6	6	–	–	–	–	–	–	10	1	–	–	–	5
Horwill	5c	5c	5c	5c	5c	5c	5c	5c	5c	5c	5c	5c	5c	5c	5c	5c	16	1	–	–	–	5
Simmons	4	4	4	4	4	4	4	4	4	4	4	4	4	4	4	4	16	2	–	–	–	10
Holmes	3	3	3	3	3	3	3	3	1R	3	3	3	3	3	–	3	15	1	–	–	–	5
S Faingaa	2	2	2R	2	2	–	2R	2	2	2	2R	2R	–	2R	2R	2R	13	–	–	–	–	0
Slipper	1	1	3R	1	1	1	1	1	3	1	–	–	1	1	3	1	14	1	–	–	–	5
Hanson	2R	2R	2	2R	2R	2	2	2	2R	2R	2	2	2	2	2	2	16	2	–	–	–	10
Daley	3R	1R	1	3R	–	–	–	–	1	3R	1	1	–	3R	1	3R	11	1	–	–	–	5
Owen	x	3R	1R	1R	3R	3R	3R	3R	3R	1R	3R	1R	–	–	–	–	11	–	–	–	–	0
O'Donoghue	5R	4R	4R	5R	4R	4R	4R	x	4R	5R	9R	4R	–	–	–	–	12	–	–	–	–	0
Robinson	6R	6R	7R	6R	6R	7	7	7	7	7R	7	7	7	7	7	7	16	1	–	–	–	5
Frisby	x	9R	9R	x	7R	x	x	x	9R	9R	x	x	x	9	9	–	7	2	–	–	–	10
A Faingaa	13R	12	x	–	13R	12R	23R	12	15R	12	–	12	12	12	–	–	11	–	–	–	–	0
Feauai-Sautia	14R	12R	13	13	–	–	–	11	14	11	12	–	–	–	–	–	8	3	–	–	–	15
Lucas	–	x	–	–	–	11R	15	15	15	14R	15R	10R	10	10	10	10	11	2	–	–	–	10
Davies	–	–	14	14	14	14	14	14	11R	14	11R	14R	14	14	14	14	14	4	–	–	–	20
Anae	–	–	–	–	1R	1R	2R	1R	–	–	1R	3R	1R	1R	1R	1R	10	1	–	–	–	5
Paraka	–	–	–	–	–	x	x	–	–	–	–	–	–	–	–	–	0	–	–	–	–	0
Browning	–	–	–	–	–	6R	6R	7R	8R	–	6	6	6	6	6	6	10	2	–	–	–	10
Taulagi	–	–	–	–	–	–	11	14R	11	11R	11	11	–	15R	x	10R	8	1	–	–	–	5
Placid	–	–	–	–	–	–	11R	–	–	–	–	–	x	–	–	–	1	–	–	–	–	0
McDuling	–	–	–	–	–	–	–	x	–	–	7R	x	6R	4R	7R	7R	5	–	–	–	–	0
Ready	–	–	–	–	–	–	–	–	–	–	–	–	x	–	–	–	0	–	–	–	–	0
Faagase	–	–	–	–	–	–	–	–	–	–	–	x	–	x	–	–	0	–	–	–	–	0
Kerevi	–	–	–	–	–	–	–	–	–	–	–	13R	12R	13	13	–	4	1	–	–	–	5
Buchanan	–	–	–	–	–	–	–	–	–	–	–	–	–	5R	–	–	1	–	–	–	–	0
Gale	–	–	–	–	–	–	–	–	–	–	–	–	–	9R	9	–	2	–	–	–	–	0
Johnson	–	–	–	–	–	–	–	–	–	–	–	–	–	–	13R	12R	2	–	–	–	–	0
Kuridrani	–	–	–	–	–	–	–	–	–	–	–	–	–	–	–	22R	1	–	–	–	–	0
Penalty try																	–	1	–	–	–	5
38 Players																	349	42	34	31	1	374

Note: ▓ = *Yellow card*

Records

CHAMPIONS: 2011

MATCH RECORDS

Biggest win	50	vs Rebels (53-3)	Brisbane	2011
Heaviest defeat	89	vs Bulls (3-92)	Pretoria	2007
Highest score	53	vs Rebels (53-3)	Brisbane	2011
Most points conceded	92	vs Bulls (3-92)	Pretoria	2007
Most tries	7	vs Blues (51-13)	Brisbane	1996
	7	vs Bulls (48-12)	Brisbane	2002
	7	vs Force (50-10)	Brisbane	2010
	7	vs Rebels (53-3)	Brisbane	2011
Most tries conceded	13	vs Bulls (3-92)	Pretoria	2007
Most points by a player	31	QS Cooper (2t, 3c, 5p) vs Crusaders	Brisbane	2010
Most tries by a player	3	RW Davies vs Blues	Brisbane	2011
Most conversions by a player	5	JA Eales on four occasions		
	5	EJ Flatley vs Stormers	Brisbane	2002
	5	QS Cooper vs Force	Brisbane	2010
	5	QS Cooper vs Rebels	Brisbane	2011
Most penalties by a player	7	QS Cooper vs Brumbies	Canberra	2011
	7	MJ Harris vs Force	Brisbane	2012
Most drop goals by a player	2	BS Barnes vs Brumbies	Canberra	2008

SEASON RECORDS

Most team points	477	from 18 matches	2011
Most points by a player	228	QS Cooper	2011
Most team tries	51	from 18 matches	2011
Most tries by a player	10	CE Latham	2002
Most conversions by a player	31	QS Cooper	2010
	31	QS Cooper	2011
Most penalties by a player	43	QS Cooper	2011
Most drop goals by a player	4	BS Barnes	2008
	4	QS Cooper	2011

CAREER RECORDS

Most appearances	123	SP Hardman	2000-2010
Most points	629	EJ Flatley	1996-2006
Most tries	41	CE Latham	1997-2008
Most conversions	92	EJ Flatley	1996-2006
Most penalties	130	EJ Flatley	1996-2006
Most drop goals	6	BS Barnes	2006-2009

VODACOM SUPER RUGBY

Western Force

Ground: NIB Stadium **Capacity:** 20526 **Address:** 310 Pier Street, Perth, WA 6000
Telephone number: + 61 8 9387 0700 **Colours:** Ocean blue jersey with black shorts and socks
Website: www.rugbywa.com.au **Head Coach:** Michael Foley
Captain: Matt Hodgson **CEO:** Mark Sinderberry **Chairman:** Dr Russel Perry
President: David Redpath

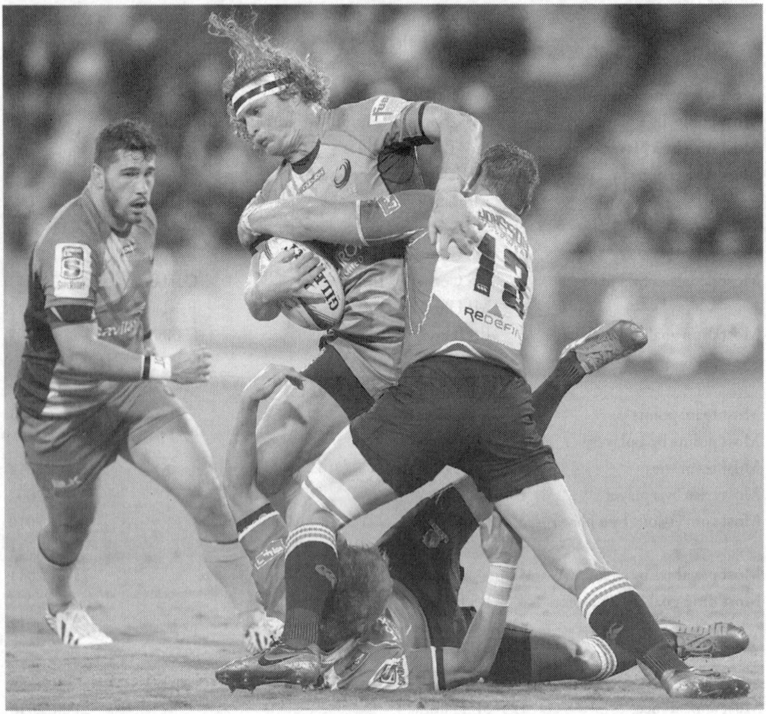

Head Coach: Michael Foley **Snr Assistant Coach:** David Wessels
Backs/Attack Coach: Kevin Foote **Skills Coach:** Dwayne Nestor
Strength & Conditioning Coach: Charlie Higgins **Asst Conditioning Coach:** Brendyn Appleby
Video Analyst: Damian Pacecca **Doctor:** Dr Mike Cadogan **Media Officer:** Nick Smith
Team Manager: Mark Calverley **Rugby Strategist:** Philip Fowler
High Performance Manager: David Joyce **Physiotherapist:** Emidio Pacceca

VODACOM SUPER RUGBY

'96	'97	'98	'99	'00	'01	'02	'03	'04	'05	'06 14th	'07 7th	'08 8th	'09 8th	'10 13th	'11 12th	'12 14th	'13 13th	'14 8th

Played	Won	Lost	Drawn	Points for	Points against	Tries for	Tries against
16	9	7	0	343	393	37	40

Date	Venue	Opponent	Result	Score	Referee	Scorers
23 Feb	Sydney	Waratahs	LOST	21-43	R Hoffman	T: Godwin, Cummins. C: Holmes. P: Holmes (3).
1 Mar	Perth	Brumbies	LOST	14-27	N Briant	T: McCalman, Hayward. C: Ebersohn (2).
8 Mar	Perth	Rebels	WON	32-7	N Briant	T: Mathewson, Cottrell, Morahan, Hodgson. C: Ebersohn (3). P: Ebersohn (2).
15 Mar	Dunedin	Highlanders	WON	31-29	G Jackson	T: McCalman, Rasolea, Charles, Ebersohn. C: Ebersohn (4). P: Ebersohn.
22 Mar	Perth	Chiefs	WON	18-15	L van der Merwe	T: Hodgson (2). C: Ebersohn. P: Ebersohn (2).
5 Apr	Brisbane	Reds	WON	32-29	G Williamson	T: McCalman, Hayward, Morahan. C: Hayward. DG: Ebersohn. P: Ebersohn.
12 Apr	Perth	Waratahs	WON	28-16	A Gardner	T: Cummins (3). C: Ebersohn (2). P: Ebersohn (3).
18 Apr	Melbourne	Rebels	LOST	16-22	A Lees	T: Cummins. C: Holmes. P: Ebersohn (3)
26 Apr	Perth	Bulls	WON	15-9	A Gardner	P: Ebersohn (5).
10 May	Bloemfontein	Cheetahs	WON	23-16	C Pollock	T: Cummins, Hayward. C: Ebersohn (2). P: Ebersohn (3).
17 May	Cape Town	Stormers	LOST	8-24	C Pollock	T: Hodgson. P: Ebersohn
24 May	Perth	Lions	WON	29-19	SR Walsh	T: Hodgson (2), Hayward, Tuatara-Morrison. C: Hayward (2), Ebersohn. P: Ebersohn.
30 May	Christchurch	Crusaders	LOST	7-30	M Fraser	T: Hayward. C: Ebersohn
28 Jun	Perth	Blues	LOST	14-40	R Hoffman	T: Charles, Stander. C: Hayward (2).
5 Jul	Perth	Reds	WON	30-20	A Gardner	T: Cummins, Charles, McCalman. C: Hayward (3). P: Hayward (3).
11 Jul	Canberra	Brumbies	LOST	25-47	SR Walsh	T: Holmes, Cowan, Tuatara-Morrison. C: Hayward, Ebersohn. P: Hayward.

‹ DID YOU KNOW? ›
The 1981 Springboks' first tour match in the USA against a Midwest side on 19 September at Roosevelt Park in Racine, Wisconsin, kicked off at 09h15 - the only time a Springbok side has ever played a match in the morning.

VODACOM SUPER RUGBY

2014 SQUAD

PLAYER	Date of Birth	Height	Weight	M	T	C	P	DG	Pts
CB (Chris) Alcock	24/06/1988	1,82	103	43	1	–	–	–	5
PD (Phoenix) Battye	28/09/1990	2,04	115	12	–	–	–	–	0
MG (Marcel) Brache	15/10/1987	1,90	92	10	–	–	–	–	0
L (Luke) Burton	17/02/1994	1,80	92	2	–	–	–	–	0
NL (Nathan) Charles	09/01/1989	1,83	103	60	4	–	–	–	20
AP (Adam) Coleman	07/10/1991	2,04	122	14	–	–	–	–	0
AJ (Angus) Cottrell	20/11/1989	1,91	105	29	1	–	–	–	5
PJM (Pekahou) Cowan	02/06/1986	1,83	109	91	4	–	–	–	20
NM (Nick) Cummins	05/10/1987	1,88	94	74	16	–	–	–	80
P (Patrick) Dellitt	21/08/1986	1,91	92	37	3	–	–	–	15
JM (Sias) Ebersohn	23/02/1989	1,75	81	59	4	58	83	5	400
T (Tetera) Faulkner	26/07/1988	1,80	114	29	–	–	–	–	0
KW (Kyle) Godwin	30/07/1992	1,87	87	27	4	3	2	–	32
DS (Dane) Haylett-Petty	18/06/1989	1,89	95	21	2	–	–	–	10
J (Jayden) Hayward	11/08/1987	1,85	95	47	4	18	22	–	122
MJ (Matt) Hodgson	25/06/1981	1,85	101	113	13	–	–	–	65
R (Ryan) Hodson	10/10/1989	1,79	99	2	–	–	–	–	0
ZA (Zac) Holmes	30/05/1990	1,75	87	23	4	10	19	–	97
O (Oli) Hoskins	06/03/1993	1,90	122	15	–	–	–	–	0
D (Dillyn) Leyds	12/09/1992	1,85	87	3	–	–	–	–	0
KA (Kieran) Longbottom	20/12/1985	1,80	107	57	–	–	–	–	0
AS (Alby) Mathewson	13/12/1985	1,73	86	106	19	–	–	–	95
B (Ben) McCalman	18/03/1988	1,92	106	65	8	–	–	–	40
HJ (Hugh) McMeniman	01/11/1983	2,01	112	42	1	–	–	–	5
L (Luke) Morahan	13/04/1990	1,89	95	53	13	–	–	–	65
IG (Ian) Prior	21/08/1990	1,79	83	44	3	–	–	–	15
J (Junior) Rasolea	29/04/1991	1,96	100	21	2	–	–	–	10
B (Brynard) Stander	27/04/1990	1,90	97	14	1	–	–	–	5
JWA (Wilhelm) Steenkamp	07/02/1985	2,00	115	67	1	–	–	–	5
HR (Heath) Tessman	03/03/1984	1,82	105	39	–	–	–	–	0
C (Chris) Tuatara-Morrison	11/09/1986	1,89	100	10	2	–	–	–	10
J (Justin) Turner	12/03/1990	1,80	85	1	–	–	–	–	0
F (Francois) van Wyk	30/07/1991	1,89	114	2	–	–	–	–	0
SL (Sam) Wykes	25/04/1988	1,95	106	74	2	–	–	–	10
TOTALS				1306	112	89	126	5	1131

VODACOM SUPER RUGBY

APPEARANCES & POINTS

PLAYER	Waratahs	Brumbies	Rebels	Highlanders	Chiefs	Reds	Waratahs	Rebels	Bulls	Cheetahs	Stormers	Lions	Crusaders	Blues	Reds	Brumbies	Apps	T	C	P	DG	Pts
Morahan	15	15	14	14	14	14	14	–	–	–	–	–	–	–	–	–	7	2	–	–	–	10
Dellit	14	14	–	–	–	–	14	–	–	14R	13R	13	–	–	–	–	6	–	–	–	–	0
Rasolea	13	13	13	13	13	13	–	–	–	–	–	–	11	13R	13	–	9	1	–	–	–	5
Godwin	12	12	12	12	12	12	12	12	12	12	–	–	–	–	–	–	10	1	–	–	–	5
Cummins	11	11	11	11	11	11	11	11	11	11	11	11	–	–	11	11	15	7	–	–	–	35
Holmes	10	10	10R	x	x	10R	14R	10R	x	10R	12R	10R	15R	x	10	10	12	1	2	3	–	18
Mathewson	9	9	9	9	9	9	9	–	–	–	–	–	–	9	–	9R	9	1	–	–	–	5
McCalman	8	8	8	8	–	8	8	8	8	8	8	8	–	8	8	8	14	4	–	–	–	20
Hodgson	7c	7c	7c	7c	7c	7c	7c	7c	7c	7c	7c	7c	7c	7c	7c	7c	16	6	–	–	–	30
Cottrell	6	4R	6	6	8	6	6	6	6	6	6	6	8	–	–	–	13	1	–	–	–	5
Steenkamp	5	5R	5	5	5	5	–	5	x	x	5R	5	5	x	5	5	12	–	–	–	–	0
Wykes	4	4	4	4	4	4	4	–	4	4	4	4	4	5	4	4	15	–	–	–	–	0
Longbottom	3	3	3	3	3	3	3	3	3	3	3	3	3	3	3	3	16	–	–	–	–	0
Charles	2	2	2	2	2	2	2	2	2	2	2	2	2	2	2	2	16	3	–	–	–	15
Faulkner	1	1	1R	1R	1R	1R	1R	1R	1R	1R	1R	–	–	x	1R	1R	13	–	–	–	–	0
Tessman	21R	2R	2R	2R	2R	2R	x	2R	2R	2R	2R	2R	2R	x	x	2R	13	–	–	–	–	0
Cowan	1R	1R	1	1	1	1	1	1	1	1	1	1	1	1	1	1	16	1	–	–	–	5
Hoskins	3R	3R	3R	x	3R	3R	3R	3R	3R	3R	3R	3R	3R	x	3R	3R	14	–	–	–	–	0
McMeniman	5R	5	–	–	6	–	–	–	–	–	–	–	–	6	6	–	5	–	–	–	–	0
Alcock	7R	6	–	–	–	–	–	–	–	–	–	–	–	–	–	–	2	–	–	–	–	0
Stander	6R	–	6R	x	6R	6R	6R	6R	6R	6R	6R	8R	6	x	x	6	12	1	–	–	–	5
Prior	x	9R	9R	9R	9R	9R	9R	9	9	9	9	9	9	x	9	9	14	–	–	–	–	0
Ebersohn	10R	10R	10	10	10	10	10	10	10	10	10	10	10	10	–	15R	15	1	17	25	1	117
Hayward	–	14R	15	15	15	15	–	–	15	15	15	15	15	15	15	15	13	4	9	5	–	53
Coleman	–	–	4R	5R	5R	4R	4R	4	5	5	5	4R	5R	5	5R	5R	14	–	–	–	–	0
Brache	–	–	12R	x	x	13R	13	13	13	13	14	–	–	13	13	–	9	–	–	–	–	0
Haylett-Petty	–	–	–	–	–	–	15	15	14	14	–	14	14	14	14	14	9	1	–	–	–	5
Tuatara-Morrison	–	–	–	–	–	15R	13R	13R	14R	13	13	12	12	12	–	–	10	2	–	–	–	10
Battye	–	–	–	–	–	–	–	5R	–	–	–	–	–	–	–	–	1	–	–	–	–	0
Turner	–	–	–	–	–	–	–	x	x	x	x	9R	x	–	x	–	1	–	–	–	–	0
Burton	–	–	–	–	–	–	–	–	–	12	12	–	–	–	–	x	2	–	–	–	–	0
van Wyk	–	–	–	–	–	–	–	–	–	–	–	1R	1R	–	–	–	2	–	–	–	–	0
Hodson	–	–	–	–	–	–	–	–	–	–	–	–	8R	–	–	–	1	–	–	–	–	0
Leyds	–	–	–	–	–	–	–	–	–	–	–	14R	x	10R	–	–	2	–	–	–	–	0
Alcock	–	–	–	–	–	–	–	–	–	–	–	–	–	–	–	8R	1	–	–	–	–	0
35 Players																	**339**	**37**	**28**	**33**	**1**	**343**

Note: ▓ = *Yellow card*

Records

MATCH RECORDS

Biggest win	41	vs Lions (55-14)	Perth	2009
Heaviest defeat	53	vs Crusaders (0-53)	Christchurch	2007
Highest score	55	vs Lions (55-14)	Perth	2009
Most points conceded	53	vs Crusaders (0-53)	Christchurch	2007
Most tries	8	vs Lions (55-14)	Perth	2009
Most tries conceded	8	vs Crusaders (0-53)	Christchurch	2007
Most points by a player	25	CB Shepherd vs Bulls (2t, 3c, 3p)	Pretoria	2007
Most tries by a player	3	SNG Staniforth vs Cats	Johannesburg	2006
	3	CB Shepherd vs Brumbies	Canberra	2009
	3	NM Cummins vs Waratahs	Perth	2014
Most conversions by a player	6	MJ Giteau vs Lions	Perth	2009
Most penalties by a player	6	JD O'Connor vs Bulls	Perth	2011
Most drop goals by a player	2	JM Ebersohn vs Bulls	Pretoria	2013

SEASON RECORDS

Most team points	343	from 16 matches	2014
Most points by a player	170	JD O'Connor	2011
Most team tries	42	from 13 matches	2009
Most tries by a player	9	SNG Staniforth	2006
Most conversions by a player	28	MJ Giteau	2009
Most penalties by a player	47	JD O'Connor	2011
Most drop goals by a player	2	JM Ebersohn	2013

CAREER RECORDS

Most appearances	113	MJ Hodgson	2006-2014
Most points	372	CB Shepherd	2006-2012
Most tries	30	CB Shepherd	2006-2012
Most conversions	55	MJ Giteau	2007-2009
Most penalties	70	JD O'Connor	2009-2011
Most drop goals	2	JM Ebersohn	2013

❰ DID YOU KNOW? ❱

Bizarrely, two Springbok matches at the 1995 World Cup started late for different reasons: the pool match vs Canada in Port Elizabeth because of a power failure, and the semi-final vs France in Durban because of a waterlogged field.

VODACOM SUPER RUGBY

Victor Matfield made a welcome return to rugby in 2014 after a two-year hiatus.

VODACOM CUP

Five-year thirst quenched

Plaudits for 'Poubloues' as tournament gets African flavour

GWK Griquas won the Vodacom Cup for the first time since 2009 when they dethroned defending champions the Golden Lions 30-6 in a surprisingly one-sided Friday-night final at GWK Park in Kimberley.

It was the home side's fifth title since the tournament's inception in 1998, drawing them level with the Lions' trophy haul in the second-tier provincial competition. Perhaps more satisfying, however, was the fact that Griquas could lay to rest the ghosts of 2012, when visitors DHL Western Province scored in the dying seconds to break their Vodacom Cup duck in spectacular fashion.

Griquas' win also soothed the pain of having been relegated from the Absa Currie Cup Premier Division at the tail-end of the 2013 season, and would have given coach Peter Engledow plenty of confidence as he prepared to plot the poubloues' potholed path back to the top flight via a new, winner-takes-all qualifying tournament involving the seven first-division sides which, as it turned out, went down to the final weekend [*see Currie Cup chapter*].

The final score might have suggested a case of one-way traffic for 80 minutes but this was hardly the case, as the Lions took a 6-3 lead with a quarter gone before the slow poison dished out by the home side's forwards began to take its toll.

Leading 9-6 with half-time fast approaching, Griquas struck a psychological blow when flyhalf Francois Brummer, who had opened his team's account with a drop goal, crossed the whitewash for his fullback, Gouws Prinsloo, to convert.

For the outgunned Gautengers, the proverbial dam wall never quite came crashing down but its cracks certainly widened as the game approached its business end and a converted try on the hour by replacement wing Danie Dames gave Griquas a 17-point cushion. This proved to be more than enough of a buffer against brave opponents who tackled for all their worth but who largely failed in their bids to bother the scoreboard operator.

Flanker Marnus Schoeman administered the last rites with a try after 67 minutes, prompting early celebrations from players and fans alike on a nippy Northern Cape night. With Griquas still smarting at having lost their top-class status just six months earlier, who could really blame the long-suffering on both sides of the four white lines for their ebullience?

As for the 17-year-old tournament, there continued to be much discussion over its role as well as its continued relevance in the South African rugby landscape. A by-product of a decision taken to field, from 1998 onwards, brand-new, American-style regional franchise outfits instead of traditional provincial teams in the then Super 12, the Vodacom Cup successfully carved out a niche during professionalism's infancy as a development platform for young players, while it provided franchises with a rich source of game time for their growing number of full-time employees, who might otherwise have had few balls to kick in anger.

However, the creation, in the short space of five years, of two high-profile, televised club tournaments – the independent, students-only Varsity Cup in 2008 and SARU's fledgling Cell C Community Cup for the country's best so-called 'open' clubs in 2013 – raised questions as to whether the Vodacom Cup still provided value for money in tough economic times, especially as all three tournaments overlapped on an increasingly congested playing calendar.

Perhaps more crucially, did the Vodacom Cup continue to provide a return on investment in the form of sufficient numbers of young black players who were ready to take the step up to franchise and international rugby?

Proponents of putting the Vodacom Cup out to pasture – in favour of possibly an expanded Community Cup or a new national club league – point to sparse crowds at most Vodacom Cup matches and the fact that the standard of club rugby has risen markedly, thereby perhaps making clubs, and not provinces, the ideal vehicles to further SARU's development objectives.

On the flipside, provinces, especially the so-called 'platteland unions', argue that without the Vodacom Cup their stadiums would remain empty for most of the year, with the resultant economic downsides. They also see the tournament as vital preparation for the Absa Currie Cup later in the season, although it can be argued that any tournament that is merely used as preparation for another, is in some way inherently flawed.

The Vodacom Cup also lost, and then regained, its international flavour after the announcement in late 2013 that Argentina's Pampas XV – champions of 2011 – would no longer take part, citing financial considerations. (They later relocated to Australasia and took part in the 2014 Pacific Rugby Cup.)

This loss was offset somewhat by the presence of a Kenyan representative team – the Tusker Simba XV – who began their hastily-arranged campaign with a shock 17-10 victory over the Eastern Province Kings. But unlike their road-running compatriots, the East Africans found the pace of the front-runners too fast and they rapidly ran out of steam, conceding 65 points against Western Province and 75 against the Free State XV en route to seventh place in the South section, which included a defeat to perennial wooden-spoonists the Border Bulldogs.

❰ DID YOU KNOW? ❱
The shortest gap between a father gaining his final Springbok cap and his son making his debut is just 17 years – SWP (Schalk) Burger snr (31 May 1986, vs NZ Cavaliers) & Schalk jnr (24 Oct 2003, vs Georgia - RWC).

VODACOM CUP

NORTH

Team	P	W	L	D	PF	PA	PD	TF	TA	LB	TB	Pts
Pumas	7	7	0	0	322	105	217	41	14	0	4	32
Griquas	7	6	1	0	259	134	125	33	12	0	3	27
Blue Bulls	7	5	2	0	313	111	202	43	10	2	4	26
Golden Lions	7	4	3	0	256	178	78	36	21	1	3	20
Leopards XV	7	3	4	0	227	178	49	29	22	2	4	18
Griffons	7	2	5	0	182	240	-58	25	35	1	3	12
Valke	7	1	6	0	180	262	-82	25	34	1	3	8
Limpopo BB	7	0	7	0	47	578	-531	6	90	0	0	0

SOUTH

Team	P	W	L	D	PF	PA	PD	TF	TA	LB	TB	Pts
Sharks XV	7	6	1	0	215	120	95	25	14	0	3	27
Free State XV	7	5	2	0	277	148	129	40	17	1	5	26
SWD	7	5	2	0	240	164	76	32	20	1	4	25
Western Province	7	5	2	0	215	138	77	32	16	0	3	23
EP Kings	7	3	4	0	171	165	6	22	20	2	1	15
Boland	7	2	5	0	158	197	-39	20	26	1	2	11
Tusker Simba XV	7	1	6	0	102	283	-181	14	45	2	1	7
Border	7	1	6	0	124	287	-163	15	42	0	1	5

Note: LB = Losing Bonus, TB = Try Bonus

Griquas celebrate their Vodacom Cup victory over the Lions in Kimberley.

⟨ **DID YOU KNOW?** ⟩

The first Springbok head – traditionally awarded to the first team to defeat a Springbok touring side – was handed to the Welsh club Newport after they beat the Springboks 9-3 on 24 October 1912.

VODACOM CUP

PLAY-OFFS

Quarter-finals: Free State XV lost to Blue Bulls 21-22 *(Bloemfontein)*, Pumas beat WP 13-8 *(Nelspruit)*, Sharks XV lost to Golden Lions 20-27 *(Durban)*, Griquas beat SWD 84-15 *(Kimberley)*.
Semi-finals: Blue Bulls lost to Golden Lions 15-16 *(Pretoria)*, Pumas lost to Griquas 14-15 *(Nelspruit)*.

Final: GWK Park, Kimberley, Friday 16 May. Referee: Jaco van Heerden.
Griquas 30 *(Tries: Brummer, M Schoeman, Dames. Conversions: Prinsloo 3. Penalties: Prinsloo 2. Drop goal: Brummer)*
Golden Lions 6 *(Penalty: Du Plessis. Drop goal: Du Plessis)*

Griquas: Gouws Prinsloo, Ederies Arendse *(Howard Mnisi, 69)*, Jonathan Francke, Wayne Stevens (c), Rocco Jansen *(Danie Dames, 56)*, Francois Brummer, Tian Meyer *(Dustin Jinka, 67)*, Burger Schoeman *(RJ Liebenberg, 72)*, Jaco Nepgen, Marnus Schoeman, Hilton Lobberts *(Stephan Greeff, 66)*, Jonathan Adendorff, Ewald van der Westhuizen, Martin Bezuiedenhout *(Simon Westraadt, 67)*, Steph Roberts *(Janro van Niekerk, 55)*.
Golden Lions: Vainon Willis *(Marais Schmidt, 22)*, JR Esterhuizen, Stokkies Hanekom, Harold Vorster, Selom Gavor *(Caswell Khoza, 72)*, Willie du Plessis, Ricky Schroeder *(c, Michael Bondesio, 52)*, Lourens Erasmus, Cyle Brink, Stephan de Wit *(Thabo Mabuza, 67)*, Hugo Kloppers, Thabo Mamojele *(Chris van Zyl, 52)*, Charles Marais *(Nico du Plessis, 72)*, Malcolm Marx *(Mark Pretorius, 72)*, Dylan Smith.

LEADING SCORERS

50 POINTS OR MORE

PLAYER	PROVINCE	T	C	P	DG	PTS
JC Roos	Pumas	1	21	21	0	110
Gouws Prinsloo	Griquas	3	24	14	0	105
Willie du Plessis	Golden Lions	1	26	11	1	93
Karlo Aspeling	SWD	0	22	11	2	83
Gerhard Nortier	Leop XV	1	22	9	1	79
Tian Schoeman	Blue Bulls	1	17	7	0	60
Tim Swiel	Sharks XV	2	11	7	0	53
Riaan Smit	Free State XV	2	12	5	0	52
Ntabeni Dukisa	EP Kings	2	11	6	0	50

5 TRIES OR MORE

9	George Tossel	Leopards XV	5	Carel Greeff	Griquas
9	Devon Williams	WP	5	Duwayne Smart	SWD
7	Sampie Mastriet	Blue Bulls	5	Hentzwill Pedro	SWD
6	Alshaun Bock	SWD	5	Martin Sithole	Griffons
6	Ederies Arendse	Griquas	5	Nicky Steyn	Griffons
6	Nico Lee	Free State XV	5	Rayn Smid	WP
6	Rohan Kitshoff	WP	5	Ruaan Lerm	Golden Lions
6	Zingisa April	Free State XV	5	Stephan de Wit	Golden Lions

Vodacom Cup Records

CHAMPIONS

Year	Champion	Year	Champion	Year	Champion
1998	Griquas	2004	Golden Lions	2010	Blue Bulls
1999	Golden Lions	2005	Griquas	2011	Pampas XV
2000	Cheetahs	2006	Valke	2012	Western Province
2001	Blue Bulls	2007	Griquas	2013	Golden Lions
2002	Golden Lions	2008	Blue Bulls	2014	Griquas
2003	Golden Lions	2009	Griquas		

RESULTS OF FINALS

Year	Winner	Score	Loser	Score	Venue
1998	Griquas	57	Golden Lions	0	Kimberley
1999	Golden Lions	73	Griquas	7	Johannesburg
2000	Free State	44	Griquas	24	Bloemfontein
2001	Blue Bulls	42	Boland Cavaliers	24	Pretoria
2002	Golden Lions	54	Blue Bulls	38	Johannesburg
2003	Blue Bulls	17	Golden Lions	26	Pretoria
2004	Golden Lions	35	Blue Bulls	16	Johannesburg
2005	Griquas	27	Leopards	25	Kimberley
2006	Valke	25	KwaZulu-Natal	17	Brakpan
2007	Griquas	33	Blue Bulls	29	Kimberley
2008	Blue Bulls	25	Free State	21	Pretoria
2009	Blue Bulls	19	Griquas	28	Pretoria
2010	Blue Bulls	31	Free State	29	Pretoria
2011	Pampas XV	14	Blue Bulls	9	Potchefstroom
2012	Griquas	18	Western Province	20	Kimberley
2013	Pumas	28	Golden Lions	42	Nelspruit
2014	Griquas	30	Golden Lions	6	Kimberley

MATCH RECORDS

Most points by a team
161   Golden Lions vs Limpopo BB   2013

Biggest winning margin
158   GL vs Limpopo BB (161-3)   2013

Most tries by a team
25   Golden Lions vs Lim BB (161-3)   2013

Most points by a player
47   AA Volmink (9t, 1c), Golden Lions vs Limpopo BB   2013

Most tries by a player
9   AA Volmink, Lions vs Limpopo BB   2013

Most conversions by a player
15   WNF du Plessis, Blue Bulls vs Limpopo BB   2013
15   WNF du Plessis, Golden Lions vs Limpopo BB   2014

VODACOM CUP

Most penalties by a player
9	E Herbert, Griffons vs Pumas	2001

Most drop goals by a player
2	GS du Toit, Griquas vs Cheetahs	1998
2	J Benade, Pumas vs Valke	1999
2	A Hough, Griffons vs Border	2006
2	F Brummer, Blue Bulls vs Leopards	2009
2	F Brummer, Blue Bulls vs FS Cheetahs	2010

SEASON RECORDS

Most points by a team
731	Griquas		1998

Most points by a player
236	GS du Toit	Griquas	1998

Most tries by a team
109	Griquas		1998

Most tries by a player
15	J Daniels	Boland Cavaliers	1998

Most conversions by a player
72	GS du Toit	Griquas	1998

Most penalties by a player
44	E Herbert	Griffons	2001

Most drop goals by a player
6	BK Francis	Blue Bulls	2008
6	F Brummer	Blue Bulls	2010

CAREER RECORDS

MOST POINTS BY A PLAYER — 682 — J Peach, EP, Boland

Most tries by a player
63	J Daniels	Boland, Lions

Most conversions by a player
110	J Peach	EP, Boland

Most penalties by a player
119	J Peach	EP, Boland

Most drop goals by a player
16	F Brummer	Blue Bulls, Griquas

⟨ DID YOU KNOW? ⟩
1995 Rugby World Cup winner Mark Andrews was the first Springbok to reach 50 Test caps.

VODACOM CUP

Blue Bulls

'98	'99	'00	'01	'02	'03	'04	'05	'06	'07	'08	'09	'10	'11	'12	'13	'14
9th	7th	4th	**1st**	3rd	1st	4th	1st	3rd	3rd	**1st**	2nd	**1st**	2nd	4th	3rd	5th

Played	Won	Lost	Drawn	Points for	Points against	Tries for	Tries against
9	6	3	0	350	148	46	13

Date	Venue	Opponent	Result	Score	Referee	Scorers
8 Mar	Pretoria	Griquas	LOST	24-26	M vd Westhuizen	T: Small-Smith, Penalty try. C: Fouche. P: Fouche (4).
15 Mar	Nelspruit	Pumas	LOST	20-22	T Ntshakaza	T: Kriel, Bullbring. C: Fouche (2). P: Fouche (2).
22 Mar	Pretoria	Golden Lions	WON	22-20	C Joubert	T: Kriel, Blommetjies, Davids. C: Fouche, Jantjies. P: Jantjies.
29 Mar	Leeudoringstad	Leopards	WON	30-26	T Ntshakaza	T: Mastriet, Small-Smith, Tobias, Hugo. C: Stander (2). P: Fouche (2).
4 Apr	Pretoria	Valke	WON	54-7	S Berry	T: Mastriet (2), Van der Walt (2), Murray, T Schoeman, R Nell. C: T Schoeman (5). P: T Schoeman (3).
11 Apr	Welkom	Griffons	WON	49-10	F Anseimi	T: Blommetjies (2), Van Wyk (2), Mastriet, Odendaal, Nell. C: T Schoeman (3), Stander. P: T Schoeman (2).
25 Apr	Pretoria	Limpopo BB	WON	114-0	E Nel	T: Mastriet (3), Odendaal (2), Liebenberg (2), Blommetjies, Murray, Kriel, Jacobs, Davids, Hugo, Bulbring, Van Wyk, Van Wyk, Mahlo, Stander. C: T Schoeman (8), Stander (4).

QUARTER-FINAL

| 3 May | Bloemfontein | Free State XV | WON | 22-21 | R Boneparte | T: Jacobs. C: T Schoeman. P: Jantjies (3), T Schoeman (2). |

SEMI-FINAL

| 10 May | Pretoria | Golden Lions | LOST | 15-16 | Q Immelman | T: Odendaal, Smit. C: Jantjies. P: Jantjies. |

Note: ■ = *Champion*

⟨ DID YOU KNOW? ⟩

Michael du Plessis (2 Sep 1989, vs World XV) was the last player to score a four-point try for the Springboks, while fellow centre Danie Gerber (15 Aug 1992, vs NZ) was the first to score a five-point try.

VODACOM CUP

2014 SQUAD

PLAYER	BLUE BULLS CAREER						OTHER UNIONS						VODACOM CUP TOTAL					
	A	T	C	P	DG	Pts	A	T	C	P	DG	Pts	A	T	C	P	DG	Pts
C (Clayton) Blommetjies	27	11	0	0	0	55	0	0	0	0	0	0	27	11	0	0	0	55
DJ (David) Bulbring	9	2	0	0	0	10	26	4	0	0	0	20	35	6	0	0	0	30
CE (Clyde) Davids	9	2	0	0	0	10	0	0	0	0	0	0	9	2	0	0	0	10
CP (Christiaan) de Bruin	4	0	0	0	0	0	0	0	0	0	0	0	4	0	0	0	0	0
JJ (Jacques) Engelbrecht	1	0	0	0	0	0	24	4	0	0	0	20	25	4	0	0	0	20
LDVZ (Louis) Fouche	8	0	6	11	0	45	0	0	0	0	0	0	8	0	6	11	0	45
JN (Neethling) Fouche	1	0	0	0	0	0	0	0	0	0	0	0	1	0	0	0	0	0
R (Reniel) Hugo	6	2	0	0	0	10	2	0	0	0	0	0	8	2	0	0	0	10
TK (Travis) Ismaiel	12	6	0	0	0	30	0	0	0	0	0	0	12	6	0	0	0	30
WJ (Luaan) Jacobs	15	2	0	0	0	10	0	0	0	0	0	0	15	2	0	0	0	10
NJ (Nico) Janse van Rensburg	2	0	0	0	0	0	0	0	0	0	0	0	2	0	0	0	0	0
R (Rohan) Janse van Rensburg	7	4	0	0	0	20	0	0	0	0	0	0	7	4	0	0	0	20
AS (Tony) Jantjies	13	3	30	22	0	141	0	0	0	0	0	0	13	3	30	22	0	141
JA (Jesse) Kriel	7	3	0	0	0	15	0	0	0	0	0	0	7	3	0	0	0	15
WA (Wian) Liebenberg	18	10	0	0	0	50	0	0	0	0	0	0	18	10	0	0	0	50
KS (Kefentse) Mahlo	3	1	0	0	0	5	0	0	0	0	0	0	3	1	0	0	0	5
BG (Bandise) Maku	31	1	0	0	0	5	0	0	0	0	0	0	31	1	0	0	0	5
S (Sampie) Mastriet	30	26	0	0	0	130	0	0	0	0	0	0	30	26	0	0	0	130
WM (Waylon) Murray	8	2	0	0	0	10	9	0	0	0	0	0	17	2	0	0	0	10
NM (Mox) Mxoli	1	0	0	0	0	0	0	0	0	0	0	0	1	0	0	0	0	0
RD (Ryan) Nell	7	2	0	0	0	10	0	0	0	0	0	0	7	2	0	0	0	10
MB (Burger) Odendaal	7	4	0	0	0	20	0	0	0	0	0	0	7	4	0	0	0	20
M (Marvin) Orie	6	0	0	0	0	0	0	0	0	0	0	0	6	0	0	0	0	0
R (Rudy) Paige	8	0	0	0	0	0	10	0	0	0	0	0	18	0	0	0	0	0
JL (Juan) Schoeman	7	0	0	0	0	0	0	0	0	0	0	0	7	0	0	0	0	0
P (Pierre) Schoeman	2	0	0	0	0	0	0	0	0	0	0	0	2	0	0	0	0	0
CF (Tian) Schoeman	5	1	17	7	0	60	0	0	0	0	0	0	5	1	17	7	0	60
BG (Basil) Short	16	2	0	0	0	10	0	0	0	0	0	0	16	2	0	0	0	10
WT (William) Small-Smith	6	3	0	0	0	15	0	0	0	0	0	0	6	3	0	0	0	15
RA (Roelof) Smit	7	3	0	0	0	15	0	0	0	0	0	0	7	3	0	0	0	15
JT (Joshua) Stander	4	1	7	0	0	19	0	0	0	0	0	0	4	1	7	0	0	19
S (Sidney) Tobias	7	1	0	0	0	5	21	2	0	0	0	10	28	3	0	0	0	15
PW (Wimpie) van der Walt	5	2	0	0	0	10	15	5	0	0	0	25	20	7	0	0	0	35
PS (Schalk) van Heerden	12	0	0	0	0	0	0	0	0	0	0	0	12	0	0	0	0	0
R (Rudi) van Rooyen	4	0	0	0	0	0	0	0	0	0	0	0	4	0	0	0	0	0
A (Arno) van Wyk	2	1	0	0	0	5	0	0	0	0	0	0	2	1	0	0	0	5
HJ (Hencus) van Wyk	14	4	0	0	0	20	0	0	0	0	0	0	14	4	0	0	0	20
GJ (Jaco) Visagie	7	0	0	0	0	0	0	0	0	0	0	0	7	0	0	0	0	0

VODACOM CUP

APPEARANCES & POINTS

PLAYER	Griquas	Pumas	Golden Lions	Leopards XV	Valke	Griffons	Limpopo BB	Free State XV	Golden Lions	Apps	T	C	P	DG	Pts
Clayton Blommetjies	15	15	14	11	15	15	15	15	15	9	4	–	–	–	20
Travis Ismaiel	14	14	11	–	11	–	–	–	11	5	–	–	–	–	0
William Small-Smith	13	13	13	13	–	–	–	–	–	4	2	–	–	–	10
Waylon Murray	12	12	12	–	13	13	13	13	13	8	2	–	–	–	10
Jesse Kriel	11	11	15	15	–	11	11	11	–	7	3	–	–	–	15
Louis Fouche	10	10	10	10	–	–	–	–	–	4	–	4	8	–	32
Rudy Paige	9	9	9	9	–	–	–	–	–	4	–	–	–	–	0
Clyde Davids	8	8	8	8	8	8	8	8	8	9	2	–	–	–	10
Christiaan de Bruin	7	7	–	–	–	7	–	–	7	4	–	–	–	–	0
Wiaan Liebenberg	6	6	8R	7	7	6	6	6	6	9	2	–	–	–	10
David Bullbring	5c	5c	5c	5c	5c	5c	5c	5c	4c	9	2	–	–	–	10
Schalk van Heerden	4	4	4	4	4	4	4	4	–	8	–	–	–	–	0
Hencus van Wyk	3	3	3	3	3	3	3	3	3	9	3	–	–	–	15
Bandise Maku	2	–	2	2	–	–	–	–	–	3	–	–	–	–	0
Pierre Schoeman	1	1	–	–	–	–	–	–	–	2	–	–	–	–	0
Juan Schoeman	–	–	1	1	1	1	1	1	1	7	–	–	–	–	0
Sidney Tobias	x	2R	–	2R	2	2	2	2	2	7	1	–	–	–	5
Johan Fouche	3R	–	–	–	–	–	–	–	–	1	–	–	–	–	0
N Janse van Rensburg	6R	4R	–	–	–	–	–	–	–	2	–	–	–	–	0
Wimpie van der Walt	7R	6R	6	6	6	–	–	–	–	5	2	–	–	–	10
Lohan Jacobs	9R	9R	x	9R	9	9	9	9	9	8	2	–	–	–	10
Joshua Stander	x	x	–	10R	12R	10R	10R	–	–	4	1	7	–	–	19
R Janse van Rensburg	12R	–	–	–	–	–	–	–	–	1	–	–	–	–	0
Jaco Visagie	–	2	2R	–	2R	2R	–	–	–	4	–	–	–	–	0
Mox Mxoli	–	1R	–	–	–	–	–	–	–	1	–	–	–	–	0
Ryan Nell	–	12R	12R	15R	11R	14R	12R	x	14R	7	2	–	–	–	10
Jacques Engelbrecht	–	–	7	–	–	–	–	–	–	1	–	–	–	–	0
Basil Short	–	–	3R	1R	3R	1R	3R	1R	3R	7	–	–	–	–	0
Reniel Hugo	–	–	4R	8R	8R	–	7	7	5R	6	2	–	–	–	10
Tony Jantjies	–	–	10R	–	–	–	–	10R	10	3	–	2	5	–	19
Sampie Mastriet	–	–	–	14	14	14	14	14	14	6	7	–	–	–	35
Burger Odendaal	–	–	–	12	12	12	12	12	12	6	4	–	–	–	20
Marvin Orie	–	–	–	4R	4R	4R	4R	4R	5	6	–	–	–	–	0
Tian Schoeman	–	–	–	–	10	10	10	10	10R	5	1	17	7	–	60
Rudi van Rooyen	–	–	–	–	9R	–	–	–	–	1	–	–	–	–	0
Roelof Smit	–	–	–	–	–	7R	8R	7R	7R	4	1	–	–	–	5
Kefentse Mahlo	–	–	–	–	–	15R	9R	x	9R	3	1	–	–	–	5
Arno van Wyk	–	–	–	–	–	–	2R	x	2R	2	1	–	–	–	5
Penalty try	–	–	–	–	–	–	–	–	–	0	1	–	–	–	5
38 Players										**191**	**46**	**30**	**20**	**0**	**350**

VODACOM CUP

Blue Bulls Limpopo

'13 16th | '14 16th

Played	Won	Lost	Drawn	Points for	Points against	Tries for	Tries against
7	0	7	0	47	578	6	90

Date	Venue	Opponent	Result	Score	Referee	Scorers
8 Mar	Bultfontein	Griffons	LOST	10-62	J Kotze	T: Maphaqa, Cronje.
15 Mar	Polokwane	Leopards XV	LOST	10-71	G de Bruin	T: N Johnson. C: Huysamen. P: Huysamen.
21 Mar	Kimberley	Griquas	LOST	13-68	M Jonker	T: N Johnson. C: Huysamen. P: Huysamen (2).
29 Mar	Sasolburg	Valke	LOST	14-65	A Sehlako	T: Janse van Rensburg, Mathonsi. C: Huysamen (2).
5 Apr	Polokwane	Pumas	LOST	0-88	O Rametsi	
12 Apr	Polokwane	Golden Lions	LOST	0-110	G de Bruin	
25 Apr	Pretoria	Blue Bulls	LOST	0-114	E Nel	

‹ DID YOU KNOW? ›

The first Springbok to score a try against the All Blacks was Attie van Heerden in the first Test of the 1921 series (13 Aug, Dunedin). He also represented South Africa as a sprinter at the 1920 Olympic Games in Antwerp, Belgium.

2014 SQUAD

PLAYER	LIMPOPO BB CAREER						OTHER UNIONS						VODACOM CUP TOTAL					
	A	T	C	P	DG	Pts	A	T	C	P	DG	Pts	A	T	C	P	DG	Pts
AJS (Barnie) Boonzaaier	6	0	0	0	0	0	0	0	0	0	0	0	6	0	0	0	0	0
JM (Johan) Coetzer	13	0	0	0	0	0	0	0	0	0	0	0	13	0	0	0	0	0
D (Divan) Cronje	3	1	0	0	0	5	0	0	0	0	0	0	3	1	0	0	0	5
LL (Louw) Davel	10	0	0	0	0	0	0	0	0	0	0	0	10	0	0	0	0	0
CA (Nollie) Davel	8	0	0	0	0	0	0	0	0	0	0	0	8	0	0	0	0	0
A (Andries) du Plessis	1	0	0	0	0	0	0	0	0	0	0	0	1	0	0	0	0	0
H (Hans) du Plessis	5	0	0	0	0	0	0	0	0	0	0	0	5	0	0	0	0	0
JLR (Johan) du Plooy	1	0	0	0	0	0	0	0	0	0	0	0	1	0	0	0	0	0
RV (Robin) Goliath	12	0	0	0	0	0	0	0	0	0	0	0	12	0	0	0	0	0
SE (Sven) Hedin	1	0	0	0	0	0	0	0	0	0	0	0	1	0	0	0	0	0
AR (Andy) Huysamen	7	0	4	3	0	17	0	0	0	0	0	0	7	0	4	3	0	17
KB (Koning) Janse van Rensburg	5	1	0	0	0	5	0	0	0	0	0	0	5	1	0	0	0	5
AM (Arno) Johnson	3	0	0	0	0	0	0	0	0	0	0	0	3	0	0	0	0	0
N (Niyass) Johnson	7	2	0	0	0	10	0	0	0	0	0	0	7	2	0	0	0	10
RL (Renier) Labuschagne	2	0	0	0	0	0	0	0	0	0	0	0	2	0	0	0	0	0
DG (Duran) Law	7	0	0	0	0	0	0	0	0	0	0	0	7	0	0	0	0	0
WJ (Willem) Louw	5	0	0	0	0	0	0	0	0	0	0	0	5	0	0	0	0	0
DL (Lloyd) Malatje	7	0	0	0	0	0	0	0	0	0	0	0	7	0	0	0	0	0
S (Sinethemba) Maphaqa	7	1	0	0	0	5	0	0	0	0	0	0	7	1	0	0	0	5
MT (Malope) Masemola	2	0	0	0	0	0	0	0	0	0	0	0	2	0	0	0	0	0
TD (Thulani) Mathonsi	13	1	0	0	0	5	0	0	0	0	0	0	13	1	0	0	0	5
SA (Sinthamdile) Memese	3	0	0	0	0	0	0	0	0	0	0	0	3	0	0	0	0	0
S (Shane) Mienie	6	0	0	0	0	0	0	0	0	0	0	0	6	0	0	0	0	0
R (Ruan) Muller	7	1	0	0	0	5	0	0	0	0	0	0	7	1	0	0	0	5
MP (Fanie) Nkuna	9	0	0	0	0	0	0	0	0	0	0	0	9	0	0	0	0	0
AM (Alwyn) Olivier	1	0	0	0	0	0	0	0	0	0	0	0	1	0	0	0	0	0
W (Walter) Pretorius	7	0	0	0	0	0	0	0	0	0	0	0	7	0	0	0	0	0
WW (Wade) Schoor	4	0	0	0	0	0	0	0	0	0	0	0	4	0	0	0	0	0
RS (Robert) Siebert	7	0	0	0	0	0	0	0	0	0	0	0	7	0	0	0	0	0
EE (Egnatius) Thomas	6	0	0	0	0	0	0	0	0	0	0	0	6	0	0	0	0	0
O (Odwa) Tinise	2	0	0	0	0	0	0	0	0	0	0	0	2	0	0	0	0	0
TG (Thabo) Tladi	1	0	0	0	0	0	0	0	0	0	0	0	1	0	0	0	0	0
PJ (Wiehann) Uys	10	0	0	0	0	0	0	0	0	0	0	0	10	0	0	0	0	0
RJ (Ruan) Venter	6	0	0	0	0	0	0	0	0	0	0	0	6	0	0	0	0	0
L (Leslie) Venton	1	0	0	0	0	0	0	0	0	0	0	0	1	0	0	0	0	0
WT (Wickus) Visser	1	0	0	0	0	0	0	0	0	0	0	0	1	0	0	0	0	0
PJH (Peet) Vorster	4	0	0	0	0	0	2	1	0	0	0	5	6	1	0	0	0	5
DH (Duggie) Weller-Blaber	2	0	0	0	0	0	0	0	0	0	0	0	2	0	0	0	0	0

VODACOM CUP

APPEARANCES & POINTS

PLAYER	Griffons	Leopards XV	Griquas	Valke	Pumas	Golden Lions	Blue Bulls	Apps	T	C	P	DG	Pts
Robin Goliath	15	15	15	13	14	15	11	7	–	–	–	–	0
Sinethemba Maphaqa	14	11	13	14R	13	13	13	7	1	–	–	–	5
Hans du Plessis	13	13	12	12	–	12	–	5	–	–	–	–	0
Andy Huysamen	12	12	10	10	10	12R	10	7	–	4	3	–	17
Koning Janse van Rensburg	11	14	11	11	–	11	–	5	1	–	–	–	5
Duran Law	10	10	10R	10R	15R	10	12R	7	–	–	–	–	0
Niyaas Johnson	9	9	9	9	9	9	9R	7	2	–	–	–	10
Willie Louw	8	8	–	–	8	8	–	4	–	–	–	–	0
Peet Vorster	7c	1c	1c	2c	–	–	–	4	–	–	–	–	0
Barnie Boonzaaier	6	2	2	6	2	–	6	6	–	–	–	–	0
Divan Cronje	5	6	6	–	–	–	–	3	1	–	–	–	5
Wade Schoor	4	4	8	5	–	–	4R	5	–	–	–	–	0
Johann du Plooy	3	–	–	–	–	–	–	1	–	–	–	–	0
Odwa Tinise	2	–	–	–	8R	–	–	2	–	–	–	–	0
Shane Mienie	1	–	3R	–	3	–	–	3	–	–	–	–	0
Ruan Venter	8R	–	8R	1R	1R	3R	1	6	–	–	–	–	0
Thulani Mathonsi	3R	3	3	3	–	3	3	6	1	–	–	–	5
Johan Coetzer	1R	18R	–	1	1	1	1R	6	–	–	–	–	0
Walter Pretorius	2R	7R	5R	–	5R	–	4	5	–	–	–	–	0
Andries du Plessis	11R	x	–	–	–	–	–	1	–	–	–	–	0
Robert Siebert	13R	12R	12R	9R	12R	10R	12	7	–	–	–	–	0
Lloyd Malatji	10R	13R	14R	14	11	14	14	7	–	–	–	–	0
Arno Johnson	–	7	7	8	–	–	–	3	–	–	–	–	0
Wiehann Uys	–	5	4	4	5c	5c	5c	6	–	–	–	–	0
Phanuel Nkuna	–	4R	5	5R	4	4	–	5	–	–	–	–	0
Elmo Thomas	–	10R	14	15	15	11R	15	6	–	–	–	–	0
Wickus Davel	–	–	6R	–	7	7	8	4	–	–	–	–	0
Dennis Weller-Blaber	–	–	–	7	12	–	–	2	–	–	–	–	0
Renier Labuschagne	–	–	–	x	–	2R	2	2	–	–	–	–	0
Alwyn Olivier	–	–	–	15R	–	–	–	1	–	–	–	–	0
Sven Hedin	–	–	–	–	6	–	–	1	–	–	–	–	0
Ruan Muller	–	–	–	–	6R	–	–	1	–	–	–	–	0
Nollie Davel	–	–	–	–	9R	9R	9	3	–	–	–	–	0
Snthemdile Memese	–	–	–	–	6	7	–	2	–	–	–	–	0
Wickus Visser	–	–	–	–	2	–	–	1	–	–	–	–	0
Malope Masemda	–	–	–	–	8R	x	–	1	–	–	–	–	0
Thabo Tladi	–	–	–	–	–	8R	–	1	–	–	–	–	0
Leslie Venton	–	–	–	–	–	2R	–	1	–	–	–	–	0
38 Players								**151**	**6**	**4**	**3**	**0**	**47**

Boland

'98	'99	'00	'01	'02	'03	'04	'05	'06	'07	'08	'09	'10	'11	'12	'13	'14
6th	3rd	8th	2nd	2nd	7th	8th	2nd	6th	6th	5th	11th	3rd	11th	9th	15th	12th

Played	Won	Lost	Drawn	Points for	Points against	Tries for	Tries against
7	2	5	0	158	197	20	26

Date	Venue	Opponent	Result	Score	Referee	Scorers
8 Mar	Cape Town [1]	WP	LOST	8-16	L Legoete	T: September. P: Zana
15 Mar	Malmesbury	Free State XV	LOST	20-28	Q Immelman	T: Constant, Roberts. C: Zana (2). P: Zana (2).
22 Mar	Swellendam	SWD	LOST	17-46	T Nshakaza	T: Rust, Radyn. C: Zana, Rust. P: Zana
29 Mar	Cape Town [1]	Tusker Simba XV	WON	24-19	C Jadezweni	T: C Pretorius (3), Zana. C: Zana (2).
5 Apr	Ceres	Sharks XV	LOST	27-43	J Kotze	T: Fortuin (2), Demas. C: Zana (2), Rust. P: Zana (2).
11 Apr	Port Elizabeth	EP Kings	LOST	21-28	J Sylvestre	T: Klaasen, Astle. C: Rust. P: Rust (3).
26 Apr	Piketberg	Border	WON	41-17	D Fortuin	T: Rust (2), Trytsman, Fortuin, Lewis, September.

[1] City Park

DID YOU KNOW?
Gerhard Morkel was the first Springbok to kick a drop goal in a Test. He slotted the kick during the second Test of the 1921 series, in Auckland. In those days, a drop goal was worth four points!

VODACOM CUP

2014 SQUAD

PLAYER	BOLAND CAREER						OTHER UNIONS						VODACOM CUP TOTAL					
	A	T	C	P	DG	Pts	A	T	C	P	DG	Pts	A	T	C	P	DG	Pts
KM (Keenan) Abrahams	2	–	–	–	–	0	–	–	–	–	–	0	2	–	–	–	–	0
BT (Brandon) April	23	9	–	–	–	45	17	6	–	–	–	30	40	15	–	–	–	75
GG (Garth) April	6	–	2	–	–	4	5	2	–	–	–	10	11	2	2	–	–	14
J (Junaid) Arendse	2	–	–	–	–	0	–	–	–	–	–	0	2	–	–	–	–	0
JC (John-Charles/JC) Astle	6	1	–	–	–	5	–	–	–	–	–	0	22	1	–	–	–	5
C (Christopher) Bosch	5	–	–	–	–	0	1	–	–	–	–	0	6	–	–	–	–	0
A (Andre) Coetzee	1	–	–	–	–	0	–	–	–	–	–	0	1	–	–	–	–	0
RJ (Ryno) Conradie	1	–	–	–	–	0	–	–	–	–	–	0	1	–	–	–	–	0
A (Ashton) Constant	30	4	–	–	–	20	–	–	–	–	–	0	54	7	–	–	–	35
J (Jovelian) de Koker	4	–	–	–	–	0	–	–	–	–	–	0	4	–	–	–	–	0
D (Danwel) Demas	5	1	–	–	–	5	–	–	–	–	–	0	20	9	–	–	–	45
MC (Martin) Dreyer	4	–	–	–	–	0	6	–	–	–	–	0	10	–	–	–	–	0
AF (Arno) Fortuin	3	3	–	–	–	15	–	–	–	–	–	0	3	3	–	–	–	15
PF (Francois) Hanekom	11	–	–	–	–	0	1	–	–	–	–	0	12	–	–	–	–	0
APM (Marnus) Hugo	10	–	–	–	–	0	21	1	–	–	–	5	31	1	–	–	–	5
JJ (Hanno) Kitshoff	9	–	–	–	–	0	–	–	–	–	–	0	9	–	–	–	–	0
HJ (Harlon) Klaasen	2	1	–	–	–	5	–	–	–	–	–	0	2	1	–	–	–	5
J (Jason) Kriel	1	–	–	–	–	0	–	–	–	–	–	0	1	–	–	–	–	0
R (Rossouw) Kruger	18	2	–	–	–	10	–	–	–	–	–	0	18	2	–	–	–	10
VE (Victor) Kruger	5	–	–	–	–	0	3	–	–	–	–	0	8	–	–	–	–	0
C (Clemen) Lewis	32	4	–	–	–	20	–	–	–	–	–	0	32	4	–	–	–	20
E (Evan) Liedeman	2	–	–	–	–	0	–	–	–	–	–	0	2	–	–	–	–	0
DK (Dumisane) Meslane	5	–	–	–	–	0	20	3	–	–	–	15	25	3	–	–	–	15
K (Khwezi) Mkhafu	7	–	–	–	–	0	24	–	–	–	–	0	31	3	–	–	–	15
C (Conway) Pretorius	5	3	–	–	–	15	–	–	–	–	–	0	5	3	–	–	–	15
U de B (Ulrich) Pretorius	8	4	–	–	–	20	–	–	–	–	–	0	8	4	–	–	–	20
T (Tiaan) Radyn	2	1	–	–	–	5	–	–	–	–	–	0	2	1	–	–	–	5
CD (Cheslyn) Roberts	9	2	–	–	–	10	–	–	–	–	–	0	9	2	–	–	–	10
HC (Christian) Rust	6	3	7	4	–	41	–	–	–	–	–	0	6	3	7	4	–	41
JP (Juwell) Samuels	5	–	–	–	–	0	–	–	–	–	–	0	5	–	–	–	–	0
E (Edwin) Sass	4	–	–	–	–	0	–	–	–	–	–	0	4	–	–	–	–	0
FJ (Franzel) September	35	12	–	–	–	60	–	–	–	–	–	0	36	12	–	–	–	60
AM (Albert) Trytsman	10	2	–	–	–	10	–	–	–	–	–	0	10	2	–	–	–	10
AG (Poena) van Niekerk	2	–	–	–	–	0	–	–	–	–	–	0	2	–	–	–	–	0
PJ (PJ) van Zyl	28	3	–	–	–	15	–	–	–	–	–	0	28	3	–	–	–	15
BCG (Ben) Venter	8	–	–	–	–	0	11	1	–	–	–	5	19	1	–	–	–	5
SP (SP) Wessels	2	–	–	–	–	0	–	–	–	–	–	0	2	–	–	–	–	0
C (Chaney) Willemse	3	–	–	–	–	0	–	–	–	–	–	0	3	–	–	–	–	0
C (Cheswin) Williams	6	–	–	–	–	0	–	–	–	–	–	0	6	–	–	–	–	0
ES (Eric) Zana	5	1	7	6	–	37	10	–	1	8	–	26	15	1	8	14	–	63

VODACOM CUP

APPEARANCES & POINTS

PLAYER	WP	Free State XV	SWD	Simba XV	Sharks XV	EP	Border	Apps	T	C	P	DG	Pts
Eric Zana	15	15	15	15	15	–	–	5	1	7	6	–	37
Danwel Demas	14	14	14	14	14	–	–	5	1	–	–	–	5
Cheswin Williams	13	10R	–	–	–	–	–	2	–	–	–	–	0
Albert Trytsman	12	12	12	12	12	12	12	7	1	–	–	–	5
Cheslyn Roberts	11	11R	11	–	–	14	–	4	1	–	–	–	5
Christian Rust	10	–	13R	10	10	10	10	6	3	7	4	–	41
Evan Liedeman	9	–	9R	–	–	–	–	2	–	–	–	–	0
PJ van Zyl	8	7	7R	7	7	8R	7	7	–	–	–	–	0
Hanno Kitshoff	7	4R	7	5	4R	4	4	7	–	–	–	–	0
Franzel September	6	–	6	6c	6	6	6	6	2	–	–	–	10
JC Astle	5c	5c	5c	–	5c	5c	5c	6	1	–	–	–	5
Victor Kruger	4	5R	4	4	4	–	–	5	–	–	–	–	0
Martin Dreyer	3	–	–	–	3	3	3	4	–	–	–	–	0
Clemen Lewis	2	2R	2	2	2	2	2	7	1	–	–	–	5
Khwezi Mkhafu	1	8R	1	1	1	1	1	7	–	–	–	–	0
Ashton Constant	1R	1	8R	1R	–	–	–	4	1	–	–	–	5
Francois Hanekom	3R	3	3	3	3R	–	–	5	–	–	–	–	0
Ben Venter	8R	4	–	–	–	–	–	2	–	–	–	–	0
Dumisane Meslane	x	6	–	8R	18R	7R	7R	5	–	–	–	–	0
Jovelian de Koker	9R	9R	–	9R	9R	–	–	4	–	–	–	–	0
Christopher Bosch	x	13	13	11R	15R	–	14	5	–	–	–	–	0
Garth April	10R	–	15R	–	–	–	–	2	–	–	–	–	0
Jason Kriel	–	11	–	–	–	–	–	1	–	–	–	–	0
Tiaan Radyn	–	10	10	–	–	–	–	2	1	–	–	–	5
Juwell Samuels	–	9	–	–	–	x	9R	2	–	–	–	–	0
Andre Coetzee	–	8	–	–	–	–	–	1	–	–	–	–	0
Ulrich Pretorius	–	2	5R	–	2R	–	2R	4	–	–	–	–	0
Marnus Hugo	–	–	9	9	9	9	9	5	–	–	–	–	0
Conway Pretorius	–	–	8	8	8	8	8	5	3	–	–	–	15
Rossouw Kruger	–	–	1R	–	–	–	–	1	–	–	–	–	0
Edwin Sass	–	–	–	13	13	13	13	4	–	–	–	–	0
Brandon April	–	–	–	11	–	x	–	1	–	–	–	–	0
Poena van Niekerk	–	–	–	12R	14R	–	–	2	–	–	–	–	0
Keenan Abrahams	–	–	–	3R	–	3R	–	2	–	–	–	–	0
Chaney Willemse	–	–	–	5R	–	7	4R	3	–	–	–	–	0
Arno Fortuin	–	–	–	–	11	11	11	3	3	–	–	–	15
Harlon Klaasen	–	–	–	–	–	15	15	2	1	–	–	–	5
Junaid Arendse	–	–	–	–	–	12R	12R	2	–	–	–	–	0
SP Wessels	–	–	–	–	–	6R	3R	2	–	–	–	–	0
Ryno Conradie	–	–	–	–	–	–	14R	1	–	–	–	–	0
40 players								**150**	**20**	**14**	**10**	**0**	**158**

VODACOM CUP

Border

'98	'99	'00	'01	'02	'03	'04	'05	'06	'07	'08	'09	'10	'11	'12	'13	'14
12th	11th	9th	11th	3rd	8th	6th	13th	13th	13th	13th	10th	9th	15th	10th	13th	15th

Played	Won	Lost	Drawn	Points for	Points against	Tries for	Tries against
7	1	6	0	124	287	15	42

Date	Venue	Opponent	Result	Score	Referee	Scorers
7 Mar	East London	Sharks XV	LOST	24-46	F Pretorius	T: Maphimpi, Waka, Putuma. C: Taljard (3). P: Taljard.
15 Mar	Grahamstown	EP Kings	LOST	6-60	L Legoete	P: Taljard (2).
22 Mar	East London	Tusker Simba XV	WON	18-17	S Geldenhuys	T: Maphimpi, Taljard. C: Taljard. P: Taljard (2).
28 Mar	East London	WP	LOST	16-29	C du Preez	T: Noordman. C: Taljard. P: Taljard (2); N Jacobs.
5 Apr	Bloemfontein	Free State XV	LOST	17-54	R Boneparte	T: Ralarala, Nofemele, Putuma. C: Kobese.
11 Apr	East London	SWD	LOST	26-40	J van Heerden	T: Nofemele, Maphimpi, Mkokeli, Makase. C: Kobese (2), Noordman.
26 Apr	Piketberg	Boland	LOST	17-41	D Fortuin	T: Waka, Jonker. C: Kobese (2). P: Kobese.

‹ DID YOU KNOW? ›

The Springboks wore white shorts for the first time in the third Test vs New Zealand in 1928 in Port Elizabeth, so that referee Boet Neser could differentiate the teams. South Africa permanently settled for white shorts in 1949.

2014 SQUAD

PLAYER	BORDER CAREER						OTHER UNIONS						VODACOM CUP TOTAL					
	A	T	C	P	DG	Pts	A	T	C	P	DG	Pts	A	T	C	P	DG	Pts
CA (Cody) Basson	2	0	0	0	0	0	0	0	0	0	0	0	2	0	0	0	0	0
AL (Ludwe) Booi	2	0	0	0	0	0	0	0	0	0	0	0	2	0	0	0	0	0
OS (Onke) Dubase	11	2	0	0	0	10	0	0	0	0	0	0	11	2	0	0	0	10
C (Cheslin) Goeda	2	0	0	0	0	0	0	0	0	0	0	0	2	0	0	0	0	0
AJ (Anthonie) Gronum	12	0	0	0	0	0	21	1	0	0	0	5	33	1	0	0	0	5
N (Neill) Jacobs	11	1	0	1	0	8	2	0	0	0	0	0	13	1	0	1	0	8
R (Ruan) Jacobs	8	0	0	0	0	0	8	1	0	0	0	5	16	1	0	0	0	5
JGA (Johannes) Jonker	7	1	0	0	0	5	0	0	0	0	0	0	7	1	0	0	0	5
C (Curtis) Kleinhans	2	0	0	0	0	0	0	0	0	0	0	0	2	0	0	0	0	0
B (Bangi) Kobese	3	0	5	1	0	13	0	0	0	0	0	0	3	0	5	1	0	13
GE (Gareth) Krause	24	2	0	0	0	10	26	7	0	0	0	35	50	9	0	0	0	45
BJ (Blake) Kyd	21	0	0	0	0	0	0	0	0	0	0	0	21	0	0	0	0	0
W (Wayne) Lemley	8	0	0	0	0	0	0	0	0	0	0	0	8	0	0	0	0	0
AG (Alvandre) Maart	1	0	0	0	0	0	1	0	0	0	0	0	2	0	0	0	0	0
M (Michael) Makase	7	1	0	0	0	5	0	0	0	0	0	0	7	1	0	0	0	5
M (Makazole) Maphimpi	7	3	0	0	0	15	0	0	0	0	0	0	7	3	0	0	0	15
S (Skhangele) Mateza	3	0	0	0	0	0	0	0	0	0	0	0	3	0	0	0	0	0
S (Siya) Mdaka	13	0	0	0	0	0	0	0	0	0	0	0	13	0	0	0	0	0
L (Lester) Mgwadleka	3	0	0	0	0	0	0	0	0	0	0	0	3	0	0	0	0	0
TM (Thembani) Mkokeli	39	8	0	0	0	40	0	0	0	0	0	0	39	8	0	0	0	40
M (Mihlali) Mpafi	5	0	0	0	0	0	0	0	0	0	0	0	5	0	0	0	0	0
B (Bonga) Mtunjani	5	0	0	0	0	0	0	0	0	0	0	0	5	0	0	0	0	0
S (Siya) Ngande	2	0	0	0	0	0	0	0	0	0	0	0	2	0	0	0	0	0
MN (Mondi) Nkosi	2	0	0	0	0	0	0	0	0	0	0	0	2	0	0	0	0	0
S (Sipho) Nofemele	5	2	0	0	0	10	0	0	0	0	0	0	5	2	0	0	0	10
N (Nkosi) Nofuma	7	0	0	0	0	0	0	0	0	0	0	0	7	0	0	0	0	0
M (Mario) Noordman	6	1	1	0	0	7	0	0	0	0	0	0	6	1	1	0	0	7
S (Siya) Pati	1	0	0	0	0	0	0	0	0	0	0	0	1	0	0	0	0	0
W (Wandile) Putuma	7	2	0	0	0	10	0	0	0	0	0	0	7	2	0	0	0	10
LS (Lundi) Ralarala	3	1	0	0	0	5	0	0	0	0	0	0	3	1	0	0	0	5
BM (Bryce) Rennie	3	0	0	0	0	0	0	0	0	0	0	0	3	0	0	0	0	0
R (Walla) Schoeman	17	0	0	0	0	0	0	0	0	0	0	0	17	0	0	0	0	0
A (Anele) Sibeko	1	0	0	0	0	0	0	0	0	0	0	0	1	0	0	0	0	0
JJ (Jeff) Taljard	11	1	6	10	0	47	15	2	9	9	0	55	26	3	15	19	0	102
LY (Lolo) Waka	12	3	0	0	0	15	3	1	0	0	0	5	15	4	0	0	0	20
L (Lindo) Welemu	5	0	0	0	0	0	0	0	0	0	0	0	5	0	0	0	0	0
Y (Yanga) Xakalashe	6	0	0	0	0	0	0	0	0	0	0	0	6	0	0	0	0	0
O (Oliver) Zono	2	0	0	0	0	0	0	0	0	0	0	0	2	0	0	0	0	0

VODACOM CUP

APPEARANCES & POINTS

PLAYER	Sharks XV	EP Kings	Simba XV	WP	Free State XV	SWD	Boland	Apps	T	C	P	DG	Pts
Curtis Kleinhans	15	11R	–	–	–	–	–	2	–	–	–	–	0
Michael Makase	14	14	15	15	15	13R	11R	7	1	0	0	0	5
Makazole Maphimpi	13	13	14	14	14	14	14	7	3	0	0	0	15
Jeff Taljard	12	12	12	12	–	–	–	4	1	5	7	0	36
Lolo Waka	11	11	–	–	–	11	11	4	2	0	0	0	10
Thembani Mkokeli	10	10	10	10	–	10	–	5	1	0	0	0	5
Skhangele Mateza	9	9	x	9R	–	–	–	3	–	–	–	–	0
Bonga Mntunjani	8	8	8	7R	8	–	–	5	–	–	–	–	0
Cody Basson	7	7	–	–	–	–	–	2	–	–	–	–	0
Siya Mdaka	6c	6c	6c	6c	7c	7c	7c	7	–	–	–	–	0
Antonie Gronum	5	5	–	–	–	–	5	3	–	–	–	–	0
Wandile Putuma	4	4	5R	5R	5R	4R	4	7	2	–	–	–	10
Johannes Jonker	3	3	3	3	3	3	3	7	1	–	–	–	5
Mihlali Mpafi	2	2	2	2	2	–	–	5	–	–	–	–	0
Blake Kyd	1	1	1	1	1	2	2	7	–	–	–	–	0
Cheslin Goeda	2R	2R	–	–	–	–	–	2	–	–	–	–	0
Yanga Xakalashe	3R	3R	3R	1R	–	1	1	6	–	–	–	–	0
Siyamthanda Ngande	8R	–	–	–	3R	x	–	2	–	–	–	–	0
Wayne Lemley	5R	4R	5	5	5	5	–	6	–	–	–	–	0
Nkosi Nofuma	7R	7R	8R	7	8R	5R	8	7	–	–	–	–	0
Mario Noordman	9R	–	9	9	9	9	9R	6	1	1	–	–	7
Mondi Nkosi	15R	15	–	–	–	–	–	2	–	–	–	–	0
Alvandre Maart	–	9R	–	–	–	–	–	1	–	–	–	–	0
Niell Jacobs	–	10R	12R	12R	10	x	–	4	–	–	1	–	3
Ruan Jacobs	–	–	13	13	15R	–	–	3	–	–	–	–	0
Sipho Nofemele	–	–	11	11	11	15	15	5	2	–	–	–	10
Gareth Krause	–	–	7	8	–	8	–	3	–	–	–	–	0
Lindokuhle Welemu	–	–	4	4	4	4	5R	5	–	–	–	–	0
Bryce Rennie	–	–	2R	2R	2R	–	–	3	–	–	–	–	0
Siya Pati	–	–	x	11R	–	–	–	1	–	–	–	–	0
Lundi Ralarala	–	–	–	–	13	13	13	3	1	–	–	–	5
Lithabile Mgwadleka	–	–	–	–	12	12	12	3	–	–	–	–	0
Onke Dubase	–	–	–	–	6	6	6	3	–	–	–	–	0
Bongihlombe Kobese	–	–	–	–	9R	9R	9	3	–	5	1	–	13
Oliver Zono	–	–	–	–	10R	–	10	2	–	–	–	–	0
Ludwe Booi	–	–	–	–	–	1R	2R	2	–	–	–	–	0
Renier Schoeman	–	–	–	–	–	–	3R	1	–	–	–	–	0
Anele Sibeko	–	–	–	–	–	–	8R	1	–	–	–	–	0
Saneliso Ngoma	–	–	–	–	–	–	x	0	–	–	–	–	0
39 Players								**149**	**15**	**11**	**9**	**0**	**124**

VODACOM CUP

Eastern Province

'98	'99	'00	'01	'02	'03	'04	'05	'06	'07	'08	'09	'10	'11	'12	'13	'14
8th	9th	7th	10th	11th	11th	13th	12th	12th	8th	12th	14th	14th	10th	5th	5th	10th

Played	Won	Lost	Drawn	Points for	Points against	Tries for	Tries against
7	3	4	0	171	165	22	20

Date	Venue	Opponent	Result	Score	Referee	Scorers
8 Mar	Cape Town	Tusker Simba XV	LOST	10-17	R Bonaparte	T: Tshidibi, Stemmet.
15 Mar	Grahamstown	Border	WON	60-6	L Legoete	T: Banda (2), Barnard (2), Skosana, Barnard, Kelly, Du Preez, Majola, Davids. C: Dukisa (5), Kelly. P: Dukisa.
22 Mar	Cape Town	WP	LOST	22-56	R Bonaparte	T: Killian, Sonkosi, Davids. C: Dukisa (2). P: Dukisa.
29 Mar	Cradock	Free State XV	LOST	3-31	J van Heerden	P: Whitehead.
4 Apr	George	SWD	LOST	21-23	B Crouse	T: Du Preez, Dukisa. C: Banda. P: Banda (3).
11 Apr	Port Elizabeth	Boland	WON	28-21	J Sylvestre	T: Linday, Punguzwa, Penalty try. C: Dukisa (2). P: Dukisa (3).
25 Apr	Durban	Sharks XV	WON	27-11	F Anselmi	T: Petersen, Dukisa, Skosana. C: Dukisa (2), Van Zyl. P: Dukisa, Van Zyl.

⟨ DID YOU KNOW? ⟩

In 1933, for the first and only time in rugby history, the Springboks hosted a five-Test series, against the Wallabies. South Africa won the series 3-2.

VODACOM CUP

2014 SQUAD

PLAYER	EP CAREER						OTHER UNIONS						VODACOM CUP TOTAL					
	A	T	C	P	DG	Pts	A	T	C	P	DG	Pts	A	T	C	P	DG	Pts
M (Masixole) Banda	5	2	1	3	0	21	0	0	0	0	0	0	5	2	1	3	0	21
EP (Eben) Barnard	6	2	0	0	0	10	0	0	0	0	0	0	6	2	0	0	0	10
RM (Rynier) Bernardo	8	0	0	0	0	0	0	0	0	0	0	0	8	0	0	0	0	0
MRG (Michael) Bernhardt	2	0	0	0	0	0	0	0	0	0	0	0	2	0	0	0	0	0
T (Thembelani) Bholi	7	0	0	0	0	0	0	0	0	0	0	0	7	0	0	0	0	0
OA (Ofentse) Boloko	2	0	0	0	0	0	0	0	0	0	0	0	2	0	0	0	0	0
S (Selvyn) Davids	4	2	0	0	0	10	0	0	0	0	0	0	4	2	0	0	0	10
A (Aidon) Davis	8	0	0	0	0	0	0	0	0	0	0	0	8	0	0	0	0	0
AJ (Albe) de Swardt	7	0	0	0	0	0	1	0	0	0	0	0	8	0	0	0	0	0
FT (Francois) du Plessis	3	0	0	0	0	0	0	0	0	0	0	0	3	0	0	0	0	0
IJ (Ivan-John) du Preez	5	2	0	0	0	10	0	0	0	0	0	0	5	2	0	0	0	10
N (Ntabeni) Dukisa	11	3	12	7	0	60	13	0	10	16	0	68	24	3	22	23	0	128
LJ (Louis) Fourie	2	0	0	0	0	0	0	0	0	0	0	0	2	0	0	0	0	0
LP (Lizo) Gqoboka	13	1	0	0	0	5	0	0	0	0	0	0	13	1	0	0	0	5
S (Siyanda) Grey	19	10	0	0	0	50	0	0	0	0	0	0	19	10	0	0	0	50
FJ (Jaco) Grobler	1	0	0	0	0	0	2	0	0	0	0	0	3	0	0	0	0	0
BRE (Brendan) Hector	2	0	0	0	0	0	0	0	0	0	0	0	2	0	0	0	0	0
MJ (Morne) Hugo	2	0	0	0	0	0	0	0	0	0	0	0	2	0	0	0	0	0
MAE (Malcolm) Jaer	1	0	0	0	0	0	0	0	0	0	0	0	1	0	0	0	0	0
A (Andile) Jho	7	0	0	0	0	0	0	0	0	0	0	0	7	0	0	0	0	0
D (Dwayne) Kelly	8	1	1	0	0	7	0	0	0	0	0	0	8	1	1	0	0	7
S (Simon) Kerrod	2	0	0	0	0	0	2	0	0	0	0	0	4	0	0	0	0	0
M (Michael) Killian	29	11	0	0	0	55	12	4	0	0	1	23	41	15	0	0	1	78
KX (Kalvano) King	1	0	0	0	0	0	0	0	0	0	0	0	1	0	0	0	0	0
C (Cameron) Lindsay	3	1	0	0	0	5	0	0	0	0	0	0	3	1	0	0	0	5
L (Lance) Louw	3	0	0	0	0	0	0	0	0	0	0	0	3	0	0	0	0	0
SQ (Sonwabo) Majola	2	1	0	0	0	5	0	0	0	0	0	0	2	1	0	0	0	5
S (Tiger) Mangweni	19	1	0	0	0	5	52	16	0	1	1	86	71	17	0	1	1	91
SNP (Siphu) Msutwana	3	0	0	0	0	0	0	0	0	0	0	0	3	0	0	0	0	0
L (Luan) Nieuwoudt	1	0	0	0	0	0	0	0	0	0	0	0	1	0	0	0	0	0
BH (Brenden) Olivier	9	0	0	0	0	0	0	0	0	0	0	0	9	0	0	0	0	0
TW (Tyler) Paul	2	0	0	0	0	0	0	0	0	0	0	0	2	0	0	0	0	0
S (Sergeal) Petersen	2	1	0	0	0	5	0	0	0	0	0	0	2	1	0	0	0	5
SQ (Siphe) Punguzwa	5	1	0	0	0	5	0	0	0	0	0	0	5	1	0	0	0	5
P (Paul) Schoeman	10	2	0	0	0	10	0	0	0	0	0	0	10	2	0	0	0	10
MB (Brian) Skosana	9	2	0	0	0	10	0	0	0	0	0	0	9	2	0	0	0	10
MG (Mzuvukile) Sofisa	5	0	0	0	0	0	0	0	0	0	0	0	5	0	0	0	0	0
K (Kuhle) Sonkosi	2	1	0	0	0	5	0	0	0	0	0	0	2	1	0	0	0	5
SS (Siviwe) Soyizwapi	4	1	0	0	0	5	0	0	0	0	0	0	4	1	0	0	0	5
PF (Pieter) Stemmet	5	1	0	0	0	5	1	1	0	0	0	5	6	2	0	0	0	10

Squad continued overleaf

VODACOM CUP

2014 SQUAD (CONT.)

PLAYER	EP CAREER						OTHER UNIONS						VODACOM CUP TOTAL					
	A	T	C	P	DG	Pts	A	T	C	P	DG	Pts	A	T	C	P	DG	Pts
CK (Claude) Tshidibi	1	1	0	0	0	5	2	0	0	0	0	0	3	1	0	0	0	5
S (Scott) van Breda	15	6	7	16	0	92	0	0	0	0	0	0	15	6	7	16	0	92
DR (Dane) van der Westhuyzen	9	0	0	0	0	0	0	0	0	0	0	0	9	0	0	0	0	0
KD (Kayle) van Zyl	9	1	6	2	0	23	0	0	0	0	0	0	9	1	6	2	0	23
CJ (Cyril-John) Velleman	3	0	0	0	0	0	0	0	0	0	0	0	3	0	0	0	0	0
GA (George) Whitehead	1	0	0	1	0	3	8	1	2	3	0	18	9	1	2	4	0	21
S (Stefan) Willemse	7	3	0	0	0	15	0	0	0	0	0	0	7	3	0	0	0	15
S (Stephan) Zaayman	3	0	0	0	0	0	0	0	0	0	0	0	3	0	0	0	0	0

APPEARANCES & POINTS

PLAYER	Simba XV	Border	WP	Free State XV	SWD	Boland	Sharks XV	Apps	T	C	P	DG	Pts
Siwiwe Soyizwapi	15	–	–	–	–	–	–	1	–	–	–	–	0
Eben Barnard	14	14	–	–	14	14	14	5	2	–	–	–	10
Scott van Breda	13	–	–	–	–	–	–	1	–	–	–	–	0
Tiger Mangweni	12	12	12	–	11R	–	–	4	–	–	–	–	0
Lance Louw	11	11	11	–	–	–	–	3	–	–	–	–	0
Ntabeni Dukisa	10	10	10	15R	10	10	10	7	2	11	6	–	50
Kalvano King	9	–	–	–	–	–	–	1	–	–	–	–	0
Stephan Zaayman	8c	5c	–	4	–	–	–	3	–	–	–	–	0
Claude Tshidibi	7	–	–	–	–	–	–	1	1	–	–	–	5
Thembelani Bholi	6	6	6	6	6	6	6	7	–	–	–	–	0
Brendan Hector	5	–	5	–	–	–	–	2	–	–	–	–	0
Kuhle Sonkosi	4	–	4	–	–	–	–	2	1	–	–	–	5
Mzu Sofisa	3	3	3	3	3R	–	–	5	–	–	–	–	0
Albie de Swardt	2	2	2	2	2c	2c	2c	7	–	–	–	–	0
Brenden Olivier	1	1	1	–	–	–	–	3	–	–	–	–	0
Francois du Plessis	2R	2R	2R	–	–	–	–	3	–	–	–	–	0
Pieter Stemmet	1R	1R	–	–	3	3	3	5	1	–	–	–	5
Ivan-John du Preez	8R	8	8	–	8	–	7R	5	2	–	–	–	10
Sipho Phunguzwa	4R	7R	–	6R	7R	6R	7	6	1	–	–	–	5
Dwayne Kelly	9R	9	9	–	9	9	9	6	1	1	–	–	7
Brian Skosana	14R	13	13	13	13	11R	13R	7	2	–	–	–	10
Selvyn Davids	11R	11R	11R	11	–	–	–	4	2	–	–	–	10
Masixole Banda	–	15	15	15	15	15	–	5	2	1	3	–	21
CJ Velleman	–	7	5R	–	7	–	–	3	–	–	–	–	0
Rynier Bernardo	–	4	–	5	–	–	–	2	–	–	–	–	0
Aidon Davis	–	5R	8R	8	–	8	8	5	–	–	–	–	0
Sonwabo Majola	–	14R	9R	12R	–	–	–	3	1	–	–	–	5

VODACOM CUP

APPEARANCES & POINTS (CONT.)

PLAYER	Simba XV	Border	WP	Free State XV	SWD	Boland	Sharks XV	Apps	T	C	P	DG	Pts
Siphu Msutwana	–	13R	13R	11R	14R	–	–	4	–	–	–	–	0
Michael Killian	–	–	14	–	–	–	–	1	1	–	–	–	5
Paul Schoeman	–	–	7c	7c	–	–	–	2	–	–	–	–	0
Lizo Gqoboka	–	–	1R	1	1	1	1	5	–	–	–	–	0
Sergeal Petersen	–	–	–	14	–	–	11	2	1	–	–	–	5
Luan Nieuwoudt	–	–	–	12	–	–	–	1	–	–	–	–	0
George Whitehead	–	–	–	10	–	–	–	1	–	–	–	1	3
Jaco Grobler	–	–	–	9	–	–	–	1	–	–	–	–	0
Dane van der Westhuyzen	–	–	–	2R	2R	7R	2R	4	–	–	–	–	0
BG Uys	–	–	–	3R	–	–	–	1	–	–	–	–	0
Tyler Paul	–	–	–	4R	4R	4R	x	3	–	–	–	–	0
Andile Jho	–	–	–	–	12	12	12	3	–	–	–	–	0
Ofense Boloko	–	–	–	–	11	11	–	2	–	–	–	–	0
Cameron Lindsay	–	–	–	–	5	5	5	3	1	–	–	–	5
Louis Fourie	–	–	–	–	4	4	–	2	–	–	–	–	0
Kayle van Zyl	–	–	–	–	9R	13R	14R	3	–	1	1	–	5
Michael Bernardt	–	–	–	–	–	13	13	2	–	–	–	–	0
Stefan Willemse	–	–	–	–	–	7	4	2	–	–	–	–	0
Simon Kerrod	–	–	–	–	–	3R	3R	2	–	–	–	–	0
Morne Hugo	–	–	–	–	–	15R	10R	2	–	–	–	–	0
Malcolm Jaer	–	–	–	–	–	–	15	1	–	–	–	–	0
Penalty try	–	–	–	–	–	–	–	0	1	–	–	–	5
48 Players								**153**	**21**	**14**	**11**	**0**	**171**

⟨ **DID YOU KNOW?** ⟩

The 1953 Wallabies were the first touring team to fly to and from South Africa. When the 1956 Springboks went to Australia and New Zealand, they became the first Springbok team to fly to the country in which they were to tour.

Free State XV

'98	'99	'00	'01	'02	'03	'04	'05	'06	'07	'08	'09	'10	'11	'12	'13	'14
11th	12th	**3rd**	4th	5th	2nd	2nd	5th	8th	4th	2nd	6th	2nd	7th	11th	10th	4th

Played	Won	Lost	Drawn	Points for	Points against	Tries for	Tries against
8	5	3	0	298	170	42	18

Date	Venue	Opponent	Result	Score	Referee	Scorers
8 Mar	Bloemfontein [1]	SWD	WON	52-47	M Jonker	T: Greyling, Mlondobozi, Lee, Marais, Smit, Ganto. C: Smit (3), Marais (2). P: Smit (2), Marais (2).
15 Mar	Malmesbury	Boland	WON	28-20	Q Immelman	T: Basson, Mlondobozi, Smith, April. C: Marais. P: Marais (2).
21 Mar	Bloemfontein [1]	Sharks XV	LOST	22-23	Q Immelman	T: Botha, Lee, Mlondobozi. C: Marais (2). P: Marais.
29 Mar	Cradock	EP Kings	WON	31-3	J van Heerden	T: Brandt (2), Lee, Mohojé. C: Marais (4). P: Marais.
5 Apr	Bloemfontein	Border	WON	54-17	R Boneparte	T: Coetzee (2), Smith (2), Cyster, Claassen, Lee, Smit. C: Smit (7).
12 Apr	Cape Town [2]	WP	LOST	15-28	B Crouse	T: Stevens, Botha. C: Smit. P: Smit.
26 Apr	Bloemfontein	Tusker Simba XV	WON	75-10	M vd Westhuizen	T: April (4), Coetzee (2), Lee (2), Greyling, Engelbrecht, Dolo, Botha, Burger. C: De Wet (5)

QUARTER-FINAL

Date	Venue	Opponent	Result	Score	Referee	Scorers
3 May	Bloemfontein	Blue Bulls	LOST	21-22	R Boneparte	T: Dolo, April. C: Smit. P: Smit (3).

[1] *Clive Solomon Stadium, Heidedal*
[2] *City Park*

Note: ■ = *Champion*

⟨ DID YOU KNOW? ⟩

Norman Sanson of Scotland made history when he became the first neutral referee in a Test match in South Africa. Sanson took charge of both home internationals against France in 1975.

VODACOM CUP

2014 SQUAD

PLAYER	FS CAREER						OTHER UNIONS						VODACOM CUP TOTAL					
	A	T	C	P	DG	Pts	A	T	C	P	DG	Pts	A	T	C	P	DG	Pts
ZN (Zingisa) April	7	6	–	–	–	30	–	–	–	–	–	0	7	6	–	–	–	30
LA (Logan) Basson	3	1	–	–	–	5	16	6	8	2	–	52	19	7	8	2	–	57
R (Renier) Botha	8	3	–	–	–	15	–	–	–	–	–	0	8	3	–	–	–	15
A (Alvin) Brandt	4	2	–	–	–	10	–	–	–	–	–	0	4	2	–	–	–	10
M (Marnus) Briedenhann	8	–	–	–	–	0	28	2	–	–	–	10	36	2	–	–	–	10
HW (Heinrich) Brussow	1	–	–	–	–	0	11	7	–	–	–	35	12	7	–	–	–	35
MA (Tienie) Burger	2	1	–	–	–	5	–	–	–	–	–	0	2	1	–	–	–	5
N (Neil) Claassen	5	1	–	–	–	5	10	1	–	–	–	5	13	2	–	–	–	10
FP (Peet) Coetzee	5	4	–	–	–	20	–	–	–	–	–	0	5	4	–	–	–	20
L (Luke) Cyster	8	1	–	–	–	5	–	–	–	–	–	0	8	1	–	–	–	5
L (Luan) de Bruin	5	–	–	–	–	0	–	–	–	–	–	0	5	–	–	–	–	0
PR (Rossouw) de Klerk	8	1	–	–	–	5	11	–	–	–	–	0	19	1	–	–	–	5
P-S (Pieter-Steyn) de Wet	7	–	5	–	–	10	5	–	13	6	1	47	12	–	18	6	1	57
MS (Maputhla) Dolo	7	2	–	–	–	10	–	–	–	–	–	0	7	2	–	–	–	10
P (Philip) du Preez	3	–	–	–	–	0	–	–	–	–	–	0	3	–	–	–	–	0
OJJ (Jacques) du Toit	1	–	–	–	–	0	–	–	–	–	–	0	1	–	–	–	–	0
GJ (Joubert) Engelbrecht	11	5	–	–	–	25	12	8	–	–	–	40	23	13	–	–	–	65
S (Sino) Ganto	6	1	–	–	–	5	5	1	–	–	–	5	11	2	–	–	–	10
H (Henco) Greyling	7	2	–	–	–	10	–	–	–	–	–	0	7	2	–	–	–	10
AJ (Abrie) Griesel	4	–	–	–	–	0	–	–	–	–	–	0	4	–	–	–	–	0
N (Nhlanhla) Hlongwane	1	–	–	–	–	0	–	–	–	–	–	0	1	–	–	–	–	0
JP (Joubert) Horn	2	–	–	–	–	0	6	–	–	–	–	0	8	–	–	–	–	0
JNO (Nicolaas) Immelman	1	–	–	–	–	0	–	–	–	–	–	0	1	–	–	–	–	0
CL (Cameron) Jacobs	4	–	–	–	–	0	3	–	–	–	–	0	7	–	–	–	–	0
M (Marco) Klopper	1	–	–	–	–	0	–	–	–	–	–	0	1	–	–	–	–	0
NJ (Nico) Lee	8	6	–	–	–	30	–	–	–	–	–	0	8	6	–	–	–	30
HJ (Hercu) Liebenberg	11	–	–	–	–	0	26	–	–	–	–	0	37	–	–	–	–	0
DR (Niel) Marais	12	1	9	6	–	41	–	–	–	–	–	0	12	1	9	6	–	41
MV (Mosoeu) Maruping	1	–	–	–	–	0	–	–	–	–	–	0	1	–	–	–	–	0
ND (Don) Mlondobozi	6	3	–	–	–	15	–	–	–	–	–	0	6	3	–	–	–	15
TS (Oupa) Mohoje	7	3	–	–	–	15	–	–	–	–	–	0	7	3	–	–	–	15
CW (Chase) Morison	4	–	–	–	–	0	–	–	–	–	–	0	4	–	–	–	–	0
SAS (Sihle) Ngxabi	0	–	–	–	–	0	–	–	–	–	–	0	0	–	–	–	–	0
GJ (Gerhard) Olivier	2	–	–	–	–	0	–	–	–	–	–	0	1	–	–	–	–	0
RM (Kholo) Ramashala	12	4	–	–	–	20	–	–	–	–	–	0	12	4	–	–	–	20
NP (Nick) Schonert	3	–	–	–	–	0	11	–	–	–	–	0	14	–	–	–	–	0
AJ (Riaan) Smit	10	3	23	9	1	91	24	12	12	6	–	102	34	15	35	15	1	193
WL (Wayven) Smith	6	3	–	–	–	15	–	–	–	–	–	0	6	3	–	–	–	15
E-J (Earl) Snyman	3	–	–	–	–	0	–	–	–	–	–	0	3	–	–	–	–	0
KB (Kevin) Stevens	8	1	–	–	–	5	31	1	–	–	–	5	39	2	–	–	–	10

Squad continued overleaf

VODACOM CUP

2014 SQUAD (CONT.)

PLAYER	FS CAREER						OTHER UNIONS						VODACOM CUP TOTAL					
	A	T	C	P	DG	Pts	A	T	C	P	DG	Pts	A	T	C	P	DG	Pts
S (Sethu) Tom	7	2	–	–	–	10	–	–	–	–	–	0	7	2	–	–	–	10
TG (Torsten) van Jaarsveld	8	–	–	–	–	0	25	3	–	–	–	15	31	3	–	–	–	15
JA (Johan) van Niekerk	2	–	–	–	–	0	–	–	–	–	–	0	2	–	–	–	–	0
HP (Henco) Venter	2	–	–	–	–	0	–	–	–	–	–	0	2	–	–	–	–	0
PV (Waltie) Vermeulen	11	–	–	–	–	0	–	–	–	–	–	0	25	–	–	–	–	0

APPEARANCES & POINTS

PLAYER	SWD	Boland	Sharks XV	EP	Border	WP	Simba XV	Blue Bulls	Apps	T	C	P	DG	Pts
Luke Cyster	15	15	15	15	15	15	15	15	8	1	–	–	–	5
Don Mlondobozi	14	14	14	–	14	14R	13R	–	6	3	–	–	–	15
Nico Lee	13	13	13	13	13	13	13	13	8	6	–	–	–	30
Niel Marais	12c	12c	10c	12c	12c	12c	–	–	6	1	9	6	–	41
Sino Ganto	11	11	11	–	–	11	14	11	6	1	–	–	–	5
Riaan Smit	10	–	–	–	10	10	–	10	4	2	12	6	–	52
Renier Botha	9	9	9	9	9	9	9R	9	8	3	–	–	–	15
Henco Greyling	8	8	8	6	7R	–	7R	8R	7	2	–	–	–	10
Zingisa April	7	7	7	–	6	6	7	7	7	6	–	–	–	30
Wayven Smith	6	6	7R	7	7	7	–	–	6	3	–	–	–	15
Waltie Vermeulen	5	5	5	5	5	5	–	5	7	–	–	–	–	0
Philip du Preez	4	4R	–	–	–	x	5R	–	3	–	–	–	–	0
Johan van Niekerk	3	3	–	–	–	–	–	–	2	–	–	–	–	0
Torsten van Jaarsveld	2	2	2	2	2	2	–	–	6	–	–	–	–	0
Kevin Stevens	1	1	1	1	1	1	1	1	8	1	–	–	–	5
Marco Klopper	22R	x	x	–	–	–	–	–	1	–	–	–	–	0
Chase Morison	3R	3R	3R	x	–	–	3R	–	4	–	–	–	–	0
Joubert Horn	4R	–	4R	–	–	–	–	–	2	–	–	–	–	0
Nicolaas Immelman	6R	–	–	–	–	–	–	–	1	–	–	–	–	0
Abrie Griesel	13R	9R	9R	9R	–	–	–	x	4	–	–	–	–	0
Alvin Brandt	14R	x	x	11R	14R	14	–	–	4	2	–	–	–	10
Earl Snyman	10R	10R	–	–	–	–	14R	x	3	–	–	–	–	0
Logan Basson	–	10	14R	x	11R	–	–	–	3	1	–	–	–	5
Marnus Briedenhann	–	4	4	x	–	–	–	–	2	–	–	–	–	0
Sihle Ngxabi	–	x	–	–	–	–	–	–	0	–	–	–	–	0
Joubert Engelbrecht	–	–	12	–	–	22R	12	12	4	1	–	–	–	5
Oupa Mohoje	–	–	6	4	–	–	–	–	2	1	–	–	–	5
Nick Schonert	–	–	3	–	1R	1R	–	–	3	–	–	–	–	0
Cameron Jacobs	–	–	–	14	11	–	–	–	2	–	–	–	–	0

VODACOM CUP

APPEARANCES & POINTS (CONT.)

PLAYER	SWD	Boland	Sharks XV	EP	Border	WP	Simba XV	Blue Bulls	Apps	T	C	P	DG	Pts
Sethu Tom	–	–	–	11	–	–	–	–	1	–	–	–	–	0
Pieter-Steyn de Wet	–	–	–	10	12R	–	10	–	3	–	5	–	–	10
Peet Coetzee	–	–	–	8	8R	6R	8	8	5	4	–	–	–	20
Luan de Bruin	–	–	–	3	3	3	3	3	5	–	–	–	–	0
Gerhard Olivier	–	–	–	8R	8	–	–	–	2	–	–	–	–	0
Jacques du Toit	–	–	–	x	–	–	2R	x	1	–	–	–	–	0
Neil Claassen	–	–	–	–	4	4	5	–	3	1	–	–	–	5
Liebenberg, Hercu	–	–	–	–	2R	2R	2c	2c	4	–	–	–	–	0
Heinrich Brussow	–	–	–	–	–	8	–	–	1	–	–	–	–	0
Nhlanhla Hlongwane	–	–	–	–	–	x	9	–	1	–	–	–	–	0
Maphutla Dolo	–	–	–	–	–	–	11	14	2	2	–	–	–	10
Henco Venter	–	–	–	–	–	–	6	6R	2	–	–	–	–	0
Tienie Burger	–	–	–	–	–	–	4	4	2	1	–	–	–	5
Mosoeu Maruping	–	–	–	–	–	–	–	6	1	–	–	–	–	0
Rossouw de Klerk	–	–	–	–	–	–	–	3R	1	–	–	–	–	0
Kholo Ramashala	–	–	–	–	–	–	–	x	–	–	–	–	–	0
45 Players									**161**	**42**	**26**	**12**	**0**	**298**

⟨ DID YOU KNOW? ⟩

South Africa have played Tests vs 25 different opponents since 1891, six of which are not countries: British & Irish Lions (& fore-runners), World XV, South America, S America & Spain, New Zealand Cavaliers & Pacific Islanders.

VODACOM CUP

Golden Lions

'98	'99	'00	'01	'02	'03	'04	'05	'06	'07	'08	'09	'10	'11	'12	'13	'14
2nd	1st	5th	8th	1st	3rd	1st	3rd	4th	11th	7th	8th	5th	2nd	5th	1st	8th

Played	Won	Lost	Drawn	Points for	Points against	Tries for	Tries against
10	6	4	0	305	243	40	28

Date	Venue	Opponent	Result	Score	Referee	Scorers
7 Mar	Potchefstroom	Leopards	WON	18-16	Q Immelman	T: Mabuza (2). C: G Cronje. P: G Cronje, Du Plessis.
15 Mar	Johannesburg	Valke	WON	23-22	C du Preez	T: Du Plessis, Volmink, Lerm. C: G Cronje. P: Du Plessis (2).
22 Mar	Pretoria	Blue Bulls	LOST	20-22	C Joubert	T: Willis, Brink. C: Jantjies (2). P: Jantjies (2).
29 Mar	Johannesburg	Griffons	WON	40-37	M vd Westhuyzen	T: Lerm (2), Qinisile (2), Esterhuizen, Erasmus. C: Du Plessis (5).
5 Apr	Kimberley	Griquas	LOST	18-33	J Peyper	T: De Wit, Penalty try. C: Du Plessis. P: Du Plessis (2).
12 Apr	Polokwane	Limpopo	WON	110-0	G de Bruin	T: Botha (2), Nel (2), Brink (2), De Wit (2), N du Plessis (2), Hanekom, Gavor, Lerm, Erasmus, Qinisile, Khoza. C: W du Plessis (15).
26 Apr	Alberton	Pumas	LOST	27-48	B Crouse	T: Gavor, Lerm, De Wit, Kloppers, Nel. C: Du Plessis.

QUARTER-FINAL

2 May	Durban	Sharks XV	WON	27-20	F Pretorius	T: Willis, Hanekom, De Wit. C: Du Plessis (3). P: Du Plessis (2).

SEMI-FINAL

10 May	Pretoria	Blue Bulls	WON	16-15	Q Immelman	T: Gavor. C: Du Plessis. P: Du Plessis (3).

FINAL

16 May	Kimberley	Griquas	LOST	6-30	J van Heerden	P: Du Plessis. D: Du Plessis.

Note: ■ = *Champion*

⟨ **DID YOU KNOW?** ⟩

Ockert Antonie 'Tonie' Roux, the Northern Transvaal utility back, never tasted victory in his seven Tests from 1969-1974. Incredibly, Roux was an unused substitute for a further 13 Tests - of which the Springboks lost only one!

VODACOM CUP

2014 SQUAD

PLAYER	GOLDEN LIONS CAREER						OTHER UNIONS						VODACOM CUP TOTAL					
	A	T	C	P	DG	Pts	A	T	C	P	DG	Pts	A	T	C	P	DG	Pts
M (Michael) Bondesio	17	4	0	0	0	20	13	5	0	0	0	25	30	9	0	0	0	45
CA (Crysander) Botha	9	7	1	0	0	37	15	6	26	18	0	136	24	13	27	18	0	173
CJ (Cyle) Brink	8	3	0	0	0	15	0	0	0	0	0	0	8	3	0	0	0	15
A (Andries) Coetzee	3	2	5	0	0	20	0	0	0	0	0	0	3	2	5	0	0	20
RJ (Ruan) Combrinck	6	3	0	0	0	15	1	0	0	0	0	0	7	3	0	0	0	15
G (Guy) Cronje	11	2	26	10	0	92	12	2	16	4	0	54	23	4	42	14	0	146
JJ (Kobus) de Kock	4	0	1	0	0	2	8	7	7	0	0	49	12	7	8	0	0	51
D (Dylan) des Fountain	9	2	0	0	0	10	9	2	0	0	0	10	18	4	0	0	0	20
AB (Bobby) de Wee	4	0	0	0	0	0	0	0	0	0	0	0	4	0	0	0	0	0
AS (Stephan) de Witt	14	6	0	0	0	30	0	0	0	0	0	0	14	6	0	0	0	30
NV (Nico) du Plessis	3	2	0	0	0	10	0	0	0	0	0	0	3	2	0	0	0	10
WNF (Willie) du Plessis	10	1	26	11	1	93	7	4	33	0	0	86	17	5	59	11	1	179
LJ (Lourens) Erasmus	9	2	0	0	0	10	0	0	0	0	0	0	9	2	0	0	0	10
J-RA (JR) Esterhuizen	11	4	0	0	0	20	0	0	0	0	0	0	11	4	0	0	0	20
S (Selmo) Gavor	5	3	0	0	0	15	0	0	0	0	0	0	5	3	0	0	0	15
LS (Lambert) Groenewald	1	0	0	0	0	0	14	1	0	0	0	5	15	1	0	0	0	5
NJ (Stokkies) Hanekom	10	2	0	0	0	10	0	0	0	0	0	0	10	2	0	0	0	10
GG (Deon) Helberg	10	2	0	0	0	10	10	4	0	0	0	20	20	6	0	0	0	30
B (Brandan) Hewitt	1	0	0	0	0	0	0	0	0	0	0	0	1	0	0	0	0	0
AWCJ (Alwyn) Hollenbach	15	2	0	0	0	10	14	5	0	0	0	25	29	7	0	0	0	35
R (Ruan) Janse van Rensburg	2	0	0	0	0	0	0	0	0	0	0	0	2	0	0	0	0	0
ET (Elton) Jantjies	3	0	3	2	0	12	0	0	0	0	0	0	3	0	3	2	0	12
CS (Caswell) Khoza	4	1	0	0	0	5	0	0	0	0	0	0	4	1	0	0	0	5
PH (Hugo) Kloppers	12	1	0	0	0	5	4	0	0	0	0	0	16	1	0	0	0	5
TA (Ashley) Kohler	3	0	0	0	0	0	0	0	0	0	0	0	3	0	0	0	0	0
R (Ruaan) Lerm	17	6	0	0	0	30	0	0	0	0	0	0	17	6	0	0	0	30
ST (Thabo) Mabuza	6	2	0	0	0	10	0	0	0	0	0	0	6	2	0	0	0	10
T (Thabo) Mamojele	5	0	0	0	0	0	8	2	0	0	0	10	13	2	0	0	0	10
CM (Charles) Marais	10	0	0	0	0	0	15	0	0	0	0	0	25	0	0	0	0	0
MJ (Malcolm) Marx	6	0	0	0	0	0	0	0	0	0	0	0	6	0	0	0	0	0
MD (Martin) Muller	2	0	0	0	0	0	17	1	0	0	0	5	19	1	0	0	0	5
T (Tyson) Mulumba	1	0	0	0	0	0	0	0	0	0	0	0	1	0	0	0	0	0
AR (Ruhan) Nel	7	4	0	0	0	20	0	0	0	0	0	0	7	4	0	0	0	20
M (Mark) Pretorius	6	0	0	0	0	0	0	0	0	0	0	0	6	0	0	0	0	0
SL (Siphatho) Qinisile	3	3	0	0	0	15	0	0	0	0	0	0	3	3	0	0	0	15
TJ (Theuns) Reynolds	1	0	0	0	0	0	0	0	0	0	0	0	1	0	0	0	0	0
JS (Bees) Roux	1	0	0	0	0	0	25	2	0	0	0	10	26	2	0	0	0	10
D (Marais) Schmidt	8	1	10	7	0	46	0	0	0	0	0	0	8	1	10	7	0	46
PE (Pieter) Scholtz	1	0	0	0	0	0	0	0	0	0	0	0	1	0	0	0	0	0
RD (Ricky) Schroeder	10	0	0	0	0	0	6	0	0	0	0	0	16	0	0	0	0	0

Squad continued overleaf

2014 SQUAD (CONT.)

PLAYER	GOLDEN LIONS CAREER						OTHER UNIONS						VODACOM CUP TOTAL					
	A	T	C	P	DG	Pts	A	T	C	P	DG	Pts	A	T	C	P	DG	Pts
CD (Courtnall) Skosan	1	0	0	0	0	0	12	7	0	0	0	35	13	7	0	0	0	35
DT (Dylan) Smith	8	0	0	0	0	0	0	0	0	0	0	0	8	0	0	0	0	0
JH (Jannie) Stander	4	0	0	0	0	0	0	0	0	0	0	0	4	0	0	0	0	0
J (Jacques) van Rooyen	10	0	0	0	0	0	0	0	0	0	0	0	10	0	0	0	0	0
CM (Chris) van Zyl	10	0	0	0	0	0	0	0	0	0	0	0	10	0	0	0	0	0
RC (Ruan) Venter	1	0	0	0	0	0	2	0	0	0	0	0	3	0	0	0	0	0
A (Anthony) Volmink	18	20	1	0	0	102	2	1	0	0	0	5	20	21	1	0	0	107
HW (Harold) Vorster	11	1	0	0	0	5	0	0	0	0	0	0	11	1	0	0	0	5
VS (Vainon) Willis	9	2	0	0	0	10	25	3	0	0	0	15	34	5	0	0	0	25

APPEARANCES & POINTS

PLAYER	Leopards XV	Valke	Blue Bulls	Griffons	Griquas	Limpopo BB	Pumas	Sharks XV	Blue Bulls	Griquas	Apps	T	C	P	DG	Pts
Deon Helberg	15	13R	–	–	13	–	–	–	–	–	3	–	–	–	–	0
Vainon Willis	14	14	14	11	14	–	15	15	15	15	9	2	–	–	–	10
Courtnall Skosan	13	–	–	–	–	–	–	–	–	–	1	–	–	–	–	0
Dylan des Fountain	12	–	–	–	–	–	–	–	–	–	1	–	–	–	–	0
Anthony Volmink	11	11	11	–	11	–	–	–	–	–	4	1	–	–	–	5
Willie du Plessis	10	12	13R	10	10	10	10	10	10	10	10	1	26	11	1	93
Ricky Schroeder	9c	9c	9c	9c	9c	9c	9c	9c	9c	9c	10	–	–	–	–	0
Ruaan Lerm	8	8	8	8	8	8	8	8	8	–	9	5	–	–	–	25
Cyle Brink	7	–	7	7	–	7	7	7	7	7	8	3	–	–	–	15
Thabo Mabuza	6	6	6	6	–	–	7R	x	6R	–	6	2	–	–	–	10
Hugo Kloppers	5	–	5	5	5	–	5	5	5	5	8	1	–	–	–	5
Ruan Venter	4	–	–	–	–	–	–	–	–	–	1	–	–	–	–	0
Pieter Scholtz	3	–	–	–	–	–	–	–	–	–	1	–	–	–	–	0
Malcolm Marx	2	2	–	–	–	2R	2	2	2	2	6	–	–	–	–	0
Jacques van Rooyen	1	3	3	–	3	–	–	–	–	–	4	–	–	–	–	0
Mark Pretorius	x	2R	–	–	2	2R	–	2R	x	2R	5	–	–	–	–	0
Charles Marais	3R	1	1	1	1	1R	1	3	3	3	10	–	–	–	–	0
Martin Muller	4R	5	–	–	–	–	–	–	–	–	2	–	–	–	–	0
Thabo Mamojele	x	–	–	–	6R	–	5R	4	4	4	5	–	–	–	–	0
Guy Cronje	12R	10	9R	9R	9R	–	–	–	–	–	5	–	2	1	–	7
Nico Hanekom	15R	13	13	13	–	13	13	13	13	13	9	2	–	–	–	10
JR Esterhuizen	x	15R	–	14	x	14	14	14	14	14	7	1	–	–	–	5
Crysander Botha	–	15	15	–	15	15	–	–	–	–	4	2	–	–	–	10
Stephan de Witt	–	7	–	–	7	6	6	6	6	6	7	5	–	–	–	25
Chris van Zyl	–	4	4	4	4	5	4	–	–	4R	7	–	–	–	–	0
Dylan Smith	–	1R	1R	–	1R	1	3R	1	1	1	8	–	–	–	–	0

VODACOM CUP

APPEARANCES & POINTS (CONT.)

PLAYER	Leopards XV	Valke	Blue Bulls	Griffons	Griquas	Limpopo BB	Pumas	Sharks XV	Blue Bulls	Griquas	Apps	T	C	P	DG	Pts
Bobby de Wee	–	5R	6R	–	6	8R	–	–	–	–	4	–	–	–	–	0
Lourens Erasmus	–	6R	4R	4R	4R	4	4R	4R	5R	8	9	2	–	–	–	10
Ruan Janse van Rensburg	–	x	–	–	–	9R	9R	–	–	–	2	–	–	–	–	0
Alwyn Hollenbach	–	–	12	–	12	–	–	–	–	–	2	–	–	–	–	0
Elton Jantjies	–	–	10	–	–	–	–	–	–	–	1	–	2	2	–	10
Theuns Reynolds	–	–	2	–	–	–	–	–	–	–	1	–	–	–	–	0
Siphatho Qinisile	–	–	x	2	–	2	2	–	–	–	3	3	–	–	–	15
Andries Coetzee	–	–	12R	–	–	–	–	–	–	–	1	–	–	–	–	0
Ruhan Nel	–	–	–	15	–	12	11R	–	–	–	3	3	–	–	–	15
Kobus de Kock	–	–	–	12	–	–	–	–	–	–	1	–	–	–	–	0
Nico du Plessis	–	–	–	3	–	3	–	x	x	3R	3	2	–	–	–	10
Ashley Kohler	–	–	–	2R	5R	–	–	–	–	–	2	–	–	–	–	0
Tyson Mulumba	–	–	–	3R	–	–	–	–	–	–	1	–	–	–	–	0
Lambert Groenewald	–	–	–	6R	–	–	–	–	–	–	1	–	–	–	–	0
Brandan Hewitt	–	–	–	10R	–	–	–	–	–	–	1	–	–	–	–	0
Caswell Khoza	–	–	–	14R	–	11R	14R	x	x	11R	4	1	–	–	–	5
Ruan Combrinck	–	–	–	–	15R	–	–	–	–	–	1	–	–	–	–	0
Selmo Gavor	–	–	–	–	–	11	11	11	11	11	5	3	–	–	–	15
Jannie Stander	–	–	–	–	–	5R	–	–	–	–	1	–	–	–	–	0
Harold Vorster	–	–	–	–	–	12R	12	12	12	12	5	–	–	–	–	0
Bees Roux	–	–	–	–	–	–	3	–	–	–	1	–	–	–	–	0
Michael Bondesio	–	–	–	–	–	–	9R	9R	9R	–	3	–	–	–	–	0
Marais Schmidt	–	–	–	–	–	–	–	15R	x	15R	2	–	–	–	–	0
Penalty try	–	–	–	–	–	–	–	–	–	–	0	1	–	–	–	5
49 Players											**207**	**40**	**30**	**14**	**1**	**305**

‹ DID YOU KNOW? ›

Rugby World Cup winner Chester Williams scored eight of his 14 Test tries at Ellis Park in Johannesburg, including his famous foursome during the Springboks' 1995 World Cup quarter-final against Western Samoa.

VODACOM CUP

Griffons

'98	'99	'00	'01	'02	'03	'04	'05	'06	'07	'08	'09	'10	'11	'12	'13	'14
13th	13th	13th	9th	13th	14th	14th	14th	11th	14th	13th	12th	12th	10th	12th	11th	11th

Played	Won	Lost	Drawn	Points for	Points against	Tries for	Tries against
7	2	5	0	182	240	25	35

Date	Venue	Opponent	Result	Score	Referee	Scorers
8 Mar	Bultfontein	Limpopo BB	WON	62-10	J Kotze	T: Le Roux (2), Nel (2), Steyn (2), Erasmus (2). Sithole, Nelson. C: Pienaar (5), Maarman.
15 Mar	Kimberley	Griquas	LOST	12-20	O Rametsi	P: Strydom (4).
21 Mar	Welkom	Pumas	LOST	5-69	C du Preez	T: Maarman.
29 Mar	Johannesburg[1]	Golden Lions	LOST	37-40	M vd Westhuizen	T: Sithole (2), Steyn (2), Groenewald. C: Strydom (2), Du Toit. P: Strydom (2).
4 Apr	Welkom	Leopards XV	LOST	15-35	S Geldenhuys	T: Nel, Le Roux. C: Du Toit. P: Du Toit.
11 Apr	Welkom	Blue Bulls	LOST	10-49	F Anselmi	T: Mbotho. C: Du Toit. P: Du Toit.
25 Apr	Kempton Park	Valke	WON	41-17	J Sylvestre	T: Pienaar (2), Sithole (2), Kritzinger, Steyn. C: Du Toit (3), Pienaar. P: Du Toit.

[1] *Bill Jardine Stadium*

⟨ DID YOU KNOW? ⟩

Only two players have played Tests for two different countries against the Springboks: Patricio Noriega (Argentina 1993-94, Australia 1999-2003) & Shane Howarth (New Zealand 1994, Wales 1998-99).

VODACOM CUP

2014 SQUAD

PLAYER	GRIFFONS CAREER						OTHER UNIONS						VODACOM CUP TOTAL					
	A	T	C	P	DG	Pts	A	T	C	P	DG	Pts	A	T	C	P	DG	Pts
M (Mlungisi) Bali	13	–	–	–	–	0	–	–	–	–	–	0	13	–	–	–	–	0
J-F (Jan-Francois) Bester	2	–	–	–	–	0	–	–	–	–	–	0	2	–	–	–	–	0
PW (Pieter-Willem) Botha	5	–	–	–	–	0	–	–	–	–	–	0	5	–	–	–	–	0
J (Jan) Breedt	5	–	–	–	–	0	–	–	–	–	–	0	5	–	–	–	–	0
RM (Rudi) Britz	12	–	–	–	–	0	–	–	–	–	–	0	12	–	–	–	–	0
L (Wikus) Davis	2	–	–	–	–	0	–	–	–	–	–	0	2	–	–	–	–	0
FC (Franna) du Toit	5	–	6	3	–	21	1	1	–	–	–	5	6	1	6	3	–	26
S (Sheldon) Erasmus	4	2	–	–	–	10	–	–	–	–	–	0	4	2	–	–	–	10
GP (Deon) Gouws	2	–	–	–	–	0	–	–	–	–	–	0	2	–	–	–	–	0
W (Werner) Griesel	46	4	–	–	–	20	–	–	–	–	–	0	46	4	–	–	–	20
H (Dirk) Grobbelaar	3	–	–	–	–	0	–	–	–	–	–	0	3	–	–	–	–	0
WR (Wilmar) Groenewald	9	1	–	–	–	5	–	–	–	–	–	0	9	1	–	–	–	5
C (Colin) Herbert	9	1	1	–	–	7	–	–	–	–	–	0	9	1	1	–	–	7
DN (Niell) Jordaan	2	–	–	–	–	0	4	–	–	–	–	0	6	–	–	–	–	0
A (Armandt) Koster	8	–	–	–	–	0	2	–	–	–	–	0	10	–	–	–	–	0
IM (Inus) Kritzinger	4	1	–	–	–	5	4	1	–	–	–	5	8	2	–	–	–	10
AJ (AJ) le Roux	7	3	–	–	–	15	11	–	–	–	–	0	18	3	–	–	–	15
HF (Erik) le Roux	12	–	–	–	–	0	1	–	–	–	–	0	13	–	–	–	–	0
H (Henru) Liebenberg	1	–	–	–	–	0	–	–	–	–	–	0	1	–	–	–	–	0
W (Werner) Lourens	4	–	–	–	–	0	–	–	–	–	–	0	4	–	–	–	–	0
T (Tertius) Maarman	36	9	3	–	–	51	–	–	–	–	–	0	36	9	3	–	–	51
BB (Bren) Marais	2	–	–	–	–	0	–	–	–	–	–	0	2	–	–	–	–	0
V (Vuyo) Mbotho	14	3	–	–	–	15	12	2	–	–	–	10	26	5	–	–	–	25
AN (Aubrey) McDonald	9	3	–	–	–	15	1	–	–	–	–	0	10	3	–	–	–	15
DS (Devin) Montgomery	1	–	–	–	–	0	–	–	–	–	–	0	1	–	–	–	–	0
J (Japie) Nel	26	8	–	–	–	40	18	–	–	–	–	0	44	8	–	–	–	40
NT (Norman) Nelson	7	1	–	–	–	5	42	21	–	–	–	105	49	22	–	–	–	110
O (Oshwill) Nortjie	17	3	–	–	–	15	–	–	–	–	–	0	17	3	–	–	–	15
M (Pro) Ntshoko	2	–	–	–	–	0	–	–	–	–	–	0	2	–	–	–	–	0
WC (Wynand) Pienaar	7	2	6	–	–	22	–	–	–	–	–	0	7	2	6	–	–	22
HR (Heinrich) Roelfse	16	–	–	–	–	0	–	–	–	–	–	0	16	–	–	–	–	0
SM (Martin) Sithole	19	8	–	–	–	40	14	–	–	–	–	0	33	8	–	–	–	40
NPJ (Nicky) Steyn	34	20	–	–	–	100	18	9	–	–	–	45	52	29	–	–	–	145
LI (Louis) Strydom	9	1	13	21	–	94	37	2	67	75	–	378	46	3	80	96	3	472
DJ (Danie) van der Merwe	7	2	–	–	–	10	1	–	–	–	–	0	8	2	–	–	–	10
FJ (Franco) van der Merwe	4	–	–	–	–	0	2	–	–	–	–	0	6	–	–	–	–	0

VODACOM CUP

APPEARANCES & POINTS

PLAYER	Limpopo BB	Griquas	Pumas	Golden Lions	Leopards XV	Blue Bulls	Valke	Apps	T	C	P	DG	Pts
Wynand Pienaar	15	15	15	15	15	15	15	7	2	6	–	–	22
Vuyo Mbotho	14	14	14	14	14	14	14	7	1	–	–	–	5
Werner Griesel	13	13	13	13	15R	15R	14R	7	–	–	–	–	0
Japie Nel	12	12	–	12	12	12	12	6	3	–	–	–	15
Norman Nelson	11	11	11	11	13	13	13	7	1	–	–	–	5
Tertius Maarman	10	–	9R	9R	9R	9R	11R	6	1	1	–	–	7
Oshwill Nortje	9	9R	9	9	9	9	9	7	–	–	–	–	0
Nicky Steyn	8	8	8	8	8	–	8	6	5	–	–	–	25
Jan Breedt	7	7	4	4R	4R	–	–	5	–	–	–	–	0
Martin Sithole	6	6	6	7	7	–	6	6	5	–	–	–	25
Mlungisi Bali	5	5	5	–	5	4	5	6	–	–	–	–	0
Mayizukiswe Ntskoko	4	x	4R	–	–	–	–	2	–	–	–	–	0
Heinrich Roelfse	3	3	3	3	3	3	3	7	–	–	–	–	0
AJ le Roux	2c	2c	2c	2c	2c	2c	2c	7	3	–	–	–	15
Rudi Britz	1	1	1R	3R	3R	–	–	5	–	–	–	–	0
Jan-Francois Bester	3R	x	3R	–	–	–	–	2	–	–	–	–	0
PW Botha	1R	1R	1	1	1	–	–	5	–	–	–	–	0
Henru Liebenberg	6R	–	–	–	–	–	–	1	–	–	–	–	0
Wilmar Groenewald	4R	7R	6R	6	6	–	4R	6	1	–	–	–	5
Sheldon Erasmus	14R	x	12R	13R	11	–	–	4	2	–	–	–	10
Colin Herbert	10R	x	12	–	–	–	–	2	–	–	–	–	0
Bren Marais	10R	–	–	–	–	–	–	1	–	–	–	–	0
Louis Strydom	–	10	10	10	10R	–	–	4	–	2	6	–	22
Inus Kritzinger	–	9	–	–	–	–	9R	2	1	–	–	–	5
Werner Lourens	–	4	–	4	–	5	4	4	–	–	–	–	0
Niell Jordaan	–	–	7	–	–	8	–	2	–	–	–	–	0
Franna du Toit	–	–	10R	10R	10	10	10	5	–	6	3	–	21
Armandt Koster	–	–	–	5	4	7	–	3	–	–	–	–	0
Erik Le Roux	–	–	–	5R	7R	6	7	4	–	–	–	–	0
Franco van der Merwe	–	–	–	1R	1R	3R	1R	4	–	–	–	–	0
Aubrey McDonald	–	–	–	–	–	11	11	2	–	–	–	–	0
Danie vd Merwe	–	–	–	–	–	1	1	2	–	–	–	–	0
Dirk Grobbelaar	–	–	–	–	–	6R	–	1	–	–	–	–	0
David Montgomery	–	–	–	–	–	4R	–	1	–	–	–	–	0
Deon Gouws	–	–	–	–	–	2R	2R	2	–	–	–	–	0
Wickus Davis	–	–	–	–	–	5R	7R	2	–	–	–	–	0
36 Players								**150**	**25**	**15**	**9**	**0**	**182**

Griquas

'98	'99	'00	'01	'02	'03	'04	'05	'06	'07	'08	'09	'10	'11	'12	'13	'14
1st	2nd	1st	3rd	10th	9th	12th	3rd	9th	2nd	4th	1st	6th	4th	2nd	6th	3rd

Played	Won	Lost	Drawn	Points for	Points against	Tries for	Tries against
10	9	1	0	388	169	47	15

Date	Venue	Opponent	Result	Score	Referee	Scorers
8 Mar	Pretoria[1]	Blue Bulls	WON	26-24	M vd Westhuizen	T: Arendse, Meyer. C: Scheepers (2) P: J Jansen (2), Brummer. DG: Brummer.
15 Mar	Kimberley	Griffons	WON	20-12	O Rametsi	T: M Schoeman, R Jansen. C: J Jansen (2). P: J Jansen (2).
21 Mar	Kimberley	Limpopo BB	WON	68-13	M Jonker	T: Clarke (3), Nepgen (2), C Greeff, Prinsloo, Kebe, Westraadt, Molefe. C: Jinka (7), Prinsloo (2).
28 Mar	Nelspruit	Pumas	LOST	16-25	L Legoete	T: M Schoeman, Prinsloo. P: J Jansen (2).
5 Apr	Kimberley	Golden Lions	WON	33-18	J Peyper	T: C Greeff, Arendse, Van der Westhuizen. C: Prinsloo (3). P: Prinsloo (4).
11 Apr	Kimberley	Valke	WON	64-34	R Rasivhenge	T: C Greeff (3), Arendse (2), Jinka, Adendorff, R Jansen, Landman, Meyer. C: J Jansen (3), Prinsloo (3), Brummer
26 Apr	Klerksdorp	Leopards XV	WON	32-8	L vd Merwe	T: B Schoeman, Arendse, Prinsloo, Karemaker. C: Prinsloo (3). P: Prinsloo. DG: Brummer.
Quarter-final						
3 May	Kimberley	SWD	WON	84-15	C du Preez	T: Van der Westhuizen (2), Francke (2), Meyer (2), B Schoeman, Dames, Arendse, Adendorff, R Jansen. C: Prinsloo (10). P: Prinsloo (3).
Semi-final						
9 May	Nelspruit	Pumas	WON	15-14	L Legoete	P: Prinsloo (4). DG: Brummer.
Final						
16 May	Kimberley	Golden Lions	WON	30-6	J van Heerden	T: Brummer, Dames, M Schoeman. C: Prinsloo (3). P: Prinsloo (2). DG: Brummer.

[1] Loftus Versfeld B field
Note: ■ = Champion

VODACOM CUP

2014 SQUAD

PLAYER	GRIQUAS CAREER						OTHER UNIONS						VODACOM CUP TOTAL					
	A	T	C	P	DG	Pts	A	T	C	P	DG	Pts	A	T	C	P	DG	Pts
JW (Jonathan) Adendorf	25	4	–	–	–	20	5	–	–	–	–	0	30	4	–	–	–	20
E (Ederies) Arendse	9	6	–	–	–	30	11	3	–	–	–	15	20	9	–	–	–	45
RJ (Ryno) Barnes	19	1	–	–	–	5	26	2	–	–	–	10	45	3	–	–	–	15
MJ (Martin) Bezuidenhout	10	–	–	–	–	0	10	1	–	–	–	0	20	1	–	–	–	5
F (Francois) Brummer	21	3	17	2	4	67	22	4	37	55	12	295	43	7	54	57	16	362
HM (Hilford) Clarke	1	3	–	–	–	15	–	–	–	–	–	0	1	3	–	–	–	15
HDP (Danie) Dames	8	2	–	–	–	10	22	5	–	–	–	25	30	7	–	–	–	35
JC (Jonathan) Francke	9	2	–	–	–	10	19	8	–	–	–	40	28	10	–	–	–	50
CFK (Carel) Greeff	7	5	–	–	–	25	–	–	–	–	–	0	7	5	–	–	–	25
S (Stephan) Greeff	6	–	–	–	–	0	7	–	–	–	–	0	13	–	–	–	–	0
J (Jacquin) Jansen	4	–	5	6	–	28	28	7	19	16	–	121	32	7	24	22	–	149
RR (Rocco) Jansen	32	13	–	–	–	65	25	21	–	–	–	105	57	34	–	–	–	170
D (Dustin) Jinka	7	1	7	–	–	19	12	1	2	1	–	12	19	2	9	1	–	31
L (Leon) Karemaker	37	21	–	–	–	105	13	5	–	–	–	25	50	26	–	–	–	130
NL (Ntando) Kebe	2	–	–	–	–	0	26	–	–	–	–	0	28	5	–	–	–	25
L (Luxolo) Koza	4	–	–	–	–	0	–	–	–	–	–	0	4	–	–	–	–	0
RJ (Rynard) Landman	11	6	–	–	–	30	17	1	–	–	–	5	28	7	–	–	–	35
RJ (RJ) Liebenberg	3	–	–	–	–	0	–	–	–	–	–	0	3	–	–	–	–	0
H (Hilton) Lobberts	6	–	–	–	–	0	41	5	–	–	–	25	47	5	–	–	–	25
TC (Tian) Meyer	8	4	–	–	–	20	19	5	–	–	–	25	27	9	–	–	–	45
XH (Howard) Mnisi	5	–	–	–	–	0	3	1	–	–	–	5	8	1	–	–	–	5
T (Thabang) Molefe	3	1	–	–	–	0	5	33	10	–	–	50	36	11	–	–	–	55
J (Jaco) Nepgen	39	3	–	–	–	15	–	–	–	–	–	0	39	3	–	–	–	15
JG (Gouws) Prinsloo	8	3	24	14	–	105	20	5	28	30	–	171	28	8	52	44	–	276
WAS (Steph) Roberts	56	1	–	–	–	5	14	–	–	–	–	0	70	1	–	–	–	5
JN (Nico) Scheepers	1	–	2	–	–	4	10	3	12	5	–	54	11	3	14	5	–	58
DB (Burger) Schoeman	20	4	–	–	–	20	–	–	–	–	–	0	20	4	–	–	–	20
M (Marnus) Schoeman	24	17	–	–	–	85	12	3	–	–	–	15	36	20	–	–	–	100
WJ (Willem) Serfontein	3	–	–	–	–	0	35	2	–	–	–	10	38	2	–	–	–	10
FL (Frans) Sisita	1	–	–	–	–	0	–	–	–	–	–	0	1	–	–	–	–	0
IW (Wayne) Stevens	10	–	–	–	–	0	–	–	–	–	–	0	35	3	–	–	–	15
E (Ewald) vd Westhuizen	10	3	–	–	–	15	–	–	–	–	–	0	10	3	–	–	–	15
JL (Janro) van Niekerk	23	4	–	–	–	20	41	3	–	–	–	15	64	7	–	–	–	35
PJ (PJ) Vermeulen	18	3	1	–	–	17	32	7	–	–	–	35	50	10	1	–	–	52
S (Simon) Westraadt	40	10	–	–	–	50	5	–	–	–	–	0	45	10	–	–	–	50

⟨ DID YOU KNOW? ⟩

Gerrie Sonnekus holds the record for the longest wait between Tests. He made his debut on 13 July 1974 against the all-conquering Lions and had to wait nine years & 325 days before his second cap, against England on 2 June 1984.

VODACOM CUP

APPEARANCES & POINTS

PLAYER	Blue Bulls	Griffons	Limpopo BB	Pumas	Golden Lions	Valke	Leopards XV	SWD	Pumas	Golden Lions	Apps	T	C	P	DG	Pts
Jacquin Jansen	15	15	–	15	x	15	–	–	–	–	4	–	5	6	–	28
Ederies Arendse	14	14R	15	–	14	14	14	14	14	14	9	6	–	–	–	30
Jonathan Francke	13	13	–	13	13	12	13	13	13	13	9	2	–	–	–	10
Wayne Stevens	12c	12c	12R	12c	12c	12R	12c	12c	12c	12c	10	–	–	–	–	0
Nico Scheepers	11	–	–	–	–	–	–	–	–	–	1	–	2	–	–	4
Francois Brummer	10	10	–	10	10	10	10	10	10	10	9	1	1	1	4	22
Tian Meyer	9	9	–	9	9	9	9	9	9	9	8	4	–	–	–	20
Leon Karemaker	8	8R	–	8	4R	8	8	8	–	–	7	1	–	–	–	5
Jonathan Adendorf	7	7	7	7	4	4	4	4	4	4	10	2	–	–	–	10
Marnus Schoeman	6	6	–	6	6	–	5R	6R	6	6	8	3	–	–	–	15
Jaco Nepgen	5	5	5R	5	7	7	7	7	7	7	10	2	–	–	–	10
Hilton Lobberts	4	4	–	–	–	–	5	5	5	5	6	–	–	–	–	0
Ewald vd Westhuizen	3	3	1R	3	3	3	3	3	3	3	10	3	–	–	–	15
Martin Bezuidenhout	2	2	2R	2R	2	2R	2	2	2	2	10	–	–	–	–	0
Steph Roberts	1	1	–	1	–	1R	1	1	1	1	8	–	–	–	–	0
Simon Westraadt	2R	2R	2	–	2R	2	–	2R	2R	2R	8	1	–	–	–	5
Luxolo Koza	1R	1R	1	x	1	–	–	–	–	–	4	–	–	–	–	0
Willem Serfontein	4R	4R	4	–	–	–	–	–	–	–	3	–	–	–	–	0
Carel Greeff	7R	–	6R	7R	8	6	6	6	–	–	7	5	–	–	–	25
Burger Schoeman	6R	8	8c	6R	–	–	6R	8R	8	8	8	2	–	–	–	10
Dustin Jinka	x	9R	10	–	x	9R	9R	9R	9R	9R	7	1	7	–	–	19
Danie Dames	11R	14	13R	14	–	–	14R	10R	14R	11R	8	2	–	–	–	10
Rocco Jansen	–	11	11	11	11	11R	11	11	11	11	9	3	–	–	–	15
Hilford Clarke	–	x	14	–	–	–	–	–	–	–	1	3	–	–	–	15
PJ Vermeulen	–	–	13	–	12R	13	–	–	–	–	3	–	–	–	–	0
Thabang Molefe	–	–	12	–	–	–	–	–	–	–	1	1	–	–	–	5
Ntando Kebe	–	–	9	9	–	–	–	–	–	–	2	1	–	–	–	5
RJ Liebenberg	–	–	6	–	–	–	–	–	8R	8R	3	–	–	–	–	0
Stephan Greeff	–	–	5	4	4R	4R	–	–	17R	5R	6	–	–	–	–	0
Janro van Niekerk	–	–	3	1R	1R	1	3R	1R	3R	1R	8	–	–	–	–	0
Gouws Prinsloo	–	–	9R	15R	15	15R	15	15	15	15	8	3	24	12	1	105
Ryno Barnes	–	–	–	2	–	2R	–	–	–	–	2	–	–	–	–	0
Howard Mnisi	–	–	–	12R	–	12R	13R	13R	14R	–	5	–	–	–	–	0
Rynard Landman	–	–	–	–	5	5c	–	–	–	–	2	1	–	–	–	5
Frank Sisita	–	–	–	–	5R	–	–	–	–	–	1	–	–	–	–	0
35 players											**215**	**47**	**39**	**19**	**5**	**388**

VODACOM CUP

Sharks XV

'98	'99	'00	'01	'02	'03	'04	'05	'06	'07	'08	'09	'10	'11	'12	'13	'14
4th	4th	12th	5th	9th	4th	4th	12th	1st	9th	9th	3rd	4th	5th	5th	2nd	2nd

Played	Won	Lost	Drawn	Points for	Points against	Tries for	Tries against
8	6	2	0	235	147	27	17

Date	Venue	Opponent	Result	Score	Referee	Scorers
7 Mar	East London	Border	WON	46-26	F Pretorius	T: Graaff, Maritz, Esterhuizen, Marais, Herbst, Du Toit. C: Zeilinga (5). P: Zeilinga (2).
15 Mar	Durban	WP	WON	25-7	J van Heerden	T: Esterhuizen, Daniel, Botes. C: Zeilinga (2). P: Zeilinga (2).
21 Mar	Bloemfontein	Free State XV	WON	23-22	Q Immelman	T: Venter, Downey. C: Zeilinga (2). P: Zeilinga (3).
29 Mar	Durban	SWD	WON	27-10	Q Immelman	T: Swiel, Hadebe, Maritz. C: Swiel (3). P: Swiel (2).
5 Apr	Ceres	Boland	WON	43-27	J Kotze	T: Daniel (2), Van Tonder, Maseko, Swiel, Meyer. C: Swiel (5). P: Swiel.
12 Apr	Cape Town	Tusker Simba XV	WON	40-3	F Pretorius	T: Maritz, Meyer, Du Toit, Du Plessis. C: Swiel (3), Du Plessis. P: Swiel (4).
25 Apr	Durban	EP	LOST	11-27	F Anselmi	T: Maseko. P: Du Plessis (2).

QUARTER-FINAL

2 May	Durban	Golden Lions	LOST	20-27	F Pretorius	T: Nokwe, Meyer. C: Van Tonder, Campbell. P: Van Tonder (2).

❰ DID YOU KNOW? ❱

1986 Springbok wing, the late Jaco Reinach, held the national 400m record of 45.01sec from 1983-98. His son, Cobus, made his Test debut in 2014 at Newlands – the same ground where his dad played his first Test.

VODACOM CUP

2014 SQUAD

PLAYER	SHARKS XV CAREER						OTHER UNIONS						VODACOM CUP TOTAL					
	A	T	C	P	DG	Pts	A	T	C	P	DG	Pts	A	T	C	P	DG	Pts
KWC (Keelin) Bastew	2	0	0	0	0	0	0	0	0	0	0	0	2	0	0	0	0	0
HN (Nikolai) Blignaut	28	2	0	0	0	10	8	1	0	0	0	5	36	3	0	0	0	15
LJ (Jacques) Botes	3	1	0	0	0	5	12	2	0	0	0	10	15	3	0	0	0	15
D (Duncan) Campbell	1	0	1	0	0	2	0	0	0	0	0	0	1	0	1	0	0	2
T (Tonderai) Chavhanga	4	0	0	0	0	0	11	3	0	0	0	15	15	3	0	0	0	15
Q (Quinton) Crocker	4	0	0	0	0	0	7	1	0	0	0	5	11	1	0	0	0	5
KR (Keegan) Daniel	11	7	0	0	0	35	0	0	0	0	0	0	11	7	0	0	0	35
J (Justin) Downey	22	4	0	0	0	20	18	2	0	0	0	10	40	6	0	0	0	30
J-L (Jean-Luc) du Plessis	1	0	0	2	0	6	0	0	0	0	0	0	1	0	0	2	0	6
TJ (Thomas) du Toit	7	2	0	0	0	10	0	0	0	0	0	0	7	2	0	0	0	10
AP (Andre) Esterhuizen	10	3	1	0	0	17	0	0	0	0	0	0	10	3	1	0	0	17
JPJ (Hansie) Graaff	2	1	0	0	0	5	10	1	12	4	1	44	12	2	12	4	1	49
MS (Monde) Hadebe	27	1	0	0	0	5	0	0	0	0	0	0	27	1	0	0	0	5
WJ (Wiehan) Herbst	28	1	0	0	0	5	0	0	0	0	0	0	28	1	0	0	0	5
EW (Edwin) Hewitt	8	0	0	0	0	0	20	1	0	0	0	5	28	1	0	0	0	5
AM (Alcino) Izaacs	7	0	0	0	0	0	0	0	0	0	0	0	7	0	0	0	0	0
F (Francois) Kleinhans	25	2	0	0	0	10	0	0	0	0	0	0	25	2	0	0	0	10
SM (Sandile) Kubeka	5	0	0	0	0	0	0	0	0	0	0	0	5	0	0	0	0	0
K (Khaya) Majola	16	0	0	0	0	0	0	0	0	0	0	0	16	0	0	0	0	0
FS (Franco) Marais	16	1	0	0	0	5	0	0	0	0	0	0	16	1	0	0	0	5
PC (Peet) Marais	31	1	0	0	0	5	0	0	0	0	0	0	31	1	0	0	0	5
NK (Neil) Maritz	6	3	0	0	0	15	0	0	0	0	0	0	6	3	0	0	0	15
SS (Sizo) Maseko	15	7	0	0	0	35	0	0	0	0	0	0	15	7	0	0	0	35
JG (Johan) Meyer	13	3	0	0	0	15	0	0	0	0	0	0	13	3	0	0	0	15
DJ (Daniel) Mienie	15	0	0	0	0	0	0	0	0	0	0	0	15	0	0	0	0	0
KJ (Khwezi) Mona	4	0	0	0	0	0	0	0	0	0	0	0	4	0	0	0	0	0
LS (Lubabalo) Mtembu	18	4	0	0	0	20	0	0	0	0	0	0	18	4	0	0	0	20
SM (Mox) Mxoli	25	0	0	0	0	0	14	0	0	0	0	0	39	0	0	0	0	0
JL (Jongi) Nokwe	1	1	0	0	0	5	23	14	0	0	0	70	24	15	0	0	0	75
SMK (Shannon) Rick	5	0	0	0	0	0	0	0	0	0	0	0	5	0	0	0	0	0
SJ (Sean) Robinson	5	1	0	0	0	5	0	0	0	0	0	0	5	1	0	0	0	5
TG (Tim) Swiel	5	2	11	7	0	53	8	2	3	0	1	19	13	4	14	7	1	72
S (Stefan) Ungerer	7	0	0	0	0	0	0	0	0	0	0	0	7	0	0	0	0	0
J (Jaco) van Tonder	12	3	1	2	0	23	0	0	0	0	0	0	12	3	1	2	0	23
HC (Hanco) Venter	14	2	0	0	0	10	0	0	0	0	0	0	14	2	0	0	0	10
JA (Johannes) Vosloo	1	0	0	0	0	0	0	0	0	0	0	0	1	0	0	0	0	0
MvZ (Marco) Wentzel	4	0	0	0	0	0	18	1	0	0	0	5	22	1	0	0	0	5
H (Heimar) Williams	24	2	0	0	0	10	0	0	0	0	0	0	24	2	0	0	0	10
FJ (Fred) Zeilinga	22	3	39	34	0	195	0	0	0	0	0	0	22	3	39	34	0	195

VODACOM CUP

APPEARANCES & POINTS

PLAYER	Border	WP	Free State XV	SWD	Boland	Simba XV	EP	Golden Lions	Apps	T	C	P	DG	Pts
Hansie Graaff	15	15	–	–	–	–	–	–	2	1	–	–	–	5
Sizo Maseko	14	14	14	14	14	14	14	–	7	2	–	–	–	10
Neill Maritz	13	13	14R	13R	–	12	14R	–	6	3	–	–	–	15
Andre Esterhuizen	12	11	–	12	12	–	12	12	6	2	–	–	–	10
Alcino Izaacs	11	–	11R	14R	11R	14R	11	11	7	–	–	–	–	0
Fred Zeilinga	10	10	10	–	–	–	–	–	3	–	9	7	–	39
Stefan Ungerer	9	9	–	–	–	–	–	9	3	–	–	–	–	0
Lubabalo Mtembu	8c	–	–	–	8	–	–	–	2	–	–	–	–	0
Francois Kleinhans	7	–	7	7	–	6R	7R	7	6	–	–	–	–	0
Khaya Majola	6	6	6	6	6	6	6	6	8	–	–	–	–	0
Edwin Hewitt	5	5	4	4	5R	4c	4	4	8	–	–	–	–	0
Peet Marais	4	4	5	5R	4	5R	5R	5	8	1	–	–	–	5
Wiehan Herbst	3	3	3	3	–	3	3	3	7	1	–	–	–	5
Monde Hadebe	2	2	2c	2c	2c	2R	2c	2c	8	1	–	–	–	5
Sangoni Mxoli	1	–	–	–	1	1	–	1	4	–	–	–	–	0
Franco Marais	2R	2R	2R	2R	2R	2	–	2R	7	–	–	–	–	0
Thomas du Toit	1R	1R	1	1	1R	1R	1	–	7	2	–	–	–	10
Marco Wentzel	5R	–	4R	5	5	–	–	–	4	–	–	–	–	0
Johan Meyer	7R	8R	8	8R	8R	8	8	8	8	3	–	–	–	15
Hanco Venter	9R	9R	9	9	9	9R	9R	–	7	1	–	–	–	5
Tim Swiel	11R	15R	–	10	10	10	–	–	5	2	11	7	–	53
Keelin Bastew	15R	11	–	–	–	–	–	–	2	–	–	–	–	0
Keegan Daniel	–	8c	–	–	7	–	–	–	2	3	–	–	–	15
Jacques Botes	–	7	–	8	–	–	–	–	2	1	–	–	–	5
Khwezi Mona	–	1	3R	1R	–	–	1R	–	4	–	–	–	–	0
Nikolai Blignaut	–	5R	–	–	5	5	5	4R	4	–	–	–	–	0
Sandile Kubeka	–	13R	13	13	–	–	12R	12R	5	–	–	–	–	0
Jaco van Tonder	–	–	15	15	15	–	–	10	4	1	1	2	–	13
Heimar Williams	–	–	12	–	–	–	–	–	1	–	–	–	–	0
Tonderai Chavhanga	–	–	11	11	11	11	–	–	4	–	–	–	–	0
Justin Downey	–	–	6R	–	–	7	7	6R	4	1	–	–	–	5
Johannes Vosloo	–	–	15R	–	–	–	–	–	1	–	–	–	–	0
Shannon Rick	–	–	–	9R	9R	9	9	–	4	–	–	–	–	0
Quinton Crocker	–	–	–	13	13	13	13	–	4	–	–	–	–	0
Danie Mienie	–	–	–	3	–	–	–	1R	2	–	–	–	–	0
Sean Robinson	–	–	–	15R	15	15	15	–	4	–	–	–	–	0
Jean-Luc du Plessis	–	–	–	–	–	10R	10	–	2	1	1	2	–	13
Jacques Taylor	–	–	–	–	–	2R	–	–	1	–	–	–	–	0
Jongi Nokwe	–	–	–	–	–	–	–	14	1	1	–	–	–	5
Cameron Wright	–	–	–	–	–	–	–	x	0	–	–	–	–	0
Duncan Campbell	–	–	–	–	–	–	–	10R	1	–	1	–	–	2
41 Players									**175**	**27**	**23**	**18**	**0**	**235**

VODACOM CUP

Leopards XV

'98	'99	'00	'01	'02	'03	'04	'05	'06	'07	'08	'09	'10	'11	'12	'13	'14
14th	14th	9th	12th	6th	4th	7th	4th	12th	7th	6th	4th	8th	13th	10th	9th	9th

Played	Won	Lost	Drawn	Points for	Points against	Tries for	Tries against
7	3	4	0	227	178	29	22

Date	Venue	Opponent	Result	Score	Referee	Scorers
7 Mar	Potchefstroom	Golden Lions	LOST	16-18	Q Immelman	T: Beukman. C: Nortier. P: Nortier (2), Oosthuizen.
15 Mar	Polokwane	Limpopo BB	WON	71-10	G de Bruin	T: Jacobs, Liebenberg, Tossel, Vermaak, Deysel, Jenkinson, Beukman, Niemand, Bezuidenhout, Mhlongo, Oosthuizen. C: Nortier (8).
22 Mar	Kempton Park	Valke	WON	40-29	L Legoete	T: Tossel (3), Jacobs. C: Nortier (4), P: Nortier (4).
29 Mar	Leeudoringstad	Blue Bulls	LOST	26-30	T Ntshakaza	T: Tossel, Nortier, Niemand. C: Nortier. P: Nortier. DG: Nortier, Botha.
4 Apr	Welkom	Griffons	WON	35-15	S Geldenhuys	T: Liebenberg, Tossel, Van der Merwe, Beukman, Mhlongo. C: Nortier (4), Tossel.
12 Apr	Middelburg	Pumas	LOST	31-44	Q Immelman	T: Tossel (2), Vermaak, Oosthuizen. C: Nortier (4). P: Nortier.
26 Apr	Klerksdorp	Griquas	LOST	8-32	L vd Merwe	T: Tossel. P: Nortier.

⟨ DID YOU KNOW? ⟩
Transvaal flyhalf Tony Harris is the only person to have played a rugby and cricket Test at Ellis Park in Johannesburg. He scored a try against the Lions in July 1938, and scored 6 and 1 not out against England in February 1949.

VODACOM CUP

2014 SQUAD

PLAYER	LEOPARDS XV CAREER						OTHER UNIONS						VODACOM CUP TOTAL					
	A	T	C	P	DG	Pts	A	T	C	P	DG	Pts	A	T	C	P	DG	Pts
RE (Rowanyne) Beukman	7	3	–	–	–	15	–	–	–	–	–	0	7	3	–	–	–	15
SM (Stephan) Bezuidenhout	9	1	–	–	–	5	8	–	–	–	–	0	17	1	–	–	–	5
JJ (Justin) Botha	3	–	–	–	1	3	–	–	–	–	–	0	3	–	–	–	1	3
ME (Molotsi) Bouwer	7	–	–	–	–	0	–	–	–	–	–	0	7	–	–	–	–	0
J (Jaco) Buys	3	–	–	–	–	0	–	–	–	–	–	0	3	–	–	–	–	0
LR (Lucien) Cupido	2	–	–	–	–	0	–	–	–	–	–	0	2	–	–	–	–	0
J (Johan) Deysel	4	1	–	–	–	5	–	–	–	–	–	0	4	1	–	–	–	5
A (Arno) Ebersohn	5	–	–	–	–	0	–	–	–	–	–	0	5	–	–	–	–	0
M (Morne) Hanekom	11	4	–	–	–	20	9	2	–	–	–	10	20	6	–	–	–	30
AJ (Adri) Jacobs	7	2	–	–	–	10	–	–	–	–	–	0	7	2	–	–	–	10
JR (John-Roy) Jenkinson	2	1	–	–	–	5	–	–	–	–	–	0	2	1	–	–	–	5
DB (Danie) Jordaan	2	–	–	–	–	0	1	–	–	–	–	0	3	–	–	–	–	0
RA (Robert) Kruger	13	2	–	–	–	10	9	1	–	–	–	5	22	3	–	–	–	15
A (Armandt) Liebenberg	7	2	–	–	–	10	7	–	–	–	–	0	14	2	–	–	–	10
E (Edgar) Marutlulle	8	–	–	–	–	0	11	3	–	–	–	15	19	3	–	–	–	15
TL (Leon) Meyer	2	–	–	–	–	0	–	–	–	–	–	0	2	–	–	–	–	0
SS (Sithembiso) Mhlongo	6	2	–	–	–	10	–	–	–	–	–	0	6	2	–	–	–	10
SJ (SJ) Niemand	6	2	–	–	–	10	–	–	–	–	–	0	6	2	–	–	–	10
GJ (Gerhard) Nortier	7	1	22	9	1	79	4	–	1	–	–	2	11	1	23	9	1	81
S (Siya) November	2	–	–	–	–	0	–	–	–	–	–	0	2	–	–	–	–	0
JC (JC) Oberholzer	2	–	–	–	–	0	4	–	–	–	–	0	6	–	–	–	–	0
WS (Wynand) Olivier	1	–	–	–	–	0	–	–	–	–	–	0	1	–	–	–	–	0
SW (SW) Oosthuizen	5	2	–	1	–	13	2	–	2	–	–	4	7	2	2	1	–	17
JA (Jaap) Pienaar	1	–	–	–	–	0	–	–	–	–	–	0	1	–	–	–	–	0
AH (Henri) Scharneck	2	–	–	–	–	0	1	–	–	–	–	0	3	–	–	–	–	0
CB (Chriswill) September	2	–	–	–	–	0	–	–	–	–	–	0	2	–	–	–	–	0
D (Dillon) Smit	1	–	–	–	–	0	3	–	–	–	–	0	4	–	–	–	–	0
SJP (Pieter) Smith	2	–	–	–	–	0	–	–	–	–	–	0	2	–	–	–	–	0
BM (Brendon) Snyman	14	–	–	–	–	0	56	8	–	–	–	40	70	8	–	–	–	40
M (Malherbe) Swart	8	1	–	–	–	5	–	–	–	–	–	0	8	1	–	–	–	5
SL (Sergio) Torrens	7	–	–	–	–	0	–	–	–	–	–	0	7	–	–	–	–	0
G de la R (George) Tossel	14	9	1	–	–	47	3	–	1	1	–	5	17	9	2	1	–	52
DM (Malan) van der Merwe	–	–	–	–	–	0	3	1	–	–	–	0	5	1	–	–	–	5
ED (Elardus) Venter	9	–	–	–	–	0	–	–	–	–	–	0	9	–	–	–	–	0
JJC (Jacques) Vermaak	10	4	–	–	–	20	–	–	–	–	–	0	10	4	–	–	–	20

❰ DID YOU KNOW? ❱

Former Junior Springbok, the late Gerbrand Grobler, is the only player to have represented his province – Northern Transvaal – in a Currie Cup final in both rugby and cricket.

APPEARANCES & POINTS

PLAYER	Golden Lions	Limpopo BB	Valke	Blue Bulls	Griffons	Pumas	Griquas	Apps	T	C	P	DG	Pts
SW Oosthuizen	15	15	–	15	–	15	15	5	2	–	1	–	13
Rowayne Beukman	14	14	14	14	14	14	14	7	3	–	–	–	15
Sergio Torrens	13	13	13	13	13	13	13	7	–	–	–	–	0
George Tossel	12	12	12	12	12	12	12	7	9	1	–	–	47
Adri Jacobs	11	11	11	11	11	11	11	7	2	–	–	–	10
Gerhard Nortier	10	10	10	10	10	10	10	7	1	22	9	1	79
Malherbe Swart	9	9	9	9	9	–	–	5	–	–	–	–	0
Morne Hanekom	8c	8c	8c	8c	–	–	–	4	–	–	–	–	0
Molotsi Bouwer	7	7	7R	6R	4R	4	7R	7	–	–	–	–	0
Robert Kruger	6	–	7	7	7	7	7	6	–	–	–	–	0
Brendon Snyman	5	5	5	5	5	5	5	7	–	–	–	–	0
Sithembiso Mhlongo	4	4	4	4	4	–	4	6	2	–	–	–	10
Stephan Bezuidenhout	3	3	3	3	3c	3c	3c	7	1	–	–	–	5
Edgar Marutlulle	2	2	2	2	2	2	2	7	–	–	–	–	0
Henri Scharneck	1	1	–	–	–	–	–	2	–	–	–	–	0
JC Oberholzer	2R	–	–	–	x	–	–	1	–	–	–	–	0
John-Roy Jenkinson	1R	1R	–	–	–	–	–	2	1	–	–	–	5
Siya November	7R	4R	–	–	–	–	–	2	–	–	–	–	0
Armandt Liebenberg	8R	6	6	6	6	6	6	7	2	–	–	–	10
Leon Meyer	9R	9R	–	–	–	–	–	2	–	–	–	–	0
Justin Botha	x	–	10R	10R	10R	x	–	3	–	–	–	1	3
Johan Deysel	13R	12R	12R	14R	–	–	–	4	1	–	–	–	5
Jaap Pienaar	–	13R	–	–	–	–	–	1	–	–	–	–	0
Jacques Vermaak	–	2R	2R	2R	–	2R	2R	5	2	–	–	–	10
SJ Niemand	–	6R	8R	8R	8	8	8	6	2	–	–	–	10
Malan vd Merwe	–	–	15	–	15	–	–	2	1	–	–	–	5
Arno Ebersohn	–	–	1	1	1	1	1	5	–	–	–	–	0
Elardus Venter	–	–	1R	3R	x	1R	1R	4	–	–	–	–	0
Chriswill September	–	–	x	9R	9R	x	–	2	–	–	–	–	0
Wynand Olivier	–	–	–	–	11R	–	–	1	–	–	–	–	0
Jaco Buys	–	–	–	–	8R	7R	6R	3	–	–	–	–	0
Pieter Smith	–	–	–	–	–	9	9	2	–	–	–	–	0
Danie Jordaan	–	–	–	–	–	4R	4R	2	–	–	–	–	0
Lucien Cupido	–	–	–	–	–	13R	11R	2	–	–	–	–	0
Dillon Smit	–	–	–	–	–	–	9R	1	–	–	–	–	0
35 Players								148	29	23	10	2	227

VODACOM CUP

Mpumalanga Pumas

'98	'99	'00	'01	'02	'03	'04	'05	'06	'07	'08	'09	'10	'11	'12	'13	'14
5th	5th	10th	14th	8th	12th	10th	7th	5th	5th	11th	9th	9th	6th	3rd	2nd	1st

Played	Won	Lost	Drawn	Points for	Points against	Tries for	Tries against
9	8	1	0	349	128	43	15

Date	Venue	Opponent	Result	Score	Referee	Scorers
7 Mar	Kempton Park	Valke	WON	26-6	J van Heerden	T: J Pretorius (2). C: Roos (2). P: Roos (4).
15 Mar	Nelspruit	Blue Bulls	WON	22-20	T Ntshakaza	T: Bothma. C: Roos. P: Roos (3), Van Staden (2).
21 Mar	Welkom	Griffons	WON	69-5	C du Preez	T: J Pretorius (2), Isbell (2), Cassiem (2), Bothma, Shabangu, Steenkamp, D Pretorius. C: Roos (7), Van Staden. P: Roos.
29 Mar	Nelspruit	Griquas	WON	25-16	L Legoete	T: Steenkamp. C: Roos. P: Roos (6).
5 Apr	Polokwane	Limpopo BB	WON	88-0	O Rametsi	T: Scott (3), Bouwer (2), Botha, Le Roux, Terblanche, Pretorius, Skorbinski, J Pretorius, Sibiya, Mathee, Herne. C: Van Staden (5), J Pretorius (3), Botha.
12 Apr	Middelburg	Leopards XV	WON	44-31	Q Immelman	T: Mathee (2), Momberg, Isbell, Bothma. C: Roos (5). P: Roos (3).
26 Apr	Alberton	Golden Lions	WON	48-27	B Crouse	T: Bothma (2), Steenkamp, Skorbinski, Roos, Mtyanda, Van Rooyen, Isbell. C: Roos (4).

QUARTER-FINAL

Date	Venue	Opponent	Result	Score	Referee	Scorers
2 May	Nelspruit	Western Province	WON	13-8	S Geldenhuys	T: Bell. C: Roos. P: Van Wyk, Roos

SEMI-FINAL

Date	Venue	Opponent	Result	Score	Referee	Scorers
9 May	Nelspruit	Griquas	LOST	14-15	L Legoete	T: Steenkamp. P: Roos 3.

⟨ DID YOU KNOW? ⟩

Percy Montgomery became the first Springbok to play 100 Tests when he appeared against the All Blacks in a Tri-Nations match at Newlands, Cape Town, on 16 August 2008.

VODACOM CUP

2014 SQUAD

PLAYER	PUMAS CAREER						OTHER UNIONS						VODACOM CUP TOTAL					
	A	T	C	P	DG	Pts	A	T	C	P	DG	Pts	A	T	C	P	DG	Pts
JW Bell	16	6	–	–	–	30	–	–	–	–	–	0	22	7	–	–	–	35
Bernado Botha	6	2	1	–	–	12	8	4	–	–	–	20	14	6	1	–	–	32
Renaldo Bothma	24	10	–	–	–	50	6	1	–	–	–	5	30	11	–	–	–	55
Jaco Bouwer	38	24	–	–	–	120	11	2	–	–	–	10	49	26	–	–	–	130
Uzair Cassiem	18	6	–	–	–	30	4	–	–	–	–	0	22	6	–	–	–	30
Marius Coetzer	28	4	–	–	–	20	6	–	–	–	–	0	34	4	–	–	–	20
Frank Herne	17	6	–	–	–	30	14	2	–	–	–	10	31	8	–	–	–	40
Ruwellyn Isbell	7	4	–	–	–	20	–	–	–	–	–	0	7	4	–	–	–	20
RW Kember	25	1	–	–	–	5	29	1	–	–	–	5	54	2	–	–	–	10
Vincent Koch	16	5	–	–	–	25	3	1	–	–	–	5	19	6	–	–	–	30
Stephan Kotze	1	–	–	–	–	0	–	–	–	–	–	0	6	–	–	–	–	0
Marco Kruger	1	–	–	–	–	0	–	–	–	–	–	0	1	–	–	–	–	0
Christo Le Roux	30	4	–	–	–	20	7	3	–	–	–	15	37	7	–	–	–	35
Wilmaure Louw	18	–	–	–	–	0	23	7	–	–	–	35	41	7	–	–	–	35
Rudi Mathee	18	4	–	–	–	20	22	6	–	–	–	30	40	10	–	–	–	50
Jacques Momberg	18	1	–	–	–	5	2	–	–	–	–	0	20	1	–	–	–	5
Lubabalo Mtyanda	8	1	–	–	–	5	–	–	–	–	–	0	50	4	–	–	–	20
Sabelo Nhlapo	7	–	–	–	–	0	20	–	–	–	–	0	27	–	–	–	–	0
Sino Nyoka	8	–	–	–	–	0	19	1	–	–	–	5	27	1	–	–	–	5
Dewald Pretorius	12	6	–	–	–	30	14	6	–	–	–	30	26	12	–	–	–	60
Jerome Pretorius	14	6	–	–	–	30	22	8	–	–	–	40	36	14	–	–	–	70
Johan Pretorius	1	1	3	–	–	11	–	–	–	–	–	0	1	1	3	–	–	11
JC Roos	16	1	44	44	0	225	1	–	–	–	1	3	17	1	44	44	1	228
Marcello Sampson	3	–	–	–	–	0	14	3	–	–	–	15	17	3	–	–	–	15
Ashwin Scott	14	4	–	–	–	20	11	1	–	–	–	5	25	5	–	–	–	25
Brian Shabangu	4	1	–	–	–	5	2	–	–	–	–	0	6	1	–	–	–	5
Pule Sibiya	1	1	–	–	–	5	–	–	–	–	–	0	1	1	–	–	–	5
Hennie Skorbinski	7	2	–	–	–	10	–	–	–	–	–	0	9	3	–	–	–	15
Corne Steenkamp	61	14	–	–	–	70	–	–	–	–	–	0	61	14	–	–	–	70
DJ Terblanche	41	3	–	–	–	15	–	–	–	–	–	0	41	3	–	–	–	15
Drew van Coller	9	1	–	–	–	5	–	–	–	–	–	0	9	1	–	–	–	5
Reynier van Rooyen	15	1	–	–	–	5	–	–	–	–	–	0	15	1	–	–	–	5
Justin van Staden	6	–	6	2	–	18	8	–	6	17	1	66	14	–	12	19	1	84
Coenie van Wyk	26	11	27	11	–	142	8	2	8	1	–	29	34	13	35	12	–	171
Ruan Venter	2	–	–	–	–	0	–	–	–	–	–	0	3	–	–	–	–	0

VODACOM CUP

APPEARANCES & POINTS

PLAYER	Valke	Blue Bulls	Griffons	Griquas	Limpopo BB	Leopards XV	Golden Lions	WP	Griquas	Apps	T	C	P	DG	Pts
JW Bell	15	15	15	15	–	15	15	15	14	8	1	–	–	–	5
Jerome Pretorius	14	14	14	14	–	14	14	14	–	7	4	–	–	–	20
Wilmaure Louw	13	13	13	13	–	13	13	13	13	8	–	–	–	–	0
Hennie Skorbinski	12	–	–	12	13	12	12	12	12	7	2	–	–	–	10
Ruwellyn Isbell	11	x	11	–	15	11	11	11	11	7	4	–	–	–	20
JC Roos	10	10	10	10	–	10	10	10	10	8	1	21	21	–	110
Sino Nyoka	9	9	9	9	–	9	9	9	9	8	–	–	–	–	0
Renaldo Bothma	8	8	8	8	–	8	8	8	8	8	4	–	–	–	20
Uzair Cassiem	7	7	7	7	–	7	7	7	7	8	2	–	–	–	10
Corne Steenkamp	6c	6c	6c	6c	–	6c	6c	6c	6c	8	4	–	–	–	20
Marius Coetzer	5	5	5	5	–	5	5	5	5	8	–	–	–	–	0
Lubabalo Mtyanda	4	4	4	4	–	5R	4	4	4	8	1	–	–	–	5
Drew van Coller	3	3	3	3	–	3	3	–	–	6	–	–	–	–	0
Jacques Momberg	2	2	2	2	10R	2	2	2	2	9	1	–	–	–	5
Vincent Koch	1	1	1	–	–	–	1	1	1	6	–	–	–	–	0
Frank Herne	2R	2R	2R	2R	2	2R	2R	2R	2R	9	1	–	–	–	5
DJ Terblanche	3R	3R	3R	3R	3	3R	3R	3	3	9	1	–	–	–	5
RW Kember	5R	6R	4R	8R	6R	8R	5R	5R	8R	9	–	–	–	–	0
Brian Shabangu	6R	–	6R	6R	6	–	–	–	–	4	1	–	–	–	5
Reynier van Rooyen	9R	9R	9R	9R	9	9R	9R	9R	9R	9	1	–	–	–	5
Justin van Staden	15R	10R	10R	11R	10	10R	–	–	–	6	–	6	2	–	18
Bernado Botha	11R	11	12R	11	13R	12R	–	–	–	6	2	1	–	–	12
Dewald Pretorius	–	12	12	–	12	–	–	–	x	3	2	–	–	–	10
Sabelo Nhlapo	–	5R	–	1	1	1	1R	1R	1R	7	–	–	–	–	0
Ruan Venter	–	–	–	4R	4	–	–	–	–	2	–	–	–	–	0
Ashwin Scott	–	–	–	–	14	–	–	–	–	1	3	–	–	–	15
Marcello Sampson	–	–	–	–	11	–	10R	14R	x	3	–	–	–	–	0
Christo Le Roux	–	–	–	–	8	–	–	–	–	1	1	–	–	–	5
Jaco Bouwer	–	–	–	–	7c	–	–	6R	5R	3	2	–	–	–	10
Rudi Mathee	–	–	–	–	5	4	–	–	–	2	3	–	–	–	15
Stephan Kotze	–	–	–	–	3R	–	–	–	–	1	–	–	–	–	0
Marco Kruger	–	–	–	–	4R	–	–	–	–	1	–	–	–	–	0
Johan Pretorius	–	–	–	–	9R	–	–	–	–	1	1	3	–	–	11
Pule Sibiya	–	–	–	–	11R	–	–	–	–	1	1	–	–	–	5
Coenie van Wyk	–	–	–	–	–	–	15R	10R	15	3	–	–	1	–	3
35 Players										195	43	31	24	0	349

VODACOM CUP

South Western Districts

'98	'99	'00	'01	'02	'03	'04	'05	'06	'07	'08	'09	'10	'11	'12	'13	'14
3rd	8th	14th	7th	12th	13th	9th	8th	14th	12th	10th	5th	13th	11th	15th	12th	6th

Played	Won	Lost	Drawn	Points for	Points against	Tries for	Tries against
8	5	3	0	255	248	34	31

Date	Venue	Opponent	Result	Score	Referee	Scorers
8 Mar	Bloemfontein [1]	Free State XV	LOST	47-52	M Jonker	T: Zito (2), Pedro, Dyantyi, Smart, Penalty try. C: Aspeling (4). P: Aspeling (2). DG: Aspeling.
15 Mar	Cape Town [2]	Tusker Simba XV	WON	51-7	S Geldenhuys	T: Roberts (2), Smart (2), Du Plessis, Pedro, Stander, Du Toit, Raubenheimer. C: Aspeling (3).
22 Mar	Swellendam	Boland	WON	46-17	T Ntshakaza	T: Smart (2), Du Plessis, Pedro, Petzer, Raubenheimer. C: Aspeling (4), Rhoode. P: Rhoode (2).
29 Mar	Durban	Sharks XV	LOST	10-27	Q Immelman	T: Bester. C: Aspeling. P: Aspeling.
4 Apr	George	SWD	WON	23-21	B Crouse	T: Bock, Raubenheimer. C: Aspeling (2). P: Aspeling (2). G: Aspeling.
11 Apr	East London	Border	WON	40-26	J van Heerden	T: Bock (4), Pedro, Bester. C: Aspeling (5).
25 Apr	George	WP	WON	23-14	R Rasivhenge	T: Bock, Roberts. C: Aspeling (2). P: Aspeling (3).

QUARTER-FINAL

3 May	Kimberley	Griquas	LOST	15-84	C du Preez	T: Pedro, Raubenheimer. C: Aspeling. P: Aspeling.

[1] *Clive Solomon Stadium*

[2] *City Park*

⟨ **DID YOU KNOW?** ⟩

Australia wing/centre Stirling Mortlock holds the record for the most points scored by a player in a Test against the Springboks - he scored 29 points for the Wallabies in a Tri-Nations match in Melbourne in 2000.

VODACOM CUP

2014 SQUAD

PLAYER	SWD CAREER						OTHER UNIONS						VODACOM CUP TOTAL					
	A	T	C	P	DG	Pts	A	T	C	P	DG	Pts	A	T	C	P	DG	Pts
KG (Karlo) Aspeling	8	–	22	11	2	83	7	–	6	18	–	66	15	0	28	29	2	149
A (Alwyn/Junior) Bester	8	2	–	–	–	10	23	1	–	–	–	5	31	3	–	–	–	15
AG (Alshaun) Bock	16	11	–	–	–	55	30	18	–	–	–	90	46	29	–	–	–	145
AS (Ashley) Buys	27	–	–	–	–	0	27	1	–	–	–	5	54	1	–	–	–	5
LC (Lionel) Cornelius	5	–	–	–	–	0	21	4	10	11	–	73	26	4	10	11	–	73
LA (Layle) Delo	12	–	–	–	–	0	–	–	–	–	–	–	12	–	–	–	–	–
CJ (Christo) du Plessis	16	4	–	–	–	20	–	–	–	–	–	–	16	4	–	–	–	20
OM (Martin) du Toit	14	2	–	–	–	10	–	–	–	–	–	–	14	2	–	–	–	10
M (Mzo) Dyantyi	31	4	–	–	–	20	8	–	–	–	–	–	39	4	–	–	–	20
DC (Danie) Faasen	6	–	–	–	–	–	12	2	–	–	–	10	18	2	–	–	–	10
J (Hannes) Franklin	31	5	–	–	–	25	33	2	–	–	–	10	64	7	–	–	–	35
LL (Lyndon) Hartnick	27	4	–	–	–	20	–	–	–	–	–	–	27	4	–	–	–	20
EG (Eldred) James	1	–	–	–	–	–	–	–	–	–	–	–	1	–	–	–	–	–
GD (Grant) Kemp	9	1	–	–	–	5	–	–	–	–	–	–	9	1	–	–	–	5
W (Wayne) Khan	16	–	–	–	–	–	3	–	–	–	–	–	19	–	–	–	–	–
G (Grant) le Roux	19	1	–	–	–	5	17	3	–	–	–	15	36	4	–	–	–	20
SW (Schalk) Oelofse	5	–	–	–	–	–	1	–	–	–	–	–	6	–	–	–	–	–
HN (Hentzwill) Pedro	8	5	–	–	–	25	–	–	–	–	–	–	8	5	–	–	–	25
AQ (Quinten) Petzer	5	1	–	–	–	5	–	–	–	–	–	–	5	1	–	–	–	5
S (Shaun) Raubenheimer	23	7	–	–	–	35	9	1	–	–	–	5	32	8	–	–	–	40
DE (Deroy) Rhoode	32	3	12	2	–	45	–	–	–	–	–	–	32	3	12	2	–	45
DC (Daniel) Roberts	10	3	–	–	–	15	–	–	–	–	–	–	10	3	–	–	–	15
DE (Duwayne) Smart	10	9	–	–	–	45	–	–	–	–	–	–	12	10	–	–	–	50
D C-L (Dillin) Snell	2	–	–	–	–	–	–	–	–	–	–	–	2	–	–	–	–	–
JH (Janneman) Stander	6	1	–	–	–	5	1	–	–	–	–	–	7	1	–	–	–	5
AP (Peet) van der Walt	2	–	–	–	–	–	5	–	–	–	–	–	7	–	–	–	–	–
E (Elric) van Vuuren	11	3	8	11	–	64	16	2	–	–	–	10	27	5	8	11	–	74
A (Anver) Venter	7	–	–	–	–	–	–	–	–	–	–	–	7	–	–	–	–	–
MR (Mzwanele) Zito	8	2	–	–	–	10	–	–	–	–	–	–	9	2	–	–	–	10

‹ DID YOU KNOW? ›

In 123 years, no player has ever managed to score a hat-trick in a Test against the Springboks. Of the more than 30 times whereby a player scored two tries, All Black Christian Cullen achieved the feat an incredible four times!

VODACOM CUP

APPEARANCES & POINTS

PLAYER	Free State XV	Simba XV	Boland	Sharks XV	EP	Border	WP	Griquas	Apps	T	C	P	DG	Pts
Daniel Roberts	15	13	13	13	13	15	13	13	8	3	–	–	–	15
Hentzwill Pedro	14	14	14	14	14	14	14	14	8	5	–	–	–	25
Anver Venter	13	9R	10R	11R	x	13	11R	13R	7	–	–	–	–	0
Martin du Toit	12	12	12	12	12	–	12	12	7	1	–	–	–	5
Duwayne Smart	11	11	11	11	–	–	–	–	4	5	–	–	–	25
Karlo Aspeling	10	10	10	10	10	10	10	10	8	–	22	11	2	83
Deroy Rhoode	9	15	15	15	15R	15R	x	13R	7	1	–	–	–	2
Christo du Plessis	8	7R	8R	8R	8	–	8	7	7	2	–	–	–	10
Lyndon Hartnick	7	–	7R	7R	7	7	6	–	6	–	–	–	–	0
Shaun Raubenheimer	6	6	6	6	6	6	–	6	7	4	–	–	–	20
Mzwanele Zito	5	5	5	5	5	5	5	5	8	2	–	–	–	10
Schalk Oelofse	4	4	4	4	4	–	–	–	5	–	–	–	–	0
Grant Kemp	3c	1c	1c	1c	1c	1c	1c	1c	8	–	–	–	–	0
Hannes Franklin	2	2	2	2	2	2	–	–	6	–	–	–	–	0
Layle Delo	1	–	–	3R	3R	3R	2R	2R	6	–	–	–	–	0
Wayne Khan	2R	2R	2R	2R	2R	2R	2	2	8	–	–	–	–	0
Ashley Buys	1R	3	3	3	3	3	3	3	8	–	–	–	–	0
Grant le Roux	4R	4R	4R	4R	4R	4	4	4	8	–	–	–	–	0
Alwyn Bester	7R	8	8	8	8R	8	7	8	8	2	–	–	–	10
Mzo Dyantyi	9R	9R	9R	9R	–	9R	–	9R	6	1	–	–	–	5
Lionel Cornelius	13R	12R	–	–	12R	–	–	–	3	–	–	–	–	0
Eldred James	12R	–	–	–	–	–	–	–	1	–	–	–	–	0
Danie Faasen	–	9	9	9	9	–	9	9	6	–	–	–	–	0
Janneman Stander	–	7	7	7	–	6R	6R	7R	6	1	–	–	–	5
Quinten Petzer	–	3R	3R	–	–	7R	3R	3R	5	1	–	–	–	5
Elric van Vuuren	–	–	–	–	15	12	15	15	4	–	–	–	–	0
Alshaun Bock	–	–	–	–	11	11	11	11	4	6	–	–	–	30
Dillin Snell	–	–	–	–	9R	9	x	–	2	–	–	–	–	0
Peet van der Walt	–	–	–	–	–	–	4R	4R	2	–	–	–	–	0
Penalty try	–	–	–	–	–	–	–	–	–	1	–	–	–	5
29 Players									**173**	**34**	**23**	**11**	**2**	**255**

Tusker Simba XV

'14
16th

Played	Won	Lost	Drawn	Points for	Points against	Tries for	Tries against
7	1	6	0	102	283	14	45

Date	Venue	Opponent	Result	Score	Referee	Scorers
8 Mar	Cape Town	EP	WON	17-10	R Boneparte	T: Mugaisi (2), Kangu. C:Andola.
15 Mar	Cape Town	SWD	LOST	7-51	S Geldenhuys	T: Kopondo. C: Andola.
22 Mar	East London	Border	LOST	17-18	S Geldenhuys	T: Mugaisi, Ogutu. C: Andola (2). P: Andola.
29 Mar	Cape Town	Boland	LOST	19-24	C Jadezweni	T: Osinde, Omondi, Nyikali. C: Mukidza (2).
5 Apr	Cape Town	WP	LOST	29-65	T Ntshakaza	T: Opondo (2), Ogutu, Chisanga. C: Andola (3). P: Andola.
11 Apr	Cape Town	Sharks XV	LOST	3-40	F Pretorius	P: Andola.
26 Apr	Bloemfontein	Free State XV	LOST	10-75	M vd Westhuizen	T: Amusala. C: Kochieng. P: Andola.

{ DID YOU KNOW? }

All Black legend Jonah Lomu, who scored 37 tries in 63 Tests for New Zealand, never managed to score a try in a dozen matches against the Springboks.

2014 SQUAD

PLAYER	TUSKER SIMBA CAREER						OTHER UNIONS						VODACOM CUP TOTAL					
	A	T	C	P	DG	Pts	A	T	C	P	DG	Pts	A	T	C	P	DG	Pts
E (Edwin) Achayo Otieno	6	0	0	1	0	3	0	0	0	0	0	0	6	0	0	1	0	3
M (Max) Adaka Kangu	6	1	0	0	0	5	0	0	0	0	0	0	6	1	0	0	0	5
I (Isaac) Adimo	4	0	0	0	0	0	0	0	0	0	0	0	4	0	0	0	0	0
E (Eden) Agero Kochieng	6	0	2	0	0	4	0	0	0	0	0	0	6	0	2	0	0	4
M (Moses) Amusala	5	1	0	0	0	5	0	0	0	0	0	0	5	1	0	0	0	5
KR (Kenny) Andola	6	0	7	3	0	23	0	0	0	0	0	0	6	0	7	3	0	23
R (Robert) Aringo	5	0	0	0	0	0	0	0	0	0	0	0	5	0	0	0	0	0
L (Lyle) Asiligwa	2	0	0	0	0	0	0	0	0	0	0	0	2	0	0	0	0	0
S (Nick) Barasa	5	0	0	0	0	0	0	0	0	0	0	0	5	0	0	0	0	0
D (Davis) Chenge	5	1	0	0	0	5	0	0	0	0	0	0	5	1	0	0	0	5
J (Joshua) Chisanga	5	1	0	0	0	5	0	0	0	0	0	0	5	1	0	0	0	5
AM (Austine) Gumo	3	0	0	0	0	0	0	0	0	0	0	0	3	0	0	0	0	0
J (James) Kang'ethe	5	0	0	0	0	0	0	0	0	0	0	0	5	0	0	0	0	0
J (Joseph) Kang'ethe	4	0	0	0	0	0	0	0	0	0	0	0	4	0	0	0	0	0
W (Wilson) Kopondo	4	1	0	0	0	5	0	0	0	0	0	0	4	1	0	0	0	5
CK (Cyprian) Kuto	3	0	0	0	0	0	0	0	0	0	0	0	3	0	0	0	0	0
C (Curtis) Lilako	6	0	0	0	0	0	0	0	0	0	0	0	6	0	0	0	0	0
O (Oliver) Mang'eni Kizito	6	0	0	0	0	0	0	0	0	0	0	0	6	0	0	0	0	0
E (Emmanuel) Mavala	5	0	0	0	0	0	0	0	0	0	0	0	5	0	0	0	0	0
L (Leonard) Mugaisi	7	3	0	0	0	15	0	0	0	0	0	0	7	3	0	0	0	15
D (Dennis) Muhanji Osinde	6	1	0	0	0	5	0	0	0	0	0	0	6	1	0	0	0	5
D (Darwin) Mukidza	4	0	1	0	0	2	0	0	0	0	0	0	4	0	1	0	0	2
T (Tony) Mutai	2	0	0	0	0	0	0	0	0	0	0	0	2	0	0	0	0	0
D (Duncan) Mwangi Gachichi	2	0	0	0	0	0	0	0	0	0	0	0	2	0	0	0	0	0
R (Ronnie) Mwenesi	1	0	0	0	0	0	0	0	0	0	0	0	1	0	0	0	0	0
BW (Brian) Nyikuli	6	0	0	0	0	0	0	0	0	0	0	0	6	0	0	0	0	0
M (Michael) Okombe Shitindo	6	0	0	0	0	0	0	0	0	0	0	0	6	0	0	0	0	0
F (Fabian) Olando Ogutu	5	2	0	0	0	10	0	0	0	0	0	0	5	2	0	0	0	10
TD (Tony) Onyango Opondo	4	2	0	0	0	10	0	0	0	0	0	0	4	2	0	0	0	10
E (Edward) Oseko	3	0	0	0	0	0	0	0	0	0	0	0	3	0	0	0	0	0
M (Martin) Owila	6	1	0	0	0	5	0	0	0	0	0	0	6	1	0	0	0	5
NN (Samuel) Warui	2	0	0	0	0	0	0	0	0	0	0	0	2	0	0	0	0	0

VODACOM CUP

APPEARANCES & POINTS

PLAYER	EP	SWD	Border	Boland	WP	Sharks XV	Free State XV	Apps	T	C	P	DG	Pts
Adimo Wamamba	15	15	15	10R	–	–	–	4	–	–	–	–	0
Leonard Mugaisi	14	14	14	13	14	14	14	7	3	0	0	0	15
Fabian Ogutu	13	13R	13	–	13	–	13	5	2	0	0	0	10
Nick Barasa	12	–	12	–	12	12	13R	5	–	–	–	–	0
Dennis Osinde	11	13	–	11	11	13	11	6	1	0	0	0	5
Kenny Andola	10	10R	10	–	10	10	10	6	0	7	4	0	26
Edwin Otieno	9	x	9	9R	9	9	9	6	–	–	–	–	0
Joshua Chisanga	8	8	8	–	8	8	–	5	1	0	0	0	5
Brian Nyikali	7	–	7	7	6c	7c	6c	6	1	–	–	–	5
Michael Shitindo	6	6	6	7R	7	6	–	6	–	–	–	–	0
Wilson Kopondo	5c	4c	4c	4c	–	–	–	4	1	0	0	0	5
Oliver Kizito	4	–	5	5R	4	4	5	6	–	–	–	–	0
James Kangethe	3	–	3	–	3	3	3	5	–	–	–	–	0
Maxwell Kangu	2	x	2	2R	2	2R	2R	6	1	0	0	0	5
Joseph Kangethe	1	–	1	–	1	1	–	4	–	–	–	–	0
Edward Oseko	x	2	x	2	2R	–	x	3	–	–	–	–	0
Moses Amusala	1R	3R	–	1	5R	–	1	5	1	0	0	0	5
Tonny Mutai	4R	5	x	–	–	–	–	2	–	–	–	–	0
Davis Chenge	6R	7	–	6	–	7R	7	5	0	0	0	0	0
Lyle Asiligwa	x	9	9R	–	–	–	–	2	–	–	–	–	0
Eden Kochieng	10R	10	–	10	10R	15R	10R	6	0	1	0	0	2
Darwin Mukidza	x	11	–	13R	13R	11R	–	4	0	2	0	0	4
Austine Gumo	–	12	–	12	–	–	12	3	–	–	–	–	0
Duncan Gachichi	–	3	–	3	–	–	–	2	–	–	–	–	0
Curtis Lilako	–	1	1R	3R	1R	3R	3R	6	–	–	–	–	0
Emmanuel Mavala	–	5R	–	5	5	5	4	5	–	–	–	–	0
Martin Omondi	–	8R	6R	8	6R	8R	8	6	1	0	0	0	5
Robert Aringo	–	9R	–	9R	9R	9R	9R	5	–	–	–	–	0
Cyprian Kuto	–	–	11	14	–	11	–	3	–	–	–	–	0
Tony Opondo	–	–	x	15	15	15	15	4	2	0	0	0	10
Samuel Warui	–	–	–	–	–	2	2	2	–	–	–	–	0
Ronnie Mwenes	–	–	–	–	–	–	4R	1	–	–	–	–	0
32 Players								**145**	**14**	**10**	**4**	**0**	**102**

VODACOM CUP

Valke

'98	'99	'00	'01	'02	'03	'04	'05	'06	'07	'08	'09	'10	'11	'12	'13	'14
7th	6th	2nd	13th	4th	6th	4th	9th	**2nd**	9th	9th	13th	12th	11th	12th	14th	14th

Played	Won	Lost	Drawn	Points for	Points against	Tries for	Tries against
7	1	6	0	180	262	26	41

Date	Venue	Opponent	Result	Score	Referee	Scorers
7 Mar	Kempton Park	Pumas	LOST	6-26	J van Heerden	P: Dumond (2).
15 Mar	Johannesburg	Golden Lions	LOST	22-23	C du Preez	T: Hendricks. C: Dumond. P: Cleophas (3), Dumond (2).
22 Mar	Kempton Park	Leopards	LOST	29-40	L Legoete	T: Ngcobo, Janke, Richter, Van Wyk. P: Cleophas (3).
29 Mar	Sasolburg	Limpopo	WON	65-14	A Sehlako	T: Verwey (3), Cronje (2), Van Wyk (2), Ngcobo, Gwavu, Richter, Am. C: Hendricks (2), Cleophas (2), Poley.
4 Apr	Pretoria	Blue Bulls	LOST	7-54	S Berry	T: Hope. C: Dumond.
11 Apr	Kimberley	Griquas	LOST	34-64	R Rasivhenge	T: Ngcobo (2), Kirkwood, Vorster, Richter. C: Cleophas (2), Gardner. P: Cleophas.
25 Apr	Kempton Park	Griffons	LOST	17-41	J Sylvestre	T: Gwavu, Hope, Taljaard. C: Hendricks.

Note: ■ = *Champion*

⟨ DID YOU KNOW? ⟩

When Jonathan Kaplan refereed SA vs Namibia in 2007, he became only the fourth South African after Johan Gouws, Steve Strydom and Fransie Muller to blow a Springbok Test since neutral referees were introduced in 1977.

VODACOM CUP

2014 SQUAD

PLAYER	VALKE CAREER						OTHER UNIONS						VODACOM CUP TOTAL					
	A	T	C	P	DG	Pts	A	T	C	P	DG	Pts	A	T	C	P	DG	Pts
GDJ (Jacques) Alberts	19	0	0	0	0	0	0	0	0	0	0	0	19	0	0	0	0	0
L (Luke) Am	2	1	0	0	0	5	2	0	0	0	0	0	4	1	0	0	0	5
FJ (Frederick) Binneman	5	0	0	0	0	0	1	0	0	0	0	0	6	0	0	0	0	0
RS (Ryan) Carmichael	1	0	0	0	0	0	0	0	0	0	0	0	1	0	0	0	0	0
AA (Angus) Cleophas	7	0	4	7	0	29	0	0	0	0	0	0	7	0	4	7	0	29
WW (Wesley) Cloete	5	0	0	0	0	0	7	0	0	0	0	0	12	0	0	0	0	0
CF (Coert) Cronje	25	10	0	0	0	50	0	0	0	0	0	0	25	10	0	0	0	50
C (Cecil) Dumond	5	0	2	4	0	16	13	0	4	10	1	41	18	0	6	14	1	57
W (Wayne) Gardner	1	0	1	0	0	2	0	0	0	0	0	0	1	0	1	0	0	2
LV (Vincent) Gwavu	10	2	0	0	0	10	21	2	0	0	0	10	31	4	0	0	0	20
C (Kyle) Hendricks	32	10	12	6	0	92	0	0	0	0	0	0	32	10	12	6	0	92
D (Devlin) Hope	6	2	0	0	0	10	0	0	0	0	0	0	6	2	0	0	0	10
GD (Grant) Janke	6	1	0	0	0	5	10	0	0	0	0	0	16	1	0	0	0	5
SM (Shane) Kirkwood	3	1	0	0	0	5	3	1	0	0	0	5	6	2	0	0	0	10
D (David) Kuatu	2	0	0	0	0	0	0	0	0	0	0	0	2	0	0	0	0	0
E (Ernst) Ladendorf	2	0	0	0	0	0	3	0	0	0	0	0	5	0	0	0	0	0
JPF (JP) Mostert	10	4	0	0	0	20	9	0	0	0	0	0	19	4	0	0	0	20
B (Bruce) Muller	3	0	0	0	0	0	0	0	0	0	0	0	3	0	0	0	0	0
SC (Sandile) Ncgobo	11	5	0	0	0	25	0	0	0	0	0	0	11	5	0	0	0	25
TS (Thulani) Ngidi	14	0	0	0	0	0	0	0	0	0	0	0	14	0	0	0	0	0
WA (Willie) Odendaal	23	4	0	0	0	20	0	0	0	0	0	0	23	4	0	0	0	20
F (Friedle) Olivier	13	1	0	0	0	5	0	0	0	0	0	0	13	1	0	0	0	5
AP (Arno) Poley	24	3	1	0	1	20	0	0	0	0	0	0	24	3	1	0	1	20
JH (Juan) Pretorius	5	0	0	0	0	0	10	2	0	0	0	10	15	2	0	0	0	10
N (Nico) Pretorius	21	0	0	0	0	0	0	0	0	0	0	0	21	0	0	0	0	0
A (Anrich) Richter	18	5	0	0	0	25	0	0	0	0	0	0	18	5	0	0	0	25
JP (Jaco) Snyman	17	2	0	0	0	10	5	0	0	0	0	0	22	2	0	0	0	10
E (Etienne) Taljaard	1	1	0	0	0	5	0	0	0	0	0	0	1	1	0	0	0	5
D (Dandre) van der Westhuizen	4	0	0	0	0	0	2	0	0	0	0	0	6	0	0	0	0	0
MP (Marco-Pierre) van Eeden	10	1	0	0	0	5	0	0	0	0	0	0	10	1	0	0	0	5
AJD (Andrew) van Wyk	7	3	0	0	0	15	4	0	0	0	0	0	11	3	0	0	0	15
TJ (Jacques) Verwey	5	3	0	0	0	15	3	0	0	0	0	0	8	3	0	0	0	15
PJH (Peet) Vorster	2	1	0	0	0	5	4	0	0	0	0	0	6	1	0	0	0	5
ME (Marlyn) Williams	7	0	0	0	0	0	0	0	0	0	0	0	7	0	0	0	0	0

❰ DID YOU KNOW? ❱
The first Springbok to receive a yellow card was Percy Montgomery, from Australian Peter Marshall vs New Zealand at Ellis Park in 1997. In those days it only meant a formal caution. Ten-minute 'sin bins' were introduced in 2000.

VODACOM CUP

APPEARANCES & POINTS

PLAYER	Pumas	Golden Lions	Leopards XV	Limpopo BB	Blue Bulls	Griquas	Griffons	Apps	T	C	P	DG	Pts
Kyle Hendricks	15	11	11	11	11	11	15	7	1	3	–	–	11
Sandile Ngcobo	14	x	14	14	14	14	14	6	4	–	–	–	20
Grant Janke	13	13	13	10R	13R	–	13	6	1	–	–	–	5
Willie Odendaal	12	–	–	–	–	12	–	2	–	–	–	–	0
Andrew van Wyk	11	14	13R	13	13	13	11	7	3	–	–	–	15
Cecil Dumond	10	10	10	–	10	–	10	5	–	2	4	–	16
Jaco Snyman	9	9	9	9c	9	9c	–	6	–	–	–	–	0
Juan Pretorius	8c	8c	8c	–	8c	–	8c	5	–	–	–	–	0
Jacques Verwey	7	7	7	7	7	–	–	5	3	–	–	–	15
Vincent Gwavu	6	6	–	6R	7R	6	6	6	2	–	–	–	10
JP Mostert	5	5	6	6	–	5R	5R	6	–	–	–	–	0
Jacques Alberts	4	4	4	4	4	–	4	6	–	–	–	–	0
Nico Pretorius	3	3	–	–	–	–	–	2	–	–	–	–	0
Devlin Hope	2	2	2	2	2	–	2	6	2	–	–	–	10
Thulani Ngidi	1	1	1R	1	1	–	3R	6	–	–	–	–	0
FJ Binneman	3R	2R	2R	2R	–	2R	–	5	–	–	–	–	0
David Kuatu	1R	–	1	–	–	–	–	2	–	–	–	–	0
Marlyn Williams	5R	1R	5	5	5	5	5	7	–	–	–	–	0
Friedle Olivier	8R	7R	7R	8	5R	7R	–	6	–	–	–	–	0
Anrich Richter	9R	x	9R	9R	10R	15R	9	6	3	–	–	–	15
Angus Cleophas	15R	15	15	10	15R	10R	10R	7	–	4	7	–	29
Coert Cronje	13R	12	12	12	12	–	12	6	2	–	–	–	10
Wesley Cloete	–	3R	3	3	1R	1R	–	5	–	–	–	–	0
Arno Poley	–	15R	15R	15	15	15	–	5	–	1	–	–	2
MP van Eeden	–	–	5R	–	6	8	–	3	–	–	–	–	0
Dandre vd Westhuizen	–	–	–	1R	3	1	1	4	–	–	–	–	0
Shane Kirkwood	–	–	–	5R	–	4	4R	3	1	–	–	–	5
Lukhanyo Am	–	–	–	14R	–	12R	–	2	1	–	–	–	5
Bruce Muller	–	–	–	2R	2	2R	–	3	–	–	–	–	0
Wayne Gardner	–	–	–	–	10	–	–	1	–	1	–	–	2
Ernst Ladendorf	–	–	–	–	7	7	–	2	–	–	–	–	0
Peet Vorster	–	–	–	–	3	3	–	2	1	–	–	–	5
Ryan Carmichael	–	–	–	–	–	9R	–	1	–	–	–	–	0
Etienne Taljaard	–	–	–	–	–	13R	–	1	1	–	–	–	5
34 Players								**152**	**25**	**11**	**11**	**0**	**180**

W.P. RUGBY

Western Province

'98	'99	'00	'01	'02	'03	'04	'05	'06	'07	'08	'09	'10	'11	'12	'13	'14
10th	10th	6th	6th	14th	10th	11th	5th	7th	1st	3rd	7th	7th	3rd	**1st**	4th	7th

Played	Won	Lost	Drawn	Points for	Points against	Tries for	Tries against
8	5	3	0	223	151	33	17

Date	Venue	Opponent	Result	Score	Referee	Scorers
9 Mar	Cape Town¹	Boland	WON	16-8	L Legoete	T: Williams (2) P: Van Aswegen (2).
15 Mar	Durban	Sharks XV	LOST	7-25	J van Heerden	T: Lewis. C: Van Aswegen.
22 Mar	Cape Town¹	EP Kings	WON	56-22	R Boneparte	T: Smid (3), Williams, Lewis, Lombard, Kitshoff, Notshe. C: Van Aswegen (5). P: Van Aswegen (2).
28 Mar	East London	Border	WON	29-16	C du Preez	T: Smid (2), Lewis, Williams, Roberts. C: Van Aswegen, Roberts.
5 Apr	Cape Town	Simba XV	WON	65-29	T Ntskakaza	T: Williams (4), Kitshoff (3), Du Preez (2), Van Wyk, Kotze. C: Coleman (3), Van Aswegen (2).
12 Apr	Cape Town¹	Free State XV	WON	28-15	B Crouse	T: Williams, Jones, R du Preez. C: Coleman (2). P: Coleman (3).
26 Apr	George	SWD	LOST	14-23	R Rasivhenge	T: Van Aswegen, Kitshoff. C: Du Preez (2).

QUARTER-FINAL

Date	Venue	Opponent	Result	Score	Referee	Scorers
2 May	Nelspruit	Pumas	LOST	8-13	S Geldenhuys	T: Kitshoff. P: Van Aswegen.

¹ *City Park*

Note: ■ = *Champion*

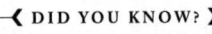

⟨ DID YOU KNOW? ⟩

Photographic evidence shows that South Africa first wore numbers on the back of their jerseys in 1906, on the first Springbok tour of the UK. Interestingly, up until 1976 the left wing wore 13 and centres 11 & 12.

2014 SQUAD

PLAYER	WP CAREER						OTHER UNIONS						VODACOM CUP TOTAL					
	A	T	C	P	DG	Pts	A	T	C	P	DG	Pts	A	T	C	P	DG	Pts
J (Justin) Ackerman	1	–	–	–	–	0	–	–	–	–	–	0	1	–	–	–	–	0
L (Liam/Tiger) Bax	10	1	–	–	–	5	–	–	–	–	–	0	10	1	–	–	–	5
E (Eital) Bredenkamp	6	–	–	–	–	0	–	–	–	–	–	0	6	–	–	–	–	0
L (Lungelo) Chonco	1	–	–	–	–	0	–	–	–	–	–	0	1	–	–	–	–	0
DG (Deacon) Chowles	4	–	–	–	–	0	–	–	–	–	–	0	4	–	–	–	–	0
SH (Stephan) Coetzee	10	–	–	–	–	0	–	–	–	–	–	0	10	–	–	–	–	0
KK (Kurt) Coleman	27	6	27	21	–	147	–	–	–	–	–	0	27	6	27	21	0	147
MR (Ridhaa) Damon	3	1	–	–	–	5	–	–	–	–	–	0	3	1	–	–	–	5
JC (Jan) de Klerk	4	–	–	–	–	0	–	–	–	–	–	0	4	–	–	–	–	0
HC (Carel) du Preez	10	2	–	–	–	10	–	–	–	–	–	0	10	2	–	–	–	10
RJ (Robert) du Preez	3	1	2	–	–	9	–	–	–	–	–	0	3	1	2	–	–	9
D (Dylon) Frylinck	5	–	–	–	–	0	–	–	–	–	–	0	5	–	–	–	–	0
MG (Taz) Fuzani	12	–	–	–	–	0	–	–	–	–	–	0	12	–	–	–	–	0
JA (Ian) Groenewald	2	–	–	–	–	0	–	–	–	–	–	0	2	–	–	–	–	0
JJ (Janco) Gunter	3	–	–	–	–	0	–	–	–	–	–	0	3	–	–	–	–	0
S (Stephan/Os) Hamman	1	–	–	–	–	0	–	–	–	–	–	0	1	–	–	–	–	0
RB (Reuben) Johannes	11	3	–	–	–	15	–	–	–	–	–	0	11	3	–	–	–	15
HRF (Huw) Jones	2	1	–	–	–	5	–	–	–	–	–	0	2	1	–	–	–	5
GJ (Gerhard) Jordaan	1	–	–	–	–	0	–	–	–	–	–	0	1	–	–	–	–	0
JM (Joshua) Katzen	1	–	–	–	–	0	–	–	–	–	–	0	1	–	–	–	–	0
M (Michael) Kennedy	3	–	–	–	–	0	–	–	–	–	–	0	3	–	–	–	–	0
R (Rohan) Kitshoff	19	13	–	–	–	65	25	5	–	–	–	25	44	18	–	–	–	90
J-B (Johnny) Kotze	6	1	–	–	–	5	–	–	–	–	–	0	6	1	–	–	–	5
JP (Jean-Paul/JP) Lewis	8	3	–	–	–	15	–	–	–	–	–	0	8	3	–	–	–	15
K (Kyle) Lombard	6	1	–	–	–	5	–	–	–	–	–	0	6	1	–	–	–	5
RJ (Renier) Marais	1	–	–	–	–	0	–	–	–	–	–	0	1	–	–	–	–	0
GHD (Godlen) Masimla	9	–	–	–	–	0	–	–	–	–	–	0	9	–	–	–	–	0
FJ (Freddie) Muller	4	–	–	–	–	0	–	–	–	–	–	0	4	–	–	–	–	0
FJ (Jean) Nel	4	–	–	–	–	0	–	–	–	–	–	0	4	–	–	–	–	0
S (Sikumbuzo) Notshe	14	3	–	–	–	15	–	–	–	–	–	0	14	3	–	–	–	15
N (Neil) Rautenbach	1	–	–	–	–	0	–	–	–	–	–	0	1	–	–	–	–	0
AD (Adrian) Roberts	2	1	1	–	–	7	–	–	–	–	–	0	2	1	1	–	–	7
JD (John/JD) Schickerling	1	–	–	–	–	0	–	–	–	–	–	0	1	–	–	–	–	0
SMS (Sti) Sithole	3	–	–	–	–	0	–	–	–	–	–	0	3	–	–	–	–	0
R (Rayn) Smid	14	7	–	–	–	35	–	–	–	–	–	0	14	7	–	–	–	35
C (Chad) Solomon	2	–	–	–	–	0	–	–	–	–	–	0	2	–	–	–	–	0
JCE (Entienne) Swanepoel	6	–	–	–	–	0	–	–	–	–	–	0	6	–	–	–	–	0
J-F (Jan) Uys	8	–	–	–	–	0	–	–	–	–	–	0	0	–	–	–	–	0
GJ (Gary) van Aswegen	11	1	14	13	2	78	–	–	–	–	–	0	11	1	14	13	2	78
MG (Michael) van der Spuy	23	5	–	–	–	25	–	–	–	–	–	0	23	5	–	–	–	25

Squad continued overleaf

VODACOM CUP

2014 SQUAD (CONT.)

PLAYER	WP CAREER						OTHER UNIONS						VODACOM CUP TOTAL					
	A	T	C	P	DG	Pts	A	T	C	P	DG	Pts	A	T	C	P	DG	Pts
CC (Chevandre) van Schoor	2	–	–	–	–	0	–	–	–	–	–	0	2	–	–	–	–	0
CJ (Christo) van Wyk	4	1	–	–	–	5	5	–	–	–	–	0	9	1	–	–	–	5
AF (Alistair) Vermaak	14	1	–	–	–	5	3	–	–	–	–	0	17	1	–	–	–	5
R (Ruan) Vermaak	1	–	–	–	–	0	–	–	–	–	–	0	1	–	–	–	–	0
ME (Michael) Willemse	8	–	–	–	–	0	–	–	–	–	–	0	8	–	–	–	–	0
DF (Devon) Williams	15	11	–	–	–	55	–	–	–	–	–	0	15	11	–	–	–	55
LT (Lihleli) Xoli	2	–	–	–	–	0	–	–	–	–	–	0	2	–	–	–	–	0

APPEARANCES & POINTS

PLAYER	Boland	Sharks XV	EP	Border	Simba XV	Free State XV	SWD	Pumas	Apps	T	C	P	DG	Pts
Liam Bax	15	15	15	10R	15	15	–	–	6	–	–	–	–	0
JP Lewis	14	14	14	14	14	14	14	14	8	3	–	–	–	15
Johnny Kotze	13	13	13	13	13	–	–	13	6	1	–	–	–	5
Michael van der Spuy	12	12	12	–	–	12	12	–	5	–	–	–	–	0
Devon Williams	11	11	11	11	11	11	–	15	7	9	–	–	–	45
Gary van Aswegen	10	10	10	10	10	–	10	10	7	1	9	5	–	38
Godlen Masimla	9	–	–	–	–	–	–	–	1	–	–	–	–	0
Rayn Smid	8	8	8	8	–	–	–	8	5	5	–	–	–	25
Sikumbuzo Notshe	7	7	7	–	–	7	7	7	6	1	–	–	–	5
Rohan Kitshoff	6c	6c	6c	6c	6c	6c	6c	6c	8	6	–	–	–	30
Jan Uys	5	5	5	5	5	4R	4R	5R	8	–	–	–	–	0
Taz Fuzani	4	4	4	–	–	4	4	4	6	–	–	–	–	0
Entienne Swanepoel	3	3	–	–	3	3	3	3	6	–	–	–	–	0
Stephan Coetzee	2	–	–	–	–	2	–	–	2	–	–	–	–	0
Alistair Vermaak	1	1	1	1	1	1	–	1	7	–	–	–	–	0
Eital Bredenkamp	2R	2	–	–	7R	8R	2R	8R	6	–	–	–	–	0
Stephan Hamman	3R	–	–	–	–	–	–	–	1	–	–	–	–	0
JD Schickerling	4R	–	–	–	–	–	–	–	1	–	–	–	–	0
Carel du Preez	8R	4R	8R	4	8	8	8	–	7	2	–	–	–	10
Reuben Johannes	6R	6R	7R	7	–	–	–	–	4	–	–	–	–	0
Dylon Frylinck	9R	9	9	9	–	–	–	9	5	–	–	–	–	0
Kyle Lombard	11R	12R	12R	12	12	–	12R	–	6	1	–	–	–	5
Chad Solomon	–	14R	–	2R	–	–	–	–	2	–	–	–	–	0
Christo van Wyk	–	3R	3	3R	3R	–	–	–	4	1	–	–	–	5
Gerhard Jordaan	–	9R	–	–	–	–	–	–	1	–	–	–	–	0
Adrian Roberts	–	10R	–	15	–	–	–	–	2	1	1	–	–	7

VODACOM CUP

APPEARANCES & POINTS

PLAYER	Boland	Sharks XV	EP Kings	Border	Simba XV	Free State XV	SWD	Pumas	Apps	T	C	P	DG	Pts
Michael Kennedy	–	–	2	2	2	–	–	–	3	–	–	–	–	0
Deacon Chowles	–	–	3R	3	–	3R	–	3R	4	–	–	–	–	0
Renier Marais	–	–	2R	–	–	–	–	–	1	–	–	–	–	0
Janco Gunter	–	–	13R	12R	–	15R	–	–	3	–	–	–	–	0
Ridhaa Damon	–	–	9R	–	–	–	–	–	1	–	–	–	–	0
Ian Groenewald	–	–	–	7R	5R	–	–	–	2	–	–	–	–	0
Freddie Muller	–	–	–	9R	9	9R	19R	–	4	–	–	–	–	0
Ruan Vermaak	–	–	–	8R	–	–	–	–	1	–	–	–	–	0
Lungelo Chonco	–	–	–	–	7	–	–	–	1	–	–	–	–	0
Jan de Klerk	–	–	–	–	4	5	5	5	4	–	–	–	–	0
Kurt Coleman	–	–	–	–	13R	10	–	–	2	–	5	3	–	19
Michael Willemse	–	–	–	–	2R	2R	2	2R	4	–	–	–	–	0
Sithembiso Sithole	–	–	–	–	1R	–	1	1R	3	–	–	–	–	0
Jean Nel	–	–	–	–	9R	9	9	9R	4	–	–	–	–	0
Huw Jones	–	–	–	–	–	13	13	–	2	1	–	–	–	5
Robert du Preez	–	–	–	–	–	12	15	13R	3	1	2	–	–	9
Chevandre van Schoor	–	–	–	–	–	14R	11	–	2	–	–	–	–	0
Lihleli Xoli	–	–	–	–	–	–	11R	11	2	–	–	–	–	0
Justin Ackerman	–	–	–	–	–	–	1R	–	1	–	–	–	–	0
Joshua Katzen	–	–	–	–	–	–	8R	–	1	–	–	–	–	0
Neil Rautenbach	–	–	–	–	–	–	–	2	1	–	–	–	–	0
47 Players									**176**	**33**	**17**	**8**	**0**	**223**

〈 DID YOU KNOW? 〉
The first-ever Springbok substitutes were Tiny Neethling, Don Walton, HO de Villiers and Piet Uys, who warmed the bench against the 1968 British Lions.

It's WP by a whisker!

Newlands faithful rewarded after 13-year wait

By Simon Borchardt, Editor: SA Rugby magazine

THE repositioning of the Absa Currie Cup as an important development tournament, rather than one that determines which team has bragging rights over the summer, was confirmed in 2014.

No sooner had the Castle Lager Rugby Championship ended than the South African Rugby Union (SARU) announced that its 20 contracted Springboks would play no part in the latter stages of the Currie Cup – as they usually would have done – and instead attend a training camp in Stellenbosch. For the first time in a non-World Cup year, therefore, Currie Cup teams would not be at full-strength for the play-off stage.

The reaction from fans on social media was overwhelmingly positive. After a year in which they had played Vodacom Super Rugby, the June Incoming Tests and the Rugby Championship, the Springboks clearly needed a break before their four-match end-of-year tour, while their absence allowed other players to excel in South Africa's premier domestic competition and put themselves in contention for Super Rugby selection.

The main criticism of SARU's decision was that they should have used common sense and allowed certain contracted Springboks to play in the Currie Cup. JJ Engelbrecht, for example, was called up to the training camp despite not having played Test rugby in 2014 and despite being in serious need of game time of any sort. On the other hand, Handré Pollard, the Springboks' first-choice flyhalf, was released to play for the Blue Bulls, as he did not have a national contract.

SARU, though, probably found it easier to withdraw all the contracted Springboks rather than release some players – a move which would have pleased some unions and upset others.

In recent years, Currie Cup crowds have been below par during the regular season, when the Rugby Championship takes centre stage, only for the fans to flock back for the full-strength play-offs when the Springboks are available. Even without the Test stars present, that was again the case in 2014, with 35,523 and 29,857 people attending the semi-finals at Ellis Park and Newlands respectively, and 44,505 the Cape Town final.

While the decider between DHL Western Province and the Xerox Golden Lions

ABSA CURRIE CUP

The Currie Cup will spend 2015 in the Western Province trophy cabinet.

lacked the intensity of the 2013 final – when WP and the Sharks selected their Springboks – it made up for it in tension and drama.

There was no doubt that the best two teams in the tournament had reached the final. WP had topped the Premier Division log after winning eight of their 10 matches, with the Lions finishing second with seven victories.

Both teams had played entertaining rugby throughout the tournament. The Lions scored 44 tries during the league stage and then another six in the 50-20 semi-final thrashing of the Sharks. WP crossed the line 40 times during the regular season, and scored three tries in the 31-23 semi-final win against the Blue Bulls.

The final was too close to call. WP had beaten the Lions 27-14 at Newlands, but had lost 35-33 in the return fixture at Ellis Park. Province would have home-ground advantage, but many believed the Lions had played the better rugby during the tournament and would prove that an expansive, ball-in hand approach could produce silverware.

The Lions, though, failed to take into account the nature of a pressure-cooker final and by half-time they found themselves 13-0 behind. The visitors played too much rugby in their own half and behind the gainline, instead of looking for field position and then putting pressure on the opposition. That is what WP did to great effect, with Demetri Catrakilis showing why he had been preferred at flyhalf ahead of Kurt Coleman, a player more suited to an expansive approach.

Two Catrakilis penalties and a Jaco Taute five-pointer saw WP take charge, but the Lions fought back well, with a couple of Marnitz Boshoff penalties and a counter-attacking try, started and finished by Jaco van der Walt, levelling the scores after 57 minutes.

Another two penalties from Catrakilis and a long-range effort from Ruan Combrinck made it 19-16, before Boshoff had a chance to take the game into extra time with a 40-metre penalty on the right-hand touchline. The flyhalf had uncharacteristically missed three earlier penalty goal attempts, and as his fourth went wide of the left-hand upright,

Province players and fans began to celebrate their second title in three years and 33rd overall.

The victory was particularly satisfying for WP captain Juan de Jongh, who enjoyed an outstanding campaign at outside centre and became the first player of colour to lift the golden trophy, and coach Allister Coetzee, who had been heavily criticised during the Stormers' disappointing Super Rugby campaign.

Apart from the Springboks' withdrawal, the 2014 Currie Cup Premier Division will be remembered for another change in format. The number of teams increased from six to eight (having been reduced from eight to six at the end of the 2011 season), with the addition of the Eastern Province Kings – now a Super Rugby anchor union – and Griquas, who finished top of the log in the qualifying tournament, with six wins out of six, including a 33-32 victory over their closest rivals, the Leopards, in Kimberley.

The eight Premier Division teams were divided into two groups, based on their 2013 positions, with Western Province, the Golden Lions, Blue Bulls and EP Kings in Section X and the Sharks, Free State Cheetahs, Pumas and Griquas in Section Y. Teams played those in their section twice, home and away, and those in the other section once, either home or away. It soon become apparent that WP and the Lions were the teams to beat and it was no surprise when they went on to reach the final.

The Sharks, who had won the South African Super Rugby conference trophy that these days determines the best domestic team, missed their Springbok contingent and while they finished third on the log they never looked like defending their title. The Blue Bulls, with Frans Ludeke back as their Currie Cup coach, made a poor start to the tournament before sneaking into the semi-finals, while the Cheetahs won just three matches to finish fifth.

The Pumas initially impressed upon their return to the top flight, winning four of their first five games – including two against the Cheetahs, home and away, and against the Sharks, in Nelspruit – but fell away badly during the cross-section matches when their lack of depth was exposed.

The EP Kings were the biggest disappointment, winning just one match, but because of their Super Rugby anchor union status, it is Griquas, who finished 10 log points clear of the Kings, who will play in the qualifying tournament in 2015.

- *In the six-team First Division, the Leopards topped the log after winning eight of their 10 matches, only to suffer a shock 34-21 home semi-final defeat to the fourth-placed Valke in Potchefstroom.*

    The men from Kempton Park then travelled to Welkom for a final against the second-placed Griffons, who had edged the SWD Eagles 45-43 in their semi-final.

    Both sides would score two tries in an entertaining final, with scrumhalf Boela Abrahams' 73rd-minute drop goal ensuring Griffons captain Nicky Steyn lifted the trophy. Abrahams' reward was an invitation to attend the Springboks' pre-tour training camp in Stellenbosch.

- *In the domestic age-group finals* [see junior provincial pages for a comprehensive review and statistics], *played as curtain-raisers to the Currie Cup final at Newlands, the Blue Bulls Under-21s scored two late tries to beat Western Province 20-10, while the WP U19s crossed the line with four minutes remaining to claim a 33-26 win against the Blue Bulls.*

ABSA CURRIE CUP – PREMIER DIVISION
LOG

Team	P	W	L	D	PF	PA	PD	TF	TA	BP	Pts
Western Province	10	8	2	0	335	206	129	40	23	7	39
Golden Lions	10	7	3	0	362	206	156	44	21	8	36
KZN Sharks	10	7	2	1	287	222	65	26	20	3	33
Blue Bulls	10	6	4	0	271	235	36	27	23	4	28
Free State Cheetahs	10	3	6	1	249	294	-45	28	33	7	21
Mpumalanga Pumas	10	4	6	0	237	269	-32	25	28	4	20
Griqualand West	10	3	7	0	220	332	-112	25	41	4	16
Eastern Province Kings	10	1	9	0	206	403	-197	27	53	2	6

LEADING SCORERS

50 POINTS OR MORE

		T	C	P	DG	Pts
Jacques-Louis Potgieter	Blue Bulls	0	15	31	0	123
Demetri Catrakilis	WP	0	30	20	1	123
Ruan Combrinck	Golden Lions	6	20	12	0	106
Justin van Staden	Pumas	3	11	21	0	100
Willie du Plessis	Free State	2	15	18	1	97
Fred Zeilinga	Sharks	1	6	24	0	89
Lionel Cronje	Sharks	1	12	14	0	71
Marnitz Boshoff	Golden Lions	0	13	14	1	71
Gouws Prinsloo	Griquas	0	3	15	0	51

5 TRIES OR MORE

9	Jaco Kriel	Golden Lions	5	Cheslin Kolbe	WP
7	Marnus Schoeman	Griquas	5	Ederies Arendse	Griquas
7	Sarel Pretorius	Free State	5	Kobus van Wyk	WP
6	Ruan Combrinck	Golden Lions	5	Shane Gates	EP Kings
6	Juan de Jongh	WP			

PLAY-OFF RESULTS

SEMI-FINALS:
Golden Lions bt Sharks 50-20 (Johannesburg). **Western Province bt Blue Bulls 31-23** (Cape Town)
2014 ABSA CURRIE CUP FINAL:
DHL Newlands, Cape Town, Saturday 25 October 2014. Referee: Craig Joubert. Crowd: 44 505
WP 19 (13) *(Try: Taute. Conversion: Catrakilis. Penalties: Catrakilis 4)*
Golden Lions 16 (0) *(Try: Van der Walt. Conversion: Boshoff. Penalties: Boshoff 2, Combrinck)*
WP: Cheslin Kolbe, Kobus van Wyk, Juan de Jongh *(Capt)*, Jaco Taute, Seabelo Senatla, Demetri Catrakilis *(Kurt Coleman, 75)*, Nick Groom, Nizaam Carr, Michael Rhodes *(Sikhumbuszo Notshe, 77)*, Rynhardt Elstadt, Manuel Carizza *(Gerbrandt Grobler, 49-51, 70)* Jean Kleyn, Pat Cilliers *(Brok Harris, 51)*, Scarra Ntubeni *(Neil Rautenbach, 70)*, Alistair Vermaak. UNUSED SUBS: Louis Schreuder, Michael van der Spuy.
Golden Lions: Jaco van der Walt, Ruan Combrinck, Lionel Mapoe, Howard Mnisi *(Harold Vorster, 67)*, Courtnall Skosan, Marnitz Boshoff, Ross Conje *(Mark Richards, 75)*, Warren Whiteley *(Capt)*, Derick Minnie *(Warwick Tecklenburg, 64)*, Jaco Kriel *(Kwagga Smith, 64)*, Franco Mostert, Martin Muller *(Willie Britz, 64)*, Ruan Dreyer *(Julian Redelinghuys, 53)*, Robbie Coetzee *(Akker van der Merwe, 59)*, Schalk van der Merwe.

ABSA CURRIE CUP

Records

CHAMPIONS

1892	Western Province	1956	Northern Transvaal	1989	Northern Transvaal
1894	Western Province	1957-59	Western Province		& Western Province
1895	Western Province	1964	Western Province	1990	Natal
1897	Western Province	1966	Western Province	1991	Northern Transvaal
1898	Western Province	1968	Northern Transvaal	1992	Natal
1899	Griqualand West	1969	Northern Transvaal	1993	Transvaal
1904	Western Province	1970	Griqualand West	1994	Transvaal
1906	Western Province	1971	Northern Transvaal	1995	Natal
1908	Western Province		& Transvaal	1996	Natal
1911	Griqualand West	1972	Transvaal	1997	Western Province
1914	Western Province	1973	Northern Transvaal	1998	Blue Bulls
1920	Western Province	1974	Northern Transvaal	1999	Golden Lions
1922	Transvaal	1975	Northern Transvaal	2000	Western Province
1925	Western Province	1976	Orange Free State	2001	Western Province
1927	Western Province	1977	Northern Transvaal	2002	Blue Bulls
1929	Western Province	1978	Northern Transvaal	2003	Blue Bulls
1932	Western Province	1979	Northern Transvaal	2004	Blue Bulls
	& Border		& Western Province	2005	Free State
1934	Western Province	1980	Northern Transvaal	2006	Free State & Blue Bulls
	& Border	1981	Northern Transvaal	2007	Free State
1936	Western Province	1982	Western Province	2008	Sharks
1939	Transvaal	1983	Western Province	2009	Blue Bulls
1946	Northern Transvaal	1984	Western Province	2010	Sharks
1947	Western Province	1985	Western Province	2011	Golden Lions
1950	Transvaal	1986	Western Province	2012	Western Province
1952	Transvaal	1987	Northern Transvaal	2013	Sharks
1954	Western Province	1988	Northern Transvaal	2014	Western Province

Note: Western Province won the SA Rugby Board Trophy at the tournament in Kimberley in 1889

MOST TITLES

33	Western Province (four times shared)	last 2014		4	Free State (once shared)	last 2007
23	N Tvl/Blue Bulls (four times shared)	last 2009		3	Griqualand West	last 1970
10	Transvaal/Golden Lions (once shared)	last 2011		2	Border (twice shared)	last 1934
7	Natal/Sharks	last 2013				

⟨ DID YOU KNOW? ⟩
The most conversions in a Currie Cup final is 6 – Gavin Johnson for Transvaal (56-33 vs Free State in 1994).

ABSA CURRIE CUP

FINAL RECORDS

Most points scored by a team
56   Transvaal vs Free State (1994, score 56-33)

Most tries scored by a team
7   Lions vs Free State on 1 October 1994

Most points scored by a player
26   Derick Hougaard, Blue Bulls vs Lions, 2002 (1try, 5 penalties, 2 drop goals)

Most conversions scored by a player
6   Gavin Johnson, Lions vs Cheetahs, 1994

Most penalty goals scored by a player
6   Thierry Lacroix, Natal vs WP, 1995
6   Patrick Lambie, Sharks vs WP, 2012

Most drop goals scored by a player
4   Naas Botha, Northern Transvaal vs Transvaal, 1987

Most appearances in finals

11	Burger Geldenhuys	Northern Transvaal	1977-1989
11	Naas Botha	Northern Transvaal	1977-1991

Most points scored by a player in finals

138	Naas Botha	1t, 10c, 20p, 18dg	1977-1991

Most tries scored by a player in finals

4	Ettienne Botha	Blue Bulls	2003-2004

Oldest and youngest winning captains

35 years 138 days	Thys Lourens	Northern Transvaal	1978
22 years 217 days	Naas Botha	Northern Transvaal	1980

Most wins as Coach

11 *	Brigadier Buurman van Zyl	Northern Transvaal	1968-1981

* including two draws

Most finals as a referee
7   Andre Watson (Valke/SARU)

Youngest winning coach
32 years 351 days   Johan Erasmus (FS Cheetahs in 2005)

YOUNGEST WINNING COACH — 32 YEARS 351 DAYS — J Erasmus FS Cheetahs 2005

MATCH RECORDS

Most points scored by a team

147	Blue Bulls vs SWD (147-8)		1996

Biggest winning margin by a team

139	Blue Bulls vs SWD (147-8)		1996

Most tries by a team

23	Blue Bulls vs SWD (147-8)		1996

Most points by a player

46	Jannie de Beer (3t, 14c, 1p)	FS vs NFS	1997

ABSA CURRIE CUP

Most tries tries by a player
7	Jacques Olivier	Blue Bulls vs SWD (147-8)	1996

Most conversions by a player
14	Tjaart Marais	W-Tvl vs Eastern Free State	1988
14	MJ Smith	Free State vs SWD	1996
14	Lance Sherrell	Blue Bulls vs SWD	1996
14	Jannie de Beer	FS vs NFS	1997
14	Nel Fourie	Pumas vs SWD	2001

Most penalty goals by a player
9	Eric Herbert	NFS vs Valke	
9	Derick Hougaard	BB vs WP	

Five drop goals by a player
5	Naas Botha	N Transvaal vs Natal	1992

SEASON RECORDS

Most points by a team
792	Natal	15 matches	1996

Most tries by a team
112	Natal	15 matches	1996

Most points by a player
268	Johan Heunis	N Transvaal	1989

Most tries by a player
21	Bjorn Basson	Griquas	2010

Most conversions by a player
62	Louis Koen	WP	1997

Most penalties by a player
50	Willem de Waal	WP	2010

Most drop goals by a player
20	Naas Botha	N Transvaal	1985

MOST MATCHES IN A CAREER 156 J Botes Pumas & Sharks 2002-2014

CAREER RECORDS

Most matches
156	Jacques Botes	Pumas & Sharks	2002-2014

Most points
1699	Naas Botha	N Transvaal	1977-1992

Most tries
77	John Daniels	Boland & Lions	1998-2008

Most drop goals
135	Naas Botha	Northern Transvaal	1977-1992

ABSA CURRIE CUP

CURRIE CUP FINAL PLAYERS 1939 - 2014

	PLAYER	Province	First & last final	Matches	Won	Lost	Drawn	Winning %
1	Ackermann DSP (Dawie)	Western Province	1954	1	1	0	0	100%
2	Adams HJ (Heini)	Blue Bulls	2006	1	0	0	1	0%
3	Aitken AD (Andrew)	Natal	1990, 97	2	2	0	0	100%
4	Alberts FNF (Frannie)	Northern Transvaal	1969-70	2	1	1	0	50%
5	Alberts WS (Willem)	Natal	2010-13	4	2	2	0	50%
6	Allan J (John)	Natal	1992-93, 95	3	2	1	0	67%
7	Anderson W (Billy)	Western Province	1939	1	0	1	0	0%
8	Andrews KS (Keith)	Western Province	1986, 88, 97	3	2	1	0	67%
9	Andrews MG (Mark)	Natal	1993, 95-96, 00	4	2	2	0	50%
10	Aplon GG (Gio)	Western Province	2010, 12-13	3	1	2	0	33%
11	Armand D (Don)	Western Province	2012	1	1	0	0	100%
12	Arnold P (Peet)	Western Province	1997	1	1	0	0	100%
13	Atherton S (Steve)	Natal	1990, 92-93, 96, 99	5	3	2	0	60%
14	Aucamp C (Cobus)	Natal	1984	1	0	1	0	0%
15	Aucamp JJ (Floors)	Northern Transvaal	1973	1	1	0	0	100%
16	Badenhorst AJ (Adri)	Western Province	2000	1	1	0	0	100%
17	Badenhorst C (Chris)	Orange Free State	1994, 97	2	0	2	0	0%
18	Badenhorst CJ	Transvaal	1939	1	1	0	0	100%
19	Badenhorst DS (Daan)	Transvaal	1986-87	2	0	2	0	0%
20	Bands RE (Richard)	Blue Bulls	2002, 04	2	2	0	0	100%
21	Barnard JH (Jannie)	Transvaal	1968-69, 71	3	0	2	1	0%
22	Barnard RW (Robbie)	Transvaal	1968, 71	2	0	1	1	0%
23	Barrit BM (Bradley)	Natal	2008	1	1	0	0	100%
24	Barry D (De Wet)	Western Province	2000-01	2	2	0	0	100%
25	Bartmann WJ (Wahl)	Transvaal	1986-87, 90, 92-93	5	2	3	0	40%
26	Basson S (Stefan)	Blue Bulls	2006	1	0	0	1	0%
27	Basson WW (Wium)	Blue Bulls	1998	1	1	0	0	100%
28	Bates AJ (Albie)	Northern Transvaal	1973-74	2	2	0	0	100%
29	Bayvel PCR (Paul)	Transvaal	1972, 74	2	1	1	0	50%
30	Beck JJ (Colin)	Western Province	1980, 82	2	1	1	0	50%
31	Bekker H (Manie)	Western Province	1947	1	1	0	0	100%
32	Bekker HJ (Hennie)	Orange Free State	1977-80, 82-85	8	4	3	1	50%
33	Bekker HPJ (Jaap)	Northern Transvaal	1954	1	0	1	0	0%
34	Bekker MJ (Martiens)	Northern Transvaal	1954, 56	2	1	1	0	50%
35	Bekker RP (Dolf)	Northern Transvaal	1956	1	1	0	0	100%
36	Bekker S (Schutte)	Blue Bulls	1998	1	1	0	0	100%
37	Benade JJ	Transvaal	1939	1	1	0	0	100%
38	Beneke JI (Izak)	Northern Transvaal	1983	1	0	1	0	0%
39	Benjamin RS (Ryno)	Golden Lions	2007	1	0	1	0	0%
40	Bennet RG (Russell)	Natal	1999	1	0	1	0	0%
41	Bestbier A (André)	Orange Free State	1973	1	0	1	0	0%
42	Bester F	Boland	1952	1	0	1	0	0%
43	Bester J	Western Province	1939	1	0	1	0	0%
44	Beukes JHT (Joe)	Orange Free State	1994	1	0	1	0	0%
45	Beyers N (Nellis)	Western Province	1946	1	0	1	0	0%
46	Bezuidenhoudt NSE (Nic)	Northern Transvaal	1975, 77	2	2	0	0	100%

CURRIE CUP FINAL PLAYERS 1939 - 2014

	PLAYER	Province	First & last final	Matches	Won	Lost	Drawn	Winning %
47	Bezuidenhout MJ (Martin)	Transvaal	2011	1	1	0	0	100%
48	Bierman P (Peet)	Eastern Transvaal	1972	1	0	1	0	0%
49	Blair R (Robbie)	Western Province	1979-80	2	0	1	1	0%
50	Blakeway AD (Andrew)	Natal	1992-93	2	1	1	0	50%
51	Blom LF (Louis)	Western Province	1995, 97	2	1	1	0	50%
52	Boer P (Piet)	Blue Bulls	1998	1	1	0	0	100%
53	Bolton WJC (Willie)	Orange Free State	1981	1	0	1	0	0%
54	Bolus RVM (Rob)	Western Province	1980	1	0	1	0	0%
55	Bondesio M (Michael)	Transvaal	2011	1	1	0	0	100%
56	Boome CS (Selborne)	Western Province	1998	1	0	1	0	0%
57	Booyens V (Vic)	Northern Transvaal	1973	1	1	0	0	100%
58	Booysen J (Jaco)	Golden Lions	2002	1	0	1	0	0%
59	Bosch GR (Gerald)	Transvaal	1972, 74	2	1	1	0	50%
60	Bosch PW (Paul)	Western Province	2010	1	0	1	0	0%
61	Bosch RG	Transvaal	1947	1	0	1	0	0%
62	Boshoff JH (Jannie)	Golden Lions	2007	1	0	1	0	0%
63	Boshoff L (Leon)	Golden Lions	1999	1	1	0	0	100%
64	Boshoff ML (Marnitz)	Golden Lions	2014	1	0	1	0	0%
65	Bosman HM (Meyer)	Free State	2005-07, 09, 12	5	2	2	1	40%
66	Bosman P (Piet)	Transvaal	1968, 72	2	1	1	0	50%
67	Botes LJ (Jacques)	Natal	2008, 10, 13	3	3	0	0	100%
68	Botes PJ (Paul)	Northern Transvaal	1985	1	0	1	0	0%
69	Botha A (Attie)	Northern Transvaal	1946	1	1	0	0	100%
70	Botha AA (André)	Natal	1984, 90	2	1	1	0	50%
71	Botha BJ	Natal	2003	1	0	1	0	0%
72	Botha DS (Darius)	Northern Transvaal	1978-82	5	3	1	1	60%
73	Botha E (Ettienne)	Blue Bulls	2003-04	2	2	0	0	100%
74	Botha G v G (Gary)	Blue Bulls	2002-06	5	3	1	1	60%
75	Botha HE (Naas)	Northern Transvaal	1977-81, 85, 87-91	11	7	2	2	64%
76	Botha JF (Jan)	Northern Transvaal	1946	1	1	0	0	100%
77	Botha JF (Johan)	Orange Free State	1973	1	0	1	0	0%
78	Botha JJ (Koos)	Transvaal	1952	1	1	0	0	100%
79	Botha JP (Bakkies)	Blue Bulls	2002, 04-05, 09	4	3	1	0	75%
80	Bothma A (Arnold)	Transvaal	1974	1	0	1	0	0%
81	Boyes RE	Western Province	1950	1	0	1	0	0%
82	Brand CP (Piet)	Northern Transvaal	1969-70	2	1	1	0	50%
83	Breedt JC (Jannie)	Northern Transvaal	1981-83, 86-87, 91-92	7	1	6	0	14%
84	Breedt N (Nico)	Free State	2009	1	0	1	0	0%
85	Bresler A (Anton)	Natal	2010, 12	2	1	1	0	50%
86	Brewis JD (Hansie)	Northern Transvaal	1946, 54	2	1	1	0	50%
87	Breytenbach CL (Conrad)	Blue Bulls	1998	1	1	0	0	100%
88	Brink RA (Rob)	Western Province	1995, 00	2	1	1	0	50%
89	Brink S (Stephen)	Natal	2000	1	0	1	0	0%
90	Brits J (Johan)	Eastern Transvaal	1972	1	0	1	0	0%
91	Britz GJJ (Gerrie)	Free State	2004	1	0	1	0	0%
92	Britz S (Stefan)	Blue Bulls	1998	1	1	0	0	100%

CURRIE CUP FINAL PLAYERS 1939 - 2014

	PLAYER	Province	First & last final	Matches	Won	Lost	Drawn	Winning %
93	Britz WS (Willie)	Golden Lions	2014	1	0	1	0	0%
94	Britz WK (Warren)	Natal	1999, 01	2	0	2	0	0%
95	Broderick F (Frans)	Transvaal	1952	1	1	0	0	100%
96	Brooks JZ (Jannie)	Blue Bulls	1998	1	1	0	0	100%
97	Brosnihan WG (Warren)	Natal	2000-01, 04	3	1	2	0	33%
98	Brown CG (Cliffie)	Northern Transvaal	1982	1	0	1	0	0%
99	Brunow HL (Harry)	Western Province	1939	1	0	1	0	0%
100	Brüssow HW (Heinrich)	Free State	2006-07, 09	3	1	1	1	33%
101	Buchler JU (Johnny)	Transvaal	1950	1	1	0	0	100%
102	Burden C B (Craig)	Natal	2010-12	3	1	2	0	33%
103	Burger J (Hannes)	Northern Transvaal	1956	1	1	0	0	100%
104	Burger J (Jan)	Boland	1952	1	0	1	0	0%
105	Burger JM (Kobus)	Western Province	1985, 88-89	3	1	1	1	33%
106	Burger MB (Thys)	Northern Transvaal	1978-81	4	3	0	1	75%
107	Burger NJ (Niel)	Western Province	1982, 84-85	3	3	0	0	100%
108	Burger PB (Philip)	Free State	2005-06	2	1	0	1	50%
109	Burger SW (Schalk) snr	Western Province	1985, 88	2	1	1	0	50%
110	Burger SWP (Schalk) jnr	Western Province	2010, 13	2	0	2	0	0%
111	Burger SWP (Schalk) snr	Western Province	1984-86	3	3	0	0	100%
112	Butler BL (Basil)	Western Province	1946	1	0	1	0	0%
113	Cabannes L (Laurent)	Western Province	1995	1	0	1	0	0%
114	Calldo JG (Cobus)	Free State	2007	1	1	0	0	100%
115	Carey F (Fraser)	Transvaal	1947	1	0	1	0	0%
116	Carizza M (Manuel)	Western Province	2014	1	1	0	0	100%
117	Carr N (Nizaam)	Western Province	2014	1	1	0	0	100%
118	Carstens P-D (Deon)	Natal	2001, 03, 08, 12	4	2	2	0	50%
119	Carstens W (Cassie)	Western Province	1998	1	0	1	0	0%
120	Catrakilis D (Demetri)	Western Province	2012-14	3	2	1	0	67%
121	Cilliers PM (Pat)	Golden Lions	2011, 13-14	3	2	1	0	67%
122	Claassen K (Koos)	Transvaal	1968	1	0	1	0	0%
123	Claassen W (Wynand)	Northern Transvaal	1975, 77, 79, 84	4	2	1	1	50%
124	Claassens JH (Jacques)	Free State	2004	1	0	1	0	0%
125	Claassens JP (Jannie)	Northern Transvaal	1990-91	2	1	1	0	50%
126	Claassens M (Michael)	Free State	2004-06	3	1	1	1	33%
127	Clarke TA (Bossie)	Western Province	1976, 79-80	3	0	2	1	0%
128	Cloete A (Abe)	Northern Transvaal	1954	1	0	1	0	0%
129	Cockrell CH (Charlie)	Western Province	1969	1	0	1	0	0%
130	Cockrell RJ (Robert)	Western Province	1976, 80	2	0	2	0	0%
131	Cockrell WJ (William)	Western Province	1986	1	1	0	0	100%
132	Coetzee D (Danie)	Blue Bulls	2002, 04-05	3	2	1	0	67%
133	Coetzee DA (Deon)	Northern Transvaal	1982	1	0	1	0	0%
134	Coetzee EL (Eduard)	Natal	2003	1	0	1	0	0%
135	Coetzee J (Johan)	Eastern Transvaal	1972	1	0	1	0	0%
136	Coetzee JH (Johan)	Orange Free State	1981	1	0	1	0	0%
137	Coetzee JHH (Jan-Boland)	Western Province	1969, 76, 79	3	0	2	1	0%
138	Coetzee JJ (Jaco)	Orange Free State	1994	1	0	1	0	0%

CURRIE CUP FINAL PLAYERS 1939 - 2014

	PLAYER	Province	First & last final	Matches	Won	Lost	Drawn	Winning %
139	Coetzee JL (Koot)	Northern Transvaal	1978	1	1	0	0	100%
140	Coetzee MC (Marcell)	Natal	2011-13	3	1	2	0	33%
141	Coetzee RL (Robbie)	Golden Lions	2014	1	0	1	0	0%
142	Coetzer JH (Joe)	Transvaal	1974	1	0	1	0	0%
143	Coleman KK (Kurt)	Western Province	2013-14	2	1	1	0	50%
144	Combrinck GJ (Gerhard)	Transvaal	1994	1	1	0	0	100%
145	Combrinck J (James)	Griquas	1970	1	1	0	0	100%
146	Combrinck RJ (Ruan)	Golden Lions	2014	1	0	1	0	0%
147	Conradie JHJ (Bolla)	Western Province	2001	1	1	0	0	100%
148	Cooper KL (Kyle)	Natal	2012-13	2	1	1	0	50%
149	Craig BK (Pat)	Transvaal	1947	1	0	1	0	0%
150	Cronjé G (Geo)	Blue Bulls	2002-03	2	2	0	0	100%
151	Cronjé J (Jacques)	Blue Bulls	2003-05, 07	4	2	2	0	50%
152	Cronjé L (Lionel)	Western Province	2010	1	0	1	0	0%
153	Cronje PA (Peter)	Transvaal	1971-72	2	1	0	1	50%
154	Cronjé R (Ross)	Natal	2011, 14	2	0	2	0	0%
155	Cupido W (Wilfred)	Western Province	1983	1	1	0	0	100%
156	Dalton J (James)	Transvaal	1996	1	0	1	0	0%
157	Daniel KR (Keegan)	Natal	2008, 10-13	5	3	2	0	60%
158	Daniels JI (John)	Golden Lions	2002	1	0	1	0	0%
159	Daniller HJ (Hennie)	Free State	2009	1	0	1	0	0%
160	Dannhauser G (Gert)	Transvaal	1947, 50	2	1	1	0	50%
161	Dannhauser T (Toy)	Transvaal	1968	1	0	1	0	0%
162	Davids Q (Quinton)	Western Province	2000-01	2	2	0	0	100%
163	Davidson CD (Craig)	Natal	1999-03	4	0	4	0	0%
164	Dawson M (Murray)	Natal	1984	1	0	1	0	0%
165	De Allende D (Damian)	Western Province	2012-13	2	1	1	0	50%
166	De Beer JH (Jannie)	Free State	1997	1	0	1	0	0%
167	De Beer MC	Northern Transvaal	1954	1	0	1	0	0%
168	De Beer RC (Ski-Hi)	Northern Transvaal	1954, 56	2	1	1	0	50%
169	De Bruyn MJ (Tewis)	Free State	2007, 09	2	1	1	0	50%
170	De Jager SHF (Frans)	Northern Transvaal	1956	1	1	0	0	100%
171	De Jongh JL (Juan)	Western Province	2010, 12-14	4	2	2	0	50%
172	De Klerk IJ (Sakkie)	Transvaal	1968	1	0	1	0	0%
173	De Klerk KBH (Kevin)	Transvaal	1971-72, 74	3	1	1	1	33%
174	De Klerk PR (Rossouw)	Blue Bulls	2009	1	1	0	0	100%
175	De Klerk WP (Moffie)	Northern Transvaal	1973	1	1	0	0	100%
176	De Kock C (Con)	Western Province	1946	1	0	1	0	0%
177	De Kock D (Deon)	Golden Lions	2002	1	0	1	0	0%
178	De Kock NA (Neil)	Western Province	2001	1	1	0	0	100%
179	De Meyer OA (Oeloff)	Northern Transvaal	1969, 75	2	2	0	0	100%
180	De Villiers AP (Apie)	Western Province	1939	1	0	1	0	0%
181	De Villiers DJ (David)	Free State	2009	1	0	1	0	0%
182	De Villiers H (Dirkie)	Western Province	1947	1	1	0	0	100%
183	De Villiers HO	Western Province	1969	1	0	1	0	0%
184	De Villiers J (Hannes)	Northern Transvaal	1946	1	1	0	0	100%

CURRIE CUP FINAL PLAYERS 1939 - 2014

	PLAYER	Province	First & last final	Matches	Won	Lost	Drawn	Winning %
185	De Villiers J (Jean)	Western Province	2010, 13	2	0	2	0	0%
186	De Vos DJJ (Dirk)	Transvaal	1968, 73-74	3	2	1	0	67%
187	De Waal W (Willem)	Free State	2004-07, 10	5	2	2	1	40%
188	De Wet A (Bertie)	Western Province	1983-84	2	2	0	0	100%
189	De Wet DJ (Daan)	Orange Free State	1973	1	0	1	0	0%
190	De Wet P	Western Province	1939	1	0	1	0	0%
191	De Wet PJ (Piet)	Western Province	1939	1	0	1	0	0%
192	Delaporte C (Dollie)	Transvaal	1939	1	1	0	0	100%
193	Delport GM (Thinus)	Golden Lions	1999	1	1	0	0	100%
194	Delport M (Marius)	Blue Bulls	2006, 08	2	0	1	1	0%
195	Demas D (Danwel)	Free State	2009	1	0	1	0	0%
196	Dercksen B (Bennie)	Eastern Transvaal	1972	1	0	1	0	0%
197	Des Dountain D (Dylan)	Transvaal	2011	1	1	0	0	100%
198	Deuchar B (Butch)	Western Province	1976	1	0	1	0	0%
199	Deysel JR (Jean)	Natal	2008, 11-12	3	1	2	0	33%
200	Dirks CA (Chris)	Transvaal	1993	1	1	0	0	100%
201	Dixon PJ (Peter)	Western Province	2000-01	2	2	0	0	100%
202	Dorrington I (Ivor)	Western Province	1954	1	1	0	0	100%
203	Downes G (Graham)	Natal	1984	1	0	1	0	0%
204	Dreyer JN (Jannie)	Northern Transvaal	1983	1	0	1	0	0%
205	Dreyer KL (Kon)	Transvaal	1972	1	1	0	0	100%
206	Dreyer RM (Ruan)	Golden Lions	2014	1	0	1	0	0%
207	Drotské AE (Naka)	Orange Free State	1994-97, 04-05	4	1	3	0	25%
208	Dryburgh RG (Roy)	Western Province	1950, 54, 56	3	1	2	0	33%
209	Du Plessis AJ (Tiny)	Orange Free State	1976	1	1	0	0	100%
210	Du Plessis BW (Bismarck)	Natal	2008, 10-11, 13	4	3	1	0	75%
211	Du Plessis CJ (Carel)	Western Province	1982-84, 86-89	7	4	2	1	57%
212	Du Plessis DC (Daan)	Northern Transvaal	1973-75, 77-79	6	5	0	1	83%
213	Du Plessis DF (Francois)	Northern Transvaal	1991	1	1	0	0	100%
214	Du Plessis F (Felix)	Transvaal	1947	1	0	1	0	0%
215	Du Plessis F (Francois)	Northern Transvaal	1982-83	2	0	2	0	0%
216	Du Plessis JN (Jannie)	Free State	2005-08, 10-13	8	5	2	1	63%
217	Du Plessis M (Morné)	Western Province	1976, 79	2	0	1	1	0%
218	Du Plessis M (Thys)	Western Province	1950	1	0	1	0	0%
219	Du Plessis MJ (Michael)	Western Province	1982, 84-85, 87-89	6	3	2	1	50%
220	Du Plessis PG (Piet)	Northern Transvaal	1971	1	0	0	1	0%
221	Du Plessis TD (Tommy)	Northern Transvaal	1975, 77-82, 85	8	5	2	1	63%
222	Du Plessis W (Willie)	Western Province	1979-80, 82	3	1	1	1	33%
223	Du Plooy TJ (Boela)	Free State	2004	1	0	1	0	0%
224	Du Preez FCH (Frik)	Northern Transvaal	1968-71	4	2	1	1	50%
225	Du Preez GJD (Delarey)	Golden Lions	2002	1	0	1	0	0%
226	Du Preez PF (Fourie) jnr	Blue Bulls	2003-05, 08-09	5	3	2	0	60%
227	Du Preez PF (Fourie) snr	Northern Transvaal	1968-70	3	2	1	0	67%
228	Du Preez RJ (Robert)	Northern Transvaal	1988-92	5	3	1	1	60%
229	Du Preez WH (Wian)	Free State	2005-07, 09	4	2	1	1	50%
230	Du Rand D (Salty)	Transvaal	1974	1	0	1	0	0%

CURRIE CUP FINAL PLAYERS 1939 - 2014

	PLAYER	Province	First & last final	Matches	Won	Lost	Drawn	Winning %
231	Du Rand HGJ (Hennie)	Northern Transvaal	1968, 75	2	2	0	0	100%
232	Du Rand JA (Salty)	Western Province	1947, 54	2	1	1	0	50%
233	Du Randt JP (Os)	Orange Free State	1994, 97, 04-05	4	1	3	0	25%
234	Du Toit FP (Pikkie)	Orange Free State	1973, 75	2	0	2	0	0%
235	Du Toit GS (Gaffie)	Natal	2000-01, 06	3	0	2	1	0%
236	Du Toit J (John)	Western Province	1954	1	1	0	0	100%
237	Du Toit JC (Jan)	Orange Free State	1981	1	0	1	0	0%
238	Du Toit PA (Fonnie)	Northern Transvaal	1946, 54	2	1	1	0	50%
239	Du Toit PG (Hempies)	Western Province	1979-80, 83, 85	4	2	1	1	50%
240	Du Toit PS (Pieter-Steph)	Natal	2013	1	1	0	0	100%
241	Du Toit T (Tobias)	Transvaal	1968, 71	2	0	1	1	0%
242	Duffett D	Western Province	1950	1	0	1	0	0%
243	Duffy G (Gavin)	Natal	1956	1	0	1	0	0%
244	Dukas D	Western Province	1950	1	0	1	0	0%
245	Duncan R (Rory)	Free State	2006-07	2	1	0	1	50%
246	Durr J (Johan)	Western Province	1983	1	1	0	0	100%
247	Duvenhage DO (Dewaldt)	Western Province	2010	1	0	1	0	0%
248	Duvenhage FP (Floris)	Transvaal	1939	1	1	0	0	100%
249	East M (Mike)	Western Province	1954	1	1	0	0	100%
250	Edmunds P (Peter)	Natal	1984	1	0	1	0	0%
251	Edwards P (Pierre)	Northern Transvaal	1977-83	7	4	2	1	57%
252	Ellis CE (Clark)	Western Province	1986	1	1	0	0	100%
253	Eloff MC (Giel)	Northern Transvaal	1973	1	1	0	0	100%
254	Els WW (Braam)	Orange Free State	1994, 97	2	0	2	0	0%
255	Elstadt R (Rynhardt)	Western Province	2014	1	1	0	0	100%
256	Engelbrecht G (Giel)	Boland	1952	1	0	1	0	0%
257	Engelbrecht K (Kobus)	Golden Lions	1999	1	1	0	0	100%
258	Engels J (Jaco)	Blue Bulls	2006	1	0	0	1	0%
259	Erasmus J (Johan)	Free State	1997, 04	2	0	2	0	0%
260	Esterhuizen G (Grant)	Golden Lions	2002	1	0	1	0	0%
261	Esterhuizen J (Johan)	Transvaal	1972	1	1	0	0	100%
262	Esterhuizen WC (Willa)	Northern Transvaal	1956	1	1	0	0	100%
263	Etzebeth E (Eben)	Western Province	2012-13	2	1	1	0	50%
264	Faure CL (Chris)	Natal	1984	1	0	1	0	0%
265	Ferreira AP (Fief)	Northern Transvaal	1971	1	0	0	1	0%
266	Ferreira FC (Freddie)	Western Province	1985-86, 88-89	4	2	1	1	50%
267	Ferreira PS (Kulu)	Western Province	1984	1	1	0	0	100%
268	Fitchet C (Christo)	Orange Free State	1981	1	0	1	0	0%
269	Fleck RF (Robbie)	Western Province	1998, 00	2	1	1	0	50%
270	Flemix JF (Jan)	Northern Transvaal	1968	1	1	0	0	100%
271	Floors L (Kabamba)	Free State	2005-07, 09	4	2	1	1	50%
272	Fondse AR (Adriaan)	Western Province	2010	1	0	1	0	0%
273	Fortuin BA (Bevin)	Free State	2005-06	2	1	0	1	50%
274	Fourie A (Braam)	Griquas	1970	1	1	0	0	100%
275	Fourie AJ (Stompie)	Transvaal	1991	1	0	1	0	0%
276	Fourie BG (Bernard)	Transvaal	1993-94	2	2	0	0	100%

CURRIE CUP FINAL PLAYERS 1939 - 2014

	PLAYER	Province	First & last final	Matches	Won	Lost	Drawn	Winning %
277	Fourie DA (Deon)	Western Province	2010, 12-13	3	1	2	0	33%
278	Fourie J (Jaque)	Golden Lions	2002	1	0	1	0	0%
279	Fourie MJ (Pote)	Northern Transvaal	1987-91	5	3	1	1	60%
280	Fourie SA (Andries)	Transvaal	1986	1	0	1	0	0%
281	Fourie TT (Polla)	Northern Transvaal	1968, 70	2	1	1	0	50%
282	Fredericks ER (Eddie)	Free State	2004-05, 07	3	2	1	0	67%
283	Fredericks KP (Keegan)	Blue Bulls	2004	1	1	0	0	100%
284	Frederickson CA (Dave)	Transvaal	1974	1	0	1	0	0%
285	Froneman DC (Dirk)	Orange Free State	1976, 78	2	1	1	0	50%
286	Fry DJ (Dennis)	Western Province	1946-47, 50	3	1	2	0	33%
287	Fry SP (Stephen)	Western Province	1946-47, 50	3	1	2	0	33%
288	Fuls HT (Heinrich)	Transvaal	1992	1	0	1	0	0%
289	Fynn EE (Etienne)	Natal	1999-01	3	0	3	0	0%
290	Fyvie WS (Wayne)	Natal	1995-96, 99	3	2	1	0	67%
291	Garvey AC (Adrian)	Natal	1995-96	2	2	0	0	100%
292	Geel PJ (Flip)	Northern Transvaal	1946	1	1	0	0	100%
293	Geffin AO (Okey)	Transvaal	1947, 50	2	1	1	0	50%
294	Geldenhuys A (Adri)	Northern Transvaal	1987, 89	2	1	0	1	50%
295	Geldenhuys J (Jan)	Western Province	1980	1	0	1	0	0%
296	Geldenhuys SB (Burger)	Northern Transvaal	1977-83, 85, 87-89	11	6	3	2	55%
297	Gerber HJ (Hendrik)	Western Province	2000-01	2	2	0	0	100%
298	Gerber LJ (Len)	Northern Transvaal	1974-75	2	2	0	0	100%
299	Gerber R (Rayno)	Free State	2004, 06, 08	3	0	2	1	0%
300	Germishuys JS (Gerrie)	Orange Free State	1973, 75-77	4	1	3	0	25%
301	Geyer C (Chris)	Northern Transvaal	1954	1	0	1	0	0%
302	Gibson B	Boland	1952	1	0	1	0	0%
303	Gie W	Western Province	1939	1	0	1	0	0%
304	Gillingham JW (Joe)	Transvaal	1996, 99	2	0	2	0	0%
305	Gioia L (Lieb)	Northern Transvaal	1956	1	1	0	0	100%
306	Goodes B (Barry)	Free State	2005	1	1	0	0	100%
307	Gous R (Riaan)	Western Province	1989	1	0	0	1	0%
308	Gouws JJ (Koos)	Northern Transvaal	1989	1	0	0	1	0%
309	Grace R (Bobby)	Transvaal	1968	1	0	1	0	0%
310	Gradwell DV (Dudley)	Northern Transvaal	1971	1	0	0	1	0%
311	Greeff WW (Werner)	Western Province	2001	1	1	0	0	100%
312	Greyling PJF (Piet)	Transvaal	1971-72	2	1	0	1	50%
313	Griffiths W (Billy)	Western Province	1946	1	0	1	0	0%
314	Grobbelaar DJE (Derrick)	Blue Bulls	1998	1	1	0	0	100%
315	Grobbelaar PJJ (Cobus)	Golden Lions	2007, 11	2	1	1	0	50%
316	Grobler CJ (Kleintjie)	Orange Free State	1973, 75	2	0	2	0	0%
317	Grobler G (Gerbrand)	Northern Transvaal	1987-91, 94	6	4	1	1	67%
318	Grobler G (Gerbrandt)	Western Province	2014	1	1	0	0	100%
319	Grobler RN (Renier)	Northern Transvaal	1969	1	1	0	0	100%
320	Groom NJ (Nick)	Western Province	2012-14	3	2	1	0	67%
321	Grundlingh HEW (Henk)	Northern Transvaal	1971	1	0	0	1	0%
322	Haarhoff RA (Ronnie)	Natal	1984	1	0	1	0	0%

CURRIE CUP FINAL PLAYERS 1939 - 2014

	PLAYER	Province	First & last final	Matches	Won	Lost	Drawn	Winning %
323	Habana BG (Bryan)	Blue Bulls	2005, 08-10, 12	5	2	3	0	40%
324	Hall DB (Dean)	Golden Lions	1999	1	1	0	0	100%
325	Halstead TM (Trevor)	Natal	1999-01	3	0	3	0	0%
326	Hamilton G (Greg)	Natal	1984	1	0	1	0	0%
327	Hankinson RG (Rob)	Natal	1984	1	0	1	0	0%
328	Harding G (Gerard)	Natal	1990, 92	2	2	0	0	100%
329	Hargreaves AJ (Alistair)	Natal	2010-11	2	1	1	0	50%
330	Harris J (Brok)	Western Province	2010, 12-14	4	2	2	0	50%
331	Harris TA (Tony)	Transvaal	1939	1	1	0	0	100%
332	Hattingh SJ (Ian)	Transvaal	1994, 96	2	1	1	0	50%
333	Henderson S (Skip)	Eastern Transvaal	1972	1	0	1	0	0%
334	Hendriks P (Pieter)	Transvaal	1991-94	4	2	2	0	50%
335	Herbert E (Eric)	Orange Free State	1994	1	0	1	0	0%
336	Herbst C (Freddie)	Transvaal	1952	1	1	0	0	100%
337	Herbst WJ (Wiehann)	Natal	2012-13	2	1	1	0	50%
338	Heunis JW (Johan)	Northern Transvaal	1981, 83, 87, 89	4	2	1	1	50%
339	Heymans JH (Dougie)	Orange Free State	1994	1	0	1	0	0%
340	Heynecke J (Johnny)	Northern Transvaal	1954	1	0	1	0	0%
341	Hinrichsen W	Western Province	1939	1	0	1	0	0%
342	Hirst H (Dummy)	Transvaal	1939	1	1	0	0	100%
343	Hoffman D (Dirk)	Northern Transvaal	1981-82	2	1	1	0	50%
344	Hoffman RS (Steve)	Boland	1952	1	0	1	0	0%
345	Hoffman T (Teddy)	Western Province	1969	1	0	1	0	0%
346	Hoffmann CF (Carel)	Natal	2011	1	0	1	0	0%
347	Hollenbach AWCJ (Alwyn)	Free State	2005, 07, 11	3	3	0	0	100%
348	Holtzhausen C (Christo)	Eastern Transvaal	1972	1	0	1	0	0%
349	Honiball HW (Henry)	Natal	1992, 95-96	3	3	0	0	100%
350	Horn H (Hendrik)	Eastern Transvaal	1972	1	0	1	0	0%
351	Hougaard DJ (Derick)	Blue Bulls	2002, 04-06	4	2	1	1	50%
352	Hougaard F (Francois)	Blue Bulls	2009	1	1	0	0	100%
353	Hugo DP (Niel)	Western Province	1986, 88-89	3	1	1	1	33%
354	Hugo WJ (Wouter)	Orange Free State	1975-78	4	1	3	0	25%
355	Human AWJ (Andries)	Blue Bulls	2003, 05	2	1	1	0	50%
356	Human PR (Flip)	Transvaal	1950, 52	2	2	0	0	100%
357	Human WA (Wylie)	Blue Bulls	2002, 07	2	1	1	0	50%
358	Hurter MH (Marius)	Western Province	1998	1	0	1	0	0%
359	Immelman K (Kobus)	Western Province	1976	1	0	1	0	0%
360	Irvine B (Brian)	Natal	1956	1	0	1	0	0%
361	Jacklin B (Brian)	Natal	1956	1	0	1	0	0%
362	Jacobs AA (Adrian)	Natal	2008, 11	2	1	1	0	50%
363	James AD (Butch)	Natal	2000, 03, 11	3	1	2	0	33%
364	Jamieson CM (Craig)	Natal	1984, 90	2	1	1	0	50%
365	Jansen E (Eben)	Orange Free State	1976-77	2	1	1	0	50%
366	Jansen JS (Joggie)	Orange Free State	1976, 78	2	1	1	0	50%
367	Jantjes CA (Conrad)	Western Province	2010	1	0	1	0	0%
368	Jantjies ET (Elton)	Transvaal	2011	1	1	0	0	100%

CURRIE CUP FINAL PLAYERS 1939 - 2014

	PLAYER	Province	First & last final	Matches	Won	Lost	Drawn	Winning %
369	Januarie ER (Enrico)	Western Province	2010	1	0	1	0	0%
370	Johnson AF (Ashley)	Free State	2009	1	0	1	0	0%
371	Johnson GK (Gavin)	Transvaal	1993-94, 96	3	2	1	0	67%
372	Johnstone B (Brett)	Golden Lions	1999	1	1	0	0	100%
373	Jonker JW	Free State	2006	1	0	0	1	0%
374	Jordaan GJ (Gert)	Orange Free State	1981	1	0	1	0	0%
375	Jordaan N (Norman)	Blue Bulls	2002-03	2	2	0	0	100%
376	Jordaan PA (Paul)	Natal	2012	1	0	1	0	0%
377	Jordaan RP (Jorrie)	Northern Transvaal	1946	1	1	0	0	100%
378	Joubert AJ (André)	Natal	1993, 95-96, 99	4	2	2	0	50%
379	Joubert CHB (Tiaan)	Blue Bulls	2002	1	1	0	0	100%
380	Joubert E (Ernst)	Golden Lions	2007	1	0	1	0	0%
381	Joubert J (Joos)	Natal	1995-96	2	2	0	0	100%
382	Joubert J-P (J P)	Free State	2009	1	0	1	0	0%
383	Joubert MC (Marius)	Free State	2007, 11	2	1	1	0	50%
384	Juries FM (Fabian)	Free State	2009	1	0	1	0	0%
385	Kahts WJH (Willie)	Northern Transvaal	1974-75, 77-80, 82	7	5	1	1	71%
386	Kamana J (James)	Transvaal	2011	1	1	0	0	100%
387	Kankowski R (Ryan)	Natal	2008, 10-11	3	2	1	0	67%
388	Kayser DJ (Deon)	Natal	2000-01, 03	3	0	3	0	0%
389	Kebble GR (Guy)	Western Province	1988-90, 93	4	1	2	1	25%
390	Kempson RB (Rob)	Natal	1995-96, 00-01	4	4	0	0	100%
391	Killian M (Michael)	Transvaal	2011	1	1	0	0	100%
392	Kirchner Z (Zane)	Blue Bulls	2008-09	2	1	1	0	50%
393	Kirkham TA (Tobie)	Orange Free State	1994	1	0	1	0	0%
394	Kirkham WH (Liaan)	Transvaal	1986-87	2	0	2	0	0%
395	Kirsten JJN (Kobus)	Western Province	1989	1	0	0	1	0%
396	Kirsten JM (Michael)	Western Province	1995	1	0	1	0	0%
397	Kitshoff S (Steven)	Western Province	2012-13	2	1	1	0	50%
398	Kleyn J (Jean)	Western Province	2014	1	1	0	0	100%
399	Klopper C (Chris)	Natal	1956	1	0	1	0	0%
400	Klopper J	Transvaal	1939	1	1	0	0	100%
401	Knoetze F (Faffa)	Western Province	1985-86, 88-89	4	2	1	1	50%
402	Knoetze MJ (Martin)	Transvaal	1991	1	0	1	0	0%
403	Knoetze NJ (Kallie)	Northern Transvaal	1974	1	1	0	0	100%
404	Knox J (John)	Northern Transvaal	1973-74, 77-79	5	4	0	1	80%
405	Koch AC (Chris)	Boland	1952	1	0	1	0	0%
406	Koch B (Agie)	Western Province	1980	1	0	1	0	0%
407	Koch HV (Bubbles)	Western Province	1946-52	2	0	2	0	0%
408	Koch W (Willem)	Boland	1952	1	0	1	0	0%
409	Koch WJ (Wilhelm)	Golden Lions	2007	1	0	1	0	0%
410	Kockott RM (Rory)	Natal	2008, 10	2	2	0	0	100%
411	Koen LJ (Louis)	Western Province	1997	1	1	0	0	100%
412	Kokoali TC (Tsepo)	Free State	2004	1	0	1	0	0%
413	Kolbe C (Cheslin)	Western Province	2013-14	2	1	1	0	50%
414	Kolisi S (Siya)	Western Province	2013	1	0	1	0	0%

CURRIE CUP FINAL PLAYERS 1939 - 2014

	PLAYER	Province	First & last final	Matches	Won	Lost	Drawn	Winning %
415	Kotze GJM (Gert)	Western Province	1969	1	0	1	0	0%
416	Kotze JJ (Jimmy)	Transvaal	1947, 50	2	1	1	0	50%
417	Krantz EFW (Edrich)	Orange Free State	1976-78, 80	4	2	2	0	50%
418	Krause J (Jackie)	Transvaal	1991	1	0	1	0	0%
419	Krause P (Piet)	Blue Bulls	2003	1	1	0	0	100%
420	Kriel JA (Jaco)	Golden Lions	2014	1	0	1	0	0%
421	Kriel PB (Piet)	Boland	1952	1	0	1	0	0%
422	Kriel PC (Piet)	Western Province	1939, 46, 50	3	0	3	0	0%
423	Krige CPJ (Corné)	Western Province	1997-98, 00-01	4	3	1	0	75%
424	Kritzinger JC	Western Province	2010	1	0	1	0	0%
425	Kritzinger JL (Klippies)	Transvaal	1974-76	3	1	2	0	33%
426	Kruger CR (Chris)	Free State	2004-05	2	1	1	0	50%
427	Kruger GHJ (Gert)	Transvaal	1950, 52	2	2	0	0	100%
428	Kruger HC (Herkie)	Natal	2001	1	0	1	0	0%
429	Kruger HE (Hendrik)	Northern Transvaal	1985, 87, 90	3	1	2	0	33%
430	Kruger PE (Piet)	Northern Transvaal	1982-83, 86-87	4	0	4	0	0%
431	Kruger T (Tjaart)	Eastern Transvaal	1972	1	0	1	0	0%
432	Kruger W (Werner)	Blue Bulls	2008-09	2	1	1	0	50%
433	Kuün GWF (Derick)	Blue Bulls	2006, 08-09	3	1	1	1	33%
434	La Grange G (Doppies)	Transvaal	2011	1	1	0	0	100%
435	La Marque D (Derek)	Natal	1984	1	0	1	0	0%
436	Labuschagne C (Cas)	Natal	1956	1	0	1	0	0%
437	Labuschagne JJ (Jannes)	Golden Lions	1999, 02	2	1	1	0	50%
438	Labuschagne L (Lappies)	Natal	1956	1	0	1	0	0%
439	Labuschagne WA (Lappies)	Transvaal	1986, 91-92	3	0	3	0	0%
440	Lacroix T (Thierry)	Natal	1995	1	1	0	0	100%
441	Laing B (Balfour)	Natal	1956	1	0	1	0	0%
442	Lambie P (Patrick)	Natal	2010-13	4	2	2	0	50%
443	Lamprecht JC (Johann)	Northern Transvaal	1985, 87-90	5	2	2	1	40%
444	Lategan MT (Tjol)	Western Province	1947	1	1	0	0	100%
445	Laubscher TG (Tommie)	Western Province	1995, 97	2	1	1	0	50%
446	Lawless GE (Gavin)	Transvaal	1996	1	0	1	0	0%
447	Lawless MJ (Mike)	Western Province	1969	1	0	1	0	0%
448	Lawton TA (Tom)	Natal	1990	1	1	0	0	100%
449	Le Roux A-H (Ollie)	Orange Free State	1994-95, 00-01, 03, 05-06	7	2	4	1	29%
450	Le Roux HP (Hennie)	Transvaal	1992-94, 96, 99	5	3	2	0	60%
451	Le Roux JHS (Johan)	Transvaal	1991	1	0	1	0	0%
452	Le Roux M (Martiens)	Orange Free State	1973, 75-78, 81	6	1	5	0	17%
453	Lensing G (Kees)	Blue Bulls	2004-05	2	1	1	0	50%
454	Leonard A (Anton)	Blue Bulls	2002-05	4	3	1	0	75%
455	Lewies JST (Stephan)	Natal	2013	1	1	0	0	100%
456	Lightfoot W (Wessel)	Western Province	1988	1	0	1	0	0%
457	Linee M (Tinus)	Western Province	1995	1	0	1	0	0%
458	Lobberts H (Hilton)	Blue Bulls	2006	1	0	0	1	0%
459	Lochner GP (Flappie)	Western Province	1939	1	0	1	0	0%
460	Lock J L (Jan)	Northern Transvaal	1985, 87-88, 90	4	2	2	0	50%

CURRIE CUP FINAL PLAYERS 1939 - 2014

	PLAYER	Province	First & last final	Matches	Won	Lost	Drawn	Winning %
461	Lockyear RJ (Dick)	Western Province	1954	1	1	0	0	100%
462	Lombaard P (Piet)	Western Province	1950	1	0	1	0	0%
463	Lötter D (Deon)	Western Province	1986, 91, 93	3	2	1	0	67%
464	Lotz JW (Jan)	Transvaal	1939, 47	2	1	1	0	50%
465	Loubscher H (Hennie)	Western Province	1954	1	1	0	0	100%
466	Loubser J (Kootjie)	Boland	1952	1	0	1	0	0%
467	Lourens JP (Johnnie)	Northern Transvaal	1946	1	1	0	0	100%
468	Lourens MJ (Thys)	Northern Transvaal	1968-69, 71, 73-75, 77-78	8	7	0	1	88%
469	Louw FH (Hottie)	Western Province	1998, 00-01, 06	4	2	1	1	50%
470	Louw L-FP (Francois)	Western Province	2010	1	0	1	0	0%
471	Louw MJ (Martiens)	Transvaal	1971	1	0	0	1	0%
472	Louw P (Pierre)	Western Province	1939	1	0	1	0	0%
473	Louw RJ (Rob)	Western Province	1979-80, 82-85	6	4	1	1	67%
474	Louw SC (Fanie)	Transvaal	1939	1	1	0	0	100%
475	Luck A (Aubrey)	Western Province	1969	1	0	1	0	0%
476	Ludik L (Louis)	Golden Lions	2007, 10, 12-13	4	2	2	0	50%
477	Lurie M (Max)	Transvaal	1947	1	0	1	0	0%
478	Luther CF (Chris)	Northern Transvaal	1970-71, 74	3	1	1	1	33%
479	Maartens C (Chris)	Transvaal	1968	1	0	1	0	0%
480	Macdonald I (Ian)	Transvaal	1991-93, 96	4	1	3	0	25%
481	Maku BG (Bandise)	Blue Bulls	2009, 11	2	2	0	0	100%
482	Malan AW (Adolf)	Northern Transvaal	1983, 85, 87-91	7	3	3	1	43%
483	Malan P (Piet)	Transvaal	1947, 50	2	1	1	0	50%
484	Malherbe JF (Frans)	Western Province	2012-13	2	1	1	0	50%
485	Mallet NVH (Nick)	Western Province	1982-84	3	3	0	0	100%
486	Mametsa SJ (John)	Blue Bulls	2003, 08	2	1	1	0	50%
487	Mapoe LG (Lionel)	Free State	2009, 14	2	0	2	0	0%
488	Marais C (Charlie)	Western Province	1980, 89	2	0	1	1	0%
489	Marais CF (Charl)	Western Province	1998, 00-01	3	2	1	0	67%
490	Marais DD (Dawie)	Northern Transvaal	1983	1	0	1	0	0%
491	Marais FP (Buks)	Boland	1952	1	0	1	0	0%
492	Marais JA (Jandré)	Natal	2012	1	0	1	0	0%
493	Marais JH (Johan)	Northern Transvaal	1981-82, 85	3	1	2	0	33%
494	Marais L (Toetie)	Orange Free State	1981	1	0	1	0	0%
495	Marais PC (Peet)	Natal	2013	1	1	0	0	100%
496	Marais SP	Natal	2013	1	1	0	0	100%
497	Marchant AR (Reg)	Northern Transvaal	1983	1	0	1	0	0%
498	Marinos AWN (Andy)	Western Province	1998	1	0	1	0	0%
499	Maritz A (Dries)	Transvaal	1986	1	0	1	0	0%
500	Markgraaff AT (André)	Western Province	1983	1	1	0	0	100%
501	Marshall F (Frank)	Natal	1956	1	0	1	0	0%
502	Martens HJ (Hentie)	Orange Free State	1994-99	2	0	2	0	0%
503	Masina M (Mac)	Golden Lions	1999	1	1	0	0	100%
504	Matfield V (Victor)	Blue Bulls	2002, 04-05, 08-09	5	3	2	0	60%
505	Mather D (Doug)	Western Province	1976	1	0	1	0	0%
506	McCallum RJ (Roy)	Western Province	1979	1	0	0	1	0%

CURRIE CUP FINAL PLAYERS 1939 - 2014

	PLAYER	Province	First & last final	Matches	Won	Lost	Drawn	Winning %
507	McKechnie R (Richard)	Eastern Transvaal	1972	1	0	1	0	0%
508	McLean DA (Des)	Natal	1984	1	0	1	0	0%
509	McLeod C (Charl)	Natal	2010, 12-13	3	2	1	0	67%
510	McLeod-Henderson BM (Brad)	Natal	2003	1	0	1	0	0%
511	Meiring FA	Northern Transvaal	1991	1	1	0	0	100%
512	Meiring J (Koos)	Northern Transvaal	1968	1	1	0	0	100%
513	Mellish FCB (Francis)	Western Province	1946-47	2	1	1	0	50%
514	Mellish HT	Western Province	1939	1	0	1	0	0%
515	Mendez FEA (Fredrico)	Natal	1996	1	1	0	0	100%
516	Menter MA (Alan)	Northern Transvaal	1968	1	1	0	0	100%
517	Mentz H (Henno)	Natal	2003	1	0	1	0	0%
518	Meyer HP (Hendrik)	Free State	2006-07	2	1	0	1	50%
519	Meyer W (Willie)	Free State	1997, 99, 02	3	1	2	0	33%
520	Meyer W (Wim)	Blue Bulls	1998	1	1	0	0	100%
521	Michalak F (Frederic)	Natal	2008, 11	2	1	1	0	50%
522	Mills PMG (Pat)	Northern Transvaal	1956	1	1	0	0	100%
523	Minnaar W (Walter)	Golden Lions	1999	1	1	0	0	100%
524	Minnie DJ (Derrick)	Golden Lions	2011, 14	2	1	1	0	50%
525	Mnisi XH (Howard)	Golden Lions	2014	1	0	1	0	0%
526	Möller JD	Western Province	2010	1	0	1	0	0%
527	Monkley D (Duane)	Western Province	1998	1	0	1	0	0%
528	Montgomery PC (Percy)	Western Province	1997-98, 00-01	4	3	1	0	75%
529	Moolman LC (Louis)	Northern Transvaal	1975, 77-83, 85	9	5	3	1	56%
530	Moore N (Nick)	Golden Lions	1999	1	1	0	0	100%
531	Mordt RH (Ray)	Northern Transvaal	1983, 85	2	0	2	0	0%
532	Morkel CT (Charlie)	Western Province	1954	1	1	0	0	100%
533	Morkel J (Hannes)	Western Province	1939, 46-47, 50	4	1	3	0	25%
534	Mostert FJ (Franco)	Golden Lions	2014	1	0	1	0	0%
535	Mostert M (Marius)	Golden Lions	1999	1	1	0	0	100%
536	Moyle BS (Brent)	Natal	1999-00	2	0	2	0	0%
537	Mtawarira T (Tendai)	Natal	2008, 10-13	5	3	2	0	60%
538	Muir DJ (Dick)	Natal	1990, 92-93, 96-97	5	4	1	0	80%
539	Mulder JC (Japie)	Transvaal	1991, 93-94, 96	4	2	2	0	50%
540	Mulder K (Koos)	Eastern Transvaal	1972	1	0	1	0	0%
541	Müller GH (Gert)	Western Province	1969, 72, 74	3	1	2	0	33%
542	Muller GJ (George)	Transvaal	1950	1	1	0	0	100%
543	Muller GJ (Johann)	Natal	2008	1	1	0	0	100%
544	Müller GP (Jorrie)	Golden Lions	2002	1	0	1	0	0%
545	Müller HL (Helgard)	Orange Free State	1994, 97	2	0	2	0	0%
546	Muller HSV (Hennie)	Transvaal	1947, 50	2	1	1	0	50%
547	Müller LF (Louis)	Northern Transvaal	1969-70, 75	3	2	1	0	67%
548	Müller LJJ (Lood)	Natal	1992-93	2	1	1	0	50%
549	Müller MD (Martin)	Golden Lions	2014	1	0	1	0	0%
550	Müller PG (Pieter)	Natal	1992-93	2	1	1	0	50%
551	Murray WM (Waylon)	Natal	2008	1	1	0	0	100%
552	Mvovo LN (Lwazi)	Natal	2010-13	4	2	2	0	50%

CURRIE CUP FINAL PLAYERS 1939 - 2014

	PLAYER	Province	First & last final	Matches	Won	Lost	Drawn	Winning %
553	Myburgh JL (Mof)	Northern Transvaal	1968-71	4	2	1	1	50%
554	Myburgh K (Kat)	Griquas	1970	1	1	0	0	100%
555	Naudé FS (Frikkie)	Orange Free State	1973, 79	2	0	1	1	0%
556	Naudé J (Johan)	Boland	1952	1	0	1	0	0%
557	Naudé SW (Schalk)	Transvaal	1986-87	2	0	2	0	0%
558	Ndungane AZ (Akona)	Blue Bulls	2005-06	2	0	1	1	0%
559	Ndungane OM (Odwa)	Natal	2008, 10-13	5	3	2	0	60%
560	Neethling JB (Tiny)	Western Province	1969	1	0	1	0	0%
561	Nel C (Christo)	Western Province	1976	1	0	1	0	0%
562	Nel GP (Giepie)	Northern Transvaal	1982, 85, 87, 89	4	1	2	1	25%
563	Nel HJ (Hennie)	Northern Transvaal	1956	1	1	0	0	100%
564	Nel J (Johan)	Northern Transvaal	1991	1	1	0	0	100%
565	Nel JP	Blue Bulls	2002-06	5	3	1	1	60%
566	Nel JT	Western Province	1939	1	0	1	0	0%
567	Nel PJL (Pieter)	Northern Transvaal	1987-88	2	2	0	0	100%
568	Nel S (Soon)	Griquas	1970	1	1	0	0	100%
569	Nel WP	Free State	2009	1	0	1	0	0%
570	Nell DP (Darron)	Free State	2006-07	2	1	0	1	50%
571	Nell H (Hekkie)	Transvaal	1968	1	0	1	0	0%
572	Neuhoff CM (Mauritz)	Northern Transvaal	1968	1	1	0	0	100%
573	Newham C (Charlie)	Transvaal	1947	1	0	1	0	0%
574	Nieuwoudt G (Bill)	Western Province	1984, 86	2	2	0	0	100%
575	Noble CD (Christie)	Natal	1990	1	1	0	0	100%
576	Nomis SH (Syd)	Transvaal	1968	1	0	1	0	0%
577	Nortjé BD (Bennie)	Golden Lions	2002	1	0	1	0	0%
578	Norwood ST (Simon)	Transvaal	1971-72	2	1	0	1	50%
579	Notshe S (Sikhumbuzo)	Western Province	2014	1	1	0	0	100%
580	Ntubeni S (Siyabonga)	Western Province	2012-14	3	2	1	0	67%
581	Oberholzer AF (Anton)	Transvaal	1971-72, 74	3	1	1	1	33%
582	Oberholzer JH (Jan)	Northern Transvaal	1978-82	5	3	1	1	60%
583	Ochse JK (Chum)	Western Province	1950, 54	2	1	1	0	50%
584	Oelofse JSA (Hansie)	Transvaal	1952	1	1	0	0	100%
585	Oelschig NH (Noël)	Free State	2004-07	4	2	1	1	50%
586	Olivier E (Eben)	Western Province	1969	1	0	1	0	0%
587	Olivier J (Jacques)	Northern Transvaal	1991, 98	2	2	0	0	100%
588	Olivier W (Wynand)	Blue Bulls	2005, 08-09	3	1	2	0	33%
589	Oosthuizen CV (Coenie)	Free State	2009	1	0	1	0	0%
590	Oosthuizen JJ (Johan)	Western Province	1976	1	0	1	0	0%
591	Oosthuizen JP de V (Jan)	Northern Transvaal	1971	1	0	0	1	0%
592	Oosthuizen OW (Okkie)	Northern Transvaal	1980-81	2	2	0	0	100%
593	Oosthuizen P (Pierre)	Western Province	1979	1	0	0	1	0%
594	Oosthuizen S (Schalk)	Orange Free State	1981	1	0	1	0	0%
595	Oosthuysen DE (Deon)	Northern Transvaal	1988-91	4	2	1	1	50%
596	Opperman RJ (Ryno)	Orange Free State	1994, 97	2	0	2	0	0%
597	Otto K (Krynauw)	Blue Bulls	1998	1	1	0	0	100%
598	Oxlee K (Keith)	Natal	1956	1	0	1	0	0%

CURRIE CUP FINAL PLAYERS 1939 - 2014

	PLAYER	Province	First & last final	Matches	Won	Lost	Drawn	Winning %
599	Passens GA (Gavin)	Blue Bulls	2002-04, 06-07	5	4	0	1	80%
600	Patterson AC (Andrew)	Western Province	1989	1	0	0	1	0%
601	Paulse BJ (Breyton)	Western Province	1998, 00-01	3	2	1	0	67%
602	Pawson AL (André)	Orange Free State	1994	1	0	1	0	0%
603	Payne S (Shaun)	Natal	1999	1	0	1	0	0%
604	Peens PWS (Pierre)	Northern Transvaal	1980	1	1	0	0	100%
605	Pelser E (Eugene)	Northern Transvaal	1983	1	0	1	0	0%
606	Pelser PA (Piet)	Transvaal	1952	1	1	0	0	100%
607	Perry M (Floris)	Northern Transvaal	1946	1	1	0	0	100%
608	Piater HW (Hein)	Northern Transvaal	1977	1	1	0	0	100%
609	Pickard JAJ (Jan)	Western Province	1954	1	1	0	0	100%
610	Pienaar JA (Japie)	Orange Free State	1973	1	0	1	0	0%
611	Pienaar JF (Francois)	Transvaal	1991-94, 96	5	2	3	0	40%
612	Pienaar R (Ruan)	Natal	2008	1	1	0	0	100%
613	Pienaar ZMJ (Gysie)	Orange Free State	1976-78	3	1	2	0	33%
614	Pieterse BH (Barend)	Free State	2004-07	4	2	1	1	50%
615	Pieterse C (Charles)	Transvaal	1987	1	0	1	0	0%
616	Pietersen J (Joe)	Western Province	2012	1	1	0	0	100%
617	Pietersen J-PR (J P)	Natal	2008, 11-12	3	1	2	0	33%
618	Pitout CA (Anton)	Free State	2004	1	0	1	0	0%
619	Pitzer G (Gys)	Northern Transvaal	1968-70	3	2	1	0	67%
620	Platford S (Shaun)	Natal	1992	1	1	0	0	100%
621	Plumtree J (John)	Natal	1990, 96	2	2	0	0	100%
622	Pope CF (Chris)	Western Province	1976	1	0	1	0	0%
623	Potgieter DJ (Dewald)	Blue Bulls	2008-09	2	1	1	0	50%
624	Potgieter HL (Hermanus)	Orange Free State	1975, 77-78	3	0	3	0	0%
625	Potgieter J-L (Jacques-Louis)	Free State	2009	1	0	1	0	0%
626	Potgieter R (Ronnie)	Northern Transvaal	1968-71	4	2	1	1	50%
627	Potgieter WC (Wilhelm)	Orange Free State	1975	1	0	1	0	0%
628	Povey SA (Shaun)	Western Province	1979, 82-86	6	5	0	1	83%
629	Powell JD (Neil)	Blue Bulls	2006	1	0	0	1	0%
630	Pretorius AS (André)	Golden Lions	2002, 10	2	1	1	0	50%
631	Pretorius JC (Jaco)	Golden Lions	2002, 07, 09	3	1	2	0	33%
632	Pretorius JJD (Jannie)	Transvaal	1987	1	0	1	0	0%
633	Pretorius PIL (Piet)	Northern Transvaal	1991	1	1	0	0	100%
634	Pretorius WJJ (Fatty)	Transvaal	1939	1	1	0	0	100%
635	Putt KB (Kevin)	Natal	1993, 95-96	3	2	1	0	67%
636	Pypers CG (Corrie)	Transvaal	1974	1	0	1	0	0%
637	Rademeyer HN (Hempas)	Transvaal	1986-87	2	0	2	0	0%
638	Rahn JA (Jackie)	Transvaal	1952	1	1	0	0	100%
639	Ralepelle MC (Chiliboy)	Blue Bulls	2008	1	0	1	0	0%
640	Ras A (Abel)	Northern Transvaal	1954	1	0	1	0	0%
641	Ras WJ de W (De Wet)	Orange Free State	1975-78, 81	5	1	4	0	20%
642	Rautenbach N (Neil)	Western Province	2014	1	1	0	0	100%
643	Rautenbach SJ (Faan)	Western Province	2000	1	1	0	0	100%
644	Redelinghuys J (Julian)	Golden Lions	2014	1	0	1	0	0%

CURRIE CUP FINAL PLAYERS 1939 - 2014

	PLAYER	Province	First & last final	Matches	Won	Lost	Drawn	Winning %
645	Reece-Edwards HM (Hugh)	Natal	1984, 90, 92	3	2	1	0	67%
646	Reinach JM (Cobus)	Natal	2012-13	2	1	1	0	50%
647	Rens IJ (Natie)	Transvaal	1952	1	1	0	0	100%
648	Retief DF (Daan)	Northern Transvaal	1946, 54	2	1	1	0	50%
649	Reynecke E (Ethienne)	Golden Lions	2007	1	0	1	0	0%
650	Rheeder G (Gert)	Western Province	1954	1	1	0	0	100%
651	Rhodes MK (Michael)	Golden Lions	2011, 13-14	3	2	1	0	67%
652	Ribbens PJ (Pierre)	Blue Bulls	1998	1	1	0	0	100%
653	Richards M (Mark)	Golden Lions	2014	1	0	1	0	0%
654	Richter AH (Adriaan)	Northern Transvaal	1991	1	1	0	0	100%
655	Robbie JC (John)	Transvaal	1986-87	2	0	2	0	0%
656	Roberts H (Harry)	Transvaal	1991-92	2	0	2	0	0%
657	Robertson P (Preston)	Western Province	1969	1	0	1	0	0%
658	Robinson J (Johnny)	Transvaal	1950	1	1	0	0	100%
659	Rodgers PH (Heinrich)	Northern Transvaal	1985, 87-90, 92-93	7	3	3	1	43%
660	Rodriguez L (Len)	Western Province	1954	1	1	0	0	100%
661	Roets J (Johan)	Blue Bulls	2003-06	4	2	1	1	50%
662	Rogers CD (Chris)	Transvaal	1986-87	2	0	2	0	0%
663	Roos GJ	Transvaal	1939	1	1	0	0	100%
664	Rose EE (Earl)	Golden Lions	2007	1	0	1	0	0%
665	Rossouw C le C (Chris)	Transvaal	1996, 00	2	0	2	0	0%
666	Rossouw C (Charles)	Transvaal	1994	1	1	0	0	100%
667	Rossouw C (Chris)	Western Province	2000-01	2	2	0	0	100%
668	Rossouw DJ (Danie)	Blue Bulls	2004-06, 08-09	5	2	2	1	40%
669	Rossouw PWG (Pieter)	Western Province	1995, 97-98, 00-01	5	3	2	0	60%
670	Roumat O (Olivier)	Natal	1995	1	1	0	0	100%
671	Roux C (Chean)	Western Province	1998	1	0	1	0	0%
672	Roux F du T (Mannetjies)	Griquas	1970	1	1	0	0	100%
673	Roux F (Francois)	Northern Transvaal	1954	1	0	1	0	0%
674	Roux JP (Johan)	Northern Transvaal	1991, 93-94, 96	4	3	1	0	75%
675	Roux OA (Tonie)	Northern Transvaal	1970-71	2	0	1	1	0%
676	Roux WG (Wessel)	Blue Bulls	2002-05	4	3	1	0	75%
677	Russell RB (Brent)	Natal	2003	1	0	1	0	0%
678	Sauerman A (Archie)	Boland	1952	1	0	1	0	0%
679	Sauermann JT (Theo)	Transvaal	1971-72, 74	3	1	1	1	33%
680	Scheepers G (Gert)	Griquas	1970	1	1	0	0	100%
681	Schlebusch JJJ (Jan)	Orange Free State	1973, 75, 77	3	0	3	0	0%
682	Schmidt BO (Barry)	Transvaal	1950, 52	2	2	0	0	100%
683	Schmidt UL (Uli)	Northern Transvaal	1985, 87-91, 93-94	8	5	2	1	63%
684	Schoeman BJ (Barry)	Orange Free State	1981	1	0	1	0	0%
685	Scholtz AW (Dries)	Blue Bulls	2002, 06	2	1	0	1	50%
686	Scholtz CP (Christiaan)	Transvaal	1994	1	1	0	0	100%
687	Scholtz H (Hendro)	Free State	2004-05, 07	3	2	1	0	67%
688	Scholtz NB (Calla)	Western Province	1983-86, 88	5	4	1	0	80%
689	Schreuder L (Louis)	Western Province	2012-13	2	1	1	0	50%
690	Schutte GA (Gert)	Transvaal	1971	1	0	0	1	0%

CURRIE CUP FINAL PLAYERS 1939 - 2014

	PLAYER	Province	First & last final	Matches	Won	Lost	Drawn	Winning %
691	Schutte PJW (Phillip)	Northern Transvaal	1990-91, 94	3	2	1	0	67%
692	Scriba HM (Hans)	Western Province	1985, 89	2	1	0	1	50%
693	Scrooby CW (Chris)	Transvaal	1939	1	1	0	0	100%
694	Senatla SM (Seabelo)	Western Province	2014	1	1	0	0	100%
695	Sephaka LD (Lawrence)	Golden Lions	2002, 07	2	0	2	0	0%
696	Serfontein DJ (Divan)	Western Province	1976, 79-80, 82-84	6	3	2	1	50%
697	Sherrell R (Reg)	Natal	1956	1	0	1	0	0%
698	Simpson B (Barry)	Natal	1956	1	0	1	0	0%
699	Sinclair DJ (Des)	Transvaal	1950	1	1	0	0	100%
700	Sinclair J (Jebb)	Western Province	2012	1	1	0	0	100%
701	Skeate RC (Ross)	Natal	2011	1	0	1	0	0%
702	Skene AL (Alan)	Western Province	1954	1	1	0	0	100%
703	Skinner A (André)	Northern Transvaal	1981-82, 87, 88, 90	5	2	3	0	40%
704	Skinstad RB (Bob)	Western Province	1997-98, 01	3	2	1	0	67%
705	Skosan CS (Courtnall)	Golden Lions	2014	1	0	1	0	0%
706	Slade J (John)	Natal	1999	1	0	1	0	0%
707	Smal GP (Gert)	Western Province	1985-86, 88-89	4	2	1	1	50%
708	Small JT (James)	Transvaal	1991-93, 95-97	6	3	3	0	50%
709	Smit BC (Chris)	Western Province	1986	1	1	0	0	100%
710	Smit FC	Western Province	1995	1	0	1	0	0%
711	Smit GA (Gert)	Northern Transvaal	1956	1	1	0	0	100%
712	Smit JW (John)	Natal	1999-01, 08	4	1	3	0	25%
713	Smit PL (Phillip)	Natal	2001, 03	2	0	2	0	0%
714	Smit WJ	Transvaal	1939	1	1	0	0	100%
715	Smith J	Eastern Transvaal	1972	1	0	1	0	0%
716	Smith JH (Juan)	Free State	2004-05	2	1	1	0	50%
717	Smith K (Kat)	Western Province	1969	1	0	1	0	0%
718	Smith AS (Kwagga)	Golden Lions	2014	1	0	1	0	0%
719	Smith MJ	Free State	1997	1	0	1	0	0%
720	Smith P (Peet)	Griquas	1970	1	1	0	0	100%
721	Smith PF (Franco)	Orange Free State	1994, 98	2	1	1	0	50%
722	Smith RF (Rodger)	Natal	2000-01	2	0	2	0	0%
723	Smith T (Tos)	Griquas	1970	1	1	0	0	100%
724	Snyman AH (André)	Blue Bulls	1998, 01, 03	3	1	2	0	33%
725	Snyman DSL (Dawie)	Western Province	1976	1	0	1	0	0%
726	Snyman JCP (Jackie)	Orange Free State	1973	1	0	1	0	0%
727	Sonnekus GHH (Gerrie)	Orange Free State	1975-78, 81	5	1	4	0	20%
728	Sonnekus PJ (Pieter)	Northern Transvaal	1983	1	0	1	0	0%
729	Sowerby RS (Shaun)	Natal	2000-01, 03	3	0	3	0	0%
730	Spangenberg JC (Christo)	Northern Transvaal	1987-89	3	2	0	1	67%
731	Spies JJ (Johan)	Northern Transvaal	1968-71	4	2	1	1	50%
732	Spies PJ (Pierre) jnr	Blue Bulls	2006, 08-09	3	1	1	1	33%
733	Spies PJ (Pierre) snr	Northern Transvaal	1975, 77	2	2	0	0	100%
734	Stander B (Ben)	Eastern Transvaal	1972	1	0	1	0	0%
735	Stander JCJ (Rampie)	Orange Free State	1973, 76, 78	3	1	2	0	33%
736	Stapelberg WP (Willem)	Northern Transvaal	1968, 73-74	3	3	0	0	100%

CURRIE CUP FINAL PLAYERS 1939 - 2014

	PLAYER	Province	First & last final	Matches	Won	Lost	Drawn	Winning %
737	Steenkamp GG (Gurthrö)	Free State	2004, 08-09	3	1	2	0	33%
738	Steenkamp MD (De Kock)	Western Province	2010, 12-13	3	1	2	0	33%
739	Stegmann GJ (Deon)	Blue Bulls	2008-09	2	1	1	0	50%
740	Steinhobel J (Tiny)	Transvaal	1947	1	0	1	0	0%
741	Stewart JC (Christian)	Western Province	1988, 95, 98	3	0	3	0	0%
742	Steyn FPL (Francois)	Natal	2008, 13	2	2	0	0	100%
743	Steyn M (Morné)	Blue Bulls	2005-06, 08-09	4	1	2	1	25%
744	Stofberg MTS (Theuns)	Orange Free State	1976-80, 82-83	7	4	2	1	57%
745	Stoltz W (Willem)	Golden Lions	2002	1	0	1	0	0%
746	Stolz T (Thys)	Western Province	2000-01	2	2	0	0	100%
747	Straeuli RAW (Rudolf)	Northern Transvaal	1990, 93, 96	3	1	2	0	33%
748	Stransky JT (Joel)	Natal	1990, 93, 95	3	1	2	0	33%
749	Strauss AJ (Andries)	Natal	2010	1	1	0	0	100%
750	Strauss CP (Tiaan)	Western Province	1986, 88-89, 95	4	1	2	1	25%
751	Strauss CR (Richardt)	Free State	2006-07, 09	3	1	1	1	33%
752	Strauss JA (Adriaan)	Blue Bulls	2006, 09	2	0	1	1	0%
753	Strauss JA (Attie)	Western Province	1984	1	1	0	0	100%
754	Strauss JC	Northern Transvaal	1981, 83	2	1	1	0	50%
755	Strauss JHP (Johan)	Transvaal	1974	1	0	1	0	0%
756	Strauss JZ (Joshua)	Transvaal	2011	1	1	0	0	100%
757	Strydom A (Andries)	Eastern Transvaal	1972	1	0	1	0	0%
758	Strydom A (Basie)	Transvaal	1968	1	0	1	0	0%
759	Strydom GJ (Gert)	Transvaal	1972, 74	2	1	1	0	50%
760	Strydom JJ (Hannes)	Transvaal	1993, 96, 99	3	2	1	0	67%
761	Strydom LI (Louis)	Blue Bulls	2003, 07	2	1	1	0	50%
762	Strydom LJ (Louis)	Northern Transvaal	1946	1	1	0	0	100%
763	Strydom PA (Piet)	Orange Free State	1975	1	0	1	0	0%
764	Strydom WT (Willie)	Orange Free State	1973	1	0	1	0	0%
765	Swanepoel R (Riaan)	Natal	2010	1	1	0	0	100%
766	Swanepoel W (Werner)	Free State	1997	1	0	1	0	0%
767	Swart FJ (Francois)	Blue Bulls	2003	1	1	0	0	100%
768	Swart IS de V (Balie)	Western Province	1989, 92-94	4	2	1	1	50%
769	Swart JC (Jakes)	Orange Free State	1973	1	0	1	0	0%
770	Swart JS (Justin)	Western Province	1995, 97, 99, 01, 03	5	1	4	0	20%
771	Swartz B (Buddy)	Griquas	1970	1	1	0	0	100%
772	Swartz E (Enrico)	Natal	2003	1	0	1	0	0%
773	Sykes SR (Steven)	Natal	2008, 10, 12	3	2	1	0	67%
774	Symington A (George)	Northern Transvaal	1946	1	1	0	0	100%
775	Symons TAW (Tommy)	Transvaal	1971-72, 74	3	1	1	1	33%
776	Taute JJ (Jaco)	Golden Lions	2011, 14	2	2	0	0	100%
777	Taylor P (Peter)	Natal	1956	1	0	1	0	0%
778	Taylor T (Tich)	Natal	1956	1	0	1	0	0%
779	Tecklenburg WJ (Warwick)	Golden Lions	2014	1	0	1	0	0%
780	Teichmann GH (Gary)	Natal	1992-93, 95-96, 99	5	3	2	0	60%
781	Terblanche CS (Stefan)	Natal	2000-01, 08, 10-11	5	2	3	0	40%
782	Thiart D (Danie)	Blue Bulls	2006	1	0	0	1	0%

CURRIE CUP FINAL PLAYERS 1939 - 2014

	PLAYER	Province	First & last final	Matches	Won	Lost	Drawn	Winning %
783	Thomson JRD (Jeremy)	Natal	1990, 92, 95-96	4	3	1	0	75%
784	Thoresson KR (Keith)	Northern Transvaal	1975	1	1	0	0	100%
785	Thorne B (Bruce)	Golden Lions	1999	1	1	0	0	100%
786	Thorne GS (Grahame)	Northern Transvaal	1971	1	0	0	1	0%
787	Tiedt JA (Jannie)	Transvaal	1986	1	0	1	0	0%
788	Townsend A (Ashton)	Transvaal	1952, 56	2	1	1	0	50%
789	Tromp JA (Kleinjan)	Golden Lions	2002	1	0	1	0	0%
790	Truscott JA (Andries)	Blue Bulls	1998	1	1	0	0	100%
791	Truter HJ (Hendrik)	Transvaal	1991, 94	2	0	2	0	0%
792	Trytsman JW (Johnny)	Western Province	1998	1	0	1	0	0%
793	Turner FG (Freddie)	Western Province	1939	1	0	1	0	0%
794	Tyibilika S (Solly)	Natal	2003	1	0	1	0	0%
795	Uys CJ (Corné)	Free State	2009	1	0	1	0	0%
796	Uys P de W (Piet)	Northern Transvaal	1968-70	3	2	1	0	67%
797	Van As HP (Hugo)	Transvaal	1986-87	2	0	2	0	0%
798	Van Aswegen HJ (Henning)	Orange Free State	1977, 79-80, 82-83, 85	6	3	2	1	50%
799	Van Aswegen J (Jannie)	Griquas	1970-71	2	1	0	1	50%
800	Van Biljon L (Lukas)	Natal	2001, 03	2	0	2	0	0%
801	Van Blerk JAR	Western Province	1947	1	1	0	0	100%
802	Van Blommenstein J (Johan)	Northern Transvaal	1969-70	2	1	1	0	50%
803	Van den Berg DS (Derek)	Western Province	1969, 76	2	0	2	0	0%
804	Van den Berg PA (Albert)	Natal	2000-01, 08	3	1	2	0	33%
805	Van den Heever DJ (Daantjie)	Northern Transvaal	1956	1	1	0	0	100%
806	Van den Heever GJ (Gerhard)	Blue Bulls	2009, 12-13	3	2	1	0	67%
807	Van der Berg CR (Riaan)	Blue Bulls	2005	1	0	1	0	0%
808	Van der Linde A (Toks)	Western Province	1995, 97-98, 00-01	5	3	2	0	60%
809	Van der Linde CJ	Free State	2004-05, 11	3	2	1	0	67%
810	Van der Merwe AHP (Akker)	Golden Lions	2014	1	0	1	0	0%
811	Van der Merwe AJ (Bertus)	Boland	1952	1	0	1	0	0%
812	Van der Merwe BS (Fiks)	Northern Transvaal	1946	1	1	0	0	100%
813	Van der Merwe CE (Erik)	Golden Lions	1999	1	1	0	0	100%
814	Van der Merwe F (Franco)	Golden Lions	2007, 11	2	1	1	0	50%
815	Van der Merwe G (Tjokkie)	Northern Transvaal	1978-80	3	2	0	1	67%
816	Van der Merwe HS (Heinke)	Golden Lions	2007	1	0	1	0	0%
817	Van der Merwe P (Piet)	Western Province	1954	1	1	0	0	100%
818	Van der Merwe RC (Ryno)	Free State	2005-06	2	1	0	1	50%
819	Van der Merwe SW (Schalk)	Golden Lions	2014	1	0	1	0	0%
820	Van der Ryst FE (Franz)	Transvaal	1950, 52	2	2	0	0	100%
821	Van der Schyff PJ (Johan)	Transvaal	1968	1	0	1	0	0%
822	Van der Spuy SJ (Fanie)	Transvaal	1939	1	1	0	0	100%
823	Van der Walt J (Jaco)	Golden Lions	2014	1	0	1	0	0%
824	Van der Walt JA (Jannie)	Transvaal	1996, 99	2	1	1	0	50%
825	Van der Walt JJ	Northern Transvaal	1988-89	2	1	0	1	50%
826	Van der Walt JN (Nicky)	Blue Bulls	1998	1	1	0	0	100%
827	Van der Walt K (Kobus)	Blue Bulls	2003	1	1	0	0	100%
828	Van der Walt L (Louis)	Northern Transvaal	1974	1	1	0	0	100%

CURRIE CUP FINAL PLAYERS 1939 - 2014

	PLAYER	Province	First & last final	Matches	Won	Lost	Drawn	Winning %
829	Van der Watt AE (Andy)	Western Province	1969	1	0	1	0	0%
830	Van der Westhuizen JF (Cabous)	Natal	1992-93, 95	3	2	1	0	67%
831	Van der Westhuizen JH (Joost)	Blue Bulls	1998, 02	2	2	0	0	100%
832	Van der Westhuyzen JNB (Jaco)	Blue Bulls	2002	1	1	0	0	100%
833	Van Deventer J (Jannie)	Transvaal	1968, 71-72	3	1	1	1	33%
834	Van Deventer JD (Doerie)	Northern Transvaal	1946	1	1	0	0	100%
835	Van Deventer PI (Piet)	Griquas	1970	1	1	0	0	100%
836	Van Dyk JJ (Kobus)	Western Province	2014	1	1	0	0	100%
837	Van Dyk S (Stompie)	Western Province	1946	1	0	1	0	0%
838	Van Dyk SWA (Schalk)	Northern Transvaal	1956	1	1	0	0	100%
839	Van Greuning K (Kapstok)	Transvaal	1996	1	0	1	0	0%
840	Van Heerden FJ (Fritz)	Western Province	1995-97	2	1	1	0	50%
841	Van Heerden HJN (Herman)	Orange Free State	1981	1	0	1	0	0%
842	Van Heerden JJ (Goggie)	Western Province	1984, 86	2	2	0	0	100%
843	Van Heerden JL (Moaner)	Northern Transvaal	1973-74, 77, 80, 82	5	4	1	0	80%
844	Van Heerden JL (Wikus)	Golden Lions	2002, 08, 11	3	1	2	0	33%
845	Van Heerden N (Nols)	Western Province	1947	1	1	0	0	100%
846	Van Heerden PJL (Wickus)	Natal	1995-96	2	2	0	0	100%
847	Van Jaarsveld CJ (Hoppy)	Transvaal	1947, 52	2	1	1	0	50%
848	Van Niekerk JC (Joe)	Golden Lions	2002	1	0	1	0	0%
849	Van Niekerk O (Otto)	Transvaal	1939, 46-47	3	2	1	0	67%
850	Van Niekerk P (Pietman)	Golden Lions	2002	1	0	1	0	0%
851	Van Niekerk W (Willouw)	Western Province	1982	1	1	0	0	100%
852	Van Reenen A	Boland	1952	1	0	1	0	0%
853	Van Reenen JNR (Ross)	Orange Free State	1975-78	4	1	3	0	25%
854	Van Renen GL (George)	Western Province	1946-47	2	1	1	0	50%
855	Van Rensburg AG (Deon)	Transvaal	2011	1	1	0	0	100%
856	Van Rensburg C (Clinton)	Natal	1999	1	0	1	0	0%
857	Van Rensburg CQ (Charl)	Natal	1999-01, 03	4	0	4	0	0%
858	Van Rensburg D (Deon)	Eastern Transvaal	1972	1	0	1	0	0%
859	Van Rensburg JCJ (J C)	Golden Lions	2007, 11	2	1	1	0	50%
860	Van Rensburg JTJ (Theo)	Northern Transvaal	1990, 92	2	0	2	0	0%
861	Van Rensburg PJ (Vuile)	Northern Transvaal	1946	1	1	0	0	100%
862	Van Schalkwyk D (Danie)	Blue Bulls	1998	1	1	0	0	100%
863	Van Schalkwyk HJ (Jaco)	Free State	2004	1	0	1	0	0%
864	Van Schouwenburg FJ (Francois)	Blue Bulls	2006	1	0	0	1	0%
865	Van Staden E (Eugene)	Natal	2010-11	2	1	1	0	50%
866	Van Staden F (Fred)	Northern Transvaal	1971	1	0	0	1	0%
867	Van Staden HJ (Fancy)	Transvaal	1950	1	1	0	0	100%
868	Van Staden JA (André)	Northern Transvaal	1969-71, 73-74	5	3	1	1	60%
869	Van Straaten AJJ (Braam)	Western Province	2000-01	2	2	0	0	100%
870	Van Vollenhoven KT (Tom)	Northern Transvaal	1954	1	0	1	0	0%
871	Van Vuuren BJJ (Koos)	Northern Transvaal	1956	1	1	0	0	100%
872	Van Wyk CJ (Basie)	Transvaal	1950, 52	2	2	0	0	100%
873	Van Wyk J (Johan)	Western Province	1997-98	2	1	1	0	50%
874	Van Wyk J-H (Jan-Harm)	Free State	1997	1	0	1	0	0%

CURRIE CUP FINAL PLAYERS 1939 - 2014

	PLAYER	Province	First & last final	Matches	Won	Lost	Drawn	Winning %
875	Van Wyngaardt JJM (Johan)	Transvaal	1971, 74	2	0	1	1	0%
876	Van Zyl A (Anton)	Golden Lions	2007, 10	2	0	2	0	0%
877	Van Zyl CC (Corniel)	Free State	2005, 07	2	2	0	0	100%
878	Van Zyl DJ (Dan)	Western Province	1998, 00	2	1	1	0	50%
879	Van Zyl JFF (Freddie)	Golden Lions	2007	1	0	1	0	0%
880	Van Zyl MC (Thys)	Northern Transvaal	1956	1	1	0	0	100%
881	Van Zyl P (Pierre)	Northern Transvaal	1973, 79	2	1	0	1	50%
882	Van Zyl PA (Piet)	Orange Free State	1973	1	0	1	0	0%
883	Venter AG (André)	Orange Free State	1994, 97	2	0	2	0	0%
884	Venter AJ	Free State	1997, 99-01, 03	5	1	4	0	20%
885	Venter B (Brendan)	Orange Free State	1994, 97	2	0	2	0	0%
886	Venter J (Hannes)	Blue Bulls	1998	1	1	0	0	100%
887	Venter JA (Barabas)	Transvaal	1986-87, 91	3	0	3	0	0%
888	Venter W (Walter)	Golden Lions	2007	1	0	1	0	0%
889	Venter W (Wickus)	Golden Lions	1999	1	1	0	0	100%
890	Vermaak AF (Alistair)	Western Province	2014	1	1	0	0	100%
891	Vermaak BS (Bian)	Free State	2006	1	0	0	1	0%
892	Vermaak J (Jano)	Golden Lions	2007	1	0	1	0	0%
893	Vermeulen DJ (Duane)	Free State	2007, 10, 12-13	4	2	2	0	50%
894	Vermeulen R (Ruan)	Blue Bulls	2002-03	2	2	0	0	100%
895	Verster JJP (Basie)	Orange Free State	1975	1	0	1	0	0%
896	Victor DP (Dennis)	Northern Transvaal	1956	1	1	0	0	100%
897	Vijoen EJ (Ernest)	Orange Free State	1981	1	0	1	0	0%
898	Viljoen FJN (Frans)	Free State	2009	1	0	1	0	0%
899	Viljoen JF (Joggie)	Griquas	1970	1	1	0	0	100%
900	Viljoen L (Lucas)	Northern Transvaal	1973	1	1	0	0	100%
901	Viljoen R (Joggie)	Western Province	1997	1	1	0	0	100%
902	Villet JV (John)	Western Province	1982-83	2	2	0	0	100%
903	Vintcent AN (Nellis)	Western Province	1947	1	1	0	0	100%
904	Visagie GP (Gawie)	Natal	1984	1	0	1	0	0%
905	Visagie IJ (Cobus)	Western Province	1998, 01	2	1	1	0	50%
906	Visagie JC	Transvaal	1952	1	1	0	0	100%
907	Visagie PJ (Piet)	Griquas	1970	1	1	0	0	100%
908	Visagie RG (Vleis)	Orange Free State	1981, 90	2	1	1	0	50%
909	Visser B (Broekies)	Western Province	1954	1	1	0	0	100%
910	Visser J de V (De Villiers)	Western Province	1979-80, 82, 88-89	5	1	2	2	20%
911	Visser J (Jan)	Western Province	1950	1	0	1	0	0%
912	Visser JG	Western Province	1950	1	0	1	0	0%
913	Visser M (Mornay)	Western Province	1995, 99	2	0	2	0	0%
914	Von Hoeslin DJB (Dave)	Natal	2001, 03	2	0	2	0	0%
915	Von Wezel SA (Syd)	Transvaal	1947	1	0	1	0	0%
916	Vorster D (Denys)	Griquas	1970	1	1	0	0	100%
917	Vorster HW (Harold)	Golden Lions	2014	1	0	1	0	0%
918	Vos AN (André)	Golden Lions	2002	1	0	1	0	0%
919	Vos JJ (Jack)	Western Province	1946-47	2	1	1	0	50%
920	Wagenaar C (Christo)	Northern Transvaal	1975, 77-79, 81	5	4	0	1	80%

CURRIE CUP FINAL PLAYERS 1939 - 2014

	PLAYER	Province	First & last final	Matches	Won	Lost	Drawn	Winning %
921	Wagner IJ (Sias)	Blue Bulls	2002-03	2	2	0	0	100%
922	Wahl JJ (Ballie)	Western Province	1946-47, 50	3	1	2	0	33%
923	Waldeck J (John)	Griquas	1970	1	1	0	0	100%
924	Wannenburg PJ (Pedrie)	Blue Bulls	2002-06, 09	6	4	1	1	67%
925	Wasserman JG (Johan)	Blue Bulls	2002-03, 05	3	2	1	0	67%
926	Watson AC (Tony)	Natal	1990, 92	2	2	0	0	100%
927	Watson K (Ken)	Western Province	1950	1	0	1	0	0%
928	Watson LA (Luke)	Natal	2003	1	0	1	0	0%
929	Weber JJ (Hans)	Northern Transvaal	1974	1	1	0	0	100%
930	Wegner CA (Callie)	Orange Free State	1981	1	0	1	0	0%
931	Wegner GN (Nico)	Natal	1999	1	0	1	0	0%
932	Welsh BF (Frikkie)	Blue Bulls	2003-04	2	2	0	0	100%
933	Wepener FW (Willie)	Golden Lions	2007	1	0	1	0	0%
934	Wessels FH (Frans)	Northern Transvaal	1985	1	0	1	0	0%
935	Wessels HJ (Japie)	Orange Free State	1978	1	0	1	0	0%
936	Whipp PJM (Peter)	Western Province	1976, 79	2	0	1	1	0%
937	Whitehead T (Tim)	Natal	2012	1	0	1	0	0%
938	Whiteley WR (Warren)	Golden Lions	2011, 14	2	1	1	0	50%
939	Wiese JJ (Kobus)	Transvaal	1991-94, 96	5	2	3	0	40%
940	Wilkens V (Vic)	Northern Transvaal	1954	1	0	1	0	0%
941	Wilkenson B (Boesman)	Eastern Transvaal	1972	1	0	1	0	0%
942	Williams CM (Chester)	Western Province	1995, 98, 99	3	1	2	0	33%
943	Williams H (Heimar)	Natal	2013	1	1	0	0	100%
944	Williams JG (John)	Northern Transvaal	1973-75	3	3	0	0	100%
945	Williamson A (Andrew)	Northern Transvaal	1987	1	1	0	0	100%
946	Winter RG (Russell)	Golden Lions	1999, 02	2	1	1	0	50%
947	Wolmarans BJ (Barry)	Orange Free State	1975-78	4	1	3	0	25%
948	Wright GD (Garth)	Transvaal	1992	1	0	1	0	0%
949	Zeeman W (Willie)	Western Province	1976	1	0	1	0	0%
950	Zietsman DW (Dave)	Western Province	1976	1	0	1	0	0%

⟨ DID YOU KNOW? ⟩

The most drop goals in a Currie Cuup final is 4 – by Naas Botha for Northern Transvaal vs Transvaal in 1987.

CURRIE CUP FINAL CAPTAINS 1939 - 2014

	PLAYER	Province	First & last final	Matches	Won	Lost	Drawn	Winning %
1	Andrews MG (Mark)	Natal	2000	1	0	1	0	0%
2	Bartmann WJ (Wahl)	Natal	1992-93	2	1	1	0	50%
3	Bates AJ (Albie)	Northern Transvaal	1973	1	1	0	0	100%
4	Bekker HJ (Hennie)	Western Province	1980	1	0	1	0	0%
5	Botha G v G (Gary)	Blue Bulls	2006	1	0	0	1	0%
6	Botha HE (Naas)	Northern Transvaal	1980-91	7	5	2	0	71%
7	Breedt JC (Jannie)	Transvaal	1986-92	4	0	4	0	0%
8	Brewis JD (Hansie)	Northern Transvaal	1954	1	0	1	0	0%
9	Burger J (Jan)	Boland	1952	1	0	1	0	0%
10	Burger SWP (Schalk)	Western Province	2010	1	0	1	0	0%
11	Claassen W (Wynand)	Natal	1984	1	0	1	0	0%
12	Daniel KR (Keegan)	Natal	2011-13	3	1	2	0	33%
13	Dannhauser T (Toy)	Transvaal	1968	1	0	1	0	0%
14	De Jongh JL (Juan)	Western Province	2014	1	1	0	0	100%
15	De Wet DJ (Daan)	Orange Free State	1973	1	0	1	0	0%
16	Drotské AE (Naka)	Orange Free State	2005	1	1	0	0	100%
17	Du Plessis CJ (Carel)	Western Province	1986-89	3	1	1	1	33%
18	Du Plessis DC (Daan)	Northern Transvaal	1979	1	0	0	1	0%
19	Du Plessis M (Morné)	Western Province	1976-79	2	0	1	1	0%
20	Du Preez FCH (Frik)	Northern Transvaal	1971	1	0	0	1	0%
21	Duncan R (Rory)	Free State	2007	1	1	0	0	100%
22	Erasmus J (Johan)	Free State	2004	1	0	1	0	0%
23	Fourie DA (Deon)	Western Province	2012-13	2	1	1	0	50%
24	Geel PJ (Flip)	Northern Transvaal	1946	1	1	0	0	100%
25	Geldenhuys SB (Burger)	Northern Transvaal	1983-89	2	0	1	1	0%
26	Greyling PJF (Piet)	Transvaal	1971-72	2	1	0	1	50%
27	Henderson S (Skip)	Eastern Transvaal	1972	1	0	1	0	0%
28	Hugo WJ (Wouter)	Orange Free State	1976-78	3	1	2	0	33%
29	Jamieson CM (Craig)	Natal	1990	1	1	0	0	100%
30	Joubert E (Ernst)	Golden Lions	2007	1	0	1	0	0%
31	Kriel PC (Piet)	Western Province	1946	1	0	1	0	0%
32	Krige CPJ (Corné)	Western Province	2000-01	2	2	0	0	100%
33	Kritzinger JL (Klippies)	Orange Free State	1975	1	0	1	0	0%
34	Le Roux A-H (Ollie)	Orange Free State	2006	1	0	0	1	0%
35	Le Roux M (Martiens)	Orange Free State	1981	1	0	1	0	0%
36	Leonard A (Anton)	Blue Bulls	2003-05	3	2	1	0	67%
37	Lotz JW (Jan)	Transvaal	1947	1	0	1	0	0%
38	Lourens MJ (Thys)	Northern Transvaal	1974-78	4	4	0	0	100%
39	Louw SC (Fanie)	Transvaal	1939	1	1	0	0	100%
40	Matfield V (Victor)	Blue Bulls	2008-09	2	1	1	0	50%
41	Morkel J (Hannes)	Western Province	1950	1	0	1	0	0%
42	Muir DJ (Dick)	Western Province	1997	1	1	0	0	100%

ABSA CURRIE CUP

CURRIE CUP FINAL CAPTAINS 1939 - 2014

	PLAYER	Province	First & last final	Matches	Won	Lost	Drawn	Winning %
43	Muller GJ (Johann)	Natal	2008	1	1	0	0	100%
44	Müller HL (Helgard)	Orange Free State	1994-97	2	0	2	0	0%
45	Muller HSV (Hennie)	Transvaal	1950	1	1	0	0	100%
46	Neethling JB (Tiny)	Western Province	1969	1	0	1	0	0%
47	Nel HJ (Hennie)	Northern Transvaal	1956	1	1	0	0	100%
48	Oberholzer AF (Anton)	Transvaal	1974	1	0	1	0	0%
49	Oberholzer JH (Jan)	Northern Transvaal	1982	1	0	1	0	0%
50	Pickard JAJ (Jan)	Western Province	1954	1	1	0	0	100%
51	Pienaar JF (Francois)	Transvaal	1993-96	3	2	1	0	67%
52	Roux F du T (Mannetjies)	Griquas	1970	1	1	0	0	100%
53	Serfontein DJ (Divan)	Western Province	1982-84	3	3	0	0	100%
54	Skinstad RB (Bob)	Western Province	1998	1	0	1	0	0%
55	Smit JW (John)	Natal	2001	1	0	1	0	0%
56	Sowerby RS (Shaun)	Natal	2003	1	0	1	0	0%
57	Strauss CP (Tiaan)	Western Province	1995	1	0	1	0	0%
58	Strauss JA (Adriaan)	Free State	2009	1	0	1	0	0%
59	Strauss JZ (Joshua)	Golden Lions	2011	1	1	0	0	100%
60	Strydom JJ (Hannes)	Transvaal	1999	1	1	0	0	100%
61	Taylor P (Peter)	Natal	1956	1	0	1	0	0%
62	Teichmann GH (Gary)	Natal	1995-99	3	2	1	0	67%
63	Terblanche CS (Stefan)	Natal	2010	1	1	0	0	100%
64	Turner FG (Freddie)	Western Province	1939	1	0	1	0	0%
65	Uys P de W (Piet)	Northern Transvaal	1968-70	3	2	1	0	67%
66	Van Aswegen HJ (Henning)	Western Province	1985	1	1	0	0	100%
67	Van der Westhuizen JH (Joost)	Blue Bulls	1998-02	2	2	0	0	100%
68	Van Renen GL (George)	Western Province	1947	1	1	0	0	100%
69	Van Wyk CJ (Basie)	Transvaal	1952	1	1	0	0	100%
70	Vos AN (André)	Golden Lions	2002	1	0	1	0	0%
71	Whiteley WR (Warren)	Golden Lions	2014	1	0	1	0	0%

⟨ DID YOU KNOW? ⟩

The most appearances in a Currie Cup final is 11 — by Burger Geldenhuys (1977-89) & Naas Botha (1977-91).

ABSA CURRIE CUP – PREMIER DIVISION

Blue Bulls Rugby Union

Founded: 1938 (as Northern Transvaal) **Ground:** Loftus Versfeld **Capacity:** 50 000
Address: Kirkness Street, Sunnyside, Pretoria, 0002
Postal address: PO Box 27856, Sunnyside, Pretoria, 0132 **Telephone Number:** 012-420 0700
Website: www.thebulls.co.za **Colours:** Sky blue jersey and socks, navy shorts
Head coach: Frans Ludeke **Currie Cup Coach:** Pine Pienaar **Captain:** Deon Stegmann
President: Louis Nel **Company CEO:** Barend van Graan **Union CEO:** Dr Eugene Hare

'96	'97	'98	'99	'00	'01	'02	'03	'04	'05	'06	'07	'08	'09	'10	'11	'12	'13	'14
2nd	5th	2nd	5th	10th	7th	4th	1st	1st	1st	2nd	4th	2nd	3rd	4th	5th	4th	5th	4th

Played	Won	Lost	Drawn	Points for	Points against	Tries for	Tries against
11	6	5	0	294	266	29	26

Date	Venue	Opponent	Result	Score	Referee	Scorers
9 Aug	Johannesburg	Golden Lions	LOST	13-41	J van Heerden	T: Mastriet. C: Potgieter. P: Potgieter (2).
16 Aug	Cape Town	WP	LOST	17-41	R Rashivhenge	T: Mbonambi. P: Potgieter (4).
23 Aug	Pretoria	EP Kings	WON	30-25	L Legoete	T: Ndungane (2), Kriel, Stegmann. C: Jantjies (2). P: Jantjies (2).
30 Aug	Pretoria	WP	LOST	18-23	C Joubert	T: Mastriet, Du Plessis. C: Stander. P: Schoeman (2).
6 Sep	Pretoria	Golden Lions	WON	36-26	M vd Westhuizen	T: Beyers, Odendaal, Hattingh. C: Potgieter (3). P: Potgieter (5).
12 Sep	Port Elizabeth	EP Kings	WON	28-13	Q Immelman	T: Small-Smith, Basson, Stegmann. C: Potgieter (2). P: Potgieter (3).
20 Sep	Pretoria	Sharks	LOST	15-26	Q Immelman	P: Potgieter (5).
26 Sep	Bloemfontein	Cheetahs	WON	31-22	M vd Westhuizen	T: Mastriet (2), Hattingh. C: Potgieter (2). P: Potgieter (4).
3 Oct	Nelspruit	Pumas	WON	37-6	J Peyper	T: Du Plessis, Stegmann, Greyling, Van Zyl. C: Pothieter (3), Schoeman. P: Potgieter (3).
11 Oct	Pretoria	Griquas	WON	46-12	L Legoete	T: Basson (3), Ndungane, Stegmann, Pollard. C: Potgieter (3), Pollard (2). P: Potgieter (2).
SEMI-FINAL						
18 Oct	Cape Town	WP	LOST	23-31	L Legoete	T: Greyling, Visagie. C: Potgieter, Pollard. P: Potgieter (3).

Note: ■ = *Champion,* * *Played as Northern Transvaal*

ABSA CURRIE CUP – PREMIER DIVISION

APPEARANCES & POINTS FOR BLUE BULLS IN 2014 CURRIE CUP

PLAYER	Lions	WP	EP	WP	Lions	EP	Sharks	F-State	Pumas	Griquas	WP (SF)	Apps	T	C	P	DG	Pts
Jurgen Visser	15	15	–	–	–	–	–	–	–	–	–	2	–	–	–	–	0
Akhona Ndungane	14	14	14	14	–	14	–	14	14	14	14	9	3	0	0	0	15
JJ Engelbrecht	13	13	–	–	13	–	13R	13	13	–	–	6	–	–	–	–	0
Burger Odendaal	12	12	12	12	12	12	12	12	12	12	–	10	1	0	0	0	5
Sampie Mastriet	11	11	11	11	14	–	14	11	11	–	14R	9	4	0	0	0	20
Jacques-Louis Potgieter	10	10	–	–	10	10	10	10	10	10	10	9	0	15	31	0	123
Piet van Zyl	9	9	9R	9	9R	9	9R	9	9R	9	9R	11	1	0	0	0	5
Jacques Engelbrecht	8	7R	–	6R	8R	4R	7R	–	–	–	–	6	–	–	–	–	0
Jono Ross	7	8	8	8	8	8	8c	8	8	8	8	11	–	–	–	–	0
Deon Stegmann	6c	6c	6c	6c	6c	6c	–	6c	6c	6c	6c	10	4	0	0	0	20
Grant Hattingh	5	5	5	5	5	5	5	5	5	5	5	11	2	0	0	0	10
Paul Willemse	4	4	4	4	4	4	4	4	4	4	4	11	–	–	–	–	0
Werner Kruger	3	3	3R	3	3	3	3	3	3	3R	3	11	–	–	–	–	0
Callie Visagie	2	1	–	2	2R	–	2	2R	2	2R	2R	9	1	0	0	0	5
Dean Greyling	1	–	1	1	1	1	1	1	1	1	1	10	2	0	0	0	10
Bongi Mbonambi	2R	2R	2	2R	2	2	2R	2	2R	2	2	11	1	0	0	0	5
Marcel van der Merwe	3R	1	3	–	–	–	–	–	3	3R	–	5	–	–	–	–	0
Nico Janse van Rensburg	5R	4R	4R	7R	7R	7R	4R	4R	7R	5R	7R	11	–	–	–	–	0
Wiaan Liebenberg	6R	–	6R	–	–	6	6R	8R	6R	8R	–	7	–	–	–	–	0
Rudy Paige	9R	9R	9	9R	9	9R	9	9R	9	9R	9	11	–	–	–	–	0
Tony Jantjies	13R	10R	10	–	x	x	–	–	–	–	–	3	0	2	2	0	10
Jesse Kriel	11R	14R	15	15	–	–	15	12R	15R	12R	10R	9	1	0	0	0	5
Jacques du Plessis	–	7	7	7	7	7	7	7	7	7	7	10	2	0	0	0	10
Hencus van Wyk	–	3R	–	3R	–	–	–	–	–	–	–	2	–	–	–	–	0
William Small-Smith	–	–	13	13	–	13	13	–	–	13	13	6	1	0	0	0	5
Bandise Maku	–	–	2R	–	–	2R	–	–	–	–	–	2	–	–	–	–	0
Ulrich Beyers	–	–	14R	–	15	15	–	15	15	15	15	7	1	0	0	0	5
Joshua Stander	–	–	x	10	–	–	–	–	–	–	–	1	0	1	0	0	2
Tian Schoeman	–	–	–	10R	–	–	x	x	10R	–	–	2	0	1	2	0	8
Ryan Nell	–	–	–	14R	x	15R	–	–	–	–	–	2	–	–	–	–	0
Jamba Ulengo	–	–	–	–	11	–	–	–	–	–	–	1	–	–	–	–	0
Basil Short	–	–	–	–	1R	1R	–	–	–	–	–	2	–	–	–	–	0
Bjorn Basson	–	–	–	–	–	11	11	–	–	11	11	4	4	0	0	0	20
Morne Mellett	–	–	–	–	–	1R	1R	1R	–	–	–	3	–	–	–	–	0
Handre Pollard	–	–	–	–	–	–	–	–	–	10R	12	2	1	3	0	0	11
35 Players												**236**	**29**	**22**	**35**	**0**	**294**

⟨ DID YOU KNOW? ⟩

Western Province have won the Currie Cup 33 times – 10 times more than the Blue Bulls. Both WP and the Blue Bulls have shared the famous trophy on four occasions.

CURRIE CUP SQUAD – CAREER CURRIE CUP APPEARANCES

PLAYER	BLUE BULLS						OTHER UNIONS						TOTAL					
	A	T	C	P	DG	Pts	A	T	C	P	DG	Pts	A	T	C	P	DG	Pts
BA (Bjorn) Basson	19	17	0	0	0	85	37	33	0	0	0	165	56	50	0	0	0	250
U (Ulrich) Beyers	20	1	0	0	0	5	0	0	0	0	0	0	20	1	0	0	0	5
WHJ (Jacques) du Plessis	20	3	0	0	0	15	0	0	0	0	0	0	20	3	0	0	0	15
JJ (JJ) Engelbrecht	15	0	0	0	0	0	25	13	0	0	0	65	40	13	0	0	0	65
JJ (Jacques) Engelbrecht	14	0	0	0	0	0	46	5	0	0	0	25	60	5	0	0	0	25
MD (Dean) Greyling	45	6	0	0	0	30	0	0	0	0	0	0	45	6	0	0	0	30
GN (Grant) Hattingh	29	2	0	0	0	10	0	0	0	0	0	0	29	2	0	0	0	10
NJ (Nico) Janse van Rensburg	11	0	0	0	0	0	0	0	0	0	0	0	11	0	0	0	0	0
A (Tony) Jantjies	7	0	6	9	0	39	0	0	0	0	0	0	7	0	6	9	0	39
JA (Jesse) Kriel	9	1	0	0	0	5	0	0	0	0	0	0	9	1	0	0	0	5
W (Werner) Kruger	97	5	0	0	0	25	0	0	0	0	0	0	97	5	0	0	0	25
WA (Wiaan) Liebenberg	16	2	0	0	0	10	0	0	0	0	0	0	16	2	0	0	0	10
BG (Bandise) Maku	41	2	0	0	0	10	23	1	0	0	0	5	64	3	0	0	0	15
S (Sampie) Mastriet	18	5	0	0	0	25	0	0	0	0	0	0	18	5	0	0	0	25
MT (Bongi) Mbonambi	22	1	0	0	0	5	0	0	0	0	0	0	22	1	0	0	0	5
MM (Morne) Mellet	13	0	0	0	0	0	0	0	0	0	0	0	13	0	0	0	0	0
AZ (Akona) Ndungane	64	28	0	0	0	140	29	20	0	0	0	100	93	48	0	0	0	240
RD (Ryan) Nell	2	0	0	0	0	0	2	0	0	0	0	0	4	0	0	0	0	0
MB (Burger) Odendaal	10	1	0	0	0	5	0	0	0	0	0	0	10	1	0	0	0	5
R (Rudi) Paige	25	2	0	0	0	10	1	0	0	0	0	0	26	2	0	0	0	10
H (Handre) Pollard	8	1	13	13	1	73	0	0	0	0	0	0	8	1	13	13	1	73
J-L (Jacques-Louis) Potgieter	35	3	46	67	0	208	32	6	57	48	5	303	67	9	103	115	5	511
JM (Jono) Ross	23	1	0	0	0	5	0	0	0	0	0	0	23	1	0	0	0	5
CF (Tian) Schoeman	2	0	1	2	0	8	0	0	0	0	0	0	2	0	1	2	0	8
BG (Basil) Short	2	0	0	0	0	0	0	0	0	0	0	0	2	0	0	0	0	0
WT (William) Small-Smith	10	3	0	0	0	15	0	0	0	0	0	0	10	3	0	0	0	15
JT (Joshua) Stander	1	0	1	0	0	2	0	0	0	0	0	0	1	0	1	0	0	2
GJ (Deon) Stegmann	63	11	0	0	0	55	0	0	0	0	0	0	63	11	0	0	0	55
JI (Jamba) Ulengo	1	0	0	0	0	0	0	0	0	0	0	0	1	0	0	0	0	0
M (Marcel) van der Merwe	13	1	0	0	0	5	27	9	0	0	5	45	40	10	0	0	5	50
HJ (Hencus) van Wyk	2	0	0	0	0	0	0	0	0	0	0	0	2	0	0	0	0	0
PE (Piet) van Zyl	11	1	0	0	0	5	22	4	0	0	0	20	33	5	0	0	0	25
C-T (Callie) Visagie	11	1	0	0	0	5	12	0	0	0	0	0	23	1	0	0	0	5
PJ (Jurgen) Visser	32	2	1	4	0	24	0	0	0	0	0	0	32	2	1	4	0	24
P (Paul) Willemse	21	3	0	0	0	15	1	0	0	0	0	0	22	3	0	0	0	15
35 Players	732	103	68	95	1	839	257	91	57	48	10	728	989	194	125	143	11	1567

ABSA CURRIE CUP – PREMIER DIVISION

FIRST-CLASS APPEARANCES FOR BLUE BULLS IN 2014 – ALL MATCHES

PLAYER	VODACOM CUP						CURRIE CUP						2014 TOTAL						CAREER MATCHES					
	A	T	C	P	DG	Pts	A	T	C	P	DG	Pts	A	T	C	P	DG	Pts	A	T	C	P	DG	Pts
BA (Bjorn) Basson	0	0	0	0	0	0	4	4	0	0	0	20	4	4	0	0	0	20	19	17	0	0	0	85
U (Ulrich) Beyers	0	0	0	0	0	0	7	1	0	0	0	5	7	1	0	0	0	5	34	4	1	0	1	25
CA (Clayton) Blommetjies	9	4	0	0	0	20	0	0	0	0	0	0	9	4	0	0	0	20	41	12	0	0	0	60
DJ (David) Bullbring	9	2	0	0	0	0	0	0	0	0	0	0	9	2	0	0	0	0	15	3	0	0	0	15
CE (Clyde) Davids	9	2	0	0	0	10	0	0	0	0	0	0	9	2	0	0	0	10	9	2	0	0	0	10
CP (Christiaan) de Bruin	4	0	0	0	0	0	0	0	0	0	0	0	4	0	0	0	0	0	4	0	0	0	0	0
WHJ (Jacques) du Plessis	0	0	0	0	0	0	10	2	0	0	0	10	10	2	0	0	0	10	22	4	0	0	0	20
JJ (JJ) Engelbrecht	0	0	0	0	0	0	6	0	0	0	0	0	6	0	0	0	0	0	15	0	0	0	0	0
JJ (Jacques) Engelbrecht	1	0	0	0	0	0	6	0	0	0	0	0	7	0	0	0	0	0	15	0	0	0	0	0
JN (Johan) Fouche	1	0	0	0	0	0	0	0	0	0	0	0	1	0	0	0	0	0	1	0	0	0	0	0
L (Louis) Fouche	4	0	4	8	0	32	0	0	0	0	0	0	4	0	4	8	0	32	28	1	2	67	63	5	308
MD (Dean) Greyling	0	0	0	0	0	0	10	2	0	0	0	10	10	2	0	0	0	10	79	9	0	0	0	45
GN (Grant) Hattingh	0	0	0	0	0	0	11	2	0	0	0	10	11	2	0	0	0	10	29	2	0	0	0	10
DP (Reniel) Hugo	6	2	0	0	0	10	0	0	0	0	0	0	6	2	0	0	0	10	6	2	0	0	0	10
TK (Travis) Ismaiel	5	0	0	0	0	0	0	0	0	0	0	0	5	0	0	0	0	0	15	7	0	0	0	35
WJ (Lohan) Jacobs	8	2	0	0	0	10	0	0	0	0	0	0	8	2	0	0	0	10	23	2	0	0	0	10
NJ (Nico) Janse van Rensburg	2	0	0	0	0	0	11	0	0	0	0	0	13	0	0	0	0	0	13	0	0	0	0	0
R (Rohan) Janse van Rensburg	1	0	0	0	0	0	0	0	0	0	0	0	1	0	0	0	0	0	7	4	0	0	0	20
A (Tony) Jantjies	3	0	2	5	0	19	3	0	2	2	0	10	6	0	4	7	0	29	20	3	36	31	0	180
JA (Jesse) Kriel	7	3	0	0	0	15	9	1	0	0	0	5	16	4	0	0	0	20	16	4	0	0	0	20
W (Werner) Kruger	0	0	0	0	0	0	11	0	0	0	0	0	11	0	0	0	0	0	123	7	0	0	0	35
WA (Wiaan) Liebenberg	9	2	0	0	0	10	7	0	0	0	0	0	16	2	0	0	0	10	34	12	0	0	0	60
KS (Kefentse) Mahlo	3	1	0	0	0	5	0	0	0	0	0	0	3	1	0	0	0	5	3	1	0	0	0	5
BG (Bandise) Maku	3	0	0	0	0	0	2	0	0	0	0	0	5	0	0	0	0	0	74	3	0	0	0	15
S (Sampie) Mastriet	6	7	0	0	0	35	9	4	0	0	0	20	15	11	0	0	0	55	49	31	0	0	0	155
MT (Bongi) Mbonambi	0	0	0	0	0	0	11	1	0	0	0	5	11	1	0	0	0	5	30	1	0	0	0	5
MM (Morne) Mellet	0	0	0	0	0	0	3	0	0	0	0	0	3	0	0	0	0	0	26	2	0	0	0	10
WM (Waylon) Murray	8	2	0	0	0	10	0	0	0	0	0	0	8	2	0	0	0	10	14	2	0	0	0	10
NM (Mox) Mxoli	1	0	0	0	0	0	0	0	0	0	0	0	1	0	0	0	0	0	1	0	0	0	0	0
AZ (Akhona) Ndungane	0	0	0	0	0	0	9	3	0	0	0	15	9	3	0	0	0	15	71	30	0	0	0	150
RD (Ryan) Nell	7	2	0	0	0	10	2	0	0	0	0	0	9	2	0	0	0	10	9	2	0	0	0	10
MB (Burger) Odendaal	6	4	0	0	0	20	10	1	0	0	0	5	16	5	0	0	0	25	17	5	0	0	0	25
M (Marvin) Orie	6	0	0	0	0	0	0	0	0	0	0	0	6	0	0	0	0	0	6	0	0	0	0	0
R (Rudi) Paige	4	0	0	0	0	0	11	0	0	0	0	0	15	0	0	0	0	0	33	2	0	0	0	10
H (Handre) Pollard	0	0	0	0	0	0	2	1	3	0	0	11	2	1	3	0	0	11	10	1	19	14	1	88
J-L (Jacques-Louis) Potgieter	0	0	0	0	0	0	9	0	15	31	0	123	9	0	15	31	0	123	64	7	101	112	4	585
JM (Jono) Ross	0	0	0	0	0	0	11	0	0	0	0	0	11	0	0	0	0	0	33	2	0	0	0	10
JL (Juan) Schoeman	7	0	0	0	0	0	0	0	0	0	0	0	7	0	0	0	0	0	9	0	0	0	0	0
P (Pierre) Schoeman	2	0	0	0	0	0	0	0	0	0	0	0	2	0	0	0	0	0	2	0	0	0	0	0
CF (Tian) Schoeman	5	1	17	7	0	60	2	0	1	2	0	8	7	1	18	9	0	68	7	1	18	9	0	68
BG (Basil) Short	7	0	0	0	0	0	2	0	0	0	0	0	9	0	0	0	0	0	18	2	0	0	0	10

ABSA CURRIE CUP – PREMIER DIVISION

FIRST-CLASS APPEARANCES FOR BLUE BULLS IN 2014 – ALL MATCHES

PLAYER	VODACOM CUP					CURRIE CUP					2014 TOTAL					CAREER MATCHES				
	A	T	C	P	DG Pts	A	T	C	P	DG Pts	A	T	C	P	DG Pts	A	T	C	P	DG Pts
WT (William) Small-Smith	4	2	0	0	0 10	6	1	0	0	0 5	10	3	0	0	0 15	16	6	0	0	0 30
RA (Roelof) Smit	4	1	0	0	0 5	0	0	0	0	0 0	4	1	0	0	0 5	7	3	0	0	0 15
JT (Joshua) Stander	4	1	7	0	0 19	1	0	1	0	0 2	5	1	8	0	0 21	5	1	8	0	0 21
GJ (Deon) Stegmann	0	0	0	0	0 0	10	4	0	0	0 20	10	4	0	0	0 20	67	12	0	0	0 60
SM (Sidney) Tobias	7	1	0	0	0 5	0	0	0	0	0 0	7	1	0	0	0 5	8	1	0	0	0 5
JI (Jamba) Ulengo	0	0	0	0	0 0	1	0	0	0	0 0	1	0	0	0	0 0	1	0	0	0	0 0
M (Marcel) van der Merwe	0	0	0	0	0 0	5	0	0	0	0 0	5	0	0	0	0 0	13	1	0	0	0 5
PW (Wimpie) van der Walt	5	2	0	0	0 10	0	0	0	0	0 0	5	2	0	0	0 10	5	2	0	0	0 10
PS (Schalk) van Heerden	8	0	0	0	0 0	0	0	0	0	0 0	8	0	0	0	0 0	12	0	0	0	0 0
R (Rudi) van Rooyen	1	0	0	0	0 0	0	0	0	0	0 0	1	0	0	0	0 0	4	0	0	0	0 0
A (Arno) van Wyk	2	1	0	0	0 5	0	0	0	0	0 0	2	1	0	0	0 5	2	1	0	0	0 5
HJ (Hencus) van Wyk	9	3	0	0	0 15	2	0	0	0	0 0	11	3	0	0	0 15	16	4	0	0	0 20
PE (Piet) van Zyl	0	0	0	0	0 0	11	1	0	0	0 5	11	1	0	0	0 5	11	1	0	0	0 5
C-T (Callie) Visagie	0	0	0	0	0 0	9	1	0	0	0 5	9	1	0	0	0 5	13	1	0	0	0 5
GJ (Jaco) Visagie	4	0	0	0	0 0	0	0	0	0	0 0	4	0	0	0	0 0	8	0	0	0	0 0
PJ (Jurgen) Visser	0	0	0	0	0 0	2	0	0	0	0 0	2	0	0	0	0 0	39	7	2	5	0 54
P (Paul) Willemse	0	0	0	0	0 0	11	0	0	0	0 0	11	0	0	0	0 0	23	3	0	0	0 15

58 Players

Juinor Springbok Jesse Kriel on the charge for the Blue Bulls against Griquas.

‹ DID YOU KNOW? ›

The most points scored by a team in a Currie Cup final is 56, by Transvaal, when they beat Free State 56-33 in the 1994 final at Springbok Park cricket ground in Bloemfontein, while the Free State Stadium underwent renovation.

ABSA CURRIE CUP – PREMIER DIVISION

Eastern Province Rugby Union

Founded: 1888 **Ground:** Nelson Mandela Bay Stadium **Capacity:** 45 000
Address: 70 Prince Alfred Road, North End, Port Elizabeth, 6001
Postal address: PO Box 13111, Humewood, 6013 **Telephone Number:** 041-408 8902
Email: info@eprugby.co.za **Colours:** Red and black hooped jersey, black shorts, red and black socks
Currie Cup Coach: Carlos Spencer **Captain:** Luke Watson, Steven Sykes, Ronnie Cooke,
Darron Nell **President:** Cheeky Watson **Company CEO (acting):** Charl Crous

'96	'97	'98	'99	'00	'01	'02	'03	'04	'05	'06	'07	'08	'09	'10	'11	'12	'13	'14
9th	14th	9th	7th	9th	11th	11th	11th	13th	12th	12th	10th	14th	12th	10th	10th	7th	8th	14th

Played	Won	Lost	Drawn	Points for	Points against	Tries for	Tries against
10	1	9	0	206	403	27	33

Date	Venue	Opponent	Result	Score	Referee	Scorers
8 Aug	Port Elizabeth	WP	LOST	16-35	J Peyper	T: Watson, Luiters. P: Van Breda (2).
16 Aug	Johannesburg	Golden Lions	LOST	19-60	C Joubert	T: Van Breda, Cooke, Davis. C: Van Breda, Van Aswegen.
23 Aug	Pretoria	Blue Bulls	LOST	25-30	L Legoete	T: Gates, Gqoboka, Van Vuuren (4). C: Van Breda (2). P: Van Breda (2).
30 Aug	Port Elizabeth	Golden Lions	LOST	22-41	M vd Westhuizen	T: Gates, Soyizwapi, Penalty try. C: Van Breda (2). D: G Whitehead.
5 Sep	Cape Town	WP	LOST	14-49	S Berry	T: T Whitehead, Schoeman. C: Van Breda (2).
12 Sep	Port Elizabeth	Blue Bulls	LOST	13-28	Q Immelman	T: Nell. C: Botes. P: Van Breda (2).
20 Sep	Port Elizabeth	Cheetahs	LOST	22-37	M Jonker	T: Grey, Dukisa, Jenner. C: Van Aswegen, Van Breda. P: Van Aswegen.
27 Sep	Durban	Sharks	LOST	24-53	C Crouse	T: T Whitehead, Gates, Schoeman. C: Van Aswegen (3). P: Van Aswegen.
4 Oct	Kimberley	Griquas	LOST	25-45	S Berry	T: Gates (2), Penalty try. C: Van Aswegen, G Whitehead. P: Van Aswegen (2).
10 Oct	Port Elizabeth	Pumas	WON	26-25	M Jonker	T: Van Breda, Cooke, Botes, Schoeman. C: Van Aswegen (3).
INTERNATIONAL						
10 Jun	Port Elizabeth	Wales	LOST	12-34	L van der Merwe	T: Soyizwapi, Kerrod. C: Whitehead.

Team: H Graaff, S Soyizwapi, R Cooke, S Gates, S van Breda, G Whitehead, K Luiters, P Schoeman, D Oosthuizen, T Bholi, C Lindsay, D Nell[c], C du Plessis, E Marutlulle, L Gqoboka. R: A de Swardt (on for #2), BG Uys(1), S Kerrod (3), S Cummins (4), S Willemse (7), J Grobler (9), D Jenner (12), N Dukisa (15).

APPEARANCES & POINTS FOR EP IN 2014 CURRIE CUP

PLAYER	WP	G Lions	B Bulls	G Lions	WP	B Bulls	Cheetahs	Sharks	Griquas	Pumas	Apps	T	C	P	DG	Pts
Scott van Breda	15	15	15	15	15	15	11R	x	x	15	8	2	8	6	0	44
Ronnie Cooke	14	14c	14	13	14	14	13	14	14c	14	10	2	0	0	0	10
Tim Whitehead	13	13	13	–	13	13	–	13	13	13	8	2	0	0	0	10
Shane Gates	12	12	12	12	12R	12	12	12	12	12	10	5	0	0	0	25
Siviwe Soyizwapi	11	11	11	11	11	11	15	15	15	11	10	1	0	0	0	5
Gary van Aswegen	10	10	10	–	–	10	10	10	10	10	8	0	9	4	0	30
Tobie Botes	9	9	–	x	10R	9R	10R	9	9	9	8	1	1	0	0	7
Luke Watson	8c	–	8c	–	–	–	–	–	–	–	2	1	0	0	0	5
Stefan Willemse	7	7	6	6R	7R	6R	6R	6	–	–	8	–	–	–	–	0
Thembelani Bholi	6	6	8R	6	6R	–	–	8R	6R	x	7	–	–	–	–	0
David Bulbring	5	5	5	5	5	5	–	–	–	–	6	–	–	–	–	0
Steven Cummins	4	4	5R	–	–	–	4R	5	5	4R	7	–	–	–	–	0
Tom Botha	3	3	3	3	3	–	3	–	–	–	6	–	–	–	–	0
Edgar Marutlulle	2	2	2	2	2	2	–	–	–	2R	7	–	–	–	–	0
Lizo Gqoboka	1	1	1	–	1	1	1	–	–	1R	7	1	0	0	0	5
Albe de Swardt	2R	17R	–	–	–	–	8R	6R	2R	–	5	–	–	–	–	0
CJ van der Linde	3R	1R	–	–	3R	3	3R	3	3	–	7	–	–	–	–	0
Darron Nell	5R	–	–	–	–	4R	5	5c	x	4c	5	1	0	0	0	5
Aidon Davis	8R	8	–	8	8	–	–	–	–	–	4	1	0	0	0	5
Kevin Luiters	9R	–	9	9	9	9	9	9R	9R	–	8	1	0	0	0	5
George Whitehead	x	10R	x	10	10	–	–	–	10R	–	4	0	1	0	1	5
Ntabeni Dukusa	x	15R	–	x	–	15R	11	11	11	15R	6	1	0	0	0	5
Steven Sykes	–	5R	4	4c	4c	4c	4c	–	–	–	6	–	–	–	–	0
Shaun McDonald	–	6R	–	7R	6	6	6	–	–	–	5	–	–	–	–	0
Jaco Grobler	–	9R	9R	–	–	–	–	–	–	9R	3	–	–	–	–	0
Paul Schoeman	–	–	7	7	7	8	8	8	6	6	8	3	0	0	0	15
Mike van Vuuren	–	–	2R	2R	2R	2R	–	–	–	–	4	1	0	0	0	5
Charles Marais	–	–	3R	1R	–	–	–	1	1	–	4	–	–	–	–	0
Siyanda Grey	–	–	13R	14	x	–	14	–	–	–	3	1	0	0	0	5
BG Uys	–	–	–	1	–	1R	–	–	–	1	3	–	–	–	–	0
Dwayne Jenner	–	–	–	x	12	–	12R	–	–	–	2	1	0	0	0	5
Devin Oosthuizen	–	–	–	–	–	7	7	7	7	7	5	–	–	–	–	0
Simon Kerrod	–	–	–	–	–	3R	–	–	–	3	2	–	–	–	–	0
Martin Ferreira	–	–	–	–	–	–	2	2	2	2	4	–	–	–	–	0
Charl du Plessis	–	–	–	–	–	–	3R	3R	3R	–	3	–	–	–	–	0
Cameron Lindsay	–	–	–	–	–	–	–	4R	4	5	3	–	–	–	–	0
Tim Agaba	–	–	–	–	–	–	7R	8	8	–	3	–	–	–	–	0
Penalty try	–	–	–	–	–	–	–	–	–	–	0	2	0	0	0	10
37 Players											**209**	**27**	**19**	**10**	**1**	**206**

ABSA CURRIE CUP – PREMIER DIVISION

CURRIE CUP SQUAD – CAREER CURRIE CUP APPEARANCES

PLAYER	EP						OTHER UNIONS						TOTAL					
	A	T	C	P	DG	Pts	A	T	C	P	DG	Pts	A	T	C	P	DG	Pts
TEVK (Tim) Agaba	13	2	0	0	0	10	0	0	0	0	0	0	13	2	0	0	0	10
T (Thembelani) Bholi	11	0	0	0	0	0	0	0	0	0	0	0	11	0	0	0	0	0
WT (Tobie) Botes	8	1	1	0	0	7	22	3	1	0	0	17	30	4	2	0	0	24
T (Tom) Botha	6	0	0	0	0	0	0	0	0	0	0	0	6	0	0	0	0	0
DJ (David) Bulbring	8	0	0	0	0	0	13	1	0	0	0	5	21	1	0	0	0	5
RJ (Ronnie) Cooke	14	2	0	0	0	10	27	10	0	0	0	50	41	12	0	0	0	60
S (Steven) Cummins	7	0	0	0	0	0	0	0	0	0	0	0	7	0	0	0	0	0
A (Aidon) Davis	8	3	0	0	0	15	0	0	0	0	0	0	8	3	0	0	0	15
AJ (Albe) de Swardt	16	0	0	0	0	0	0	0	0	0	0	0	16	0	0	0	0	0
CF (Charl) du Plessis	12	0	0	0	0	0	26	0	0	0	0	0	38	0	0	0	0	0
N (Ntabeni) Dukisa	19	3	5	7	1	49	9	5	8	16	0	89	28	8	13	23	1	138
M (Martin) Ferreira	4	0	0	0	0	0	23	6	0	0	0	30	27	6	0	0	0	30
S (Shane) Gates	11	6	0	0	0	30	0	0	0	0	0	0	11	6	0	0	0	30
LP (Lizo) Gqoboka	23	1	0	0	0	5	0	0	0	0	0	0	23	1	0	0	0	5
S (Siyanda) Grey	9	4	0	0	0	20	0	0	0	0	0	0	9	4	0	0	0	20
FJ (Jaco) Grobler	3	0	0	0	0	0	4	0	0	0	0	0	7	0	0	0	0	0
D (Dwayne) Jenner	2	1	0	0	0	5	13	2	0	0	0	10	15	3	0	0	0	15
SJ (Simon) Kerrod	2	0	0	0	0	0	1	0	0	0	0	0	3	0	0	0	0	0
C (Cameron) Lindsay	3	0	0	0	0	0	0	0	0	0	0	0	3	0	0	0	0	0
K (Kevin) Luiters	8	1	0	0	0	5	4	1	0	0	0	5	12	2	0	0	0	10
CL (Charles) Marais	4	0	0	0	0	0	1	0	0	0	0	0	5	0	0	0	0	0
E (Edgar) Marutlulle	7	0	0	0	0	0	26	7	0	0	0	35	33	7	0	0	0	35
S (Shaun) McDonald	5	0	0	0	0	0	0	0	0	0	0	0	5	0	0	0	0	0
DP (Darron) Nell	29	6	0	0	0	30	39	5	0	0	0	25	68	11	0	0	0	55
DA (Devin) Oosthuizen	32	5	0	0	0	25	0	0	0	0	0	0	32	5	0	0	0	25
P (Paul) Schoeman	8	3	0	0	0	15	0	0	0	0	0	0	8	3	0	0	0	15
SS (Siwiwe) Soyizwapi	16	4	0	0	0	20	0	0	0	0	0	0	16	4	0	0	0	20
SR (Steven) Sykes	12	3	0	0	0	15	87	5	0	0	0	25	99	8	0	0	0	40
BG (BG) Uys	3	0	0	0	0	0	36	4	0	0	0	20	39	4	0	0	0	20
GJ (Gary) van Aswegen	8	0	9	4	0	30	9	0	11	8	0	46	17	0	20	12	0	76
S (Scott) van Breda	22	3	35	35	0	190	0	0	0	0	0	0	22	3	35	35	0	190
CJ (CJ) van der Linde	7	0	0	0	0	0	50	4	0	0	0	20	57	4	0	0	0	20
MT (Mike) van Vuuren	4	1	0	0	0	5	3	0	0	0	0	0	7	1	0	0	0	5
LA (Luke) Watson	19	11	0	0	0	55	66	28	0	0	0	140	85	39	0	0	0	195
GA (George) Whitehead	27	3	26	7	1	91	1	0	0	0	0	0	28	3	26	7	1	91
TJ (Tim) Whitehead	8	2	0	0	0	10	27	1	0	0	0	5	35	3	0	0	0	15
S (Stefan) Willemse	19	5	0	0	0	25	0	0	0	0	0	0	19	5	0	0	0	25
37 Players	417	70	76	53	2	667	487	82	20	24	0	522	904	152	96	77	2	1189

ABSA CURRIE CUP – PREMIER DIVISION

FIRST-CLASS APPEARANCES FOR EP IN 2014 – ALL MATCHES

PLAYER	VODACOM CUP						INTERNATIONAL TOUR MATCH						CURRIE CUP						2014 TOTAL						CAREER MATCHES					
	A	T	C	P	DG	Pts	A	T	C	P	DG	Pts	A	T	C	P	DG	Pts	A	T	C	P	DG	Pts	A	T	C	P	DG	Pts
TEVK (Tim) Agaba	0	0	0	0	0	0	0	0	0	0	0	0	3	0	0	0	0	0	3	0	0	0	0	0	15	2	0	0	0	10
M (Masixole) Banda	5	2	1	3	0	21	0	0	0	0	0	0	0	0	0	0	0	0	5	2	1	3	0	21	5	2	1	3	0	21
EP (Eben) Barnard	5	2	0	0	0	10	0	0	0	0	0	0	0	0	0	0	0	0	5	2	0	0	0	10	9	2	0	0	0	10
R (Rynier) Bernardo	2	0	0	0	0	0	0	0	0	0	0	0	0	0	0	0	0	0	2	0	0	0	0	0	19	0	0	0	0	0
MRG (Michael) Bernardt	2	0	0	0	0	0	0	1	0	0	0	0	0	0	0	0	0	0	2	0	0	0	0	0	2	0	0	0	0	0
T (Thembelani) Bholi	7	0	0	0	0	0	0	0	0	0	0	0	7	0	0	0	0	0	15	0	0	0	0	0	19	0	0	0	0	0
OA (Ofense) Boloko	2	0	0	0	0	0	0	0	0	0	0	0	0	0	0	0	0	0	2	0	0	0	0	0	2	0	0	0	0	0
WT (Tobie) Botes	0	0	0	0	0	0	0	0	0	0	0	0	8	1	1	0	0	7	8	1	1	0	0	7	8	1	1	0	0	7
T (Tom) Botha	0	0	0	0	0	0	0	0	0	0	0	0	6	0	0	0	0	0	6	0	0	0	0	0	6	0	0	0	0	0
DJ (David) Bulbring	0	0	0	0	0	0	0	0	0	0	0	0	6	0	0	0	0	0	6	0	0	0	0	0	30	1	0	0	0	5
RJ (Ronnie) Cooke	0	0	0	1	0	0	0	0	0	0	0	0	10	2	0	0	0	10	11	2	0	0	0	10	15	2	0	0	0	10
S (Steven) Cummins	0	0	0	0	0	0	1	0	0	0	0	0	7	0	0	0	0	0	8	0	0	0	0	0	8	0	0	0	0	0
S (Selvyn) Davids	4	2	0	0	0	10	0	0	0	0	0	0	0	0	0	0	0	0	4	2	0	0	0	10	4	2	0	0	0	10
A (Aidon) Davis	5	1	0	0	0	5	0	0	0	0	0	0	4	1	0	0	0	5	9	1	0	0	0	5	16	3	0	0	0	15
AJ (Albe) de Swardt	7	0	0	0	0	0	0	1	0	0	0	0	5	0	0	0	0	0	13	0	0	0	0	0	24	0	0	0	0	0
CF (Charl) du Plessis	0	0	0	0	0	0	1	0	0	0	0	0	3	0	0	0	0	0	4	0	0	0	0	0	31	0	0	0	0	0
FT (Francois) du Plessis	3	0	0	0	0	0	0	0	0	0	0	0	0	0	0	0	0	0	3	0	0	0	0	0	3	0	0	0	0	0
N (Ntabeni) Dukisa	7	2	11	6	0	50	0	0	0	0	0	0	6	1	0	0	0	5	14	3	11	6	0	55	32	6	17	14	1	109
IJ (Ivan-John) du Preez	5	2	0	0	0	10	0	0	0	0	0	0	0	0	0	0	0	0	5	2	0	0	0	10	5	2	0	0	0	10
M (Martin) Ferreira	0	0	0	0	0	0	0	0	0	0	0	0	4	0	0	0	0	0	4	0	0	0	0	0	4	0	0	0	0	0
LJ (Louis) Fourie	2	0	0	0	0	0	0	0	0	0	0	0	0	0	0	0	0	0	2	0	0	0	0	0	2	0	0	0	0	0
S (Shane) Gates	0	0	0	0	0	0	1	0	0	0	0	0	10	5	0	0	0	25	11	5	0	0	0	25	21	7	0	0	0	35
LP (Lizo) Gqoboka	5	0	0	0	0	0	0	0	0	0	0	0	7	1	0	0	0	5	13	1	0	0	0	5	43	3	0	0	0	15
JPJ (Hansie) Graaff	0	0	0	0	0	0	0	0	0	0	0	0	1	0	0	0	0	0	1	0	0	0	0	0	1	0	0	0	0	0

ABSA CURRIE CUP – PREMIER DIVISION

FIRST-CLASS APPEARANCES FOR EP KINGS IN 2014 - ALL MATCHES

PLAYER	VODACOM CUP					INTERNATIONAL TOUR MATCH					CURRIE CUP					2014 TOTAL					CAREER MATCHES				
	A	T	C	P	DG	Pts	A	T	C	P	DG	Pts	A	T	C	P	DG	Pts	A	T	C	P	DG	Pts	A	T	C	P	DG	Pts
S (Siyanda) Grey	0	0	0	0	0	0	0	0	0	0	0	0	3	1	0	0	0	5	3	1	0	0	0	5	33	15	0	0	0	75
FJ (Jaco) Grobler	1	0	0	0	0	0	1	0	0	0	0	0	3	0	0	0	0	0	5	0	0	0	0	0	5	0	0	0	0	0
BRE (Brendan) Hector	2	0	0	0	0	0	0	0	0	0	0	0	0	0	0	0	0	0	2	0	0	0	0	0	2	0	0	0	0	0
MJ (Morne) Hugo	2	0	0	0	0	0	0	0	0	0	0	0	0	0	0	0	0	0	2	0	0	0	0	0	2	0	0	0	0	0
MAE (Malcolm) Jaer	1	0	0	0	0	0	0	0	0	0	0	0	0	0	0	0	0	0	1	0	0	0	0	0	1	0	0	0	0	0
D (Dwayne) Jenner	0	0	0	0	0	0	0	0	0	0	0	0	2	1	0	0	0	5	2	1	0	0	0	5	2	1	0	0	0	5
A (Andile) Jho	3	0	0	0	0	0	0	0	0	0	0	0	0	0	0	0	0	0	3	0	0	0	0	0	9	0	0	0	0	0
D (Dwayne) Kelly	6	1	1	0	0	7	0	0	0	0	0	0	0	0	0	0	0	0	6	1	1	0	0	7	18	1	1	0	0	7
SJ (Simon) Kerrod	2	0	0	0	0	0	1	0	0	0	0	0	2	1	0	0	0	5	5	1	0	0	0	5	5	1	0	0	0	5
M (Michael) Killian	1	1	0	0	0	5	0	0	0	0	0	0	0	0	0	0	0	0	1	1	0	0	0	5	84	28	0	0	0	140
KX (Kalvano) King	1	0	0	0	0	0	0	0	0	0	0	0	0	0	0	0	0	0	1	0	0	0	0	0	1	0	0	0	0	0
C (Cameron) Lindsay	3	1	0	0	0	5	1	0	0	0	0	0	3	0	0	0	0	0	7	1	0	0	0	5	7	1	0	0	0	5
L (Lance) Louw	3	0	0	0	0	0	0	0	0	0	0	0	0	0	0	0	0	0	3	0	0	0	0	0	3	0	0	0	0	0
K (Kevin) Luiters	0	0	0	0	0	0	1	0	0	0	0	0	8	1	0	0	0	5	9	1	0	0	0	5	9	1	0	0	0	5
SQ (Sonwabo) Majola	3	1	0	0	0	5	0	0	0	0	0	0	0	0	0	0	0	0	3	1	0	0	0	5	3	1	0	0	0	5
S (Tiger) Mangweni	4	0	0	0	0	0	0	0	0	0	0	0	0	0	0	0	0	0	4	0	0	0	0	0	68	11	0	0	0	55
CL (Charles) Marais	0	0	0	0	0	0	0	0	0	0	0	0	4	0	0	0	0	0	4	0	0	0	0	0	4	0	0	0	0	0
E (Edgar) Marutlulle	0	0	0	0	0	0	1	0	0	0	0	0	7	0	0	0	0	0	8	0	0	0	0	0	8	0	0	0	0	0
S (Shaun) McDonald	0	0	0	0	0	0	0	0	0	0	0	0	5	0	0	0	0	0	5	0	0	0	0	0	5	0	0	0	0	0
SNP (Siphu) Msutwana	4	0	0	0	0	0	0	0	0	0	0	0	0	0	0	0	0	0	4	0	0	0	0	0	4	0	0	0	0	0
DP (Darron) Nell	0	0	0	0	0	0	1	0	0	0	0	0	5	1	0	0	0	5	6	1	0	0	0	5	56	10	0	0	0	50
L (Luan) Niewoudt	1	0	0	0	0	0	0	0	0	0	0	0	0	0	0	0	0	0	1	0	0	0	0	0	1	0	0	0	0	0
BH (Brenden) Olivier	3	0	0	0	0	0	0	0	0	0	0	0	0	0	0	0	0	0	3	0	0	0	0	0	20	0	0	0	0	0
DA (Devin) Oosthuizen	0	0	0	0	0	0	1	0	0	0	0	0	5	0	0	0	0	0	6	0	0	0	0	0	58	10	0	0	0	50

ABSA CURRIE CUP – PREMIER DIVISION

FIRST-CLASS APPEARANCES FOR EP KINGS IN 2014 – ALL MATCHES

PLAYER	VODACOM CUP						INTERNATIONAL TOUR MATCH						CURRIE CUP						2014 TOTAL						CAREER MATCHES					
	A	T	C	P	DG	Pts	A	T	C	P	DG	Pts	A	T	C	P	DG	Pts	A	T	C	P	DG	Pts	A	T	C	P	DG	Pts
TW (Tyler) Paul	3	0	0	0	0	0	0	0	0	0	0	0	0	0	0	0	0	0	3	0	0	0	0	0	3	0	0	0	0	0
S (Sergeal) Petersen	2	1	0	0	0	5	0	0	0	0	0	0	0	0	0	0	0	0	2	1	0	0	0	5	5	1	0	0	0	5
SA (Sipho) Phunguzwa	6	1	0	0	0	5	0	0	0	0	0	0	0	0	0	0	0	0	6	1	0	0	0	5	6	1	0	0	0	5
P (Paul) Schoeman	2	0	0	0	0	0	0	0	0	0	0	0	0	0	0	0	0	0	2	0	0	0	0	0	3	0	0	0	0	0
MBJ (Brian) Skosana	7	2	0	0	0	10	1	0	0	0	0	0	8	3	0	0	0	15	11	3	0	0	0	15	19	5	0	0	0	25
MG (Mzu) Sofisa	2	0	0	0	0	0	0	0	0	0	0	0	6	1	0	0	0	5	6	1	0	0	0	5	19	3	0	0	0	15
K (Kuhle) Sonkosi	5	0	0	0	0	0	0	0	0	0	0	0	2	0	0	0	0	0	7	0	0	0	0	0	19	0	0	0	0	0
SS (Siviwe) Soyizwapi	2	1	0	0	0	5	1	0	0	0	0	0	5	3	0	0	0	15	8	4	0	0	0	20	21	6	0	0	0	30
PF (Pieter) Stemmet	5	1	0	0	0	5	0	0	0	0	0	0	0	0	0	0	0	0	5	1	0	0	0	5	5	1	0	0	0	5
SR (Steven) Sykes	1	0	0	0	0	0	1	0	0	0	0	0	10	1	0	0	0	5	12	1	0	0	0	5	12	3	0	0	0	15
CK (Claude) Tshidibi	1	1	0	0	0	5	0	0	0	0	0	0	5	0	0	0	0	0	6	1	0	0	0	5	6	1	0	0	0	5
BG (BG) Uys	1	0	0	0	0	0	1	0	0	0	0	0	5	1	0	0	0	5	7	1	0	0	0	5	7	1	0	0	0	5
GJ (Gary) van Aswegen	0	0	0	0	0	0	1	0	0	0	0	0	5	1	0	0	0	5	6	1	0	0	0	5	6	1	0	0	0	5
S (Scott) van Breda	1	0	0	5	0	30	0	0	0	0	0	0	8	2	8	6	0	44	9	2	8	11	0	74	9	4	10	51	0	287
CJ (CJ) van der Linde	1	0	0	0	0	0	1	0	0	0	0	0	8	2	0	0	0	10	10	2	0	0	0	10	49	10	0	0	0	49
DR (Dane) van der Westhuyzen	4	0	0	0	0	0	0	0	0	0	0	0	3	0	0	0	0	0	7	0	0	0	0	0	7	0	0	0	0	0
MT (Mike) van Vuuren	0	0	0	0	0	0	0	0	0	0	0	0	4	1	0	0	0	5	4	1	0	0	0	5	4	1	0	0	0	5
KD (Kayle) van Zyl	3	0	0	0	0	0	1	0	0	0	0	0	0	0	0	0	0	0	4	0	0	0	0	0	18	3	7	2	0	35
CJ (CJ) Velleman	3	0	0	0	0	0	0	0	0	0	0	0	0	0	0	0	0	0	3	0	0	0	0	0	3	0	0	0	0	0
LA (Luke) Watson	0	0	0	0	0	0	0	0	0	0	0	0	2	0	0	0	0	0	2	0	0	0	0	0	29	8	0	0	0	125
GA (George) Whitehead	1	0	0	3	0	0	0	0	0	0	0	0	4	0	2	1	0	10	5	0	2	1	0	10	45	0	61	28	1	249
TJ (Tim) Whitehead	1	0	0	0	0	0	0	0	0	0	0	0	6	2	0	0	0	10	8	2	0	0	0	10	8	2	0	0	0	10
S (Stefan) Willemse	2	0	0	0	0	0	0	0	0	0	0	0	0	0	0	0	0	0	2	0	0	0	0	0	2	0	0	0	0	0
S (Stefan) Zaayman	3	0	0	0	0	0	0	0	0	0	0	0	0	0	0	0	0	0	3	0	0	0	0	0	5	0	0	0	0	0

72 Players

ABSA CURRIE CUP – PREMIER DIVISION

Free State Rugby Union

Founded: 1895 (as Orange Free State) **Ground:** Free State Stadium **Capacity:** 46 000
Address: Att Horak St, Bloemfontein, 9300 **Postal address:** PO Box 15, Bloemfontein, 9300
Telephone Number: 051-407 1700 **Website:** www.fscheetahs.co.za
Colours: White jersey with orange stripes, black shorts **Currie Cup Coach:** Rory Duncan
Captain: Torsten van Jaarsveld **President:** Lindsay Mould **Company CEO:** Harold Verster
Union CEO: Lindsay Mould

'96	'97	'98	'99	'00	'01	'02	'03	'04	'05	'06	'07	'08	'09	'10	'11	'12	'13	'14
3rd	3rd	5th	3rd	4th	4th	2nd	5th	3rd	**4th**	**1st**	**1st**	3rd	4th	3rd	3rd	6th	3rd	5th

Played	Won	Lost	Drawn	Points for	Points against	Tries for	Tries against
10	3	6	1	249	294	28	33

Date	Venue	Opponent	Result	Score	Referee	Scorers
9 Aug	Nelspruit	Pumas	LOST	21-28	M vd Westhuizen	T: Benjamin (2). C: W du Plessis. P: W du Plessis (3).
16 Aug	Bloemfontein	Griquas	WON	34-27	M Jonker	T: Rhule (2), Watts, Benjamin, Pretorius. C: Watts (2), W du Plessis. P: Watts.
23 Aug	Durban	Sharks	LOST	16-19	R Rasivhenge	T: Blommetjies. C: W du Plessis. P: W du Plessis (3).
30 Aug	Kimberley	Griquas	WON	36-25	J van Heerden	T: Blommetjies, Uys, Cook, Benjamin, Burger. C: De Wet (3), W du Plessis. P: W du Plessis.
6 Sep	Bloemfontein	Pumas	LOST	17-31	C Joubert	T: JP du Plessis, Pretorius. C: De Wet (2). P: De Wet.
13 Sep	Bloemfontein	Sharks	DREW	30-30	S Berry	T: Pretorius (2), Burger. C: W du Plessis (3). P: W du Plessis (3).
20 Sep	Port Elizabeth	EP Kings	WON	37-22	M Jonker	T: F Venter, Rhule, Pretorius, W du Plessis. C: W du Plessis (3), De Wet. P: W du Plessis
26 Sep	Bloemfontein	Blue Bulls	LOST	22-31	M vd Westhuizen	T: Pretorius. C: W du Plessis. P: W du plessis (4). DG: W du Plessis.
4 Oct	Bloemfontein	WP	LOST	29-34	M Jonker	T: F Venter, Engelbrecht, Labuschagne, W du Plessis. C: W du Plessis (3). P: W du Plessis.
11 Oct	Johannesburg	Golden Lions	LOST	7-47	S Berry	T: Pretorius. C: W du Plessis.

Note: ■ = Champion

ABSA CURRIE CUP – PREMIER DIVISION

APPEARANCES & POINTS FOR FREE STATE IN 2014 CURRIE CUP

PLAYER	Pumas	Griquas	Sharks	Griquas	Pumas	Sharks	EP Kings	Blue Bulls	WP	Golden Lions	Apps	T	C	P	DG	Pts
AJ Coertzen	15	15	–	–	15	9R	–	13R	14		6	–	–	–	–	0
Ryno Benjamin	14	14	14	14	14	15	–	14	–	–	7	4	–	–	–	20
Francois Venter	13	13	13	13	12	13	13	13	13	–	9	2	–	–	–	10
Joubert Engelbrecht	12	12	12	12	x	12	12	12	12	12	9	1	–	–	–	5
Raymond Rhule	11	11	11	11	11	–	11	11	11	11	9	3	–	–	–	15
Willie du Plessis	10	10R	10	10	10R	10	10	10	10	10	10	2	15	18	1	97
Sarel Pretorius	9	9	9	9	9	9	9	9	9	9	10	7	–	–	–	35
Boom Prinsloo	8	8	–	–	–	–	–	–	–	–	2	–	–	–	–	0
Neil Claassen	7	8R	7	7	7	7	7	8R	7	7	10	–	–	–	–	0
Tienie Burger	6	6	6	6	6	6	6	6	6	6	10	2	–	–	–	10
Francois Uys	5	5	5	5	5	5	5	5	5	5	10	1	–	–	–	5
Carl Wegner	4	4	4	–	–	–	–	–	–	–	3	–	–	–	–	0
Luan de Bruin	3	3	–	–	–	–	–	–	–	–	2	–	–	–	–	0
Torsten van Jaarsveld	2c	2c	2c	2c	2c	2c	2c	2c	2c	2c	10	–	–	–	–	0
Kevin Stevens	1	1	1	1	1	–	–	–	–	–	5	–	–	–	–	0
Hercu Liebenberg	x	–	–	–	–	–	x	x	2R		1	–	–	–	–	0
Bees Roux	3R	–	–	–	–	–	–	–	–	–	1	–	–	–	–	0
Waltie Vermeulen	7R	x	–	5R	–	–	–	–	–	–	2	–	–	–	–	0
Henco Venter	8R	–	4R	4	4	4	4	4	4R	4R	9	–	–	–	–	0
Renier Botha	x	–	–	–	–	–	–	–	–	–	0	–	–	–	–	0
Elgar Watts	10R	10	–	–	–	–	–	–	–	–	2	1	2	1	–	12
JP du Plessis	12R	14R	12R	12R	13	11	14	14R	14	13	10	1	–	–	–	5
Jean Cook	–	7	8	8	8	–	–	8	–	–	5	1	–	–	–	5
Rudolph Botha	–	3R	3	3	3	1R	3R	–	–	–	6	–	–	–	–	0
AJ le Roux	–	17R	x	1R	2R	x	2R	–	–	–	4	–	–	–	–	0
Shaun Venter	–	15R	14R	9R	11R	14R	14R	x	14R	14R	8	–	–	–	–	0
Clayton Blommetjies	–	–	15	15	15	–	15	15	15	15	7	2	–	–	–	10
George Marich	–	–	3R	3R	1R	3	3	3	3	1R	8	–	–	–	–	0
Vincent Jobo	–	–	x	8R	8R	8R	8R	–	x	–	4	–	–	–	–	0
Pieter-Steyn de Wet	–	–	x	10R	10	x	10R	x	x	10R	4	–	6	1	–	15
Werner Lourens	–	–	–	–	4R	x	–	4R	4	–	3	–	–	–	–	0
Maphutha Dolo	–	–	–	–	–	14	–	–	–	x	1	–	–	–	–	0
Pieter Labuschagne	–	–	–	–	–	8	8	7	8	8	5	1	–	–	–	5
Caylib Oosthuizen	–	–	–	–	–	1	1	3R	3R	1	5	–	–	–	–	0
Brendon Groenewald	–	–	–	–	–	–	4R	–	–	–	1	–	–	–	–	0
Coenie Oosthuizen	–	–	–	–	–	–	1	1	–		2	–	–	–	–	0
Toboho Mohoje	–	–	–	–	–	–	–	–	–	7	1	–	–	–	–	0
Lood de Jager	–	–	–	–	–	–	–	–	–	4	1	–	–	–	–	0
Trevor Nyakane	–	–	–	–	–	–	–	–	–	3	1	–	–	–	–	0
39 Players											**203**	**28**	**23**	**20**	**1**	**249**

ABSA CURRIE CUP – PREMIER DIVISION

CURRIE CUP SQUAD – CAREER CURRIE CUP APPEARANCES

PLAYER	FREE STATE						OTHER UNIONS						TOTAL					
	A	T	C	P	DG	Pts	A	T	C	P	DG	Pts	A	T	C	P	DG	Pts
RS (Ryno) Benjamin	28	7	–	–	–	35	60	46	–	–	–	230	88	53	–	–	–	265
C (Clayton) Blommetjies	7	2	–	–	–	10	14	1	–	–	–	5	21	3	–	–	–	15
PR (Dolph) Botha	6	–	–	–	–	0	–	–	–	–	–	0	6	–	–	–	–	0
R (Renier) Botha	0	–	–	–	–	0	–	–	–	–	–	0	0	–	–	–	–	0
MA (Tienie) Burger	10	2	–	–	–	10	–	–	–	–	–	0	10	2	–	–	–	10
N (Neil) Claassen	10	–	–	–	–	0	–	–	–	–	–	0	10	–	–	–	–	0
AJ (AJ) Coertzen	6	–	–	–	–	0	–	–	–	–	–	0	6	–	–	–	–	0
JG (Jean) Cook	5	1	–	–	–	5	6	1	–	–	–	5	11	2	–	–	–	10
L (Luan) de Bruin	2	–	–	–	–	0	–	–	–	–	–	0	2	–	–	–	–	0
L (Lood) de Jager	11	–	–	–	–	0	–	–	–	–	–	0	11	–	–	–	–	0
PS (Pieter-Steyn) de Wet	4	–	6	1	–	15	4	–	7	2	–	20	8	–	13	3	–	35
MS (Maphutha) Dolo	1	–	–	–	–	0	–	–	–	–	–	0	1	–	–	–	–	0
PJS (JP) du Plessis	10	1	–	–	–	5	9	2	–	–	–	10	19	3	–	–	–	15
WNF (Willie) du Plessis	19	2	18	18	1	103	–	–	–	–	–	0	19	2	18	18	1	103
GJ (Joubert) Engelbrecht	10	1	–	–	–	5	29	6	5	1	–	43	39	7	5	1	–	48
B (Brendon) Groenewald	1	–	–	–	–	0	–	–	–	–	–	0	1	–	–	–	–	0
VT (Vincent) Jobo	4	–	–	–	–	0	–	–	–	–	–	0	4	–	–	–	–	0
PHC (Pieter) Labuschagne	42	10	–	–	–	50	–	–	–	–	–	0	42	10	–	–	–	50
AJ (AJ) le Roux	12	–	–	–	–	0	5	1	–	–	–	5	17	1	–	–	–	5
HJ (Hercu) Liebenberg	31	–	–	–	–	0	13	1	–	–	–	5	44	1	–	–	–	5
W (Werner) Lourens	3	–	–	–	–	0	4	–	–	–	–	0	7	–	–	–	–	0
G (George) Marich	8	–	–	–	–	0	–	–	–	–	–	0	8	–	–	–	–	0
TS (Oupa) Mohoje	12	–	–	–	–	0	5	–	–	–	–	0	17	–	–	–	–	0
TN (Trevor) Nyakane	25	–	–	–	–	0	1	–	–	–	–	0	26	–	–	–	–	0
CR (Caylib) Oosthuizen	8	–	–	–	–	0	2	–	–	–	–	0	10	–	–	–	–	0
CV (Coenie) Oosthuizen	51	9	–	–	–	45	–	–	–	–	–	0	51	9	–	–	–	45
SJ (Sarel) Pretorius	34	14	–	–	–	70	71	26	–	–	–	130	105	40	–	–	–	200
JG (Boom) Prinsloo	26	8	–	–	–	40	–	–	–	–	–	0	26	8	–	–	–	40
RK (Raymond) Rhule	37	18	–	–	–	90	–	–	–	–	–	0	37	18	–	–	–	90
JS (Bees) Roux	1	–	–	–	–	0	43	–	–	–	–	0	44	–	–	–	–	0
KB (Kevin) Stevens	5	–	–	–	–	0	36	2	–	–	–	10	41	2	–	–	–	10
FJ (Francois) Uys	59	6	–	–	–	30	1	–	–	–	–	0	60	6	–	–	–	30
TG (Torsten) van Jaarsveld	10	–	–	–	–	0	38	4	–	–	–	20	48	4	–	–	–	20
HP (Henco) Venter	10	–	–	–	–	0	–	–	–	–	–	0	10	–	–	–	–	0
JF (Francois) Venter	9	2	–	–	–	10	31	9	–	–	–	45	40	11	–	–	–	55
SH (Shaun) Venter	8	–	–	–	–	0	61	16	–	–	–	80	69	16	–	–	–	80
PV (Waltie) Vermeulen	31	–	–	–	–	0	–	–	–	–	–	0	31	–	–	–	–	0
EG (Elgar) Watts	13	5	10	10	–	75	61	23	65	39	–	362	74	28	75	49	–	437
C (Carl) Wegner	10	–	–	–	–	0	–	–	–	–	–	0	10	–	–	–	–	0
39 Players	**579**	**88**	**34**	**29**	**1**	**598**	**494**	**138**	**77**	**42**	**0**	**970**	**1063**	**226**	**111**	**71**	**1**	**1568**

ABSA CURRIE CUP – PREMIER DIVISION

FIRST-CLASS APPEARANCES FOR FREE STATE CHEETAHS IN 2014 – ALL MATCHES*

PLAYER	CURRIE CUP						CAREER MATCHES					
	A	T	C	P	DG	Pts	A	T	C	P	DG	Pts
RS (Ryno) Benjamin	7	4	–	–	–	20	26	6	–	–	–	30
C (Clayton) Blommetjies	7	2	–	–	–	10	7	2	–	–	–	10
PR (Dolph) Botha	6	–	–	–	–	0	6	–	–	–	–	0
R (Renier) Botha	0	–	–	–	–	0	0	–	–	–	–	0
MA (Tienie) Burger	10	2	–	–	–	10	10	2	–	–	–	10
N (Neil) Claassen	10	–	–	–	–	0	10	–	–	–	–	0
AJ (AJ) Coertzen	6	–	–	–	–	0	6	–	–	–	–	0
JG (Jean) Cook	5	1	–	–	–	5	5	1	–	–	–	5
L (Luan) de Bruin	2	–	–	–	–	0	2	–	–	–	–	0
L (Lood) de Jager	1	–	–	–	–	0	11	–	–	–	–	0
PS (Pieter-Steyn) de Wet	4	–	6	1	–	15	4	–	6	1	–	15
MS (Maphutha) Dolo	1	–	–	–	–	0	1	–	–	–	–	0
PJS (JP) du Plessis	10	1	–	–	–	5	10	1	–	–	–	5
WNF (Willie) du Plessis	10	2	15	18	1	97	19	2	18	18	1	103
GJ (Joubert) Engelbrecht	9	1	–	–	–	5	10	1	–	–	–	5
B (Brendon) Groenewald	1	–	–	–	–	0	9	2	–	–	–	10
VT (Vincent) Jobo	4	–	–	–	–	0	4	–	–	–	–	0
PHC (Pieter) Labuschagne	5	1	–	–	–	5	44	11	–	–	–	55
AJ (AJ) le Roux	4	–	–	–	–	0	11	1	–	–	–	5
HJ (Hercu) Liebenberg	1	–	–	–	–	0	58	–	–	–	–	0
W (Werner) Lourens	3	–	–	–	–	0	3	–	–	–	–	0
G (George) Marich	8	–	–	–	–	0	8	–	–	–	–	0
TS (Oupa) Mohoje	1	–	–	–	–	–	12	–	–	–	–	0
TN (Trevor) Nyakane	1	–	–	–	–	0	38	2	–	–	–	10
CR (Caylib) Oosthuizen	5	–	–	–	–	0	8	–	–	–	–	0
CV (Coenie) Oosthuizen	2	–	–	–	–	0	55	11	–	–	–	55
SJ (Sarel) Pretorius	10	7	–	–	–	35	32	14	–	–	–	70
JG (Boom) Prinsloo	2	–	–	–	–	0	33	9	–	–	–	45
RK (Raymond) Rhule	9	3	–	–	–	15	31	18	–	–	–	90
JS (Bees) Roux	1	–	–	–	–	0	1	–	–	–	–	0
KB (Kevin) Stevens	5	–	–	–	–	0	11	–	–	–	–	0
FJ (Francois) Uys	10	1	–	–	–	5	68	8	–	–	–	40
TG (Torsten) van Jaarsveld	10	–	–	–	–	0	10	–	–	–	–	0
HP (Henco) Venter	9	–	–	–	–	0	10	–	–	–	–	0
JF (Francois) Venter	9	2	–	–	–	10	9	2	–	–	–	10
SH (Shaun) Venter	8	–	–	–	–	0	8	–	–	–	–	0
PV (Waltie) Vermeulen	2	–	–	–	–	0	46	–	–	–	–	0
EG (Elgar) Watts	2	1	2	1	–	12	13	5	10	10	–	75
C (Carl) Wegner	3	–	–	–	–	0	8	–	–	–	–	0
39 Players (of which 38 players made an appearance)	203	28	23	20	1	249	657	98	34	29	1	648

*Free State's Vodacom Cup matches were also first-class but they played as the 'Free State XV', which the FSRU considers a completely different team. This table shows first-class matches played by the 'Free State Cheetahs' only. See Vodacom Cup section for Free State XV info.

ABSA CURRIE CUP – PREMIER DIVISION

Golden Lions Rugby Union

Founded: 1889 **Ground:** Ellis Park) **Capacity:** 60 000
Address: South Office Block, Johannesburg Stadium, 124 Van Beek Street, Doornfontein 2094
Postal address: PO Box 15724, Doornfontein, 2028 **Telephone Number:** 011-402 2960
Website: www.lionsrugby.co.za **Colours:** White and red trim jersey, black shorts and black socks
Currie Cup Coach: Johan Ackermann **Captain:** Warren Whiteley
President: Kevin de Klerk **Company CEO:** Rudolf Straeuli

'96	'97	'98	'99	'00	'01	'02	'03	'04	'05	'06	'07	'08	'09	'10	'11	'12	'13	'14
4th	4th	8th	**1st**	3rd	3rd	3rd	4th	4th	2nd	5th	3rd	4th	6th	3rd	**1st**	3rd	4th	2nd

Played	Won	Lost	Drawn	Points for	Points against	Tries for	Tries against
12	8	4	0	428	245	51	25

Date	Venue	Opponent	Result	Score	Referee	Scorers
9 Aug	Johannesburg	Blue Bulls	WON	41-13	J van Heerden	T: Hanekom, Combrinck, Kriel, Tecklenburg. C: Boshoff (2), Van der Walt. P: Boshoff (2), Van der Walt (2). D: Boshoff.
16 Aug	Johannesburg	EP Kings	WON	60-19	C Joubert	T: Kriel (2), A Coetzee, R Coetzee, Hanekom, Combrinck, Minnie, Britz, Smith. C: Van der Walt (6). P: Van der Walt.
23 Aug	Cape Town	WP	LOST	14-27	C Joubert	T: A Coetzee. P: Combrinck (3).
30 Aug	Port Elizabeth	EP Kings	WON	41-22	M vd Westhuizen	T: Kriel, Mostert, Dreyer, S vd Merwe, Minnie. C: Combrinck (5). P: Combrinck.
6 Sep	Pretoria	Blue Bulls	LOST	26-36	M vd Westhuizen	T: Muller, Smith. C: Combrinck (2). P: Combrinck (4).
13 Sep	Johannesburg	WP	WON	35-33	J Peyper	T: Mapoe, Kriel, Mostert, A van der Merwe, S van der Merwe. C: Combrinck (5).
19 Sep	Johannesburg	Pumas	WON	29-15	J van Heerden	T: Hanekom, Skosan, Mostert, Dreyer. C: Combrinck (3). D: Van der Walt.
27 Sep	Kimberley	Griquas	WON	46-8	J Peyper	T: Kriel (2), A Coetzee, Combrinck, Mostert, Smith. C: Combrinck (5). P: Combrinck (2).
3 Oct	Durban	Sharks	LOST	23-26	L Legoete	T: Combrinck, Hanekom. C: Boshoff (2). P: Boshoff (3).
11 Oct	Johannesburg	Cheetahs	WON	47-7	S Berry	T: Combrinck, Mnisi, Minnie, Kriel, A van der Merwe, Tecklenburg. C: Boshoff (4). P: Boshoff (3).

ABSA CURRIE CUP – PREMIER DIVISION

Date	Venue	Opponent	Result	Score	Referee	Scorers
SEMI-FINAL						
18 Oct	Johannesburg	Sharks	WON	50-20	J van Heerden	T: Combrinck, Mnisi, Cronje, Whiteley, Kriel, A van der Merwe. C: Boshoff (4). P: Boshoff (4).
FINAL						
25 Oct	Cape Town	WP	LOST	16-19	C Joubert	T: Van der Walt. C: Boshoff. P: Boshoff (2), Combrinck.

Note: ■ = *Champion*

APPEARANCES & POINTS FOR GOLDEN LIONS IN 2014 CURRIE CUP

PLAYER	B.Bulls	EP	WP	EP	B.Bulls	WP	Pumas	Griquas	Sharks	Cheetahs	Sharks (SF)	WP (F)	Apps	T	C	P	Do	Pts
Andries Coetzee	15	15	15	10	15	15	15	15	–	–	–	–	8	3	0	0	0	15
Lionel Mapoe	14	14	13	14c	14	13c	13c	13c	13c	13	13	13	12	1	0	0	0	5
Nico Hanekom	13	13	10	13	13	12	12	13R	12	–	–	–	9	4	0	0	0	20
Harold Vorster	12	12	12	–	–	–	–	–	13R	12R	12R		6	–	–	–	–	0
Ruan Combrinck	11	11	11	15	11	14	14	14	14	14	14	14	12	6	20	12	0	106
Marnitz Boshoff	10	–	–	–	–	–	10R	15	10	10	10		6	0	13	14	1	71
Ross Cronje	9	9	9	9	9	–	–	9	9	9	9	9	10	1	0	0	0	5
Warren Whiteley	8c	8c	–	–	–	–	8	–	8c	8c	8c		6	1	0	0	0	5
Derick Minnie	7	7	6c	8R	8c	–	6R	–	6R	7	7	7	10	3	0	0	0	15
Jaco Kriel	6	6	7R	6	6	6	6	6	6	6	6	6	12	9	0	0	0	45
Franco Mostert	5	5	5	5	5	5	5	5	5	5	5	5	12	4	0	0	0	20
MB Lusaseni	4	4	4	4	4	4	–	–	–	–	–	–	6	–	–	–	–	0
Ruan Dreyer	3	3	3	3	3	3	3R	3	3	3	3		12	2	0	0	0	10
Robbie Coetzee	2	2	2	–	–	–	2R	2	2	2	2		8	1	0	0	0	5
Schalk van der Merwe	1	1	1	1	1	1	1	–	1	1	1	1	11	2	0	0	0	10
Armand van der Merwe	2R	2R	2R	2	2R	2	2	2	2R	2R	2R	2R	12	3	0	0	0	15
Jacques van Rooyen	3R	1R	1R	1R	1R	1R	1R	1	1R	–	–		10	–	–	–	–	0
Willie Britz	4R	5R	8	8	7R	8	8	5R	8	5R	5R	4R	12	1	0	0	0	5
Warwick Tecklenburg	7R	6R	7	7	7	6R	7R	7	7	6R	4R	7R	12	2	0	0	0	10
Ricky Schroeder	9R	–	–	11R	–	9	9	–	–	–	–	–	4	–	–	–	–	0
Jaco van der Walt	10R	10	–	–	10	10	10	10	15	15	15		10	1	7	3	1	31
Howard Mnisi	14R	13R	14R	12R	10R	11R	12R	12	12R	12	12	12	12	2	0	0	0	10
Albertus Smith	–	14R	5R	7R	8R	7	7	7R	7R	–	6R	6R	10	3	0	0	0	15
Guy Cronje	–	9R	12R	–	–	–	–	–	–	–	–	–	2	–	–	–	–	0
Courtnall Skosan	–	–	14	11	–	11	11	11	11	11	11	11	9	1	0	0	0	5
Martin Muller	–	–	4R	4R	4R	4R	4	4	4	4	4	4	10	1	0	0	0	5
Alwyn Hollenbach	–	–	–	–	12	12	–	–	–	–	–	–	2	–	–	–	–	0
Willie Wepener	–	–	–	–	2R	2	–	2R	–	–	–	–	3	–	–	–	–	0
Mark Richards	–	–	–	–	–	9R	9R	9R	9R	9R	9R	9R	8	–	–	–	–	0
Malcolm Marx	–	–	–	–	–	–	2R	–	–	–	–	–	1	–	–	–	–	0
Julian Redelinghuys	–	–	–	–	–	3R	–	3	3R	3R	1R	3R	6	–	–	–	–	0
Chris van Zyl	–	–	–	–	–	–	4R	–	–	–	–	–	1	–	–	–	–	0
32 Players													**264**	**51**	**40**	**29**	**2**	**428**

CURRIE CUP SQUAD – CAREER CURRIE CUP APPEARANCES

PLAYER	GOLDEN LIONS						OTHER UNIONS						TOTAL					
	A	T	C	P	DG	Pts	A	T	C	P	DG	Pts	A	T	C	P	DG	Pts
ML (Marnitz) Boshoff	17	2	33	28	1	163	13	0	2	2	0	10	30	2	35	30	1	173
WS (Willie) Britz	32	4	0	0	0	20	17	5	0	0	0	25	49	9	0	0	0	45
A (Andries) Coetzee	26	6	1	0	0	32	0	0	0	0	0	0	26	6	1	0	0	32
RL (Robbie) Coetzee	18	2	0	0	0	10	3	0	0	0	0	0	21	2	0	0	0	10
RJ (Ruan) Combrinck	21	10	20	14	0	132	0	0	0	0	0	0	21	10	20	14	0	132
G (Guy) Cronje	10	0	1	0	0	2	6	0	3	0	0	6	16	0	4	0	0	8
R (Ross) Cronje	26	2	0	0	0	10	14	0	0	0	0	0	40	2	0	0	0	10
RM (Ruan) Dreyer	25	4	0	0	0	20	0	0	0	0	0	0	25	4	0	0	0	20
NJ (Nico) Hanekom	10	5	0	0	0	25	0	0	0	0	0	0	10	5	0	0	0	25
AWCJ (Alwyn) Hollenbach	35	8	0	0	0	40	27	6	0	0	0	30	62	14	0	0	0	70
JA (Jaco) Kriel	35	16	0	0	0	80	0	0	0	0	0	0	35	16	0	0	0	80
L (MB) Lusaseni	6	0	0	0	0	0	29	2	0	0	0	10	35	2	0	0	0	10
LG (Lionel) Mapoe	32	6	0	0	0	30	9	3	0	0	0	15	41	9	0	0	0	45
MJ (Malcolm) Marx	1	0	0	0	0	0	0	0	0	0	0	0	1	0	0	0	0	0
DJ (Derick) Minnie	70	22	0	0	0	110	0	0	0	0	0	0	70	22	0	0	0	110
XH (Howard) Mnisi	12	2	0	0	0	10	17	3	0	0	0	15	29	5	0	0	0	25
FJ (Franco) Mostert	12	4	0	0	0	20	4	1	0	0	0	5	16	5	0	0	0	25
MD (Martin) Muller	10	1	0	0	0	5	24	1	0	0	0	5	34	2	0	0	0	10
J (Julian) Redelinghuys	9	0	0	0	0	0	8	0	0	0	0	0	17	0	0	0	0	0
M (Mark) Richards	8	0	0	0	0	0	4	1	0	0	0	5	12	1	0	0	0	5
RD (Ricky) Schroeder	4	0	0	0	0	0	10	0	0	0	0	0	14	0	0	0	0	0
CD (Courtnall) Skosan	9	1	0	0	0	5	0	0	0	0	0	0	9	1	0	0	0	5
AS (Kwagga) Smith	10	3	0	0	0	15	0	0	0	0	0	0	10	3	0	0	0	15
WJ (Warwick) Tecklenburg	23	3	0	0	0	15	13	3	0	0	0	15	36	6	0	0	0	30
AHP (Akker) van der Merwe	12	3	0	0	0	15	11	0	0	0	0	0	23	3	0	0	0	15
SW (Schalk) van der Merwe	11	2	0	0	0	10	20	3	0	0	0	15	31	5	0	0	0	25
J (Jaco) van der Walt	10	1	7	3	1	31	0	0	0	0	0	0	10	1	7	3	1	31
J (Jacques) van Rooyen	21	2	0	0	0	10	0	0	0	0	0	0	21	2	0	0	0	10
CM (Chris) van Zyl	8	0	0	0	0	0	0	0	0	0	0	0	8	0	0	0	0	0
HW (Harold) Vorster	6	0	0	0	0	0	0	0	0	0	0	0	6	0	0	0	0	0
FW (Willie) Wepener	43	7	0	0	0	35	55	4	0	0	0	20	98	11	0	0	0	55
WR (Warren) Whiteley	47	6	0	0	0	30	5	1	0	0	0	5	52	7	0	0	0	35
32 Players	619	122	62	45	2	875	289	33	5	2	0	181	908	155	67	47	2	1056

ABSA CURRIE CUP – PREMIER DIVISION

FIRST-CLASS APPEARANCES FOR GOLDEN LIONS IN 2014 – ALL MATCHES*

PLAYER	CURRIE CUP						CAREER MATCHES					
	A	T	C	P	DG	Pts	A	T	C	P	DG	Pts
ML (Marnitz) Boshoff	6	0	13	14	1	71	17	2	33	28	1	163
WS (Willie) Britz	12	1	0	0	0	5	32	4	0	0	0	20
A (Andries) Coetzee	8	3	0	0	0	15	26	6	1	0	0	32
RL (Robbie) Coetzee	8	1	0	0	0	5	18	2	0	0	0	10
RJ (Ruan) Combrinck	12	6	20	12	0	106	21	10	20	14	0	132
G (Guy) Cronje	2	0	0	0	0	0	10	0	1	0	0	2
R (Ross) Cronje	10	1	0	0	0	5	26	2	0	0	0	10
RM (Ruan) Dreyer	12	2	0	0	0	10	25	4	0	0	0	20
NJ (Nico) Hanekom	9	4	0	0	0	20	10	5	0	0	0	25
AWCJ (Alwyn) Hollenbach	2	0	0	0	0	0	35	8	0	0	0	40
JA (Jaco) Kriel	12	9	0	0	0	45	35	16	0	0	0	80
L (MB) Lusaseni	6	0	0	0	0	0	6	0	0	0	0	0
LG (Lionel) Mapoe	12	1	0	0	0	5	32	6	0	0	0	30
MJ (Malcolm) Marx	1	0	0	0	0	0	1	0	0	0	0	0
DJ (Derick) Minnie	10	3	0	0	0	15	70	22	0	0	0	110
XH (Howard) Mnisi	12	2	0	0	0	10	12	2	0	0	0	10
FJ (Franco) Mostert	12	4	0	0	0	20	12	4	0	0	0	20
MD (Martin) Muller	10	1	0	0	0	5	10	1	0	0	0	5
J (Julian) Redelinghuys	6	0	0	0	0	0	9	0	0	0	0	0
M (Mark) Richards	8	0	0	0	0	0	8	0	0	0	0	0
RD (Ricky) Schroeder	4	0	0	0	0	0	4	0	0	0	0	0
CD (Courtnall) Skosan	9	1	0	0	0	5	9	1	0	0	0	5
AS (Kwagga) Smith	10	3	0	0	0	15	10	3	0	0	0	15
WJ (Warwick) Tecklenburg	12	2	0	0	0	10	23	3	0	0	0	15
AHP (Akker) van der Merwe	12	3	0	0	0	15	12	3	0	0	0	15
SW (Schalk) van der Merwe	11	2	0	0	0	10	11	2	0	0	0	10
J (Jaco) van der Walt	10	1	7	3	1	31	10	1	7	3	1	31
J (Jacques) van Rooyen	10	0	0	0	0	0	21	2	0	0	0	10
CM (Chris) van Zyl	1	0	0	0	0	0	8	0	0	0	0	0
HW (Harold) Vorster	6	0	0	0	0	0	6	0	0	0	0	0
FW (Willie) Wepener	3	0	0	0	0	0	43	7	0	0	0	35
WR (Warren) Whiteley	6	1	0	0	0	5	47	6	0	0	0	30
32 Players	264	51	40	29	2	428	619	122	62	45	2	875

*The Golden Lions' Vodacom Cup matches were also first-class but they played as a separate team. This table shows first-class matches played by the 'Golden Lions' only. See Vodacom Cup section for Golden Lions XV info.

⟨ DID YOU KNOW? ⟩
The most points scored by a player in a Currie Cup final is 26 – by Derick Hougaard for the Blue Bulls against the Golden Lions in the 2002 final (1 try, 5 penalties, 2 drop goals).

Griqualand West Rugby Union

Founded: 1886 **Ground:** GWK Park, Kimberley **Capacity:** 11 000
Address: Jacobus Smit Avenue, New Park, Kimberley
Postal address: PO Box 110825, Hadison Park, Kimberley 8306 **Telephone Number:** 053-832 8773
Website: www.griquasrugby.co.za **Colours:** Peacock blue and white hooped jersey, black shorts
Currie Cup Coach: Hawies Fourie **Captain:** Wayne Stevens **President:** Jannie Louw
Company CEO: Arni van Rooyen

'96	'97	'98	'99	'00	'01	'02	'03	'04	'05	'06	'07	'08	'09	'10	'11	'12	'13	'14
6th	6th	1st	6th	8th	8th	7th	7th	6th	7th	6th	6th	6th	5th	6th	6th	5th	6th	7th

Played	Won	Lost	Drawn	Points for	Points against	Tries for	Tries against
10	3	7	0	220	332	25	41

Date	Venue	Opponent	Result	Score	Referee	Scorers
9 Aug	Kimberley	Sharks	LOST	24-31	C Joubert	T: C Greeff, Arendse, M Schoeman. C: Scheepers (3). P: Scheepers.
16 Aug	Bloemfontein	Free State	LOST	27-34	M Jonker	T: M Schoeman (2), Arendse, Stevens. C: Scheepers, Schmidt. P: Schmidt.
22 Aug	Nelspruit	Pumas	LOST	15-33	Q Immelman	T: M Schoeman, Grant. C: Grant. P: Grant.
30 Aug	Kimberley	Free State	LOST	25-36	J van Heerden	T: Arendse, Beszuidenhout, Meyer. C: Grant (2). P: Grant (2).
6 Sep	Durban	Sharks	WON	21-18	L vd Merwe	P: Gouws (6), DG: Brummer.
13 Sep	Kimberley	Pumas	WON	31-27	C Joubert	T: Vermeulen. C: Prinsloo. P: Prinsloo (8).
20 Sep	Cape Town	WP	LOST	12-36	L Legoete	T: Lerm, Griesel. C: Grant
27 Sep	Kimberley	Golden Lions	LOST	8-46	J Peyper	T: C Greeff. P: Prinsloo.
4 Oct	Kimberley	EP Kings	WON	45-25	S Berry	T: M Schoeman (3), Vermeulen (2), Van Niekerk, Beszuidenhout. C: Grant (3), Prinsloo (2),
11 Oct	Pretoria	Blue Bulls	LOST	12-46	L Legoete	T: Arendse (2). C: Jansen.

Note: ■ = *Champion*

ABSA CURRIE CUP – PREMIER DIVISION

APPEARANCES & POINTS FOR GRIQUAS IN 2014 CURRIE CUP

PLAYER	Sharks	Free State	Pumas	Free State	Sharks	Pumas	WP	G Lions	EP	B Bulls	Apps	T	C	P	DG	Pts
Nico Scheepers	15	15	–	–	–	–	–	–	–	–	2	–	4	1	–	11
Danie Dames	14	–	–	–	–	–	11R	11R	14	14	5	–	–	–	–	0
Jonathan Francke	13	13R	13	13	13	13	13	13	13	12	10	–	–	–	–	0
Wayne Stevens	12c	12c	12c	12c	–	–	–	12c	12c	–	6	1	–	–	–	5
Rocco Jansen	11	11	–	11R	–	–	–	–	–	–	3	–	–	–	–	0
Francois Brummer	10	10	15	15	10c	10c	10c	–	–	10c	8	–	–	–	1	3
Tian Meyer	9	9	9	9	9	9	9	9	9	9	10	1	–	–	–	5
Carel Greeff	8	8	8	8	7	7	6R	8	7	–	9	2	–	–	–	10
Hilton Lobberts	7	–	–	–	4	4	4	4	–	–	5	–	–	–	–	0
Marnus Schoeman	6	6	6	6	6	6	6	6R	6	6	10	7	–	–	–	35
Jaco Nepgen	5	5	5	5	5	5	–	7	5	5	9	–	–	–	–	0
Willem Serfontein	4	4	–	–	–	–	–	–	–	–	2	–	–	–	–	0
Maks van Dyk	3	1R	1R	–	3R	3R	3	3	3	3	9	–	–	–	–	0
Ryno Barnes	2	2	2R	1R	2R	4R	2R	3R	2R	17R	10	–	–	–	–	0
Steph Roberts	1	1	1	1	1	1	1	–	–	–	7	–	–	–	–	0
Simon Westraadt	2R	–	–	–	–	–	1R	1R	1	–	4	–	–	–	–	0
Ewald vd Westhuizen	3R	3	3	3	3	3	–	–	–	–	6	–	–	–	–	0
Hugo Kloppers	4R	4R	x	5R	5R	6R	5	5	4	4	9	–	–	–	–	0
RJ Liebenberg	7R	7	8R	–	7R	7R	–	8R	4R	6R	8	–	–	–	–	0
Abrie Griesel	x	x	x	9R	x	11R	9R	9R	–	–	4	1	–	–	–	5
Marais Schmidt	14R	15R	–	–	–	–	–	–	–	–	2	–	1	1	–	5
Ederies Arendse	11R	14	14	14	14	14	14	14	12R	11	10	5	–	–	–	25
PJ Vermeulen	–	13	11	11	11	11	11	11	11	13	9	3	–	–	–	15
Martin Bezuidenhout	–	2R	2	2	2	2	2	2	2	2	9	2	–	–	–	10
Burger Schoeman	–	x	–	4R	8R	8R	8	–	–	–	4	–	–	–	–	0
Dean Grant	–	–	10	10	x	12R	15R	10	10	10R	7	1	7	3	–	28
Ruaan Lerm	–	–	7	7	8	8	7	6	8	8	8	1	–	–	–	5
Jonathan Adendorf	–	–	4	4	–	–	8R	–	7R	7	5	–	–	–	–	0
Niel Marais	–	–	10R	–	–	–	–	–	–	–	1	–	–	–	–	0
Doppies la Grange	–	–	12R	12R	12	12	12	–	–	14R	6	–	–	–	–	0
Janro van Niekerk	–	–	–	3R	–	–	1R	1	1	–	4	1	–	–	–	5
Gouws Prinsloo	–	–	–	–	15	15	15	15	15	–	5	–	3	15	–	51
Jaquin Jansen	–	–	–	–	–	–	–	15R	15R	15	3	–	1	–	–	2
Dustin Jinka	–	–	–	–	–	–	–	–	10R	–	1	–	–	–	–	0
Wesley Cloete	–	–	–	–	–	–	–	–	3R	–	1	–	–	–	–	0
Rudi van Rooyen	–	–	–	–	–	–	–	–	9R	–	1	–	–	–	–	0
Wendal Wehr	–	–	–	–	–	–	–	–	4R	–	1	–	–	–	–	0
37 Players											213	25	16	20	1	220

ABSA CURRIE CUP – PREMIER DIVISION

CURRIE CUP SQUAD – CAREER CURRIE CUP APPEARANCES

PLAYER	GRIQUAS						OTHER UNIONS						TOTAL					
	A	T	C	P	DG	Pts	A	T	C	P	DG	Pts	A	T	C	P	DG	Pts
JW (Jonathan) Adendorf	13	1	–	–	–	5	–	–	–	–	–	0	13	1	–	–	–	5
E (Ederies) Arendse	13	7	–	–	–	35	–	–	–	–	–	0	13	7	–	–	–	35
RJ (Ryno) Barnes	80	9	–	–	–	45	30	3	–	–	–	15	110	12	–	–	–	60
MJ (Martin) Bezuidenhout	13	3	–	–	–	15	33	1	–	–	–	5	46	4	–	–	–	20
F (Francois) Brummer	37	2	31	32	3	177	26	1	23	33	1	153	63	3	54	65	4	330
WW (Wesley) Cloete	1	–	–	–	–	0	14	–	–	–	–	0	15	–	–	–	–	0
HDP (Danie) Dames	8	–	–	–	–	0	46	17	–	–	–	85	54	17	–	–	–	85
JC (Jonathan) Francke	17	2	–	–	–	10	26	4	–	–	–	20	43	6	–	–	–	30
D (Dean) Grant	7	1	7	3	–	28	–	–	–	–	–	0	7	1	7	3	–	28
CFK (Carel) Greeff	25	12	–	–	–	60	–	–	–	–	–	0	25	12	–	–	–	60
S (Stephan) Greeff	5	–	–	–	–	0	4	–	–	–	–	0	9	–	–	–	–	0
AJ (Abrie) Griesel	4	1	–	–	–	5	–	–	–	–	–	0	4	1	–	–	–	5
J (Jacquin) Jansen	7	–	1	–	–	2	25	8	33	13	–	145	32	8	34	13	–	147
RR (Rocco) Jansen	50	18	–	–	–	90	8	7	–	–	–	35	58	25	–	–	–	125
D (Dustin) Jinka	4	–	–	–	–	0	12	–	–	–	–	0	16	–	–	–	–	0
PH (Hugo) Kloppers	9	–	–	–	–	0	4	–	–	–	–	0	13	–	–	–	–	0
L (Luxolo) Koza	1	–	–	–	–	0	–	–	–	–	–	0	1	–	–	–	–	0
G (Doppies) la Grange	6	–	–	–	–	0	88	22	–	–	–	110	94	22	–	–	–	110
RJ (Rynard) Landman	17	2	–	–	–	10	35	5	–	–	–	25	52	7	–	–	–	35
RS (Ruaan) Lerm	8	1	–	–	–	5	–	–	–	–	–	0	8	1	–	–	–	5
RJ (RJ) Liebenberg	20	–	–	–	–	0	–	–	–	–	–	0	20	–	–	–	–	0
H (Hilton) Lobberts	12	1	–	–	–	5	46	3	–	–	–	15	58	4	–	–	–	20
DR (Niel) Marais	1	–	–	–	–	0	–	–	–	–	–	0	1	–	–	–	–	0
TC (Tian) Meyer	16	4	–	–	–	20	27	5	–	–	–	25	43	9	–	–	–	45
XH (Howard) Mnisi	17	3	–	–	–	15	12	2	–	–	–	10	29	5	–	–	–	25
J (Jaco) Nepgen	33	3	–	–	–	15	1	–	–	–	–	0	34	3	–	–	–	15
JG (Gouws) Prinsloo	18	1	20	36	–	153	3	–	–	–	–	0	21	1	20	36	–	153
WAS (Steph) Roberts	74	3	–	–	–	15	–	–	–	–	–	0	74	3	–	–	–	15
JN (Nico) Scheepers	13	2	18	17	–	97	16	4	20	30	–	150	29	6	38	47	–	247
D (Marais) Schmidt	6	–	1	1	–	5	–	–	–	–	–	0	6	–	1	1	–	5
DB (Burger) Schoeman	37	6	–	–	–	30	1	2	–	–	–	10	38	8	–	–	–	40
M (Marnus) Schoeman	43	26	–	–	–	130	–	–	–	–	–	0	43	26	–	–	–	130
WJ (Boela) Serfontein	7	1	–	–	–	5	30	–	–	–	–	0	37	1	–	–	–	5
IW (Wayne) Stevens	11	1	–	–	–	5	27	10	–	–	–	50	38	11	–	–	–	55
E (Ewald) van der Westhuizen	11	–	–	–	–	0	–	–	–	–	–	0	11	–	–	–	–	0
NJJ (Maks) van Dyk	14	1	–	–	–	5	–	–	–	–	–	0	14	1	–	–	–	5
JL (Janro) van Niekerk	15	1	–	–	–	5	69	3	–	–	–	15	84	4	–	–	–	20
R (Rudi) van Rooyen	3	–	–	–	–	0	–	–	–	–	–	0	3	–	–	–	–	0
PJ (PJ) Vermeulen	19	5	–	–	–	25	30	5	–	–	–	25	49	10	–	–	–	50
W (Wendal) Wehr	1	–	–	–	–	0	15	2	–	–	–	10	16	2	–	–	–	10
S (Simon) Westraadt	25	–	–	–	–	0	1	–	–	–	–	0	26	–	–	–	–	0
41 Players	721	117	78	89	3	1017	629	104	76	76	1	903	1350	221	154	165	4	1920

ABSA CURRIE CUP – PREMIER DIVISION

FIRST-CLASS APPEARANCES FOR GRIQUAS IN 2014 – ALL MATCHES

PLAYER	VODACOM CUP						CURRIE CUP QUALIFIERS						CURRIE CUP						2014 TOTAL						GRIQUAS CAREER					
	A	T	C	P	DG	Pts	A	T	C	P	DG	Pts	A	T	C	P	DG	Pts	A	T	C	P	DG	Pts	A	T	C	P	DG	Pts
JW (Jonathan) Adendorf	10	2	0	0	0	10	4	1	0	0	0	5	5	0	0	0	0	0	19	3	0	0	0	15	38	5	0	0	0	25
E (Ederies) Arendse	9	6	0	0	0	30	3	2	0	0	0	10	10	5	0	0	0	25	22	13	0	0	0	65	22	13	0	0	0	65
RJ (Ryno) Barnes	2	0	0	0	0	0	6	2	0	0	0	10	10	0	0	0	0	0	18	2	0	0	0	10	100	11	0	0	0	55
MJ (Martin) Bezuidenhout	10	0	0	0	0	0	4	1	0	0	0	5	9	2	0	0	0	10	23	3	0	0	0	15	23	3	0	0	0	15
F (Francois) Brummer	9	1	1	4	0	22	6	1	9	0	0	23	8	0	0	1	0	3	23	2	10	1	0	48	56	5	48	34	7	244
HM (Hilford) Clarke	1	3	0	0	0	15	0	0	0	0	0	0	0	0	0	0	0	0	1	3	0	0	0	15	1	3	0	0	0	15
WW (Wesley) Cloete	0	0	0	0	0	0	0	0	0	0	0	0	0	0	0	0	0	0	0	0	0	0	0	0	1	0	0	0	0	0
HDP (Danie) Dames	8	2	0	0	0	10	3	0	0	0	0	0	5	0	0	0	0	0	16	2	0	0	0	10	16	2	0	0	0	10
JC (Jonathan) Francke	9	2	0	0	0	10	6	2	0	0	0	10	10	0	0	0	0	0	25	4	0	0	0	20	26	4	0	0	0	20
D (Dean) Grant	0	0	0	0	0	0	0	0	0	0	0	0	7	1	7	3	0	28	7	1	7	3	0	28	7	1	7	3	0	28
CFK (Carel) Greeff	7	5	0	0	0	25	6	6	0	0	0	30	9	2	0	0	0	10	22	13	0	0	0	65	30	16	0	0	0	80
S (Stephan) Greeff	6	0	0	0	0	0	0	0	0	0	0	0	5	0	0	0	0	0	11	0	0	0	0	0	11	0	0	0	0	0
AJ (Abrie) Griesel	0	0	0	0	0	0	0	0	0	0	0	0	4	1	0	0	0	5	4	1	0	0	0	5	4	1	0	0	0	5
J (Jacquin) Jansen	4	0	5	6	0	28	4	0	0	0	0	0	3	0	1	0	0	2	11	0	6	6	0	30	11	0	6	6	0	30
RR (Rocco) Jansen	9	3	0	0	0	15	2	0	0	0	0	0	3	0	0	0	0	0	14	3	0	0	0	15	79	31	0	0	0	155
D (Dustin) Jinka	7	1	7	0	0	19	3	0	0	0	0	0	1	0	0	0	0	0	11	1	7	0	0	19	11	1	7	0	0	19
L (Leon) Karemaker	7	1	0	0	0	5	0	0	0	0	0	0	0	0	0	0	0	0	7	1	0	0	0	5	66	24	0	0	0	120
NL (Ntando) Kebe	2	1	0	0	0	5	0	0	0	0	0	0	0	0	0	0	0	0	2	1	0	0	0	5	2	1	0	0	0	5
PH (Hugo) Kloppers	0	0	0	0	0	0	0	0	0	0	0	0	9	0	0	0	0	0	9	0	0	0	0	0	9	0	0	0	0	0
L (Luxolo) Koza	4	0	0	0	0	0	0	0	0	0	0	0	1	0	0	0	0	0	5	0	0	0	0	0	5	0	0	0	0	0
G (Doppies) la Grange	0	0	0	0	0	0	0	0	0	0	0	0	6	0	0	0	0	0	6	0	0	0	0	0	6	0	0	0	0	0
RJ (Rynard) Landman	2	1	0	0	0	5	0	0	0	0	0	0	0	0	0	0	0	0	2	1	0	0	0	5	26	8	0	0	0	40
RS (Ruaan) Lerm	0	0	0	0	0	0	0	0	0	0	0	0	8	1	0	0	0	5	8	1	0	0	0	5	8	1	0	0	0	5
RJ (RJ) Liebenberg	3	0	0	0	0	0	1	0	0	0	0	0	8	0	0	0	0	0	12	0	0	0	0	0	21	0	0	0	0	0

ABSA CURRIE CUP – PREMIER DIVISION

FIRST-CLASS APPEARANCES FOR GRIQUAS IN 2014 – ALL MATCHES

PLAYER	VODACOM CUP						CURRIE CUP QUALIFIERS						CURRIE CUP						2014 TOTAL						GRIQUAS CAREER					
	A	T	C	P	DG	Pts	A	T	C	P	DG	Pts	A	T	C	P	DG	Pts	A	T	C	P	DG	Pts	A	T	C	P	DG	Pts
H (Hilton) Lobberts	6	0	0	0	0	0	3	1	0	0	0	5	5	0	0	0	0	0	14	1	0	0	0	5	18	1	0	0	0	5
DR (Niel) Marais	0	0	0	0	0	0	0	0	0	0	0	0	1	0	0	0	0	0	1	0	0	0	0	0	1	0	0	0	0	0
TC (Tian) Meyer	8	4	0	0	0	20	6	3	0	0	0	15	10	1	0	0	0	5	24	8	0	0	0	40	24	8	0	0	0	40
XH (Howard) Mnisi	5	0	0	0	0	0	4	2	0	0	0	10	0	0	0	0	0	0	9	2	0	0	0	10	20	3	0	0	0	15
T (Thabang) Molefe	1	1	0	0	0	5	0	0	0	0	0	0	0	0	0	0	0	0	1	1	0	0	0	5	1	1	0	0	0	5
J (Jaco) Nepgen	10	2	0	0	0	10	5	1	0	0	0	5	9	0	0	0	0	0	24	3	0	0	0	15	72	7	0	0	0	35
JG (Gouws) Prinsloo	8	3	24	12	1	105	2	1	6	2	0	23	5	0	3	15	0	51	15	4	33	29	1	179	24	4	41	43	0	237
WAS (Steph) Roberts	8	0	0	0	0	0	6	0	0	0	0	0	7	0	0	0	0	0	21	0	0	0	0	0	132	4	0	0	0	20
JN (Nico) Scheepers	1	0	2	0	0	4	4	1	9	4	0	35	2	0	4	1	0	11	7	1	15	5	0	50	14	2	20	17	0	101
D (Marais) Schmidt	0	0	0	0	0	0	0	0	0	0	0	0	6	1	0	0	0	5	6	1	0	0	0	5	6	1	0	1	0	5
DB (Burger) Schoeman	8	2	0	0	0	10	6	3	0	0	0	15	4	0	0	0	0	0	18	5	0	0	0	25	55	10	0	0	0	50
M (Marnus) Schoeman	8	3	0	0	0	15	6	7	0	0	0	35	10	7	0	0	0	35	24	17	0	0	0	85	65	42	0	0	0	210
WJ (Boela) Serfontein	3	0	0	0	0	0	5	1	0	0	0	5	2	0	0	0	0	0	10	1	0	0	0	5	10	1	0	0	0	5
FL (Frans) Sisita	1	0	0	0	0	0	0	0	0	0	0	0	0	0	0	0	0	0	1	0	0	0	0	0	1	0	0	0	0	0
IW (Wayne) Stevens	10	0	0	0	0	0	5	0	0	0	0	0	6	1	0	0	0	5	21	1	0	0	0	5	21	1	0	0	0	5
E (Ewald) van der Westhuizen	10	3	0	0	0	15	4	0	0	0	0	0	6	0	0	0	0	0	20	3	0	0	0	15	21	3	0	0	0	15
NJJ (Maks) van Dyk	0	0	0	0	0	0	5	1	0	0	0	5	9	0	0	0	0	0	14	1	0	0	0	5	14	1	0	0	0	5
JL (Janro) van Niekerk	8	0	0	0	0	0	2	0	0	0	0	0	4	1	0	0	0	5	14	1	0	0	0	5	36	5	0	0	0	25
R (Rudi) van Rooyen	0	0	0	0	0	0	2	0	0	0	0	0	1	0	0	0	0	0	3	0	0	0	0	0	3	0	0	0	0	0
PJ (PJ) Vermeulen	3	0	0	0	0	0	4	0	0	0	0	0	9	3	0	0	0	15	16	3	0	0	0	15	37	8	1	0	0	42
W (Wendal) Wehr	0	0	0	0	0	0	0	0	0	0	0	0	1	0	0	0	0	0	1	0	0	0	0	0	1	0	0	0	0	0
S (Simon) Westraadt	8	1	0	0	0	5	2	0	0	0	0	0	4	0	0	0	0	0	14	1	0	0	0	5	68	10	0	0	0	50
46 players	215	47	39	19	5	388	130	36	24	6	0	246	213	25	16	20	1	220	558	108	79	45	6	854	1223	241	127	108	7	1806

ABSA CURRIE CUP – PREMIER DIVISION

KwaZulu-Natal Rugby Union

Founded: 1890 (as Natal Rugby Union) **Ground:** Kings Park **Capacity:** 53 000
Address: Jacko Jackson Drive, Stamford Hill, Durban
Postal address: PO Box 307, Durban, 4000 **Telephone Number:** 031-308 8400
Website: www.sharksrugby.co.za **Colours:** Black and white jersey and socks, white shorts
Currie Cup Coach: Brad MacLeod-Henderson **Captain:** Tera Mtembu
President: Graham McKenzie **Company CEO:** John Smit **Union CEO:** Peter Smith

'96	'97	'98	'99	'00	'01	'02	'03	'04	'05	'06	'07	'08	'09	'10	'11	'12	'13	'14
1st	2nd	3rd	2nd	1st	2nd	1st	2nd	5th	5th	4th	2nd	1st	1st	1st	2nd	1st	2nd	3rd

Played	Won	Lost	Drawn	Points for	Points against	Tries for	Tries against
11	7	3	1	307	272	29	26

Date	Venue	Opponent	Result	Score	Referee	Scorers
9 Aug	Kimberley	Griquas	WON	31-24	C Joubert	T: Sithole, Jordaan, Zeilinga. C: Zeilinga (2). P: Zeiliga (4).
15 Aug	Durban	Pumas	WON	34-17	C du Preez	T: SP Marais, Mtembu, Botes, Hadebe. C: Lambie (3), Zeilinga. P: Zeilinga (2).
23 Aug	Durban	Cheetahs	WON	19-16	R Rasivhenge	T: Chavhanga. C: Zeilinga. P: Zeilinga (4).
29 Aug	Nelspruit	Pumas	LOST	22-32	B Crouse	T: SP Marais. C: Zeilinga. P: Zeilinga (5).
6 Sep	Durban	Griquas	LOST	18-21	L vd Merwe	T: Adriaanse, T du Toit. C: Cronje. P: Zeilinga, Cronje.
13 Sep	Bloemfontein	Cheetahs	DREW	30-30	S Berry	T: Sithole, Esterhuizen, Mtembu. C: Cronje (3). P: Cronje (3).
20 Sep	Pretoria	Blue Bulls	WON	26-15	Q Immelman	T: Sithole, Mvovo. C: Cronje (2). P: Cronje (2), Marais (2).
27 Sep	Durban	EP Kings	WON	53-24	B Crouse	T: Jordaan (2), Esterhuizen, Mvovo, Cronje, Adriaanse, Lewies. C: Cronje (6). P: Cronje (2).
3 Oct	Durban	Golden Lions	WON	26-23	L Legoete	T: Esterhuizen. P: Zeilinga (7).
11 Oct	Cape Town	WP	WON	28-20	J Peyper	T: Sithole, Adriaanse. P: Cronje (5), Zeilinga.
SEMI-FINAL						
18 Oct	Johannesburg	Golden Lions	LOST	20-50	J van Heerden	T: Marais, Mvovo, Mtembu. C: Zeilinga. P: Cronje.

Note: ■ = *Champion*

APPEARANCES & POINTS FOR SHARKS IN 2014 CURRIE CUP

PLAYER	Griquas	Pumas	Cheetahs	Pumas	Griquas	Cheetahs	B Bulls	EP	G Lions	WP	G Lions (SF)	Apps	T	C	P	DG	Pts
SP Marais	15	15	15	15	–	14R	15	15	15	15	15	10	3	0	2	0	21
Odwa Ndungane	14	14	14	14	14	14	–	–	–	–	–	6	–	–	–	–	0
Sibusiso Sithole	13	13	13	13	11	13	14	14	14	13	13	11	4	0	0	0	20
Paul Jordaan	12	12	12	12	13	–	13	13	13	–	–	8	3	0	0	0	15
Tonderai Chavhanga	11	11	11	11	–	11	x	21R	–	14	14	8	1	0	0	0	5
Fred Zeilinga	10	10	10	10	10	x	–	–	13R	10R	10R	8	1	6	24	0	89
Cameron Wright	9	9	9	9R	12R	9R	9	9	9	–	9R	10	–	–	–	–	0
Lubabalo Mtembu	8c	8c	8c	8c	8c	8c	8c	8c	8c	8c	8c	11	3	0	0	0	15
Etienne Oosthuizen	7	7	4	4	7	7	7	7	7	7	7	11	–	–	–	–	0
Jacques Botes	6	6	6	6	6	6	6	–	6	6	6	10	1	0	0	0	5
Stephan Lewies	5	–	4R	5R	5	5	–	4R	4	4	4	9	1	0	0	0	5
Marco Wentzel	4	5	5	–	x	4	5	5	5	5	5	9	–	–	–	–	0
Lourens Adriaanse	3	3	3R	3R	3	3	3	3	3	3R	3R	11	3	0	0	0	15
Kyle Cooper	2	2	2	2	2	2	2	2	2	–	2	10	–	–	–	–	0
Thomas du Toit	1	1	1R	–	1	–	–	–	1	1	1	7	1	0	0	0	5
Monde Hadebe	x	2R	–	–	x	x	–	–	2R	2	2R	4	1	0	0	0	5
Dale Chadwick	1R	–	1	1	–	1	1	1	1R	1R	1R	9	–	–	–	–	0
Matt Stevens	3R	1R	3	3	3R	–	–	–	3R	3	3	8	–	–	–	–	0
JC Astle	5R	4	–	5	–	–	4	4	4R	4R	4R	8	–	–	–	–	0
Francois Kleinhans	7R	4R	7	7	–	–	–	–	–	–	–	4	–	–	–	–	0
Hanco Venter	9R	9R	–	–	–	9R	–	–	–	–	–	3	–	–	–	–	0
Lionel Cronje	14R	13R	15R	10R	10R	10	10	10	10	10	10	11	1	12	14	0	71
Johan Meyer	–	7R	–	7R	7R	7R	x	6R	–	–	–	5	–	–	–	–	0
Patrick Lambie	–	10R	–	–	–	–	–	–	–	–	–	1	0	3	0	0	6
Franco Marais	–	–	x	4R	–	–	2R	2R	–	2R	–	4	–	–	–	–	0
Conrad Hoffmann	–	–	9R	9	9	9	–	9R	9R	9R	9	8	–	–	–	–	0
Heimar Williams	–	–	12R	13R	12	–	–	–	–	–	–	3	–	–	–	–	0
Jaco van Tonder	–	–	–	–	15	–	–	–	–	–	–	1	–	–	–	–	0
Wiehan Hay	–	–	–	–	4	–	–	–	–	–	–	1	–	–	–	–	0
Tim Swiel	–	–	–	15R	15	x	15R	–	–	–	–	3	–	–	–	–	0
Andre Esterhuizen	–	–	–	–	–	12	12	12	12	12	12	6	3	0	0	0	15
Danie Mienie	–	–	–	–	–	1R	1R	1R	–	–	–	3	–	–	–	–	0
Khaya Majola	–	–	–	–	–	x	4R	6	7R	7R	7R	5	–	–	–	–	0
Lwazi Mvovo	–	–	–	–	–	–	11	11	11	11	11	5	3	0	0	0	15
Cobus Reinach	–	–	–	–	–	–	–	–	9	–	–	1	–	–	–	–	0
35 Players												232	29	21	40	0	307

CURRIE CUP SQUAD – CAREER CURRIE CUP APPEARANCES

PLAYER	SHARKS						OTHER UNIONS						TOTAL					
	A	T	C	P	DG	Pts	A	T	C	P	DG	Pts	A	T	C	P	DG	Pts
LC (Lourens) Adriaanse	11	3	0	0	0	15	31	3	0	0	0	15	42	6	0	0	0	30
J-C (JC) Astle	8	0	0	0	0	0	19	1	0	0	0	5	27	1	0	0	0	5
LJ (Jacques) Botes	129	43	0	0	0	215	27	3	0	0	0	15	156	46	0	0	0	230
DM (Dale) Chadwick	43	2	0	0	0	10	0	0	0	0	0	0	43	2	0	0	0	10
T (Tonderai) Chavhanga	8	1	0	0	0	5	36	12	0	0	0	60	44	13	0	0	0	65
KL (Kyle) Cooper	48	2	0	0	0	10	0	0	0	0	0	0	48	2	0	0	0	10
L (Lionel) Cronje	11	1	12	14	0	71	22	2	12	2	0	40	33	3	24	16	0	111
TJ (Thomas) du Toit	7	1	0	0	0	5	0	0	0	0	0	0	7	1	0	0	0	5
AP (Andre) Esterhuizen	6	3	0	0	0	15	0	0	0	0	0	0	6	3	0	0	0	15
MS (Monde) Hadebe	17	1	0	0	0	5	0	0	0	0	0	0	17	1	0	0	0	5
W (Wiehan) Hay	1	0	0	0	0	0	0	0	0	0	0	0	1	0	0	0	0	0
CF (Conrad) Hoffmann	18	1	0	0	0	5	22	3	0	0	0	15	40	4	0	0	0	20
PA (Paul) Jordaan	19	6	0	0	0	30	0	0	0	0	0	0	19	6	0	0	0	30
F (Francois) Kleinhans	11	0	0	0	0	0	0	0	0	0	0	0	11	0	0	0	0	0
P (Patrick) Lambie	29	6	50	63	2	325	0	0	0	0	0	0	29	6	50	63	2	325
SJ (Stephan) Lewies	14	1	0	0	0	5	0	0	0	0	0	0	14	1	0	0	0	5
K (Khaya) Majola	5	0	0	0	0	0	0	0	0	0	0	0	5	0	0	0	0	0
FS (Franco) Marais	5	0	0	0	0	0	0	0	0	0	0	0	5	0	0	0	0	0
SP (SP) Marais	21	7	0	2	0	41	14	13	3	0	0	71	35	20	3	2	0	112
JG (Johan) Meyer	5	0	0	0	0	0	0	0	0	0	0	0	5	0	0	0	0	0
DJ (Danie) Mienie	9	0	0	0	0	0	0	0	0	0	0	0	9	0	0	0	0	0
LS (Tera) Mtembu	22	4	0	0	0	20	0	0	0	0	0	0	22	4	0	0	0	20
LN (Lwazi) Mvovo	61	28	0	0	0	140	0	0	0	0	0	0	61	28	0	0	0	140
OM (Odwa) Ndungane	84	29	1	0	0	147	36	18	0	0	0	90	120	47	1	0	0	237
E (Etienne) Oosthuizen	11	0	0	0	0	0	3	0	0	0	0	0	14	0	0	0	0	0
JM (Cobus) Reinach	27	4	0	0	0	20	0	0	0	0	0	0	27	4	0	0	0	20
SCT (Sibusiso) Sithole	30	8	0	0	0	40	0	0	0	0	0	0	30	8	0	0	0	40
MJH (Matt) Stevens	8	0	0	0	0	0	0	0	0	0	0	0	8	0	0	0	0	0
TG (Tim) Swiel	3	0	0	0	0	0	1	0	0	0	0	0	4	0	0	0	0	0
J (Jaco) van Tonder	7	0	0	0	0	0	7	0	0	0	0	0	14	0	0	0	0	0
HC (Hanco) Venter	3	0	0	0	0	0	0	0	0	0	0	0	3	0	0	0	0	0
M van Z (Marco) Wentzel	14	1	0	0	0	5	40	6	0	0	0	30	54	7	0	0	0	35
H (Heimar) Williams	12	4	0	0	0	20	0	0	0	0	0	0	12	4	0	0	0	20
CR (Cameron) Wright	10	0	0	0	0	0	0	0	0	0	0	0	10	0	0	0	0	0
FJ (Fred) Zeilinga	18	2	19	41	3	180	0	0	0	0	0	0	18	2	19	41	3	180
35 Players	737	158	82	120	5	1329	258	61	15	2	0	341	995	219	97	122	5	1670

ABSA CURRIE CUP – PREMIER DIVISION

FIRST-CLASS APPEARANCES FOR SHARKS IN 2014 – ALL MATCHES*

PLAYER	CURRIE CUP						CAREER MATCHES					
	A	T	C	P	DG	Pts	A	T	C	P	DG	Pts
LC (Lourens) Adriaanse	11	3	0	0	0	15	11	3	0	0	0	15
J-C (JC) Astle	8	0	0	0	0	0	8	0	0	0	0	0
LJ (Jacques) Botes	10	1	0	0	0	5	130	43	0	0	0	215
DM (Dale) Chadwick	9	0	0	0	0	0	43	2	0	0	0	10
T (Tonderai) Chavhanga	8	1	0	0	0	5	8	1	0	0	0	5
KL (Kyle) Cooper	10	0	0	0	0	0	48	2	0	0	0	10
L (Lionel) Cronje	11	1	12	14	0	71	11	1	12	14	0	71
TJ (Thomas) du Toit	7	1	0	0	0	5	7	1	0	0	0	5
AP (Andre) Esterhuizen	6	3	0	0	0	15	6	3	0	0	0	15
MS (Monde) Hadebe	4	1	0	0	0	5	17	1	0	0	0	5
W (Wiehan) Hay	1	0	0	0	0	0	1	0	0	0	0	0
CF (Conrad) Hoffmann	8	0	0	0	0	0	18	1	0	0	0	5
PA (Paul) Jordaan	8	3	0	0	0	15	19	6	0	0	0	30
F (Francois) Kleinhans	4	0	0	0	0	0	11	0	0	0	0	0
P (Patrick) Lambie	1	0	3	0	0	6	29	6	50	63	2	325
SJ (Stephan) Lewies	9	1	0	0	0	5	14	1	0	0	0	5
K (Khaya) Majola	5	0	0	0	0	0	5	0	0	0	0	0
FS (Franco) Marais	4	0	0	0	0	0	5	0	0	0	0	0
SP (SP) Marais	10	3	0	2	0	21	21	7	0	2	0	41
JG (Johan) Meyer	5	0	0	0	0	0	5	0	0	0	0	0
DJ (Danie) Mienie	3	0	0	0	0	0	9	0	0	0	0	0
LS (Tera) Mtembu	11	3	0	0	0	15	22	4	0	0	0	20
LN (Lwazi) Mvovo	5	3	0	0	0	15	62	28	0	0	0	140
OM (Odwa) Ndungane	6	0	0	0	0	0	84	29	1	0	0	147
E (Etienne) Oosthuizen	11	0	0	0	0	0	11	0	0	0	0	0
JM (Cobus) Reinach	1	0	0	0	0	0	27	4	0	0	0	20
SCT (Sibusiso) Sithole	11	4	0	0	0	20	30	8	0	0	0	40
MJH (Matt) Stevens	8	0	0	0	0	0	8	0	0	0	0	0
TG (Tim) Swiel	3	0	0	0	0	0	3	0	0	0	0	0
J (Jaco) van Tonder	1	0	0	0	0	0	7	0	0	0	0	0
HC (Hanco) Venter	3	0	0	0	0	0	3	0	0	0	0	0
M van Z (Marco) Wentzel	9	0	0	0	0	0	14	1	0	0	0	5
H (Heimar) Williams	3	0	0	0	0	0	12	4	0	0	0	20
CR (Cameron) Wright	10	0	0	0	0	0	10	0	0	0	0	0
FJ (Fred) Zeilinga	8	1	6	24	0	89	18	2	19	41	3	180
35 Players	232	29	21	40	0	307	737	158	82	120	5	1329

* The Sharks' Vodacom Cup matches were also first-class but they played as a separate team, namely the 'Sharks XV'. This table shows first-class matches played by the 'Sharks' only. See Vodacom Cup section for Sharks XV info.

❰ DID YOU KNOW? ❱

The most penalties kicked by a player in a Currie Cup final is 6 –achieved twice by Natal/Sharks players, and both times against Western Province. They are Thierry Lacroix (1995 final) and Pat Lambie (2012 final).

ABSA CURRIE CUP – PREMIER DIVISION

Mpumalanga Rugby Union

Founded: 1969 (as South Eastern Transvaal) **Ground:** Mbombela Stadium
Capacity: 43 500 **Address:** 1 Bafana Bafana Str, Nelspruit
Postal address: Box 1574, Witbank 1035 **Telephone Number:** 013-7574600
Email: arrie@pumas.co.za **Colours:** Dove grey, black and pink jersey, shorts and socks
Currie Cup Coach: Jimmy Stonehouse **Captain:** Corne Steenkamp
President: Hein Mentz **Company CEO:** Koos Kruger

'96	'97	'98	'99	'00	'01	'02	'03	'04	'05	'06	'07	'08	'09	'10	'11	'12	'13	'14
7th	9th	11th	9th	7th	6th	6th	6th	7th	10th	8th	12th	12th	9th	9th	7th	8th	7th	6th

Played	Won	Lost	Drawn	Points for	Points against	Tries for	Tries against
10	4	6	0	237	269	25	28

Date	Venue	Opponent	Result	Score	Referee	Scorers
9 Aug	Nelspruit	Free State	WON	28-21	M v/d Westhuizen	T: Bell, Steenkamp, Jonker. C: Van Staden (2). P: Van Staden (3).
15 Aug	Durban	Sharks	LOST	17-34	C du Preez	T: Spies, Bothma. C: Van Staden, Roos. P: Roos.
22 Aug	Nelspruit	Griquas	WON	33-15	Q Immelman	T: Pretorius (2), Steenkamp, Bothma. C: Van Staden, Roos. P: Van Staden (2), Roos.
29 Aug	Nelspruit	Sharks	WON	32-22	B Crouse	T: Van Staden, Mtyanda, Bothma, Watermeyer. C: Roos (2), Van Staden. P; Van Staden (2).
6 Sep	Bloemfontein	Free State	WON	31-17	C Joubert	T: Skorbinski, Coetzer, Specman. C: Van Staden, Roos. P; Van Staden (4).
13 Sep	Kimberley	Griquas	LOST	27-31	C Joubert	T: Jonker, Van Rooyen. C: Van Staden. P: Van Staden (4), Roos.
19 Sep	Johannesburg	Pumas	LOST	15-29	J van Heerden	T: Watermeyer, Koch. C: Roos. P: Van Staden.
26 Sep	Nelspruit	WP	LOST	23-37	J van Heerden	T: Van Staden, Watermeyer. C: Van Staden (2). P: Roos (2), Van Staden.
3 Oct	Nelspruit	Blue Bulls	LOST	6-37	J Peyper	P; Van Staden (2).
10 Oct	Port Elizabeth	EP Kings	LOST	25-26	M Jonker	T: Herne, Van Staden, Watermeyer. C: Van Staden (2). P: Van Staden.

Note: ■ = *Champion*

APPEARANCES & POINTS FOR PUMAS IN 2014 CURRIE CUP

PLAYER	F.State	Sharks	Griquas	Sharks	F.State	Griquas	G.Lions	WP	B.Bulls	EP	Apps	T	C	P	DG	Pts
JW Bell	15	15	–	15	15	11R	15R	15	15	14	9	1	–	–	–	5
Jerome Pretorius	14	14	14	14	14	14	14	14R	12R	14R	10	2	–	–	–	10
JW Jonker	13	13	13	13	13	13	13	13	13	13	10	2	–	–	–	10
Stefan Watermeyer	12	12	12	12	–	12	12	12	12	12	9	4	–	–	–	20
Ruwellyn Isbell	11	11	11	–	–	–	–	14	14	–	5	–	–	–	–	0
Justin van Staden	10	10	10	10	10	10	10	10R	10	10	10	3	11	21	–	100
Reynier van Rooyen	9	9	9	9R	9R	9	9R	9	9	9	10	1	–	–	–	5
Renaldo Bothma	8	8	8	8	8	8	8	8	8	–	9	3	–	–	–	15
Jaco Bouwer	7	7	7R	7R	6R	18R	7R	7	7	–	9	–	–	–	–	0
Corne Steenkamp	6c	6c	6c	6c	6c	6c	6c	6c	6c	6c	10	2	–	–	–	10
Marius Coetzer	5	5R	4R	4R	4R	4R	4R	5	5	5	10	1	–	–	–	5
Frikkie Spies	4	4	4	4	4	4	4	–	–	5R	8	1	–	–	–	5
DJ Terblanche	3	3	1R	1R	5R	1R	3R	1R	3R	1R	10	–	–	–	–	0
Francois du Toit	2	2	2	2	2	2	2	2R	2R	2R	10	–	–	–	–	0
Vincent Koch	1	1	3	3	3	3	3	3	3	3	10	1	–	–	–	5
Frank Herne	2R	2R	2R	2R	2R	2R	2R	2	2	2	10	1	–	–	–	5
Corne Fourie	1R	1R	1	1	1	1	1	1	1	1	10	–	–	–	–	0
Lubabalo Mtyanda	3R	5	5	5	5	5	5	4	4	4	10	1	–	–	–	5
Uzair Cassiem	4R	7R	7	7	7	7	7	4R	6R	7R	10	–	–	–	–	0
Sino Nyoka	6R	–	–	–	9R	–	–	–	–	–	2	–	–	–	–	0
JC Roos	14R	10R	15R	10R	10R	10R	10R	10	–	10R	9	–	6	5	–	27
Heinrich Steyl	11R	15R	15	–	–	–	–	–	–	–	3	–	–	–	–	0
Rosco Speckman	–	11R	11R	11	11	11	11	11	11	11	9	1	–	–	–	5
Dylon Frylinck	–	–	R9	9	9	–	9	9R	9R	9R	7	–	–	–	–	0
Coenie van Wyk	–	–	–	15R	12R	15	15	–	10R	15	6	–	–	–	–	0
Hennie Skorbinski	–	–	–	–	12	–	–	–	–	–	1	1	–	–	–	5
RW Kember	–	–	–	–	–	–	–	7R	8R	8	3	–	–	–	–	0
Brian Shabangu	–	–	–	–	–	–	–	–	–	7	1	–	–	–	–	0
28 Players											220	25	17	26	0	237

⟨ DID YOU KNOW? ⟩

The most tries scored by a team in a Currie Cup final was 7 – Transvaal did it against Free State in the 1994 final in Bloemfontein, which they won 56-33. Fittingly, the match took place at the Springbok Park cricket stadium!

CURRIE CUP SQUAD – CAREER CURRIE CUP APPEARANCES

PLAYER	PUMAS						OTHER UNIONS						TOTAL					
	A	T	C	P	DG	Pts	A	T	C	P	DG	Pts	A	T	C	P	DG	Pts
JW (JW) Bell	28	11	–	–	–	55	8	1	–	–	–	5	36	11	–	–	–	55
R (Renaldo) Bothma	20	7	–	–	–	35	8	2	–	–	–	10	28	9	–	–	–	45
WJ (Jaco) Bouwer	60	11	–	–	–	55	20	6	–	–	–	30	80	17	–	–	–	85
U (Uzair) Cassiem	25	3	–	–	–	15	–	–	–	–	–	–	25	3	–	–	–	15
M (Marius) Coetzer	57	5	–	–	–	25	28	–	–	–	–	0	85	5	–	–	–	25
F (Francois) du Toit	22	1	–	–	–	5	3	–	–	–	–	–	25	1	–	–	–	5
C (Corne) Fourie	30	2	–	–	–	10	3	–	–	–	–	–	33	2	–	–	–	10
D (Dylon) Frylinck	7	–	–	–	–	–	–	–	–	–	–	–	7	–	–	–	–	0
F (Frank) Herne	25	4	–	–	–	20	9	2	–	–	–	10	34	6	–	–	–	30
RM (Ruwellyn) Isbel	5	–	–	–	–	–	–	–	–	–	–	–	5	–	–	–	–	0
JW (JW) Jonker	23	3	–	–	–	15	50	17	–	–	–	85	73	20	–	–	–	100
RW (RW) Kember	31	9	–	–	–	45	59	11	–	–	–	55	90	20	–	–	–	100
VP (Vincent) Koch	28	2	–	–	–	10	–	–	–	–	–	–	28	2	–	–	–	10
L (Lubabalo) Mtyanda	30	3	–	–	–	15	24	5	–	–	–	25	54	8	–	–	–	40
S (Sino) Nyoka	2	–	–	–	–	–	19	–	–	–	–	–	21	–	–	–	–	0
J (Jerome) Pretorius	21	5	–	–	–	25	–	–	–	–	–	–	21	5	–	–	–	25
J-C (JC) Roos	19	–	27	24	–	132	1	–	1	1	–	5	20	–	28	25	–	137
SB (Brian) Shabangu	1	–	–	–	–	–	11	2	–	–	–	10	12	2	–	–	–	10
AH (Hennie) Skorbinski	1	1	–	–	–	5	13	2	–	–	–	10	14	3	–	–	–	15
RS (Rosco) Speckman	27	14	–	–	–	70	1	–	–	–	–	–	28	14	–	–	–	70
FA (Frikkie) Spies	8	1	–	–	–	5	40	2	–	–	–	10	48	3	–	–	–	15
CJ (Corne) Steenkamp	100	19	–	–	–	95	–	–	–	–	–	–	100	19	–	–	–	95
HD (Heinrich) Steyl	3	–	–	–	–	–	2	–	–	–	–	–	5	–	–	–	–	0
DJ (De-Jay) Terblanche	69	4	–	–	–	20	–	–	–	–	–	–	69	4	–	–	–	20
R (Reynier) van Rooyen	17	2	–	–	–	10	–	–	–	–	–	–	17	2	–	–	–	10
J (Justin) van Staden	10	3	11	21	–	100	12	1	24	25	2	134	22	4	35	46	2	234
CG (Coenie) van Wyk	34	14	8	10	–	116	–	–	–	–	–	–	34	14	8	10	–	116
S (Stefan) Watermeyer	26	10	–	–	–	50	29	9	–	–	–	45	55	19	–	–	–	95
28 Players	729	134	46	55	0	933	340	60	25	26	2	434	1069	193	71	81	2	1362

ABSA CURRIE CUP – PREMIER DIVISION

FIRST-CLASS APPEARANCES FOR PUMAS IN 2014 – ALL MATCHES

PLAYER	VODACOM CUP						CURRIE CUP PREMIER DIV.						2014 TOTAL						PUMAS CAREER					
	A	T	C	P	DG	Pts	A	T	C	P	DG	Pts	A	T	C	P	DG	Pts	A	T	C	P	DG	Pts
JW (JW) Bell	8	1	0	0	0	5	9	1	0	0	0	5	17	2	0	0	0	10	42	17	0	0	0	85
(Bernado) Botha	6	2	1	0	0	12	0	0	0	0	0	0	6	2	1	0	0	12	6	2	1	0	0	12
R (Renaldo) Bothma	8	4	0	0	0	20	9	3	0	0	0	15	17	7	0	0	0	35	54	22	0	0	0	110
WJ (Jaco) Bouwer	3	2	0	0	0	10	9	0	0	0	0	0	12	2	0	0	0	10	109	46	0	0	0	230
U (Uzair) Cassiem	8	2	0	0	0	10	10	0	0	0	0	0	18	2	0	0	0	10	51	13	0	0	0	65
M (Marius) Coetzer	8	0	0	0	0	0	10	1	0	0	0	5	18	1	0	0	0	5	85	2	0	0	0	10
F (Francois) du Toit	0	0	0	0	0	0	10	0	0	0	0	0	10	0	0	0	0	0	20	1	0	0	0	5
C (Corne) Fourie	0	0	0	0	0	0	10	0	0	0	0	0	10	0	0	0	0	0	62	6	0	0	0	30
D (Dylon) Frylinck	0	0	0	0	0	0	7	0	0	0	0	0	7	0	0	0	0	0	7	0	0	0	0	0
F (Frank) Herne	9	1	0	0	0	5	10	1	0	0	0	5	19	2	0	0	0	10	40	10	0	0	0	50
RM (Ruwellyn) Isbell	7	4	0	0	0	20	5	0	0	0	0	0	12	4	0	0	0	20	12	4	0	0	0	20
JW (JW) Jonker	0	0	0	0	0	0	10	2	0	0	0	10	10	2	0	0	0	10	56	23	0	0	0	115
RW (RW) Kember	9	0	0	0	0	0	3	0	0	0	0	0	12	0	0	0	0	0	70	16	0	0	0	80
VP (Vincent) Koch	6	0	0	0	0	0	10	1	0	0	0	5	16	1	0	0	0	5	46	7	0	0	0	35
S (Stephan) Kotze	1	0	0	0	0	0	0	0	0	0	0	0	1	0	0	0	0	0	6	0	0	0	0	0
M (Marco) Kruger	1	0	0	0	0	0	0	0	0	0	0	0	1	0	0	0	0	0	1	0	0	0	0	0
C (Christo) le Roux	1	1	0	0	0	5	0	0	0	0	0	0	1	1	0	0	0	5	98	15	0	0	0	75
WD (Wilmaure) Louw	8	0	0	0	0	0	0	0	0	0	0	0	8	0	0	0	0	0	32	1	0	0	0	5
R (Rudi) Mathee	2	3	0	0	0	15	0	0	0	0	0	0	2	3	0	0	0	15	52	7	0	0	0	35
CJ (Jacques) Momberg	9	1	0	0	0	5	0	0	0	0	0	0	9	1	0	0	0	5	26	3	0	0	0	15
L (Lubabalo) Mtyanda	8	1	0	0	0	5	10	1	0	0	0	5	18	2	0	0	0	10	36	4	0	0	0	20
S (Sabelo) Nhlapo	7	0	0	0	0	0	0	0	0	0	0	0	7	0	0	0	0	0	7	0	0	0	0	0

ABSA CURRIE CUP – PREMIER DIVISION

FIRST-CLASS APPEARANCES FOR PUMAS IN 2014 – ALL MATCHES

PLAYER	VODACOM CUP						CURRIE CUP PREMIER DIV.						2014 TOTAL						PUMAS CAREER					
	A	T	C	P	DG	Pts	A	T	C	P	DG	Pts	A	T	C	P	DG	Pts	A	T	C	P	DG	Pts
S (Sino) Nyoka	8	0	0	0	0	0	9	0	0	0	0	0	17	0	0	0	0	0	47	3	0	0	0	15
DP (Dewald) Pretorius	3	2	0	0	0	10	0	0	0	0	0	0	3	2	0	0	0	10	3	9	0	0	0	45
J (Jerome) Pretorius	7	4	0	0	0	20	10	2	0	0	0	10	17	6	0	0	0	30	42	13	0	0	0	65
JW (Johan) Pretorius	1	0	0	0	0	0	0	0	0	0	0	0	1	0	0	0	0	0	1	1	3	0	0	11
J-C (JC) Roos	1	0	3	0	0	11	0	0	0	0	0	0	1	0	3	0	0	11	1	1	3	0	0	11
MED (Marcello) Sampson	8	1	21	21	0	110	9	0	5	0	0	27	17	1	26	0	0	137	47	3	105	89	1	495
AH (Ashwin) Scott	3	0	0	0	0	0	0	0	0	0	0	0	3	0	0	0	0	0	3	0	0	0	0	0
SB (Brian) Shabangu	1	3	0	0	0	15	0	0	0	0	0	0	1	3	0	0	0	15	14	14	0	0	0	70
P (Pule) Sibiya	4	0	0	0	0	0	1	0	0	0	0	0	5	0	0	0	0	0	5	0	0	0	0	0
AH (Hennie) Skorbinski	1	1	0	0	0	5	0	0	0	0	0	0	1	1	0	0	0	5	1	1	0	0	0	5
RS (Rosco) Speckman	1	0	0	0	0	0	0	0	0	0	0	0	1	0	0	0	0	0	3	1	0	0	0	5
FA (Frikkie) Spies	7	2	0	0	0	10	1	0	0	0	0	0	8	2	0	0	0	10	51	14	0	0	0	70
CJ (Corne) Steenkamp	0	0	0	0	0	0	8	1	0	0	0	5	8	1	0	0	0	5	8	1	0	0	0	5
HD (Heinrich) Steyl	0	4	0	0	0	20	0	0	0	0	0	0	0	4	0	0	0	20	34	24	0	0	0	120
DJ (De-Jay) Terblanche	0	0	0	0	0	0	10	0	0	0	0	0	10	0	0	0	0	0	10	0	0	0	0	0
D (Drew) van Goller	0	0	0	0	0	5	9	1	0	0	0	5	9	1	0	0	0	5	28	2	0	0	0	10
R (Reynier) van Rooyen	0	0	0	0	0	0	3	0	0	0	0	0	3	0	0	0	0	0	7	0	0	0	0	0
J (Justin) van Staden	6	1	0	0	0	5	3	1	0	0	0	5	9	2	0	0	0	10	32	3	0	0	0	15
CG (Coenie) van Wyk	6	0	0	2	0	18	10	3	11	21	0	100	16	3	17	23	0	118	73	32	35	23	0	293
RC (Ruan) Venter	3	0	0	0	0	3	6	0	0	0	0	0	9	0	0	1	0	3	17	17	21	0	0	118
S (Stefan) Watermeyer	2	0	0	0	0	0	4	0	0	0	0	20	2	4	0	0	0	20	13	0	0	0	0	65
43 Players	195	43	31	24	0	349	220	25	17	26	0	237	415	68	48	50	0	586	636	363	161	133	1	2539

ABSA CURRIE CUP – PREMIER DIVISION

W.P. RUGBY

Western Province RFU

Founded: 1883 **Ground:** Newlands **Capacity:** 49 000
Address: 11 Boundary Road, Newlands **Postal address:** PO Box 66, Newlands 7725
Telephone Number: 021-659 4500 **Website:** www.wprugby.com
Colours: Royal blue & white hoops, black shorts & socks
Currie Cup Coach: Allister Coetzee **Captain:** Juan de Jongh
President: Thelo Wakefield **Company MD:** Rob Wagner **Union CEO:** Theuns Roodman

'96	'97	'98	'99	'00	'01	'02	'03	'04	'05	'06	'07	'08	'09	'10	'11	'12	'13	'14
5th	1st	4th	11th	2nd	1st	5th	3rd	2nd	3rd	3rd	5th	5th	2nd	2nd	4th	3rd	1st	1st

Played	Won	Lost	Drawn	Points for	Points against	Tries for	Tries against
12	10	2	0	385	245	44	26

Date	Venue	Opponent	Result	Score	Referee	Scorers
8 Aug	Port Elizabeth	EP Kings	WON	35-16	J Peyper	T: Kolbe, Van der Spuy, Carr, Howard. C: Catrakilis (3). P: Catrakilis (3).
16 Aug	Cape Town	Blue Bulls	WON	41-17	R Rasivhenge	T: Senatla (2), De Jongh, Rhodes, Carr, Cilliers. C: Catrakilis (4). P: Catrakilis.
23 Aug	Cape Town	Golden Lions	WON	27-14	C Joubert	T: Van Wyk (2), Taute. C: Catrakilis (2), Coleman. P: Catrakilis (2).
30 Aug	Pretoria	Blue Bulls	WON	23-18	C Joubert	T: Senatla, Van Wyk. C: Catrakilis (2). P: Coleman (2), Catrakilis.
5 Sep	Cape Town	EP Kings	WON	49-14	S Berry	T: De Jongh (2), Kolisi (2), Kolbe, Van Wyk, Elstadt. C: Catrakilis (5), Coleman (2).
13 Sep	Johannesburg	Golden Lions	LOST	33-35	J Peyper	T: De Jongh, Geduld, Rhodes. C: Kolbe, Catrakilis, Coleman. P: Coleman (4).
20 Sep	Cape Town	Griquas	WON	36-12	L Legoete	T: Notshe (2), Harris, Kolbe, Geduld. C: Catrakilis (3), Coleman. P: Catrakilis
26 Sep	Nelspruit	Pumas	WON	37-23	J van Heerden	T: Carr (2), Notshe, Van der Spuy. C: Catrakilis (4). P: Catrakilis (3).
4 Oct	Bloemfontein	Free State	WON	34-29	M Jonker	T: De Jongh (2), Van Wyk, Ntubeni. C: Catrakilis (3), Coleman. P: Catrakilis (2).
11 Oct	Cape Town	Sharks	LOST	20-28	J Peyper	T: Coleman, Howard. C: Coleman (2). P: Coleman (2).
SEMI-FINAL						
18 Oct	Cape Town	Blue Bulls	WON	31-23	L Legoete	T: Kolbe (2), Groom. C: Catrakilis (2). P: Catrakilis (2). DG: Catrakilis
FINAL						
25 Oct	Cape Town	Golden Lions	WON	19-16	C Joubert	T: Taute. C: Catrakilis. P: Catrakilis (4).

Note: ■ = *Champion*

ABSA CURRIE CUP – PREMIER DIVISION

APPEARANCES & POINTS FOR WP IN 2014 CURRIE CUP

PLAYER	EP	B Bulls	G Lions	B Bulls	EP	B Lions	Griquas	Pumas	F State	Sharks	B Bulls (SF)	G Lions (F)	Apps	T	C	P	DG	Pts
Cheslin Kolbe	15	15	15	15	15	15	15	15	–	–	15	15	10	5	1	–	–	27
Kobus van Wyk	14	14	14	14	14	14	14	14	14	–	14	14	11	5	–	–	–	25
Juan de Jongh	13c	13c	13c	13c	13c	13c	13c	13c	13c	–	13c	13c	11	6	–	–	–	30
Michael van der Spuy	12	12	12	–	–	–	–	15R	12R	12	12	x	7	2	–	–	–	10
Seabelo Senatla	11	11	11	11	–	–	–	–	–	–	11	11	6	3	–	–	–	15
Demetri Catrakilis	10	10	10	10	10	10R	10	10	10	–	10	10	11	–	30	20	1	123
Nick Groom	9	9	9	9	9R	–	9R	9	–	9	9	9	9	1	–	–	–	5
Nizaam Carr	8	8	8	8	8	8	8	8	8	–	8	8	11	4	–	–	–	20
Michael Rhodes	7	7	7	7	7	7	7	7	7	–	7	7	11	2	–	–	–	10
Siya Kolisi	6	6	6	6	6	6	–	–	–	–	–	–	6	2	–	–	–	10
Manuel Carizza	5	5	5	5	4R	4R	4R	5R	5	–	5	5	11	–	–	–	–	0
Jean Kleyn	4	4	4	4	4	4	4	4	–	–	4	4	10	–	–	–	–	0
Pat Cilliers	3	3	3	3	3R	3	3R	3	3	–	3	3	11	1	–	–	–	5
Tiaan Liebenberg	2	–	–	–	–	–	–	–	–	–	–	–	1	–	–	–	–	0
Alistair Vermaak	1	1	1	1	1	1	1	1	1	–	1	1	11	–	–	–	–	0
Stephan Coetzee	2R	2	2	2	2	2	–	–	2R	–	–	–	7	–	–	–	–	0
Frans Malherbe	1R	–	–	–	–	–	–	–	–	–	–	–	1	–	–	–	–	0
Eben Etzebeth	4R	–	–	–	–	–	–	–	–	–	–	–	1	–	–	–	–	0
Sikhumbuszo Notshe	5R	–	–	–	6R	6	6	6	8	8R	7R	–	8	3	–	–	–	15
Louis Schreuder	9R	9R	9R	9R	9	9	9	9	x	9	9R	x	10	–	–	–	–	0
Robert du Preez	10R	–	–	–	–	–	–	–	–	–	–	–	1	–	–	–	–	0
Patrick Howard	14R	–	–	11R	11	–	11	13	–	–	–	–	6	2	–	–	–	10
Neil Rautenbach	–	2R	2R	2R	2R	–	2R	x	2R	2	2R	2R	9	–	–	–	–	0
Brok Harris	–	1R	3R	1R	3	3R	3	3R	3R	3c	3R	3R	11	1	–	–	–	5
Ruan Botha	–	5R	5R	5R	5	5	5	5	–	–	–	–	7	–	–	–	–	0
Rynhardt Elstadt	–	4R	8R	6R	8R	–	–	–	4	7	6	6	8	1	–	–	–	5
Kurt Coleman	–	10R	10R	10R	10R	10	10R	12R	10R	10	15R	10R	11	1	8	8	–	45
Jaco Taute	–	12R	12R	12	12	12	12	12	–	–	–	12	9	2	–	–	–	10
Justin Geduld	–	–	–	–	15R	14R	11	11	–	–	–	–	4	2	–	–	–	10
Siyabonga Ntubeni	–	–	–	–	–	2R	2	2	2	–	2	2	6	1	–	–	–	5
Godlen Masimla	–	–	–	–	–	9R	11R	–	–	9R	–	–	3	–	–	–	–	0
Oliver Kebble	–	–	–	–	–	–	1R	–	1R	1	1R	–	4	–	–	–	–	0
Rohan Kitshoff	–	–	–	–	–	–	7R	4R	–	6	–	–	3	–	–	–	–	0
Dillyn Leyds	–	–	–	–	–	–	–	–	15	15	–	–	2	–	–	–	–	0
Jurie van Vuuren	–	–	–	–	–	–	–	–	4R	4	–	–	2	–	–	–	–	0
EW Viljoen	–	–	–	–	–	–	–	–	14	6R	–	–	2	–	–	–	–	0
Devon Williams	–	–	–	–	–	–	–	–	11	–	–	–	1	–	–	–	–	0
Gerbrandt Grobler	–	–	–	–	–	–	–	–	5	–	5R	–	2	–	–	–	–	0
Anton van Zyl	–	–	–	–	–	–	–	–	5R	–	–	–	1	–	–	–	–	0
Gavin Annandale	–	–	–	–	–	–	–	–	4R	–	–	–	1	–	–	–	–	0
Pat O'Brien	–	–	–	–	–	–	–	–	7R	–	–	–	1	–	–	–	–	0
Justin Ackerman	–	–	–	–	–	–	–	–	1R	–	–	–	1	–	–	–	–	0
Chevandre van Schoor	–	–	–	–	–	–	–	–	x	–	–	–	0	–	–	–	–	0
43 Players (of which 42 made an appearance)													259	44	39	28	1	385

ABSA CURRIE CUP – PREMIER DIVISION

CURRIE CUP SQUAD – CAREER CURRIE CUP APPEARANCES

PLAYER	WP						OTHER UNIONS						TOTAL					
	A	T	C	P	DG	Pts	A	T	C	P	DG	Pts	A	T	C	P	DG	Pts
J (Justin) Ackerman	1	–	–	–	–	0	–	–	–	–	–	0	1	–	–	–	–	0
GB (Gavin) Annandale	1	–	–	–	–	0	22	1	–	–	–	5	23	1	–	–	–	5
R (Ruan) Botha	7	–	–	–	–	0	–	–	–	–	–	0	7	–	–	–	–	0
MN (Manuel) Carizza	11	–	–	–	–	0	–	–	–	–	–	0	11	–	–	–	–	0
N (Nizaam) Carr	27	8	–	–	–	40	–	–	–	–	–	0	27	8	–	–	–	40
D (Demetri) Catrakilis	39	1	79	97	8	478	–	–	–	–	–	0	39	1	79	97	8	478
PM (Pat) Cilliers	23	1	–	–	–	5	50	9	–	–	–	45	68	10	–	–	–	50
SH (Stephan) Coetzee	7	–	–	–	–	0	–	–	–	–	–	0	7	–	–	–	–	0
KC (Kurt) Coleman	25	1	17	29	–	126	–	–	–	–	–	0	25	1	17	29	–	126
JL (Juan) de Jongh	48	19	–	–	–	95	–	–	–	–	–	0	48	19	–	–	–	95
RJ (Robert) du Preez	1	–	–	–	–	0	–	–	–	–	–	0	1	–	–	–	–	0
R (Rynhardt) Elstad	22	1	–	–	–	5	–	–	–	–	–	0	22	1	–	–	–	5
E (Eben) Etzebeth	7	–	–	–	–	0	–	–	–	–	–	0	7	–	–	–	–	0
JG (Justin) Geduld	4	2	–	–	–	10	–	–	–	–	–	0	4	2	–	–	–	10
DG (Gerbrandt) Grobler	9	–	–	–	–	0	–	–	–	–	–	0	9	–	–	–	–	0
NJ (Nic) Groom	38	4	–	–	–	20	–	–	–	–	–	0	38	4	–	–	–	20
J (Brok) Harris	113	15	–	–	–	75	–	–	–	–	–	0	113	15	–	–	–	75
PB (Patrick) Howard	11	3	–	–	–	15	–	–	–	–	–	0	11	3	–	–	–	15
OR (Oliver) Kebble	4	–	–	–	–	0	–	–	–	–	–	0	4	–	–	–	–	0
R (Rohan) Kitshoff	14	–	–	–	–	0	33	7	–	–	–	35	47	7	–	–	–	35
J (Jean) Kleyn	10	–	–	–	–	0	–	–	–	–	–	0	10	–	–	–	–	0
C (Cheslin) Kolbe	22	8	1	–	–	42	–	–	–	–	–	0	22	8	1	–	–	42
S (Siya) Kolisi	23	6	–	–	–	30	–	–	–	–	–	0	23	6	–	–	–	30
DY (Dillyn) Leyds	2	–	–	–	–	0	–	–	–	–	–	0	2	–	–	–	–	0
CR (Tiaan) Liebenberg	59	6	–	–	–	30	49	4	–	–	–	20	108	10	–	–	–	50
JF (Frans) Malherbe	30	–	–	–	–	0	–	–	–	–	–	0	30	–	–	–	–	0
GHD (Godlen) Masimla	3	–	–	–	–	0	–	–	–	–	–	0	3	–	–	–	–	0
S (Sikumbuzo) Notshe	8	3	–	–	–	15	–	–	–	–	–	0	8	3	–	–	–	15
S (Scarra) Ntubeni	31	2	–	–	–	10	–	–	–	–	–	0	31	2	–	–	–	10
P (Patrick) O'Brien	1	–	–	–	–	0	–	–	–	–	–	0	1	–	–	–	–	0
N (Neil) Rautenbach	9	–	–	–	–	0	–	–	–	–	–	0	9	–	–	–	–	0
MK (Michael) Rhodes	21	5	–	–	–	25	39	6	–	–	–	30	60	11	–	–	–	55
L (Louis) Schreuder	43	2	–	–	–	10	–	–	–	–	–	0	43	2	–	–	–	10
SM (Seabelo) Senatla	6	3	–	–	–	15	–	–	–	–	–	0	6	3	–	–	–	15
JJ (Jaco) Taute	9	2	–	–	–	10	31	13	–	1	–	68	40	15	–	1	–	78
MG (Michael) van der Spuy	13	2	–	–	–	10	–	–	–	–	–	0	13	2	–	–	–	10
JG (Jurie) van Vuuren	2	–	–	–	–	0	–	–	–	–	–	0	2	–	–	–	–	0
JP (Kobus) van Wyk	11	5	–	–	–	25	–	–	–	–	–	0	11	5	–	–	–	25
A (Anton) van Zyl	32	2	–	–	–	10	33	3	–	–	–	15	65	5	–	–	–	25
AF (Alistair) Vermaak	11	–	–	–	–	0	–	–	–	–	–	0	11	–	–	–	–	0
EW (EW) Viljoen	2	–	–	–	–	0	–	–	–	–	–	0	2	–	–	–	–	0
DF (Devon) Williams	1	–	–	–	–	0	–	–	–	–	–	0	1	–	–	–	–	0
42 Players	761	101	97	126	8	1101	257	43	0	1	0	218	1013	144	97	127	8	1319

ABSA CURRIE CUP – PREMIER DIVISION

FIRST-CLASS APPEARANCES FOR WP IN 2014 – ALL MATCHES

PLAYER	VODACOM CUP						CURRIE CUP						2014 TOTAL						WP CAREER					
	A	T	C	P	DG	Pts	A	T	C	P	DG	Pts	A	T	C	P	DG	Pts	A	T	C	P	DG	Pts
J (Justin) Ackerman	1	0	0	0	0	0	1	0	0	0	0	0	2	0	0	0	0	0	2	0	0	0	0	0
GB (Gavin) Annandale	0	0	0	0	0	0	1	0	0	0	0	0	1	0	0	0	0	0	1	0	0	0	0	0
L (Liam) Bax	6	0	0	0	0	0	0	0	0	0	0	0	6	0	0	0	0	0	11	1	0	0	0	5
R (Ruan) Botha	0	0	0	0	0	0	7	0	0	0	0	0	7	0	0	0	0	0	8	1	0	0	0	5
E (Eital) Bredenkamp	6	0	0	0	0	0	0	0	0	0	0	0	6	0	0	0	0	0	6	0	0	0	0	0
MN (Manuel) Carizza	0	0	0	0	0	0	11	0	0	0	0	0	11	0	0	0	0	0	11	0	0	0	0	0
N (Nizaam) Carr	0	0	0	0	0	0	11	4	0	0	0	20	11	4	0	0	0	20	28	5	0	0	0	25
D (Demetri) Catrakilis	0	0	0	0	0	0	11	1	30	20	1	123	11	1	30	20	1	123	51	1	96	131	9	617
L (Lungelo) Chonco	1	0	0	0	0	0	0	0	0	0	0	0	1	0	0	0	0	0	1	0	0	0	0	0
DG (Deacon) Chowles	4	0	0	0	0	0	0	0	0	0	0	0	4	0	0	0	0	0	4	0	0	0	0	0
PM (Pat) Cilliers	0	0	0	0	0	0	11	1	0	0	0	5	11	1	0	0	0	5	23	1	0	0	0	5
SH (Stephan) Coetzee	2	0	0	0	0	0	7	0	0	0	0	0	9	0	0	0	0	0	17	0	0	0	0	0
KC (Kurt) Coleman	2	0	5	3	0	19	11	1	8	8	0	45	13	1	13	11	0	64	52	6	44	50	0	273
MR (Ridhaa) Damon	1	0	0	0	0	0	0	0	0	0	0	0	1	0	0	0	0	0	3	1	0	0	0	5
JL (Juan) de Jongh	0	0	0	0	0	0	11	6	0	0	0	30	11	6	0	0	0	30	50	20	0	0	0	100
JC (Jan) de Klerk	4	0	0	0	0	0	0	0	0	0	0	0	4	0	0	0	0	0	4	0	0	0	0	0
HC (Carel) du Preez	7	2	0	0	0	10	0	0	0	0	0	0	7	2	0	0	0	10	10	2	0	0	0	10
RJ (Robert) du Preez	3	1	2	0	0	9	1	0	0	0	0	0	4	1	2	0	0	9	4	1	2	0	0	9
R (Rynhardt) Elstad	0	0	0	0	0	0	8	1	0	0	0	5	8	1	0	0	0	5	32	1	0	0	0	5
E (Eben) Etzebeth	0	0	0	0	0	0	1	0	0	0	0	0	1	0	0	0	0	0	7	0	0	0	0	0
D (Dylon) Frylinck	5	0	0	0	0	0	0	0	0	0	0	0	5	0	0	0	0	0	5	0	0	0	0	0
MG (Tazz) Fuzani	6	0	0	0	0	0	0	0	0	0	0	0	6	0	0	0	0	0	15	0	0	0	0	0
JG (Justin) Geduld	0	0	0	0	0	0	4	2	0	0	0	10	4	2	0	0	0	10	4	2	0	0	0	10
DG (Gerbrandt) Grobler	0	0	0	0	0	0	2	0	0	0	0	0	2	0	0	0	0	0	17	0	0	0	0	0
JA (Ian) Groenewald	2	0	0	0	0	0	0	0	0	0	0	0	2	0	0	0	0	0	2	0	0	0	0	0
NJ (Nic) Groom	0	0	0	0	0	0	9	1	0	0	0	5	9	1	0	0	0	5	58	8	0	0	0	40
JJ (Janco) Gunter	3	0	0	0	0	0	0	0	0	0	0	0	3	0	0	0	0	0	3	0	0	0	0	0

ABSA CURRIE CUP – PREMIER DIVISION

FIRST-CLASS APPEARANCES FOR WP IN 2014 – ALL MATCHES

PLAYER	VODACOM CUP						CURRIE CUP						2014 TOTAL						WP CAREER*					
	A	T	C	P	DG	Pts	A	T	C	P	DG	Pts	A	T	C	P	DG	Pts	A	T	C	P	DG	Pts
S (Stephan) Hamman	1	0	0	0	0	0	0	0	0	0	0	0	1	0	0	0	0	0	1	0	0	0	0	0
J (Brok) Harris	0	0	0	0	0	0	11	1	0	0	0	5	11	1	0	0	0	5	120	15	0	0	0	75
PB (Patrick) Howard	0	0	0	0	0	0	6	2	0	0	0	10	6	2	0	0	0	10	20	5	0	0	0	25
RB (Reuben) Johannes	4	0	0	0	0	0	0	0	0	0	0	0	4	0	0	0	0	0	7	0	0	0	0	0
HR (Huw) Jones	2	1	0	0	0	5	0	0	0	0	0	0	2	1	0	0	0	5	2	1	0	0	0	5
GJ (Gerhard) Jordaan	1	0	0	0	0	0	0	0	0	0	0	0	1	0	0	0	0	0	1	0	0	0	0	0
JM (Joshua) Katzen	1	0	0	0	0	0	0	0	0	0	0	0	1	0	0	0	0	0	3	0	0	0	0	0
OR (Oliver) Kebble	0	0	0	0	0	0	4	0	0	0	0	0	4	0	0	0	0	0	5	0	0	0	0	0
M (Michael) Kennedy	3	0	0	0	0	0	0	0	0	0	0	0	3	0	0	0	0	0	3	0	0	0	0	0
R (Rohan) Kitshoff	8	6	0	0	0	30	3	0	0	0	0	0	11	6	0	0	0	30	33	13	0	0	0	65
J (Jean) Kleyn	0	0	0	0	0	0	10	0	0	0	0	0	10	0	0	0	0	0	10	0	0	0	0	0
C (Cheslin) Kolbe	0	0	0	0	0	0	10	5	1	0	0	27	10	5	1	0	0	27	29	12	1	0	0	62
S (Siya) Kolisi	0	0	0	0	0	0	6	2	0	0	0	10	6	2	0	0	0	10	29	7	0	0	0	35
J-B (Johnny) Kotze	6	1	0	0	0	5	0	0	0	0	0	0	6	1	0	0	0	5	6	0	0	0	0	0
J-P (JP) Lewis	8	3	0	0	0	15	0	0	0	0	0	0	8	3	0	0	0	15	8	3	0	0	0	15
DY (Dillyn) Leyds	0	0	0	0	0	0	2	0	0	0	0	0	2	0	0	0	0	0	4	1	0	0	0	5
CR (Tiaan) Liebenberg	6	1	0	0	0	5	0	0	0	0	0	0	6	1	0	0	0	5	62	6	0	0	0	30
K (Kyle) Lombard	0	0	0	0	0	0	1	0	0	0	0	0	1	0	0	0	0	0	6	1	0	0	0	5
JF (Frans) Malherbe	1	0	0	0	0	0	0	0	0	0	0	0	1	0	0	0	0	0	34	0	0	0	0	0
RJ (Renier) Marais	1	0	0	0	0	0	0	0	0	0	0	0	1	0	0	0	0	0	1	0	0	0	0	0
GHD (Godlen) Masimla	0	0	0	0	0	0	3	0	0	0	0	0	3	0	0	0	0	0	13	0	0	0	0	0
FJ (Freddie) Muller	4	0	0	0	0	0	0	0	0	0	0	0	4	0	0	0	0	0	4	0	0	0	0	0
FJ (Jean) Nel	4	0	0	0	0	0	0	0	0	0	0	0	4	0	0	0	0	0	4	0	0	0	0	0
S (Sikumbuzo) Notshe	6	1	0	0	0	5	8	3	0	0	0	15	14	4	0	0	0	20	23	6	0	0	0	30
S (Scarra) Ntubeni	0	0	0	0	0	0	6	1	0	0	0	5	6	1	0	0	0	5	38	2	0	0	0	10
P (Patrick) O'Brien	0	0	0	0	0	0	1	0	0	0	0	0	1	0	0	0	0	0	1	0	0	0	0	0
N (Neil) Rautenbach	1	0	0	0	0	0	9	0	0	0	0	0	10	0	0	0	0	0	10	0	0	0	0	0

ABSA CURRIE CUP – PREMIER DIVISION

FIRST-CLASS APPEARANCES FOR WP IN 2014 – ALL MATCHES

PLAYER	VODACOM CUP						CURRIE CUP						2014 TOTAL						WP CAREER					
	A	T	C	P	DG	Pts	A	T	C	P	DG	Pts	A	T	C	P	DG	Pts	A	T	C	P	DG	Pts
MK (Michael) Rhodes	0	0	0	0	0	0	11	2	0	0	0	10	11	2	0	0	0	10	22	4	0	0	0	20
AD (Adrian) Roberts	2	1	0	0	0	0	0	0	0	0	0	0	2	1	0	0	0	0	2	1	0	0	0	7
JD (JD) Schickerling	1	0	0	0	0	0	0	0	0	0	0	0	1	0	0	0	0	0	1	0	0	0	0	0
L (Louis) Schreuder	0	0	0	0	0	0	10	0	0	0	0	0	10	0	0	0	0	0	54	3	0	0	0	15
SM (Seabelo) Senatla	0	0	0	0	0	0	6	3	0	0	0	15	6	3	0	0	0	15	6	3	0	0	0	15
SMS (Sti) Sithole	3	0	0	0	0	0	0	0	0	0	0	0	3	0	0	0	0	0	3	0	0	0	0	0
R (Rayn) Smid	5	5	0	0	0	25	10	1	0	0	0	5	15	6	0	0	0	25	15	6	0	0	0	35
C (Chad) Solomon	2	0	0	0	0	0	0	0	0	0	0	0	2	0	0	0	0	0	2	0	0	0	0	0
JCE (Entienne) Swanepoel	6	0	0	0	0	0	0	0	0	0	0	0	6	0	0	0	0	0	6	0	0	0	0	0
JJ (Jaco) Taute	0	0	0	0	0	0	2	0	0	0	0	0	2	0	0	0	0	0	15	2	0	0	0	10
J-F (Jan) Uys	8	0	0	0	0	0	1	0	0	0	0	0	9	0	0	0	0	0	9	0	0	0	0	0
GJ (Gary) van Aswegen	7	1	9	5	0	38	0	0	0	0	0	0	8	1	9	5	0	38	8	1	25	21	2	124
MG (Michael) van der Spuy	5	0	0	0	0	0	7	0	0	0	0	0	12	0	0	0	0	0	36	7	0	0	0	35
CC (Chevandre) van Schoor	2	0	0	0	0	0	0	0	0	0	0	0	2	0	0	0	0	0	2	0	0	0	0	0
JG (Jurie) van Vuuren	0	0	0	0	0	0	2	0	0	0	0	0	2	0	0	0	0	0	2	0	0	0	0	0
CJ (Christo) van Wyk	4	1	0	0	0	5	0	0	0	0	0	0	4	1	0	0	0	5	4	1	0	0	0	5
JP (Kobus) van Wyk	0	0	0	0	0	0	11	5	0	0	0	25	11	5	0	0	0	25	16	8	0	0	0	40
A (Anton) van Zyl	0	0	0	0	0	0	1	0	0	0	0	0	1	0	0	0	0	0	46	2	0	0	0	10
AF (Alistair) Vermaak	7	0	0	0	0	0	11	0	0	0	0	0	18	0	0	0	0	0	25	1	0	0	0	5
R (Ruan) Vermaak	1	0	0	0	0	0	1	0	0	0	0	0	2	0	0	0	0	0	2	0	0	0	0	0
EW (EW) Viljoen	0	0	0	0	0	0	2	0	0	0	0	0	2	0	0	0	0	0	2	0	0	0	0	0
DF (Devon) Williams	7	9	0	0	0	45	1	1	0	0	0	5	8	10	0	0	0	45	16	11	0	0	0	55
ME (Michael) Willemse	4	0	0	0	0	0	4	0	0	0	0	0	4	0	0	0	0	0	10	1	0	0	0	0
LT (Lihleli) Xoli	2	0	0	0	0	0	0	0	0	0	0	0	2	0	0	0	0	0	2	0	0	0	0	0
78 Players	176	33	17	8	0	223	259	44	39	28	1	385	435	77	56	36	1	608	1216	174	169	202	11	1852

ABSA CURRIE CUP – 1ST DIVISION

LOG

Team	P	W	L	D	PF	PA	PD	TF	TA	BP	Pts
Leopards	10	8	2	0	514	254	260	75	32	10	42
Griffons	10	6	4	0	314	330	-16	41	44	8	32
SWD Eagles	10	6	4	0	296	317	-21	38	39	6	30
Valke	10	5	5	0	303	323	-20	40	43	6	26
Boland Cavaliers	10	4	6	0	275	278	-3	36	37	9	25
Border	10	1	9	0	211	411	-200	27	62	4	8

Note: Log includes matches played in the Currie Cup Qualifiers (see following section)

LEADING SCORERS

30 POINTS OR MORE

PLAYER	PROVINCE	T	C	P	DG	Pts
Elric van Vuuren	SWD	1	19	15	0	88
Jaun Kotze	Valke	0	13	11	0	59
Louis Strydom	Griffons	0	13	8	2	56
Andre Pretorius	Leopards	1	16	4	0	49
Eric Zana	Boland	2	8	3	1	38
Masixole Banda	Border	1	6	7	0	38

4 TRIES OR MORE

5	Tertius Maarman	Griffons	4	Kyle Hendricks	Valke
4	Boela Abrahams	Griffons	4	Norman Nelson	Griffons
4	Dirk Dippenaar	Valke	4	Sylvain Mahuza	Leopards
4	Johan Deysel	Leopards			

PLAY-OFF RESULTS

SEMI-FINALS:
Griffons bt SWD Eagles 45-43 (Welkom). **Leopards lost to Valke 24-31** (Potchefstroom).
2014 ABSA FIRST DIVISION FINAL:
North West Stadium, Welkom, Friday, 17 October 2014. Referee: Ben Crouse. Crowd: 3500
Griffons 23 *(Tries: Abrahams, Nelson. Conversions: Strydom 2. Penalties: Strydom 2. Drop goal: Abrahams).*
Valke 21 *(Tries Richter, Verwey. Conversion: Kotze. Penalties: Kotze 2. Drop goal: Swart)*
Griffons: Tertius Maarman, Norman Nelson *(Wynand Pienaar, 45)*, Vuyo Mbotho, Japie Nel, Aubrey McDonald, Louis Strydom, Boela Abrahams, Nicky Steyn *(Capt)*, Armandt Koster, Frans Sisita *(Martin Sithole, 69)*, Johan van der Hoogt, Chris Ehlers *(Erik le Roux, 67)*, Heinrich Roelfse, Elandre Huggett, Gerard Baard *(Danie van der Merwe, 72)*. UNUSED SUBS: Hannes Snyman, Oshwill Nortjie, Franna du Toit.
Valke: Jaun Kotze, Dirk Dippenaar, Andrew van Wyk, Willie Odendaal, Coert Cronje, Clinton Swart *(Kyle Hendricks, 63)*, Anrich Richter, Ernst Ladendorf, Jacques Verwey *(Capt)*, JP Jonck *(JP Mostert, 62)*, Jacques Alberts *(Marlyn Williams, 62)*, Shane Kirkwood, Nico Pretorius, Dean Muir, Bruce Muller, Nico Pretorius *(Thulani Ngidi, 69)*, Dean Muir, Bruce Muller. UNUSED SUBS: Devlin Hope, Jaco Snyman, Dewald Pretorius.

ABSA CURRIE CUP – 1ST DIVISION

Boland Rugby Union

Founded: 1939 **Ground:** Boland Stadium **Capacity:** 11 000
Address: 50 Fontein Street, Wellington **Postal address:** PO Box 127, Wellington, 7654
Telephone Number: 021-873 2317 **Website:** www.bolandrugby.com
Colours: Pink, black and white jersey, black shorts
Currie Cup Coach: Abe Davids **Captain:** Franzel September
President: Ivan Pekeur **CEO:** Willie Small

'96	'97	'98	'99	'00	'01	'02	'03	'04	'05	'06	'07	'08	'09	'10	'11	'12	'13	'14
8th	7th	10th	12th	5th	9th	12th	10th	9th	6th	10th	7th	7th	8th	11th	9th	12th	11th	13th

Played	Won	Lost	Drawn	Points for	Points against	Tries for	Tries against
5	2	3	0	138	143	19	18

Date	Venue	Opponent	Result	Score	Referee	Scorers
30 Aug	Wellington	Griffons	LOST	19-27	L vd Merwe	T: C Lewis, Lawson, Jordaan. C: Zana, Hugo.
6 Sep	Potchefstroom	Leopards	LOST	32-54	F Anselmi	T: Rust, De Koker, Lawson, Kruger. C: Zana, Hugo. P: Hugo (2)
13 Sep	Wellington	Valke	LOST	25-32	L Legote	T: Zana (2), Trytsman, Kruger. C: Hugo. P: Hugo.
20 Sep	George	SWD	WON	35-24	B Crouse	T: Demas (2), Williams, Jordaan. C: Zana (3). P: Zana (2). DG: Zana.
26 Sep	Wellington	Border	WON	27-6	L Legoete	T: Williams, Demas, E Lewis, Pretorius. C: Zana (2). P: Zana.

ABSA CURRIE CUP – 1ST DIVISION

APPEARANCES & POINTS FOR BOLAND IN 2014 1ST DIVISION

PLAYER	Griffons	Leopards	Valke	SWD	Border	Apps	T	C	P	DG	Pts
Eric Zana	15	11R	15	15	15	5	2	8	3	1	38
Duwayne Smart	14	–	–	–	–	1	–	–	–	–	0
Richard Lawson	13	13	–	–	13R	3	2	–	–	–	10
Edwin Sass	12	12	11R	–	–	3	–	–	–	–	0
Sino Ganto	11	–	–	–	–	1	–	–	–	–	0
Morne Hugo	10	10	10	10R	10R	5	–	3	3	–	15
Marnus Hugo	9	9R	9R	9	–	4	–	–	–	–	0
Zandre Jordaan	8	8	8	8	8	5	2	–	–	–	10
Chaney Willemse	7	–	–	–	–	1	–	–	–	–	0
Franzel September	6c	–	6R	6c	–	3	–	–	–	–	0
Victor Kruger	5	5c	5c	–	5	4	2	–	–	–	10
Hanno Kitshoff	4	4	4	–	–	3	–	–	–	–	0
Martin Dreyer	3	3R	3	3	–	4	–	–	–	–	0
Clemen Lewis	2	2R	2	2	2c	5	1	–	–	–	5
Khwezi Mkhafu	1	1	1	1	1	5	–	–	–	–	0
Ulrich Pretorius	2R	2	2R	7R	6R	5	1	–	–	–	5
Francois Hanekom	3R	3	–	–	–	2	–	–	–	–	0
Jason Fraser	4R	7	7	4R	8R	5	–	–	–	–	0
Dumisane Meslane	7R	6	6	6R	6	5	–	–	–	–	0
Jovelian de Koker	9R	9	9	9R	9	5	1	–	–	–	5
Cheswin Williams	10R	–	13	14	14	4	2	–	–	–	10
Christian Rust	14R	15	14	–	–	3	1	–	–	–	5
Danwel Demas	–	14	–	11	11	3	3	–	–	–	15
Earl Lewis	–	11	10R	10	10	4	1	–	–	–	5
Gavin Annandale	–	7R	4R	4	4	4	–	–	–	–	0
Christopher Bosch	–	14R	–	13	13	3	–	–	–	–	0
Ryno Coetzee	–	4R	–	7	–	2	–	–	–	–	0
Albert Trytsman	–	–	12	12	12	3	1	–	–	–	5
Chevandre van Schoor	–	–	11	11R	14R	3	–	–	–	–	0
Ashton Constant	–	–	1R	3R	3	3	–	–	–	–	0
Yves Bashiya	–	–	5	7	–	2	–	–	–	–	0
Keenan Abrahams	–	–	–	–	1R	1	–	–	–	–	0
Kelvin Fikster	–	–	–	–	2R	1	–	–	–	–	0
33 Players						110	19	11	6	1	138

ABSA CURRIE CUP – 1ST DIVISION

CURRIE CUP 1ST DIV. SQUAD - CAREER CURRIE CUP APPEARANCES

PLAYER	BOLAND						OTHER UNIONS						CURRIE CUP TOTAL					
	A	T	C	P	DG	Pts	A	T	C	P	DG	Pts	A	T	C	P	DG	Pts
KM (Keenan) Abrahams	2	–	–	–	–	0	–	–	–	–	–	0	2	–	–	–	–	0
GB (Gavin) Annandale	10	–	–	–	–	0	13	1	–	–	–	5	23	1	–	–	–	5
J-C (JC) Astle	19	1	–	–	–	5	8	–	–	–	–	0	27	1	–	–	–	5
YMT (Yves) Bashiya	5	–	–	–	–	0	13	1	–	–	–	5	18	1	–	–	–	5
C (Christopher) Bosch	5	–	–	–	–	0	–	–	–	–	–	0	5	–	–	–	–	0
R (Ryno) Coetzee	8	2	–	–	–	10	–	–	–	–	–	0	8	2	–	–	–	10
A (Ashton) Constant	16	2	–	–	–	10	39	4	–	–	–	20	55	6	–	–	–	30
J (Jovelian) de Koker	5	1	–	–	–	5	–	–	–	–	–	0	5	1	–	–	–	5
D (Danwel) Demas	23	23	–	–	–	115	30	11	–	–	–	55	53	34	–	–	–	170
MC (Martin) Dreyer	8	1	–	–	–	5	11	1	–	–	–	5	19	2	–	–	–	10
KW (Kelvin) Fikster	2	–	–	–	–	0	–	–	–	–	–	0	2	–	–	–	–	0
AF (Arno) Fortuin	4	1	–	–	–	5	–	–	–	–	–	0	4	1	–	–	–	5
J-C (Jason) Fraser	8	–	–	–	–	0	–	–	–	–	–	0	8	–	–	–	–	0
S (Sino) Ganto	1	–	–	–	–	0	14	3	–	–	–	15	15	3	–	–	–	15
PF (Francois) Hanekom	20	–	–	–	–	0	–	–	–	–	–	0	20	–	–	–	–	0
APM (Marnus) Hugo	37	4	–	–	–	20	37	–	–	–	–	0	74	4	–	–	–	20
MJ (Morne) Hugo	7	–	6	8	1	39	–	–	–	–	–	0	7	–	6	8	1	39
Z (Zandré) Jordaan	37	11	–	–	–	55	–	–	–	–	–	0	37	11	–	–	–	55
JJ (Hanno) Kitshoff	14	–	–	–	–	0	–	–	–	–	–	0	14	–	–	–	–	0
HJ (Harlon) Klaasen	1	1	–	–	–	5	–	–	–	–	–	0	1	1	–	–	–	5
VE (Victor) Kruger	5	2	–	–	–	10	4	–	–	–	–	0	9	2	–	–	–	10
RJ (Richard) Lawson	8	2	–	–	–	10	20	3	–	–	–	15	28	5	–	–	–	25
C (Clemen) Lewis	84	5	–	–	–	25	–	–	–	–	–	0	84	5	–	–	–	25
EC (Earl) Lewis	7	1	–	–	–	5	2	–	–	–	–	0	9	1	–	–	–	5
NGP (Nathaniel) Manuel	2	1	–	–	–	5	–	–	–	–	–	0	2	1	–	–	–	5
DK (Dumisani) Meslane	5	–	–	–	–	0	35	5	–	–	–	25	40	5	–	–	–	25
K (Khwezi) Mkhafu	11	1	–	–	–	5	30	3	–	–	–	15	41	4	–	–	–	20
UD (Ulrich) Pretorius	22	4	–	–	–	20	–	–	–	–	–	0	22	4	–	–	–	20
DE (Deroy) Rhoode	5	–	–	–	–	0	24	1	1	–	–	5	29	1	1	–	–	5
HC (Christian) Rust	9	2	1	–	–	12	–	–	–	–	–	0	9	2	1	–	–	12
E (Edwin) Sass	6	–	–	–	–	0	–	–	–	–	–	0	6	–	–	–	–	0
FJ (Franzel) September	33	10	–	–	–	50	–	–	–	–	–	0	33	10	–	–	–	50
DE (Duwayne) Smart	5	1	–	–	–	5	11	3	–	–	–	15	16	4	–	–	–	20
AM (Albert) Trytsman	9	1	–	–	–	5	–	–	–	–	–	0	9	1	–	–	–	5
C (Chevandre) van Schoor	3	–	–	–	–	0	–	–	–	–	–	0	3	–	–	–	–	0
PJ (PJ) van Zyl	23	4	–	–	–	20	–	–	–	–	–	0	23	4	–	–	–	20
BCG (Ben) Venter	13	–	–	–	–	0	12	–	–	–	–	0	25	–	–	–	–	0
C (Chaney) Willemse	3	–	–	–	–	0	–	–	–	–	–	0	3	–	–	–	–	0
C (Cheswin) Williams	15	5	–	–	–	25	–	–	–	–	–	0	15	5	–	–	–	25
ES (Eric) Zana	24	7	33	16	1	152	15	–	–	–	–	0	39	7	33	16	1	152
40 Players	**524**	**93**	**40**	**24**	**2**	**623**	**318**	**36**	**1**	**0**	**0**	**180**	**842**	**129**	**41**	**24**	**2**	**803**

ABSA CURRIE CUP – 1ST DIVISION

FIRST-CLASS APPEARANCES FOR BOLAND IN 2014 – ALL MATCHES

PLAYER	VODACOM CUP						CURRIE CUP QUALIFIERS						CURRIE CUP 1ST DIV.						2014 TOTAL						CAREER MATCHES					
	A	T	C	P	DG	Pts	A	T	C	P	DG	Pts	A	T	C	P	DG	Pts	A	T	C	P	DG	Pts	A	T	C	P	DG	Pts
KM (Keenan) Abrahams	2	–	–	–	–	0	1	–	–	–	–	0	–	–	–	–	–	–	3	–	–	–	–	0	4	–	–	–	–	0
GB (Gavin) Annandale	–	–	–	–	–	–	6	–	–	–	–	0	4	–	–	–	–	0	10	–	–	–	–	0	10	–	–	–	–	0
BT (Brandon) April	1	–	–	–	–	0	–	–	–	–	–	–	–	–	–	–	–	–	1	–	–	–	–	0	67	34	–	–	–	170
GG (Garth) April	2	–	–	–	–	0	–	–	–	–	–	–	2	–	–	–	–	0	2	–	–	–	–	0	6	2	–	–	–	4
J (Junaid) Arendse	2	–	–	–	–	0	1	–	–	–	–	0	2	–	–	–	–	0	2	–	–	–	–	0	25	2	–	–	–	10
J-C (JC) Astle	6	1	–	–	–	5	6	3	–	–	–	15	–	–	–	–	–	–	12	4	–	–	–	20	5	–	–	–	–	0
YMT (Yves) Bashiya	–	–	–	–	–	–	3	–	–	–	–	0	2	–	–	–	–	0	5	–	–	–	–	0	10	–	–	–	–	0
C (Christopher) Bosch	5	–	–	–	–	0	2	–	–	–	–	0	3	–	–	–	–	0	10	–	–	–	–	0	10	–	–	–	–	0
A (Andre) Coetzee	1	–	–	–	–	0	–	–	–	–	–	–	–	–	–	–	–	–	1	–	–	–	–	0	1	–	–	–	–	0
R (Ryno) Coetzee	–	–	–	–	–	–	6	2	–	–	–	10	2	–	–	–	–	0	8	2	–	–	–	10	8	2	–	–	–	10
RJ (Ryno) Conradie	–	–	–	–	–	–	–	–	–	–	–	–	–	–	–	–	–	–	–	–	–	–	–	–	7	–	–	–	–	0
A (Ashton) Constant	4	1	–	–	–	5	3	–	–	–	–	0	3	–	–	–	–	0	10	1	–	–	–	5	58	7	–	–	–	35
J (Jovellan) de Koker	4	–	–	–	–	0	–	–	–	–	–	–	5	1	–	–	–	5	9	1	–	–	–	5	9	1	–	–	–	5
D (Danwel) Demas	5	1	–	–	–	5	3	3	–	–	–	15	3	–	–	–	–	0	15	8	–	–	–	20	27	25	–	–	–	125
MC (Martin) Dreyer	4	–	–	–	–	0	4	1	–	–	–	5	4	–	–	–	–	0	12	1	–	–	–	5	12	1	–	–	–	5
KW (Kelvin) Fikster	–	–	–	–	–	–	1	–	–	–	–	0	1	–	–	–	–	0	2	–	–	–	–	0	2	–	–	–	–	0
AF (Arno) Fortuin	3	3	–	–	–	15	4	1	–	–	–	5	–	–	–	–	–	–	7	4	–	–	–	20	7	4	–	–	–	20
J-C (Jason) Fraser	–	–	–	–	–	–	3	–	–	–	–	0	5	–	–	–	–	0	8	–	–	–	–	0	8	–	–	–	–	0
S (Sino) Ganto	1	–	–	–	–	0	–	–	–	–	–	–	1	–	–	–	–	0	–	–	–	–	–	–	1	–	–	–	–	0
PF (Francois) Hanekom	5	–	–	–	–	0	6	–	–	–	–	0	2	–	–	–	–	0	13	–	–	–	–	0	45	–	–	–	–	0
APM (Marnus) Hugo	5	–	–	–	–	0	6	–	–	–	–	0	4	4	–	–	–	20	15	4	–	–	–	20	47	4	–	–	–	20
MJ (Morne) Hugo	1	–	–	–	–	0	2	–	–	5	1	24	5	–	6	8	–	39	7	–	6	8	1	39	7	–	6	8	1	39
Z (Zandré) Jordaan	–	–	–	–	–	–	3	–	3	–	–	0	5	2	–	–	–	10	8	2	–	–	–	10	74	23	–	–	–	115
JJ (Hanno) Kitshoff	7	–	–	–	–	0	5	–	–	–	–	0	3	–	–	–	–	0	15	–	–	–	–	0	30	–	–	–	–	0
HJ (Harlon) Klaasen	2	1	–	–	–	5	1	1	–	–	–	5	–	–	–	–	–	–	3	2	–	–	–	10	3	2	–	–	–	10
J (Jason) Kriel	–	–	–	–	–	–	–	–	–	–	–	–	–	–	–	–	–	–	–	–	–	–	–	–	2	2	–	–	–	10
R (Rossouw) Kruger	1	–	–	–	–	0	–	–	–	–	–	–	–	–	–	–	–	–	1	–	–	–	–	0	42	3	–	–	–	15
VE (Victor) Kruger	5	–	–	–	–	0	1	–	–	–	–	0	4	2	–	–	–	10	10	2	–	–	–	10	10	2	–	–	–	10

ABSA CURRIE CUP – 1ST DIVISION

FIRST-CLASS APPEARANCES FOR BOLAND IN 2014 – ALL MATCHES

PLAYER	VODACOM CUP					CURRIE CUP QUALIFIERS					CURRIE CUP 1ST DIV.					2014 TOTAL					CAREER MATCHES					
	A	T	C	P	DG	Pts	A	T	C	P	DG	Pts	A	T	C	P	DG	Pts	A	T	C	P	DG	Pts	A	T	C	P	DG	Pts
RJ (Richard) Lawson	–	–	–	–	–	0	5	–	–	–	–	5	3	2	–	–	–	10	8	2	–	–	–	10	8	2	–	–	–	10
C (Clemen) Lewis	7	1	–	–	–	5	5	5	–	–	–	5	5	1	–	–	–	5	17	2	–	–	–	10	119	9	–	–	–	45
EC (Earl) Lewis	1	–	–	–	–	0	3	3	–	–	–	3	4	–	–	–	–	0	5	–	–	–	–	0	7	–	–	–	–	5
E (Evan) Liedeman	2	–	–	–	–	0	–	–	–	–	–	–	5	–	–	–	–	5	7	1	–	–	–	5	7	1	–	–	–	5
NGP (Nathaniel) Manuel	–	–	–	–	–	0	–	–	–	–	–	–	2	–	–	–	–	0	2	–	–	–	–	0	2	–	–	–	–	0
DK (Dumisani) Meslane	5	–	–	–	–	0	–	3	–	–	–	5	5	–	–	–	–	0	10	1	–	–	–	5	3	1	–	–	–	5
K (Khwezi) Mkhafu	7	–	–	–	–	0	6	–	–	–	–	–	5	–	–	–	–	0	18	–	–	–	–	0	18	–	–	–	–	0
C (Conway) Pretorius	5	3	–	–	–	15	–	–	–	–	–	–	5	–	–	–	–	0	10	3	–	–	–	15	5	3	–	–	–	15
UD (Ulrich) Pretorius	4	–	–	–	–	0	–	–	–	–	–	–	5	–	–	–	–	5	14	2	–	–	–	10	30	8	–	–	–	40
T (Tiaan) Radyn	2	1	–	–	–	5	–	–	–	–	–	–	1	–	–	–	–	0	2	1	–	–	–	5	5	1	–	–	–	5
DE (Deroy) Rhoode	–	–	–	–	–	0	5	–	–	–	–	–	–	–	–	–	–	0	5	–	–	–	–	0	18	1	–	–	–	5
CD (Cheslyn) Roberts	4	1	–	–	–	5	–	–	–	–	–	–	–	–	–	–	–	0	4	1	–	–	–	5	15	2	–	–	–	10
HC (Christian) Rust	6	3	7	4	–	41	6	1	–	1	–	7	3	1	5	–	–	15	15	5	8	4	0	53	15	5	8	4	0	53
JP (Juwell) Samuels	2	–	–	–	–	0	–	–	–	–	–	–	2	–	–	–	–	0	2	–	–	–	–	0	2	–	–	–	–	0
E (Edwin) Sass	4	–	–	–	–	0	3	–	–	–	–	0	3	–	–	–	–	10	10	–	–	–	–	10	10	–	–	–	–	10
FJ (Franzel) September	6	2	–	–	–	10	6	3	–	–	–	15	3	–	–	–	–	0	15	5	–	–	–	25	80	29	–	–	–	145
DE (Duwayne) Smart	–	–	–	–	–	0	4	1	–	–	–	5	–	–	–	–	–	0	5	1	–	–	–	5	5	1	–	–	–	5
AM (Albert) Trytsman	7	1	–	1	–	5	1	–	–	–	–	–	–	–	–	–	–	0	–	–	–	–	–	5	5	1	–	–	–	5
AG (Poena) van Niekerk	7	–	–	–	–	5	6	1	–	–	–	5	3	1	–	–	–	5	16	2	–	–	–	10	19	2	–	–	–	10
C (Chevandre) van Schoor	2	–	–	–	–	0	–	–	–	–	–	–	–	–	–	–	–	0	2	–	–	–	–	0	3	–	–	–	–	0
PJ (PJ) van Zyl	–	–	–	–	–	0	–	–	–	–	–	–	–	–	–	–	–	0	–	–	–	–	–	0	65	10	–	–	–	50
BCG (Ben) Venter	7	1	–	–	–	5	1	–	–	–	–	1	–	–	–	–	–	0	3	1	–	–	–	5	21	–	–	–	–	0
SP (SP) Wessels	2	–	–	–	–	0	–	–	–	–	–	–	–	–	–	–	–	0	2	–	–	–	–	0	7	–	–	–	–	0
C (Chaney) Willemse	2	–	–	–	–	0	–	2	–	–	–	10	–	–	–	–	–	0	–	–	–	–	–	10	2	–	–	–	–	10
C (Cheswin) Williams	3	–	–	–	–	0	–	–	–	–	–	–	–	–	–	–	–	0	3	–	–	–	–	0	6	–	–	–	–	0
ES (Eric) Zana	2	–	–	–	–	0	–	–	–	–	–	–	–	–	–	–	–	0	–	–	–	–	–	0	2	–	–	–	–	0
54 Players	150	20	14	10	0	158	129	17	11	10	1	140	110	19	11	6	1	138	389	56	36	26	2	436	1047	205	58	38	2	1261

ABSA CURRIE CUP – 1ST DIVISION

Border Rugby Football Union

Founded: 1891 **Ground:** BCM Stadium (formerly the Basil Kenyon Stadium)
Capacity: 15 000 **Address:** Recreation Road, East London, 5201
Postal address: PO Box 75, East London, 5200 **Telephone Number:** 043-743 5998
Website: www.borderbulldogs.co.za **Colours:** Brown jersey with white, red and green stripes and white shorts with green stripes. Brown socks with two white stripes.
Head Coach: Paul Flanaghan **Captain:** Gareth Krause **President:** Phumlani Mkolo
CEO: Lefty Ngece

'96	'97	'98	'99	'00	'01	'02	'03	'04	'05	'06	'07	'08	'09	'10	'11	'12	'13	'14
9th	14th	9th	7th	9th	11th	11th	11th	13th	12th	12th	10th	14th	12th	10th	10th	7th	8th	14th

Played	Won	Lost	Drawn	Points for	Points against	Tries for	Tries against
5	1	4	0	98	143	12	22

Date	Venue	Opponent	Result	Score	Referee	Scorers
29 Aug	East London	Valke	WON	19-14	S Berry	T: Ndlela, Mphafi. P: Banda (3).
6 Sep	Welkom	Griffons	LOST	32-37	M Jonker	T: Ralarala, Mgwadleka, Banda, Van Wyk. C: Banda (2), Graaff. P: Banda, Graaff.
12 Sep	George	Eagles	LOST	22-31	L van der Merwe	T: Maphimpi, Ralarala, Mgwadleka. C: Banda (2). P: Banda.
19 Sep	East London	Leopards	LOST	19-34	J Peyper	T: Van Wyk (2), Maphimpi. C: Banda (2).
26 Sep	Wellington	Cavaliers	LOST	6-27	L Legoete	P: Banda (2).

APPEARANCES & POINTS FOR BORDER IN 2014 1ST DIVISION

PLAYER	Valke	Griffons	Eagles	Leopards	Cavaliers	Apps	T	C	P	DG	Pts
Masixole Banda	15	10	15	15	15	5	1	6	7	0	38
Lindani Ndlela	14	11	–	–	–	2	1	0	0	0	5
Lundi Ralarala	13	13	13	13	13	5	2	0	0	0	10
Lithabile Mgwadleka	12	12	12	12	–	4	2	0	0	0	10
Makazole Maphimpi	11	14	14	14	14	5	2	0	0	0	10
Thembani Mkokeli	10	–	10	10	10	4	–	–	–	–	0
Ntando Kebe	9	9c	9	9	9	5	–	–	–	–	0
Rynardt van Wyk	8	8	8	8	8	5	3	0	0	0	15
Siya Mdaka	7	7	7	7	7	5	–	–	–	–	0
Lukhanyo Nomzanga	6	6	–	6	6	4	–	–	–	–	0
Anthonie Gronum	5	5	–	–	–	2	–	–	–	–	0
Wayne Lemley	4	4	4	4	–	4	–	–	–	–	0
Buhle Mxunyelwa	3	3	3	3	3	5	–	–	–	–	0
Mihlali Mpafi	2	–	2	2	–	3	1	0	0	0	5
Blake Kyd	1c	–	1c	1c	1c	4	–	–	–	–	0
Ludwe Booi	2R	3R	x	x	2	3	–	–	–	–	0
Yanga Xakalashe	3R	1	3R	3R	3R	5	–	–	–	–	0
Wandile Putuma	5R	5R	5	5	5	5	–	–	–	–	0
Nkosikhana Nofuma	7R	4R	4R	4R	4	5	–	–	–	–	0
Onke Dubase	x	7R	6	–	6R	3	–	–	–	–	0
Mario Noordman	x	9R	x	x	–	1	–	–	–	–	0
Oliver Zono	10R	–	–	x	10R	2	–	–	–	–	0
Hansie Graaff	–	15	x	–	–	1	0	1	1	0	5
Martin Ferreira	–	2	–	–	–	1	–	–	–	–	0
Simon Kerrod	–	1R	–	–	–	1	–	–	–	–	0
Joe Seerane	–	14R	11	x	–	2	–	–	–	–	0
Athenkosi Manentsa	–	–	6R	x	7R	2	–	–	–	–	0
Ruan Jacobs	–	–	10R	–	12	2	–	–	–	–	0
Michael Makase	–	–	–	11	11	2	–	–	–	–	0
Bryce Rennie	–	–	–	–	2R	1	–	–	–	–	0
Lindekuhle Welemu	–	–	–	–	4R	1	–	–	–	–	0
Bangi Kobese	–	–	–	–	9R	1	–	–	–	–	0
32 Players						100	12	7	8	0	98

ABSA CURRIE CUP – 1ST DIVISION

CURRIE CUP 1ST DIV. SQUAD – CAREER CURRIE CUP APPEARANCES

PLAYER	BORDER						OTHER UNIONS						TOTAL					
	A	T	C	P	DG	Pts	A	T	C	P	DG	Pts	A	T	C	P	DG	Pts
M (Masixole) Banda	11	2	16	13	0	81	0	0	0	0	0	0	11	2	16	13	0	81
AL (Ludwe) Booi	9	0	0	0	0	0	0	0	0	0	0	0	9	0	0	0	0	0
OS (Onke) Dubase	15	1	0	0	0	5	0	0	0	0	0	0	15	1	0	0	0	5
M (Martin) Ferreira	1	0	0	0	0	0	26	6	0	0	0	30	27	6	0	0	0	30
JPJ (Hansie) Graaff	1	0	1	1	0	5	2	0	0	0	0	0	3	0	1	1	0	5
AJ (Anthonie) Gronum	13	0	0	0	0	0	35	1	0	0	0	5	48	1	0	0	0	5
R (Ruan) Jacobs	17	0	0	0	0	0	2	0	1	0	0	2	19	0	1	0	0	2
JGA (Johann) Jonker	4	1	0	0	0	5	0	0	0	0	0	0	4	1	0	0	0	5
NL (Ntando) Kebe	27	0	0	0	0	0	14	1	0	0	0	5	41	1	0	0	0	5
S (Simon) Kerrod	1	0	0	0	0	0	2	0	0	0	0	0	3	0	0	0	0	0
N (Naythan) Knoetze	1	0	0	0	0	0	0	0	0	0	0	0	1	0	0	0	0	0
B (Bangi) Kobese	7	1	0	0	0	5	0	0	0	0	0	0	7	1	0	0	0	5
GE (Gareth) Krause	52	10	0	0	0	50	67	12	0	0	0	60	119	22	0	0	0	110
BJ (Blake) Kyd	17	1	0	0	0	5	0	0	0	0	0	0	17	1	0	0	0	5
W (Wayne) Lemley	14	1	0	0	0	5	0	0	0	0	0	0	14	1	0	0	0	5
M (Michael) Makase	6	1	0	0	0	5	0	0	0	0	0	0	6	1	0	0	0	5
A (Athenkosi) Manentsa	4	0	0	0	0	0	0	0	0	0	0	0	4	0	0	0	0	0
M (Makazole) Maphimpi	10	2	0	0	0	10	0	0	0	0	0	0	10	2	0	0	0	10
S (Siya) Mdaka	23	0	0	0	0	0	4	0	0	0	0	0	27	0	0	0	0	0
L (Lithabile) Mgwadleka	9	2	0	0	0	10	0	0	0	0	0	0	9	2	0	0	0	10
TM (Thembani) Mkokeli	61	9	0	1	0	48	0	0	0	0	0	0	61	9	0	1	0	48
M (Mihlali) Mpafi	8	1	0	0	0	5	0	0	0	0	0	0	8	1	0	0	0	5
B (Buhle) Mxunyelwa	26	1	0	0	0	5	3	0	0	0	0	0	29	1	0	0	0	5
LN (Lindani) Ndlela	4	3	0	0	0	15	0	0	0	0	0	0	4	3	0	0	0	15
S (Siyamthanda) Ngande	2	0	0	0	0	0	0	0	0	0	0	0	2	0	0	0	0	0
N (Nkosi) Nofuma	7	0	0	0	0	0	0	0	0	0	0	0	7	0	0	0	0	0
LW (Lukhanyo) Nomzanga	9	0	0	0	0	0	0	0	0	0	0	0	9	0	0	0	0	0
M (Mario) Noordman	2	0	0	0	0	0	0	0	0	0	0	0	2	0	0	0	0	0
W (Wandile) Putuma	10	0	0	0	0	0	0	0	0	0	0	0	10	0	0	0	0	0
LS (Lundi) Ralarala	9	4	0	0	0	20	0	0	0	0	0	0	9	4	0	0	0	20
BM (Bryce) Rennie	1	0	0	0	0	0	0	0	0	0	0	0	1	0	0	0	0	0
J (Johannes) Seerane	2	0	0	0	0	0	0	0	0	0	0	0	2	0	0	0	0	0
RI (Rynardt) van Wyk	25	6	0	0	0	30	0	0	0	0	0	0	25	6	0	0	0	30
LY (Lolo) Waka	13	7	0	0	0	35	0	0	0	0	0	0	13	7	0	0	0	35
L (Lindokuhle) Welemu	6	0	0	0	0	0	0	0	0	0	0	0	6	0	0	0	0	0
Y (Yanga) Xakalashe	10	1	0	0	0	5	0	0	0	0	0	0	10	1	0	0	0	5
O (Oliver) Zono	7	1	0	0	0	5	0	0	0	0	0	0	7	1	0	0	0	5
37 Players																		

ABSA CURRIE CUP – 1ST DIVISION

FIRST-CLASS APPEARANCES FOR BORDER IN 2014 – ALL MATCHES

PLAYER	VODACOM CUP						CURRIE CUP QUALIFIERS						CURRIE CUP 1ST DIV.						2014 TOTAL						CAREER MATCHES					
	A	T	C	P	DG	Pts	A	T	C	P	DG	Pts	A	T	C	P	DG	Pts	A	T	C	P	DG	Pts	A	T	C	P	DG	Pts
M (Masixole) Banda	0	0	0	0	0	0	6	1	10	6	0	43	5	1	6	7	0	38	11	2	16	13	0	81	11	2	16	13	0	81
CA (Cody) Basson	2	0	0	0	0	0	0	0	0	0	0	0	0	0	0	0	0	0	2	0	0	0	0	0	2	0	0	0	0	0
AL (Ludwe) Booi	2	0	0	0	0	0	5	0	0	0	0	0	3	0	0	0	0	0	10	0	0	0	0	0	12	0	0	0	0	15
OS (Onke) Dubase	3	0	0	0	0	0	2	0	0	0	0	0	3	0	0	0	0	0	8	0	0	0	0	0	27	3	0	0	0	15
M (Martin) Ferreira	0	0	0	0	0	0	0	0	0	0	0	0	1	0	0	0	0	0	1	0	0	0	0	0	1	0	0	0	0	0
C (Cheslin) Goeda	2	0	0	0	0	0	0	0	0	0	0	0	0	0	0	0	0	0	2	0	0	0	0	0	2	0	0	0	0	0
JPJ (Hansie) Graaff	0	0	0	0	0	0	0	0	0	0	0	0	1	1	0	0	0	5	1	1	0	0	0	5	1	1	0	0	0	5
AJ (Anthonie) Gronum	3	0	0	0	0	0	1	0	0	0	0	0	2	0	0	0	0	0	6	0	0	0	0	0	40	0	0	0	0	0
N (Niell) Jacobs	4	0	0	1	0	3	0	0	0	0	0	0	0	0	0	0	0	0	4	0	0	1	0	3	35	3	1	2	0	23
R (Ruan) Jacobs	3	0	0	0	0	0	0	0	0	0	0	0	0	0	0	0	0	0	8	0	0	0	0	0	31	4	0	0	0	20
JGA (Johann) Jonker	7	1	0	0	0	5	4	1	0	0	0	5	0	0	0	0	0	0	11	2	0	0	0	10	11	2	0	0	0	10
NL (Ntando) Kebe	0	0	0	0	0	0	5	0	0	0	0	0	5	4	0	0	0	20	10	4	0	0	0	20	52	4	0	0	0	20
S (Simon) Kerrod	0	0	0	0	0	0	0	0	0	0	0	0	1	0	0	0	0	0	1	0	0	0	0	0	1	0	0	0	0	0
C (Curtis) Kleinhans	2	0	0	0	0	0	0	0	0	0	0	0	0	0	0	0	0	0	2	0	0	0	0	0	2	0	0	0	0	0
N (Naythan) Knoetze	0	0	0	0	0	0	1	0	0	0	0	0	0	0	0	0	0	0	1	0	0	0	0	0	1	0	0	0	0	0
B (Bangi) Kobese	3	0	5	1	0	13	6	1	0	0	0	5	1	0	0	0	0	0	10	1	5	1	0	18	10	1	5	1	0	18
GE (Gareth) Krause	3	1	0	0	0	5	3	0	0	0	0	0	0	0	0	0	0	0	6	1	0	0	0	5	84	14	0	0	0	70
BJ (Blake) Kyd	3	0	0	0	0	0	6	1	0	0	0	5	4	0	0	0	0	0	17	2	0	0	0	10	50	2	0	0	0	10
W (Wayne) Lemley	6	0	0	0	0	0	4	1	0	0	0	5	4	0	0	0	0	0	14	1	0	0	0	5	21	1	0	0	0	5
AG (Alvandre) Maart	1	0	0	0	0	0	0	0	0	0	0	0	0	0	0	0	0	0	1	0	0	0	0	0	1	0	0	0	0	0
M (Michael) Makase	7	1	0	0	0	5	2	0	0	0	0	0	2	0	0	0	0	0	13	2	0	0	0	10	13	2	0	0	0	10
A (Athenkosi) Manentsa	0	0	0	0	0	0	2	0	0	0	0	0	2	0	0	0	0	0	4	0	0	0	0	0	4	0	0	0	0	0
M (Makazole) Maphimpi	7	3	0	0	0	15	5	0	0	0	0	0	5	2	0	0	0	10	17	5	0	0	0	25	17	5	0	0	0	25
S (Skhangele) Mateza	3	0	0	0	0	0	0	0	0	0	0	0	0	0	0	0	0	0	3	0	0	0	0	0	3	0	0	0	0	0
S (Siya) Mdaka	7	0	0	0	0	0	6	0	0	0	0	0	5	1	0	0	0	5	18	1	0	0	0	5	38	1	0	0	0	5
L (Lithabile) Mgwadleka	3	0	0	0	0	0	5	0	0	0	0	0	4	2	0	0	0	10	12	2	0	0	0	10	12	2	0	0	0	10

ABSA CURRIE CUP – 1ST DIVISION

FIRST-CLASS APPEARANCES FOR BORDER IN 2014 – ALL MATCHES

PLAYER	VODACOM CUP						CURRIE CUP QUALIFIERS						CURRIE CUP 1ST DIV.						2014 TOTAL						CAREER MATCHES					
	A	T	C	P	DG	Pts	A	T	C	P	DG	Pts	A	T	C	P	DG	Pts	A	T	C	P	DG	Pts	A	T	C	P	DG	Pts
TM (Thembani) Mkokeli	5	1	0	0	0	5	6	2	0	0	0	10	4	0	0	0	0	0	15	3	0	0	0	15	105	18	0	1	0	93
B (Bonga) Mtunjani	5	0	0	0	0	0	0	0	0	0	0	0	0	0	0	0	0	0	5	0	0	0	0	0	40	4	0	0	0	20
M (Mihlali) Mpafi	5	0	0	0	0	0	5	0	0	0	0	0	3	1	0	0	0	5	13	1	0	0	0	5	13	1	0	0	0	5
B (Buhle) Mxunyelwa	0	0	0	0	0	0	4	0	0	0	0	0	5	0	0	0	0	0	9	0	0	0	0	0	28	2	0	0	0	10
LN (Lindani) Ndlela	0	0	0	0	0	0	2	2	0	0	0	10	2	1	0	0	0	5	4	3	0	0	0	15	4	3	0	0	0	15
S (Siyamthanda) Ngande	2	0	0	0	0	0	2	0	0	0	0	0	0	0	0	0	0	0	4	0	0	0	0	0	4	0	0	0	0	0
MN (Mondi) Nkosi	2	0	0	0	0	0	0	0	0	0	0	0	0	0	0	0	0	0	2	0	0	0	0	0	2	0	0	0	0	0
S (Sipho) Nofemele	5	2	0	0	0	10	4	1	0	0	0	5	0	0	0	0	0	0	9	3	0	0	0	15	9	3	0	0	0	15
N (Nkosi) Nofuma	7	0	0	0	0	0	2	0	0	0	0	0	5	0	0	0	0	0	14	0	0	0	0	0	14	0	0	0	0	0
LW (Lukhanyo) Nomzanga	0	0	0	0	0	0	5	0	0	0	0	0	4	0	0	0	0	0	9	0	0	0	0	0	9	0	0	0	0	0
M (Mario) Noordman	6	1	1	0	0	7	1	0	0	0	0	0	1	0	0	0	0	0	8	1	1	0	0	7	8	1	1	0	0	7
S (Siya) Pati	1	0	0	0	0	0	0	0	0	0	0	0	0	0	0	0	0	0	1	0	0	0	0	0	1	0	0	0	0	0
W (Wandile) Putuma	7	2	0	0	0	10	5	0	0	0	0	0	5	0	0	0	0	0	17	2	0	0	0	10	17	2	0	0	0	10
LS (Lundi) Ralarala	3	1	0	0	0	5	4	2	0	0	0	10	5	2	0	0	0	10	12	5	0	0	0	25	12	5	0	0	0	25
BM (Bryce) Rennie	3	0	0	0	0	0	0	0	0	0	0	0	1	0	0	0	0	0	4	0	0	0	0	0	4	0	0	0	0	0
R (Walla) Schoeman	1	0	0	0	0	0	0	0	0	0	0	0	1	0	0	0	0	0	2	0	0	0	0	0	41	6	0	0	0	30
J (Johannes) Seerane	0	0	0	0	0	0	0	0	0	0	0	0	2	0	0	0	0	0	2	0	0	0	0	0	12	6	0	0	0	30
A (Anele) Sibeko	1	0	0	0	0	0	0	0	0	0	0	0	0	0	0	0	0	0	1	0	0	0	0	0	1	0	0	0	0	0
JJ (Jeff) Taljard	4	1	5	7	0	36	0	0	0	0	0	0	0	0	0	0	0	0	4	1	5	7	0	36	37	7	28	35	0	196
RI (Rynardt) van Wyk	0	0	0	0	0	0	6	1	0	0	0	5	5	3	0	0	0	15	11	4	0	0	0	20	38	8	0	0	0	40
LY (Lolo) Waka	4	2	0	0	0	10	2	0	0	0	0	0	0	0	0	0	0	0	6	2	0	0	0	10	12	2	0	0	0	10
L (Lindokuhle) Welemu	5	0	0	0	0	0	5	1	0	0	0	5	1	0	0	0	0	0	11	1	0	0	0	5	11	1	0	0	0	5
Y (Yanga) Xakalashe	6	0	0	0	0	0	0	0	0	0	0	0	10	1	0	0	0	5	16	1	0	0	0	5	16	1	0	0	0	5
O (Oliver) Zono	2	0	0	0	0	0	5	1	0	0	0	5	2	0	0	0	0	0	9	1	0	0	0	5	9	1	0	0	0	5
50 Players	149	15	11	9	0	124	131	16	10	6	0	118	100	12	7	8	0	98	380	43	28	23	0	340	929	110	52	53	0	813

www.sarugby.co.za

ABSA CURRIE CUP – 1ST DIVISION

Griffons Rugby Union

Founded: 1968 (as Northern Free State) **Ground:** North West Stadium, Welkom
Capacity: 8 500 **Address:** Rugby Street, Welkom **Postal address:** PO Box 631, Welkom 9460
Telephone Number: 057-352 6482 **Email:** rugbybond@icon.co.za
Colours: Purple and yellow jersey, white shorts **Currie Cup Coach:** Oersond Gorgonzola
Captain: Nicky Steyn **President:** Randall September
Company CEO: Eugene van Wyk

'96	'97	'98	'99	'00	'01	'02	'03	'04	'05	'06	'07	'08	'09	'10	'11	'12	'13	'14
12th	12th	14th	13th	14th	13th	14th	14th	14th	11th	14th	11th	9th	11th	12th	12th	9th	12th	10th

Played	Won	Lost	Drawn	Points for	Points against	Tries for	Tries against
7	5	2	0	223	224	27	27

Date	Venue	Opponent	Result	Score	Referee	Scorers
30 Aug	Wellington	Boland	WON	27-19	L v/d Merwe	T: Abrahams, Sisita, Nelson. C: Srydom (3). P: Strydom, Du Toit.
6 Sep	Welkom	Border	WON	37-32	M Jonker	T: Nel (2), McDonald, Van der Hoogt, Steyn. C: Strydom (2), Du Toit. P: Strydom (2).
13 Sep	Welkom	Leopards	WON	37-31	M v/d Westhuizen	T: Abrahams (2), Mbotho, Pienaar, McDonald. C: Du Toit (2), Strydom. P: Strydom, Du Toit.
20 Sep	Kempton Park	Valke	LOST	27-36	F Anselmi	T: Maarman (2), Mbotho. C: Du Toit (2), Strydom. P: Du Toit (2).
27 Sep	Welkom	SWD	LOST	27-42	Q Immelman	T: Maarman (2), Ehlers, Pienaar. C: Du Toit (2). P: Du Toit.
SEMI-FINAL						
3 Oct	Welkom	SWD	WON	45-43	B Crouse	T: Nelson (2), Ehlers, Maarman, Pienaar. C: Strydom (4). P: Strydom (2). DG: Strydom (2).
FINAL						
17 Oct	Welkom	Valke	WON	23-21	B Crouse	T: Abrahams, Nelson. C: Strydom (2). P: Strydom (2). DG: Abrahams

ABSA CURRIE CUP – 1ST DIVISION

APPEARANCES & POINTS FOR GRIFFONS IN 2014 1ST DIVISION

PLAYER	Boland	Border	Leopards	Valke	SWD	SWD (SF)	Valke (F)	Apps	T	C	P	DG	Pts
Tertius Maarman	15	15	15	14	14	15	15	7	5	–	–	–	25
Aubrey McDonald	14	14	11	11	11	11	11	7	2	–	–	–	10
Vuyo Mbotho	13	13	13	13	–	13	13	6	2	–	–	–	10
Japie Nel	12	12	12	12	–	12	12	6	2	–	–	–	10
Norman Nelson	11	11	14	–	–	14	14	5	4	–	–	–	20
Louis Strydom	10	10	10	10R	12R	10	10	7	–	13	8	2	56
Boela Abrahams	9	9	9	–	9	9	9	6	4	–	–	1	23
Nicky Steyn	8c	8c	8c	8c	8c	8c	8c	7	1	–	–	–	5
Erik le Roux	7	–	4R	7	–	6R	4R	5	–	–	–	–	0
Frans Sisita	6	6	–	–	6	6	6	5	1	–	–	–	5
Johan van der Hoogt	5	5	5	5	5	5	5	7	1	–	–	–	5
Armandt Koster	4	4R	7	4	7	7	7	7	–	–	–	–	0
Heinrich Roelfse	3	3	3	3	1R	3	3	7	–	–	–	–	0
Elandre Huggett	2	2R	2	2	x	2	2	6	–	–	–	–	0
Danie van der Merwe	1	1	–	–	1	3R	1R	5	–	–	–	–	0
Hannes Snyman	x	2	x	2R	2	x	x	3	–	–	–	–	0
PW Botha	1R	1R	–	–	–	–	–	2	–	–	–	–	0
Jan Breedt	5R	–	7R	4R	–	–	–	3	–	–	–	–	0
Martin Sithole	8R	7	6	6	6R	7R	6R	7	–	–	–	–	0
Andre van der Walt	9R	x	9R	9	–	–	–	3	–	–	–	–	0
Franna du Toit	10R	10R	10R	10	10	14R	x	6	–	7	5	–	29
Wynand Pienaar	15R	15R	15R	15	15	15R	14R	7	3	–	–	–	15
Chris Ehlers	–	4	4	–	4	4	4	5	2	–	–	–	10
Dirk Grobbelaar	–	6R	–	–	–	–	–	1	–	–	–	–	0
Gerard Baard	–	–	1	1	3	1	1	5	–	–	–	–	0
Franco van der Merwe	–	–	x	3R	–	–	–	1	–	–	–	–	0
Oshwill Nortjie	–	–	9R	9R	9R	x	–	3	–	–	–	–	0
Wilmar Groenewald	–	–	6R	–	–	–	–	1	–	–	–	–	0
Colin Herbert	–	–	13R	12	–	–	–	2	–	–	–	–	0
Werner Griesel	–	–	–	–	13	–	–	1	–	–	–	–	0
Rudi Britz	–	–	–	–	3R	–	–	1	–	–	–	–	0
Wikus Davis	–	–	–	–	4R	–	–	1	–	–	–	–	0
32 Players								145	27	20	13	3	223

ABSA CURRIE CUP – 1ST DIVISION

CURRIE CUP 1ST DIV. SQUAD - CAREER CURRIE CUP APPEARANCES

PLAYER	GRIFFONS						OTHER UNIONS						TOTAL					
	A	T	C	P	DG	Pts	A	T	C	P	DG	Pts	A	T	C	P	DG	Pts
YW (Boela) Abrahams	12	5	–	–	1	28	5	–	–	–	–	0	17	5	–	–	1	28
G (Gerard) Baard	6	–	–	–	–	0	–	–	–	–	–	0	6	–	–	–	–	0
M (Mlungisi) Bali	12	–	–	–	–	0	–	–	–	–	–	0	12	–	–	–	–	0
PW (PW) Botha	6	–	–	–	–	0	–	–	–	–	–	0	6	–	–	–	–	0
J (Jan) Breedt	7	–	–	–	–	0	–	–	–	–	–	0	7	–	–	–	–	0
RM (Rudi) Britz	9	–	–	–	–	0	–	–	–	–	–	0	9	–	–	–	–	0
L (Wikus) Davis	1	–	–	–	–	0	–	–	–	–	–	0	1	–	–	–	–	0
P-S (Pieter-Steyn) de Wet	4	–	7	2	–	20	4	–	6	1	–	15	8	–	13	3	–	35
FC (Franna) du Toit	12	–	19	11	–	71	–	–	–	–	–	0	12	–	19	11	–	71
C-E (Chris) Ehlers	19	3	–	–	–	15	13	1	–	–	–	5	32	4	–	–	–	20
GJ (Joubert) Engelbrecht	14	2	5	1	–	23	25	5	–	–	–	25	39	7	5	1	–	48
W (Werner) Griesel	57	15	–	–	–	75	1	1	–	–	–	5	58	16	–	–	–	80
H (Dirk) Grobbelaar	1	–	–	–	–	0	–	–	–	–	–	0	1	–	–	–	–	0
WR (Wilmar) Groenewald	11	2	–	–	–	10	–	–	–	–	–	0	11	2	–	–	–	10
C (Colin) Herbert	6	–	3	1	–	9	–	–	–	–	–	0	6	–	3	1	–	9
E (Elandre) Huggett	15	2	–	–	–	10	3	1	–	–	–	5	18	3	–	–	–	15
CL (Cameron) Jacobs	6	–	–	–	–	0	10	3	–	–	–	15	16	3	–	–	–	15
DN (Niell) Jordaan	1	–	–	–	–	0	–	–	–	–	–	0	1	–	–	–	–	0
A (Armandt) Koster	13	3	–	–	–	15	–	–	–	–	–	0	13	3	–	–	–	15
IM (Inus) Kritzinger	11	4	5	–	–	30	–	–	–	–	–	0	11	4	5	–	–	30
AJ (AJ) le Roux	5	–	–	–	–	0	4	1	–	–	–	5	9	1	–	–	–	5
HF (Erik) le Roux	22	5	–	–	–	25	–	–	–	–	–	0	22	5	–	–	–	25
W (Werner) Lourens	4	–	–	–	–	0	3	–	–	–	–	0	7	–	–	–	–	0
T (Tertius) Maarman	45	16	2	–	–	84	–	–	–	–	–	0	45	16	2	–	–	84
V (Vuyo) Mbotho	20	3	–	–	–	15	10	5	–	–	–	25	28	8	–	–	–	40
AN (Aubrey) McDonald	17	2	–	–	–	10	–	–	–	–	–	0	17	2	–	–	–	10
J (Japie) Nel	57	26	–	–	–	130	16	4	–	–	–	20	73	30	–	–	–	150
NT (Norman) Nelson	16	13	–	–	–	65	69	51	–	–	–	255	85	64	–	–	–	320
O (Oshwill) Nortjie	19	2	–	–	–	10	–	–	–	–	–	0	19	2	–	–	–	10
WC (Wynand) Pienaar	11	3	–	–	–	15	6	1	–	–	–	5	17	4	–	–	–	20
HR (Heinrich) Roelfse	17	–	–	–	–	0	–	–	–	–	–	0	17	–	–	–	–	0
FL (Frans) Sisita	10	1	–	–	–	5	–	–	–	–	–	0	10	1	–	–	–	5
SM (Martin) Sithole	24	5	–	–	–	25	23	6	–	–	–	30	47	11	–	–	–	55
JJ (Hannes) Snyman	13	–	–	–	–	0	–	–	–	–	–	0	13	–	–	–	–	0
KB (Kevin) Stevens	35	2	–	–	–	10	6	–	–	–	–	0	41	2	–	–	–	10
NPJ (Nicky) Steyn	57	20	–	–	–	100	–	–	–	–	–	0	57	20	–	–	–	100
LI (Louis) Strydom	36	4	50	53	2	285	103	6	172	134	7	797	139	10	222	187	9	1082
NJ (Nico) van der Hoogt	7	1	–	–	–	5	–	–	–	–	–	0	7	1	–	–	–	5
DJ (Danie) van der Merwe	23	1	–	–	–	5	–	–	–	–	–	0	23	1	–	–	–	5
FJF (Franco) van der Merwe	1	–	–	–	–	0	–	–	–	–	–	0	–	–	–	–	–	0
AJ (Andre) van der Walt	3	–	–	–	–	0	–	–	–	–	–	0	3	–	–	–	–	0
41 Players	665	140	91	68	3	1095	301	85	178	135	7	1207	963	225	269	203	10	2302

ABSA CURRIE CUP – 1ST DIVISION

FIRST-CLASS APPEARANCES FOR GRIFFONS IN 2014 – ALL MATCHES

PLAYER	VODACOM CUP						CURRIE CUP QUALIFIERS						CURRIE CUP 1ST DIV.						2014 TOTAL						CAREER MATCHES					
	A	T	C	P	DG	Pts	A	T	C	P	DG	Pts	A	T	C	P	DG	Pts	A	T	C	P	DG	Pts	A	T	C	P	DG	Pts
YW (Boela) Abrahams	0	0	0	0	0	0	4	1	0	0	0	5	6	4	0	0	1	23	10	5	0	0	1	28	14	5	0	0	1	28
G (Gerard) Baard	0	0	0	0	0	0	1	0	0	0	0	0	5	0	0	0	0	0	6	0	0	0	0	0	6	0	0	0	0	0
M (Mlungisi) Bali	6	0	0	0	0	0	6	0	0	0	0	0	0	0	0	0	0	0	12	0	0	0	0	0	25	0	0	0	0	0
J-F (Jan-Francois) Bester	2	0	0	0	0	0	0	0	0	0	0	0	0	0	0	0	0	0	2	0	0	0	0	0	2	0	0	0	0	0
PW (PW) Botha	5	0	0	0	0	0	4	0	0	0	0	0	2	0	0	0	0	0	11	0	0	0	0	0	11	0	0	0	0	0
J (Jan) Breedt	5	0	0	0	0	0	4	0	0	0	0	0	3	0	0	0	0	0	12	0	0	0	0	0	12	0	0	0	0	0
RM (Rudi) Britz	5	0	0	0	0	0	0	0	0	0	0	0	1	2	0	0	0	10	6	2	0	0	0	10	36	2	0	0	0	10
L (Wikus) Davis	2	0	0	0	0	0	0	0	0	0	0	0	1	0	0	0	0	0	3	0	0	0	0	0	3	0	0	0	0	0
P-S (Pieter-Steyn) de Wet	0	0	0	0	0	0	4	0	7	2	0	20	0	0	0	0	0	0	4	0	7	2	0	20	4	0	7	2	0	20
FC (Franna) du Toit	5	0	6	3	0	21	2	0	2	6	0	22	6	0	6	5	0	29	13	0	14	14	0	72	17	0	24	14	0	92
C-E (Chris) Ehlers	0	0	0	0	0	0	5	0	0	0	0	0	0	0	0	0	0	0	5	0	0	0	0	0	5	0	0	0	0	0
GJ (Joubert) Engelbrecht	0	0	0	0	0	0	5	1	0	0	0	5	0	0	0	0	0	0	5	1	0	0	0	5	37	5	0	0	0	25
S (Sheldon) Erasmus	0	0	0	0	0	0	0	0	0	0	0	0	5	2	0	0	0	10	5	2	0	0	0	10	14	2	5	1	0	23
GP (Deon) Gouws	4	2	0	0	0	10	0	0	0	0	0	0	0	0	0	0	0	0	4	2	0	0	0	10	4	2	0	0	0	10
W (Werner) Griesel	2	0	0	0	0	0	0	0	0	0	0	0	0	0	0	0	0	0	2	0	0	0	0	0	3	0	0	0	0	0
H (Dirk) Grobbelaar	7	0	0	0	0	0	0	0	0	0	0	0	2	0	0	0	0	0	9	0	0	0	0	0	123	26	0	0	0	130
WR (Wilmar) Groenewald	1	0	0	0	0	0	0	0	0	0	0	0	1	0	0	0	0	0	2	0	0	0	0	0	4	0	0	0	0	0
C (Colin) Herbert	6	1	0	0	0	5	3	0	0	0	0	0	1	0	0	0	0	0	10	1	0	0	0	5	25	3	0	0	0	15
E (Elandre) Huggett	2	0	0	0	0	0	3	1	0	0	0	5	2	0	0	0	0	0	7	1	0	0	0	5	16	2	0	0	0	10
CL (Cameron) Jacobs	6	1	0	0	0	5	6	1	0	0	0	5	0	0	0	0	0	0	12	1	3	0	0	9	15	1	4	1	0	16
DN (Niell) Jordaan	0	0	0	0	0	0	3	0	0	0	0	0	0	0	0	0	0	0	3	0	0	0	0	0	14	0	0	0	0	0
A (Armandt) Koster	2	0	0	0	0	0	1	0	0	0	0	0	0	0	0	0	0	0	3	0	0	0	0	0	3	0	0	0	0	0
IM (Inus) Kritzinger	3	0	0	0	0	0	6	3	0	0	0	15	7	0	0	0	0	0	16	3	0	0	0	15	27	3	0	0	0	15
AJ (AJ) le Roux	2	1	0	0	0	5	1	0	0	0	0	0	0	0	0	0	0	0	3	1	0	0	0	5	22	7	5	0	0	45
HF (Erik) le Roux	7	3	0	0	0	15	0	0	0	0	0	0	1	0	0	0	0	0	8	3	0	0	0	15	17	5	0	0	0	25
H (Henry) Liebenberg	4	0	0	0	0	0	5	2	0	0	0	10	5	0	0	0	0	0	14	2	0	0	0	10	43	4	0	0	0	10
W (Werner) Lourens	1	0	0	0	0	0	0	0	0	0	0	0	0	0	0	0	0	0	0	0	0	0	0	0	0	0	0	0	0	0
W (Werner) Lourens	4	0	0	0	0	0	4	0	0	0	0	0	0	0	0	0	0	0	8	0	0	0	0	0	8	0	0	0	0	0
T (Tertius) Maarman	6	1	1	0	0	7	6	2	0	0	0	10	7	5	0	0	0	25	19	8	1	0	0	42	89	28	5	0	0	150

ABSA CURRIE CUP – 1ST DIVISION

FIRST-CLASS APPEARANCES FOR GRIFFONS IN 2014 – ALL MATCHES

PLAYER	VODACOM CUP						CC QUALIFIERS						CC FIRST DIVISION						2014 TOTAL						CAREER MATCHES					
	A	T	C	P	DG	Pts	A	T	C	P	DG	Pts	A	T	C	P	DG	Pts	A	T	C	P	DG	Pts	A	T	C	P	DG	Pts
BB (Bren) Marais	1	0	0	0	0	0	0	0	0	0	0	0	0	0	0	0	0	0	1	0	0	0	0	0	2	0	0	0	0	0
V (Vuyo) Mbotho	7	1	0	0	0	5	0	0	0	0	0	0	3	0	0	0	0	0	10	1	0	0	0	5	34	6	0	0	0	30
AN (Aubrey) McDonald	0	0	0	0	0	0	0	0	0	0	0	0	5	1	0	0	0	5	5	1	0	0	0	5	5	1	0	0	0	5
DS (Devin) Montgomery	2	0	0	0	0	0	2	0	0	0	0	0	0	0	0	0	0	0	4	0	0	0	0	0	26	5	0	0	0	25
J (Japie) Nel	1	0	0	0	0	0	0	0	0	0	0	0	0	0	0	0	0	0	1	0	0	0	0	0	1	0	0	0	0	0
NT (Norman) Nelson	6	3	0	0	0	15	6	6	0	0	0	30	6	2	0	0	0	10	18	8	0	0	0	40	96	39	0	0	0	195
O (Oshwill) Nortje	1	0	0	0	0	0	5	4	0	0	0	20	7	3	0	0	0	15	18	7	0	0	0	35	23	14	0	0	0	70
M (Mayi) Ntshoko	0	0	0	0	0	0	0	0	0	0	0	0	2	0	0	0	0	0	9	1	0	0	0	5	40	6	0	0	0	30
WC (Wynand) Pienaar	7	2	0	0	0	22	4	0	0	0	0	0	0	0	0	0	0	0	2	0	0	0	0	0	2	0	0	0	0	0
HR (Heinrich) Roelfse	7	0	0	0	0	0	5	0	0	0	0	0	0	0	0	0	0	0	14	0	6	0	0	37	18	5	6	0	0	37
FL (Frans) Sisita	0	0	0	0	0	0	0	0	0	0	0	0	3	0	0	0	0	0	18	5	0	0	0	0	10	0	0	0	0	0
SM (Martin) Sithole	6	5	0	0	0	25	7	1	0	0	0	10	5	1	0	0	0	5	17	7	0	0	0	35	10	1	0	0	0	55
JJ (Hannes) Snyman	0	0	0	0	0	0	1	0	0	0	0	0	0	0	0	0	0	0	1	0	0	0	0	0	1	0	0	0	0	0
KB (Kevin) Stevens	6	0	0	0	0	0	4	0	0	0	0	0	3	0	0	0	0	0	17	0	5	0	0	25	55	19	0	0	0	95
NPJ (Nicky) Steyn	0	0	0	0	0	0	1	0	0	0	0	0	1	0	0	0	0	0	6	1	0	0	0	0	30	1	0	0	0	5
LI (Louis) Strydom	4	2	0	2	0	25	5	2	1	1	0	7	7	1	13	8	2	56	19	5	15	11	2	85	73	3	62	74	3	380
NJ (Nico) van der Hoogt	0	0	0	0	0	0	6	1	0	0	0	7	1	0	0	0	0	0	18	8	0	0	0	40	106	46	0	0	0	230
DJ (Danie) van der Merwe	2	0	0	0	0	0	0	0	0	0	0	0	0	0	0	0	0	0	2	0	0	0	0	0	3	0	0	0	0	0
FJF (Franco) van der Merwe	0	0	0	0	0	0	0	0	0	0	0	0	5	1	0	0	0	5	5	1	0	0	0	5	31	3	0	0	0	15
AJ (Andre) van der Walt	0	0	0	0	0	0	0	0	0	0	0	0	3	0	0	0	0	0	3	0	0	0	0	0	7	1	0	0	0	5
Penalty try																														
48 Players	150	25	15	9	0	182	126	25	14	10	0	183	145	27	19	13	3	223	421	77	48	32	3	588	1235	252	118	92	4	1776

ABSA CURRIE CUP – 1ST DIVISION

Leopards Rugby Union

Founded: 1920 (as Western Transvaal) **Ground:** Profert Olen Park
Capacity: 22 000 **Address:** Cnr James Moroka & Piet Bosman Streets
Postal address: PO Box 422, Potchefstroom 2520 **Telephone Number:** 018-297 5304/5
Email: karen@leopardsrugby.co.za **Colours:** Green & red jersey, white shorts
Currie Cup Coach: Robert du Preez **Captain:** André Pretorius
President: Adv. André May
Company CEO: Eugene Fourie

'96	'97	'98	'99	'00	'01	'02	'03	'04	'05	'06	'07	'08	'09	'10	'11	'12	'13	'14
13th	13th	13th	14th	12th	10th	12th	9th	11th	8th	9th	13th	10th	7th	8th	8th	10th	9th	9th

Played	Won	Lost	Drawn	Points for	Points against	Tries for	Tries against
6	3	3	0	214	177	32	24

Date	Venue	Opponent	Result	Score	Referee	Scorers
29 Aug	George	SWD	LOST	21-29	L Legoete	T: Hanekom (2). C: Pretorius. P: Pretorius (3).
6 Sep	Potchefstroom	Boland	WON	54-32	F Anselmi	T: Maritz (3), Deysel (2), Tossel (2), Vermaak. C: Pretorius (7).
13 Sep	Welkom	Griffons	LOST	31-37	M vd Westhuizen	T: Swart, Deysel, Welgemoed, Mahuza. C: Pretorius (4). P: Pretorius.
19 Sep	East London	Border	WON	34-19	J Peyper	T: Jacobs (2), Pretorius, Deysel, Welgemoed, Smith. C: Pretorius (2).
27 Sep	Potchefstroom	Valke	WON	50-29	M Jonker	T: Smit (2), Jacobs, Carney, Swart, Torrens, Mahuza, Pen try. C: Smith (5)

SEMI-FINAL

Date	Venue	Opponent	Result	Score	Referee	Scorers
3 Oct	Potchefstroom	Valke	LOST	24-31	Q Immelman	T: Smith (2), Mahuza (2). C: Pretorius (2).

APPEARANCES & POINTS FOR LEOPARDS IN 2014 1ST DIVISION

PLAYER	Valke	Griffons	Eagles	Leopards	Cavaliers		Apps	T	C	P	DG	Pts
Hoffman Maritz	15	13	–	–	13		3	3	–	–	–	15
Sylvian Mahuza	14	15	14	14	14	14	6	4	–	–	–	20
Rowayne Beukman	13	11	–	–	–		2	–	–	–	–	0
George Tossel	12	12	13	–	13R	–	4	2	–	–	–	10
Luther Obi	11	–	11	–	–	11	3	–	–	–	–	0
Andre Pretorius	10c	10c	10c	10c	10c	10c	6	1	16	4	–	49
Dillon Smit	9	–	–	9	9	9	4	2	–	–	–	10
Morne Hanekom	8	8	8	–	–	8	4	2	–	–	–	10
Rhyk Welgemoed	7	6R	6	6	6	6	6	2	–	–	–	10
Juan Language	6	–	–	–	–	6R	2	–	–	–	–	0
Danie Jordaan	5	5	–	5	5	5	5	–	–	–	–	0
Ruan Venter	4	4	4	4	4	4	6	–	–	–	–	0
John Roy Jenkinson	3	3	3	3	3	3	6	–	–	–	–	0
Jacques Vermaak	2	2	2R	x	2R	2R	5	1	–	–	–	5
Joe Smith	1	1	1	1	1	1	6	–	–	–	–	0
Marius Fourie	2R	2R	–	–	–	–	2	–	–	–	–	0
Stephan Bezuidenhout	1R	1R	1R	x	3R	x	4	–	–	–	–	0
Schalk van Heerden	5R	5R	4R	8R	–	–	4	–	–	–	–	0
HP Swart	7R	7	7	7	8	7	6	2	–	–	–	10
Vian van der Watt	9R	9	9	x	9R	x	4	–	–	–	–	0
Kobus de Kock	11R	11R	15	x	–	–	3	–	–	–	–	0
Johan Deysel	12R	14R	12	12	12	12	6	4	–	–	–	20
Lucien Cupido	–	14	–	–	–	–	1	–	–	–	–	0
Johan Wessels	–	6	6R	6R	–	–	3	–	–	–	–	0
Percy Williams	–	x	x	–	–	–	0	–	–	–	–	0
Francois Robertse	–	–	5	–	–	–	1	–	–	–	–	0
JC Oberholzer	–	–	2	2	2	2	4	–	–	–	–	0
Ryno Smith	–	–	15R	15	15	15	4	3	5	–	–	25
Sergio Torrens	–	–	8R	13	13	11R	4	1	–	–	–	5
Adri Jacobs	–	–	–	11	11	10R	3	3	–	–	–	15
PJ Uys	–	–	–	8	7	4R	3	–	–	–	–	0
Warren Gilbert	–	–	–	x	10R	–	1	–	–	–	–	0
Deon Carney	–	–	–	–	7R	–	1	1	–	–	–	5
Molotsi Bouwer	–	–	–	–	4R	–	1	–	–	–	–	0
Penalty try	–	–	–	–	–	–	–	1	–	–	–	5
34 Players (of which 33 made an appearance)							123	32	21	4	0	214

ABSA CURRIE CUP – 1ST DIVISION

1ST DIVISION SQUAD – CAREER CURRIE CUP APPEARANCES

PLAYER	LEOPARDS						OTHER UNIONS						TOTAL					
	A	T	C	P	DG	Pts	A	T	C	P	DG	Pts	A	T	C	P	DG	Pts
RE Rowayne) Beukman	2	–	–	–	–	0	–	–	–	–	–	0	2	–	–	–	–	0
SM (Stephan) Bezuidenhout	21	1	–	–	–	5	–	–	–	–	–	0	21	1	–	–	–	5
ME (Molotsi) Bouwer	4	–	–	–	–	0	–	–	–	–	–	0	4	–	–	–	–	0
D (Deon) Carney	1	–	–	–	–	0	–	–	–	–	–	0	1	–	–	–	–	0
LR (Lucien) Cupido	1	–	–	–	–	0	–	–	–	–	–	0	1	–	–	–	–	0
JJ (Kobus) de Kock	9	4	–	–	–	20	2	–	–	–	–	0	11	4	–	–	–	20
PA (Philip) de Wet	20	7	–	–	–	35	–	–	–	–	–	0	20	7	–	–	–	35
J (Johan) Deysel	6	4	–	–	–	20	–	–	–	–	–	0	6	4	–	–	–	20
AE (Adriaan) Engelbrecht	21	2	49	21	–	171	–	–	–	–	–	0	21	2	49	21	–	171
M (Marius) Fourie	9	–	–	–	–	0	–	–	–	–	–	0	9	–	–	–	–	0
WJ (Warren) Gilbert	7	–	–	–	–	0	–	–	–	–	–	0	7	–	–	–	–	0
M (Morne) Hanekom	27	7	–	–	–	35	2	–	–	–	–	0	29	7	–	–	–	35
AJ (Adri) Jacobs	3	3	–	–	–	15	2	–	–	–	–	0	5	3	–	–	–	15
JR (John Roy) Jenkinson	18	1	–	–	–	5	2	–	–	–	–	0	20	1	–	–	–	5
DB (Danie) Jordaan	6	–	–	–	–	0	–	–	–	–	–	0	6	–	–	–	–	0
RA (Robert) Kruger	19	1	–	–	–	5	3	–	–	–	–	0	22	1	–	–	–	5
JM (Juan) Language	8	6	–	–	–	30	–	–	–	–	–	0	8	6	–	–	–	30
MC (Mashudu) Mafela	6	–	–	–	–	0	–	–	–	–	–	0	6	–	–	–	–	0
S (Sylvian) Mahuza	14	15	–	–	–	75	–	–	–	–	–	0	14	15	–	–	–	75
HVH (Hoffman) Maritz	20	10	–	–	–	50	–	–	–	–	–	0	20	10	–	–	–	50
M (Tsotsho) Mbovane	2	–	–	–	–	0	–	–	–	–	–	0	2	–	–	–	–	0
S (Sthembiso) Mhlongo	2	1	–	–	–	5	9	1	–	–	–	5	11	2	–	–	–	10
N (Nhalanhla) Ngcamu	5	–	–	–	–	0	–	–	–	–	–	0	5	–	–	–	–	0
JC (JC) Oberholzer	14	–	–	–	–	0	–	–	–	–	–	0	14	–	–	–	–	0
LBS (Luther) Obi	23	18	–	–	–	90	–	–	–	–	–	0	23	18	–	–	–	90
AS (Andre) Pretorius	12	1	52	6	1	130	43	4	105	57	14	443	55	5	157	63	15	573
F (Francois) Robertse	7	3	–	–	–	15	–	–	–	–	–	0	7	3	–	–	–	15
D (Dillon) Smit	10	6	–	–	–	30	2	–	–	–	–	0	12	6	–	–	–	30
J (Joe) Smith	14	–	–	–	–	0	–	–	–	–	–	0	14	–	–	–	–	0
RC (Rhyno) Smith	4	3	5	–	–	25	–	–	–	–	–	0	4	3	5	–	–	25
HP (HP) Swart	20	3	–	–	–	15	–	–	–	–	–	0	20	3	–	–	–	15
SL (Sergio) Torrens	10	1	–	–	–	5	–	–	–	–	–	0	10	1	–	–	–	5
GD (George) Tossel	36	13	1	1	–	70	–	–	–	–	–	0	36	13	1	1	–	70
PJJ (PJ) Uys	3	–	–	–	–	0	–	–	–	–	–	0	3	–	–	–	–	0
AHP (Armand) van der Merwe	11	–	–	–	–	0	12	3	–	–	–	15	23	3	–	–	–	15
V (Vian) van der Watt	6	–	–	–	–	0	–	–	–	–	–	0	6	–	–	–	–	0
PS (Schalk) van Heerden	4	–	–	–	–	0	–	–	–	–	–	0	4	–	–	–	–	0
RC (Ruan) Venter	11	–	–	–	–	0	2	–	–	–	–	0	13	–	–	–	–	0
JC (Jacques) Vermaak	15	1	–	–	–	5	–	–	–	–	–	0	15	1	–	–	–	5
R (Rhyk) Welgemoed	13	3	–	–	–	15	–	–	–	–	–	0	13	3	–	–	–	15
PJ (Johan) Wessels	3	–	–	–	–	0	29	3	–	–	–	15	32	3	–	–	–	15
K (Percy) Williams	4	–	–	–	–	0	–	–	–	–	–	0	4	–	–	–	–	0
42 Players	451	114	107	28	1	871	108	11	105	57	14	478	559	125	212	85	15	1349

ABSA CURRIE CUP – 1ST DIVISION

FIRST-CLASS APPEARANCES FOR LEOPARDS IN 2014 - ALL MATCHES*

PLAYER	CURRIE CUP QUALIFIERS						CURRIE CUP 1ST DIV.						2014 TOTAL						CAREER MATCHES					
	A	T	C	P	DG	Pts	A	T	C	P	DG	Pts	A	T	C	P	DG	Pts	A	T	C	P	DG	Pts
RE (Rowayne) Beukman	2	0	0	0	0	0	0	0	0	0	0	0	2	0	0	0	0	0	2	0	0	0	0	0
SM (Stephan) Bezuidenhout	4	0	0	0	0	0	1	0	0	0	0	0	5	0	0	0	0	0	43	1	0	0	0	5
ME (Molotsi) Bouwer	1	0	0	0	0	0	3	0	0	0	0	0	4	0	0	0	0	0	4	0	0	0	0	0
D (Deon) Carney	0	0	1	1	0	5	0	0	0	0	0	0	1	0	1	1	0	5	1	1	1	1	0	5
LR (Lucien) Cupido	1	0	0	0	0	0	0	0	0	0	0	0	1	0	0	0	0	0	1	0	0	0	0	0
JJ (Kobus) de Kock	3	0	0	0	0	0	6	4	0	0	0	20	9	4	0	0	0	20	9	4	0	0	0	20
PA (Philip) de Wet	0	0	0	0	0	0	3	2	0	0	0	10	3	2	0	0	0	10	32	15	0	0	0	75
J (Johan) Deysel	6	4	0	0	0	20	0	0	0	0	0	0	6	4	0	0	0	20	6	4	0	0	0	20
AE (Adriaan) Engelbrecht	0	0	0	0	0	0	6	0	0	6	0	18	6	0	0	6	2	18	42	9	54	25	0	228
M (Marius) Fourie	2	0	0	0	0	0	0	0	0	0	0	0	2	0	0	0	0	0	3	1	0	0	0	5
WJ (Warren) Gilbert	1	0	0	0	0	0	0	0	0	0	0	0	1	0	0	0	0	0	7	0	1	0	0	2
M (Morne) Hanekom	4	2	0	0	0	10	3	1	0	0	0	5	7	3	0	0	0	15	36	8	0	0	0	40
AJ (Adri) Jacobs	3	3	0	0	0	15	0	0	0	0	0	0	3	3	0	0	0	15	3	3	0	0	0	15
JR (John Roy) Jenkinson	6	0	0	0	0	0	5	1	0	0	0	5	11	1	0	0	0	5	27	1	0	0	0	5
DB (Danie) Jordaan	5	0	0	0	0	0	0	0	0	0	0	0	5	0	0	0	0	0	7	0	0	0	0	0
RA (Robert) Kruger	0	0	0	0	0	0	3	0	0	0	0	0	3	0	0	0	0	0	36	2	0	0	0	10
JM (Juan) Language	2	0	0	0	0	0	6	6	0	0	0	30	8	6	0	0	0	30	8	6	0	0	0	30
MC (Mashudu) Mafela	0	0	0	0	0	0	6	0	0	0	0	0	6	0	0	0	0	0	6	0	0	0	0	0
S (Sylvian) Mahuza	6	4	0	0	0	20	5	10	0	0	0	50	11	14	0	0	0	70	14	15	0	0	0	75
HVH (Hoffman) Maritz	3	3	0	0	0	15	5	4	0	0	0	20	8	7	0	0	0	35	37	16	0	0	0	80
M (Tsotsho) Mbovane	0	0	0	0	0	0	2	0	0	0	0	0	2	0	0	0	0	0	2	0	0	0	0	0
S (Sthembiso) Mhlongo	0	0	0	0	0	0	2	1	0	0	0	5	2	1	0	0	0	5	2	1	0	0	0	5
N (Nhlanhla) Ngcamu	0	0	0	0	0	0	5	0	0	0	0	0	5	0	0	0	0	0	5	0	0	0	0	0

ABSA CURRIE CUP – 1ST DIVISION

FIRST-CLASS APPEARANCES FOR LEOPARDS IN 2014 - ALL MATCHES*

PLAYER	CURRIE CUP QUALIFIERS						CURRIE CUP 1ST DIV.						2014 TOTAL						CAREER MATCHES					
	A	T	C	P	DG	Pts	A	T	C	P	DG	Pts	A	T	C	P	DG	Pts	A	T	C	P	DG	Pts
JC (JC) Oberholzer	4	0	0	0	0	0	6	0	0	0	0	0	10	0	0	0	0	0	18	0	0	0	0	0
LBS (Luther) Obi	3	0	0	0	0	0	6	10	0	0	0	50	9	10	0	0	0	50	23	18	0	0	0	90
AS (Andre) Pretorius	6	1	16	4	0	49	6	0	37	2	1	83	12	1	53	6	1	132	12	1	53	6	1	132
F (Francois) Robertse	1	0	0	0	0	0	6	3	0	0	0	15	7	3	0	0	0	15	7	3	0	0	0	15
D (Dillon) Smit	4	2	0	0	0	10	6	4	0	0	0	20	10	6	0	0	0	30	10	6	0	0	0	30
J (Joe) Smith	6	0	0	0	0	0	6	0	0	0	0	0	12	0	0	0	0	0	15	0	0	0	0	0
RC (Rhyno) Smith	4	3	5	0	0	25	0	0	0	0	0	0	4	3	5	0	0	25	4	3	5	0	0	25
HP (HP) Swart	6	2	0	0	0	10	5	0	0	0	0	0	11	2	0	0	0	10	24	4	0	0	0	20
SL (Sergio) Torrens	4	1	0	0	0	5	6	0	0	0	0	0	10	1	0	0	0	5	10	1	0	0	0	5
GD (George) Tossel	4	2	0	0	0	10	6	4	0	0	0	20	10	6	0	0	0	30	41	11	2	2	0	75
PJJ (PJ) Uys	3	0	0	0	0	0	0	0	0	0	0	0	3	0	0	0	0	0	3	0	0	0	0	0
AHP (Armand) van der Merwe	0	0	0	0	0	0	2	0	0	0	0	0	2	0	0	0	0	0	11	0	0	0	0	0
V (Vian) van der Watt	4	0	0	0	0	0	2	0	0	0	0	0	6	0	0	0	0	0	6	0	0	0	0	0
PS (Schalk) van Heerden	4	0	0	0	0	0	0	0	0	0	0	0	4	0	0	0	0	0	4	0	0	0	0	0
RC (Ruan) Venter	6	0	0	0	0	0	5	0	0	0	0	0	11	0	0	0	0	0	11	0	0	0	0	0
JC (Jacques) Vermaak	5	1	0	0	0	5	4	0	0	0	0	0	9	1	0	0	0	5	15	1	0	0	0	5
R (Rhyk) Welgemoed	6	2	0	0	0	10	5	1	0	0	0	5	11	3	0	0	0	15	13	0	0	0	0	0
PJ (Johan) Wessels	3	0	0	0	0	0	0	0	0	0	0	0	3	0	0	0	0	0	3	0	0	0	0	0
K (Percy) Williams	0	0	0	0	0	0	4	0	0	0	0	0	4	0	0	0	0	0	4	0	0	0	0	0
Penalty try	0	1	0	0	0	5	0	0	0	0	0	0	0	1	0	0	0	5	0	0	0	0	0	0
42 Players	123	32	21	4	0	214	130	51	43	4	1	356	253	83	64	8	1	570	567	135	115	33	1	1017

The Leopards' Vodacom Cup matches were also first-class but they played as the 'Leopards XV', which the LRU considers a completely different team. This table shows first-class matches played by the 'Leopards' only. See Vodacom Cup section for Leopards XV info.

ABSA CURRIE CUP – 1ST DIVISION

South Western Districts Rugby Football Union

Founded: 1899 **Ground:** Outeniqua Park **Capacity:** 7500
Address: CJ Langenhoven Road, George **Postal address:** PO Box 10471, George 6530
Telephone Number: 044-873 0137 **Email:** rugby@swdeagles.co.za
Colours: White & green jersey, white shorts and green socks
Currie Cup Coach: Bevin Fortuin **Captain:** Roy Godfrey
President: Hennie Baartman **Union CEO:** Johan Prinsloo

'96	'97	'98	'99	'00	'01	'02	'03	'04	'05	'06	'07	'08	'09	'10	'11	'12	'13	'14
14th	8th	7th	4th	6th	14th	9th	8th	8th	13th	11th	9th	11th	10th	9th	11th	11th	10th	11th

Played	Won	Lost	Drawn	Points for	Points against	Tries for	Tries against
6	3	3	0	188	174	21	20

Date	Venue	Opponent	Result	Score	Referee	Scorers
29 Aug	George	Leopards	WON	29-21	L Legoete	T: Bock, Du Toit. C: Van Vuuren (2). P: Van Vuuren (5).
6 Sep	Kempton Park	Valke	LOST	19-24	R Rasivhenge	T: Bock, C: Van Vuuren. P: Van Vuuren (4).
12 Sep	George	Border	WON	31-22	L vd Merwe	T: Roberts (2), Bock, Parks, Kelly. C: Van Vuuren (3)
20 Sep	George	Boland	LOST	24-35	B Crouse	T: Skosana, Eksteen, Zito. C: Van Vuuren (3). P: Van Vuuren.
27 Sep	Welkom	Griffons	WON	42-27	Q Immelman	T: Kelly (2), Bester, Skosana, Van Vuuren, Godfrey
SEMI-FINAL						
3 Oct	Welkom	Griffons	LOST	43-45	B Crouse	T: Wagman (2), Scott, Du Plessis. C: Van Vuuren (4). P: Van Vuuren (5).

ABSA CURRIE CUP – 1ST DIVISION

APPEARANCES & POINTS FOR SWD IN 2014 1ST DIVISION

PLAYER	Leopards	Valke	Border	Boland	Griffons	Griffons (SF)	Apps	T	C	P	DG	Pts
Daniel Roberts	15	15	15	–	10R	10R	5	2	–	–	–	10
Clinton Wagman	14	14	14	11R	14	14	6	2	–	–	–	10
Elric van Vuuren	13	13	13	12	15	15	6	1	19	15	–	88
Luzuko Vulindlu	12	12	–	–	–	–	2	–	–	–	–	0
Alshaun Bock	11	11	11	11	–	11R	5	3	–	–	–	15
Martin du Toit	10	–	–	–	10	10	3	1	–	–	–	5
Dwayne Kelly	9	9	9	9	9	9	6	3	–	–	–	15
Christo du Plessis	8	8	8	8	8	8	6	1	–	–	–	5
Alwyn Bester	7	7	6R	6	6	6	6	1	–	–	–	5
Shaun Raubenheimer	6	–	–	–	–	–	1	–	–	–	–	0
Mzwanele Zito	5	4R	5	5	5	5	6	1	–	–	–	5
Schalk Oelofse	4	4	–	–	–	–	2	–	–	–	–	0
Grant Kemp	3	3	3	3	3	3	6	–	–	–	–	0
Kurt Haupt	2	2	2	2	2	2	6	–	–	–	–	0
Roy Godfrey	1c	1c	1c	1c	1c	1c	6	1	–	–	–	5
Wayne Khan	2R	2R	2R	2R	2R	2R	6	–	–	–	–	0
Ashley Buys	3R	–	3R	–	–	–	2	–	–	–	–	0
Peet van der Walt	5R	5	4R	–	–	–	3	–	–	–	–	0
Davon Raubenheimer	7R	6R	7	7	7	7	6	–	–	–	–	0
Mzo Dyantyi	9R	9R	–	–	–	–	2	–	–	–	–	0
Gerrit Smith	12R	15R	12	15	12	12	6	–	–	–	–	0
Brian Skosana	11R	12R	14R	13	11R	–	5	2	–	–	–	10
Leighton Eksteen	–	10	10	10	9R	9R	5	1	–	–	–	5
Buran Parks	–	6	6	–	4R	7R	4	1	–	–	–	5
Dexter Fahey	–	3R	–	–	–	–	1	–	–	–	–	0
Grant le Roux	–	–	4	4	4	4	4	–	–	–	–	0
Layle Delo	–	–	1R	1R	1R	3R	4	–	–	–	–	0
Ashwin Scott	–	–	15R	13R	13	13	4	1	–	–	–	5
Hentzwill Pedro	–	–	–	14	11	11	3	–	–	–	–	0
Lyndon Hartnick	–	–	–	4R	8R	4R	3	–	–	–	–	0
Janneman Stander	–	–	–	7R	–	–	1	–	–	–	–	0
Marcel Groenewald	–	–	–	8R	–	–	1	–	–	–	–	0
32 Players							**132**	**21**	**19**	**15**	**0**	**188**

ABSA CURRIE CUP – 1ST DIVISION

1ST DIVISION SQUAD – CAREER CURRIE CUP APPEARANCES

PLAYER	SWD						OTHER UNIONS						TOTAL					
	A	T	C	P	DG	Pts	A	T	C	P	DG	Pts	A	T	C	P	DG	Pts
KG (Karlo) Aspeling	5	–	11	3	–	31	13	1	5	5	1	33	18	1	16	8	1	64
A (Alwyn) Bester	11	2	–	–	–	10	35	9	–	–	–	45	46	11	–	–	–	55
AG (Alshaun) Bock	24	23	–	–	–	115	27	11	–	–	–	55	51	34	–	–	–	170
AS (Ashley) Buys	45	4	–	–	–	20	44	–	–	–	–	0	89	4	–	–	–	20
JA (Jarryd) Buys	2	–	–	–	–	0	8	4	1	–	–	22	10	4	1	–	–	22
LA (Layle) Delo	19	2	–	–	–	10	–	–	–	–	–	0	19	2	–	–	–	10
CJ (Christo) du Plessis	27	5	–	–	–	25	–	–	–	–	–	0	27	5	–	–	–	25
OM (Martin) du Toit	20	4	1	–	–	22	–	–	–	–	–	0	20	4	1	–	–	22
M (Mzo) Dyantyi	20	2	–	–	–	10	2	–	–	–	–	0	22	2	–	–	–	10
L (Leighton) Eksteen	5	1	–	–	–	5	–	–	–	–	–	0	5	1	–	–	–	5
DC (Danie) Faasen	4	–	–	–	–	0	12	1	–	–	–	5	16	1	–	–	–	5
DS (Dexter) Fahey	5	–	–	–	–	0	–	–	–	–	–	0	5	–	–	–	–	0
RAM (Roy) Godfrey	27	6	–	–	–	30	–	–	–	–	–	0	27	6	–	–	–	30
MB (Marcel) Groenewald	3	–	–	–	–	0	–	–	–	–	–	0	3	–	–	–	–	0
LL (Lyndon) Hartnick	36	6	–	–	–	30	6	–	–	–	–	0	42	6	–	–	–	30
KS (Kurt) Haupt	12	3	–	–	–	15	–	–	–	–	–	0	12	3	–	–	–	15
D (Dwayne) Kelly	12	7	–	–	–	35	–	–	–	–	–	0	12	7	–	–	–	35
GD (Grant) Kemp	21	1	–	–	–	5	–	–	–	–	–	0	21	1	–	–	–	5
W (Wayne) Khan	16	–	–	–	–	0	–	–	–	–	–	0	16	–	–	–	–	0
D (Dwayne) Kelly	12	7	–	–	–	35	–	–	–	–	–	0	12	7	–	–	–	35
G (Grant) le Roux	18	1	–	–	–	5	24	–	–	–	–	0	42	1	–	–	–	5
SW (Schalk) Oelofse	19	1	–	–	–	5	–	–	–	–	–	0	19	1	–	–	–	5
BJ (Buran) Parks	19	2	–	–	–	10	–	–	–	–	–	0	19	2	–	–	–	10
HN (Hentzwill) Pedro	9	2	–	–	–	10	–	–	–	–	–	0	9	2	–	–	–	10
DS (Davon) Raubenheimer	50	2	–	–	–	10	59	3	–	–	–	15	109	5	–	–	–	25
S (Shaun) Raubenheimer	41	19	–	–	–	95	18	3	–	–	–	15	59	22	–	–	–	110
DC (Daniel) Roberts	17	3	–	–	–	15	–	–	–	–	–	0	17	3	–	–	–	15
AR (Ashwin) Scott	31	12	–	–	–	60	31	7	–	–	1	38	62	19	–	–	1	98
MB (Brian) Skosana	11	6	–	–	–	30	10	1	–	–	–	5	21	7	–	–	–	35
GPJ (Gerrit) Smith	22	3	11	2	–	43	1	–	–	–	–	0	23	3	11	2	–	43
JH (Janneman) Stander	2	–	–	–	–	0	–	–	–	–	–	0	2	–	–	–	–	0
AP (Peet) van der Walt	6	–	–	–	–	0	12	–	–	–	–	0	18	–	–	–	–	0
E (Elric) van Vuuren	22	4	56	29	–	219	17	6	2	2	–	40	39	10	58	31	–	259
A (Anver) Venter	3	2	–	–	–	10	–	–	–	–	–	0	3	2	–	–	–	10
L (Luzuko) Vulindlu	10	1	–	–	–	5	9	1	–	–	–	5	19	2	–	–	–	10
CA (Clinton) Wagman	25	6	–	–	–	30	–	–	–	–	–	0	25	6	–	–	–	30
MR (Mzwanele) Zito	24	4	–	–	–	20	–	–	–	–	–	0	24	4	–	–	–	20
37 Players	655	141	79	34	0	965	328	47	8	7	2	278	983	188	87	41	2	1243

ABSA CURRIE CUP – 1ST DIVISION

FIRST-CLASS APPEARANCES FOR SWD IN 2014 – ALL MATCHES

PLAYER	VODACOM CUP						CURRIE CUP QUALIFIERS						CURRIE CUP 1ST DIV.						2014 TOTAL						SWD CAREER					
	A	T	C	P	DG	Pts	A	T	C	P	DG	Pts	A	T	C	P	DG	Pts	A	T	C	P	DG	Pts	A	T	C	P	DG	Pts
KG (Karlo) Aspeling	8	0	22	11	2	83	5	0	11	3	0	31	0	0	0	0	0	0	13	0	33	14	2	114	13	0	33	14	2	114
A (Alwyn) Bester	8	2	0	0	0	10	5	1	0	0	0	5	6	1	0	0	0	5	19	4	0	0	0	20	54	33	0	0	0	165
AG (Alshaun) Bock	4	6	0	0	0	30	4	3	0	0	0	15	5	3	0	0	0	15	13	12	0	0	0	60	48	41	0	0	0	205
AS (Ashley) Buys	8	0	0	0	0	0	3	0	0	0	0	0	2	0	0	0	0	0	13	0	0	0	0	0	71	3	0	0	0	15
JA (Jarryd) Buys	0	0	0	0	0	0	0	0	0	0	0	0	0	0	0	0	0	0	0	0	0	0	0	0	2	0	0	0	0	0
LC (Lionel) Cornelius	3	0	0	0	0	0	0	0	0	0	0	0	0	0	0	0	0	0	3	0	0	0	0	0	5	0	0	0	0	0
LA (Layle) Delo	6	0	0	0	0	0	0	0	0	0	0	0	4	0	0	0	0	0	10	0	0	0	0	0	37	2	0	0	0	10
CJ (Christo) du Plessis	7	2	0	0	0	10	3	1	0	0	0	5	6	1	0	0	0	5	16	4	0	0	0	20	49	9	0	0	0	45
OM (Martin) du Toit	7	1	0	0	0	5	6	0	0	0	0	0	3	1	0	0	0	5	16	2	0	0	0	10	38	6	0	0	0	30
M (Mzo) Dyantyi	6	1	0	0	0	5	2	0	0	0	0	0	2	0	0	0	0	0	10	1	0	0	0	5	65	8	0	0	0	40
L (Leighton) Eksteen	0	0	0	0	0	0	5	1	0	0	0	5	0	0	0	0	0	0	5	1	0	0	0	5	5	1	0	0	0	5
DC (Danie) Faasen	6	0	0	0	0	0	4	0	0	0	0	0	0	0	0	0	0	0	10	0	0	0	0	0	10	0	0	0	0	0
DS (Dexter) Fahey	0	0	0	0	0	0	4	0	0	0	0	0	1	0	0	0	0	0	5	0	0	0	0	0	5	0	0	0	0	0
J (Hannes) Franklin	6	0	0	0	0	0	0	0	0	0	0	0	0	0	0	0	0	0	6	0	0	0	0	0	64	18	0	0	0	90
RAM (Roy) Godfrey	0	0	0	0	0	0	6	1	0	0	0	5	6	0	0	0	0	0	12	1	0	0	0	5	26	6	0	0	0	30
MB (Marcel) Groenewald	0	0	0	0	0	0	2	0	0	0	0	0	1	0	0	0	0	0	3	0	0	0	0	0	3	0	0	0	0	0
LL (Lyndon) Hartnick	6	0	0	0	0	0	3	0	0	0	0	0	3	0	0	0	0	0	12	0	0	0	0	0	68	9	0	0	0	45
KS (Kurt) Haupt	0	0	0	0	0	0	6	3	0	0	0	15	6	0	0	0	0	0	12	3	0	0	0	15	12	3	0	0	0	15
EG (Eldred) James	1	0	0	0	0	0	0	0	0	0	0	0	0	0	0	0	0	0	1	0	0	0	0	0	2	0	0	0	0	0
D (Dwayne) Kelly	0	0	0	0	0	0	6	4	0	0	0	20	6	3	0	0	0	15	12	7	0	0	0	35	12	7	0	0	0	35
GD (Grant) Kemp	8	0	0	0	0	0	5	0	0	0	0	0	6	0	0	0	0	0	19	0	0	0	0	0	43	4	0	0	0	20
W (Wayne) Khan	8	0	0	0	0	0	6	0	0	0	0	0	6	0	0	0	0	0	20	0	0	0	0	0	27	0	0	0	0	0
G (Grant) le Roux	8	0	0	0	0	0	4	0	0	0	0	0	4	0	0	0	0	0	16	0	0	0	0	0	48	3	0	0	0	15
SW (Schalk) Oelofse	5	0	0	0	0	0	5	0	0	0	0	0	2	0	0	0	0	0	12	0	0	0	0	0	23	1	0	0	0	5

ABSA CURRIE CUP – 1ST DIVISION

FIRST-CLASS APPEARANCES FOR SWD IN 2014 – ALL MATCHES

PLAYER	VODACOM CUP						CURRIE CUP QUALIFIERS						CURRIE CUP 1ST DIV.						2014 TOTAL						SWD CAREER					
	A	T	C	P	DG	Pts	A	T	C	P	DG	Pts	A	T	C	P	DG	Pts	A	T	C	P	DG	Pts	A	T	C	P	DG	Pts
BJ (Buran) Parks	0	0	0	0	0	0	0	0	0	0	0	0	5	0	0	0	0	5	5	0	0	0	0	5	30	2	0	0	0	10
HN (Hentzwill) Pedro	8	5	0	0	0	25	6	3	0	0	0	0	5	0	0	0	0	0	19	0	0	0	0	0	31	0	0	0	0	0
AQ (Quinten) Petzer	5	1	0	0	0	5	3	0	0	0	0	0	0	0	0	0	0	0	8	1	0	0	0	5	16	7	0	0	0	35
DS (Davon) Raubenheimer	0	0	0	0	0	0	0	0	0	0	0	0	6	1	0	0	0	5	6	1	0	0	0	5	5	1	0	0	0	5
S (Shaun) Raubenheimer	7	4	0	0	0	20	5	2	0	0	0	10	0	0	0	0	0	0	12	6	0	0	0	30	72	26	0	0	0	130
DE (Deroy) Rhoode	7	0	1	0	0	2	6	0	0	0	0	0	0	0	0	0	0	0	13	0	1	0	0	2	60	4	13	3	0	55
DC (Daniel) Roberts	8	3	0	0	0	15	4	1	0	0	0	5	5	2	0	0	0	10	17	6	0	0	0	30	27	6	0	0	0	30
AR (Ashwin) Scott	0	0	0	0	0	0	6	4	0	0	0	20	4	0	0	0	0	0	10	4	0	0	0	20	43	12	0	0	1	63
MB (Brian) Skosana	0	0	0	0	0	0	6	2	0	0	0	10	5	0	0	0	0	0	11	2	0	0	0	10	11	2	0	0	0	10
DE (Duwayne) Smart	4	5	0	0	0	25	0	0	0	0	0	0	0	0	0	0	0	0	4	5	0	0	0	25	43	12	0	0	0	63...

43 Players

ABSA CURRIE CUP – 1ST DIVISION

Valke Rugby Union

Founded: 1947 (as Eastern Transvaal) **Ground:** Barnard Stadium, Kempton Park
Capacity: 7 000 **Address:** CR Swart Avenue, Kempton Park
Postal address: PO Box 12703, Edleen 1625 **Telephone Number:** 011-975 2822/2487
Email: valke@global.co.za **Colours:** Red jersey, shorts and socks
Currie Cup Coach: John Williams **Captain:** Jacques Verwey
President: Vivian Lottering
CEO: Jurie Coetzee

'96	'97	'98	'99	'00	'01	'02	'03	'04	'05	'06	'07	'08	'09	'10	'11	'12	'13	'14
11th	10th	6th	10th	11th	5th	8th	12th	12th	9th	7th	8th	8th	14th	12th	11th	12th	14th	12th

Played	Won	Lost	Drawn	Points for	Points against	Tries for	Tries against
7	4	3	0	187	187	25	24

Date	Venue	Opponent	Result	Score	Referee	Scorers
29 Aug	East London	Bulldogs	LOST	14-19	S Berry	T: Hendricks, Mostert. C: Kotze (2).
6 Sep	Kempton Park	Eagles	WON	24-19	R Rasivhenge	T: Muller, Cronje. C: Kotze. P: Kotze (4).
13 Sep	Wellington	Cavaliers	WON	32-25	P Legoete	T: Hendricks (2), Verwey, Muller, Penalty try. C: Kotze (2). P: Kotze.
20 Sep	Kempton Park	Griffons	WON	36-27	F Anselmi	T: Hendricks, Dippenaar, Olivier, Kirkwood. C: Kotze (2). P: Kotze (4).
27 Sep	Potchefstroom	Leopards	LOST	29-50	M Jonker	T: Dippenaar, Richter, Van Tonder, Verwey, Penalty try. C: Kotze (2).
SEMI-FINAL						
3 Oct	Potchefstroom	Leopards	WON	31-24	Q Immelman	T: Dippenaar (2), Richter, Mostert, Muller. C: Kotze (3).
FINAL						
17 Oct	Welkom	Griffons	LOST	21-23	B Crouse	T: Richter, Verwey. C: Kotze. P: Kotze (2). D: Swart.

ABSA CURRIE CUP – 1ST DIVISION

APPEARANCES & POINTS FOR VALKE IN 2014 1ST DIVISION

PLAYER	Bulldogs	Eagles	Cavaliers	Griffons	Leopards	Leopards (SF)	Griffons (F)	Apps	T	C	P	DG	Pts
Jaun Kotze	15	10	10	10	10	15	15	7	0	13	11	0	59
Dirk Dippenaar	14	–	–	14	14	14	14	5	4	0	0	0	20
Willie Odendaal	13	12	12	–	12	12	12	6	–	–	–	–	0
Jaco Oosthuizen	12	–	–	–	–	–	–	1	–	–	–	–	0
Kyle Hendricks	11	11	15	15	15	13R	10R	7	4	0	0	0	20
Cecil Dumond	10	–	–	–	–	–	–	1	–	–	–	–	0
Anrich Richter	9	9	9	9	9	9	9	7	3	0	0	0	15
Ernst Ladendorf	8	–	8	–	–	8R	8	4	–	–	–	–	0
Jacques Verwey	7c	7c	7c	7c	7c	–	7c	6	3	0	0	0	15
Andrew van Tonder	6	8	–	–	8	8c	–	4	1	0	0	0	5
Jacques Alberts	5	–	5R	5R	5R	5	5	6	–	–	–	–	0
Shane Kirkwood	4	4	4	4	4	4	4	7	1	0	0	0	5
Nico Pretorius	3	3	3	3	3	3	3	7	–	–	–	–	0
Devlin Hope	2	–	–	–	–	–	x	1	–	–	–	–	0
Dandre van der Westhuizen	1	1	1	1	1	1	–	6	–	–	–	–	0
Bruce Muller	2R	1R	1R	1R	1R	1R	1	7	3	0	0	0	15
Thulani Ngidi	3R	3R	3R	3R	3R	3R	3R	7	–	–	–	–	0
Marlyn Williams	5R	5	5	5	5	5R	5R	7	–	–	–	–	0
JP Mostert	6R	5R	8R	6R	–	7	6R	6	2	0	0	0	10
Andrew van Wyk	x	13	13	13	13	13	13	6	–	–	–	–	0
Arno Poley	14R	14	11	11R	–	–	–	4	–	–	–	–	0
Wayne Gardner	10R	15	10R	–	–	–	–	3	–	–	–	–	0
Juan-Pierre Jonck	–	6	6	–	6	6	6	5	–	–	–	–	0
Dean Muir	–	2	2	2	2	2	2	6	–	–	–	–	0
Friedle Olivier	–	7R	–	8	7R	–	–	3	1	0	0	0	5
Sinovuyo Nyoka	–	9R	–	–	–	–	–	1	–	–	–	–	0
Coert Cronje	–	15R	14	11	11	11	11	6	1	0	0	0	5
Dewald Pretorius	–	13R	13R	12	12R	12R	x	5	–	–	–	–	0
Jaco Snyman	–	–	9R	9R	9R	9R	x	4	–	–	–	–	0
Brian Shabangu	–	–	–	6	–	–	–	1	–	–	–	–	0
Clinton Swart	–	–	–	13R	13R	10	10	4	0	0	0	1	3
Penalty try	–	–	–	–	–	–	–	–	2	0	0	0	10
31 Players								150	25	13	11	1	187

1ST DIVISION SQUAD – CAREER CURRIE CUP APPEARANCES

PLAYER	VALKE						OTHER UNIONS						TOTAL					
	A	T	C	P	DG	Pts	A	T	C	P	DG	Pts	A	T	C	P	DG	Pts
GDJ (Jacques) Alberts	20	0	0	0	0	0	0	0	0	0	0	0	20	0	0	0	0	0
RA (Riaan) Arends	5	5	0	0	0	25	0	0	0	0	0	0	5	5	0	0	0	25
RS (Ryan) Carmichael	2	0	0	0	0	0	0	0	0	0	0	0	2	0	0	0	0	0
CF (Coert) Cronje	42	20	0	0	0	100	0	0	0	0	0	0	42	20	0	0	0	100
DHF (Dirk) Dippenaar	5	4	0	0	0	20	0	0	0	0	0	0	5	4	0	0	0	20
C (Cecil) Dumond	4	1	0	0	0	5	32	2	16	23	1	114	36	3	16	23	1	119
GP (Gerhard) Engelbrecht	3	0	0	0	0	0	0	0	0	0	0	0	3	0	0	0	0	0
W (Wayne) Gardner	4	0	0	0	0	0	0	0	0	0	0	0	4	0	0	0	0	0
K (Kyle) Hendricks	44	24	7	4	0	146	0	0	0	0	0	0	44	24	7	4	0	146
D (Devlin) Hope	6	0	0	0	0	0	0	0	0	0	0	0	6	0	0	0	0	0
GD (Grant) Janke	4	1	0	0	0	5	1	0	0	0	0	0	5	1	0	0	0	5
J-P (Juan-Pierre) Jonck	8	0	0	0	0	0	0	0	0	0	0	0	8	0	0	0	0	0
SM (Shane) Kirkwood	22	3	0	0	0	15	0	0	0	0	0	0	22	3	0	0	0	15
J (Jaun) Kotze	32	8	68	30	7	287	0	0	0	0	0	0	32	8	68	30	7	287
EFE (Ernst) Ladendorf	10	0	0	0	0	0	0	0	0	0	0	0	10	0	0	0	0	0
J-PF (JP) Mostert	25	7	0	0	0	35	9	1	0	0	0	5	34	8	0	0	0	40
D (Dean) Muir	6	0	0	0	0	0	14	2	0	0	0	10	20	2	0	0	0	10
B (Bruce) Muller	20	6	0	0	0	30	0	0	0	0	0	0	20	6	0	0	0	30
TS (Thulani) Ngidi	24	0	0	0	0	0	0	0	0	0	0	0	24	0	0	0	0	0
S (Sinovuyo) Nyoka	1	0	0	0	0	0	20	0	0	0	0	0	21	0	0	0	0	0
WA (Willie) Odendaal	37	8	0	0	0	40	0	0	0	0	0	0	37	8	0	0	0	40
F (Friedle) Olivier	8	1	0	0	0	5	0	0	0	0	0	0	8	1	0	0	0	5
J (Jaco) Oosthuizen	8	1	0	0	0	5	0	0	0	0	0	0	8	1	0	0	0	5
AP (Arno) Poley	19	1	0	0	0	5	0	0	0	0	0	0	19	1	0	0	0	5
DP (Dewald) Pretorius	19	4	0	0	0	20	28	3	0	0	0	15	47	7	0	0	0	35
N (Nico) Pretorius	32	0	0	0	0	0	1	0	0	0	0	0	33	0	0	0	0	0
CJ (Chris) Richardson	6	1	0	0	0	5	0	0	0	0	0	0	6	1	0	0	0	5
A (Anrich) Richter	29	13	0	0	0	65	0	0	0	0	0	0	29	13	0	0	0	65
AS (Andries) Schutte	5	0	0	0	0	0	0	0	0	0	0	0	5	0	0	0	0	0
SP (Brian) Shabangu	1	0	0	0	0	0	11	2	1	0	0	12	12	2	1	0	0	12
JP (Jaco) Snyman	31	6	0	0	0	30	0	0	0	0	0	0	31	6	0	0	0	30
CR (Clinton) Swart	4	0	0	0	1	3	0	0	0	0	0	0	4	0	0	0	1	3
E (Etienne) Taljaard	5	1	0	0	0	5	0	0	0	0	0	0	5	1	0	0	0	5
L (Lenience) Tambwera	1	0	0	0	0	0	0	0	0	0	0	0	1	0	0	0	0	0
D (Dandre) vd Westhuizen	19	0	0	0	0	0	0	0	0	0	0	0	19	0	0	0	0	0
AS (Andrew) van Tonder	9	1	0	0	0	5	0	0	0	0	0	0	9	1	0	0	0	5
AJD (Andrew) van Wyk	12	1	0	0	0	5	13	5	0	0	0	25	25	6	0	0	0	30
TJ (Jacques) Verwey	24	4	0	0	0	20	3	0	0	0	0	0	27	4	0	0	0	20
PJH (Peet) Vorster	3	0	0	0	0	0	3	0	0	0	0	0	6	0	0	0	0	0
ME (Marlyn) Williams	11	1	0	0	0	5	0	0	0	0	0	0	11	1	0	0	0	5
40 Players	570	122	75	34	8	886	135	15	17	23	1	181	705	137	92	57	9	1067

ABSA CURRIE CUP – 1ST DIVISION

FIRST-CLASS APPEARANCES FOR VALKE IN 2014 – ALL MATCHES

PLAYER	VODACOM CUP						CURRIE CUP QUALIFIERS						CURRIE CUP 1ST DIV.						2014 TOTAL						CAREER MATCHES					
	A	T	C	P	DG	Pts	A	T	C	P	DG	Pts	A	T	C	P	DG	Pts	A	T	C	P	DG	Pts	A	T	C	P	DG	Pts
GDJ (Jacques) Alberts	6	0	0	0	0	0	4	0	0	0	0	0	6	0	0	0	0	0	16	0	0	0	0	0	48	1	0	0	0	5
L (Lukhanyo) Am	2	1	0	0	0	5	0	0	0	0	0	0	0	0	0	0	0	0	2	1	0	0	0	5	2	1	0	0	0	5
RA (Riaan) Arends	0	0	0	0	0	0	5	5	0	0	0	25	0	0	0	0	0	0	5	5	0	0	0	25	5	5	0	0	0	25
FJ (FJ) Binneman	5	0	0	0	0	0	0	0	0	0	0	0	0	0	0	0	0	0	5	0	0	0	0	0	5	0	0	0	0	0
RS (Ryan) Carmichael	1	0	0	0	0	0	2	0	0	0	0	0	0	0	0	0	0	0	3	0	0	0	0	0	3	0	0	0	0	0
AA (Angus) Cleophas	7	0	4	7	0	29	0	0	0	0	0	0	0	0	0	0	0	0	7	0	4	7	0	29	7	0	4	7	0	29
WW (Wesley) Cloete	5	0	0	0	0	0	0	0	0	0	0	0	0	0	0	0	0	0	5	0	0	0	0	0	5	0	0	0	0	0
CF (Coert) Cronje	6	2	0	0	0	10	3	2	0	0	0	10	6	1	0	0	0	5	15	5	0	0	0	25	72	31	0	0	0	155
DHF (Dirk) Dippenaar	0	0	0	0	0	0	0	0	0	0	0	0	5	4	0	0	0	20	5	4	0	0	0	20	5	4	0	0	0	20
C (Cecil) Dumond	5	0	2	4	0	16	3	1	0	0	0	5	1	0	0	0	0	0	9	1	2	4	0	21	9	1	2	4	0	21
GP (Gerhard) Engelbrecht	0	0	0	0	0	0	3	0	0	0	0	0	0	0	0	0	0	0	3	0	0	0	0	0	3	0	0	0	0	0
W (Wayne) Gardner	1	0	1	0	0	2	1	0	0	0	0	0	3	0	0	0	0	0	5	0	1	0	0	2	5	0	1	0	0	2
LV (Vincent) Gwavu	6	2	0	0	0	10	4	0	0	0	0	0	0	0	0	0	0	0	20	3	0	0	0	10	20	3	0	0	0	15
K (Kyle) Hendricks	7	1	3	0	0	11	4	1	0	0	0	5	7	4	0	0	0	20	18	6	3	0	0	36	79	34	19	10	0	238
D (Devlin) Hope	6	2	0	0	0	10	4	0	0	0	0	0	1	0	0	0	0	0	11	2	0	0	0	10	12	2	0	0	0	10
GD (Grant) Janke	6	1	0	0	0	5	4	1	0	0	0	5	0	0	0	0	0	0	10	2	0	0	0	10	10	2	0	0	0	10
J-P (Juan-Pierre) Jonck	0	0	0	0	0	0	3	0	0	0	0	0	5	0	0	0	0	0	8	0	0	0	0	0	8	0	0	0	0	0
SM (Shane) Kirkwood	3	1	0	0	0	5	6	1	0	0	0	5	7	1	0	0	0	5	16	3	0	0	0	15	25	4	0	0	0	20
J (Jaun) Kotze	0	0	0	0	0	0	6	5	19	8	2	93	7	0	13	11	0	59	13	5	32	19	2	152	55	13	98	46	8	423
TMK (David) Kuatu	2	0	0	0	0	0	0	0	0	0	0	0	0	0	0	0	0	0	2	0	0	0	0	0	2	0	0	0	0	0
EFE (Ernst) Ladendorf	2	0	0	0	0	0	6	0	0	0	0	0	4	0	0	0	0	0	12	0	0	0	0	0	12	0	0	0	0	0
J-PF (JP) Mostert	6	0	0	0	0	0	5	1	0	0	0	5	6	2	0	0	0	10	17	3	0	0	0	15	37	11	0	0	0	55
D (Dean) Muir	0	0	0	0	0	0	0	0	0	0	0	0	6	0	0	0	0	0	6	0	0	0	0	0	6	0	0	0	0	0
B (Bruce) Muller	3	0	0	0	0	0	1	0	0	0	0	0	7	3	0	0	0	15	11	3	0	0	0	15	29	7	0	0	0	35
SC (Stix) Ngcobo	6	4	0	0	0	20	0	0	0	0	0	0	6	4	0	0	0	20	6	4	0	0	0	20	36	10	0	0	0	50

ABSA CURRIE CUP – 1ST DIVISION

FIRST-CLASS APPEARANCES FOR VALKE IN 2014 – ALL MATCHES

PLAYER	VODACOM CUP						CURRIE CUP QUALIFIERS						CURRIE CUP 1ST DIV.						2014 TOTAL						CAREER MATCHES					
	A	T	C	P	DG	Pts	A	T	C	P	DG	Pts	A	T	C	P	DG	Pts	A	T	C	P	DG	Pts	A	T	C	P	DG	Pts
TS (Thulani) Ngidi	6	0	0	0	0	0	4	0	0	0	0	0	7	0	0	0	0	0	17	0	0	0	0	0	40	0	0	0	0	0
S (Sinovuyo) Nyoka	0	0	0	0	0	0	0	0	0	0	0	0	1	0	0	0	0	0	1	0	0	0	0	0	1	0	0	0	0	0
WA (Willie) Odendaal	2	0	0	0	0	0	5	0	0	0	0	0	6	0	0	0	0	0	13	0	0	0	0	0	76	14	0	0	0	70
F (Friedle) Olivier	6	0	0	0	0	0	3	0	0	0	0	0	3	1	0	0	0	5	12	1	0	0	0	5	21	2	0	0	0	10
J (Jaco) Oosthuizen	6	0	0	0	0	0	2	0	0	0	0	0	1	0	0	0	0	0	3	0	0	0	0	0	19	4	0	0	0	20
AP (Arno) Poley	5	0	1	0	0	2	2	1	0	0	0	5	4	0	0	0	0	0	11	1	1	0	0	7	54	4	2	0	1	27
DP (Dewald) Pretorius	0	0	0	0	0	0	0	0	0	0	0	0	5	0	0	0	0	0	5	0	0	0	0	0	19	4	0	0	0	20
JH (Juan) Pretorius	5	0	0	0	0	0	0	0	0	0	0	0	0	0	0	0	0	0	5	0	0	0	0	0	5	0	0	0	0	0
N (Nico) Pretorius	2	0	0	0	0	0	0	0	0	0	0	0	7	0	0	0	0	0	9	0	0	0	0	0	62	1	0	0	0	5
CJ (Chris) Richardson	0	0	0	0	0	0	6	1	0	0	0	5	0	0	0	0	0	0	6	1	0	0	0	5	6	1	0	0	0	5
A (Anrich) Richter	6	3	0	0	0	15	6	2	0	0	0	10	7	3	0	0	0	15	19	8	0	0	0	40	62	23	0	0	0	115
AS (Andries) Schutte	0	0	0	0	0	0	5	0	0	0	0	0	0	0	0	0	0	0	5	0	0	0	0	0	5	0	0	0	0	0
SP (Brian) Shabangu	0	0	0	0	0	0	0	0	0	0	0	0	1	0	0	0	0	0	1	0	0	0	0	0	1	0	0	0	0	0
JP (Jaco) Snyman	6	0	0	0	0	0	2	0	0	0	0	0	4	0	0	0	0	0	12	0	0	0	0	0	58	8	0	0	0	40
CR (Clinton) Swart	0	0	0	0	0	0	0	0	0	0	0	0	4	0	0	0	1	3	4	0	0	0	1	3	4	0	0	0	1	3
E (Etienne) Taljaard	1	1	0	0	0	5	5	1	0	0	0	5	0	0	0	0	0	0	6	2	0	0	0	10	6	2	0	0	0	10
L (Lenience) Tambwera	0	0	0	0	0	0	1	0	0	0	0	0	0	0	0	0	0	0	1	0	0	0	0	0	1	0	0	0	0	0
D (Dandre) vd Westhuizen	4	0	0	0	0	0	3	0	0	0	0	0	6	0	0	0	0	0	13	0	0	0	0	0	27	0	0	0	0	0
MP (Marco) van Eeden	3	0	0	0	0	0	5	0	0	0	0	0	5	0	0	0	0	0	3	0	0	0	0	0	20	1	0	0	0	5
AS (Andrew) van Tonder	0	0	0	0	0	0	5	0	0	0	0	0	4	1	0	0	0	5	9	1	0	0	0	5	9	1	0	0	0	5
AJD (Andrew) van Wyk	7	3	0	0	0	15	6	1	0	0	0	5	6	3	0	0	0	20	19	4	0	0	0	20	19	4	0	0	0	20
TJ (Jacques) Verwey	5	3	0	0	0	15	6	3	0	0	0	15	6	3	0	0	0	15	17	7	0	0	0	35	29	7	0	0	0	35
PJH (Peet) Vorster	2	1	0	0	0	5	3	0	0	0	0	0	0	0	0	0	0	0	5	1	0	0	0	5	5	1	0	0	0	5
ME (Marlyn) Williams	7	0	0	0	0	0	4	1	0	0	0	5	7	0	0	0	0	0	18	1	0	0	0	5	18	1	0	0	0	5
49 Players																														

ABSA CURRIE CUP – QUALIFIERS

LOG

Team	P	W	L	D	PF	PA	PD	TF	TA	BP <7	BP 4	Pts
Griquas – **QUALIFIED**	6	6	0	0	246	101	145	36	14	0	4	28
Leopards	6	5	1	0	356	141	215	51	16	1	6	27
Griffons	6	3	3	0	183	213	-30	25	30	1	5	18
SWD	6	3	3	0	163	245	-82	23	33	0	3	15
Boland	6	2	4	0	140	156	-16	17	21	2	2	12
Valke	6	2	4	0	193	223	-30	25	31	0	2	10
Border	6	0	6	0	118	320	-202	16	48	1	1	2

Note: LB = Lost Bonus, TB = Try Bonus

LEADING SCORERS

30 POINTS OR MORE

PLAYER	PROVINCE	T	C	P	DG	Pts
Jaun Kotze	Valke	5	19	8	2	93
Andre Pretorius	Leopards	0	37	2	0	83
Luther Obi	Leopards	10	0	0	0	50
Sylvain Mahuza	Leopards	10	0	0	0	50
Eriz Zana	Boland	4	7	5	0	49
Masixole Banda	Border	1	10	6	0	43
Marnus Schoeman	Griquas	7	0	0	0	35
Nico Scheepers	Griquas	1	9	4	0	35
Karlo Aspeling	SWD	0	11	3	0	31
Carel Greeff	Griquas	6	0	0	0	30
Juan Language	Leopards	6	0	0	0	30
Norman Nelson	Griffons	6	0	0	0	30

4 TRIES OR MORE

5	Tertius Maarman	Griffons	4	Kyle Hendricks	Valke
4	Boela Abrahams	Griffons	4	Norman Nelson	Griffons
4	Dirk Dippenaar	Valke	4	Sylvain Mahuza	Leopards
4	Johan Deysel	Leopards			

ABSA CURRIE CUP – QUALIFIERS

Boland

Played	Won	Lost	Drawn	Points for	Points against	Tries for	Tries against
6	2	4	0	140	156	17	21

Date	Venue	Opponent	Result	Score	Referee	Scorers
7 Jun	Welkom	WP	LOST	25-27	L Legoete	T: Zana, U Pretorius. C: Zana (2). P: Zana (2).
14 Jun	Wellington	Griquas	LOST	3-21	B Crouse	P: Zana.
20 Jun	East London	Border	**WON**	37-12	B Crouse	T: September (2), Fortuin, Zana, Klaasen, Dreyer. C: Zana, Rust. P: Zana.
28 Jun	Wellington	SWD	LOST	17-21	J van heerden	T: Mkhafu, Zana. C: Zana (2). P: Zana.
5 Jul	Kempton Park	Valke	**WON**	35-20	L Legoete	T: Coetzee (2), Manuel, Smart. C: Morne Hugo (3). P: Morne Hugo (2). DG: Morne Hugo.
12 Jul	Wellington	Leopards	LOST	23-55	R Rasivhenge	T: Rust, September. C: Zana (2). P: Morne Hugo (3).

APPEARANCES & POINTS IN 2014 CURRIE CUP QUALIFIERS

PLAYER	Griffons	Griquas	Border	SWD	Valke	Leopards	Apps	T	C	P	DG	Pts
Christian Rust	15	10	10	10	11R	10R	6	1	1	–	–	7
Duwayne Smart	14	14	–	–	11	11R	4	1	–	–	–	5
Richard Lawson	13	13	13	13	13	–	5	–	–	–	–	0
Albert Trytsman	12	12	12	12	12	12	6	–	–	–	–	0
Arno Fortuin	11	11	11	11	–	–	4	1	–	–	–	5
Eric Zana	10	15	15	15	15	15	6	4	7	5	–	49
Marnus Hugo	9	9	9	9	9	9	6	–	–	–	–	0
Ryno Coetzee	8	8	8R	8	7R	7	6	2	–	–	–	10
Gavin Annandale	7	7	7	7	6R	7R	6	–	–	–	–	0
Franzel September	6c	6c	6c	6c	6c	6c	6	3	–	–	–	15
JC Astle	5	5	5	5	5	5	6	–	–	–	–	0
Hanno Kitshoff	4	4	4	4	4	–	5	–	–	–	–	0
Francois Hanekom	3	3	3R	3R	3	3	6	–	–	–	–	0
Clemen Lewis	2	2	2	2	2	–	5	–	–	–	–	0
Khwezi Mkhafu	1	1	1	1	1	1	6	1	–	–	–	5
Ulrich Pretorius	2R	7R	2R	–	2R	2	5	1	–	–	–	5
Martin Dreyer	3R	1R	3	3	–	–	4	1	–	–	–	5
Yves Bashiya	4R	–	–	4R	–	5R	3	–	–	–	–	0
Jason-Colin Fraser	7R	–	–	7R	7	–	3	–	–	–	–	0
Deroy Rhoode	9R	14R	–	13R	9R	9R	5	–	–	–	–	0
Edwin Sass	12R	12R	13R	–	–	–	3	–	–	–	–	0
Nathaniel Manuel	x	–	11R	x	–	–	1	–	–	–	–	0
Chaney Willemse	–	6R	4R	–	–	–	2	–	–	–	–	0
Ben Venter	–	4R	–	–	–	–	1	–	–	–	–	0
PJ van Zyl	–	x	–	–	–	–	0	–	–	–	–	0
Harton Klaasen	–	–	14	–	–	–	1	1	–	–	–	5
Zandre Jordaan	–	–	8	–	8	8	3	–	–	–	–	0
Earl Lewis	–	–	12R	14	–	11	3	–	–	–	–	0
Ashton Constant	–	–	1R	4R	2R	–	3	–	–	–	–	0
Christopher Bosch	–	–	10R	13R	–	–	2	–	–	–	–	0
Nathaniel Manuel	–	–	–	14	14	–	2	1	–	–	–	5
Morne Hugo	–	–	–	10	10	–	2	–	3	5	1	24
Cheswin Williams	–	–	–	–	13	–	1	–	–	–	–	0
Victor Kruger	–	–	–	–	4	–	1	–	–	–	–	0
Kelvin Fikster	–	–	–	–	1R	–	1	–	–	–	–	0
35 Players							129	17	11	10	1	140

ABSA CURRIE CUP – QUALIFIERS

Border

Played	Won	Lost	Drawn	Points for	Points against	Tries for	Tries against
6	0	6	0	118	320	16	48

Date	Venue	Opponent	Result	Score	Referee	Scorers
6 Jun	Kimberley	Griquas	LOST	5-52	C du Preez	T: Nofemele.
20 Jun	East London	Boland	LOST	12-37	B Crouse	T: Jonker, Xakalashe. C: Banda.
28 Jun	Kempton Park	Valke	LOST	40-54	M vd Westhuizen	T: Mkokeli (2), Ndlela, Lemley, Krause, Zono. C: Banda (5).
4 July	East London	SWD	LOST	31-33	J van Heerden	T: Banda, Ralarala, Ndlela. C: Banda (2). P: Banda (4).
11 Jul	East London	Griffons	LOST	15-41	L Legoete	T: Ralarala, Van Wyk. C: Banda. P: Banda.
19 July	Potchefstroom	Leopards	LOST	15-103	B Crouse	T: Makase, Kobese. C: Banda. P: Banda.

APPEARANCES & POINTS IN 2014 CURRIE CUP QUALIFIERS

Player	Griquas	Boland	Valke	SWD	Griffons	Leopards	Apps	T	C	P	DG	Pts
Masixole Banda	15	15	15	15	15	15	6	1	10	6	0	43
Sipho Nofemele	14	14	–	–	11	11	4	1	0	0	0	5
Makazole Maphimpi	13	13	13	12	–	12	5	–	–	–	–	0
Lithabile Mgwadleka	12	12	12	–	12	11R	5	–	–	–	–	0
Lolo Waka	11	11	–	–	–	–	2	–	–	–	–	0
Oliver Zono	10	x	10R	10R	10R	10	5	1	0	0	0	5
Ntando Kebe	9	9	9	9	–	9	5	–	–	–	–	0
Rynardt van Wyk	8	8	8	8	8	8	6	1	0	0	0	5
Nkosi Nofuma	7	–	–	8R	–	–	2	–	–	–	–	0
Siya Mdaka	6	7	7	7	7	7	6	–	–	–	–	0
Wayne Lemley	5	5	5	–	4	–	4	1	0	0	0	5
Gareth Krause	4	–	4	4	–	–	3	1	0	0	0	5
Buhle Mxunyelwa	3	–	–	3	3	3	4	–	–	–	–	0
Mihlali Mpafi	2	2	2	2	2	–	5	–	–	–	–	0
Blake Kyd	1c	1c	1c	1c	1c	2c	6	–	–	–	–	0
Ludwe Booi	2R	2R	2R	–	2R	2R	5	–	–	–	–	0
Yanga Xakalashe	3R	3R	3R	1R	–	1	5	1	0	0	0	5
Johann Jonker	1R	3	3	3R	–	–	4	1	0	0	0	5
Lindokuhle Welemu	5R	4	–	4R	4R	5R	5	–	–	–	–	0
Onke Dubase	7R	–	6R	–	–	–	2	–	–	–	–	0
Bongi Kobese	11R	9R	9R	9R	9	9R	6	1	0	0	0	5
Thembani Mkokeli	10R	10	10	10	10	10R	6	2	0	0	0	10
Lukhanyo Nomzanga	–	6	6	6	6	6	5	–	–	–	–	0
Wandile Putuma	–	5R	5R	5	5	4	5	–	–	–	–	0
Naythan Knoetze	–	6R	–	–	–	–	1	–	–	–	–	0
Ruan Jacobs	–	14R	–	12R	13R	–	3	–	–	–	–	0
Michael Makasa	–	–	14	14	14	14	4	1	0	0	0	5
Lindani Ndlela	–	–	11	11	–	–	2	2	0	0	0	10
Lundi Ralarala	–	–	11R	13	13	13	4	2	0	0	0	10
Siyamthanda Ngande	–	–	–	–	1R	1R	2	–	–	–	–	0
Athenkosi Manentsa	–	–	–	–	8R	8R	2	–	–	–	–	0
Mario Noordman	–	–	–	–	9R	–	1	–	–	–	–	0
Anthonie Gronum	–	–	–	–	–	5	1	–	–	–	–	0
33 Players							131	16	10	6	0	118

ABSA CURRIE CUP – QUALIFIERS

Griffons

Played	Won	Lost	Drawn	Points for	Points against	Tries for	Tries against
6	3	3	0	183	213	25	30

Date	Venue	Opponent	Result	Score	Referee	Scorers
7 Jun	Welkom	Boland	WON	27-25	L Legoete	T: Nelson, Penalty try. C: Du Toit P: Du Toit (5).
13 Jun	George	SWD	LOST	37-40	C du Preez	T: Huggett, Le Roux, Nel, Nelson, Mbotho. C: Herbert (2), Du Toit. P: Du Toit, Herbert.
28 Jun	Welkom	Griquas	LOST	24-43	R Rasivhenge	T: Van der Merwe, Nel, Nelson, Maarman. C: Herbert, De Wet.
5 Jul	Potchefstroom	Leopards	LOST	25-70	M vd Westhuizen	T: Nelson (2), Koster, Steyn. C: De Wet. P: De Wet.
11 Jul	East London	Border	WON	41-15	L Legoete	T: Koster, Abrahams, Engelbrecht, Steyn, Nelson, Maarman. C: De Wet (4). P: De Wet.
18 Jul	Welkom	Valke	WON	29-20	Q Immelman	T: Nel (2), Koster, E le Roux. C: Strydom (2), De Wet. P: Strydom.

APPEARANCES & POINTS IN 2014 CURRIE CUP QUALIFIERS

Player	Boland	SWD	Griquas	Leopards	Border	Valke	Apps	T	C	P	DG	Pts
Wynand Pienaar	15	9R	–	10R	15R	–	4	–	–	–	–	0
Cameron Jacobs	14	14	14	–	–	–	3	–	–	–	–	0
Joubert Engelbrecht	13	–	13	13	13	13	5	1	–	–	–	5
Japie Nel	12	12c	12	12	–	12	5	4	–	–	–	20
Norman Nelson	11	11	11	11	11	11	6	6	–	–	–	30
Franna du Toit	10	10	–	–	–	–	2	–	2	6	–	22
Inus Kritzinger	9c	–	–	–	–	–	1	–	–	–	–	0
Nicky Steyn	8	–	8c	8c	8c	8c	5	2	–	–	–	10
Jan Breedt	7	7	5R	–	4R	–	4	–	–	–	–	0
Erik Le Roux	6	8	7	7	–	7	5	2	–	–	–	10
Mlungisi Bali	5	5	5	5	5	5	6	–	–	–	–	0
Werner Lourens	4	–	–	7R	4	4R	4	–	–	–	–	0
Heinrich Roelfse	3	3	–	3	3	3	5	–	–	–	–	0
Hannes Snyman	2	2R	2R	2R	–	x	4	–	–	–	–	0
Danie van der Merwe	1	1	3	1	1	1	6	1	–	–	–	5
Elandre Huggett	2R	2	2	2	2	2	6	1	–	–	–	5
PW Botha	7R	1R	1	–	1R	x	4	–	–	–	–	0
Armandt Koster	4R	4	4	4	7	4	6	3	–	–	–	15
Frans Sisita	6R	6	6	–	–	6R	4	–	–	–	–	0
Oshwil Nortjie	9R	9	9	x	11R	x	4	–	–	–	–	0
Louis Strydom	x	–	–	–	–	10R	1	–	2	1	–	7
Tertius Maarman	15R	15	15	15	15	15	6	2	–	–	–	10
Vuyo Mbotho	–	13	14R	14	14	14	5	1	–	–	–	5
Colin Herbert	–	10R	10	x	7R	–	3	–	3	1	–	9
Wilmar Groenewald	–	4R	–	5R	6R	–	3	–	–	–	–	0
Niell Jordaan	–	5R	–	–	–	–	1	–	–	–	–	0
Aubrey McDonald	–	14R	–	–	–	14R	2	–	–	–	–	0
Gerard Baard	–	–	1R	–	–	–	1	–	–	–	–	0
Martin Sithole	–	–	6R	6	6	6	4	–	–	–	–	0
Pieter-Steyn de Wet	–	–	10R	10	10	10	4	–	7	2	–	20
Boela Abrahams	–	–	9R	9	9	9	4	1	–	–	–	5
Kevin Stevens	–	–	–	1R	–	–	1	–	–	–	–	0
Werner Griesel	–	–	–	–	12	–	1	–	–	–	–	0
AJ Le Roux	–	–	–	–	2R	–	1	–	–	–	–	0
Penalty try	–	–	–	–	–	–	–	1	–	–	–	5
34 Players							126	25	14	10	0	183

ABSA CURRIE CUP – QUALIFIERS

Griquas

Played	Won	Lost	Drawn	Points for	Points against	Tries for	Tries against
6	6	0	0	246	101	36	14

Date	Venue	Opponent	Result	Score	Referee	Scorers
6 Jun	Kimberley	Border	WON	52-5	C du Preez	T: M Schoeman (3), B Schoeman, C Greeff, Nepgen, Francke, Bezuidenhout. C: Prinsloo (6).
14 Jun	Wellington	Boland	WON	21-3	B Crouse	T: Prinsloo, Lobberts, Mnisi. P: Prinsloo (2).
21 Jun	Kimberley	Leopards	WON	33-32	M Jonker	T: B Schoeman, M Schoeman, Scheepers. C: Scheepers (3). P: Scheepers (4).
28 Jun	Welkom	Griffons	WON	43-24	R Rasivhenge	T: C Greeff (3), Arendse, Brummer, Mnisi, Adendorff. C: Brummer (2), Scheepers (2).
12 Jul	Kimberley	Valke	WON	40-25	B Crouse	T: M Schoeman (2), Meyer (2), Serfontein, B Schoeman. C: Brummer (5).
19 Jul	George	SWD	WON	57-12	L vd Merwe	T: Barnes (2), C Greeff (2), Arendse, Francke, Van Dyk, M Schoeman, Meyer. C: Scheepers (4), Brummer (2).

APPEARANCES & POINTS IN 2014 CURRIE CUP QUALIFIERS

	Border	Boland	Leopards	Griffons	Valke	SWD	Apps	T	C	P	DG	Pts
Gouws Prinsloo	15	15	–	–	–	–	2	1	6	2	–	23
Ederies Arendse	14	–	–	11	x	14	3	2	–	–	–	10
Jonathan Francke	13	13	13	13	13	13	6	2	–	–	–	10
Wayne Stevens	12c	12c	–	12R	12c	12c	5	–	–	–	–	0
Danie Dames	11	14	11	–	–	–	3	–	–	–	–	0
Francois Brummer	10	10	10c	10c	10	10	6	1	9	–	–	23
Tian Meyer	9	9	9	9R	9	9	6	3	–	–	–	15
Burger Schoeman	8	8	8	8	8	8R	6	3	–	–	–	15
Jaco Nepgen	7	–	7	7	5	5	5	1	–	–	–	5
Marnus Schoeman	6	6	6	5R	6	6	6	7	–	–	–	35
Willem Serfontein	5	4R	–	5	4	4	5	1	–	–	–	5
Jonathan Adendorf	4	7	4	4	–	–	4	1	–	–	–	5
Janro van Niekerk	3	3R	–	–	–	–	2	–	–	–	–	0
Martin Bezuidenhout	2	2	2	2	–	–	4	1	–	–	–	5
Steph Roberts	1	1	1	1	1	1	6	–	–	–	–	0
Ryno Barnes	2R	2R	2R	2R	2	2	6	2	–	–	–	10
Luxolo Koza	3R	–	–	–	–	–	1	–	–	–	–	0
Stephan Greeff	5R	4	–	4R	4R	4R	5	–	–	–	–	0
Carel Greeff	8R	6R	6R	6	7	8	6	6	–	–	–	30
Dustin Jinka	9R	10R	x	9	–	–	3	–	–	–	–	0
Marais Schmidt	10R	15R	14R	–	–	10R	4	–	–	–	–	0
Howard Mnisi	13R	12R	12	12	–	–	4	2	–	–	–	10
Jacquin Jansen	–	11	15	15	15	–	4	–	–	–	–	0
Hilton Lobberts	–	5	5	–	–	7	3	1	–	–	–	5
Maks van Dyk	–	3	3	3	3	3	5	1	–	–	–	5
Nico Scheepers	–	–	14	14	15R	15	4	1	9	4	–	35
Ewald van der Westhuizen	–	–	3R	3R	3R	3R	4	–	–	–	–	0
Rynard Landman	–	–	5R	–	–	–	1	–	–	–	–	0
PJ Vermeulen	–	–	12R	14R	14	14R	4	–	–	–	–	0
Rocco Jansen	–	–	–	–	11	11	2	–	–	–	–	0
Simon Westraadt	–	–	–	–	2R	2R	2	–	–	–	–	0
RJ Liebenberg	–	–	–	–	7R	–	1	–	–	–	–	0
Rudi van Rooyen	–	–	–	–	9R	9R	2	–	–	–	–	0
33 Players							130	36	24	6	0	246

ABSA CURRIE CUP – QUALIFIERS

Leopards

Played	Won	Lost	Drawn	Points for	Points against	Tries for	Tries against
6	5	1	0	356	141	51	16

Date	Venue	Opponent	Result	Score	Referee	Scorers
7 Jun	Potchefstroom	SWD	WON	51-23	B Crouse	T: Language (2, Mahuza (2), Obi, De Wet, Welgemoed. C: Pretorius (5). P: Pretorius. DG: Pretorius.
13 Jun	Kempton Park	Valke	WON	45-22	R Rasivhenge	T: De Kock (2), Robertse, Tossel, Language, Mhlongo. C: Pretorius (6). P: Pretorius.
21 Jun	Kimberley	Griquas	LOST	32-33	M Jonker	T: Tossel, Language, Obi, Mahuza. C: Engelbrecht (3). P: Engelbrecht (2).
5 Jul	Potchefstroom	Griffons	WON	70-25	M vd Westhuizen	T: Obi (2), Mahuza (2), Maritz (2), Smit, Robertse, Jenkinson, De Wet. C: Pretorius (8), Engelbrecht (2).
12 Jul	Wellington	Boland	WON	55-23	R Rasivhenge	T: Smit (2), Language (2), Obi (2), Maritz, De Kock, Mahuza. C: Pretorius (4), Engelbrecht.
19 Jul	Potchefstroom	Border	WON	103-15	B Crouse	T: Mahuza (4), Obi (4), Tossel (2), Smit, Robertse, Maritz, De Kock, Hanekom. C: Pretorius (14).

APPEARANCES & POINTS IN 2014 CURRIE CUP QUALIFIERS

Player	SWD	Valke	Griquas	Griffons	Boland	Border	Apps	T	C	P	DG	Pts
Kobus de Kock	15	14	15	15R	15R	15R	6	4	–	–	–	20
Sylvain Mahuza	14	–	14	14	14	14	5	10	–	–	–	50
Adriaan Engelbrecht	13	12	12	13	13	13	6	–	6	2	–	18
George Tossel	12	13R	15R	12	12	12	6	4	–	–	–	20
Luther Obi	11	11	11	11	11	11	6	10	–	–	–	50
Andre Pretorius	10c	10c	10c	10c	10c	10c	6	–	37	2	1	83
Dillon Smit	9	9	9	9	9	9	6	4	–	–	–	20
Rhyk Welgemoed	8	8	8	–	8R	6R	5	1	–	–	–	5
Robert Kruger	7	4	4	–	–	–	3	–	–	–	–	0
Juan Language	6	6	6	7	7	6	6	6	–	–	–	30
Francois Robertse	5	5	5	5	5	5	6	3	–	–	–	15
Ruan Venter	4	–	4R	4	4	4	5	–	–	–	–	0
Nhlanhla Ngcamu	3	3	3	3	3	–	5	–	–	–	–	0
JC Oberholzer	2	2R	7R	2	2	2	6	–	–	–	–	0
Mashudu Mafela	1	1	1	1	1	1	6	–	–	–	–	0
Jacques Vermaak	2R	–	–	2R	2R	2R	4	–	–	–	–	0
John-Roy Jenkinson	3R	3R	3R	3R	x	3	5	1	–	–	–	5
Sithembiso Mhlongo	8R	8R	–	–	–	–	2	1	–	–	–	5
Philip de Wet	4R	7R	x	6	–	–	3	2	–	–	–	10
Vian van der Watt	9R	9R	–	–	–	–	2	–	–	–	–	0
Sergio Torrens	12R	13	13R	12R	12R	12R	6	–	–	–	–	0
Tshotso Mbovane	13R	15R	–	–	–	–	2	–	–	–	–	0
Hoffman Maritz	–	15	13	15	15	15	5	4	–	–	–	20
HP Swart	–	7	7	8R	6	7	5	–	–	–	–	0
Akker van der Merwe	–	2	2	–	–	–	2	–	–	–	–	0
Percy Williams	–	–	14R	9R	9R	9R	4	–	–	–	–	0
Morne Hanekom	–	–	–	8	8	8	3	1	–	–	–	5
Molotsi Bouwer	–	–	–	6R	4R	7R	3	–	–	–	–	0
Stephan Bezuidenhout	–	–	–	–	–	1R	1	–	–	–	–	0
29 Players							130	51	43	4	1	356

ABSA CURRIE CUP – QUALIFIERS

SWD

Played	Won	Lost	Drawn	Points for	Points against	Tries for	Tries against
6	3	3	0	163	245	23	33

Date	Venue	Opponent	Result	Score	Referee	Scorers
7 Jun	Potchefstroom	Leopards	LOST	23-51	B Crouse	T: Bock, Haupt. C: Aspeling (2). P: Aspeling (3).
13 Jun	George	Griffons	WON	40-37	C du Preez	T: Bock, Bester, Kelly, Haupt, Vulindlu, S Raubenheimer. C: Aspeling (5).
20 Jun	George	Valke	LOST	34-52	Q Immelman	T: Bock, Venter, Skosana, Kelly, Zito. C: Aspeling (3). P: Van Vuuren.
28 Jun	Wellington	Boland	WON	21-17	J van Heerden	T: Skosana, Roberts, Kelly. C: Van Vuuren (2), Aspeling.
4 Jul	East London	Border	WON	33-31	J van Heerden	T: Skosana, Kelly, Pedro, Haupt, S Raubenheimer. C: Van Vuuren (4).
19 Jul	George	Griquas	LOST	12-57	L vd Merwe	T: Skosana, Du Plessis. C: Van Vuuren.

APPEARANCES & POINTS IN 2014 CURRIE CUP QUALIFIERS

	Leopards	Griffons	Valke	Boland	Border	Griquas	Apps	T	C	P	DG	Pts
Jarryd Buys	15	15	–	–	–	–	2	–	–	–	–	0
Luzuko Vulindlu	14	14	–	–	13	13	4	1	–	–	–	5
Elric van Vuuren	13	13	15	15	15	15	6	–	7	1	–	17
Martin du Toit	12	12	12	12	10	10	6	–	–	–	–	0
Alshaun Bock	11	11	11	11	–	–	4	3	–	–	–	15
Karlo Aspeling	10	10	10	10	12R	–	5	–	11	3	–	31
Danie Faasen	9	9	9R	9	–	–	4	–	–	–	–	0
Davon Raubenheimer	8	8	8	8	4R	8	6	–	–	–	–	0
Alwyn Bester	7	7	7	7	–	7	5	1	–	–	–	5
Marcel Groenewald	6	6	–	–	–	–	2	–	–	–	–	0
Mzwanele Zito	5	5	5	5	–	5	5	1	–	–	–	5
Schalk Oelofse	4	4	4	–	4	4	5	–	–	–	–	0
Grant Kemp	3	3R	3	–	3R	3R	5	–	–	–	–	0
Wayne Khan	2	2	2R	2R	2	2R	6	–	–	–	–	0
Roy Godfrey	1c	1c	1c	1c	1c	1c	6	–	–	–	–	0
Kurt Haupt	2R	2R	2	2	2R	2	6	3	–	–	–	15
Dexter Fahey	3R	–	3R	3	3	–	4	–	–	–	–	0
Grant le Roux	4R	–	4R	4	5	–	4	–	–	–	–	0
Peet van der Walt	6R	6R	–	–	–	5R	3	–	–	–	–	0
Dwayne Kelly	9R	9R	9	9R	9	9	6	4	–	–	–	20
Brian Skosana	13R	14R	13	14	14	14	6	4	–	–	–	20
Daniel Roberts	11R	–	x	13	13R	12R	4	1	–	–	–	5
Ashley Buys	–	3	–	3R	–	3	3	–	–	–	–	0
Shaun Raubenheimer	–	15R	6	6	6	6	5	2	–	–	–	10
Lyndon Hartnick	–	7R	7R	4R	–	–	3	–	–	–	–	0
Anver Venter	–	–	14	14R	–	–	2	1	–	–	–	5
Clinton Wagman	–	–	14R	–	–	11R	2	–	–	–	–	0
Christo du Plessis	–	–	–	6R	8	7R	3	1	–	–	–	5
Gerrit Smith	–	–	–	10R	12	12	3	–	–	–	–	0
Hentzwill Pedro	–	–	–	–	11	11	2	1	–	–	–	5
Janneman Stander	–	–	–	–	6	–	1	–	–	–	–	0
Buran Parks	–	–	–	–	6R	–	1	–	–	–	–	0
Mzo Dyantyi	–	–	–	–	9R	9R	2	–	–	–	–	0
33 Players							131	23	18	4	0	163

ABSA CURRIE CUP – QUALIFIERS

Valke

Played	Won	Lost	Drawn	Points for	Points against	Tries for	Tries against
6	2	4	0	193	223	25	31

Date	Venue	Opponent	Result	Score	Referee	Scorers
13 Jun	Kempton Park	Leopards	LOST	22-45	R Rasivhenge	T: Arends (2), Poley. C: Kotze (2). D: Kotze.
20 Jun	George	Eagles	WON	52-34	Q Immelman	T: Arends (2), Kotze, Richter, Mostert, Williams, Kirkwood. C: Kotze (4). P: Kotze (3).
28 Jun	Kempton Park	Bulldogs	WON	54-40	M vd Westhuizen	T: Kotze, Cronje, Janke, Dumond, Richter, Verwey, Richardson, Taljaard. C: Kotze (7).
5 Jul	Kempton Park	Cavaliers	LOST	20-35	L Legoete	T: Kotze, Cronje. C: Kotze (2). P: Kotze (2).
12 Jul	Kimberley	Griquas	LOST	25-40	B Crouse	T: Van Wyk, Arends, Kotze. C: Kotze (2). P: Kotze. DG: Kotze.
18 Jul	Welkom	Griffons	LOST	20-29	Q Immelman	T: Hendricks, Kotze. C: Kotze (2). P: Kotze (2).

APPEARANCES & POINTS IN 2014 CURRIE CUP QUALIFIERS

Player	Leopards	Eagles	Border	Boland	Griquas	Griffons	Apps	T	C	P	DG	Pts
Arno Poley	15	15	–	–	–	–	2	1	0	0	0	5
Etienne Taljaard	14	14	11R	–	15R	14	5	1	0	0	0	5
Grant Janke	13	12	11	–	–	13	4	1	0	0	0	5
Willie Odendaal	12c	–	12c	12	12c	12	5	–	–	–	–	0
Riaan Arends	11	11	–	11	11	11	5	5	0	0	0	25
Jaun Kotze	10	10	15	15	10	10	6	5	19	8	2	93
Anrich Richter	9	9	9	9	9	9	6	2	0	0	0	10
Ernst Ladendorf	8	8	8	8	8	8	6	–	–	–	–	0
JP Mostert	7	7	–	8R	7	8R	5	1	0	0	0	5
Andrew van Tonder	6	6c	–	6c	6R	6c	5	–	–	–	–	0
Marlyn Williams	5	5	5	5	–	–	4	1	0	0	0	5
Shane Kirkwood	4	4	4	4	4	4	6	1	0	0	0	5
Thulani Ngidi	3	3	3	3	–	–	4	–	–	–	–	0
Bruce Muller	2	–	–	–	–	–	1	–	–	–	–	0
Dandre v/d Westhuizen	1	1	–	–	–	1R	3	–	–	–	–	0
Chris Richardson	2R	2	2	2	2R	2R	6	1	0	0	0	5
Andries Schutte	3R	1R	1	1	1	–	5	–	–	–	–	0
Friedle Olivier	4R	7R	6R	–	–	–	3	–	–	–	–	0
Jacques Verwey	6R	8R	7	7	7R	7	6	1	0	0	0	5
Ryan Carmichael	9R	9R	x	–	–	–	2	–	–	–	–	0
Lenience Tambwera	14R	–	–	–	–	–	1	–	–	–	–	0
Andrew van Wyk	12R	13	13	13	13	12R	6	1	0	0	0	5
Devlin Hope	–	2R	2R	x	2	2	4	–	–	–	–	0
Cecil Dumond	–	11R	10	10	–	–	3	1	0	0	0	5
Coert Cronje	–	15R	14	14	–	–	3	2	0	0	0	10
Juan-Pierre Jonck	–	–	6	–	6	6R	3	–	–	–	–	0
Gerhard Engelbrecht	–	–	1R	–	3	3	3	–	–	–	–	0
Jacques Alberts	–	–	5R	5R	5	5	4	–	–	–	–	0
Kyle Hendricks	–	–	10R	10R	14	15	4	1	0	0	0	5
Peet Vorster	–	–	–	3R	1R	1	3	–	–	–	–	0
Jaco Snyman	–	–	–	x	9R	9R	2	–	–	–	–	0
Waylon Thompson	–	–	–	x	–	–	0	–	–	–	–	0
Wayne Gardner	–	–	–	–	15	–	1	–	–	–	–	0
Jaco Oosthuizen	–	–	–	–	14R	14R	2	–	–	–	–	0
34 Players							**128**	**25**	**19**	**8**	**2**	**193**

ABSA U21 & U19 PROVINCIAL CHAMPIONSHIPS

Old foes share junior titles

Blue Bulls, WP dominate yet again

A LATE try by Jesse Kriel confirmed the Vodacom Blue Bulls' dominance of their Absa Under-21 Provincial Championship final against defending champions DHL Western Province at Newlands, resulting in a 20-10 win.

The visitors played with more purpose in the second half of a tight game in which their great defence and forward pack chipped away at the home team's resolve. The Blue Bulls also used the rolling maul to great effect and in the end won going away.

The first half proved to be a classic north-south encounter with the Blue Bulls hammering away with their forwards and WP creating turnovers and counter-attacks.

Robert du Preez, for the home side, cancelled out an earlier Joshua Stander penalty to get WP on the board, but after Stander kicked a second penalty, the visitors claimed bragging rights after the first 40 minutes of hard and uncompromised action.

The second half was equally sapping. Du Preez scored and converted his own try to put WP 10-6 up, but by now the Blue Bulls machine was truly lit. Some impact from their reserve bench also added some spark and when captain Ruan Steenkamp was worked over for his team's first try in the 70th minute, the heads started to hang in the WP camp.

Their dominance was confirm when Kriel, who had a try disallowed in the first half, crashed through a number of tackles to seal the fate of the defending champions. Kobus Marais, who replaced Stander during the second half, kicked both conversions.

Steenkamp praised his side's first phase play afterwards. "We drove and scrummed well all season and decided not to change that for the final. We stuck to our guns and it worked out again for us today. We worked hard for this and this win will be remembered by all," he said.

Western Province will be disappointed with the result, having topped the seven-team log after the double-round-robin group stages, followed by the Blue Bulls, Golden Lions and Free State.

WP dispatched their Cheetahs counterparts in 41-17 in the semi-final to set up a Newlands final, while the Blue Bulls edged their Lions rivals 23-19 in the other knock-out match to advance.

ABSA U21 & U19 PROVINCIAL CHAMPIONSHIPS

Celebration time for the Blue Bulls' Under-21 team.

There was a clear gap between the top four sides and the rest, with 10 points separating Free State and the fifth-placed Sharks, and another 10 between the KZN side and the sixth-placed Leopards.

The Sharks juniors were particularly disappointing, winning just five of their 12 matches, with the Leopards victorious in just two encounters.

But they had nothing on the performances of an outclassed Border side, who not only went winless but scored only 59 points in 12 matches, while conceding an incredible 1131, including five centuries of which their 143-0 away loss to the Blue Bulls in round one was the heaviest. It was also, on reflection, a hint of what was to come.

Absa Under-19 Championship

AS in the Under-21 final, a late converted try helped DHL Western Province to a 33-26 win over defending Absa Under-19 champions, the Vodacom Blue Bulls, in the 2014 final at Newlands.

The home side were still trailing by three points with nine minutes to go, but a long-range penalty by flyhalf Ernst Stapelberg equalled matters before flanker Christo van der Merwe kicked through to score the winning try. Stapelberg converted from the touchline to seal a memorable afternoon with the boot, kicking three conversions and four penalties.

Stapelberg kicked two penalties in the opening minutes before the Blue Bulls found some rhythm in attack, Abongile Nonkontwana racing through for the opening try.

It was just a matter of minutes though before WP struck again, this time using the pace of their backline, with fullback Khanyo Ngcukana finishing after some good phase play. Warrick Gelant scored the visitors' second try but another Stapelberg penalty added to the score and WP led 16-12 at the break. The second 35 minutes provided even more drama.

ABSA U21 & U19 PROVINCIAL CHAMPIONSHIPS

Western Province's Under-19 team celebrate their title at Newlands.

Prop Francois van der Merwe scored shortly after the restart and Stapelberg's conversion saw his side enjoying a 10-point lead. Some replacements saw the Blue Bulls erase that deficit via tries by Menzi Nhlabathi and Dewald Human.

With the scores level and five minutes left, the final play belonged to Van der Merwe who hacked a loose ball ahead, regathered and dived for glory.

The Blue Bulls will look back on their campaign with disappointment, having topped the seven-team log convincingly after the double-round-robin stages.

The Pretoria side won nine of their 12 matches to finish on 47 points, six ahead of Free State and WP, on 41, with the Sharks 15 points adrift on 32.

The Blue Bulls then made light work of their semi-final against the Durban side, running out comfortable 43-20 winners to advance to the final. In the other semi, WP then shocked Free State 29-22 in Bloemfontein to set up a Newlands showdown against their great foes.

ABSA UNDER-21 CUP
SECTION A PLAY-OFF RESULTS

SEMI-FINALS:
WP bt Free State 41-17 (Cape Town); **Blue Bulls bt Golden Lions 23-19** (Pretoria)
FINAL - SECTION A
DHL Newlands Rugby Stadium, Cape Town. Saturday, 25 October. Referee: Lesego Legoete
WP 10 *(Try: Du Preez. Con: Du Preez. Pen: Du Preez).*
Blue Bulls 20 *(Tries: J Kriel, Steenkamp. Cons: Marais 2. Pens: Stander 2).*
WP: Justin Geduld, EW Viljoen, Johnny Kotzé, Kyle Lombard *(Lihleli Xoli, 73)*, JP Lewis, Robert du Preez, Frederick Nel, Carel du Preez, Justin Benn, Eital Bredenkamp *(Capt, Tapiwa Tsomondo, 12-20)*, Jan Uys, Jurie van Vuuren, Deacon Chowles *(Niel Oelofse, 69)*, Michael Willemse *(Michael Kennedy, 55)*, John-Hubert Meyer. UNUSED SUBS: Jade Kriel, SP Ferreira, Huw Jones.

ABSA U21 & U19 PROVINCIAL CHAMPIONSHIPS

Blue Bulls: Duncan Matthews, Kefentse Mahlo, Jesse Kriel, Rohan Janse van Rensburg *(Dan Kriel, 71)*, Joshua Stander *(Kobus Marais, 47)*, Carlo Engelbrecht, Jannes Kirsten *(Roelof Smit, 55)*, Jacques du Plessis, Ruan Steenkamp *(Capt, Marquit September, 71)*, Marvin Orie, Irne Herbst *(Nico Janse van Rensburg, 55)*, Neethling Fouche *(Dayaan van der Westhuizen, 49)*, Jan Enslin *(Arno van Wyk, 69)*, Pierre Schoeman.

U21 SECTION B PLAY-OFF RESULTS
SEMI-FINALS:
EP Kings bt Limpopo Blue Bulls 28-26 (Port Elizabeth); **SWD bt Boland 40-33** (Wellington)
FINAL - SECTION B
North West Stadium, Welkom. Friday, 17 October. Referee: Archie Sehlako
EP Kings 46 *(Tries: Davis, Velleman, Ueckermann, Davids, Petersen, Msutwana. Cons: Davids 5. Pens: Davids 2)*.
SWD 3 *(Pen: Eksteen)*.
EP Kings: Selvyn Davids, Sergeal Petersen, Sipho Msutwana, Riaan Esterhuizen *(Jaco Bernardo, 63)*, Aya Dlepu *(Warren Swarts, 66)*, Malcolm Jaer, Franswa Ueckermann, *(Sonwabo Majola, 66)*, Ivan-John du Preez *(Frans Gerber, 66)*, Aidon Davis, CJ Velleman, Stephan Zaayman *(Brendon Hector, 66)*, Kevin Kaba *(Capt)*, Mzu Sofisa, John-Henry Schmitt *(Warrick Venter, 61)*, Nicolas Roebeck *(Matthew Moore, 69)*.
SWD: Luzanne Williams *(Lee-Roy Pojie, 71)*, Marcelino Marais *(Fizell Fredericks, 57)*, Creswin Josephs, Juandre Fourie, Kirsten Heyns, Leighton Eksteen, Dillin Snell *(Kerwin Apollis, 48)*, Andisa Ntsila, Joshwine Cornelius, *(Capt, Lungi Dube, 71)*, Janneman Stander, Achmad Salie, Ansley Theunissen *(Wikus Oosthuizen, 66)*, JP Ellard *(Bradley Jumaats, 48)*, Brianton Booysen, Raeez Salie *(Nathan Gogela, 39)*.

U21 LOGS

Section A	P	W	L	D	PF	PA	Diff	TF	TA	BP	BP7	PTS
Western Province	12	11	1	0	580	268	312	83	36	0	10	54
Blue Bulls	12	9	3	0	600	225	375	81	27	2	8	46
Golden Lions	12	8	4	0	543	262	281	79	31	1	9	42
Free State	12	7	5	0	429	273	156	59	36	1	6	35
Sharks	12	5	7	0	413	376	37	56	50	0	5	25
Leopards	12	2	10	0	353	442	-89	49	56	2	5	16
Border	12	0	12	0	59	1131	-1072	4	175	0	0	0
Section B	P	W	L	D	PF	PA	Diff	TF	TA	BP	BP7	PTS
EP Kings	7	7	0	0	261	90	171	35	12	0	6	34
Boland	7	6	1	0	305	162	143	47	23	0	6	30
SWD	7	5	2	0	202	171	31	27	22	0	3	23
Limpopo Blue Bulls	7	3	4	0	230	177	53	37	24	3	5	20
Griquas	7	3	4	0	136	190	-54	18	28	2	2	16
Valke	7	3	4	0	173	212	-39	23	30	1	2	15
Pumas	7	1	6	0	136	212	-76	21	31	1	2	7
Griffons	7	0	7	0	133	362	-229	17	55	1	0	1

Note: BP = Bonus point, BP7 = Less than 7

ABSA U21 & U19 PROVINCIAL CHAMPIONSHIPS

U21 LEADING SCORERS

60 POINTS OR MORE

PLAYER	PROVINCE	T	C	P	DG	PTS
Kobus Marais	Blue Bulls	4	35	15	1	138
Robert du Preez	Western Province	3	37	16	0	137
Selvyn Davids	EP Kings	10	15	8	0	104
Joshua Stander	Blue Bulls	3	22	13	0	98
Ryno Smith	Leopards	11	10	4	0	87
Brendon Cope	Sharks	2	28	5	0	81
Pieter Jordaan	Free State	5	16	7	0	78
Harlon Klaasen	Boland	15	0	0	0	75
Fizell Fredericks	SWD	7	10	6	0	73
JJ du Plessis	Leopards	1	24	5	1	71
Hanco Deale	Golden Lions	4	17	4	0	66
Eital Bredenkamp	Western Province	13	0	0	0	65

TRIES

Harlon Klaasen	Boland	15	Ruan Steenkamp	Blue Bulls	9
Eital Bredenkamp	Western Province	13	CJ Coetzee	Free State	8
Ryno Smith	Leopards	11	JP Lewis	Western Province	8
Koch Marx	Golden Lions	11	Selom Gavor	Golden Lions	8
Selvyn Davids	EP Kings	10	Valentino Wellman	Boland	8
Damian Engledoe	Golden Lions	9			

ABSA UNDER-19 CUP
SECTION A PLAY-OFF RESULTS

SEMI-FINALS:
Western Province bt Free State 29-22 (Bloemfontein). **Blue Bulls bt Sharks 43-20** (Pretoria)
FINAL
DHL Newlands Rugby Stadium, Cape Town, Saturday, 25 October. Referee: Rodney Bonaparte.
Western Province 33 *(Tries: C van der Merwe, F van der Merwe, Ngcukana. Cons: Stapelberg 3. Pens: Stapelberg 4).*
Blue Bulls 26 *(Tries: Nonkontwana, Human, Nhlabathi, Gelant. Cons: Human 3).*
Western Province: Khanyo Ngcunkana *(Adriaan Carelse, 62)*, Grant Hermanus *(Jarryd Sage, 24-32)*, Heinrich Buhr, Ryan Oosthuizen *(Jarryd Sage, 62)*, Leolin Zas, Ernst Stapelberg, Justin Phillips, Rikus Bothma *(Capt)*, Luke Stringer *(Graham Geldenhuys, 62)*, Christo van der Merwe, David Ribbans, Johan Momsen, Francois van der Merwe *(Kyle White, 62)*, Paul Wipplinger, Frans van Wyk. UNUSED SUBS: Hanno Snyman, Lebohang Mdakane, Ruaan du Preez, Vrendon Nell.
Blue Bulls: Warrick Gelant, Matji Molapo, Jurie Linde, Adrian Maebane, Duhan van der Merwe, Dewald Human, Ivan van Zyl, Hanro Liebenberg *(Capt)*, Abongile Nonkontwana *(Calvonn Allison, 48)*, Francois Steyn *(Menzi Nhlabathi, 46)*, RG Snyman, Jason Jenkins, Matthys Basson *(Stefaan Grundlingh, 47)*, Jan van der Merwe, Njabula Gumede *(Johan van Wyk, 47)*. UNUSED SUBS: Vuyo Khathide, Theo Maree, Wyatt Murphy, Willem Louw.

ABSA U21 & U19 PROVINCIAL CHAMPIONSHIPS

U19 SECTION B PLAY-OFF RESULTS

SEMI-FINALS:
Valke bt Pumas 35-19 (Kempton Park). **Boland bt Limopo Blue Bulls** 35-30 (Wellington)
FINAL
North West Stadium, Welkom, Friday, 17 October. Referee: Lourens van der Merwe.
Valke 17 *(Tries: Botha, Wessels. Cons: Kotze 2. Pen: Kotze).*
Boland 42 *(Tries: Williams 3, Arendse, Carstens. Cons: Lubbe 4. Pens: Lubbe 3).*
Valke: Ruhann Ferreira, Jacqone de Villiers, Arno Kotzé, Ruan Neethling, Boela Croukamp *(Ryan Solomons, 64)*, Dudley Thopmpson *(Igno Venter, 21/Francois Pretorius, 54)*, Brandon Rieck, Philip Terblanche, Marco Botha, El-Dean Baker *(Rholane Ngubuka, 45)*, Gideon Roux, Ruhan Bouwer *(Elandre Strauss, 69)*, Nico van Tonder *(Donovan Venter, 4-5/Johan Vreugdenburg, 69)*, Johan Swart *(Capt)*, Zane Wessels *(Donovan Venter, 60)*.
Boland: Lohan Lubbe, Esteban van der Merwe, Killian von Mollendorff, Etienne Swarts *(Mishaun Arendes, 30)*, Warren Williams, Chemandre van Schalkwyk *(Jaydrin Kotze, 44)*, Gervin Rossouw *(Gerdwill le Fleur, 44)*, Denvor Cloete *(Corbin Larey, 45)*, Cheslyn Korasie *(Capt)*, Gareth Cilliers, Le Curt Wessels, Kenan Cronje, Hendrik Carstens *(Lance Korabie, 67)*, JC Genade *(Ray-Niel de Jager, 67)*, Ruan Laubscher *(Willem de Kock, 67)*.

U19 LOGS

Section A	P	W	D	L	PF	PA	Diff	TF	TA	BP	BP7	PTS
Blue Bulls	12	9	3	0	387	282	105	53	34	2	9	47
Free State	12	8	4	0	310	204	106	45	23	2	7	41
Western Province	12	9	3	0	332	270	62	38	36	0	5	41
Sharks	12	6	6	0	287	256	31	35	33	4	4	32
Golden Lions	12	4	8	0	222	313	-91	28	44	3	3	22
EP Kings	12	4	8	0	227	253	-26	25	32	3	2	21
Leopards	12	2	10	0	243	430	-187	38	60	2	5	15
Section B	P	W	D	L	PF	PA	Diff	TF	TA	BP	BP7	PTS
Valke	7	7	0	0	246	118	128	28	14	0	5	33
Boland	7	6	1	0	244	128	116	33	12	0	4	28
Limpopo Blue Bulls	7	5	2	0	228	181	47	33	24	1	4	25
Pumas	7	4	3	0	220	252	-32	32	38	0	5	21
Griffons	7	3	4	0	217	228	-11	26	34	2	3	17
SWD	7	2	5	0	179	154	25	25	18	2	2	12
Griquas	7	1	6	0	146	160	-14	22	21	3	1	8
Border	7	0	7	0	103	362	-259	17	55	0	2	2

Note: BP = Bonus point, BP7 = Less than 7

‹ DID YOU KNOW? ›
Naas Botha has scored more points in Currie Cup finals than any other player. In his 11 appearances between 1977 and 1991, Botha scored 138 points made up of a try, 10 conversions, 20 penalties and an incredible 18 drop goals!

ABSA U21 & U19 PROVINCIAL CHAMPIONSHIPS

U19 LEADING SCORERS

50 POINTS OR MORE

PLAYER	PROVINCE	T	C	P	DG	PTS
Ernst Stapelberg	Western Province	1	34	34	0	175
Arno Kotze	Valke	9	22	24	0	161
Innocent Radebe	Sharks	4	24	17	1	122
Lohan lubbe	Boland	1	27	18	1	116
Dewald Human	Blue Bulls	4	28	13	0	115
Malcolm Jaer	EP Kings	8	11	14	0	104
Jaya Juries	Griffons	4	18	11	0	89
Andre Swarts	Free State	1	29	8	0	87
Warren Williams	Boland	16	0	0	0	80
Dylan du Buison	Pumas	2	17	11	0	77
Shaun Reynolds	Golden Lions	4	15	8	0	74
Jurie Linde	Blue Bulls	10	0	0	0	50

TRIES

Warren Williams	Boland	16	Duhan van der Merwe	Blue Bulls	8
Jurie Linde	Blue Bulls	10	Dylan Pieterse	Pumas	7
Arno Kotze	Valke	9	Hanro Liebenberg	Blue Bulls	7
Jasper Wiese	Free State	9	Jean-Luc du Preez	Sharks	7
Malcolm Jaer	EP Kings	8	Mishaun Arendse	Boland	7

Ernst Stapelberg.

YOUTH WEEKS

Junior Kings revive spirit of '77

WP teams dominate Youth Weeks once again

By Zeena Isaacs

EASTERN Province took the honours as the unofficial champions of the Coca-Cola Craven Week for the first time in 37 years, in a season once again dominated by Western Province's junior teams.

WP, who registered a clean-sweep of Youth Weeks victories in 2013, once again dominated the series of tournaments as they won the final match at the Under-13 Craven Week, Under-16 Grant Khomo Week and the Under-18 Academy Week. Their sister union, Boland, meanwhile took top honours at the LSEN Week.

With the Under-18 Craven Week, held in Middelburg, marking the final tournament on the Youth Week calendar there were high hopes among the WP players and management that they could repeat the heroics of 2013. But a defeat against SWD in their second match at HTS Middelburg dashed these hopes.

Instead it was EP and SWD who progressed through the first few days of Craven Week unbeaten thanks to their fine form, and they rightfully earned their places in the final match. This marked the first time in 14 years that one of South Africa's current franchise unions failed to feature in the final match of the tournament.

Eastern Province rose to the challenge early in the closing match as they forced their way through the determined SWD defence twice in the first half, while flyhalf Curwin Bosch slotted two penalties to build up a morale-boosting 20-0 lead at the break.

EP added another try two minutes into the second half to extend their lead to 25-0. SWD fought back with intent and spent several minutes in Eastern Province's half, but their efforts bore only one try as the tenacious EP defence held, earning the side a convincing 25-7 victory.

The result was particularly significant as it marked the first time since 1977 that the Eastern Cape side finished the tournament as the last team standing. Interestingly, that year EP toppled Western Province in the final match, with legendary Springbok Danie Gerber featuring strongly.

WP, meanwhile, took the honours as the unofficial champions at the **Under-16 Grant Khomo Week** for the third successive time as they registered a convincing 26-11 victory against hosts, the Blue Bulls, at the Tshwane University of Technology in

YOUTH WEEKS

Eastern Province Under-18 celebrate a Craven Week to remember.

Pretoria. The Cape side built on their victories against Border and the Golden Lions on the opening two days by delivering another impressive attacking performance against the Blue Bulls on the final day, which they supported with a solid defensive effort to secure the victory.

The team was in top form thanks to an effective game plan which involved retaining possession on attack and applying intense pressure on the hosts. With their pack and backline functioning well, the Cape side spent most of the match in the hosts' half and penetrated the Blue Bulls' defence at will, which earned them four well-worked tries. Such was the Blue Bulls' struggle to make their presence felt they earned only a penalty in the first half for their efforts, while they managed to score a try and another penalty in the second half to take their score into double figures.

The match was a repeat of the final game of 2013, which Western Province won 22-15, while WP pipped Free State 10-7 in the 2012 tournament.

In the **Under-13 Craven Week** held at Glenwood High School in Durban, Western Province emerged as the top team after claiming a 29-14 victory over Border in a pulsating final match. The final day's matches were played at Growth-Point Kings Park.

The win over an impressive Border team left the Cape side as the only unbeaten team. Equally impressive was the abundance of talent spread right across the country, with a number of so-called platteland regions performing very well against the metropolitan provinces.

Three teams were still undefeated at the beginning of day four, but after the Leopards fell to Eastern Province, it was up to either Border or WP to walk away undefeated.

In the end it was WP, who scored 126 points and only conceded 27 in four matches, who proved their mettle. They also had the final say in the **Academy Week** as they beat KwaZulu-Natal 38-7 on the final day at HTS Drostdy in Worcester to establish themselves as the top side.

The emphatic win over a highly rated KZN side confirmed the credentials of a WP

YOUTH WEEKS

side who had brushed aside the challenges of Free State and the Blue Bulls earlier in the week. WP remained unbeaten, as did the Golden Lions, Blue Valke and Boland XV on a final day that again saw plenty of tries.

In the **LSEN (Learners with Special Education Needs) Week** hosted in Potchefstroom, Boland took top honours as they defeated SWD 45-3 after beating the Blue Bulls and Eastern Province respectively on the opening two days.

The win capped off a fantastic tournament for the side as they won all their matches with 40-point scores, which ensured bonus points in each match. Such was the quality of the team's performance that they scored 18 tries in their three matches and conceded only eight. The Valke also had a memorable tournament as they were the only other unbeaten team at its conclusion.

COCA-COLA UNDER-18 CRAVEN WEEK RESULTS

DAY ONE: July 14

Limpopo BB (13) 25 – *T: Kgetho Mabokela (2), Diederick Oberholzer, Mitch Mametsa. C: Oberholzer. P: Oberholzer.* **Griquas CD (19) 19** – *T: André Share, Dian Dry, Elmo Jantjies. C: Coennie Lamprecht (2).*

EP CD (39) 54 – *T: Bradley Christian (2), Craig Williams, Ethan September, Joshua Shelly, Nicolaas Oosthuizen, Xandré Vos. C: Cameron Hertz (5). P: Hertz (3).* **Zimbabwe (17) 43** – *T: Matthew Ushewokunze (2), Tawanda Ngosi (2), Brian Mhuriyengwe, Tinashe Gonese. C: Campbell Nyakudya (5). P: Nyakudya.*

Griffons (42) 47 – *T: Erik Knoetze (2), Ezrick Alexander (2), Francois Stemmet, Jaywinn Juries, Johann Vermaak. C: Juries (6).* **Border (6) 20** – *T: Courtney Winnaar, Jerry Danquah. C: Morgan Steyn, Winnaar. P: Steyn.*

SWD (12) 18 – *T: Ruan Barnard, Shadward Fillies. C: JT Jackson. P: Jackson (2).* **KZN (13) 13** – *T: Morné Joubert. C: Tristan Tedder. P: Tedder (2).*

WP (30) 33 – *T: Duncan Saal (2), Jaco Willemse. C: Tiaan Swanepoel (3). P: Swanepoel (4).* **Pumas (15) 32** – *T: Barend Smit, Driaan Bester, Mfundo Ndlovu, Stephan Enslin. C: Müller Joubert (3). P: Joubert (2).*

DAY TWO: July 15

Griquas (49) 96 – *T: Daniello Huyster (2), Gerco Nortjé (2), JD Swanepoel (2), J-P Abrahams (2), Leon Becker, Brandon de Melim, Gloucester Hugo, Keaton Gordon, Rikus Zwart. C: Nortjé (13).* **Border CD 0**.

Leopards (15) 53 – *T: Gerhard Steenekamp (2), Markus Coetzer (2), Edmund Rheeder, Garann Kriek, Thabang Phatudi, Stefan van Vuuren. C: Coetzer (5). P: Coetzer.* **Namibia (6) 13** – *T: Armando van Wyk. C: PW Steenkamp. P: Steenkamp (2).*

Valke (17) 30 – *T: Jimmy Mpailane, Marco Jansen van Vuuren, Martin van Wyk. C: Forrest Roos (3). P: Roos (3).* **Boland (14) 24** – *T: Adriaan de Waal, André-Pierre Gouws, Conal Brown, Earl Dowrie. C: Raylinn Philander (3).*

EP (06) 26 – *T: Athenkosi Mayinje, Curwin Bosch. C: Bosch. P: Bosch (4).* **Blue Bulls (16) 25** – *T: Etteinne Matthys. C: Thinus de Beer. P: De Beer (6).*

Free State (10) 33 – *T: Alexander Jonker, Shirwin Cupido, Victor Maruping. C: Lourens Steenkamp (3). P: Steenkamp (4).* **Golden Lions (10) 20** – *T: Wikus van Biljon, Armandt Grobler, Gavin Delport. C: Van Biljon (2). P: Ralton October, Van Biljon.*

DAY THREE: July 16

Griquas CD (14) 26 – *T: Cobus Wiese, Coennie Lamprecht, Denvill Joseph, Dillon Magerman. C: Lamprecht (3).* **Zimbabwe (20) 20** – *T: Brian Muntanga, Daniel Nyamugama, Stephen Bhasera. C: Shaun Snyder. P: Snyder.*

Border (54) 78 – *T: David Brits (3), Jerry Danquah (3), Michale Brink (3), Reinhardt Engelbrecht, Robert Lyons, Yamkela Myalambisa. C: Morgan Steyn (9).* **Limpopo BB (0) 17** – *T: Armand Davies, Diederick Oberholzer, Dumisani Mushwana. C: Benhard Janse van Rensburg.*

YOUTH WEEKS

Griffons (19) 33 – *T:* Siya Ngxesha (2), Johann Vermaak (2), Francois Stemmet. *C:* Johan van Zyl (4). **EP CD (3) 15** – *T:* Bradley Christian, Daveron Cameron. *C:* Cameron Hertz. *P:* Hertz.
KZN (24) 38 – *T:* Jakobus Coetzee (2), Morné Joubert, Curtis Jonas. *C:* Jonas (5). *P:* Jonas. **Pumas (5) 27** – *T:* Chrisjan Steynberg (2), Mfundo Ndlovu, Siyabonga Masuku, Barend Smit. *C:* Smit.
SWD (5) 38 – *T:* JT Jackson (2), Shadward Fillies (2), Niven Langdown, Le Roux Baard. *C:* Jackson (4). **WP (6) 23** – *T:* Aidynn Cupido, Mervano Da Silva. *C:* Tiaan Swanepoel (2). *P:* Cupido (2).

DAY FOUR: July 17
Namibia (24) 69 – *T:* Adriaan Booysen (3), Divan Rossouw (2), Milan van Wyk (2), Jandré du Toit, PW Steenkamp, Stefan Potgieter, Umassa Kavita. *C:* Steenkamp (4), Stiaan van der Merwe (2), Booysen. **Border CD 0**.
Griquas (20) 38 – *T:* Brandon de Melim, Gerhard Holtzhauzen, J-P Abrahams, Robbie Petzer. *C:* Petzer (3). *P:* Petzer (4). **Boland (10) 27** – *T:* Iver Aanhuizen, André-Pierre Gouws, Conal Brown, Handré Ontong. *C:* Adriaan van der Bank (2). *P:* Van der Bank.
Leopards (13) 26 – *T:* Brenden Esterhuizen, Markus Coetzer. *C:* Coetzer (2). *P:* Coetzer (4).
Valke (20) 20 – *T:* Martin van Wyk, Darren de Bruin. *C:* Forrest Roos (2). *P:* Roos (2).
Blue Bulls (21) 21 – *T:* Juandré Michau, Ruan de Beer, Stedman Gans. *C:* Thinus de Beer (3).
Golden Lions (3) 10 – *T:* Constant Beckerling. *C:* Ralton October. *P:* Wikus van Biljon.
EP (19) 19 – *T:* Athenkosi Mayinje, Darren Lottering, Keanu Vers. *C:* Curwin Bosch (2). **Free State (0) 5** – *T:* Julian Jordaan.

DAY FIVE: July 19
Griquas CD (17) 60 – *T:* Denvill Joseph (2), Erik Jordaan (2), Reinhard Hayes (2), Joe-Lythen Willemse, David du Toit, Etienne Kruger, Gert Nel. *C:* Coenie Lamprecht (5). **Border CD (14) 21** – *T:* Chuma Tukela, Mpumelelo Velem, Phelane Macingwane. *C:* Siyambonga Mxhaka (3).
Namibia (15) 38 – *T:* Jandré van Wyk (2), Divan Rossouw (2), Hans Breedt, Herlé Otto. *C:* Stiaan van der Merwe (2), PW Steenkamp (2).
Zimbabwe (9) 25 – *T:* Ackim Sibanda, Bradley Crause, Daniel Nyamugama, Matthew Ushewokunze. *C:* Ngoni Zinyama. *P:* Shaun Snyder.
Golden Lions (17) 39 – *T:* Willem Massyn (3), Gavin Delport, Jaco Holtzhausen, Preston Karstens. *C:* Ralton October (3). *P:* October.
Pumas (0) 24 – *T:* Siyabonga Masuku (2), Chrisjan Steynberg, Penalty try. *C:* Masuku (2).
WP (22) 37 – *T:* Duncan Saal (2), Jondré Williams, Justin Heunis, Mogamat Davids. *C:* Tiaan Swanepoel (3). *P:* Swanepoel (2). **Free State (10) 29** – *T:* Julian Jordaan (2), De Wet Bezuidenhout, Shirwin Cupido. *C:* Jéandré Christian (3). *P:* Christian.
Border (29) 55 – *T:* David Brits (2), Henning Coetzee, Jason Steyn, Jerry Danquah, Michael Brink, Morgan Steyn, Pierre Bester, Reinhadrt Engelbrecht. *C:* M Steyn (5). **Griquas (26) 26** – *T:* Geo Davel, Keaton Gordon, Robbie Petzer, Wilfred Bowers. *C:* Petzer (3).
Boland (15) 56 – *T:* Jaydrin Kotzé (3), Earl Dowrie, Handré Ontong, Iver Aanhuizen, Morné van Wyk, Raylinn Philander, Robert Hunt. *C:* André-Pierre Gouws (2), Adriaan van der Bank, Ontong. *P:* Ontong. **Limpopo BB (17) 24** – *T:* John-John van der Kolf (2), Diederick Oberholzer, Thapelo Molapo. *C:* Benhard Janse van Rensburg (2).
Valke (14) 35 – *T:* Martin van Wyk (3), Ntshepe Kokong, Forrest Roos. *C:* Roos (5). **EP CD (8) 13** – *T:* Arno le Roux, Josiah Twum-Boafo. *C:* Cameron Hertz.
Griffons (27) 44 – *T:* Johann Vermaak (2), Johan van Zyl, Jaywinn Juries, Ezrick Alexander. *C:* Juries (5). *P:* Juries (3). **Leopards (12) 24** – *T:* Douglas Bruce-Smith, Keanu van der Merwe, Jano Smith, Roodt van Zyl. *C:* Markus Coetzer (2).
Blue Bulls (15) 36 – *T:* Thinus de Beer (2), Embrose Papier, Eduan Keyter, Aston Fortuin. *C:* T de Beer (4). *P:* T de Beer. **KZN (10) 15** – *T:* Jakobus Coetzee, James Hall. *C:* Curtis Jonas. *P:* Tristan Tedder.
EP (20) 25 – *T:* Athenkosi Mayinje, Johann van Niekerk, Stephanus Nieuwoudt. *C:* Curwin Bosch (2). *P:* Bosch (2). **SWD (0) 7** – *T:* Dominic Smith. *C:* JT Jackson.

YOUTH WEEKS

BLUE BULLS U/18

No.	Name	School	Town	ID Number	Weight	Height (m)
1	Michael Kumbirai	St. Alban's College	Pretoria	9605095092083	118	1.87
2	Jan-Henning Campher (C)	Garsfontein HS	Pretoria	9612105046083	102	1.86
3	Sarel-Marco Smith	Edloraigne HS	Pretoria	9601085065080	120	1.90
4	Ashton Fortuin	Southdowns College	Pretoria	9601465101080	103	1.94
5	Etteinne Matthys	Centurion HS	Pretoria	9609075023084	104	1.95
6	P-J Toerien	Garsfontein HS	Pretoria	9602175053085	95	1.87
7	Juandré Michau	Waterkloof HS	Pretoria	9609025151084	87	1.84
8	Eduan Lubbe	Afrikaans HS	Pretoria	9708125089085	100	1.90
9	Embrose Papier	Garsfontein HS	Pretoria	9602175053085	77	1.76
10	Thinus de Beer	Waterkloof HS	Pretoria	9601245050089	83	1.78
11	Andell Loubser	Menlo Park HS	Pretoria	9703035206085	93	1.89
12	Franco Naudé	Garsfontein HS	Pretoria	9603285193084	97	1.86
13	Stedman Gans	Waterkloof HS	Pretoria	9703195125083	73	1.82
14	Conreree Poole	Garsfontein HS	Pretoria	9612035190084	82	1.78
15	Eduan Keyter	Afrikaans HS	Pretoria	9606135048085	93	1.85
16	Jungqo Hennings	Menlo Park HS	Pretoria	9602085101081	97	1.82
17	Luyolo Qinela	Southdowns College	Pretoria	9702135390088	120	1.76
18	Rohan Goosen	Menlo Park HS	Pretoria	9610185124085	115	1.88
19	Arnold Gerber	Menlo Park HS	Pretoria	9610055459082	94	1.89
20	Justin Meintjies	Menlo Park HS	Pretoria	9608275019082	95	1.84
21	Eddie Fouché	Afrikaans HS	Pretoria	9709045016083	91	1.84
22	Ruan de Beer	Menlo Park HS	Pretoria	9601132050085	90	1.84

TEAM MANAGERS: Ofentse Moeng **COACHES:** Piet van Wyk, Jan Mollentze **PERMANENT REPRESENTATIVE:** Ferdi Niemand.

BOLAND U/18

No.	Name	School	Town	ID Number	Weight	Height (m)
1	Roy Brink	Drostdy THS	Worcester	96052050840	118	1.87
2	Adriaan de Waal	Augsburg AHS	Clanwilliam	9602095182089	90	1.76
3	Robert Hunt	Drostdy THS	Worcester	9608165152084	116	1.83
4	Willem Augustyn	Drostdy THS	Worcester	9602235320086	98	1.85
5	Christie van der Merwe	Piketberg HS	Piketberg	9609095134085	106	1.98
6	Handley Hendricks	Montague HS	Montague	9604305019085	95	1.83
7	Conal Brown	Klein Nederburg HS	Paarl	9609305051087	92	1.92
8	Iver Aanhuizen (C)	Klein Nederburg HS	Paarl	9604255205080	94	1.84
9	Gerwin Rossouw	Swartland HS	Malmesbury	9611195227082	74	1.77
10	Fabio Africa	Weston HS	Saldanha	9605025121085	70	1.72
11	Jaydrin Kotzé	Augsburg AHS	Clanwilliam	9603195219086	72	1.71
12	André-Pierre Gouws	Hermanus HS	Hermanus	9607305264080	83	1.79
13	Stephan Borman	Swartland HS	Malmesbury	9601225130083	82	1.76
14	Earl Dowrie	Drostdy THS	Worcester	9712115161086	80	1.81
15	Raylinn Philander	Hugenote HS	Wellington	9601265244083	76	1.74
16	Tiaan Smuts	Drostdy THS	Worcester	9603125147084	91	1.74
17	Adriaan Oberholzer	Augsburg AHS	Clanwilliam	9602295062081	93	1.77
18	Stephan Fourie	Overberg HS	Caledon	9702065096085	113	1.79
19	Morné van Wyk	Montague HS	Montague	9608125116088	81	1.87
20	Handré Ontong	Montague HS	Montague	9602205240082	65	1.65
21	Gilroy Farmer	Klein Nederburg HS	Paarl	9604115314080	60	1.65
22	Adriaan van der Bank	Worcester Gymnasium	Worcester	9702085062083	75	1.80

TEAM MANAGERS: Mervin Petersen **COACHES:** Wylie Seroot, Johan Thalwitzer **PERMANENT REPRESENTATIVE:** David Coert

YOUTH WEEKS

BORDER COUNTRY DISTRICTS U/18

No.	Name	School	Town	ID Number	Weight	Height (m)
1	Simphiwe Matanzima	Queens College	Queenstown	9708185451084	102	1.82
2	Philela Mabandla	Maclear HS	Maclear	9703115942088	81	1.79
3	Qhawe Bula	Queens College	Queenstown	9709305218081	102	1.78
4	Siphosakhe Mameza	Maclear HS	Maclear	9601016154086	78	1.84
5	Sinoxolo Gaba	CHB HS	Libode	9607155823084	84	1.84
6	Akhona Makwahla	Mt. Packard	Mqanduli	9601255854081	80	1.87
7	Esethu Mdenge	Mt. Packard	Mqanduli	9601266524087	75	1.87
8	Mpumelelo Velem			961213	80	1.84
9	Anele Nonkala	Tyelinzima SSS	Mqanduli	9709146397085	70	1.72
10	Sinegugu Lituka (c)	Maclear HS	Maclear	9701175709084	78	1.75
11	Thabo Dlebedlebe	Dalibaso HS	Mqanduli	9705145667080	80	1.86
12	Onele Nogoxo	Tyelinzima SSS	Mqanduli	9603186102085	75	1.62
13	Shivaan Johnson	THS	Queenstown	9607305172085	69	1.73
14	Luvo Magagu	Maclear HS	Maclear	9606266399083	65	1.72
15	Vuyisanani Mtshengulana	Maclear HS	Maclear	9610096037087	70	1.83
16	Onezwa Gasayi	Sibabale HS	Ugie	9706175484081		
17	Phelane Macingwane			960826	80	1.77
18	Amahle Bhungeni	Dalibaso HS	Mqanduli	9607075707086	90	1.90
19	Ayanda Mvimbi	Maclear HS	Maclear	9702055822086	79	1.76
20	Siyambonga Mxhaka					
21	Babalo Ketwa	Maclear HS	Maclear	9607185404087	71	1.80
22	Chuma Tukela	Maclear HS	Maclear	9612215928089	74	1.75
23	Yawosei Penxe			9704035271087		
24	Lukhanyo Matshoba			9701285489088		

TEAM MANAGERS: M.S. Nani **COACHES:** M.M. Madlalisa, R. Pretorius

BORDER U/18

No.	Name	School	Town	ID Number	Weight	Height (m)
1	Siyavuya Milwayo	Queen's College	Queenstown	9603245383080	92	1.70
2	Tango Balekile (C)	Selborne College	East London	9603075482085	98	1.83
3	Kuhle Makhoabane	Dale College	King William's Town	9605105209081	98	1.70
4	Robert Lyons	Selborne College	East London	9606265140082	106	1.88
5	Henning Coetzee	Grens HS	East London	9607295169083	104	1.88
6	Adrian Greig	Selborne Colleg	East London	9605105315086	95	1.78
7	Nico Grobler	Grens HS	East London	9707285194081	94	1.88
8	Jason Steyn	Selborne College	East London	9602205204088	101	1.85
9	Siyamthanda Mgubo	Dale College	King William's Town	9710166043088	80	1.68
10	Morgan Steyn	Selborne College	East London	9706125245087	89	1.77
11	Jerry Danquah	Queen's College	Queenstown	9601196252080	92	1.78
12	David Brits	Selborne College	East London	9704275016085	95	1.80
13	Avela Jubase	Queen's College	Queenstown	9602265220081	85	1.81
14	Yamkela Nyalambisa	Dale College	King William's Town	9602236217083	84	1.80
15	Courtney Winnaar	Dale College	King William's Town	9703275032084	83	1.86
16	Sango Mtotywa	Dale College	King William's Town	9601215274081	95	1.70
17	Curtley du Preez	Grens HS	East London	9605015093088	113	1.84
18	Pierre Bester	Grens HS	East London	9604145133088	98	1.78
19	Alno Schultz	Grens HS	East London	9601235208085	85	1.72
20	Reinhardt Engelbrecht	Grens HS	East London	9701145474081	74	1.70
21	Michael Brink	Grens HS	East London	9609245047088	87	1.82
22	Luyolo Khuse	Dale College	King William's Town	9703065462087	84	1.78

TEAM MANAGERS: Sivuyile Vakele **COACHES:** Anton Jacobs, Phiwe Nomlomo **PERMANENT REPRESENTATIVE:** Mtobeli Kweliti

YOUTH WEEKS

E.P. COUNTRY DISTRICTS U/18

No.	Name	School	Town	ID Number	Weight	Height (m)
1	Xandré Vos	Graeme College	Grahamstown	9609305090085	95	1.76
2	Johannes le Roux	Marlow AHS	Cradock	9702085247080	85	1.77
3	Nicolaas Oosthuizen	Marlow AHS	Cradock	9611195088088	110	1.82
4	Cristoffel Viljoen	Marlow AHS	Cradock	9608305184088	94	1.94
5	Phillip Crouse	Volkskool	Graaff-Reinet	9608295145081	95	1.90
6	Erwin Ittershagen-Straus	Volkskool	Graaff-Reinet	9604245114087	91	1.85
7	Evert Potgieter	Gill College	Somerset East	9605105067083	88	1.84
8	Luigy van Jaarsveld (C)	Marlow AHS	Cradock	9608215132086	98	1.90
9	Craig Williams	Graeme College	Grahamstown	960721505708	68	1.68
10	Joshua Shelly	Kingswood	Grahamstown	9603056099080	83	1.78
11	Kwesi Ansa	Union HS	Graaff-Reinet	9703165161084	72	1.83
12	Cameron Hertz	Kingswood	Grahamstown	9604295156087	90	1.87
13	Davron Cameron	Kingswood	Grahamstown	9606085152085	70	1.67
14	Fabio Mapaling	Graeme College	Grahamstown	9610205082081	72	1.75
15	Bradley Christian	Graeme College	Grahamstown	9601195126087	74	1.69
16	Jacques-Pierre Barkhuizen	Port Alfred	Port Alfred	9609285083084	96	1.78
17	MC Van Damme	Burgersdorp	Burgersdorp	9707095414083	90	1.77
18	Chuma Mboxwana	Cradock HS	Cradock	9612215504088	84	1.77
19	Ethan September	Graeme College	Grahamstown	9604015178080	105	1.80
20	Ryan Calitz	Graeme College	Grahamstown	9610045027080	80	1.78
21	Estiaan von Solms	Volkskool	Graaff-Reinet	9604165304080	77	1.81
22	Josiah Twum-Boafo	Graeme College	Grahamstown	H2278226	96	1.80

TEAM MANAGERS: George Lamani **COACHES:** Allan Miles, Gert van Wyk **PERMANENT REPRESENTATIVE:** John de Vos

EASTERN PROVINCE U/18

No.	Name	School	Town	ID Number	Weight	Height (m)
1	Lupumlo Mguca	Daniel Pienaar THS	Uitenhage	9704255257089	109	1.78
2	Alandré van Rooyen	Nico Malan HS	Humansdorp	9608235115087	103	1.80
3	Erich De Jager	Brandwag H	Uitenhage	9602295075083	110	1.84
4	Stefan Janse van Vuuren	Brandwag HS	Uitenhage	9612105288081	93	1.93
5	Wihan Coetzer	Framesby HS	Port Elizabeth	9608305314081	90	1.95
6	Stephanus Niewoudt	Framesby HS	Port Elizabeth	9608275137082	84	1.78
7	Johann Van Niekerk (C)	Grey High	Port Elizabeth	9601305141083	95	1.80
8	Junior Sipato Pokomela	Grey High	Port Elizabeth	9612106444089	95	1.90
9	Rouchè Nel	Framesby HS	Port Elizabeth	9603265083081	76	1.75
10	Curwin Bosch	Grey High	Port Elizabeth	9706255336086	82	1.84
11	Darren Lottering	Humansdorp SS	Humansdorp	9601235237084	80	1.79
12	Heino Bezuidenhout	Daniel Pienaar THS	Uitenhage	9703135041085	85	1.85
13	Jeremy Ward	Grey High	Port Elizabeth	9601105037085	84	1.84
14	Athenkosi Mayinje	Grey High	Port Elizabeth	9601185263080	85	1.82
15	Keanu Vers	Grey High	Port Elizabeth	9602045832080	85	1.77
16	Robin Stevens	Grey High	Port Elizabeth	9602285145086	87	1.75
17	Kaden Prince	Brandwag HS	Uitenhage	9610075069085	115	1.79
18	Roché Van Zyl	Framesby HS	Port Elizabeth	9606145026089	104	1.80
19	Morney Moos	Brandwag HS	Uitenhage	9605105118084	87	1.84
20	Nathan Augustus	Pearson High	Port Elizabeth	9610155099085	70	1.65
21	Tiaan Stander	Framesby HS	Port Elizabeth	9601265123089	90	1.85
22	Lunathi Nxele	Muir College	Uitenhage	9602175268089	79	1.70

TEAM MANAGERS: Relton Hermanus **COACHES:** Louis Gerber, Patdro Somerset, Christiaan van Schalkwyk
PERMANENT REPRESENTATIVE: Willem October

YOUTH WEEKS

FREE STATE U/18

No.	Name	School	Town	ID Number	Weight	Height (m)
1	Ruben Terblanche	Grey College	Bloemfontein	9602215255088	105	1.79
2	JC Janse van Vuuren	Grey College	Bloemfontein	9601035146089	97	1.74
3	Janu Botha	Grey College	Bloemfontein	9603065122089	110	1.75
4	Jurie Burger	Grey College	Bloemfontein	9710205020089	104	1.93
5	Ruben Schoema	Grey College	Bloemfontein	9603145031086	118	1.97
6	De Wet Bezuidenhout	Grey College	Bloemfontein	9609105385081	94	1.83
7	Victor Maruping	Louis Botha TH	Bloemfontein	9608245686085	95	1.85
8	Alexander Jonker (c)	Grey College	Bloemfontein	9607235185082	95	1.80
9	Shirwin Cupido	Louis Botha THS	Bloemfontein	9610155285080	60	1.60
10	DP de Lange	Sentraal HS	Bloemfontein	960304	81	1.70
11	Dale Koopman	Louis Botha THS	Bloemfontein	9604105093082	85	1.79
12	Michael Andrade	Grey College	Bloemfontein	9602275243081	86	1.80
13	Julian Jordaan	Grey College	Bloemfontein	9601025175080	82	1.80
14	Patrick Mbangi	Louis Botha THS	Bloemfontein	9601206397081	80	1.72
15	Lourens Steenkamp	Grey College	Bloemfontein	9702185131085	82	1.81
16	Greydon Wenn	Louis Botha THS	Bloemfontein	9610095114085	98	1.80
17	Khanya Gela	Louis Botha THS	Bloemfontein	9704165355080	103	1.83
18	Ignatius Prinsloo	Grey College	Bloemfontein	9704045027081	122	1.90
19	Kian Skipper	Louis Botha THS	Bloemfontein	9702055121089	100	1.89
20	Dian Badenhorst	Grey College	Bloemfontein	9608085121086	80	1.72
21	Sentle Lehoko	Grey College	Bloemfontein	970816	82	1.79
22	Jéandré Christian	Louis Botha THS	Bloemfontein	9608255366081	65	1.64

TEAM MANAGERS: Jimmy Jimlongwe **COACHES:** Dirkie Groenewald, Corné Erasmus, Wessels du Plessis
PERMANENT REPRESENTATIVE: Michael Barker

GOLDEN LIONS U/18

No.	Name	School	Town	ID Number	Weight	Height (m)
1	Franco van den Berg	Randburg HS	Randburg	9610315024080	101	1.83
2	Justin Brandon	Monument HS	Krugersdorp	9708095090089	80	1.78
3	Jaco Holtzhausen	Monument HS	Krugersdorp	9601125072088	108	1.86
4	Rhyno Herbst	Monument HS	Krugersdorp	9607055022084	106	1.97
5	Reinhard Nothnagel	Monument HS	Krugersdorp	9709255210087	98	2,01
6	Gavin Delport (C)	Monument HS	Krugersdorp	9601265173084	90	1.83
7	Constant Beckerling	Helpmekaar College	Johannesburg	9604145106084	96	1.80
8	Juan Lemmer	Monument HS	Krugersdorp	9610275087085	97	1.84
9	Ralton October	Florida HS	Florida	9606205264083	74	1.72
10	Wikus van Biljon	Monument HS	Krugersdorp	9609275285087	65	1.74
11	S'busiso Nkosi	Jeppe BHS	Johannesburg	9601215259082	98	1.83
12	Tshepo Thulo	Jeppe BHS	Johannesburg	9608215054082	91	1.84
13	Ashley Lindewaal	Florida HS	Florida	9604185476082	81	1.78
14	Justin Bahna	Florida HS	Florida	9606195259085	74	1.79
15	Preston Karstens	Florida HS	Florida	9602275347080	76	1.88
16	Willem du Plessis	King Edward VII	Johannesburg	9604245172085	92	1.78
17	Ricky Nwagbara	Jeppe BHS	Johannesburg	9712205139083	93	1.71
18	Bradley van Waardhuizen	Jeppe BHS	Johannesburg	9603175936089	113	1.78
19	Nyasha Tarusenga	St Beneddict's	Johannesburg	75-2021644E-07	80	1.85
20	Willem Massyn	Monument HS	Krugersdorp	9705215023081	92	1.92
21	Odwa Nkujane	Monument HS	Krugersdorp	9602135334088	75	1.76
22	Armandt Grobler	Monument HS	Krugersdorp	9604095105086	78	1.78
23	Adriaan van Blerk	Helpmekaar College	Johannesburg	9605295053083	83	1.83
24	Sibusiso Mngomezulu	Jeppe BHS	Johannesburg	9601085412084	88	1.70

TEAM MANAGERS: Richard van Rensburg **COACHES:** Stephan Louwrens, Marius Swanepoel **PERMANENT REPRESENTATIVE:** Tinus Diedericks

YOUTH WEEKS

GRIFFONS U/18

No.	Name	School	Town	ID Number	Weight	Height (m)
1	Fanie Vermaak	Welkom Gymnasium	Welkom	9701085575086	113	1.80
2	Nick Fortuin	Welkom Gymnasium	Welkom	9601165312089	93	1.79
3	Armand Van Wyk	Bothaville HS	Bothaville	9606045295081	106	1.73
4	Wesley McMaster	Welkom Gymnasium	Welkom	9601255192086	91	1.92
5	Frederik Knoetze	Afrikaans HS	Kroonstad	9602235018086	85	1.88
6	Juan-Pierre Kalp	Afrikaans HS	Kroonstad	9605045113088	90	1.82
7	Henry Searle	Afrikaans HS	Kroonstad	9602135018087	95	1.87
8	Francois Stemmet (C)	Afrikaans HS	Kroonstad	9606115014081	98	1.91
9	Jaywinn Juries	Hentie Cilliers HS	Virginia	9610095245087	70	1.70
10	Luan James	Hentie Cilliers HS	Virginia	9701165214085	77	1.80
11	Jonathan April	Hentie Cilliers HS	Virginia	9603255143085	74	1.73
12	Johann Vermaak	Voortrekker HS	Bethlehem	9601025095080	93	1.85
13	Siya Ngxesha	Hentie Cilliers HS	Virginia	9705075926084	81	1.81
14	Nazo Nkala	Welkom Gymnasium	Welkom	9603015339080	87	1.83
15	Ezrick Alexander	Hentie Cilliers HS	Virginia	9609265212083	77	1.84
16	Harold Hills	Afrikaans HS	Kroonstad	9611055255082	105	1.82
17	Neo Mohapi	Hentie Cilliers HS	Virginia	9705275144082	107	1.88
18	Niel Janse van Rensburg	Voortrekker HS	Bethlehem	9605245252082	105	1.75
19	Nathan Kemp	Hentie Cilliers HS	Virginia	9606045256083	89	1.83
20	Jason Olivier	Hentie Cilliers HS	Virginia	9702125261083	66	1.67
21	Kobus Kleyn	Afrikaans HS	Kroonstad	9606275177082	91	1.80
22	Johan Van Zyl	Voortrekker HS	Bethlehem	9603085102087	83	1.79

TEAM MANAGERS: Wilfred Berling **COACHES:** Kassie Kasselman, Roean Bezuidenhout **PERMANENT REPRESENTATIVE:** Victor Campher

GRIQUAS COUNTRY DISTRICTS U/18

No.	Name	School	Town	ID Number	Weight	Height (m)
1	David du Toit	Duineveld HS	Upington	9709175010088	100	1.85
2	Erlu Jonck	Kalahari HS	Kuruman	9607025159081	95	1.77
3	Stefan Hanekom	Duineveld HS	Upington	9710175242085	99	1.86
4	Cobus Wiese	Upington HS	Upington	9706025180087	94	1.97
5	Ryno Karstens (C)	Duineveld HS	Upington	9608285015088	94	1.92
6	Dian Dry	Upington HS	Upington	9705015182087	90	1.82
7	Erik Jordaan	Duineveld HS	Upington	9701095012088	81	1.86
8	Rynard Hayes	Upington HS	Upington	9709015086082	85	1.78
9	André Share	Upington HS	Upington	9703095012084	59	1.65
10	Coennie Lamprecht	Duineveld HS	Upington	9610095244080	85	1.83
11	Marcel van der Westhuizen	Upington HS	Upington	9704305170084	65	1.70
12	Dillon Magerman	Upington HS	Upington	9608085224088	85	1.68
13	Ettiene Kruger	Duineveld HS	Upington	9610045550081	70	1.68
14	Joe-Lythen Willemse	Upington HS	Upington	9708115061086	68	1.71
15	Renaldo Theron	Namakwaland HS	Springbok	9609055086085	79	1.86
16	Gert Nel	Upington HS	Upington	9601185030083	75	1.74
17	Sergio Boer	Upington HS	Upington	9608255138084	89	1.80
18	Wynand Terblanche	Upington HS	Upington	9710205331080	90	1.85
19	Garth-Lee Young	Steinkopf HS	Steinkopf	9601055066084	87	1.83
20	Denvil Joseph	Steinkopf HS	Steinkopf	9703295234082	75	1.80
21	Naziem van Wyk	Concordia HS	Concordia	9609195200083	68	1.67
22	Elmo Jantjies	Duineveld HS	Upington	9701045176082	70	1.67

TEAM MANAGERS: Leonardo de Wet **COACHES:** Emile Neethling, J-Ell Slabbert

YOUTH WEEKS

GRIQUALAND WEST U/18

No.	Name	School	Town	ID Number	Weight	Height (m)
1	Boan Venter	De Aar HS	De Aar	9704125123081	110	1.88
2	Brandon Smith	Dinamika HS	Kimberley	9607155146080	99	1.74
3	FC Swart	Jacobsdal AHS	Jacobsdal	9605145268089	108	1.82
4	Rikus Zwart	Noord Kaap HS	Kimberley	9603295086088	106	1.97
5	Teubus Brits	Jacobsdal AHS	Jacobsdal	9611195289082	101	1.98
6	Damian van den Bergh	Noord Kaap HS	Kimberley	9611155017085	88	1.85
7	Nardus Bosman	Dinamika HS	Kimberley	9604255039083	92	1.92
8	Georg Sieberhagen	De Aar HS	De Aar	9609065145087	86	1.84
9	Brandon de Melim	Noord Kaap HS	Kimberley	9612235574087	75	1.73
10	Robbie Petzer	Noord Kaap HS	Kimberley	9602135126088	86	1.84
11	J-P Abrahams	Dinamika HS	Kimberley	9605125195088	85	1.85
12	Gerhard Holtshauzen	Noord Kaap HS	Kimberley	9611145178088	85	1.87
13	JD Swanepoel	Dinamika HS	Kimberley	9603105051082	82	1.73
14	Leon Becker	Noord Kaap HS	Kimberley	9601015209089	85	1.85
15	Wilfred Bowers	Noord Kaap HS	Kimberley	9601095072085	70	1.80
16	Geo Davel	Noord Kaap HS	Kimberley	9603145264083	95	1.89
17	Gloucester Hugo	De Aar HS	De Aar	9607055052081	85	1.80
18	Ulric Sellar	Noord Kaap HS	Kimberley	9601045170087	100	1.82
19	Ruan Willemse	Prieska HS	Prieska	9611145131087	75	1.71
20	Gerco Nortjé	Dinamika HS	Kimberley	9704055176083	84	1.80
21	Daniello Heyster	Noord Kaap HS	Kimberley	9702055111084	83	1.80
22	Keaton Gordon	Dinamika HS	Kimberley	9707075215088	70	1.79

TEAM MANAGERS: Adam Botha **COACHES:** Derrick de Clerk, Shaun Huygen

KWAZULU-NATAL U/18

No.	Name	School	Town	ID Number	Weight	Height (m)
1	Kenneth van Niekerk	Glenwood HS	Durban	9601295013086	101	1.80
2	Bradley Roberts	Michaehouse	Balgowan	9601045098080	90	1.74
3	Jakobus Tredoux	Glenwood HS	Durban	9602235174087	106	1.81
4	Tristan Dixon	Kearsney College	Botha's Hill	9704235210083	104	1.94
5	Kevin du Randt	Glenwood HS	Durban	9602155271087	94	1.90
6	James Venter	Glenwood HS	Durban	9608215173080	92	1.82
7	McMillan Müller	Glenwood HS	Durban	9608055236088	105	1.80
8	Jakobus Coetzee (C)	Glenwood HS	Durban	9606105058080	102	1.88
9	James Hall	Kearsney College	Botha's Hill	9601025054087	78	1.70
10	Tristan Tedder	Kearsney College	Botha's Hill	9604175067081	73	1.80
11	Ilunga Mukendi	Glenwood HS	Durban	9705076350268	83	1.82
12	Wayne Smith	Westville BHS	Durban	9603075034084	90	1.80
13	Tristan Blewett	Hilton College	Hilton	9608265010083	84	1.77
14	Xolisa Guma	Maritzburg College	Pietermaritzburg	9701295826089	78	1.85
15	Morné Joubert	Glenwood HS	Durban	9601195049081	80	1.80
16	Percy Mngadi	Glenwood HS	Durban	9601196040089	102	1.71
17	Ngonidzashe Chidoma	Northwood HS	Durban	63-2001045 G 24	117	1.84
18	Cody Thomas	Westville BHS	Durban	9603015271085	112	1.86
19	Bandisa Ndlovu	Voortrekker HS	Pietermaritzburg	9610125144086	95	1.80
20	Kwazi Khanyile	Glenwood HS	Durban	9612225152084	73	1.63
21	Curtis Jonas	Glenwood HS	Durban	9608275180082	72	1.70
22	Philani Ngcobo	Glenwood HS	Durban	9604135253086	73	1.78

TEAM MANAGERS: Dean Moodley, Deon Gericke **COACHES:** Barend Steyn, Grant Bell **PERMANENT REPRESENTATIVE:** Gerald Pyoos

YOUTH WEEKS

LEOPARDS U/18

No.	Name	School	Town	ID Number	Weight	Height (m)
1	Charl le Roux	Rustenburg HS	Rustenburg	9602075087084	107	1.79
2	Roodt van Zyl	Schweizer Reneke HS	Schweizer Reneke	9602285082081	90	1.75
3	Thabiso Khanye	Potchefstroom BHS	Potchefstroom	9606155236081	130	1.86
4	Oratile Mabusela	Potchefstroom BHS	Potchefstroom	971135098088	90	1.84
5	Jaco Swanepoel (C)	Schweizer Reneke HS	Schweizer Reneke	9602235141086	92	1.99
6	Brenden Esterhuizen	Rustenburg HS	Rustenburg	9605015122085	91	1.88
7	Gerhard Steenekamp	Potchefstroom Gymnasium	Potchefstroom	9704095024087	116	1.70
8	Edmund Rheeder	Klerksdorp HS	Klerksdorp	9702055188082	93	1.87
9	Thabang Phatudi	Klerksdorp HS	Klerksdorp	9602285318089	67	1.66
10	Hein Claase	Rustenburg HS	Rustenburg	9603205088083	80	1.80
11	Paul Maluleke	Klerksdorp HS	Klerksdorp	9604055554083	85	1.87
12	Stefan van Vuuren	Lichtenburg HS	Lichtenburg	9601205075084	94	1.86
13	Markus Coetzer	Bergsig Academy	Rustenburg	9605145417082	94	1.89
14	Mogau Mphahlele	Potchefstroom BHS	Potchefstroom	9612045497081	90	1.85
15	Jano Smith	Schweizer Reneke HS	Schweizer Reneke	9607235023085	80	1.79
16	Ryno Visagie	Volkskool HS	Potchefstroom	9705065071081	103	1.80
17	Neo Thekiso	Potchefstroom BHS	Potchefstroom	9608035081083	80	1.75
18	Douglas Bruce-Smith	Klerksdorp HS	Klerksdorp	9708015021081	116	1.83
19	Moses Makhubelo	Potchefstroom BHS	Potchefstroom	9611185466084	95	1.92
20	Garann Kriek	Potchefstroom Gymnasium	Potchefstroom	9601155140086	76	1.78
21	Keanu van der Merwe	Potchefstroom Gymnasium	Potchefstroom	9604075029082	80	1.80

TEAM MANAGERS: Johnnie Robbetze **COACHES:** Koot Booysen, Gary Middleton
PERMANENT REPRESENTATIVE: Japie van Rooyen

LIMPOPO BLUE BULLS U/18

No.	Name	School	Town	ID Number	Weight	Height (m)
1	Kgetho Mabokela	Ben Vorster HS	Tzaneen	9607155640082	107	1.85
2	Mitch Mametsa (C)	Ben Vorster HS	Tzaneen	9604295791081	105	1.83
3	Arthur-Henry Jones	Hans Strijdom HS	Mookgopong	9609145130083	119	1.88
4	JR Visagie	Pietersburg HS	Polokwane	9609205067084	94	1.94
5	Dumisani Mushwana	Ben Vorster HS	Tzaneen	9701255252086	87	1.97
6	Armand Davies	Frikkie Meyer HS	Thabazimbi	9606115244084	78	1.79
7	Willem Dreyer	Hans Strijdom HS	Mookgopong	9605215373082	86	1.76
8	Hendrik du Plessis	Frikkie Meyer HS	Thabazimbi	9611125037080	100	1.90
9	Diederick Oberholzer	Ben Vorster HS	Tzaneen	9605235478085	78	1.75
10	Benhard Janse van Rensburg	Frikkie Meyer HS	Thabazimbi	9701146261080	80	1.83
11	Thapelo Molapo	Ben Vorster HS	Tzaneen	9705215045084	85	1.87
12	BJ Vorster	Ben Vorster HS	Tzaneen	9607265053085	75	1.79
13	Vukasi Mabuza	Ben Vorster HS	Tzaneen	9604235845088	80	1.80
14	Damian Strauss	Frikkie Meyer HS	Thabazimbi	9603315145088	76	1.77
15	Vandré Rolls	Ben Vorster HS	Tzaneen	9612035288086	79	1.87
16	Dirk Coetzee	Ben Vorster HS	Tzaneen	9710295163088	83	1.79
17	Hanco Taljaard	Ben Vorster HS	Tzaneen	9708155040081	101	1.85
18	John-John van der Kolf	Piet Potgieter HS	Makopane	9604195134085	95	1.85
19	Theo Mahlo	Ben Vorster HS	Tzaneen	9605095492085	87	1.86
20	Tiaan Vorster	Ben Vorster HS	Tzaneen	9703265177089	80	1.89
21	Nick Enslin	Pietersburg HS	Polokwane	9609265282086	78	1.73
22	Ansten Mokgokolo	Pietersburg HS	Polokwane	9603275455089	87	1.79

TEAM MANAGERS: Dirk Oosthuizen, David Mathabatha **COACHES:** Andre Hay, Hennie van Vuuren, Ian van Heerden
PERMANENT REPRESENTATIVE: Eben Lingenfelder

YOUTH WEEKS

MPUMALANGA U/18

No.	Name	School	Town	ID Number	Weight	Height (m)
1	Bheki Shongwe	Barberton HS	Barberton	9609205033086	111	1.80
2	Marinus Enslin	Nelspruit HS	Nelspruit	9606135116080	88	1.82
3	Wiehan Steyn	Nelspruit HS	Nelspruit	9604195087085	100	1.81
4	Ian Joubert	Standerton HS	Standerton	9609016323080	95	1.94
5	Driaan Bester	Middelburg THS	Middelburg	9605255019082	103	1.91
6	Chrisjan Steynberg	Middelburg THS	Middelburg	9701165009089	86	1.84
7	Bernhard Kotzenberg	Middelburg THS	Middelburg	9612255030085	85	1.82
8	Oscar Shuld	Nelspruit HS	Nelspruit	9609225087088	95	1.85
9	Stephan Enslin	Middelburg THS	Middelburg	9603255043087	82	1.84
10	Müller Joubert	Ligbron HS	Ermelo	9608165017089	73	1.72
11	Siyabonga Nkosi	Piet Retief HS	Piet Retief	9606025957080	85	1.71
12	Cyprian Nkomo	Middelburg HS	Middelburg	9712016383086	92	1.76
13	Telvin Mhlongo	Middelburg HS	Middelburg	9705156381084	69	1.69
14	Mfundo Ndlovu	Standerton HS	Standerton	9704055239089	74	1.78
15	Barend Smit (C)	Middelburg THS	Middelburg	9602125015085	94	1.85
16	Marnus van der Merwe	Nelspruit HS	Nelspruit	9702175116088	112	1.92
17	Cauwen Mashaba	Generaal Hertzog HS	Witbank	9602035287089	88	1.69
18	Ruan Groenewald	Middelburg THS	Middelburg	9604225082080	95	1.77
19	Riaan le Roux	Nelspruit HS	Nelspruit	9603075152084	91	1.92
20	Mphumelelo Matias	Middelburg HS	Middelburg	9711115020086	75	1.70
21	Siyabonga Masuku	Piet Retief HS	Piet Retief	9608015989081	76	1.80
22	Siyabonga Khaliswhayo	Piet Retief HS	Piet Retief	9703095508081	82	1.74

TEAM MANAGER: Koos de Jager **COACHES:** Gert van der Westhuizen, Cobus van Dyk **PERMANENT REPRESENTATIVE:** Dolf Jonker

NAMIBIA U/18

No.	Name	School	Town	ID Number	Weight	Height (m)
1	Hans Breedt	Tsumeb Gymnasium	Tsumeb	04/07/96	110	1.80
2	Jandré van Wyk	Elnatan HS	Stampriet	25/01/96	95	1.70
3	Norman Erasmus	Walvisbaai HS	Walvis Bay	26/02/97	98	1.77
4	Thomas van der Westhuizen	Windhoek Gymnasium	Windhoek	23/05/96	85	1.86
5	Conraad Willemse	WAP	Windhoek	24/05/96	91	1.89
6	Valarius de Vries	Windhoek Gymnasium	Windhoek	24/06/96	85	1.80
7	Camaron McNab	Dr Lemmer HS	Rehobot	14/04/96	92	1.85
8	Adriaan Booysen (C)	Elnatan HS	Stampriet	17/05/96	93	1.90
9	Stefan Potgieter	Tsumeb Gymnasium	Tsumeb	30/04/96	75	1.68
10	PW Steenkamp	Elnatan HS	Stampriet	11/12/97	72	1.75
11	Milan van Wyk	Windhoek Gymnasium	Windhoek	30/04/96	87	1.68
12	Jandré du Toit	Elnatan HS	Stampriet	26/08/96	75	1.76
13	Divan Rossouw	Windhoek Gymnasium	Windhoek	12/03/96	85	1.87
14	Umassa Kavita	Windhoek HS	Windhoek	14/01/96	73	1.74
15	Stiaan van der Merwe	Elnatan HS	Stampriet	01/04/96	81	1.85
16	Wildré Smith	Windhoek Gymnasium	Windhoek	05/08/96	82	1.74
17	Vincent Tjombe	Windhoek THS	Windhoek	04/04/96	116	1.78
18	Marino Goagoseb	Windhoek HS	Windhoek	07/08/97	113	1.83
19	Herlé Otto	Windhoek Gymnasium	Windhoek	04/09/96	87	1.83
20	Armando van Wyk	WAP	Windhoek	09/04/97	74	1.80
21	Brandon Groenewaldt	Windhoek Gymnasium	Windhoek	14/02/97	85	1.82
22	Allistair Miller	Walvisbaai HS	Walvis Bay	30/04/97	78	1.78

TEAM MANAGERS: Thys Reynecke **COACHES:** Johan Adriaanse, A. Arries **PERMANENT REPRESENTATIVE:** Hendrie Kemp

YOUTH WEEKS

SOUTH WESTERN DISTRICTS U/18

No.	Name	School	Town	ID Number	Weight	Height (m)
1	Samuel Odendaal	Oakdale AHS	Riversdale	9601195122086	105	1.84
2	Le Roux Baard (C)	Outeniqua HS	George	9602275158081	92	1.77
3	Wynand de Necker	Outeniqua HS	George	9605075127081	122	1.86
4	Anton Smit	Outeniqua HS	George	9608055193081	101	1.94
5	Eduan Zandberg	Outeniqua HS	George	9602145143081	115	2.01
6	Christopher Roelofse	Outeniqua HS	George	9601035149083	86	1.75
7	Armand Heunis	Oakdale AHS	Riversdale	9601315015087	90	1.80
8	Navada Jacobs	Langenhoven Gymnasium	Oudtshoorn	9709215130086	78	1.85
9	Dominic Smit	Oudtshoorn HS	Oudtshoorn	9601315162087	70	1.73
10	Christo Hamman	Oakdale AHS	Riversdale	9708315134089	83	1.84
11	Shadward Fillies	Sao Bras HS	Mossel Bay	9604195198080	80	1.79
12	John Thomas Jackson	Oakdale AHS	Riversdale	9607105087087	94	1.89
13	Curtley Prins	Outeniqua HS	George	9609295121080	88	1.87
14	Immanuel Libbok	Outeniqua HS	George	9707156356082	76	1.84
15	Ruan Barnard	Oakdale AHS	Riversdale	9601135109086	82	1.75
16	Vogien Talmaggies	Oakdale AHS	Riversdale	9602095200089	94	1.70
17	Andrew Kühn	Outeniqua HS	George	9705075120084	110	1.85
18	Roux Swart	Outeniqua HS	George	9708175080083	110	1.88
19	André Smith	Oakdale AHS	Riversdale	9706045022087	102	2.01
20	Levuju Ndevu	Outeniqua HS	George	9711135111089	90	1.77
21	Niven Langdown	Outeniqua HS	George	9607035528085	65	1.65
22	J-P Duvenhage	Outeniqua HS	George		85	1.81

TEAM MANAGERS: Rodney Thomas **COACHES:** Stephan Joubert **PERMANENT REPRESENTATIVE:** Gerrit Rudolph

VALKE U/18

No.	Name	School	Town	ID Number	Weight	Height (m)
1	Hanriël Coetzee	Hans Moore HS	Benoni	9610145709082	104	1.86
2	Nico Peyper	EG Jansen HS	Boksburg	9701165058086	90	1.85
3	Donavan Venter	Vereniging Gymnasium	Vereeniging	9607085258088	102	1.81
4	Quinton Van Der Schyff	EG Jansen HS	Boksburg	9601285054082	93	1.85
5	Hendrè Stassen	EG Jansen HS	Boksburg	9712296336085	108	200
6	Juanrè Van Der Walt	Kempton Park HS	Kempton Park	9607175065088	90	1.81
7	Simangaliso Moalusi	Benoni HS	Benoni	9705095074089	81	172
8	Warren Brits	EG Jansen HS	Boksburg	9701215153085	103	195
9	Marco Jansen Van Vuuren	Transvalia HS	Vanderbijlpark	9606145147083	87	1.84
10	Forrest Roos	EG Jansen HS	Boksburg	9601215107083	72	1.82
11	Darren De Bruin	Jeugland HS	Kempton Park	9606115196086	65	1.79
12	Jimmy Mpailane	Kempton Park HS	Kempton Park	9608165171084	78	1.88
13	Erich Cronje	EG Jansen HS	Boksburg	9701015144086	92	1.87
14	Irvin Ali	EG Jansen HS	Boksburg	9710265259080	76	1.82
15	Martin Van Wyk	EG Jansen HS	Boksburg	9601235136088	76	1.70
16	Stefan Jacobs	Transvalia HS	Vanderbijlpark	9608275036086	97	1.80
17	Lesego Sereme	Suiderlig HS	Vanderbijlpark	9607045245084	101	1.80
18	Thokozani Skhosana	St. Dunstans HS	Benoni	9702125151086	97	1.88
19	Motlatsi Khoza	Voortrekker HS	Boksburg	9609195453088	81	1.87
20	Charl Barkhuizen	EG Jansen HS	Boksburg	9601015152081	80	1.80
21	Ntshepe Kokong	Vereeniging Gymnasium	Vereeniging	9703025303082	65	1.74
22	Joas Narre	Kempton Park HS	Kempton Park	9604115587081	71	1.75

TEAM MANAGERS: Kwagga Loubser **COACHES:** Phillip Lemmer, Schalk Snyman **PERMANENT REPRESENTATIVE:** Doom Gouws

YOUTH WEEKS

WESTERN PROVINCE U/18

No.	Name	School	Town	ID Number	Weight	Height (m)
1	Gavin van den Berg	Paark Gymnasium	Paarl	9601105140087	120	1.87
2	Jacques van Zyl	Paul Roos Gymnasium	Stellenbosch	9602135218083	100	1.78
3	Jean-Pierre Smith	Diocesan College	Cape Town	9706185141085	119	1.85
4	Jaco Willemse	Paark Gymnasium	Paarl	9603145018083	126	2.00
5	Ruben de Villiers	Paarl BHS	Paarl	9703225046085	105	2.00
6	Mervano Da Silva	Diocesan College	Cape Town	9609065131087	82	1.78
7	Mogamat Davids	Rondebosch BHS	Cape Town	9705045104085	101	1.85
8	Saud Abrahams	Diocesan College	Cape Town	9601045227085	95	1.86
9	Herschel Jantjies	Paul Roos Gymnasium	Stellenbosch	9604225232081	73	1.67
10	Aidynn Cupido	Paul Roos Gymnasium	Stellenbosch	9609045044087	80	1.78
11	Edwill van der Merwe	Paul Roos Gymnasium	Stellenbosch	9604125107086	78	1.78
12	Edrich Venter (C)	Paul Roos Gymnasium	Stellenbosch	9607185038083	96	1.90
13	Justin Heunis	Diocesan College	Cape Town	9602165420088	87	1.89
14	Duncan Saal	Kasselsvlei HS	Bellville	9610245013088	79	1.77
15	Gerard Pieterse	Diocesan College	Cape Town	9610245023087	86	1.86
16	Shane Farmer	Tygerberg HS	Parow	9704245070089	93	1.75
17	Wikus Groenewad	Paarl BHS	Paarl	9701235092081	115	1.86
18	Jerome Korff	Paul Roos Gymnasium	Stellenbosch	9602056347085	120	1.88
19	Emile Cloete	Paul Roos Gymnasium	Stellenbosch	9603155200084	102	1.94
20	Jondré Williams	Boland AHS	Paarl	9703205191083	76	1.77
21	Tiaan Swanepoel	Stellenberg HS	Bellville	9606045650087	87	1.77
22	Ryan Müller	Bellville HS	Bellville	9706125064082	80	1.78

TEAM MANAGERS: Petrie Stofberg **COACHES:** Hein Kriek, Peter Links **PERMANENT REPRESENTATIVE:** Kervin Grové

ZIMBABWE U/18

No.	Name	School	Town	ID Number	Weight	Height (m)
1	Justin Mendelsohn	CBC	Bulawayo		117	1.80
2	Lebogang Ngwenya	St George's	Harare		87	1.78
3	Stephen Bhasera (C)	Falcon	Esigodini		115	1.81
4	Tinashe Gonese	Hillcrest	Mutare		91	1.90
5	Eli Snyman	St John's	Harare		105	2.01
6	Jeff Makoni	Prince Edward	Harare		91	1.76
7	Cole Bond	St John's	Harare		90	1.86
8	Daniel Nyamugama	St Georges	Harare		94	1.84
9	Campbell Nyakudya	Kyle	Masvingo		67	1.65
10	Angus Bruce	St George's	Harare		81	176
11	Brian Mhuriyengwe	Falcon	Esigodini		84	1.86
12	Mattthew Ushewokunze	Falcon	Esigodini		75	1.75
13	Tapiwa Mazorodze	St George's	Harare		84	1.81
14	Tawanda Ngosi	MCC	Gweru		79	1.83
15	Tarisai Mapfumo	St George's	Harare		70	1.69
16	Brian Muntanga	Falcon	Esigodini		84	1.71
17	Bradley Crause	St John's	Harare		92	1.83
18	Ackim Sibanda	Falcon	Esigodini		95	1.79
19	Muchineripi Mangenje	Prince Edward	Harare		98	1.89
20	Ngoni Zinyama	St George's	Harare		80	1.69
21	Shaun Snyder	Falcon	Esigodini		101	1.92
22	Dean Mcroberts	Peterhouse	Marondera		79	1.77

TEAM MANAGERS: Tunga Mashungu **COACHES:** Godwin Murambiwa, Brendon Brider

Miners strike gold in George

Impala provide timeous cheer for strike-torn Rustenburg

WHEN Rustenburg Impala appointed Hugh Reece-Edwards in late 2013, with the express purpose to win the ambitious club's first-ever national title, few thought that a soutie from Durban – even one who had played for South Africa and had coached at Vodacom Super Rugby level – was the right man for the job.

But they say that opposites attract, and Reece-Edwards, the flip-flop-wearing 53-year-old former Springbok fullback, proved this emphatically when Impala, in a nailbiting match played in pouring rain at Outeniqua Park in George, held off surprise finalists Roodepoort to lift the priceless Gold Cup.

The 13-11 victory could not have come at a better time for the North West miners, with the club and its players part of a Rustenburg community paralysed by a strike at the Lonmin mine that was to become the longest running in the country's history.

For Reece-Edwards, a man without airs or graces, the opportunity to coach Impala came about following a cleanout at the Sharks, which included the sacking of head coach John Plumtree and Reece-Edwards himself.

He spent his months in Rustenburg in a one-roomed flat, only occasionally travelling back and forth to the coast to see his family. The coach's attitude earned him respect from players and officials but also allowed him to live through an unprecedented period in the history of the club and the city.

"The players who are parents are telling me that only 20 percent of people at their school can afford their kids' fees," Reece-Edwards told this writer in Rustenburg, ahead of his team's pool match against Western Province's Hamiltons. "Guys are getting their cars repossessed. Go to the mall and it's deserted. Things are really, really bad."

Against this backdrop, it's astounding that Impala barely functioned at all, let alone won three of their four pool matches – the loss coming at home to Hammies – en route to the play-offs and claiming the biggest club prize of them all.

In the awful conditions that George seems to specialise in, both sides scored their only tries in the first half, with two penalties and a conversion from former Griquas and WP flyhalf Naas Olivier giving the Rustenburgers a 13-8 half-time lead.

Impala players celebrate their long-awaited national title after hanging on to beat Roodepoort.

Those 13 points proved however to be enough, with Roodepoort flyhalf Hennie Oosthuizen's 56th-minute penalty the only score of the second period for either side.

Roodepoort, who were also chasing history, having last won a national club title 25 years previously, hinted at something special in the quarter-finals when they knocked out defending champions Despatch.

The West Rand club might have won the final in the dying seconds when they were awarded a five-metre scrum with their pack in dominant form.

But Impala's defence held – just – and it was the miners who celebrated a famous victory.

POOL STAGES

The eight-team field for the George play-offs was only confirmed after a dramatic final round, which saw the identity of the final quarter-finalist only decided in the dying seconds of the 40th and final pool match.

The major shock was the elimination of 2013 bronze medallists and many people's pre-tournament favourites, Valke champions Brakpan, after they drew 32-all against Centurion – the Blue Bulls' representatives' second deadlock following their 26-all result against Roses United.

With both sides finishing on 15 log points, it was Centurion, coached by former Springbok prop Christo Bezuidenhout, who advanced on points difference.

And while it might have been the end of the road for the 12 non-qualifiers, a number of clubs took heart from their performances. Free State's top open club, Bloemfontein Crusaders, featuring brothers Griffin, Darren and Brandon Colby in their starting line-up, beat Welkom 62-22 to finish a creditable third in Pool B and 10th overall.

Griquas champions Sishen could also hold their heads high. The men from Kathu, under the guidance of amongst others former Springbok flyhalf Boeta Wessels, finished their campaign with a resounding 52-10 victory over Wesbank that saw them finish third in Pool D and 11th overall.

And at the New Brighton Oval, Spring Rose, who had played defending champions Despatch in the tournament's televised opening match, ended a disappointing campaign on a superb note when they overcame a 24-point deficit at half-time against Mossel Bay Barbarians to score 27 unanswered second-half points to run out 32-29 winners and so finish 12th overall.

• *In the final day's other matches, tournament debutantes and the country's oldest club, Hamiltons, registered a 27-18 victory against 2013 runners-up College Rovers in light rain to finish in third place, and in the dry matches GAP Management Despatch thumped Roses United 57-21 for their fifth-place finish while Refreshhh! Centurion beat Kempston Old Selbornians 42-14 to finish seventh.*

AFRICA CUP

NOT satisfied with their Community Cup title, Impala won their maiden international tournament in style when they beat Nigeria 86-10 at the Botswana National Stadium in Gaborone in June to cap off an unbeaten Africa Cup 1C campaign.

Impala, who were invited by the Confederation of African Rugby to represent South Africa at the IRB-sanctioned tournament that also featured hosts Botswana, Mauritius, Swaziland and Zambia, finished top of the six-team log with a full house of 15 points.

The miners, without Reece-Edwards – he had accepted an offer to coach in Japan after the Community Cup – opened their campaign with a 61-17 win over Mauritius on the opening day and followed it up with a 54-9 victory over their hosts in their second match.

Mauritius and Botswana both finished the tournament on 10 points, but thanks to a better points difference it is the Indian Ocean islanders who will be promoted to the 1B group for the next cycle of African Rugby World Cup qualifying, where they will meet, amongst others, Senegal and Ivory Coast.

"Impala were great ambassadors for South African rugby and it was wonderful to see our club players being given a chance to test themselves against international opposition," said SARU CEO, Jurie Roux. "I think this would also have helped those African countries they played against, as they will now go back home and identify ways to improve.

"South Africa has a duty to help raise the level of rugby across the continent and perhaps in years to come we might look back on Impala's involvement in Gaborone as the start of something positive."

FULL RESULTS
15 JUNE:
Rustenburg Impala 61-17 Mauritius, Botswana 87-0 Swaziland, Nigeria 20-30 Zambia
18 JUNE:
Botswana 9-54 Rustenburg Impala, Nigeria 61-10 Swaziland, Zambia 17-54 Mauritius
21 JUNE:
Rustenburg Impala 86-10 Nigeria, Botswana 66-14 Zambia, Mauritius 134-0 Swaziland

Cell C Community Cup

LOG

Pool A	P	W	L	D	PF	PA	PD	TF	TA	LB	TB	Pts
Despatch	4	4	0	0	147	34	113	20	3	0	3	19
Old Selbornians	4	3	1	0	109	84	25	13	11	0	2	14
Spring Rose	4	2	2	0	77	90	-13	9	11	1	1	10
Barbarians	4	1	3	0	86	106	-20	12	15	1	2	7
Bridgton	4	0	4	0	44	149	-105	6	20	1	0	1

Pool B	P	W	L	D	PF	PA	PD	TF	TA	LB	TB	Pts
College Rovers	4	4	0	0	230	48	182	35	6	0	4	20
Roodepoort	4	3	1	0	151	89	62	18	11	0	1	13
Bfn Crusaders	4	2	2	0	122	140	-18	17	20	1	2	11
Rovers	4	1	3	0	106	108	-2	15	12	1	2	7
Welkom	4	0	4	0	38	262	-224	4	40	0	0	0

Pool C	P	W	L	D	PF	PA	PD	TF	TA	LB	TB	Pts
Roses United	4	3	0	1	161	109	52	22	14	0	4	18
Centurion	4	2	0	2	162	100	62	18	14	0	3	15
Brakpan	4	2	1	1	141	104	37	19	11	1	4	15
Boksburg	4	1	3	0	121	169	-48	14	20	0	2	6
Noordelikes	4	0	4	0	78	181	-103	9	23	0	0	0

Pool D	P	W	L	D	PF	PA	PD	TF	TA	LB	TB	Pts
Hamiltons	4	4	0	0	198	61	137	28	8	0	4	20
Impala	4	3	1	0	148	84	64	21	9	0	4	16
Sishen	4	2	2	0	113	116	-3	15	16	0	2	10
Ferros	4	1	3	0	91	162	-71	11	24	1	1	6
Wesbank	4	0	4	0	49	176	-127	8	26	0	1	1

LEADING SCORERS

50 POINTS OR MORE

	TEAM	T	C	P	DG	Pts
Monty Dumond	Despatch	5	26	10	0	107
Shane Vallender	Hamiltons	0	22	14	1	89
Steven Moir	Centurion	1	23	10	0	81
Ryan Julies	Roses United	0	22	5	2	65
Jors Dannhauser	College Rovers	1	25	3	0	64
Naas Olivier	Rustenburg Impala	1	20	6	0	63
Hennie Oosthuizen	Roodepoort	0	10	1	0	56
Ashley Buchler	Boksburg	0	12	9	0	51
Elcardo Mintoor	Despatch	10	0	0	0	50

5 TRIES OR MORE

Elcardo Mintoor (Despatch)	10	Monty Dumond (Despatch)	5
Earl Lewis (Rustenburg Impala)	7	Jan du Plessis (Hamiltons)	5
Jaun Shaw (Roodepoort)	7	Jesse Geyer (Roodepoort)	5
Wikus van der Berg (Brakpan)	7	Tommy Damba (Brakpan)	5
Shaun Nieuwenhuyzen (Rovers)	6	Quinton Crocker (College Rovers)	5
Brendon April (Roses United)	6	Shannon Rick (College Rovers)	5
Christiaan Burger (Centurion)	6	Tiaan Ramat (Roses United)	5
Jean Pretorius (College Rovers)	6		

EASTER PLAY-OFFS - GEORGE

Thursday, 17 April:
Roodepoort beat Despatch 26-20
College Rovers beat Old Selbornians 36-13
Rustenburg Impala beat Roses United 66-13
Hamiltons beat Centurion 40-10

Saturday, 19 April:
Roses United beat Old Selbornians 39-31
Despatch beat Centurion 23-21
Rustenburg Impala beat College Rovers 32-13
Roodepoort beat Hamiltons 20-18

Monday, 21 April:
Centurion beat Old Selbornians 42-14
Despatch beat Roses United 57-21
Hamiltons beat College Rovers 27-18

Rustenburg Impala beat **Roodepoort 13-11** (FINAL)
Rustenburg Impala 13 *(Try: Du Plessis. Conversion: Olivier. Penalties: Olivier, De Wet)*
Roodepoort 11 *(Try: Shaw. Penalties: Oosthuizen 2)*
RUSTENBURG IMPALA: Wilco de wet, Earl Lewis, Dumisani Matyeshane, Mzivukile Duma, Michael Nienaber, Naas Olivier *(Morne Jooste, 41)*, Leon du Plessis *(Nelis Nel, 75)*, Wendal Wehr, Victor Joubert *(capt)*, Tiaan Nel, Hendrik Huyser *(Morne Basson, 69)*, Zander de Kock, Gavin Williamson *(Giovani Fourie, 66)*, Louis Hollamby. UNUSED SUBS: Paul Groenewald, Jermaine Apollis, Linton Terblanche, Rynhardt Steenkamp.
ROODEPOORT: Chanley Williams, Lesego Malau, Jesse Geyer, Byron Godfrey, Leander Rademeyer, Hennie Oosthuizen, Andre Esterhuizen, Gerhard Scholtz *(capt)*, Junior Gray, Jaun Shaw, Gareth Hemingway *(Ronald Goodman, 63)*, Nicky Cronje, Jaco Vermeulen, Thys de Villiers, Mauritz van Rooyen. UNUSED SUBS: Gabriel Grobler, Mike Vermeulen, Zuki Japhta, Shane Agrella, Andre Botha, Ruan Basson, Johan Prins.

CELL C COMMUNITY CUP - POOL A

Despatch

Played	Won	Lost	Drawn	Points for	Points against	Tries for	Tries against
7	6	1	0	247	102	33	12

Date	Venue	Opponent	Result	Score	Referees	Scorers
8 Mar	WJ de Wet Stadium, Despatch	Spring Rose	WON	24-6	Christie du Preez	T: Mintoor, Bekker. C: Dumond. P: Dumond (4).
15 Mar	Bridgton Sports Ground, Oudtshoorn	Bridgton	WON	54-7	Ruhan Meiring	T: McBean (3), Dyer, Mintoor, Ligman, Dumond, Van Tonder. C: Dumond (7).
22 Mar	WJ de Wet Stadium, Despatch	Barbarians	WON	31-5	Lusanda Jam	T: De Doncker, Dumond, Erasmus, Deyzel. C: Dumond (4). P: Dumond.
5 Apr	Kempston Park, East London	Old Selbornians	WON	38-16	Daniel Fortuin	T: Mintoor (4), Slabbert, Dumond. C: Dumond (4).

QUARTER FINAL 1

Date	Venue	Opponent	Result	Score	Referees	Scorers
17 Apr	Outeniqua Park, George	Roodepoort	LOST	20-26	Juan Sylvestre	T: Russel, Dumond. C: Dumond (2). P: Dumond (2).

LOSERS MATCH 2

Date	Venue	Opponent	Result	Score	Referees	Scorers
19 Apr	Outeniqua Park, George	Centurion	WON	23-21	Cwengile Jadezweni	T: Van Tonder, Dyer, Mintoor. C: Dumond. P: Dumond (2).

PLAY-OFF 5TH/6TH

Date	Venue	Opponent	Result	Score	Referees	Scorers
21 Apr	Outeniqua Park, George	Roses United	WON	57-21	Rametsi Oregopotse	T: Mintoor (3), Deyzel, Ligman, Luiters, Van Tonder, Dumond. C: Dumond (7). P: Dumond.

❰ DID YOU KNOW? ❱

The fastest Springbok Test try hat-trick was scored in just seven minutes by Pieter Rossouw during their record 96-13 demolition of Wales at Loftus Versfeld in June 1998, in the 39th, 42nd and 46th minute.

CELL C COMMUNITY CUP - POOL A

2014 APPEARANCES & POINTS

PLAYER	Spring Rose	Bridgton	Barbarians	Old Selbornians	Roodepoort	Centurion	Roses Utd	Apps	T	C	P	DG	Pts	Career Apps
Ryan Brown	15	–	–	–	–	–	–	1	–	–	–	–	0	8
Billy Mintoor	14	14	14	14	14	14R	14	7	10	–	–	–	50	14
Jaco Bekker	13	13	13	13	13	13	13	7	1	–	–	–	5	11
Basil de Doncker	12	–	12	12	12	12	12	6	1	–	–	–	5	13
Baldwin McBean	11	11	11	15	15	11	15	7	3	–	–	–	15	14
Monty Dumond	10	10	10	10	10	10	10	7	5	26	10	–	107	13
Marlon Lewis	9	9	9	9	9	9R	9R	7	–	–	–	–	0	14
Jaco Swanepoel	8	8	8	8	8	8	8	7	–	–	–	–	0	14
Michael Vermaak	7	7	7	4	4	–	–	5	–	–	–	–	0	5
Elroy Ligman	6c	6c	6c	7c	7c	6c	6c	7	2	–	–	–	10	14
Stephan Deyzel	5	5	5	4R	5R	7	7	7	2	–	–	–	10	7
Trichardt van Tonder	4	4	–	5	5	5	5	6	3	–	–	–	15	13
Ayanda Nogampula	3	3R	1R	3	3	1R	1R	7	–	–	–	–	0	14
Bobby Dyer	2	2	2	2R	2	2	2	7	2	–	–	–	10	14
Dylan Lamprecht	1	1R	–	1	1	3	3	6	–	–	–	–	0	12
Robert Slabbert	2R	–	2R	2	x	2R	2R	5	1	–	–	–	5	5
Kobus vd Westhuizen	3R	–	–	–	x	x	3R	2	–	–	–	–	0	2
Michael Ferreira	7R	–	–	–	–	–	–	1	–	–	–	–	0	1
Renier Erasmus	8R	7R	8R	6	6	–	–	5	1	–	–	–	5	5
Ashley Viviers	5R	4R	4	6R	6R	5R	4R	7	–	–	–	–	0	14
Lesley Luiters	9R	15R	9R	–	9R	9	9	6	1	–	–	–	5	6
Francois Nel	12R	12R	15	–	x	x	12R	4	–	–	–	–	0	4
Virgil Russel	–	15	–	11R	14R	15	–	4	1	–	–	–	5	5
Rossouw Prinsloo	–	12	–	–	–	–	–	1	–	–	–	–	0	7
Pierre Bouwer	–	3	3	–	–	–	–	2	–	–	–	–	0	2
Dewald Barnard	–	1	1	3R	1R	1	1	6	–	–	–	–	0	13
Marius Oosthuizen	–	8R	–	–	–	–	–	1	–	–	–	–	0	1
Darren van Winkel	–	–	7R	–	–	6R	5R	3	–	–	–	–	0	7
Deon Booysen	–	–	15R	9R	–	–	11R	3	–	–	–	–	0	5
Maijavi Kapara	–	–	14R	11	11	14	11	5	–	–	–	–	0	5
Sinjin Greyvenstein	–	–	–	5R	–	4	4	3	–	–	–	–	0	3
31 Players								152	33	26	10	0	247	265

CELL C COMMUNITY CUP - POOL A

Old Selbornians

Played	Won	Lost	Drawn	Points for	Points against	Tries for	Tries against
7	3	4	0	167	201	20	27

Date	Venue	Opponent	Result	Score	Referees	Scorers
15 Mar	New Brighton Oval, Epakeni, PE	Spring Rose	WON	20–19	Cwengile Jadezweni	T: Shone, Alberts, Amui. C: Shone. P: Shone.
22 Mar	Kempston Park, East London	Bridgton	WON	43–7	Archie Sehlako	T: Birkholtz (2), Gombert (2), Kleinhans. C: Shone (3). P: Shone (4).
29 Mar	D'Almeida Stadium, Mossel Bay	Barbarians	WON	30–20	Renier Vermeulen	T: Birkholtz, Gulwa, Smith, Tyokowana. C: Rielly (2). P: Rielly (2).
5 Apr	Kempston Park, East London	Despatch	LOST	16–38	Daniel Fortuin	T: Le Marquand. C: Rielly. P: Rielly (3).
QUARTER-FINAL 2						
17 Apr	Outeniqua Park, George	College Rovers	LOST	13–36	Federico Anselmi	T: Hammond, Pieterse. P: Shone.
LOSERS' MATCH 1						
19 Apr	Outeniqua Park, George	Roses United	LOST	31–39	Federico Anselmi	T: Kleinhans (2), Van Coller, Hammond. C: Shone (3), Kleinhans. P: Kleinhans.
PLAY-OFF 7TH/8TH						
21 Apr	Outeniqua Park, George	Centurion	LOST	14–42	Tahla Ntshakaza	T: Green. P: Shone (2), Rielly.

⟨ DID YOU KNOW? ⟩
Danie Gerber scored the fastest hat-trick from the start of a Test after scoring his third try against England in 1984 after just 32 minutes.

CELL C COMMUNITY CUP - POOL A

2014 APPEARANCES & POINTS

PLAYER	Spring Rose	Bridgton	Barbarians	Despatch	College Rovers	Roses Utd	Centurion	Apps	T	C	P	DG	Pts	Career Apps
Warren Rielly	15	15	15	15	15	–	15	6	–	3	6	–	24	6
Lindani Gulwa	14	–	14	14	–	14	13R	5	1	–	–	–	5	7
André van Niekerk	13	12	12	12	13	–	–	5	–	–	–	–	0	5
MJ le Marquand	12	10	10	10	12	12R	12	7	1	–	–	–	5	11
Michael Amui	11	11	–	–	–	–	14R	3	1	–	–	–	5	3
Jack van Coller	10	13	–	14R	13R	13	13	6	1	–	–	–	5	6
Craig Shone	9	9	–	–	9	9	9	5	1	7	8	–	43	9
Craig Green	8	6	7	7	x	8	8	6	1	–	–	–	5	10
Duran Alberts	7c	7c	4c	4c	4c	5R	–	6	1	–	–	–	5	10
Peter Smith	6	–	6	6	6	6	6	6	1	–	–	–	5	10
Alister Keet	5	–	5	5	5	4R	5	6	–	–	–	–	0	6
Richard Osner	4	4	5R	5R	–	4	5R	6	–	–	–	–	0	6
Ryan Pietersen	3	3	3R	3R	3R	3	3R	7	1	–	–	–	5	11
Ludwe Booi	2	2	2	2	2	1R	2	7	–	–	–	–	0	11
Smash Tyokolwana	1	1	3	–	3	3R	3	6	1	–	–	–	5	6
Craig Pederson	1R	–	–	–	–	–	–	1	–	–	–	–	0	4
Manelisi Tyala	x	–	–	–	–	–	2R	1	–	–	–	–	0	1
Craig Gombert	8R	5	6R	–	2R	5	4	6	2	–	–	–	10	6
Roy Bursey	4R	8	8	8	8	7R	–	6	–	–	–	–	0	6
Wade Bailey	14R	9R	–	–	10R	12	9R	5	–	–	–	–	0	8
Felix Godlo	10R	13R	–	–	–	–	–	2	–	–	–	–	0	5
Gareth Catherine	x	–	x	–	–	–	–	0	–	–	–	–	0	1
Bradley Birkholtz	–	14	11	11	11	11	11	6	3	–	–	–	15	6
Curtis Kleinhans	–	11R	13	13	10	10	10	6	3	1	1	–	20	9
Dylan Pieterse	–	1R	1	1	1	2c	1c	6	–	–	–	–	0	10
Delarey du Preez	–	2R	–	3	–	–	–	2	–	–	–	–	0	2
JP Opperman	–	4R	–	–	–	–	–	1	–	–	–	–	0	1
Paul Warner	–	–	9	9	9R	15	–	4	–	–	–	–	0	8
Codey Basson	–	–	8R	7R	5R	7	6R	5	–	–	–	–	0	5
Dylan Swartz	–	–	14R	15R	14	8R	14	5	–	–	–	–	0	5
Akona Makalima	–	3R	x	2R	1R	1	19R	5	–	–	–	–	0	5
Marc Hammond	–	–	–	6R	7	19R	7	4	2	–	–	–	10	6
32 Players								**152**	**20**	**11**	**15**	**0**	**167**	**205**

CELL C COMMUNITY CUP - POOL A

Spring Rose

Played	Won	Lost	Drawn	Points for	Points against	Tries for	Tries against
4	2	2	0	77	90	9	11

Date	Venue	Opponent	Result	Score	Referees	Scorers
8 Mar	WJ de Wet Stadium, Despatch	Despatch	LOST	6-24	Christie du Preez	P: Meki (2).
15 Mar	New Brighton Oval, Epakeni, PE	Old Selbornian	LOST	19-20	Cwengile Jadezweni	T: Moyake, Makwabe. P: Meki (3).
29 Mar	Bridgton Sports Grounds, Oudtshoorn	Bridgton	WON	20-17	Lusanda Jam	T: Ngqolombe, Makwaba. C: Tom (2). P: Tom (2).
5 Apr	New Brighton Oval, Epakeni, PE	Barbarians	WON	32-29	Christie du Preez	T: Mtaba (2), Tsotsobe, Moyake, Faba. C: Meki (2). P: Tom.

⟨ DID YOU KNOW? ⟩

George Daneel is the only Test-playing Springbok to have reached a 100th birthday. He played eight Tests from 1928-32. He was a Dutch Reformed Church minister and was chief chaplain to the South African forces during WWII.

CELL C COMMUNITY CUP - POOL A

2014 APPEARANCES & POINTS

PLAYER	Despatch	Old Selb.	Bridgton	Barbarians	Apps	T	C	P	DG	Pts	Career Apps
Langa Tsotsobe	15	–	13R	14	3	1	–	–	–	5	3
Gugu Makwabe	14	14	14	13	4	1	–	–	–	5	4
Luvuyo Mhlobiso	13	12	–	–	2	–	–	–	–	0	2
Mteteleli Stick	12	13	10	10R	4	–	–	–	–	0	4
Siviwe Moyake	11	11	11	11	4	3	–	–	–	15	4
Thulani Meki	10	10	12	12	4	–	2	5	–	19	4
Pumlani Mnikina	9	9	9R	9	4	–	–	–	–	0	4
Lusindiso Meleni	8	8	8	8	4	–	–	–	–	0	4
Bongani Ngqolombe	7	5R	5	–	3	1	–	–	–	5	3
Lizwi Maxela	6	7	6	–	3	–	–	–	–	0	3
Africa Rala	5	5	x	5	3	–	–	–	–	0	3
Thembekile Mtaba	4	4	4	4	4	2	–	–	–	10	4
Zolani Faba	3	3	1	3	4	1	–	–	–	5	4
Lubabalo Mpongoshe	2c	2c	2c	6c	4	–	–	–	–	0	4
Luthando Menze	1	1	3	–	3	–	–	–	–	0	3
Thulani Jacobs	2R	1R	6R	2	4	–	–	–	–	0	4
Sonwabile Ntezo	1R	–	3R	1	3	–	–	–	–	0	3
Lonwabo Zonke	x	4R	7R	7	3	–	–	–	–	0	3
Simphiwe January	5R	6	7	–	3	–	–	–	–	0	3
Sidima Kondile	9R	–	9	x	2	–	–	–	–	0	2
Pumezo Tom	15R	15	15	15	4	–	2	3	–	13	4
Brian Louw	x	–	–	14R	1	–	–	–	–	0	1
Mziwamadoda Yako	–	2R	–	x	1	–	–	–	–	0	1
Lulama Mkwakwi	–	15R	13	–	2	–	–	–	–	0	2
Mzwandile Makhunga	–	9R	–	–	1	–	–	–	–	0	1
Luthando Foster	–	x	x	10	1	–	–	–	–	0	1
Andile Faku	–	–	–	7R	1	–	–	–	–	0	1
Unathi Lubambo	–	–	–	x	0	–	–	–	–	0	0
Phumlani Blaauw	–	–	–	x	0	–	–	–	–	0	0
29 Players					**79**	**9**	**4**	**8**	**0**	**77**	**79**

CELL C COMMUNITY CUP - POOL A

Mossel Bay Barbarians

Played	Won	Lost	Drawn	Points for	Points against	Tries for	Tries against
4	1	3	0	86	106	12	15

Date	Venue	Opponent	Result	Score	Referees	Scorers
8 Mar	D'Almeida Stadium, Mossel Bay	Bridgton	WON	32-13	Ruhan Meiring	T: Fillies, Erasmus, Arendse, Hendricks, Antony. C: Buis (2). P: Buis.
22 Mar	WJ de Wet Stadium, Despatch	Despatch	LOST	5-31	Lusanda Jam	T: Fillies.
29 Mar	D'Almeida Stadium, Mossel Bay	Old Selbornian	LOST	20-30	Renier Vermeulen	T: Fillies, Buys. C: Buys (2). P: Buys (2).
5 Apr	New Brighton Oval, Epakeni, PE	Spring Rose	LOST	29-32	Christie du Preez	T: Fillies, Treurnicht, Arendse, Hendricks. C: Buys (3). P: Buys.

‹ DID YOU KNOW? ›

The Springboks' worst losing run is seven Tests, beginning with the loss to France in Springs in July 1964 and ending with their 19-16 victory over New Zealand in the 3rd Test at Christchurch on 4 September 1965.

CELL C COMMUNITY CUP - POOL A

2014 APPEARANCES & POINTS

PLAYER	Bridgton	Despatch	Old Selbornians	Spring Rose	Apps	T	C	P	DG	Pts	Career Apps
Wahlon Antony	15	15	15	15	4	1	–	–	–	5	4
Jerome Fillies	14	14	14	14	4	4	–	–	–	20	4
Anwar Fillis	13	13	12R	13	4	–	–	–	–	0	4
Leslie London	12	12	12	13R	4	–	–	–	–	0	4
Logan Hendricks	11	11	11	11	4	2	–	–	–	10	4
Francois Smith	10	–	10	10	3	–	–	–	–	0	3
Morné Buis	9	9	9	9	4	1	7	4	–	31	4
Winston Seconds	8	8	8	–	3	–	–	–	–	0	3
Fernando Fourie	7	7	7	–	3	–	–	–	–	0	3
Morné Kannemeyer	6	7R	–	7	3	–	–	–	–	0	3
Lance Andrews	5	4R	5	4	4	–	–	–	–	0	4
Kosie Jackson	4	5	4	6	4	1	–	–	–	5	4
Alvizo Erasmus	3	–	3	3	3	1	–	–	–	5	3
Raimothy du Preez	2c	2c	2c	2c	4	–	–	–	–	0	4
Cardio Jones	1	3	x	1R	3	–	–	–	–	0	3
Anthony Scheepers	2R	3R	x	4R	3	–	–	–	–	0	3
Alistair Thyssen	1R	1	–	–	2	–	–	–	–	0	2
Carlo Klaasen	3R	4	6R	5	4	–	–	–	–	0	4
Isaac Treurnicht	6R	6	6	8	4	–	–	–	–	0	4
Macdelin Saayman	10R	10	x	–	2	–	–	–	–	0	2
Jaco Arendse	13R	13R	13	12	4	2	–	–	–	10	4
Clint Miller	11R	14R	–	–	2	–	–	–	–	0	2
Dayle Brandt	–	1R	1	1	3	–	–	–	–	0	3
Curshwon Mono	–	11R	x	15R	2	–	–	–	–	0	2
Daniel Papah	–	–	1R	18R	2	–	–	–	–	0	2
Chestlon Palmer	–	–	–	x	0	–	–	–	–	0	0
Shaun London	–	–	–	x	0	–	–	–	–	0	0
27 Players					**82**	**12**	**7**	**4**	**0**	**86**	**82**

CELL C COMMUNITY CUP - POOL A

Bridgton

Played	Won	Lost	Drawn	Points for	Points against	Tries for	Tries against
4	0	4	0	44	149	6	20

Date	Venue	Opponent	Result	Score	Referees	Scorers
8 Mar	D'Almeida Stadium, Mossel Bay	Barbarians	LOST	13-32	Ruhan Meiring	T: Erasmus, Malgas. P: Booysen.
15 Mar	Bridgton Sports Grounds, Oudtshoorn	Despatch	LOST	7-54	Ruhan Meiring	T: Waarts. C: Booysen.
22 Mar	Kempston Park, East London	Old Selbornians	LOST	7-43	Archie Sehlako	T: G September. C: Booysen.
29 Mar	Bridgton Sports Grounds, Oudtshoorn	Spring Rose	LOST	17-20	Lusanda Jam	T: Arries, Plaatjies. C: Booysen (2). P: Booysen.

‹ DID YOU KNOW? ›

All three flyhalves on the 1956 Springbok tour to Australia and New Zealand were provincial cricketers:
Clive Ulyate for Eastern Province and Transvaal, Brian Pfaff for Western Province and PeeWee Howe for Border.

CELL C COMMUNITY CUP - POOL A

2014 APPEARANCES & POINTS

PLAYER	Barbarians	Despatch	Old-Selbornians	Spring Rose	Apps	T	C	P	DG	Pts	Career Apps
Warren Malgas	15	9R	9	11R	4	–	–	–	–	0	4
Frelimo September	14	14	11	11	4	–	–	–	–	0	4
Rhupino Plaatjies	13	12R	13	12	4	1	–	–	–	5	4
André Fielies	12	11R	12	x	3	–	–	–	–	0	3
Charlie Ewerts	11	11	–	–	2	–	–	–	–	0	2
Adriaan Booysen	10	13	15	10	4	1	4	2	–	19	4
Grahame September	9	9	9R	9	4	1	–	–	–	5	4
Algernon Waarts	8c	8c	8c	8c	4	1	–	–	–	5	4
David Goliaths	7	–	–	–	1	–	–	–	–	0	1
Ronald Bratz	6	6	6	6	4	–	–	–	–	0	4
Ruahl Lewis	5	–	5	5	3	–	–	–	–	0	3
Jan Simmers	4	4	4R	4	4	–	–	–	–	0	4
Wesley le Roux	3	3	3	3	4	–	–	–	–	0	4
Cheslyn September	2	3R	3R	3R	4	–	–	–	–	0	4
Enzo Erasmus	1	1	–	1	3	1	–	–	–	5	3
Regan Behrends	2R	2	2	2	4	–	–	–	–	0	4
Samuel Mokhehle	x	1R	1	2R	3	–	–	–	–	0	3
Ricardo Davids	4R	4R	–	–	2	–	–	–	–	0	2
Monde Stofile	7R	5R	4	4R	4	–	–	–	–	0	4
Roderick January	x	–	12R	–	1	–	–	–	–	0	1
Hadley Arries	13R	15	14	15	4	1	–	–	–	5	4
Joseph Saptou	12R	10	10	x	3	–	–	–	–	0	3
Lionel Prinsloo	–	12	–	13	2	–	–	–	–	0	2
Wayne Julies	–	7	7	7	3	–	–	–	–	0	3
Jaco Manewil	–	5	–	–	1	–	–	–	–	0	1
Jolin Saptou	–	–	5R	5R	2	–	–	–	–	0	2
Leroi Nimrod	–	–	11R	14	2	–	–	–	–	0	2
Ashley Loff	–	–	2R	–	1	–	–	–	–	0	1
28 Players					**84**	**6**	**4**	**2**	**0**	**44**	**84**

CELL C COMMUNITY CUP - POOL B

College Rovers

Played	Won	Lost	Drawn	Points for	Points against	Tries for	Tries against
7	5	2	0	297	120	43	15

Date	Venue	Opponent	Result	Score	Referees	Scorers
8 Mar	KP3, Kings Park, Durban	Welkom	WON	85-0	Blake Beattie	T: Rick (3), Wilkinson (2), Crocker (2), Micklewood, Pretorius, Dannhauser, Adam, Blignaut, Venter. C: Micklewood (5), Dannhauser (5).
22 Mar	Clive Solomon Stadium, Heidedal	Crusaders	WON	78-14	Jaco Kotzé	T: Noble (3), Pretorius (2), Chiocchetti, Small, Mkize, Crocker, Rick, Randall, Twine. C: Dannhauser (9).
29 Mar	Rand Leases Sports Ground, Roodepoort	Roodepoort	WON	41-20	Jan Venter	T: Nokwe (2), Noble, Twine, Phillips, Micklewood. C: Dannhauser (3), Micklewood. P: Dannhauser.
5 Apr	KP3, Kings Park, Durban	Rovers	WON	26-14	Archie Sehlako	T: Nokwe, Wilkinson, Jones, Strydom. C: Dannhauser (3).
QUARTER-FINAL 2						
17 Apr	Outeniqua Park, George	Old Selbornians	WON	36-13	Federico Anselmi	T: Pretorius (3), Bester, Rick. C: Dannhauser (4). P: Small.
SEMI-FINAL 1						
19 Apr	Outeniqua Park, George	Impala	LOST	13-32	Quinton Immelman	T: Crocker. C: Dannhauser. P: Dannhauser (2).
PLAY-OFF 3RD/4TH						
21 Apr	Outeniqua Park, George	Hamiltons	LOST	18-27	Juan Sylvestre	T: Venter, Crocker. C: Micklewood. P: Micklewood (2).

〈 DID YOU KNOW? 〉

Former Springbok No 8 and coach Nick Mallett was an Oxford University double blue for cricket and rugby.

CELL C COMMUNITY CUP - POOL B

2014 APPEARANCES & POINTS

PLAYER	Welkom	Crusaders	Roodepoort	W Rovers	Old Selbornians	Impala	Hamiltons	Apps	T	C	P	DG	Pts	Career Apps
Jors Dannhauser	15	15	15	15	15	15	15	7	1	25	3	–	64	14
Dusty Noble	14	14	14	–	14	14	14	6	4	–	–	–	20	6
Kyle Wilkinson	13	13	14R	13	13	13	11	7	3	–	–	–	15	10
Quinton Crocker	12	12	12	–	12	12	12	6	5	–	–	–	25	6
Jongi Nokwe	11	–	11	11	11	11	–	5	3	–	–	–	15	5
Chris Micklewood	10	–	10	10c	–	10	10	5	2	7	2	–	30	11
Shannon Rick	9	9	–	–	9	9	9R	5	5	–	–	–	25	5
Kelvin Adam	8	–	8	–	–	–	–	2	1	–	–	–	5	2
Liam O'Connell	7	7	7	–	–	–	–	3	–	–	–	–	0	3
Jean Pretorius	6	6	6	–	6	6	6	6	6	–	–	–	30	6
Nikolai Blignaut	5c	5c	5c	–	5c	5	5	6	1	–	–	–	5	13
Simba Bwanya	4	4	5R	4	4	4	4	7	–	–	–	–	0	12
Njabulo Mkize	3	3	–	3	3R	3	3R	6	1	–	–	–	5	6
Warrick Venter	2	2	2R	2R	2	2	2	7	2	–	–	–	10	7
Matthew Jones	1	1	–	1	1	1R	1	6	1	–	–	–	5	9
Duan Coertzen	2R	2R	2	–	2R	2R	2R	6	–	–	–	–	0	6
Luciano Santos	3R	3R	1R	3R	–	–	–	4	–	–	–	–	0	4
Edlyn Serge	4R	4R	4	–	5R	x	4R	5	–	–	–	–	0	5
Mesuli Mncwango	8R	8	–	6	6R	8R	8	6	–	–	–	–	0	6
Warren Randall	15R	9R	9	9	x	x	9	5	1	–	–	–	5	5
Jeandré Small	13R	10	13R	10R	10	x	13R	6	1	–	1	–	8	6
Kobus Lourens	14R	13R	15R	12	x	–	15R	5	–	–	–	–	0	5
Jared Chiocchetti	–	11	–	14	–	–	–	2	1	–	–	–	5	2
Matthew Phillips	–	12R	13	13R	12R	11R	13	6	1	–	–	–	5	6
Kirk Twine	–	6R	7R	8	8	8	6R	6	2	–	–	–	10	6
Louis Hazelhurst	–	–	–	7	–	–	–	1	–	–	–	–	0	1
Sanele Sibanda	–	–	–	5	–	–	–	1	–	–	–	–	0	1
Chris Kemp	–	–	–	2	–	–	–	1	–	–	–	–	0	8
Richard Strydom	–	–	–	14R	–	–	–	1	1	–	–	–	5	1
Jason Kankowski	–	–	–	6R	–	–	–	1	–	–	–	–	0	1
Paul Bester	–	–	–	7R	7	7	7	4	1	–	–	–	5	4
Sangoni Mxoli	–	–	3	–	3	x	3	3	–	–	–	–	0	8
Jarrett Crouch	–	–	1	–	1R	1	1R	4	–	–	–	–	0	4
33 Players								**151**	**43**	**32**	**6**	**0**	**297**	**194**

CELL C COMMUNITY CUP - POOL B

Roodepoort

Played	Won	Lost	Drawn	Points for	Points against	Tries for	Tries against
7	5	2	0	208	140	24	14

Date	Venue	Opponent	Result	Score	Referees	Scorers
8 Mar	Rand Leases Sports Ground, Roodepoort	Crusaders	WON	19-17	Renier Vermeulen	T: Williams, Geyer. P: Oosthuizen (3).
15 Mar	Griffons Stadium B-Field, Welkom	Welkom	WON	75-0	AJ Jacobs	T: Shaw (3), Malau (2), Williams, Scholtz, Geyer, Gray, Cronjé, De Villiers. C: Williams (5), Oosthuizen (5).
22 Mar	Rovers Rugby Club, Welkom	Rovers	WON	37-31	Enrico van Rooyen	T: Shaw (2), Geyer. C: Williams (2). P: Williams (5). DG: Esterhuizen.
29 Mar	Rand Leases Sports Ground, Roodepoort	College Rovers	LOST	20-41	Jan Venter	T: Esterhuizen, Geyer. C: Oosthuizen (2). P: Oosthuizen (2).
QUARTER-FINAL 1						
17 Apr	Outeniqua Park, George	Despatch	WON	26-20	Juan Sylvestre	T: Shaw, Malau, Vermeulen. C: Oosthuizen. P: Oosthuizen (3).
SEMI-FINAL 2						
19 Apr	Outeniqua Park, George	Hamiltons	WON	20-18	Oregopotse Rametsi	T: Scholtz, Geyer. C: Oosthuizen (2). P: Oosthuizen (2).
CUP FINAL						
21 Apr	Outeniqua Park, George	Impala	LOST	11-13	Quinton Immelman	T: Shaw. P: Oosthuizen (2).

⟨ DID YOU KNOW? ⟩

Four Springbok internationals have had four first names: Pieter Albertus Ryno Otto Nel; Noel Richard Frank George Howe-Brown; Willem Ferdinand van Rheede van Oudtshoorn Bergh; Arthur Frederick William Douglas Marsberg.

2014 APPEARANCES & POINTS

CELL C COMMUNITY CUP - POOL B

PLAYER	Crusaders	Welkom	W Rovers	Coll Rovers	Despatch	Hamiltons	Impala-Final	Apps	T	C	P	DG	Pts	Career Apps
Chanley Williams	15	15	10	15	15	15	15	7	2	7	5	–	39	14
Lesego Malau	14	14	14	14	14	14	14	7	3	–	–	–	15	14
Jesse Geyer	13	13	13	13	13	13	13	7	5	–	–	–	25	14
Byron Godfrey	12	12	12	–	12	12	12	6	–	–	–	–	0	13
Leander Rademeyer	11	11	11	11	11	11	11	7	–	–	–	–	0	14
Hennie Oosthuizen	10	10	–	10	10	10	10	6	–	10	12	–	56	12
André Esterhuizen	9	9	9	9	9	9	9	7	1	–	–	1	8	13
Gerhard Scholtz	8c	8c	8c	8c	8c	8c	8c	7	2	–	–	–	10	14
Junior Gray	7	7	7	7	7	7	7	7	1	–	–	–	5	13
Jaun Shaw	6	6	6	6	6	6	6	7	7	–	–	–	35	10
Gareth Hemingway	5	–	5	5	5	5	5	6	–	–	–	–	0	10
Nicky Cronjé	4	4	4	4	4	4	4	7	1	–	–	–	5	14
Jaco Vermeulen	3	3	3	3	3	3	3	7	1	–	–	–	5	13
Thys de Villiers	2	2	2	2	2	2	2	7	1	–	–	–	5	14
Mauritz van Rooyen	1	1	–	1	1	1	1	6	–	–	–	–	0	11
Gabriel Grobler	2R	2R	x	2R	6R	–	x	4	–	–	–	–	0	4
Mike Vermeulen	1R	1R	1	x	1R	6R	x	5	–	–	–	–	0	5
Ronnie Goodman	6R	5	–	6R	5R	5R	5R	6	–	–	–	–	0	6
Zukisa Japhtha	x	4R	x	–	x	x	x	1	–	–	–	–	0	1
Jarryd Hettema	x	–	9R	–	–	–	–	1	–	–	–	–	0	1
Ruan Basson	x	11R	15R	12	14R	–	x	4	–	–	–	–	0	4
André Botha	x	10R	15	14R	x	x	x	3	–	–	–	–	0	3
Wi-André Erasmus	–	6R	x	–	–	6R	x	2	–	–	–	–	0	2
Shane Agrella	–	9R	x	9R	x	x	x	2	–	–	–	–	0	2
Johan Prins	–	–	1R	1R	2R	3R	x	4	–	–	–	–	0	11
Liam MacKay	–	–	–	10R	–	x	–	1	–	–	–	–	0	1
26 Players								134	24	17	17	1	208	233

CELL C COMMUNITY CUP - POOL B

Bloemfontein Crusaders

Played	Won	Lost	Drawn	Points for	Points against	Tries for	Tries against
4	2	2	0	122	140	17	20

Date	Venue	Opponent	Result	Score	Referees	Scorers
8 Mar	Rand Leases Sports Ground, Roodepoort	Roodepoort	LOST	17-19	Renier Vermeulen	T: G Colby. P: Taljaard (3), B Colby.
15 Mar	Rovers Rugby Club, Welkom	Rovers	WON	29-21	Lebohang Raleteng	T: Viljoen, Taljaard, Job, Boucher. C: Taljaard (2), G Colby. DG: Job.
22 Mar	Clive Solomon Stadium, Heidedal	College Rovers	LOST	14-78	Jaco Kotzé	T: Job, Boucher. C: Taljaard (2).
5 Apr	Griffons Stadium B-Field, Welkom	Welkom	WON	62-22	AJ Jacobs	Boucher (2), Tsoeu (2), Viljoen (2), Manus, Ball, G Colby, Van Rooyen. C: G Colby (5), Taljaard.

⟨ DID YOU KNOW? ⟩

The oldest Springbok on debut is Deon Lötter on 3 July 1993 against France in Johannesburg, aged 36 years and 235 days.

CELL C COMMUNITY CUP – POOL B

APPEARANCES & POINTS

PLAYER	Roodepoort	W Rovers	Coll Rovers	Welkom	Apps	T	C	P	DG	Pts	Career Apps
Griffin Colby	15	15	–	15	3	2	6	–	–	22	7
Perry Appies	14	14	14R	6R	4	–	–	–	–	0	4
Phumzile Mafika	13	13	10R	13	4	–	–	–	–	0	4
Deon Taljaard	12	12	13	12	4	1	5	3	–	24	4
Brandon Colby	11	11	11	11	4	–	–	1	–	3	8
Isak Job	10	10	10	10	4	2	–	–	1	13	4
Blaine Tlhapane	9	12R	9R	14	4	–	–	–	–	0	7
Gustav Muller	8	8	–	–	2	–	–	–	–	0	6
Donavan Ball	7	7	7	7	4	1	–	–	–	5	8
Randall Nelson	6c	6c	6c	6c	4	–	–	–	–	0	7
Erick van Niekerk	5	5	5	–	3	–	–	–	–	0	3
Moises Mpande	4	4	4	4R	4	–	–	–	–	0	8
Corné Stemmet	3	–	–	3R	2	–	–	–	–	0	2
Don Marnus	2	3	2	2	4	1	–	–	–	5	4
Gavin Pitt	1	–	3	–	2	–	–	–	–	0	5
Arno Visagie	2R	2	–	5	2	–	–	–	–	0	2
Johannes van Niekerk	3R	1	1	3	4	–	–	–	–	0	4
Lebohang Tsoeu	5R	5R	4R	4	4	2	–	–	–	10	4
Daniel Viljoen	8R	4R	8	8	4	3	–	–	–	15	4
Darren Colby	9R	9	9	9	4	–	–	–	–	0	8
Jonathan Boucher	13R	13R	12	12R	4	4	–	–	–	20	8
Emmanuel Papgis	14R	–	–	–	1	–	–	–	–	0	1
Bjorn van Wyk	–	14R	14	11R	3	–	–	–	–	0	3
Mangaliso Matakane	–	x	1R	1	2	–	–	–	–	0	2
Lebogang Gabole	–	x	7R	2R	2	–	–	–	–	0	2
Franco van der Merwe	–	–	15	–	1	–	–	–	–	0	1
Lovelint Hgxabazi	–	–	2R	–	1	–	–	–	–	0	1
Jacques van Rooyen	–	–	–	13R	1	1	–	–	–	5	1
28 Players					85	17	11	4	1	122	122

CELL C COMMUNITY CUP - POOL B

Welkom Rovers

Played	Won	Lost	Drawn	Points for	Points against	Tries for	Tries against
4	1	3	0	106	108	15	12

Date	Venue	Opponent	Result	Score	Referees	Scorers
15 Mar	Rovers Rugby Club, Welkom	Crusaders	LOST	21-29	Lebohang Raleteng	T: S Nieuwenhuyzen (2), Van Tonder. P: S Nieuwenhuyzen (2).
22 Mar	Rovers Rugby Club, Welkom	Roodepoort	LOST	31-37	Enrico van Rooyen	T: S Nieuwenhuyzen, Strydom, Ntlantsana, Van Staden. C: Strydom (4). P: Strydom.
29 Mar	Rovers Rugby Club, Welkom	Welkom	WON	40-16	Oregopotse Rametsi	T: S Nieuwenhuyzen (2), Mateus, Van Tonder, Kekana, Mabomba. C: Strydom (5).
5 Apr	KP3, Kings Park, Durban	College Rovers	LOST	14-26	Archie Sehlako	T: S Nieuwenhuyzen, Kekana. C: Strydom (2).

❰ DID YOU KNOW? ❱

The least experienced Springbok bench was for the 1st Test vs the 1974 British Lions in Cape Town. Gerrie Germishuys, Gerald Bosch, Paul Bayvel, Rampie Stander, André Bestbier & Dugald MacDonald did not have a single cap between them!

CELL C COMMUNITY CUP - POOL B

2014 APPEARANCES & POINTS

PLAYER	Crusaders	Roodepoort	Welkom	Goll Rovers	Apps	T	C	P	DG	Pts	Career Apps
Willem van Vuuren	15	11R	15	15	4	–	–	–	–	0	8
Stephan Kekana	14	13	13	13	4	2	–	–	–	10	4
Shaun Nieuwenhuyzen	13	12	12	12	4	6	–	2	–	36	4
Wessel Pretorius	12	–	x	12R	2	–	–	–	–	0	4
Robbie Ntlantsana	11	11	11	11	4	1	–	–	–	5	4
Pieter Strydom	10	10	10	10	4	1	11	1	–	30	7
Jaco Pretorius	9	9	9	9	4	–	–	–	–	0	8
LC Lieb van Tonder	8c	8c	8c	8c	4	2	–	–	–	10	8
Wayne Ludick	7	7	7	7	4	1	–	–	–	5	8
Ivan de Klerk	6	6	6	6	4	–	–	–	–	0	8
Donavan Nieuwenhuyzen	5	5	5	5	4	–	–	–	–	0	4
Niekie Pretorius	4	–	–	–	1	–	–	–	–	0	5
Willem van Staden	3	3	3	3	4	–	–	–	–	0	4
Brummer Marais	2	2R	2	2	4	–	–	–	–	0	4
Johannes Barnard	1	1	1	1	4	–	–	–	–	0	4
Andries Kruger	2R	2	–	–	2	–	–	–	–	0	2
John Lonergan	1R	x	3R	1R	3	–	–	–	–	0	3
Jean-Jacques Muller	5R	3R	4R	–	3	–	–	–	–	0	7
Johnnie Fourie	7R	–	–	–	1	–	–	–	–	0	2
Thembelani Mabomba	12R	5R	5R	x	3	1	–	–	–	5	3
Frank Mateus	15R	x	2R	2R	3	1	–	–	–	5	3
Dillan Laurent	10R	14R	15R	14R	4	–	–	–	–	0	8
Ryno Venter	–	15	11R	x	2	–	–	–	–	0	4
Wynand Venter	–	14	14	14	3	–	–	–	–	0	5
Alex van Staden	–	4	4	4	3	–	–	–	–	0	7
Div Tertius de Villiers	–	–	–	5R	1	–	–	–	–	0	2
26 Players					**83**	**15**	**11**	**3**	**0**	**106**	**130**

CELL C COMMUNITY CUP - POOL B

Welkom

Played	Won	Lost	Drawn	Points for	Points against	Tries for	Tries against
4	0	4	0	38	262	4	40

Date	Venue	Opponent	Result	Score	Referees	Scorers
8 Mar	KP3, Kings Park, Durban	College Rovers	LOST	0-85	Blake Beattie	
15 Mar	Griffons Stadium B-Field, Welkom	Roodepoort	LOST	0-75	AJ Jacobs	
29 Mar	Rovers Rugby Club, Welkom	Rovers	LOST	16-40	Oregopotse Rametsi	T: Fullagar. C: Barnard. P: Till. DG: Barnard (2).
5 Apr	Griffons Stadium B-Field, Welkom	Crusaders	LOST	22-62	AJ Jacobs	T: Boshoff, Till, Davis. C: Till (2). DG: Barnard.

‹ DID YOU KNOW? ›

The most experienced Springbok bench was for the 2007 World Cup pool match vs Tonga in Lens. John Smit, BJ Botha, Victor Matfield, Juan Smith, Bryan Habana, Francois Steyn & Percy Montgomery boasted 311 Test caps between them!

CELL C COMMUNITY CUP - POOL B

2014 APPEARANCES & POINTS

PLAYER	College Rovers	Roodepoort Rovers	Rovers	Crusaders	Apps	T	C	P	DG	Pts	Career Apps
Malcolm-Kerr Till	15	15	15	15	4	1	2	1	–	12	4
Patrick Kampher	14	14	14	14	4	–	–	–	–	0	4
Neill Fullagar	13	x	12	x	2	1	–	–	–	5	2
Freddie Wepener	12	13	13	13	4	–	–	–	–	0	4
Bongi Qabathe	11	11	–	–	2	–	–	–	–	0	2
Heinrich Bronkhorst	10	11R	–	–	2	–	–	–	–	0	2
Dwayne Burger	9	9	9	9	4	–	–	–	–	0	4
Hendrik Venter	8	8	8	8	4	–	–	–	–	0	4
Werner Jonker	7	7	7	4	4	–	–	–	–	0	4
Christiaan Pelser	6	6	6	6	4	–	–	–	–	0	4
Egmond de Villiers	5	5	–	–	2	–	–	–	–	0	2
Shaun Botha	4	4	–	–	2	–	–	–	–	0	2
Sarel Louw	3c	3c	3c	3c	4	–	–	–	–	0	4
Gerhard van der Merwe	2	2	–	4R	3	–	–	–	–	0	3
Kobus Kalp	1	1	2R	x	3	–	–	–	–	0	3
Quintin Davis	2R	2R	2	2	4	1	–	–	–	5	6
André van Zyl	x	–	–	–	0	–	–	–	–	0	0
Charles Barnard	7R	7R	4	–	3	–	–	–	–	0	3
Jacee Cloete	4R	5R	5	5	4	–	–	–	–	0	4
Juan Davis	11R	–	11R	x	2	–	–	–	–	0	4
Lesley Abrahams	x	–	–	–	0	–	–	–	–	0	0
Walter Magadlela	14R	4R	11	11	4	–	–	–	–	0	4
Michael Pienaar	–	12	12R	12R	3	–	–	–	–	0	3
Heinrich Barnard	–	10	10	10	3	–	1	–	3	11	3
David Wiid	–	x	1R	1R	2	–	–	–	–	0	2
Jobrey Fortuin	–	–	14R	12	2	–	–	–	–	0	2
Christo Boshoff	–	–	1	1	2	1	–	–	–	5	2
Pieter Boshoff	–	–	4R	7	2	–	–	–	–	0	2
Jaco Louw	–	–	3R	2R	2	–	–	–	–	0	2
29 Players					**81**	**4**	**3**	**1**	**3**	**38**	**85**

CELL C COMMUNITY CUP - POOL C

Roses United

Played	Won	Lost	Drawn	Points for	Points against	Tries for	Tries against
7	4	2	1	234	263	32	34

Date	Venue	Opponent	Result	Score	Referees	Scorers
8 Mar	Pelican Park, Wellington	Brakpan	WON	27-26	Ben Crouse	T: Willemse, Cilliers, Appollis, Ramat. C: Lubbe, Julies. P: Lubbe.
15 Mar	Prince George Park, Boksburg	Boksburg	WON	50-36	Ruaan du Preez	T: April (2), Ramat (2), Fortuin, Ellman, Penalty Try. C: Julies (6). DG: Julies.
22 Mar	Pelican Park, Wellington	Centurion	DREW	26-26	Daniel Fortuin	T: Marsh (3), Fikster. C: Julies (3).
5 Apr	Noordelikes Rugby Club, Polokwane	Noordelikes	WON	58-21	Richard Schwulst	T: Jacobs (2), April (2), Moses (2), Ramat. C: Julies (7). P: Julies (3).
QUARTER-FINAL 3						
17 Apr	Outeniqua Park, George	Impala	LOST	13-66	Cwengile Jadezweni	T: Ramat. C: Julies. P: Julies. DG: Julies.
LOSERS' MATCH 1						
19 Apr	Outeniqua Park, George	Old Selbornians	WON	39-31	Federico Anselmi	T: Fikster (2), Marsh, Ellman, April, Penalty Try. C: Julies: (3). P: Julies.
PLAY-OFF 5TH/6TH						
21 Apr	Outeniqua Park, George	Despatch	LOST	21-57	Rametsi Oregopotse	T: Ellman, April, Cilliers. C: Lubbe (2), Julies.

‹ DID YOU KNOW? ›

Naas Botha is the only Springbok to have scored points in all 28 Tests he played in. Percy Montgomery scored points in 26 consecutive Tests he played in between 2004 and 2006.

CELL C COMMUNITY CUP - POOL C

2014 APPEARANCES & POINTS

PLAYER	Brakpan	Boksburg	Centurion	Noordelikes	Impala	Old Selbornians	Despatch	Apps	T	C	P	DG	Pts	Career Apps
Ryan Julies	15	15	15	15	15	10	10R	7	–	19	4	2	56	11
Brendon April	14	14	14	14	14	14	11R	7	6	–	–	–	30	7
Renaldo Petersen	13	13	13	13	13	12	13	7	–	–	–	–	0	11
Gerswin Moses	12	12	12	12	12	–	12	6	2	–	–	–	10	8
Clinton Oncker	11	11	–	–	–	–	–	2	–	–	–	–	0	2
Lohan Lubbe	10	10	10	10	10	–	10	6	–	6	2	–	18	6
Tiaan Ramat	9	9	9	9	9	9	–	6	5	–	–	–	25	6
Thurlow Marsh	8	8	8	8c	8	8	8	7	4	–	–	–	20	9
Chaney Willemse	7	7	7	7	7	7c	7	7	1	–	–	–	5	7
Geoffrey Allies	6c	6c	6c	–	6c	6R	6c	6	–	–	–	–	0	10
Reinart Ellmann	5	4	5	5	4	4	5	7	3	–	–	–	15	7
Gerhardus Goosen	4	–	–	4R	5	5R	4	5	–	–	–	–	0	9
Keenan Abrahams	3	3	3	3	–	–	–	4	–	–	–	–	0	4
Kelvin Fikster	2	2	2	2	2	2	2R	7	3	–	–	–	15	11
Stephan Wessels	1	1	1	1	1	1	1R	7	–	–	–	–	0	7
Martin Nel	2R	2R	2R	x	2R	x	2	5	–	–	–	–	0	7
Yagyaa Crook	6R	1R	1R	3R	1R	x	1	6	–	–	–	–	0	10
Lee-Heino Appollis	4R	4R	4R	5R	5R	5	–	6	1	–	–	–	5	9
Gareth Cilliers	17R	6R	6R	6	6R	6	6R	7	2	–	–	–	10	7
Michael Abrahams	x	8R	8R	6R	8R	22R	8R	6	–	–	–	–	0	9
Adriaan Jacobs	10R	10R	10R	10R	10R	15	15	7	2	–	–	–	10	7
Denver Fortuin	12R	11R	11	12R	11R	13	15R	7	1	–	–	–	5	11
Lgnacio Korabie	–	5	4	4	–	–	–	3	–	–	–	–	0	6
Gavoran Sherman	–	–	12R	11	11	13R	11	5	–	–	–	–	0	6
John-Ross Hofmeester	–	–	–	–	3	x	3R	2	–	–	–	–	0	4
Ayyoob Moerat	–	–	–	–	3R	3	3	3	–	–	–	–	0	3
Valentino Wellman	–	–	–	–	–	11	14	2	–	–	–	–	0	2
Percival Williams	–	–	–	–	–	9R	9	2	–	–	–	–	0	6
Penalty Try	–	–	–	–	–	–	–	–	2	–	–	–	10	
28 Players								152	32	25	6	2	234	202

CELL C COMMUNITY CUP - POOL C

Centurion

Played	Won	Lost	Drawn	Points for	Points against	Tries for	Tries against
7	3	2	2	235	177	29	23

Date	Venue	Opponent	Result	Score	Referees	Scorers
15 Mar	Centurion Rugby Club, Centurion	Noordelikes	WON	46-22	Wilko Esterhuizen	T: C Pieterse, Jacobs, Stroh, R Coetzee, Booysen, Keyter. C: Moir (4), Twiname. P: Moir, Twiname.
22 Mar	Pelican Park, Wellington	Roses United	DREW	26-26	Daniel Fortuin	T: Burger (2). C: Moir (2). P: Moir (2), Twiname (2).
29 Mar	Prince George Park, Boksburg	Boksburg	WON	58-20	Pieter Maritz	T: Burger (3), Olivier, Horn, Twiname, Oosthuizen. C: Moir (7). P: Moir (3).
5 Apr	Centurion Rugby Club, Centurion	Brakpan	DREW	32-32	Ricus van der Hoven	T: Van der Merwe, R Coetzee, Njomba, Moir. C: Moir (3). P: Moir, Twiname.

QUARTER-FINAL 4

17 Apr	Outeniqua Park, George	Hamiltons	LOST	10-40	Tahla Ntshakaza	T: B Coetzee. C: Moir. P: Moir.

LOSERS' MATCH 2

19 Apr	Outeniqua Park, George	Despatch	LOST	21-23	Cwengile Jadezweni	T: Burger, Bashiya, Jacobs. C: Moir (3).

PLAY-OFF 7TH/8TH

21 Apr	Outeniqua Park, George	Old Selbornians	WON	42-14	Tahla Ntshakaza	T: Twiname (3), Van der Merwe, Olivier, Bashiya. C: Moir (3). P: Moir (2).

⟨ DID YOU KNOW? ⟩

Up until 1995, South Africa had 22 rugby provinces. The eight that didn't survive the switch to professionalism were North West Cape, North East Cape, Far North, Eastern Free State, Stellaland, Northern Natal, Vaal Triangle and Lowveld.

CELL C COMMUNITY CUP - POOL C

2014 APPEARANCES & POINTS

PLAYER	Noordelikes	Roses United	Boksburg	Brakpan	Hamiltons	Despatch	Old Selbornians	Apps	T	C	P	DG	Pts	Career Apps
Cornel Pieterse	15	15	–	14R	15	11	12R	6	1	–	–	–	5	6
Neill Pieterse	14	11	11	11	11	–	11	6	–	–	–	–	0	6
Gerhard van der Merwe	13	–	13	13	13	13	13	6	2	–	–	–	10	6
Stanley Twiname	12	12	12	12	12	12	12	7	4	1	4	–	34	7
Wilmar Keyter	11	–	–	–	14	14	–	3	1	–	–	–	5	3
Steven Moir	10	10	10	10	10	10	10	7	1	23	10	–	81	7
Jacques Olivier	9	9	9	9	9	9	9R	7	2	–	–	–	10	7
Ryno Coetzee	8c	8c	8c	8c	8c	8c	8c	7	2	–	–	–	10	7
EJ Jooste	7	7	–	–	7	–	6R	4	–	–	–	–	0	4
Sibongile Njomba	6	6	6	6	7	6	–	7	1	–	–	–	5	14
Rohann Stroh	5	5	5	5	5	5R	5	7	1	–	–	–	5	7
Yves Bashiya	4	4	4	4	4	4	4	7	2	–	–	–	10	7
Jean-Philip Pike	3	3	3	–	–	–	–	3	–	–	–	–	0	3
Sylvester Booysen	2	2	2	2	2	2R	2	7	1	–	–	–	5	7
Paul Jacobs	1	1	1	1	1	1R	1	7	2	–	–	–	10	7
Christiaan de Klerk	1R	1R	1R	x	2R	2	–	5	–	–	–	–	0	5
Zac Oosthuizen	3R	1R	3R	3	3	3	1R	7	1	–	–	–	5	7
Stefan Nel	4R	4R	4R	4R	7R	5	5R	7	–	–	–	–	0	7
Bertus Coetzee	6R	6R	7	6	6R	6	–	6	1	–	–	–	5	6
Quentin Horn	9R	14R	14	14	–	11R	14	6	1	–	–	–	5	6
Christiaan Burger	14R	13	15	15	11R	15	15	7	6	–	–	–	30	7
Siphamandla Madlala	x	x	–	–	–	–	–	0	–	–	–	–	0	0
Adriaan Pretorius	–	14	–	–	–	–	–	1	–	–	–	–	0	1
Jacques de Villiers	–	15R	x	x	9R	x	9	3	–	–	–	–	0	3
Armandt Pryor	–	–	7R	7R	–	7R	7	4	–	–	–	–	0	4
Cornelius Rautenbach	–	–	x	–	–	–	–	0	–	–	–	–	0	0
Fano Ntsala	–	–	x	x	x	x	14R	1	–	–	–	–	0	1
Nico van den Heever	–	–	–	3R	3R	3R	3	4	–	–	–	–	0	4
Pieter Kilian	–	–	–	–	1R	1	3R	3	–	–	–	–	0	3
Wentzel van Zyl	–	–	–	–	–	–	2R	1	–	–	–	–	0	1
30 Players								146	29	24	14	0	235	153

CELL C COMMUNITY CUP - POOL C

Brakpan

Played	Won	Lost	Drawn	Points for	Points against	Tries for	Tries against
4	2	1	1	141	104	19	11

Date	Venue	Opponent	Result	Score	Referees	Scorers
8 Mar	Pelican Park, Wellington	Roses United	LOST	26-27	Ben Crouse	T: Van der Berg (2), Lotter, Horn. C: Horn (3).
20 Mar	Bosman Stadium, Brakpan	Boksburg	WON	48-23	Jaco Pretorius	T: Damba (2), Van der Merwe, Strydom, Van der Berg. C: Horn (4). P: Horn (5).
29 Mar	Bosman Stadium, Brakpan	Noordelikes	WON	35-22	AJ Jacobs	T: Van der Berg (3), Damba (2). C: Horn (2). P: Horn, Cronjé.
5 Apr	Centurion Rugby Club, Centurion	Centurion	DREW	32-32	Ricus van der Hoven	T: Damba, Van der Berg, Strydom, Booysen, Ueckermann. C: Horn (2). P: Horn.

‹ DID YOU KNOW? ›

Danie Gerber's 19 Test tries was a South African record until James Small broke it against Scotland on 6 December 1997. Gerber also held the first-class record of 158 tries when the mark was broken by Chris Badenhorst in 1998.

CELL C COMMUNITY CUP - POOL C

2014 APPEARANCES & POINTS

PLAYER	Roses Utd	Boksburg	Noordelikes	Centurion	Apps	T	C	P	DG	Pts	Career Apps
Tobie Strydom	15	11	–	11	3	2	–	–	–	10	9
Langa Damba	14	15	15	15	4	5	–	–	–	25	4
Thinus Ueckermann	13	–	13	14R	3	1	–	–	–	5	3
Christo Joubert	12	12	–	12	3	–	–	–	–	0	10
Zolile Mtshali	11	14	11	14	4	–	–	–	–	0	4
Gido Horn	10	10	11R	10	4	1	11	7	–	48	10
Ryno Hendrikz	9	9	9R	9	4	–	–	–	–	0	4
Theo Mynhardt	8	8	–	8	3	–	–	–	–	0	10
Jacques Nieuwenhuis	7	7	7c	–	3	–	–	–	–	0	9
Wikus van der Berg	6	6	6	7	4	7	–	–	–	35	10
Francois Robbertse	5c	5c	–	6c	3	–	–	–	–	0	10
Dean van der Merwe	4	4	4	4	4	1	–	–	–	5	11
Rudolf van Loggenberg	3	3	3	3	4	–	–	–	–	0	9
Jaco Lotter	2	2	2R	2	4	1	–	–	–	5	11
Jason Arundel	1	1	1R	1	4	–	–	–	–	0	10
Vernon du Preez	R	1R	2	1R	4	–	–	–	–	0	10
Roan Helberg	R	x	1	2R	3	–	–	–	–	0	9
Dwane Morrison	R	4R	5	5	4	–	–	–	–	0	4
Thabo Molete	R	13R	x	4R	3	–	–	–	–	0	3
Theo Becker	R	8R	8	8R	4	–	–	–	–	0	4
Ronwin Roets	R	12R	12	–	3	–	–	–	–	0	3
Cornelius de Villiers	R	–	14	–	2	–	–	–	–	0	2
Franco Booysen	–	13	–	13	2	1	–	–	–	5	8
Ian Evans	–	9R	9	9R	3	–	–	–	–	0	3
Hein Cronjé	–	–	10	10R	2	–	–	1	–	3	2
Wesley Pretorius	–	–	8R	–	1	–	–	–	–	0	1
Dauw Steyn	–	–	14R	–	1	–	–	–	–	0	1
27 Players					**86**	**19**	**11**	**8**	**0**	**141**	**174**

CELL C COMMUNITY CUP - POOL C

Boksburg

Played	Won	Lost	Drawn	Points for	Points against	Tries for	Tries against
4	1	3	0	121	169	14	20

Date	Venue	Opponent	Result	Score	Referees	Scorers
8 Mar	Noordelikes Rugby Club, Polokwane	Noordelikes	WON	42-13	T Correira	T: Adams, Erasmus, Bester, Vermeulen, Havenga. C: Buchler (4). P: Buchler (3).
15 Mar	Prince George Park, Boksburg	Roses United	LOST	36-50	Ruaan du Preez	T: Adams, Jantjes, Swart, Taljaard, Venter. C: Buchler (4). P: Buchler.
20 Mar	Bosman Stadium, Brakpan	Brakpan	LOST	23-48	Jaco Pretorius	T: Adams, Matthee. C: Buchler (2). P: Buchler (3).
29 Mar	Prince George Park, Boksburg	Centurion	LOST	20-58	Pieter Maritz	T: Swart, Rhodes. C: Buchler (2). P: Buchler (2).

⟨ DID YOU KNOW? ⟩

When the South African Rugby Board was formed in 1889, a tournament was held in Kimberley in the same year. The first official provincial game under the auspices of the Board took place on 28 August 1889 between EP and WP.

CELL C COMMUNITY CUP - POOL C

APPEARANCES & POINTS

PLAYER	Noordelikes	Roses Utd	Brakpan	Centurion	Apps	T	C	P	DG	Pts	Career Apps
Ashwill Adams	15	15	15	15	4	3	–	–	–	15	4
Dean Swart	14	14	14	14	4	2	–	–	–	10	4
Marius Matthee	13	13	13	13	4	1	–	–	–	5	4
Theo Rhodes	12	–	12	12	3	1	–	–	–	5	3
Willem Vlok	11	–	–	–	1	–	–	–	–	0	1
Ashley Buchler	10	10	10	10	4	–	12	9	–	51	4
Diederik Burger	9	9	9	9	4	–	–	–	–	0	4
Wayne Havenga	8	–	8	–	2	1	–	–	–	5	2
Calvin Jantjies	7	8	7R	8	4	1	–	–	–	5	4
Juan Bester	6	6	7R	6	4	1	–	–	–	5	4
Dirk Bloem	5c	5c	5c	5c	4	–	–	–	–	0	4
Gian Vorster	4	4	4	4	4	–	–	–	–	0	4
Dwayne Korff	3	3	1R	1R	4	–	–	–	–	0	4
Rudi Willemse	2	2	2	2	4	–	–	–	–	0	4
Wikus Coetzer	1	1	3	1	4	–	–	–	–	0	4
Karel Vermeulen	2R	8R	7	–	3	1	–	–	–	5	3
Coenrad Nolte	3R	–	–	–	1	–	–	–	–	0	1
Stanley Peacock	x	1R	1	–	2	–	–	–	–	0	2
Wesley van Rooyen	6R	4R	–	7	3	–	–	–	–	0	3
Wian Engelbrecht	9R	–	9R	–	2	–	–	–	–	0	2
Ernst Behr	13R	12	x	–	2	–	–	–	–	0	2
Ferdinand Erasmus	11R	11R	–	15R	3	1	–	–	–	5	3
Etienne Taljaard	–	11	11	11	3	1	–	–	–	5	3
Jacques van der Walt	–	7	6	–	2	–	–	–	–	0	2
Wynand Venter	–	9R	–	–	1	1	–	–	–	5	1
Jacques Stierlin	–	17R	–	–	1	–	–	–	–	0	1
Antonie Vlok	–	12R	–	12R	2	–	–	–	–	0	2
Andries Engelbrecht	–	–	2R	3	2	–	–	–	–	0	2
Noel Rhodes	–	–	x	14R	1	–	–	–	–	0	1
Jacobus van Zyl	–	–	–	4R	1	–	–	–	–	0	1
Juan Vorster	–	–	–	6R	1	–	–	–	–	0	1
Evurne du Plooy	–	–	–	2R	1	–	–	–	–	0	1
32 Players					85	14	12	9	0	121	85

CELL C COMMUNITY CUP - POOL C

Noordelikes

Played	Won	Lost	Drawn	Points for	Points against	Tries for	Tries against
4	0	4	0	78	181	9	23

Date	Venue	Opponent	Result	Score	Referees	Scorers
8 Mar	Noordelikes Rugby Club, Polokwane	Boksburg	LOST	13-42	T Correira	T: De Beer, Varela. P: Byleveldt.
15 Mar	Centurion Rugby Club, Centurion	Centurion	LOST	22-46	Wilko Esterhuizen	T: De Beer, Van der Merwe, Jongbloed. C: Byleveldt (2). P: Byleveldt.
29 Mar	Bosman Stadium, Brakpan	Brakpan	LOST	22-35	AJ Jacobs	T: Van der Merwe. C: Byleveldt. P: Byleveldt (5).
5 Apr	Noordelikes Rugby Club, Polokwane	Roses United	LOST	21-58	Richard Schwulst	T: Smith (2), Jongbloed. C: Byleveldt (3).

‹ DID YOU KNOW? ›

The first Currie Cup final took place in 1939 - prior to that the team on top of the log won the trophy. Originally the Currie Cup final did not take place every year, but since 1968 a final has been played each season.

CELL C COMMUNITY CUP - POOL C

2014 APPEARANCES & POINTS

PLAYER	Boksburg	Centurion	Brakpan	Roses Utd	Apps	T	C	P	DG	Pts	Career Apps
Zander Byleveldt	15	15	15	15	4	–	6	7	–	33	8
Sias van Wyk	14	14	14	14	4	–	–	–	–	0	4
Mynhardt Smith	13c	13c	13c	13c	4	2	–	–	–	10	7
Gert van der Merwe	12	12	12	12	4	2	–	–	–	10	5
Johannes van Niekerk	11	15R	10R	x	3	–	–	–	–	0	4
Johan de Beer	10	10	10	10	4	2	–	–	–	10	8
Theyman Jongbloed	9	9	9	9	4	2	–	–	–	10	5
Tienie Janse van Rensburg	8	8	8	8	4	–	–	–	–	0	8
Sinthamdile Memese	7	7	7	7	4	–	–	–	–	0	6
Cornelius van Greyn	6	6	6	6	4	–	–	–	–	0	8
Malopo Masemola	5	5	5	5	4	–	–	–	–	0	8
Thabo Tladi	4	4	4	4	4	–	–	–	–	0	6
Wickus Visser	3	3	3	2R	4	–	–	–	–	0	8
Nicolaas Els	2	2	2	–	3	–	–	–	–	0	6
Jan Jacobs	1	1	–	–	2	–	–	–	–	0	2
Webster Mugadi	2R	–	1R	1R	3	–	–	–	–	0	3
Ricardo Valera	1R	3R	2R	3	4	1	–	–	–	5	8
Dustin Hoffmann	5R	4R	4R	3R	4	–	–	–	–	0	4
Willie Roberts	14R	12R	–	x	2	–	–	–	–	0	2
Lufuno Ramoyada	6R	7R	7R	7R	4	–	–	–	–	0	4
JP Vermeulen	x	11	–	–	1	–	–	–	–	0	5
Jacques Els	11R	11R	11	11	4	–	–	–	–	0	4
Leslie Venton	–	1R	1	1	3	–	–	–	–	0	3
Zanru Fuchs	–	–	11R	x	1	–	–	–	–	0	1
Arno Venter	–	–	14R	2	2	–	–	–	–	0	2
25 Players					**84**	**9**	**6**	**7**	**0**	**78**	**129**

CELL C COMMUNITY CUP - POOL D

Rustenburg Impala

Played	Won	Lost	Drawn	Points for	Points against	Tries for	Tries against
7	6	1	0	259	121	34	12

Date	Venue	Opponent	Result	Score	Referees	Scorers
8 Mar	Rustenburg Impala RC, Rustenburg	Sishen	WON	29-17	Stephan Geldenhuys	T: Visser (2), Du Plessis, Joubert. C: Olivier (3). P: Olivier.
15 Mar	Puma Stadium, Emalahleni	Ferros	WON	41-17	Terence Westcott	T: Wheeler (2), Lewis, Du Plessis, Jooste. C: Olivier (5). P: Olivier (2).
29 Mar	Wesbank Sports Ground, Mamesbury	Wesbank	WON	50-7	Francois Pretorius	T: Kok (2), Apollis, St.Jerry, Du Plessis, Terblanché, Joubert, De Kock. C: Olivier (4), De Wet.
5 Apr	Rustenburg Impala RC, Rustenburg	Hamiltons	LOST	28-43	Lesego Legoete	T: Lewis (3), Nienaber. C: De Wet. P: Kok (2).

QUARTER-FINAL 3

| 17 Apr | Outeniqua Park, George | Roses United | WON | 66-13 | Cwengile Jadezweni | T: Lewis (2), Matyeshana, Nienaber, Kok, Joubert, Wheeler, Wehr. C: Olivier (5), De Wet, Lewis. P: Olivier (2), De Wet (2). |

CUP SEMI-FINAL 1

| 19 Apr | Outeniqua Park, George | College Rovers | WON | 32-13 | Quinton Immelman | T: Nienaber (2), Lewis, Olivier. C: Olivier (2), De Wet. P: De Wet. DG: Kok. |

CUP FINAL

| 21 Apr | Outeniqua Park, George | Roodepoort | WON | 13-11 | Quinton Immelman | T: Du Plessis. C: Olivier. P: Olivier, De Wet. |

⟨ DID YOU KNOW? ⟩

François Steyn became the youngest recipient of a RWC winners' medal in 2007. Steyn, born on 14 May 1987, was 20 years and 159 days old on 20 October 2007 when South Africa beat England to win the 2007 World Cup Final.

CELL C COMMUNITY CUP - POOL D

2014 APPEARANCES & POINTS

PLAYER	Sishen	Ferros	Wesbank	Hamiltons	Roses Utd	Coll Rovers	Roodepoort	Apps	T	C	P	DG	Pts	Career Apps
Linton Terblanché	15	15	15	–	10R	x	x	4	1	–	–	–	5	9
Berty Visser	14	14	–	–	–	–	–	2	2	–	–	–	10	6
Dumisani Matyeshana	13	13	13	13	13	13	13	7	1	–	–	–	5	7
Justin St Jerry	12	12	12	12	12	–	–	5	1	–	–	–	5	11
Morné Jooste	11	11	11	–	–	x	10R	4	1	–	–	–	5	4
Naas Olivier	10	10	10	10	10	10	10	7	1	20	6	–	63	14
Willie Kok	9	9	9	9	9	9	9	7	3	–	2	1	24	12
Justin Wheeler	8	7	7	7	7	8	–	6	3	–	–	–	15	6
Wendal Wehr	7	–	7R	–	8R	7	7	5	1	–	–	–	5	7
Victor Joubert	6c	6c	6c	6c	6c	6c	6c	7	3	–	–	–	15	11
Tiaan Nel	5	5	5	5	5	5	5	7	–	–	–	–	0	13
Lehan Koekemoer	4	4	4	4	4	–	–	5	–	–	–	–	0	5
Musa Tukela	3	–	–	–	–	–	–	1	–	–	–	–	0	4
Gavin Williamson	2	2	2	2	2	2	2	7	–	–	–	–	0	13
Louis Hollamby	1	1	1	1	1	1	1	7	–	–	–	–	0	14
Alfred Ries	2R	–	–	2R	–	–	–	2	–	–	–	–	0	9
Zander de Kock	3R	3	3	3	3	3	3	7	1	–	–	–	5	10
Henro Huyser	4R	4R	5R	7R	–	4	4	6	–	–	–	–	0	12
Leon du Plessis	7R	8	8	8	8	8R	8	7	4	–	–	–	20	14
Jermaine Apollis	9R	12R	9R	13R	12R	9R	x	6	1	–	–	–	5	10
McDonald Duma	13R	9R	12R	9R	9R	12	12	7	–	–	–	–	0	14
Earl Lewis	15R	14R	14	14	14	14	14	7	7	1	–	–	37	12
Giovano Fourie	–	2R	2R	–	5R	2R	2R	5	–	–	–	–	0	12
Paul Groenewald	–	x	3R	3R	3R	3R	x	4	–	–	–	–	0	4
Morné Basson	–	x	–	5R	4R	4R	4R	4	–	–	–	–	0	4
Wilco de Wet	–	–	10R	15	15	15	15	5	–	4	4	–	20	5
Michael Nienaber	–	–	–	11	11	11	11	4	4	–	–	–	20	10
Nelis Nel	–	–	–	8R	–	–	8R	2	–	–	–	–	0	6
Rynardt Steenkamp	–	–	–	–	1R	1R	x	2	–	–	–	–	0	2
29 Players								**149**	**34**	**25**	**12**	**1**	**259**	**260**

CELL C COMMUNITY CUP - POOL D

Hamiltons

Played	Won	Lost	Drawn	Points for	Points against	Tries for	Tries against
7	6	1	0	283	109	36	13

Date	Venue	Opponent	Result	Score	Referees	Scorers
15 Mar	Stephan Oval, Green Point, Cape Town	Sishen	WON	48-9	Daniel Fortuin	T: Giliomee (2), Van Jaarsveld, Botha, Bartels, De Villiers, Jacobs. C: Vallender (5). P: Vallender.
22 Mar	Wesbank Sports Ground, Mamesbury	Wesbank	WON	41-12	Cwengile Jadezweni	T: Tsomondo (2), Winter. Pheiffer, Bartels, Burch, Cleghorn. C: Van Zyl (2), Vallender.
29 Mar	Stephan Oval, Green Point, Cape Town	Ferros	WON	66-12	Daniel Fortuin	T: Du Plessis (2), Burch (2), Winter, Purdon, Bartels, Van Zyl, Cleghorn, Tsomondo. C: Vallender (8).
5 Apr	Rustenburg Impala RC, Rustenburg	Impala	WON	43-28	Lesego Legoete	T: Du Plessis, Burch, Van Zyl, Jacobs. C: Vallender (4). P: Vallender (4). DG: Vallender.
QUARTER FINAL 4						
17 Apr	Outeniqua Park, George	Centurion	WON	40-10	Tahla Ntshakaza	T: Du Plessis (2), Jacobs, Lawson, Van Zyl. C: Vallender (3). P: Vallender (3).
CUP SEMI FINAL 2						
19 Apr	Outeniqua Park, George	Roodepoort	LOST	18-20	Oregopotse Rametsi	P: Vallender (6).
PLAY-OFF 3RD/4TH						
21 Apr	Outeniqua Park, George	College Rovers	WON	27-18	Juan Sylvestre	T: Bartels, Jacobs, Botha. C: Van Zyl (2), Vallender. P: Van Zyl (2).

⟨ DID YOU KNOW? ⟩

South Africa's first international took place on Thursday, 30 July 1891 vs Great Britain on the Port Elizabeth Cricket Club Ground - 20 years after the very first international rugby match in 1871 between England & Scotland.

CELL C COMMUNITY CUP - POOL D

2014 APPEARANCES & POINTS

PLAYER	Sishen	Wesbank	Ferros	Impala	Centurion	Roodepoort	College Rovers	Apps	T	C	P	DG	Pts	Career Apps
Pierre Cronjé	15	15	9	15	–	15	9	6	–	–	–	–	0	6
Terry Jacobs	14	14	14	14	14	14	14	7	4	–	–	–	20	7
Jandré du Plessis	13	13	13	13	13	13	13	7	5	–	–	–	25	7
Morgan Newman	12	12	12c	–	12	12	11R	6	–	–	–	–	0	6
Richard Lawson	11	–	–	–	12R	12R	12	4	1	–	–	–	5	4
Shane Vallender	10	10	10	10	10	10	10	7	–	22	14	1	89	7
Charlie Purdon	9	9	9R	9	9	9	–	6	1	–	–	–	5	6
Jody Burch	8	8	8	8	8	8	8	7	4	–	–	–	20	7
Waldo Prinsloo	7	–	–	–	7	7	7	4	–	–	–	–	0	4
Gareth Rowe	6	6	6	6	6	6	–	6	–	–	–	–	0	6
Tian Fick	5	5	5	5	5	–	4	6	–	–	–	–	0	6
Henk Franken	4	4	–	4	4	4	5	6	–	–	–	–	0	6
Attie Winter	3	3	3	3	3	3	2R	7	2	–	–	–	10	7
JG Giliomee	2c	2c	3R	2c	2c	2c	2c	7	2	–	–	–	10	7
Christo McNish	1	3R	1	1	1	1	3	7	–	–	–	–	0	7
Gregory van Jaarsveld	3R	2R	2	3R	1R	1R	3R	7	1	–	–	–	5	7
Denzel Riddles	1R	1	1R	–	3R	3R	1	6	–	–	–	–	0	6
Kudu Herman Botha	4R	4R	4	7R	–	5	7R	6	2	–	–	–	10	6
Niel Cleghorn	6R	7	7	–	–	5R	6	5	2	–	–	–	10	5
Pieter de Villiers	9R	9R	15	9R	15	–	15	6	1	–	–	–	5	6
Craig Pheiffer	11R	11	–	–	11	9R	13R	5	1	–	–	–	5	5
Iewan Bartels	14R	14R	11	11R	x	x	11	5	4	–	–	–	20	5
Janno van Zyl	–	11R	14R	11	9R	11	10R	6	3	4	2	–	29	6
Taps Tsomondo	–	8R	8R	7	5R	–	–	4	3	–	–	–	15	4
Sandile Buthelezi	–	–	5R	5R	6R	8R	4R	5	–	–	–	–	0	5
Jason Morrison	–	–	12R	12	–	–	–	2	–	–	–	–	0	2
Jonathan Raphael	–	–	–	2R	2R	x	1R	3	–	–	–	–	0	3
Calvin Kotze	–	–	–	12R	–	–	–	1	–	–	–	–	0	1
28 Players								**154**	**36**	**26**	**16**	**1**	**283**	**154**

CELL C COMMUNITY CUP - POOL D

Sishen

Played	Won	Lost	Drawn	Points for	Points against	Tries for	Tries against
4	2	2	0	113	116	15	16

Date	Venue	Opponent	Result	Score	Referees	Scorers
8 Mar	Rustenburg Impala RC, Rustenburg	Impala	LOST	17-29	Stephan Geldenhuys	T: Meyer (2). C: Bloem, Coetzer. P: Bloem.
15 Mar	Stephan Oval, Green Point, Cape Town	Hamiltons	LOST	9-48	Daniel Fortuin	P: Bloem (3).
22 Mar	Sivos Rugby Stadium, Kathu	Ferros	WON	35-29	Nico Schmahl	T: Bloem, Tities, Zwiegelaar, Van Aarde, Grobler. C: Bloem (2). P: Bloem. DG: Le Roux.
5 Apr	Sivos Rugby Stadium, Kathu	Wesbank	WON	52-10	Nico Schmahl	T: Le Roux (2), De Villiers, Coetzee, Du Plessis, Zwiegelaar, Poolman, Penalty Try. C: Le Roux (6).

‹ DID YOU KNOW? ›

South Africa's first victory came in their seventh Test, namely the fourth at Newlands vs Great Britain on 5 September 1896. South Africa won 5-0. South Africa wore green jerseys for the first time in this Test.

CELL C COMMUNITY CUP - POOL D

2014 APPEARANCES & POINTS

PLAYER	Impala	Hamiltons	Ferros	Wesbank	Apps	T	C	P	DG	Pts	Career Apps
Andries Bloem	15	15	15	–	3	1	3	5	–	26	3
Johan Myburgh	14	11R	11R	–	3	–	–	–	–	0	6
Stevie Meyer	13	12	12	13	4	2	–	–	–	10	6
Prince Mofokeng	12	14R	6R	12R	4	–	–	–	–	0	4
Aubrene Tities	11	11	11	14	4	1	–	–	–	5	4
Tiaan le Roux	10	9	9	9	4	2	6	–	1	25	8
Sarel du Plessis	9	–	–	–	1	–	–	–	–	0	4
Jamie Zwiegelaar	8	8	8	8	4	2	–	–	–	10	8
Anthony de Villiers	7	4	4	7	4	1	–	–	–	5	4
Ruan Grobler	6	6	6	6	4	1	–	–	–	5	5
Arnold Coetzee	5	5	5	5	4	1	–	–	–	5	8
Leon Poolman	4	–	7R	4	3	1	–	–	–	5	7
Nicolaas Steyn	3	3	3	3	4	–	–	–	–	0	4
BW van Dyk	2c	2c	2c	2c	4	–	–	–	–	0	8
Pieter van Aarde	1	1	1	1	4	1	–	–	–	5	4
Dawid Roux	2R	2R	2R	2R	4	–	–	–	–	0	4
Darryl Dawson	1R	1R	3R	1R	4	–	–	–	–	0	7
Johannes Peenze	4R	–	–	–	1	–	–	–	–	0	3
Attie du Plessis	8R	7	7	5R	4	1	–	–	–	5	4
Brendon Coetzer	15R	10	10	10	4	–	1	–	–	2	4
Johan Peens	12R	12R	12R	12	4	–	–	–	–	0	8
Lithando Noko	14R	13	–	–	2	–	–	–	–	0	2
Khangelani Mbekela	–	14	14	11	3	–	–	–	–	0	3
André Roberts	–	6R	4R	6R	3	–	–	–	–	0	6
Arno de Blom	–	7R	–	–	1	–	–	–	–	0	1
Len le Roux	–	–	13	13R	2	–	–	–	–	0	2
Henco Olivier	–	–	–	15	1	–	–	–	–	0	5
Heinrich van der Walt	–	–	–	11R	1	–	–	–	–	0	1
Penalty Try	–	–	–	–	0	1	–	–	–	5	0
28 Players					**88**	**15**	**10**	**5**	**1**	**113**	**133**

CELL C COMMUNITY CUP - POOL D

Ferros

Played	Won	Lost	Drawn	Points for	Points against	Tries for	Tries against
4	1	3	0	91	162	11	24

Date	Venue	Opponent	Result	Score	Referees	Scorers
8 Mar	Puma Stadium, Emalahleni	Wesbank	WON	33-20	Ricus van der Hoven	T: Sibiya (2), Collen. C: Pieters (3). P: Pieters (4).
15 Mar	Puma Stadium, Emalahleni	Impala	LOST	17-41	Terence Westcott	T: Botha, W van der Merwe. C: Pieters (2). P: Pieters.
22 Mar	Sivos Rugby Stadium, Kathu	Sishen	LOST	29-35	Nico Schmahl	T: Botes (2), Ngozo, Collen. C: Pieters (3). P: Pieters.
29 Mar	Stephan Oval, Green Point, Cape Town	Hamiltons	LOST	12-66	Daniel Fortuin	T: Botha, Ngozo. C: Pieters.

❰ DID YOU KNOW? ❱

When Harry Walker (1953-56), the son of Alf Walker (1921-24), was selected for South Africa, they become the first father and son to play for the Springboks.

CELL C COMMUNITY CUP - POOL D

2014 APPEARANCES & POINTS

PLAYER	Wesbank	Impala	Sishen	Hamiltons	Apps	T	C	P	DG	Pts	Career Apps
Dewald Pieters	15	15	13	10	4	–	9	6	–	36	4
Letlakwe Mpanya	14	14	14	14R	4	–	–	–	–	0	4
Tommie Collen	13	13	12	13	4	2	–	–	–	10	4
Jean Botha	12	12	–	12	3	2	–	–	–	10	3
Pule Sibiya	11	11	–	14	3	2	–	–	–	10	3
Christo Nelson	10	22R	10	x	3	–	–	–	–	0	3
Wayne Dreyer	9	9	9	9	4	–	–	–	–	0	4
Izan Green	8	8	8	8	4	–	–	–	–	0	4
Willie van der Merwe	7c	2c	2c	2c	4	1	–	–	–	5	4
Jackie Smit	6	6	6	6	4	–	–	–	–	0	4
Brandon Snell	5	4	4	–	3	–	–	–	–	0	3
Werno Smit	4	5	5	5	4	–	–	–	–	0	4
Willem van Niekerk	3	–	–	–	1	–	–	–	–	0	1
Jaco Marneweck	2	1	1	1	4	–	–	–	–	0	4
MC Botes	1	3	3	3	4	2	–	–	–	10	4
Waldo Nelson	2R	–	2R	6R	3	–	–	–	–	0	3
Morné Pretorius	3R	x	–	–	1	–	–	–	–	0	1
Chris van Leeuwen	4R	4R	8R	4	4	–	–	–	–	0	4
Petrus Prinsloo	x	8R	4R	5R	3	–	–	–	–	0	3
Jean-Di Oosthuizen	5R	7	7	–	3	–	–	–	–	0	3
Jan van der Merwe	10R	10	15	–	3	–	–	–	–	0	3
Siphesihle Barnabas	x	9R	9R	–	2	–	–	–	–	0	2
Lesley Orton	–	5R	5R	7	3	–	–	–	–	0	3
Drikus Fourie	–	1R	–	–	1	–	–	–	–	0	1
Nkululeko Ngozo	–	–	11	11	2	2	–	–	–	10	2
Willie Muller	–	–	1R	3R	2	–	–	–	–	0	2
Jaco de Beer	–	–	14R	11R	2	–	–	–	–	0	2
Barnard Janse van Vuuren	–	–	–	15	1	–	–	–	–	0	1
Emilio Skosana	–	–	–	1R	1	–	–	–	–	0	1
29 Players					**84**	**11**	**9**	**6**	**0**	**91**	**84**

CELL C COMMUNITY CUP - POOL D

Wesbank

Played	Won	Lost	Drawn	Points for	Points against	Tries for	Tries against
4	0	4	0	49	176	8	26

Date	Venue	Opponent	Result	Score	Referees	Scorers
8 Mar	Puma Stadium, Emalahleni	Ferros	LOST	20-33	Ricus van der Hoven	T: S Coetzee, A Coetzee, N Solomons, Wellman.
22 Mar	Wesbank Sports Ground, Mamesbury	Hamiltons	LOST	12-41	Jadezweni Gwengile	T: Swarts, Penalty Try. C: Jonkers.
29 Mar	Wesbank Sports Ground, Mamesbury	Impala	LOST	7-50	Francois Pretorius	T: Stander. C: Jonkers.
5 Apr	Sivos Rugby Stadium, Kathu	Sishen	LOST	10-52	Nico Schmahl	T: Slabber. C: Nelson. P: Jonkers.

DID YOU KNOW?
The first penalty try awarded to South Africa in a Test was vs Australia at Newlands on 10 August 1963, when Tommy Bedford was obstructed by Beres Ellwood during a chase following a kick by Jannie Engelbrecht.

CELL C COMMUNITY CUP - POOL D

2014 APPEARANCES & POINTS

PLAYER	Ferros	Hamiltons	Impala	Sishen	Apps	T	C	P	DG	Pts	Career Apps
Rodville Jonkers	15	15	15	15	4	–	2	1	–	7	4
Sedwell Diedericks	14	11	14	–	3	–	–	–	–	0	3
Johannes Slabber	13	13	13	13	4	1	–	–	–	5	4
Nadius Solomons	12	12R	12R	–	3	1	–	–	–	5	3
Salmon Coetzee	11	14	–	–	2	1	–	–	–	5	2
Theodore Marinus	10	15R	10R	10R	4	–	–	–	–	0	4
Dashton Wellman	9	10	10c	10	4	1	–	–	–	5	4
Emgee Fredericks	8	8	–	–	2	–	–	–	–	0	2
Arno Hendriks	7c	7c	–	5	3	–	–	–	–	0	3
Westley Isaacs	6	7R	6	–	3	–	–	–	–	0	3
André Coetzee	5	–	–	8c	2	1	–	–	–	5	2
Tiaan Breytenbach	4	4	4	–	3	–	–	–	–	0	3
Alwyn Liebenberg	3	–	–	–	1	–	–	–	–	0	1
Mario Samson	2	–	–	2	2	–	–	–	–	0	2
Petro Louw	1	1	1	1	4	–	–	–	–	0	4
Vincent Fredericks	x	–	2	x	1	–	–	–	–	0	1
André van Reenen	1R	3	3	–	3	–	–	–	–	0	3
Ghriswin Swarts	5R	5R	4R	–	3	–	–	–	–	0	3
Johan September	6R	6	8	7	4	–	–	–	–	0	4
Edwill Solomons	10R	9	–	–	2	–	–	–	–	0	2
Nevin Edas	12R	–	–	–	1	–	–	–	–	0	1
Anton Stander	15R	12	12	–	3	1	–	–	–	5	3
Morris Moses	–	5	5	–	2	–	–	–	–	0	2
Stuart Halvorsen	–	2	2R	–	2	–	–	–	–	0	2
Jacquinn Ruthford	–	8R	7	4R	3	1	–	–	–	5	3
Angelo Johnson	–	11R	11	11R	3	–	–	–	–	0	3
Braison Albertus	–	2R	3R	3	3	–	–	–	–	0	3
Evan Liedeman	–	–	9	9	2	–	–	–	–	0	2
Melvin Laserus	–	–	7R	7	2	–	–	–	–	0	2
Magnum Nelson	–	–	9R	12R	2	–	1	–	–	2	2
Anvon Davids	–	–	–	14	1	–	–	–	–	0	1
Franklin Barendse	–	–	–	12	1	–	–	–	–	0	1
Stallone Scott	–	–	–	11	1	–	–	–	–	0	1
Daryl Losper	–	–	–	4	1	–	–	–	–	0	1
Jeremiah Titus	–	–	–	3R	1	–	–	–	–	0	1
Manfred Doman	–	–	–	7R	1	–	–	–	–	0	1
Penalty Try	–	–	–	–	–	1	–	–	–	5	–
36 Players					86	8	3	1	0	49	86

FNB VARSITY CUP

UCT in 'greatest comeback of all time'

Indefatigable Ikeys claim second Varsity title on the road

IT was, quite simply, a revival that would have made Lazarus' rise from the dead appear decidedly humdrum by comparison.

'The greatest comeback/choke of all time in rugby (or sport)' was how SuperSport described the night of 7 April on their YouTube online viewing channel. Such hyperbole is not uncommon in the world of sport, especially when the sweeping statement comes from a partisan broadcaster with an active interest in the match, but few who watched those final seven minutes – 158,000 had done so at the time of writing – would argue that this was precisely the stuff that had spawned any number of cheesy Hollywood sports movies.

In the build-up to the match, Kevin Musikanth, the Ikeys' soft-spoken but intense and obsessively driven coach, had agonised over how best to motivate his players against a side, coached by former Springbok scrumhalf Robert du Preez, who had finished top of the log and who, on their home ground, seemed a shoe-in for a long overdue maiden title.

Musikanth, as told to this writer, then had a brainwave. So comprehensively were UCT being written off that he thought it pointless to appeal to his team using fire-and-brimstone tactics. So instead the eccentric coach employed the services of a magician, who attended a team training the previous week. "He told the guys, believe in magic and anything is possible," said Musikanth. "By the time the game rolled around, they believed exactly that."

Not that the Ikeys have historically ever lacked faith in their own abilities. Their never-say-die attitude and ability to win games at the death through audacious running rugby stretches back decades. But this was an altogether different challenge, and Musikanth, perhaps sensing this, sensibly chose to take all the pressure off his charges.

The outcome, as they say, is history. Trailing 33-15 with less than six minutes remaining, the Cape Town students threw caution to the wind as only they know how.

What followed was perhaps not broadcaster hyperbole after all: a try by eighthman Michael Botha after 74 minutes and 20 seconds, converted by flyhalf Dean Grant, cut the deficit to 10 points and yet, with the sands of time fast running out, few saw the score as anything other than a well-deserved consolation try.

The Ikeys celebrate their second Varsity Cup title – one that will live long in the memory.

The momentum appeared to swing from the restart, when the visitors launched yet another sweeping movement down the left-hand touchline that ended with centre Huw Jones, who had opened the scoring 70 minutes earlier, being bundled into touch just five metres short.

But by the time Pukke hooker Akker van der Merwe found his jumper from the resultant lineout, less than two minutes remained and the thousands of home fans who had packed the Fanie du Toit Sports Grounds like sardines were already celebrating.

Cue Musikanth's magic. Somehow the lineout was turned over, a succession of drives for the line reclaimed the momentum, and Grant danced through a gaping hole to make it 33-31.

Home-town flyhalf Johnny Welthagen – who was about to play an central role in the drama that was unfolding – restarted with 30 seconds left on the clock, and Pukke looked to have done enough when they fed a scrum after a last-gasp Ikeys attack broke down. The clock indicated 80 minutes and 55 seconds.

At that moment, all that stood between Pukke and the title was a quick heel and a hoof into the highest row of the stands. What happened next will go down in rugby folklore: for some inexplicable reason, eightman Juan Language picked up, passed left, and, in doing so, kept the ball alive when all it needed to do was go dead. The die was cast.

At 81 minutes and 14 seconds, reserve scrumhalf Dillon Smit passed back to Welthagen who, in his desperation to now end the match, had positioned himself for a drop-goal – when all that was needed yet again was a kick into touch. But Welthagen made a fatal error: he positioned himself too flat and the inevitable charge-down came. And from it, the Ikeys surged upfield once more, stretching their surprised opponents left and right before striking the killer below down the grandstand touchline, reserve hooker Chad Solomon lobbing inside to another replacement, wing Nate Nel, who stepped inside and, upon realising he had a clear 50-metre dash to glory, could not contain his emotions as he dived over.

"Nate told me he was crying before he even touched down," said Musikanth. "He said it was because he had dreamed earlier in the week that he'd come off the bench and score the winning try. He believed it with all his heart. He said he had a vision that he was going to win the game. And then he did. Was that magic?"

Spare a thought, too, for Pukke coach Du Preez, who, less than a year earlier, had suffered a similar gut-wrenching defeat when GAP Despatch snatched the inaugural Cell C Community Cup title out of the grasp of his Jonsson College Rovers team, thanks to an injury-time penalty by Monty Dumond.

The final, its place in rugby folklore assured, was just what the doctor ordered for a tournament which seemed to be approaching a crossroads, with critics pointing out that, during the course of its seven-year existence, the Varsity Cup had moved away from its student ethos and had become simply another professionalised layer in an increasingly congested tournament calendar.

The tournament organisers clearly have some tough decisions to make in the coming seasons if they are to stay true to their original intentions, and to this end UCT's cavalier approach proved a timely reminder that the public *want* to watch student rugby for its rebellious, swashbuckling style. What they clearly *don't* want is simply another clinical professional tournament dressed up as student rugby.

The 2014 Varsity Cup will also be remembered for defending champions Tuks' poor run, the Pretoria students managing just three wins from seven matches en route to sixth place in the standings. Interestingly, the three Gauteng-based sides – Tuks, UJ and Wits – finished sixth, seventh and eighth respectively.

At the top of the log, Pukke deserved their number-one position, while the continued resurgence of NMMU saw them reach the semi-finals for the second year running. But the Port Elizabeth side seemingly found little acknowledgement from the rugby gods for their sterling efforts: having lost 16-15 away to Maties in the 2013 semi-finals, they went down 19-18 to Pukke in Potchefstroom, a season's worth of good work undone by a 79th-minute penalty slotted by home-side replacement, Ryno Smith.

A fortnight later, however, it was Pukke who would be wondering just how they had snatched defeat from the wide-open jaws of victory.

- In the Varsity Shield, CUT beat UKZN 35-26 in the final having topped the log convincingly in regular-season play. The Bloemfontein students will now join neighbours Shimlas in the Cup in 2015, with Wits, who finished at the foot of the Cup table, automatically relegated to the Shield.

- Seventh-placed UJ retained their Cup status when they beat Shield runners-up UKZN 42-8 in a promotion-relegation match.

- Bottom-placed TUT of Pretoria retained their Shield status when they beat NWU Vaal 39-26 in a promotion-relegation match.

BACK OF THE TOURNAMENT: Sylvain Mahuza (NWU-Pukke)
FORWARD OF THE TOURNAMENT: Shaun McDonald (UCT)
OVERALL PLAYER OF THE TOURNAMENT: Robert du Preez (Maties)

FNB VARSITY CUP

LOG

	P	W	L	D	PF	PA	PD	TF	TA	LB	TB	Pts
NWU-Pukke	7	6	1	0	226	130	96	30	16	0	3	27
UCT	7	5	2	0	186	141	45	26	21	0	4	24
Maties	7	4	2	1	174	159	15	23	22	0	3	21
NMMU	7	4	3	0	165	177	-12	22	23	1	2	19
Shimlas	7	3	3	1	164	173	-9	23	24	0	4	18
UP-Tuks	7	3	3	1	156	120	36	21	14	0	2	16
UJ	7	1	5	1	135	191	-56	17	26	2	2	10
Wits	7	0	7	0	78	193	-115	12	28	2	0	2

Note: LB = Losing bonus, TB = Try bonus

LEADING SCORERS

50 POINTS OR MORE

	TEAM	T	C	P	DG	Pts
Robert du Preez	Maties	5	17	4	0	84
Dean Grant	UCT	1	20	6	0	77
Adriaan Engelbrecht	Pukke	1	21	3	0	74
Gavin Hauptfleisch	NMMU	1	13	5	0	54
Gouws Prinsloo	Shimlas	1	15	2	0	54

5 TRIES OR MORE

8	Chris Cloete	NMMU	5	Lihleli Xoli	UCT
6	Sylvian Mahuza	NWU-Pukke	5	Luther Obi	NWU-Pukke
5	Robert du Preez	Maties	5	Ross Jones-Davies	UCT

PLAY-OFF RESULTS

SEMI-FINALS:
NWU-Pukke beat NMMU 19-18 (Potchefstroom) ; **UCT beat Maties 20-08** (Cape Town).
FINAL:
Fanie du Toit Sport Grounds, Potchefstroom, Monday 7 April.
Referees: Marius van der Westhuizen & Cwengile Jadezweni
NWU-PUKKE: 33 (13) *(Tries: Van der Merwe, Smit, Robertse, Obi, Welgemoed. Conversion: Smit, Dorfling. P: Smit)*
UCT 39 (10) *(Tries: Grant, Jones, Klaasen, Botha, Nel, Stewart. Conversions: Grant, Alexander)*
NWU-PUKKE: Sylvian Mahuza, Edmar Marais, Jaap Pienaar, Johan Deysel, Luther Obi, Johnny Welthagen, Tiaan Dorfling *(c, Dillon Smit, 23)*, Juan Language, Henro Swart *(Philip de Wet, 60)*, Rhyk Welgemoed, Francois Robertse, Peet van der Walt, Nhlanlhla Ngcamu *(John-Roy Jenkinson, 63)*, Akker van der Merwe, Mashudu Mafela. UNUSED SUBS: Marius Fourie, Joe Smith, Danie Jordaan, Ryno Smith, Lucien Cupido.
UCT: Ross Jones-Davies, Richard Stewart, Huw Jones, Guy Sckwikkerd *(Martin Sauls, 67)*, Lihleli Xoli *(Nate Nel, 73)*, Dean Grant, Liam Slatem *(c, James Alexander, 70)*, Michael Botha, Vincent Jobo *(Guy Alexander, 67)*, Jason Klaasen, James Kilroe *(Kyle Kriel, 72)*, Shaun McDonald, Digby Webb, Neil Rautenbach *(Chad Solomon, 72)*, Joel Carew *(Robin Murray, 72)*. UNUSED SUB: David Maasch.

Maties

2014 APPEARANCES & POINTS

PLAYER	NMMU	UCT	PUK	Wits	Shimlas	UJ	UP-Tuks	UCT-SF	Apps	T	C	P	DG	Pts	Previous seasons	Career Apps
Craig Barry	15	15	15	15	15	15	15	15	8	2	–	–	–	10	9	17
Clearance Khumalo	14	14	14	14	14	14	–	–	6	1	–	–	–	5	16	22
Mark Hodgskiss	13	13	14R	13	13	13	13	14	8	2	–	–	–	10	9	17
Louis Jordaan	12	13R	12	12	12	–	12	12	7	1	–	–	–	5	18	25
Caleb Smith	11	11	11	11	11	11	11	–	7	1	–	–	–	5	0	7
Chris CH Smith	10	x	15R	10R	x	14R	15R	15R	6	1	1	–	–	8	0	6
Jean Nel	9	9R	9	9	9	9	9	9	8	2	–	–	–	10	6	14
Tertius Daniller	8c	8c	8c	8c	8c	8c	8c	8c	8	–	–	–	–	0	14	22
Jurgen Streicher	7	–	–	–	–	–	–	–	1	–	–	–	–	0	5	6
Beyers de Villiers	6	6	6	6	6	6	–	–	6	3	–	–	–	15	5	11
Wilhelm van der Sluys	5	5	5	5	5	5	5	5	8	–	–	–	–	0	8	16
Jan de Klerk	4	4	4	4	4	4	4	4	8	2	–	–	–	10	7	15
Brendan Pitzer	3	–	–	–	–	–	–	–	1	–	–	–	–	0	9	10
Freddie Kirsten	2	2	2	2	2	–	–	–	5	1	–	–	–	5	3	8
Wesley Adonis	1	1R	1R	1R	1R	17R	1	1	8	–	–	–	–	0	0	8
Charl de Villiers	2R	2R	2R	2R	2R	2	2	2	8	–	–	–	–	0	9	17
Boeta Kleinhans	1R	–	–	–	1	–	–	–	2	–	–	–	–	0	0	2
Reinier Ehlers	5R	–	–	–	–	–	–	–	1	1	–	–	–	5	0	1
Lungelo Chonco	7R	7	7R	7	–	–	6R	6R	6	–	–	–	–	0	8	14
Gerhard Jordaan	9R	–	–	–	–	–	–	–	1	–	–	–	–	0	0	1
Robert du Preez	10R	10	10	10	10	10	10	10	8	5	17	4	–	84	0	8
Johnny Kotzé	12R	12	13	12R	–	–	–	–	4	2	–	–	–	10	0	4
Liam Hendricks	3R	3R	3R	3R	3R	3R	3R	3	8	–	–	–	–	0	0	8
Louis Nel	–	9	9R	9R	–	–	–	–	3	–	–	–	–	0	0	3
Nicol Heyns	–	3	3	3	3	3	3	3R	7	–	–	–	–	0	0	7
Chippie Oelofse	–	1	1	1	–	1	1R	1R	6	–	–	–	–	0	6	12
Ian Groenewald	–	4R	4R	4R	5R	4R	4R	4R	7	–	–	–	–	0	0	7
Justin Benn	–	7R	–	7R	7	7	6	6	6	–	–	–	–	0	0	6
Helmut Lehmann	–	–	7	–	6R	7R	7	7	5	–	–	–	–	0	25	30
Bjorn Bernado	–	–	–	–	x	x	9R	x	1	–	–	–	–	0	0	1
Koos Loubser	–	–	–	–	12R	12	11R	13	4	–	–	–	–	0	0	4
Neethling Gericke	–	–	–	–	–	2R	2R	x	2	–	–	–	–	0	5	7
JW Durr	–	–	–	–	–	12R	14	11	3	–	–	–	–	0	0	3
Tebogo Letlape	–	–	–	–	–	–	–	x	0	–	–	–	–	0	0	0
34 Players									177	24	18	4	0	182	162	339

Note: ■ = *Yellow card*

FNB VARSITY CUP

UP-Tuks

2014 APPEARANCES & POINTS

PLAYER	UJ	Wits	Shimlas	UCT	PUK	NMMU	Maties	Apps	T	C	P	DG	Pts	Previous seasons	Career Apps
Warrick Gelant	15	15	15	15	15	15	15	7	2	1	–	–	13	0	7
Jade Stighling	14	14	14	14	14	14	11	7	1	–	–	–	5	0	7
Dries Swanepoel	13	13	13	13	13	13	13	7	3	–	–	–	15	0	7
Rohan Janse van Rensburg	12	–	–	–	–	–	14R	2	1	–	–	–	5	0	2
Kefentse Mahlo	11	11	11	11	11	11	15R	7	–	–	–	–	0	0	7
Francois Tredoux	10	13R	12R	12R	12R	12R	–	6	–	–	–	–	0	0	6
Carlo Engelbrecht	9	9	9	9	9R	9	9	7	–	–	–	–	0	0	7
Jono Janse van Rensburg	8	–	–	4R	–	–	–	2	–	–	–	–	0	3	5
Rudolph Smith	7	8	8	–	7	7	7	6	1	–	–	–	5	0	6
Roelof Smit	6	6	6	6	6	–	–	5	1	–	–	–	5	0	5
Reniel Hugo	5c	5c	5c	8c	8c	8c	8c	7	2	–	–	–	10	19	26
Dennis Visser	4	4	4	5	4	5	5	7	–	–	–	–	0	0	7
Basil Short	3	3	3	–	3	3	3	6	1	–	–	–	5	15	21
Jaco Visagie	2	–	–	–	2R	–	–	2	–	–	–	–	0	9	11
Juan Schoeman	1	1	1	1	1R	1	1	7	1	–	–	–	5	18	25
Sidney Tobias	2R	2	2	–	–	–	–	3	–	–	–	–	0	1	4
Brummer Badenhorst	1R	1R	1R	1R	1	1R	1R	7	1	–	–	–	5	8	15
Jannes Kirsten	8R	4R	8R	7	19R	7R	7R	7	–	–	–	–	0	0	7
Leneve Damens	x	8R	4R	7R	6R	6R	5R	6	–	–	–	–	0	0	6
Emile Temperman	9R	9R	9R	9R	9	9R	9R	7	–	–	–	–	0	6	13
Tian Schoeman	10R	10	10	10	10	10	10	7	–	14	3	–	48	4	11
Jacques Rossouw	x	15R	15R	–	–	–	–	2	–	–	–	–	0	0	2
Andrew Beerwinkel	3R	3R	3R	3	3R	3R	3R	7	1	–	–	–	5	2	9
Ryan Nell	–	12	12	12	12	12	–	5	–	–	–	–	0	25	30
Wiaan Liebenberg	–	7	7	–	–	–	–	2	2	–	–	–	10	7	9
Corniel Els	–	2R	2R	2	2	2	2	6	–	–	–	–	0	0	6
Irné Herbst	–	–	–	4	5	4	4	4	–	–	–	–	0	0	4
Arno van Wyk	–	–	–	2R	2R	–	2R	3	1	–	–	–	5	0	3
Duncan Matthews	–	–	–	11R	11R	11R	14	4	2	–	–	–	10	0	4
Neethling Fouché	–	–	–	3R	–	–	–	1	–	–	–	–	0	0	1
Chris Massyn	–	–	–	–	–	6	6	2	1	–	–	–	5	0	2
Burger Odendaal	–	–	–	–	–	–	12	1	–	–	–	–	0	1	2
32 Players								159	21	15	3	0	156	118	277

Note: ▉ = *Yellow card*

❰ DID YOU KNOW? ❱

In 1937 when Ebbo Bastard was chosen for the Springbok side to Aus & NZ, they received a telegram: 'Best of luck. You are the most representative side ever to have left our shores: 16 Afrikaners, 10 Englishmen, one Jew and a Bastard!'

FNB VARSITY CUP

UJ

2014 APPEARANCES & POINTS

PLAYER	UP-Tuks	NMMU	Wits	Shimlas	UCT	Maties	PUK	Apps	T	C	P	DG	Pts	Previous seasons	Career Apps
Marais Schmidt	15	15	15	15	15	15	10	7	–	13	2	–	43	–	7
JR Esterhuizen	14	–	–	–	–	–	–	1	–	–	–	–	0	–	16
Robert de Bruyn	13	–	–	–	–	–	–	1	1	–	–	–	5	–	1
Harold Vorster	12	12	12	12	12	12	12	7	1	–	–	–	5	–	7
Jacques Nel	11	13	13	13	13	13	13	7	1	–	–	–	5	–	7
Jaco van der Walt	10	10	10	10	10	10	15R	7	1	1	–	–	8	–	7
Jacques Pretorius	9c	9c	9c	9c	9c	9c	9R	7	1	–	–	–	5	–	31
Kobus Porter	8	8	–	8	8	6	6	6	–	–	–	–	0	–	14
Victor Sekekete	7	7	5R	7	7	7	7	7	–	–	–	–	0	–	7
Tiaan Macdonald	6	6	6	6	6	–	–	5	2	–	–	–	10	–	5
David Antonites	5	5	5	5	5	5	5	7	3	–	–	–	15	–	15
Shane Kirkwood	4	4	4R	4	4	4	4	7	–	–	–	–	0	–	30
Van Zyl Botha	3	3	3	3	3	3	3	7	1	–	–	–	5	–	8
Francois du Toit	2	2	2	–	2	–	–	4	–	–	–	–	0	–	17
Wiseman Kamanga	1	1	1	1	1	1R	1R	7	–	–	–	–	0	–	15
Jannes Snyman	2R	2R	2R	2R	2R	2	2	7	–	–	–	–	0	–	7
Devon Martinus	1R	1R	1R	1R	1R	1	1	7	–	–	–	–	0	–	7
Fabian Booysen	x	x	–	7R	7R	7R	5R	4	–	–	–	–	0	–	9
Dylan Peterson	7R	8R	7	6R	6R	8	8	7	1	–	–	–	5	–	8
Lukas van Zyl	x	x	9R	11R	x	–	–	2	–	–	–	–	0	–	3
Jaun Kotzé	x	x	15R	10R	10R	10R	–	4	–	–	–	–	0	–	4
PJ Peter-John Walters	13R	14	14	14	14	14	14	7	2	–	–	–	10	–	7
Ryan Plasket	3R	–	–	–	–	–	–	1	–	–	–	–	0	–	1
Michal Haznar	–	11	11	11	11	11	11	6	3	–	–	–	15	–	6
Pieter Morton	–	x	12R	14R	13R	13R	13R	5	–	–	–	–	0	–	5
Henna Bredenkamp	–	3R	3R	3R	3R	3R	3R	6	–	–	–	–	0	–	6
Rynardt van Wyk	–	–	8	–	–	–	–	1	–	–	–	–	0	–	1
Jeremy Jordaan	–	–	4	–	–	–	–	1	–	–	–	–	0	–	1
Mark Pretorius	–	–	–	2	–	–	–	1	–	–	–	–	0	–	1
Siphatho Qinisile	–	–	–	–	–	x	x	0	–	–	–	–	0	–	0
JP Swanepoel	–	–	–	–	–	8R	8R	2	–	–	–	–	0	–	2
Vian van der Watt	–	–	–	–	–	9R	9	2	–	–	–	–	0	–	9
Jayn Kotzé	–	–	–	–	–	–	15	1	–	–	–	2	4	–	1
33 Players								**151**	**17**	**14**	**2**	**2**	**135**		**265**

‹ DID YOU KNOW? ›

Centre Jaque Fourie scored a try in each of his first three Tests, at the 2003 World Cup. In 2010, Willem Alberts, like Fourie a Monument High old boy, also scored tries in his first three Tests. Incredibly, Alberts came on as a sub in all three Tests!

FNB VARSITY CUP

NMMU

2014 APPEARANCES & POINTS

PLAYER	Maties	UJ	UCT	PUK	Wits	UP-Tuks	Shimlas	PUK SF	Apps	T	C	P	DG	Pts	Previous seasons	Career Apps
Jarryd Buys	15	–	–	15	10	15	15	15	6	–	4	–	1	14	–	22
Ayabulela Dlepu	14	13R	x	14	14	–	–	–	4	–	–	–	–	0	–	4
Michael Bernardt	13	13	13	13	13	13	13	13	8	4	–	–	–	20	–	8
Andile Jho	12	12	12	12R	12R	12	12	12	8	–	–	–	–	0	–	8
Tythan Adams	11	14	14	–	–	14	14	14	6	2	–	–	–	10	–	23
Gavin Hauptfleisch	10	10	10	10	15R	10	10	10	8	1	13	5	–	54	–	8
Enrico Acker	9	9	9	9	9	9	9	9	8	2	–	–	–	10	–	8
Tim Agaba	8	8	8	8	8	x	8	x	6	1	–	–	–	5	–	17
Marcel Groenewald	7	7	–	7	7	8	7	8	7	–	–	–	–	0	–	8
Chris Cloete	6	6	6	6	6	6	6	6	8	8	–	–	–	40	–	8
Cameron Lindsay	5	5	–	–	–	5	5	5	5	–	–	–	–	0	–	5
Stefan Willemse	4	4	4	4	4	7	4	7	8	–	–	–	–	0	–	16
Dexter Fahey	3	3	–	–	3	3	3	3	5	–	–	–	–	0	–	18
Martin Ferreira	2	2	2	2	2	2R	2R	2	8	1	–	–	–	5	–	28
Roy Godfrey	1c	1c	1c	1c	1c	1c	1c	1c	8	1	–	–	–	5	–	23
Gregory Bauer	6R	2R	–	–	–	–	–	–	2	–	–	–	–	0	–	2
Nicolas Roebeeck	1R	–	–	–	–	–	–	–	1	–	–	–	–	0	–	1
Louis Fourie	4R	4R	5	5	5	4	4R	4	8	1	–	–	–	5	–	24
Wade Elliot	8R	7R	7	4R	–	8R	8R	6R	7	–	–	–	–	0	–	7
Ivan Ludick	9R	9R	x	9R	–	–	–	–	3	–	–	–	–	0	–	3
Fanie Booysen	13R	15R	x	12	–	–	–	–	3	–	–	–	–	0	–	3
Donnovan Marais	15R	15	15	–	–	–	–	–	3	1	–	–	–	5	–	3
Abongile Mnyaka	3R	1R	x	3R	3R	x	x	x	4	–	–	–	–	0	–	4
Yamkela Ngam	–	11	11	11	11	11	11	11	7	2	–	–	–	10	–	7
Simon Kerrod	–	3R	3	3	3	3R	3R	3R	7	–	–	–	–	0	–	7
Jody Reyneke	–	–	2R	x	2R	2	2	x	4	–	–	–	–	0	–	4
Matthew Tweddle	–	–	4R	–	–	–	–	–	1	–	–	–	–	0	–	1
André Barnard	–	–	7R	6R	7R	–	–	–	3	–	–	–	–	0	–	3
Kewan Voysey	–	–	x	–	–	–	–	–	0	–	–	–	–	0	–	0
Sinakho Mafu	–	–	–	10R	x	x	x	x	1	–	–	–	–	0	–	1
Laurence Christie	–	–	–	x	x	–	–	–	0	–	–	–	–	0	–	0
Kayle van Zyl	–	–	–	–	15	x	10R	x	2	–	–	–	–	0	–	2
Devon Lailvaux	–	–	–	–	12	x	13R	13R	3	–	–	–	–	0	–	11
Robert Louw	–	–	–	–	x	–	–	–	0	–	–	–	–	0	–	0
34 Players									162	24	17	5	1	183		287

❮ DID YOU KNOW? ❯

Danie Gerber & Chester Williams both scored tries in six successive Tests. Gerber achieved the feat between 1982 & 1984, including two hat-tricks. Williams' streak lasted from Argentina in 1994 to the 1995 World Cup quarter-final vs Samoa.

Pukke

2014 APPEARANCES & POINTS

PLAYER	UCT	Shimlas	Maties	NMMU	UP-Tuks	Wits	UJ	NMMU	UCT	Apps	T	C	P	DG	Pts	Previous seasons	Career Apps
Sylvain Mahuza	15	15	13	15	15	15	–	15	15	8	6	–	–	–	30	–	14
Edmar Marais	14	14	14	14	14	14	14	14	14	9	2	–	–	–	10	–	9
Jaap Pienaar	13	13	–	–	–	–	–	13	13	4	–	–	–	–	0	–	4
Adriaan Engelbrecht	12	12	12	12	12	12	12	12	–	8	1	21	3	–	74	–	8
Luther Obi	11	11	11	11	11	11	11	11	11	9	5	–	–	–	25	–	16
Johnny Weltagen	10	10	10	10	10	10	10	10	10	9	1	–	–	1	7	–	9
Tiaan Dorfling	9c	9c	9c	9c	9c	9c	9c	9c	9c	9	1	5	–	–	20	–	30
Juan Language	8	8	–	8	8	–	8	8	8	7	2	–	–	–	10	–	7
HP Henro-Pierre Swart	7	7	7	7	7	–	7	–	7	7	1	–	–	–	5	–	13
Rhyk Welgemoed	6	6	8	6	6	8	6	7	6	9	2	–	–	–	10	–	9
Francois Robertse	5	5	5	5	5	–	5	5	5	8	3	–	–	–	15	–	8
Peet van der Walt	4	4	4	–	–	4	5	4	4	7	–	–	–	–	0	–	7
Elardus Venter	3	3	3	3R	3R	3R	3R	–	–	7	–	–	–	–	0	–	7
Akker van der Merwe	2	2	2	2	–	2R	2	2	2	8	3	–	–	–	15	–	10
Mashudu Mafela	1	1	1R	1	1	1	1	1	1	9	–	–	–	–	0	–	18
Marius Fourie	2R	2R	–	–	–	2R	2	2R	x	5	–	–	–	–	0	–	16
Joe Smith	1R	1R	1	1R	1R	1R	1R	1R	x	8	1	–	–	–	5	–	8
Danie Jordaan	4R	5R	4R	4	4	4R	4	x	x	7	2	–	–	–	10	–	13
Philip de Wet	8R	–	–	8R	6R	6	6R	6	7R	7	3	–	–	–	15	–	21
Dillon Smit	9R	x	9R	9R	9R	9R	10R	10R	9R	8	2	1	1	–	15	–	8
Ryno Smith	11R	13R	15	10R	15R	x	15	12R	x	7	–	–	1	–	2	–	7
Lucien Cupido	14R	x	x	14R	11R	x	11R	x	x	4	–	–	–	–	0	–	4
Lucky Ngcamu	3R	3R	3R	3	3	3	3	3	3	9	–	–	–	–	0	–	9
Robey Labuschagne	–	7R	6	7R	8R	7	7R	6R	–	7	–	–	–	–	0	–	10
Jacques Vermaak	–	–	2R	2R	2R	2	–	–	–	4	1	–	–	–	5	–	4
Jaco Buys	–	–	7R	–	–	7R	–	–	–	2	–	–	–	–	0	–	2
Johan Deysel	–	–	15R	–	–	–	–	–	12	2	–	–	–	–	0	–	4
Hoffman Maritz	–	–	–	13	13	13	13	–	–	4	1	–	–	–	5	–	11
AK Akhona Nela	–	–	–	–	–	–	13R	–	–	1	–	–	–	–	0	–	1
John-Roy Jenkinson	–	–	–	–	–	–	–	3R	3R	2	–	–	–	–	0	–	2
30 Players										195	37	27	5	1	278		289

{ DID YOU KNOW? }

Schutte Bekker replaced Gary Teichmann for a blood bin for only two minutes vs Australia at Loftus Versfeld on 23 August 1997 to win his only Test cap. His is the shortest-ever Springbok Test career in terms of playing time.

Shimlas

2014 APPEARANCES & POINTS

PLAYER	Wits	PUK	UP-Tuks	UJ	Maties	UCT	NMMU	Apps	T	C	P	DG	Pts	Previous seasons	Career Apps
AJ Coertzen	15	15	15	–	–	–	–	3	–	–	–	–	0	–	3
Divandré Strydom	14	x	14R	11R	x	11	x	4	2	–	–	–	10	–	24
Robbie van Schalkwyk	13	13	13	–	–	–	–	3	–	–	–	–	0	–	17
Joubert Engelbrecht	12	12	12c	12c	12c	12c	12c	7	3	–	–	–	15	–	15
Sethu Tom	11	11	11	11	11	11R	11	7	2	–	–	–	10	–	8
Gouws Prinsloo	10	10	10	10	10	15	10	7	1	15	2	–	54	–	7
André van der Walt	9	–	–	–	–	–	–	1	–	–	–	–	0	–	1
Niell Jordaan	8	8	8	5R	8R	8R	8R	7	2	–	–	–	10	–	9
Henco (Hendrik) Venter	7	–	–	–	–	–	–	1	–	–	–	–	0	–	6
Tienie Burger	6	6	6	6	6	6	6	7	–	–	–	–	0	–	7
Niel Claasen	5	5	5	5	5	5	5	7	3	–	–	–	15	–	7
Teboho Mohoje	4	7	7	7	7	7	7	7	1	–	–	–	5	–	22
Nick Schonert	3	3	3	–	–	–	–	3	–	–	–	–	0	–	8
Elandré Hugget	2c	2c	–	–	–	–	–	2	–	–	–	–	0	–	8
Rudolph Botha	1	1	–	1R	–	–	–	3	–	–	–	–	0	–	3
Ockert du Toit	2R	2R	2	2	2	2	2	7	2	–	–	–	10	–	8
Gideon Bruwer	1R	1R	1R	–	–	1R	1R	5	–	–	–	–	0	–	5
Fanie van der Walt	7R	4	4R	–	–	–	–	3	1	–	–	–	5	–	16
Andile Ngxabi	8R	–	–	–	–	–	–	1	–	–	–	–	0	–	1
Kevin Luiters	9R	9	9	9	9	9	9	7	–	–	–	–	0	–	17
Franna du Toit	15R	–	–	–	–	10R	15R	3	–	–	–	–	0	–	21
Maphuthla Dolo	11R	14	14	14	14	14	14	7	3	–	–	–	15	–	14
Justin Pappin	3R	3R	3R	3	3	3	3	7	1	–	–	–	5	–	7
Johan van der Hoogt	–	8R	6R	7R	4R	6R	x	5	–	–	–	–	0	–	11
Gerhard Olivier	–	x	–	8	8	8	8	4	–	–	–	–	0	–	4
Kay-Kay Hlongwane	–	x	x	9R	x	x	x	1	–	–	–	–	0	–	7
Pieter-Steyn de Wet	–	15R	11R	12R	15R	10	–	5	–	–	–	–	0	–	11
Armand Koster	–	–	4	4	4	4	4	5	–	–	–	–	0	–	14
Frans van der Merwe	–	–	1	1	1	1	1	5	–	–	–	–	0	–	5
Luan de Bruin	–	–	2R	3R	3R	3R	3R	5	–	–	–	–	0	–	11
Ludwig Erasmus	–	–	–	15	15	–	15	3	–	–	–	–	0	–	3
Tertius Kruger	–	–	–	13	13	13	13	4	1	–	–	–	5	–	4
Markus Odendaal	–	–	–	2R	x	x	x	1	–	–	–	–	0	–	1
Deon Bruwer	–	–	–	1R	–	–	–	1	1	–	–	–	5	–	1
34 Players									148	23	15	2	0	164	306

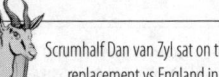

DID YOU KNOW?

Scrumhalf Dan van Zyl sat on the bench for eight full Tests and won his only Test cap when he came on as 75th-minute replacement vs England in 2000 for Joost vd Westhuizen. Van Zyl's Test career therefore lasted just five minutes!

FNB VARSITY CUP

UCT

2014 APPEARANCES & POINTS

PLAYER	PUK	Maties	NMMU	UP-Tuks	UJ	Shimlas	Wits	Maties	PUK	Apps	T	C	P	DG	Pts	Previous seasons	Career Apps
Ross Jones-Davies	15	15	12R	15	15	15	10R	15	15	9	4	–	–	–	25	–	16
Richard Stewart	14	14	14	14	14	14	14	14	14	9	5	–	–	–	20	–	18
Huw Jones	13	13	13	12R	13	13	13	13	13	9	2	–	–	–	10	–	9
Guy Schwikkard	12	12	–	–	–	12	12	12	12	6	–	–	–	–	0	–	6
Lihleli Xoli	11	11	11	11	11	11	11	11	11	9	5	–	–	–	25	–	16
Dean Grant	10	10	10	10	10	10	10	10	10	9	1	20	6	–	77	–	18
Liam Slatem	9c	9c	9c	9c	9R	9c	9R	9c	9c	9	3	–	–	–	15	–	22
Guy Alexander	8	8	8	8	7R	8R	8	–	7R	8	1	–	–	–	5	–	8
Vince Jobo	7	7	x	7	8	7	7	7	7	8	1	–	–	–	5	–	8
Shaun McDonald	6	5R	7	8R	7	4	4	4	4	9	4	–	–	–	20	–	11
Jan-Frederick Uys	5	4	4	4	4	–	–	–	–	5	–	–	–	–	0	–	5
James Kilroe	4	5	5	5	5	5	5	5	5	9	–	–	–	–	0	–	22
Digby Webb	3	3	3	3	3	3	3	3	3	9	–	–	–	–	0	–	20
Neil Rautenbach	2	2	2R	2	2R	2	2	2	2	9	–	–	–	–	0	–	16
Joel Carew	1	1	–	–	1	1	1	1	1	6	–	–	–	–	0	–	9
Chad Solomon	2R	2R	2	2R	2	2R	–	x	2R	7	–	–	–	–	0	–	7
David Maasch	x	3R	1R	1R	3R	3R	4R	x	x	6	–	–	–	–	0	–	6
Kyle Kriel	5R	–	–	–	8R	4R	7R	4R	5R	6	–	–	–	–	0	–	13
Jason Klaasen	6R	6	6	6	6	8R	6	6	6	9	4	–	–	–	20	–	16
James Alexander	9R	9R	9R	9R	9c	9R	9c	x	9R	8	–	1	–	–	3	–	20
Suwilanji Chibale	11R	–	x	x	11R	–	–	–	–	2	–	–	–	–	0	–	2
Martin Sauls	12R	15R	15	13	12R	12R	15	x	12R	8	–	–	–	–	0	–	8
Robin Murray	1R	1R	1	1	1	1R	1R	1R	1R	9	–	–	–	–	0	–	9
Tinotenda Zakeyo	–	4R	x	x	–	–	–	–	–	1	–	–	–	–	0	–	1
David Strachan	–	12R	–	–	–	–	–	–	–	1	–	–	–	–	0	–	1
Nic Holton	–	–	12	12	12	–	–	–	–	3	–	–	–	–	0	–	4
Michael Kennedy	–	–	x	x	–	–	–	–	–	0	–	–	–	–	0	–	0
Michael Botha	–	–	–	–	–	8	6	8	8	4	2	–	–	–	10	–	5
Mzisi Zondi	–	–	–	–	x	–	15R	–	–	1	–	–	–	–	0	–	2
Nate Nel (Michael)	–	–	–	–	11R	14R	x	–	11R	3	2	–	–	–	10	–	5
Gareth Ehret	–	–	–	–	–	–	x	–	–	0	–	–	–	–	0	–	0
31 Players										191	34	21	6	0	245		303

< DID YOU KNOW? >

Ray Mordt is the only Springbok to score hat-tricks in consecutive Tests - he achieved this in the third and final Test of the 1981 series against New Zealand, and followed it up with three tries against the USA.

Wits

2014 APPEARANCES & POINTS

PLAYER	Shimlas	UP-Tuks	UJ	Maties	NMMU	PUK	UCT	Apps	T	C	P	DG	Pts	Previous seasons	Career Apps
Ruhan Nel	15	15	15	15	15	15	15	7	2	–	–	–	10	–	7
Joshua Jarvis	14	11	11	11	11	x	14	6	–	–	–	–	0	–	6
Mandla Dube	13	12	12	14	14	14	13	7	–	–	–	–	0	–	11
Brent Crossley	12	–	–	12	12	12	12	5	1	–	–	–	5	–	7
Divan Ferguson	11	13	11R	13	13	13	–	6	–	–	–	–	0	–	6
Ashlon Davids	10	10	10	10	10	10	10	7	2	1	–	–	13	–	7
Matt Torrance	9	9	9	9	9	9	9	7	1	3	3	–	20	–	14
Jason-Collin Fraser	8	8	6R	8	8	8	8	7	2	–	–	–	10	–	13
JJ Breet	7	7	–	5	–	–	–	3	1	–	–	–	5	–	9
Juan-Pierre Jonck	6	6	7	6	–	6	6	6	1	–	–	–	5	–	7
Rendani Ramovha	5	4R	5	4R	6R	5	5	7	–	–	–	–	0	–	7
Devin Montgomery	4c	4c	4c	4c	4c	4c	4c	7	–	–	–	–	0	–	14
Gideon Muller	3	3	3	x	x	3	3	5	–	–	–	–	0	–	5
Ashleigh Kohler	2	2	2	2	2	2	2	7	–	–	–	–	0	–	7
Hannes Ludick	1	–	1	1	1	1	1	6	2	–	–	–	10	–	13
James Marx	x	x	x	2R	x	6R	–	2	–	–	–	–	0	–	2
Kyle Wood	3R	1	23R	3R	3R	3R	3R	7	–	–	–	–	0	–	7
Senna Estherhuizen	5R	8R	8	7	7	7	7R	7	–	–	–	–	0	–	7
Thato Mavundla	x	6R	1R	6R	6	–	7	5	–	–	–	–	0	–	11
Nkululeko Gamede	12R	14R	13	x	11R	–	–	4	–	–	–	–	0	–	5
Wilton Pietersen	x	14	–	–	–	9R	14R	3	–	–	–	–	0	–	3
Peter van Biljon	x	x	6	–	x	7R	6R	3	–	–	–	–	0	–	4
Ferdinand Kelly	x	3R	3R	3	3	17R	17R	6	–	–	–	–	0	–	9
Rinus Bothma	–	5	–	–	5	–	–	2	–	–	–	–	0	–	8
Ish Nkolo	–	x	x	x	x	x	x	0	–	–	–	–	0	–	0
Jacques Erasmus	–	–	14	–	–	–	–	1	–	–	–	–	0	–	8
Conor-Terrah Brocksmidt	–	–	x	7R	8R	5R	x	3	–	–	–	–	0	–	3
Riaan Arends	–	–	–	–	–	11	11	2	–	–	–	–	0	–	9
Allistair Ballantyne	–	–	–	–	–	–	x	0	–	–	–	–	0	–	0
29 Players								138	12	4	3	0	78		209

⟨ DID YOU KNOW? ⟩

Joost van der Westhuizen is the only Springbok captain to score a hat-trick — against Uruguay at the 2003 RWC.

FNB Varsity Shield

LOG

Team	P	W	L	D	PF	PA	PD	TF	TA	LB	TB	Pts
CUT	8	6	2	0	255	171	84	35	21	1	6	31
UKZN	8	4	3	1	246	171	75	32	21	3	4	25
UFH	8	4	3	1	215	217	-2	27	28	0	4	22
UWC	8	3	5	0	199	240	-41	24	30	1	3	16
TUT	8	2	6	0	184	300	-116	23	41	2	3	13

Note: LB = Losing bonus, TB = Try bonus

LEADING SCORERS

50 POINTS OR MORE

	TEAM	T	C	P	DG	Pts
Duan Pretorius	CUT	5	17	6	0	88
Freddie Muller	UWC	1	19	11	0	84
Morne Hugo	TUT	0	19	5	1	69
Oliver Zono	UFH	5	9	8	0	68
Duncan Campbell	UKZN	2	15	2	0	59

5 TRIES OR MORE

6	Shayne Makombe	UKZN	5	Calvin Ngcungama	UKZN	
5	Duan Pretorius	CUT	5	Danie van der Merwe	CUT	
5	Oliver Zono	UFH	5	Stefan van Schalkwyk	UKZN	

FINAL RESULT

CUT Rugby Stadium, Bloemfontein. Monday 31 March. Referee: Quinton Immelman

CUT 35 *(Tries: Mhlanga, Pretorius, Coetzer, Griesel. Conversion: Pretorius 3. Penalties: Pretorius 2. Drop goal: Marx)*

UKZN 26 *(Tries: Muir, Carney, Campbell. Conversions: Campbell 3. Penalty: Campbell)*

CUT: Charles Hitchcock, Alex Mhlanga, Johan van Schalkwyk, Duan Pretorius, Kholo Ramashala (c), Noel Marx, Stephen Griesel, Dean Kouprihanoff, Mosoeu Maruping, Frans Sisita *(Moekoa Bolofo, 54)*, Lyvette Shikwambana *(Johann Grundlingh, 70)*, Stefanus Coetzer, Danie van der Merwe *(Gerard Baard, 35-37)*, Deon Gouws *(Danie de Jager, 59)*, Len Noort. UNUSED SUBS: Marius Grobler, Louis Nel, Theunis Truter, Johannes Liebenberg.

UKZN: Hendrik Groenewald *(Gavin Nyawata, 76)*, Shayne Makombe *(Yandisa Mdolomba, 6-20)*, Brandon Bailing, Kurt Mavrodaris, Hendrik Lategan, Duncan Campbell, Cameron Wright, Deon Carney, Njabulo Zondi, Calvin Ngcungama (c, *Sanele Malwane, 65)*, Johan Wagenaar *(Gideon Koegelenberg, 50)*, Ado Wessels, Stefan van Schalkwyk *(Bart le Roux, 54)*, Dean Muir *(Mikyle Webster, 65)*, Henri Boshoff *(Sizwe Kubheka, 75)*. UNUSED SUB: Sibusiso Makhanye.

BACK OF THE TOURNAMENT: Shayne Makombe (UKZN)
FORWARD OF THE TOURNAMENT: Calvin Ngcungama (UKZN)
OVERALL PLAYER OF THE TOURNAMENT: Onke Dubase (UFH)

AMATEUR TOURNAMENTS

Leopards are amateur interprovincial kings

Last-gasp drop goal gives North West side victory

THE Leopards showed nerves of steel in the national Amateur Provincial Championship (APC) final against Emerging Western Province in Potchefstroom for a 33-30 victory and the title.

The overall APC champions are crowned each year following a round-robin series between the winners of the Central, South and North Amateur Provincial competitions.

The match, hosted at Profert Olen Park, saw the Leopards hold a narrow 15-13 lead at the break. The second half followed the same pattern as the first, with neither team giving an inch, which left the teams level at 30-30 with seconds left on the clock.

However, a late drop goal by the Leopards' replacement scrumhalf, Francois Nel, secured the national title for the home team.

The Sharks Club XV qualified for the play-offs by claiming the **APC Central** title in style with an emphatic 62-12 victory against the Griffons in Margate.

The final day's play proved to be thrilling with the KZN Wildebeest thumping Griquas Rural 36-5 to win the Plate final, while Griffons Rural and Free State Rural played to a 24-24 draw in the opening match. Free State, meanwhile, registered a narrow 39-35 victory against Griquas Central to finish the tournament in third place. But the Sharks Club XV stole the spotlight as they cruised to a 50-point victory to win the title.

Western Province continued their dominance in the **APC South** tournament by defeating SWD 13-7 in Humansdorp for a hat-trick of titles. The Cape side registered a 28-19 victory against the self-same SWD in the 2013 final, while they also won the title in 2012.

The Leopards claimed the **APC North** title with a 27-10 victory against the Valke at the Old Peter Mokaba Stadium in Polokwane to complete a fantastic run of form in the tournament. The victory followed an emphatic 57-13 drubbing of the Pumas and a 30-21 win over defending champions the Blue Bulls.

APC CENTRAL RESULTS: Griffons Rural 24-24 Free State Rural (7th/8th place playoff), Griquas Rural 5-36 KZN Wildebeest (Plate Final), Free State 39-35 Griquas Central (3rd/4th place playoff), Sharks Club XV 62-12 Griffons Amateur (Final)

APC SOUTH RESULTS: Western Province 13-7 SWD (Final), EP Urban 51-7 EP Rural (Plate Final), Boland 67-5 Border (3rd/4th place playoff), Border Rural 51-29 EP Invitational (7th/8th place playoff)

APC NORTH RESULTS: Pumas 18-17 Limpopo Blue Bulls (7th/8th place playoff), Lions 47-45 Blue Bulls (3rd/4th place playoff), Blue Bulls XV 55-17 Pumas Lowveld (Plate Final), Leopards 27-10 Falcons (Final)

AMATEUR TOURNAMENTS

MISCELLANEOUS 2014 AMATEUR TOURNAMENT RESULTS:

• THE BLUE Bulls men's and Border A women's teams were crowned the **SARU Interprovincial Sevens** champions at West Coast School in Saldanha in November. The tournament featured 16 men's and 18 women's teams.
DAY-TWO RESULTS:
CUP FINALS: Blue Bulls 40 – 28 Leopards (Men), Border A 33 – 0 Free State (Women). **PLATE FINALS:** SWD 22 – 21 Lions (Men), Griquas 7 – 5 SA Students (Women). **CUP SEMI-FINALS:** Leopards 14 – 7 Boland (Men), Blue Bulls 28 – 21 Western Province (Men), Border A 24 – 0 Blue Bulls (Women), KZN 14 – 21 Free State (Women). **PLATE SEMI-FINALS:** Pumas 21 – 24 Lions (Men), SWD 21 – 7 Lowveld (Men), Griffons 7 – 15 SA Students (Women), Griquas 17 – 7 Boland (Women)

• WESTERN Province took top honours at the **Sub-Union South** tournament in Kimberley after a hard-fought final won 34-25 against the KZN Wildebeest, which denied the opposition back-to-back titles. The Leopards won the **Sub-Union North** tournament in Potchefstroom after a 31-25 victory in over the Valke in the final.
SUB-UNION SOUTH RESULTS: Free State 12 – 36 Border (7th/8th place play-off), Griquas 21 – 46 Eastern Province (Plate Final), SWD 39 – 46 Boland (3rd/4th place play-off), KZN Wildebeest 25 – 34 Western Province (Final).
SUB-UNION NORTH RESULTS: Pumas 52-18 Pumas Lowveld (7th/8th place play-off), Blue Bulls 33-7 Lions (3rd/4th place play-off), Griffons 45-34 Limpopo Blue Bulls (Plate Final), Leopards 31-25 Valke Cup (Final).

• THE South African Under-18 Sevens team did the country proud in June by winning the gold medal at the **African Youth Games** in Botswana for the second year running. **THE GOLD MEDAL WINNERS ARE:** Edrich Venter (Paul Roos Gym), Herschelle Jantjies (Paul Roos Gym), Edwill van der Merwe (Paul Roos Gym), Jaco Coetzee (Glenwood), Morne Joubert (Glenwood), Tshepiso Mahasa (Ben Vorster), Luigy van Jaarsveld (Marlow Landbou), Ivan Kunz (Tygerberg), Eduan Kuyter (Afrikaans Seuns), Grant Williams (Paarl Gym), PJ Toerien (Garsfontein), Marco Janse van Vuuren (Transvalia). Coach: Gavin Beresford (Tygerberg).

• WESTERN Province won the **SARU Under-18 Sevens** at Hoërskool Monument in Krugersdorp by beating SWD 31-24 in a thrilling final. Boland won the Plate Final, KwaZulu-Natal the Bowl final and Griquas the Shield final, while the Leopards defeated the Limpopo Blue Bulls to finish the competition in third position.
DAY 2 RESULTS:
BOWL QUARTER-FINALS: KwaZulu-Natal 33 – 12 Eastern Province, Namibia 28 - 22 Border, Free State 45 - 17 Griffons, Golden Lions 34 – 27 Griquas. **CUP QUARTER-FINALS:** Valke 10 - 12 Leopards, SWD 17 - 12 Boland, WP 32-21 Blue Bulls, Pumas 12 - 45 Limpopo Blue Bulls. **SHIELD SEMI-FINALS:** Eastern Province 0 – 12 Border, Griffons 19 – 54 Griquas. **BOWL SEMI-FINALS:** KwaZulu-Natal 17 – 12 Namibia, Free State 34 – 12 Golden Lions. **PLATE SEMI-FINALS:** Valke 7 – 22 Boland, Blue Bulls 31 – 19 Pumas. **CUP SEMI-FINALS:** Leopards 0 – 39 SWD, WP 29 – 24 Limpopo Blue Bulls. **SHIELD FINAL:** Border 7 - 40 Griquas. **PLATE 3RD/4TH PLACE PLAY-OFF:** Valke 24 - 19 Pumas. **BOWL FINAL:** KwaZulu-Natal 26 - 21 Free State. **PLATE FINAL:** Boland 52 - 12 Blue Bulls. **CUP 3RD/4TH PLACE PLAY-OFF:** Leopards 31 - 14 Limpopo Blue Bulls. **CUP FINAL:** SWD 24 - 31 WP.

• EASTERN Province and Western Province stamped their authority on the **SARU Girls' Under-16 Inter-Provincial Series** in Durban in July, with both sides finishing the 16-team tournament unbeaten. With the objective of the tournament being to grow women's rugby and to develop players for senior provincial and national rugby, the tournament is similar to the Coca-Cola Youth Weeks in that no official winner is named at its conclusion.
RESULTS – DAY 1: Border 27-5 Limpopo Blue Bulls, Western Province 29-5 Border CD, Free State 7-12 Leopards, Eastern Province 15-0 Blue Bulls, Boland 10-5 Golden Lions, SWD 76-0 KwaZulu-Natal XV, Pumas 12-7 Griffons, KZN 12-5 Griquas.
RESULTS – DAY 2: Eastern Province 29-0 Leopards, Blue Bulls 49-0 KZN XV, Boland 12-10 Pumas, Griffons 51-5 Free State,

AMATEUR TOURNAMENTS

Border 45-0 KZN, Border CD 20-7 Golden Lions, Western Province 31-5 SWD, Griquas 12-14 Limpopo Blue Bulls.
RESULTS – DAY 3: Griffons 7-7 Border CD, KZN XV 5-12 Free State, Pumas 5-22 Leopards, Griquas 17-3 Blue Bulls, KZN 20–0 Boland, Limpopo Blue Bulls 31-0 Golden Lions, SWD 0-20 Eastern Province, Western Province 26-19 Border

• KWAZULU-NATAL cruised to victory in the **SARU Girls' Under-18 North Sevens** Inter-Provincial tournament in July, after toppling the Blue Bulls in the final to remain unbeaten in the two-day series. Western Province won the corresponding South tournament in Uitenhage thanks to a resounding 43-0 victory in the final against Boland.
NORTH RESULTS – DAY 1: Blue Bulls A 5-5 Golden Lions, Blue Bulls B 0-36 Leopards, Limpopo Blue Bulls 0-25 KZN, Pumas 12-10 Griffons, Blue Bulls A 20-10 Leopards, Blue Bulls B 5-34 Golden Lions, Limpopo Blue Bulls 7-10 Griffons, Pumas 0-19 KZN, Blue Bulls A 37-0 Blue Bulls B, Golden Lions 5-31 Leopards, Limpopo Blue Bulls 26-17 Pumas, KZN 17-5 Griffons
NORTH RESULTS – DAY 2: Blue Bulls A 20-5 Griffons, Leopards 0-12 KZN, Golden Lions 19-19 Pumas, Blue Bulls B 0-22 Limpopo Blue Bulls, Blue Bulls B 5-10 Pumas, Golden Lions 10-7 Limpopo Blue Bulls, Griffons 0-22 Leopards (bronze play-off), Blue Bulls A 5-17 KZN (final)
SOUTH RESULTS – DAY 1: Western Province 38 - 0 SWD, Border 45 - 0 Free State, Boland 19 - 10 Border CD, Griquas 5 - 19 Eastern Province, Western Province 48 - 0 Free State, Border 30 - 7 SWD, Boland 7 - 0 Eastern Province, Griquas 17 - 12 Border CD, Western Province 19 - 7 Border, SWD 39 - 0 Free State, Boland 5 - 0 Griquas, Border CD 7 - 26 Eastern Province
SOUTH RESULTS – DAY 2: Western Province 19 - 10 Eastern Province, Border 5 - 17 Boland, SWD 10 - 7 Griquas, Free State 30 - 0 Border CD, Griquas 7 - 5 Free State, SWD 12 - 20 Border CD, Eastern Province 0 - 29 Border, Western Province 43 - 0 Boland

• WINTER ROSE of Mdantsane in the Eastern Cape won the **Women's Club Invitational Championship** at the City Park Stadium in Cape Town in October with a 20-10 victory over local club Busy Bees in an exciting final to close off the two-day tournament. The tournament, which brought down the curtain on the 2014 women's inter-provincial season, featured eight club teams from Border, Blue Bulls, Eastern Province, KwaZulu-Natal, Limpopo and the Western Cape. The tournament was made possible by funding from the Department of Sport and Recreation. **RESULTS – DAY 1, ROUND 1:** Busy Bees 39 - 0 Pelicans, Middelburg Stormers 7 - 19 College Rovers, Kwaru 33 - 5 Soshanguve, Winter Roses 60 - 0 Nkowa-Nkowa. **RESULTS – DAY 1, ROUND 2:** Busy Bees 34 - 0 College Rovers (Cup semi-final), Winter Roses 10 - 8 Kwaru (Cup semi-final), Middelburg Stormers 19 – 3 Pelicans (Plate semi-final), Soshanguve 29 – 7 Nkowa-Nkowa (Plate semi-final). **RESULTS – DAY 2:** Winter Roses 20 - 10 Busy Bees (Cup Final), Soshanguve 25 - 5 Middelburg Stormers (Plate final), Kwaru 14 - 5 College Rovers (3rd/4th place-playoff), Pelicans 24 - 21 Nkowa-Nkowa (7th /8th place-playoff).

• GAUTENG came out tops in the **SA National Defence Force Rugby Week** held from 30 June to 4 July in Potchefstroom, beating South Eastern Cape 34-8 in the final match. Western Province beat Free State 33-19 in the bronze-medal match. The tournament featured six senior, four President and four women's teams. Northern Cape beat KZN 32-9 to win the President division while Western Province were winners of the women's division.

• SEA Harvest retained their **SARU Fish Factory** title in Velddrif in October, beating West Point 13-8 in the 27th edition of the famous tournament. The South African Fish Industries tournament was the brainchild of the late Dr Danie Craven, former Springbok centre Ian Kirkpatrick and former Proteas skipper Dougie Dyers, and was first held in Saldanha Bay in 1987 with the aim of providing players working in the fishing industry with an opportunity to wear the colours of their employers.
RESULTS – DAY 1: Gansbaai 8, Elandsbaai 7; Cerebos A 30, Sea Vuna 14; Mykonos 23, Lucky Star 3; Sea Harvest 14, I & J 7; Gansbaai 13, Pioneer Fishing 10; Cerebos A 19, Marine Products 10; Mykonos 19, Cerebos B 7; West Point 8, Sea Harvest 0; Pioneer Fishing 7, Elandsbaai 6; Sea Vuna 13, Marine Products 0; Lucky Star 10, Cerebos B 6; West Point 7, I & J 3.
RESULTS – DAY 2: Bowl Semifinals: Elandsbaai 15, I & J 7; Cerebos B 16, Marine Products 12. Bowl Final: Elandsbaai 28, Cerebos 3. Plate Semifinals: Lucky Star 21, Gansbaai 17; Sea Vuna 23, Pioneer Fishing 8. Plate Final: Sea Vuna 28, Lucky Star 0. Cup Quarterfinals: Sea Harvest 27, Gansbaai 5; Cerebos A 10, Lucky Star 3; Mykonos 12, Sea Vuna 10; West Point 10, Pioneer Fishing 3. Cup Semifinals: Sea Harvest 8, Cerebos A 3; West Point 12, Mykonos 11. Cup Final: Sea Harvest 13, West Point 8.

Obituaries

By Paul Dobson
Additional contributions by Albertus Kennedy & Frikkie van Rensburg, as credited

Harry Abrahams (1929-2014)
Refereeing pioneer, dedicated schoolmaster
HARRY Abrahams, a great man of rugby, died at his home on 19 June 2014, three weeks after his wife Gwen. He was 84.

Harry Francis Abrahams was born in Humansdorp on 19 September 1929. The family moved to Somerset West when he was small and he went to St George's Primary School and Trafalgar High School in Cape Town. In the community and at Trafalgar he acquired a love of rugby that lasted him all his life.

A small man, he was a scrumhalf. He played provincial rugby for Somerset Board and then became a referee. He refereed the Final of the Gold Cup in 1967 and a Test between the Federation and the African Springboks at Athlone Stadium in 1971, at which time he was a Federation national selector and helped in picking the team that played against England in 1972.

Abrahams was a schoolmaster and later taught at UWC. His passion for rugby took him into coaching and he coached the Tygerberg provincial team. It was in refereeing that Abrahams probably made his biggest contribution to the game. A Test referee, he went on to become the chairman of TRASA, SARU's refereeing body in pre-unification days. He led his referees into unification as the leader of the 10 representatives of the five SARU units in the Western Province area. He was vice-chairman to Piet Robbertse on the new national body and vice-chairman of the new Western Province Referees where he took on the task of appointments.

In 2010, Abrahams was made a life member of South African Referees. A vast knowledge of rugby, its history and its players has died with him.

Thys Adams (1944-2014)
Boland rugby player & cricketer, teacher, son of Wellington
THYS Adams was a man of Wellington. He was born there, played rugby there, worked there and in 2014 died nearby, an important part of the community.

Adams was at Bergrivier as a schoolboy, the son of a schoolmaster. After school he went off to the training college in Oudtshoorn and then for his third year to Hewat Training College in Cape Town. But he was a hard-working man and eventually obtained a BComm through Unisa. He taught first in Wolseley but then in 1970 went back to Bergrivier where he ended his career as the deputy principal. In his playing days Adams played for Roslins, a club over a century old when it amalgamated with Rosebuds to form Roses United, who are amongst the best clubs in the country. A tall, thin loose forward whose nickname was Mossie, he captained Roslins and Boland. Adams stopped playing in 1978 and after that coached Roslins and Boland.

When in matric he noticed a younger pupil and asked her what her age was; she said 15. In 1970 Thys and Wilma were married, both schoolteachers. When Adams became ill he was taken to hospital in Paarl and died there of internal organ failure.

❖ *Thys Adams was born in Wellington on 24 August 1944 and died in Paarl on 20 March 2014, survived by Wilma, children Graham, Jackie, Rozelle, Bradley and Gillian, and 12 grandchildren.*

Pietman Basson (1945-2014)
Ceres legend
PIETMAN Basson was a remarkably popular man, part of the heart and soul of the Boland town of Ceres.

He played sport, administered sport and sport was a part of his business – AJ Rankins Uitrusters and Basson Sports. His widow, Christine, said of him that he had no boundaries: he treated everybody in the same kindly way. One of his last acts was to provide a set of jerseys for Bella Vista Rugby Club of Ceres.

Pietman Retief, who played flank for Boland and was the first general manager of South African rugby, said of his friend: "Pietman was an honest, jovial man who wanted only to make those about him happy. He was an outstanding sportsman and administrator, a community person and a wonderful family man."

Basson came from a sporting family. His father Ewie played for Western Province and Boland. His brother Adri also played flank for Boland and his sister Rennie captained South Africa at hockey. When Basson left Hoërskool Montagu, he went to Stellenbosch where he read geology, played rugby and increased his circle of friends, but then Ceres became his home.

As player his great involvement was at flank for Boland in 24 matches from 1969-72 – slight of build but fast. In today's parlance he was a fetcher but also a creative player, one capable of breaking open a game.

Boland were strong in those days. His first match was against EP in Port Elizabeth which Boland won. They beat the touring Wallabies 12-3 and it took a last-minute conversion from touch to deny them the Currie Cup when WP beat them 13-11 at Newlands. In 1970, he played against Brian Lochore's All Blacks who beat Boland 35-9. In 1971, Basson was chosen for SA Country, the year he scored a try in Boland's 13-6 victory over Llanelli. But a back injury ended his career.

He then got involved in sports administration, not just at the rugby club where his involvement reached all facets of club management. He was a good tennis player and became chairman of the North Boland Tennis Federation. He was a good golfer and captain of Ceres Golf Club. He was also

OBITUARIES

chairman of Witzenberg Bird Club. And he did it all with his ready smile.

❖ *Pieter Joubert Basson, known as Pietman, was born in Montagu on 2 January 1945. He underwent a replacement of a heart valve and was at home recuperating when he died on 4 July 2014, survived by wife Christine, son Peter, daughters Patrys, who played netball for South Africa, and Justine, who is married to former Springbok captain Corné Krige, and seven grandchildren.*

Whitey Basson (1928-2013)
Decorated scientist, Northern Transvaal flanker

WHITEY Basson was a remarkably brainy man who also played sport at a high level.

Basson matriculated from Paul Roos Gymnasium at 14. At 17 he received a BSc degree and at 19 an MSc from Stellenbosch. He then headed north and received his doctorate from the University of Pretoria at 24.

Basson became one of South Africa's leading nuclear physicists, a medical pioneer in the field of medical use of isotopes and radiation in South Africa and a pioneer in the development of radiation technology in mining and other industries. He was much honoured for his achievements: the State Award of the Order for Meritorious Service, Class 1 Gold, for his contribution to medical research in 1988; the Salus medal from the then Dept of Health & Population Development for his pioneering work in radiation technology in 1986; and the MT Steyn Medal from the South African Academy for Science and Art in 1991 for his work in the creation of a safe South African nuclear industry.

Incredibly, Basson also found the time to play rugby, hockey and baseball. He played 105 times for Northern Transvaal at baseball and in 1962 was named the best baseballer in South Africa.

It was hard for him to get his rugby career going. When he was in matric, he captained the Under-14 side at Paul Roos – and took a Std 4 (Grade 6) girl to the matrics' farewell function! From Paul Roos he went to Stellenbosch but was caught in a sporting catch-22 – too young at 15 to play with the students and not allowed, as a student, to play for the school. Instead, he played waterpolo and baseball. Basson played for Oostelikes in Pretoria, a club started originally for former Tukkies, and in 1954 played No. 8 for Northern Transvaal in one match.

❖ *Johan Kristof Basson was born on 21 February 1928. His health was not good for the last 12 years of his life after two strokes. Because he was handicapped, he had a special car to get around but was killed in an accident at Buffels Bay on 28 December 2013. He is survived by wife Helga, sons Kristof & Peter, daughter Lise & five grandchildren.*

Koos Claassen (1937-2014)
Junior Springbok, farmer

KOOS Claassen was a fiery flank forward. There is a story that he was playing for Tukkies against Defence in days before replacements for injuries. Tukkies had lost two players to injury and Claassen ordered his men to kick up and-unders so that he could get amongst the soldiers and even numbers out. In the end, 13 Tukkies beat the 12 of Defence.

In 1958 he played four matches for Northern Transvaal as a flank. In 1965 he did not make the team but Danie Craven saw him playing for Potgietersrus, as Mokopane then was, and invited him to the Springbok trials ahead of the ill-fated tour to Australasia, and that year he was picked for the Junior Springboks (then a senior Springbok 'B' team) in their famous match at Ellis Park against the Argentinian team which had just acquired the nickname Pumas. The Pumas won 11-6, scoring three tries to two.

In 1966, Claassen joined Diggers and played for Transvaal 14 times from 1966-69. One of those was against the 1968 Lions which Transvaal won 14-6.

At the time of his death, Claassen was living on his farm Stirrup Glen Horse and Game Farm. He allowed walkers of the first Walker Charity Walk to use the farm as their base, but Claassen did not live to see it. The walk took place in June, a month after he died.

❖ *Jacobus Andries Claassen, always called Koos, was born at Steynsrust in the Free State on 10 February 1937 and went to school there. After school he went to Tukkies and graduated with a BSc in agriculture. He became a farmer. He had bypass surgery but did not recover well and died on his farm near Eikenhof, south of Johannesburg, on 13 May 2014. He was 77 and survived by wife Jessica, son Johan, daughter Tina and three grandchildren.*

Gerry Cresswell (1928-2014)
Sporting all-rounder, Lowveld legend

GERRY Cresswell was an all-rounder of the old-fashioned kind, playing provincial rugby and cricket – impossible in this age when seasons no longer exist.

Cresswell was ever grateful to Pretoria Boys' High for many things, including the development of his sporting talents. He was head of Solomon House and joint Head Boy in 1946. Cresswell began boarding school at nine till he finished school. Six of those years were when his father was fighting in World War II. Like many boys at boarding school, sport is the great escape. For Cresswell, this meant rugby, cricket, boxing, tennis, squash, shooting and soccer.

After school he played for Pretoria Harlequins and in 1950 played one match at flyhalf for Northern Transvaal – where the incumbent was the great Hansie Brewis. He had a longer career at cricket. He captained North Eastern Transvaal Schools and was chosen for a South African Schools XI in 1946. In 1947, he played for North Eastern Transvaal against the MCC and in 1948 played against Australia.

Married, he and wife Verna, who were married for 66 years, settled in the Lowveld where he became a prominent member of the community. Later the Cresswells moved to White River.

❖ *Gerald Andrew Cresswell was born in Johannesburg on 4 September 1928 and died in Nelspruit on 15 July 2014, survived by Verna, sons Andy, Chris and Vernon, and their families.* – Frikkie van Rensburg

Archer Dames (1948-2013)
Northern Transvaal centre, sports administrator

IN 1971, Archer Dames, a member of the Police club, played four times for Northern Transvaal. Police were strong that year, ending second in the Carlton League, and Northern Transvaal went unbeaten. That year the Springboks were touring Australia and while they were away André van Staden captained the team. On the return of the Springboks Frik du Preez, in his last season, took

OBITUARIES

over the captaincy. Dames played his four matches while the Springboks were away and coach Buurman van Zyl had Graham Thorne, the All Black, in the centre. That year Northern Transvaal and Transvaal drew the Currie Cup Final 14-all.

Son Jaco said of his Dad: "He always reached out to less fortunate people, giving where sometimes he couldn't afford to give. He lived to put smiles on people's faces. He made a difference wherever he went."

❖ *Archer Dames was born in Vanrhynsdorp on 6 April 1948. He went to the Police College in Pretoria and later became the director of sport & recreation in the Vaal Triangle. He died of heart failure in Vereeniging on 21 December 2013, survived by wife Magda, sons Jaco, Conrad and Rudi, and a grandchild.*

Uys de Jager (1949-2014)
Western Province & Boland flanker

UYS de Jager came from South West Africa to school in Uitenhage, then Stellenbosch, then Moorreesburg, then Ceres, then Worcester and finally Malmesbury. And he played a lot of rugby along the way. His father was a railway policeman in SWA who was transferred to Uitenhage where Uys went to Die Brandwag, played for EP Schools at Craven Week and then went to Stellenbosch to study agriculture.

While he was there he played in the first team of the modern era called the Victorians. Western Province had allowed Stellenbosch two teams in the Grand Challenge and their second team they called the Victorians, as in early days the institution that became Stellenbosch University was named Victoria College. De Jager also played one match on the flank for Western Province, in 1972. In 1974 he moved to Moorreesburg and played 19 times for Boland till he retired in 1977, captaining them on occasion. De Jager was in the team that the 1974 Lions thumped 33-6 but they went on to win six of their seven Currie Cup matches, losing only to Transvaal.

After his playing days De Jager stayed involved in rugby, a Boland selector, playing for veterans' teams, coaching and serving on committees. His laughing boast was that he had made Tommy Laubscher a Springbok for he had coached the strong prop at the Malmesbury club. De Jager worked for Kaap Agri where he was a manager.

❖ *Uys de Jager was born in Usakos in Namibia, which was then called South West Africa, on 17 March 1949. He died in Malmesbury on 15 January 2014. He had suffered heart problems for some time and had undergone a bypass. He is survived by wife Anita, who was a provincial athlete when at Stellenbosch, children Charlotte, Vicus and Hermanus, and four grandchildren.*

Jack Dolomba (1943-2014)
Pioneering African Springbok

JACK Dolomba, who in his day played for and captained the African Springboks and went on a tour of Italy with them, died in Ginsberg Township in King William's Town where he was born.

Dolomba started playing at Charles Morgan Primary School where Zukile Gcilitshe was the coach. Then he was a scrumhalf or a wing. In 1962, the school's old boys formed a club, Star of Hope, which soon became one of the strongest in the Eastern Cape, at its best from 1965-74. Dolomba joined as a 20-year old and changed to hooker because of a shortage, after which he then hooked for Border from 1966-74. This was a time when four national bodies were running rugby – the SA Rugby Board, the SA Coloured Rugby Board (and then SARU), the SA Rugby Football Federation and the SA African Rugby Board. All four bodies were choosing national teams!

Dolomba made his debut for the African Rugby Board's African Springboks in 1971 against the Federation's Proteas at Athlone Stadium, a match won 10-3 by the Africans. They won the return match in Port Elizabeth as well – 13-6, when Dolomba scored a try off a pass from Morgan Cushe. In 1972, he was on the bench when the African Springboks lost 36-3 to England at Wolfson Stadium. It was a big disappointment to him that he did not play but Thompson Magxala was the hooker – the tallest man in the side and their main source of line-out ball. Dolomba played against Italy in Port Elizabeth and went on the African Springboks' tour to Italy where they played six matches in 15 days. Dolomba captained the side in the Test against Italy in Brescia when the home side won 25-10, Dolomba's fifth and last Test.

The newspaper *Imvo Zabantsundu*, which covered rugby extensively, said that Dolomba was "a fast striker and very active in the loose". He was also "terrier-like and at times gets to broken play before the loose trio".

At the time of his death Dolomba was working for the Buffalo City Municipality.

❖ *Khebi Jack Dolomba died after a short illness in Bhisho in the Eastern Cape on 16 August 2014, survived by his wife, a daughter, two grandchildren and a great-grandchild. On the Saturday after his death, a minute's silence in his honour was observed at matches around South Africa.*

Eddie Dorey (1938-2014)
Teacher extraordinaire, eccentric champion sportsman

EDDIE Dorey was a famous schoolmaster at Pretoria Boys' High, a legend in fact, partly because he was eccentric and partly for his remarkable strength. He was on the staff from the age of 24 in 1959 till he was made redundant in 1992 – save for two years, 1967-68, when he taught English in Japan to sustain himself while he learnt karate, returning with the title *sensei* and the ability to be South African champion, after being the national judo champion for five years. Schoolboys saw him as a tough guy with a strange sense of humour, and they loved him.

His father was a policeman and therefore subject to many transfers, and so he was a boarder at Potchefstroom Volkskool till 1953 from where he went to the Normal College in Pretoria. Paul Anthony, an Old Boy and former teacher at the school but now a coach at the Blue Bulls, said: "At first we were all petrified of this colossal man with his hawk-like features. Yet when he smiled his face would light up and his thick moustache would shake as he shared his jokes and wisdom with us."

At school Dorey coached the 1st XV, as he was well qualified to do: he played for Oostelikes and in 1958 played prop for Northern Transvaal.

❖ *Charles Edward Dorey was born in Ficksburg in 1938 and died at his home in Lynnwood, Pretoria, on 26 May 2014, survived by wife Eline and their adopted son, a farmer in the Lydenburg District.*

Louis du Pisanie (1933-2014)
Free State centre, financial manager

HIS family called him Louis, his friends Dup

OBITUARIES

and the rugby public Oupa and for four seasons he played centre for Free State in the time of Ian Kirkpatrick, Nelie Smith and Louis Luyt. He managed this despite living in Welkom, where he played for Rovers.

In those days there was just one Orange Free State, except for the years when it was the Orange Free State & Basutoland Rugby Football Union. Fragmentation did not come till 1968 when the two sub-unions of Northern Free State and Eastern Free State became unions. He played six matches for Free State from 1957-60. Du Pisanie made his debut in Windhoek when he partnered Bok Fourie and the Free State, captained by Ben Klopper, won 12-9. His second match was also a victory, 9-8, over EP, the first time Luyt captained the side. In his last match, defeat at the hands of Eastern Transvaal in Springs, he partnered Ian Kirkpatrick in the centre.

❖ *Louis du Pisanie was born in Steytlerville on 6 January 1933 and educated there. From there he went to Stellenbosch where he did two years towards a BComm degree. Then he headed for the goldfields as a financial manager. He died in Jeffreys Bay on 1 August of emphysema, survived by Blondie, his wife of 56 years, three children - Leonie, Christel and Louise - three grandchildren and a great grandson. His daughter Louise became the first Free State woman to represent South Africa at rugby when she played in the Women's World Cup in Canada in 2006.*

Roy Gamble (1948-2014)
Loyal Northern Transvaal administrator
ROY Gamble played for Correctional Services in Pretoria and stayed loyal to the club till his death. He was chairman for eight years and on the committee when he died. He also served cheerfully on the committees of the Northern Transvaal/Blue Bulls Rugby Union. Known as the Red Baron, he was vice-president of the Union from 1985-88.

❖ *Robert Edward Gamble was born on 23 January 1948 and died on 18 June 2014 after a long illness, survived by wife Ina, children Robert and Kevin, and grandchildren.*

Nico Geldenhuys (1953-2014)
Oudtshoorn club legend
NICO Geldenhuys was coach of Oudtshoorn who dominated South Western Districts club rugby in the 1990s. He died there on 20 September 2014, aged 61.

After matriculating at Tygerberg High he joined the Police in 1972 and left the service in 1989 with the rank of captain and Officer Commanding of the Dog Unit in Oudtshoorn. He bought the *Headlines* Restaurant and managed this well-known landmark until he died there after suffering a heart attack.

Geldenhuys, who took over as coach from Jan Lotz – who also died in 2014 at the age of 91 *[see separate entry]* – won the SWD Grand Challenge for the first time in 1988. He had further successes in 1989, 90, 92, 93, 96, 97, 98, 99, 2000 and 2001. In 1997 the SA Rugby Football Union introduced a new-look club championship, with the club champions of each of the fourteen affiliates competing. With Geldenhuys at the helm, Oudtshoorn represented SWD from 1997-2001. A personal highlight in his career came in August 1999 when Oudtshoorn beat Maties 30-13 in Oudtshoorn.

In the 1980s and 1990s he also coached the Southern Cape Police team that participated in the annual national tournament, as well as the SWD 'A' team that participated in the SA Cup. He also served on the SWDRFU Executive Committee.

❖ *Nicolaas Johannes Jacobus (Nico) Geldennhuys was born in Parow on 21 February 1953. He is survived by wife Hannetjie, daughters Ilze & Sonet, and son Marthinus.* – Albertus Kennedy

Ray Griesel (1930-2014)
Legendary lock forward, gentle giant
THE tight forwards tend to be the strong, silent men of rugby who can get on with the job of exerting domination. Ray Griesel was one of those: a tall, unyielding, undemonstrative lock who played for Eastern Province for 13 successive seasons – till he was 35.

He was born in the Free State and then the family migrated to the Transvaal, where he played for Transvaal Under-19. Then the family moved to Uitenhage. He qualified at the Technical College (now one of the campuses of Port Elizabeth College), and joined the technical division of South African Railways in Uitenhage.

Griesel played for Swifts whom he captained for many years. The club, founded in 1890, was very successful during Griesel's time, winning the EP Grand Challenge in 1962 & 1965 and the Burch Cup when the team won 18 consecutive matches from 1964-66.

Griesel was first chosen for EP in 1953 and he had played over 80 matches for them when he retired in 1967. He played against the 1953 Wallabies, the 1955 Lions and the 1960 All Blacks. The 1955 match was astonishing for Eastern Province won 20-0.

He started coaching Swifts' Under-20 side and in 1969 became an EP Under-20 selector. In 1970 he became coach of the senior side.

Griesel loved animals and his hobby was building models of cars and boats, all to perfect scale. And the big, tough lock had a fine collection of teddybears.

❖ *Raymond Nevarre Griesel was born on 6 October 1930 near Winburg in the Free State. When he retired he and wife Val settled on a smallholding in Sardinia Bay, south of Port Elizabeth. Griesel died there on 10 January 2014.*

Joranda Hattingh (1980-2014)
Blue Bulls women's flyhalf, schoolteacher
HER team-mates called her Naas. After all she played flyhalf for the Blue Bulls and was a remarkable kicker. But then Joranda Hattingh had taken to rugby from childhood, born when Botha was such a force. She retired in 2013 after playing for the Blue Bulls for two years. Before that she played for the Golden Lions.

As far back as she could remember, Hattingh played with and kicked a rugby ball. When her grandmother asked her what she wanted for her 11th birthday, she asked for a pair of boots, which she did not get. Hattingh was at Hoërskool Secunda where she excelled at hockey and discus and was awarded colours in Grade 11. At the time of her death she was the sports co-ordinator at Lynnwood Ridge Primary School in Pretoria. There she did her best to persuade girls to play rugby.

❖ *Johanna Gertruida Hattingh, called Joranda by combining the two names, was born in Brits on 25 August 1980. She died in Pretoria on 10 February 2014, survived by her mother, brother Gerhard and sister, Madelyn.*

OBITUARIES

Sarel Herbst (1939-2013)
West Rand legend
SAREL Herbst, universally known as Ouboet, was a big man who loved rugby and he passed that love on to his family. In 1955, when he was at Hoërskool Monument, he played for Transvaal schools. His son, Danie, was a star at Monnas. Danie's dad was a lock but Danie was a wing and one of the best goal-kickers the great rugby school has ever had. Ouboet played for Transvaal Schools from 1979-80, and then for Transvaal Under-20. Barend Herbst, Danie's son, was also at Monument when he was chosen for the Golden Lions at the 2012 Craven Week. He was a fullback. In 2013 he played for Lions U19 & U21. Danie's other son, Rhyno, already taller than his grandfather, played for Monnas and the Lions in 2013 and 2014. And that is not all. Ouboet Herbst's younger son, Sarel, played eighthman for Transvaal Schools in 1995, 40 years after his father.

Grandfather Ouboet played lock for West Rand for 10 years in partnership with Toy Dannhauser, who captained Transvaal for two seasons. Herbst was kept out of the side largely by Piet Botha, the Springbok lock, who played 93 times for Transvaal. Ouboet and Toy played together for Transvaal six times. Herbst was also a remarkable goal-kicker.

❖ *Sarel Martinus Herbst, a rigger, was born in Krugersdorp on 28 October 1939 and went to school there. After a long illness Herbst died in Krugersdorp on 31 December 2013, aged 77, survived by second wife Julliana (his first wife died of cancer), four children – Danie, Daleen, Juanita and Sarel – and seven grandchildren. The Volle Evangelie Kerk Krugersdorp West was packed for his funeral.*

Fanie Kuhn (1935-2014)
Springbok prop
FANIE Kuhn, a great and famous Springbok prop, was born in Krugersdorp, went to school there, played his club rugby there and died there. But his fame spread throughout South Africa and in major rugby countries throughout the world, for he played in 19 Tests and 18 tour matches in an international career that lasted from 1960-65. His playing career for Transvaal was longer: from 1956-65, 79 matches in all.

Kuhn made his international debut in 1960. He played against Wilson Whineray's All Blacks four times – the Junior Springboks, beaten 20-6 in Durban, Transvaal, beaten 19-3 at Ellis Park, and in the last two Tests of the four-match series. In the third Test – a dramatic 11-all draw in Bloemfontein – he replaced the great Chris Koch and then played in Port Elizabeth when the Springboks won 8-3 to clinch the series. His immediate opponent was Whineray. Later in 1960 he embarked on the Springbok tour to the UK, Ireland and France. Kuhn played in all five Tests and in 16 other matches. In 1961, he was in the team that beat Ireland at Newlands and Australia at Ellis Park and in Port Elizabeth. In 1962, the British & Irish Lions toured. Kuhn played against them in all four Tests: the drawn first Test and the three Springbok victories. He also played against them for Transvaal. In 1963, he was dropped for the first time, playing the first three Tests against the Wallabies before being replaced by Mof Myburgh for the last Test when the Springboks managed to draw the series. He actually played against them twice in a week – on the Monday for Transvaal and on the Saturday for South Africa.

Kuhn's last hurrah was a damp squib. The underprepared Springboks went on a rushed five-match tour of Ireland and Scotland and failed to win a single match. Kuhn played for West Rand which later changed its name to Krugersdorp. In his time Toy Dannhauser was the captain and main man and Springboks Basie van Wyk and Lofty Nel were also there. The club won the Pirates Grand Challenge five times, including in 1964 when Kuhn played for them.

❖ *Stephanus Petrus Kuhn was born on 12 June 1935. He went to Central High School in Krugersdorp, now called Hoërskool Jan de Klerk and worked for South African Breweries. He had a fall and spent three weeks in hospital before he died on 21 January 2014, survived by wife Lulu (Louisa) and children Eben, Sonja and Francois.*

Mervyn Lawton (1922-2014)
Currie Cup champion, fighter pilot, mining engineer
MERVYN Lawton did many things in many places: born in Cape Town, studied and played rugby in Johannesburg, fought in North Africa and Italy, worked on mines in South Africa, Canada and the USA, and died in the USA.

Lawton was born on 7 July 1922. His father, known as Dendy, was a 1937 Springbok, a wing who scored the most tries on that most famous tour. Like his father, Mervyn went to Bishops and was there from 1931-40, playing for the 1st XV in his last year.

From Bishops he went to Wits to study mining engineering but there was a war on and he went, becoming a Spitfire pilot in North Africa and Italy. In later life he wrote to his friend John Heuton: "In 1941 I was at Wits...however at mid-year I could not take it any longer and went across to Roberts Heights [now Voortrekkerhoogte] to start my career of being a fighter pilot. I felt that I would rather operate in England, as there would be an invasion by the British or visa versa by Germany and I wanted to be in the thick of things. Our ship, scheduled to take us to England, was sunk on its way to Cape Town. Roberts Heights could not wait for another ship so our group was sent to the Middle East to operate under the control of the RAF."

War over, Major Lawton returned to Wits and started his mining career in that area of opportunity. He played wing for Transvaal from 1947-50. He was in the team that lost 6-3 to the 1949 All Blacks and played for Northern Universities whom the New Zealanders beat 17-3. In 1950 he won the Currie Cup.

In 1957, he and his wife, Penny, went to Canada to work on an uranium mine in northern Ontario. Then he went further north to a copper mine in Saskatchewan. In 1971, he moved south to Moab, Utah, as the mine manager of Rio Algom mine. Lawton enjoyed Moab as the vegetation reminded him of the Cape. After his retirement he raised sheep and looked after rescued animals.

❖ *Mervyn Hector Dendy Lawton, born on 7 July 1922, died on 9 January 2014, survived by ex-wife Penny, their five children – Wendy, Antonia, Gillian, Jane and Bruce – and five grandchildren.*

Jan Lotz (1922-2014)
Legend of SWD rugby
YOU just had to look at that craggy face with a jaw that could plough a field, and you knew that

OBITUARIES

Jan Lotz was a powerful man. And you had just to look into those twinkly eyes to know that this strong man was kind and filled with happiness and humour. He was the big personality in South Western Districts rugby over a great number of years – the 'Danie Craven of SWD' – especially in his home town, Oudtshoorn, the capital of the ostrich world.

He wandered from Oudtshoorn for a while – up to the Witwatersrand and down to Cape Town. In Johannesburg, he played for Rand Leases, later Roodepoort. And he was chosen on the wing for Transvaal in 1948. He is sometimes confused with Jan Lotz, the 1937 Springbok hooker, who was captaining Transvaal when Jan Lotz of SWD was playing wing and centre.

The next year he went down to Cape Town and played for Gardens for whom Ryk van Schoor was in the centre; Gardens won the Grand Challenge. In 1950 Lotz went back to SWD, joined Oudtshoorn and was immediately made captain. From 1950-58 he led them to the Grand Challenge four times. For the next six decades he was an active player, coach, selector, chairman and honorary life president.

In 1953, he was on the wing when the Wallabies beat SWD 34-11 in Oudtshoorn and he was in the centre in 1955 when the great Lions won 22-3, also in Oudtshoorn. He coached his club from 1960-77, a period in which they won the Grand Challenge seven times. In 2012, he was honoured with a lifetime achievement award by the SWD Sports Council.

❖ *Jan Melchior Petrus Lotz was born in Prince Albert on 22 October 1922. He was a health inspector. His wife Marie died in 2005 and he died in Oudtshoorn on 17 June 2014, aged 91, after a stroke. He is survived by son Jan, daughters Dojema, Gerda and Marietjie, and seven grandchildren* – additional information by Albertus Kennedy.

Johnny Lourens (1924-2014)
Currie Cup try-scoring hero
JOHNNY Lourens, forever a hero when the Currie Cup's past is mentioned, died on the night of 12 February 2014. He was 89.

He will always be remembered as the man who scored the try that won the Currie Cup for the first time for Northern Transvaal, a union then just eight years old.

While Lourens was a hero, spare a thought for Con de Kock, the Western Province fullback. Time was up, WP were leading 9-8 when in desperation Hansie Brewis, who had dropped two goals for the eight points, kicked downfield and 22-year-old Lourens chased. The ball was rolling to touch when tall, bronzed, handsome De Kock came smiling across to foot the ball into touch and take the Currie Cup back to Newlands. But the ball is oval and the kick went wrong, and Lourens, at the age of 86, told what had happened. "Hansie kicked the ball and as soon as he did, I started to chase. The ball landed near the Western Province 25 and Con de Kock tried to kick it into touch. Instead, he kicked it straight to me and I ran in for the try. There was chaos at Loftus as we won 11-9.

"Very few people knew, but the final was supposed to be in Cape Town, but was moved to Pretoria after the Northern Transvaal Rugby Union offered to bring the WP team north on the Blue Train. The poor Con went back to Cape Town on his own. He never played again."

De Kock played in lower leagues in the Boland the following year. Lourens later worked for National Intelligence. He tells of a chance meeting: "In 1983, while I was on duty in Cape Town, I bumped into Con. We had coffee, but did not talk about rugby!"

Lourens played for Northern Transvaal 22 times from 1944-52. He played for Tukkies and then for Police. In 1946 he set a season record of 13 tries for Northern Transvaal. Lourens was the last living player from the 1946 final following the deaths of Attie Botha of Northern Transvaal and Francis Mellish of WP.

❖ *John Petrus Lourens was born on 9 August 1924. He died on 12 February 2014.*

Phil Minnaar (1946-2014)
Blue Bull sculptor
IT started as a cartoon of a player, then it became a union's name and then it became a powerful bronze image by a world-famous sculptor.

The player was tough Louis Schmidt with the extravagant moustache. In *Die Vaderland*, cartoonist Victor Ivanoff produced a cartoon of Schmidt with fierce eyes and a massive moustache sweeping forward like the horns of an aggressive bull. Schmidt played for Northern Transvaal, who wore blue, and so the bull became a blue bull with Schmidt as the prototype.

Calling forwards *bulle* is still common. Northern Transvaal had powerful forwards, *bulle*. Blou Bulle, Blue Bulls was not a big step. But when unions in the North started changing their names for some reason, Northern Transvaal neatly became the Blue Bulls Rugby Union. A cartoon had become a name – a proud name. Then they got Phil Minnaar to make a life-size bull in bronze outside the stadium – a powerful, muscular animal-machine. The sculptor of that had been a schoolmaster before turning to bronze statuary with famous figures including Nelson Mandela, Paul Kruger, Oliver Tambo (standing at OR Tambo Airport), FW de Klerk, a wounded soldier, General De la Rey and more – altogether some 165 busts and 86 monuments.

Minnaar's large intestine was operated on on 1 March 2014 and he went home to recuperate. But Ria, his wife of 42 years, saw that he was not looking well. She called an ambulance but when it arrived he was already dead.

❖ *Phil Minnaar died at his home in Pretoria on 23 March 2014, survived by Ria.*

Gordon Osterloh (1941-2013)
West Rand, Diggers & Transvaal centre, mining executive
GORDON Osterloh, so the story goes, changed clubs for a change of career. He was at Krugersdorp High where he excelled at sport, especially gymnastics, athletics, swimming and finally rugby, a sport which would become his passion.

He started playing for the school's first team in Standard 8 (Grade 10 nowadays) and was granted special permission by his parents to play for the senior West Rand Club at 17. After school he continued to play for West Rand till he was offered a job at General Mining provided that he play for Diggers, which he did – and thus began a business career.

Both West Rand and Diggers were powerful in those days. West Rand, captained by Toy Dannhauser, won the Pirates Grand Challenge in 1956, 1964 and 1965. Diggers won more often:

OBITUARIES

1958-62, 1966 and 1968. Osterloh played centre for Transvaal from 1964-66. In 1964, he played when they were beaten by Michel Crauste's French in an unedifying match at Ellis Park. Often plagued by injury, Osterloh continued to play well into his 30s. He retained a great love for rugby when his playing days were over and passed that love onto his family.

Osterloh's business career started as a sub-accountant at a bank in Krugersdorp. He joined General Mining Corporation in 1966, which ultimately became Billiton. As an executive, Osterloh travelled extensively internationally over a period of more than 30 years before retiring as Marketing Director of Ingwe Coal Corporation in 1999. He continued consulting for more than five years after retiring. During this period he was appointed to the board of Eyesizwe Coal, whose formation he was involved in facilitating. It would later merge with Kumba to form Exxaro.

❖ *Gordon Patrick Osterloh was born in Johannesburg on 10 October 1941 and died there on 12 December 2013, survived by wife Monica and sons Patrick and Sean, his first wife Janet and their children, Rory, Gareth and Sheena, and three grandchildren.*

Hambly Parker (1934-2014)
1965 Springbok prop, prolific businessman

HAMBLY Parker was not just a big prop; he was also a generous man who did remarkably well in business.

Parker played for Crusaders, the second oldest club in Eastern Province, and for EP. In 1965, he was chosen for the tour to Australasia in the belief that he would do well in New Zealand. Ironically, the only two Tests he played in were two defeats in Australia in the worst year in our rugby history, when the Springboks went on a run of seven defeats. Parker was a remarkable scrummager on the loosehead and excellent protection in the lineout but he was extraordinarily slow about the field and so rarely of any use outside of the set phases. In his history of the tour, *Now is the Hour*, AC Parker (no relation) wrote: "The stiff-legged Eastern Province man had obvious limitations once the scrum was over. Hambly, nevertheless, was a loyal team man who made many friends with his reserved, courteous ways."

Apart from his two Tests, Parker played 12 other matches on the tour. Robert and Roley, Hambly's younger brothers, also played in the front row for Eastern Province. The three, numbers 3, 4 and 5 of the seven sons, were all in the front row and all were remarkable for their sense of humour.

Parker's father, a descendant of 1820 settlers, was a farmer in Somerset East. Hambly went into the business but accumulated greater wealth in property development and other entrepreneurial undertakings. He owned various properties and businesses in Port Elizabeth. Hambly was married to Rose, the owner of the highly successful Ascot Stud. Parker's second wife was a widow with two sons when she married him in 1987. The one son, a top veterinarian, Dr Ashley Parker, runs the stud just outside Port Elizabeth and the other son Brett has a successful car business.

❖ *Walter Hambly Parker was born on 13 April 1934 in Somerset East, one of seven sons, and was educated there, at Gill College. He died on 19 September 2014 in Port Elizabeth. He is survived by wife Rose, first wife Elinor, daughter Dianne, sons Ian, Michael and David, stepsons Ashley and Brett and 24 grandchildren.*

Jan Pienaar (1951-2014)
Loyal servant of refereeing

JAN Pienaar, chairman of Griffons referees, loved sport and particularly refereeing, where he made a great contribution over the course of 30 years.

He started refereeing in Kroonstad in 1985 and eventually became chairman of the Griffons Referees' Society, a popular man who did much to develop referees in the province.

From Hartswater Primary, Pienaar went to what is now called Hoërskool Noord-Kaap in Kimberley. After school he went to Potchefstroom, ending with a BComm degree and embarking on a career as an accountant. But Pukke meant also playing rugby and cricket and doing athletics. He was a provincial athlete, representing Western Transvaal. He played 1st league cricket in Bloemfontein (Ramblers), Kroonstad and Welkom. He stopped refereeing in 2006 when cancer struck for the first time, attacking his pancreas and kidneys. Then he was more and more involved in committee work for referees and for the Union. He was in remission but then was diagnosed with leukaemia in December 2013, and still he went on doing his rugby work. He had been the referees' chairman for four years when he died, still in office.

❖ *Jan Gysbert Pienaar was born in Hartswater on 4 March 1951 and died on 7 June 2014, survived by wife Martie, children Jan and Lettie, and two grandchildren.*

John Rooiland (1948-2014)
SARU wing, councillor, son of Postmasburg

JOHN Rooiland of Postmasburg was a rugby player and after retiring from the Postmasburg municipality a councillor representing the Democratic Alliance in Postmasburg and surrounding areas.

Postmasburg is about 170km east of Upington and famous for its manganese mine in a world full of all sorts of mines in the Northern Cape. Rooiland was born there and went to school at Glosam, a mining town near to Postmasburg. He was playing on the wing for Griqualand West when chosen for two Tests for SARU against the SA Africans in 1969, the only Griquas player chosen for the team captained by Winsie Pieterse. In the first of those Tests, at Green Point Track, the African Springboks were leading 9-0 when scrumhalf Cassiem Jabaar broke down the blindside on a long run. Jabaar passed to Keith Lentoor who passed to right wing Rooiland who opened the scoring for SARU – who went on to win 40-19. Only the 1974 Lions scored more points against the African Springboks than SARU did that day. The second Test at Wolfson Stadium in Port Elizabeth was a much closer affair. SARU won 9-8, thanks to a try under the posts by Raymond Killian, converted by Mogamat Theunissen's left boot.

Rooiland worked for the Postmasburg municipality and when he retired he became a DA councillor, a post he held to his death.

❖ *John Rooiland was born in Postmasburg on 11 June 1948. He fell seriously ill in Postmasburg and was transferred to Kimberley where he died on 5 November 2014, survived by wife Nannie, children Ursula, Riaan and Raylene, 10 grandchildren and a great grandchild.*

OBITUARIES

Sakkie Sauerman (1944-2014)
Diggers, Transvaal & Springbok prop, farmer

SAKKIE Sauermann was born in Alberton on the East Rand and went to school at Amsterdam Agricultural High in the small town of Amsterdam, in a sheepfarming district on the Swaziland Border. After school he worked on the mines and when his rugby career was over he headed back to the Lowveld and became a farmer, a quiet life for a big, tough prop.

In some ways the best memory of Sauermann is from the 1971 Currie Cup Final at Ellis Park. Northern Transvaal's Chris Luther goaled a penalty to put his side 14-9 ahead with little time remaining. Transvaal kicked off and Piet Greyling, Simon Norwood and Gert Schutte drove forward. The ball popped to Sauermann who dived over for a try. 14-12. Jannie van Deventer converted, the final whistle sounded and the two sides shared the golden trophy. Sauerman, who was also known as Theo, played 55 times for Transvaal from 1969-74. His club was Diggers, founded on 11 April 1892, a club that won the Pirates Grand Challenge 28 times, including 1968, 1970 and 1972. In his debut season, Toy Dannhauser was the captain and the team included Martiens Louw, Piet Greyling, Peter Swanson, Piet Botha and Robbie Barnard, all Springboks. Hugh Bladen, the popular commentator, was also in the team. There were Springboks in his last team as well – Gerald Bosch, Gert Müller, Kevin de Klerk, Johan Strauss, Paul Bayvel, Dave Frederickson, Klippies Kritzinger and – of course – Theo Sauerman.

In 1969, he played for Transvaal when they beat the Wallabies 23-10. In 1970, he played for the Gazelles when they came to close to beating the All Blacks in Potchefstroom. In 1971, he was invited to an extensive series of Springbok trials. He started in the B team, ended in the A team and was chosen for both Tests against France, the first at the Free State Stadium when the Springboks won 22-9, the second in Durban when the match was drawn 8-all.

Sauermann was one of seven Transvalers chosen to tour Australia. Despite the vigour of anti-apartheid demonstrations, that touring team is the only one to have won all its matches – 13 of them. The Springboks were soon brought back to earth with a thump when a mediocre England beat them at Ellis Park – mediocre in southern hemisphere eyes, its power disguised by the rise in power of British and Irish rugby. This became clear in 1974 when the Springboks failed to win a Test against the touring Lions. Sauermann played in just the first Test at Newlands, which the Lions won 12-3. Nic Bezuidenhout took Sauerman's place in the other three Tests.

In all Sauermann played in five Tests and six tour matches. In 1972, Transvaal, captained by Piet Greyling, won the Currie Cup, beating Eastern Transvaal 25-19 after leading 18-3 at half-time.

Sauermann retired from rugby in 1974, stopped being a mine clerk and went farming in the Lowveld which he loved so much, ending his days on a farm near Hoedspruit on the banks of the Olifants.

❖ *Johannes Theodorus Sauermann was born on 16 November 1944. He died on 16 June 2014, survived by wife Cecilia and four children, Adelé, Theo, Paul and Manfred.*

LM Smit (1912-2014)
Last surviving original Blue Bull

LM Smit played for Northern Transvaal in their very first match – against Transvaal on Monday 18 April 1938. He died gently on 8 December 2014, three weeks short of his 102nd birthday.

Northern Transvaal had been a sub-union of Transvaal in those days and so Smit had played for Transvaal in 1937. But in 1938 Northern Transvaal was upgraded to a union and he was chosen at prop. Those were years of few provincial matches but the tough man played prop or flank for 10 times, ending his provincial career in 1942. There were a number of Springboks in that first Northern Transvaal team: Ferdie Bergh, who captained the side, Roger Sherriff, Ben du Toit, Lukas Strachan, Tallie Broodryk, Nic Bierman and scrumhalf Danie Craven, who captained the Springboks that year and in fact took over the Northern Transvaal captaincy after that first match. Transvaal, who boasted five Springboks, won 22-9.

Lourens Martinus Smit, generally known as LM, was born in Perdeberg west of Kimberley, site of a critical battle in the South African War, and attended high school in Hopetown where he learnt to play rugby. After school he worked as a labourer on the railways and, as a 17-year-old, played for Lichtenburg before becoming a travelling salesman and moving to Pretoria where he joined Harlequins. Later he bought a farm in the Dullstroom district and carried on playing rugby, first for Machadodorp and then for Belfast, finally hanging up his boots in 1950.

In 1971, Smit left the farm Waaikraal in Mpumalanga and settled his family in Middelburg where he lived in his own house well into his nineties before his health required him to have greater care. His wife Lizzie had died in 1985 and he is survived by his four sons – At, Fanus, Louwtjie and Gert – six grandchildren and two great-grandchildren.

Smit's great rugby disappointment was that he never played for South Africa, missing out on two notable occasions. In 1938, he was a favourite for a Test place against the touring Lions but was on a train going to investigate farming opportunities in Northern Rhodesia (now Zambia) and the selectors could not contact him. The second time was when he was told he would be chosen but suffered a bout of malaria. Going to Zambia did him no favours and he never did farm there.

LM Smit's death ends an era.

Nicky Smit (1979-2014)
EP, Border, Boland & Toulon lock

NICKY Smit succumbed to a brain tumour and died, only 35 years of age. He had had an operation on the tumour in Paris in May 2012 and had returned to South Africa for the second operation.

Smit was a lock from Worcester who played for three provinces before moving to France. At school at HTS Drostdy in Worcester he went to the 1997 Craven Week as part of the Boland Academy team. Two years later he was in the Boland Under-21 team and in 2001 he made his Currie Cup debut for Eastern Province. He played for them 19 times that year and the next year played for Border 19 times before returning to Boland in 2003, for whom he played 66 times before moving to Toulon in 2006.

At that time Toulon were in Pro D2, the sec-

OBITUARIES

ond division of professional rugby in France, but they won promotion to the Top 14 and he played for them then – 44 times in all. He then moved to Massy in the Federal League. He played for them 81 times before the operation on the tumour ended his career, even though the tumour turned out to be non-cancerous.

Smit, who considered coming back to South Africa to become a tour guide, then became a coach at the club.

❖ *Nicolaas Machiel Smit was born in Worcester on 30 October 1979. He died at his parents' home in Rawsonville on 14 November 2014, survived by his French wife Caroline and by parents Pollie and Ronelle.*

Simon Sokutu (1935-2014)
KWARU & SARU prop

SIMON Sokutu played in four Tests for two different national bodies. Those were the days when there were first three and then four 'national' bodies running rugby in South Africa: the SA Rugby Board, the SA Coloured Rugby Board, the SA African Rugby Board and the SA Rugby Football Federation. That became more complicated when the SA Coloured Rugby Board closed down and the SA Rugby Union was formed in its place. This has become more complicated since the unification of rugby in South Africa and the foundation of the SA Rugby Football union, which has subsequently changed its name to the South African Rugby Union, one of the components of unification.

Sokutu belonged to Spring Rose in Port Elizabeth. In 1971, one of their members, the great Eric Majola, was killed in a car crash and the club wanted their Saturday fixture postponed. The Union refused and so they left and, as KWARU (KwaZakhele Rugby Union), joined SARU, causing a huge rift in African rugby. All of this explains why Sokutu played his Tests for different unions.

In 1957, he was in the African Springbok team, captained by Norris Singapi, that played the Coloured Springboks, captained by Fatty Bohardien, at the Showgrounds in Port Elizabeth and lost 18-11. His next match was again against the Coloured Springboks at Green Point Track in 1963. This time Fanie Headbush's Africans won 9-3. In 1969, the African Springboks played SARU twice, losing the first heavily and then playing the second at Wolfson Stadium in Port Elizabeth. Sokutu played in the second match which the Africans won 9-8. Sokutu was 37 when he played his last representative match, this time for SARU (who refused to play 'racial' Tests) against an Invitation XV, which ended in a 13-all draw.

Sokutu was a prop – a kind man off the field but one filled with explosive aggression on it. He was coached by Dan Qeqe and Mona Bodela.

❖ *Born in 1935, Simon Charles Sokutu died in Port Elizabeth on 13 January 2014, survived by his daughter and a grandchild. His funeral was in KwaZakhele Township.*

Jeffrey Stevens
Exhilarating wing, coach

JEFFREY Stevens, nicknamed Bolle, was not big but he was exceedingly fast, and something of a boy wonder. He was not a great defender but brilliant on attack and a crowd favourite. When the ball was on its way in his direction there was a frisson of excitement in the crowd. When he was at Drostdy in Worcester, he went to Craven Week for Boland and was chosen for South African Schools in 1995 and 1996. He had been on overseas tours before he left school – to Romania with SA Schools in 1995 and to Italy in 1996.

That year he was the youngest member of the SA Barbarians Sevens team in France and the SA Sevens in Dubai. He had five seasons with the SA Sevens. In 1997, the year after he left school, he made his debut for the Boland senior team. He played for them for two years and won 14 caps before moving to Western Province for whom he played in 1999, 2000 and 2002 – 40 times in all before catching the Kimberley train to Griquas in 2003 and then moving back to Boland in 2004. In 1998, he played for SA U21 and in 2000 for SA U23. In 2002, he played three times for the Stormers in Super Rugby. His playing career over, Stevens went into coaching, got himself qualified and was a popular, enthusiastic coach of the University of the Western Cape at 15s and Sevens. He started coaching in 2000 when he was still playing.

Jan Steyn (1928-2013)
Judge, referee, administrator

JAN Steyn did many great things and was a greatly admired man till his death just after Christmas in 2013. He was a judge, head of the Urban Foundation, head of the Independent Development Trust, and a fighter for the rights of the voiceless, even if they were convicts.

He was ombudsman for the Long-Term Insurance Industry, a trustee of NICRO, on the board of Communicare, the international president of Reach to Recovery (an international volunteer breast cancer NGO) and a board member of companies such as Anglo American and Barclays Bank, and then also the chairman of Western Province Cricket Club, President of Rondebosch Golf Club and a rugby referee.

He was an active, remarkably talented man who received honorary doctorates from five South African universities – UCT, Stellenbosch, Wits, Natal and the Medical University of South Africa, whose chancellor he was for 10 years. He also served on the Councils of UCT and UNISA. He served briefly as an Acting Judge of Appeal in Lesotho and in 1990 was appointed to the Lesotho Court of Appeal where he served eight years as a member and subsequently 10 years as president. He also served for seven years on the Court of Appeal of Botswana and until 2007 as a Judge of Appeal of Swaziland's highest court.

Steyn was a first-league rugby referee in Western Province.

❖ *Jan Hendrik Steyn was born in Cape Town on 4 March 1928. He went to school at Hoërskool Jan van Riebeeck and then read law at Stellenbosch University. He was admitted to the bar in 1950 and became a judge at the age of 36. He died in Cape Town on 30 December 2013, survived by his wife Ann, four children, three step-children, 15 grandchildren and three great-grandchildren.*

John Tshona (1967-2014)
Victim of catastrophic injury

JOHN Tshona was the victim of the saddest side of rugby football, a catastrophic injury, one that left him with 16 years as a quadriplegic.

He was 31, an electrician's assistant, play-

OBITUARIES

ing hooker for Strand Tigers when he sustained an injury described as 'C6 complete'. That was on 22 February 1998 when he was the father of two daughters. He was taken to Conradie Hospital and spent the next 16 years in a wheelchair, unable to work. Tshona was the recipient of help from the Chris Burger Petro Jackson Players' Fund, established in 1980 to help severely injured rugby players and their families. The Fund helped him in various ways – from providing and maintaining his wheelchair to medical supplies, a monthly allowance, and renovations to his home. And when he died the Fund helped with the cost of his funeral in the Eastern Cape. Tshona was married twice, the second time to Sange in 2012. They had been boyfriend and girlfriend at school, Sange's first boyfriend. His first wife moved off to Port Elizabeth where she remarried.

❖ *Mfusi John Tshona was born on 25 November 1967. He died on 2 February 2014 in Khayelitsha. He is survived by wife Sange, his former wife and their two daughters and a grandson.*

Schalk van Dyk (1931-2014)
1956 Currie Cup-winning eighthman, cattle farmer
SCHALK van Dyk, who had been a student at the University of Pretoria (Tukkies), was playing for Pretoria, the oldest club in Pretoria, in 1955 when he was chosen to play in the Northern Transvaal trials. He made a pledge the night before the trials that he would keep off alcoholic spirits for the rest of his life if he was chosen. He was chosen and when he died 59 years later he was still keeping that promise he had made to himself.

That year Van Dyk was at eighthman for Northern Transvaal when they played the great 1955 Lions who beat the Blue Bulls 14-11 when Cliff Morgan broke and Jeff Butterfield scored the winning try with a matter of minutes left.

In 1956, the Springboks went on tour to New Zealand and, as was largely true in 2014, the Springboks were not playing in the Currie Cup. Northern Transvaal beat Transvaal 9-6 at Ellis Park and Natal beat Western Province 11-10 at Newlands, and the Currie Cup final was played at Kingsmead in Durban.

Five minutes before the final whistle Van Dyk burst over for a try with defenders clinging to him and Northern Transvaal won 9-8. In all Van Dyk was a loose forward in the Northern Transvaal team 25 times between 1955 and 1958, on one occasion dropping a goal.

The next year Van Dyk went off to Harrismith in the Free State to farm cattle. In three seasons he played 25 matches for Orange Free State, including the 9-8 victory over the All Blacks in 1960, Louis Luyt's last match. Van Dyk captained the side once – against Transvaal in Kroonstad when Free State won 20-8. After he gave up farming, Van Dyk had garages in which he was actively involved till he turned 80.

❖ *Schalk Wilhelm Albertus van Dyk was born in Amersfoort in what is now Mpumalanga on 25 August 1931 and died of heart failure in Polokwane on 17 July 2014, survived by partner Erna Lister, former wife Rey, children Deon and Michele Young and Michele's two children.*

Gawie Visagie (1955-2014)
Larger-than-life Springbok
GAWIE Visagie, one of the most popular Springboks ever, died in Durban after a long battle against cancer. He was 59. Gawie's brother, Piet, was eight years older and played the last of his 25 Tests in 1971, a decade before Gawie became a Springbok.

A strong and talented player, Gawie never played in a Test. He travelled to New Zealand to replace Barry Wolmarans, who was said to be injured. Getting to Greymouth, where he joined the team, took Gawie 58 hours – via Johannesburg, London, Zurich, Singapore, Auckland and Christchurch. But Wolmarans recovered and played on, leaving Gawie just three matches on the tour – against Nelson Bays, which the Springboks won 83-0, and against North Auckland, which the tourists won 19-10. On the USA leg of the tour Gawie played one match – against Mid-West which the Springboks won 46-12.

Gawie was a skilled, strong, all-round player, perhaps too much of an all-rounder for his own good as he was not chosen just at scrumhalf. On that remarkable 1979 SA Barbarians tour to England, Scotland and Wales with Chick Henderson as manager and Dougie Dyers as coach, he played in four different positions, from fullback to scrumhalf. He was what Oubaas Markötter called a 'footballer'.

It was the first racially-mixed South African team to tour abroad. They did well on and off the field and their management were impressive in dealing with difficult political questions. That year Gawie was voted one of South Africa's five Promising Players of the Year.

The 1984 Currie Cup was remarkable for Natal. They were in the B Section and had lost their promotion-relegation match to Northern Free State when they had to play Free State the following week. Free State were second in the A Section, Natal the winners of the B Section. A Free State victory was regarded as a foregone conclusion, so much so that Free State had handed out their allotment of Final tickets before they played Natal. But the Banana Boys won 26-15. That took them to the Final at Newlands. Gawie was at flyhalf outside Craig Jamieson. Gawie kicked two drop goals and Hugh Reece-Edwards slotted a penalty to give Natal a 9-3 lead at half-time.

WP scored three tries in the second half and won 19-9. Like Piet, Gawie was originally a Griqua, educated at HTS Kimberley. He played 39 times for Griquas from 1977-80 and then moved to Durban, playing 42 times for Natal from 1981-85. He played for Ammasol, Durban Collegians and Dallas Harlequins. A third brother, Johan, played wing for Eastern Free State from 1968-74. Gawie had his own business in Durban – GV Agencies – supplying sports equipment and accessories and workwear.

❖ *Gabriel Pieter Visagie was born in Vereeniging on 31 March 1955, his names those of his father. He died at his home in Durban on the morning of 19 November 2014, survived by his wife Janet and their two children.*

André Vosloo (1946-2014)
Eastern Province flyhalf, broker, marathoner
ANDRé Vosloo was an all-round sportsman who shone particularly at rugby when a young man.

He played at his school, Victoria Park High, and then for Olympics in Port Elizabeth. An outstanding handler of the ball, he played flyhalf for Eastern Province, notably against the 1968 Lions, the 1970 All Blacks and, in 1971, against Western

OBITUARIES

Province when Eastern Province had a rare – just the second – victory over WP at Newlands. The Lions won 23-14 when each side scored a try but the All Blacks gave the home side a 49-9 hammering. Being a flyhalf, it is no surprise that he played cricket as well – for Pirates in Port Elizabeth. Vosloo was an insurance broker, transferred to Cape Town in 1980 where he established his own brokerage. While there he joined Celtic Harriers and in their colours ran 13 Two Oceans marathons and three Comrades.

❖ *André Vosloo was born in Port Elizabeth on 24 December 1946. He developed cancer which he suffered from for two years before dying at his Claremont home on 30 April 2014, survived by wife Rita, son Clint, daughter Hayley Harrod and five grandchildren. Vosloo matriculated in 1965. The next year Rita Evans was the head girl at Victoria Park. Rita captained Eastern Province at hockey for several years. Andre and Rita married in 1970. They both died in 2014, Rita just 67 days after André.*

Douw Wessels (1937-2014)
SWD player & administrator extraordinaire

DOUW Wessels, a colourful individual who left a huge legacy as a player, administrator and schools coach, died of cancer in Oudtshoorn on 11 March 2014, aged 76.

Wessels, who was educated at Heidelberg High and Stellenbosch, made his debut for South Western Districts in 1957 as a member of the Heidelberg Club at the age of 19. As a centre and flyhalf he played for the Maties first team from 1958-61 before returning to the SWD where he started his teaching career at Oudtshoorn Commercial School in 1962. He also joined Oudtshoorn where he played until 1970. Besides captaining the club he again represented SWD from 1962-65. In 1962, he played against the Lions of Arthur Smith and in 1963 against the touring Wallabies of John Thornett. For many years, he was the coach of the school's first XV and served SWD Schools rugby as secretary, chairman and manager of various Craven Week teams.

❖ *Douw Wessels was born at Heidelberg in the Western Cape on 5 May 1937 and is survived by wife Amanda and three children, Isabel, Douw (jnr) and Bernard. His son, Douw (jnr) represented SWD at Craven Week from 1988-89 and Boland U23 from 1993-94. His son-in-law, Johan, played for SWD at schools and senior level as well as for WP U20 in 1989 whilst his grandson, JP Duvenage, represented SWD Schools at U13, U16 and U19 level.* – Albertus Kennedy

Koos Wessels (1928-2013)
Legendary teacher & coach, Free State centre

WESSELS is a good Free State rugby name. In fact there have been 24 players with the surname Wessels who have played for Free State – not counting Wessel Lightfoot! The first Wessels to play did so in 1894, a year before the Union was officially formed.

When Koos Wessels died on the last day of 2013, he was 86, born in 1928 when the Union was only 33. In 2014, the Union was 119 years old. Koos Wessels' life had run parallel to most of the Union's life. After school in Brandfort, Wessels went to Bloemfontein Teachers' College and then to the University of the Free State where he graduated with a BCom degree. He played rugby and boxed for the University and then went teaching, for two years in Kroonstad and then for 37 years at Hoërskool Wessel Maree in Odendaalsrus, where he became a legend. It is also where he met his wife, for they were both in the *koshuis*. Not only did he teach accountancy but he also coached rugby. His most famous Springbok old boy was Jannie de Beer. Wessels coached the 1st XV at the school for 20 years. He made his Free State debut against Natal in Bethlehem in 1952, a match which Free State, captained by Basie Viviers, won 24-8. When Free State beat Transvaal 17-15 Wessels scored a try. In all he played 11 times for Free State, once on the wing.

Wessels' son Japie had an even more illustrious career. He first played for Free State in 1978. He played for Transvaal in 1981 and 1982, came back to the Free State and then played for WP at the end of his career. In all he played 145 times for them. In 1986, Japie became captain and captained them 42 times in all, ending in 1988.

After retiring from teaching, Wessels lived in Bloemfontein but, as he and his wife had done for nearly 60 years, he went back every week to the family farm *Skanskraal* near Thaba Nchu where he grew up. His interest in rugby stayed sharp and, an old centre, he disapproved of skip passes and no-look passes.

❖ *Jacobus Lamprecht Wessels was born near Thaba Nuchu on 5 September 1928 and died in Bloemfontein on 31 December 2013, survived by his wife Francine, their son Japie, their daughter Henriëtte, five grandchildren and two great grandchildren.*

Tony Wessels (1938-2014)
Currie Cup referee, all-round sportsman

ONE of the keenest of referees, Tony Wessels of KwaZulu-Natal was a keen sportsmen all his life. At Maritzburg College he played flyhalf for the 1st XV, in 1955 when they were unbeaten and in 1956 when their only defeat was against Umtali in Rhodesia. After leaving College he played for the 1st XV of Wasp Wanderers in Pietermaritzburg and then went on to referee. He played cricket for Natal from 1958-59 and also played hockey, golf and finally bowls, made an honorary life member of Lynwood Bowling Club in Pietermaritzburg.

As a referee he attained Currie Cup status in 1974 when the only other Natal referee on panels was Ian Gourlay, the Test referee. Wessels served rugby after hanging up the whistle – as chairman of the Maritzburg Rugby Referees' Sub-Society and president of the Maritzburg Sub-Union, which later made him an honorary life member. He served on the executive committee of the Natal Rugby Union and became an honorary life vice-president.

Wessels's three sons – Gary, Keith and Mike – all became referees. Gary reached a national panel but has stopped refereeing though Keith and Mike still referee. Like their father, both Gary and Keith have been chairmen of the Maritzburg Rugby Referees' Sub-Society. In fact, Keith is the incumbent.

❖ *Anthony John Wessels was born in Pietermaritzburg on 17 August 1938. He was not just a sportsman but earned his living as the manager of the Pietermaritzburg branch of Kings Sports. He suffered from Parkinson's for the last 15 years of his life, but was still very active on the bowling greens until about two years before his death. He died in Pietermaritzburg on 10 October 2014, survived by his first wife Rose and three sons, Gary, Michael and Keith, daughters Sharon and Lee-Anne and nine grandchildren.*